THE GREAT
CONTEMPORARY
ISSUES

CHINA

THE GREAT
CONTEMPORARY
ISSUES

CHINA

𝕿𝖍𝖊 𝕹𝖊𝖜 𝖄𝖔𝖗𝖐 𝕿𝖎𝖒𝖊𝖘

ARNO PRESS

NEW YORK/1972

O. EDMUND CLUBB

Advisory Editor

Copyright © 1972 by The New York Times Company.
Library of Congress Catalog Card Number: 72-5108.
ISBN 0-405-04162-4.
Manufactured in the United States of America by Arno Press, Inc.

The editors express special thanks to The Associated Press, United Press International, and Reuters for permission to include in this series of books a number of dispatches originally distributed by those news services.

A HUDSON GROUP BOOK
Produced by Morningside Associates. Edited by Joanne Soderman.

Contents

A Publisher's Note About the Series

It would take even an accomplished speed-reader, moving at full throttle, some three and a half solid hours a day to work his way through all the news THE NEW YORK TIMES prints. The sad irony, of course, is that even such indefatigable devotion to life's carnival would scarcely assure a decent understanding of what it was really all about. For even the most dutiful reader might easily overlook an occasional long-range trend of importance, or perhaps some of the fragile, elusive relationships between events that sometimes turn out to be more significant than the events themselves.

This is why "The Great Contemporary Issues" was created—to help make sense out of some of the major forces and counterforces at large in today's world. The philosophical conviction behind the series is a simple one: that the past not only can illuminate the present but must. ("Continuity with the past," declared Oliver Wendell Holmes, "is a necessity, not a duty.") Each book in the series, therefore, has as its subject some central issue of our time that needs to be viewed in the context of its antecedents if it is to be fully understood. By showing, through a substantial selection of contemporary accounts from THE NEW YORK TIMES, the evolution of a subject and its significance, each book in the series offers a perspective that is available in no other way. For while most books on contemporary affairs specialize, for excellent reasons, in predigested facts and neatly drawn conclusions, the books in this series allow the reader to draw his own conclusions on the basis of the facts as they appeared at virtually the moment of their occurrence. This is not to argue that there is no place for events recollected in tranquility; it is simply to say that when fresh, raw truths are allowed to speak for themselves, some quite distinct values often emerge.

For this reason, most of the articles in "The Great Contemporary Issues" are reprinted in their entirety, even in those cases where portions are not central to a given book's theme. Editing has been done only rarely, and in all such cases it is clearly indicated. (Such an excision occasionally occurs, for example, in the case of a Presidential State of the Union Message, where only brief portions are germane to a particular volume, and in the case of some names, where for legal reasons or reasons of taste it is preferable not to republish specific identifications.) Similarly, typographical errors, where they occur, have been allowed to stand as originally printed.

"The Great Contemporary Issues" inevitably encompasses a substantial amount of history. In order to explore their subjects fully, some of the books go back a century or more. Yet their fundamental theme is not the past but the present. In this series the past is of significance insofar as it suggests how we got where we are today. These books, therefore, do not always treat a subject in a purely chronological way. Rather, their material is arranged to point up trends and interrelationships that the editors believe are more illuminating than a chronological listing would be.

Each volume in this series contains an index; cumulative indexes to the entire series will be issued from time to time. Each volume also contains a selective bibliography.

"The Great Contemporary Issues" series will ultimately constitute an encyclopedic library of today's major issues. Long before editorial work on the first volume had even begun, some fifty specific titles had already been either scheduled for definite publication or listed as candidates. Since then, events have prompted the inclusion of a number of additional titles, and the editors are, moreover, alert not only for new issues as they emerge but also for issues whose development may call for the publication of sequel volumes. We will, of course, also welcome readers' suggestions for future topics.

China in the Twentieth Century

In the 19th century, under the battering of alien influences, China strove to maintain the ancient Confucian order of things, in which the peasant masses supported the state apparatus headed by the Son of Heaven, the emperor, who pretended to universal rule. There had indeed been movements directed at reform, even at social revolution; but all had proved largely fruitless.

As the 20th century began, China was embroiled in the turmoil of the Boxer Rebellion. The xenophobic excesses of that "rebellion" led to foreign intervention and new defeat by the Powers of the proud empire. It also effectively marked the entry of the decadent Manchu rule into its final stage. A modest new reform movement begun by Tzu-hsi, the reactionary Empress Dowager, proved to be too little and too late. It was only another mark of China's weakness that the land battles of the Russo-Japanese War of 1904–05 were fought on Chinese soil.

The Emperor and Empress Dowager died within a day of each other in 1908, and the infant Pu-yi succeeded to the throne. In the face of a rising Chinese revolutionary nationalism directed against the alien rule, power began to slip from the weak hands of the regent. In October 1911, a revolution began against the corrupt, anachronistic rule. After 268 years, the dynasty ended with abdication of the last Manchu monarch in February of the following year.

Not only a dynasty ended, but also the Confucian imperial system; a Republic was born. But the transformation was far from complete. The strong man who came to power, Yuan Shih-kai, was an official of the old autocratic tradition. His "modernity" was largely limited to the military field. China had only entered the stage viewed by Chinese historiographers as the dynastic interregnum—the period of political turmoil and contest intervening between two stable rules.

The World War I period added to China's instability. Japan took advantage of the war to assume Germany's special privilege in Shantung province—and went on to present China with demands infringing seriously upon the latter's sovereignty. The Yuan government acceded to most of them, thereby laying the foundation for modern Chinese nationalism; for when Japan, at the 1919 Versailles Conference, demanded legal confirmation of the position it had won from Germany in China, a wave of anger whipped up by Chinese intellectuals swept the country, and the May Fourth Movement was born. The Chinese people's deeply ingrained provincialism was supplanted, on that memorable occasion, by nationalism directed against a common foe. The nation's jealous, perfervid concern with its "sovereign rights" would constitute a major factor in its foreign relations in the years ahead.

The new, non-Confucian ideas that had been penetrating China over the past decades began to show their effect. In the wake of the May Fourth Movement, Sun Yat-sen revived the Kuomintang (Nationalist Party), which had been organized in 1912 but soon outlawed by Yuan. And the Russian Revolution of 1917 began to exert an influence. In 1921, by the inspiration of Comintern agents, the Chinese Communist Party (CCP) was born—with 57 members. One of its organizers was Mao Tse-tung.

The Kuomintang (KMT), which had enlisted a number of ambitious military men under its banner, and the infant CCP joined forces at Canton to overthrow the warlord regime seated at Peking. The basic program of political action was embodied in the Three People's Principles (nationalism, democracy and the people's livelihood) as finally formulated by Sun Yat-sen with the help of a Soviet adviser. Soviet aid went beyond political advice: the USSR also supplied arms and military advisers. The collaboration begun in 1923 was so effective that it proved feasible to launch a Northern Expedition in mid-1926. Time-serving military men joined the ranks of the revolutionaries.

But there were different kinds and degrees of revolutionary fervor present in the coalition, as well as clashing political ambitions. In mid-1927, still only halfway to their goal, the KMT right and left split apart and both turned on the far left—the Communists. The Russian advisers were sent home; CCP members were hunted down and killed, and the remnant Communists, after several abortive attempts to spur a revolutionary wave, took refuge in the deep mountains of Kiangsi province. Those dissident elements were the nuclei of future rebellion; from them Chu Teh and Mao Tse-tung organized the Workers' and Peasants' Red Army.

The shattered Kuomintang pulled itself together under the leadership of four outstanding military men, and in June 1928 their combined efforts brought about the overthrow of the warlord regime at Peking. A new National government was established at Nanking in October 1928. Sun Yat-sen had not lived to see that day; he had died in February 1925. The one who came out on top in 1928 was the military man Chiang Kai-shek.

Chiang, like Yuan Shih-kai, proposed unification of the country through force of arms, and his regime waged successive civil wars against KMT rivals. With the emphasis on military action there was corresponding neglect of Sun Yat-sen's third principle—the people's livelihood. The explosive land tenure problem was effectively ignored, for Chiang depended for much of his support on the wealthy landowning class. He was no social revolutionary. The Communists, viewed by the KMT regime as "Red bandits," consequently found ripe occasion to undertake revival of the revolution through mobilization of popular discontents. Chiang's government found cause to wage successive "bandit-suppression" campaigns in response.

Circumstances strengthened national discontents and armed Chiang's enemies. In 1931, the Japanese invaded Manchuria and in 1932 set up there a puppet state, Manchukuo, to serve their imperial purposes. The left-wing revolutionaries had been able to make little progress by exploitation of peasant distress, but the aroused patriotism of the bourgeoisie created new potential allies for the anti-government forces. The Red Army in 1934 was driven from its Kiangsi base areas and forced to take up the Long March to a haven of (relative) safety in the northwest. The CCP in 1935 adopted a united-front policy; now all discontented elements, regardless of their degree of social radicalism, were viewed as potential allies. A climax was reached in December 1936 when, as the result of the kidnapping of Chiang Kai-shek by a fellow KMT general at Sian on the eve of a sixth "bandit-suppression" campaign against the Communist rebels, Chiang himself was more or less forcibly committed to a policy of resisting any further Japanese advance.

Nationalism was served. War with Japan began in July 1937, and the Nationalists and Communists once more entered upon an alliance against a common foe. The USSR came to the aid of the political combine fighting its potential enemy, Japan. But the stronger Japanese within a year occupied most of the main towns and communications lines of north and eastern China, and drove the National government from Nanking and into the deep hinterland; it finally settled in Chungking in west China as wartime capital. It continued in existence there until the Japanese attack on Pearl Harbor in December 1941 automatically endowed "Free China" with major new allies: the United States, Britain and the Netherlands.

The chief of those, in Chungking's estimation, was the United States; and the Nationalists now bent their main efforts to serve their selfish power interests. This policy led to growing conflict with both the USSR in foreign affairs and the Chinese Communists in the domestic realm. Finally, given the manifest predilection of the Nationalists for the playing of safe power games in preference to fighting the Japanese, a major conflict developed between the Nationalists and their American allies. But the factor of prime significance for China's future was that, as the Nationalists became more corrupt, the Communists developed both their political influence and their military capacities.

Victory over the Japanese came in 1945. The Nationalists continued to indulge their old habits, and the manifestations of greedy carpetbagging that attended their return to the coastal areas and Manchuria (ex-Manchukuo) alienated many. Increasing numbers of the population were estranged as inflation became rampant—reminiscent of the situation that prevailed in Germany after World War I.

And the issue of power remained outstanding. The Kuomintang had originally been committed to renunciation of its dictatorship (its "tutelage" of the nation) after a specified period, but had always found reason in crisis not to open the door to China's democratic stage. Again crisis threatened: the Communists, grown strong, demanded a share in power. Chiang was intent still upon national unification on his terms, by force if need be. With the issue unresolved, China after V-J Day drifted rapidly toward a state of civil war.

The United States endeavored to reconcile the irreconcilables. The first American mediator, Maj. General Patrick J. Hurley, threw in the towel soon after the war was over. The Marshall Mission took up the task in December 1945. General George C. Marshall made a heroic effort, but each Chinese side endeavored to manipulate American intervention to its own ends. The mediatory effort failed, and the "third revolutionary civil war" began in July 1946. The outcome of the struggle between the corrupt and inefficient *ancien régime* and the disciplined and newly strong revolutionaries was determined by a fundamental shift in the disillusioned nation's allegiance from the Nationalists to the Communists. In 1949, the Nationalist power structure crumbled under the blows of the politically motivated (Communist) People's Liberation Army, and a new government was established in Peking; the remnant Nationalist forces fled the mainland and took refuge on Taiwan. Mao Tse-tung's New Democracy was based upon political, economic and social principles that differed radically from those employed by the military dictatorship of Chiang Kai-shek. Was this then the end of the dynastic interregnum?

In the beginning, the Communists still served the united-front principle. This was the period of the People's Democratic Dictatorship, the period of consolidation of power, and the rule was in theory based upon the collaboration of the workers, peasants, petty bourgeoisie and national bourgeoisie. But the Chinese Communist Party dominated the scene and dictated the nation's new directions.

The new Peking government demonstrated confidence in its destiny when, even as it embarked upon the herculean task of rehabilitating the war-torn country, it intervened massively in the Korean War and simultaneously moved to restore the Chinese rule in Tibet. In both martial and peaceful pursuits, it depended heavily for support upon agreements reached with the USSR in early 1950. Incidental to the outbreak of the Korean War in June of that year, the United States extended a protecting wing over the Nationalists on Taiwan, and thus again took sides in the still not-quite-finished Chinese civil war. The amity with the USSR appeared consolidated, and enmity with the United States crystallized, as Peking, with peace restored in Korea, took up the work of "constructing socialism."

From its beginnings, the regime made repeated use of movements to achieve its ends of purging the nation of unwanted elements and of inculcating in human material judged malleable the social disciplines desired for service of the new order. The petty and national bourgeoisie were naturally marked for early extinction. China, by the concepts of Mao Tse-tung, was to be pushed by the process of uninterrupted revolution into the ultimate stage of communism, incidentally attaining to the rank of major economic power by the year 2000. It was easy to read between the Chinese lines: by that date also, China should have recovered Middle Kingdom preeminence in world affairs. For all this, it was necessary to change the nature of Chinese Man.

A major beginning was accomplished. Rapid advances were made in the industrial field, thanks in good measure to Soviet aid, during the period of the first Five-Year Plan (1953–57). In agriculture, there was a drive toward collectivization—with the process accelerated in 1955. But the Hundred Flowers episode of 1956–57 demonstrated clearly that the Communist regime had not succeeded in changing fundamentally the thought processes of the Chinese people—and particularly of the Chinese intelligentsia. The Party leadership,

seemingly to its considerable consternation, came under wide attack by the nation's intellectuals for its policies in general and its dictatorial procedures in particular. In sum, China's non-Party thinkers found the regime lacking in the democratic element it professed to serve so faithfully.

Mao Tse-tung had much earlier condemned bourgeois "liberalism," and the Hundred Flowers dissidents were roughly put down in an anti-rightest movement. The trend toward authoritarianism accelerated. The Thought of Mao Tse-tung in due course came to be identified as "Marxism-Leninism of the present era": thus the contemporary Chinese ideology, like Confucianism in the past, was viewed as having universal applicability. Mao Tse-tung in revolutionary warfare had proved himself a great leader in destroying the class adversary; he showed himself less competent in solving the problems of peace.

There was no weakness in Mao's imagination: he gave full rein to *his* version of Marxism-Leninism—a version imbued with illuminism and voluntarism. He believed that the Chinese masses, under his leadership, could perform miracles. His weakness was shown in that defiance of reality. Mao's impatient romanticism led him finally into calamitous undertakings—the Great Leap Forward of 1958, the effort openly undertaken in 1960 to bend the more powerful Soviet Union to Mao's imperious will and the Great Proletarian Cultural Revolution of 1966–68 designed to purge the Party of his opponents.

As a result of those Maoist ventures, massive changes were indeed wrought in China. Hundreds of millions of peasants were herded from collectives into agricultural communes, and the process of regimentation was strengthened by mobilization of approximately one-third of the total population, male and female, into the people's militia. But the Great Leap Forward in the end proved to be an economic disaster. And the quarrel picked with the Soviet Union brought a withdrawal of all Soviet economic aid. China's economic advance, already interrupted by the Great Leap Forward, was now consciously slowed to put primary emphasis on the agricultural effort necessary to feed China's rapidly growing population.

China consequently continued marked by fundamental weaknesses. The living conditions of the people were in all truth markedly improved over what they had known under previous conditions of "feudalistic" exploitation, but it became evident that China was not going to attain its goal of modernization rapidly. While Third World countries had looked upon China as offering patterns to follow in the 1950's, that admiration flagged by the 1960's. Peking's efforts to provide revolutionary leadership to Third World countries and thus to build up a world power structure capable of contending with both the United States and the Soviet Union were stepped up in the 1963–65 period, but failed ignominiously.

The Great Proletarian Cultural Revolution (GPCR), staged as China wrestled with obdurate domestic and foreign problems, further weakened the country at home and abroad. Mao Tse-tung indeed succeeded in purging the Party of many of his opponents, including chief of state Liu Shao-chi, but this meant eliminating able men whose chief sins were pragmatism and opposition to Mao's policies. The existing Party and governmental structures were largely destroyed and had to be rebuilt—in accordance with Mao's specifications. Nominally, the rule had now assumed the form of a Dictatorship of the Proletariat, but in reality the machinery of democratic centralism designed as a means for expression of "the will of the masses" had been dismantled, and the leadership principle operated instead.

The movement had failed to create a "revolutionary generation" to constitute the political succession when the Long March veterans should depart the stage. Instead it was found necessary to use the People's Liberation Army (PLA) to suppress youthful rebels who had responded all too enthusiastically to the Chairman's directive that "to rebel is good." The Maoist personality cult attained new peaks, and Mao Tse-tung was acclaimed in terms reminiscent of those addressed in the imperial past to the Son of Heaven. Mao even proposed to fix the succession to power. At the Ninth Party Congress of April 1969, Defense Minister Lin Piao was designated as Mao's "close comrade-in-arms and successor." The action was a mark of the enhanced position enjoyed by the PLA in the Communist hierarchical structure by reason of the critical role it had played in the GPCR.

The Cultural Revolution had once more dislocated economic processes, and the nation's progress toward the creation of a solid power base was again slowed down. Worse, China's foreign relations were pushed into a steep decline, and a major crisis had developed in China's relations with the USSR over border conflicts. But detente was speedily introduced into the country's foreign relations when China turned from Mao's "revolutionary diplomacy" back to the policy of peaceful coexistence and once more presented a bland countenance to the outside world.

The revised policy paid off handsomely. From October 1970 to February 1972, 25 new states accorded diplomatic recognition to the Peking regime. In October 1971, Peking scored a major victory by wresting China's UN seat from the Nationalists in the face of a strong American opposition that had persisted for a full decade. Just four months later President Richard M. Nixon visited Peking, long viewed by American statesmen as the seat of America's irreconcilable enemy.

The CCP achievement after nearly a quarter century of rule is manifestly incomplete. For all of its imperial ambitions, China remains an agricultural society and Mao Tse-tung's dream of the country's becoming an economic power by the end of the century is far from realization. The post-Cultural Revolution political reconstruction is still incomplete. That instability persists at the top of the CCP hierarchy was shown in September 1971, when Mao found it necessary to purge his "close comrade-in-arms and successor" Lin Piao, thus rendering succession less certain than ever. In the realm of international affairs, while moved by the strong urge to resume the prominent role once played as Middle Kingdom, China finds itself encircled by three great powers governed by ideologies that Peking deems inimical to Maoism—the United States, Japan and the Soviet Union. Maoist doctrine demands that the leadership identify the country's principal enemy and subordinate other antagonisms to the primary "contradiction." But Peking in 1971 showed itself frustrated and apparently divided by the problem. For China was manifestly without the power to manipulate any one of its major antagonists against another.

Communist China thus stands at the beginning of the 1970's at an important crossroads discovered earlier on the imperial way: how should the nation attain to wealth and power in a hostile world? If Great Helmsman Mao Tse-tung found the Marxist "democratic centralism" unsatisfactory as a principle of government in "socialist" China, and was unable to provide a "revolutionary succession" for his personal rule, what principles of government will be evolved by the men who rule after him? How shall China advance from Mao's "socialism" into the stage of communism? And how finally shall the nation, discontented with its recent past and its historical lot, fit into a world of warring states that denies the preeminence of Chinese orthodoxy? One thing seems certain at the beginning of the 1970's: the process of change that began in the 19th century has not yet ended.

O. Edmund Clubb

THE GREAT
CONTEMPORARY
ISSUES

CHINA

CHAPTER 1

End of the Imperial Era
1900–11

*U.S. Marines defend legation
quarters at Peking during
the Boxer Rebellion.*

AN ULTIMATUM TO CHINA

Powers Demand Suppression of the Society of Boxers.

Will Land Troops Unless This Is Done Within Two Months — Minister Conger Must Act Alone.

LONDON, April 7.—A special dispatch from Shanghai announces that the American, British, German, and French Ministers have sent a joint note to the Chinese Foreign Office demanding the total suppression of the Society of Boxers within two months, and announcing that, otherwise, the powers mentioned will land troops and march into the interior northern provinces, Shan-Tung and Chi-Li, in order to secure the safety of foreigners.

According to the same dispatch the American, Italian, and French Legations are now provided with naval guards from the large gathering of warships at Taku.

WASHINGTON, April 7.—It is said at the State Department that nothing has been heard from United States Minister Conger within the last few days to indicate any substantial change in the situation in Shan-Tung. The Minister has not informed the department of the reported concerted action of the representatives of the foreign powers at Peking. It is known here that so far as the United States Minister is concerned, nothing has been done by him to commit the United States Government to action in the combination with the powers.

Mr. Conger's instructions enable him to make as strong a presentation as he may deem necessary of the desire of his Government that full protection should be extended to the American residents in China. It was entirely competent for him to couch this demand in strong language, and even to intimate the intention of the United States Government to undertake, through its own agencies, to supply the needed protection to our citizens, should the Chinese Government fail in its duty in that matter. In doing this, Mr. Conger might have acted in precisely the same line as representatives of some of the great European powers at Peking, but the officials are confident that he did not become a party to any concert of action.

The United States Minister was specifically instructed on this point, that he must act on his own responsibility, and, while his course might lie parallel to that followed by the other Ministers resident in Peking, he must under no circumstances join with them in concert.

Just how far the Minister has gone in the direction indicated is at present unknown here. The naval officers do not believe that he has yet summoned a naval force from Admiral Watson's command to guard his Legation at Peking, for in such case they assume that the naval commander addressed would have notified the Navy Department by cable. The Minister appears to have anticipated the necessity for something of the kind, however, for a month ago he suggested to the State Department the expediency of having a warship from Admiral Watson's fleet sent to a point as near Peking as possible.

The Wheeling was accordingly dispatched from Manila to Taku, which lies at the mouth of the Pei-Ho River. The Wheeling, from her light draught, may easily ascend the river as far as Tien-Tsin, one of the storm centres at this moment, and a point giving easy access by rail to Peking. It was over this route that marines were sent to Peking from one of the United States warships about a year ago.

CHINESE CAPITAL MENACED

"Boxers" March on Peking— Train Service to Tien-Tsin Ceases.

DIPLOMATIC CORPS MEETS

Foreign Guards to be Brought to the Capital—Admiral Kempff at Taku.

PEKING, May 28.—The Diplomatic Corps is now in session considering the situation caused by the "Boxers."

The foreign guards will certainly be brought here.

The position of affairs is alarming.

Railway communication with Tien-tsin is interrupted.

TIEN-TSIN, May 28.—The "Boxers" burned the Liulino Station, on the Luhan Railway, twenty-nine miles from Peking, last night. They also wrecked the track, destroyed a number of cars, and murdered several Chinese employes.

The "Boxers" are marching on Peking.

The British and Belgians have left Fingtai and the "Boxers" are expected there to-day. A relief train is bringing the refugees to Tien-Tsin.

Train service between Peking and Tien-Tsin has been suspended since noon to-day.

The United States cruiser Newark and a French man-of-war have arrived at Taku.

SHANGHAI, May 28.—The troubles arising from the defeat of the Government troops by the "Boxers" have extended to Luhan, where work on the railway is almost completely stopped.

Five hundred refugees have sought protection in the French Cathedral at Peking.

It is reported that while retreating several Belgians and their families were cut off at Chang-Hsin-Tein, ten kilometres from Feng-Tai. They are now defending themselves on a hill.

The "Boxers" are now burning Feng-Tai.

Several missionaries have been cut off at Pao-Ting-Fu.

THE REBELLION IN CHINA

"Boxers" Said to Have Support of the Imperial Troops.

MASSACRE AT PEKING FEARED

Rebels Massed Outside—Foreign Envoys Call for Guards—Nine Methodist Missionaries Killed.

LONDON, May 30.—The Daily Express has the following from Shanghai, dated Tuesday:

"The rebellion continues to grow in intensity, and the gravest fears are entertained of its ultimate extent. The foreign envoys at Peking, fearing a massacre within the capital, have decided to bring up the guards of the legations.

"The rebels are now massing outside of Peking, and their numbers are reported to be constantly augmenting. Fresh contingents of armed malcontents are coming up almost hourly from the north.

"The imperial troops who were sent to disperse the rebels found themselves hopelessly outnumbered. Several hundreds were killed, and two guns and many rifles were captured, after which the greater part of the remaining troops went over to the rebels. They are now marching side by side.

"It is believed that the 'Boxers' have the sympathy of the entire Manchu Army in the anti-foreign crusade; and there is no doubt that they have the countenance of the Empress Dowager and of Prince Ching.

"The Belgian Minister, escorted by a strong body guard, has gone to obtain an audience of the Tsung-li-Yamen, a number of his countrymen, with their families, having been cut off by the rebels at Chang-hsin-tien.

"The position of the missionaries is one of extreme peril, unless aid is speedily forthcoming. It is feared that they will meet with the same fate as their unfortunate converts, whom the 'Boxers' are ruthlessly murdering."

Another dispatch from Shanghai says:

"It is believed that Russia is about to land troops at Taku from Port Arthur, where 20,000 men are in readiness. The Chinese are reported to be sending large masses of troops overland from Hu-nan and Kiang, but the Generalissimo refuses to assume command on the plea of sickness.

"The 'Boxers' assert that they are confident of receiving support from the Dowager Empress, Princes Kang-yi and Ching-Tuan, and the entire Manchu army. Throughout the North the 'Boxers' are enlisting hordes of desperadoes. They are intent upon expelling everything foreign."

The Peking correspondent of The Times, telegraphing Tuesday, says:

"The foreign guards have been summoned by the legations and will arrive immediately. This decision was well taken. The opinion is widespread that the powers should compel China to defray the cost of a measure which the apathy of the Chinese Government necessitates. All the French engineers and their families are reported safe."

The Times, commenting upon the situation in Peking, says:

"We must follow the excellent example set us by the Americans and must lose no time in telling the Tsung-li-Yamen that, unless they re-establish security for the life and property of our fellow-subjects in China without delay we shall take strong measures on our part."

The Times expresses the opinion that Great Britain will have to intervene vigorously for the defense of the elementary rights of British subjects.

SHANGHAI, May 29.—The Russian Minister at Peking has telegraphed asking that all the available gunboats be sent to Taku.

TIEN-TSIN, May 29.—A hundred American marines from the United States cruiser Newark are expected here at 11 o'clock to-night.

An armed rescue party of Frenchmen and Germans started this afternoon to try to relieve the besieged Belgians. The Viceroy, under the pressure of the French Consul, has permitted the rescuers to travel by railroad to Feng-tai, where Chinese protection ends.

A detachment of 200 Chinese soldiers has cleared the railway between here and Peking, and the ordinary service was resumed at noon.

Thirty Japanese have arrived from the gunboat Atagokan. The French flagship and the gunboat Surprise have left Taku.

PEKING, May 29.—The relief party has returned from Chang-hsin-tien, bringing twenty-five persons, including several women and children.

MINISTER CONGER ASKS AID.

Authorization Sent Him to Call on Nearest American Naval Vessel.

WASHINGTON, May 29.—Such advices as have reached here indicate that the situation in China has assumed a very critical phase, and one calculated to tax the entire resources of the Chinese Government. The State Department has been in close communication wi h Mr. Conger, the Minister at Peking, and the Navy Department is doing its share, having placed the flagship Newark as far up the Pei-ho River as the Taku forts, which is the nearest point to Peking that the ship can reach.

The operations of the "Boxers" are increasing in magnitude. Their demonstrations are no longer local, and they appear to be governed in their movements by some well-settled design. They have murdered nine Methodist missionaries in one province, at the town of Pachow, and have closed in on Peking. Meanwhile the Chinese Army is suspected of disloyalty, this belief being strengthened by wholesale desertions of the soldiers to the "Boxers."

Minister Conger has appealed to the State Department for the protection of a marine guard for his legation. The department has promptly sent him an authorization to call upon the nearest United States naval vessel for assitance. It is not known yet whether he has availed himself of the permission. The ship he would naturally look to would be the Newark, and it is assumed that he has already communicated with Admiral Kempff on board that flagship.

According to reports, the Chinese Government has done everything in its power to meet the demands of the diplomatic body at Peking for the dispersion of the "Boxers," but it appears that the uprising is more serious than was at first apprehended, and even the resident Ministers at Peking are inclined to admit that the task is not an easy one for the Chinese Government.

So far all of the measures taken by the State Department look merely to the protection of the American Legation at Peking, the American Consulates in the vicinity, and the lives of such Americans as may be obliged to take refuge therein in the event of general rioting. The State Department is closely adhering to the practice it has always observed of non-interference in the Chinese disturbances, and it is not contemplated that the American forces shall take any part in the contest between the Chinese Government and the "Boxers," though it is assumed that Rear Admiral Remey, the Commander in Chief of the Asiatic Station, will take immediate steps to supply Rear Admiral Kempff, the senior squadron commander, with such naval force as he may need for safeguarding American interests at the treaty ports.

MAY HAVE TO SEND TROOPS

American Soldiers Likely to be Necessary in China.

Administration Realizes that Marines Will, Perhaps, Be Insufficient, and May Draw on Men at Manila.

WASHINGTON, June 15.—It seems probable that, after all, the United States troops in the Philippines will be called upon to furnish a contingent to assist in the rescue of the foreign missionaries in China and in the protection of the foreign embassies and legations.

A great change has come over the Administration in this regard, for as late as yesterday there was a firm determination not to go beyond the employment of marines and sailors. There was still such a purpose when the Cabinet met this morning, and there is even now a disposition to limit the United States forces employed to the navy if sufficient force can be secured from that branch of the service. So inquiries are being made of the Navigation Bureau and of Admiral Remey to see to what extent the United States forces in China can be augmented. It is realized that the small force now engaged is entirely disproportionate, when compared with the foreign contingents, to the interests and duty of the United States.

The newspaper reports that the Chinese imperial troops are opposing the progress of the relief column have given great concern and without doubt have had as much to do with bringing about the determination to increase the United States contingent as have the direct appeals of the friends of the missionaries in the United States.

There is reason to believe, however, that the navy has done all that it can do with safety in China at this stage and that recourse must be had to the army. Already Admiral Remey has indicated that he cannot spare more marines, and he is looking to the Navy Department for another battalion to replace the men he has been obliged to withdraw from the naval station at Cavite to assist Admiral Kempff.

Therefore it is admitted that the Cabinet is seriously considering the dispatch of troops to Tien-Tsin, and it is understood that inquiries are being made, probably directed to Gen. MacArthur, as to the number of troops that can be spared for this emergency and the possibility of securing transportation for them.

The troops could not be gotten to Tien-Tsin in less than a week, even if the order for their employment should go forward to-day.

That the crisis is by no means past, but on the contrary, is rather more acute, is evidenced by a cablegram received by the State Department this morning from the United States Consul at Tien-Tsin, Mr. Ragsdale. He says that the mobs are in control of the native city of Tien-Tsin, and the authorities do not seem to be able to do anything with them. He adds that the foreigners in Tien-Tsin are still safe.

The surprising feature of this telegram is the announcement that the Boxers are operating freely under the very guns of the men of war, for it is understood that several Russian gunboats are lying off Tien-Tsin, which is also the depot of the relief column. Fortunately the Nashville and Monocacy are just about due at Taku, and one or both of these vessels will soon be able to command the situation at Tien-Tsin.

The records of the War Department show that there are now in the City of Manila and vicinity the Fourteenth and Twentieth Infantry, and one battery each of the

Third. Fourth. Fifth, and Sixth Artillery, less than 3,000 soldiers altogether. There are, however, no less than 57,000 soldiers distributed among the various commands outside of Manila, and some of these would certainly be called upon to furnish garrisons for the city in case the beforementioned troops should be sent to China.

Owing to the natural reluctance to employ troops save as a last resort, and the disinclination of the War Department to supply such troops except under pressure, the officials to-day were considering an alternative proposition. This contemplated the putting out of commission of several of the big ships attached to Admiral Remey's fleet, notably the Oregon, and the addition of the sailors and marines so released to Admiral Kempff's landing force. The big ships carry, on an average, more than three hundred men apiece.

There is a growing belief that it will be necessary to organize another expeditionary force at Tien-Tsin to maintain the communications of Admiral Seymour's column, which with limited supplies will be in severe need very shortly unless it can force its way through to Peking.

The Monocacy arrived this afternoon at Taku, and, if there were an emergency, by pushing up the river she could have reached Tien-Tsin before dark. The Monocacy on such a short trip could easily carry fully 500 men in addition to her own crew, so that the safety of the foreigners at Tien-Tsin is probably assured.

The navy has arranged with Quartermaster General Ludington for a battalion of marines, composed of 220 men and eight officers, to Manila on the transport Grant, which sails from San Francisco on July 1.

Should it be decided to send troops from Manila to China, there are now available at Manila the big transports Logan and Warren, with a capacity of about 3,000 troops. The Sherman is due at Manila July 1, and the Pennsylvania and Indiana and several other small craft are also available.

The Cabinet meeting to-day lasted until after 1 o'clock. Much of the time was devoted to the discussion of the Chinese situation. The severance of communication with Peking and the failure to hear from Minister Conger for sixty hours naturally creates considerable anxiety, and the complications in connection with possible future contingencies were talked over. No effort will be spared, should the occasion arise, to protect the lives and property of American citizens.

Secretary Long said there were still 800 marines at Cavite who were available in case of necessity.

Secretary Root declines to discuss the military aspect of the situation. To the newspaper men this afternoon he admitted that the general Chinese situation was discussed at the Cabinet meeting to-day, and that Secretary Hay furnished all the information he had on the subject.

The Secretary was asked whether it had been finally decided to send any troops to China from the Philippines, and replied that it had not. To a further question as to whether there was any prospect of such action, he said he would not undertake to talk about it. He was willing, however, to make the broad, general assertion that troops would be sent to China in case it were found that there was greater necessity for them there than in the Philippines. To another leading question he said that, so far as he was advised, there was nothing in the present situation in China to call for the immediate dispatch of troops from the Philippines.

Information that the United States would probably augment its military force in China was received with very general satisfaction, particularly in British and Japanese circles. Mr. Nabashima, the Japanese Chargé, pointed out that the forwarding of a large military force by any one of the European powers would excite suspicion and opposition, whereas such a course by the United States was absolutely above suspicion. While no joint request had been made on this Government to act, yet, he said, the other powers would speedily acquiesce in the action and applaud its disinterestedness.

The Chinese Minister showed the deepest interest in the course of the United States relative to the dispatch of troops, but in the absence of advices from his Government indicating its policy with regard to such movements, he did not wish to discuss the effect of the action. The Peking Government is maintaining absolute silence throughout the agitation.

GERMAN MINISTER REPORTED KILLED

The Legations in Peking Said to Have Been Destroyed.

CATHOLIC CHURCH BURNED

Battle Between British Marines and Imperial Troops.

Incendiary Fires at Tien-Tsin, Which is Now Cut Off—Chinese Soldiers Join the Boxers.

LONDON, June 17.—A special dispatch received yesterday from Hongkong says all the Peking legations have been destroyed.

It adds that the German Minister, Baron von Ketteler, has been killed.

The latest Chinese reports state that the British marines and sailors fought the troops of Gen. Jung-Fuh-Siangs several hours. Many Chinese were killed.

There is at present no confirmation of either of these reports.

Dispatches from Shanghai dated last evening state that Admiral Seymour's force is in a tight place, between Lang-Fang and Yung-Sun, with enormous masses of soldiery in front, while the Boxers, with more soldiery, are cutting the railway in the rear. The column is reported short of provisions and water. Kiang-Nan Arsenal, outside of Shanghai, is sending vast quantities of munitions north.

A special dispatch from Shanghai, dated yesterday, says that it is reported that after the audience of Sir Claude MacDonald, British Minister to China, with the Tsung-li-Yamen, five foreign Ministers demanded a safe conduct for their servants and their people, notifying the Tsung-li-Yamen that they could no longer maintain relations with the Government.

The answer was: "Certainly not. What other answer could be expected in a civilized country?"

This was followed by an increase of the forces round the gates, and, the next night, widespread incendiarism.

This incendiarism prevailed among the foreign residencies. The massacre of native Christians and other friends of the foreigners was also common.

The buildings of the American missions, the Customs, the mess quarters, and a number of other structures were destroyed. The guards alone saved the foreigners, who, it is stated, are huddled in legations, are very short of food, and are deserted by the native servants.

The last reports which came through Tien-Tsin said that the Boxers had massacred a number of native converts and servants of foreigners in the East City of Peking, besides burning the Catholic Cathedral at Peking.

Dispatches from Tien-Tsin received in Berlin state that the Boxers entered Peking on the evening of June 13, destroyed several missions, and attacked the legations, but were repulsed with the aid of Maxims. No Europeans were reported killed. The attitude of the Chinese troops toward the Boxers was uncertain.

A dispatch from Shanghai, dated June 16, says:

"Last night advices from Tien-Tsin report that large incendiary fires occurred in the eastern part of the city, where three English and American churches were burned, besides the residences of many foreigners.

"Telegraphic communication is interrupted, the poles having been burned, and there is no hope of immediate repairs being made."

According to information received at Shanghai, 10,000 imperial troops which were between Peking and the international forces advancing on that city have disbanded and joined the Boxers.

It is asserted that the Government of China does not consider itself responsible for any encounter which may take place.

All is quiet at Shanghai, but trade has been disrupted. It is stated there that seven thousand Americans are coming from Manila, and that large forces of Japanese are also en route.

Latest Chinese reports state that the Empress has ordered Liu-Kung-Yin, Chang-Chi-Tung, and Li Hung Chang to hasten to Peking. They will probably find an excuse for declining.

The latest edict against the rioters especially avoids mentioning the Boxers.

A Cabinet meeting held to-day under the Presidency of Lord Salisbury was concerned almost wholly with the situation in China.

Berlin and St. Petersburg dispatches assert that Russia and Germany have combined for common action in China. It is reported that a high Russian personage is going to Berlin to arrange details, and that Russia does not wish to compromise hopelessly her relations with China by a rupture which would only be to the advantage of other powers.

SHANGHAI, June 16.—The train conveying the relieving party with food and ammunition for the international force was obliged to return, being unable to reach Lang-Fang, where detachments of foreign troops, dispatched on Sunday last, are now endeavoring to repair the line.

The native banks at Chin-Kiang closed business yesterday, fearing trouble from the "Boxers."

Excitement prevails in the Yang-Tsze Valley, but all is quiet at Chee-Foo, in spite of alarming rumors to the contrary.

HONGKONG, June 16.—Trouble is brewing near West River. Riots have broken out at Bun-Chow, whence over a hundred refugees arrived at Wu-Chow on June 12.

About 5,000 rebels have assembled at Kwei-li-Sien. Bodies of Canton troops passed through Wu-Chow on June 11 on their way to meet the rebels.

According to a special dispatch from Vienna, on the other hand, it is stated in diplomatic circles there that the question of intervention is under discussion by the powers. It is proposed that Japan act as mandatory of the powers, and re-establish order in Peking and elsewhere. This suggestion, it is said, emanates from Great Britain, and is supported by Germany and Austria, but it is doubtful if Russia and France will agree to the proposition.

LONDON TOPICS OF THE WEEK

Thorough Analysis of the Cause of the Peking Reign of Terror.

ADMIRALS TOO PRECIPITATE

Kempff's Foresight Appreciated in the Light of Subsequent Events.

Patience and Diplomacy Might Have Saved the Situation—Russia the Jealous Obstacle in the Way of Japan's Intervention.

Special Cable to THE NEW YORK TIMES.
Copyright, 1900.

LONDON, July 7.—One little ray of light from out the gloom has come to us this week, and I allude to it first, as the rest of my tale is so gloomy. Sir Frederic M. Hodgson, Governor of the Gold Coast Colony, has escaped from Kumassi, and may be expected at Cape Coast Castle almost immediately. This unhappily does not mean that the black uprising in that country has been quashed, but it may imply the beginning of a return to order and settled government.

We have hardly given thought to this petty trouble so absorbed are we in the horrors of China. What to believe of the tales pouring in upon us, we know not, but in spite of an eager desire to believe the best, we begin to fear the worst. Hitherto everybody has tried to keep his courage up by saying, "Oh, that tale comes from Shanghai. You know nothing but lies ever generate there." Or, "Oh, that is a Che-Foo tale. How can they know anything there about what is doing in Peking?"

When, however, day after day stories that substantially agree with each other repeat the same harrowing information of Europeans massacred, Embassies stormed and burned, the Manchu Government overthrown with its Emperor dead and its usurping Empress dying, it is impossible to resist the dread that the worst may be true. Should authentic news reach Europe that all the whites in Peking have been murdered, or all who could not escape through the friendly co-operation of natives, then I fear the most uncontrollable storm of indignation will arise in this country against Russia, a storm all the greater because we ourselves are in no small measure to blame for the precipitate manner in which the rebellion has laid hold of China in the north and threatens to overwhelm it in the Middle Kingdom and the south.

RUSSIA BLAMED.

Had it not been for the obstruction of Russia it is contended that Japanese troops in sufficient numbers might have been landed on the coast of China in time to overawe the Chinese rabble and troops, and rescue the Europeans in the capital. Russia is still, it seems, obstructing action by Japan, which has an army ready for transport, having foreseen the storm before anybody in Europe had the slightest suspicion of it. We have gone as far as to intimate to Japan that we are perfectly willing for her to intervene and endeavor to put an end to the troubles until Europe can bring her forces up to bear upon them. Russia stands in the way, is jealous of Japan, and prefers, apparently, that thousands of lives should be sacrificed rather than allow Japan a foothold on the mainland and the chance of establishing her claim to Korea or to other territory there when the division of the spoil comes.

It will be a great pity should angry passions arise in this manner at the very outset of these troubles, but it never requires much to inflame us against Russia. Our habitual attitude of mind is jealousy of her. In our heat, we have altogether overlooked the fact that if the English Admiral on the spot had taken up the position adopted by your Admiral Kempff an outbreak of popular fury might have been postponed.

∴

MURAVIEFF'S ADVICE.

You know the story of how the late Count Muravieff, the Russian Foreign Minister, counseled that a show of force should make the pretext that the Chinese were laying torpedoes in the mouth of the river at Taku to enable the Admirals to send an ultimatum. This was sent, and, being disregarded, gave them the requisite excuse to open bombardment upon these forts preparatory to their capture. From the moment the first shot was fired by the European fleets the populace between the coast and Peking—all over North China, we may say—got completely out of hand and it is now not merely Europeans who are hunted but the Manchus.

It may be that our action has overthrown the Manchu dynasty, and that of itself would undoubtedly be a blessing for China, but it has done more. It has put an end to any semblance of order in the empire, and it has opened the door to the lawless in every province to arise against the authorities and put them at defiance, to wreak their vengeance not only on foreigners but on personal enemies, creditors, Viceroys, and functionaries of every description. And Europe is totally unprepared to cope with this upheaval. It will be no more prepared within another three months, during which time over the greater part of the Chinese Empire lawlessness may prevail unchecked.

∴

VAIN HOPE IN THE VICEROYS.

It is vain to cling to the hope that the Viceroys in the Yang-Tse Provinces can keep order, can force their troops to quell disturbances. In all probability these Viceroys will soon be trembling for their lives. We have kindled a fire in short that we are totally without the means to quench, and how far it will burn, how much it will destroy, no human being can forecast. Had the Admirals restrained their hands, abstained from attacking the forts at the mouth of the Pei-Ho River, put up with insults and with preparations for vigorous defense by winking at them all, and, had

they at the same time diligently applied diplomatic pressure upon the authorities in Peking to open the way for the Envoys to come to the coast—to bankers, to Europeans in the Imperial Maritimes Customs Service, to tourists, in fact, to everybody in danger—it is possible that we might now be in a position to stand calmly by while the Manchu Governors and the Chinese governed had it out with each other in and around the capital. That is the painful reflection in many peoples' minds to-day.

We were too precipitate in striking the blow and in attempting to descend upon Peking with forces so absolutely inadequate to maintain any position captured, as to cause every subsequent step to appear in the eyes of the Chinese as defeat to the hated foreigners. Our conduct has thus stimulated the rebellion from the beginning unto this hour, and vainly do walls come to us for help from Shanghai, from Canton, from every treaty port almost where Englishmen have settled and do business.

No help can come in time to most of these places unless Russia gives way and allows the active, vigorous Jap to be our savior. We have no men apart from our Indian native troops, and few of these could be mustered without grave inconvenience to Indian finance. If it comes to that, all the powers, except perhaps you, are confoundedly hard up at the present time, caught unawares with their resources engaged upon extensive projects of naval expansion or internal industrial development.

∴

HOW EUROPE IS HANDICAPPED.

Russia, as an example, has already spent more than £50,000,000 on her Siberian Railway, and it will cost her quite another £50,000,000 before it is completed. Germany is in the throes of an industrial crisis, as you well know, has been wrestling with it for more than a year back, and has not mastered it yet. France is again wealthy, though her people are, as a Government, chronically hard up. If Germany, France, and ourselves are each to put 20,000 men in China, as one story has it, all the budgets will be disarranged by the effort, and the 60,000 men are of no use whatever. It will take 500,000 soldiers to master the coast and the river provinces of China, if the rebellion spreads and gets any headway. Russia has men enough, but very little money, just like the rest of us. Japan, too, is poor enough, if it come to that, but, being handily placed, could do more than any European power at less cost, and it would be worth a high price to get her services as a relief to the pressure otherwise thrown upon the budgets of European powers.

It is profitless, however, to discuss what is to be done just yet. We are sick about it and are much at sea and incapable of making up our minds, groping more or less in the dark after a policy, seeking for somebody to sacrifice as a stop to popular resentment, and amid all clinging to the hope that the actual worst may be better than the lurid pictures of it, coming over to us almost hourly, force us to dread.

I need say nothing about South Africa this week. It stands much where it did—marching and counter-marchings and convergings to surround De Wet, peace one day and fighting the next, the Boers giving up their arms and coming in and other Boers nabbing up patrols, stealing provisions of our armies, and generally floundering about the country with the energy of men in despair, yet determined not to submit.

ALLIES' ADVANCE BEGUN.

BRUSSELS, Aug. 1.—M. de Favereau, Minister of Foreign Affairs, has received the following dispatch, dated Shanghai, Aug. 1, from M. de Cartier de Marchienne, Secretary of the Belgian Legation, now acting as Belgian Chargé d'Affaires at Shanghai:

"The allies are marching on Peking. They are eighteen miles from Tien-Tsin and should reach Peking in eight days."

———

LONDON, Aug. 2.—"The allies began the advance from Tien-Tsin this morning," announced an agency bulletin dated at Shanghai at 11:10 A. M. yesterday. It is assumed that the Americans, British, and Japanese are taking part in this forward movement, whether other nationalities are or not. An advanced base will probably be established twenty or thirty miles nearer Peking, and supplies will be assembled preparatory to a direct stroke at the capital.

Gen. Sir Alfred Gaselee is quoted as saying on July 28 that he was ready to advance, although lacking in artillery. Col. Daggett, commanding the Americans at Tien-Tsin, is also credited with a similar statement on the same date, although utterly without transportation, not even having a horse for himself.

Reinforcements are reported to have been sent to the Chinese at Yang-Tsun, where strong intrenchments have been thrown up to bar the advance of the allies.

Of the 60,000 allies debarked at Pe-chi-Li ports, British military observers consider that 30,000 are available for an advance beyond Tien-Tsin. The Chinese forces, according to the vague gatherings of the allies' intelligence officers, were up to July 27 disposed in a great arc thirty miles long. The numbers and exact location of the several divisions are unknown. The Pei-ho is blockaded by sunken stone-laden junks for twenty miles beyond Tien-Tsin, and further up, according to Chinese spies of the allies, a dam has been constructed for the purpose of flooding the low-lying expanse of country.

Information was brought to Tien-Tsin on Wednesday, July 25, by a Chinese missionary student who was sent to the British Legation at Peking. He was unable to deliver the message intrusted to him, and left Peking on July 18. He saw a few troops between Peking and Yang-Tsun. No works had been constructed. Food in Peking was scarce, and the student said the city would be quite unable to endure a siege.

ALLIED TROOPS ARE IN PEKING

Enter City from the East and Surround Legations.

THE EMPRESS A FUGITIVE

She and Tuan Said to Have Fled to Hsian-Foo.

Japanese Report Says Chinese Resisted at Peking Obstinately — British Troops to Land at Shanghai To-day.

The United States Consul at Che-Foo, reporting information received from the Japanese Admiral, sent word in a cablegram received last evening that the allies attacked Peking from the east last Wednesday.

After an obstinate resistance, the Japanese in the evening entered the city "with the other forces."

The allies immediately surrounded the legations, the inmates of which were safe.

Admiral Remey, in a dispatch received at about the same time, says he has received word that Peking was captured on Aug. 15, and that the legations are safe.

The Dowager Empress, with Prince Tuan and the greater part of the army, are reported to have fled to Hsian-Foo. Some reports say that the Emperor was taken there against his will.

The British troops sent to Shanghai are to be landed there to-day.

THE ENVOYS LIBERATED.

WASHINGTON, Aug. 17.—The Acting Secretary of State to-night made public the following telegram, received from the United States Consul at Che-Foo:

Che-Foo, Aug. 17, 1900. (Received Aug. 17, 7:55 P. M.)

Secretary of State, Washington.

Seventeenth.—Japanese Admiral reports allies attacked Peking, east, 15th. Obstinate resistance. Evening, Japanese entered capital with other forces. Immediately surrounded legations. Inmates safe. Japanese loss over 100. Chinese, 300.

FOWLER.

The Navy Department to-night received the following cablegram from Admiral Remey:

Taku, Aug. 17, 1 A. M.

Bureau Navigation, Washington.

Just received telegram from Tien-Tsin dated 16th, 10 P. M.: "Peking was captured on Aug. 15. Foreign legations are safe. Details follow shortly."

Remey.

LONDON, Aug. 18.—" Peking was relieved on the night of the 15th."

This message was received last evening at the Imperial Customs Office in London from the Commissioner of Customs in Che-Foo. It is the only official message that has reached England in confirmation of the earlier reports, Admiral Remey's dispatch not having arrived in time for publication in the London morning papers.

The first report of the relief of the envoys came from the German Consul at Shanghai, who wired to the Foreign Office at Berlin as follows:

" The allies have entered Peking without fighting. The legations are relieved, and the foreigners are liberated."

The Morning Post, which is the only paper printing the Che-Foo message, says editorially:

" To-day is not only a day of national rejoicing; it is also a day of congratulation for all the powers of the world."

The collapse of Chinese resistance is explained in dispatches from Shanghai as being due to the failure of the Chinese to flood the country below Tung-Chow. The earthworks connected with the dam of the Pei-Ho were unfinished, and the canal at Tung-Chow was full of water, facilitating boat transport when the allies arrived there.

Signals between the allies and the legationers holding part of the wall of Peking were exchanged during the morning of Aug. 15.

BERLIN, Aug. 17.—The news regarding the entrance of the allies into Peking was further confirmed to-day by two telegrams received by the Japanese Legation in Berlin.

One, dated Aug. 14, said the allied forces were only ten li (three and one-third miles) from the capital, and the other briefly announced that they had entered the city.

EMPRESS FLEES TO HSIAN-FOO.

LONDON, Aug. 18.—A dispatch from Shanghai says:

" The allies entered Peking Aug. 15.

" It is believed that Yuan-Shi-Kai's troops have gone thence to Shen-Si to protect the Empress, who, according to reports received by local officials here, with Tuan, the imperial household, and the bulk of the army and Boxers, left Peking on Aug. 7 for Hsian-Foo.

Other Shanghai dispatches say that Emperor Kwang-Su accompanied the Empress Dowager to Hsian-Foo much against his will. Prince Tuan, it is added, commanded the rear guard of the imperial escort, of

which Boxers formed 65 per cent. It was expected that Gen. Tung-Fu-Siang would follow after the arrival of the allies.

All the palace treasures were sent to Hsian-Foo.

POWERS' TASK NOT ENDED.

BERLIN, Aug. 17.—The German press, while expressing joy at the happy discharge of one part of the China programme in the relief of the envoys, points out that there is much left to be done. The Berliner Post says:

" A great thing has been done, but a greater must be done before the allied powers will be satisfied. It remains to obtain redress for the attacks upon the legations and other wrongs, particularly the assassination of the German Minister, and to install a government which will punish the guilty and give ample guarantees against the recurrence of similar crimes."

The National Zeitung, the Freisinnige Zeitung, and the Vossische Zeitung express themselves in a similar strain.

Germany, beyond any doubt, is preparing for an Autumn and Winter campaign in China.

One striking evidence of this is the fact that a slow steamer has been chartered for December to carry to China material for a sixty-mile field railroad.

Referring to a number of special dispatches appearing in German papers, which claim that the United States Government, now that the members of the Peking legations are relieved, is about to withdraw from the international undertaking, a high official of the German Foreign Office said this evening:

" The Washington Government has assured the other powers of its willingness to co-operate in carrying out a joint programme. This assurance has sufficed so far, and will continue to suffice, in spite of newspaper stories to the contrary."

John B. Jackson, United States Chargé d'Affaires, said:

" The United States Government has acted with the greatest harmony regarding China from the outset. In fact, up to Peking the powers are all agreed; but beyond that no agreement has even been attempted. The future must be left to new diplomatic negotiations."

LONDON, Aug. 18.—Discussing the probabilities of a cessation of hostilities in China, The Morning Post assumes that the United States is willing to abandon any idea of further aggressive action, but it questions the disposition of Germany and the other powers to agree to such a course.

The Berlin correspondent of The Morning Post says that he learns that no formal request for an armistice has yet reached the powers, and that it is improbable that any such request would be granted.

The other papers comment guardedly upon the general situation, owing to the lack of definite news when the editorials were written. Most of them advocate a stern inquisition regarding outrages, and the punishment of the leaders, even if they have to be pursued all over China.

CONVERTS TO BE PROTECTED.

WASHINGTON, Aug. 17.—A Cabinet official said to-day that unquestionably the native Christians in China, said to number several thousand, will be included in any arrangement made between this Government and China incident to the cessation of hostilities.

At the present stage of the Chinese situation this subject has not been seriously discussed by the Cabinet, but there is no doubt, according to this member, that the United States is honor bound to protect them, and will sacredly look out for their security.

" What will be done with them?" was asked.

" That has not been decided," was the reply, " but rest assured that in their disposition the honor of the United States will be fully preserved. It may be arranged for them to go to the Philippines, or one of many other plans that are available may be adopted."

It also was stated that, while the matter has not been formally considered, the indemnity to be collected by the United States will be not only for the families of the victims, but also probably to compensate this Government for the expense to which it has been put in prosecuting the campaign.

" It has not been a heavy expense, compared to the Spanish war." the same official said, "but it will be sufficient, together with the indemnity to the families of missionaries and other victims, and for all loss to property of the United States Government or of American citizens, to make it a very serious matter, financially, to China."

HISTORY OF THE SIEGE.

The siege of the foreigners in the Chinese capital lasted fifty-six days. The bombardment of the legations, in which, with the exception of some of the Roman Catholic missionaries, all the aliens in Peking had assembled for safety, was begun on June 20. Previous to this, however, the Europeans, Americans, and Japanese had been virtually prisoners for three weeks. News that the Japanese Chancellor of Legation had been killed was received on June 12, and five days later it was learned that the German Minister, Baron von Ketteler, had been assassinated by members of Dowager Empress Tse-Hsi-An's bodyguard.

It was on May 29 in response to urgent requests from the envoys that an international force of marines was landed at Taku. They were at once sent on to Peking. They went by train, and found little obstruction on the way. The force consisted of 350 officers and men, made up of marines of the six principal powers. Three days after their arrival at Peking, on June 3, all railroad traffic between Peking and Tien-Tsin was suspended, and communication with the legations was cut off. An attempt had been made to keep this open by means of a line of marines along the railway, but the Boxers, on June 5, attacked and defeated the men guarding the line.

Then began the period of terrible suspense, with continual reports of the killing of all the foreigners in the city, which only ended on July 30, when unmistakably authentic cipher messages were received from three of the Ministers.

The full history of the siege and bombardment of the legations cannot, of course, be told till the rescued men and women shall have been able to communicate fully with Europe and America. It appears, however, that about the middle of June the Chinese Imperial Government—or those who had usurped its power—ordered the Ministers to leave Peking in twenty-four hours. This they refused to do. A very few days afterward the greater portion of the legation buildings had been demolished by bombardment. The Italian, Dutch, Spanish, Russian, Austrian, German, Japanese, and part of the French Legations are believed to have been destroyed.

All the women and children belonging to the legations took refuge in the British building, which is the largest of the legation structures and the best situated for defense, as it is surrounded by a large inclosure, which has prevented the Chinese approaching near enough to set fire to it.

Whether the legations were supplied with food by the Chinese is as yet unknown to the outside world, but it is considered probable that some prominent Chinamen, sympathizers with the foreigners, found means to send supplies.

To attempt to give even an outline of the multitude of "imperial edicts" dealing with the legationers would be impossible in limited space. To say that these were contradictory is hardly to describe them. They contained an amount of tergiversation which has amazed even those who are familiar with the tortuous character of Chinese diplomacy, and it was this, more than the silence of the envoys, which made the world believe the worst as to their fate.

On July 16 civilized mankind was horrified to read a ghastly and detailed account of the alleged massacre in Peking. It was sent from Shanghai to The Daily Mail of London, and seemed to leave no room for doubt that all the foreigners, 1,000 in number, including nearly 400 soldiers, 100 members of the Chinese customs staff, and a number of women and children, had been killed. The report even went the length of stating that the defenders of the legations had shot the women and children to prevent them falling into the hands of the Chinese.

On June 11 a relief force commanded by Admiral Seymour set out from the coast. It comprised 1,944 marines of various nationalities. This force was stopped at Lang-Fang by a large Chinese army, and was compelled to retreat to Tien-Tsin, short of provisions and harassed by Chinese hordes.

The movement which has resulted in the relief of the legations began on Aug. 2, when the advance guard of 16,000 allies began their march from Tien-Tsin. The history of this movement is too recent to need recapitulation.

CHINA IS LIKELY TO ACCEPT ALLIES' TERMS

But Execution of the Princes Is Believed to be Impossible.

JAPAN'S MYSTERIOUS MOVES

Li Made Generalissimo of Northern Army—Sir Robert Hart to Arrange Indemnities.

LONDON, Nov. 14.—Dr. Morrison, wiring to The Times, expresses the opinion that China will "readily accede to all the terms of the conjoint note except the execution of the Princes and officials, which it will be impossible to fulfill while the Court is in the hands of these very officials."

"Considerable curiosity is felt at Tien-Tsin," says the Shanghai correspondent of The Times, "as to the whereabouts of the Japanese forces, which, though not leaving the country, are disappearing from Peking and Tien-Tsin. It is not known whither."

It is asserted in Shanghai that the Empress Dowager has appointed Sir Robert Hart, Director of Chinese Imperial Maritime Customs, to arrange the indemnity question with the powers.

An imperial edict appoints Li-Hung-Chang to replace Gen. Yung-Lu as Generalissimo of the northern army.

The London morning papers are again agitated concerning the stability of the concert of powers. The attitudes of Germany and the United States meet with disapproval, the former because Count von Waldersee has sent a column to destroy the Ming tombs, an act which is regarded as needlessly vindictive, and the latter because it threatens to break up the concert. The Times says:

"The United States accepted the German note demanding the punishment of Prince Tuan and the other guilty officials, and it will not be harder to secure the punishment of eleven officials than of the three whose names were originally indicated by the State Department. Therefore it is difficult to see how America could justify in her own eyes a refusal to join with the other powers in steps needful to secure this result."

The Daily Chronicle comments strongly upon the American attitude as a "feeble compromise which it is impossible to accept."

The Morning Post says: "It would be unreasonable for the United States to break up the concert because they do not desire

indemnity. The powers would probably be willing to consider America's objections. If, however, the United States have in view some new combination of powers, it would be necessary for Great Britain and Germany to agree upon a common policy to be pursued in the absence of a general agreement."

The Standard, which dismisses the subject with a mere reference, says: "American opinion on the Chinese problem is too uncertain to be considered seriously."

BERLIN, Nov. 13.—A semi-official dispatch from Peking, dated yesterday, gives the text of the conjoint note of the powers to China, confirming the terms as published yesterday. Among the additional stipulations, the note requires China to erect expiatory monuments in every foreign or international burial ground where graves have been profaned.

WASHINGTON, Nov. 13.—The Chinese question was discussed by the Cabinet to-day in a general way. It was stated by one member that the Government had received no confirmation of the story cabled by Dr. Morrison to The London Times to the effect that the Ministers had formulated demands on the Chinese Government.

Another member, discussing this dispatch said that previous advices to this Government indicated that Dr. Morrison's dispatch was a very fair exposition of the demands that had been formulated by the Ministers. He said, however, that there was considerable doubt as to the ability of the Chinese Government as now constituted to enforce the execution of the eleven powerful officials indicated in the dispatch.

In addition to the points said to be agreed upon at Peking as a basis for settlement with China, it is understood that several other points are likely to receive attention when the matter is taken up with the Chinese envoys. One of these is as to making the City of Peking an "open port," for, while it is not on the seacoast, the purpose is to extend to it that freedom of commerce and intercourse with foreigners which now applies only to those open ports designated by treaties with China.

Another point which may be proposed is that capital punishment, by beheading or otherwise, shall not occur in future by imperial edict alone, but only after a trial such as is given in civilized countries, the accused having an opportunity to be heard. This does not apply to the executions made necessary by the Boxer movement.

ST. PETERSBURG, Nov. 13.—The Novoe Vremya says it believes that the powers are becoming convinced that China is unable to pay a war indemnity and that this discovery will cool the Anglo-German war fever.

In the first of a series of articles on the relations between Japan and Russia the Novoe Vremya makes the prediction—probably inspired—that the estrangement between the two countries will be transient. The article recalls the former testimonials of Russian friendship for Japan and the pedagogic services rendered the Mikado's army and navy by Russia. The Novoe Vremya asserts that the differences existing between the two Governments are due to West European powers, who inspired the Japanese ambition to acquire Korea.

The Bourse Gazette demands that Russia, the United States, France, and Japan shall open peace negotiations with China.

EMPRESS PLAYED AND LOST

Chinese Ruler's Fatal Mistake in Not Restraining the Boxers.

PLANNED ORGANIZED RISING

Imperial Edicts Worthless — Probable Dethronement—Evidence that She Actuated the Anti-Foreign Movement.

Foreign Correspondence NEW YORK TIMES.

PEKING, Oct. 13.—Chinese diplomacy stops at nothing, under one reading of the imperial edict, decreeing the punishment of the anti-foreign leaders. If read another way the edict means that the Dowager Empress sees an opportunity, which she is glad to embrace, to rid herself of a member of her household, in Prince Tuan, who could soon compass her own downfall.

Royal secrets are not yet sufficiently disclosed to explain the dominant influence of this man. Perhaps the Empress needed no prompting in the anti-foreign movement. There is reason to believe that she initiated it. But when she named Prince Tuan's son as the next Emperor she had a prompter. Since then Tuan has outgrown every figure at court. If the Empress felt herself dwindling beside him, she might well have feared that next year, when the lad will be old enough to be crowned, her career would end, if Tuan were about. She has not played at politics all her life to so little purpose as to be eased by that prospect. Tuan's exile might bar the succession, or install the new Emperor as her tool, whichever suited her.

To what lengths the present military policy of the allies may lead no one predicts. It would seem to point to the dethronement of the Dowager Empress, if nothing more serious befalls her; to the restoration of the Emperor, with a liberal Cabinet of advisers, and to severe punishment, probably by death, of the leaders in the anti-foreign movement. If the military forces be unhampered, as practically they have been so far, they will force those demands to some conclusion.

Suggestions from the Ministers, while civilly received, get little encouragement, except as they fall in with military notions. While it is commonly recognized that civil authority may at any time become supreme, it has been so far unmistakably subordinate, as if the commanders had been given to understand from home that there would be no interference with them until further notice. That understanding suits them so well that they scout propositions to stop short of the plans outlined as a pretense for inviting further trouble in order that another expedition may be sent here, to make two jobs, when one should be sufficient.

When the negotiators, now here and trying to appear industrious, can positively report progress, pending the execution of the military plans, it will be time to believe that the home Governments have directed another course in Chinese affairs than that followed unvaryingly and consistently up to this time. Appearances may mislead, because in a few weeks the weather will forbid large military movements, while rumor is as impervious to cold in China as elsewhere. Hence things accomplished rather than proposed should alone be accepted without reserve.

ORIGIN OF THE RISING.

The dethronement of the Empress is forecast on the ground that she actuated the anti-foreign movement. Evidence in that line is cumulative and seems not to lack plausibility. She has held upon power a grasp too firm to make it conceivable that such a movement could have advanced against her will. The story is that after the seizure of Kiau-Chow by the Germans, three years ago, and the subsequent demands resulting in the lease of Port Arthur and Ta-lien-wan to Russia—which was also sending garrisons into Manchuria—Wei-Hai-Wei to England, and the Bay of Kwang-Chau-Wan, with its islands, to France, she concluded that the foreigners were taking advantage of China's weakened condition, following the Japanese war, and that these leases were the beginning of territorial encroachments designed to leave her without an empire.

She summoned her Generals in the northern provinces, and through them took vigorous measures to strengthen the defenses and to improve the efficiency of the army with the primary view of resisting the invasion which she feared, and in the hope that she might be prepared to carry this policy as far as circumstances required, even to the expulsion of all foreigners from China. Her Generals took measures in accordance with her instructions, and fresh orders for arms and ammunition went forward to Europe on a large scale.

The Boxer Society was one of many patriotic bodies, something on the Know-Nothing order, but not distinctively so until the widespread military activity and the leakage of imperial wishes vitalized it for the purposes that afterward made it notorious. Responsibility for the leakage may not be assigned to individual betrayal, but rather to the bustle of military preparation which charged the atmosphere with anti-foreign sentiment. There could hardly have been distinct avowal to the Boxer leaders that the Empress favored the policy of exclusion, but they understood without being told that they might safely develop their principles along practical lines.

Something like a craze for the thing was started. It appealed not only to fanaticism, prevalent in the northwest among the Mohammedans, but a mystic quality which invested it made it specially attractive to thousands. The creed that devotees of Boxer rites became invulnerable found believers among the multitudes, and even natives who rank as highly intelligent subscribed to it; evidence to the contrary proving to the native mind merely that the victims lacked faith or were not sufficiently advanced in the order to enjoy its full benefits.

This society was not discouraged, because it suited the general plan of exclusion. Its activities, manifested first in Shan-Tung, when Yü-Hsien was Viceroy, furnished the designation for a movement much broader in its inception than the work of a non-official society could have become. Army preparations had not advanced to the point of readiness for aggression when the Shan-Tung murders occurred, and of course the Empress had excuses ready and a basket of regrets for every foreign complaint regarding them. The demand for Yü-Hsien's removal from office, however, was met in a different way. The Empress sent him from Shan-Tung, where he had done about as much mischief as was possible, to govern Shan-Si, where many helpless foreigners resided. He spared none whom he could kill, boasted of his work, was continued in power, and if the Empress did not thank him by official promulgation, she could hardly have omitted later to express in person her pleasure over what he had done, for she was his guest when she passed through his province on her recent trip westward.

Boxer depredations might well have excited imperial displeasure, because the zeal shown in them and the extent to which they were carried on, brought a foreign fleet to the north coast in advance of the readiness of the army for the work mapped out for it. Capture of the Taku forts and Admiral Seymour's advance precipitated an official movement. It was imperial troops who drove him back, who afterward made such hot work for the allies at Tien-Tsin, and who, in such numbers as could be spared from escort duty in the imperial flight, opposed the march to this city and its occupation. Boxers were along, but the regular army men did the hard fighting.

Had the Boxers been restrained long enough for the completion of imperial plans, foreign losses, considerable as they were, must have been much greater. If the Boxers had waited for the Chinese troops to make the first attack at Tien-Tsin, the foreign settlement could not have been saved, or any one in it. The Boxers warned the foreigners that they were coming by first setting fire to foreign churches in the native city. When they had finished gloating over this destruction and made their raid, the foreigners were ready for them. Troops must certainly have had sense enough to let the churches wait until after the massacre, which would have taken the foreign settlement unawares and have been easily accomplished. This would have added to the mortality list 800 whites and from 1,000 to 1,500 friendly natives quartered there.

FOREIGNERS BLIND TO DANGER.

Of all the marvelous happenings hereabout in late Spring and early Summer the failure to appreciate the situation by those who should have been well informed is most amazing. Even the British Minister, on the eve of the legation siege, when murders had become common and missionaries were seeking safety in flight, laid the troubles to a dry season, and saw no reason why rains should not end them. The Ministers generally held similar views. Intelligent Chinese, whose friendliness and sincerity were undoubted, could not believe that anything graver than an insurrection was possible. Yet all this time the common, ignorant coolies knew what was coming. House servants with families out of the settlements gave up their employment to go home and look after them. Both of these classes warned the foreigners and no one believed them.

With this hold on the credulity of people here and personally observant of affairs, the Empress may well have counted on befooling the outside world, with telegrams declaring that she was protecting the legations, when there were sharpshooters in every vantage point watching for chances to pick off foreigners; guns throwing shells into the legation quarter which destroyed scores of buildings; men prowling about at night to apply the torch, and men digging underground so that the explosion of mines might make certain work where other agencies fell short. All this time she was assuring Europe of her protecting care over the legations, possibly in the hope that the powers might trust the Ministers to her guardianship and not send troops to relieve them. As despatches have reported, provisions and ammunition were nearly exhausted when the troops arrived. Attack could have been resisted only a few days longer.

Diplomatic and military opinion agrees almost without dissent that when the Empress failed to restrain the Boxers, she lost the stake for which she was playing, and exhibited herself as an opportunist rather than as a strategist. Since her troops were to be engaged, she missed it in not taking care that they held others back until they were ready, for then the work might have been thorough. In this view, she was so set on foreign extermination that every life taken or every bit of property destroyed was a move toward the object sought, unmindful of the major plays necessary to win the game. Had she felt that the army was not prepared to resist invasion, but might become so, she might have lulled suspicion everywhere by letting her troops escort and pilot the way here instead of opposing it, and have remained herself to welcome the relief column and bid it godspeed on its early departure, leaving to diplomatic or special agents the indemnity settlements. That course might have left her hope of a renewal of preparations to get rid of foreigners, while now, it is asserted, she has lost that chance forever, unless the troops withdraw from her declared programme unfinished.

Those who urge extreme measures with her have no faith in her edicts. They believe that she will do what may seem to her to be to her personal or immediate advantage and nothing else. Some believe her so heedless of every other consideration that rather than comply with all that is demanded, she will hold the capital at Sian-Foo and let the powers do with Northeastern China as they like, perhaps hoping that they may get into a fight among themselves over it. Her own safety and continuance in power are thought so much to outweigh everything else with her, that she is believed to be willing to chance the resignation of the Viceroys of Nanking, Hankow, Shan-Tung, and the loss of revenue from those rich sources, as are threatened unless the Court is re-established here.

It is upon these grounds that the demands rest. Those who persist in them declare that only in this way can foreign lives or property have any future assurance of safety in China. Indemnity settlements are held to be quite apart from the effective punishment of those responsible for what has occurred. The Boxer rabble cuts small figure in this calculation. Things known to be accomplished will alone be believed, and edicts pass as mere words, which, if authentic, should be placed in parallel columns with the earlier professions regarding the safety of the Ministers.

FREDERICK W. EDDY.

December 9, 1900

8

WHAT CHINA HAS TO PAY.

The Indemnity and Interest Will Amount Altogether to Over $700,000,000, All to be Paid by 1940.

PEKING, July 26.—The Ministers of the Powers, after to-day's meeting, dispatched a note to the Chinese Peace Commissioners formally accepting the recent Chinese offer, which was in anticipation of the Ministers' plan for the payment of 450,000,000 taels as indemnity at 4 per cent. interest, the final payment to be made in 1940.

The total payments of principal and interest will be 1,000,000,000 taels (over $700,-000,000).

The portions of Chinese revenue that are now applied to foreign debts previously incurred will be devoted to the payment of this indemnity whenever those debts be extinguished.

Unless China in the meantime incurs other obligations, she will be free of foreign debt in 1940.

The Ministers of the powers are hopeful that the protocol will be signed in a fortnight.

The subjects of punishments and examinations were practically closed to-day, the Ministers accepting the Chinese statement of what has been accomplished as the best settlement obtainable, although not satisfactory.

Advises Lenient Treatment of China.

PARIS, July 26.—M. Pichon, ex-Minister to China, who is now in Paris, in an interview published to-day, urges the considerate treatment of the Chinese. He believes a policy of violence will lead to even more serious uprisings than the recent troubles. M. Pichon says he does not believe in an immediate "Yellow Peril," as he thinks it will be a long time before the Chinese become dangerous to Europe. Referring to the Japanese, he says this is another matter, and that their progress inspired him with anxiety.

July 27, 1901

CHINESE EDUCATIONAL REFORM.

Edict Abolishing Essay Examinations Promulgated in Su-Chow.

LONDON TIMES—NEW YORK TIMES
Special Cablegram.

LONDON, Oct. 19.—A Chinese Imperial decree, abolishing the literary essay examinations and introducing radical reforms in education, has, says the Shanghai correspondent of The Times, been introduced in Su-Chow. The results of this edict, as affording a test of the sincerity of the Government in connection with the whole subject of reform, are awaited with much interest.

A party of Chinese officials have left Su-Chow for Nanking, from whence they will go to Japan to witness the military manoeuvres, at the invitation of the Mikado.

October 19, 1901

CHINA PROTOCOL IS SIGNED.

Troops of the Powers to Evacuate Public Places in Peking Before Sept. 17.

PEKING, Sept. 7.—The settlement protocol between China and the powers was signed this morning at the Spanish Legation. The Chinese representatives, Li-Hung-Chang and Prince Ching, came in chairs, with a large following of horsemen. Li-Hung-Chang was so feeble that he had to be lifted out of his chair by two men.

The doyen of the Diplomatic Corps, Señor de Cologan, made a brief speech in behalf of the Ministers. He expressed the hope that the signing of the protocol would begin a new era for China in her relations with the powers.

Prince Ching replied that he was glad the horrors of the past year were ended, and trusted there would never be another breach between China and the powers. China, he said, would fulfill all her obligations.

Under the agreement the troops must evacuate public places, including the Forbidden City and the Summer Palace, before Sept. 17, and all the expeditionary troops in the provinces, except the permanent garrisons, must be withdrawn by Sept. 22. The Americans and British are permitted to occupy the temples until their barracks are completed.

Mr. Rockhill, the special representative of the United States, leaves here to-morrow and will embark on board the Empress of China on Oct. 3 at Yokohama.

September 8, 1901

China to Send Students Abroad.

WASHINGTON, Nov. 23.—The State Department has received from Minister Conger, at Peking, translations of two imperial edicts, providing for the establishing of schools throughout the Chinese empire and ordering the Viceroys and Governors to select and send students abroad to be educated in special branches of industrial science. The student, on his return, passes on to the Board of Foreign Affairs, and if this board finds him thoroughly equipped, it is to memorialize the throne and request that honors be conferred upon the student.

November 24, 1901

THE COURT BACK IN PEKING

PEKING, Jan. 7.—The entry of the Emperor and Empress Dowager into Peking to-day was the most remarkable episode in the annals of Kwang-Su's reign, save the fright of the Court when Peking was bombarded by the allied forces.

The spectacular phases of the return of the Court exceeded expectations. The cortège was a sort of glorified Lord Mayor's show, and was a bewildering and barbaric exhibition of Oriental tinseled splendor. The most significant feature of the arrangements was the complete effacement of the traditional deification of Chinese royalty. Greater facilities to witness the ceremonial were given to foreigners than would have been afforded to them at most European Courts.

The scene at the Chien-Men Gate when the Emperor and the Dowager Empress entered the Temples to offer thanks for their safe journey were nothing less than revolutionary when viewed in the light of all Chinese customs. The horseshoe wall around the ancient gate was crowded with Europeans—diplomats, army officers, missionaries, women, photographers, and correspondents. When the Emperor and the Dowager Empress arrived at the temple the procession halted, and their Majesties alighted from their chairs, which were covered with imperial yellow silk and lined with sable.

The Emperor proceeded to the Temple of the God of War, on the west side of the plaza, with hundreds of foreigners peering down only forty feet above him. Dozens of cameras were focused upon the Son of Heaven. When he returned, his chair was borne through the gate.

Then the chair of the Dowager Empress was brought to the doorway of the Temple of the Goddess of Mercy, on the east side of the plaza, and the Dowager Empress appeared. Amid a great scuffling of attendants she proceeded into the temple, resting on the arms of two officials and followed by a company of Buddhist priests bearing offerings. The spectators then heard the booming of the temple bell.

EMPRESS BOWS TO FOREIGNERS.

After an interval of five minutes the Dowager Empress reappeared. Standing in the doorway of the temple, she looked upward. Directly overhead were the German Minister, Dr. Mumm von Schwartzenstein; the Secretaries of the German Legation, and the officers of the American garrison and some American women. The Dowager Empress saw the foreigners, and bowed low. She advanced a few steps and bowed again in acknowledgment of the salutations of the foreigners. She then returned to her chair looking upward at the semicircle of foreign faces and bowing repeatedly.

In the meantime the Chinese soldiers, Manchu bannermen, and minor officials, who had crowded the Plaza, were reverently kneeling. The two arches at the sides of the ancient gateway framed the faces of hundreds of Chinese coolies, who, emboldened by the presence of the foreigners, ventured to gaze upon their rulers. This incident constituted a most sharp contrast with the old régime, when neither diplomats nor natives were permitted to view the passage of royal personages along the streets.

The expression of the Dowager Empress seemed almost appealing as she faced those who had humbled her from her former arrogance, and confirmed the impression that she is returning to Peking with anxiety for her safety.

The streets from the Machiapo Station to the gateway of the Forbidden City, a distance of four miles, were swept and garnished early this morning. The great plaza between the Temples of Heaven and Agriculture was sprinkled with yellow sand. Residents were compelled to remain indoors. The soldiers and the police formed a close cordon along both sides of the entire route. A sharp wind, bringing sand from the Mongolian Desert, blinded the spectators.

The special train bearing the Emperor and Empress Dowager, composed of twenty-two cars, was preceded by a pilot engine, and arrived shortly after noon. The engine and the Emperor's cars had been decorated with yellow silk dragons by the British railroad officers. Two companies of Chinese cavalry mounted on white horses and two companies astride horses from Australia were drawn up at the sides of the station. Two thousand officials, Princes, Viceroys, and Taotais—a kaleidoscopic field of silks and furs, in which gleamed an occasional yellow jacket—were massed upon the platform.

When the Emperor appeared the entire assemblage prostrated itself and remained kneeling until his Majesty had taken his place in his chair. At the station the Dowager Empress summoned Traffic Manager Foley and Superintendent Moffat of the railroad, the latter having driven the engine which drew the special train, and presented them to the Emperor, who thanked them for their services.

THE IMPERIAL PROCESSION.

The imperial cavalcade then moved off at a swift trot, the Chinese cavalry in the lead. Then followed the great body of officials, riding shaggy Mongolian ponies, the Manchu bannermen, the umbrella bearers, the spearmen, Viceroy Yuan-Shi-Kai in his newly bestowed yellow jacket, and the Emperor, with eight bearers carrying his chair, and a guard of infantrymen marching on either side. Then came the Empress Dowager with an equally conspicuous entourage. She was followed by the Boxer chief and Prime Minister Jung-Lu in a yellow chair. The Dowager Empress, Prince Chun, and the lesser officials were carried in yellow and green chairs.

While their Majesties passed the soldiers lining the route of the procession knelt, holding their guns at present arms, and the buglers sounded their instruments continuously. Although the streets were kept empty, thousands of Chinese crowded the elevations along the line of march, a thing never permitted before.

The soldiers of the American garrison stationed here witnessed the spectacle from the parade ground opposite the entrance to the palace. The soldiers of the British garrison, including the officers, were kept in their quarters. This occasioned much lamenting. The majority of the foreign Ministers, including the British, American, French, and Russian representatives, absented themselves from the spectacle, but the ladies of the legations were entertained by Chinese officials on balconies along the line of march.

It appears that the Empress Dowager ordered that every courtesy be extended to the foreigners here, and that the efforts to exclude them from witnessing the passage of the imperial cortège emanated from local officials.

LONDON, Jan. 8.—It is announced in a dispatch from Peking that an Imperial edict has been issued, conferring yellow jackets on Viceroy Yuan-Shi-Kai and on Tsen-Chun-Hsuan, Governor of Shen-Si, who protected the Chinese rulers in their flight from Peking.

Both these officials are privileged to ride on horseback in the Forbidden City.

The Chinese Court has been absent from the capital of the empire for almost seventeen months. The legations in Peking were rescued on Aug. 14, 1900, and the Court fled from the city as soon as it was evident that Peking would be captured by the allies. Just before the flight the Empress Dowager ordered three officials who advised surrender to be beheaded.

Prince Su, who accompanied the Emperor and Dowager Empress in their flight as far as Tai-yuen-Foo, has given an account of the journey. According to his statement, the day the Court left Peking the Emperor, Dowager Empress, and their attendants traveled in carts to Kuan-Shi, twenty miles to the north, escorted by 3,000 soldiers of various commands. This army pillaged and murdered along the whole route.

At Kuan-Shi mule litters were supplied for their Majesties, and thereafter the flight was continued at the rate of twenty miles daily. At Hsuan-hua-Foo, 120 miles from Peking, a halt was made, the journey up to there having been of the most panic-stricken and disorderly nature. The soldiers even stole the meals prepared for the Emperor and Dowager Empress. A proposition to remain at Hsuan-hua was negatived, the court still being in fear of capture by the foreigners. The Dowager Empress did little but weep and rail at those who were responsible for her situation. The Emperor reviled every one.

A long wait was made at Tai-yuen-Foo, but ultimately the Court settled at Sian-Foo, the old capital of the empire, and now the capital of Shen-Si. There some kind of order was restored, and gradually the Court regained the power among the native officials that it seemed at one time in danger of losing altogether.

That the Court would ever return to Peking has been doubted by many foreigners, and it took all the persuasion of Li Hung-Chang and others to induce the Empress Dowager to decide on the step. It is understood that she required specific assurances that she would not be molested by the foreigners before she would venture back to the capital. Even then the journey was several times broken, and threats were made that the Court would remain at some point between Sian-Foo and Peking.

WAR IN FAR EAST FEARED

Japanese Again Take a Gloomy View of the Situation

Indications That a Decisive Development Is Near—Rumor That Negotiations with Russia Have Been Broken Off.

YOKOHAMA, Oct. 21.—The Ministerial conferences, naval preparations, and, notably, the appointment of Vice Admiral Toga, known as a "fighting Admiral," to command the standing squadron, have led to a renewal of the anticipations of a conflict with Russia.

Some decided development in the crisis is expected shortly.

The steamship and railroad companies have, it is reported, been notified to be in readiness for emergencies.

LONDON, Oct. 22.—A Reuter dispatch from Tokio says:

"Russian military activity on the Korean frontier is unabated.

"The important newspapers take a gloomy view. They are inclined to believe that Russia does not intend to fulfil her repeated promises and declarations, in which case it will be incumbent on Japan to take decisive steps for the sake of her very existence.

"The Japanese gunboat Chiokai was to have wintered at Niu-Chwang, but this arrangement has been countermanded."

A report was in circulation on the Stock Exchange yesterday that the negotiations between Russia and Japan had been broken off, but the Foreign Office officials here said they had not heard anything confirmatory of the rumor. This statement was made subsequent to a visit paid by Baron Hayashi, the Japanese Minister, to Lord Lansdowne yesterday afternoon. The officials of the Foreign Office added that the report was contrary to the general trend of information.

BERLIN, Oct. 21.—The German Government takes a cheerful view of the Russo-Japanese difficulties. Russia has conveyed assurances to Germany that she will keep strictly on the defensive, even if Japan occupies Korean ports in force. Japan may act aggressively toward Korea without Russia being affronted thereby or making a counterstroke. The only limitations Russia places on Japan's action is that she must not cross the Yalu River.

January 8, 1902

October 22, 1903

JAPAN TO LAND TROOPS TO-DAY

Tokio Advices Say Korea Will be Seized

DID NOT WAIT FOR NOTE

Diplomatic Relations Were Broken Because She Was Weary of Waiting for an Answer.

TOKIO, Feb. 7—The severance of diplomatic relations between Russia and Japan appears to be only a step toward war, although when the Ministers of Russia and Japan withdraw from their respective posts quick and decisive action is expected.

When Minister of Foreign Affairs Komura on Saturday notified Baron de Rosen, the Russian Minister, of Japan's determination to sever diplomatic relations, he is reported to have declared to him that Japan is tired of Russia's delays, evasions, and insincerity, and has decided to take independent action for the conservation of Japan's Oriental interests.

During the final negotiations Japan's repeated requests for an answer were treated in a most unsatisfactory manner. Japan waited until convinced that it was useless to wait longer, and has now ended the discussion.

The indications are that there will be no formal declaration of war. Japan will publicly define its position and purposes, and the Foreign Office has prepared a new statement, which will probably be announced to-night.

On Monday Japan will unquestionably seize Korea, and although Russia has previously intimated that it would not interfere in view of that country's present attitude, developments are eagerly awaited.

EXPECT WAR TO-DAY.

LONDON, Feb. 8.—Telegrams from Tokio published here this morning announce that an emergency Council of Ministers was held Sunday and that Marquis Ito and Field Marshal Oyama had an audience of the Emperor.

The Tokio correspondent of The Standard reports the utmost activity on the part of the railroads, which are rapidly conveying troops to ports of embarkation. The streets of the capital are full of animation and the coming and going of soldiers. The people are calm and confident, the correspondent continues, and there is no excitement.

Cabling from Tokio, the correspondent there of The Daily Telegraph gives a report that Russian troops have already crossed the Korean frontier, and that an official declaration of war is expected Monday. He adds that Russian interests in Japan have been placed in the hands of the Austrian Minister, the Italian Minister having declined to undertake this mission.

JAPAN CHARTERS STEAMSHIPS.

Baron de Rosen had a brief interview with Baron Komura Sunday, The Daily Telegraph correspondent continues, and Baron Komura afterward had an audience of the Emperor. The Government has chartered steamships of the Nippon-Yusen, Osaka-Shosen, and Mitsui-Bussan Lines.

A correspondent of The Daily Mail at Söul says he learns that Japan has warned noncombatants to withdraw from Song-ching, and has advised those north of Chongju and Gensan to come south. This is supposed to indicate Japan's intention to strike through Northern Korea in the direction of Harbin and the Manchurian Railroad.

RUSSIANS RETIRE AFTER HOT FIGHT

Have 3 Killed and 16 Wounded near Chong-Yu.

THE JAPANESE ALSO SUFFER.

Russians Attack Japanese Infantry and Cavalry, but are Forced to Retire, Though in Good Order

ST. PETERSBURG, March 29.—Gen. Kuropatkin in his first report to the Emperor from the scene of war announces that offensive land operations took place yesterday against the Japanese upon the sixth anniversary of the occupation of Port Arthur by the Russians.

These operations took the form of a cavalry attack by six companies of Cossacks, led personally by Gen. Mishtchenko, against four squadrons of Japanese cavalry, which the General believed to be beyond Chong-Ju, but which he found to be in occupation of that town.

Despite a cross fire which Gen. Mishtchenko directed against the enemy, he pays a tribute to their tenacity and bravery, the Japanese only ceasing to fire after a combat which lasted for half an hour.

Before the Russians could follow up their advantage three Japanese squadrons galloped toward the town, which two of them succeeded in entering, while the third was driven back in disorder, men and horses falling. The fire maintained upon the town was so destructive that the Japanese were unable to make an effective return.

Further Japanese reinforcements arrived an hour later, and, in view of the superiority of the enemy, Gen. Mishtchenko determined to retire, doing so without embarrassment, although he carried with him three killed and sixteen wounded.

Gen. Mishtchenko's Cossacks have been endeavoring for some days to come in contact with the Japanese patrols, but the latter refused the combat.

The skirmish of to-day will have the effect of fixing the policy of the Russians to retard as much as possible the advance of the Japanese Army.

Gen. Kuropatkin's dispatch reporting Gen. Mishtchenko's operations does not give the place of its origin, but it is presumed that the Commander in Chief is either at Liao-Yang or en route to Niu-Chwang.

Gen. Kuropatkin's report is as follows:

"I have the honor to respectfully communicate to your Majesty the report of Gen. Mistchenko, dated March 28, at 10 P. M., which says:

"'For three consecutive days our small outposts attempted to draw the Japanese cavalry into action, but their patrols, after contact was established, retired beyond Chong-Ju, (about fifty miles northwest of Ping-Yang.)

" 'Having learned that four squadrons of the enemy were posted five versts beyond Chong-Ju, on March 27, six companies marched toward Kasan, and on March 28 reached Chong-Ju at 10:30 A. M. As soon as our scouts approached the town the enemy opened fire from behind the wall. Two squadrons promptly dismounted and occupied the heights 600 yards distant. An engagement ensued.

" 'In the town a company of infantry and a squadron of cavalry were lying in ambush. Our men were reinforced by three companies, and attacked the Japanese with a cross fire. Notwithstanding this and our commanding position, the Japanese gallantly held their ground, and it was only after a fierce fight of half an hour's duration that the Japanese ceased fire and sought refuge in the houses. The Japanese hoisted the Red Cross flag at two points.

" 'Soon afterward three squadrons of the enemy were seen advancing along the Kasam road at full gallop toward the town, which two of the squadrons succeeded in entering, while the third fell back in disorder under repeated volleys from our troops. A number of men and horses were seen to fall.

" 'For an hour afterward companies continued to fire on the Japanese in the town, preventing them from leaving the streets and houses.

" 'An hour and a half after the beginning of the engagement four companies were seen on the Kasan road hastening to attack. I gave the order to mount, and the entire force, with a covering squadron, advanced in perfect order and formed in line behind the hill. The wounded were placed in front and the retirement was carried out with the deliberation of a parade.

" 'The Japanese squadron which was thrown into disorder was evidently unable to occupy the hill which we had evacuated, and their infantry arrived too late.

" 'The detachment protecting our rear guard arrived quietly at Kasan (?) where we halted for two hours in order to give attention to our wounded. At 9 P. M. our force reached Noo-San.

" 'It is supposed that the Japanese had heavy losses in men and horses. On our side, unfortunately, three officers were severely wounded—Stepanoff and Adroonko in the chest and Vaselevitch in the stomach. Schilnikoff was less seriously wounded in the arm, but did not leave the field. Three Cossacks were killed and twelve were wounded, including five seriously.

" Gen. Mistchenko bears witness to the excellent conduct and gallantry of the officers and Cossacks, and especially praises the Third Company of the Argunsk Regiment, commanded by Krasnostanoff."

LONDON, March 30.—No Japanese report of the land operations in Korea has yet been received here, and there is much speculation as to the size of the opposing armies, regarding which there is no reliable information.

A correspondent at Russian headquarters in Mukden telegraphs that, according to reports received there, about 10,000 Japanese have crossed the river at Chin-Chan-gau and 5,000 have advanced north from Chong-Ju.

The Chronicle's Shanghai correspondent asserts that practically the whole Japanese Army in Korea, consisting of 100,000 men, is concentrated at Pak-Chen and An-ju, only small detachments being left in Southern Korea to maintain communications.

A St. Petersburg special says that a Russian division of 25,000 men from Southern Ussuri is advancing in two columns through Korea. The main column, coming along the east coast road, reached Puk-Chang, 180 miles from the Tumen River, and the flanking column, consisting of Cossacks and mountain artillery, coming along the Valley of the Tumen River towards its source, had reached the coast of Lake Tadji. This column reports that the Japanese are advancing north from Won-san, and that their advance guard is encamped at Ohong-Ping. It is probable, however, that none of these various reports can be accepted as authentic.

COSSACKS FIGHT BANDITS.

Twenty-eight Killed and Six Captured Near Bidzevo.

LIAO-YANG, March 29.—In the rear of Bidzevo, fifty Cossacks encountered a strong band of Chinese bandits and charged upon them, killing 28 and capturing 6.

Three Cossacks were killed and 6 wounded.

FIRST SHOT OF THE WAR.

Korietz Fired It, but in Reply to Three Japanese Torpedoes.

ST. PETERSBURG, March 29.—According to a letter received from an officer of the Russian gunboat Korietz, which was destroyed by the Japanese at Che-mul-pho, his ship technically fired the first shot of the war, but this shot was not fired until after the Japanese had fired three torpedoes in an effort to sink the Korietz.

The officer writes that on Feb. 8, without knowing that there had been even a rupture of diplomatic relations, the Korietz left Che-mul-pho for Port Arthur and met the Japanese cruiser and torpedo squadron while still in neutral waters. The Korietz steamed between the two divisions of the squadron with the tarpaulins still covering her guns when it was noticed that the cruisers were training their guns on the Russian vessel. It was then decided to put back into the harbor.

While the Korietz was going about the Japanese launched a torpedo, which passed astern. The Japanese launched another torpedo, but it was only when a third torpedo was seen coming directly for the Korietz's beam that the command was given to open fire, and two shots were fired. The third torpedo sank just before reaching the Korietz.

100,000 JAPANESE CROSSING THE YALU

Russians Say Passage of River Is Practically Unopposed.

TOWN ABOVE AN-TUNG SEIZED

Reports from Various Sources of Great Battle and Russian Defeat Discredited in St. Petersburg.

ST. PETERSBURG, April 30.—All news from the front indicates that the armies of Gen. Kuroki and Gen. Oki, comprising about 100,000 men, are being rapidly pushed forward and will be thrown across the Yalu as speedily as possible. Japanese transports have also appeared at the mouth of the river, and, supported by a few warships, will assist in the operations.

The Japanese seem to be following closely the tactics pursued by them during the Chino-Japanese war, having already occupied Kulien-Cheng, above An-tung, where they crossed in 1895.

An official dispatch has been received at headquarters concerning affairs on the Yalu up to April 28. It is as follows:

" Official reports received during the last few days state that on April 22 a movement was seen among the Japanese troops on the Yalu, small detachments moving on the left bank. On April 23 larger bodies concentrated opposite Wi-ju, and the Japanese proceeded to cross by small detachments. About two companies, with a small body of cavalry, crossed at Sjaopoussikhe.

" From the evening of April 24 onward reports began to come in to the effect that the enemy was preparing to cross at Wi-ju, Turen-Cheng, and Tphao-Chen-Ling.

" On the following day the Japanese endeavored to throw bridges across the eastern arm of the Yalu opposite Kulien-Cheng and Siaopoussikhe. Toward 3 o'clock in the afternoon they occupied the Island of Somalinda, and spent the night of April 26 on an island north of Sandakou.

Met by Fire of Cavalry.

"The Japanese, who numbered 1,500, were received by the fire of our light cavalry, who, being numerically inferior, took boats and crossed to the right bank, whence they kept up a lively fire, occupying a narrow path along the bank, sheltered by a sharp ascent. Our light cavalry lost the chief of the detachment, Lieut. Semenoff, and eighteen men wounded, but their severe fire at short range against the Japanese in close formation must have inflicted considerable losses.

" At 3:30 A.M. April 26 by their firing on the island opposite Turen-Cheng our guns destroyed the bridge across the eastern branch of the Yalu toward the Island of Somalinda, forcing the Japanese to continue their passage of the river by pontoons south of Wi-ju. Toward midday a detachment of Japanese with a battery of artillery began a march upon Kulien-Cheng, but, meeting with the fire of our artillery, they retired in disorder and confusion toward the place of their passage. The Japanese battery did not have time even to come into action.

" At 9 o'clock in the evening of April 27 some three battalions of Japanese crossed the Yalu at the village of Matoutseo, over the eastern branch of the river. The night of April 27-28 passed quietly.

Another Island Occupied.

" On the morning of April 28 our scouts reported that the Japanese had occupied an island opposite the village of Sandakou, having screened advanced posts on the left bank of the river.

" Our troops continue to occupy their position on the right bank of the river."

The Emperor has received a telegram from Gen. Kuropatkin, under to-day's date, as follows:

" Gen Sassulitch reports that the night of April 28-29 passed quietly. Small bodies of Japanese are moving on the right bank of the Yalu, at the mouth of which steamers are arriving.

" On April 28 at about 2 in the afternoon, Japanese columns were seen going from Yong-am-pho toward Wi-ju, and a party of Japanese scouts was seen on a mountain to the southward of Sindiaju.

" The Japanese have not yet undertaken any active operations."

'I AM SURROUNDED' SAYS KUROPATKIN

LONDON TIMES—NEW YORK TIMES
Special Cable. Copyright, 1905.

ST. PETERSBURG, Saturday, March 11.—The latest telegram from Kuropatkin, presumably brought by messenger to Tie Pass, reached Tsarskoe Selo last (Friday) night. It stated laconically:

" I am surrounded."

This telegram, which is believed to have been dispatched early yesterday morning, inspires the worst fears. In view of the previous news of the approach of an eastern flanking force, there is no longer scope for optimism. The gravest fears are entertained for the safety of the army, as the Russians have been compelled to leave Mukden, which has been occupied by the Japanese.

Kuropatkin's Last Stand.

Kuropatkin is delivering a last desperate blow against the enemy, who are surrounding him on every side.

Such is the picture of the situation given in the latest Russian dispatches. These, as well as the Tokio reports of the surrounding of 200,000 men, were stopped by the censorship. Consequently the general public is still unaware of the gravity of the situation and continues to enjoy itself after the customary fashion in carnival week.

It was late last evening when official news of the surrender of Mukden appeared. The last unofficial messages transmitted by the Mukden telegraph office yesterday said that a decisive battle was proceeding north of the city, that Oku's forces were constantly increasing, that the men had lost all hope of victory, and were going

out to fight with the conviction that they were being sacrificed to save the rest of the army.

Mukden Cut Off Thursday.

Telegraphic and railway communication with Mukden was finally severed late Thursday. That is regarded as a sign that the Japanese are gradually hemming in Kuropatkin and gaining a permanent foothold on the railway.

According to an account of the final operations furnished by an officer of the General Staff, Gen. Kaulbars has been reinforced by several corps belonging to Linevitch and Bilderling, and has been withstanding Oku's onslaught.

Gen. Kuropatkin has been personally directing the battle. Demobvsky's corps was engaged Wednesday night north of Fu-Ling, (eight miles east of Mukden,) and sustained terrible losses. The Seventeenth Corps, which was sent in support, succeeded in repulsing the enemy.

This is was hoped would enable Kuropatkin to extricate the army under cover of a terrific sandstorm which prevailed Thursday, but Oku resumed the battle a few hours later, and Kuropatkin was again compelled to send his best troops to engage the foe.

The fiercest fighting was at San-tai-Tse, six miles northeast, and Wanchen-Tun, seven miles north of Mukden.

Japanese Destroy Railway.

The proximity of the latter point to the railway enabled the Japanese to destroy the track and shell the Mandarin Road.

Official reports put the Russian losses up to Thursday morning at 65,000.

Officers of the General Staff refuse to consider Kuropatkin's position hopeless. They believe a decisive engagement is still in progress, but that whatever the result, Kuropatkin will extricate the army, even if at the sacrifice of several corps.

It is persistently reported that the Fourth Army Corps has reached Tie Pass, whence it will make a diversion to relieve the pressure on Kuropatkin.

WAR LASTED 18 MONTHS, BIGGEST BATTLE KNOWN

Engagement at Mukden Unparalleled in World's Conflicts.

RUSSIANS WON NO VICTORY

Admiral Togo's Ships Opened and Closed Hostilities–Czar's Navy Wiped Out–Russian Miscalculation.

The war that has been ended by the "Peace of Washington"–the treaty will probably be signed in Washington–began on Feb. 8, 1904. The period of hostilities, therefore, has been 1 year 6 months and 21 days.

Two days before the war began the Japanese had severed diplomatic relations with Russia at the end of negotiations covering many months. Even at the last moment Russia did not believe that Japan meant to fight, and when, on Feb. 9, the news came that Admiral Togo's fleet had made a night attack on the Russian squadron at Port Arthur, it astounded the Russians.

The first Japanese blow was a severe one. Togo's torpedo flotilla badly damaged the battleships Czarevitch and Retvizan and the cruiser Pallada. On the following day the naval action was renewed, and one Russian battleship (the Poltava) and three cruisers were injured.

Meanwhile Admiral Uriu's squadron had appeared off Che-mul-Pho, Korea, and had engaged and sunk the Russian cruiser Variag and the gunboat Korietz.

Japan began to hurry troops to Korea and the Russians sent reinforcements to the Far East by way of the Trans-Siberian Railway. Viceroy Alexieff, who is regarded as having been chiefly responsible for the "forward" policy which resulted in the war, left Port Arthur for Harbin. Admiral Makaroff was appointed Commander in Chief of the Czar's naval forces in the Orient, and, on Feb. 21, Gen. Kuropatkin was appointed Commander in Chief on land. Korea, in an astonishingly short time, was dominated by the Japanese. The authorities at Sŏul were for the most part pro-Russian, but in spite of this a treaty was signed with Japan by which she received permission to send troops to Korea, and practically, to do anything she liked in the country.

On March 12 Gen. Kuropatkin left St. Petersburg amid the cheers of an enormous crowd. A week later the Japanese and Russian outposts were in touch in Northern Korea. On April 6 the Russians, who had continually retreated, crossed the Yalu, and the Japanese were, in a military sense, masters of Korea.

Togo's successes had continued. The first great Russian disaster of the war occurred on April 13, when Japanese cruisers decoyed Admiral Makaroff out of Port Arthur and Togo caught him in a trap. The Japanese led the Russians over mines they had previously laid, and in their hasty return Makaroff's flagship, the Petropavlovsk, was blown up, the Admiral and 600 men going down with her. Verestchagin, the most famous of all Russian artists, was among the drowned.

Several attempts were made by the Japanese to block the entrance of Port Arthur. None was permanently successful, but it is supposed that they had some effect in confining the Russian vessels to the harbor.

The first great land battle of the war was fought on April 30 and the following two days. The Japanese Army under Gen. Kuroki obtained a complete victory. The Russians were forced far north of the Yalu, Kiu-lien-Cheng was captured by the Japanese, and the Russians lost many men and guns.

The worst Japanese disaster of the war occurred on May 15, 1904. The battleship Hatsuse was sunk by a mine near Port Arthur and the cruiser Yoshino was sunk in a collision with the cruiser Kasuga.

In the beginning of May a Japanese army landed on the Liao-Tung Peninsula. The Port Arthur army moved forward to meet it, and on May 27 the battle of Kin-Chow was fought. The Japanese stormed Nan-Shan Hill and at enormous sacrifice routed the Russians and captured 78 guns. The siege of Port Arthur proper began with this date, and at the same time Togo's blockade of the southern end of the Liao-Tung Peninsula became effective. On May 30 the Russians occupied Dalny, the mushroom city which had been built at an outlay of many million dollars, designed by the Russians to be the chief seaport of that part of Asia.

The Siege of Port Arthur.

There followed Kuropatkin's disastrous attempt to relieve Port Arthur, made, it was said, against his advice on an imperative order from the Czar. The Russians were defeated with a loss of 7,000 men and 16 guns, and were all but cut off from retreat.

The weeks following saw almost constant fighting, repeated Japanese successes, but no great battle. On July 6 Field Marshal Oyama, the Japanese Commander in Chief, started for the front. On July 25 Gen. Oku won an important victory at Tashi-Chao, and at the end of July the Russians, after extraordinary efforts on the part of the besiegers, had been driven from the outlying lines of defense at Port Arthur and had retired on the main fortifications.

On Aug. 10 the Port Arthur fleet made a disastrous sortie. Admiral Wittsoeft was killed, a number of the best vessels were badly damaged, and some of the Russian ships took refuge in neutral ports, where they were interned.

On Aug. 12 the Czarevitch was born, and the Russian people hailed the event as an omen of a turn in the tide of war. But it did not prove a true omen. Defeats on land and sea continued. Point after point outside Port Arthur was taken, more ships were lost, including the gallant little cruiser Novik, and the only Russian success was the defeat on Aug. 24 of the first general attack on Port Arthur.

The following day the Japanese began an advance on Liau-Yang. The fighting continued until Sept. 4, when Ovama entered the city, after one of the greatest battles in the history of the world. A flank movement was chiefly responsible for the Japanese victory. For two days the result had appeared to be in doubt. The Japanese made attack after attack on the Russian works, but were beaten back. Then, suddenly, Kuroki appeared to the northeast of the Russian position, and Kuropatkin, seeing himself outmanoeuvered, ordered a general retreat.

It took both armies several weeks to recover from the effects of the battle. Finally, Kuropatkin considered that the Russians were strong enough to begin an offensive movement. From Oct. 9 to Oct. 24 the battle of the Sha River was fought. Again there were enormous losses on both sides and again the Russians were defeated. They were driven back across the Sha River, but the Japanese did not, as it was expected that they would do, press their advantage. Instead they built strong works and both armies in Manchuria settled down to inactivity for the Winter.

On Oct. 15 the Baltic fleet under Admiral Rojestvensky left Libau for the Far East. A few days later it began its career on the seas by firing at some English fishing boats. The incident nearly led to war between Great Britain and Russia, but in the end an international inquiry board was appointed which settled the question in a manner satisfactory to both parties.

On Nov. 20 the Japanese at Port Arthur, who had pushed on in spite of terrible slaughter, captured 203-Meter Hill, and this was the beginning of the end for the Russian garrison. During December the position of the Russians grew more and more desperate. Once the inner line of fortifications had been pierced the town and harbor were at the mercy of the besiegers. The damaged warships could not escape, and the terribly accurate Japanese fire further damaged several of them. The Russians' stock of ammunition was running low, a large portion of the defending force was hors de combat, and at last Gen. Stoessel decided to give in. On Jan. 1, 1905 he accepted the terms of surrender laid down by Gen. Nogi, and, after sinking their ships, the Russians gave up the fortress.

In February the battle of Mukden was fought—the greatest battle in the history of the world so far as is known. It lasted from Feb. 23 to March 10, when the Japanese entered Mukden. The Russian retreat from the city was more or less disorganized, and the victors captured enormous quantities of trophies and supplies. Oyama pressed his success to the point of pursuing the Russians to Tie Pass. Later he moved further north, but the battle of Mukden was the last great land battle of the war.

On May 14, 1905, the Baltic fleet left Hon-Kohe Bay for the north, and on May 27 and 28 it was engaged in Tsu-Shima Strait and the Sea of Japan by the fleet under Admiral Togo. The complete disaster suffered by the Russians is so recent that the details need not be recapitulated. Practically every one of the Russian ships was destroyed or captured and Rojestvensky was taken prisoner.

A week later President Roosevelt began the negotiations which have resulted in ending the war.

August 30, 1905

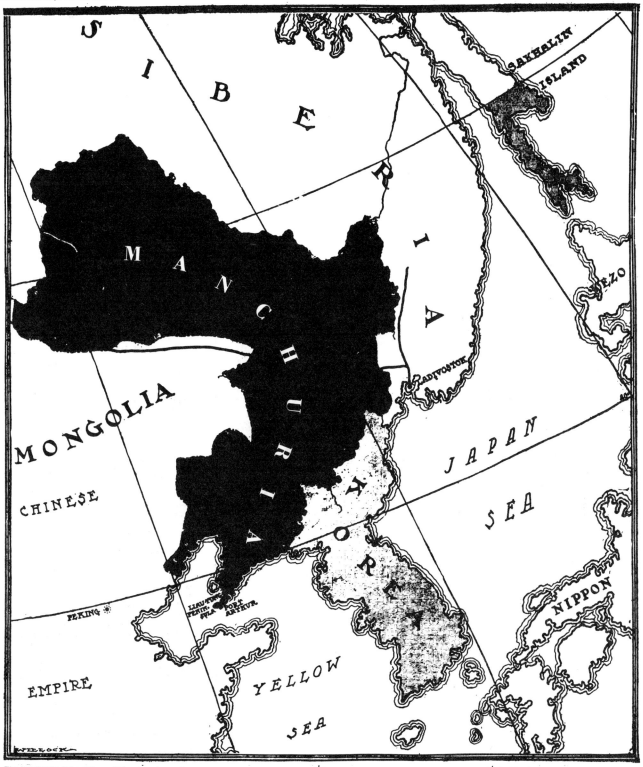

The lightly shaded portions of the above map show the territory which Japan gains as a result of the war. Korea will not be hers nominally, as, it is understood, she promises not to disturb the ruling dynasty of that country. Practically, however, it is recognized that Japan will be in complete control of Korea, and that it will in a short time be a Japanese colony. Japan also gets the leases of the Liao-Tung Peninsula, including Port Arthur and Dalny, and the absolute possession of the southern half of the Island of Sakhalin. This half of the island is by far the more valuable portion of it.

The heavily shaded portion of the map shows the Manchurian provinces which are to be returned to China as a result of the war.

BEST CHINESE BEHIND AMERICAN BOYCOTT---WU

Symptom of Progress Toward Real Nationality for China.

WANTS GRIEVANCES SETTLED

His Plan to Keep Coolies Out of United States—Seeks to Open Hawaii and Philippines.

PEKING, Aug. 9.—Wu Ting-Fang, formerly the Minister of China at Washington, in an interview to-day on the exclusion laws of the United States, declared that the spread of the boycott on American goods was a symptom of extraordinary progress toward a real nationality. He pointed out that the movement against Americans, though thoroughly organized by the best and most representative Chinese, was altogether pacific and not directed against persons or property.

The extent of the movement and the depth of feeling manifested not only by the mercantile classes, but by the students and even the women, Mr. Wu said, surprised him. Such an expression of public sentiment was indicative of a new spirit in China. He trusted that the boycott would soon be rendered unnecessary by satisfactory settlement of the grievances.

Mr Wu's attention was called to the fact that he was credited with directing the boycott and he indignantly repudiated the suggestion. He said it would be as unreasonable to expect that his Government had the ability to compel the Chinese to purchase goods as to believe that the United States Government was able to prevent the Chicago strikes.

The Chinese, he said, agreed to the exclusion of coolies, and this point presented no difficulty. The existing regulations pressed with severity on other classes. Merchants, travelers for pleasure, students, and others who, while nominally admissible to the United States, were forced to undergo examinations, which, though possibly necessary, were generally rendered very objectionable by the manner of enforcement. A clearer definition of the term "laborer" for one thing was essential.

"A superior Chinaman arriving in San Francisco, for example," said Mr. Wu, "is detained by the authorities while his credentials are being examined, and this detention frequently involves consorting with a low class of coolies in a common shed. He is unable to communicate with friends and is subjected to inconveniences and indignities to which Americans would refuse to submit.

"Moreover, he is not allowed to retain the services of any one to protect his interests, and if the immigration authorities decide against him there is no possibility of appeal. That these grievances are well founded is demonstrated by the necessity for President Roosevelt's stringent order that courtesy be shown the Chinese by the immigration officials under pain of dismissal. There have been numberless instances of harsh treatment which the Americans themselves have been forced to admit."

Mr. Wu admitted that European immigrants could not have lawyers during their examinations, but he rejected this argument because, he said, the treatment of Chinese in other respects was entirely different from that of Europeans.

The admission of coolies to Hawaii, he said, he regarded as of the utmost importance. Hawaii was greatly in need of laborers, and, since the exclusion of the Chinese, industries on the islands had suffered. At all events, the Chinese there could not compete with American labor. The Philippines had long been a natural field for Chinese industry, but the application of the Exclusion act to the islands had changed this. Regarding the desirability of Chinese labor Mr. Wu instanced the prosperity of Singapore and the adjacent country. He added:

"I regret that so little progress has been made in the negotiations for a new convention. Should the American Government permit the wishes of China to be embodied in this convention it would practically have no effect on the United States, as Hawaii and the Philippines do not concern American labor. I suggest that an educational test would be the most effective means of preventing the ingress of coolies, besides eliminating undesirable class distinction."

CHINESE ANNOUNCE DEATH OF EMPEROR

Dowager Said to Have Collapsed on Hearing News—Death Chair Ready.

REFORM ELEMENT RULES

Prince Chun Said to Favor Progress— Japan Not to Act Without Consulting Powers.

PEKING, Nov. 14.—Emperor Kwang-Hsu died shortly after 5 o'clock this evening. This information came from the palace after another day of wild speculation as to the occurrences there.

At the moment of the death of the Emperor, the Dowager Empress's own death-chamber chair was waiting in the courtyard. She, too, had been in a serious condition, and word that was brought to her earlier in the day that the Emperor was dying caused her to collapse. This has prevented her from assuming the relationship of grandmother to the successor to the throne, which, according to the Chinese system, would enormously augment her authority.

There is little indication of emotion among the people over the events which have been transpiring. The Emperor's death and the probable death of the Dowager Empress within a very short time have had but little effect upon the Chinese, who are pursuing the even tenor of their way without signs of mourning.

Victory for the Reformers.

Public attention was largely centred to-day on the new Government for China as indicated by the edict promoting Prince Chun to the Regency and his infant son, Pu Wei, to be heir presumptive. The edict granted Prince Chun precedence over all other Princes.

The appointment has made a good impression. It satisfies the reformers and appeals to the sentiments held by the people for Kwang-Hsu, because it respects the close blood ties in the matter of the succession and introduces a new and more modern element into the Government of the empire. The appointment is an evidence of victory for the reformers.

The Government to-day notified the American Legation officially that Prince Chun had been made Regent, and that he was therefore the head of the State. This was recognition of the retirement of the Dowager Empress.

Kwang-Hsu's later life was a pitiable spectacle to his attendants. His feebleness had rendered him a mere puppet, and he had suffered long from ill health, which was combined with fear and despair. Latterly he showed marked signs of mental disturbance, and even went so far last August as to declare himself mad.

Emperor's Plea for Help.

During recent audiences with foreign representatives he was unable to sit upon

THE EMPRESS OF CHINA, THE DOWAGER EMPRESS
AND THE WOMEN OF THE ROYAL HOUSEHOLD

the throne or even in an erect position. It was evident for a long time that he would be unable to withstand a crisis which sooner or later must develop in the disease from which he was suffering. A recent edict issued in his name says:

Since last Autumn we have been ill. The physicians recommended by the Government have not been successful in curing us. We are weak and without spirit, racked by pain, without appetite, cold and feverish, and it has been impossible for us to sleep. We are anxious to permit the Viceroys and the Governors to send other physicians to us quickly, and we will give extraordinary rewards to the physicians or officials who help us.

Recent climatic extremes caused the development of fatal complications that resulted in his death.

The difficulty of getting news from the palace yesterday and to-day lies largely in the fact that it has been the custom of the Chinese Court to make a secret of any imperial death. The Foreign Board was busily engaged last night and to-day in issuing ardent denials of the reported death of the Emperor, and at 9 o'clock last night it issued a statement to the effect that he showed some slight improvement. While the foreign residents in Peking were confused to-day, and had no means of ascertaining the truth as against the practices of misstatement of the Court, the belief was general here that the Emperor was dead—that he might have died last night, or even before.

TSI-AN, RULER OF CHINA, DEAD

Special Cable to THE NEW YORK TIMES.

LONDON, Nov. 15.—A dispatch to The London Times from Peking says the death of the Empress Dowager, which occurred to-day, following so closely upon the death of the Emperor Saturday, arouses suspicions of foul play. The new Empress Dowager, it is added, is a complete nonentity.

Neurasthenia was the direct cause of the Emperor's death. His Majesty refused to allow himself, when the end was approaching, to be removed to the Pavilion of Peaceful Longevity, thus violating the precedents which prescribe the place of death of the rulers of China.

Eventually he expired without having donned the robes proper to the occasion.

PEKING, Nov. 15.—Tsi-An, the Dowager Empress of China, the autocratic head of the Government, which she had direct-

ed without successful interference since 1861, and without protest since 1881, died at 2 o'clock this afternoon.

The announcement of the Dowager Empress's death was official and followed closely upon the announcement that Kwang-Hsu, the Emperor, had died yesterday at 5 o'clock in the afternoon, but it is believed that the deaths of both the Emperor and the Dowager Empress occurred a considerable time before that set down in the official statements.

An edict issued at 8 o'clock this morning placed upon the throne Prince Pu-Yi, the three-year-old son of Prince Chun, the Regent of the Empire, in accordance with a promise given by the Dowager Empress soon after the marriage of Prince Chun, in 1908. An edict issued on Friday made Pu-Yi heir presumptive.

Troops Held in Readiness.

The foreign legations were notified this morning by the Foreign Board of the death of the Emperor and the succession of Prince Pu-Yi. Troops have been in readiness for several days to quell any disorders that might arise on the death of Kwang-Hsu, and the possibility of uprisings was made greater because of the fact that the death of the Dowager Empress was known to be close at hand. Two divisions of troops have been held in reserve, and these are now stationed in various quarters of the city. Twenty gendarmes were dispatched to guard the approaches to the legations, but up to the present the duties of the forces have been slight. It was announced that the legation guard was ordered out at "the special call of the legations on account of the Emperor's death."

Prince Chun, the Regent, has ordered the Viceroys and Governors to take precautions for the continuation of the administration of the provinces as heretofore, and he has commanded a hundred days of mourning. The Court will go into mourning for three years.

Peking has already been greatly transformed; all red objects have been removed and blue substituted. The people learned this evening of the death of the Dowager Empress, and, although the Chinese are in no way emotional, they showed that they were profoundly impressed by the passing of their powerful ruler. The foreigners in the city are watching the strange ceremonies with great interest. At the palace elaborate rites are being observed, and a flood of edicts has been sent forth.

Emperor and Empress Died Alone.

Deathbed observances of three thousand years ago marked the passing of the Emperor and Dowager. They died alone and unattended,, although surrounded by circles of abject spectators, who remained a rod distant, as, on account of the sacred persons of their Majesties, they could not be approached. The Emperor died as he had lived, without ministration of any kind or scientific aid. For months he had refused to permit the services of foreign physicians, and although it was stated that he had gone back to the old form of medical treatment, it is believed that latterly he received no treatment at all.

The Government has given out that the Dowager Empress in a lucid interval on Friday last received Prince Ching, who is a Manchu and a member of the royal family, and approved the edicts declaring Prince Pu-Yi, heir presumptive, and Prince Chun Regent of the Empire. Prince Ching was at the beginning of the Boxer outbreak Lord Chamberlain of the Court and Commander of the Peking field force. It was on Prince Ching that the foreign officials hung hopes of the safety of the envoys. He has held many official positions and was high in imperial favor.

Regent Chun Progressive Man.

That the Dowager Empress took this step is discredited. Nevertheless Prince Ching is believed to have established successfully the Chun régime, which is the Manchu régime, without obstacle, and the opinion is held here that this solution of the difficulty which has necessarily confronted the Government is the best possible.

Until word of the Dowager's death is spread broadcast, no general disorders are apprehended. China is quieter now than at any time since 1900. Local disorders in the South are possible on any pretext, but the North is more inclined to peace. There are few signs of antagonism to foreigners and there is no manner of doubt that Prince Chun will be able to meet the situation, as he is recognized as thoroughly progressive, and he

is the most acceptable man to those most disposed to cause trouble, the reformers. Antagonism on the part of the conservatives and even an insurrectionary movement are conceivable because the death of the powerful woman who dominated all and the weakling Emperor sweeps away the old palace corruptionists.

The foreign troops have taken measures to safeguard the interests of their respective countrymen here. The British guard has been increased by the arrival of fifty highlanders from Tientsin.

SHANGHAI, Nov. 15.—On account of the death of the Emperor and the Dowager Empress Tuan Fang, the Viceroy of Nanking, has left the scene of the manoeuvres and will proceed at once to Peking with troops.

THINK FOUL PLAY UNLIKELY.

Chinese Legation Says Regency Was Arranged by Late Emperor.

Special to The New York Times.

WASHINGTON, Nov. 15.—Though the State Department is silent with regard to the changes likely to follow the death of the Emperor yesterday afternoon and—still more important—the death of the Empress Dowager this afternoon, a general feeling of safety is manifested at the Chinese Legation that under the regency of young Prince Chun the present policy of the empire will be maintained. His influence, it is confidently asserted at the legation to-night, will be on the side of the progressive reform. The death of the Empress Dowager was officially announced to the legation to-night in the following dispatch from the Board of Foreign Affairs:

This is to announce the death of Her Imperial Majesty the Empress Dowager at 2 o'clock this afternoon. The legation is requested to notify the Department of State.

That is the sum of the official knowledge possessed by Chinese diplomats here as to the way the Empress Tsi-An came to her end, and if they have any suspicion of foul play of the familiar palace revolution variety they keep it, with Oriental discretion, to themselves.

The legation announced to-night that further advices are expected in the morning.

As against the probability of foul play is pointed out the fact that the Government remains in the hands of those selected by the late Emperor, and is expected to be carried on according to a plan agreed on at least two years ago. The first step in that plan was the appointment of young Prince Chun, then only 28 years old, to the Grand Council of the Empire.

That appointment, according to a statement made at the legation to-night, was by way of preparation for the position he now holds. His son, who was then only a year old, was selected by the arbitrary will of the Emperor to be his successor. The selection of the little Prince's father to be Regent followed in the natural course of events.

Prince Chun, it is said, is not a man of striking attainments, but his near relation to the late Emperor has on more than one occasion brought him to the fore, and he has always acquitted himself satisfactorily. His first important mission was his visit to Berlin in 1901 to express on behalf of his imperial brother the regret of China for the killing of the German Ambassador. He was then not quite 20. On his return from that mission he began to interest

himself in the internal policy of the nation, and aligned himself easily with the progressive element. At the legation to-night it is said that he will continue, along the lines already laid down, to work for a constitutional Government, modern equipment of the army and navy, and eventually a representative assembly.

This last innovation, said a Chinese high in authority here, is expected to become a reality with a few years, long before the little Prince comes to the throne. As twenty years is the generally accepted age for the recognition in China of the prerogatives of manhood, Prince Chun will have seventeen years as Regent, and during that time the heir apparent is expected to be reared along those progressive lines to which as Emperor he will be expected to give his sanction.

At the legation here no changes are expected in the membership of the Grand Council. That is an appointive body, but its membership is practically permanent. Prince Chun has been an active member of it for two years, and is said to be in perfect harmony with its other members, while the portfolios, according to the local legation, are expected to remain in charge of the men now constituting the Imperial Ministry.

EMPRESS DOWAGER'S CAREER.

Tsi-An, Empress Dowager of China, takes rank as one of the women who from time to time utilize the chances of marriage to force themselves upon the Government of a great State. Like Catherine de Medici and Elizabeth of Russia she gained and held her position only by unwavering cruelty, and, like them, she remained to the last a good deal of an enigma to those around her.

The empire over which this remarkable woman held despotic sway for so long, covered with its dependencies an area of 4,225,000 square miles, or about one-fifteenth of the total land surface of the globe. The population of that empire is estimated at about 400,000,000, or more than a fourth of the total population of the world.

There are many stories of the birth and family of the Empress. It is not doubted, however, that she is a Manchu, and therefore comes of the race which invaded China from the North in the seventeenth century and imposed its customs and rule on the true Chinese.

Tsi-An is generally said to have been born in 1835, the daughter of a Manchu, in Canton. He met with reverses and sold her when she was 3 years old to a rich merchant. She was even then remarkable for her cleverness, and at the age of 8 could read and write.

Becomes Hien-fung's Wife.

In 1848 an imperial proclamation was issued directing all Manchu girls between the ages of 15 and 18 to present themselves in Pekin as candidates for the hand of the Emperor Hien-fung. Tsi-An was then chosen to be one of the secondary wives of the Emperor. Wu Ting-fang, the Chinese Minister at Washington, has, however, given another version of this story and has declared that she was the daughter of a Peking official.

In 1861 Hien-fung died and left the kingdom by will to his son, Tung Chih, who happened to be the son of Tsi-An. This at once, according to Chinese custom, elevated the mother to a position of great importance, and she began her career of intrigue. She suggested to Prince Kung, the brother of the late Emperor, that it would be better to suppress the Council of Regency and to appoint herself and the first wife of Hien-fung to look after the young Emperor while all real power was left in the hands of the Prince himself.

Kung fell in with her scheme and for twelve years the two Empresses acted as joint Regents at Peking. Then in 1875 Tung Chih passed away, not, it is hinted in Chinese court circles, without the connivance of the Empresses. His wife soon followed him, and then the Empresses made a happy discovery. They came across a document naming Kwang-Hsu, whose death occurred last Saturday, as the successor to the throne. He was only 3 years old and in consideration of his tender years the document went on to nominate the two Empresses as Regents until he reached years of discretion.

Becomes Virtual Sole Ruler.

Six years later the elder Empress died, or, as the Chinese Court phrase had it, "ascended to be a guest on high," and once more there were whispers about the part the Empress Dowager might have had in this promotion. But now she was in undisputed power, and it went hardly with those who dared to oppose her wishes. The Chinese Empire has always maintained itself by arbitrary and cruel measures, and the Dowager Empress had no hesitation whatever in removing from her path any one who would not bend to her will.

In 1884 she dismissed Prince Kung from all his offices, and made him retire into obscurity. She found in Prince Chung, the father of the Emperor, and Li Hung-Chang more plastic instruments of her power. To all suggestions of reform or of the introduction of railroads and other products of European civilization the Empress turned a deaf ear. She tried to keep the empire standing still, careless of the Western world knocking at her doors.

For a short period about the year 1889 it did indeed seem that she might move forward with the times. Li Hung-Chang was in favor of some concessions to Western ideas, and it was understood that his imperial mistress was behind him. But the extreme reformers went too fast for those bred in all the prejudices of China, and the Empress became alarmed. She suddenly changed her position and steadfastly refused to allow any innovations in the Flowery Kingdom.

Fable of Chinese Power Exploded.

This obduracy of hers had the most unhappy effects for all China. When she first ruled alone the fable of Chinese power had not yet been exploded. European nations dreaded to arouse the empire, and it was generally believed that there was a vast reserve of latent power to be called forth by any attack. If the Dowager Empress had foreseen the trend of events and realized that she must allow her people to embrace modern ideas she would have been spared many later humiliations.

It was Japan which opened the eyes of the world to the real powerlessness of the empire. In 1894 war broke out between the two Far Eastern powers over the Korean question, and in a few months China had to sue for peace, which was granted by the treaty of Shimonoseki. Forthwith all the great Western powers cast covetous eyes upon China and began to intrigue to gain concessions of territory and commercial privileges.

Against this situation even the Empress Dowager could not fight successfully. Her régime was evidently a failure. Japan had torn away all China's authority over Korea and had nearly taken Peking itself. England had seized Wei-Hai-Wei. Germany had established herself at Kiao-Chow. Russia was steadily encroaching on the western frontier, and France had obtained a foothold in Annam and Tonkin.

The more enlightened Chinese turned in despair to the Emperor and endeavored to set him up as the real ruler of the empire. In the Summer of 1898 they prevailed upon him to issue a remarkable series of edicts. He ordered the foundation of a university at Peking; he directed the Tsung-li-Yamen to undertake the en-

couragement of agriculture; he declared his intention of sending around the world an Imperial Commission consisting of Princes of the blood to observe the progress of modern civilization and to report on what might be introduced into China.

Late Emperor's Attempted Reforms.

A few days later the literary examinations which had kept Chinese officialdom in the thrall of Confucianism were abolished, and political economy and international law were decreed as the subjects by which promotion must be earned. The Ministers were severely censured for delay in pushing on the university, and it was ordered that the Lu-Han Railway should be expedited.

Other decrees dealt with the reformation of the army and the substitution of modern weapons and tactics for the traditional drill and armament and with the establishment of naval academies and training ships. Useless officials were dismissed; the Emperor disgraced two Presidents and four Vice Presidents of the Board of Rites for preventing the delivery of memorials to the Emperor unopened, and three Governorships were abolished as useless expenses to the people.

China was to be opened to foreign trade, imperial decrees ordered local officials to do all they could to foster commerce, a post system was established, and steps were taken to develop the great mineral wealth of the empire.

In three months enough decrees had been issued to pave the way for a repetition in China of the marvelous awakening which had taken place in Japan. As in that country, the true Emperor had stepped from seclusion to take the power from the hands of the actual ruler, the Shogun, so in China it seemed as though the Emperor would crush the usurping Dowager Empress and bring about a new era.

But Tsi-An had no intention of losing her authority. While the Emperor had been issuing decrees which he could not enforce she had been intriguing against him. In September, 1898, she regained all her old ascendancy over him and made him sign a decree which practically amounted to an abdication. He transferred all his authority to the Dowager Empress and explained that he was too sick in mind and body to take active control of affairs.

From this time on the Emperor became practically of no account. He existed but did not rule. It was often difficult to discover whether he was not already dead. Many of the reformers took alarm at once at the new situation, and fled for their lives. Many were captured and executed, and Kang Yu-Wei, the Cantonese, who had been the leader of the reform movement, only just managed to escape into exile.

Yet even in China there exists a public opinion, and this made itself felt at this juncture. On Jan. 24, 1900, it seemed to the Empress Dowager that the time had come to dethrone once and for all the puppet Emperor. She caused him to sign an actual abdication in favor of the six-year-old child of Prince Tuan. There seemed no doubt that she could have enforced this decree, but throughout the empire there arose the mutterings of discontent. A petition was presented against the dethronement of the Emperor, and the Dowager Empress had to give way. She marked out a few of those who had thus opposed her will for destruction, but she recognized that she could not make headway against the widespread feeling against her.

Lesson of Boxer Uprising.

A few months later the Boxer outrages broke out throughout the empire. Missionaries, foreign traders, and native Christians were murdered wherever they were found. To this work of massacre the Empress is said to have given 100,000 taels from her private fortune. Apparently she dreamed of consolidating her

power on the basis of the old policy of the exclusion of all the foreign devils.

The swift vengeance of the Western nations followed. An international force under command of Marshal von Waldersee marched on Peking, relieved the legations, which were closely besieged, and forced their way into the heart of the Forbidden City. The Court and the Empress were driven to seek safety in flight, and were not able to return until 1902.

The allies refused to permit the deposition of the Emperor, and the Dowager Empress had to assent to his restoration. It really mattered little to her. She still continued to be the power behind the throne, and to the day of her death it has been her will and determination not to give in to Western ways which has hampered the awakening of China.

In her last years there were indeed signs that she felt a pressure from outside too great to be altogether withstood. She assented to the reorganization of the military forces of China on Western lines. She consented to receive the ladies connected with the embassies at Peking and gave audience to the then Miss Alice Roosevelt during her trip to the East with Mr. Taft and his party.

American Woman Paints Portrait.

She even allowed her portrait to be painted by an American artist, Miss Katherine Carl. For nearly a year the artist lived in the imperial palace, sharing in the life of the inmates. She has published a description of her experience, in which she describes the Empress as a "kindly-looking lady, so remarkably youthful in appearance, with so winning a smile," that it was impossible to believe that this was really the redoubtable Dowager Empress.

"She was clothed," goes on Miss Carl, "in a gown of imperial yellow brocaded with the wistaria vine in realistic colors and richly embroidered in pearls. It was made in the graceful Manchu fashion, in one piece, reaching from the neck to the floor, and fastened from the right shoulder to the hem with jade buttons. The stuff of the gown was a stiff, transparent silk, and was worn over a softer undergown of the same color and length. From the top button from the right shoulder hung a string of eighteen enormous pearls, separated by flat pieces of brilliant transparent green jade. From the same button was suspended a large carved pale ruby, which had yellow silk tassels terminating in two immense pear-shaped pearls of great beauty."

Hated and Feared by Chinese.

Among the Chinese the Dowager Empress was hated and feared. She was known to be keeping the Emperor in practical imprisonment, and the people as a whole deeply resented it. She was in as little actual touch with the needs of her own countrymen as she was with the world beyond her dominions. Nearly all communications with her had to be carried on through the little band of favorites with whom she had surrounded herself.

Yet it was said that, in spite of her deficient education, she was a woman of parts. She possessed something more than the grim determination and ruthless cruelty which kept her in power. She is said to have been a poet of some merit, and to have had real artistic ability. She had the gift of humor, and at times convulsed her court by her sallies.

"The Old Buddha" was the nickname by which she was known in Peking, and her officials had a lively apprehension of her terrible temper. Yet she did not seem to grow harsher with age, but rather gave way a little to the influences about her. To the last she was mistress of all her circle, and she kept a strict control of even the marriages and betrothals of the members of her Court.

China Is On a New Road.

Much importance must be ascribed to the recently issued edict of the Chinese Government, proclaiming as a settled policy of the future that the Emperor will be Commander in Chief of the Army, and that during the minority of the present Emperor the Prince Regent will perform the duties and accept the responsibilities of the new position. This may or may not mean much, immediately, as to the competence with which the Chinese Army will be trained and led, but it does show that hereafter the military profession in China, instead of being held the lowest in the social system, and viewed with contempt by all classes down to the laborers at unskilled trades, will have something like the esteem it has in other countries.

When the half divine Emperor himself is a soldier, other soldiers cannot be despised. In this matter China has always been the exact antithesis of Japan. In the latter country, from the beginning of history, and even of legend, the fighting man has always been held in the highest honor. Limitless courage and devotion have been expected of him, and therefore both have developed in him, while the tradesman and artisan have passed for—and consequently been—beings with distinctly inferior standards. The result can be seen in the widely different reputations now possessed by Chinese and Japanese merchants—a difference which is one of the greatest difficulties encountered by the Japanese in their effort to meet the Occidental nations on their own ground.

Whether the change will mean the elevation or the depression of the Chinese character is a question to which varying answers will be given, in accordance with the prophet's liking or dislike for the military spirit and characteristics, but undoubtedly it will tend to make harder the coercion of China by foreigners, for it will sooner or later create among the Chinese the feeling of national unity and patriotism which until recently seemed to be almost entirely lacking in them. The Chinaman's interests and sympathies will no longer be limited to his own family, and the shades of his ancestors will probably soon miss some of the reverence they have been accustomed to receive.

CHINA REVOLT GROWING FAST

HANKOW, Oct. 12.— The revolution which has been hanging over China for months past and of which the rising in the province of Sze-Chuen was only a small part has begun in earnest. It is a concerted movement to take the empire and declare a republic. The noted exiled revolutionist, Dr. Sun Yat Sen, leader of the anti-Manchu party, if the plans do not miscarry, is to be elected President. He was the delegate of the revolutionary party to the United States in 1910 and is believed, during that tour, to have made arrangements for the financing of the movement.

Sun Yu, a brother of Dr. Sun Yat Sen, who is now in Hankow, has been elected President of the Provincial Assembly, and Tang Hua Lung, the retiring President of the Assembly and a well-known scholar, has been elected Governor of Hu-Peh.

The whole Assembly has seceded from the imperial Government. The rebels are well organized and financially strong. They have confiscated the local treasures and banks and are issuing their own paper money, redeeming the Government notes with this, as the foreign banks are refusing the Government notes.

The revolutionaries who two days ago captured Wu-Chang have crossed the Yang-Tse River and occupied the native section—comprising the whole city except the foreign concessions of Hankow and Han-Yang. All are adjoining cities in Hu-Peh Province. Chang-Sha, capital of Hu-Peh, is reported to have risen in revolt, and Nanking, capital of the Province of Kiang-Su, is on the verge of a rising, several public buildings having been destroyed, including the yamens of the Viceroy and the Tartar General.

Thousands of soldiers have joined the mutiny in Hu-Peh.

Twenty miles of the Peking & Hankow Railway has been torn up and the bridges burned.

Many Manchus have been killed and the terrified people are fleeing from the cities into the country, carrying their belongings. The prisons have been opened and the criminals liberated. There has been fighting in the streets, but the most stringent orders have been issued that the lives of foreigners and their property shall be respected.

An American expedition which was dispatched from Hankow to Wu-Chang for the purpose of aiding the missionaries there returned here to-day with all the missionaries, with the exception of Miss R. A. Kemp of the Episcopal Society, the members of the Roman Catholic mission, including the sisters and the London mission, who declined to depart.

There was a brief exchange of shots to-day between the Wu-Chang forts and a loyal Chinese cruiser. The firing ceased after the British and Japanese officials had protested that it endangered the foreign concessions.

When the revolutionists swept across the river they followed their previous policy in Wu-Chang, avoiding any attack on the foreign concessions. The Methodist missionaries in Wu-Chang escaped over the walls and are known to be safe.

A special proclamation issued by the rebel General in charge of the forces in Hu-Peh states that the penalty for any interference with foreigners or with commerce shall be instant death. The proclamation further declares: "This is the army of the people. We will overthrow the tyrant Manchu dynasty and revive the rights of the real Chinese."

The foreigners of Hankow, Wu-Chang, and Han-Yang have been assembled and were entering the foreign concessions this evening. They report that they received every attention and consideration at the hands of the revolutionists.

The capture of Han-Yang, which is a town of perhaps 100,000 just north of Hankow, has delivered into the hands of the revolutionists the arsenal and the important Han-Yang iron works. The revolutionists had no trouble in Han-Yang, overwhelmingly outnumbering the local troops. Gen. Chang Piao escaped by flight, and the members of the local Government were dispersed.

The popularity of the revolutionary movement all along the river and in the interior is indicated by apparently authentic reports that several near-by cities have fallen. Where resistance was offered the rebel forces, the towns appear to have been put to the torch.

The losses in the fighting aggregate several hundred, but practically all the dead are Manchus. The slogan of the movement, which is guided by shrewd and temperate leaders, is evidently "down with the Manchus."

PEKING SENDS TROOPS.

Two Divisions Ordered to Hankow— Navy Also Ordered There.

PEKING, Oct. 12.—The Chinese Government has awakened to the danger of the revolution in Hu-Peh Province. Gen. Yin Tchang, the Minister of War, left hurriedly this evening for Pao-Ting-Fu, 100 miles to the south of Peking, where the Sixth Division of the army is making hasty preparations to leave to-morrow for Hankow. An imperial edict issued to-day ordered the immediate dispatch of two divisions of troops to the disaffected provinces. About 20,000 of the troops are Manchus. It is against the Manchus that the revolutionaries have risen.

April 6, 1911

At the same time orders have been issued for the assembling of a fleet of warships in the Yang-tse-Kiang, which are to unite with the land forces against the rebels, now in possession of Wu-Chang, Hankow, and Han-Yang. According to the official report, at least 10,000, and possibly 15,000, troops have mutinied in the province of Hu-Peh alone. It is said that they captured thirty modern guns at Wu-Chang. There is an unconfirmed rumor that the revolutionists occupied Chang-Sha on Oct. 10.

The rebels occupied Sui-Ting-Fu yesterday. It is believed they will attempt to destroy the railway and prevent the transport into Hu-Peh Province of the troops that were concentrated in Sze-Chuen last month.

Meantime elaborate military precautions have been taken to prevent any sympathetic revolutionary uprising in this city, and the palaces are guarded by troops of proved loyalty. The advices received here indicate that three regiments of the army took part in the revolt at Wu-Chang.

An edict cashiers the Viceroy of Wu-Chang, who fled before the rebels, but at the same time orders him to return to his post and retrieve his reputation. He is threatened with severe punishment if he fails to recapture Wu-Chang.

It is expected that the revolutionists will dynamite the bridges of the Peking & Hankow Railroad to prevent the early arrival of troops. Extraordinary precautions are being enforced here. Chinese passengers are forbidden to travel on the Peking & Hankow Railroad beyond Chu-matient, Hu-Nan Province, in either direction.

A dispatch to the British Legation from Chung-King says that the rebels of Sze-Chuen hold the Min River and the country west, and confirms also earlier reports of daily fighting in that vicinity.

A telegram from Hankow states that at the most four battalions remain loyal. It is known that three Wu-Chang regiments of infantry and one regiment of artillery revolted.

The American gunboat Helena and the Japanese cruiser Tsushima were expected at Hankow to-day. Several British warships have been ordered to proceed thither. The women and children living on the water front slept aboard the merchant steamers in the harbor last night.

According to Chinese rumors, Kang Yu Wei, who was adviser to the late Emperor until 1898, when the coup of the Dowager Empress restored her regency and drove the Emperor's adviser into exile, has arrived at Hankow. The missionaries at Wu-Chang are safe.

A dispatch from Cheng-tu says that the insurgents in Sze-Chuen Province hold all the country west of the Min River between Kia-ting, which is eighty-five miles south of Cheng-Tu, to Kwanhsien, fifteen miles north and thirty-five miles west of Cheng-tu. Five hundred troops have joined the rebels and the fighting continues daily.

WASHINGTON, Oct. 12.—At the Chinese Legation to-night it was stated that, while the imperial Government regards the revolution now raging in China as very serious, there has been no intimation in advices from Peking that the uprising is a concerted movement to supplant the empire by a republic.

It was said that messages received at the legation have contained but little information not carried in press dispatches. The legation has been informed that the Cabinet has delegated the Ministers of the Boards of War and Navy to make a personal investigation of the situation and report to the Government.

UPRISING AGAINST MANCHUS.

Chinese Moving to Abolish Domination Which Has Lasted 300 Years.

The term Hankow native city is applied to that part of the town which is occupied by Chinese as distinct from the foreign concessions. The British, German, French, Russian, and Japanese concessions stretch along the river bank for a distance of two miles. As the foreigners have adopted a neutral attitude, the possession of the "native city," as reported, constitutes the capture of Hankow.

Accordingly the rebels may now be said to be in control of Wu-Chang, Hankow, and Han-Yang, three important cities close together in Hu-Peh Province; and in the neighboring province of Sze-Chuen, to hold Kia-Ting, Sui-Ting-Fu, and several villages. There are about forty-nine foreign missionaries stationed at Wu-Chang, fifty-four at Hankow, and sixteen at Han-Yank.

Much of the unrest and political disaffection in China in recent years has been due to the underlying current of race hatred which the native Chinese have had for the Manchu dynasty and its empire-wide network of officials. Although the Manchus swept down from the north and took possession of the Chinese throne nearly 300 years ago, there has been little mixing of their blood with that of the native Chinese, and the two peoples have existed side by side, two continually clashing elements.

The Manchus were originally called in to assist in suppressing internal troubles which threatened the overthrow of the Ming dynasty. Their work done, they refused to withdraw, but proceeded to conquer the country for themselves. In 1643 they proclaimed the son of their own ruler as the first Emperor of a new dynasty, the tenth Emperor of which now reigns.

The Manchus have ruled China on Chinese lines of polity, and in recent years have made many efforts to conciliate the natives. A few years ago it was stated that of the 144 officials then forming the Supreme Government of the empire, only thirty-two were Manchus. In the provincial administrations the proportion of Manchus chosen in the last five years has not been more than one-fifth of the whole number.

The real reason for this change, however, may be undoubtedly found in the marked superiority of the Chinese in mental equipment and in capacity for administration. Practically all the high Chinese officials rise through a long course of promotions from the junior ranks, and most of the Manchus have found themselves outstripped early in the race by the Chinese.

The recent widespread movement for the cutting off of the queue or pigtail appears to be a part of the native crusade against Manchu domination. The wearing of the queue is one of the few really distinctive Manchu customs which the conquerors enforced upon the Chinese people.

The Episcopal Board of Missions to-day received the following cable from Bishop Logan H. Roots of Hankow, China, who has charge of the Episcopal missionary work in that part of the empire:

"Missionaries are safe and well. Everything is now quiet. Can remain here."

CHINA'S DESTINY IN YUAN'S HANDS

He Wavers Between Throne's Bait of Premiership and Republicans' Offer of Presidency.

TALK OF SPLITTING EMPIRE

South of Yangtze to be Republican, Manchuria and Chi-Li Monarchical, and Provinces as They Choose.

PEKING, Nov. 12.—The fate of the Throne apparently rests on the action of Yuan Shi-Kai. The latest message from Yuan, who has been conducting negotiations with the rebel leader, Gen. Li Yuen-Heng, indicates that a compromise is possible, that Gen. Li was becoming less irreconcilable, but that there was a difference of opinion between Gen. Li and his colleagues on the matter of policy.

Pending this message from Yuan, the Throne and Government alternated between hope and despair. First came a telegram from Yuan, in which he stated that he was unable to come to Peking, and expressed a pessimistic view of the situation. A second message coming several hours later struck a more cheerful note. In his first message Yuan Shi-Kai said:

"The outlook is decidedly gloomy. I do not expect to be able to effect the desired pacification. Moreover, my health is so feeble that I am unable to come to Peking and assume the post of Premier."

Gloom settled deeper over the official family when this was read, for they had in mind yesterday's announcement of the Chinese papers that Yuan Shi-Kai had been invited by Gen. Li Yuen-Heng, the leader of the revolutionists, to become President of the Republic of China pending the assembling of a Parliament. It seemed as though the last prop of the Throne had given way, for the expectation that Gen. Chang Shao-Tsen, who, as the real commander of the Twentieth Division of the imperial troops, holds the key to the situation in the North, might come to Peking and renew his allegiance to the Government rested upon the assumption that he would meet in conference Yuan Shi-Kai and Hsi-Liang, the former Viceroy of Manchuria.

Accordingly a pleasant surprise was caused when Yuan's second telegram arrived. This message informed the Foreign Board that the sender's negotiations with Gen. Li Yuen-Heng had taken a turn for the better, and that Gen. Li had showed signs of becoming less irreconcilable and possibly would agree to a peaceful compromise in order to avert further bloodshed. Yuan added that Li's colleages differed on matters of policy so that trouble might arise among them.

According to foreign official telegrams from Hankow last evening, Gen. Li, failing to exact better terms, might perhaps be prepared to agree to the partition of China, that portion of the country south of the Yang-tse becoming republican, Manchuria and Chi-Li remaining monarchical, and the other provinces making their own choice.

Many of Li's followers demand the overthrow of the Government and scout the idea of dividing the empire. This is supposed to be the reason why Gen. Li asked delegates from other provinces to meet at Wu-Chang, and appointed Huang-Sing, the noted revolutionary leader, commander in chief, and retained for himself the Governor Generalship, which gives him greater freedom in administrative affairs. Huang-Sing is making Hanyang his headquarters, where he is superintending the rebel defenses.

Prince Ching, the Acting Premier, and other high officials have guaranteed Gen. Chang's safety, if he will go to Peking. Gen. Chang has not yet agreed to do this, but remains at Lanchau with his troops, awaiting definite results from the Wu-Chang negotiations. Gen. Chang has not been permitted to resign his command, but has been granted so-called "sick leave."

October 13, 1911

21

The revolutionaries in Tien-Tsin do not consider it wise at the present time to force the issue. They take this attitude because of the presence of the troops at Lanchau, whose sympathies are doubtful.

The Provincial Assembly at Mukden has vetoed the Russian loan, and has informed the Viceroy that if it is taken up they will declare independence.

AMOY, China, Nov. 11.—Attacks by robber bands in different quarters threw the city into a panic early to-day. The authorities, self-constituted, dealt with the situation as best they could. The water patrol captured a piratical junk and its crew of sixteen men await decapitation.

Taotai Chang assumes office to-day. A conference of officials with representatives of the Conservative and the Radical elements was held to determine a course of action. The officials and the Conservatives proposed establishing a temporary independence for the city and the adoption of a neutral attitude toward the revolution. The Radicals, however, favored surrendering the city to the revolutionists, and this policy probably will prevail.

Chang-Chow, a city with a population estimated as high as 1,000,000, situated twenty-four miles west by north of Amoy, reports that the rebels announce that the city will be occupied on Nov. 20. The people are fleeing from the place, fearing a repetition of the experiences of the Taiping rebellion. Foreigners are in no danger.

FOO-CHOW, Nov. 11.—The Manchus who were defeated yesterday have concentrated at the Governor's palace. Robbers are burning and looting. The whole city is in disorder.

PRINCE CHUN DROPS REGENCY OF CHINA

Succeeded by a Manchu and a Chinese—Latter First to Hold Such a Place in 300 Years.

BUT YUAN IS REAL RULER

Rebels Believe He Is Only Awaiting Proper Time to Declare for Republic—Armistice Extended.

PEKING, Dec. 6.—An edict announcing the resignation of the Regent, Prince Chun, father of the child Emperor, was issued to-day by the Empress Dowager. It is also signed by the members of the Cabinet, and points out that the administration has been unpopular, and that a constitutional Government has not yet been established, explaining that owing to this complications arose, the peoples' hearts were broken, and the country was thrown into turmoil. The Regent, it is stated, regrets that his repentance came too late, and feels that if he continued in power his commands would soon be disregarded. The edict continues:

He wept and prayed to resign the Regency, at the same time expressing his earnest intention to abstain from politics. I, the Empress Dowager, living in the palace, am ignorant of the state of affairs, but I know that rebellion exists and fighting continues, causing disaster everywhere, while the commerce of friendly nations suffers. The Regent is honest, though ambitious. Being misled, he has harmed the people. Therefore his resignation is accepted.

The edict demands loyalty to the Ministers from the people, who " must now realize that the Court does not object to the surrender of the power vested in the Throne."

The retiring Regent is to receive a grant of 50,000 taels (about $30,000) annually from the Imperial household allowances. His place as guardian of the throne is to be taken jointly by Shi-Hsu, a Manchu Prince and ex-President of the National Assembly, and Hsu Shi-Chang, Vice President of the Privy Council. Both were formerly Grand Councilors.

The edict exhorts all the Princes to retire peacefully, which may indicate that there was some truth in the reports often current that the youthful Princes desired

to attack the foreigners, hoping to create foreign complications which might benefit the Manchus.

The Regent sacrificed himself in a last effort to save the Throne for his son, but, unless all evidences fail, it is too late. Some of the legations sympathize with the Regent. They pity but do not blame him. It is pointed out that he was far from selfish; that he sought the best for the Throne and the country, but was incapable. The palace, where avarice and intrigue prevail, is hopeless as a seat of government.

The administration remains for the present in the hands of the Premier, Yuan Shi-Kai, while the Empress Dowager and the Emperor continue to hold audiences and carry out ceremonial functions.

Yuan is now entirely powerful within the limitations of the disrupted Government. The rebels say that they expect him to manipulate the regiments until the Manchus are no longer capable of disturbing the capital, and then the Shanghai assembly of representatives of the loyal and rebel provinces, soon to be held, will decide in favor of a republic. The Premier has promised to abide by the assembly's decision, which, it is admitted, will be for a republic.

It is believed that the Premier desires foreign mediation in order to insure the safety of the Court and the granting of pensions. Yuan Shi-Kai has let Peking know that he has taken the British Minister, Sir John Jordan, into his confidence. He has told the Minister his plans, and says he hopes much from Sir John's mediation.

The rebels describe Yuan as a master statesman, because he is accomplishing the transition from the Manchu dynasty to a republic without a massacre or an attack on the legations.

The legations of the larger powers are increasing their guards to between 300 and 500 men. The court seems to have lost hope when the loan it asked was definitely denied.

Mail advices which have just arrived from Sian-Foo, dated Nov. 14, make brief mention of the attack on foreigners at that place some time previously. The letters say that Philip Manners, the German postal clerk who was reported killed, was alive on Nov. 14, and that W. Henne, District Postmaster at Sian-Foo, was recovering from injuries. No mention is made of other foreigners having been injured, but there are indications that the rebels have been censoring the letters.

As the imperial and revolutionary leaders at Hankow have not yet come to an understanding, the armistice has been extended for three more days.

Rebels Still Demand Republic.

SHANGHAI, Dec. 6.—The southern revolutionaries are apparently more than ever determined upon the effacement of the Manchu administration as the only terms upon which peace can be established. The abdication of the Regent is regarded with suspicion, according to the revolutionary leaders seen to-night, and the dual guardianship is unsatisfactory.

Notwithstanding the peace negotiations at Wu-Chang and Shanghai, those at the head of the republican movement at a meeting to-night decided to float the first issue of republican war bonds, covering a patriotic and sympathetic loan amounting to 10,000,000 taels. The bonds will be issued in denominations of 100, 50, 10, and 5 taels, the issue price being 80 per cent. of the face value, and the average rate of interest 12 per cent. The bonds are repayable in six years by the agents of the new Republican Bank, which has a capital of 5,000,000 taels at the present time, subscribed entirely by Chinese.

The hope was expressed at the meeting that Americans could be induced to subscribe. One speaker said that the United States was the only country to which China looked for sympathetic assistance, because the United States was the only disinterested friend of China's millions of starving and oppressed people.

Arrangements have practically been completed for a meeting of delegates representing the Shanghai Republicans and representatives of Yuan Shi-Kai in order to discuss terms of peace. Wu Ting-Fang, Secretary of Foreign Affairs in the Republican Government, was invited to go to Wu-Chang to join in the peace negotiations there, but has declined. He considers the negotiations at Wu-Chang unofficial, as the centre of the Republican Government has been transferred to Shanghai, pending the declaration of Nanking as the capital of the republic.

The most significant circumstance in connection with the abdication of Prince Chun is that his place is taken, not by one or more Manchus, but by a Manchu and a Chinese. Shi-Hsu is a Manchu, while Hsu Shi-Chang is a Chinese. Yesterday's events in Peking mean that, for the first time since the Manchu conquest nearly 300 years ago, a Chinese shares the Imperial power.

To determine whether a man is a Chinese or a Manchu is easy. The Manchus are distinguished from the Chinese by the fact that they do not use their family or surnames, which belong rather to the clan than to the individual; but, in order to conform to the requirements of Chinese life, the personal name is made to do duty instead. Foreigners distinguish Chinese from Manchu names by a certain disposition of hyphens. Thus, Li Hung-Chang is at once seen to be the name of a Chinese, the surname Li being isolated from the personal name Hung-Chang. Jui-Lin and Na-Tung are by the same system recognized as the names of Manchus.

Prince Chun is the father of the infant Emperor Pu-Yi, who was born in February, 1906, and succeeded his uncle, the late Emperor Kwang-Su, in November, 1908. After Kwang-Su and the much more influential Empress Dowager Tsi-An died, within a few days of each other, Prince Chun, in the resulting confusion, proved to be the most competent and clearest headed of the Manchu Princes and became the ruler of the empire.

Chun's Stormy Regency.

His regency was a stormy one from the first. He tried to hold a middle ground which pleased neither the Manchu reactionaries nor the native progressives. He has handled the existing crisis with perhaps something less than his old-time vigor, and recent reports have hinted that his mind was weakening.

Wu Ting-Fang, formerly Minister at Washington, who is now one of the revolutionary leaders in Shanghai, a few days ago issued an appeal to Prince Chun urging him to abdicate in favor of the republic. It was reported later from Peking that Chun was willing to accept a pension and retire to Je-Hol if his personal safety were assured.

DR. SUN IS ELECTED PRESIDENT OF CHINA

Unanimously Chosen by the Assembly at Nanking—Court to Quit Peking.

MANCHUS' OFFER REJECTED

Rebels Not Satisfied by Convention Plan—Buddhist Kutuktu Proclaimed Khan of Mongolia.

NANKING, Friday, Dec. 29.—Dr. Sun Yat-Sen has been unanimously elected President of the Republic of China.

SHANGHAI, Dec. 28.—Sun Yat-Sen's election as President of the Republic by the Nanking conference to-day means that the peace conference between Wu Ting Fang and Tang Shao Yi is closed. The President will assume charge of all negotiations. The continuance of these negotiations with Yuan Shi Kai as the representative of the retiring Manchu royalty will depend entirely upon the immediate withdrawal of all the so-called imperial troops from all points of contact with the revolutionaries.

Under these conditions the armistice will be extended for ten days in order to give President Sun time to issue the terms under which the Manchus must lay down their arms and to decide upon pensions and other preliminary details.

The President, or head of the military government now established, with the capital at Nanking, will treat the Court as a thing of the past, because eighteen provinces have already voted in favor of a republic in a properly constituted convention, and the edict recently issued at Peking says that if a representative convention favors a republic the throne will abdicate.

[Dr. Sun Yat-Sen, who left this country some months ago for England and France, where he continued his campaign on behalf of the Chinese revolutionary cause, has been a thorn in the flesh of the Manchu dynasty for many years. In 1895 a price was put upon his head, but he slipped noiselessly about the world, escaping the nets of the imperial authorities.

Sun Yat-Sen was educated in Honolulu, where his father was a merchant of considerable means. It was while a medical student in Hongkong that he met many of his fellow-countrymen who had returned to China from other countries and desired a change in the Government. Out of this element was formed the Chinese Reform Association. This Spring and Summer Dr. Sun spent many months in San Francisco, where he induced the Chinese to contribute largely to the revolutionary cause.]

LONDON, Friday, Dec. 29.—A telegram from Tien-Tsin to the Exchange Telegram Company says that the imperial family has decided to leave Peking.

The Daily Telegraph's Peking correspondent notes a remarkable change in the attitude of the semi-official press, foreshadowing the establishment of a republic, and adds that Tang Shao-Yi has resigned and seceded to the Republicans.

Another remarkable development, he says, is that the provincial generalissimos have begun to order back to Peking the metropolitan officials who followed the generalissimos to their native provinces. This alone, says the correspondent, breaks up the Central Government and renders the Manchu position absolutely desperate.

PARIS, Dec. 28.—A Peking dispatch received here says:

"Disgusted at the refusal of the imperial clan to contribute to the war chest, Yuan Shi-Kai to-night took sick leave. It is believed that this presages his early retirement from the premiership. He bitterly resents the bad faith of Wu Ting-Fang and his party in proposing a national congress and now insisting upon a rump, not a representative congress.

"Yuan fears that a republic means the country's dissolution and believes that the only sane solution is to fight it out, but he is handicapped by lack of money."

Throne Accepts Yuan's Plan.

The Throne to-day agreed to Premier Yuan Shi-Kai's suggestion that the question of the future Government of China be referred to a National convention, and consented to abide by the decision of the convention whatever it may be. The Dowager Empress, Premier Yuan, and the Manchu Princes of the imperial clan debated throughout the entire morning on the scheme. Prince Ching, ex-Premier and Minister of Foreign Affairs, stoutly urged the acceptance of the proposal. Prince Yu-Lang, member of the Grand Council, and Prince Tsai-Tao, ex-Minister of War, and brother of the Prince Regent, on the other hand, strenuously opposed the scheme.

Those among the Manchu Princes present who were in favor of the acceptance of the proposition finally prevailed and the decision was reached to leave the settlement of the future form of government in the hands of the delegates selected by the nation.

Premier Yuan explained to the Princes that he could continue the Government and retain the country north of the Yangtse only by having funds placed at his disposal. He asked the Princes to empower him to obtain money. He explained that $10,000,000 would meet the payments for the soldiers for five months, after which the south would become disunited and province after province would return to its allegiance to the throne.

But the Princes were unmoved. They pleaded lack of money, although most of them are very wealthy. None has given any substantial amount to aid the Government with the exception of Prince Ching, who has handed over more than $100,000 for that purpose. The Dowager Empress wept and Yuan Shi-Kai showed signs of distress. Then he declared that he could not desert her and the child Emperor, and agreed to continue in office.

The decision taken at the meeting was followed quickly by an imperial edict in the following terms:

Dr. Wu Ting-Fang, the chief of the revolutionary delegates to the peace conference at Shanghai, and others contend that the people of China desire a republic. This question neither the Government nor a section of the people is able to decide. Therefore a National conference is necessary. The Princes and the members of the imperial clan agree to let the Cabinet inform the revolutionaries and then frame regulations for a conference and arrange for an extension of the armistice. The Empress Dowager sanctions the calling together of a conference, as she is desirous to avoid bloodshed and to bring happiness to the people of China according to the wishes of the majority.

The Cabinet has been instructed to draw up the regulations which shall govern the national convention and to inform the delegates to the peace conference at Shanghai that the Throne is willing to abide by the decision of a representative convention, no matter what form of government it may choose.

The action of the Throne leaves no room for doubt that the advisers of the Regent and the Emperor are prepared for abdication should that course prove to be the only way of settlement.

CHAPTER 2

Post-Dynastic Interregnum 1912–49

Mao Tse-tung and
Chiang Kai-shek, 1945.

YUAN, FEARING RUIN, WANTS TO RESIGN

Tells Wu He Can't Control Chinese Situation and Urges Sun Yat-Sen for President.

WILL STAY UNTIL RELIEVED

Meantime Asks Aid from the Republican War Ministers to Quell the Disturbances in Manchuria.

SHANGHAI, Feb. 17.—Yuan Shi-Kai telegraphed to-day to Dr. Wu Ting-fang, Republican Minister of Justice, and to Tang-Shao-Yi, his representative, urging them to try to obtain the election of Dr. Sun Yat Sen as President of the republic in his place. In his dispatch he said:

"I am unable to control the involved situation in China, as I am suffering from impaired health. Now that the aims of the republicans have been attained I have accomplished my duty. The post of President of the republic would only serve to lead to my ruin. I ask your kind offices and interest with the people of the country to elect Dr. Sun Yat Sen, to whom credit should be given. I will wait here until I am relieved. Then I will return to my home and resume my work as a husbandman."

Yuan-Shi-Kai also telegraphed to Nanking requesting Huang Sing, War Minister in the Republican Cabinet, to dispatch troops to the north to help quell disturbances in Manchuria.

The new Constitution of the provisional Government will be approved by the Assembly at Nanking Monday, after which it will be notified by a delegation which will start for the north.

Gen. Homer Lea, the American officer who has been acting as military adviser to Dr. Sun Yat Sen and has been seriously ill, has now rallied and may recover.

Dr. Sun Yat Sen, in an interview to-day, urged that an appeal be made to foreigners to contribute to the relief of the famine in China. He said that owing to the life-and-death struggle for freedom which has been going on in China, the administration was at present helpless, but he hoped that hereafter it would not be necessary for China to make any appeal abroad.

ASK AMERICA'S RECOGNITION.

Thousand Members of China Society from New York See the President.

WASHINGTON, Feb. 17.—A delegation of the China Society of America, including 1,000 Chinese-American residents of New York, appeared before the President, the Senate Foreign Relations Committee, the House Foreign Affairs Committee, and the Chinese Ambassador, and urged immediate recognition by the United States of the Republic of China.

Major Lewis Livingston Seaman, President of the society; V. K. Wellington Koo, Secretary, and Marcus M. Marke called at the White House, where they presented a resolution which "earnestly requests the President of the United States to be the first among the representatives of foreign nations to accord recognition to the republican Government in China."

The committee was well satisfied with its interview with President Taft and members of Congress. Major Seaman said he was convinced that the disposition of the American Government toward the new Chinese Government was kindly. The President, he said, was hopeful of an opportune time of manifesting it. The delegation found the Chinese Ambassador enthusiastic over the prospects of the new Government.

FEAR POWERS PUSH CHINA TOWARD RUIN

Franco-Russian Intrigues to Prevent Success of Loan Helped by British Foreign Office.

FINANCE MINISTER DESPAIRS

Threatens to Resign, Which Would Wreck the Cabinet and Perhaps Cause Republic's Downfall.

Special Cable to THE NEW YORK TIMES.
LONDON, Monday, Feb. 17.—The Daily Telegraph's Peking correspondent in a long dispatch on the loan situation asserts that serious consequences will follow soon unless the British Government reconsiders its determination to force China to the last extremity. He says:

"The sextuple group, having failed to keep any of their promises, are to-day more hopelessly at sea than ever regarding the arrangement of their differences and carrying out of their engagements.

"A week ago the Minister of Finance, Tchow-Hsueh-Hsi, realizing that the postponement was indefinite, made arrangements with the sextuple group, with the approval of the British Minister, to the effect that China might contract an independent £10,000,000 ($50,000,000) loan, to be issued immediately, if security could be found other than the salt revenues.

"The Finance Minister, therefore, offered the land transfer tax and stamp tax, amounting together to £2,000,000 ($10,000,000) annually.

"These negotiations were proceeding smoothly and successfully in London until last Thursday, when the Foreign Office suddenly raised new objections, positively refusing to sanction any issue until after the six-power loan was floated.

"The British financiers, though prepared to issue the loan and finance the Chinese Government generally, will not act without the sanction of the Foreign Office, and on Friday they telegraphed to this effect.

"Faced by this new collapse, the Finance Minister, finding his position intolerable and being unable to turn in any direction for help, purposes to resign immediately, and depart from Peking, which would bring about the fall of the entire Cabinet."

With reference to France's objection to the three Chinese nominees as auditors under the sextuple agreement, the correspondent says:

"I am in a position to assert that the French protest, though technically directed against all three alike, would certainly be made on some other score, no matter what names were substituted, as absolute instructions have been conveyed to the Russian and French Legations not to permit any financial help to China until the autonomy of Mongolia is fully recognized.

"The attitude of the British Foreign Office is undoubtedly due to French and Russian representations, and China is menaced with ruin for base political reasons."

The Russian pressure is steadily growing, says the correspondent, but the Chinese Army and the political parties are determined to stand firm on the question of Mongolia, holding that Peking would be untenable if Mongolia was lost. He continues:

"The French proposal to substitute French and Russian auditors is regarded as a deliberate and carefully calculated insult, for even if the Peking Government accepted it, the provinces would revolt, throw off Peking's authority, and assemble the Parliament at Nanking.

"The final circumstance lies in the fact that if the large amounts of Chinese Treasury bills in the hands of foreign bankers and maturing next month are not redeemed, or renewed, China can be proclaimed officially bankrupt and armed intervention must come.

"Many observers already believe that if the present conditions continue for a few days longer, the whole provisional Government, including President Yuan Shi Kai, must drive to the legation quarter and declare that the work of the Government has become impossible."

After stating that from an instrument destined to accomplish Chinese regeneration the sextuple loan had been changed to a weapon to effect China's ruin, the correspondent condemns England's indorsement of this reactionary policy, adding:

"If in the face of all these circumstances the British Foreign Office disregards the warnings and persists in ignoring the realities of the situation, it is said here that the culpability for any tragedy in China will rest on its shoulders. I repeat that unless an adequate British loan is arranged promptly the Chinese situation will break the two."

PEKING, Feb. 16.—Present returns from the general elections held throughout China indicate that President Yuan Shi Kai will be returned to office by a substantial majority.

CHINA LOAN SIGNED, REBELLION FEARED

Agreement Concluded at Daybreak in Spite of Parliament's Protests.

$125,000,000 IS INVOLVED

Dominant Political Party Opposes Yuan Shih Kai's Compact with Five-Power Group.

PEKING, April 27.—China's day of prayer did not prove entirely peaceful, because of dissension over the five-power loan. The loan, which is for $125,000,000, was signed just before daybreak, the Chinese and foreign signatories having assembled late last evening to conclude the details.

A delegation from the Senate and House of Representatives gathered outside the British Bank, where the representatives of the Government and the five-power group met. The Vice President of the Senate acted as spokesman for the delegation, and, when an opportunity was given to him to confer with the signatories, he explained that the majority in the Parliament considered the loan illegal.

Since the days of the monarchy the question of a loan has been discussed in various forms, and it threatens now to bring about another revolution similar to that caused by the Hu-Kuang loan.

The situation is about as follows: The five-power bankers and the Chinese Government have arranged the loan practically for Yuan Shih Kai's Cabinet, which Yuan Shih Kai completely dominates. The Cabinet contends that the Government has a right to conclude such a contract because the permanent Assembly has not yet been constituted, and therefore approval of the six-power loan by the Provisional Assembly holds good. In addition to the withdrawal of the United States from the combination, however, other alterations have been made in the contract since the Assembly approved it.

The Kwo Ming Tang Party, which is the dominating political party, would remove Yuan Shi Kai by parliamentary means or by force, but neither is possible while the President controls the army at Peking. The adherents of the Kwo Ming Tang Party do not desire to withdraw to Nanking for the purpose of establishing a Parliament there, because such action would result in disruption of the North from the South.

The deadlock is at present complete. Members of the Kwo Ming Tang express the fear that some of the powers represented in the loan—Great Britain, France, Germany, Russia, and Japan—now that the loan is concluded with Yuan Shih Kai may strengthen his hands by recognizing the republic at an early date. In this connection an interesting question arises as to whether the United States will anticipate these powers, in spite of the fact that the Chinese House of Representatives has again failed to elect a Speaker.

It is probable that the Southern party will seek to cancel the loan as a test of their strength against Yuan Shih Kai.

April 28, 1913

PEKING EXPECTS RECOGNITION TO-DAY

State Department Reticent as to Proposed Acknowledgment of Republic of China.

COMPLIES WITH CONDITIONS

Constitutional Assembly Has Organized as Required by This Government—Luncheon for Legation Staff.

PEKING, May 1.—The United States will recognize the Republic of China to-morrow. The Chinese Government will testify its appreciation by an elaborate reception and luncheon to the legation staff at the Winter Palace.

Special to The New York Times.

WASHINGTON, May 1.—State Department officials were not prepared to-night to discuss the announcement from Peking that the United States would recognize the new Chinese republic to-morrow. They explained that the formal recognition of the republic would be the automatic result of arrangements carefully made weeks ago by President Wilson and Secretary Bryan. The plan of recognition was simply that Edward T. Williams, Secretary of the American Legation at Peking and Chargé d'Affaires, was to represent to the provisional Government of China that the United States would recognize the republic when certain conditions had been met.

Among these conditions was the organization of the Constitutional Assembly by the election of its presiding officers. Some days ago the Senate chose its President. To-day Mr. Williams advised the State Department that the lower house had selected its presiding officer. There has been consideration of the idea of including as a condition the election by the Parliament of the Provisional President of the republic. But that action was not made an indispensable condition precedent to recognition.

The act of recognition will be essentially simple, but State Department officials would not speak of the details, nor state whether or not a communication from President Wilson would be presented to the houses of the Chinese Parliament.

May 2, 1913

WE GAIN IN CHINA AND ENGLAND LOSES

Resentment at British Opium Traffic—Feeling of Gratitude Toward America.

OUR GOODS ARE PREFERRED

Gen. Chang, President of Opium Prohibition Commission, in England on Educational Mission.

By Marconi Transatlantic Wireless Telegraph to The New York Times.

LONDON, Tuesday, May 13.—Gen. Chang, President of the Chinese National Opium Prohibition Commission, has arrived in England. He is delegated to place before the British people the plain facts of the opium-suppression movement and to appeal, on behalf of the men of all parties and provinces in China, for a complete release from the obligations imposed by existing treaties in respect to the Indian traffic.

Gen. Chang, discussing the British policy in an interview in The Daily News, referred to the effect of the opium traffic on Anglo-Chinese commercial relations, saying:

"Now that the Chinese people generally have realized the evil that opium is doing to the country, they find it hard to forgive England for insisting on its importation. The poorer people are learning to read, and many of hte new vernacular newspapers are very bitter.

"It would be going too far to say that there is a definite boycott against British goods, but certainly the tendency is not to buy them when something else will do as well.

"From many points of view British influence in China is decreasing, solely on account of the resentment against the opium traffic. As long as your Shanghai stocks keep coming in these strained relations will, I am afraid, continue.

"How far this tendency has penetrated you will see from an amusing conversation I had recently with one of my servants. He had been sent to buy some kerosene oil, and came back with an unusual brand. Questioned why he had chosen this, he explained that one kind had a trade mark which he thought British and the other was American, and he unhesitatingly chose the American.

"You see," the General concluded, "America gave us back her share of the Boxer indemnity, and she has given us recognition. Great Britain has given us opium. Can you wonder that America gains in our developing markets what Great Britain loses?"

May 13, 1913

SUN YAT SEN'S WARNING.

Declares That Chinese Loan May Cause Civil War.

PARIS, May 9.—The full text of the document sent out from Shanghai by Dr. Sun Yat Sen and addressed to the Governments and peoples of foreign powers reads as follows:

"As a result of careful investigation by officials appointed by the Government to inquire into the recent murder of the Nationalist leader, Sung Chiaoyu, in Shanghai, the fact is clearly established that the Peking Government is seriously implicated in the crime.

"Consequently the people are extremely indignant, and the situation has become so serious that the nation is on the verge of the most acute and dangerous crisis yet experienced.

"The Government, conscious of its guilt and the enormity of its offense, and realizing the strength of the wave of indignation sweeping over the nation as a direct result of its criminal deeds and its wicked betrayal of the trust reposed in it, and perceiving that it is likely to lead to its downfall, suddenly and unconstitutionally concluded a loan for £25,000,000 with the quintuple group, despite the vigorous protests of the representatives of the nation now assembled in Peking.

"This high-handed and unconstitutional action of the Government instantly accentuated the intense indignation which had been caused by the foul murder of Sung Chiaoyu, so that at the present time the fury of the people is worked up to white heat, and a terrible convulsion appears almost inevitable.

"Indeed, so acute has the crisis become that the widespread smoldering embers may burst forth in a devastating conflagration at any moment. From the date of the birth of the republic I have striven for unity, peace, concord, and prosperity. I recommended Yuan Shih Kai for the Presidency because there appeared reasons for believing that by doing so the, unification of the nation and the dawn of an era of peace and prosperity would thereby be hastened.

"Ever since then I have done all I could to evolve peace, order, and government out of the chaos created by the revolution. I earnestly desire to preserve peace throughout the republic, but my efforts will be ineffective if the financiers supply the Peking Government with money that would, and probably will, be used in waging a war against the people.

"If the country is plunged into war at this juncture, it will inevitably inflict terrible misery and suffering upon the people, who are just beginning to recover from the dislocation of trade and the losses of various funds caused by the revolution.

"For the establishment of the Republic they have sacrificed much, and are now determined to preserve it at all costs. If all the people are now forced into a life and death struggle for the preservation of the republic, not only will it entail terrible suffering to the masses, but will inevitably also adversely affect all the foreign interests in China.

"If the Peking Government is kept without funds there is every prospect of a compromise between it and the people being effected, while the immediate effect of a liberal supply of money will probably be the precipitation of a terrible and disastrous conflict.

"In the name and for the sake of humanity — which civilization holds sacred—I therefore appeal to you to exert your influence in preventing bankers from making the loan to the Peking Government."

NEW CIVIL WAR BEGUN IN CHINA

Eight Southern Provinces Preparing to Declare an Independent Confederacy.

JAPANESE PLOTS ALLEGED

Southerners Declare That They Have Received Promises of Support from the Mikado's Officers.

SHANGHAI, July 16.—The revolt along the Yang-tse Kiang is spreading, and there is fighting along the Tien-Tsin—Pu-Kow Railway.

Proclamations are being circulated here, setting forth that a punitive expedition has been undertaken for the purpose of bringing President Yuan Shih-Kai to justice for the murder of Gen. Sung Chiao-Jen, the ex-Minister of Education, who was killed at Shanghai last March, and for violating the Constitution.

The Yang-tse Kiang towns are going over to the proposed Southern Confederacy, and it is stated that Yuan Shih-Kai has ordered a general advance of his troops against them.

PEKING, July 16.—The Provinces of Kiang-Si, Kiang-Su, Kwang-Si, Fo-Kien, Sze-Chuen, Hu-Nan, Ngan-Hwei, and Kwang-Tung are preparing to declare their independence and to form a Southern Chinese Confederacy, according to apparently authoritative reports current here.

Fighting continues in the Province of Kiang-Si, and large numbers of Northern troops are proceeding there.

The attitude of the Japanese is bitterly discussed here. The Chinese believe they are stirring up strife everywhere, and Japanese officers are said to be fighting on the side of the rebels, the presence of Japanese gunboats in the fighting zone being taken as lending color to the belief that they are aiding the revolt. The Southerners openly declare that they have received assurances of Japanese support.

Commenting on an alleged speech by the Japanese Minister designate to China, in which Yuan Shih-Kai's administration was criticised, the newspapers pointedly refer to the recall of Charles R. Crane after he had been appointed United States Minister to China, and intimate that similar action would be advisable in the case of Enjire Yamaza.

The German consulate at Nanking was surrounded to-day by insurgents. It was stated that in the event of an attack the Germans intended to adopt their own measures for their protection. The trouble apparently arose because the Germans recently permitted the extradition of two revolutionaries who had taken refuge in the German concession at Han-Kow.

CHINA'S OUTLOOK BRIGHT, HE SAYS

American Agent Asserts Wonderful Development Will Follow Present Revolution.

SAW THE TROUBLE START

Fanaticism of the Cantonese Aroused by the Murder of Two Manchu Generals.

W. H. Reich, who represents an American firm in Hongkong, and who has lived there or in the Far East for twenty years, believes that business in China will be upset by the present revolution for a long time to come.

"It is my opinion," said Mr. Reich at the Wolcott yesterday, "that until something like real peace is established things in a commercial way will be in a state of paralysis. I have lived among the Cantonese for many years. They have been a timid race in their dealings with another nation, but when they start to fight one another they don't know when to stop.

"It was a student who had come back from the United States who started the trouble. He stationed himself on the roof of a house on one of the narrow streets of Canton before a Manchu General passed to witness a balloon ascension. He let fall a bomb, and it got not only the General, but a dozen of his retinue. Three months afterward a new Manchu General was appointed, and it was three months after that before he arrived in Hongkong on the way to his post. He went up the Pearl River on a gunboat, landed at Canton, and got into a sedan chair, and though as a precaution all his suite wore the same sort of clothes he did the bomb thrower picked him out on his way to the palace. These two happenings seemd to work a change in the whole character of the Cantonese. They were always fanatical, but these killings seemed to give them courage.

"I was in Hongkong when news came of the fall of Peking. Within less than five minutes after the telegram arrived the streets swarmed with Chinamen, who were buying packages of firecrackers, and for hours they ran through the streets yelling like mad and shooting off the crackers in their hands. They rode in the street cars without paying fares, and the English authorities had to call out the militia to quiet them.

"When things once quiet down there will be a wonderful development in China. The Chinese are great for taking up Western ways. Not long ago my office man, who has been with me twelve years, made his appearance in the office one morning with a smile on his face.

"'Mr. Reich,' he said, 'I bought myself yesterday one of your American spring beds. I tried it last night, and it's fine. I didn't know what I was missing.'

"Early in the last revolution I was held up in Canton. As our train approached that city it stopped at every little station, and at each place a squad of half a dozen men stood with fixed bayonets. At Canton we heard the crack of rifles, and there was a great commotion. When we alighted at the station, I asked the station master about getting a ricksha to take me to the European settlement.

"'You can't take a ricksha anywhere,' he informed me. Five thousand discharged troops have refused to give up their arms, and are now fighting. There are 300 dead in the streets.'

"'I guess I had better take a train straight back to Hongkong,' I suggested.

"'There is no certainty of your getting there,' he returned. 'The rails may have been torn up.'

"Finally, upon his suggestion, I managed to get a sampan, which was driven by a motor. I had Wing, my office man, with me, and we started out. We could hear fighting on the shore, and the bullets came shrieking over the water.

" 'You'd better bend down,' cautioned Wing. 'Those bullets have no eyes, and they can't tell that you are not a Chinaman.'

"We got to the foreign concession safely, passing boatloads of troops going up the river. I heard later that the Federal troops had taken between 3,000 and 4,000 of the rebels in the fighting, and then, because it was too much trouble and expense to feed them, they tied their hands and feet, took them out in boats, and dumped them overboard.

"Sun Yat-sen is popular among the Cantonese, who hate President Yuan Shih-kai."

August 13, 1913

CANTON REVOLTS FROM YUAN'S RULE

China's Great Southern Province, Kwang-tung, Declares Its Independence.

PREDICT MORE DEFECTIONS

Belief in Shanghai That This Action Points to Probable Downfall of the Executive.

SHANGHAI, China, April 7.—The independence of Canton and the Province of Kwang-tung was formally declared yesterday afternoon, after a conference of military and naval officers and leading citizens with Lung Chi-kuang, the Governor of the province. No fighting took place.

The secession is considered important here, as observers of the situation regard it as pointing to the probable downfall of Yuan Shih-kai. It is expected to lead to the defection of other southern provinces and strengthen the hands of the southern leaders in their reiterated demand for Yuan's retirement and the restoration of the Nanking Constitution.

The influence at Peking of Vice President Li Yuan-hung and Secretary of State Hsu Shih-chang and Marshal Tuan Chi-jui, it is thought possible, may result in the peaceful solution of the situation that the southerners ardently desire, but information from a usually well-informed foreign source in Peking is to the effect that Yuan Shih-kai will fight bitterly.

The China Merchant Steamship Company has refused to transport northern troops to Canton. Lack of tonnage available was given as the reason.

The United States cruiser Cincinnati is on her way to Amoy. The Galveston is due at Swatow tomorrow, when the Wilmington will sail for Canton.

It is considered noteworthy that there are no apprehensions for the safety of foreigners.

PEKING, China, April 7.—Paul R. Josselyn, American Vice Consul at Canton, telegraphed to the American Minister, Dr. Paul Reinsch, today that no disturbances had occurred in Canton following the declaration of the independence of Kwang-tung Province. Both the civil and military Governors of the province proclaimed its independence.

Kwang-tung is an important province of China, in the southeastern part of the empire, on the China Sea. Its capital is Canton. Its population is estimated at between 22,000,000 and 30,000,000.

EXPECTS NANKING TO REBEL.

Hwang Sing, Refugee Here, Says Yuan Is About Bankrupt.

General Hwang Sing, for several years a political refugee because his political differences with Yuan Shih-kai, the President of China, said yesterday at his home, 404 West 115th Street, where he has been living with his suite since he came to this country two years ago, that he had received a cablegram from China announcing the secession from Yuan's rule of the Province of Kwang-tung. General Hwang made the following statement through his secretary, who acted as interpreter:

"This declaration of independence simply goes to show the ill-feeling and spirit of rebellion which most of the people of China are nursing toward their President, the would-be Emperor. Yuan Shih-kai has proved to be inordinately ambitious. After saying that the Chinese were not suited to a republican form of government he deliberately set about to wreck the Republic and establish himself as Emperor.

"When the nation found out that an Emperor's rule was not what it wanted the wily Yuan Shih-kai came forth with the declaration that he would gladly revert to the republican government and call himself President.

"The people of Kwang-tung have been rapidly getting tired of misrule and despotism. Kwang-tung, you know, has a population of more than 25,000,000. It is important, likewise commercially and strategically, because of its arsenal and port. Millions in Government funds are kept there, but better, almost all of the officers of the Chinese navy are natives of the Province and in sympathy with its every move. Yuan Shih-kai, then, cannot depend on the navy to aid him much.

"The secession of Kwang-tung only presages to my mind the formal declaration of independence on the part of several other provinces. The people of the city of Nanking are very much in sympathy with the action of their compatriots and from a trustworthy source I have been informed that a definite move may be expected from them very soon.

"Yuan Shih-kai has practically no resources now whatever. The well-known six-Power loan, which was borrowed ostensibly for constructive purposes, has been squandered, the money being paid out for the annihilation of the ruler's enemies, in bribery and the like. I sincerely hope there is nothing to the report that there is to be another loan made him by American capitalists to aid in carrying on his despotism, as such a loan would only be repudiated by the republicans.

"If money went from this country now for the support of Yuan Shih-kai it might prove disastrous to the friendly relations existing at present between the Chinese and this country. One of my objects in coming here from Japan, where I was a refugee for some time, was to see what could be done to set this loan matter right."

General Hwang said that his information concerning the political affairs of his native country came to him at first hand, as he was in receipt of almost daily messages.

April 8, 1916

YUAN SHIH-KAI DIES; CHINA PEACE NEAR

Death of President in Palace at Peking Is Expected to Pacify Rebels.

LI YUAN-HUNG SUCCESSOR

Vice President Will Take Oath of Office Today—Capital Tranquil at News.

WAS FEARED AS DICTATOR

Dead Leader Antagonized the Southern Provinces by His Ambition for Power.

PEKING, June 6.—Yuan Shih-kai, President of the Chinese Republic, died today. Premier Tuan Chi-jui immediately advised Li Yuan-hung, the Vice President, of his succession to the Presidency. Yuan Shih-kai had been ill for several days with stomach trouble, which was followed by a nervous breakdown. It was reported last week that he had been poisoned, but this was later officially denied.

Quiet prevailed in the capital. The death of the President apparently solves the heated political crisis. Li Yuanhung's succession to the Presidency meets the demands of the leaders in the southern provinces.

Yuan Shih-kai died at 1 o'clock this morning in the Palace, surrounded by his wives and older children. Rumors that he committed suicide were denied stoutly by high officials.

The commandants of the legation guards, including the German and Austrian, met today and discussed the situation here, coming to the decision that rioting was unlikely. The American and British commandants advised their nationals living outside the legation quarter that it was safe to remain there for the present.

Li Yuan-hung will take the Presidential oath tomorrow.

SHANGHAI, June 6.—The opinion was expressed here today that the death of Yuan Shih-kai might have an unfortunate effect on political conditions, and that it was most inopportune for the southerners. Negotiations were on the eve of successful completion on the basis of the retirement of Yuan Shih-kai in favor of Li Yuan-hung and the formation of a coalition Cabinet, in which the southerners expected to obtain a predominating position. The southerners were to guarantee the safety of Yuan Shih-kai and his monarchist partisans.

The death of the President, which, under the Constitution, results in the succession of Li Yuan-hung, robs the southerners of all grounds of hostility to the north, but it also leaves them nothing with which to bargain for power. Premier Tuan Chi-jui, supported by the troops, may be able to set up a quasi-military Government, in which the southerners, if represented at all, will be in the minority.

Chang Soulin, Governor of Mukden Province, and the former Manchu General Chang Shun, may make an attempt to reinstate the Manchu dynasty. It is also believed that Feng Kuo-chang, Governor of Nanking, aspires to the Presidency.

REBELS FAVOR SUCCESSOR.

Li Yuan-hung Has Public Confidence and a Record of War Service.

Li Yuan-hung, who becomes President of China, in the regular course of events would remain in office until October of next year, when the term of five years for which Yuan Shih-kai was elected will expire. Owing to the disturbed political conditions in China, however, his tenure of office is uncertain.

Li Yuan-hung is reported to have been in sympathy with the rebel movement, although little has been heard of his activities in recent months. The State Department at Washington was advised on May 17 that he had been elected President of four seceding provinces in Southern China.

Li Yuan-hung is 52 years old. He served on a cruiser during the Chino-Japanese War and later entered the army, holding several commands and spending two years in Japan for the study of fortifications. On the outbreak of the revolution at Wuchang he was coerced into accepting command of the revolutionary forces, whose operations he directed. He was mainly instrumental in arranging for the Shanghai peace conference, and after the abdication of the Manchus was elected Vice President of the republic and appointed Chief of the General Staff. He was made a General, and in October of 1913 was re-elected Vice President.

YUAN FEARED BY HIS FOES.

Services to China During Crisis Were Forgotten as He Got Power.

Yuan Shih-kai's admirers have always contended that all his work was consecrated to the betterment of his country, and that his ambition for supreme power were merely means to this end. His detractors have merely seen in his career selfish ambition, treason, and absolutism. Yuan found his supporters in the merchant and professional classes and his enmies in the Viceroy of the old régime and students who had been educated abroad. Indeed, it was all these contending elements which finally pushed him into prominence at the time of the great revolution six years ago.

As early as 1908 the throne had promised a constitution and an elected Parliament, but the realization was postponed by a number of makeshifts of apparently liberal tendencies—the appointment of a cabinet instead of the Grand Council, for example. Floods and famine and a weak, shortsighted Government made a general rising to demand at once a liberal Government facile. When it came the Regent saw only one man who, he thought, could save the Empire and dynasty. That man was Yuan Shih-kai, who three years before, in 1908, he had banished from the councils of State. By the edict of Oct. 14, 1911, Yuan was made Viceroy of Hupeh and Human and Generalissimo of the Imperial forces.

Yuan was born in Hunan Province in 1858. He was educated in law, religion, and military affairs. He served as a soldier in Korea in 1882, and three years later became Imperial Resident at the Korean Court, a post he retained until the outbreak of the Chino-Japanese War in 1894. In 1897 he was Judicial Commissioner of Chihli, and the following year he was placed in command of an army corps.

His acquaintances among foreigners was large and he had the reputation of being a reformer. For this fact the Emperor Kuang Hsu sought his aid, but Yuan sided with the Empress Dowager, and helped carry through the great coup d'état in 1898. Under the patronage of the Dowager Empress, he then became Junior Vice President of the

Board of Works in 1899. When the Boxer rebellion broke out in that year he was Governor of Shantung, and afforded protection to foreigners.

On the death of Li Hung-chang he became Viceroy of Chihli, December, 1901, with the honorary title of Junior Guardian of the heir apparent. At Chihli he laid the foundation of China's modern army. He was at the height of his influence under the old régime in 1907. But two years later, on the death of the Empress Dowager and the Emperor Kuang Hsu and the assumption of the Regency by Prince Chun, Yuan was dismissed from office and sent to his home in Hunan in disgrace.

Recalled from Obscurity.

It was from this obscurity that the Regent recalled him in October, 1911. Yuan took the field, but found himself face to face with well-organized mutiny on every side; still, by compromises, he managed to have it appear that the Imperial troops were winning. The armed rebellion rather subsided than was put down, while the revolutionary movement continued to gain in strength and to insist on a constitution, which was finally drawn up.

Prince Chun, as Regent, abdicated in December, 1911, and Yuan became Premier with almost dictatorial powers

YUAN SHIH-KAI.

—both the throne and the revolutionists, for opposite reasons, placed their faith in him. Preparations were made for a National Convention which would either turn the Government into a constitutional monarchy or a republic.

There were many Republicans, however, who did not believe in the apparent liberal proclivities of Yuan; among them was Dr. Sun Yat-sen, who succeeded in reviving the revolution in the southern provinces. He had conducted an elaborate propaganda from abroad. Early in 1912 delegates of fourteen provinces elected him "President of the Chinese Republic."

This movement in the southern provinces against the various forms of government which have succeeded one another at Peking has been active until the present day. The death of Yuan may consolidate the close constructionists of the north and the broad constructionists of the south, since the latter's opposition to Yuan has been chiefly personal, due to his alleged monarchical tendencies.

On Feb. 12, 1912, the Manchu dynasty came to an end. The Imperial edict declared that sovereignty henceforth was to be possessed by the whole people and that the form of government was to be republican. Yuan Shih-kai was nominated "with full powers" to organize a provisional republican government. The Emperor was to retain his title and receive an annuity, but he was also to retain his religious offices and the functions thereof.

For a time the southern provinces accepted the situation. Dr. Sun Yat-sen resigned and Yuan was elected by the Nanking Council Provisional President of the republic. General Li Yuan-hung became Vice President, and a provisional constitution was adopted by the Council on March 10, 1912, the day on which Yuan took the oath of office in Peking.

On Oct. 6, 1913, Yuan Shih-kai was chosen President for a term of five years by a large majority of both houses of the Chinese Parliament. The other candidates were Dr. Sun Yat-sen and Dr. Wu Ting-fang, former Ambassador at Washington.

Almost from the beginning of his administration Yuan was accused of seeking dictatorial powers and a monarchical title. Last Summer he let it be known that he contemplated assuming Imperial office and title on the ground that the strong centralized government which China needed could be obtained in no other way. His coronation was set for February. In the meantime the southern provinces again revolted and such strong opposition came from other quarters to the Imperial idea that Yuan declared that if the country could show itself worthy of being a republic he would be the last to think of fastening an empire on it.

This was the situation at the time of the death of Yuan Shih-kai and its meaning is best shown in an article from a neutral Chinese source which appeared in a recent number of the Peking Gazette. Here are a few pertinent extracts:

"The reason must have been known to a select few among the Chinese from the very beginning, but it was not until the monarchy campaign was in full blast that it became apparent that Yuan's indisposition was due to disapproval of the President's desire to elevate himself to the throne. We all remember that some of the leading provincial Governors visited Peking in the Summer, and that the monarchical press loudly proclaimed that they had all come to urge a reluctant and overmodest President to take the essential step of restoring the monarchy, with himself as Emperor. As a matter of fact, most of these high personages, as we have recently learned, came to urge the exact contrary. Feng Kuo-chang, in particular, warned the President of the inexpediency of such a step at such a time, and had the pleasure of seeing the Peking press report that Yuan Shih-kai had rebuked him for supporting the project, when in fact he was strongly opposing it.

"The monarchists in Peking are cock-a-whoop, in the belief that the prospective success of the Government armies will mean a revival of the monarchy scheme. That, however, is not the view in responsible quarters. The belief is that Yuan Shih-kai perceives that a mistake has been made, and that he will not pursue the matter, although he may take no further steps to announce his abandonment of it until he has defeated the rebels. What has stopped him from proceeding with his coronation—apart from the question of the foreign advice—is not the rebellion, but the fact that many of his best friends have dropped away from him on this account, and because practically all the prominent men in the country have manifested their disapproval, although not necessarily going so far as to join the rebels. Any resumption of the monarchy program might lead these disapprovers to take some active step in opposition."

June 7, 1916

REBEL PROVINCES YIELD.

China's Unity Assured Under Li by Action—May Change Laws.

PEKING, June 9.—The provinces of Sze-chuen, Hunan, Che-kiang, and Shen-si have rescinded their declarations of independence and reasserted their loyalty to the Peking Government.

President Li Yuan-hung has received from President Wilson a message of condolence with Mme. Yuan Shih-kai and the Chinese people, and expressing wishes for the continued prosperity of China under the new régime. President Li Yuan-hung replied, thanking the American Executive, and expressing the hope that under his guidance American ideals would be realized and the nation prosper.

———

Special to The New York Times.

WASHINGTON, June 9.—The Chinese situation was today reported to the State Department in a cablegram from Minister Reinsch at Peking to be steady and satisfactory, following the death of Yuan Shih-kai and the elevation of Vice President Li Yuan-hung to the Presidency. On the basis of Minister Reinsch's message, Secretary Lansing authorized the following announcement:

"The Department is in receipt of a telegram, dated June 9, from the American Legation at Peking, saying that the succession of Li Yuan-hung to the Presidency has been accepted by all the Northern provinces, including Chekiang, and that as the Southern provinces had already proclaimed him as the rightful President, he holds the reins of Government without opposition. The telegram states further that it is expected, however, that the Southern provinces will ask that changes be made in the personnel of the Cabinet."

Unofficial information received here indicates that it is the purpose of the new President to make changes in the personnel of the Cabinet in an effort to strengthen the Government by giving representation to the various elements in China in the affairs of the Central Government.

———

TOKIO, Saturday, June 10.—Japan is augmenting her troops at Tien-Tsin and Peking by one battalion, which was withdrawn from Dairen, on the Liaotung Peninsula, near Port Arthur.

June 10, 1916

CHINA: A REPUBLIC ON TRIAL FOR ITS LIFE

Boldest Democratic Experiment in History Has Not Yet Proved Itself

By THEODORE E. BURTON

Ex-United States Senator from Ohio

IN the last nine years changes have occurred in China, the land of conservatism and calm, quite as startling as in storm-tossed Europe. After an unbroken imperial régime lasting for more than 4,000 years, an insurrection against the Manchu dynasty and in support of a republic broke out at Wuchang, opposite Hankow, on the Yangtze River, on Oct. 10, 1911. In the contest which ensued, two classes of soldiers took part; the imperial troops under the direction of the central Government at Peking, and the provincial troops under the control of the local authorities of the twenty-two provinces of China. A majority of the latter, especially in South China, supported the insurrection.

After a brief conflict, in which there were varying successes, the revolutionists prevailed, capturing the prominent cities of Hankow, Shanghai, Nanking and Canton. A provisional constitution was promulgated at Nanking, and Mr. Sun Yat-sen was chosen as President of the newly established republic on Dec. 29, 1911.

Prior to the outbreak, there had been two opposing schools of thought in China: one supporting a republic, the other a constitutional monarchy. The Dowager Empress of China, a woman of great force but of reactionary ideas, was in practically absolute control for many years until her death in 1908. Early in this century she recognized the necessity for sweeping reforms.

In 1907, a commission was chosen, including a Prince of the blood, to study the institutions of other countries. The Dowager Empress realized that other peoples could no longer be regarded as barbarians of the outer world, but that their methods must be considered in the government of China.

In 1909, after her death, Provincial Assemblies were established, and a promise was made that a National Assembly should be convened in the year 1915; a date which later was changed to 1913. In the year 1910, a National Assembly of 200 members styled an "Advice Board" was called together, half of whom were chosen by the Imperial Government, and half by the Provincial Assemblies. It was no doubt anticipated that, by reason of the appointment of half the members, the whole body would be under the control of the sovereign; but this expectation was disappointed, as those chosen by the Provincial Assemblies included many radicals who were so much more assertive and able than the hand-picked members that their influence prevailed.

It was thought that these reforms, present and prospective, would satisfy the aspirations of China. During the course of the insurrection, Yuan Shih-kai, who had been called from banishment to support the throne, seemed to favor the continuance of the monarchy with constitutional reforms, and appointed delegates to confer with the southern rebels. The negotiations failed, however, and on Feb. 12, 1912, the child Emperor of China, after having made a pitiful appeal in which he admitted his weakness and mistakes, abdicated, and the Manchu sovereignty came to an end.

The causes of the overthrow of the monarchy are not difficult to explain. In the first place, there had been an infusion of new ideas by reason of larger contact with the outside world, the education of numerous Chinese abroad and in missionary and other foreign schools in China. Again, as in Russia, the final overthrow of the dynasty was largely due to its weakness and inefficiency. Those who had the welfare of China at heart regarded the imperial rulers with more or less contempt, and as utterly incapable of grappling with the problems confronting the country. The domination of the alien Manchu race had caused deeply rooted resentment. For centuries secret political societies, which are numerous in China, had existed, one of the most prominent of which was the so-called Ku-Ming-Tong, an anti-Manchu organization, said to include in its membership 390,000 at home and abroad.

The unrest was intensified by one of the serious periodical floods which occurred in the Winter of 1910-11, as a result of which millions of people were starving and dying.

Still further, an attempt was made to nationalize railroads, which those in the separate provinces claimed should be under their control. The doctrine of States' rights, then as now, is particularly strong in China.

The republic was destined from its very beginning to a stormy career. Selfish ambitions, intrigues, plots and counterplots have been all too manifest. Immediately after the abdication of the Emperor, Sun Yat-sen, evidently influenced by patriotic motives and desiring to unite the whole country, resigned and asked that Yuan Shih-kai be chosen as President. The latter was elected as Provisional President at Nanking, Feb. 15, 1912, and then for a definite term of five years, at Peking on Oct. 6, 1913.

A National Assembly, representing all provinces of the country, was elected and convened at Peking April 6, 1913. Its first task was to frame a Constitution, but its only achievement was provision for the election of a President and Vice President. It was dissolved by President Yuan in the month following his election. In the month of December, 1915, he issued a proclamation declaring his intention to assume the position of Emperor. This was immediately followed by uprisings in some of the provinces, and he withdrew his proclamation in the following March.

There is great difference of opinion among Chinese and foreigners familiar with China as to the character and aims of Yuan Shih-kai. It is universally conceded that he was one of the ablest as well as one of the strongest men in China. He showed a disposition to adopt progressive ideas in education and in administrative reforms. One of his many protégés, now Governor of one of the leading provinces, stated to me last Autumn that his action in seeking to become Emperor indicated that failing health had impaired his mental vigor; because Yuan had repeatedly told him that his one ambition was to be the

"George Washington of China" and that the republic must be established on perpetual foundations, but failing health and the importunity of favorites led him to make the abortive attempt to assume the imperial title. It is alleged that he became convinced a republic was impossible and that the sooner a monarchy was restored the better for China.

On the other hand, many of his actions are clearly condemnatory of him and indicate that instead of being a patriot he was a shrewd and resourceful self-seeker. When given control by the Manchu rulers, his loyalty to them was doubtful and the most obvious interpretation of his course is that he was scheming to become the head of the republic as a stepping-stone to the foundation of a new dynasty with himself as its first sovereign. It is certain that his brief rule was at the same time more forceful and more absolute than that of the dynasty which was overthrown. He died in July, 1916, after having ruled most of the time in the absence of any legislative assembly.

His successor, President Li Yuanhung, who had taken a prominent part in support of the revolution, reconvened the Assembly on Aug. 1, 1916. During the following year, an attempt was made by a Chinese General to restore the Manchu dynasty. He gained possession of Peking and restored the child Emperor to power for the brief period of eleven days, from July 1 to July 12, 1917, when he was overthrown.

President Li, patriotic and universally trusted as a friend of the republic, but disgusted by the constant friction between himself and his Cabinet, and apparently lacking in firmness, dissolved the National Assembly in June, 1917, and resigned on the occasion of the Manchu restoration. He is now living

in a beautiful home in the English concession at Tientsin. In an interesting interview with him, he expressed the utmost concern for the future of China and for the friendship of the United States. He is still vigorous, resembling somewhat the late President Roosevelt. Every one seems to have a good word for him, but many express the opinion that he failed in time of emergency.

As a result of this dissolution and the course of events at Peking, provinces and parts of provinces centring around Canton seceded and established a separate Government at Canton, with five Commissioners exercising the executive power, among them being Sun Yat-sen, Wu Ting-fang, well known in the United States, where he was twice Minister from China, and Tang Shao-yi, one of the most intelligent Chinese, educated at Columbia.

Since that time there have been two Governments in China and two Parliaments; one at Peking, the other at Canton. The Northern Parliament is made up of members chosen since the dissolution by President Li; the Southern, of members chosen at the original election in 1913. Repeated efforts have been made to bring the two sections together, but thus far the efforts have failed. I visited the Northern Parliament at Peking last October. It seemed much like other legislative bodies.

Chinese boast that they are in advance of the United States in that they have a budget system. One day the budget was under consideration, there was a large attendance, a number of brief speeches were made, and votes on each successive paragraph were taken by raising of the hands. At a later time, on meeting a delegation including the presiding officers of the two houses, the one dominant note, as in all interviews with the Chinese, was a supreme desire for the aid and co-operation of the United States, the country which they trust.

In the following month I met and addressed some 400 members of the Southern Parliament at Canton. They were intensely anxious to hear a friendly voice from America. At the close of the formal addresses of welcome and some remarks made to them an effort was made to show that the Southern Parliament was representative of all China. Members came forward for introduction, first from Manchuria in North China, among whom was the presiding officer of the House of Representatives; then delegates from Mongolia, of a distinctive physical type, very stalwart, with a marked resemblance to the North American Indians; then the delegates from Tibet and later the delegation from Shantung.

President Li was succeeded by the Vice President, Feng Kuo-chang, who died recently. He occupied the position until August, 1918, when the incumbent, Hsu Shih-chang, was chosen as President, a dignified and well-preserved man of about sixty-five, who was an official under the old Manchu régime and is highly respected for his fairness and his attainments as a scholar. It is universally conceded that in a time of peaceful development he would be a model executive.

Future Still in Doubt.

What will be the future of popular government in China, now divided into two opposing sections; the one representing the conservative north, less influenced by modern ideas and seriously accused of undue partiality to Japan; the other the more progressive south, which for centuries has furnished most of the emigrants who have gone abroad and is much more radical and ready for innovations?

No experiment in popular government of quite so bold a nature or involving so radical changes has ever been tried as in the establishment of a republic in China. In the first place, it must be noted that it is not so much the substitution of a republic for a monarchy that is attempted, as the creation of an efficient Government for a vast empire scattered over an immense area, inhabited by a people of 300,000,000 to 400,000,000, individualistic and provincial in their aspirations, and without that cohesion essential for a strong and efficient central Government. The Chinese Empire under the Manchus was little more than a shell, a shadowy image of a Government, maintaining great pomp and display within the Forbidden City in Peking, but absolutely out of touch with the people. There were no great public enterprises; there were no forward-looking ideas; contact with the people was limited to hated forms of taxation for the maintenance of the army and the support of the imperial court.

Then, it is obvious, there is an absence of that training and preparation which are so essential for efficient popular government.

The most enthusiastic advocate of the rule of the people must pause when he considers the obstacles in the path of the new republic. Adequate means of communication, so necessary for exchange of thought and unity of action, are lacking. It was stated by several of the members of the Southern Parliament at Canton that it required five weeks to reach that city from their homes.

Factors For and Against Success.

One main desire of the more fortunate class among the Chinese is to avoid the payment of taxes. These, though burdensome, were light under imperial rule, but a centralized Government, competent to perform its proper functions and develop China, would require greatly increased taxes. Again, the Chinese, like other Orientals, for long centuries have been accustomed to the rule of despots. Their respect is for force. They are not accustomed to submission to elected rulers chosen from among them, nor have they yet reconciled themselves to the necessary principle which must prevail in all popular governments that majorities must rule. Provinces are loath to submit to central authority. There is a lack of adequate electoral machinery for the selection of representatives and executive officials. In the elections thus far held the qualifications of voters as to property or education are extremely severe. In the choice of the members of the House of Representatives it has been estimated that barely one in one hundred of the population is eligible as a voter.

On the other hand, there are not lacking favorable indications. The two attempts to restore a monarchy failed most disastrously. There is a disposition to acquiesce in existing conditions and to be peaceable and law-abiding. Indications of a moral awakening are to be found in movements such as a crusade against opium and efforts to do away with gambling. Then, too, there is a feeling on the part of those capable of leadership that China must assert herself as a nation and take a place among the countries of the world. As was well said by the Civil Governor of Shantung Province in his address to the Provincial Assembly last Autumn: " The responsibility rests upon us to develop and safeguard our country. Should we fail in this, other nations will gain control and fulfill the duties which we should perform."

CHINA MAKES PLEA TO GREAT BRITAIN

Japanese, Germans, and British Are Violating Her Neutrality, Peking Legations Are Told.

JAPAN LANDS MORE MEN

Open Zone Extended, but China Asserts She Will Defend Her Rights Outside the New Limits.

PEKING, Sept. 8.—The exact number of Japanese troops ashore at Lung-kow, the Chinese port north of Tsing-tau, cannot be definitely determined here. It is believed, however, that no fewer than 6,000 men already are on shore and that 24,000 more are coming.

The Chinese officials of Lung-kow politely protested against the landing of Japanese forces. The Japanese accepted the protest with equal politeness, and then proceeded to disregard it. There was no hostile incident during the Lung-kow landing.

The Foreign Office has formally protested to the Japanese and British Legations here against the violation of China's neutrality, involved in the landing at Lung-kow, which, being 100 miles from Tsing-tau, is approximately 70 miles beyond the confines of the German leased territory. Knowing, however, that its protest would be useless, the Foreign Office at the same time requested the British and Japanese authorities to confine their operations to the zone extending on the north from Lung-kow to Lia-chow, and on the south to the previously prescribed fighting area. Neither legation, however, accepted these limitations.

The British regiments which are expected to take part in the investment of Tsing-tau are still at Tien-tsin.

The Foreign Office later in the day notified the foreign diplomats here that Germany, Japan, and Great Britain were transgressing Chinese neutrality in Shan-tung Province, and at the same time expressed regret that China was unable to prevent such transgression. The note asserted that China would continue to enforce its regulations respecting neutrality outside the zone bounded by Lung-kow and Lia-chow on the north, and the breadth of the Kiao-Chau neutral sphere on the south. The note concludes with these words:

"But it is still incumbent upon the belligerent powers to respect the territorial and administrative rights of China, and all persons and properties within the area defined above."

SECRET JAPANESE DEMANDS ON CHINA?

Memorandum to the Powers Said to Have Omitted Important Features.

VETO POWER FOR JAPAN

Suppressed Stipulations Said to Give Her Right to Exclude Others from Concessions.

PEKING, Feb. 17.—If information from presumably well-informed sources, both foreign and Chinese, is correct, the memorandum recently given by the Japanese Legation to the diplomatic representatives here of the United States, Great Britain, France, and Russia respecting the demands of the Tokio Government on China, omits certain of the requirements originally presented to Peking.

These negotiations, which began late in January, had for their object the determination of the future status of Japan's relations with China and a decision respecting certain questions regarding the future development of the Chinese Republic. Their course has been guarded with great secrecy.

The Peking Government did not conceal its concern over the situation thus brought about, and on Feb. 6 Sun Pao-chi, the Chinese Foreign Secretary, in conference with the Japanese Minister at Peking, rejected Japan's proposals on the ground that they were incompatible with China's sovereignty, and conflicted with existing treaties between China and other foreign powers. The Japanese Minister then asked for an acceptance in principle, stating that the detailed negotiations could be conducted later; but the Peking Government returned the same answer as to the principles involved.

The original demands, according to information from Peking sources, were twenty-one in number, and were far-reaching both in their political and commercial aspects. But it is not known whether the original demands were made orally or in a formal written communication. The memorandum as handed to the Legations of the United States, Great Britain, France, and Russia is understood to contain but eleven demands, substantially as follows:

Demands German Concessions.

In relation to Shantung, Japan asks that China transfer to her all rights and concessions previously enjoyed by Germany, and requires China to consult Japan on all matters previously agreed upon between Germany and China in the Province of Shantung.

China is to agree not to alienate or lease Shantung or any part of the coast on any pretext to any foreign Government; and similarly, no island near Shantung is to be leased to any foreign power.

China is asked to grant to Japan the right to construct a railroad from Kiao-Chau to Chi-fu.

It is demanded that certain cities in the Province of Shantung shall be opened as treaty ports.

In southern Manchuria and Mongolia the extension is asked of the terms of the lease of the Kwangtung (Port Arthur and Darien) and the Manchurian and Mukden railroads.

In the same region, Japan asks for the acquisition by Japanese of the

rights of residence and ownership of land and the grant of mining rights.

In the same region of southern Manchuria and Mongolia the following four requests are made:

Before granting railroad concessions to any third power, China must agree to consult Japan in advance.

Before endeavoring to obtain capital for loans from any third power, China must consult Japan.

Before choosing any foreign, political, military or financial advisers, China must consult Japan.

The transfer of the management and control of the Changchin railroad is to be made to the Japanese.

China is obligated not to alienate or lease any ports or bays on any island near the coast of Formosa.

Some Demands Suppressed?

Among the stipulations said to have been originally presented by Japan which are not included in the memorandum as handed to certain of the foreign legations are the following:

That if China employs foreigners as controlling advisers in police, military or financial departments of the entire country, Japanese shall be preferred; that one-half of the ammunition and arms hereafter used by China must be purchased from Japan, otherwise an arsenal must be established in China employing Japanese experts and materials; that China must grant to Japan the same privileges as other nations to establish missions, schools, and churches throughout the country with the privilege of propagating Buddhism; that mining concessions conflicting with existing concessions at Hanang, Tayeh, and Pingsiang shall not be granted to other foreigners if a Chino-Japanese company hereafter to be formed, shall disapprove; that certain railroad concessions from Nanchang to Chao Chow Fu, from Nanchang to Kukiang, from Nanchang to Wuchang, and from Nanchang to Hangchow shall be granted; that foreigners other than Japanese shall be excluded from future railroad, mining, and dock building concessions unless Japan shall give her consent.

China's Counter Proposals.

It is learned that China has made three counter proposals respecting that portion of the Japanese demands which concerns concessions in Manchuria, Mongolia, and Shantung. The Chinese Government also has signified its willingness to make a public declaration that China shall never cede a port, harbor, or island to another power, but it has declined to pledge itself to that effect to Japan.

The statute of the negotiations is now rather clouded. Two opinions prevail in Chinese Government circles—one that Japan will press for her demands in full, and the other that Japan cannot insist upon any stipulation beyond the eleven set forth in the communications to the foreign Governments.

BERLIN, (via London,) Feb. 17.—The political demands which Japan is reported to have made upon China during the last fortnight are attracting much attention in German newspapers.

The Kölnische Zeitung says the most important step ever undertaken by Japan occurs at a time when all the great powers of Europe are rending each other, and the United States is playing a rôle which was never expected of her. The Zeitung regrets the "blindness of Germany's enemies, who permit such a catastrophe to threaten the white race."

LONDON, Feb. 17.—" Gloom in Europe is sunshine for Japan, so Japan is making hay," is the comment of The Manchester Guardian on the demands made by Japan upon China, which The Guardian declares "in some ways are scarcely compatible with the declared object of the Anglo-Japanese alliance to insure the independence and integrity of China."

The Guardian contends that in meeting Japan's very comprehensive projects in Manchuria, Shantung Province, Eastern Mongolia, the Yangtse Valley and in Fukien, China, has none of the advantages which she had before August of last year. Her European friends are occupied, the paper says, and the United States, which is one of the guarantors of the "open door" policy, has urgent business closer home.

CHINA DECLARES WAR ON CENTRAL POWERS

LONDON, Aug. 14.—Reuter's Limited has been officially informed that China has declared war against Germany and Austria-Hungary, the declaration dating from 10 o'clock this morning.

WASHINGTON, Aug. 4.—Official notice of China's declaration of war on Germany and Austria-Hungary was received today at the Chinese Legation in cable dispatches from Peking.

China is the seventeenth nation to array itself against the Central Powers. The decision of the Chinese Cabinet to declare war on Germany and Austria-Hungary was reached Aug. 2, and the action of the members of the Ministry was approved by Feng Kwochang, the acting President of the republic

August 15, 1917

CHINA'S MAN POWER AIDS FRANCE IN WAR

The pick of Chinese skilled and partly skilled laborers is being sent from Tien-tsin, China, to France, at the rate of more than 1,000 a week, and from Indo-China to France in at least equal numbers, mainly to work in French munition factories, according to a representative of one of the largest British manufacturing and trading concerns in China, now on a visit to the New York branch of the company.

"They are carried over to France at the rate of between 2,000 and 3,000 a ship," he said. "It does not take a large ship to carry 2,000 Chinese, for they go practically as freight. A Chinese can flourish in a space that would hardly do a white man for his grave.

"Only the best selected stock is going to France from Tien-tsin. A large percentage of the men are six feet tall. For the most part they are Chinese who have learned something about machinery in British mills and factories or in construction camps. Some are agricultural laborers, taken to France to increase food production.

"The exportation of Chinese to France has been going on at Tien-tsin for considerably more than a year, and the number of Chinese now in France, including those from French China, is probably considerably more than 100,000.

"Before they can be induced to leave China these Chinamen all insist on a contract providing not only for their wages, which are small enough, but binding the French Government to ship their bodies back to China for burial if they die in France. It also provides in detail for the apparatus of a Chinese burial. Every Chinese who dies must have a new set of clothing for his appearance in the future world and for the food which goes for the spirit of a Chinese of his class, from rice to roast goose and pig. He must be assured that other funeral ceremonies will be faithfully observed, such as the burning of a string of tin foil imitations of Chinese money, the burning of a paper house and of a paper chair or carriage.

"In our factories in China we pay Chinese workingmen who have some mechanical knowledge 12½ cents a day American money. The contract which induces them to go to France provides for wages of 20 or 25 cents a day, and that is enough to recruit the Chinese as fast as ships can be found to carry them out.

"There is no doubt of the great value of these Chinese in adding to the man-power of France. They are hard workers and, while they have not quite the stamina of Europeans, they are willing to put in long hours and live on very little. Only those are taken who are found to be of better intelligence than the average Chinese workman. I should say that, generally speaking, three of them would be the equal of two Europeans in the less skilled labor connected with making munitions. They rank even higher as agricultural laborers.

"There is an inexhaustible stock of Chinese fit to meet the required standards, and the loss of those who have gone has hardly been perceptible on industries in China.

"With each shipment of Chinese go several Europeans, usually Englishmen, who talk Chinese. They act as gang foremen to interpret orders to the Chinese workmen. The Chinese, however, is quick, when he is in a foreign country, to get enough of the language to enable him to do without an interpreter.

"The English and French officers and civilians who are recruiting Chinese in Tien-tsin and thereabout have no difficulty getting all the men they want. No trickery or shanghaing has ever been resorted to.

"It is almost certain that before the war is over Chinese colonies will have established themselves in France, and possibly in every European country. While the Chinese who go to a foreign land always intends eventually to return to China, and often do, they have always stuck to new lands, where they have once got a foothold, as in the United States. After settling for some time they usually send home for women, and there is soon a younger generation with a good deal of the Oriental worn off. No women, however, have accompanied the Chinese who have left Tien-tsin so far.

"While a large number of the Annamites imported by France from Indo-China have been soldiers, and have gone to the front, I understand they are now leaving French China for France in large numbers to labor in munition factories and on farms."

February 25, 1917

What China Is Doing and Can Do in the War

Camp of Chinese Laborers Employed at Road Making and Trench Building in France.

ON its surface the movement to lend money to China presents some of the aspects of international comedy. The sum commonly mentioned in Washington dispatches is $50,000,000, which is just about the amount the United States is spending every day in this war. Yet never was there such a pother over what is, in world finance, a bagatelle; never did the mountain labor so to give forth a mouse.

But beneath the surface stirred something graver than comedy—something which involved a diplomatic about-face for this country, and the promise of moving developments in the Far East. For the United States, contrary to precedent, now offered to put itself squarely behind the lenders; and Frank L. Polk, Acting Secretary of State, in his official announcement not long since regarding that attitude, partly explained the reversal of policy when he said that "this Government has felt a special interest in the desire of China so to equip herself as to be of more specific assistance in the war against the Central Powers."

We are not accustomed to think of China even as a possible factor in this conflict. Prior to the foreign intrusion upon her in the nineteenth century, she had all but forgot the arts of war. The soldier was despised there. That man was a hero who, like "pious Aeneas," displayed conspicuous filial devotion, but did it peacefully. And so the world, forgetful that this good-natured and industrious race was not known as warlike simply because it was not quarrelsome, still regarded China as no fighting nation, and, therefore, of no particular account in whipping Germany.

Of late years the bitter necessity of armies and armament has been borne in on China, but that made no difference; the old opinion prevailed in spite of it, and found verification in the fact that China had sent to France no military units. How was the world to know that Lieut. Gen. Tang Tsai-li, Vice Minister of the Chinese Chief of Staff, had established military headquarters in Paris; that Chinese officers were at the front, and that at home 40,000 of China's sturdiest troops were awaiting eagerly the call to active service? How was the world to know that this peaceful people had a standing army 900,000 strong—forty-five divisions, nearly three-fourths of them well-equipped and well drilled, according to European standards—versed in the use of the spitfire machine gun?

It can be said that China is eager to put into France 200,000 stalwart soldiers. She is only waiting for the necessary money and the necessary ships. Let those who are furrowing their brows over man power statistics consider that fact, and the further fact that those 200,000 would hail from the world's vastest national reservoir of humanity, a population more than thrice that of the United States. If ever a flow of men starts from China into France and Siberia, Berlin may as well quit computing man power.

It is to be expected that Berlin will sneer at the Chinese, just as Berlin belittled the American menace, but with more foundation in fact. For there are whole provinces in China which have never heard of this war, and even when they have learned what it is and where it is, and why it is being fought, they may be expected to move slowly. Of all countries none is more reactionary, none shrinks more from change.

But account must be taken of China's immediate danger from Germany since Russia collapsed; of the fact that China learned something of German rapacity when Berlin, upon the pretext of the murder of two missionaries, seized the Bay of Kiao-Chau—a possession wrested from her, since the war began, by the Japanese—and of the fact that the Chinese learned something of German savagery during the Boxer rebellion. So

that, although rent by civil war, China knows the greater danger from without, and by reason of that danger may hope to quiet her warring factions. The menace of German penetration may act as a counterirritant. A cable from Peking says Pao-Kuci-ching, the Tuchun of Sei Lung-kiang, has been appointed commander of the expedition to Vladivostok, and that French and Annamite companies in China have already set forth.

China is Russia's nearest eastern neighbor, and for 570 miles of its length the Trans-Siberian Railroad traverses Manchuria. There is not likely to be joint intervention without China. Her forces will accompany the Japanese and other allied troops whenever a military expedition may be undertaken. Germany's predacious eye has long been fixed on her territory, and "Berlin-to-Peking" is a watch-cry as seductive to the *Geschaeftsmann's* ears as "Berlin-to-Bagdad."

China's navy, a substantial and considerable fighting arm, is not needed by the Allies, it happens, because the "Grand Fleet" is securely corked in the North Sea; and it is not available, either, because Admiral Ching, commanding it, has thrown in his fortunes with the southern revolutionists. It should be explained that the two factions are at odds on a technical constitutional question, not an issue involving property rights nor direct political spoils; so that this conscientious internal strife, hinting at a stubborn Scot stuff in the Oriental makeup, speaks volumes for their qualities when aroused.

China's response to the allied call for workers was an earnest of what she can do in the way of fighting men. Not the Canton coolie type were they, but bronzed six-footers from Northern Shantung and Chihli, capable, any one of them, of carrying 200 pounds ten miles, able to work harder and longer than the sturdiest Continental peasant. China sent 125,000 of them as readily and easily as a New York subway contractor would order out a gang. Tagged with metal identification disks, shaven of their queues, 3,000 of these superb physical specimens were sent to Mesopotamia, others to South Africa, still others in greater numbers to France; all in military order, with their own regimental organization, drilling in obedience to commands in English. And the Germans got an inkling of their temper during the offensive in Picardy last Spring when, caught by the Teuton onrush, some of them stemmed the tide until French reserves could turn it back. Those alien laborers of old Cathay, born of a civilization which was ancient when Germany was the home of Genseric's barbarian hordes, flung aside their shovels, seized the nearest rifles, and fought for all the world like a bunch of American engineers.

But China as a military factor is prospective. The loan would but open the sluice-gate. Consider what the nation already has done and is doing in the war. Chinese hides and leather are reducing an acute allied shortage. Chinese coal, sent when the fuel famine came to the Western Hemisphere, is being burned along the Pacific Coast of the United States and Canada. That need surprise no German, because Germany knows

what China's wealth in coal amounts to. She has appraised it. Did not Baron von Richtofen estimate that in Southern Shansi alone there was coal enough to last the whole world for several thousand years? That coal field is 30,000 square miles in extent and yields both bituminous and anthracite.

Consider also antimony, a metal vital to the munition maker. The world's greatest supply of it, so far as is known, is in China, and Chung Yu-wang wrote in 1909 a volume about its uses and properties which is still a textbook for students. In the first half of 1916 China exported from Shanghai and Hongkong $330,000 worth of antimony to the United States, and her exports have increased greatly since then, although exact figures are not at hand. Antimony is valuable in making bearings for machines and cannon. It hardens chilled shot, and is used in shrapnel bullets. As a rule it must be an alloy of other metals, usually tin and copper.

China has pledged her food to the Allies, and she produces enormous quantities of wheat and beef, little of which is consumed at home. (Chinese famines, it should be explained, are due to lack of distribution facilities rather than lack of food.) The Chinese have for export, too, beans and pork and eggs.

Nor must China depend wholly upon the Allies for the ships in which to transport these things. She is building ships—not many, to be sure, but some. Since the war began new yards have been constructed, and vessels of wood and steel are taking to the Eastern waters manned by Chinese crews. Chairman Hurley of our Shipping Board recently contracted for $30,000,000 worth of vessels to be built in the Government yard at Shanghai.

This is China's first attempt to build vessels of 10,000 tons. The yard of the Kiagnon Dock and Engineering Works at Shanghai, which has twelve ways and a dry dock capable of taking 544-foot craft, is large enough. It employs 1,500 men, others at Shanghai 3,500, and those at Hongkong 10,000. All are thoroughly modernized, and there is an abundance of trained labor. The only need is steel, which the United States is now supplying.

But China, although the mightiest nation in population and potentially perhaps the richest, is one of the most helpless. Its industries, its commerce, and its government are unorganized. This hoary civilization is, as a republic, but seven years old. It is in its political swaddling clothes. That its present plight is in some measure due to the ambition of its people for the ballot must touch the sympathy even of those Americans who take their franchise rather as a matter of course. Washington, you may be sure, is not insensible of it. Washington has finally taken helpful action. Diplomatic precedents are seldom upset over night.

The precedent was established soon after President Wilson assumed office. He issued an announcement then that a group of American bankers had asked whether the Government wanted them to participate in a proposed loan to China. This was what was known as the "six-power " loan, including bankers of Great Britain, France, Japan, Russia, and Germany. Mr. Wilson said that American bankers participating in such a loan must do so at their own risk, without hope of formal recognition of the transaction or support of it by the Government.

Mr. Wilson added that the United States was earnestly desirous of aiding China. He manifested unmistakably his advocacy of the open door in the Far East, of China for the Chinese. But the " six-power " loan carried certain political conditions of which apparently he could not approve. In the circumstances now prevailing this objection evidently has been removed.

The conviction is growing that the door in China cannot be kept open if the United States stand aloof. America has come to realize that its individual business men and bankers cannot undertake operations in China unless the United States accepts membership in a coalition whose basis is the maintenance of China's political and territorial integrity.

Individuals cannot act solely on their own initiative in China, because, as William J. Calhoun expressed it when he was Minister to Peking, " there are no courts to which the foreigner can appeal—his only protection is to appeal to his Government for diplomatic support."

This war brought the situation home to the State Department with the necessary emphasis, and created the necessary international community of interests. China must be made " of more specific assistance." And so a group of bankers was summoned to Washington, and a series of conferences began, which resulted in Mr. Polk's announcement. Parts of it are worth repeating here:

Until the present time the engagements of the United States in preparing to exert effectively its strength in the European theatre of war have operated to prevent specific constructive steps to help China realize her desires. Recently, however, this Government felt that, because of the approach to Chinese territory of the scenes of disorder, a special effort should be made to place proper means at the disposal of China. Consequently, a number of American bankers, who had been interested in the past in making loans to China and who had had experience in the Orient, were called to Washington and asked to become interested in the matter. The bankers responded very promptly, and an agreement has been reached between them and the Department of State which has the following salient features:

First—The formation of a group of American bankers to make a loan or loans and to consist of representatives from different parts of the country.

Second—An assurance on the part of the bankers that they will co-operate with the Government and follow the policies outlined by the Department of State.

Third—Submission of the names of the banks which will compose the group for approval by the Department of State.

Fourth—Submission of the terms and conditions of any loan or loans for approval by the Department of State.

Fifth—Assurances that, if the terms and conditions of the loan are accepted by this Government and by the Government to which the loan is made, in order to encourage and facilitate the free intercourse between American citizens and foreign States which is mutually advantageous, the Government will be willing to aid in every way possible and to make prompt and vigorous representations and to take every possible step to insure the execution of equitable contracts made in good faith by its citizens in foreign lands.

It is hoped that the American group will be associated with bankers of Great Britain, Japan, and France. Negotiations are now in progress between the Government of the United States and those Governments which it is hoped will result in their co-operation and in the participation by the bankers of those countries in equal parts in any loan which may be made.

August 11, 1917

CHINA SENDS TROOPS TO SIBERIAN BORDER

WASHINGTON, Aug. 19.—The Chinese Government has sent a large force of troops to the Siberian border to prevent a threatened invasion of Chinese territory by German and Hungarian prisoners of war who joined with the Red Guard and other elements of the Bolsheviki against the Czechoslovaks in the Trans-Baikal region.

The sending of the Chinese force was taken to mean that everything possible to extend relief to the Czechoslovaks was being done by the allied powers. The active participation of the Chinese Army on the Siberian border may have an important bearing on developments there within a few days, according to officials here.

That the large army of prisoners who were set free by the Bolsheviki, armed and equipped, and enlisted to fight against the Czechoslovaks, are menacing the Chinese border has been known for several days. If permitted to cross the border they would be able to manoeuvre to far better advantage. This, however, China has declared she will not permit, and if Chinese territory is violated a battle is promised, with all the advantages resting with the Chinese.

It was said today at the State Department that the American troops were to be governed by military necessities and were not bound by orders to any particular field of action. It is safe to assume that the troops of the British, French and other allied nations at Vladivostok have similarly elastic instructions.

PEKING, Aug. 19, (Associated Press.) —The movement of Japanese troops from Chang-Chun, on the Mukden-Harbin Railroad, to the Manchuria-Siberian front has been further delayed. This delay is due to the demand made by the Japanese that they guard and virtually control the operations of the Chinese Eastern Railway.

The Chinese officials, supported by the Entente allied representatives in Peking, have declined to consent to the taking over of the railroad by Japan.

August 20, 1918

VOID ISHII-LANSING DEAL, CHINA URGES

By CHARLES A. SELDEN.

Copyright, 1919, by The New York Times Company.
Special Cable to THE NEW YORK TIMES.

PARIS, Feb. 6.—So true and generally accepted is the fact that America came into the war without any desire for gain that it has been taken for granted also that America has done nothing in the past in the way of agreements, secret or otherwise, with other countries that will have to be set aside by the Peace Conference as inconsistent with Wilson's fourteen principles.

But there is one blemish, at least, in the opinion of the Chinese delegation on America's otherwise clean slate. Because of the general assumption that nothing contrary to Wilson's points will be left standing after peace is signed and the League of Nations established, China assumes that the Ishii-Lansing agreement, entered into by the Japanese Baron and the American Secretary of State in March, 1917, will be nullified automatically, thus meeting the fate of the various agreements between European States which America disapproves.

Part of this Ishii-Lansing arrangement was, briefly, that the United States recognized that Japan had a special interest in China. Such recognition in itself was and is seriously resented by China, but what made it far worse in her opinion was that it was entered into secretly at Washington by Baron Ishii and Secretary Lansing without consulting the Chinese Minister to America or the Government in Peking.

The first China knew of this agreement, which virtually concerned herself, was when it was announced from Tokio as an accomplished fact. China filed a memorandum of protest at Washington, and then the matter was dropped for the time being.

The United States was then about to go into the war and concentrate all her energies on the European western front, and for that reason, a Chinese statesman in Paris said today, China did not wish to embarrass America by trying to upset the agreement that Japan had determined to get.

China now bases her case against this agreement especially on the first of Wilson's fourteen points and in general on the spirit of the whole Wilson program.

But China, regardless of the fact that she thinks she got a blow in the face from her best friend, still regards the United States as that best friend and is not inclined to embarrass President Wilson at the Peace Conference by formally demanding that he repudiate the specific act of a member of his Cabinet, if she feels assured that the agreement will simply die automatically because of inability to live in the new atmosphere of fairness among nations and open covenants.

Furthermore, China assumes that the Ishii-Lansing agreement will go by the board along with two other matters against which she has filed specific protests with the Peace Conference. One of these is the group of twenty-one demands to which Japan forced China to accede at the very opening of the European war, and the effect of which was to take away from China railroad and commercial rights in her own country till the year 2007, and practically give Japan control of the Gulf of Pechili as well as the land approaches to Peking and Tientsin. Naturally China wants all the twenty-one demands wiped out of existence and asks the Peace Conference to do it for her.

She insists upon the assurance also that Kiao-Chau, which was taken by Japan from Germany at the outset of the war, shall be restored to China as agreed, and quickly, instead of being held by Japan, which is something China fears is being arranged against her.

China is not oversanguine of her success at Paris, but she made a beginning in getting representation, for that was against the wishes of Japan, as is a matter of record.

The suggestion of Japan was that she represent both China and herself at the conference. Japan's argument was that, as China was divided in her internal politics by a struggle between north and south, she could not claim national unity for herself at Paris.

China's countermove to that was selection by the north as one of the five delegates to the conference of C. A. Wing, a leading statesman of South China. He represents both sections of the country by common consent and selection of both parts. Moreover, there is now in session in Shanghai a conference of ten representatives of North China and as many of South China on the work of restoring harmony.

"If China," said my Chinese informant, "does not find herself freed by this Peace Conference from all Japanese domination and all handicaps and humiliations put upon her by arrangement among the other countries, the Chinese people will rise in protest. The temper of my people is no longer what it was. We have thrown off the Manchu yoke and have since survived two movements to restore the monarchy. This has taught us that abject submission need no longer be our part in the world."

February 8, 1919

PEKING IS CUT OFF FROM ALL CABLES

Wireless from Reinsch to Washington Confirms Reports of Rioting Over Shantung.

INTENSE FEELING SHOWN

WASHINGTON, May 8.—The State Department received word today that cable communication with Peking, China, had been cut off. A radiogram was received from Minister Reinsch confirming press reports of disturbances in the capital due to indignation over the action in Paris regarding Shantung Province.

A report reached here that Chinese residents of Shantung Peninsula have organized to oppose the cession to the Japanese and are asking all Chinese to join the movement.

The plan is to hold meetings, petition the powers, and refuse to submit to the authority of Japan. It is not the intention to start armed opposition, but to hold demonstrations like those in Korea.

Much concern is felt in official circles here over the agitation in China.

Japanese warning to Chinese authorities, it is felt, may be the prelude to action, should any Japanese subject suffer violence.

PEKING, May 5, (Associated Press.)—National sentiment has been aroused in Peking and China over the Peace Conference decision regarding Shantung and Kiao-Chau. The press is united in demanding that the territory be returned unfettered to China.

Parliament today adopted a resolution, addressed to the Peace Conference, deprecating the decision to give the disputed territory temporarily to Japan. A boycott of Japanese goods is being discussed in official circles here.

When yesterday students purned the home of Tsao Yu-lin, Minister of Communications, and severely beat Chang Tsung-hsiang, ex-Minister to Japan, who was a guest at Tsao Yu-lin's house, the police observed an attitude of "benevolent neutrality," but made several arrests after urgent orders were received from Police Headquarters.

May 9, 1919

WHAT GERMANS LOSE TO JAPAN IN CHINA

PARIS, May 19. (Associated Press.)—The peace treaty clause concerning the Shantung settlement contains no provision respecting its return to China, which, it is understood, lies in an agreement of some character, possibly a verbal agreement between President Wilson, Premier Lloyd George and Baron Makino. The text follows:—

"Germany renounces in favor of Japan all her rights, title, and privileges, particularly those concerning the territory of Kiao-Chau, railways, mines, and submarine cables, which she acquired by virtue of the treaty concluded by her with China March 6, 1898, and of all other arrangements relative to the province of Shantung.

"All German rights in the Tsing-tao-Tsinan Fu Railway, including its branch lines, together with its subsidiary property of all kinds, stations, shops, fixed rolling stock, mines, plant and material for the exploitation of mines are to remain acquired by Japan, together with all rights and privileges attaching thereto.

"The German submarine cables from Tsing-tao to Shanghai and from Tsing-tao to Chi-Fu, with all rights, privileges and properties attached thereto, are similarly acquired by Japan free and clear of all charges and incumbrances.

"Movable and immovable property owned by the German State in the territory of Kiao-Chau, as well as all rights which Germany might claim in consequence of works or improvements made or other expenses incurred by her, directly or indirectly, in connection with this territory, are and remain acquired by Japan, free and clear of all charges and encumbrances.

"Germany shall hand over to Japan within three months from the coming into force of the present treaty the archives, registers, title deeds and documents of every kind, wherever they may be, relating to the administration, civil or military, financial or judicial, or other, of the territory of Kiao-Chau.

"Within the same period Germany shall give particulars to Japan of all treaties, arrangements, and agreements relating to the rights, title, and privileges referred to in the two preceding articles."

May 20, 1919

CHINESE APPEAL TO SENATE GIVEN OUT

The text of a petition sent to the United States Senate early in May by the Chinese representatives at the Paris conference urging that the Senate assist in securing a revision of the Shantung settlement "by speedily passing a resolution affirming the same to be inconsistent with the national honor and interests of America, an incredible injustice to China and a danger to world peace," was made public here last night by the China Society of America.

In the communication to the Senate, Eugene Chen, one of China's representatives in Paris, says that "the only fair and just settlement of the existing situation is that all Germany's rights in Shantung be acquired by the Council of Prime Ministers and be referred to the League for disposal according to the findings of an international commission, appointed by the Conference after visiting Shantung and investigating the situation on the spot."

Andrew B. Humphrey, director of the society, announced that the original petition sent by cable was received by the Foreign Relations Committee of the Senate, but was not made public because, under the rules, a petition from aliens cannot be received and published in the record except by unanimous consent, which was denied. The text made public by mail and is as follows:

"Important meeting representative of Chinese assembled at Paris decided to appeal to Senate to assist in securing revision of Shantung settlement by speedily passing resolution affirming same to be inconsistent with national honor and interests of America, besides incredible injustice to China and danger to world peace.

"President's counsel finally brought about China's entrance into war. On him as trustee of American honor China rested hope of settlement enabling her to live untrammeled and unthreatened by Japanese imperialism. Aug. 14, 1917, China declared war. American and allied Governments assured her of their solidarity, friendship, and support, and promised to do all that rests with them to insure that China shall enjoy in her international relations a position and a regard due to a great country.

"Proposed settlement is a denial of this and a violation of well-defined aim of American foreign policy. Apart from Monroe Doctrine, America committed nowhere except in China through the Hay doctrine of the open door with its necessary guarantee of territorial integrity and political independence of China.

Root Agreement Is Cited.

"Doctrine confirmed in Root-Takahira agreement, reaffirmed by Lansing-Ishii agreement, which introduced, according to a statement issued by Lansing Nov. 6, 1917, principle of non-interference with sovereignty and territorial integrity of China, which, generally applied, is essential to perpetual peace, as clearly declared by President Wilson and which is the very foundation also of Pan Americanism as interpreted by this Government.

"This principle of non-interference was stated in terms denying that America and Japan had any purpose to infringe in any way on the independence or territorial integrity of China, and also in terms declaring that they are opposed to the acquisition by any Government of any special rights or privileges that would affect the independence or territorial integrity of China or that would deny the subjects or citizens of any country full enjoyment and equal opportunity in the commerce and industry of China.

"The proposed settlement of the Shantung question is a direct violation of this principle, and nothing better established than the German system as to Shantung, which included or later consisted of special rights and privileges that affected the independence and the territorial integrity of China besides denying the subjects of other countries the full enjoyment of equal opportunity in the commerce and industry of China in the Province of Shantung.

"Despite this precise provision of the Lansing-Ishii agreement and the notorious character of the German servitude of Shantung, the American member of the Council of Three has consented to the inclusion in the Peace Treaty of two special articles drafted by the Japanese granting more than originally asked of China and providing that all German rights in Shantung are and remain acquired by Japan free and acquitted of all charges.

"This injustice is more glaring when it is remembered that regrets [concessions?] whose acquisition by Japan is ordered by the Council of Three ceased to exist since China declared war on the 14th of August, 1917. In the Chinese declaration of war all treaties of whatever nature between China and Germany are expressly abrogated. Notice of abrogation was given to America and the allied powers, and none questioned the validity of this act of abrogation.

"These reasons of high policy, as well as your Philippine and Pacific interests, your historic trade relations with China, your cultural influence exercised through American-educated Chinese who are missionaries of the American idea in China, all witness the necessity of envisaging the Chinese Republic as the political child of the American people and emphasizing that the just settlement of the Shantung question is of more consequence to America than Fiume or Danzig, and that not in Europe, but in Asia is the American interest great.

Pan Asiatic Peril Invoked.

"Such a settlement is also opposed to world interests, because a Pan Asiatic solution of the Chinese question is rendered a certainty. The Chinese question involves the issue of whether the manpower and resources of China are to be developed in the interest of the world

and human progress or are to be exploited and used for selfish Asiatic ends.

"If China is free to co-operate with America and the West, the Chinese question will be solved in the interests of the world as a whole. If China is prevented from developing in co-operation with the West, the Chinese question will be solved in the sense desired by the Pan Asiatics under the political and military leadership of Japan.

"Pan Asiatic development of China is inevitable if the policy embodied in the twenty-one demands continues in operation. The dominant feature of this policy is Japan's claim to be the beneficiary of German ruthlessness in Shantung. As one of the Allied Associated States China has been claiming that the destruction of the German system cannot be limited to Europe, Africa, and the Pacific, but must be extended to the Far East. But the proposed Shantung settlement perpetuates the German system in China in circumstances which result in grave and added danger because it replaces Germany, whose strength is based on Europe, by Japan, at the very threshold of China.

"The meaning of the Pan Asiatic or Japanese development of China is indicated in the Korean claim for liberation from Japan and the reconstitution of Korea as an independent State filed last week. China arraigns Japan as a power whose soul is mediaeval, but whose methods are Prussian in their ruthlessness and efficiency.

"China points out that Japan is ejecting the white man from Korea, and that this policy reveals continued fidelity to that instant execution which in the past found expression in her rigidly guarded exclusion and which today expresses itself in the attempt to exclude the foreigner from Far Asia through a false Monroe Doctrine for the Far East.

"Attention is next directed to the formidable danger lying in Japan's Continental policy, which is defined as aiming at the seizure of Asiatic hegemony through dominating the resources of China in order ultimately to secure the mastery of the Pacific as the sole means of compassing unrestricted entrance for the Japanese immigrant into Australasia and America.

Japan's Policy in Korea.

"Korean claim tabulates series of facts showing that this Japanese world conquest has already found expression inter alia Japan's two successful wars against China and Russia, which have made her the greatest military power in Asia in much the same way that Prussia's two wars against Austria and France made her the greatest military power in Europe.

"The annexation of Korea and the Japanese possession of the South Sea Islands north of the equator bring Japan nearly 2,000 miles closer to Australia, giving Japanese navy base, dominating practically the entire land areas of the Pacific. The growing subjection of China to Japanese domination through the same methods made the annexation of Korea, in spite of solemn treaties, a political necessity.

"This process of subjection will be powerfully assisted by the proposed Shantung settlement, which will enable Japan to intrench herself in a vitally strategic area in intramural China, just as she has already intrenched herself outside the Great Wall in South Manchuria, through which lies the quite historic road of invasion into China. In the past Asiatic invaders have entered China from the north, and it was through the Manchuria gate that the last invaders crossed into the great plains of Northern China.

"It is said that China had to be abandoned in the belief that the President's insistence on a just settlement of the Shantung question might have wrecked

the conference and destroyed the League. But this event was only a possibility, [in the event of?] Great Britain reversing her policy for an Anglo-Saxon entente and aligning herself definitely with Japan against America in China, where Anglo-American interests are faced by Japan's aggressive rivalry.

"It is also said the whole future relationship between China and Japan will fall under guarantee of the League regarding territorial integrity and political independence. But if the Senate opposes Article X. or otherwise, the same forces that enabled Japan to triumph today may be expected to enable her to triumph in China though the League exists. This is almost a certainty, in view of China's exclusion from the Executive Council of the League, despite strong Chinese expectation that the President would secure for China and the representative small power of China one of the four seats allottable to the small powers of the world.

"The covenant of the League shows it is possible for Japan to contend that her consent is necessary before China could submit twenty-one demands set forth in the treaties and notes of 1915 for the consideration of the League under Article XIX.

"In a statement communicated to the American press on the Shantung settlement it was represented there is vested in Japan only the rights of economic concessionaire; but no one with any knowledge of the subject can doubt succession to the German rights in Shantung. At the meeting of the Five-Power Council on Jan. 27, although conquest expressly denied, application made for disposal of the possessions absolutely Germany—for instance, German colonies to which mandatories applied, settlement governed by the principle of conquest in spite of the fact that property rights belonging to China and only held on lease by Germany involved therein.

"Settlement if ratified would compromise national honor and vital interests of the American people in that same particular, because:

"Proposed Shantung settlement inherently unjust acquire rights belonging to China by every consideration of justice and sound policy, and perpetuates German system in China under American and allied sanction and authority.

"Settlement violates every principle of peace formulated by the President and agreed to by warring powers, and will be interpreted by Asia as an Anglo-Saxon and Latin renunciation of great thoughts greatly uttered at bidding of an Asiatic power that is summoning an ancient East to struggle for world supremacy.

"Settlement only justified on the principle of conquest, which indeed is the precise ground whereon Baron Makino claimed Japan's right to concessionaire of Shantung, which will be the real figure of conquest in China.

"Entire mischief due to detaching issue and viewing it without the menacing background of the Japanese policy thrown across China today.

"Holding fast faith in America, we appeal to your Senate to say that the decision of the Council of Three against China shall not be ratified by the American people in Congress assembled for the reasons set forth herein and because it involves the violation of the pledged word of the American Government to China and the chief, if not only aim of American foreign policy outside the Americas.

"From this view, therefore, the equitable settlement of the Shantung question is as much a war aim of America as of China.

"The only fair and just settlement of the existing circumstances is that all Germany's rights in Shantung acquired by the Council of Prime Ministers be referred to the League for disposal according to the findings of an international commission appointed by the conference after visiting Shantung and investigating the situation on the spot.

SMALL CONCESSION WILL TURN CHINA

By CHARLES A. SELDEN.

Copyright, 1919, by The New York Times Company.

Special Cable to THE NEW YORK TIMES.

PARIS, July 2.—The peace delegation from China, which may be soon the only nation still at war with Germany, are awaiting instructions from Peking as to what attitude they shall take toward the treaty with Austria. China declared war on Austria and Germany on the same day. She has refused to make peace with Germany because of the conference's refusal to allow her to sign the treaty with a reservation as to Shantung clauses or make a declaration of protest before signing.

The feeling of the Chinese in Paris since Saturday when the delegates refused to go to Versailles, has been one of satisfaction that they had sufficient backbone to break away from the traditional policy of China to submit to everything demanded of her, regardless of her own rights and dignity. That feeling is shared by others of the powers, who feel that their yielding to Japan in the Shantung matter was only an expedient to keep Japan in the League of Nations is justified, perhaps, by the Japanese promise to do the right thing by China later on in restoring her sovereignty in Shantung.

Underlying all this Shantung situation, there has been a misunderstanding by which A. J. Balfour, who has been largely responsible for the Peace Conference's attitude toward China, was led by Japan to believe that the Chinese delegates were only bluffing when they declared that they would not sign without reservations. The Japanese delegation had given a strong impression that the Chinese had been secretly instructed by Peking to sign anyway, if at the last moment they found that reservations were forbidden. This intimation from the Japanese is more effective than the reiterated statement from the Chinese that they would not and could not sign without reservations. So the English and French delegates at Versailles on Saturday were genuinely surprised when the Chinese failed to appear, thereby proving the sincerity of their declarations.

The attitude of America in this matter has been that it was best to yield to Japan as a matter of expediency to keep her in the League, trusting to her promises of future restitution to China. But the real sympathy of America is best indicated, perhaps, by the remark of one delegate from the United States who said that it was a great relief to him because the Chinese refused to go to Versailles at the last moment, thereby showing their determination not to submit to national humiliation.

The last effort of the Chinese to get what they held to be proper recognition was on Saturday noon three hours before the Versailles meeting, when Hoo Pi Teh, Chinese Minister to France, called at the Foreign Office to present a protest to Clemenceau and ask that it be officially recognized as an essential preliminary to China's signing of the German treaty. This protest, signed by Tsiang and Wang, Chinese plenipotentiaries, was as follows:

"Paris, June 28, 1919.

"His Excellency, Georges Clemenceau, President of the Peace Conference:

"In proceeding to sign the treaty of peace with Germany today, the under-

signed, plenipotentiaries of the Republic of China, considering as unjust Articles 156, 157, and 158, therein, which purport to transfer German rights in the Chinese province of Shantung to Japan instead of restoring them to China, the rightful sovereign over the territory and a loyal co-partner in war on the side of the allied and associated powers, hereby declare in the name and on behalf of their Government, that their signing of the treaty is not to be understood as precluding China from demanding at a suitable moment the reconsideration of the Shantung question, to the end that the injustice to China may be rectified in the interest of permanent peace in the Far East.

"LOU TSENG THIANG,

"CHENTING THOMAS WANG."

M. Dutasta, Secretary of the General Peace Conference, who received Hoo at the Foreign Office, said that Clemenceau was not there. Clemenceau at that moment was at President Wilson's home in the Place Des Etats Unis. M. Dutasta telephoned the contents of the final Chinese protest to Clemenceau, who evidently repeated them to Wilson. In a few minutes M. Dutasta reported that neither Clemenceau nor Wilson approved allowing China to make the suggested protest as a preliminary to signing. In the mean time the same letter had been submitted to Lloyd George with the same result. Now the Chinese delegates are awaiting instructions from Peking about signing the Austrian treaty. They take it for granted that they will be told to sign it, thereby qualifying for immediate membership in the League of Nations.

Furthermore, China would also sign the German treaty if Japan would make two concessions; first, to say when she will carry out the agreement to restore Chinese sovereignty at Kiao Chau; second, to withdraw her police from the Shantung Railways. As to the first proposition, China would be content if Japan would restore sovereignty in a year.

July 4, 1919

PRESS CHINA ON SHANTUNG.

TOKIO, April 24 (Associated Press).—The Japanese Foreign Office recently instructed Minister Obata at Peking again to open negotiations with the Chinese Government for the return of Shantung province direct to China by Japan, it was semi-officially stated today.

Foreign Minister Uchida, according to the semi-official account, made this statement to the Cabinet yesterday. The instructions were sent, the Minister said, as a period of three months since the signing of the peace treaty with Germany had elapsed on April 9, and Germany's rights in Shantung, according to the Shantung clause of the treaty, then vested in Japan.

April 30, 1920

CHINA'S DELEGATES START.

Dr. Yen, Foreign Minister, Will Be Chief Representative in Washington.

PEKING, Sept. 29. (Associated Press) —China's delegation to the conference on limitation of armaments and Far East questions left this city for Shanghai today on its way to Washington, intending to make the voyage across the Pacific on the steamer Hawkeye State. Dr. W. W. Yen, Foreign Minister, who has been expected to be chief of the delegation, did not start today, but it was said he would follow, provided China's Shantung policy was determined and initiated soon enough for him to reach the American capital for the opening of the conference.

Three prominent Chinese diplomats were members of the party which left today. They were Chow Tzechi, former Minister of Finance, and at one time Secretary of the Chinese Legation in Washington; Wang Ta-shieh, leader of the Progressive Party and former Minister of Foreign Affairs, and Dr. M. T. Liang, former Minister of Foreign Affairs and a prominent diplomat during the latter years of the Manchu dynasty.

Dr. Yen on Tuesday evening telegraphed Dr. C. C. Wu, son of Dr. Wu Ting-fang, former Chinese Minister to the United States, and a Cantonese member of the Chinese delegation in the Paris Peace Conference, offering him an associate delegateship. It is believed that Dr. Wu will accept.

September 30, 1921

UPHOLD CHINA STAND ON SHANTUNG ISSUE

PEKING, Nov. 5 (Associated Press). —Native and foreign newspapers in north China generally express satisfaction over the latest Chinese note to Japan on the question of Shantung. Some of them consider it a diplomatic victory over Japan.

The British owned and edited Peking and Tien-tsin Times considers that the honors are with China in the second exchange of notes and that in dialectics China always will be superior to Japan regarding the question of Shantung, since Japan's claims are based on might rather than on right. The newspaper asserts that some of the other powers for expediency's sake have recognized these claims based on might, but that this does not turn might into right.

The Peking Leader says the Chinese memorandum brought out clearly the exact points of difference between China and Japan, namely, conflicting viewpoints regarding the Versailles Treaty, on the disposition of the Shantung Railway and on the disposal of public property in Tsing-tao. The Leader thinks that Japan had better stop the discussion of the treaty, thus simplifying the opening of negotiations between China and Japan on a specific, practical basis. It also expresses the hope that Japan will make a specific proposal regarding the disposition of public property in Tsing-tao.

"This," the newspaper continues, "would leave the Shantung railway the sole important issue, the question being, shall Japan share in the railway's management and control or shall China have complete control while buying out the Japanese interest in the line? The issues involved can legitimately come under the Pacific discussion at the Washington Conference in connection with a clear definition of the application of the open door. With Japan controlling the railway, Shantung's door would not be open; with the railway under China, the door would be open.

"If Japan really is sincere in desiring to restore Shantung to China, she must take her hands off the railway. If Japan does not like the Chinese proposal, she is obligated to suggest other terms, which must involve complete withdrawal if one of the sorest spots in the Far East is to be removed.

"It would be well if a settlement could be reached before the Pacific Conference, otherwise the conference almost necessarily will be obliged to take up the question."

SHANGHAI, China, Nov. 3 (Associated Press)—A meeting of the British Chambers of Commerce in China today passed a resolution on the Shantung controversy, as follows:

"This conference is convinced that any settlement of the Shantung question leaving Japan in a privileged position in that province will constitute a negation of the policy of the 'open door' and equal trade opportunity in China, to which the British Government is committed."

November 7, 1921

Japanese Deny Peking Right To Speak for All of China

WASHINGTON, Nov. 20 (Associated Press).—Japan has no positive program concerning the general question of China, which will be discussed this week, it was learned today, but as various points are presented Japan will explain her position as clearly as possible.

In Japanese circles some anxiety was apparent tonight as to the concrete questions which China might bring before the conference. Emphasis was laid on the Japanese contention that the Chinese delegates represent only the Peking Government, which does not control a great part of China, and that the delegates, therefore, do not represent the Chinese people as a whole.

November 21, 1921

CHINA'S STAND FIRM ON THE 21 DEMANDS

Dr. Wang States at Final Committee Session Reasons Why They Should Be Re-examined.

Special to The New York Times.

WASHINGTON, Feb. 3.—The final session of the Committee on Pacific and Far Eastern Questions today adopted the Nine-Power Treaty to stabilize conditions in the Far East, completing the last of the treaties before the conference.

After this, the Twenty-one Demands, which were before the committee yesterday, were brought up by Dr. Wang, replying to the offer of Baron Shidehara of three modifications in the demands, including withdrawal of Group V.

Dr. Wang expressed pleasure over the offer and regretted that Japan did not volunteer to renounce the other claims set up in the treaties and notes of 1915. After reviewing the events that led up to the presentation of the Twenty-one Demands and the results thereof, Dr. Wang said:

"Because of the essential injustice of these provisions, the Chinese delegation, acting in behalf of the Chinese Government and of the Chinese people, has felt itself in duty bound to present to this conference, representing the powers with substantial interests in the Far East, the question as to equity and justice of these agreements and therefore as to their fundamental validity.

"If Japan is disposed to rely solely upon a claim as to the technical or juristic validity of the agreements of 1915, as having been actually signed in due form by the two Governments, it may be said that so far as this conference is concerned, the contention is largely irrelevant, for this gathering of the representatives of the nine powers has not had for its purpose the maintenance of the legal status quo.

"Upon the contrary, the purpose has been, if possible, to bring about such changes in existing conditions upon the Pacific and in the Far East, as might be expected to promote that enduring friendship among the nations of which

the President of the United States spoke in his letter of invitation to the powers to participate in this conference.

Reasons for Asking Abrogation.

"For the following reasons, therefore, the Chinese Delegation is of the opinion that the Sino-Japanese treaties and exchange of notes of May 25, 1915, should from the subject of impartial examination with a view to their abrogation.

"1. In exchange for the concessions demanded of China, Japan offered no 'quid pro quo.' The benefits derived from the agreements were wholly unilateral.

"2. The agreements, in certain respects, are in violation of treaties between China and the other powers.

"3. The agreements are inconsistent with the principles relating to China which have been adopted by the conference.

"4. The agreements have engendered constant misunderstandings between China and Japan, and, if not abrogated, will necessarily tend, in the future, to disturb friendly relations between the two countries, and will thus constitute an obstacle in the way of realizing the purpose for the attainment of which this conference was convened. As to this, the Chinese delegation, by way of conclusion, can, perhaps, do no better than quote from a resolution introduced in the Japanese Parliament in June, 1915, by Mr. Hara, later Premier of Japan, a resolution which received the support of some 140 members of Parliament. The resolution reads:

Resolved, That the negotiations carried on with China by the present Government have been inappropriate in every respect; that they are detrimental to the amicable relationship between the two countries, and provocative of suspicions on the part of the powers; that they have the effect of lowering the prestige of the Japanese Empire, and that, while far from capable of establishing the foundation of peace in the Far East, they will form the source of future trouble.

"The foregoing declaration has been made in order that the Chinese Government may have upon record the view which it takes, and will continue to take, regarding the Sino-Japanese treaties and exchange of notes of May 25, 1915."

Hughes States Our Position.

Secretary Hughes then explained the position of the United States in reference to Japan's attitude toward China as embraced in the twenty-one demands,

quoting the note sent by the American Government to Japan on May 13, 1915. He said that this note was in accord with the historic policy of the United States.

Reviewing the Twenty-one Demands, Mr. Hughes said that Group I had been wiped out by the settlement of the Shantung issue and that Group V would not be pressed, while many of the rigid features in the other demands had been modified by Japan's offer made yesterday through Baron Shidehara.

Concerning the express statement of Japan's readiness not to insist upon the right of option, granted exclusively in favor of Japanese capital with regard to loans for the construction of railroads in South Manchuria and Eastern Inner Mongolia, and loans secured on the taxes of those regions, but to throw them open to the joint activity of the international consortium, Mr. Hughes remarked:

"It is doubtless the fact that any enterprise of the character contemplated which may be undertaken in these regions by foreign capital would in all probability be undertaken by the consortium. But it should be observed that existing treaties would leave the opportunity for such enterprises open on terms of equality to the citizens of all nations. It can scarcely be assumed that this general right of the treaty powers in China can be effectively restricted to the nationals of those countries which are participants in the work of the consortium, or that any of the Governments which have taken part in the organization of the consortium would feel themselves to be in a position to deny all rights in the matter to any save the members of the respective national groups in that organization. I, therefore, trust that it is in this sense that we may properly interpret the Japanese Government's declaration of willingness to relinquish its claim under the 1915 treaties to any exclusive position with respect to railway construction and to financial operations secured."

Secretary Hughes here noted that the treaty rights between China and Japan were distinct from the question of the treaty rights of the United States under its treaties with China.

He concluded:

"I may say that it is with especial pleasure that the Government of the United States finds itself now engaged in the act of reaffirming and defining, and I hope, I may add, revitalizing, by the proposed Nine-Power Treaty, these policies (the open door and equality of all nationals) with respect to China."

At the suggestion of Mr. Hughes the speeches bearing on the Twenty-One Demands will be spread on the proceedings of the conference, the Chinese delegates reserving the right to seek a solution of the questions on future occasions.

February 4, 1922

CHINA FORMS NEW CABINET.

Li Yuan-Hung Puts Tuan Chi-jui at Head of Ministry.

PEKING, China, June 30.—Li Yuan-hung, the President of the Chinese Republic, today announced the formation of a compromise Cabinet. The Ministry is headed by Tuan Chi-jui, who takes the War portfolio in addition to the Premiership, and the direction of foreign affairs is assumed by Tang Shao-yi, who was Premier under the late President Yuan Shih-kai.

The composition of the Cabinet is as follows: Premier and Minister of War, Tuan Chi-jui; Foreign Affairs, Tang Shao-yi; Interior, Hsu Shih-ying; Navy, Chen Pih-kuan; Commerce and Agriculture, Chang Kuo-kan; Justice, Chang Yaoo-tseng; Education, Sung Hung-yi; Communications, Wang Ta-hsien; Finance, Chen Chin-tao.

July 1, 1916

PEKING NOW EXPECTS PEACEFUL SETTLEMENT

Secessionist Sentiment Waning —President Calls for Elections for a New Parliament.

WASHINGTON, June 20.—Peaceful settlement of China's internal troubles is forecast in an official dispatch to the Chinese Embassy from Peking.

The message, dated today, says that the provinces of Yunnan and Kwantung, which formed the backbone of the southern secessionist movement, have notified the Central Government that they favor co-operation toward a peaceful settlement and are ready to do everything possible to clear up the situation. Several other provinces are said to be about to take similar action.

President Li Yuan Hung, who complied with the revolting Military Governors' demand for a dissolution of Parliament, has issued another decree, calling for an immediate new election. The old Parliament, elected in 1913, was held to be unrepresentative, and failed to draw up a satisfactory constitutional draft. The new body, which cannot be convoked within a period of several months, owing to the complicated electoral machinery, is expected to be more closely in touch with public opinion.

During the interim the present Government, it is expected, will continue in power under President Li. General Chang-Haun, the Military Governor of Anhwei Province and originally head of the seceding Military Governors, who came to Peking after the President dissolved Parliament, will probably stay in Peking some time.

TOKIO, June 19, (delayed.)—The situation in China is not so serious as might be believed, according to the opinion understood to have been expressed by the Japanese Government in its reply to the American note inviting Japan to associate herself with the action of the United States in asking the rival factions in China to compose their differences.

The Japanese reply gives courteous recognition of the sincerity and high-mindedness of America's motives in seeking to assist China, but sets forth the belief that China is not endangered gravely. Moreover, it is said conditions have changed since the American note was presented, and Japan therefore submits her belief that it is not desirable that she shall forward a note to China similar to that sent by the United States.

June 21, 1917

Chinese Dictator Restores Throne; Hsun Tung Emperor

LONDON, July 2.—General Chang Hsun, says a Reuter dispatch from Peking, has informed President Li Yuan-Hung that he must retire; as the Manchu Emperor, Hsun Tung, has been restored to the throne.

Another Reuter dispatch from Peking says that Hsun Tung issued a mandate Saturday morning announcing his succesison to the throne of China.

July 2, 1917

CHINESE ARMIES MARCH ON PEKING TO OUST DICTATOR

Special Cable to THE NEW YORK TIMES.
TIENTSIN, July 5, (Dispatch to The London Morning Post.)—The Manchu restoration appears to be on the verge of collapse. By midnight Tuan Chi-jui, the new Premier, will, it is expected, have 20,000 troops between Peking and Tientsin, and large forces are also advancing from the south and along the Hankow railway.

Altogether 50,000 troops are converging on Peking, where Chang Hsun has only some 30,000.

Tuan Chi-jui today sent an ultimatum to Chang Hsun's troops, promising them lenient treatment if they would lay down their arms. The northern members of the militant party do not expect fighting to take place, as they believe that Chang Hsun will be deserted by his own troops when the strength of the republican force is realized.

Offer Shanghai as Capital.

SHANGHAI, July 5.—At a conference of military and naval leaders and other prominent men here today, a resolution was adopted in favor of the transfer of the central republican government to Shanghai, instead of the establishment of a provisional government here. A telegram was sent to President Li Yuan-hung, who took refuge in the Japanese Legation on his escape from the palace following the proclamation of the Manchu dynasty's restoration, inviting him to come to Shanghai forthwith. It is believed here that if Li Yuan-hung comes the situation will assume a far more serious aspect.

The conference was attended by Admirals Chen Pi-kwan and Sah Chan-ping, ex-Minister of the Navy; General Lu Yun-hsiang, General Ma Hung-lieh, Dr Sun Yat-sen, the revolutionary leader; Tang Shao-yi, former Premier; Sun Hung-yi, former Minister of Education; Quo Ti-chi, former Secretary to President Li Yuan-hung, and Eugene Chen, formerly editor of the Peking Gazette. Tang Shao-yi said that until the monarchy was recognized by the powers the republic would be the only legal government.

Disaffection in Peking.

TIENTSIN, July 5.—A military clash in China is imminent. The troops of Peking are showing signs of opposition to General Chang Hsun's dictatorship under the guise of a monarchy. At the same time the troops of Tsao Kun, Military Governor of the province of Chihli, are mobilizing and preparing to proceed to Peking.

Tsao Kun's action followed an ultimatum sent to General Chang Hsun, giving him twenty-four hours to withdraw troops from Peking. General Chang Hsun took no notice of the demand.

Prominent officials have been put to death or imprisoned as a result of the disturbed state of affairs. Treachery and opposition to the Manchu restoration are given as reasons for this action. Among those imprisoned was Wang Shih-cheng, Minister of War under the republic. Those put to death already number nine, among the most prominent being Prince P'u Lun, Chairman of the Council of State.

A Provisional Government has been established at Nanking, capital of the Province of Ingsu. Baron Feng Kuo-chang, ex-President of the National Assembly, was named President, Lut Mung-tio Vice President, and Tuan Chi-jui Premier.

Tuan Chi-jui has issued an eloquent denunciation of the Manchu restoration, accusing General Chang Hsun of overweening ambition and of committing crimes of inconceivable magnitude. He charged that the General was betraying the Manchus themselves. Tuan Chi-jui said he had intended to remain in retirement, but saw that the Manchus were being used as catspaws for brigandage. Now he calls on all provinces to put out every ounce of strength to save China from Chang Hsun.

Sun Yat-sen Naval Chief.

SAN FRANCISCO, July 5.—Dr. Sun Yat-sen, first President of the Republic of China, has been appointed Commander in Chief of the naval forces of Chinese provinces fighting for the preservation of the republic, according to cable advices received here today by the Chinese Nationalist League. The same report states that Senators opposing the Manchus' return to power have met in Nanking and decided on war, and that the southern army, loyal to democracy, has mobilized at Shanghai.

TOKIO, July 5.—Viscount Motono, Foreign Minister, said in the Diet yesterday that the restoration movement in China was causing anxiety in Japan, but, as it concerned Chinese domestic politics, he believed peace in China would best be served by Japan remaining a spectator and refraining from interference, at least for the present.

DICTATORSHIP FACES FAILURE

State Department Learns Chang's Cause Is Waning Fast.

Special to The New York Times.
WASHINGTON, July 5.—Dispatches to the State Department from American Minister Reinsch, at Peking, state that the monarchical element in China does not seem to be receiving the support in either the North or the South which it expected and must have in order to assure the permanent success of the coup which overthrew the republic last Sunday.

Minister Reinsch reported that many Northern Chinese leaders, who had been credited with assisting the restoration, appeared now to favor the republic, and that several of them had taken the field against General Chang Hsun. Division among the Northern leaders is expected to result in considerable advantage to the Republican forces in the South, although information is still insufficient to warrant confident prediction. The military Governor at Nanking is said to have 40,000 well-trained troops under arms ready to take the field, and other Southern military chieftains are also prepared for battle.

Adhesion of many militarists to the Republican ranks is interpreted here as showing that Chang far overplayed his hand and that the greatest gamble of his adventurous life will not succeed. Nevertheless, fear is felt that he will make an active resistance with his considerable military forces, and that in an attack by the Republicans, serious damage to Peking may follow. Chang probably could maintain himself for some time behind the Peking walls, especially as artillery is lacking in China. A compromise is rendered doubtful by the execution of death sentences, particularly that of Prince P'u Lun, who through a Manchu and a cousin of the restored Emperor, has been an ardent Republican and Progressive. It appears that Chang appointed many men to office in his Cabinet who had neither accepted nor been consulted.

Dr. V. K. Wellington Koo, the Chinese Minister, called at the State Department today, but had no information

July 6, 1917

FENG KUO-CHANG NOW PRESIDENT OF CHINA

Assumes Duties Provisionally, Thus Officially Ending the Rebellion.

WASHINGTON, July 14.—The Chinese Minister transmitted to the State Department today the following proclamation, issued by Feng Kuo-chang, the new Provisional President:

" Whereas, President Li Yuan HRung is unable, for cause, to perform the duties of his office:

" Now, therefore, I, Feng Kuo-chang, do hereby proclaim to all whom it may concern that in pursuance of Article V., Section 2, of the Presidential election law, I have, on this day of the seventh month, July 6, 1917, respectfully taken up the duties of the office of the President of the Republic."

The occupation of Peking by the Republican forces, following the surrender at Fung Tai Thursday of the Monarchist army of 10,000 men, indicates the complete restoration of the republic, the Chinese Legation here declared today.

Order in the capital was restored with few casualties. Premier Tuan Chi-jui will establish Republican headquarters in Peking immediately, it was said.

TIENTSIN, July 14.—A dispatch from Peking, dated Thursday, (before Chang Hsun fled,) says that at daybreak the Republican troops began bombarding the Temple of Heaven, which is the headquarters of General Chang Hsun, the commander of the Monarchial forces. The attackers then were within a quarter of a mile of the Legation quarter of the city.

There was machine gun and rifle fire from all directions, and shrapnel was being dropped onto General Chang Hsun's retreat. The Monarchists were fighting desperately, with no sign of surrendering.

Stray bullets flying over the Legation section wounded the following Americans while they were on the city wall: A. R. Zumbrum, of Cheyenne, Wyoming; R. A. White, of Cedar Rapids, Iowa, and Private Gault, of the Marine Corps. In addition, one Japanese and one Italian were wounded. All the Legation guards were stationed at strategic positions, and civilians residing outside of the city were being brought into the foreign quarter.

Airplanes were flying over General Chang Hsun's positions, and the Republicans were rapidly surrounding the Monarchists, who were making a determined stand. It was believed that the besieged troops would have to be annihilated before they ceased fighting.

SHANGHAI, July 14.—A telegram received here today from Mien-yang, dated July 11, says:

" Fighting broke out on July 6 at Cheng-tu (capital of the Province of Sze-chuen with a population of 800,-000) between Sze-chuen and Kwei-chow troops. Fires were started in some parts of the city. The situation is critical. Most of the foreign residents of Cheng-tu have taken to the hill resorts."

July 15, 1917

Prospect of Dr. Sun's Return to Power in China

CAN Sun Yat-sen come back? An American business man, A. Masters MacDonell, just back from a four months' visit to China, during which he had several conversations with the first Provisional President of the Chinese Republic, is of the opinion that, although Sun Yat-sen is making no attempt to become President, events may easily shape themselves in such a way as to make his selection necessary, because he is the strongest available man. Mr. MacDonell, who is a New York importer and exporter, has been in close touch with the intellectual Chinese in America for the last ten years. There are about 2,000 Chinese students in this country, many of whom are his personal friends. When he went to China in the early Spring he was the bearer of letters of introduction to many influential people. He was on intimate terms with the members of the Progressive group, among whom were Sun Yat-sen, revolutionist in the most conservative land under heaven, and fugitive for fifteen years from the keenest and most relentless trailers of men; Tang Shao-yi, a Yale graduate and one of the most important men now in China, and B. C. Wise, who has held important offices under the Chinese Government.

Mr. MacDonell regards Sun Yat-sen as perhaps the master mind of China. In the interview below he gives the substance of what that romantic figure, upon whose head a price totaling $500,-000 has been offered by provisional Governments and the central authorities in Peking during the last twenty years, thinks of the present political upheaval, and the part that he believes the United States will play in the Orient. China is broadly divided into three political parties, according to Mr. MacDonell's analysis. The military, official, and reaction-

aries compose one, which he referred to as the Tories. The others are the Kuomintang, or Progressive group, and the Chinputang, a subdivision of the Kuomintang.

" At the time I left China, on June 10, half of the Chinputang, disgusted with their own party, had joined the Kuomintang," said Mr. MacDonell at his home in East Eighty-third Street. " It was generally felt that the existing Government was about to fall, and there was a strug-

Dr. Sun Yat-sen

gle between the Tories on the one hand and the Progressives on the other as to which should succeed to power. At that time Chang Hsun was an important factor in the Tory group. The Progressives, though, looked for advice and leadership to Dr. Sun Yat-sen. It was felt that the time had now come when the Progressives, representing modern ideas, were bound to come into power, as they alone would be able to preserve the republic and to develop it along up-to-date lines.

" This naturally met with the opposition of the Tories, who were well satis-

fied to let things run as they had been doing. A serious clash was imminent, and as the bulk of the people of China were in sympathy with the Progressive element, that party had every reason to believe in their ultimate success.

" Since I have left China, however, Chang Hsun, an old-fashioned chieftain, with his own army of some 40,000 pigtailed retainers and fired with the ambition to marry his daughter of tender years to the little, deposed Emperor, has endeavored to re-establish the empire, thereby hoping to found a new dynasty, of which he would be the power behind the throne. This move was bound to fail, and no one but a freebooter like Chang Hsun would imagine for a moment that it could be successful.

" The well-censored cables from China have recently announced two significant things—that Dr. Sun Yat-sen had been named Commander in Chief of the Republican Army and Navy, with headquarters in Shanghai, and that Tuan Chijui has established a capital in Nanking. This clearly indicates that the two parties—Progressive and Tory—are as far apart as ever, and that the future of the republic hangs in the balance. The strength of the Tories lies in a few provinces in the north; the Progressives control the remainder of the country and have the support of the majority of the population.

" In the case of a struggle between the two parties for supremacy, there is no doubt that the Progressives will win, which will mean a modern, enlightened, and constructive republican government that will command the respect of the world at large.

" Early in May rumors were current among all classes of Chinese that a revolution of some sort was pending. In Peking many of the coolies had begun to grow their pigtails again, giving as a reason that the Manchu Dynasty might again be established. They wished to be on the safe side. Certain stories were circulating, some of them sufficiently fantastic, but that quality in them did not interfere with their ready acceptance by the populace.

"In Shanghai, which is generally well informed, there was great uneasiness among the natives, who predicted the downfall of the Cabinet and feared civil war. Early in June the impotency of the existing Government became apparent even to the casual visitor to China; but there were no surface indications of the storm that was to break on the republic. Native business men hurriedly put their affairs in order, and the professional politicians got busy preparing for early trouble. Tuan Chi-jui assumed the leadership of the Reactionary Party, while the Liberals and Progressives found an advisor and leader in Dr. Sun Yat-sen, who had withdrawn from political life to devote his attention to the industrial development of China.

"I had the pleasure of seeing a great deal of Dr. Sun Yat-sen at this critical period. Being a modest and unassuming man, he lives in a small house in a pleasant part of the French Concession in Shanghai. The only outward sign of the importance of its occupant is the sentry box by the front door, in which an Anhamite armed policeman is always seated. From sunrise until long after dark there was a line of motors, carriages, and rickshaws standing before the house in which, as it seems to me, the master mind of China studies the tremendous problems of the country's future.

"After ringing the bell the door was quickly opened, and a noiseless secretary asked my business. I was ushered into a reception room furnished in European fashion and having a few good prints on the walls. The windows overlooked a small garden, largely lawn, on which croquet wickets were laid out. Croquet is Dr. Sun's favorite form of exercise, both he and Mrs. Sun being really good players.

"I had barely seated myself when the door opened and Dr. Sun entered. He is of medium height, and was dressed on this occasion in a semi-military suit of light-brown material. I have talked with him several times, and it was not until after I had had a number of interviews with him that I realized how, at first, one sees only his face, which, unlike that of most Orientals, is sensitive and mobile, full of expression and responsive to his thoughts. He speaks in a low and well-modulated voice, and his English is that of a cultivated American. I think it is justifiable to compare him to Napoleon in that he is both a practical man and an idealist—practical in so far as the immediate demands of his country are concerned, an idealist concerning the limitless possibilities in the future of its 400,-000,000 people.

"In a few moments the door opened again, and Mrs. Sun appeared. Instead of meeting the Chinese lady of fable and

fiction, I saw a dainty, slender brunette, dressed in soft voile of recent Paris origin, who smilingly greeted me in my mother tongue and asked for the latest news of the operas and plays in New York. She is genuinely interested in current topics. You do not feel so surprised when you learn that she was educated at Wesleyan College, and had spent much time traveling in the United States. But at first the impression created by her appearance and conversation in such surroundings is extremely piquant.

"Dr. Sun has the capacity to make a visitor feel at ease quickly, and awaits the inevitable question with calm. I had called on him to ascertain what I could of his opinion as to the causes of the present political unrest and widespread dissatisfaction in China, and when I had made this fact known Dr. Sun talked freely, though carefully weighing his observations, in view of the circumstance that I had told him I should like permission to present his ideas to the people of my country upon my return.

"Dr. Sun's summing up of the situation was about like this: The revolution of 1911 did away with the empire and paved the way for a modern system of republican government. It overthrew the power of the Manchus and made of the Chinese a united people and freed them of many of the abuses of the past. Owing, however, to the ingrained conservatism of the Chinese people, which retards all active measures, actual reform is necessarily slow.

"As in the past, the public has taken no part in the government of China, the old official class of the empire has been able to retain a certain amount of its former power, and it was expedient to give members of it high offices of state. Yuan Shi-kai, for example, belonged to the old order. He floated many loans, the proceeds of which he, in many cases, according to Dr. Sun, diverted to his own pocket, and finally, carried away by his own egotism, he tried to restore the empire by founding his own dynasty. Li Yuan-hung, his successor, a man with more modern views, has been trying to have a coalition Government, composed of old-school officials and up-to-date men. Dr. Sun said to me: 'This is like trying to mix oil and water. The result is the chaos of today. China is surrounded by her enemies, and unless something is done, and done speedily, she will succumb.'

"Dr. Sun added that China was at present undergoing a housecleaning. The old official classes had proved their incompetence—they must go, he said. The Tuchuns, relics of the past, must disband their men and retire to civil life. Both classes, he believes, realize that they are doomed; hence their last desperate fight. When China has disposed of them and established law and order, her Government must be reconstructed on civil lines. China must break down prejudices, abolish extra-territoriality—that was Dr. Sun's phrase—and assert her rights as a

modern power. She must, he believes, outline a program of internal development that will command the respect of the other great powers by reason of its logic and intelligence."

Mr. MacDonell put this question to Dr. Sun: "Would you mind giving your opinion on Chinese foreign relations?" The Chinese leader replied in the following words:

"For many years past, owing to a weak Government and an absence of a definite program for conducting China's external policies, we have been forced to part not only with territory, but with priceless public property as well—for example, railroad franchises and mining rights. Very few mining rights have been given away. We don't object to foreigners developing mines and railways, but we do object to their control of them. Our very integrity has been threatened, and, owing to our impotence, we have been unable to resist many arbitrary demands.

"As you know, I have been consistently opposed to China's entering the war. I have given my reasons to the Peking Government, and to the world at large. I am confirmed in my position by the official statements of practically all of the belligerents, who solemnly declare that this war is not one of conquest, but is being waged to preserve the integrity of weaker nations. If it is a political necessity to rehabilitate Belgium, Serbia, and Poland, and to protect their independence, it is of greater importance to do the same for China.

July 15, 1917

NEW MILITARY REGIME PROCLAIMED IN CHINA

Sun Yat Sen Made Head of Army and Navy by Malcontents Meeting at Canton.

PEKING, Monday, Sept. 3, [delayed.] Dr. Sun Yat Sen has been designated Commander in Chief of the Army and Navy of a new Military Government of China proclaimed by seventy members of the disbanded Chinese Parliament meeting in Canton. The Military Governor of Canton is supporting the Peking Government. Fighting between his troops and the forces of Sun Yat Sen is feared. Civilians in Canton are fleeing to Hongkong.

President Feng Kuo-chang says he is optimistic over the reconciliation of South China. He has informed the American Minister, Mr. Reinsch, that he will not call a Popular Council or order a Parliamentary election until he has determined positively which plan is most acceptable to the Provincial officers.

Minister Reinsch and representatives of other allied Powers, in order to give financial relief to the Peking Government, have virtually agreed to the postponement of all Boxer indemnity payments for five years.

September 8, 1917

Civil War in China Resumed by Armies of North and South

AMOY, China, Oct. 7, (Associated Press.)—Hostilities between the Northern and the Southern Governments have been resumed, numerous troops leaving this city against the southern forces stationed at Changchow.

The usual rice supply to this port has been cut.

The Chinese peace delegation at Paris was advised from Peking on Aug. 28 that Wong-I-Tong, representing the Northern Government, had begun negotiations with Tang Shao Yi of the Southern Government looking to reconciliation. On Sept. 29 further advices reported that southern representatives had refused to treat with Wong-I-Tong and a resumption of hostilities between the two factions was predicted.

October 8, 1919

ANFU FORCES COLLAPSE.

Another Chinese Militarist General Offers His Submission.

PEKING, July 22 (Associated Press)—The armies on the Feng Tai-Lang Fang sector of the Tientsin railway line of General Hsu Shu-cheng, former Resident Commissioner of Inner Mongolia and one of the Anfu leaders, are reported to be disintegrating, like the forces to the south of the capital. Ten thousand of his men, comprising the 3d division under General Sung Tzo-yang, have advised the Government that they are ready to obey the orders of the War Ministry. They were formerly part of the command of ex-President Feng Kwo-chang.

General Hsu Shu-cheng yesterday was a guest at a foreign hotel in the legation quarter here. Later he departed in the company of Japanese officers.

There is virtually no military obstacle to prevent the troops of Generals Tsao Kun and Wu-fu from entering the capital, as the army hitherto opposing them has completely disintegrated, some of the troops laying down their arms and returning to their barracks, while others fled to the hills.

The Chi Li leaders, however, have chosen to withhold their troops in the present line in view of the representations by Cabinet members and diplomats that an advance might result in disorder in the capital. The advance guard is stationed at Chang Sintien, a day's march away.

It is represented as the President's plan to accept the proffered resignation of General Tuan Chi-jui, the army commander, and abolish the Frontier Defense Force. The President, it is reported, will ask Wang Shi-chen to form a new Cabinet, eliminating Anfu influence.

July 24, 1920

TUAN, ANFU CHIEF, RESIGNS HIS POST

PEKING, July 25.—Tuan Chi-jui has tendered his resignation as Generalissimo of the army, and a group of his militarist associates yesterday started for Tientsin, authorized to accept terms providing for the punishment of General Hsu Shu-chenk (who refused to acknowledge his dismissal as Resident Commissioner of Inner Mongolia), the disbanding of the frontier force, the dissolution of Parliament and the suppression of the Anfu Club.

Tuan Chi-jui attempted to commit suicide, but was prevented from doing so. Generals Hsu Shu-cheng and Ting Shih-yuan are fugitives. The Ministers of Finance, Communications and Justice have resigned.

The troops of Chang Tso-lin, are surrounding Peking with the intention of enforcing the proposed terms of surrender. The city gates remain closed against the dispersed soldiery, opening for a short time in the morning to admit market produce. The city is practically under siege. Steps are being taken to limit profiteering and take care of the poor.

PEKING, July 25 (Associated Press).—President Hsu Shih-chang has accepted the resignation of Tsang Yu-chun, Minister of Communications; Li Shih-hao, Minister of Finance, and Chu-shen, Minister of Justice.

Tien Wen-lieh, Minister of the Interior, has been named acting Minister of Communications, and the other resigning members of the Cabinet will be succeeded by the Vice Ministers. All those who resigned belong to the Anfu faction.

Traffic with Tientsin is still restricted to military trains.

Hope for a compromise between the opposing factions is pinned on the peace mission which has arrived at Tientsin,

HONORS RESTORED TO GENERAL WU

PEKING, July 27.—The downfall of the Anfu faction is now complete. The troops of the Chi-li leaders have surrounded the city and the Anfu soldiers are being absorbed into their forces.

General Wu Ping-hsing, Chief of Police, has been summarily dismissed, and a Presidential mandate restores their ranks and honors to Tsao-kun and Wu Pei-fu.

Three Anfu Ministers are refugees at the Italian Legation.

Order is maintained in the city and there is only a little looting outside by starving soldiers.

There is evidence that the victors will not be extremely vindictive toward their enemies except in the case of half a dozen leaders.

General Wu Pei-fu's troops are close to the city on the southwest, but everything in Peking is orderly. Traffic with Tientsin, interrupted for several days, has not yet been restored.

Tung-cho, where looting and disorder were reported Sunday, is now said to be quiet. The detachment of American marines sent to bring out American residents, if necessary, is remaining there as a precautionary measure.

headed by former Premier Chin Yunpeng. It is expected that General Tsaokun, Military Governor of Chi-li Province, will also arrive soon in Tientsin from Paoting-fu.

Since Chin has the confidence of the Chi-li generals and also of General Chang Tso-lin, Military Inspector of Manchuria and Military Governor of the Province of Feng-tien, it is believed the peace mission promises success.

Reports of looting and disorder in Tung-cho have been received here. A small detachment of American marines has been sent there to bring out American residents if necessary.

TIENTSIN, July 25 (Associated Press).—General Chang Tso-lin arrived here today, to remain two or three days while Feng-tien troops complete the investment of the capital.

Ma-liang, the Anfu General from Shantung who recently captured Teh-chow, is said to have given his troops two days of looting, while General Sang-yuan, commanding the Chi-li troops opposing him, is reported also to have behaved disgracefully. After a cross-country march from Paoting-fu, the Chi-li forces attacked and drove back Ma-liang toward Teh-chow.

Unconfirmed reports from Feng-tai say that fighting on the Peking-Hankow line has ceased and that Tuan Chi-jui, the army commander, has resigned. The reports say that Tuan petitioned the President to relieve him of command of the frontier defense forces, converted by him into a "preservation-of-the-nation army," on the ground that the army had failed to carry on a successful campaign, and asked that the army be dissolved. The President declined to accept, according to the reports.

The British Admiral Duff left here yesterday afternoon for Taku, where he will remain for two days. An international military train carrying 100 Japanese to reinforce the legation guard also left here yesterday afternoon for Peking.

An airplane from Peking bombed Manchurian troops encamped at Pei-ts'ang yesterday morning, with unexpected results. The troops, never having seen an airplane before, were greatly interested, and there was no panic.

July 26, 1920

TIENTSIN, July 26 (Associated Press).—General Chang Tso-lin, Military Inspector of Manchuria and Military Governor of the Province of Feng-Tien, in an interview today declared he was compelled to act against the Anfuites "to save the country from their misdeeds and corruption." The General said he had nothing to conceal and disclaimed personal ambitions, asserting that it was his purpose to place his forces entirely at the disposal of the President.

General Chang Tso-lin said he never intended to restore the Manchus or exploit himself for the Presidency or Vice Presidency.

"I would be content," he added, "if Tuan Chi-jui went into complete retirement, but I am determined that other Anfu leaders be severely punished."

General Chang Tso-lin appealed to the foreign Powers not to shelter these leaders in foreign concessions or legation quarters.

A conference is soon to be held at Tientsin, at which representatives of Military Governors and people will decide the future policy of the country, according to General Chang Tso-lin. He said he was working only for a reunion of the nation, after which he intended to return to Mukden and devote himself to developing the immense uncultivated resources of Manchuria for the benefit of the people.

The General said he was redistributing his troops with a view to causing minimum interference with the railways.

July 28, 1920

45

ELECT SUN YAT SEN.

HONOLULU, T. H., April 7.—The Chinese Parliament, sitting at Canton, has unanimously elected Dr. Sun Yat Sen, first Provisional President of China at the time a Republican form of Government was substituted for the empire, as "President of the Chinese Republic," says a dispatch received from Canton, China, today by the Liberty News, a Chinese newspaper here.

April 8, 1921

BEGIN CHINESE CIVIL WAR.

Canton Troops, Led by Sun Yat-sen, Are Marching on Peking.

The Canton Government has declared war upon the Peking militarists and the Southern Chinese troops, led by President Sun Yat-sen in person, are beginning a drive through Kwangsi north, with Peking as their objective, according to cablegram advices received yesterday by Ma Soo, representative of the Canton Government in this country. Sun Yat-sen will leave Canton this week at the head of several divisions of Southern-Chinese troops and join the army already assembled in Kwangsi, the cablegrams state.

"The Chinese people have decided to do away with the so-called leaders in Peking, who are so in debt to foreign powers that they have become mere hirelings," said Mr. Ma Soo in New York yesterday, "and within a short time the world will see how feeble the hold these militarists and politicians have upon the China that they claim to govern."

October 12, 1921

NEW CHINESE ALLIANCE AGAINST WU-PEI-FU

Sun Yat-Sen Unites Forces With Chang Tsao-lin, Governor of Manchuria.

PEKING, April 17 (Associated Press).—American diplomatic agents here have been informed that a union between Sun Yat-sen, head of the South Chinese Government in Canton, and General Chang Tsao-lin, Governor of Manchuria, has been effected for the purpose of defeating General Wu Pei-fu, leader of Central Chinese forces. This alliance of forces, hitherto opposed, is considered likely to hasten impending changes in the Peking Government.

General Wu Pei-fu, regarded as the most powerful military genius in China, is rapidly concentrating 50,000 soldiers at the junction of the Yellow River with the Peking-Hankow Railroad. He has advanced other forces into the Province of Chi-li, in which Peking is located.

Wu Pei-fu's position is further strengthened by the sudden departure of General Tsao Kun, Military Governor of Chi-li, thus leaving Wu Pei-fu's invasion of the province unopposed except by General Chang Tsao-lin. Tsao Kun, accompanied by the Civil Governor, is supposed to have gone to Shanghai.

President Hsu Shih-chang has dispatched an envoy to Wu Pei-fu to ascertain the purpose of his military movements northward.

Jacob Gould Schurman, the American Minister, has just returned from a tour of China, coming directly from Mukden. While in Mukden he received General Chang Tsao-lin's explanation of events. The Manchurian Governor said he was sending 70,000 troops from Mukden southward merely to support contemplated changes in the Government. His purpose, he told Mr. Schurman, was to call, in Tien-Tsin or some other convenient city, within a month, a convention of political and military leaders of the country to form a new Government, revise the Constitution, summon Parliament and elect a President acceptable to all factions. He said that Wu Pei-fu would be invited, but that if he opposed the purposes of such a convention he (Chang Tsao-lin) intended to fight. He declared that Wu Pei-fu was obstructing plans for unification.

General Chang Tsao-lin assured Mr. Schurman that fighting would be avoided as long as possible, and that if it could not be avoided foreigners would be adequately protected.

April 18, 1922

CAPTURE OF CANTON MAY REUNITE CHINA

General Chen Proclaims Peking Government Supreme After Rout of Sun Yat-sen.

WINS A QUICK VICTORY

Southern Delegates Now Expected to Join Old Parliament and Support President Li.

PEKING, June 17 (Associated Press).—General Chen Chiung-ming, formerly civil Governor of Kwantung Province, whose troops seized Canton on Friday, announced today that the South China or Canton Government had been terminated and that henceforth Canton would unite with the north in recognizing the old Republican Parliament.

Dispatches from Canton describe the collapse of the Southern Government as complete, Sun's military forces crushed and the former Canton President himself a fugitive.

Advices received here vary as to the details of what are called the last hours of the Southern Constitutional Government, nor is it definitely known how much fighting preceded Sun Yat-sen's flight.

One dispatch from American sources in Canton declares that Sun's bodyguard continued to hold the Presidential Palace in the face of the assaults of Ye Chui's troops after their leader had taken refuge aboard a gunboat and departed for Whampoa.

Another report said that Chen Chiung-ming's forces, commanded by Ye Chui, suddenly surrounded Canton, seized the forts, invaded the city and marched upon the Palace.

The fall of the Southern leader is said to have been the result of an agreement between General Wu Pei-fu, dominant military chieftain of Northern China, President Li Yuan-hung and Chen Chiung-ming, formerly Sun Yat-sen's supporter, but who later came out in favor of a reunited China.

Official circles here assert that the elimination of Sun Yat-sen will mean speeding up of the plans to reunify the country. However, they issue the warning that a counter-revolution may develop if Sun is able to gather enough troops about him to launch a drive to regain Canton.

Unless Sun is able to retrieve his lost authority it is believed that Chen's coup will result in many southern members of the old Republican Parliament proceeding to Peking and constituting the necessary Government quorum to put that legislative body in legal motion again.

As the result of Chen's coup at Canton, Dr. Sun's principal army is in a precarious position. These forces are facing 12,000 of Wu's troops at Nanchang in Kiangsi Province, while the hostile army of General Chen occupies their base at Canton.

General Chang Tso-lin, the Manchurian leader, while not wholly eliminated, is in a conciliatory mood as a result of his recent defeat by Wu's Chihli army on the Chihli-Manchurian front. The opposing commanders on that front are reported to have boarded a British warship at Chinwangtao to arrange an armistice.

The situation in Manchuria has been further complicated, apparently by the proclamation through an assembly of self-government for each of the three Manchurian provinces. Dispatches said the assembly had appointed Chang Tso-lin Commander-in-Chief. It was represented as the purpose of the assembly to give Manchurian provinces separate administration, but to consider them still a part of China.

Dr. Wellington Koo, Minister to Great Britain and former Minister to the United States, today was appointed by President Li Yuan-hung to head a commission that will investigate China's financial condition with a view to reorganization.

June 18, 1922

46

China's Parliament Meets After Five Years; North and South Split Immediately Develops

PEKING, Aug. 1 (Associated Press).— The old Republican Parliament of China, dissolved by the militarists in 1917, reassembled today with a quorum and began the transaction of business. The opening of the Parliament, it is believed, will weaken the cause of Sun Yat-sen, deposed President of South China, who had attempted to prevent southern members attending its revival.

When a roll call in both houses showed that each had a quorum, it was decided to take up business at the point where it was dropped five years ago when the military sabre swept aside the constitutional gavel. Drafting of a permanent Constitution for the country is expected to be an early item on the program.

A split between the northern and southern members developed at the first session today on the attitude to be adopted toward the minority section of Parliament that established the Canton Government, as well as toward the legislative body which succeeded the Constitutional Parliament at Peking when the militarists drove out the latter.

As soon as the House convened, Speaker Wu Ching-Lien urged that the five-year lapse be considered as a recess. This course, if adopted, would totally ignore the acts of the members of the southern minority who met in Canton last year and elected Sun Yat-sen "President of China," while its apparent effect would be repudiation of Sun by the members who voted for him in the south.

When Speaker Wu asked the House to proceed to the adoption of a constitution, the debate storm broke. The southerners charged the northern members with treachery in permitting themselves to be dissolved by the militarists.

The Speaker led the orators for the north, declaring that all acts since dissolution were illegal and particularly

the election of Sun Yat-sen, which had been accomplished without a quorum.

No vote was reached today and adjournment was taken subject to the call of the Speaker.

A further test of strength between the northern and southern factions is expected when the House meets again, but in the meantime all the members feel a moral victory has been gained by the mere assembling of Parliament with a quorum and those legislators who have continued to linger at Canton are expected to hurry to Peking.

August 2, 1922

WU PEI-FU PLEDGES AID FOR SUN'S PLAN

Backs His Terms for a Free Parliament and Abolition of Tuchuns.

SUN RECONCILING FACTIONS

Representatives of Three Promise Support, as Do Shanghai Labor Organizations.

SHANGHAI, Aug. 21.—Sun Yat-sen, deposed President of China, who recently fled to this city from Canton, leaped to the front today as a pivotal figure in the reorganization of the Chinese Government with the receipt of a telegram from Wu Pei-fu, dominant military figure of North China, flatly endorsing Sun's recent manifesto and pledging his support to Sun's plan for rebuilding the Federal governmental machinery.

The Southern leader, who Peking authorities recently declared had been wiped from the slate of Chinese politics by his overthrow in Canton, has become the focal point of a series of interfactional conferences here which, his supporters say, point to an early settlement of the country's problems.

Despite the fact that Sun Yat-sen backed Chang Tso-lin, Governor of the three Eastern provinces, in his late unsuccessful tilt against Wu Pei fu, the latter's telegram today addressed to his personal representative here, General Sun Yueh, expressed unqualified endorsement of Sun Yat-sen's policies.

These include the Southerner's terms for the convocation and functioning of Parliament free from all outside interests, self-government for the provinces to replace the Tuchun, or military governorship system, and the conversion of the independent provincial armies into labor battalions to wield the hoe instead of the sword.

Another incident today pointed to the drawing together of the different factions, whose representatives have been conferring here with Sun. This was the return to Peking of Li Shu and the other spokesmen for President Li Huanhung, bringing a cordial letter from Sun to the chief executive, expressing Sun's readiness to advise and aid in the task of reconstructing and reuniting China. Whether this presages Sun's early departure for the capital, a step which President Li has repeatedly urged him to take, is not disclosed.

Three factional delegations today visited Sun and pledged their support. Representatives of twenty-seven labor organizations of Shanghai gave like assurances to the deposed Southern chieftain.

SHANGHAI, Aug. 21.—More than 100 Southern parliamentarians who have been holding out against Peking are departing for the capital to join their fellows there and are expected to provide a quorum necessary for the election of a permanent President and the promulgation of a Constitution.

The break between the President and General Wu Pei-fu is constantly widening over the division of patronage and a profound difference regarding the Constitution. General Wu desires a strong centralization of Government in Peking, while the President, with the backing of the Cantonese and General Chang, desires a loose confederacy or a semi-independent province.

General Chang's recent employment of Japanese and Russian military instructors presages another attempt to dominate Peking against General Wu.

Meanwhile, the financial situation is worse, and many leaders predict national bankruptcy, with general rebellions of the unpaid troops or some form of international financial control that would permit the peaceful disbandment of troops and their employment on national projects.

August 22, 1922

'LITTLE HSU' RAISES STANDARD OF REVOLT

Movement Believed to Be Backed by Anfu Party, Sun Yat-sen and General Chang.

PEKING, Oct. 8 (Associated Press).— General Hsu Shuh-chen, known as "Little Hsu," avowed militarist and one of the leaders of the Anfu Club, which was broken up by Wu Pei-fu and other popular leaders, has established an independent military government at Yenping, Province of Fukien, and is causing the Peking Administration no little uneasiness.

There is a distinct impression in official circles here that the developments in Fukien mark the beginnings of new disturbances to be conducted jointly by the Anfuites, or so-called pro-Japanese party headed by General Tan Chi-jui, a former Premier, the adherents of Sun Yat-sen, deposed President of South China, and Chang Tso-lin, ruler of Manchuria.

"Little Hsu," the spearpoint of the movement, has been lying low for some months. When the Anfu Club was broken up he fled for refuge to the Japanese Legation in Peking and remained under its sheltering roof for many weeks. Later he escaped. He is the only one of the Anfu movement who has not been pardoned by the Central Government.

The native money market has tightened perceptibly with the developments in Fukien, in which each of the three groups mentioned above is said to be represented.

According to the native press, "Little Hsu" issued a proclamation that he has made Yenping his headquarters, and that from there he proposes to fight for the unification of the country. He contends that Sun Yat-Sen and Tuan Chijui should assume prominent roles in the developments of the plan.

General Li's reports to the Peking Government indicate he has dispatched a column of troops against Yenping. The Peking authorities also are said to have ordered those gunboats already in Southern waters to proceed to the mouth of the Min River to support Li's offensive against "Little Hsu."

October 9, 1922

BANDITS LAY WASTE WIDE PATH IN CHINA

Outlaw Army of 30,000 Is Destroying Every Town on Its Road, Missionary Reports.

DEAD STREWN ALONG TRAIL

SHANGHAI, Nov. 21 (Associated Press).—The bandit army of Honan Province, 30,000 strong, which has kidnapped a number of foreign missionaries recently, is laying waste a path six miles wide across the province, burning every city, town and farmhouse in its line of march and leaving its trail strewn with dead bodies, according to a letter received here from H. E. Ledgard, an English missionary, who escaped.

"The bandit army," said Ledgard's letter, "is made up mostly of disbanded troops, the majority of them well mounted and well armed. It totals probably 30,000 men.

"They march over the countryside, spread across a route six miles wide, lighting their way at night by burning farmhouses. Every city and town through which they pass is burned and looted. Thousands of men, women and children are being carried away. Some of these have been ransomed, but many have been cruelly shot. Our road was strewn with bodies.

"On Nov. 10 the bandits encountered and overawed a force of Government troops near Chumatien.

"At the time I made my escape the bandits were holding captive six foreign adults and one child, seven in all, of whom four were Americans, two were French and one an Italian priest."

Mr. Ledgard's letter, written from Yencheng, Province of Honan, describing his experience said:

"Early on the morning of Oct. 28 I was awakened by rifle firing near by. The doors of our house were burst in and a band of outlaws with rifles leveled took possession of our home. They helped themselves to everything, even my wife's wedding ring, remaining all that day and part of the following.

"They compelled my wife to play the organ to amuse them in the rests they took while burning and looting the town (Shantsaihsien). Two American Lutheran ministers, the Rev. Anton Lundeen and the Rev. C. A. Forsberg, were brought in by the outlaws, and told us they had been captured two weeks previously at Yuchow Ho, where their mission had been looted. They said their wives also had been carried off but later released.

"I was informed also that two French railway men had been taken prisoner twenty days before and were being held.

"On Sunday afternoon the bandits ordered me to mount at a moment's notice despite my wife's pleadings that I be permitted to remain with her. We traveled hard all night and arrived at Shangchenghsien in the morning. The town already had been captured and given to the flames.

"In the next few days the bandits captured, sacked and burned the towns of Sengchunsien and Ingchowfu in Anhwei Province. I saw Madam and Miss Soderstrom for a few minutes at Sengchunsien. They told me they had been captured when their mission was destroyed a few days previously."

Mr. Ledgard then described the forced march across country which eventually resulted in his horse giving out, and the captive with a single guard was left far in the rear of the outlaw army. At Hsinsien, which he found in ashes, he was told of the capture of another American missionary, the Rev. Einar Borg-Breen, and his son Rolfe, 5 years old.

At this time Ledgard and his guard were far behind the main body and while passing through Hsinsien a mob of residents, whose property had been carried off or burned, shot the bandit guard dead. They were on the point of doing away with the missionary as well, thinking he, too, was an outlaw, when a native Christian intervened and saved his life.

DR. SUN YAT-SEN DIES IN PEKING

Chinese Leader Had Failed Steadily Since an Operation on Jan. 26 for Cancer.

HELPED TO OUST MANCHUS

Headed the New Government for a Time—Latterly He Had Directed the Southern Republic.

PEKING, Thursday, March 12 (Associated Press).—Dr. Sun Yat-sen, the South China leader, died this morning.

Dr. Sun for some time had been suffering from cancer of the liver. Surgeons who operated on Dr. Sun at the Rockefeller Hospital here on Jan. 26 declared his case was hopeless and gave him only ten days to live. The Chinese leader clung to life, however, the ten days passing, leaving him weaker but still alive.

On Feb. 18, against the advice of the hospital authorities, Dr. Sun was removed by friends and political associates to the headquarters of the Kuomintang (People's Party) to the former residence of Wellington Koo, former Foreign Minister. It was there that he died.

The daily bulletins issued by his physicians had shown that Dr. Sun was growing weaker and weaker, and Wednesday night it was declared he had taken bad turns for the worse. He refused to accept food and his friends expressed the fear that death was near.

As the Southern leader yesterday was slowly passing into his final sleep, his headquarters in Canton announced that his troops had occupied Swatow, in the Province of Kwangtung, whence all the rebel leaders were said to have fled without giving battle.

Career of Dr. Sun.

The name of Dr. Sun Yat-sen first began to be heard in Chinese political affairs in the late '80s, when his vigorous pronouncements against the Manchu emperors of China reached beyond the boundaries of his native land. Since that time few men in public life have known more ups and downs, more victories, more defeats, than Dr. Sun, who won the title of the "Father of the Republic." He was born in 1866.

To Dr. Sun was given the credit for having engineered the uprising by which the people retired the Manchus and proclaimed the republic in 1912.

When the revolution broke out prematurely in the Yangtze Valley in October, 1911, Dr. Sun was in England. He hurried back and was chosen head of the revolutionary Republican headquarters at Nanking, the rebels designating him "Provisional President of the Republic."

Actually and officially he never was President of China, as the Manchus had merely appointed Yuan Shi-kai, as Premier in Peking, to mediate with the rebels. The result was the formal establishment of the republic in February, 1912, with Yuan Shi-kai as President, and Dr. Sun's organization, by agreement, was disbanded.

Yuan served as President until his death in June, 1916, which occurred soon after his futile attempt to become emperor, an empty title he bestowed upon himself for 100 days. He was succeeded as President by Vice President Li Yuan-hung.

Again in 1921 the remnant of the original Chinese Republican Parliament of 1913, never having received any further mandate to sit, besides having been dissolved by Yuan Shi-kai, met in Canton and "elected" Sun Yat-sen "President of China." The real President of China was then Hsu Shieh-ch'ang, and he was in no way superseded by Sun.

However, Dr. Sun and his associates took control of affairs in South China, with headquarters in Canton, and they have administered an area with a population of about 40,000,000 people ever since. The total population of China is estimated to be 400,000,000.

Out of this assumption of power in the South grew what is called the "Republic of South China," which, however, has never been recognized by any Government in the world.

Since 1922 the Sun group has been fighting, on the battlefield and in political councils, with general Chen Chiung-min, for control of the South, resulting in constant pillage, murder and turmoil there.

Early Career of Dr. Sun.

Dr. Sun's father was a Christian farmer in Kuangtung Province, where Sun Yat-sen was born in 1866. He received his early training in an American mission school in his native district.

Under the tutelage of Dr. Kerr of the mission school, he learned English rapidly and when he determined to take up the study of medicine and started for the College of Medicine in Hongkong he was as well versed in English as the ordinary American boy starting off to college.

He went to Hongkong in 1887, graduated in 1892, and at once took up his work as an assistant at the Alice Memorial Hospital there.

A political career had a stronger appeal to him than the profession of medicine, and with the launching of the Young China Party his active work in the affairs of his country began. One of the exciting incidents in his career came in October, 1896, while he was in London. While outside the Chinese Legation he was kidnapped. The intention, it was learned afterward, was to smuggle him to China, where there was a price on his head.

He was confined in the basement of the legation; but he was able to smuggle out a letter addressed to his former teacher, Sir James Cantle, who took the note to the Foreign Office. His liberation was effected by policemen sent to the legation by Lord Salisbury.

At the first opportunity Dr. Sun appeared openly in China. This opportunity came in 1911, as outlined above.

In a report from Hongkong last April it was charged that Dr. Sun was leaning toward a Soviet form of Government. He attended a public gathering held in memory of Lenin, and it was said he made three reverent bows before a portrait of Lenin.

While in New York in 1911 Dr. Sun was dining in a prominent club with a number of international bankers. They were inclined to minimize the accounts of his constant danger, whereupon Sun asked that they accompany him to one of the upper rooms, fronting on Fifth Avenue. There, standing in the dark, they were able to look out upon the street and distinguish three evil-looking Chinese skulking in the shadows. When Sun left they disappeared.

Perhaps his narrowest escape was in Canton in 1905. One of his plots to assassinate the Manchu officials and seize the city was betrayed and a round-up of the leaders was set in motion. Dr. Sun fled with a band of hostile soldiers at his heels. Suddenly a door opened and he was drawn inside. The door closed as mysteriously as it had opened, and the pursuers passed on. A friendly servant in the house of a prominent mandarin had made the rescue. There days later the fugitive watched from a window of that same house as fifteen of his followers were put to death.

CHINA AFTER SUN YAT-SEN.

The overthrow of the Manchus and the establishment of the Chinese Republic, in which Dr. SUN YAT-SEN played a leading part, had for its consequence a break-up of Chinese unity. Death has overtaken Dr. SUN while negotiations looking toward reunification are still under way at Peking. In the chaos of Chinese politics it is unsafe to predict what the effect of his departure from the scene will be. Reunification may be hastened by the disappearance of his militant personality. On the other hand, it is doubtful whether such public opinion as exists in China will accept unity under the Manchurian Viceroy, CHANG TSO-LIN, who is now the strongest man in the country. With many vagaries, Dr. SUN did bring to the alliance with CHANG an element of idealism which is not to be sought for in the Mukden chieftain.

The reunification of China is generally understood to mean an attempt to bring together the three virtually independent sections of South China, where Dr. SUN has been the dominant figure; Central China, which nominally obeys whatever Government may happen to be in power at Peking, and Manchuria, where CHANG TSO-LIN is entrenched. But with the exception of Manchuria there is no internal unity even within the separate parts of the country. In the south Dr. SUN and General CHENG have alternately been chasing each other out of Canton. Further north we have had the hurly-burly of the last three years. The unification of China thus involves more than regional separatism. It must deal with factional and personal ambitions.

Unhappily for China, the second factor is now uppermost. Leaders of the stature of SUN YAT-SEN may couple national policy with ambition. The smaller men are actuated by the most sordid motives. China's civil wars have been largely fought with cash. Last year the task of reunification was undertaken by WU PEI-FU, whose honesty is generally recognized and whose courage has received tribute even from his Japanese opponents. For a time it seemed that he would succeed. Suddenly the situation changed. WU's chief lieutenant, the Christian General FENG, marched upon Peking, ousted the President, and declared against WU and for CHANG and SUN. Ostensibly this was done out of a desire to terminate civil warfare and to bring about the reunification of the country. Actually FENG was bought with huge sums of money raised in Manchuria. His betrayal of WU had been arranged months before WU took the field. It adds nothing to the clarity of the situation that at the present moment CHANG TSO-LIN should be extremely suspicious of General FENG. The latter is accused of not delivering the goods in return for the $5,000,000 he is supposed to have received. He had been hired to put WU out of business, and this he did. But it was not part of the Chang plan that FENG should make himself master at Peking.

At the same time it should be noted that in a country of civil strife and official banditry economic life has somehow managed to adjust itself and to carry on. The year 1922 witnessed new high points in China's foreign commerce. Exports and imports attained the respectable sum of $1,310,000,000. The following year showed a further increase of nearly $100,000,000 in exports. When the figures for 1924 are available they may show a continued growth despite the fact that it was a war year. All this helps to explain why the mass of the Chinese people remain fairly indifferent to their leaders' games.

March 13, 1925

COMMUNISTS RULE CANTON.

Disarm Last of Yuman Troops— Russians May Be Sent Out.

CANTON, June 16 (Æ).—The last stand of the Yunnanese troops, who surrendered Canton on Saturday after a week of fighting with Cantonese troops, was made yesterday.

About 3,000 of the men from Yunnan returned from the east to Canton and occupied Konyum Hill, on the outskirts of the city. There another battle took place. The Kwangtungites finally defeated and disarmed them.

Evacuation of soldiers from the city proper is expected soon. It also is reported that Russian Bolsheviki now in Canton will be required to leave.

WUHU, China, June 16 (Æ).—Anti-foreign meetings are being held here, but so far without disturbances.

Wuhu is a treaty port with a population of more than 100,000, on the Yangtse River, about fifty miles southwest of Nanking.

HONOLULU, June 16 (Æ).—China will never be greatly influenced by Soviet Russia, said S. T. Wen, a Chinese delegate to the Pan-Pacific Relations Institute, who told a group of church workers that "practically everybody in China owns something."

China, he said, was suffering from the pressure of modern industrialism, but "no matter whether the Government is good or bad the country will not be affected, because the Chinese are a patient, tolerant people, not a warring people."

June 17, 1925

CANTON WATCHES BATTLE.

More Wounded Come In as Cheng and Cheung Fight 60 Miles Away.

CANTON, Oct. 11 (Æ).—Canton, a strike-torn city for several months, turned its attention today from the immediate situation to the advancing troops of Cheng Kwing-ming, who is attempting to close in the city with anti-foreign forces.

Canton is being defended by field armies in charge of General Cheung Kai-shek. The fury of the fighting is indicated by the increasing numbers of wounded who are being returned from the battlefront sixty miles away. The local strike of Chinese against foreigners continues.

October 12, 1925

49

SOVIET ASKS CHINA TO SUBDUE CHANG

By Wireless to THE NEW YORK TIMES.

MOSCOW, Jan. 22.—Moscow is taking a grave view of the attempt by Chang Tso-lin's troops to run the Eastern Chinese Railroad in Manchuria, thus violating existing agreements.

Combined Russo-Chinese military operations against Chang are likely unless Chang manages to control his troops within the next few days.

Izvestyia, editorializing this morning, says semi-officially:

"We can again assure Chang Tso-lin that in the long run he alone will suffer the consequences of his policy. History will again use him as the example for an unpleasant lesson, with results this time decidedly unfavorable for him.

"He who stands in the way of the peaceful development of relations between China, Japan and Soviet Russia risks being crushed. Let Chang Tso-lin think.

Timely Warning Sent to Chang.

"The treaty was not signed to be torn on every convenient or inconvenient occasion. We honestly and energetically fulfill our obligations contracted in international treaties, and must demand the same from other parties to such treaties."

Ambassador Karakhan, who simultaneously with addressing a protest note to the Peking Government telegraphed to Chang to immediately stop all his troops from committing untoward acts or that he, Karakhan, could not take responsibility for the consequences, is considered here to have given the General timely warning that unless he acts immediately Soviet Russia will be forced to protect the railroad by force, presumably with Chinese cooperation.

M. Karakhan instructed M. Grandt, the Soviet Consul in Harbin, to ask the Chinese officials whether they were willing and able to stop the railroad disorders immediately, adding: "We consider every evasive answer as an aid to disorder and disorganization, the responsibility for which will fall on the Chinese authorities."

Karakhan expressed opposition to any attempts of foreign diplomats in Harbin to interfere, stating:

"We cannot allow any arbitration between the Eastern Chinese Railroad and China, since this railroad's affairs concern China and Soviet Russia only."

Fear Trains Will Be Wrecked.

Inasmuch as the Chinese soldiers who rioted are running the railroad with the signal system partly destroyed, and the trains are run by soldiers without any signals, the railroad administration authorities are fearful of a collision.

M. Ivanoff, the Soviet manager of the road, states that Chang owes the road a million rubles, adding that the General cannot expect forever to increase his indebtedness without part payment.

January 23, 1926

Changes in Canton Government.

CANTON, Jan. 24 (P).—Cheng Kai-shek has resigned the Generalship of the Kwangtung army. General Hoy Ving-yam has been appointed as his successor. M. Borrodin, Bolshevik Russian adviser to the Government here, who resigned on account of the opposition of the Whampoa Cadets, resumed his office today at the request of Government officials.

January 25, 1926

PRESIDENT TUAN DEPOSED IN PEKING

Coup at 2 A. M. Also Releases Ex-President Tsao Kun and Calls Wu Pei-fu to Power.

CHANGE IS BLOODLESS

Tuan's Guards, Deprived of $350,000 by Him, Submit Quietly to Kuominchun.

PEKING, April 10 (P).—Marshal Wu Pei-fu, leader of the Chihli Party, ousted from control of the Peking Government a year and a half ago by Marshals Chang Tso-lin and Feng Yü-hsiang, once more dominates the capital of China.

A bloodless coup d'état, carried out early today by leaders of the Kuominchun (national armies), formerly followers of Marshal Feng, placed Chief Executive Tuan Chi-jui under restraint, freed his predecessor, former President Tsao Kun, and called Marshal Wu "to restore the political situation" in Peking.

Thus Wu is able to return to the capital, backed by his own Hupeh army and acknowledged as chief by the Kuominchun, the creation of his bitter enemy, Feng, whose leadership the National Army Generals no longer admit. Feng is believed to have retired to Urga, Mongolia.

The coup means a complete realignment of the forces striving for mastery in Northern China. It breaks the anti-Kuominchun alliance between Wu and Chang Tso-lin and his Manchurian-Shantung armies. While the Kuominchun hold Peking, backed by Wu's army on the south and southwest, the Manchurian-Shantung forces, presumably hostile to the new combination, threaten the city from the east and northeast. In view of the strength of the Wu-Kuominchun alliance, Chang is not expected to take the offensive soon.

The turnover is the outgrowth of negotiations carried on for the last week between the Kuominchun leaders and Marshal Wu, who, with the Hupeh army with which he has advanced from the Yangtse River in the last two months, has been awaiting the expected call at Paoting-fu, eighty miles southwest of Peking.

Tuan's Guards Easily Disarmed.

The coup was carried out quietly at 2 o'clock this morning. The bodyguard of the Chief Executive was disarmed without a struggle and submitted to being transferred to the southern part of the Imperial City, where the members were enrolled in the Kuominchun.

The defection of this force, which was Marshal Tuan's chief reliance, is explained by the fact that 500,000 taels (about $350,000) recently made available by the Diplomatic Corps to pay the guard and Peking police, is alleged to have been retained by the Chief Executive.

Secrecy surrounded the preparations. The great gates which pierce the massive walls of Peking were closed late last night, the telephone service was cut off and the residence of the Chief Executive surrounded by the Kuominchun troops.

The delegates to the extraterritoriality conference, including Silas H. Strawn, the American delegate, were turned away by Chinese pickets when they arrived this morning at the building in the Imperial City designated for their use and in which the records of their deliberations are kept. The delegates were obliged to confer elsewhere.

Proclamation Is Issued.

After the disarming of the Chief Executive's bodyguard, a proclamation was posted by General Lu Chung-lin, one of the most prominent of the Kuominchun military chiefs and commander of the unsuccessful defense of Tientsin.

The proclamation said that Tuan Chi-jui, since his assumption of the office of Chief Executive, had done much detrimental to the people and the country. His worst offenses were called the signing of the gold franc settlement of the French Boxer indemnity, allegedly without the approval of the people, and the recent shooting by his guards of student demonstrators.

He was surrounded, the proclamation adds, by members of the Anfu Party, who abetted him in ignoring the law, furthering his own interests and stirring up warfare.

"For the sake of the people," it continues, "we are obliged to take drastic measures against him. Meanwhile we have liberated from his guard the former Chief Executive Tsao Kun and have telegraphed General Wu Pei-fu, inviting him to come to Peking immediately to handle all affairs.

"Peace and order will be maintained. The merchants and people are hereby informed of the facts, and are urged to carry on business. In the event that rumor mongers attempt to stir up strife, they will be severely dealt with."

Envoy Uncertain as to Results.

Special to The New York Times.

WASHINGTON, April 10.—The Chinese Chief Executive, Tuan Chi-jui, has been placed under "restraint" and former President Tsao Kun will again assume the Presidency of China, while Marshal Wu Pei-fu is expected to come to Peking to "assume control of the whole situation," according to advices reaching the State Department today from John Van A. MacMurray, American Minister at Peking.

By the new arrangement President Tsao Kun would be under Marshal Wu Pei-fu. Rumors afloat in Peking are to the effect that General Feng Yu-hsiang has returned to Peking from Mongolia and is taking a hand in the situation.

The telegram received from Minister MacMurray reads, in part, as follows:

"The senior Minister has just officially circularized his colleagues to the effect that former officers of ex-President Tsao Kun had called to communicate the fact that Marshal Tuan had been placed under restraint in his residence; that Tsao Kun had been freed and would resume previous office; that General Lu Chung-lin had placed him under the command of Marshal Wu Pei-fu; and that General Chang Chih-chiang in Kalgan was in agreement with this action on the part of the Kuominchun, which had manifested growing discontent with Marshal Feng.

"Soon afterward, the senior Minister was informed by Y. L. Tong of Lu's office, who had just given the same information to this Legation, that Tuan, had resigned; that his bodyguard had voluntarily disbanded; that Lu was holding himself responsible for peace and order in the capital; that Marshal Wu would be invited to come to Peking; and that Tsao Kun had been freed. * * *

"From Anfu and independent Chinese and foreign sources of highest credibility I have been informed that the coup d'etat has not been entirely successful; that the combination between Wu and Kuominchun has not been effected; that Tuan's bodyguard has taken defensive positions at his house and at the Cabinet offices and President's palace and that he himself took refuge in the Legation Quarter at midnight last night.

"The Legation was first aware of the coup d'état early this morning when the city gates were closed and telephone service was interrupted. The gates have now been opened and telephone service has been resumed. There are many extravagant rumors afloat. A report has even reached me from an ordinarily credible source that Marshal Feng has returned to Peking and taken charge.

"It is too early yet to determine definitely what has actually taken place or how Chang Tso-lin, whose troops are reported to be closing in more and more on Peking, will react to the coup d'etat if it has been successful. All is quiet in Peking."

April 11, 1926

CHINESE DICTATORS MAY RULE FOR YEARS

So Long as Regional Usurpers Remit Cash to Pay on Loans Powers Do Not Interfere.

PEKING REGIME 'A FICTION'

Chang and Wu Dicker There Over Funds Each Hopes to Obtain From Higher Tariffs.

CANTON BODY INDEPENDENT

Chen Tells American Consul Its Area Exceeds France and Italy and Has 60,000,000 People.

By THOMAS F. MILLARD.

Special Correspondence, The New York Times.

SHANGHAI, July 20.—It is commonplace nowadays to say that China has no government. Yet, as we see about us everywhere, the masses of people in this large country go along day by day living and acting according to conditions which in their relation to the average person so closely resemble government that it is hard to say where government stops and habit begins. Laws (or customs) are enforced in so far as the average person is concerned. Police go about their duties, malefactors and misdemeanants are apprehended, courts function, taxes are paid, and among the people generally "business as usual" is the rule.

It is evident that there remains Authority in China.

But in the accepted national and international meanings there is no government here. For wherever and however it may be felt, such authority as exists in China now does not reside in what, for want of a better description, continues to be called the Peking Government.

Overturns in governments are so frequent in these times that news of such events attracts only passing interest. But in most countries a downfall of one government or ministry is quickly followed by the organization of a new government or ministry to carry on. When, as often happens a dictatorship takes over authority in the name of government, something is there which can be recognized as being able for a time to have its orders obeyed. The world has become accustomed to dictators since the World War.

If one could say correctly that China now is under a dictatorship, in a sense that would be synonymous with saying this nation has a government. For some years practical people have been hoping for a real dictatorship in China and they consider that the only way to stabilize the country. Unfortunately, however (from that point of view), the dictatorship does not materialize. It remains illusive.

Sectional and local military dictatorships constitute all there is of government in this country. I am not sure whether the Chinese are better or worse off living in these conditions than they were before. They do not seem especially unhappy; nor, with some exceptions, much worried about the future of their nation. The kind of government people get under these sectional and local dictatorships depends on the characters and abilities of dictators of the moment. Some are good officials, others are fairly good, some are bad. That could have been said also with as much truth of the Mandarinate when China was an empire.

Most of the worrying about the present state and future of China is done by foreigners. Most of the worrying about injuries and sufferings of Chinese in these unsettled times is done by foreigners. Most of the international concern about the state of this nation is voiced by foreigners—by foreign offices and diplomats, by foreign writers, by foreign trade bodies, by foreign uplifters.

(It would be levity not to point out, also, that a considerable proportion of this foreign worrying about and criticism of China really is camouflaged alarm about the foreign position and interests and comforts here as they are, or are believed to be, affected by conditions and tendencies.)

Take, for example, some recent moves concerning the so-called Peking Government. Persons involved may have shifted before this article can be printed, but the situation will remain awhile.

By a turn of events Wu Pei-fu again obtained command of enough soldiers to control a section of Central China. With that as a trading point he made a deal with Chang Tso-lin to co-operate for the purpose of expelling Feng Yu-hsiang from Peking. Wu and Chang formerly were enemies, and Wu and Feng formerly were allies. That means little among Chinese militarists. The Chang-Wu alliance served well enough to eject Feng's troops from Peking and to force them to retire outside the Great Wall. That happened three months ago.

Then followed protracted "negotiations" between the new allies, Wu and Chang, conducted entirely through intermediaries because, apparently, both of the marshals were averse to "taking the chance" involved in a personal meeting. Those negotiations were, so far as expert observers can see, about nothing except how, as between Wu and Chang, the power and emoluments that go with, or may be derived from, control of the "Government" at Peking will be divided. As the negotiations are revealed in press reports they would appear to be about constitutional questions and restoration of a national government.

What actually interested Wu and Chang was the prospect that additional revenue will be obtained by tariff revision, and the political manoeuvring was about how this revenue, if it materializes, will be "split" between them. Except that a nominal government, and its "recognition" by the powers, is thought essential or convenient to making a tariff increase effective, and thereby increasing the surplus released to the Government after service of loans and other debts is taken care of, Wu and Chang probably would not care a rap if the Peking "Government" vanished.

Dictators Keep Customs Surpluses.

On the other hand, it is likely that a majority of the foreign Governments are beginning to have little interest as to whether this fiction of a government in Peking lives or dies, except that in the treaties the powers have with it are embodied the method and the organization whereby China's foreign debts are served.

Not that the provisions of those treaties, or that organized service any longer are of much security to China's foreign creditors; nor is it certain that

51

prolongation of the status quo will be possible in any case. More and more sectional dictators are holding customs and other hypothecated revenues for their own uses.

And foreign creditors of China whose principal and interest are secured by those revenues need not be especially concerned about how the surpluses are spent or by whom. As long as sectional dictators allow the Chinese Maritime Customs gabelle to function and refrain from grabbing any part of the revenues except surpluses, no international equities are violated.

There is a growing feeling among foreign officials in China that as conditions are, and seem likely to be for years, it is better to abandon the method of recognizing and dealing with Peking, and instead to carry on relations with the important sectional dictators.

(There is practical sense in that idea, too; as long as customs and salt surpluses are paid to Peking, all the sectional dictators who do not get their whack are anxious to break up the system, but if each sectional dictator gets a fair share of the surpluses he then becomes personally interested in allowing the existing customs gabelle to function. Thus their service of foreign debts may be allowed to continue for some time.)

In fact, such diplomatic contact as foreigners have with Chinese administrative authority for some time has been conducted directly with sectional dictators.

British Deal Direct with Canton.

Witness the Canton-Hongkong situation.

For more than one year the international treaties affecting the relations of China with that British colony have been waste paper. At first the colony tried to get the home Government to use strong-arm methods to intimidate Canton. Downing Street shied from that. The colony then turned to private negotiations with the "independent" Government of Canton. These have been resumed recently under somewhat extraordinary circumstances.

A new "Minister for Foreign Affairs" at Canton (Eugene Chen, a Chinese journalist who a few months ago languished in a Tientsin prison) has undertaken to reopen negotiations with Hongkong. But before doing so he asked some pertinent questions of the colony's government. Chen wanted to know whether delegates appointed by Hongkong were acting for the colony only, or if their authority was derived from the British Imperial Government, and if their acts would be accepted by it. The colony's government replied, cryptically, that its commissioners would represent both the colony and the home government.

So we actually have one foreign power through its colonial officers conducting separate negotiations with a part of China that absolutely repudiates the authority of Peking.

In the Shanghai area we have another dictatorship, headed at this time by Marshal Sun Chuan-fang, a young militarist. His bailiwick includes five provinces, but his tenure in three of them is precarious. How long he will hold on is doubtful. But while this particular military dictator exercises

authority in this section of China the foreign municipalities of Shanghai and foreign Consular officials here are forced by practical reasons to recognize and to deal with Marshal Sun. (Sun Chuan-fang, it can be said in passing, seems to be an enlightened and progressive dictator).

Lately the American Consul General in Canton (whose position has humorous aspects) had occasion to communicate with the Canton Ministry of Foreign Affairs about a matter of local American interest—the sequestration of some American hospital property. In his note the Consul General expressly stated that it was not to be construed as diplomatic recognition of the Canton Government by the American Government.

Whereupon Eugene Chen, who is some note writer himself, retorted:

"I have the honor to acknowledge receipt of your letter of June 30 in which you explain—what has already been quite clear and obvious to me—that recognition is not implied in your dispatch of June 16, acknowledging my note of June 4, acknowledging your of the abolition of the office of Commissioner of Foreign Affairs and the decision of the Ministry of Foreign Affairs to deal with all international cases in the future."

It should be understood that at each important point of contact with foreign nations the Peking Government has an official termed Commissioner of Foreign Affairs, who is the local intermediary for foreign relations. It is that representative of the Peking Government in Canton to whom Mr. Chen refers. Chen's note continues:

"Though in ordinary circumstances your letter might call for no specific reply, I believe the best interest of the American people and of the Chinese people, as represented by my Government, would be served if I make a categorical statement that while my Government (which has stabilized an independent political régime founded here nearly ten years ago and has unified a group of territories larger in area than France and Italy combined, with a population of 60,000,000) demands that it be treated with respect, it neither desires nor expects from America and other foreign powers the sort of recognition which even considerations of political realism and international dignity have not prevented them from granting to phantom governments successively set up in Peking by mandarin squeezers military plunderers and ex-bandit chiefs. The foreign powers have not yet realized that it is today but an organ of exploitation and plunder in the hands of the mandarins and northern militarists.

"As long as this fundamental fact remains ungrasped by the foreign powers the State of China must necessarily become worse and some of the ominous possibilities of the situation may become realities."

Without analyzing very deeply in a comparative sense, Mr. Chen's note, which contains a fair amount of political bunkum, does state a palpable truth as to the relation of Peking now to China as a whole.

What the effective foreign powers ought to do, and can do, to meet, or to remedy, this state of affairs, and whither these conditions tend, are, to paraphrase Kipling, other questions.

REDS TO AID CANTONESE.

Moscow International Outlines Program for Chinese Bolsheviki.

Copyright, 1926, by The New York Times Company.
By Wireless to THE NEW YORK TIMES.

RIGA, Nov. 21.—The Presidium of the Communist International has announced an enlarged plenary conference of the Executive Committee to open in Moscow tomorrow. The agenda allot considerable space to Chinese questions.

A thesis submitted to the Presidium and approved says that the basis of further revolutionary development must be extension of the influence of the national Government at Canton. The success of the Canton forces must in the near future create a foundation for combining revolutionary China.

It is necessary to combine the Chinese labor elements with the peasants, small traders and progressive bourgeoisie, but the Communist Party must direct the movement and arrange the summoning of a National Assembly to realize the national ideals of the revolution. The National Assembly must establish a Government representing the whole Chinese nation and wage war only against reactionaries, the great land owners, feudal masters and all imperialists.

November 22, 1926

'COMMITTEE RULE' PLANNED FOR CHINA

Canton Pushes Communistic Idea as the Governmental Remnant Quits in Peking.

BRITAIN READY TO ACT

Chamberlain Tells Commons of Hankow Crisis and Will Make Statement Tomorrow.

PEKING, Nov. 29 (A).—With its enemies organizing for a concerted attack upon it, the Peking Government today is once more without a Cabinet or recognized head. In telegrams sent today to the war lords, who appointed them and dictated their acts, the Cabinet members declared their determination to quit the responsibilities of office.

Daily reports have come to Peking of the successes of the armies of the Cantonese Government, of one province after another going over to the Southerners, whose battle cry is "One Government for all China and China for the Chinese."

In addition, the Kuominchun (national army) of the Peking Government, which was deposed last April, was said to be preparing to march from Kansu Province to join the Cantonese troops, which are coming north after their victories in the Yangtse Provinces over the forces of Marshals Wu Pei-fu and Sun Chuan-fang, not long ago styled dictators, respectively, of Central and Eastern China.

52

Faced with this situation, without power to enforce its orders even in the vicinity of Peking and with an empty Treasury, the Cabinet quit as a body and requested the war lords to assume responsibility for the Government, which they actually controlled.

Chang Tso-lin Chief Militarist.

The militarists who thus have the civil as well as military authority thrust upon them are:

Marshal Chang Tso-lin, dictator of Manchuria and dominant militarist of Northern China; Chang Tsung-chang, one of his chief commanders and former Governor of Shantung Province; Wu Pei-fu, from whom the Cantonese wrested China's Central Provinces; Sun Chuan-fang, who lost two of his Provinces to the Cantonese and has a slippery hold on the remaining three in Eastern Central China, and Yen Hai-shan, the "model Governor" of Shensi Province, who has been trying to prevent the Kuominchun troops from forming a junction with the Cantonese.

Meanwhile, aided by Russian money, munitions and officers, the Kuominchun from the North and the Cantonese from the South are preparing to unite under the plans of the Kuomintang (National People's Party), whose object as expressed by the Cantonese General-in-Chief, Chiang Kai-shek, is to "continue the revolution immediately over the entire country."

Cordon Isolates Peking.

The Kuominchun's recent alliance with the Kuomintang's "Red" army of the Cantonese Government, and their combined successes against the Northerners, have taken away not only what remained of the prestige and authority of the Peking Government, but have obtained actual control of more than half of the old empire.

The Kuominchun forces have not had the brilliant successes of the Cantonese, but through the alliance a cordon is created around the Peking domain. Cantonese victories have succeeded one after another in amazing rapidity.

The Southern capital is being moved from Canton into the heart of the Yangtse Valley, at Wuchang, so that the new Communistic or "committee form" of Government is gradually crowding the more conservative Administration out of the picture.

Downing Street May Act.

LONDON, Nov. 29.—Despite his cautious words, the Foreign Secretary, Sir Austen Chamberlain, clearly implied, in the House of Commons, this afternoon, that the Chinese situation is so serious that the Government is devoting especial attention to it, with the view possibly of taking important steps.

He admitted that a general strike might occur in Hankow, and hinted at a possible strengthening of the British naval forces in Chinese waters as a result of the recent serious news from that city and other Chinese centres, including Shanghai.

Chamberlain's remarks were elicited by a question from former Premier Ramsay MacDonald, who celebrated his first appearance in the House since his return from a vacation in Africa by resuming the embarrassing interrogation of the Government for which he is noted.

Replying, Sir Austen Chamberlain said:

"Serious developments in the situation have taken place during the past few weeks at Hankow, where a grave anti-foreign movement appears to be at work. A union of the lower grade employes of Chinese maritime customs was formed on Nov. 21, with the support of the Superintendent, who is a Chinese official. This union announces that its aim is to oust elements of foreign management from the service and bring it under purely Chinese control.

"The Commissioner of Customs hopes it may be possible to keep the Custom House and to maintain the right service with foreign labor; but this may be difficult if the Custom House, which is in the Chinese city, is picketed. The latest report is that the situation in this respect appears somewhat easier—the union has presented its demands, but these are understood not to be of an impossible nature, though it may be that this is only their preliminary move.

"At the same time the general strike movement has made very rapid progress. Servants of Japanese are already on strike and the Japanese have to import their food surplus from other centres.

"The Communist section is showing great activity and there is fear of a general strike being forced. This would throw out of employment thousands of lower grade workers and it would be easy for agitators to incite them to violence.

"The situation is now being considered by his Majesty's Government, and I shall be obliged if the right honorable gentleman will repeat his question on Wednesday."

To the question as to whether the Government means to reinforce its naval units in Chinese waters, Chamberlain repeated that the matter is now being considered by the Government, including the naval authorities.

This serious view of affairs is taken by The Daily News:

"There is no doubt that the position in China is worse than it has been at any time in the last eighteen months. Out of a welter of confused information there emerges the somber impression that affairs in that distracted country are on the verge of a dramatic and formidable dénouement. There is no reason to mince words about it." * * *

Hankow Native Police Are Restive.

SHANGHAI, Nov. 29.—Now the Hankow native police are threatening to join the strike, as was feared. Their unrest is believed to be due to threats of violence to their families living outside the foreign concessions.

All shipping employes there also are likely to come out.

Naval detachments have been landed to assist the Sikhs (British police) and special constables have been enrolled to defend the British concession, and especially to keep out a crowd of agitators.

Here in Shanghai the situation is calmer because of an announcement by Dr. Ting, the Mayor, that he has received a definite promise that the Shantung troops, who are coming by sea from Tsingtao, will not land here.

Some professional agitators are endeavoring to intimidate the local Chinese Chamber of Commerce into declaring a general strike here, but up to the present they have been unsuccessful.

Provided the promise about the Shantung troops is kept, it may be expected that the local situation will be fairly tranquil.

Business, however, is dead.

"Gravest Crisis" Since Boxer Days.

LONDON, Nov. 29 (Æ).—"The gravest crisis since the Boxer rebellion," is how British correspondents in China describe the present situation there, and their concern is fully reflected here in official quarters.

The Government, however, maintaining its wary attitude, which has prevailed throughout the prolonged Chinese troubles, is still declining to be hurried into any precipitate action based on what may possibly develop as inadequate information.

There is considerable interest as to what action the United States will take if the threatened general strike should affect Americans.

November 30, 1926

CHINESE REDS LINK RUSSIA AND CANTON

By WALTER DURANTY.

MOSCOW, Dec. 5.—The present session of the Communist International Executive Committee may be recorded as a great historical landmark, because it has established a practical working arrangement between the Kuomintang — the Chinese Nationalist Party of Canton—and the Chinese Communist Party, which, in turn, is closely linked up with the Communist Party of Russia. In other words, this session has established the position of the Chinese Communist Party as a liaison or bond of union between Soviet Russia and the growing Nationalist State of South China.

To appreciate the full importance of this development it is necessary briefly to review recent events in China in relation to the Chinese Communist Party and Soviet Russia. Early last Spring, the Canton Government, under heavy pressure alike from discontented non-proletarian elements within the the city and attacks from its enemies outside, suddenly swung away from the Left policy it hitherto had followed and dismissed a number of Chinese Communists and some Extremist Russian advisers. This done in virtual obedience to this injunction of the now dead Canton chief, Dr. Sun Yat-sen:

"Work with Moscow but look toward the West."

Some of the Sun Yat-sen followers felt that the overclose relations with the Communists were restricting their freedom of action and of negotiation.

Break Due to Chiang Kai-shek.

The leader of this movement was the Cantonese General, Chiang Kai-shek, at that time director of the Canton Military Academy, who thereby succeeded in removing the obstacles to his own supreme command of the Cantonese armed forces.

But he was far too sagacious to ignore the assistance of the Chinese Communists and their Russian friends. After discussions a modus operandi was attained whereby the Russian military advisers were retained, and the rules established were satisfactory to the Executive Committee of the Kuomintang and to the Chinese Communists.

At the same time the Canton army reorganized on a basis similar to that of the Red army in Russia, namely, with an infusion of "political" representatives among the higher officers and in picked regiments among the subalterns and the non-commissioned officers and even in the ranks.

As is the Russian Red army, this insured that the entire Canton force from the commanding General downward would be to a considerable extent under the control of the party executive committee.

Chiang Kai-shek might be a new Trotsky, but he couldn't be a new Napoleon.

At the same time it was expressly decided that the Chinese Communist members of the Kuomintang should obey the orders of the Kuomintang before the orders of the Chinese Communist Party, and that where said orders appeared to be in conflict the matter would be referred back to the Central Executive of the Kuomintang for discussion.

That arrangement has now been ratified here in theory if not explicitly. It is impossible to exaggerate the importance of this step at the moment when the Western nations are forced to admit the bankruptcy of any joint intervention policy against the Cantonese, and when their attempts to unite Marshal Chang Tso-lin and other Northern commanders with Wu Pei-fu and Sun Chuan-fang against the Cantonese appear equally unsuccessful to Moscow eyes. From the Russian angle the advantages thus gained fully compensate for the retreat of the "Christian General" Feng Yu-hsiang, whose close relations with Moscow are a matter of general knowledge, from his apparently impregnable position at the Nankow Pass, northwest of Peking.

Peasant Revolts Beat Feng.

THE NEW YORK TIMES is now able to state the reason for Feng's inexplicable withdrawal without a battle. There had arisen a peasant revolt behind his lines due to requisition of horses, cattle and food, for which, although he gave paper pledges of repayment, he was quite unable to pay.

It is confidently expected here that the Canton Government soon will be recognized by several important foreign powers. That opponents will be able to prevent the Cantonese occupation of Nanking with its great trade and wealth, and even perhaps of the still more important Shanghai, seems unlikely. That would mean the formation of a stable Nationalist Government for all South China with a population the equal if not the numerical superior of Soviet Russia itself.

For Semi-Proletarian Rule.

Not even the Communist International extremists here imagine that such a Government would be "Red" in the usual sense of the word. But it is hoped that the influence of the Chinese Communists on the one hand and the rapidly growing Chinese labor unions in the industrial cities of the Yangtse Kiang basin on the other will be sufficient to hold the ruling Kuomintang to a semi-proletarian variety of nationalistic type not extremely different from what now obtains in the Soviet Union. The chief difference being, it is thought here, that the military successes already achieved would make wholesale "nationalization" unnecessary and thus permit speedy cooperation with foreign capital—something which the Soviet Union in Russia is now slowly and with difficulty restoring.

Should these anticipations be fulfilled, it is felt that there would follow a period of perhaps three or four years of comparative peace in China, during which the Kuomintang influence gradually would extend northward until, possibly as the result of a fresh conflict, it finally includes Peking, and thus unite the country, with the exception of Manchuria and the northeastern provinces, which would remain in the control of Chang Tso-lin and his Japanese friends.

That such plans are shared by the Cantonese is evident from the decision to move the Cantonese Government headquarters northward to Wuchow, opposite Hankow on the Yangtse, which is expected to go into effect today.

Should Nanking fall the Government will be transferred there, but without it the power and prestige of the Kuomintang are so vastly increased by the acquisition of the Yangtse basis as to justify, it is felt here, hopes that six months ago were a sheer fantasy.

December 6, 1926

CANTON LABOR ROW KILLS 3, WOUNDS 30

Textile Factional Fight Moves Government to Forbid Strikes in Essential Industries.

DIPLOMACY IN HANKOW

American, Japanese and British Agents Go There as General Chiang Consults Russian.

Copyright, 1926, by The New York Times Company.
By Wireless to THE NEW YORK TIMES.

HONGKONG, Dec. 8. — The Canton labor troubles have led to a serious clash between the Red and White silk textile unions, which resulted in three being killed and thirty wounded.

As a result the Canton Government today declared strikes in the essential services illegal. These include arsenals, banks, food industries and railways.

Hongkong local opinion welcomes the recognition scheme of the China Committee of the British Parliament, but it feared that now it is too late. The Canton policy is summed up in an apparently inspired article in the Canton Gazette, which says:

"There is talk of recognition, but there is to be no misunderstanding about this recognition.

"The views of the Nationalists have been clearly expressed several times. Nevertheless, there seems to be a proposal, which is gaining ground among foreign imperialists, to divide this country into many local Governments and then extend to each Government a sort of recognition with such stipulations and reservations as are possible when treating with such local authorities.

"We trust that the removal of the national capital to Wuchang will end these machinations for the division of China in order to safeguard treaty rights.

"If Mr. Lampson [the new British Minister to China] meets Mr. Eugene Chen [Canton's Foreign Minister] in Hankow, he will hear about the Nationalist policy at first hand."

However, in view of the approach of Winter, together with the labor troubles and the great task still before the Cantonese of subduing the Northern armies, it is felt they may compromise.

Copyright, 1926, by The New York Times Company.
By Wireless to THE NEW YORK TIMES.

HANKOW, Dec. 8. — Representatives of the Canton Government, General Chiang Kai-shek, commander of the Cantonese Army, and their Russian advisers, now are in Kuling, the foreigners' mountain resort near Kiukiang discussing, it is understood, their future policy. The Canton Govern-

ment representatives are due here on Thursday.

Miles Lampson, British Minister to China, arrived at Kiukiang yesterday en route to Hankow, while the American and Japanese diplomatic agents are expected here tomorrow.

Hostilities are believed to be suspended on all fronts.

According to some Chinese reports, representatives of the northern leaders are also in Kuling with the object of making peace, but no value can be given to this report until it is confirmed.

The main Cantonese Army is supposed to be near Nanchang.

December 9, 1926

CHINESE CONSULT SOVIET.

Army Envoys Learn How to Interest Peasants in the Revolution.

Copyright, 1927, by The New York Times Company.
Special Cable to THE NEW YORK TIMES.

RIGA, Jan. 7.—It became known today that a special delegation of twenty-two representatives of the Chinese revolutionary army have been in Moscow for some time, and have taken part in the joint sittings of Soviet officials and delegates of the Communist International, at which technical military questions and propaganda were discussed.

It is explained that they went to Moscow in order to study Soviet organizations and establishments.

They are, it is stated, particularly interested in peasant questions, and in methods of educating the Chinese peasantry to take an important part in the Canton revolutionary movement.

The Chinese delegates, conducted by M. Orloff, representative of the Red Peasants International, yesterday visited the Agronomic Institute in Moscow, where the leader of these Chinese, in the course of a speech, promised to follow the lead of Soviet Russia in organizing the Chinese peasantry.

M. Dubnovsky, acting director of the institute, offered to place at their disposal "all Bolshevist experience, because, without enlisting the cooperation of the peasants, victory would be impossible."

M. Rotstein, a member of the Collegium of the Foreign Commissariat, in a review of the situation in China, has informed representatives of the foreign press that certain Soviet Russian officers were in the pay of the Government of South China, but that it is their private affair.

January 8, 1927

CANTONESE TROOPS TAKE SHANGHAI; ENTER NATIVE CITY AND CUT RAILROAD

LITTLE RESISTANCE MADE

Nationalists Army Routs Shantungese and Gen. Pi Flees.

FOREIGN NATIONALS CALM

Movies, Shops and Churches Remain Open as Usual Behind the Defenses.

21 WARSHIPS IN HARBOR

Reports Persist of Deal Between Chang Kai-shek and the Northern War Lords.

By The Associated Press.

SHANGHAI, Monday, March 21.—The Chinese Nationalists have entered the native city of Shanghai.

General Pi Shou-chen, commander of the Northern forces in Shanghai, is reported to have taken refuge in the French concession.

Previously they had occupied the village of Lungwha, four miles from the French Concession in Shanghai.

The capture of Lungwha, which has been Shantungese military headquarters for the Shanghai area of occupation, meant that Shanghai was virtually in Nationalist hands and that they could walk into the Chinese sections of the city whenever they desired.

Another Northern setback has also taken place in the capture of Changchow by the Cantonese, who thus have cut the Nanking-Shanghai Railway, isolating the Shantungese in the Shanghai region.

Foreign Forces Active.

Meantime there has been feverish activity in the foreign settlements. The barbed-wire barriers in the French concession on the border have all been closed. The main barriers of the International Settlement are still open, but they may be closed at any moment.

Thousands of armed and unarmed soldiers are swarming through the country outside the foreign settlements, but every precaution has been taken to keep them out.

There has thus far been no incident on the British line, which is strongly held. Seven thousand retreating Shantung soldiers arrived outside the French Concession late yesterday, but made no attempt to enter. It was their presence that caused the French to close their wire barriers.

Reports of a Deal Persist.

General Pi Shou-chen, the Shantung defender of Shanghai, was reported last night to have gone over to the Cantonese. There was no confirmation of this report, but it is stated that he sent a representative to General Ho Ying-ching, the Southern commander, to discuss the conclusion of a truce in order to avoid fighting in the Shanghai area.

This, in connection with the fact that the Shantung forces have made no attempt to hold the Southern line descending on Shanghai, tends to confirm the belief in foreign military and well-informed Chinese circles here that some arrangement has been made regarding Shanghai between General Chang Kai-shek, the Cantonese Commander-in-Chief, and General Chang Tsung-chang, Governor of Shanghai, whose whereabouts recently has been a mystery. Everything points to such an arrangement and there is even the possibility that there is an understanding between General Chang Kai-shek and Marshal Chang Tso-lin, the Manchurian war lord.

Shantung Defense Went to Pieces.

Experienced observers confess their inability to grapple with the manifold complexities the situation in China today presents. Saturdays sensational collapse of the Shantungese defenses placed Shanghai at the disposal of the Nationalists, and was only a question of hours before they could claim the prize.

However, from Hankow comes the news that the Nationalist structure, if not on the verge of collapse, is at all events having its foundations very severely tested by bitter internal strifes, the split which recently developed in the Kuomingtang Party between Chang Kai-shek's supporters and the Communist elements is now extending to the Nationalist military forces, and dispatches from Hankow, which the censor delayed, state that General Tang Shen-chin, commander of the Hunan troops who helped the Cantonese capture Wuchang, has definitely ranged himself on the side of the Communists and is replacing Chang Kai-shek's garrison at Hankow with his own troops.

In effect there has been a complete Communist coup d'état at Hankow, and the delicacy of the political situation there is illustrated by a report from a reliable source to the effect that Eugene Chen, the Cantonese Foreign Minister, who is generally regarded as belonging to Chang Kai-shek's party, has sent his family to Shanghai.

Meanwhile in Honan, Marshal Chang, Tso-lin is steadily pushing ahead with his drive down the railway toward Hankow, but the latest Peking reports suggest he is merely walking into a well-prepared trap, as Governor Yan Hsin-shan of Shensi, who is an expert fence rider but usually has been with the North, is on the point of linking up with General Feng Yuhsiang, the Christian General, with a view of bottling up this expedition beyond all hope of extrication.

Despite the prevailing uncertainty, Shanghai remains calm and unperturbed, especially in view of the presence of strong foreign naval and military forces ready to deal with any sudden emergency.

The foreign troops in Shanghai now number about 20,000 trained men, the greater portion of whom are British.

The American force consists of 1,800 marines and 2,000 bluejackets, but these men so far have been kept aboard United States warships and transports in the harbor.

The Japanese have 3,000 fighting men in Shanghai and the French a somewhat smaller force.

Twenty-one warships of five foreign countries are lying off Shanghai ready to protect foreign lives and property. Shanghai, China's biggest port, has a foreign population of nearly 40,000 persons, 3,000 of whom are Americans. There are heavy foreign investments. Chinese in the city number about 1,500,000.

March 21, 1927

TOKIO EXPECTS REDS IN CHINA TO LOSE

Believes Chang Kai-shek Will Establish His Power and Put Them Down.

FOREIGN PATIENCE URGED

Influence of Borodin Is Thought Shaken by Attack on the Nationalist General.

Special Cable to THE NEW YORK TIMES.

TOKIO, March 29.—The reaction of Japanese opinion to the Nanking incidents has been slight in volume and exemplary in moderation. It is believed that danger to foreign life and property is over for the present, Nanking being evacuated and Shanghai impregnable, and that the most important aspect of the Chinese question now is the struggle proceeding between Chang Kai-shek and the Communists.

The Tokio press published somewhat perfunctory editorials yesterday on the Nanking affair and today it is engrossed in innocuous topics such as the recent bank failure, domestic politics and the tripartite naval conference. The Asahi, in an editorial which is quite typical of the press as a whole, deplores the outrages, which leave a black stain on the South's record, but immediately expresses confidence that Chang Kai-shek will restore discipline and punish the guilty commanders.

Says Japan Will Aid Chang.

"Japan has suffered, but she will assist Chang in his efforts for adjustment," it says. "Japan will not allow herself to be carried away by impassioned feeling, but will follow her declared principle with calmness and composure. We are firmly convinced that the consistency of Japan's attitude will appease the excitement of other nations and have a good effect in China."

Other leading journals adopt a similar tone, though several seem afraid that the outrages America and England have endured may cause these nations to cooperate more closely in the future. Nowhere is there any call for strong action, but

a general admission that painful incidents are to be expected and the conviction that Japan's policy of friendly non-interference must remain unchanged.

Baron Sakatani, an active peer who has shown continual vigilance about China, has hastened to publish a statement in the Japanese press cautioning the public against the temptation to demand a strong policy. "It is easier at present to advocate strong measures than deliberation and calmness," he says. "But it would be dangerous to seek redress by force. Punishment of offenders, apologies and indemnities are all that Japan can reasonably demand. Despite unfavorable criticism of Shidehara's policy, Japan has obtained better results from it than either America or England and it must be continued."

All the evidence of public opinion obtainable shows that the Japanese people are fully satisfied with M. Shidehara's methods of dealing with the China question and there is little risk of their being stampeded by any awkward incident. The explanation of this unusual moderation is the fact that Japan suffered heavily by the Chinese boycott for some years and found military pressure only involved her in more or less injury. She is now convinced that her best policy is to befriend the Nationalist movement and endure with good grace the inevitable trouble and disorders of the revolutionary period.

To many Japanese the most important aspect of the China question at

the present moment is the struggle for supremacy between Chang and the Communists. There is extreme reluctance to admit that Chang may be overpowered and a strong predisposition to believe he will establish his power, put down the Reds and give China a Government with which Japan can have friendly relations.

Foreign Pressure Deprecated.

The Japanese who anticipate this solution of the Chinese problem point out that excessive pressure by foreign powers for reparations will play into the hands of the Communists by increasing Chang's difficulties. According to this view the powers should be guided by the consideration that the political complications in China are now a more serious risk than damage to foreign life and property. Chang is the only outstanding Nationalist who is able to save China from utter chaos. The Communists are endeavoring to effect his downfall and have penetrated the military academy Chang founded and which furnished him with trained officers.

The alternatives before China are either Chang or Russian-ridden anarchy.

The views summarized here are those of Japanese who do not speak for the Government but are well informed on the Chinese situation and Japanese policy. They believe Borodin's power is shaken by his attacks on Chang and the Right Wing and hold that only patience is needed while Chang settles his account with the Reds.

March 30, 1927

FIGHT ON REDS LED BY CHANG KAI-SHEK

PEKING, April 2.—The war on Bolshevism in the ranks of Kuomintang (National People's Party), which has set up the Nationalist Government in Hankow, is now being led personally by General Chang Kai-shek, the intrepid Chekiangese commander, who has brought the Cantonese army all the way to the Yangtse and thence down to the key position of Shanghai.

General Chang has had no sympathy with Bolshevism from the start, but when the control of the Government passed from the hands of the committee of the party into a group of three radicals dominated by Moscow he refused to be a party to the Red movement. With that declaration the movement to liberate China from the rule of feudalists and to lift from the republic the burden of the unequal treaties entered into a new phase.

The rift in the party founded by Sun Yat-sen began in February and widened greatly in early March—so much so that the whole plan of campaign was changed and the Northern militarists, who had sent tens of thousands of troops to the Yangtse Valley to try to stem the Red tide, found their own somewhat loosely allied associates drifting over to the Nationalist movement. Chang Tso-lin, the autocratic

leader of the feudalist forces, began to take stock and to get a new outlook on the picture.

Although the British had large forces ashore at Shanghai and many more at Hongkong, and the Americans, French, Japanese and Italians had bluejackets and marine to the extent of several thousand aboard ships off the Shanghai bund, Chang Tso-lin changed his viewpoint in two directions. First, he entertained a much higher respect for the able field leader of the Nationalists and, second, he began to court the foreign powers. He made a round of all the legations in Peking for a series of dinners, the two most notable of which were at the British and American legations, the latter occasion being on the evening of March 18.

Opens Fight on the Reds.

Chang Kai-shek turned the whole tide of affairs by his bold and challenging speeches at Nanchang at the time of the convention of the Kiangsi Kuomintang in the provincial capital. While he paid respect to Chang Tso-lin and his armies, he openly attacked the Communist Christian Minister, Hsu Chien, and the other Bolshevized members of the Government at Hankow. Translations of this speech are now available—they throw a great light on this sudden turn of affairs.

"At present there is a strong agitation on the part of the Kuomintang," General Chang said, "for the concentration and consolidation at Wuhan (Wuchang and Hankow) of the authority of the party. The real motive of those behind the agitation is apparently to curb the authority of others with whom they do not agree. As presiding officer of the Central Executive Committee, the Political Committee

and the Ordinary Business Committee, I yield to none in support of the authority of the party. But they have complained repeatedly that the power of the Central Executive Committee is too excessive to be resisted.

"I submit that the Central Executive Committee is the highest political organ of the Kuomintang and that if there is any organ which can compare with it in power and authority it is the Joint Committee in Hankow. But the committee has no legal basis, and if my opponents are really solicitous for the authority of the party let them scrap the Hankow committee first, otherwise I fear both the Kuomintang and the Nationalist Government will disappear.

"Let me explain: The Hankow committee tries to dictate to the Kuomintang and the Nationalist Government. The Government has ordered its dissolution, yet it defies the order and continues to call sessions. This is the way they treat the discipline of the party.

"Again I have been attacked as trying to be a dictator. Nothing could be further from the truth. So far as I am concerned, I obey nothing but the orders of the Central Executive Committee and the Nationalist Government.

Warns of Threat to Party.

"The Kuomintang is a historic party with certain definite principles. If our members do not bear this in mind and if they indulge in irresponsible attacks on each other they will descend to the level of counter-revolutionaries and eventually will bring about the downfall of the party. Any one who criticizes the party out of pure sentiment is not serving the best interests of the organization.

"I hope for the reinstatement of Wang Ching-wei [a moderate] and have personally urged him to come out of his retirement.

"I never have taken the view that I cannot cooperate with the Communists. As a matter of fact, I may rightly claim the credit for bringing the Communists into the fold of the Kuomintang.

"But I also have made it clear that, while I was opposed to the oppression of the Communists, I would check their influence as soon as they grew too powerful. Today the Communists have reached the zenith of their power as well as their arrogance, and if their activities are not checked they will bring disaster upon the Kuomintang. It is therefore obvious that I no longer can treat them as a small revolutionary group, for otherwise I would not be loyal to my own party.

"Now a word to those who accuse me of entertaining yearnings for a dictatorship. Since I am Commander-in-Chief of the revolutionary army, it is essential that I am clothed with certain powers to execute the responsibilities of my post. It will not contribute to the success of the revolution if I become the centre of suspicions and jealousy. I have a clear conscience and have no private interests to serve. If my work is not satisfactory to the party I shall be glad to retire and thereby fulfill my original wish."

General Chang made another speech at the Nanchang convention, in which he paid high tribute to the character of the Northern forces which have been sent against him.

"We should not look down upon the Mukden army," he said. "It is far better equipped than our revolutionary army; in fact, it can stand comparison with the best military unit in the Far East."

General Chang said the army of Chang Tso-lin consists of 250,000 men. Allied with it, he said, is the army of Chang Tsung-chang, Governor of Shantung, totaling 150,000.

Against these General Chang said that, excluding the 150,000 Kuominchun of the Christian General, Feng Yuhsiang, he had a total of 350,000 men. Of these, however, 150,000 are in Szechwan and Yunan Provinces, leaving 200,000 in the Provinces of Kwangtung, Kwangsi, Hunan, Hupeh, Kiangsi and Fukien, but only 50 per cent. of these at best can be concentrated. However, the troops of the Christian General in Shensi Province are counted upon to hold a major part of the forces Chang Tso-lin can put in the field as he must also guard a long line of communications and maintain his position in Manchuria and also in Peking. Even though outnumbered and facing armies far better equipped, General Chang was confident of consolidating his position in the lower Yangtse Valley.

"Why?" he exclaimed. "Because we have the revolutionary spirit, principles, discipline, and what is more, the support of the masses."

April 3, 1927

CHINESE WAR HALTS AS SOUTHERN CHIEFS GATHER AT NANKING

This Is Taken as Further Proof of a Deal Between Chiang and the Northerners.

MILITARY RULES SHANGHAI

Power of Red Groups Is Broken, With Their Arms Seized and Their Unions Suppressed.

GENERAL STRIKE A FAILURE

Raids on Communists Came After a Reported Payment to Chiang by Chinese Merchants.

By FREDERICK MOORE.

Copyright, 1927, by The New York Times Company.
Special Cable to THE NEW YORK TIMES.

SHANGHAI, April 14.—As anticipated yesterday, the guns of Pukow are silent and the Northerners' airplanes have been restrained, leaving peace to reign over Nanking for the Kuomintang conference beginning Friday. The conviction therefore grows that an agreement has been reached between General Chiang Kaishek and the Northern Generals. No foreign warship today reports troop movements or shelling across the river.

Two passenger trains from Shanghai went to Nanking yesterday. Unless a truce has been arranged for at least several days, the conferees would be in danger of being prevented from returning by the railway being cut or being bombed. Moreover, the Nationalist warships have been anchored out of action above Nanking.

Recent events have shown how wary the foreigner must be in accepting Chinese statements at their face value. Two weeks ago information was current in informed Chinese circles that Chinese bankers and merchants had sent a delegation to Chiang Kai-shek petitioning him to remain at Shanghai to maintain order, offering him a fund of 15,000,000 Shanghai dollars on condition that he suppress communist and labor activities. Shanghai is the business metropolis of China and whoever controls it can become the richest and may be the most powerful military chief.

My information that the first instalment of 3,000,000 Shanghai dollars was paid is from such sources that I have no doubt of its correctness. Furthermore, facts seem to corroborate it.

Soon after the money is alleged to have been paid, Chiang dispatched all his own troops to Nanking, leaving Shanghai controlled by General Chow Feng-chi, who recently deserted the former Northern war lord of Shanghai, Sun Chuan-fang.

Under General Chow Feng-chi the work of suppressing the armed laborers and Communists has been proceeding in the past forty-eight hours with effective results. According to the best reports 3,000 rifles, 20 machine guns. 600 pistols and nearly 1,000,000 rounds of ammunition were captured at the Commercial Press, where several fights occurred. Two thousand long-handled pikes were taken from Toongwoo Temple. One hundred and twenty armed laborers were killed, 180 wounded. How many soldiers and how many civilians is not stated.

Wang Shou-hua, Chairman of the General Labor Union has disappeared and is reported kidnapped and executed. The General Labor Union has been dissolved and the Federated Association of Labor Unions ordered to assume its place with two military men as administrators.

The battles lasted one to three hours, causing the streets to be deserted and the stores barricaded in the neighborhood, and the foreign troops, reinforced, to stand to arms at the barricades with armored cars ready for any emergency.

Chinese Quit Native City.

Thousands of Chinese from the Chapei have moved into the foreign settlement, keeping the police busy for hours searching them and their baggage as they entered through the barbed-wire gates. The exodus from Shanghai southward continues daily.

Among the places raided by the soldiers were the headquarters of the General Labor Union, one police station, the Anti-Kidnapping Society, the premises of the Door of Hope mission, the Shanghai Kuomintang headquarters, the Shanghai provincial government headquarters and a dozen others in which armed, laborers and Communists had established themselves. It is believed that the city is now in military hands.

The students, laborers and Communists have protested with mass meetings, parades and the declaration of the general strike, but the gatherings were dispersed or ignored, and the strike failed. Docilely, the laborers are returning to work, although several assassinations of foremen are reported.

The newspapers report events, but fear a display of sympathy with the defeated radicals.

But tragic as events are, they are only a repetition of what has been going on in the wealth-producing cities of China since the republic was established and military chieftains began battling one another for prizes under patriotic titles and with generous promises. One group calls itself the People's Party, that is, the Kuomintang; another, the Peace Restoration Army, that is, the Ankuochun; a third the People's Army, that is, the Nationalists, but the war lords dominate the Governments and the soldiers murder and plunder when pay is in arrears or when Bolshevists incite.

Sometimes, however, for periods of many months a city has peace by tribute funds, such as is now being collected here for General Chiang Kai-shek.

57

It is without a desire to belittle the group now gathering at Nanking to formulate a new government and make new promises, but with a sense of duty to the readers of THE TIMES's dispatches, that I state what I believe to be the facts and what I know represents the opinions of the majority of Americans here. Others besides the missionaries hope intensely that a better spirit will some day pervade the Chinese, but if those others do not permit themselves to be caught by each new promise it means only that they permit their heads to control their hearts.

Lull Reported in Fighting.

SHANGHAI, April 14 (Æ).—After several days of hectic developments that included Cantonese reverses along the Yangtse battlefront and inter-party bloodshed in Shanghai between Cantonese moderates and radicals, China's civil warfare today was comparatively quiet.

Whether it was merely the lull before the possible storm of tomorrow's scheduled meeting at Nanking, called by General Chiang Kai-shek, for the expected purpose of destroying the power of the radicals within the Cantonese régime remains to be seen.

Although Shanghai was quiet after yesterday's raids by Chiang's soldiers on the "reds" which resulted in the death of 100 Chinese and the demonstration at Chiang's military headquarters in which 20 persons were killed, reports from Hankow indicated further apprehension on the part of foreigners.

A telegram from Hankow said Frank P. Lockhart, American Consul General there, had served notice on American residents in the city that the American naval authorities at Hankow would not attempt to defend any point except the Consulate in the event of trouble.

The message added that the naval authorities felt they did not have sufficient forces available to undertake any defense except in the case of an actual evacuation, and that the American Chamber of Commerce in Han-

kow had protested against this, asking for full protection of property.

A strong force of Japanese sailors are patroling the Japanese concession of Hankow behind heavy barricades.

Persistent rumors were current that the Cantonese, who lost Pukow, across the river from Nanking, to the Northerners on Tuesday, have retaken the city. The Foreign Affairs Office of the Cantonese at Shanghai said that advices had been received reporting Pukow to be in the hands of their troops, but no confirmation of this could be obtained.

LONDON, April 14 (Æ).—Moderate Nationalists have given a decided setback to the Chinese Communists at the important ports of Amoy and Foochow, between Shanghai and Canton, say official British advices today.

The postal strikes at those ports have been called off. The messages say the moderates have popular support and that pressure has been relieved to the extent that the British residents will not be evacuated.

The British mine sweeper Marazion has been sent to Hoihow, northern port of Hainan Island, southwest of Canton, at the request of the British Consul.

April 15, 1927

NEW NANKING REGIME OUTLAWS HANKOW; ORDERS BORODIN AND OTHER REDS SEIZED

CHIANG GETS QUICK ACTION

Majority of Kuomintang Control Committee Backs His Fight.

AIM TO REUNITE THE PARTY

But a Bitter Struggle Is Likely With a New Civil War in South a Possibility.

CHEN ESCAPES THEIR WRATH

Right Wing Leaders Declare He Is Loyal, but Is Used as a Tool by the Communists.

Copyright, 1927, by The New York Times Company.
Special Cable to THE NEW YORK TIMES.

SHANGHAI, April 15.—The effectiveness of Eugene Chen's replies to the five-power notes on the Nanking incident faded this evening with the impeachment of the Hankow Government by the Central Control Committee of the Kuomintang at Nanking and the demand for the arrest of Michael Borodin and other Communist leaders in the party.

The action took the form of a resolution adopted by the committee, which is composed of the moderates and elder chiefs within the party. The committee ranks in power with the Central Executive Committee in control of the Nationalist Government's affairs.

The resolution was adopted at the instigation of General Chiang Kai-shek, according to information available here, the military leader apparently having decided to throw down the gauntlet forthwith to the Communists.

Early reports indicated that the Nanking conference had been postponed. Consequently this startling action occasioned no little surprise, even among Cantonese officials here.

Borodin's Arrest Ordered.

The resolution demands the impeachment of the Hankow Government and the arrest of the Communist leaders, including Michael Borodin, George

Hsu-chien, the Minister of Justice; Tung Ping-shan, the Minister of Agriculture; Chen To-shi, head of the Communist Party, and General Teng Yenta, Chief of the Political Bureau.

The impeachment is expected here to mark the end of the Borodin régime and the naming of the above Communists as enemies of public peace and order.

Eugene Chen's name is not included in the resolution. Chen is believed to be loyal to the Kuomintang, but to have been unduly influenced recently by the Reds. He is apparently to continue, possibly coming to Nanking as soon as possible.

The Nanking conference agenda were not made public here, but THE NEW YORK TIMES correspondent learns that their chief aim is to clarify the Communist fight and to unify the party once more without the Bolshevist element.

New Cabinet Is Expected.

Nationalist officials here are inclined to be noncommittal regarding Nanking forming a new Government and naming a new Cabinet, but there is no doubt that this action will follow the ultimatum to Hankow.

In the meantime peace prevails in the Yangtse Valley, strangely, in view of the Northerners' apparent rejuvenation, and the Nationalists are still claiming Pukow as well as the intention to continue the campaign northward as soon the the interparty fight is settled and Chiang Kai-shek's backing is assured.

Two reliable American reports from Hankow state that Eugene Chen is practically the prisoner of the Communist Party and that he is closely watched to prevent his escape like T. V. Soong, who on departing was escorted to the ship by soldiers.

Chiang Kai-shek has authorized the publication of the charges the Kuomintang has compiled against the Communist Party. The Chinese press will print the charges tomorrow with the names of those accused of intrigues and the announcement of their expulsion from the Kuomintang, these including the names of the Cabinet Ministers and other leaders mentioned above.

The fight promises to be bitter and to be of paramount importance to the future of the Nationalist movement.

April 16, 1927

'RED' CHINA OPPOSED BY SOVIET CHIEFS

Stalin and Bukharin Declare Chinese Revolution Must Be Moderate to Win.

SHOW COMPROMISE POLICY

Disclose Stand in Attacks on the Opposition for Its Fight Over China in Party Councils.

By Wireless to THE NEW YORK TIMES.

MOSCOW, April 21.—The long struggle within the high councils of the Russian Communist Party having been temporarily "liquidated" by the vote of the Plenum of the Central Committee approving the Political Bureau's report on the Soviet's policy on China, a corner of the veil is now lifted and the points at issue are revealed to the general Russian public in long statements penned by N. D. Bukharin, the

Communist Party majority's leading Marxian theorist and dialectician, and Joseph Stalin, with whose name, as he is the virtual head of the Administration, the Soviet's present Chinese policy is generally associated.

The attitude of "Radek & Co.," as M. Stalin calls them, without naming Leon Trotsky, seems somewhat paradoxical. Whereas, in general international relations the Opposition has been up to now, on the whole, working for compromise on the West in the Chinese imbroglio, it is taking an extremely radical line and it is precisely with "compromise" that it now charges M. Stalin's Administration.

For it is not only on the question of the continued participation of the Chinese Communists in the Kuomintang that the Opposition insists in order to prove that the Russians are shunting Chinese revolution down a bourgeois sidetrack, it also urges the Communist Party majority to use every means for bringing about the creation of Soviets of Chinese peasants, workers and soldiers—in fine, to imitate the Russian example of 1917 with its overthrow of Menshevism as personified by Alexander Kerensky and the reactionary militarist General Kornilof, for whom they find a parallel in Chiang Kai-shek.

Sharp Attacks on Opposition.

The Opposition's views, of course, have not been directly published in the Communist Party press, but one can deduce them from the destructive attacks launched against them by M. Bukharin, M. Stalin and other leaders—M. Bukharin in twenty-one closely printed columns of subtle and extremely theoretical polemic, with Radek overloaded with Marxian orthodoxy of the neo-Leninist stamp and M. Stalin succinctly in straight, sharp-edged phrases, every word packed with his dominant will and directed to its ends.

None the less, certain phrases of M. Bukharin's thesis indicate and bring out the acuteness of the situation within the Russian Communist Party.

"Kerensky we fought because he was fighting for the Fatherland," he says. "Our aim was to destroy the Fatherland at the time." [M. Bukharin, of course, does not mean "destroy Russia," but the Nationalists' conception of Russia's rôle.]

"But can we fight the Kuomintang, which is fighting for a reborn China and the rights of the Chinese people? Does the Opposition believe that we repudiate such forces as these in order to fight the imperialist powers?

"On the contrary, we must utilize these national forces united in the Kuomintang, with the exception of the extreme Right, which is flirting with the militarists."

These words of M. Bukharin contain the essence of the real issues at stake in this new Communist Party controversy. The majority, under the leadership of M. Stalin, believes that the revolution in China is not yet and cannot be a "Red" revolution in the sense that the Russian revolution of 1917 was Red. It is regarded a bourgeois revolution in its essence which can only be very slowly converted into a Socialist revolution.

It is noteworthy that neither M. Stalin nor M. Bukharin says that this final revolution must come. But their practical realistic attitude is concentrated on collaborating with the moderate Nationalist bourgeois element in China, which stretches from the Right of the Kuomintang to the "revolutionary workers' masses" of the extreme Left.

It is precisely that which the Opposition calls a "compromise," at the same time declaring itself to be the defender and vehicle of the true revolutionary spirit.

Certain it is that the minority derives new arguments in support of its contentions from the latest events which annihilate the influence of the Centre and Left of the Kuomintang Government at Hankow. Even the Canton source of this movement has been taken by the dreaded militarists, the "Chinese Korniloffs."

But the majority may retort that these occurrences are mere incidents which do not at all prove that the line of action which the Opposition advocates would not lead to still greater disasters.

Oppose a "Red" China as Ruinous.

In the controversies, held behind closed doors, and palely reflected in M. Bukharin's published thesis, the majority seems to have openly declared that a Red China would never obtain the capital needed for building up a modern industrial State such as a genuine proletarian country requires. A Red revolution in China, unlike the Russian revolution, would collapse because it would not find adequate preparation, organization and financial resources at its disposal. And that to attempt to force the "tempo" of the Russian revolution of 1917 on China would mean its ruin.

Undoubtedly the facts in this Communist Party polemic have an international significance of no mean importance. They disclose the "relative" nature of the Red efforts and Red propaganda in the Far East. The vast black cloud of Russo-British tension ought to shrink somewhat with the collapse of the Cantonese means of aggression against the "imperialists.."

As the main impression created by this family quarrel between the Russian Communist party chiefs is that M. Stalin is a man of compromise with a "bourgeois" China, the most modest conclusion one can draw from present events is that at least they do not tend further to embitter the relations between Britain and the Soviet Union.

April 22, 1927

CHANG SAYS CHIANG MUST JETTISON REDS

Will Never Leave Peking Alive, He Declares, While a Communist Is in Control in China.

HE AGAIN ASKS POWERS' AID

Though Doubtful of Sincerity of Yen and Chiang, He Declares North and South Must Reach Accord.

LONDON, June 10 (℗).—Marshal Chang Tso-lin, Manchurian war lord in control of the Northern Government at Peking, is quoted by the Peking correspondent of The Daily Express as saying in an interview that there must be an agreement between the North and the South "for the sake of peace in China, which must come soon." He was not completely convinced, however, respecting the attitude of the Southerners.

Chang expressed regret that foreign troops were coming to North China, because, he said, it showed the powers distrusted him, for which feeling there was no ground. He again told of his old wish that the powers would help him, suggesting that Great Britain, the United States and Japan blockade the Yangtse River and assist the North militarily, diplomatically and politically by applying pressure on the Russians on the northern borders.

Chang reiterated his unalterable hostility to Bolshevism and communism, declaring:

"I will never leave Peking alive while there is a Communist anywhere in control of affairs in China. I have received many tempting advances from the South, including Chiang Kai-shek. (Chiang is Generalissimo of the Nanking, or Moderate, Nationalists.)

Doubtful of Yen Hsi-shan.

"I believe Chiang Kai-shek is opposed to Bolshevism, but I am not completely convinced. To prove his sincerity he must get rid of those Russians around him, and that poser and liar, Eugene Chen. (Chen is leader of the Hankow, or Radical, Nationalists.)

"Even then, there are difficulties, because one of Chiang's terms of settlement is that I disown General Chang Tsung-chang (Governor of Shantung), and this I will never do.

"I am prepared to embrace the principles of Sun Yat-sen (the late Chinese Republican leader), but I am not sure whether the Kuomintang (Nationalist) flag is the banner of Sun Yat-sen or a symbol of communism. At any rate, I am sure that not all who bear it are anti-Communists, and, therefore, it shall never fly from Peking."

Referring to General Yen Hsi-shan, Governor of the Province of Shansi, Marshal Chang did not know where he stood.

"I knew yesterday," the Marshal declared, "but he flirts with one side today and the other tomorrow. I am prepared to treat him on the same basis as Chiang Kai-shek, but if he has definitely joined with Hankow he is my enemy."

Chang asserted that one of his conditions was a combined attack on Hankow.

"We must catch that rascal Borodin," he added.

(A spokesman for Marshal Chang Tso-lin said several days ago at Peking that definite negotiations were going on for peace between North and South China, and the establishment of an alliance of three of the most powerful military leaders, with the definite exclusion of Communism. The leaders named were Chang, Chiang Kai-shek and General Yen Hsi-shan.)

June 11, 1927

NATIONALIST CHINA FREE OF RED AGENTS

Men From Moscow Have Been Ousted, but Propaganda Is Still Effective.

BORODIN PROVIDES PARADOX

His Personality at Once Secret of His Success and Cause of His Failure.

By HENRY F. MISSELWITZ.
Special Correspondence of THE NEW YORK TIMES.

SHANGHAI, Dec. 22.—The Reds are gone from China. The efficient structure which they had built up in the last half dozen years tottered during the past Summer and, as the year closed, fell around about them, until now, as far, at least, as the eye can see, the whole of Nationalist China is destitute of the men from Moscow who were agents of Soviet propaganda and intrigue. Their efforts to use China "as the springboard for the world revolution," as the Russian influence in this country has been termed, have, for the moment, if not permanently, failed.

Causes for this decline of the Reds lie deeply imbedded in the political affairs of the Kuomintang revolution on the one hand and, observers are inclined to believe, none the less deeply rooted in international political manoeuvrings on the other. There always has been a group of those influential in the revolutionary party thoroughly opposed to the growing influence of the Soviet in Canton's rebellion; and it is obvious that abroad there are interests just as stanchly opposed to a powerful Russia in the Orient, China or elsewhere. Russian policy in Asia has varied little from the days of the Czar. The methods only have changed.

It will be recalled that as long ago as 1920 the leaders of the Nationalist revolution here were flirting with Moscow in their search for foreign assistance in the campaign against Peking. The late Dr. Sun Yat-sen, who roamed the world spreading the gospel of the revolution he did so much to inspire, found the new Russia only too willing to lend an attentive ear to his sayings and a flattering tongue to his ambitions. The latter went as far as persuading the Sovietized Chinese to elect Dr. Sun and Nicolai Lenin as their Presidents that year, the Chinese workers in Moscow clamorously proclaiming these men their saviors and their ideals.

Motives Disregarded.

None was so ready to treat the China of the revolution as equals as the Soviet. The basic reason for this eagerness was not considered, it would seem, the late leader of the Cantonese feeling it sufficient that here, at last, was a nation that understood him and his grand scheme for the New China. It is not a national characteristic of the Chinese to accept aid without seeking the motive of the donor. Yet it would seem that the late Dr. Sun if he thought of motives at all was willing at the time to overlook that sinister side of the alliance and take the Soviet sympathy and aid at its face value as coming from one revolutionary Government to another.

From 1920 until 1923 little was done in the way of active assistance. The Soviet was still not sure that the revolution in the South was the better faction to back. Peking was worth dallying with for a while longer. But in 1923 the men in Moscow decided to proceed with the plan that was to make the Reds in China the most powerful influence in the country, and one which, but for the firm opposition of a comparatively small group of Kuomintang leaders would doubtless today still be running the Nationalist movement.

In 1923, Michael Borodin came into the scheme of things as high adviser to whatever government Dr. Sun

60

Yat-sen and his colleagues might care to set up. Dr. Sun met the Soviet Envoy to China, the late M. Joffe, in Shanghai and they agreed on the latter's plan to provide advisers, money, arms and, in short, put the nebulous theorizings of the good "tsung-li," or leader, as Dr. Sun was universally known, into practical form. Dr. Sun had met Borodin, according to the latter's tale of how he got into the revolution, and when M. Joffe suggested Borodin take charge of the Russian advisorate, the tsung-li agreed readily enough.

Borodin Came Bearing Gifts.

So Borodin came to Canton in 1923 and set to work. He offered a scheme of government and of organization that was accepted virtually outright. He came bearing gifts in the way of men and money. His dollars were accepted eagerly and the people's revolution waxed opulent.

The Communist Party of China was at that time helpless. It was not a power. So when Borodin suggested that inasmuch as this was to be an agrarian and workmen's revolution along Communist lines, and the Kuomintang had little to fear in welcoming the notorious CP, as the Communist Party is known, nobody objected strenuously.

In the early days of the Russian Advisorate system the Communists did not accept positions in the Government. These were filled by Chinese, all members of the old Kuomintang. The party formed a government along Soviet lines, with the committe system imported from Moscow. The party was organized into committees and so was the government. The party, in theory, at all times was to direct the government. The government was subject to the party. Incidentally, this theory never worked very well. The government committees usually went ahead and did the work and consulted the presumably all-powerful party committees later. There were too many bosses otherwise.

In the period from 1923 until May, 1926, Borodin and his staff devoted themselves assiduously to the task of completely reorganizing the Canton Government. The scores of Russians he imported went into every phase of the revolution, becoming secretaries in the governmental departments, advisers to the military leaders and starting the propaganda bureaus and the now ill-famed Political Bureau which when the drive to the North began in May, 1926, functioned so ably. The Whampoa Military Academy was organized and General Chiang Kai-shek became its head.

First Sign of Break.

The first intimation of a break with the Soviet masters of the Kuomintang came in March, 1926, before the northward campaign even had got under way. A group of leaders, among whom were Dr. C. C. Wu, then Foreign Minister in the Canton régime; Sun Fo, a son of the late Dr. Sun Yat-sen, and few military men, attempted to discredit Borodin and throw off the advisorate before the Russians got too firm a hold on the revolution. Borodin went to Russia that Spring, but he was allowed to return because for one thing General Chiang Kai-shek, appointed Commander-in-Chief of the Northern Expeditionary Forces, was not willing to break with him yet.

Borodin came back with more money and, what was more important, with munitions for the expedi-

tion. It was decided to proceed with it immediately, and in May, 1926, the Nationalist revolution moved northward.

Their route took them tediously overland through Kwantung and into Kiangsi. The armies moved slowly because the men had to walk most of the distance. They moved northward all that Summer of 1926, with little opposition, and while one branch moved somewhat to the west and came to the railroad at Pingsiang in Kiangsi the other went on toward Nanchang and eventually to the Yangtze at Kiukiang.

The plan, however, was to take Hankow first. Borodin wanted to move through the interior, letting Shanghai and Nanking go until Peking had been captured. His idea was to reach Peking, gain recognition and foreign sympathy and aid to the new Nationalist Government and thus force the war lords in Shantung and Kiangsu to capitulate even more readily than they did in the Yangtze Valley.

Borodin's Prominence Resented.

Hankow was captured after a siege, Wuchang falling Oct. 10, and the other Wuhan cities, Hankow and Hanyang, at the fork of the Yangtze and Han Rivers, following forthwith. Wuchang was Marshal Wu Pei-fu's last important stand.

Then began a series of incidents that came on the heels of this rapid success. Borodin came more into prominence. His name was more before the public than the Chinese leaders of the revolution. He had organized the propaganda corps and his men told the peasants and workmen what Borodin could do for them and what they could achieve if united. Borodin made a speech at Nanchang, in Kiangsi. It was his first public appearance. He spoke to meetings of peasants and workers frequently after that. The reaction among his Chinese co-revolutionists was soon apparent. They simply did not like it.

The first international incident which was a forerunner to subsequent steps interpreted as meaning the whole Nationalist movement was anti-foreign occurred in Hankow when on Jan. 3, 1927, a mob which the newly organized Hankow Government said was out of hand took over the British Concession. Once taken over, the Hankow régime could find no way, Borodin advised, in which to turn it back without losing "face." It would be, he advised, a fatal step and one which would alienate the support of the peasants and workmen—break, in other words, the backbone of the revolution. So Eugene Chen, by this time Foreign Minister in place of Dr. Wu, who was forced to flee to the safety of the International Settlement in Shanghai after his unsuccessful Opposition movement in Canton mentioned above, said he was sorry but things like that were bound to happen in a "people's revolution," and that nothing could be done about it.

Chamberlain Memorandum Cited.

Furthermore, Sir Austen Chamberlain the previous Dec. 18, 1926, had issued his famous Memorandum in which it is stated that Britain was ready to consider giving China back all the British concessions (excluding the colony at Hongkong) and to take a more lenient attitude on the treaty revision demands, &c. Hence Mr. Chen and Mr. Borodin

thought this gave them a further right to keep the British Concession at Hankow. They did.

Mr. O'Malley from the British Legation in Peking went to see Mr. Chen in Hankow and they signed an agreement on Feb. 19 under which the concession was to remain in Chinese hands, but that it should be for the time at least under Sino-British control. Since then things occurred so rapidly that the agreement has had little effect other than to permit the Chinese to continue to keep the concession. It seems now there is little chance that Britain ever will take it back.

In the early months of 1927 Borodin went about with his advisers organizing the farmers and the workmen in the newly acquired provinces of Kiangsi, Hunan and Hupeh. Farmers' guilds were formed and the peasantry learned they were the power behind the new China. Labor unions flourished. Borodin during the first six months of the year just passing was in his prime, and it seemed, on the surface at least, nothing could stop him and his sovietization of China.

The armies had succeeded not so much by fighting as by marching into welcoming territories. The propaganda of the Kuomintang guided by Borodin paved the way. They won by the now famed "paper bullets," by the slogans, posters and tireless soapbox orations, all telling of the better days to come when the war lords were overthrown.

Great Days for Borodin.

Those were the ringing days of such slogans as "Down with the northern militarists," "Down with the foreign imperialists," "Down with the capitalists," and "Down with" anything else that might appeal to the masses. Those were gala days for Borodin and despite the break in April with General Chiang Kai-sek, Hankow was carried on the crest of its own wave of optimism and organization. In April and May of 1927 few saw the handwriting on the wall in Hankow. Things were too prosperous.

The Hankow régime under Borodin also organized the woman's movement. Women were to be emancipated overnight. Bobbed hair was the insignia of the new freedom. One sojourning in Hankow in April and May last cannot forget the meetings for women only, where they heard optimistic tales of what they could do if united. They paraded through the streets, and in Red Hunan, perhaps most affected by all this propaganda for the "agrarian revolution" there were places where youths and girls adopted the earlier Russian revolution hysteria and indulged in free love.

It was a swirling life in the revolution in those days, the hey-day of Borodinism. The High Advisor had reason to be pleased with his handiwork. He was here, there, everywhere in the direction of his revolution—and one could but admire his tireless energy, his genius for organization, his pleasant, calm manner in talking with callers who wanted to know how and why he did these things. It must be said that although one might disagree heartily with the theories and practice of Michael Borodin, revolutionist, few have met the man who have not admired him personally. This personality was in a large measure the secret of his phenomenal success—and at once the source of his rapid failure.

NEW REGIME STARTS AT NANKING TODAY

It Will Succeed Nationalist Factional Governments and Be Under Commission of 5.

7 MINISTRIES, 2 COUNCILS

Several Portfolios Are Allotted— Hankow Raid on Reds Reveals Plot to Dynamite Cities, It Is Said.

SHANGHAI, Sept. 19 (P).—A new Nationalist Government which will succeed the two Nationalist bodies which hitherto have functioned from Hankow and Nanking will assume office at Nanking tomorrow, it was announced today.

The Government will be controlled by a commission of five, consisting of Hu Han-min, former generalissimo of the Kuomintang Army; Dr. Wang Ching-wei, Chairman of the Central Executive of the Kuomintang; Tsai Yon-pei, Minister of Education in the first Republican Cabinet under Yuan Shi-kai; Tan Yen-kai, member of the Executive Committee of the Kuomintang, and Li Lieh-chun, former civil Governor of the Province of Kiangsi, also a prominent member of the Kuomintang.

In addition, seven Ministries and two Councils, on Education and Military Affairs, will carry out the Government's executive duties.

The following portfolios have been allotted: Foreign Affairs, Dr. Wu Chao-hu; Finance, Sun Fo, son of the late revolutionary leader, Dr. Sun Yat Sen; Justice, Dr. Wang Chung-hui, an authority on international law; Communications, Wang Pei-chung, and Education, Tsai Yuan-pei.

September 20, 1927

CHINESE CHIEFS DROP QUARRELS AT TOMB OF DR. SUN YAT-SEN

Military "Big Four" Report Success of Nationalism to Dead Founder.

FENG'S ARRIVAL DRAMATIC

Last-Minute Appearance After All-Night Ride Spikes Talk of Factional Disputes.

Special Cable to THE NEW YORK TIMES.

PEKING, July 6.—A dramatic culmination of the Nationalist campaign to unify China was staged this morning at the Temple of the Western Hills near Peking when the "Big Four" of the movement paid homage at the tomb of Dr. Sun Yat-sen, founder of Chinese Nationalism.

When the casket was opened Chiang Kai-shek wept long and bitterly, flinging himself on the coffin of the dead leader from which he was raised by Feng Yu-hsiang, whose arrival several hours before had greatly lightened anxiety over a possible split. Chiang, Feng, Yen Hsi-shan and Li Tsung-jen were the only persons permitted to view the body, which was preserved three years ago in a glass casket filled with oil.

The ceremonies were spectacular and impressive, blending modernism and medievalism.

They included the reading of Sun Yat-sen's will, three minutes of silent tribute, dirges by bands, burning of incense, and the Confucian observance of offering a table loaded with choice food to the memory of the dead.

The actual purpose of this meeting of the main Nationalist leaders was not apparent, since all say nothing will be settled at the conferences in Peking. Yet T. V. Soong, Finance Minister, is joining the gathering and General Li Chai-sum is en route from Canton. Well-informed foreign circles believe that determination of Manchurian policy may be the main topic.

There is a growing feeling in Nationalist circles that Manchuria must be conquered by force, but since the Tsinan-fu affair great reluctance is felt against further embroilment with Japan and Tokio is outspoken in repeating her determination not to permit the ravages of civil warfare in zones of Manchuria where her interests are important. If Manchuria is invaded it will be by way of Jehol and not Shan Haikwan, which, Japan has warned, must not be attacked.

Nationalist leaders refute rumors that the gathering of leaders here means that Peking may remain the capital.

PEKING, July 6 (P).—The four most powerful military leaders of the Nationalist movement in China today presented an accounting of their stewardship to Dr. Sun Yat-sen at the tomb of the founder of the Nationalist movement.

Nationalism's military "Big Four" united in devout homage before the remains of the dead leader, reporting to the spirit of the father of the Nationalist cause the successful completion of the military stage of the Chinese revolution as he envisioned it, and pledging to him loyal cooperation to achieve the reconstruction of their country along the lines which he had pointed out.

At the last minute, just as day was breaking, the ranks of the four were dramatically completed by the arrival of Feng Yu-hsiang, long one of the most picturesque figures among China's military chieftains. He had traveled from his headquarters all night despite illness and appeared at the scene bearded, travel-stained and tired.

A simple, moving memorial service was held at the temple, fifteen miles northwest of Peking, where Sun Yat-sen's body has rested since he died in March, 1925.

Commanders Gaze on Body.

Shortly after 8 o'clock this morning the quartet, walking abreast, climbed to the white carved marble shrine, above which fluttered the Nationalist banners, and entered the small alcove containing the heavy flowered and lacquered coffin, draped with flags, which held the body.

The four leaders bowed before this and stood in profound silence as the great gathering of Generals, officials and soldiers, which filled the courtyard outside, also bowed in homage.

Then the report to Sun Yat-sen's spirit was read before the coffin and a few moments later came a dramatic climax when the heavy wooden outer lid was raised, permitting the four commanders to gaze upon the body of their late chieftain.

Chiang Kai-shek, for many years Sun Yat-sen's chief disciple, broke down and wept, and his sobs, continuing for three or four minutes and audible in all parts of the courtyard outside, caused many others to weep in sympathy.

In the meantime military bands played dirges at intervals. The gathering had attracted to the cedar-shaded multiple courtyard a throng in varied uniforms. Troops from nearly all parts of China mingled among the sober-robed civilians and smartly tailored younger Nationalists.

The public assembling of the Big Four for the first time in the revolutionary campaign in manifest sincerity in their devotion to Sun Yat-sen is viewed in Peking as a hopeful augury calculated to allay the current rumors of imminent dissension.

The marked diversity of types was noticeable. Chiang Kai-shek, slender, youthful, self-conscious and flushed with emotion, was spick and span in the uniform of the Nationalist army, with the occidental Sam Browne belt around his waist. Feng Yu-hsiang, towering, bulky and stolid, was in a well-worn uniform, unbelted, and a stained straw hat, and with his recently grown heavy black beard, showed the effects of a three days' fast, which he recently underwent at his ancestral tombs near Paoting-fu. Yen Hsi-shan, self-effacing and with an ingratiating smile, wore a loose-fitting military tunic without any insignia of rank, while Li Tsung-jen, small, boyish and alert, was dressed in the latest military fashion, with glistening boots and spurs.

A tomb for Dr. Sun Yat-sen's body is being built by the Nanking Nationalist Government at Nanking at a cost of more than 1,000,000 yen and it is expected that the body will some day be taken south to rest in the new capital.

After today's ceremony, the four military commanders opened a conference with the questions of a drastic military reduction and a possible invasion of Manchuria as the dominating matters on the agenda.

July 7, 1928

CHANGSHA IN FLAMES AS REDS SACK CITY

10,000 Well Armed Communists Loot and Destroy Alien and Government Property.

THREE AMERICANS IN PERIL

Mutiny of Garrison Left City Helpless—All Foreign Missions Reported Wrecked.

Special Cable to The New York Times.

SHANGHAI, July 29.—Within the brief space of forty-eight hours, instead of the district being pacified by the Nanking Government's military operations, as was previously reported, the situation at Changsha, Honan Province, has developed the worst Communist excesses yet reported from the Yangtse Valley and is threatening to involve the weakly defended river cities.

As the American gunboat Palos left Changsha early this morning, the sky was streaked with red and a large part of the city was in flames following the occupation of the city by 10,000 well-armed Communists who ran riot, burning, looting and destroying the government buildings and foreign business and mission properties.

Forty-one foreigners, including Americans and British, were evacuated aboard the British gunboat Aphis which left for Yochow, but five foreigners remain in the city, comprising three Americans, W. H. Lingle and his wife, Presbyterians, and Allen H. Cameron of the Faith Mission, who refuse to leave; Miss G. Rugg, a British missionary, who lives five miles outside the city and is out of reach of assistance, and the aged Father Baima, an Italian who was captured by the Communists while seeking safety.

Changsha is a big missionary centre, and is normally populated by 300 foreigners, but most of them left before the Communist storm broke.

It is revealed that part of the Nanking Government troops mutinied on Monday night, fleeing across the Siang River, leaving the city helpless. Thereupon, the Communists, after the foreigners had evacuated, entered the city, burned the government buildings and the Governor's yamen and then turned their attention to foreign property to which they also set fire.

On Monday night the Communists announced their intention of crossing over to the tiny island in the middle of the river where the British Consulate is located and of burning it. All the foreign officials and business men have taken refuge aboard the gunboats.

Fear for Foreigners at Kuling
By HALLETT ABEND.
Special Cable to The New York Times.

PEKING, July 29.—The capture of Changsha by Communists and the approach of their armies to within ten miles of Kiukiang have thoroughly alarmed the legations here because 220 foreigners, including twenty Americans, are summering at Kuling, a mountain resort near Kiukiang, and it is doubtful if they can reach the safety zones before the fall of Kiukiang.

Many Americans are believed to be still in Hupeh, Honan, Hunan and Kiangsi, four provinces which are overrun by Communist bands. There were 239 American men and 180 women and children in this area on July 11, when they were officially warned to leave.

The Peking Foreign Office has received telegrams from Marshal Feng Yu-hsiang expressing his belief that Hankow will be taken in ten days without fighting because of the rapidity with which the generals are deserting President Chiang Kai-shek. Marshal Feng reports understandings have been reached with General Yang Hu-tsun, holding a section of the Peking-Hankow railway, and with General Yo Wei-chin, in the same zone, both of whom were formerly Nanking supporters.

One regiment of Yang's men mutinied, marched to Yehsien and joined Feng's forces, which were holding the city, but Feng disarmed the mutineers and sent them back to Yang Hu-tsun's zone, followed by their full armed equipment in carts.

The Japanese Chargé d'Affaires denies to the Peking Foreign Office the reports from Japan that the Tokyo government intends to send troops and officials to Shantung to protect Japanese interests. He says he has no fears regarding their safety under General Yen Hsi-shan's protection.

Yen Hsi-shan has wired to the Peking Foreign Office from the front lines south of Taian that there is little fighting. He says the Northerners are entrenched in strong positions and are awaiting Nanking's announced attacks.

Missions Reported Destroyed.

SHANGHAI, Wednesday, July 30 (AP).—The British North China Daily News today says all foreign missions at Changsha, capital of Hunan Province, were destroyed by the Communists, who overran the city yesterday.

Overrun by a Communist horde, the rich city of Changsha, capital of Hunan Province, was systematically sacked yesterday and burned by the invaders, but not before foreign warships had removed their nationals to safety.

Influential Chinese reiterated their belief that the Changsha raid was instigated by the Third International at Moscow. They said unless the Nanking Government was able to halt the civil war that has been ravaging the country for months and to turn its attention to the communistic activity, the Red threat was destined soon to become more grave.

The wildest rumors resulted from the raid. One was to the effect that the establishment of a Communist government south of the Yangtse River was imminent. Nationalist Government bonds declined sharply as another result of the Red activity.

After taking aboard missionaries and foreigners desiring to leave, the warships were forced by the rapidly receding river to withdraw. Millions of dollars worth of foreign property thus was left at the mercy of the Reds.

Nanking Officials Executed.

The foreigners were rescued before the sacking of the city commenced by the American warship Palos, two British and three Japanese gunboats, which also escorted foreign commercial vessels to safety and towed away floating equipment of various concerns.

Relief work done by the naval men, who risked their lives in penetrating isolated portions of the city, was warmly praised.

Advices trickling through before communications were severed with Changsha said the Reds had executed numerous Nanking and provincial officials. A brother of the Hochien Provincial Governor was beheaded.

Foreign wireless reports from Changsha said the Communists, after sacking virtually all of the city, which lies on the right bank of the Siang River, then crossed to the island opposite the town where the foreign consulates and additional foreign properties are located. An unconfirmed report said these had been looted and burned.

When the Communists entered Changsha fewer than 10,000 provincial troops under General Ho Chien, Governor of Hunan Province, guarded the city. Upon the entry of the Reds half of this force fled. Three thousand joined the Reds and the remainder, attempting to oppose the marauders, were slaughtered. Ho Chien fled to Changteh, 150 miles northwest. This city was reported to be destined to fall to the Communists.

Reds Seize River Ports.

The Communists who have long menaced Central China have renewed their activities in the Upper Yangtse valley. Dispatches yesterday told of unusual communistic activity along the middle section of the Yangtse where bands of marauders fired upon river steamers at many points in addition to capturing and looting several minor river ports.

The principal activity of this nature seemed to be in Hunan Province, near Yochow, where recently the Reds looted and burned most of the city, causing foreigners to flee. Communists concentrated in this area are attacking the few steamers which attempt to operate above Hankow. Many ships are tied up at Hankow or are operating solely between that city and Shanghai.

Chinese dispatches from Kiukiang said the provincial forces were seeking to curb Communist activities in Kiangsi Province but indicated they were meeting with only slight success. One-eighth of the province was said to be in the rebels' hands and bands of marauders were swarming in from Fukien Province.

Naval officers in Changsha believed the city would remain in the hands of the Reds for at least ten days. Due to the civil warfare, the Provincial and Nanking Government authorities are not expected to undertake immediate opposition to the Red forces, which are terrifying the populace throughout Central and Southern China.

NEW HAVEN, Conn., July 29 (AP).—Officials at the home office of Yale-in-China today had received no information from Changsha concerning the fate of the mission college's property in that city. A cablegram was being sent today to the directors of the Y. M. C. A. in Changsha in an attempt to determine what damage had resulted from the rioting.

In the absence of any official notification from the State Department it was believed here that whatever damage was done to the college property was light.

The mission college's property in Changsha includes a hospital, the middle school, and several dormitories and private residences. Fighting in the Hunan Province forced the college to close about three years ago and the mission was reopened last year.

DAVIDSON, N. C., July 29 (AP).—No word has been received from Dr. W. H. Lingle, Presbyterian missionary in China, since May 8, his brother, Dr. T. W. Lingle, Davidson College professor, said today.

A native of Rowan County, North Carolina, Dr. W. H. Lingle has been in the Chinese mission field since 1890. His wife, the former Jean Richie of Ohio, is with him. Of his two married daughters, one is in the United States and another en route to this country.

Another brother of the missionary, Dr. Walter L. Lingle, is president of Davidson College, the Presbyterian institution here.

Not Surprised Husband Stayed.

DENVER, Col., July 29 (P).—Dr. Allen N. Cameron, missionary at Changsha, has been in China as a missionary since 1895. The Faith Mission, which he represents, is a branch of the Denver Galilee Baptist Church.

Dr. Cameron was born and reared in Lawrence, Kan. His wife lives here. He is a graduate of the Moody Bible Institute of Chicago.

Mrs. Cameron, herself a missionary, said she was forced to flee eight weeks ago from China. She expressed little surprise that her husband remained in the city after it was captured.

Americans at Changsha.

The Y. M. C. A. representative at Changsha is G. G. Helde. Mr. Helde has been in China since 1916. He is a native of New Mexico. His nearest relative, records show, is Mrs. George W. Helde of Central, N. M. The record did not indicate the relationship.

R. K. Veryard, the other Y. M. C. A. representative, left China a month ago on furlough and is now in England visiting relatives. He is expected in New York in September.

The representative of the Y. W. C. A. in Changsha is Maud Russell of Hayward, Cal. Miss Russell has been in China for the Y. W. C. A. since 1919. The last direct word from her to Y. W. C. A. headquarters in New York was on June 16. At that time she was well and in no danger. Miss Russell's mother, Mrs. Thomas D. Russell, lives at Hayward.

CHANGSHA IS IN RICH AREA.

One of Leading Cities In China, It Is Famous for Its Fireworks.

Special to The New York Times.

WASHINGTON, July 29.—Changsha, China, is described in a special bulletin issued today by the National Geographic Society, as a "city of fireworks, literally and figuratively."

"The Fourth of July firecrackers used by the American small boy before the 'safe and sane Fourth,' was so widely enforced," the society stated, "were imported heavily from Changsha. The city long was a focal point for operations between the Northern and Southern armies, especially in 1922, when it was a scene of the long-delayed meeting of the two units.

"The city is the capital of the hilly province of Hunan, important because it contains enormous coal fields, many unworked, and because in it, to the north of Changsha, is the huge lake Tung-Ting Hu, which acts as a reservoir for the Yangtse floods.

"In Hunan the necromancer has exerted much power, and Changsha was so well-protected by the lucky constellation under which it was founded and by the Holy Hill which guards it that it was thought a profanation for the 'foreign devils' to enter. In 1910 there were serious riots, mainly directed against the growing commercial power of foreign firms, but the disturbance had also its astronomical accompaniments, for it was the approach of Halley's comet which touched off the explosion.

"Today Changsha is closely linked with New Haven, Conn., for there is, just outside the rapidly disappearing wall, in which the inhabitants once took great pride, one of the best known mission schools in China, which is Yale's contribution to the education of the Chinese who can not come to America.

"A large part of Hunan is an unworked field of anthracite and bituminous coal at Pinghsiang, which is connected with Changsha by railroad, there is one of the mines which furnishes fuel for the great iron works at Hanyang.

"Among the great men who have been among Changsha's chief products, the most famous was General Tsang Kuo-fan, who cooperation with 'Chinese Gordon' was largely instrumental in putting down the Taiping rebellion. General Tsang was not only a soldier and statesman, but a literary man as well, and his collected works of 156 books were edited by Li Hung-chang.

"Changsha lies on a projected line of railway between Peking and Canton and trains have already competed with the light draft steamers which make the 220-mile trip from Hankow. With about 500,000 inhabitants, it rules a province of 22,000,000 people, and is one of the cleanest cities in China.

"Many of the streets are long and straight and at one time the city itself was divided between two magistracies. The bazaars are full of life and interest, some of the candles being famous for miles around.

"The Episcopal Mission has a live Boy Scout troop and the visitor, who watched tent-pegging, fire-rescue, stretcher-making and other Boy Scout activities would marvel at China's quick changes. For until the Boxer trouble, Hunan's capital excluded the dread foreigner from its walls, whose brick battlements, rising above the site of a former wall constructed in 202 B. C., were themselves built while Shakespeare was alive."

CHINA'S COMMUNISM TAKES ON NEW FORM

No Longer Organized Movement Directed From Moscow, but a Phase of Disintegration.

AN EFFECT AND NOT A CAUSE

"Direct Action" of Peasants, if It Comes, Will Be a Result of Despair, Not of a Set of Doctrines.

By NATHANIEL PEFFER.

Into the tangled web of internal conflict in China, already untraceable to the Western eye, yet another strand has been woven. This is what is called communism. The designation is too simple.

Like everything else Western that has been introduced into China, communism has undergone subtle transformations. It has been said that, if a monkey-wrench is sent to China from Chicago and put to use in a small machine shop in Wusih, in three months that monkey-wrench will be working quite satisfactorily, quite as a monkey-wrench ought to, but it will not be the same monkey-wrench that it was when shipped from Chicago; it will not be quite like any other monkey-wrench in Chicago. It will be working just a little differently and looking just a little different. Something will have happened to it. It will have taken on a certain Chinese character.

So it is with Christianity, constitutional government, Grand Rapids furniture, fox-trots, college yells or anything else taken over from the West. All have become in some indefinable way different from what they were originally. And so it is also with what is called communism in China. For purposes of brevity in news cables, this may be described as communism, but in Chinese actuality it is something that would have to be freely translated to be recognized in Moscow.

An Earlier Communism.

This is to be distinguished as well from the communism which threatened to sweep China five years ago. Then it was a tour de force of propaganda rather than a real belief in the doctrines of Karl Marx and Moscow. On the part of the overwhelming majority of those who were following the Communist leaders and practically all those who were sympathetic, there was a hazy feeling that in some miraculous way this new party with the new name Kung Chan Tang would ease the contemporary sufferings of the people and finally end the suffering for all time.

So great has been the suffering of the Chinese in these years that a miracle-seeking psychology was easy to engender. But of any real comprehension of the meaning of communistic doctrine and its implications there was a complete lack except on the part of an infinitesimal proportion. And of these the majority blinked at the doctrine in order to get Russian support against the other powers which have imperialistic rights in China, notably Great Britain.

Nevertheless, the communism which was abroad in China then could be said to stem at least indirectly from Moscow. There were Russian advisers in the Canton Government, Chinese who had studied in Moscow and returned, and a few intellectuals in academic circles who had a reasoned belief in communism.

Now it is entirely different. In the sudden onrush of armies which are sweeping over the Yangtse basin it is hard to draw the line between what is communism and what is merely guerrilla militarism or plain banditry. And even what believes itself to be genuine communism has been sadly diluted since 1928.

For one thing there was a sharp break in 1928. It began with the process of purgation after the Kuomintang, or Nationalist party, had decided that it was necessary to sever the alliance with Moscow if the Nationalist revolution was not to come completely under Russian control. Purgation was by the simple but effective expedient of killing. Vital statistics are unreliable in China and there is no way of telling how many tens of thousands were put to death that year, but it was a wholesale affair and thousands were shot in batches who had only the remotest connection with communism. Then in 1928 China severed all diplomatic relations with Soviet Russia, and communism went underground altogether.

Leaderless Movement.

Since that time there has been a great deal of subterranean propaganda and a certain amount of organization. The disillusionment produced, especially among the student classes, by the failure of the Nanking Government to redeem the promise of unification, peace and reconstruction which seemed so bright in 1926 has given propaganda something to work on. Also the savage repression, not only of communism but of labor organizations suspected of immoderate demands, has bred a reaction. In addition, there has been the influence of the misery of the population under the curse of endless civil wars, militarist extortions and chronic, organized banditry.

Nevertheless, it can be said that the communist efforts of the last two years have been leaderless, spasmodic and not very far-reaching. Between 1924 and 1927 they were spon-

sored by the Nationalist party heads and the intellectual leaders, with all the prestige that scholarship still gives in China. Without this sponsorship communism could have got nowhere even then. Now, those same elements are inflexibly opposed to communism. However they may differ on other subjects, they are convinced that communism is repugnant to the Chinese spirit and that Russian interference in China's internal affairs is as inimical to the country's welfare as that of any of the other countries called imperialistic.

The process of purgation did leave in certain parts of the country men who had come somewhat under the influence of communistic propaganda. Most of them knew just enough of communism to interpret it as a legitimate and easy form of expropriation. This could easily be applied, as it is being applied by Generals and brigand leaders—that is, by robbery. And as conditions in China in the last few years have made tens of thousands homeless and without work, it is easy to recruit men for any purpose that promises a full rice bowl. This is also the explanation for the huge armies now overrunning the country. They can get recruits because being a soldier is one way of getting fed. Thus a great many of the so-called Communist armies have been raised.

The communism of 1930 is a phase of the underlying turmoil of China. The Nanking Government has failed in its ambition to exercise the functions of a real government. There are civil wars among three or four of the main groups, but there are also a number of what might be called private wars among guerrilla leaders all over the country. Organized authority has broken down. The last vestiges of authority exercised by the old régime disappeared with the collapse of the Northern Government before the Nationalist advance. There is little check on any form of disorder, whether going under the name of communism or something else.

Furthermore, there is the complete social confusion of the time. More than government has broken down. The whole traditional social system has dissolved. The impetus of disintegration has gathered force for twenty years. All the forces which have been playing on China for nearly fifty years have been sapping its foundations, and now the foundations have given way. It is a time of natural disorder. Any slogan, any rallying cry, any appeal, can command a following, if only because hardly anything could be worse than what is. Every traditional discipline in China has disappeared—the discipline of custom, education, family authority, government authority. All the controls of a civilization have slipped, principally because Chinese civilization has gone under.

The suffering of the Chinese people today cannot be exaggerated. Their

villages and farms have been overrun by troops for years. They have been bilked by taxation to pay the upkeep of official and unofficial armies. They have lived in terror of banditry and whole districts have been subject to looting. Fighting and banditry together have interrupted transportation of goods, so that business has been hard hit. In addition, the collapse of silver in the last year has had a disastrous economic effect, since Chinese currency is based on silver.

It is true that China is a fertile field for Communist efforts, but communism is an effect, not a cause. And it is one of the lesser effects. The city of Changsha was looted by so-called Communists and other cities have been occupied. But still others have been captured and looted in the same way by bands to which communism would mean as much as the single tax.

This is not to say that Soviet Russia has not been well aware of the possibilities for exploitation in China. The crushing blow suffered in 1928 has not laid Russian ambitions low forever. China would still be an ideal point of departure for carrying the world revolution over the whole East. If the Nanking Government should break completely and conditions get even worse, if a number of predatory armies should start looting all over the country, they might easily be gathered up by skillful Communist organizers and placed under the Russian egis. But, if the Russians were unsuccessful in 1927, when they held every position of vantage, there is not much reason to believe that they can succeed now, when there are such ponderous forces of opposition. It is more likely that all they can be is a complicating factor.

The Immediate Danger.

What threatens China much more immediately and seriously is that the civil war will come to a stalemate by the collapse of all parties, and that the peasantry, which has been the most cruelly victimized, will take to direct action and wreak its vengeance on whatever comes in its way. Had the Chinese not been a people inured to hardship and patient and law-abiding by virtue of a tradition 3,000 years old, they might long ago have risen. It may be that they will yet be goaded beyond endurance.

A hundred years of pressures of every kind—Western armies and navies, Western economic penetration, European diplomatic domination, Western ideas of democracy, individualism, speed and production by machinery—have disorganized the life of the race. The cumulative effect of these has hit China with a terrible impact these last five years, and as a result China is now reeling. At bottom the problem is not communism or anti-communism, but whether China can ever get back on its feet and regain its equilibrium. And this will be determined not by Moscow or propaganda emanating from Moscow, but by much broader considerations.

Chinese Anti-Red Campaign Faces Disaster; Desertions and Hostile Peasants Balk Moves

By HALLETT ABEND.
Special Cable to THE NEW YORK TIMES.

SHANGHAI, Jan. 19.—Nanking's anti-Communist campaign in Kiangsi Province continues to be disastrous for the government. There have been minor defeats and serious desertions on the part of the soldiers, while the solidarity with which the peasantry is giving its support to the Reds is complicating the situation.

Though President Chiang Kai-shek controls 900,000 men, a curious palsy seems to be afflicting the military arm of the government, while Communists keep up their gains. It is believed to be a disturbed political and military situation which prompts the government to maintain so many troops at present in camps.

General Shih Yu-san, who revolted against Nanking in 1929, is again a menacing figure. He has just seized five locomotives and more than 300 coaches from the Peking-Hankow Railway. The vacillating state of affairs in Szechuan Province is also unfavorable to large-scale movements elsewhere.

Marshal Chang Hsueh-Liang has returned to Mukden, it is believed, to clear up his personal affairs prior to settling down permanently in his Peking headquarters.

Tomorrow morning at 8 o'clock the American flier, G. W. Brothy, will hop alone on his airmail flight from Shanghai to Manila, with stops at Foochow and Canton. He is using a small Waco biplane, which is not equipped with either pontoons or radio.

NANKING, Jan. 19 (Æ).—It was stated in official quarters here today that the French Government had decided to transfer its legation from Peking to Nanking.

The United States and other nations with legations in Peking have contended that the city of Nanking is still too undeveloped and unprovided with modern conveniences and housing facilities, as well as too inconveniently situated, to be adaptable for legation quarters. It is also understood that the powers did not consider the Nanking Government strong or stable enough to warrant a move that might later have to be undone.

CHINESE REDS GAIN; KUOMINTANG LOSING

Nationalist Party Is Assailed in Peiping-Tientsin Area—Swing to the Left Is Wide

JAPANESE IN SHANGHAI RIOT

Two Killed in Outbreaks After Chinese Factory Is Set Afire— Police Are Mobilized.

By HALLETT ABEND.
Special Cable to THE NEW YORK TIMES.

PEIPING, Jan. 20.—Even the Peiping-Tientsin area today affords striking evidence of the degree to which the Kuomintang party has lost the confidence of the people. Students, labor unions and other elements are openly denunciatory of the Kuomintang in Peiping and Tientsin, while in Shansi Province students have established a "People's Tribunal," which now is presuming to try Kuomintang officials for alleged misdemeanors.

Everywhere a decided swing to the Left is evident, with occasional unique efforts to combine Communist methods with those of the French Revolution. The Kuomintang party never enjoyed popularity in North China. Today it is being treated as a scapegoat by the elements it sought particularly to woo when the Northern militarists accepted party domination as a momentary necessity.

This widespread tendency to attack the Kuomintang seriously weakens what is termed the "mandate" to govern the country, which is claimed by the politicians who now form the Nanking Government. In this crisis there seem only two possible trends —first, a return to regional militarism; second, the development of communism, because, thanks to the repressive policies of the Kuomintang, minority parties do not exist in China. Today, therefore, political opinions are expressed in Sun Yat-senism and communism.

In either event China seems destined to face a renewal of large-scale civil warfare with the coming of Spring, for neither the Kuomintang militarists nor the Communists will agree on basic compromises, and no one faction will be deterred from warfare by the fact that China's pretentions to existence as a genuine national entity will soon be on trial before the League of Nations commission of inquiry.

JAPANESE SEIZE MUKDEN IN BATTLE WITH CHINESE; RUSH MORE TROOPS TO CITY

TOKYO ALLEGES ATTACK

But Chinese Say Assault Was Unprovoked and Unanswered.

MANCHURIANS LIST 70 DEAD

Japanese Demand Surrender of Chinese Troops and Police— Foreigners Protected.

NAVY ORDERED ON ALERT

Warships Will Be Held Ready for Call to Ports—Some Japanese Suspect Army in Move.

By HUGH BYAS.

Wireless to THE NEW YORK TIMES.

TOKYO, Saturday, Sept. 19.—A violent clash between Chinese and Japanese soldiers in the vicinity of Mukden was followed by all-night fighting which culminated in the capture of the Mukden inner walled city by Japanese troops at 4:30 A. M. today. The fighting is still proceeding in the streets and suburbs.

Japanese reinforcements are being speeded to Mukden by special trains from Port Arthur and other points.

The affair began, according to reports available, at 10:30 o'clock last night, when three companies of Chinese troops began destroying the South Mancuhuria Railway line at Hokutaiei, a village three miles from Mukden, on the main line. A smaller number of Japanese troops posted there as guards drove the Chinese away and occupied the village.

Chinese Said to Have Reattacked.

The Chinese re-attacked with machine-guns and even field guns, it is said, and surrounded the Japanese.

At midnight Japanese troops at Mukden, numbering three battalions, began an attack on the inner walled city, which they captured after four and a half hours of fighting. The Japanese demand the surrender of the Chinese garrison and the Chinese police of Mukden.

By 6:30 A. M. the Japanese had completely occupied the walled city. Military police were detailed to preserve order, while the troops began an attack on the military airdrome and arsenal.

Telegrams from Seoul say that part of the Korean garrison has been ordered to Manchuria.

Officials do not try to conceal the extreme gravity of the affair, but there are still hopes it may prove a local incident capable of settlement as such. The atmosphere of Manchuria for weeks past has been of the kind in which guns go off of themselves.

Frontier incidents were to be expected and both governments must have expected some such affair. The agitation the army here has been conducting over the Nakamura murder has created widespread anxiety and the question all Japanese are asking is whether the affair was premeditated or is an isolated incident such as is likely to occur in a bellicose atmosphere.

Hurried inquiries here tend to show it was not foreseen and, as far as the Japanese Government is concerned, unpreventable.

The official theory is that the Mukden commander imagined an attack on the bridge at Hokutaiei, otherwise Peitayeng, was the commencement of a concerted attack on Japanese troops. Anticipating that the cutting of the bridge was the prelude to a general assault, he determined to get his blow in first, and immediately attacked Chinese Army headquarters.

The Chinese did not offer serious resistance and the casualties, it is hoped, were few.

A Mukden dispatch to the Tokyo Asahi reports that on the night of Sept. 15, when General Honjo, the new commander of the Japanese garrison in Manchuria, arrived, orders were issued to all Japanese troops in Manchuria. The test was carried out satisfactorily and the next morning troops began their march.

General Honjo, who has been touring Manchuria, addressed the troops in several places on the great increase in banditry and ordered them to take drastic measures against bandits found in the South Manchuria Railroad zone.

The Japanese forces in Manchuria at present consist of one division, at peace strength about 12,000 men, and six battalions of railroad guards.

Chinese Deny They Fought.

Special Cable to THE NEW YORK TIMES.

PEIPING, Saturday., Sept. 19.— Japanese soldiers occupied the city of Mukden, Manchuria, at 3 A. M. today. A squad of Japanese soldiers approached the north camp at Mukden at about 10 o'clock Thursday night and opened fire. This was followed by shellfire on the camp arsenal and the city from the Japanese concession.

A message received here by Vice Marshal Chang Hsueh-liang, Governor of Manchuria, stated that at 1 o'clock Friday afternoon the firing continued, one shell falling every ten minutes. Between seventy and eighty Chinese soldiers were killed. Japanese consular authorities were reported to be unable to induce the military to cease firing. The Chinese did not retaliate.

On receiving the message Marshal Chang immediately ordered all Chinese soldiers in Mukden to put their arms in the barracks and not to fire a shot or retaliate in any way. No "incident" or immediate cause for the attack was reported.

Four Japanese Wounded.

TOKYO, Saturday, Sept. 19 (Æ).— A War Department communiqué said today an attempt by Chinese troops to destroy the South Manchuria Railway bridge at Peitaying, suburb of Mukden, precipitated a clash last night between Chinese and Japanese soldiers at Mukden, in which a Japanese Lieutenant and three soldiers were wounded.

A second communiqué said the Chinese, "three or four companies strong, withdrew into their barracks after the encounter with the Japanese."

A part of the Chinese position was taken over by the Japanese troops. The Chinese were being reinforced with machine guns.

Dispatches to the Rengo News Agency and special dispatches said the Chinese used bombs to destroy part of the railway line near the Peitaying bridge. Japanese troops reinforced the handful of railway guards and some infantry fighting followed. The authorities cautioned the 20,000 Japanese inhabitants not to leave the Japanese concession in Mukden.

Japanese who had been living within the walled part of Mukden and other parts of the native city began moving to the Japanese district in all haste.

Japanese troops, according to a message to the newspaper Asahi, occupied three Chinese banks in Mukden—the Bank of the Three Eastern Provinces, the Bank of Communications and a private institution.

The Rengo Agency said that as a result of a conference of naval officials, it was decided to dispatch vessels from the Sasebo Base at Kyushu Island to assist the military should occasion arise.

It was reported that all ship commanders were ordered to prepare for emergency calls in event it was deemed necessary to protect Japanese subjects at Tsingtau, Port Arthur, Dairen and other ports.

After conferring at the War Office, high officials were called to the Imperial Palace, where the Manchurian situation was detailed to the Emperor.

An extraordinary session of the Japanese Cabinet was called here this morning to discuss the situation.

The session was called shortly after a spokesman for the Foreign Office, discussing the clash at Paitaying, said, "It is taken for granted the situation is extremely serious."

"We have not yet received detailed reports as to the object of Chinese troops in attempting to destroy a section of the South Manchuria Railway," he said. "Whatever the reason may be, we can hardly overlook such conduct, and it is natural that Japan will take proper steps to defend herself."

The Japanese authorities ordered the whole Japanese colony in areas outside the South Manchuria Railway zone to enter the zone for protection.

Chinese Police Disarmed.

Upon entering the walled city of Mukden, Rengo dispatches said, Japanese troops disarmed all Chinese police. The news agency dispatches said both sides used some artillery, and it was calculated at Mukden that the Japanese fired twelve shells. Japanese reinforcements from various near-by points were arriving at the Mukden main station, which is within the Japanese concession zone.

A dispatch to the Rengo agency from Seoul, Korea, said a Japanese air squadron was moving from Pingyang to Shingishu, on the Korean border, 125 miles from Mukden. In other places, the dispatch said, planes were ready to get under way but were awaiting orders.

News agency dispatches said a second Japanese battalion occupied the howitzer plant, outside the east gate of Mukden.

The howitzer plant is some distance from the enormous arsenal which was started by the late Chang Tso-lin when the war lord had visions of conquering all of China. As far as is known the arsenal is unoccupied.

Chinese Act in Executions.

A dispatch from Mukden to the Rengo News Agency yesterday said a Chinese General and eleven soldiers probably would be executed for having caused the shooting of a Japanese Captain and three companions.

General Jung Chun, Chief of Staff of the Manchurian Army, said the dispatch, informed Japanese Consul Morioka that proof had been obtained that Captain Shintaro Nakamura, another Japanese, a Mongolian and a Russian were shot as spies by regular troops under General Kwan Yu-heng. It was not stated whether General Kwan carried out the shooting himself or instructed troops to shoot.

The Nakamura group held certificates from Chinese authorities permitting the party to travel in Manchuria and Mongolia to make maps. The men were arrested July 26 and shot the next day.

General Jung Chin has sent fifty cavalrymen to arrest General Kwan Yu-heng and eleven others and bring them to Mukden, where it is expected they will be executed.

The Nakamura incident caused much resentment in Japan, with correspondence between the Japanese and Chinese Governments.

Relations Recently Strained.

Recent causes of irritation between Chinese and Japanese were the attacks by Chinese upon Korean irrigation workers in Manchuria and the resultant riots in Korea, in which Korean mobs killed about 100 Chinese.

The Chinese in Korea fled to Japanese police stations, where they received protection, the Japanese firing upon Korean attacking parties. The incident, however, caused considerable friction between China and Japan, the Nanking Government demanding that Japan make formal apology for the attacks upon Chinese in Korea, render compensation for loss of life and property and give guarantees against a recurrence of the outrages.

Another recent disturbance of Japanese and Chinese relations was the execution of Captain Shintaro Nakamura and three companions.

The South Manchuria Railway is a Japanese semi-governmental concern. It extends from Dairen, in the Kwantung district of Southern Manchuria, a Japanese Government leased territory, to Changchun, Manchuria, 438 miles away, where it connects with the Chinese Eastern Railway. Another section leads from Mukden to Antung, connecting with the Korean main system.

The South Manchuria Railway crosses the Hun River in entering Mukden, the capital of Manchuria, which has about 200,000 inhabitants.

September 19, 1931

NANKING INVOKES AID OF WORLD'S POWERS

Calls on League Members and Treaty Signatories to Prevent Japan Destroying Pacts.

Special Cable to THE NEW YORK TIMES.

SHANGHAI, Sunday, Jan. 31.— The Nanking Government yesterday issued a manifesto formally calling upon all members of the League of Nations and signatories to the Kellogg-Briand pact and Nine-Power treaty "to take immediate effective action in fulfillment of their sacred obligations undertaken under such pacts and treaties in order thus to prevent the dictates of right and humanity, the rules of international law and the sanctity of treaties from being completely violated and destroyed by Japanese might."

Previous to the foregoing invocation of the world's assistance, the manifesto outlined the development of the present crisis and then called attention to "the continuous indiscriminate bombardment over which twenty Japanese military bombers," although only six airplanes actually were used, and also charged that "Shanghai is now under the scourge of terrific artillery fire," although the only artillery used yesterday was that used by the Chinese in violation of the truce supposedly effective since 8 o'clock Friday evening.

Capital Moved to Honanfu.

The Nanking Government is moving to Loyang [Honanfu] in the heart of Honan Province, far north of Hankow and far out of the gun range of Japanese cruisers, according to unconfirmed but credible reports from Nanking. Chiang Kai-shek and Wang Chung-wei are said already to have departed from Nanking for Honanfu.

This move had been seriously considered in inner Chinese circles ever since the beginning of the Sino-Japanese clash in Manchuria last September.

Despatches from Nanking declare that Generals Chiang Kai-shek, Wang Chin-wei, Ho Ying-ching and other responsible leaders conferred previous to the issuance of this proclamation, deciding in the meanwhile to undertake effective action to curb the Japanese naval forces.

The military committee advising Chiang Kai-shek in this crisis, now regarded as the nation's highest military power, included Generals Feng Yu-hsiang, Yen Hsi-shan, Li Tsung-jen and Chen Ming-shu, all recently rebels against Nanking, and Chang Hsiao-liang, the defeated and discredited former Manchurian war lord. Behind this show of unification exists the shocking reality of petty intrigues, working at cross purposes.

Chiang Kai-shek, having attempted to maintain his non-resistance policy, strongly disapproved resistance of the Japanese by the Nineteenth Route Army under General Tsai Ting-chai. Therefore he sent three regiments of loyal troops from Nanking under orders to check, and if necessary, to disarm the Nineteenth Route Army. However, when the Nanking regiments reached Shanghai they disobeyed orders, joining General Tsai's army in counter-attacking the Japanese.

Sun Fo, Eugene Chen and others who recently resigned from the government, are continuously bombarding Chiang Kai-shek with telegrams demanding strong reinforcements and a positive policy, which stand is fully endorsed by many business, professional and labor organizations.

For a time there was a tendency toward a general revolt in the ranks of all military forces against continuing the passive attitude. General Tsai Ting-chai, General Tai chi, the garrison, commander at Shanghai and Woosung, have been almost hourly conferring with such prominent leaders as Feng Fug-siang, Li Tsung-jen and Chang Fak-wei, the noted ironsides commander, all of whom are strongly supporting the Nineteenth Route Army's resistance policy. This clique has now prevailed.

At Nanking T. V. Soong, with characteristic vigor, moving rapidly toward a reorganization of the disrupted finance Ministry, telegraphed to Shanghai, ordering most of the members of his old staff to proceed to Nanking immediately. Since railway service is disrupted the staff departed from Shanghai yesterday afternoon aboard a customs cruises.

Decide to Declare War.

NANKING, Jan. 30 (P).—Goaded by the Japanese invasion of Shanghai, the Chinese National Government decided today to declare war on Japan.

The formal declaration will be withheld for several days. The gov-ernment had intended to keep its decision secret, but when news of it got abroad, no denial was issued.

Meanwhile the United States authorities took precautions to protect their nationals living in Nanking. Every American citizen was ordered by the United States Consulate to be ready to get out of the city within two hours.

Concentration points were selected against the possibility of sudden emergency growing out of the disorders at Shanghai. A system of flashlight signals was arranged in order that the Consulate might keep United States naval vessels anchored in the Yangtse informed about what was going on in the city.

A large-scale troop movement toward Shanghai was carried on all during the day. Trainloads of soldiers of the Nineteenth Chinese Army left as quickly as railroad facilities permitted.

Thousands of Chinese citizens cheered the departing warriors. Demonstrators at the railroad tracks carried banners inscribed: "Resist the invaders!" and "Hold Shanghai at all costs!"

Dispatches from various parts of China indicated a tremendous public sentiment in favor of a formal declaration of hostilities. From Canton came word that the authorities were sending a squadron of airplanes to Nanking "for war against Japan."

An aviator who flew in from Chengchow said he saw a long column of soldiers en route to Nanking. In Nanking itself the whole atmosphere has changed. The fight put up by the Chinese at Chapei brought about an overwhelming sentiment for war—and a week ago there was nothing here except defeatism.

Before leaving the capital, Marshal Chiang dispatched a telegram to military commanders throughout the country, urging them to prepare China "to fight for her national existence."

Marshal Chiang offered his services "as a citizen to fight side by side with you all" in a telegram to the government.

"The more we endure, the more aggressive the Japanese become," his message said. "The fate of China is at stake, and any one with any sense of patriotism can no longer endure the Japanese oppression.

"Now is the time for all the governments of China and all the armies to defend the national honor and the very existence of the Chinese people.

"We must prepare to fight and make sacrifices rather than yield to the Japanese, who have destroyed the peace of the world.

"I have been with you through thick and thin. I am still willing to fight side by side with you all."

January 31, 1932

MUKDEN FORMALLY DECLARES FREEDOM

Jehol and Inner Mongolia Join in New State, Ankuo, With the Japanese Aiding.

PU-YI LIKELY PRESIDENT

Tokyo to Turn Over Railways and Send In 5,000,000 Colonists by 1942.

Special Cable to THE NEW YORK TIMES.

MUKDEN, Feb. 18.—The independence of Manchuria and Inner Mongolia was formally declared today by the new Northeastern Administrative Committee.

The declaration was signed by Tsang Shih-yi, Governor of Mukden; Hsi Hsia, Governor of Kirin; General Ma Chen-shan, who fought the Japanese last Autumn; Chang Ching-hui, Governor of Harbin, and two Mongolian Princes, Ling Sheng and Chi Wang. Tang Yu-lin, Governor of Jehol, also signed, thereby including Jehol within the new State.

A declaration was also issued on the future administrative policy, which denounces the régime of former Marshal Chang Hsiao-liang, while statements are being sent to all Chinese leaders as well as the governments of all foreign countries announcing the absolute independence of the new State, to be known as Ankuo.

The committee pledges its efforts to improve the administration, to wipe out the evils of the old régime and to improve the condition of the common people.

To Keep Open Door.

An exhaustive statement on the foreign policy promises to avoid anti-foreignism and declares an abhorrence of warfare. It also pledges cooperation with the world powers to maintain the open door and the equality of opportunity.

The internal policies, it is announced, are designed to make Manchuria and Mongolia prosperous, to encourage agriculture and industry, to reduce unemployment, to end class wars and to root out communism.

The same committee will meet at Changchun beginning Feb. 21, when government officials will be elected and the committee will automatically dissolve in favor of the government of its own creation.

A high Japanese official said today that the former Emperor of China, Henry Pu-yi, was the most likely choice for the first President.

Japanese Answers Questions.

After the independence proclamation was issued Chang Ching-hui received press correspondents. He was attended by a retinue of secretaries and bodyguards and one Japanese adviser, K. Kowasaki, one-time Consul General at San Francisco.

Mr. Kowasaki several times answered questions addressed to Chang Ching-hui without giving the Manchurian leader time for a translation or a reply, Chang Ching-hui often revealing that he did not understand the program when questions were asked.

The independence proclamation stresses the impossibility of relations with any Chinese government dominated by the Kuomintang. The more flowery portions declare the people desire peace as the hungry wish food and the thirsty water.

Referring to Chang Hsiao-liang's administration, the proclamation declares the people were tortured as with fire, with their tears yet undried and the poisons not yet eliminated.

General Ma Chen-shan has returned to Harbin, but is expected to attend the conference at Changchun on Sunday.

Despite the Japanese claims of the suppression of banditry and the restoration of stability, bandits are becoming stronger in the Kirin-Tunghua Railway zone, where yesterday telephone and telegraph wires were demolished. They were repaired today.

The military admits that yesterday and today Manchurian railways were broken in seventeen places. The bandit soldiers holding the city of Tunghua number 1,800 and another thousand are marching to join them, according to reports by Japanese aerial scouts. Unconfirmed reports say the Japanese army is attacking Tunghua.

The Japanese announce that the soldiers killed in Manchuria between Sept. 18 and Feb. 5 totaled 338, with the wounded numbering 698. Meanwhile, the Japanese military is slowly retiring from Manchuria. A heavy artillery corps sailed from Dairen yesterday, ostensibly for Japan.

Tokyo Holds Up Recognition.

Special Cable to THE NEW YORK TIMES.

TOKYO, Feb. 18.—The Japanese Government is not considering the recognition of the new Manchurian State and will not recognize it until it shows all the attributes of an independent political entity, a Foreign Office spokesman said tonight.

Japan will deal with the new government as she has dealt with every Manchurian Chinese Government in the past, because of her interests, but that is not intended as de facto recognition.

This announcement will disappoint those who had hoped Japan would recognize the new State as quickly as President Roosevelt recognized Panama.

"We are in no hurry," said the spokesman. "We have no canal to build."

Recognition lies within the province of the Foreign Office, which takes a longer view than the army, and evidently means to wait and see the new State show its paces.

The spokesman pointed with pride to the fact that General Ma Chenshan, who recently was Japan's bitter enemy, was participating in the new government, and predicted that even Chang Hsiao-liang would find a place in the autonomous Manchuria.

It remains to be seen whether this remark indicates the possibility Chang may be a candidate for the life Presidency, which still lures Henry Pu-yi.

NEW BATTLE STARTS IN SOUTH MANCHURIA

Chinese and Japanese Begin Fierce Fight Near Changchung, Kirin's Largest City.

PU-YI HEADS ANKUO STATE

Former "Boy Emperor" Is Believed Likely to Take Throne—Will Recognize Foreign Debts.

CHANGCHUN, Manchuria, Saturday, Feb. 20 (P).—A bitter battle raged today between Chinese and Japanese forces at Tunhua. Strategically the most important town in the Province of Kirin, which is now a part of the new federated State of Ankuo (Manchuria), called "the land of peace."

A force of 500 Chinese troops under General Wang Teh-lin, foe of the régime of Hsi Tsia, Kirin's Governor, who was one of the founder of the new state, attacked a small Japanese detachment which has been garrisoned at Tunhua since Feb. 17, when Wang Teh-lin's rebellion began to look dangerous.

Wireless to THE NEW YORK TIMES.

TOKYO, Saturday, Feb. 20.—Continuing with smoothness and celerity the process of State building, the Northeastern Executive Council today unanimously selected Henry Pu-yi as the first chief of the new State of Ankuo. His name, coupled with this announcement is now allowed to appear for the first time in the Japanese newspapers.

While the position offered to the former "boy Emperor" of China is still quasi-republican, all the members of the committee except Chang Ching-hui and Tsang Shih-yi favor the restoration of the imperial régime. Advices reaching official quarters here state that Pu-yi is disinclined to accept any seat lower than a throne.

The inauguration of the new State, the installation of its ruler and the promulgation of its Constitution are now being framed by the committee, over which Chang Ching-hui presides and are scheduled for March 1.

Pu-yi's younger brother and also his wife's younger brother are pupils in the Tokyo Peers School under Japanese names. Pu-yi's latest portrait, with his wife wearing a Japanese kimono, was published in the newspapers here this morning.

A Manchurian central bank is being established by a merger of four of the chief provincial banks. It will be capitalized at $30,000,000 silver

Associated Press Photo.

Henry Pu Yi, who reigned briefly as the Boy Emperor Hsuan Tung in China away back in 1911.

and will have silver bullion covering a note issue of $10,000,000.

The central bank alone will have the right to issue notes. Other banks' note-issuing franchises have been canceled and they have been ordered to redeem their outstanding paper. The step will cause a temporary confusion and some bank failures, but the ultimate result will be stability instead of wildly fluctuating currency backed by nothing.

To Recognize Foreign Debts.

Special Cable to THE NEW YORK TIMES.

SHANGHAI, Feb. 19.—The new Manchurian nation, while it will immediately establish its own customs service and institute a new tariff system applicable to Manchuria's needs, will not attempt to avoid payment of Manchuria's just proportion of China's foreign indebtedness secured by customs revenues. This was learned this afternoon in high Japanese official circles in Shanghai, which further emphasized that Manchuria would fully recompense all foreign creditors of the late Chang Hsiao-liang régime.

Manchuria will also immediately organize its own postal and telegraph system. When the postal service is a going concern Japan plans to abolish her own postoffices now maintained along the South Manchurian Railway as well as at Dairen and Port Arthur. Kwantung leased territory, containing these two cities, will continue to be held by Japan under her lease that expires late this century, but Japan will look to Manchuria as holding sovereign rights there.

It is emphasized that the new Manchurian State will pay British in-

February 19, 1932

vestors in the Peiping-Mukden Railroad a proportionate share of the railway's debt based on the mileage inside Manchuria's borders. Customs payments on China's foreign indebtedness will be based upon the average Manchurian contributions to those payments in the last three or five years.

Japan, it is announced, hopes to assist the new nation in the early codification of its laws and the institution of reliable modernized courts. After these have been founded, it is said, Japan will lead the way in voluntary relinquishment of extra-territoriality in Manchuria. It is emphasized that Japan hopes to assist in the establishment of stability in Manchuria quickly so that foreign capital, particularly American, will look upon Manchuria as a field for profitable investment and great development enterprises. Closing of the Open Door is declared unthinkable and undesirable and Japan hopes that foreign apprehensions on this score may be completely ended.

Now that the Manchuria coup is a fait accompli, at least in Japan's eyes, responsible Japanese have expressed a desire that it be understood abroad that what has been done there is in no sense meant as action against China, but entirely inspired by what Japan considers an urgent national necessity, that is, fortifying her position in Manchuria as a precautionary measure against another life-and-death struggle against Russia.

Favor Changchun as Capital.

Special Cable to THE NEW YORK TIMES.
DAIREN, South Manchuria, Feb. 19.—The founders of the new Manchurian State announce that they favor Changchun for a capital instead of Kirin and will probably announce a definite decision by March 1. This decision was foreshadowed by Japanese officials in Mukden last December, who considered Changchun a most important city in view of the projected extension of the Changchun-Kirin Railway eastward to Korea, where a great seaport was to be founded on the Northern Korean coast.

It is semi-officially announced from Mukden that, pending the establishment of the gold standard, there presumably will be a yen equivalent of stabilized silver currency equivalent to the Chinese dollar. It will be put into circulation by the new National Government. For this purpose a central bank with a paid-up capital of $30,000,000 in silver is being established within which will be included three semi-official banks formerly personally controlled by Chang Hsiao-liang, their confiscated assets being used to assist in bringing the depreciated Manchurian currency up to face value.

A meeting for the election of heads of the new government, originally scheduled to take place in Changchun Feb. 21, has been postponed to Feb. 25.

The new educational head announces that the twenty-six primary schools in Mukden, long closed for lack of funds, will reopen March 1. High schools and universities will follow as soon as faculties can be recruited.

JAPAN SIGNS TREATY WITH MANCHUKUO

Extends Recognition to the New Manchurian State in Accord Concluded at Changchun.

CHINESE OUTBREAK FEARED

Shanghai Holds Troops Ready to Quell Riots—Natives Are Asked to Vow Vengeance.

JAPANESE THERE WARNED

By The Associated Press.
CHANGCHUN, Manchuria, Thursday, Sept. 15.—Japan and the new Manchurian State of Manchukuo entered into a defensive alliance today which also carried with it Japanese recognition of the new government. The protocol was signed at 9:10 A. M (9:10 P. M., Wednesday, Eastern Daylight Time).

This town's single Occidental-style hotel was crowded with Japanese military officials and newspaper men last night, but native Changchun reposed in its usual Oriental calm.

Extraordinary precautions were taken to insure the safety of General Nobuyoshi Muto, special diplomatic representative of Tokyo and commander of the Japanese military forces in Manchuria, the success of which in the field made possible the establishment of the new government in place of the old Chinese Administration. The General signed the treaty for Tokyo, and Cheng Hsiaohsu, Premier of Manchukuo, signed for his government.

Changchun was not dressed up in honor of the ceremony. Neither banners nor posters were displayed. Japanese officials explained that the real celebration was to be held Sunday, the first anniversary of the beginning of the campaign which swept the former Chinese rulers from the region.

The treaty is brief, containing not more than 300 words. To accompany it officials prepared a statement explaining the significance of the document and its implication of Japan's recognition of the Manchukuo régime.

The Tokyo Foreign Office has explained that Japan will undertake internal and external defense of Manchukuo under the pact, that a defensive alliance is set up and that each government guarantees respect for the territorial sovereignty of the other.

The palace of Henry Pu Yi, former boy Emperor of China and now Regent of the new State, was selected for the ceremony.

TRUCE NEUTRALIZES BIG AREA IN CHINA; INVADERS TO LEAVE

Also, the Chinese Agree to Withdraw Below Line Ten Miles North of Peiping.

CIVIL POLICE TO CONTROL

Japanese Will Return to the Great Wall, but Keep Right to Inspect Northern Zone.

POLITICAL ISSUES PUT OFF

Governments Plan to Negotiate Directly as to Manchukuo and Other Problems.

By HALLETT ABEND.
Wireless to THE NEW YORK TIMES.
TANGKU, China, May 31.—A truce formally terminating the Chino-Japanese hostilities in North China was signed at the Japanese barracks in Tangku this morning.

The document, while containing no political provision, consists of harsh military terms imposed by the victor upon the vanquished. All questions relating to Manchukuo, an indemnity and other contentious matters were deferred for direct negotiations between the governments.

The official announcement from Japanese headquarters this afternoon consists of six paragraphs, including five terms. The announcement explained:

"The commander of the Japanese Kwantung troops received formal proposals for a truce from General Hsu Yen-mao, a staff officer of Ho Ying-ching (China's War Minister) at Miyun on May 25. Based on this proposal, Major Gen. Okamura, Vice Chief of Staff of the Kwantung troops, made and signed a truce with Hsiung Ping, a Lieutenant General of the Chinese, today."

Terms of the Armistice.

The terms, as officially worded, follow:

First. The Chinese troops shall all immediately withdraw to the districts south and west of a line connecting Yenchieng, Changping, Kaoling, Shunyi, Tungchow, Sanho, Paoti, Lintingchen, Ningho and Lutai. They shall make no advance over this line nor repeat any provocations.

NEUTRAL ZONE CREATED IN CHINA.

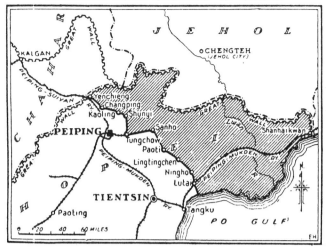

The Chinese agreed, in the armistice with Japan signed yesterday, to withdraw all troops southward from a line through the ten towns indicated. Japan, in turn, promised to send her armies back to the Great Wall, but retained the right to inspect the neutral zone to make sure the truce terms were being observed. The Chinese are to police the neutral area.

Second. The Japanese troops, in order to insure enforcement of No. 1 term, will visit these places occasionally by airplane, or otherwise, and the Chinese authorities shall afford them protection and facilities for inspection.

Third. The Japanese troops, when fully satisfied that the Chinese have carried out No. 1 term, will not continue pursuit across the above line, but will voluntarily withdraw to the Great Wall.

Fourth: Maintenance of peace and order north and east of the line specified in No. 1 term, and south of the Great Wall, shall be carried out by Chinese police authorities.

Fifth. This agreement shall come into force immediately.

The line established by the Japanese is about 250 miles long. To the west it starts at the Great Wall, passes at Tungchow within ten miles of the Peiping walls and then swings northeastward and ends about thirty-five miles north of Tientsin, at Lutai.

The Chinese delegates left Tangku this afternoon, returning to Tientsin. A portion of the Japanese delegation, including Sei-ichiro Nakayama, the Chargé d'Affaires from the Peiping Legation, is also proceding to Tientsin and Peiping this afternoon aboard a Japanese destroyer, with a convoy.

The official Japanese interpretation of the terms of the truce is that the Chinese forces must entirely evacuate the towns listed,

withdrawing to a reasonable distance southward and westward, and leaving the towns to be administered by Chinese civilian police authorities.

This establishes permanent Chinese army defense lines less than ten miles from Peiping in the Tungchow area and relinquishes Chinese military control of Changping, a town of strategic value on the Peiping-Suiyuan Railway near the southern end.

Thus Nankow Pass, through which the railway proceeds to Kalgan, would be an easy conquest for the Japanese troops if they chose to charge breach of faith.

Through train service to Mukden, Manchuria, from Lutai will soon be inaugurated, leaving only about 140 miles of the 1,800-mile Peiping-Mukden line available for Chinese troop movements.

The Chinese continue to hold Tangku, but it would be untenable if hostilities were renewed, since it is within range of Japanese naval guns.

It is anticipated that the Chinese delegates who signed the truce on behalf of the Nanking Government will soon resign.

The highest Japanese authorities admit that the terms of the truce were unmistakably those dictated by the victorious invaders, and no attempts were made to placate the sensibilities of the Chinese delegates. It is significant that the truce fails to mention the future treatment of various renegade Chinese forces now operating in the Lwan River triangle, flying the old five-barred Chinese flag.

Signed Under Japanese Guns.

On arriving at Tangku this morning at 10:40 o'clock this correspondent discovered the tensest conceivable military situation, with

Chinese soldiers posted at least every twenty feet along the railway platform, tracks and streets, supplemented by occasional gray-clad patrols. Their weapons ranged from revolvers, rifles,. Thompson automatics and machine-guns to old-style beheading swords. On the track farthest from the river stood a Chinese armored train, with its guns covering the river. Five tracks toward the river stood a special train of private coaches which arrived yesterday. At bottom of every car's steps were Chinese sentries with drawn revolvers, their fingers at the triggers.

At a distance equivalent to one city block lay two Japanese destroyers, numbered fourteen and sixteen, tied at the docks with everything in readiness for immediate hostalities, the guns and turrets manned.

After following various false trails leading to the China merchants Steamship Building and the Chutal salt offices your correspondent finally located the Chino-Japanese parley inside the Japanese barracks always maintained at Tangku. The premises were newly reinforced with barbed wire and trenches while the tops of the surrounding walls were covered with sandbags. In a semi-circle at one side of the main gate, which fronts on the railway tracks, to the other side was a newly-built concrete blockhouse loopholed for the firing of rifles and machine guns.

Delegates Kept Incommunicado.

Only two Japanese soldiers were in evidence. They were steel-helmeted and fully armed, grimly guarding the gate inside which the Chinese and Japanese delegates were then awaiting the final drafting of the truce terms.

It was evident that the details had been agreed upon days ago and that the drafting and signing was the nearest formality, carried out under the muzzles of the guns on the Japanese destroyers less than a hundred yards away.

The Japanese, evidently grimly determined to impose humiliations upon the vanquished, sent a Major General to countersign with a Chinese Lieutenant General and also arranged the venue forcing the Chinese delegates to leave their luxurious special trains and proceed afoot across the narrow, dusty roadway to enter the Japanese barracks to sign the final terms of capitulation.

While the formal signing was taking place the windows of the special trains showed the faces of scores of disconsolate, depressed Chinese secretaries, translators and other minor officials.

All of the Chinese guards and officials were exceedingly friendly on learning the identity of this correspondent and freely permitted the photographing of the guards and armored train, but when the camera was pointed toward the Japanese destroyers a dock sentry gesticulated and shouted angrily.

The precautions against communicating with any member of the Japanese delegation were stringent, but an arrangement to see General Hsiung Ping was easily made. The sentries at the gate of the Japanese barracks had been instructed from headquarters of the Kwantung army not to permit any outsider to see the delegates until the truce was signed and they were not allowed even to carry a visit-

ing card to Mr. Nakayama, the diplomatic representative. Their instructions specified that the Japanese delegates be kept incommunicado until after the truce was signed.

Wide Repercussion Expected.
Wireless to THE NEW YORK TIMES.

TIENTSIN, Thursday, June 1.— The Chinese domestic repercussions to yesterday's signing of a Japanese truce at Tangku probably are incalculable in extent. For months every governmental and Kuomintang agency has been shouting slogans of resistance—"to the last man and last bullet"—whereby enormous contributions have been obtained from the Chinese people, at home as well as abroad, but today the truce emphatically signifies the surrender of at least 25,000 Chinese troops against an invasion of at most, 25,000 Japanese.

Especially noteworthy is the utter absence of any Chinese airplanes from the skies of Northern China, although for more than a year the public has contributed large sums for the purchase of aircraft. Chiang Kai-shek and at least one Szechuan leader possess dozens of airplanes which have been ruthlessly used in anti-Communist and other civil wars in the last twenty months, but thus far not a single Chinese plane has attempted to combat the Japanese fliers except more than a year ago, when Robert Short, an American flier, was shot down and killed near Soochow fighting for the Chinese.

Conspicuously silent in a present emergency are the Northern students, who, seventeen months ago, paralyzed railway traffic between Peiping and Tientsin by lying on the tracks and demanding special trains for Nankin in order to urge anti-Japanese resistance.

Despite the defeat imposed by the superior Japanese military and mechanical equipment, China might today present a defeated but dauntless front against an enemy superiorly equipped. Instead, Feng Yu-hsiang has raised the banner of revolt within a 100 miles of the Japanese troops he is denouncing, Nanking and Canton applauding his action, while the Cantonese armies advance into the Yangtse Valley. Simultaneously devasting civil wars are racing in Szechuan, Sinkiang and other portions of the remote hinterland.

Move "Purely Military."
By The Associated Press.

NANKING, China, May 31.—The Chino-Japanese agreement signed today at Tangku is "designed to give a breathing space to the sorely tired troops and the distressed population of North China," Premier Wang Ching-wei explained.

He declared the agreement was "purely military and does not affect the nation's territorial rights or international position."

Wireless to THE NEW YORK TIMES.

MUKDEN, Manchuria, Thursday, June 1.—The Kwantung Army today announced it was ready for peace or war. It is continuing to mass troops in North China. A new unit has arrived at Yutien, sixty miles north of Tientsin.

June 1, 1933

SWEEPING CHANGE IN CHINA FORECAST

Japanese Army Chief in North Doubts Autonomous Regime Will Be Successful.

HONAN PROVINCE SOUGHT

Tokyo Believes Shantung Will Join Independent District After Shensi Acts.

Special Cable to THE NEW YORK TIMES.

TIENTSIN, Dec. 14.—The autonomous reform council, which probably will formally assume office on Monday or Tuesday, will not bring to North China sorely needed peace and prosperity and a cessation of uncertainty as to its future status. This was made plain today when General Hayao Tada, commander of the Japanese forces here, forecast Japanese dissatisfaction with the personnel and policies of the probable administration of the new régime and said frankly that if the pessimistic expectations were fulfilled radical changes would become necessary.

General Tada prefaced his revelation of the Japanese Army's disillusionment with a long résumé of Chinese history, concluding with the charge that the republican revolution had made the conditions of the common people worse. He broadly hinted that the national provincial leaders were engrossed in self-aggrandizement and were callous to the masses' fate. He expounded the Japanese conviction that the only way to prevent China from becoming communistic was to ameliorate the conditions of China's hundreds of millions.

Doubts Sung Régime's Success.

When asked if he believed General Sung Cheh-yuan and the projected autonomous council would better conditions for the people of Hopei and Chahar Provinces, General Tada hesitated and then replied:

"It is very doubtful, and if they could do so it would take a very long time. Sung Cheh-yuan and the other members of the council, after all, are from the ranks of the men who have long woefully misgoverned the country. If they prove their unfitness, the urgent task of sweeping changes will naturally become necessary."

After voicing the first Japanese official intimation of dissatisfaction with the conditions which Japan is charged with having created in North China, General Tada also expressed doubts as to whether General Han Fu-chu would become an ideal administrator in Japanese eyes for Shantung Province. He said the agreement barring Nanking's armies from North China did not apply to Shantung so he believes Governor Han will not attempt an autonomy movement until certain he will be protected from a punitive expedition from Nanking Government armies.

Spread of Autonomy Seen.

If an excellent government is established in Hopei and Chahar General Tada said wider and wider areas will seek adhesion to obtain the benefits of autonomy.

He denied direct knowledge of the beginning of a northward movement of Japanese troops from Shanhaikwan but believed it possible "because the reported northward movements of Chiang Kai-shek's troops, which caused the Japanese army mobilization along the Great Wall, apparently were grossly exaggerated."

Military trains are still held on Japanese orders on sidetracks in Tientsin, Fengtai and Tangshan but the prospects of the Japanese army moving southward, are daily more remote. The holding up of scores of coaches and many locomotives is seriously impairing traffic.

Foreign and Chinese employes of the Peiping-Shanhaikwan Railway gloomily expect to lose their positions within a few months. They expect the autonomous council will assume operation of the railway, employing Japanese advisors and ousting all employes who are suspected of anti-Japanese sympathies.

Defends Troop Increases.

By The Associated Press.

TIENTSIN, Dec. 14. — A Japanese army spokesman said tonight there was no reason for other countries to object to the strengthening of the Japanese garrison in North China "in view of Japan's special position in this area."

He said he was confident the Japanese Government would approve the increase in forces and that such an increase was not in violation of the protocol ending the Boxer rebellion.

Foreign observers estimated that 3,000 Japanese troops were along the Peiping-Shanhaikwan Railway and 7,000 along the Great Wall.

December 15, 1935

CHIANG KAI-SHEK IS PRISONER OF MUTINOUS SHENSI TROOPS, DEMANDING WAR ON JAPAN

Names Leader for Armies in Field—New Risings Feared —Students Plead for War.

By HALLETT ABEND
Wireless to THE NEW YORK TIMES.

SHANGHAI, Sunday, Dec. 13.—Generalissimo Chiang Kai-shek has been seized by General Chang Hsueh-liang in Shensi Province in an effort to force the Nanking Government to declare war against Japan.

General Chang, former Manchurian commander, guaranteed the life of the generalissimo in a telegram to military leaders throughout China. The telegram also carried these demands:

1. An immediate declaration of war against Japan.

2. A pledge by the Nanking government to recover all lost territories, including Manchuria.

3. Reorganization of the Kuomintang [Nationalist party] to readmit Communists to membership on the basis existing before the anti-Communist purge began in 1927.

Seizure Follows Mutiny

The arrest of Generalissimo Chiang followed a mutiny yesterday at Sian, the capital of Shensi Province. Part of the former Manchurian forces commanded by General Chang Hsueh-liang and part of the Shensi provincial troops commanded by General Yang Fu-cheng mutinied and presented demands for immediate cooperation with the Chinese Communists and military action to stop Japan's encroachments on China's territorial and administrative integrity.

Following the mutiny General Chang, his executive officers and General Yang sent an urgent telegram to the Executive Yuan at Nanking advocating cooperation with the Communists and formal approval of a policy of armed resistance to Japan.

When the mutiny started the generalissimo was resting at the hot springs twenty miles from Sian. When informed of the turmoil in the provincial capital he disregarded personal danger and hastened there, hoping to regain control.

Nanking Acts Swiftly

The central government moved swiftly to cope with what was admitted to be a large-scale revolt. A joint all-night meeting of the standing committee of the Central Executive Committee and the Political Council in Nanking decided on four important measures:

First—The Executive Yuan, with Finance Minister H. H. Kung as vice chairman, received full responsibility during the detention of the chairman, Generalissimo Chiang.

Second—The standing committee of the National Military Council was increased to include General Ho Ying-ching, the War Minister; General Chen Chien, the chief of staff, and Generals Li Lih-chun, Chu Pei-teh and Tang Sheng-chih and Admiral Chen Shao-kwan, the Navy Minister.

Third—Responsibility for the conduct of affairs of the National

73

Military Council, of which Generalissimo Chiang is chairman, was given to General Feng Yu-hsiang, the vice chairman, and the other members.

Fourth—Movement of the armies in the field was entrusted to the command of General Ho Ying-ching.

General Chang Hsueh-liang was dismissed from all government and military posts. Punishment by the National Military Council was recommended. The council was instructed to assume command over General Chang's forces as soon as possible.

The first intimation of trouble came yesterday morning when telegraph lines to Shensi were interrupted. It was later learned that General Chang himself had led the former Manchurian armies in revolt.

In the afternoon General Chang issued a circular telegram advocating the overthrow of the central government and adding, "I am making a last effort to persuade the generalissimo to change his policies and meanwhile am detaining him."

The order issued by the national government says in part:

"According to reports, General Chang Hsueh-liang has revolted. This is a very painful thing. This official since his assumption of office has not behaved very well, but the central government did its very best to give him every chance to improve his conduct, hoping that in the future he would render effective service to the State.

"At this critical time, when foreign aggression is menacing the nation and when the anti-Communist campaign was about to be successfully completed, Chang Hsueh-liang has misled his troops, thereby abusing his military power and also advocating injurious principles.

"Since he was entrusted with heavy responsibility his action is as bad as those of any bandit chief, for he disobeys the law and ruins discipline."

The order closes with a declaration that the former Manchurian leader must be punished.

Blow to Suiyuan Drive

This sensational revolt, accompanied by the capture of Generalissimo Chiang, who besides being Commander-in-Chief of China's armed forces is virtual Premier by the fact of his chairmanship of the executive yuan, will cripple the government's Suiyuan campaign and also will probably lead to the immediate revival of the activities of individuals and organizations favoring stronger anti-Japanese policies.

All eyes at present are turned toward the south since Generals Li Tsung-jen and Pai Chung-hsi, the Kwangsi leaders, openly declared in September's settlement of last Summer's Southwest revolt that they considered the settlement only

a truce and would wait and see what policies Generalissimo Chiang adopted before making any fresh move.

For many months a dangerous situation existed in Shensi, where General Chang's troops had been fraternizing with Communist armies. General Chang's former Manchurian troops, about 120,000 strong, had been exiled from their native land since September, 1931. Since then they have been bitterly anti-Japanese and were ready listeners when Communists began propaganda in favor of war against Japan.

Apparently the mutiny was as orderly as such a movement can be, because the telegrams from Sian declared there was no looting and made no reference to loss of life. If no violence occurred there probably was a settlement through negotiation and persuasion.

Many divisions of Generalissimo Chiang's own army are in Shensi, whither they were sent to assist in the anti-Communist campaign. Many more are eastward across the Yellow River in Shansi, whither they were sent since the beginning of the Suiyuan disturbances.

Train traffic into Shensi over the Lunghai line, the only railway, has been interrupted at Tungkwan, a strategic pass at the Honan-Shensi border.

Finance Minister H. H. Kung and Mrs. Chiang Kai-shek, both of whom have been undergoing medical treatment in Shanghai, departed for Nanking at midnight on a heavily guarded train. All the important members of the Central Government are flocking to the capital to assist in meeting the crisis.

Not since the Japanese attack on Shanghai almost five years ago has the Chinese Government faced such peril. Generalissimo Chiang's personal power and forceful personality have been the main adhesive force holding discordant elements and leaders to a semblance of unity.

If he is long detained or if his life is sacrificed, it is feared that chaos will ensue and China will find herself facing a recurrence of the conditions existing a decade ago before the Nationalist triumphs.

Japanese sources seek to minimize the anti-Japanese character of the mutiny, declaring the mutineers objected to an order to move into Fukien Province, whither part of General Chang's forces were reported sent recently when the extent of their fraternization with Communists was discovered.

Peiping Students Urge War

Wireless to THE NEW YORK TIMES.

PEIPING, Dec. 12.—Another dangerous anti-Japanese student demonstration occurred in Peiping this afternoon when 2,000 students, including 300 girls, seized control of part of Peihai Park formerly part of the "Forbidden City."

The students attempted a parade in the morning, distributing handbills and shouting anti-Japanese

FIGURES IN LATEST CHINESE AFFAIR

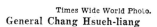

Times Wide World Photo.
General Chang Hsueh-liang

Times Wide World Photo.
General Chiang Kai-shek

slogans, but were peaceably dispersed. Late in the afternoon they gathered in Peihai Park, entering in small groups. Suddenly they unfurled anti-Japanese banners and began speeches urging war on Japan.

General Sung Cheh-yuan, head of the Hopei-Chahar Political Council, immediately sent 100 special military guards to aid the police and the meeting was dispersed without violence at 6 o'clock.

Meanwhile students from Tsinghua University, which is supported by American Boxer funds, and from Yenching University, which is supported by American missions, marched upon the city but the gates were closed. They returned to their campuses where they met and voted formal demands, including the breaking of diplomatic relations with Japan, the sending of General Sung Cheh-yuan's army to assist in the campaign against Manchukuoans and Mongols in Suiyuan and Chahar, the abolition of Yin Ju-keng's independent East Hopei régime, opposition to Japan's imperialism and the recovery of Manchuria.

Denjiro Kato, first secretary of the Japanese Embassy, called on General Sung at 7 P. M. and made

a harshly-worded protest, demanding suppression of student agitation.

Troops Try to Free Chiang

TOKYO, Sunday, Dec. 13.—Troops that remained loyal to Generalissimo Chiang Kai-shek are fighting to free him from arrest at the headquarters of General Chang Hsueh-liang, according to reports of the Domei news agency from Shanghai.

General Chang sent a telegram to Nanking at midnight guaranteeing the safety of the generalissimo. He is believed to command a large force because communications have been interrupted. Although Generalissimo Chiang commanded extensive forces in Shensi Province the rebels have control of all traffic and communications.

Japanese observers believe the rebellion is connected with the accord between General Chang Hsueh-liang and the leaders in Canton and Kwangsi Province. General Chang's first telegram, addressed to the military commanders in Kwangtung and Kwangsi Provinces, embodied their demands for war against Japan and a general reconstruction of the Nanking government.

GEN. CHIANG FREED; ARRIVES IN NANKING; EX-CAPTOR ON WAY

TERMS ARE SECRET

But Chang Is Held to Be Virtual Captive Going to 'Face the Music.'

DICTATOR SHOWS STRAIN

Japan Hears He Will Give Up Posts While Gen. Chang Goes Into Permanent Exile.

CHINA ACCLAIMS RELEASE

Generalissimo Carried Through Streets of Capital — Wild Celebrations Staged.

By HALLETT ABEND

SHANGHAI, Saturday, Dec. 26.— At what appeared the gloomiest hour of China's greatest crisis in years, Generalissimo Chiang Kai-shek, her dictator, was freed from captivity on Christmas afternoon with dramatic suddenness.

More than that, the tables were turned, and his captor, General Chang Hsueh-liang, former "young marshal" of Manchuria, surrendered himself to the generalissimo, whom he had held immured in Sian, Shensi Province, for thirteen days.

This startling revelation was made to the Chinese nation in an announcement by the Nanking government that the dictator and his "prisoner" had flown together to Loyang, on the way to the capital, accompanied by Mrs. Chiang and W. H. Donald, Australian adviser to the generalissimo.

[Generalissimo Chiang arrived in Nanking shortly after noon Saturday and was carried through the streets in a tumultuous ovation.]

The first reports that the "young marshal" had left Sian with his former captive were for a time generally discredited as too fantastic until they were officially confirmed at midnight.

It still remains to be explained how matters were arranged with Yang Fu-cheng, the other rebel commander at Sian, to permit Chang Hsueh-liang to make a safe exit. Conjecture is rife as to whether General Chang may eventually retain command of his former Manchurian armies or another will succeed him.

It was War Minister Ho Ying-chin's Christmas Eve ultimatum, telegraphed to Chang Hsueh-liang, that resulted in the "young marshal's" suddenly releasing the generalissimo and thereby probably averting a civil war of the first magnitude.

Chiang Kai-shek's first action upon alighting from his airplane at Loyang at 5:30 P. M. was to issue an order for the government troops on all the Shensi fronts to begin withdrawing immediately, thereby negativing the chances of accidental clashes. This action immediately gave rise to many and varying versions of supposed compromise agreements, but it is stated by high government officials in Shanghai that there will be no announcement by the generalissimo until he reaches Nanking today.

Chiang Kai-shek and his party flew from Sian to Loyang with a guard of three new government bombers, among those given to the generalissimo by public subscription on his fiftieth birthday anniversary, Oct. 30. The other government officials who had been imprisoned in Sian since Dec. 12 are to fly to Loyang today.

It is understood that long conversations between the "young marshal" and the generalissimo finally established an amicable settlement upon the basis that Chang Hsueh-liang's rash coup had been a result of a misunderstanding. Chang Hsueh-liang said he had believed Chiang Kai-shek intended to dismiss him from all offices and disband his entire armies. He asserted that only after he had read Chiang Kai-shek's personal diary, which he seized at the time of the imprisonment, did he realize that the generalissimo had not harbored hostile intentions.

Another ground for misunderstanding was said to be that Chang Hsueh-liang had not been receiving money from the government for support of his armies, but discussion and search of the records proved that remittances had been made regularly and a subordinate official of Chiang Hsueh-liang's staff had retained millions. This man is now under arrest in Sian.

Japanese military and naval spokesmen here expressed gratification today over Chiang Kai-shek's liberation, declaring that Japan rejoiced with China in the dramatic ending of the long-drawn-out crisis. Some Japanese voiced fears that a possible compromise had been reached upon the question of anti-Japanism and pro-communism, but a semi-official Japanese news agency in dispatches from Nanking negatived these conjectures. It quoted an official spokesman of the Chinese Government as saying China's foreign policies were remaining unchanged.

Japanese sources forecast banishment of Chang Hsueh-liang and drastic reorganization of that portion of his armies that does not join the Communists, but these forecasts are believed to be only conjectures.

100,000 Welcome Chiang

Wireless to THE NEW YORK TIMES.

NANKING, Saturday, Dec. 26.— Generalissimo Chiang Kai-shek arrived here by plane at 12:20 P. M., today. He was greeted by Lin Sen, chairman of the national government; virtually all other prominent leaders, and a colorful throng of almost 100,000, and was triumphantly carried through beflagged and bannered streets amid the din of bursting firecrackers.

Chiang Kai-shek, upon alighting from his airplane at Loyang, showed alarming evidences of the great strain he had endured. He refused to make a statement of any kind and immediately retired for a long rest.

Reports widely credited in Nanking say the generalissimo's release was unconditional. Authorities here agree that yesterday's surprise developments probably averted civil war.

The government's attitude toward General Chang Hsueh-liang is likely to be based entirely upon Chiang Kai-shek's personal report and recommendation. It is possible that the fact of the generalissimo's release before serious hostilities were begun may mitigate the rigor of such punishment as is decided to be appropriate.

Chiang's Wife With Him

By The Associated Press.

NANKING, Saturday, Dec. 26.— Generalissimo Chiang Kai-shek arrived here accompanied by his wife and by W. H. Donald, Australian adviser to the Nanking government, whose spectacular flight to deal directly with General Chang Hsueh-liang, the generalissimo's captor, at Sian was followed quickly by today's dramatic release.

Chang Hsueh-liang did not arrive here with Chiang Kai-shek, although he had been reported earlier accompanying the released leader to the capital.

The government, in a statement, had said Chang Hsueh-liang was "coming to Nanking in person to face the music—to give himself up to the national authorities, if necessary, but preferably to state clearly and openly his case to the leaders of the country."

The Foreign Office asserted that the generalissimo's release was unconditional, that no political terms had been made with his captor, who was declared to have "seen the error of his ways."

Denying reports that a huge financial settlement had been made by the generalissimo's relatives and the government with General Chang prior to the release, a spokesman of the Executive Council said:

"Not one cent of cash was involved other than the expenses of emissaries to and from Sian."

Many Nanking authorities gave major credit for the generalissimo's release to skillful negotiations carried out at Sian by Mrs. Chiang and her brother, T. V. Soong, former Finance Minister.

When the devoted wife of the Nanking leader flew to Sian two days ago to plead directly with the rebel chieftain, she had to disregard the advice of many high officials, who insisted that any negotiated settlement with General Chang would weaken the government's authority.

Tokyo Reports Conditions

Wireless to THE NEW YORK TIMES.

TOKYO, Saturday, Dec. 26. — Apart from financial considerations still undisclosed, the following three conditions are attached to Chiang Kai-shek's release, according to Japanese reports from China.

1. Chang Hsueh-liang will assume responsibility for the incident, abandon his command and go abroad permanently.

2. Chiang Kai-shek will voluntarily resign from the Nanking government [it is assumed his retirement would be only temporary].

3. Chang Hsueh-liang's army will not be disbanded or reorganized but will come under Governor Yen Hsi-shan of Shansi, representing the central military committee.

The latter condition confirms impressions that the affair was organized by Chang Hsueh-liang's young officers, who forced him to seize the dictator when they were threatened by reorganization and transfer to other districts.

December 26, 1936

CHINA AND JAPAN NEAR CLIMAX OF THEIR DRAMA

Crisis Which Is Seen Approaching Has Been Prepared by Events Since Tokyo Embarked on Her Adventure

By STERLING FISHER Jr.

The kidnapping of Chiang Kai-shek—dictator over nearly twice as many people as Stalin, Hitler and Mussolini combined—has provided a new climax for one of the great dramas of history.

It is the drama of Japan's expansion upon a vast continent and a drama that, even after five years' action, still moves with unabated pace toward an unknown end.

It is a drama directly affecting nearly one-fifth of the world's land area and one-third of all its people—the 90,000,000 of Japan, 165,000,-000 of Russia and 450,000,000 of China.

It springs from an urge of such force in Japanese minds and hearts that it has twice surged over resistance at home in mutinies and assassinations, threatening revolution.

Now, at this acute moment, is a time to pause and look back for a clearer view of the completed acts of this amazing drama—and especially of the act that began five years ago.

I—MANCHUKUO

The present chain of events began on the night of Sept. 18, 1931 at 10:30 o'clock, when a bomb exploded under the rails of the Japanese-owned South Manchuria Railway, just outside Mukden. Some skeptics, even Japanese, will tell you the bomb may have been put there by Japanese, or may not have been there at all.

Japanese troops said they saw 300 Chinese soldiers do the bombing, and added that the Chinese opened fire on them. So, at 11:20 P. M., indicating some anticipation of such a crisis, the Japanese stormed the Peitaying barracks, at 1:25 A. M. on the 19th occupied them, and an hour and a half later had seized the great modern city of Mukden. A few hours later they were in Tungtaying and

Kuanchengtze and that afternoon were in distant Nanling. It was the beginning of Manchukuo-Japanese dominance over Manchuria. Chiang Kai-sek, he who last week sat brooding and saying nothing in the hands of Chang Hsueh-liang, threatened war but made no move to wage it.

A New Emperor

Within three months virtually all Manchuria was under control. And by January 7, 1932, a "spontaneous" movement for independence among the Manchurians resulted in the announcement that they would form a new nation, comprising the three northeastern provinces of China and Jehol, in Inner Mongolia.

The Japanese found the ideal leader of this new nation in the person of Henry Pu-Yi, last of the Manchu emperors of China, who was discovered, most fortunately, living in the Japanese concession in Tientsin on land owned by Japan's garrison. He was hurried to Manchuria and on March 1, 1932, became Regent of Manchukuo, to be elevated a year later to the rank of Emperor Kangte I.

Meanwhile, anger rose among the Chinese. In every city of China, in Cuba, in Europe, in the Philippines, they raised money, demanded war and boycotted Japanese goods. In some Chinese cities they attacked, wounded and killed Japanese citizens.

Shanghai Incident

At Shanghai, the great metropolis of the East, such attacks, leaving dead two Japanese priests and several women, brought on a "war within a war" as a side-show to Manchuria. A small Japanese landing party clashed with Chinese patrols on Jan. 29. China's hot-blooded southern Nineteenth Route Army fought grimly and Japan sent over division after division. Still, Chiang kept most of his troops out,

pursuing his policy of unifying China before risking its existence in open war. At last, on March 3, the Chinese forces yielded, a twenty-mile neutral zone was created, the Shanghai war was over, and attention again turned to the North.

Closing thus the first chapter of her expansion, Japan embarked in Manchukuo on programs of intrialization, railroad and city building and immigration. On March 11, 1935, she finally crowded out the remaining Russian influence by buying the Chinese Eastern Railway. But long before that, below the Great Wall, she embarked upon the next scene in the drama.

II—BEYOND MANCHUKUO

The Chinese troops had attacked along the Great Wall; in retaliation Japanese armies marched through the gates and southward until they were almost in sight of the old capital of Peiping and the port of Tientsin. To save those cities Chiang ordered his officials to agree to the Japanese terms—all of them. This they did in the famous Tangku truce of May 31, 1933.

By that truce China agreed to withdraw most of her troops from the northern provinces, to grant Japan railway and aerial concessions, and, most important, to create a "neutral" zone, extending from just north of the two cities to the Great Wall.

Still Chiang refused to consider war; still Chinese in China and throughout the world denounced him as a traitor.

For the next two years the Japanese in China were occupied in consolidating their position in Manchukuo, and in perfecting plans for the setting up of a new automonous State consisting of the five North China provinces—Hopei, Chahar, Shantung, Shensi and Suiyuan. But they had reckoned without several of the Chinese leaders and at the last moment found unexpected resistance. Two of the provinces yielded and a "Hopei-Chahar Autonomous Council" was set up. But the five-province plan had to be held in abeyance.

In Inner Mongolia

Then early this year the autonomy drive turned westward toward Inner Mongolia.

But China had at last become well aware of the meaning of this activity. At last she offered serious resistance by force in Suiyuan.

China was aroused equally, if not more, by a new form of Japanese

drive—a diplomatic drive. This drive found its opportunity arising from the terroristic murders by Chinese in the Summer and Fall of this year of seven Japanese in widely separated parts of China.

In reparation, Tokyo's Ambassador demanded (1) suppression of all anti-Japanese movements, (2) revision of text books to eliminate anti-Japanese teachings, (3) cooperation against communism, (4) special aerial rights, (5) brigading of Japanese with Chinese troops.

Because Mongol and Manchukuoan troops invaded Suiyuan while these negotiations were in progress, China's Foreign Minister bluntly refused early this month to have anything further to do with the Japanese envoy. This was the position when the kidnapping of Chiang changed the whole aspect of the situation.

III—CHINA RESISTS

It remains now to examine what lies behind the final beginning of Chiang's open resistance, both diplomatic and military, to the Japanese. That resistance has come from the fruition of the generalissimo's policy of putting unity before all else. What, then, was he doing in those years from Sept. 18, 1931, to the present?

First, he was using judicious mixtures of money and arms to weld China into a whole. Secondly, he was striving desperately to give her a semblance of a modern army and air force.

His unification campaign was directed mainly against the Communists. A map of China of 1931 shows Red splotches scattered by scores at random; a map of today shows Red areas reduced to three, all around and in Shensi, where Chiang himself was captured.

In armament Chiang has given China nearly 850 modern fighting planes, with pilots trained by Italians and Americans; he has put the finest modern weapons into the hands of hundreds of thousands of his men, and had German officers teach them their use

Despite all these improvements, Chiang was not fully ready to go to war. He needed to wait another two years or three. But Japanese diplomatic drives, autonomy drives and military pressure have not allowed him to bide his time. When he was seized by his subordinate, Chang Hsueh-liang, he was in the north for the purpose of further unifying his front in his attempt to ring down the curtain upon the Japanese epic of expansion.

TEN VIVID SCENES IN FIVE YEARS OF THE CHINESE DRAMA

LEGEND:
- JAPANESE TERRITORY
- COMMUNIST AREAS OF CHINA
- CHAHAR AND HOPEI AUTONOMOUS AREAS
- TERRITORY UNDER NANKING CONTROL
- AREAS UNDER LOCAL WAR LORDS

Times Wide World and Black Star Photos.

Events in a people's war-torn existence—(1) September, 1931, Japan starts conquest of Manchuria, (2) January, 1932, Japanese bombard Shanghai, (3) January, 1933, Japan takes Jehol, (4) March, 1933, Emperor Kangte crowned in Hsinking, (5) May, 1933, Japan and China sign Tangku truce, (6) 1934, Chiang Kai-shek campaigns against Communists, capturing their capital, (7) December, 1935, Japan makes Hopei and Chahar autonomous, (8) July, 1936, Chiang Kai-shek and southern leaders come to terms, (9) November and December, 1936, China beats back Mongol and Manchukuoan irregulars in Suiyuan, (10) December, 1936, Chiang Kai-shek seized in Sian, Shensi. A Chinese soldier (below) and Japanese soldier (above) are shown.

December 20, 1936

JAPANESE BATTLE CHINESE AT PEIPING

Troops Use Machine Guns and Artillery Before 5-Hour Conflict Is Halted

MANY REPORTED KILLED

Tokyo Says Nanking Forces Opened Attack While Night Manoeuvres Were Staged

By HALLETT ABEND

Wireless to THE NEW YORK TIMES.

SHANGHAI, Thursday, July 8.— A threat to "wipe out" Chinese troops unless they agreed to disarm immediately terminated at 10 o'clock this morning a sanguinary five-hour clash between the Chinese and a Japanese force on the outskirts of Peiping. The Chinese retreated across the Yingting River under machine-gun and rifle fire, suffering heavy losses. Scores of bodies were reported floating downstream.

Unless the Peiping-Fengtai situation is entirely adjusted, meeting all Japanese requirements, within a few hours, there is every probability that the Japanese Army will launch a determined effort at military occupation of Peiping. This information was given out by the Japanese Embassy in Shanghai at 12:30 this afternoon after receiving detailed reports from Japanese Army headquarters in Tientsin.

Cessation of the fighting, which occurred at 10 A. M., was under a one-hour armistice with the understanding that the Japanese Army would renew the attack upon the Chinese forces unless by 11 o'clock the Chinese had entirely withdrawn beyond the west bank of the river.

The fighting started last night and was resumed with greater intensity this morning. At 8:30 A. M. Japanese troops occupied the town of Liuwangkiao. They stormed Lukuochiao and began disarming Chinese soldiers there. Japanese reinforcements were rushed from Fentai and from the legation guard in Peiping.

The threat that brought the clash to an abrupt end came from the Japanese Army headquarters in Tientsin. It was telegraphed to General Seeichi Kita, the military attaché in Shanghai.

The first machine-gun outburst came from a pillbox near the village of Yuwanmiao. The first outburst of fire killed one Japanese officer, several non-commissioned officers and privates and wounded one Japanese officer and nearly a score of privates. Hastily entrenching themselves the manoeuvring Japanese forces communicated with the Japanese legation guard at Peiping. At 1 A. M. Lieut. Col. Morita, accompanied by Foreign Affairs Commissioner Li Lien-yu of the Hopei-Chahar political council and Magistrate Wang Ling-chi, started for the scene of action intending to attempt mediation.

Before they arrived the Chinese lines, reenforced by a detachment of field artillery, reopened machine-gun and artillery fire and the Japanese began returning the fire. The battle involving several thousand forces began shortly before 5:30 o'clock. General Feng Chian, commanding the Thirty-seventh Division of General Sung Cheh-yuan's forces, fruitlessly attempted mediation. The latter hoisted a white flag and announced the neutrality of his army.

The outbreak of Chino-Japanese hostilities in the Peiping-Tientsin area occasions no surprise, for tension there has been growing during the last three months. Many experienced observers realize that the situation in North China is alarmingly akin to that existing in Manchuria before the Mukden incident of September, 1931.

During the last week Chinese police in Peiping arrested nearly 300 Chinese Korean agitators and armed plainclothes conspirators upon charges of attempting to foment disorders, and various units of the Twenty-ninth Route Army, loyal to General Sun Cheh-yuan, have been slowly converging upon Peiping's outskirts in order to be able to act quickly in case of the anticipated uprising of elements suspected of favoring a greater degree of Japanese domination.

The situation inside Peiping's walls lately has approached martial law. Police and military patrols have been doubled and pedestrians after dark are stopped and searched at the point of a bayonet. Various Chinese officials have been openly charging that plentiful evidence has been secured that Japanese army agents are scattering liberal bribes among unscrupulous agitators with the aim of creating disturbances affording grounds for active intervention.

General Sung Cheh-yuan's continued absence from Peiping, now prolonged to two months on various pretexts such as ill-health and sweeping the tombs of his ancestors, has aroused intense Japanese irritation because during General Sung's absence all attempts to conclude various projects of economic cooperation are at a complete standstill. Nanking's authority in North China has been steadily increasing during the last half-year and many high Japanese officials have been complaining that the announced Japanese policy has been misunderstood as a sign of weakness.

July 8, 1937

POWERFUL FORCES ARE PUSHING JAPAN FORWARD

By HANSON W. BALDWIN

Political and Economic Considerations Support Military Drive in China

As the fires of another undeclared war flamed around Peiping and Tientsin last week the scope of immediate Japanese ambitions in Asia became more clearly defined.

There has never been any doubt as to Japan's eventual intentions in the East. Countless announcements of Japanese statesmen, emphasized by the well-nigh inexorable course of Japanese policy, have indicated that Japan will be content with nothing less than hegemony of the Western Pacific and of the Continent of Asia. The virtual annexation by Japan of the Chinese Provinces of Manchuria and Jehol were a means to that end; the present fighting in Hopeh is another chapter in a history of conquest, for hegemony in Asia means economic and physical domination of a large part of China.

Resistance Increases

This program of encroachment has met with increasing, though sporadic, resistance, from a China more unified today (although still far from being a "nation" in the Western sense) under Chiang Kai-shek than at any time since the fall of the Manchu dynasty.

Japan, for a brief time after the conquest of Manchukuo and Jehol was content with consolidating her hold on those provinces and strengthening her Asian front against her natural enemy, Soviet Russia. But not for long. Both military and economic reasons, as well as political ambitions, dictated a further extension of her sovereignty through the five northern provinces of China—Hopeh, in which Peiping and Tientsin are situated; Chahar, to the north, between Mongolia and Manchukuo; Suiyuan, Shansi and Shantung. Her influence was gradually extended by peaceful penetration, backed by force, through Hopeh Province and Chahar until twenty-two eastern Hopeh counties became virtually a Japanese protectorate, and Hopeh and Chahar became ostensibly, at least, semi-autonomous States.

Japanese Aims

The genesis of the present fighting does not make it clear whether the latest bloody war in Asia is an attempt to extend by force through out the five provinces Japanese influence which had been checkmated by growing Chinese unity and increasing anti-Japanese spirit. Yet the progress of the fighting, confined almost entirely to Northern Hopeh and without serious attempts, so far, by the Japanese to penetrate further to the south, does indicate that Japan may be content for the present to extend her sovereignty in one form or another to the Peiping-Tientsin area and perhaps to part of Chahar and to increase her influence and strengthen her position throughout the rest of those two provinces.

But the danger of the situation—for the Chinese—lies in its very irregularity. For if the Chinese resistance stiffens too greatly—particularly, if Nanking sends material aid to the Twenty-ninth Army, which has borne the brunt of the fighting so far—the Japanese, angered by resistance, may decide to chasten China so thoroughly that she will not soon forget, and they may, in that case, revise their aims to include the five northern provinces and nearly all of the Chinese territory to the valley of the Yellow River.

Prestige Involved

In either case the Japanese have pat reasons for their actions. One is a psychological and morale reason. Japan is a pushing, "have-not" nation, committed by tradition and policy to a policy of expansion and predominance in Asia. Her people have that strange Oriental pride, often so inexplicable to Westerners, which does not permit the "loss of face" and which requires death before dishonor, war before compromise.

It is because Japan feels that it is absolutely vital to her national honor to maintain her prestige and position in Asia as the dominant nation that she visits such terrible retribution upon the Chinese who provoke or oppose her. Her nationals in China and her troops in North China are in somewhat the same position as a garrison in a hostile land. Hence, Japan feels that for her own safety, as well as for her honor and to impress upon the Chinese her dominance in Asia, even the slightest aggressive act (or opposition to Japanese aims) must be met with crushing force.

Economic Compulsion

The second and perhaps the predominant reason for Japanese expansion in North China is economic. The pressure of population in Japan (almost 1,000,000 a year increase, with a 70,000,000 population) and the need for raw materials were Japan's stock reasons for her establishment of the puppet State of Manchukuo, carved out of the Chinese Provinces of Manchuria and Jehol.

But Manchukuo has not been to date the economic "gold mine" that was so glowingly predicted. It has siphoned money from Japan (some fourteen hundred million yen have been invested in Manchukuo since 1931), and although the investment is beginning to show some returns, soy beans and kaolaing, the start of a new chemical industry, a one and a half million ton increase in the production of iron ore, a couple of million tons increase in coal production and a doubling of the oil shale output are in no sense sufficient to satisfy Japan's peoples or industries. The increased value of Japanese exports to the United States in 1935 as compared to 1934 was alone

WHERE FAR-EAST ARMIES COLLIDE

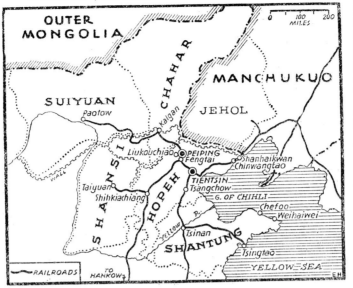

about 30 per cent the value of all the exports to Manchukuo. And Manchukuo has not proved the "colony" that Japan hoped; only 243,868 Japanese are resident there.

And so Japan has looked for richer lands to conquer, and North China, economically, offers a fertile field for her industrialists, as well as a market for Japanese manufactured products and an advanced base for exploitation of the huge Chinese market proper. Shansi Province alone contains 51 per cent of all the coal mines of China and in the northern provinces lie great cotton fields which produce cotton indispensable for the Japanese textile industry and for the manufacture of powder. China is the world's third cotton-producing country; the bulk of her export of this commodity went to Japan until China imposed restrictions on such exports. That fact, incidentally, might be one of the many reasons for the present Japanese aggression in the northern provinces.

From a military point of view the northern provinces are particularly important, primarily to cover the left flank of Japan's "Asiatic front." With the provinces of Suiyuan and Chahar as buffers against Sovietized Mongolia, the Japanese strategic position on the mainland would be considerably stronger than it now is. Suiyuan and Chahar are partly included in the Gobi Desert. The terrain is difficult, with few transportation or communication facilities, and under the Rising Sun of Japan a comparatively few well-trained, well-drilled troops might easily forestall any danger of Russian penetration of the region, and, moreover, could prevent the spread of Communist influence or the use of these areas

as bases for Communist guerrilla armies against Jehol and Manchukuo.

The Shantung Peninsula includes the rich valley of the Yellow River and the important ports of Tsingtao, Chefoo and Weihaiwei, and its possession would consolidate Japanese control of the Gulf of Chihli and the Yellow Sea. Hopeh Province, together with Shantung, and, to a lesser extent, Shansi, are the communication and transportation nerve centres of the north.

Railway Control

Control of the railroads in China means virtual control of the regions they serve. Hence the military importance to Japan of the Peiping-Tientsin area in particular. With that area firmly in her grip, her influence could easily radiate along the rail routes from Peiping northwest to the important city of Kalgan in Chahar (and thence westward to Paotow in Suiyuan) and southwestward along the Peiping-Hankow line to Shihkiachiang, where a spur road leads off to the centre of Shansi Province.

From Tientsin her influence also radiates northeastward along the coast to Chingwangtao and Shanhaikwan, gateway into Manchukuo, and could radiate southward through Tsangchow on the Tsinan-Nanking line to Tsinan and thence eastward to Tsingtao. For some months past Japan has been trying to secure Chinese permission for the construction of an east-west line across Hopeh Province from Tsangchow to Shihkiachiang, which would be of considerable military as well as economic advantage.

Peiping-Tientsin Line

The Peiping-Tientsin line, with

the important junction point at Fengtai, is already virtually in Japanese control, although Chinese troops of the Twenty-ninth Army and other Chinese forces apparently are still in a position, according to latest reports, to threaten that control. Any threat to those communications would be a threat to all of Japan's interests in North China—hence another reason, according to the Japanese view, for aggressive action around Peiping.

The vicinity of the railroad junction of Liukouchiao, south of Peiping, which controls the Peiping-Hankow railroad route into the ancient capital, was, significantly enough, the scene of some of the early fighting in the present conflict. It, too, is essential to Japan, if her domination of the Peiping area is to be complete, and to China, if she is to retain any shred of her sovereignty near there.

Thus extension of Japanese sovereignty over the five Northern Chinese provinces—or over even a part of them— would extend and consolidate the Japanese "Asiatic front," would tend to contain the projecting salient of the Sovietized Outer Mongolia, would further isolate the Soviet Maritime provinces, would further remove the danger of Soviet raids—either over land or in the air—into Manchukuo or other Japanese territory, and would considerably strengthen the Japanese strategic position on the mainland.

Japanese Unity

Such are the reasons—psychological, political, economic and military—for Japan's adventurous excursions into the ancient land of dead dynasties and forgotten glories.

Her latest adventure—prompted largely by the military, upon whom, under the Japanese system of government, there is no ready constitutional check—is probably backed, more or less wholeheartedly, by the great majority of the Japanese people. For the Japanese believe it is their manifest destiny to control the Eastern part of the continent in Asia.

The restraining influence of Japanese liberals (not to be compared in the degree of their liberalism with Western liberals) and the apparently more moderate policy of the Konoye government may cause divisions as to means but never as to the end. And when the guns begin to fire, there is a curious unanimity to which the government tolerates no opposition.

Hence, in the cockpit of Asia, a Japan which is largely united is opposing China which is still politically divided, but which is growing united because of the increasing resentment of its people against the series of Japanese aggressions.

August 1, 1937

Hirota Says Japan Demands China Enter Tokyo-Berlin Pact Against Communism

By HUGH BYAS
Wireless to THE NEW YORK TIMES.

TOKYO, Friday, Aug. 6.—Cooperation against bolshevism, to be effected by China's entering the German-Japanese pact against the Communist International, is a fundamental principle of Japan's policy on China, Foreign Minister Koki Hirota told members of the House here yesterday.

This definition was given extempore in answer to a series of questions, some of which clearly revealed the Japanese psychology in relation to China. Mr. Hirota himself would not claim it is a complete definition, since it omits Japan's demand for economic rights in North China, but it expresses the army's dominant motive, which is to obtain combined action against an extension of Soviet power in Eastern Asia.

Mr. Hirota was summoned by the committee considering the tax increase bill. Reikichi Kita of the Minseito, majority party, had said:

"The fundamental cause of the North China incident is the manner in which the Chinese reject and despise Japan. Unless China is chastised once and for all, there

cannot be a real solution. What is the Foreign Minister's view?"

Mr. Hirota replied:

"I have endeavored to eliminate this Chinese tendency to reject and despise Japan. The so-called Hirota three principles were submitted to China as a fundamental policy. But behind this idea of rejecting and despising Japan are Communism and the Comintern.

"The Sian incident is an illustration of Chinese communism, with Chiang Kai-shek in the center of the picture. But the whole of China is not permeated with anti-Japanism. Some Chinese leaders are willing to listen to Japan.

"Japan needs something from China and China needs something from Japan. My mind is occupied at present by the thought that if China will participate in the Berlin anti-Comintern agreement and communism is driven from the Orient, then the peace of the Far East will be firmly assured."

The Hirota principles emphasized the prevention of bolshevization. This point was also emphasized in seeking an agreement in North China.

August 6, 1937

Japan Prepares to Declare War To Speed Capitulation by Chinese

Pact With Italy Is Expected to Keep British Navy From Protecting Hong Kong Against Strict Blockade—Nanking Official Says Republic Cannot Be Conquered

By HUGH BYAS
Wireless to THE NEW YORK TIMES.

TOKYO, Thursday, Nov. 4.—A vitally important turning point is approaching in Japan's policy. On one hand is the possibility of an early peace; on the other hand is the serious likelihood of an aggravated, extended war with an increased risk of foreign entanglements.

With these alternatives approaching some hopes of peace before the end of the year are again heard in unofficial but well-informed quarters. They may prove to be mere wishful thinking, but one chapter of the war is ending in conditions which on Japan's side offer an opportunity to talk peace.

The factors making for peace are:

1. Japan's material objectives have been almost gained.

2. A long war is not desirable because the Japanese Army does not wish to drain its resources in China while the Soviet Union looms as the ultimate enemy.

3. An atmosphere has been created presenting the United States as a reliable neutral.

Japan will need, perhaps soon, a foreign mutual friend not to mediate but to open the way for a peace conference. When Japan last engaged in a major war that friend

was Theodore Roosevelt. A picture seems to be forming in the Japanese mind in which Franklin D. Roosevelt might acceptably repeat Theodore Roosevelt's role.

The three most striking features in the present situation are the impending establishment of imperial general headquarters, the impending announcement of an Italo-Japanese agreement and the sustained press attacks against Britain. The function of the projected imperial headquarters will be to prosecute the war with utmost vigor, sparing no means to obtain an early, complete victory.

It probably will declare war to tighten the blockade of the Chinese coasts. Foreign supplies are reaching China through Hong Kong which, being a British possession, is exempted from the blockade. A war blockade would involve interference with shipping using Hong Kong and grave friction with Britain. The value of the Italian pact would then be revealed and Premier Benito Mussolini would have an opportunity to cooperate against the spread of communism to China by adopting an attitude which would detain the British fleet in Europe.

Meantime the Italian pact is being heralded by continuous press attacks on Britain. This has been accompanied by an effort to dissociate the United States from the criticisms applied to Britain and to represent Washington as a real neutral. A desire not to burn Japan's bridges to the United States is part of her peace strategy.

Italy Can Block Britain

The Italian agreement's war strategy is directed against Britain as clearly as the German pact is directed against Russia. Mussolini has the power by Mediterranean activities to give the Japanese Navy greater freedom in the Far East, just as the anti-Communist agreement between Japan and Germany reduces the Japanese Army's fears of the Far Eastern Red Army.

The Italian agreement represents a risky departure from Japan's traditional policy. In ordinary times the Japanese press and public would have considered Mussolini's cooperation dearly bought if it made a revival of Anglo-Japanese friendship impossible, but that objection has been killed in advance by press denunciations of British hostility.

Britain and Russia, according to the press chorus—the unanimity of which is too striking to be accidental—are unreservedly assisting China. Britain is held responsible for the Geneva resolution for the Brussels conference; British munitions, it is charged, are being sold to China and British officials in Shanghai are accused of being openly anti-Japanese. Thus the way will be made smooth for the Italian pact at a moment when the new imperial general headquarters may change an incident into a full-fledged war.

The signs pointing to a possible early peace are less definite and can be felt rather than seen in Tokyo's atmosphere. The existing

situation as seen by the General Staff and the Cabinet is as follows:

The only major operation now going on, except the Shansi campaign, which is drawing to a close, is the big push at Shanghai. When that is completed the Chinese will have been driven back from Shanghai. To the Japanese high command Shanghai is only an expensive, unwanted sideshow. Japan did not want a war for Shanghai and if she smashes Nanking's best armies there she will be satisfied with moderate terms in which the other powers with interests at Shanghai can associate themselves.

North China Plan Exceeded

In North China the Japanese armies have more than they originally wanted. Suiyuan and Chahar Provinces have been completely conquered; an independent Mongolian Government has been established and a "corridor" separating China and Manchukuo from the Soviet Union has been created. Within the Great Wall Japanese armies are now near the Yellow River.

Japan's objectives have been attained, so there is a reason to terminate the war if it can be done without losing face. The Foreign Office's position, as officially stated, is that Japan will listen to any direct peace overtures from China.

Chinese Stresses Stand

By HALLETT ABEND
Wireless to THE NEW YORK TIMES.

SHANGHAI, Nov. 3. — "We fear America and Europe take too lightly our repeated declarations that we intend to continue fighting Japan indefinitely and will not accept from her any kind of a dictated peace," said one of the most powerful figures in the Chinese Government in an interview with this writer last night.

"Foreigners probably think our insistence that we intend to fight to the last man is a mere rhetorical flourish. But a common-sense, calm consideration of the situation will show there is nothing else we can do.

"Suppose we decided to negotiate for peace tomorrow—what could we expect? Japan would filch from us five Northern provinces and would force upon us some intolerable status for the whole Shanghai area.

"Some sincere friends of China advise us to sue for peace before the Japanese army advances farther up the Yangtze Delta and in North China, saying we cannot forever oppose our men against mechanical superiority. They warn that the longer we resist the harsher the final terms will be."

The speaker paused, signed a half dozen important-looking documents, lighted a cigarette and reflectively blew several smoke rings toward the ceiling.

"Suppose we stop fighting now," he continued. "Japan doubtless would impose terms forbidding our rearmament. We know she aspires to play the role of great capitalist manufacturer in the Far East and wants to reduce the Chinese people to the role of factory workers, diggers of coal, hewers of wood and drawers of water. We decline.

"China realizes fully that there is no hope of any early military victory on her part, but is firmly convinced that Japan is certain to exhaust herself if we fight long enough. Japan may take Shanghai, even Nanking, but what of it?

"We concede that if Japan launches an onslaught with the full power of her whole army and her whole navy she can take the coastal zone, but will struggle helplessly, as though caught in a morass, if she attempts to advance inland. It would require a dozen tin-hatted Japanese soldiers to sit on the lid in every village if Japan attempts a real conquest of all China.

"So, of course, we are continuing our resistance and will not listen to any peace from Japan or from any one else which would involve our giving away anything."

The government leader then discussed with considerable frankness various aspects of China's financial problems which he admitted were becoming acute as a result of the naval blockade. So far, he said, China has continued to make all interest and amortization payments on the Boxer indemnities and all other foreign loans secured by customs revenue, but he could not commit himself concerning the future.

Customs revenues, he admitted, have fallen off enormously, but he said new means were being devised to accelerate exports despite the blockade. Imports, except those needed for war activities continue to drop, he said, because the people are economizing, their incomes having been reduced.

This tendency, he declared, was healthy in a national sense, tending eventually to give China a favorable trade balance because the people have learned to live entirely upon the country's own products. Such a favorable balance, he stressed, would assist in meeting foreign obligations.

November 4, 1937

JAPANESE THREAT TO NANKING GROWS AS DEFENSES OPEN

Troops Pushing Inland in 3 Columns—Flight to Chungking Is Formally Announced

---

SOOCHOW IS EASILY SEIZED

Foreign Experts Say Clashes Among China's Leaders Are Responsible for Reverses

---

By The Associated Press.

SHANGHAI, Sunday, Nov. 21.—The Japanese drove west to new conquests today following the fall of Soochow, keypoint of China's "Hin-denburg line." The Chinese strove to form a new line to bar the invaders' progress to Nanking, from which the government yesterday formally announced the removal of the capital to Chungking in Szechwan Province.

Foreign military observers, however, expressed doubt that the Chinese would make a determined stand before Nanking. Some predicted the city would be given up after a feeble struggle. In that event, they said, Chinese troops would follow their government into the hinterland.

The new Chinese line, along which 130,000 troops were reported entrenched, stretched from Wusih, twenty-five miles north of Soochow, to Kiangyin, thirty-five miles away on the Yangtze River. Japanese drove toward the line, northwest of Shanghai, from three points.

The Japanese announced that, after a bombardment which lasted throughout the night, their marines had captured the Fushan forts, stronghold on the Yangtze River, thirty-three miles northeast of Soochow.

Farther inland, a column from Changshu was reported to have occupied Anchen, within eight miles of Wusih.

Another column, from Soochow, advanced along a railway to capture Sinan, six miles from Wusih.

Political Friction Reported

Foreign observers believed that political friction and military incompetence were largely responsible for China's reverses. Expressing only praise for the bravery of Chinese troops, foreign military authorities criticized Chinese leaders for their lack of cooperation and the breakdown of supply lines.

It was learned authoritatively that friction between the Nanking government and some Chinese generals concerning troop dispositions caused Chinese forces to be replaced in the Hangchow Bay area the day Japanese units landed there. The new Chinese units wilted before the Japanese march inland, forcing China's withdrawal from Pootung and Hungjao, Shanghai areas that previously had been successfully defended.

Soochow's Fall 'Tragi-Comic'
By HALLETT ABEND
Wireless to THE NEW YORK TIMES.

SHANGHAI, Sunday, Nov. 21.—The capture of the great city of Soochow on Friday was carried out at dawn, when fifteen Japanese infantrymen, headed by a lieutenant and wearing stormhoods partly concealing their faces, marched into the city and hoisted the Rising Sun flag, whereupon thousands of disorganized Chinese troops fled pell-mell from the city without firing a shot, according to official reports received here.

The official Japanese spokesman characterized the capture of Soochow as "the most unusual tragi-comic exploit in the history of modern warfare". He said the capture had surprised the Japanese army as much as it had surprised the Chinese.

"About midnight, from our front lines two scouting parties totaling seven or eight men each began a careful reconnoiter toward Soochow," he declared. "They stealthily followed two large bodies of Chinese troops retreating toward the city. The Soochow gates stood wide open and the Chinese forces marched in and stacked their bayoneted rifles, whereupon fifteen Japanese followed.

Not a Shot Fired

"The Japanese proceeded to the city administration building and, when dawn broke, hoisted the Japanese flag, creating an extraordinary panic among the Chinese forces within the walls, all of whom fled by every available gate, some with and some without arms, and all without firing a shot.

"Those fifteen scouts, without a single man killed or wounded, remained in undisputed possession of Soochow for the next thre hours, until other Japanese forces overtook them."

The spokesman expressed the view that the disorganized troops in Soochow had been so utterly weary from many days of fighting, marching and being subjected to aerial bombing that they probably did not know and did not care what was happening.

The news of the capture of the Soochow-Changshu line, which the Chinese contended they could hold at least six months, has reached Wusih, where, coupled with lootings by mutinous troops, it is said to have caused panic. A general exodus to the west is already reported to have begun.

Foreign military observers at Nanking report to Shanghai that twelve divisions landed at Nanking from river steamers in the last few days are poorly drilled Szechwanese, new conscripts from Yunnan and provincials from Kwangtung. None of these divisions is properly trained and equipped for modern warfare, and the foreign observers believe that flinging these men into the lines east of Nanking will not stiffen Chinese morale and resistance, but may result only in a sacrifice of thousands of lives.

November 21, 1937

JAPAN'S INVASION AIDS REDS IN CHINA

Armed Communists Now Put at 700,000—Organizers Get Free Hand in Country

---

THEIR RANGE NATION-WIDE

Astonishing Forays Are Made Into Regions Occupied by Tokyo Soldiers

---

By HALLETT ABEND

By Air Mail to THE NEW YORK TIMES

SHANGHAI, July 13.—For the last decade one of the principal worries of the Japanese Government has been the possibility of the spread and triumph of communism in China. And now, by her one year of aggressive warfare against China, Japan has done more to spread and popularize communism in this country than the Chinese Communists were able to do in the previous ten years.

When fighting began near Peiping in July of last year the Communist armed forces in China had been reduced to between 80,000 and 100,000 men and the zone of Communist occupation had been restricted to the northern part of Shensi Province and a few counties in the adjoining province of Kansu, an arid area with a very small population.

Today, according to the Japanese, the armed Communists number about 700,000 men, and their forces are widely scattered over the country. Moreover, under the unification compromise that the Kuomintang [major Chinese party] and the Communist party adopted, under pressure of Japanese military aggression, Communist propagandists and organizers are receiving a virtually free hand in all provinces not under Japanese military occupation.

Estimates Red Armies' Strength

According to statistics that the Japanese high command has gathered, the strength of the various Chinese Red armies and their present fields of activities are now as follows:

The old "regulars" of the Communists now consist of sixteen divisions of 8,000 men each, or 120,000 men, located in Shensi and Kansu Provinces and occasionally raiding into Shansi. In addition, this force has ten fresh divisions in reserve, of 10,000 men each, newly armed and trained. These reserves are in Kansu and in Southwestern Suiyuan Provinces. These former

81

regulars also have the organization and direction of 80,000 armed plainclothes men, who continually harry Japanese lines of communication.

Chu Teh is said to direct this whole "parent force," which in the matter of guerrilla activities extends from Suiyuan clear southward into Honan Province and actually administers various "Red areas" within two score miles of Peiping and Tientsin, in Hopeh Province. Chu Teh's force has two air bases—one at Lanchow, the capital of Kansu, and one at Sian, the capital of Shensi. Each of his divisions is credited with possessing eight tanks and eight field pieces—equipment entirely inadequate for positional warfare, but ample for mobile tactics.

In Kwangsi Province, in the South, because of the opposition of General Li Tsung-jen, there are no Communist forces, but in the far South, in Yunnan and in Kwangtung, there are scattered a total of fourteen Red divisions, each of 8,000 men. These are under the general command of Yeh Chien-ying of the Thirteenth Route Army.

Report Ho Lung Is Active

The Japanese contend that what is known as the National Government's Fourth Route Army, stationed in Central China, is really the augmented and reorganized Communist Eleventh Route Army. They assert that its six divisions of 10,000 men each are scattered over Fukien, Kwangsi and Chekiang Provinces, under the command of the famous Ho Lung, and that mobile bands of these troops raid behind the Japanese lines in Kiangsu and Anhwei Provinces.

In Szechwan, Hunan and Hupeh there are what the Japanese describe as "five more Red units, of 40,000 men each," which are said to be rapidly extending their spheres of influence and working at the arming and organization of the peasants.

The sources of this Japanese information are, of course, carefully guarded, but from the concern that the foregoing statistics have aroused it is obvious that the Japanese believe the figures to be approximately correct.

Hit the Peiping Region

In the Peiping-Tientsin area the Reds have been making some astonishing forays. Late in June, for instance, a considerable body of these Chinese Communist troops raided across the Peiping-Suiyuan Railways, and actually briefly occupied Changping, a large town between Peiping and Nankow. The city surrendered without resistance; the police were disarmed and many joined the Reds, and all money in the Bank of East Hopeh was seized.

A few days later the Reds raided Kupeikow and destroyed one of the bridges on the new Peiping-Jehol Railway, which the Japanese have constructed since last October. They then moved eastward into the "demilitarized" zone of East Hopeh and occupied the towns of Kihsien, Sanho, Yutien and Hsinglung. Early in July the Reds reached Paoti and Tsunhwa. These places are inland and north of Tangku, the port at the mouth of the river below Tientsin.

July 31, 1938

CHINA REDS FIGHT FORCES OF CHIANG

Battle in Kansu Is Reported Following Clashes in Other Joint Defense Areas

'UNITED FRONT' IN DANGER

Gen. Mao Charged Last Month That the Central Authorities Antagonized Communists

Wireless to THE NEW YORK TIMES.
SHANGHAI, Nov. 15—Peiping reports that are received in Shanghai with reserve declare Chinese Communist troops under General Peng Teh-hua exchanged fire with central government troops under General Chu Shao-liang in Eastern Kansu Province.

Japanese sources say that following the encounter the Communists demanded abolition of the dual Kuomintang-Communist administration in Shensi, Kansu, Ningsia and Sinkiang and the turning over of the four provinces to a single Communist administration.

Large increases in Chungking's monthly appropriation to the Communist former Eighth Route Army are also said to have been demanded.

"United Front" in Difficulties

HONG KONG, Nov. 1 (UP) (By Air Mail, Uncensored)—China's 3-year-old "united front" political combination of the Kuomintang [Nationalist party] and the Communist party must undergo a drastic overhauling if it is to be preserved for continued resistance against Japanese aggression, foreign and Chinese political observers in Chungking, the wartime capital, believe.

Although there has been no final break between the parties, friction is increasing and at least twice during the past five months hostilities broke out between contingents of the Communist and central armies.

In Chungking, last month, General Mao Tse-tung, leader of the former Eighth Route Army and now political generalissimo of the border regional government at Yenan, Shensi, charged the central authorities incited trouble between the Communists and the Central army, failing to fulfill promises to establish a democratic form of government in China, and failing to concentrate its energies on resisting Japan and preparing for a strong counter-offensive.

The accusation was published in the Hsin Hua Jih Pao, Communist newspaper at the capital. Within a few hours, government authorities confiscated that issue. The paper was banned.

General Mao accused Central government officials, notably Chang

Yin-wu of Hopeh and Chin Chi-yung of Shantung, of concentrating their energies and fighting power against the Communist armies operating in those two provinces rather than using them against the Japanese.

He referred to the Pingkiang incident, in which Central army officers arrested an officer of the Communist New Fourth Route Army, precipitating fighting between the two groups. The question was not settled for days and antagonism was aroused. The arrest occurred just before the Japanese invasion of North Hunan by way of Pingkiang, and according to reports was settled amicably only because of the Japanese threat.

General Mao also referred to the North Shensi incident which occurred early this Summer when Chinese Communist and Central Army forces fought a three-day battle for possession of a county while Japanese forces were less than 100 miles away. The affair was settled when General Chiang Ting-wen, Governor of Shensi, ordered both groups to leave the district. Three days later, the Central Army reoccupied the area.

General Mao warned that the Communists would "retaliate with similar weapons" if forced to do so. He closed the interview with an appeal for unity, political cooperation, and democracy.

"The people are ready for democracy," he said. "We have [in the border area] one of the best-administered and most efficient governments in China. It is democratic.

"To resist, the people must have something to fight for, something to unite them. The time of political tutelage is over. The people must have their own government. All parties in China must exist side by side and cooperate."

Foreign observers believe the fault lies equally with both parties. The Communists have taken advantage of the "war of resistance" to spread their doctrines of land distribution, abolition of taxes and interest on debts, and the establishment of democracy in North China. The Kuomintang claims this is in violation of the Communist pact with the Central Government. They fear any growth of a popular mass movement that might threaten the power of the Kuomintang.

The Communists believe that many of the leaders of the Kuomintang are more interested in preserving their power than in saving China from dismemberment. If this is not true, they argue, why does not the government convoke the National Peoples Assembly and place the government on a constitutional basis? Why does not the Kuomintang grant political sovereignty to the people similar to that which was "proved successful" in the border area?

Between these two extremist groups is a powerful combination led by Mme. Chiang Kai-shek, Dr. Sun Fo, president of the legislative Yuan; General Pai Chung-hsi and Colonel J. L. Huang which has a liberal viewpoint and wants to see cooperation between the two parties. But their power is offset to a great extent by the Kuomintang group headed by Chen Li-fu, Minister of Education; General Kang Tse, Dr. Chu Chia-hua, secretary-general of the party, and General Cheng Chen, who are outspoken in their criticism of the Communists.

Kang Tse, the "Mussolini" of the San Min Chu Yi Youth Corps, is attempting to build a youth movement to combat the Yenan group. During a recent visit to a girls' training camp he discovered Communist literature in the library. He ordered it confiscated. The girls appealed to Mme. Chiang, who ordered it replaced for "reference."

Early this summer, the government closed all Communist book shops and printing establishments with the exception of those at Chungking. Kuomintang leaders said the move was aimed only at shops that were sending out propaganda without authorization from Yenan and not at the Communist party.

A few weeks later, secret resolutions were drawn up by the powerful anti-Communist military and political group, demanding that the Kuomintang be established as the sole political party in China, all others be completely disbanded, the border government to be abolished and the Eighth Route Army to be incorporated as the Eighteenth Army Corps under the central army. Government officials deny that any of the resolutions, with the exception of the dissolution of the Eighth Route Army, were adopted.

Communist circles, including General Mao, contend they were secretly adopted but have not been enforced as yet.

November 16, 1939

CHINA SEES MENACE IN SOVIET ADVANCE

Aid Is Welcome, but Control of Sinkiang Causes Chungking to Become Apprehensive

AIR BASES ARE STRATEGIC

Revolutionary Technique Not Preached, but Shift in Scene Could Portend Disaster

By F. TILLMAN DURDIN
Special Correspondence, THE NEW YORK TIMES.
CHUNGKING, China, Nov. 30— In the process of helping China fight the Japanese, Russia has greatly expanded the territorial and military range of her penetration in China's Northwest.

This expansion has occurred in a region where Chinese Communists have long been entrenched and where they rule an area as large as an average-sized American State.

For Chinese who think of China's future in terms of independence of Moscow the strong position of both the Russian and the Chinese Communists is cause for deepest apprehension. It is realized that the Chinese Communists and the agencies of the Russian State are at present powerful factors in China's resistance against Japan. It is hoped that the Soviet Union will maintain them in this role and that history will record no change in policy of these forces by which they will become subversive of Chinese independence and sovereignty.

The Chinese Northwest is commonly thought of as taking in the Provinces of Shensi, Suiyuan Kansu, Chinghai, Ninghsia and Sinkiang, with a combined population of between 20,000,000 and 25,000,000.

Russian Influence Is Old

Russia's influence in this territory began in Sinkiang, westernmost and largest Chinese province, and goes back to the beginning of the modern era. The earliest treaties China signed with a Western power were agreements between Peking and Moscow over the boundaries of Sinkiang and over Czarist Russian trading privileges in the province.

Shortly after the Bolshevist revolution China signed a treaty with Moscow giving Russia the right to have consulates at Urumchi, Kashgar, Inin, Tarbagatai and Altai.

Real Soviet dominance over Sinkiang, however, dates from 1931, when the Soviets concluded a treaty with the semi-independent Chinese warlord of the province. The treaty permitted Russia to establish commercial agencies in Tihua, the capital, and in Kashgar, Inin and Tarbagatai, and in general provided for the development of Sinkiang economic life with the use of Russian equipment and experts.

Soviet influence was further strengthened in 1934 when General Sheng Shih-tsai, the present Pacification Commissioner, emerged in control of Sinkiang after a period of civil war.

Aided by refugee Chinese troops from Manchuria, who had been allowed by the Soviets to make their way through Siberia to Sinkiang after the Japanese conquest of the Northeastern Chinese provinces, General Sheng cooperated with the Russians. Penetration as a result of his policy and the Chinese Central Government's rapprochement with and dependence upon Russia during the war with Japan has been such that the Soviets now dominate most of Sinkiang almost as completely as they dominate Outer Mongolia, another section of Asia nominally a part of China.

Russian advisers are in evidence in almost every activity of the provincial government. The provincial army has been built up by Russian officers and equipped with Russian armaments. The air force is composed of Russian planes, its native pilots trained by Russian instructors.

Russia maintains garrisons of Soviet troops in probably a half dozen or more of the strategic Sinkiang cities. This is consistently denied in Chinese and Russian quarters, but foreign sources in Lanchow, Kansu capital, and Sining, Chinghai capital, insist that it is true.

Indeed, Russian troops have been in Sinkiang for several years. Despite sensational Japanese claims, they probably do not exceed a few thousand at each garrisoned city. However, they could be increased from the Turk-Sib Railway in a few days.

Control Is Indirect

Russia, of course, does not directly rule Sinkiang. Control is exercised to the end that administration is in accordance with Russian wishes. In many phases of provincial life, organization parallels that in the U. S. S. R.

Tight control of political activity and thought is maintained through policing agencies officered by Chinese educated in Moscow and organized along the lines of the NKVD. The Kuomintang is permitted, but the dominant political group is the provincial "Anti-Imperialist party," which is an instrument of Soviet influence in all walks of life.

The few independent, first-hand reports obtainable from Sinkiang indicate that free speech is permitted only in so far as it is not anti-Russian and not outside the line of Soviet policy. Political espionage abounds. The mails and press are closely censored and communication with the rest of China is rigidly supervised.

The link-up of the political machinery in Sinkiang and in Moscow is shown by the fact that purges of deviationists in Russia are accompanied by parallel clean-ups in Sinkiang. Trotskyist hunts in Moscow call for Left Opposition searches in Tihua. When Henry G. Yagoda was shot in Moscow the head of the Bureau of Public Safety in Tihua was likewise executed. He was Yagoda's man.

Sinkiang is a forbidden land to all but approved Soviet Russians and Chinese. The Chinese Government's control is only nominal, and Chungking knows only in a general way what is going on in the province. General Sheng functions with only a remote obligation of responsibility to Chungking.

All travel into Sinkiang from the rest of China is through the famous Baboon Pass on the Kansu border. Even Chinese going in are closely watched, and no non-Russian foreigner has entered Sinkiang in several years. None is likely to without the approval of Moscow or the Russian diplomatic agent in Lanchow.

When asked for a Sinkiang visa the Chungking Government confesses, in embarrassment, that a visa can be granted only if the applicant can obtain a permit from the Soviet Embassy for travel through Russia. The latter is never given in cases where passage through Sinkiang is planned.

Russian hegemony over Sinkiang has brought the territory into the Soviet economic orbit. Said to be rich in iron, saltpeter, gypsum, salt, gold, coal, oil—how rich probably only the Russians know—the province sends what quantities of these items are produced almost entirely to Russia. The foreign trade of the 3,000,000 Sinkiang natives—Chinese, Turkis, Mongols, Chinese Moslems Kazaks, Uzbeks—is chiefly with Russia.

Notable Progress Made

Hand in hand with the large measure of Russian control in Sinkiang have gone notable material progress and political modernization. Roads, small factories, arsenals and power plants have been built, cities improved. A provincial assembly advises the government and the large number of different races send delegates to province-wide conferences. Modern sports have been introduced.

While the Soviets have long been expanding their influence in Sinkiang, Russian penetration farther into China from that province is a development born of the Chino-Japanese war.

Russian agreements with China to provide the latter with aviators, airplanes and general war supplies in return for Chinese wool, wood oil, pig bristles, tea, pig intestines and camel wool called for the development of communications from Siberia through China's Northwest and the establishment of air bases.

The Northwest highway was constructed. It is, at least from the Siberian border to Lanchow, virtually a Russian road. Russian trucks, driven by Russian army men, often carrying Russians for service as fliers in China or as advisers with the Chinese Army, monopolize its 1,500-mile way. Along it, from the Russian border all the way into Shensi, hostels have been erected for the use of the Russians. These places are staffed with Russian-speaking personnel and serve Russian-style food. From the Shensi border westward on the road, signs are in Russian and Chinese.

Export agents who handle China's bartered exports to Russia are numerous at chief cities along the northwest route. Lanchow, in Kansu, is the main center for both commercial and aviation activity by the Russians, and by special arrangement with the Chinese Government the Russians maintain there a diplomatic agent.

In connection with the aviation help to China, the Russians, in co-operation with the Chinese, have built large air bases at Lanchow, Ansi, Hami, Tihua and Ili. At each of these Russian personnel totals from 20 to 300 men.

The Lanchow base has been the northwest headquarters of the Chinese Air Force.

The Russian section of the Chinese Air Force operates under its own command and almost independently of the Chinese command, excepting the Russians who have volunteered for service with the Chinese. These men occupy a status similar to that of a Chinese flier.

The string of Russian air bases, fully equipped to repair and otherwise service planes, stemming out from a big Soviet aviation center at Alma Ata, just inside the Russian border from Sinkiang, constitutes a spearhead of immense power. Russian wings could dominate China's entire northwest from these bases.

Near to Communist Base

Russian Communists along the Russo-Chinese Northwest road skirt within a few-score miles of the Chinese Communist Northwest base, the capital of which is Yenan, Shensi. By agreement with the Chinese Government, the Northwest Communist region, which takes in eighteen hsien [fourth-class towns] with a population of 1,500,000 in Shensi, Kansu and Ninghsia, enjoys a special administration.

The chairman of the so-called Shen-Kan-Ning Border Government is a Kuomintang man, but the actual chief administrator is the vice chairman, a Communist. Within this area the Chinese Communists have instituted widespread reforms and have concentrated the manifold activities of the Communist party headquarters.

The taxation burden has been lifted on the farmers, income tax made the chief source of revenue, village and district elections begun and many other steps toward democracy taken.

At Yenan, until recently, was located the famous Kang Ta, or Anti-Japanese University (now moved into Shansi), which trained men and women for participation in the unique type of guerrilla warfare that the Communists have developed in North China. At Yenan also are the Lu Hsun Art Academy, hospitals for the Communist Eighth Route Army, a medical school and many another institutions connected with Communist party and anti-Japanese activity.

Potent military agency of the Communist base at Yenan is the Eighth Route Army, whose more than 100,000 regulars and many hundreds of thousands of cooperating partisan fighters are locked in the anti-Japanese struggle in North and Eastern Shansi, most of Hopei, some of Chahar and a large part of Shantung. Technically a part of the Chinese national armies and partially supported from Chungking, the Eighth Route Army nevertheless is ultimately under the control of Yenan.

It is evident that both the Russian and Chinese Communists are strongly placed in the Northwest and in a position to co-operate militarily as well as politically if occasion demands.

Yet, on the part of neither is there at present any activity looking toward expansion of territorial spheres or promotion into political control of their ideology in areas outside their present centers. No agents of communism, Stalin vintage, either Russian or Chinese, work the Northwest exhorting the masses to rise up and establish a Marxian system of government.

Even in Sinkiang, the Russians have not attempted communization. Elsewhere in the Northwest, planned political activity by Russians is non-existent. Russian advisers with the Chinese Army all over China, aviation men, truck men and commercial agents stick to their various technical assignments and leave politics pretty much alone.

The immediate Chinese Communist party political program has been the achievement of a bourgeois democracy in China based on the principles of Dr. Sun Yat-sen. So far there is no open indication that this program is to be revised as a result of Moscow's rift with the democracies and rapproachement with fascism.

Since the start of the Japanese war, efforts of the Chinese Communists all over China have been concentrated on working toward democratic aims through liberal-leftists "united front" groups and by means of books, pamphlets and newspapers. Neither in the North-west nor elsewhere has there been organization of the workers or peasants on a revolutionary basis.

The methods and spirit of anti-Japanese resistance and national rejuvenation evolved at Yenan have impressed all progressive Chinese profoundly, and have made a particular appeal to youth. It is natural, therefore, that in the Northwest and throughout China the influence of the Shen-Kan-Ning should be extensive. Thousands of students have flocked to Yenan institutions. Left-wing intellectuals of all nationalities have extolled the merits of the Chinese Communist party.

Some Reprisals Provoked

Reaction against this wide influence has been especially severe in the Northwest where the threat to their class and economic dominance has impelled the Kuomintang and army leaders, the gentry, merchants, bankers and bureaucrats to bitter reprisals. In Shensi, especially in Sian, in Kansu, Suiyuan and Ninghsia, in districts outside the Yenan area, Communists do well to venture about and remain alive.

Sympathizers are constantly arrested, often tortured, sometimes shot. Sian authorities make every effort to prevent students from the rest of China from going through the city up to Yenan. In the war zones antagonism of the Kuomintang armies against the Eighth Route often flames into open attack.

Between the Russians along the Northwest Road and the Chinese Reds there is little direct contact. Nevertheless, Chinese Communists from Yenan do, from time to time, travel the Russian route on Russian trucks on trips to and from Moscow or Sinkiang.

While neither the Chinese nor the Russian Communists are at the moment trying to communize Northwest China, the potent position which agencies of the Soviet State have come to occupy there, viewed in the light of the entrenched position of the Chinese Reds, is causing profound concern to many Chinese.

Even those who would normally be friendly to Russia do not look without apprehension on a situation which—if the demands of Russian foreign policy dictated—could be almost overnight turned into complete political control of the Northwest.

Yet non-Communist Chinese, from General Chiang Kai-shek down realize that they must depend on Russia for continued help against the Japanese. They must trust and hope that Joseph Stalin will continue to think that Russia's best interests are served by the maintenance of a sovereign Chinese State serving as a buffer between Russia and Japan.

This trust and hope carries with it no illusions, however. Non-Communist Chinese, looking at Poland and Finland, do not for a moment doubt that if Mr. Stalin suddenly felt the interests of the Russian State — perhaps to be promoted through an anti-British or anti-American deal with the Japanese— were to be served by consolidating political control over the Northwest he would hasten to do so. And they know that he has, through the instrumentalities of his entrenched position in Sinkiang, the Russian road through the Northwest, the string of air bases down to Lanchow, and the Chinese Communist party, the potentialities for taking over.

CHIANG URGES U. S. TO GIVE QUICK AID

Chinese Generalissimo Says It Is Also Russia's Duty to Help Against Japan

HE WARNS ON INDO-CHINA

Third Anniversary of the War Today Finds Invaders Far From Conquering China

By F. TILLMAN DURDIN
Wireless to THE NEW YORK TIMES.

CHUNGKING, China, July 6— China's war position, domestically and internationally, was appraised today in statements by the nation's leaders, issued to mark the end of the third year of hostilities with Japan.

The statements express the determination to continue the fight to the end despite the grave adversities represented by the recent Japanese capture of the important transport center of Ichang and the closing of the Indo-China border and reflect a stanch belief in ultimate victory.

The United States and the Soviet Union were singled out for special reference in the day's most important message from Generalissimo Chiang Kai-shek, addressed to "friendly nations. General Chiang pointed out that the United States and Russia, because they were not yet involved in the war in Europe, were at liberty to exert themselves in China's favor and in opposition to Japan.

Sees Duty to Aid China

"Such action, I believe, is not only the bounden duty but also the responsibility and right of those two countries. * * * If America and the Soviet can speedily take adequate steps to provide China with material assistance there would be little doubt of an early clarification and stabilization of Pacific affairs such as would not by any means benefit China alone.

The Generalissimo solemnly reiterated China's determination to continue resistance "until the enemy has entirely cast off its aggressive policy and withdrawn its forces from our soil."

He urged the powers to meet "bullying Japan's threats" to Indo-China, Netherlands Indies and Burma with discernment and resolution because Japan "is powerless to make war on any third nation."

He virtually warned that China would take military action in Indo-China if Japan attacked there with the declaration:

"China will not hesitate to oppose with force any future aggressive acts by the Japanese in Indo-China or other Asiatic areas both with the view of our own security and in pursuance of our consistent policy of working against aggression."

He said "unthinkably grave" consequences would follow if Japan's threats to Indo-China, Netherlands Indies and Burma were treated with indifference and tolerance by nations friendly to China. He ended with an appeal for the organization of a strong system of collective security among the world's nations.

The soundness of China's financial outlook was stressed in a statement by Finance Minister H. H. Kung. He declared the tax burden had not increased, that China's credit was still sound, that foreign exchange was still available for legitimate needs and that the bank-note issue, though increased, was still inadequate to meet the demand.

There was little in the way of official observances scheduled for tomorrow to mark the third anniversary of the war that has cost China more than 2,000,000 military casualties, a third of her territory and incalculable civilian and material losses. It is anticipated the Japanese will again bomb Chungking and a general exodus to the country is expected.

July 7, 1940

CHIANG AND COMMUNISTS SHELVE FIGHT

By HALLETT ABEND
Special to THE NEW YORK TIMES.

WASHINGTON, March 15 — The latest dispute and open hostilities between the Chinese Government armies and those of the Chinese Communists will probably serve to clear the air. They are expected to result in a renewed stiffening of Chinese resistance against Japan, instead of leading to disruption, civil war and a collapse of China's hard-won unity.

Although much bitterness has been aroused, and although the killed and wounded in both forces were numerous when the recent clashes occurred, today both the Chungking Government and the leaders of the Communists, who have their own regime with headquarters at Yenan, in Shensi Province, are working for harmony. The Chinese are intellectually too agile not to realize that civil disturbance at this time would only play into the hands of Japan, their common enemy, and might even

January 2, 1940

result in a sharp reduction of necessary outside assistance from the United States, Great Britain and Russia.

History Repeats Itself

The origins of the recent quarrel are little different than those that caused General Chiang Kai-shek to break with the Chinese Communists fourteen years ago. Fundamentally, the Kuomintang party, which is the official party of the Chungking government, can never make up its differences with the Chinese Communist party. Their united front against Japan has been, since the Summer of 1937, what is domestically recognized as nothing more than a truce.

If China wins the war against Japan, the two parties will automatically renew their struggle for control of the country. This struggle may well lead to a renewal of active warfare of the kind the Generalissimo waged against the Communists off and on from 1927 until after he was kidnapped and held by them at Sian in December, 1936.

It was at Sian that he became convinced he could count upon them in a struggle against Japan. The truce reached there, however, did not mean a political or military compromise between the Kuomintang and the Communists.

The so-called Chinese Communists are not, properly speaking, Communists at all. Their political, social and economic and agrarian programs are not like any combination of such programs that Soviet Russia ever tried from the earliest days of Lenin's ascendancy to Joseph Stalin's one-man rule of today. The Chinese Communists aim primarily at a beneficent revision of the Chinese system of land tenure and share-cropping. They oppose the system of usury, which keeps the peasants virtually serfs. They want a rather socialistic democracy. Their program has been well likened to the liberal program of the agrarian policy of Bulgaria.

The Kuomintang party, on the other hand, has forgotten all its promises made to the peasants fifteen years ago, and fears that the Communist party may eventually become a truly peasants' party and succeed to control of the government.

But the Chinese Communist party, although it does not advocate any form of Russian communism, is nevertheless closely tied to Moscow through its leaders. These leaders take their political orders from Moscow.

This is one reason Chiang Kai-shek fought against them so long and probably deeply distrusts them to this day. After all, no head of any government would willingly tolerate the existence of an opposition political party that maintained its own standing army and took orders on domestic and international policies from the capital of another country.

The recent "mutiny" of the Communist Fourth Route Army and the hostilities that resulted when General Chiang ordered them to be disarmed had strange origins. One of these origins was a mistake of judgment in Chungking, when the Fourth Route Army was permitted to enter the provinces of Kiangsu, Chekiang and Anhui.

These are among China's richest provinces. Shanghai and Nanking are in Kiangsu. Hangchow is in Chekiang, a province that produces much silk, tea and bamboo. Anhui is on the Yangtze River, just above Nanking, and is rich in agriculture and mining.

When the Fourth Route Army entered these provinces to carry on guerrilla warfare behind the Japanese front lines it seems to have broken the promise not to carry on Communist propaganda among the peasants. Soon what are called "partisan groups" began to appear in the villages and small towns. These partisans were anti-Japanese and adopted guerrilla activities, but they were also anti-Kuomintang and began chasing out the magistrates appointed from Chungking.

Attempted Removal

In other words, the Chinese Communists were getting a strong political foothold in three provinces whose control will be vital to General Chiang if or when the Japanese are ever driven out of the country. So, of course, he ordered them to move toward the northwest, toward Communist-held territory. Equally, of course, they demurred and delayed; and when he sent Chungking forces to disarm them, of course they fought.

How strong, militarily, are the Chinese Communists today? Actually, nobody knows, not even Chungking. Estimates of their armies in their own northwest zone of administration run all the way from 70,000 to about 120,000 men. But there are also the "partisans" and the armed guerrillas to consider. Most of these are peasants. They number, roughly, between 1,500,000 and 2,000,000 good fighters, mostly without uniforms.

In the fight against the Japanese they support the Chungking government loyally. But if it came to a fight between the Communists and the Kuomintang, the majority would be likely to side with the Communists, although, if the issue were complicated, the anti-Japanese faction, continuing to resist the alien invaders, would receive overwhelming support.

Decision Lies With Others

Unhappily, the renewal and continuance of a truce and of true cooperation between Chungking's armies and those of the Chinese Communists will probably not depend entirely upon decisions made by the leaders of the various Chinese factions. Decisions made in Washington, in London and particularly in Moscow may be of vital importance, or if Britain is "made groggy" by the blows of Reichsfuehrer Hitler's anticipated Spring offensive, this too may bear upon what happens in China's hinterland.

It is felt in some quarters that if American or British aid to China should slacken, a small group of "appeasers" in Chungking might move for a negotiated peace with Japan and for Japanese aid in defeating the Chinese Communists. It is also held by some observers that if Mr. Stalin really wants a nonaggression pact, or even an alliance with Japan, he may briefly augment his assistance to Chungking, because it would give him more bargaining strength if he chose to offer Japan a complete cessation of such aid.

On the other hand, these observers say, if the enigma of the Kremlin wants Japan's downfall, he may continue and greatly increase his aid to China.

Wait Upon Germany

In any event, Mr. Stalin's ultimate attitude toward both Japan and China will probably not be determined until there is some fairly definite indication of Germany's ultimate chances for victory, stalemate or defeat.

One opinion held is that one of the best guarantees of an immediate and probably lasting truce between Chungking and the Chinese Communists would be a reaffirmation of American intention to help China against Japan in every way possible. Such a reaffirmation, its proponents say, would be an excellent antidote to Japanese Foreign Minister Yosuke Matsuoka's journey to Moscow and Berlin, would hearten all Chinese factions, and might serve to make the hours Mr. Matsuoka spends in Moscow a sheer waste of time.

March 16, 1941

U. S. ARMY MISSION WILL ASSIST CHINA

Gen. Magruder Is Named by Roosevelt to Head Group of Military Experts

By FRANK L. KLUCKHOHN
Special to THE NEW YORK TIMES.

WASHINGTON, Aug. 26—To China, engaged in a death struggle with Japan, the United States within two weeks will dispatch a military mission to arrange increased lease-lend aid and assist and advise the Chinese Army, President Roosevelt announced today.

The step, which the President declared was taken as part of "the world effort in resistance to movements of conquest by force," represented another blow at Japan. It indicated, at least, that Far Eastern tension had not lessened.

The President declared in a statement on the matter, which he read at his press conference, that "the sending of this mission is in keeping with and is on parallel lines to the sending of a similar mission to the Soviet Union."

"Strategical" Task Seen

Although the President emphasized that the mission was being sent "for the purpose of assisting in carrying out the lease-lend act," the wording of his statement made it possible for the group, to be headed by Brig. Gen. John Magruder, twice military attaché in China, to carry out broader duties. Dr. Hu Shih, the Chinese Ambassador, said following a conference with Mr. Roosevelt at the White House that he understood its task also would be "strategical."

[In Tokyo, the Japanese Government Information Bureau declined to comment on President Roosevelt's announcement of a military mission to Chungking, but a source close to the Foreign Office called it "an unfriendly act," The Associated Press reported.]

The sending of the mission to China and the preparations to send another to Moscow made it apparent that the United States was taking definite steps to play a more active part toward assuring the defeat of the Axis and that Japan's partnership in this totalitarian group was not going to be minimized.

The action made it appear that conversations in Washington and Tokyo looking toward a solution of American-Japanese difficulties had not borne much fruit. When a reporter asked the President if he cared to comment upon a statement Saturday by Admiral Kichisaburo Nomura, Japanese Ambassador, that difficulties must be bridged, Mr. Roosevelt remarked that the Secretary of State had said all there was to say on that.

Secretary of State Cordell Hull said yesterday that the American program of 1937, requiring abandonment of the use of force, must be the basis of any American-Japanese understanding.

PRESIDENT'S STATEMENT

The President's statement follows:

This government is preparing to send a military mission to China. The mission will be sent for the purpose of assisting in carrying out the purposes of the lend-lease act. It is being organized and it will operate under the direction of the Secretary of War. Its chief will be Brig. Gen. John Magruder.

The function of the mission will be to study, in collaboration with the Chinese and other authorities, the military situation in China, the need of the Chinese Government for matériel and materials; to formulate recommendations regarding types and quantities of items needed; to assist in procurement in this country and in delivery in China of such matériel and materials; to instruct in the use and maintenance of articles thus provided, and to give advice and suggestions of appropriate character toward making lend-lease assistance to China as effective as pos-

85

sible in the interest of the United States, of China, and of the world effort in resistance to movements of conquest by force.

The sending of this mission is in keeping with and is on parallel lines to the sending of a similar mission to the Soviet Union. The purposes of the two missions are identical.

General Magruder has had long experience in China, where he twice served as military attaché. He, therefore, will be working on familiar ground among people he knows well, and to whom he is well known. An adequate staff of thoroughly qualified officers will accompany General Magruder.

Broad Authority Indicated

The statement that the mission should give "advice and suggestions of an appropriate character" toward making lease-lend assistance most effective was widely interpreted as giving broad authority to the mission.

Although Mr. Roosevelt said that the purpose of the mission to Russia would be "identical," he drew one important distinction. Russia would not get lease-lend aid, he stressed. When a reporter asked why the lease-lend act would not apply to the Soviet Union, the President snapped that it just didn't.

When a reporter noted that his announcement mentioned that the function of the mission was to work with "Chinese and other authorities," Mr. Roosevelt said he could make a guess that the "and others" might involve the authorities of British Burma, through whose territory American war supplies for China are passing. He was not, however, certain about this.

The President said he was not yet ready to announce the personnel of the mission to Russia, but was emphatic in saying that no hitch had developed in the plan to send a group to Moscow.

Speaking of his talk with Mr. Roosevelt, the Chinese Ambassador said:

"The President assured me that China's needs were not left out at his historic conference on the high seas with Prime Minister Churchill of Great Britain. On the whole, we had a very satisfactory meeting."

The Ambassador asserted lease-lend aid for China was not specifically discussed and remarked that he was not able, therefore, to say what part, if any, of the next lease-lend appropriation would be earmarked for Chinese use.

In recent months General Magruder has been assigned to the First Division, largely composed of Regular Army troops, at Fort Devens, Mass. Before that he devoted himself to War Department intelligence work in Washington for a considerable period.

August 27, 1941

Gen. Stilwell Sees President Before Going to China

Special to THE NEW YORK TIMES.

WASHINGTON, Feb. 9—Major Gen. Joseph W. Stilwell conferred with President Roosevelt at the White House today, presumably to receive final instructions before departing for China, where, the White House said, he would work in close cooperation with Generalissimo Chiang Kai-shek.

The White House would give no details of Major Gen. Stilwell's mission, and referred to the War Department an inquiry as to whether he would supplement or supplant Brig. Gen. John E. Magruder, now head of the United States Military Mission to China. The War Department said that it had no information available beyond that released at the White House.

Major Gen. Stilwell has been commander of the Third Army Corps, with headquarters at the Presidio of Monterey, California. He is fifty-nine years of age.

February 10, 1942

MANDALAY CAPTURED JAPANESE CLAIM; CHINESE REPULSE FOE ON BURMA ROAD

BRITISH FALL BACK

All Troops in Mandalay Area Retire, Menaced by Flanking Threat

CHINESE CLAIM SUCCESS

Report They Inflicted Heavy Casualties Above Lashio— Japanese Bomb Akyab

By DAVID ANDERSON
Special Cable to THE NEW YORK TIMES.

LONDON, May 2—Mandalay, old capital of Burma, has been occupied by Japanese troops, according to a communiqué of Tokyo Imperial Headquarters broadcast today and inferentially confirmed by the British communiqué. The invaders, however, were said by Chungking to have been checked in their headlong rush over the Burma Road northeastward from Lashio. The Chinese reported inflicting heavy casualties on the foe at a point north of Hsenwi.

The Japanese announced that Mandalay fell yesterday. While this was not confirmed in authoritative quarters here, it was explained that "with Lashio already in enemy hands, it would not be worth while to suffer great losses to defend Mandalay."

[With Mandalay and Lashio, the Japanese hold all the strategic points in Northeast Burma—adjoining Free China — excepting Bhamo, which is eighty miles northwest of Hsenwi, and Myitkyini. Bhamo, at the head of navigation on the Irrawaddy River, is the terminus of an old and important Caravan route to Kunming, capital of Yunnan Province. Myitkyini, eighty miles north of Bhamo, is the terminus of a narrow-gauge railway from Mandalay.]

Mandalay had already been largely destroyed by Japanese air raids, and the tactical situation that developed in the area in the last few days made defense virtually impossible at any cost. The belief held here that the topography around Mandalay might favor its defense has been proved unreliable.

The enemy communiqué said the fall of Mandalay followed ten days of fighting in which "British and Chungking forces were annihilated in various places." Once the Japanese had advanced beyond Kyaukse, about twenty miles away, it was evident Mandalay was doomed since the enemy already was thrusting in the direction of Monywa on the west and from Hsipaw on the northeast.

A New Delhi communiqué today stated that "on the Mandalay front all British troops were being withdrawn from positions north of the Irrawaddy." The British headquarters in India added that the road and rail bridges across the Myitnge River had been successfully blown up. Two spans of the Ava Bridge also were demolished.

British Protect Flank

NEW DELHI, India, May 2 (U.P.) —British forces in Burma, according to today's communiqué, have been fighting in and around Monywa to protect the United Nations' flank and halt a Japanese encirclement thrust northwest of Mandalay, while the situation along the adjacent Irrawaddy sector was reported unchanged.

The Japanese obviously pushed a mobile column against Monywa in an effort to outflank the British at Mandalay and also to cut off their meager communication routes to India. General Harold Alexander, British commander, must defend these rudimentary communications lines or be forced to fall back northward where there is no usable route through the rough jungle country except toward China.

The general line of the Allied retirement at present is northward along the Irrawaddy and the narrow-gauge railroad leading almost 300 miles toward Myitkyina near the border of China.

Chinese Report Success

CHUNGKING, China, May 2 (U.P.) —A Japanese advance through the Lashio sector of Burma toward the Chinese frontier was repulsed with heavy losses, a communiqué said tonight, and Chinese troops in the Taunggyi-Loilem sector have killed 1,350 troops in a struggle to cut off reinforcements.

The communiqué said that six Japanese fourteen-ton tanks had been destroyed and much booty captured as the Chinese slashed at the Japanese rear lines in the Taunggyi area.

Travelers said that 100 British women and children refugees have been evacuated from Lashio to India aboard three United States Army transports before the Japanese reached that key communications town on the Burma Road.

A delayed dispatch from a United Press correspondent with the American Volunteer Group said that General Chiang Kai-shek on April 29 had telegraphed Major Gen. Claire Chennault, the A. V. G. commander, as follows:

"When on April 25 you shot down four Japanese planes, destroyed thirty trucks and damaged hundreds more * * * you prevented the enemy from consolidating at Lashio and thus at the most critical juncture you were instrumental in causing what may prove to be the turning of the tide in Burma. * * *

"I feel you will fight on to victory. * * * In the near future the A. V. G. will control the Burma skies as the Chinese land forces will control the Burma soil entrusted to their defense."

Akyab Reported Bombed

TOKYO, May 2 (From Japanese broadcast recorded by The United Press in San Francisco)—Imperial headquarters said late today that the strategic city of Mandalay had fallen to Japanese troops in Burma Friday afternoon.

The communiqué said the city was completely occupied.

The Domei News Agency said that the fall of Mandalay meant the wholesale retreat of British influences from East Asia and that it had virtually cut communications between Chungking and Burma, as well as severed the American supply line to China.

Tokyo radio said today that Japanese naval airplanes bombed Akyab on the Bay of Bengal Friday morning and inflicted heavy damage on the air field, hangars and runways. [Akyab is the last useful port held by the United Nations on the Burmese Coast.]

May 3, 1942

BRITISH REMNANTS ELUDE BURMA TRAP

Tengyueh Falls as Japanese Press Into Yunnan—Serious Threat to China Seen

By ROBERT P. POST
Wireless to THE NEW YORK TIMES.

LONDON, May 15—British remnants retreating from Burma were reported today to have reached the Indian frontier after having frustrated Japanese attempts to drive between them and India. New Delhi dispatches said there had been no contact with the Japanese for the past twenty-four hours.

Meanwhile the Japanese continued to push into Yunnan, with the Chinese acknowledging the fall of Tengyueh on the ancient caravan route from Bhamo.

The British withdrawal up the Chindwin valley is described here as a masterly retreat, but admittedly it is a Japanese victory. Apparently the Imperial troops not only foiled Japanese enveloping tactics but destroyed heavy equipment that they were forced to abandon because of lack of transport.

In the China campaign there was no news of a column of Japanese that was reported to have pushed forty miles along the west bank of the Salween River, by-passing Tengyueh. But there was another column that was reported to have crossed the Irawaddy near Katha, presumably to consolidate the Japanese hold on Upper Burma.

Chinese vanguards were said by Chungking to be nearing Myitkyina, northernmost town in Burma, and another Chinese column was within striking distance of Wangting. This is the border town to which the Japanese retired from the Chefang area after the Chinese last week drove them back from the Burma Road. The Japanese rear was said to be so thinly garrisoned that these two Chinese forces were meeting little resistance, but a Japanese advance into Yunnan appeared to continue.

A small number of British and Indian garrison troops who evacuated Akyab before the Japanese advance arrived in India today. They escaped on merchant ships with naval escort. They were mainly demolition troops plus some anti-aircraft units that claimed five Japanese planes,

Myitkyina Bombed Again

NEW DELHI, India, May 15 (AP) —British bombers again attacked Japanese barges on the Chindwin River, and United States Army fliers from India bombed the Myitkyina airdrome yesterday for the second day in a row, but the Japanese were busily consolidating their hold on Burma.

As the Chinese admitted loss of Tengyueh, the threat to China appeared the most serious in nearly five years of stubborn warfare against the Japanese invaders.

The Japanese appeared to be paying little attention to Chinese units still in Burma, but instead were concentrating on reinforcing their spearheads in China itself.

The Chinese expressed confidence that the situation would soon be stabilized, but the Japanese already have isolated China from her allies, have pushed 125 miles up the Burma Road and are sending other forces northward into China from the Thailand and French Indo-China border zones.

The main Japanese column was reported in combat with the Chinese at a point on the west bank of the swift Salween River.

The east bank is held in strength by the Chinese, who have destroyed the river bridges to prevent a Japanese advance toward Yungchang, fifty-five miles farther up the road from the frontier.

[Kunming, capital of Yunnan and the most important base of Free China excepting Chungking, is about 250 miles due east of Tengyueh. The northernmost part of Indo-China is about 160 miles south of Kunming. But the terrain of both the southern and western parts of Yunnan probably would provide the Japanese with the most serious problems of logistics encountered in the war. Also they would presumably be met by forces many times larger than opposed them in all Malaysia or Burma.]

Chinese Say Foe Suffers

CHUNGKING, China, Saturday, May 16 (AP)—Chinese troops battling the Japanese in the Tengyueh-Lungling areas of Yunnan Province in the past week have inflicted more than 4,000 casualties on the invaders, the Central News Agency reported today.

The Japanese were reported shelling Chinese positions on the east bank of the Salween River in a night-and-day pounding, but the agency said little damage was done.

Inside Burma, Japanese troops advancing northward along a railway from Mandalay occupied Kinu Station on May 9, a communiqué said yesterday, while a Japanese column, advancing westward from Bhamo, made a forced crossing of the Irrawaddy River on the evening of May 10, bitterly resisted by Chinese troops.

May 16, 1942

BIG RAIDS ON JAPAN SEEN IN SIX MONTHS

Chennault, Head of A. V. G., Says 2,000 U. S. Planes Could 'Wipe Out' Foe's Air Force

KUMMING, China, May 22 (U.P.) —Brig. Gen. Claire L. Chennault, commander of China's American Volunteer Group, predicted today that the United States would unleash an air offensive against the Japanese in six months. He said that 2,000 United States planes could "wipe out" the Japanese air force.

The leader of the Flying Tigers was confident that the coming offensive would be successful if the United States would earmark "even a small percentage" of the present airplane output for the Far East.

If the Japanese continue to lose as many planes as they have in the past six months, he said, they will be suffering a severe shortage before the first anniversary of their attack on Pearl Harbor.

He said the Japanese were wasting their time in striking into the interior of Chekiang Province, in hope of capturing airfields the Allies could use for bombing raids against Japan. There are too many airdromes or sites for them within striking range of Japan for all to be seized, he explained.

Japanese air activity in Burma has slackened, he said, because of bad weather, lack of profitable objectives and, above all, a shortage of planes because of heavy losses inflicted by the A. V. G.

China Air Route in Peril

AMERICAN FERRYING COMMAND HEADQUARTERS, Northeast India, May 22 (U.P.)—American pilots, who span jungles flying supplies to China, believe that a "reasonable" number of fighter planes could keep their route open, despite the threat from near-by Japanese-occupied bases in Burma.

Despite the vulnerability to attack, the American transports already have carried tons of equipment to China and have evacuated hundreds from Burma without the loss of a single plane from enemy action. But it cannot keep up forever because Japanese fighters are patrolling dangerously close to the route the Americans travel.

Pilots said that as the Japanese opened new bases in Northern Burma the small force of A. V. G. planes probably would be unable to keep this air route open.

STILWELL IS SAFE IN NORTHEAST INDIA

LONDON, May 23 (U.P.)—An Exchange Telegraph Agency correspondent reported today from Dinapur, Northeastern India, that Lieut. Gen. Joseph W. Stilwell had arrived there with 400 other persons after a strenuous trek over the mountains from Burma.

The correspondent said he met General Stilwell, who had commanded the Chinese Fifth and Sixth armies in Burma, while he was eating breakfast with his liaison officer, Major Gen. Franklin Sibert, yesterday, and that General Stilwell talked between mouthfuls of biscuit and canned cheese and gulps of tea from a thermos jug.

General Stilwell referred lightly to his trip over the mountains.

"We brought 400 with us, including an American physician, Dr. Seagrave from the American Baptist Mission, Burmese nurses, Americans, British, Chinese, Burmese and Anglo-Indians," he said. "Many joined in when they found out we had some chow.

"It was a mixed gathering but when we got a little discipline into them they were all right. There still are a lot of refugees in Burma but I think they'd do a damned sight better by staying there than by facing the toil and privations of the mountain paths."

He would not talk about the fighting in Burma or of the route he had followed to India, but he finally admitted that the going was tough.

"But we made it," he said. "It's O. K. to look back at it, but it would be no fun to face it again. I managed to pick up some supplies dropped by plane, but I don't think the Japs knew where we were. The country is beautiful to look at, but tough to live in. All our marches were forced ones, because one must force one's self to march at all."

General Stilwell said that one of his hardest tasks in Burma had been to break the ideas of Chinese generals that their armies belonged to them, to command alone, as their whims and not a preconceived plan dictated. But there finally was unity, he said.

"I didn't know there was a lot of anxiety about us," he said. "When I arrived farther down the road I found an American Army colonel and lieutenant colonel had been searching for us. It's nice to look forward to the prospect of getting food regularly and cleaning up."

WILLKIE ASKS AID FOR CHINESE NOW

Action Rather Than Words Is Needed, He Says in Surprise Speech in Town Hall

Wendell L. Willkie, in a surprise appearance last night at a China Resistance Day Rally at Town Hall, told 1,000 persons he regretted that this country had been giving China more words than action and that he hoped by the next anniversary of the outbreak between China and Japan five years ago the situation would be the other way around.

Mr. Willkie, who slipped quietly into the second row of the balcony during the early part of the program, agreed to speak after Dr. Tsune-chi Yu, Chinese Consul General here, paid him a visit in the balcony. Previous speakers had included Mayor La Guardia, Dr. Hu Shih, the Chinese Ambassador; General Hsiung Shih-fei, head of the Chinese military mission; John Gunther, and Cecil Brown.

Introduced by Clare Boothe, the 1936 Republican Presidential candidate began:

"I have a notion that in the last few weeks we have been 'saving China' largely with words. I'd feel much more like participating in this rally tonight if I knew that my own government was participating more actively in helping China.

"The only reason I came here was to add what little weight I may have to stirring up some agitation to get some more bombers for China."

'No Inconsistency in Stand.'

After the applause, Mr. Willkie went on to say that no one appreciated more fully than he the "necessity for the crushing of Hitler." Moreover, he went on, he felt he had made that appreciation clear by the number of speeches he had made along those lines.

"But I see no inconsistency," he continued, "in crushing Hitler and in saving some of the materials rolling off our assembly lines to send to those fighting Chinese."

Mr. Willkie's talk was the only one bluntly to broach the issue of additional arms for China. The Ambassador had made such an appeal in a prepared speech, which he said stood as a statement, but he did not deliver a word of it. Instead, Dr. Hu restricted himself largely to a portrayal of the traditional love of freedom, the respect for the right to doubt, of his people —as evidencing that they could

never yield to Japanese domination.

Mayor La Guardia asserted that "if it had not been for the stupidity of the British, French and United States diplomacy in failing to recognize the purpose behind the aggression of Japan in China, we would not be at war today."

He chided Americans for being poor geographers, and warned that 'as a matter of survival, we just can't let China down; for every setback that China has, it prolonged our war just that much longer. For every month of defeat that China suffers, that adds one year to our winning of the war."

Stands "Humbly Beside China"

A previous speaker, Ting Wing-Chu of the Chinese Consolidated Benevolent Association, co-sponsor of the rally with United China Relief, had declared China "stands proudly beside the United Nations," the Mayor recalled, adding:

"No, my friend, the United Nations stand humbly beside China."

He hailed Chiang Kai-shek's anniversary pronouncement of confidence, and suggested as a reply: "Forgive us, we're five years late, but we're sending you the resources, the military supplies and the weapons that your brave men will know how to use."

Speaking through an interpreter, General Hsiung outlined probable Japanese aims in China and warned of the danger of their realization to the United Nations. W. R. Herod, president of United China Relief, and Colonel Remington Orsinger, representing General Hugh A. Drum, also spoke.

After many references to the 3,000,000 Chinese war casualties, a memorial ceremony was held, built around a symbolic representation of the Chinese unknown soldier at the rear of the platform. United States Army buglers played taps while soldiers and a Chinese youth group stood at attention. Lucy Monroe and Liu Liang-Mo sang.

U.S. ARMY AND NAVY PLEDGE CHINA HELP

Stimson and Knox in First Joint Order of Day Since Dec. 7 Praise Heroic Defense

By DAVID ANDERSON
Special to THE NEW YORK TIMES.

WASHINGTON, July 7 — The first Order of the Day to be issued by the Secretaries of War and Navy since Dec. 7 today paid special tribute to the Chinese on the fifth anniversary of their resistance against the Japanese aggression and pledged "firm determination to expel the aggressor from every foot of Chinese soil."

The Order of the Day, read to all members of the armed forces on land and at sea, follows:

To the Armed Forces:

Five years ago today the Imperial Japanese Government launched a brutal and unprovoked attack on the people of China.

Lacking adequate arms and other equipment, the leaders of China have nevertheless continued their gallant resistance for five years. Today they are fighting with a tenacity and courage which are an inspiration for all defenders of democracy on every front.

Today the members of the Army and Navy of the United States salute their comrades-in-arms in China and join with them in the firm determination to expel the aggressor from every foot of Chinese soil.

HENRY L. STIMSON,
Secretary of War.
FRANK KNOX,
Secretary of the Navy.

July 8, 1942

STILWELL IS EAGER FOR THE OFFENSIVE

By BROOKS ATKINSON
Wireless to THE NEW YORK TIMES.

CHUNGKING, China, Jan. 8 (Delayed)—"Got any news," Lieutenant General Joseph W. Stilwell ironically inquired when this correspondent turned up at the house on the side of the hill this morning at an hour no gentleman would consider decent.

"You give out the news, we print it," I replied with professional punctilio.

"Hell, we never have any news around here," said the genial commander of the American Army Forces in China, Burma and India.

"How about announcing that you have got over your cold and are receiving correspondents right after breakfast?" I asked.

"That's a hot piece of news to cable half way around the world," "Uncle Joe" reported with a chuckle.

But as far as public statements are concerned that just about sums up the status of the war in China, where Brigadier General Claire L. Chennault's boys are raiding the Japanese whenever they can put their hands on the stuff and where the Chinese and Japanese forces are glowering at each other on the big, loose and spotty periphery of Free China.

Foe Not Just Sitting Around

Not that "Uncle Joe" is content to have it so. An active man with a volatile personality he dislikes to think of the Japanese consolidating their positions in Burma day after day.

"They are workers," he said, gloomily. "They don't sit around much."

But after five and a half years of war in China he is at the end of the line and committed to a world strategy that puts his job at the bottom of the list. As Chief of Staff for Generalissimo Chiang Kai-shek he is also the man in the middle who devotes a good half of his time to the annoying art of diplomacy.

Like some of the other shrewd men in this theatre of war, General Stilwell knows how the Japanese can be defeated. In the meantime he has had to fiddle with small jobs and bide his time.

Although the Chinese as well as the Americans are dissatisfied not to be waging a counter-offensive thirteen months after Pearl Harbor the present stalemate is not a total loss. It immobilizes about sixteen of Japan's seventy-five divisions; another thirty are immo-

bilized against Russia and to the north of China.

At present the Chinese armies lack all sorts of heavy equipment and even have an inadequate medical corps. But when the Chinese soldier is properly trained, equipped and led, General Stilwell says he gives a very good account of himself.

General Stilwell thinks the Chinese soldiers and people are worth anything we can do for them.

Hard Task of Recovery

On the long trek out of Burma last Spring General Stilwell was the man who said "we got a hell of a beating" there and we will have to "go back and retake it." He has not forgotten.

What China needs most urgently is overland transport. That still points the finger at Burma. What with mountains, jungles, rivers, malaria, bad roads and paths a Burma campaign is difficult, particularly for the aggressors, who would be constantly extending their lines of communication into rough country while the Japanese fell back on communication lines that would be constantly improving.

Nor have the Japanese been idle since last May. It is supposed that they have about eight divisions in Burma, Thailand and Indo-China. No one knows how many planes they have since they hide them in shelters and move them around constantly. Estimates run from 200 up.

Although the Japanese have lost considerable naval strength in the past six months they can compensate somewhat by saving from 3,500 to 5,000 miles round-trip in the voyage to Rangoon for they can land troops and supplies at Haiphong and Saigon and ship them overland by road and railroad. There was a short gap in the railroad between Indo-China and Thailand that Chinese sources think may be closed by new building, although American sources are less certain.

Day by day the Japanese positions grow stronger in Burma. And there are dark factors on the reverse of the picture. When and if the Burma Road is retaken it will have to be put back in working condition with new bridges and other repairs; and unless Rangoon is taken the road will need new feeder lines.

For the present General Stilwell is not discussing these matters, but any one with a map can figure them out for himself. In the first place reopening the Burma Road is not a simple matter depending upon the receipt of a few new planes and engine-head gaskets from America. In the second place reopening it does not win the war in China.

But General Stilwell has recovered from his cold. That's the news from the Chungking Front.

January 11, 1943

CHINA IS NETTLED AS CRITICISM GROWS

Anti-Democratic Vestiges Are Explained as Result of Military Control

By BROOKS ATKINSON
By Wireless to THE NEW YORK TIMES.

CHUNGKING, China, April 17— Although no one in the Government pretends that China is now a democratic state, increasing criticism from abroad of anti-democratic tendencies here has created considerable concern and anxiety. As one of the four leading United Nations powers, China covets her good reputation and does not like being called totalitarian, Fascist, reactionary.

Under the control of the Kuomintang party China officially passed through a period of military domination and is now in a transitional period of political tutelage on her way to democracy. One year after the war the national Congress is scheduled to meet, adopt a constitution and inaugurate democratic government.

But the size of the gendarmerie throughout China and of the police force and troops dividing Communist from Free China throws some doubt on the assertion that China has wholly emerged from military domination. The lack of free speech and a free press suggests that the current training for democratic government is inefficient.

Ever since a goodwill mission returned from Britain a month ago there has been some guarded discussion in the newspapers about the institution of the free press in Britain, where people are likely to believe what they read. Also the criticism abroad of the disputed 'thought control" regulation for students has created considerable soul-searching here.

Rumor Is Sole Guide

Since the Government conducts being called totalitarian, Fascist, occasional tight-lipped public statement, there are only rumors in Chungking to indicate what the mood of the moment may be. Just now the rumor is that the censorship may be lifted or liberalized at the next meeting of the Kuomintang's Central Executive Committee, and an attempt made to democratize the Kuomintang.

Presumably the latter means the promoting of local self-government to the point at which local officials will be elected by the people instead of being appointed by the Kuomintang. At the present time the government of all China is dominated by the party, which has lost its revolutionary spirit and progress.

When there is a choice of precedence the party invariably comes ahead of the Government. In the Chinese Government directory the Kuomintang, with Chiang Kai-

89

shek as Tsungtsai, or President, comes before the National Government, of which Generalissimo Chiang is chairman.

Of the anti-democratic tendencies in China, the controlled press is the most paralyzing. The official attitude is that the people of China are not sufficiently educated to absorb facts and opinions of a disturbing nature. It is also part of the transition period in China to write of the good and the beautiful; conventional literature here idealizes life and people. Whatever the reason, the press emerges as a sort of court calendar that portrays the public activities of a group of scholars and gentlemen who move through a polite world of highmindedness, thoughtful manners, generosity and success. The press portrait is unreal to an extreme.

Regime Isolated From Masses

The tone of the press is so uniform that any minor criticism of the government that penetrates the censorship provokes wonder, gossip and speculation. Without a free press the Government conducts its affairs in private, depending upon its own ingenuity and power to wrestle with enormous problems which increasingly baffle it.

The Government is cut off from the people, who are the source of the vitality of democratic states. Within the Kuomintang there is more and more restlessness and criticism. Dr. Sun-Fo's recent speech criticizing the Kuomintang crystallized a good deal of the discontent. But without a free press it is unlikely that the Kuomintang can acquire anything more than the passive disinterest of a people who are congenitally cynical about politics.

The next meeting of the Central Executive Committee of the Kuomintang will doubtless furiously emit solemn resolutions that recognize the validity of the criticism from abroad. The Generalissimo, who is China's only leader, will insist upon an attempt to make the tone of the Government more reassuring to foreign critics.

Although his will is supreme, his Government is not sufficiently close to the people. China is at present incapable of satisfying the criticism from foreign liberals. China is currently afflicted with so many minor problems that she cannot solve this major one, which, if faced two or three years ago, might have averted many of the intangible, bewildering troubles of today.

April 18, 1944

Indecisive War in Orient

Japanese Drive in Burma a Limited Move—British Blow at Sumatra a Raid

By HANSON W. BALDWIN

The Japanese operations against Imphal, Kohima and Dimapur in India are still indecisive and the monsoon rains are now not far off.

The enemy seems to have cut most, if not all, of the main overland supply routes to Imphal and to have virtually invested Kohima. Some of his patrols are undoubtedly nearing the important Bengal-Assam railway, but that line is still in Allied hands. The Japanese have attempted at numerous points to debouch on to the Imphal plain, twenty by thirty miles in size, but the British say the enemy is still restricted to the jungles and that the siege of Kohima has been lifted. Japanese reports have mentioned the mobilization of increasing forces against them and have stated that Admiral Lord Louis Mountbatten has been transporting sizable forces by air from the Arakan front to reinforce the Imphal area.

Allied reports have also mentioned that air-borne troops—perhaps part of the group of Wingate's Raiders or a new long-range penetration group — have shifted the scene of their operations southward to threaten the communications of the three Japanese divisions pushing into Manipur State, India. To meet this threat, the Japanese seem to have transferred one division from eastern Burma, where it was guarding against a possible offensive by the Chinese from Yunnan, to the Mandalay-Chindwin area.

Meanwhile, Lieut. Gen. Joseph W. Stilwell's Chinese-American forces in the north, aided by native levies and British and Indian troops, are pushing slowly on toward the key railhead point of Myitkyina, which gives access to the Irrawaddy Valley and which is connected by road with Bhamo and thence by another road to the Burma Road. If General Stilwell can reach Myitkyina before the monsoon he may be able to hold his position there; if not, he may have to fall back to the Ledo roadhead.

Allies Race Against Time

The Burma-Indian operations, therefore, are now in a great measure a race against time. There is no doubt that the Allies have realized only a part of our very limited ambitions in the Burma theatre in the past dry season. And there is no doubt that the limited Japanese invasion of India and the co-related enemy push in China have had a diversionary effect upon our own offensive operations and are still threatening not alone the principal supply line to our forces in northern Burma but also some of our most important bomber and transport airfields in the whole Asiatic theatre.

Despite their successes, the enemy still faces great difficulties. The main British strength in the Imphal area still must be defeated, and the Japanese are fighting time as well as the Allies. The Japanese can scarcely hope, during the monsoon season, to supply themselves completely over the long and tortuous jungle trails behind them, and they have insufficient air power to supply by air; they must probably seize and hold Imphal, Kohima and the surrounding area, if they are to hold their positions in Manipur State.

Their main objective—seizure of the Imphal airfields and cutting of the Bengal-Assam railway—main artery of supply for our air transport route to China and for our forces operating in northern Burma, still has to be accomplished. Even if the Japanese should sever it, the enemy force would have to remain astride the railway to eliminate its use by the Allies completely, and the Japanese attacking force—three divisions—is probably too small to do this.

Even if such complete severance were possible, supplies could still move to General Stilwell—though in limited quantity—up the shifting channels of the Bramhaputra River by barge and by the part-rail, part-road transportation system that closely follows both banks of the Brahmaputra. Both of these supply arteries are considerably to the west of the main Bengal-Assam railway and its junction of Dimapur, which the Japanese have been approaching.

Danger to Both Sides

India is not imperilled, therefore, but our operations in northern Burma and our limited aid to China might be crippled for some months to come if the Japanese could sever the Bengal-Assam railway. However, the Burma operations of both sides are clearly campaigns by limited forces for limited objectives. The Imphal-Kohima-Dimapur area is in danger —though perhaps not so acutely as it appeared to be some days ago —but so are the Japanese forces attacking it. And the monsoon will probably soon dim the ambitions of both sides.

But it would not interfere to an equal extent with amphibious operations in the Bay of Bengal-Indian Ocean area. The recent transfer of Admiral Mountbatten's headquarters from New Delhi, India, to Kandy, Ceylon, and a correlated shift of some subordinate commands to other areas are not only "declarations of independence" on Admiral Mountbatten's part. They represent a shift to the base from which the main effort— an amphibious effort—is likely to be made in southeast Asia.

The carrier task force raid announced yesterday—and it was probably no more than a raid— upon Japanese-held points in northern Sumatra, was the first sizeable blow mounted in this area.

The British Eastern Fleet, commanded by Admiral Sir James F. Somerville, has been recently reinforced and some of its units probably participated in the attack. The raid follows subsidiary operations, which have included submarine "strikes" against Japanese shipping in the Strait of Malacca and bombardments of the Andaman Islands. It may preface more ambitious operations against the Andamans, Malaya and Sumatra, but it seems probable that a major effort in southeast Asia is still some distance off.

April 21, 1944

Stilwell Men Gain Six Miles As Big Kohima Fight Looms

By The Associated Press.

KANDY, Ceylon, April 27—With the monsoon rains less than three weeks away, Lieut. Gen. Joseph W. Stilwell's Chinese and American forces appear to have broken the back of Japanese resistance in northern Burma. In a spectacular six-mile advance yesterday, "Uncle Joe's" infantry and tanks swept through the Mogaung Valley jungle into the village of Manpin, only ten miles from Kamaing, and no more than forty-five miles from Myitkyina, the enemy's main base of operations north of Mandalay. The campaign to open a land supply route from India to China—General Stilwell's pet project—already had carried his mixed force some 120 miles into Burma, nearly halfway to a junction with the old Burma Road at a point inside China.

The enemy's counter-invasion of India, meantime, appeared to be rushing toward a bloody climax in the 6,000-foot hills ringing the Allied base of Kohima. A report that a major battle had begun there was expected almost hourly.

Dispatches today said that Allied reinforcements of men, tanks and guns continued to stream into Kohima along the thirty-five-mile highway from Dimapur on the Bengal-Assam railway, and that an assault to break the Japanese and send them reeling back along the trails toward Burma was imminent. The Japanese hold the highest points around Kohima, and just outside the town Allied reinforcements were confronted with a large, white sign that said: "From this point you are in view of the enemy."

British and American staff officers estimated that the better part of two Japanese divisions, representing perhaps 20,000 men, already had been "chewed up" in the invasion of India.

Today's Allied communiqué said operations continued to clear the sixty-mile highway between Kohima and Imphal. The Japanese again fared badly in the air when they attempted to raid Allied air fields in India from which transports take off with supplies for China. Out of eleven enemy aircraft that appeared, Allied pilots probably destroyed three and damaged five.

Last night Allied bombers attacked Mandalay and scored many hits. The communiqué said American heavy bombers hit Monywa and Alon on the railway from Mandalay to Ye-U yesterday.

A Japanese prisoner recently taken by the Chindits—the airborne soldiers who have established a 130-mile front inside Burma behind the Japanese lines — was quoted by headquarters as saying: "We are fed up with the war and with this operation. We are hungry, badly fed, and have been collected together from anywhere and everywhere. We are thrust into the battlefront short of food and suffering from malaria and dysentery."

Foe Reports Drive on Kohima

"A Japanese general offensive has begun at Kohima," the Tokyo radio asserted in a broadcast heard in New York last night by the National Broadcasting Company.

KOHIMA BATTLE CRUCIAL

Japanese Forces Can Be Cut Off From Elements in North

By TILLMAN DURDIN

By Cable to THE NEW YORK TIMES.

ON THE DIMAPUR-KOHIMA ROAD in Northern Manipur, April 24 (Delayed)—Efforts to drive back the Japanese from northern Manipur and the Naga Hills fringing the tea garden districts of northeastern Assam are now focused in a crucial battle for full control of the little mountain center of Kohima. On the ridges of hills in and around Kohima British and Indian troops are now locked in bitter combat with a strongly entrenched Japanese force.

Our troops hold part of Kohima, a hilltop sprinkled with Western-style red-roofed bungalows, while the Japanese possess the native village and bazaar area. The Japanese have now had time to dig into bunkers, foxholes and trenches cunningly situated on slopes and hilltops naturally suited for defense. Against these positions British artillery is pounding and tanks and infantry are attacking.

In the last few days several strong Japanese bunkers have been taken out. British troops are being deployed against Kohima through a narrow bottleneck formed by steep hills that rise on each side of the road north of the town. The Japanese flank their road line of communications back to Dimapur on the Assam railway for a few miles along the eastern side.

British forces are being thrown against this enemy flank threat and an encircling movement around the northeast of Kohima

has been launched, which in turn is menacing the Japanese flank and rear. The Japanese are actually strung out north by west of Kohima through the jungle-mantled Naga Hills along a line roughly fifty miles from the railway.

The Japanese threat to the Assam railway from these scattered northern forces is believed to have been substantially reduced in the last few days.

Kohima is the key to the whole Manipur area. Five thousand feet in the Naga Hills, it is the highest point but one on the Dimapur-Imphal road. It is the radiating center for roads and trails. Into it from the east runs a motor road from Jessami over which the Japanese advanced to make their original attack. Into Kohima and north runs a road from Bokajan on the Assam railway that parallels the main Dimapur-Kohima road.

The Japanese are now established along the Bokajan road for fifteen-odd miles north of Kohima. From this road they constantly threaten to cut the British-held Dimapur road, and it is from this road that the British are seeking to dislodge the enemy by their outflanking move northeast of Kohima.

Would Cut Off Foe in North

If the British can drive the Japanese completely from the Kohima area they will have advanced a big step toward reopening of the highway from Dimapur to Imphal and cut the Japanese northern forces off from easy contact with their forces around Imphal, which they now maintain along the Imphal road through Kohima. The British have superiority in numbers and equipment.

Their light and medium artillery is rapidly silencing Japanese mountain guns. The British have tanks; the Japanese have none in this area. Threatened as they are, the British communications are much superior to the mountain trails behind the Japanese.

Through their confiscation of food from Naga villages, the Japanese seem still to be eating well enough, but their inferiority in materials of combat is beginning to determine whether they can hold in this sector.

NEW PUSH IN CHINA IS BEGUN BY ENEMY

Japanese Attack in Anhwei— American Bombers Cut Road in the Chengchow Area

By The United Press.

CHUNGKING, China, April 30—Japanese troops have started a second spring drive in Anhwei Province, about 200 miles southeast of the Chengchow fighting zone, along the Hwai River west of the Tientsin-Pukow railroad and south of the east-west Lung-Hai line, a Chinese communiqué revealed tonight.

After the arrival of reinforcements the enemy attacked last Monday in two columns, one along the river, the other over open country, the communiqué said.

The attack centered in the Showhsien-Fengtai-Yingshang triangle about 190 miles northwest of Nanking. Driving westward, the Japanese by Thursday had reached a point near Yingshang, the communiqué said, and fighting is still in progress near the city.

Yingshang is twenty-eight miles west of Fengtai, which is eight miles north of Showhsien.

Anhwei Province is east of Honan. It was indicated that the new attack was made by troops of the Japanese Eleventh Army under Gen. Masao Yokoyama, who had been expected to attack to the west in southern Honan along the Peiping-Hankow railroad.

Lieut. Gen. Joseph W. Stilwell's American planes went to the support of the Chinese in the Chengchow area. Liberators of the Fourteenth Air Force, escorted by fighters, attacked the main Yellow River bridges, which the Japanese are using for troop and supply transport. Three tons of bombs were dropped on two bridges and buildings along the north side of the river. Fires were started.

General Stilwell's Mitchells hit a 1,200-ton Japanese freighter off Hainan Island, on the China coast, and badly damaged it, and fighter-bombers gunned twenty junks on the Yangtze River south of the Honan-Anhwei areas. More than 100 Japanese were believed killed in the Yanktze attack.

Chinese planes destroyed a railroad bridge on the main Japanese supply route in the Honan offensive, the Chinese communiqué said.

Fighting continued in Honan. Tonight's communiqué said action was especially furious south and west of Mihsien, the highway

April 28, 1944

91

junction twenty miles southwest of Chengchow. Chinese forces continued their advance in counterattacks, the communiqué reported, despite heavy enemy artillery opposition.

Chinese Recapture Villages

Many villages were recaptured in a big Chinese attack yesterday morning, the communiqué said, and heavy casualties were inflicted on the Japanese.

Other Chinese units reached Kwanyintang, east of Mihsien, where they routed an enemy column containing scores of troop-laden trucks, it was said. The communiqué added that the columns routed had been sent from Chengchow to rescue the Japanese around Mihsien.

In the Hulao Pass, west of Chengchow, Japanese attacked from the south, from the direction of Szeshui village, Thursday morning. It was admitted that they had penetrated into some of the Chinese positions. However, the communiqué added that south of Szeshui the Chinese attacked Saturday and captured a number of heights.

South of Yushih, thirty-seven miles southeast of Chengchow, the Chinese continued their attacks near Manhsi and the communiqué said that brisk fighting continued.

May 1, 1944

NORTH BURMA FOE HURLED BACK AGAIN

SOUTHEAST ASIA HEADQUARTERS, Kandy, Ceylon, May 17 (AP)—Allied forces rolled the Japanese back east and west of the big enemy base of Myitkyina in north Burma today and a headquarters spokesman declared with optimism tonight that the Japanese on the eve of the monsoon period had been thrown on the defensive generally throughout the Indo-Burma theatre.

Allied planes took the offensive over a widespread area in support of the ground troops.

Lieut. Gen. Joseph W. Stilwell's Chinese Twenty-second Division in the Mogaung Valley cut the main road to the Japanese base of Kamaing at a point south of Malakawng, fifteen miles to the northwest, today's Allied communiqué announced, adding that the Japanese "fought stubbornly, and when forced back left numerous casualties and much equipment."

Earlier other Allied forces were reported in front dispatches to be only nine miles northeast of Kamaing, which is forty miles west of the Japanese main north Burma base at Myitkyina.

Ninety miles east of Myitkyina 20,000 American-trained and American-equiped Chinese smashed forward in their westward drive across the Salween River in China's Yunnan Province, the Chinese command in Chungking announcing the capture of the village of Chiaotou inside Mamien Pass. Pass.

Chinese troops also broke into the town of Tatangtzu, southeast of the pass and twenty-nine miles northeast of Tengyueh. The Chinese Command said the Japanese were resisting fiercely here, but were being encircled. Another column reached Hupan, southeast of Kunlung, and continued to advance beyond, the Chinese bulletin said.

On other sectors of this new front the Japanese counterattacked repeatedly, but were pounded by the American Fourteenth Air Force, which retained supremacy of the skies here as in North Burma.

A dispatch from the Mogaung Valley front by an Associated Press correspondent gave details of the cutting of the main road to Kamaing, which was reported only briefly in the headquarters communiqué. An undetermined number of Japanese were trapped in the village of Malakawng. The highway is the only one in the Mogaung Valley that can be used by trucks.

News of the Chinese Salween offensive toward Myitkyina was received with great satisfaction at the Mogaung front, it was reported, "because the move likely will tie up Japanese who might otherwise be used against Stilwell's forces."

"With Generalissimo Chiang Kai-shek's Chinese attacking from the east and General Stilwell's Chinese from the north and west, the Japanese in northern Burma now are in a tough spot, and prospects for reoccupation of northern Burma now seem brighter than ever," the dispatch from the Mogaung Valley said.

East of the Mogaung Valley elements of the Chinese Thirty-eighth Division, in the face of artillery opposition, closed from the southeast on Warong in the Kumon hills.

Col. Philip G. Cochran's American Air Commando Force put bombers and fighters into the air of North Burma on both sides of the Mogaung Valley, and air support also was given the Chindits in their harassing attacks against the Japanese Eighteenth Division south of Myitkyina.

May 18, 1944

FOE IN KAMAING IN TIGHTER NOOSE

Stilwell's North Burma Force Cuts Road to Mogaung, Big Japanese Base

NEW GAIN AT MYITKYINA

Chinese in Western Yunnan Go On in Mamien Pass, Aided by Return of Good Weather

SOUTHEAST ASIA HEADQUARTERS, Kandy, Ceylon, May 30 (U.P.)—Lieut. Gen. Joseph W. Stilwell's forces have cut the Kamaing-Mogaung highway in northern Burma, virtually isolating the large Japanese garrison in Kamaing and other enemy remnants in the Mogaung valley, a Southeast Asia Command communiqué announced today.

Front dispatches said Chinese troops were firmly entrenched at a road block they had established six miles southeast of Kamaing and were now attacking the village of Seton.

Forty miles to the east, Brig. Gen Frank Merrill's American and Chinese units gained a foothold inside Myitkyina after advancing 600 yards from the west. In heavy fighting Sunday night the Allies repulsed sharp Japanese counter-attacks south and southwest of the town.

Good Retreat Routes Cut

The Japanese garrison in Kamaing appeared doomed, as well as that in Myitkyina. With the only automobile road in the Mogaung Valley cut and the navigable Mogaung River east of the road denied to them, the enemy's only means of withdrawal or of receiving supplies and reinforcements during the monsoon is over mountain tracks or through the Indaw Valley to the southwest, which has a few good trails, but no all-weather road.

Latest reports said General Stilwell's main Chinese forces were advancing down the main valley road and were attacking Malakawng, fifteen miles from Kamaing. An outflanking unit, however, had cut the road south of Malakawng and was within ten miles of Kamaing.

Another Chinese force was pushing forward from the village of Sharaw, thirteen miles due north of Kamaing, and a fourth column was closing in on Manpin, at the edge of the Kumon Range, nine miles northeast of Kamaing. Still other Chinese troops were moving southward from newly captured Warong, fifteen miles northeast of Kamaing.

Desperately trying to retrieve their position in northern Burma, the Japanese were attempting to rush reinforcements up the Mandalay-Myitkyina railroad after clearing Maj. Gen. W. D. A. Lentaigne's Chindits from an air strip and road and railway block southwest of Mogaung. Other Chindit columns, however, still were operating deep inside Japanese territory, where sections of the railway north of Mandalay and important bridges have been destroyed.

The Allied air force was harassing enemy efforts to re-establish communications between central and north Burma. American, RAF and Indian air force medium bombers and long-range fighters made repeated attacks Sunday on key railroad junctions, bridges and rolling stock between Mandalay and Myitkyina.

On the Manipur front in eastern India British imperial troops eliminated several trapped Japanese pockets in the Bishenpur area, southwest of Imphal, and captured considerable booty in widespread fighting. The Allies scored new gains in attacks on Naga village, north of Kohima, and also made progress south of Kohima.

Chinese Gain in Yunnan

CHUNGKING, China, May 30 (U.P.)—Aided by a return of good weather, which opened the way for strong American air support, Chinese troops in western Yunnan Province have captured Lengshuikou, the highest village on the Mamien trail leading across the towering Kaolikung Mountains toward Burma, a Chinese communiqué said today.

During their advance the Chinese surrounded the Japanese garrison at Chaikungtang, last enemy holding on the Mamien trail, and its fall was believed imminent.

Maj. Gen. Claire L. Chennault's Fourteenth United States Air Force gave its strongest support so far to the Chinese drive west of the Salween River yesterday.

In other air operations Liberators attacked a convoy off Hainan Island, in the South China Sea, yesterday, sinking a 1,700-ton freighter and damaging a large cargo vessel.

All the planes returned.

Chinese Lose Chiaotou

CHUNGKING, China, May 30 (AP)—The Chinese High Command announced today that the Japanese had reoccupied Chiaotou, near the Burma frontier in the Shweli River Valley north of Tengyueh.

May 31, 1944

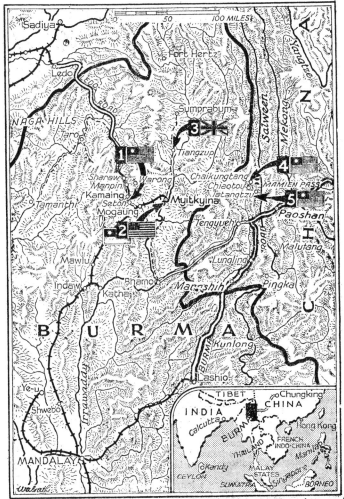

Chinese troops cut the main road between Kamaing and Mogaung (1) and attacked Seton and to the north advanced from Sharaw and approached Manpin. At Myitkyina (2) General Stilwell's Chinese and American forces advanced in an attack from the west. British native levies assaulted Tiangzup (3). On the Salween front the Chinese attacked Chaikungtang (4), last Japanese pocket on the trail out of Mamien Pass, but lost Chiaotou. Beyond Tatangtzu (5) they advanced westward.

May 31, 1944

JAPANESE NARROW RING ON CHANGSHA

CHUNGKING, China, May 30 (AP) — Japanese forces who landed on the southeastern shore of Lake Tungting have breached the Chinese second line of defense at the Milo River, forty miles north of Changsha, the Chinese High Command acknowledged tonight.

Other advances were scored by the enemy on a fifteen-mile front against the Chinese first line of defense below the Sinchiang River.

Enemy gains were reported also in supporting operations both east and west of Lake Tungting, in northern Hunan Province, and field dispatches said casualties were heavy as the Chinese battled to hold the invaders from thrice ravaged Changsha, the provincial capital.

The Japanese were estimated unofficially to have massed twelve divisions for the attempt to reconquer the whole Hankow-Canton railway, nine in the Hankow-Yochow area and three in the Canton region to the south. The three divisions in the Canton area, however, still were idle.

CHUNGKING, China, May 30 (U.P.)—Spearheaded by crack shock troops brought from Manchuria, 150,000 Japanese have now been thrown into the enemy offensive in the Hunan-Hupeh Provinces border area and the drive already has developed into the biggest in the rice-bowl area since the war started nearly seven years ago, Chinese military authorities said tonight.

Moving in the general direction of Changsha, eighty miles south of Yochow at the mouth of Lake Tungting, in their attempt to clear the Hankow-Canton Railroad, the Japanese were now on the offensive over a front of about 140 miles, from Kungan, sixty-seven miles northwest of Yochow, to Tungcheng, forty-five miles east-southeast of Yochow.

The easternmost of three Japanese offensive forces had stormed Tungcheng after moving southwestward from Tsungyang.

The central column had stormed Yingtien, roughly a midway point between Yochow and Changsha. Yingtien was attacked with the aid of troops landed on the shores of the lake from barges.

The westernmost column was attacking Nanhsien, forty-five miles west of Yochow, and Kungan, forty miles north-northwest of Nanhsien.

May 31, 1944

PACIFIC VICTORY PERILS JAPAN'S INNER DEFENSES

At the Same Time, Japanese Advance In China Is Making Our Task Harder

By SIDNEY SHALETT

WASHINGTON, June 24—The firmly established and overwhelming American superiority in the Pacific theatre was strikingly demonstrated this week when the Japanese Fleet, after suffering disastrous air losses and considerable damage to its surface ships, fled from combat with the Pacific Fleet.

The performance—hardly inspiring—of the Japanese Fleet units was extremely significant. What happened was this:

The Japanese Fleet, now about as skittish as the Italian Navy was at its worst, apparently summoned up sufficient courage to venture an offensive blow at our naval forces supporting the American offensive in the Marianas. The best available opinion is that the Japanese hoped to catch our forces when they possibly were weaker and their ammunition was low.

Instead, Japanese carrier-based planes, which carried out the initial attack, ran into an agonizingly destructive reception; 353 enemy aircraft were shot down in the worst aerial defeat the Japanese have suffered since the Battle of Midway.

Show-down Still Avoided

Then Admiral Raymond A. Spruance's Fifth Task Fleet got after the sizable force of Japanese surface ships—including battleships and carriers—that were gingerly steaming our way. Their air cover knocked out, the Japanese Navy ran so fast that our ships couldn't close the distance, so Vice Admiral Marc A. Mitscher's carrier task force planes got after them, inflicting serious damage.

The lessons were plain: The Japanese Navy is not yet ready to risk the show-down with our fleet which, our naval leaders are confident, will end in the enemy's defeat. Our power of initiative remains supreme, and we can continue our victorious, though difficult, advances, taking more and more key positions in the Pacific until the moment comes for us to strike boldly inside Japan's inner line of defenses.

Competent naval observers here indicated their regret that some of the reports on the plane-over-ship victory depicted the engagement as a major defeat for the main Japanese Fleet. As Secretary of the Navy James Forrestal pointed out, it was neither the main Japanese Fleet nor a crushing defeat.

As usual, the reaction of Japanese propagandists was so hysterical that it was almost amusing. Apparently, the harder we hit the Japanese the more "destructive" the Tokyo radio becomes in conjuring up the losses that supposedly were visited on our fleet.

This type of reckless lying also impresses trained observers here as significant, because it conveys to them that Japan must be hard

93

pressed to cover up the true fortunes of war in its reports to the home front.

Geography of the War

As we extend our conquests in the Pacific, the inter-relationship of the Pacific and the Far Eastern campaigns becomes closer. Extreme importance is placed here on conquest of the Marianas, because these islands are so situated geographically that they can strategically nullify the military usefulness of many of Japan's remaining bases in the Pacific.

When our conquest of Saipan is completed, as observers here are confident it will be, it may not even be necessary for us to attempt a land invasion of Guam, the base which Japan seized from us at the beginning of the war, unless we particularly wish to repossess the island. Planes from Saipan can neutralize any benefits the Japanese may derive from Truk, and Saipan's superior anchorage will make it possible for our fleet to straddle the sea lanes leading southward from Japan.

From the increased tempo of the Pacific war, which includes Gen. Douglas MacArthur's satisfactory advances in the southwest, it appears entirely logical that the time is nearing when a really decisive blow will be struck to establish ourselves on a major base inside Japan's inner line of defense. Informed eyes here still are turned on some corner of the Philippines; a Philippine base in our hands would make it possible for us to cut off Japan's vital oil supply in the Netherlands Indies, and also would make easier our cherished goal of establishing ourselves on the China east coast. The obviousness of this strategy may mean that we will fool the Japanese by striking elsewhere.

Toward Japan

However, it must not be assumed that because of our excellent progress in the Pacific we can move into the knock-out phase of the Pacific-Asiatic war with the same superiority. It must be remembered that the war with the Japanese is going to be ended in Japan and in the territory more immediately adjacent to the heart of the Japanese Empire.

Our Pacific gains are stepping-stones to this goal but the Japanese are working diligently to perfect their defenses along the inner lines where the final phases of the war will be fought. Their current drive into southeast China is evidence of this strategy.

Indeed, the persistent Japanese gains south of Changsha on the railway route from Hankow to Canton are the most depressing feature of the entire Pacific-Asiatic war panorama. The situation in southeast China is extremely frustrating for the Allied com

manders because for the moment there appears too be little we can do about it.

Observers here regard the south east China campaign as closely related to the Pacific war. The Japanese know that we intend ultimately to land on the east China coast to knock open a backdoor to their own islands.

Near U. S. Airbase

They also know from painful experience that air bases are vital to our advance. So they are moving south of Changsha, apparently in earnest, to deprive us of territory now valuable as advance base for Maj. Gen. Claire Chennault's United States Fourteenth Air Force. As this week neared its close the invaders were near Hengyang, which is one of our most advanced air bases in China.

The Japanese gains in China also must be viewed as a triple threat to the Allied cause in the Pacific and Far East. These threats are: (1) Make our air position more difficult; (2) set up an interior block to the back-door supply route into China that Lieut. Gen. Joseph W. Stilwell is attempting to carve, and (3) place an exceedingly serious strain on the economic and military position of the hard-pressed Chinese.

General Chennault's airmen were striking back furiously. Secretary of War Stimson pointed out this week that, in ten days, General Chennault's fliers had killed an estimated 3,000 Japanese soldiers by strafing troop columns and river traffic. However, if the Japanese are determined to take this territory, it seems inevitable that the Fourteenth Air Force's area of operations will be pushed back, which will make it more difficult for them to operate against coastal shipping and possibly to support any operations we eventually may plan against the coast of China.

The B-29 Superfortress will provide part of the answer to the problem that may be caused if our bases are pushed back. But, it is pointed out, Superfortresses take a lot of fuel, and scarcity of gasoline in that remote, inaccessible part of the world is one of the heartbreaking reasons that General Chennault's truly intrepid airmen are not able to do more than they are doing. In few sectors of the global battle front is the supply situation more difficult.

Retreat at Changsha

In the face of the Japanese advance, Chinese troops apparently did the best thing they could do by strategically withdrawing and escaping encirclement and annihilation in Changsha.

Military observers here detected this week evidence that the Japanese are determined to try to reinforce their troops in the Mo-

gaung-Myitkyina area in Burma, where they are under siege. It also was pointed out by Secretary Stimson that there is no reason to expect the Japanese to be kicked out of the Imphal area in India any time soon — though experts now consider this a mere nuisance operation against the British, valuable only for what underground activities the Japanese may be conducting in India.

One of the significant revelations of the past week regarding the Pacific war was Admiral Ernest F. King's disclosure that the United States Chiefs of Staff conferred in England recently with their opposite numbers on future plans to bring Britain's strength into the war against the Japanese just as soon as she is free to lend a hand in that part of the world.

June 25, 1944

JAPANESE CRACK ON UKHRUL FRONT

SOUTHEAST ASIA HEADQUARTERS, Kandy, Ceylon, July 10 (AP)—All organized Japanese resistance has ceased in Ukhrul, advance enemy base inside the border of northeastern India, Admiral Lord Louis Mountbatten's headquarters announced today.

More enemy positions north of the Ukhrul-Imphal road, fourteen miles from the latter city, have been cleared and villages sixteen miles northeast of Imphal also have been retaken, the announcement said.

Villages cleared of the Japanese included Chepu, Sagabung and Thawai as enemy opposition "crumbled with the isolation, dispersion and destruction of rear guards left to cover the withdrawal of his Thirty-first and Fifteenth Divisions," the communiqué from Admiral Mountbatten's headquarters said.

An indication that Lieut. Gen. Joseph W. Stilwell's American and Chinese forces had virtually completed the hard conquest of Myitkyina in north Burma was found in the communiqué statement that two Japanese fighters "attempting to strafe the Myitkyina area" were destroyed. Chinese south of the rain-soaked bastion made minor gains and straightened their line, killing ninety Japanese.

To the west in the Mogaung Valley, Chinese advancing down the main road reached within five miles of other Chinese occupying that base.

Many Japanese were reported killed in offensive patrolling in Arakan, far to the south on the Bay of Bengal approaches to Akyab.

CHUNGKING, China, July 10 (AP)—Chinese troops on the Yunnan front have fought to the walls of the big Japanese base of Tengyueh which blocks the way to a junction with Allied forces in Burma, the Chinese High Command announced today.

The objective of the Yunnan drive is to erase the enemy core of resistance at Tengyueh and facilitate a union with Lieut. Gen. Joseph W. Stilwell's forces fighting in Myitkyina, in northern Burma, ninety-five miles to the northwest. Advance elements of these two forces last were reported only twenty-six miles apart.

Tengyueh was a scene of confusion, with Chinese attacking from nearly all sides a Japanese force that was resisting fiercely on three sides of the city and which was attacking in turn a core of Chinese resistance inside the city.

Fighting continued for positions commanding the Burma Road west of the Salween River, while other Chinese forces were reorganizing for an assault on the strongly held Yunnan base of Lungling. The Chinese captured the town a few weeks ago but had to withdraw.

The Tokyo radio yesterday broadcast an Imperial Headquarters announcement claiming that Japanese air forces in the Burma theatre had "destroyed or set ablaze" a total of thirty-nine planes in an attack on Allied-held Myitkyina airfield on July 7.

Similar in tone to previous Japanese claims of Allied losses that later proved to be completely false or highly exaggerated, the announcement made the usual assertion that "all our planes returned safely."

The broadcast was recorded by the Federal Communications Commission.

July 11, 1944

CHINA AND INDIA AID PUT AT $1,400,000,000

WASHINGTON, July 16 (AP)—Leo T. Crowley, Foreign Economic Administrator, reported today that almost $1,400,000,000 worth of lend-lease goods were sent to the China-Burma-India theatre from the beginning of the war to May 1, 1944.

Three-quarters of the total, he said, consisted of planes, tanks, guns and other war material for the Chinese, British and Indian forces.

In addition, more than $217,000,000 in war materials had been consigned to Lieut. Gen. Joseph W. Stilwell for transfer to Chinese forces. The greater part of this was ordnance, accounting for almost $134,000,000; tanks and other vehicles, $63,000,000.

Major items in the general China-Burma-India distribution were ordnance, $216,319,000; aircraft, $269,404,000; tanks and vehicles, $270,187,000; industrial items, $322,328,000.

Help moved both ways, Mr. Crowley said, illustrating this with a report of tens of thousands of Indians working with American engineers building India bases for the giant B-29 bombing planes, and an estimated 400,000 Chinese laboring with crude tools or bare hands to create the surfaces from which the B-29's take off against Japan.

July 17, 1944

U. S. FLIERS PIN FOE INSIDE HENGYANG

CHUNGKING, China, Aug. 10 (U.P.)—The Chinese High Command today confirmed the fall of Hengyang, strategic Hunan Province rail junction town, but Chinese and American air men, intensifying their slashing attacks against the enemy there, have pinned the Japanese forces down and denied them the opportunity to exploit their success, a communiqué from Gen. Joseph W. Stilwell's headquarters reported.

Killed "virtually to the last man" in last-ditch street battles within the burned and battered town, the heroic Chinese garrison was overwhelmed on Tuesday after an epic defense that stalled the Japanese drive south along the Changsha-Canton rail line for more than six weeks, a Chinese communiqué said.

Japanese forces holding Hengyang, now under assault from all sides by Gen. Hsueh Yueh's vengance bent Chinese troops of the Ninth Corps Area, are unable to move supplies into the area in daylight or expand the ground they control, due to the Fourteenth American Air Force's continuous pounding of their positions and communications, today's reports showed.

Meanwhile the furious see-saw battles for position on the flanks of the Hunan Province battle, east and west of the Siang River, continued to rage unabated, the Chungking war bulletin reported.

The Chinese High Command has no knowledge of the fate of the commander of the annihilated forces within Hengyang, it said. Although the Japanese claim to have captured Gen. Fang Hsienchueh, ranking officer of the garrison, reports received here indicate that he probably died at the head of his surviving troops in the rubble of the blazing town.

[The Tokyo Radio yesterday reported that Emperor Hirohito sent a congratulatory message to the Japanese troops for their "successful campaigns" at Hengyang. The broadcast, recorded by the Federal Communications Commission, said the imperial commendations had been conveyed to the Japanese units in a "solemn ceremony" yesterday.]

Maj. Gen. Claire L. Chennault's airmen, in addition to their relentless attacks against the enemy in the Hengyang region, ranged north to smash at Japanese shipping on the Yangtze River between Lake Tungting and Hankow. They shot down nine Japanese fighters and damaged four more out of a flight of sixteen that attempted interception. Airfields in the Tungting Lake area also were attacked.

American Mitchell bombers plastered targets on the Yangtze near Kiukiang, southeast of Hankow, sinking two large boats and also bombed the Hankow airdrome.

Heavy damage was inflicted by American bombers striking at Amoy, on the southeast coast of China. A large steamer was damaged, docks hit, a seaplane hangar damaged and a radio station strafed.

Supply dumps at Swatow, a port southwest of Amoy, were raided and large fires started, General Stillwell's communiqué added.

August 11, 1944

CHINESE RETAKE BURMA ROAD BASE

Japanese Pull Out of Lungling —No B-29 Hit in Foe's Blow at Field, Stilwell Says

CHUNGKING, China, Sept. 18 (AP) — Chinese forces have reoccupied the important Burma Road base of Lungling and the Japanese garrison is withdrawing to the vicinity of Mangshih, thirteen miles to the southwest, where the enemy has begun work on defensive positions east and northeast of the city, the Chinese High Command said today.

Chinese troops are still fighting to reoccupy positions northeast of Lungling at Sankuanpo which have changed hands several times, but have taken the village of Nanchang near Lungling.

Gen. Joseph W. Stilwell's headquarters refuted a Tokyo claim that forty B-29's had been destroyed in an attack on American bases in China on Sept. 9. A small force of Japanese medium bombers attacked the bases that day, but caused no real damage and there were no losses of American aircraft, headquarters said.

KANDY, Ceylon, Sept. 18 (AP)—Troops of the Fifth Indian Division developed their crossings of the Manipur River in the Burma border area today while mountain fighting raged in the coastal Province of Arakan.

The southeast Asia communiqué said Fourteenth Army troops had occupied another strategic hill in the Mayu range in Arakan.

Accurate shelling dispersed Japanese raiding parties striking south of Maungdaw. Closely coordinated air support aided Allied troops fighting in Arakan.

Following up attacks yesterday on rail communications in north and south Burma, fighter-bombers of the Eastern Air Command attacked oil storage dumps in the central part. Stormy weather limited air operations in north Burma.

September 19, 1944

COMMUNISTS' BASE AIDS CHINESE ARMY

Uniforms and Arms Are Made and Wounded Are Treated in Remote District

By Wireless to THE NEW YORK TIMES.

QUARTERMASTER BASE OF EIGHTH ROUTE ARMY, in Shansi-Suiyuan Military Area, Aug. 29 (Delayed) —The writer is unable to give the location of this base except to say that to reach it he had to travel 250 miles horseback from Yenan in Shensi through mountainous country and that the main features of the vicinity are the Yellow River and the Great Wall.

The brisk life here is geared directly to the immediate day-by-day needs of the war. Here, guarded by peasant militia, are supply dumps, repair shops, equipment factories, evacuation hospitals and the plant of the regional newspaper, the Resistance War Daily.

Here also is the answer to the question of whether the Communist-led Eighth Route Army, fighting in the rear of the Japanese, is a loosely organized guerrilla formation or a regular military force. The answer is that it is a highly integrated regular army, employing guerrilla tactics in coordination with guerrilla detachments that can be ordered from place to place and with the defense militia, who fight only in the vicinity of their own towns and villages.

Rails Provide Arsenal's Steel

The raw materials warehouse for the near-by repair arsenal has a courtyard piled high with rails from Japanese railways, the Army's chief source of steel. The rails, cut into short lengths, are transported by mules to the rear. There were

hundreds of feet of pipe, ripped out of railway stations and great numbers of unexploded Japanese shells.

Large wooden crates overflowed with old Chinese copper coins with square holes, bought up from conservative local residents who had hoarded them since the fall of the empire. These hoards would be a numismatist's paradise. Some were issued 1,000 years ago. These treasures are to be made into shell cases.

The weapons warehouse had more enemy material, mortars, machine guns, rifles, ammunition, tear and blister gas cylinders, field radio and telephone equipment, some broken and some still fit for use.

The uniforms warehouse was filled with piles of old cotton-padded clothing and fur-lined leather tunics and pants used by the Eighth Route Army cavalry in Mongolia. Much is salvaged from these items. The old cotton padding is washed, refluffed and requilted. The old cloth is pressed and made into thick soles for shoes.

In other warehouses were bales of regulation gray-blue cloth, largely woven by the army itself and dyed with materials obtained from local plants. New cotton-quilted uniforms were baled, ready for the annual issue to the troops. Mules were being loaded with them for journeys over mountain trails to various unit headquarters.

Wounded Veterans Are Tailors

This base has thirty sewing machines and 130 tailors, mostly wounded veterans. Many of them were plying their needles, sitting cross-legged in traditional tailor fashion. This plant turns out 200 winter suits and many caps and shoes daily.

To save metal and enamel, buttons are lathe turned from local hardwood and insignia are made of porcelain with the design baked in. As in Yenan the soldier workers have a trade union and their own clubs. They work ten hours daily and study one hour under the army's plan to eliminate illiteracy.

This small base has seven hospital units, accommodating more than 1,000 patients. One unit has 110 men, many of whom were wounded in an engagement three weeks ago. They were carried for twelve days by peasant litter bearers.

The wounded men said it was much easier to fight the Japanese now because the best units had been withdrawn, that garrisons consisted largely of old men and boys and that the spirit of the enemy's new puppet troops was wavering.

There was one woman patient, a pretty twenty-four-year-old political worker, whose arm had been shattered above the elbow by a rifle bullet in a surprise encirclement. She said the doctors had promised that she would soon have partial use of her arm, after which she intended to return to the front.

October 14, 1944

STILWELL RECALL BARES RIFT WITH CHIANG

LONG SCHISM SEEN

Stilwell Break Stems From Chiang Refusal to Press War Fully

By BROOKS ATKINSON

Gen. Joseph W. Stilwell, relieved of his command in China, Burma and India, before leaving Chungking on Oct. 21 made a final swift tour of some of the military bases in his command and then flew directly toward Washington in his silver-colored transport plane facetiously dubbed "Uncle Joe's Chariot."

For the last two months negotiations had been going on between President Roosevelt's personal representative, Maj. Gen. Patrick J. Hurley, and Generalissimo Chiang Kai-shek to give General Stilwell full command of the Chinese ground and air forces under the Generalissimo and to increase China's participation in the counter-offensive against Japan.

Although the Generalissimo at first was inclined to agree to General Stilwell's appointment as commander, he decided later that he would accept any American commander except General Stilwell.

Pressed for Reform

His attitude toward the American negotiations became stiff and hostile. At a private meeting of the standing committee of the Kuomintang [National party] Central Executive Committee this month he announced the terms of his personal ultimatum to Americans who were pressing him for military and governmental reform. He declared that General Stilwell must go, that the control of American lend-lease materials must be put in his hands and that he would not be coerced by Americans into helping to unify China by making terms with the Chinese Communists. If America did not yield on these points, he said China would go back to fighting the Japanese alone, as she did before Pearl Harbor.

President Roosevelt agreed to the Generalissimo's demand for General Stilwell's recall. Dividing the huge China-Burma-India war sector in two, the War Department appointed Maj. Gen. Albert G. Wedemeyer, now Deputy Chief of Staff to Admiral Lord Louis Mountbatten, as Commander of United States Army Forces in China and Lieut. Gen. Daniel I. Sultan, General Stilwell's Chief of Staff in India, as Commander of United States Army Forces in India and Burma.

After a career of more than twenty years largely devoted to military affairs in China and two years and eight months as commander of the United States Army Forces in China, Burma and India and as Allied Chief of Staff to the Generalissimo, "Vinegar Joe" Stilwell has now concluded a busy and constantly frustrated attempt to help China stay in the war and to improve the combat efficiency of the Chinese forces.

Uncle Joe speaks Chinese. He knows more about China than most foreigners. He is more intimately acquainted with the needs and capacities of the Chinese Army than the Generalissimo and Gen. Ho Ying-chin, Minister of War and Chief of Staff, because he has repeatedly been in the field with the troops.

He is commonly regarded as the ablest field commander in China since "Chinese" Gordon. The second retreat with Stilwell seemed the final one. It was not from the enemy but from an ally.

The decision to relieve General Stilwell has the most profound implications for China as well as American policy toward China and the Allied war effort in the Far East. It may mean that the United States has decided from now on to discount China's part in a counter-offensive.

Inside China it represents the political triumph of a moribund anti-democratic regime that is more concerned with maintaining its political supremacy than in driving the Japanese out of China. America is now committed at least passively to supporting a regime that has become increasingly unpopular and distrusted in China, that maintains three secret police services and concentration camps for political prisoners, that stifles free speech and resists democratic forces.

The Main Difference

The fundamental difference between the Generalissimo and General Stilwell has been that the latter has been eager to fight the Japanese in China without delay and the Generalissimo has hoped that he would not have to.

In no other way is it possible to understand the long series of obstructions and delays that have made it impossible for General Stilwell to fulfill his original mission of equipping and training the "unlimited manpower" resources of the Chinese Army.

The Generalissimo has one positive virtue for which America is now indebted; he has never made peace with the Japanese, although there have been times when his Ministers thought the future looked hopeless. But the technique of preserving his ticklish balance of political power in China keeps him a passive man.

Although he is the acknowledged leader of China, he has no record of personal military achievement and his basic ideas for political leadership are those of a war lord. He conceives of armies as political forces.

In an enormous, loosely strung country populated chiefly by ignorant peasantry he maintains his authority by preventing any group from becoming too powerful. A few well equipped armies under a command not entirely loyal to him personally might upset the military and political balance inside China and curtail his authority.

The Chinese Communists, whom the generalissimo started trying to liquidate in 1927, have good armies that are now fighting guerrilla warfare against the Japanese in northeast China. The generalissimo regards these armies as the chief threat to his supremacy. For several years he has immobilized 300,000 to 500,000 (no one knows just how many) Central Government troops to blockade the Communists and keep them from expanding.

Distrusting the Communists, the generalissimo has made no sincere attempt to arrange at least a truce with them for the duration of the war. The generalissimo's regime, based on the support and subservience of General Ho, Dr. H. H. Kung, Minister of Finance, and Dr. Chen Li-fu, Minister of Education, has remained fundamentally unchanged over a long period and has become bureaucratic, inefficient and corrupt.

Most of the armies are poorly fed and shockingly maltreated. In some parts of the country the peasants regard the armies as bandits and thieves. In Honan last Spring the peasants turned against the Chinese armies during the Japanese offensive in revenge for the ruthlessness with which the armies collected rice during the famine years.

Most of China's troubles now are the result of her having been at war with Japan for more than seven years and totally blockaded for two and one-half.

The reason nothing is done to alleviate the miseries is that the generalissimo is determined to maintain his group of aging reactionaries in power until the war is over, when, it is commonly believed, he will resume his war against the Chinese Communists without distraction.

Bewildered and alarmed by the rapidity with which China is now falling apart, he feels secure only with associates who obey him implicitly. His rages become more and more ungovernable and attack the symptoms rather than the causes of China's troubles.

Since the negotiations with General Hurley began the generalissimo's attitude toward America has become more resentful and American criticisms of China is hotly rebuked. Relieving General Stilwell and appointing a successor has the effect of making us acquiesce in an unenlightened, cold-hearted autocratic political regime.

Into this stagnant, baleful atmosphere General Stilwell came in February, 1942, animated by the single idea of fighting the Japanese immediately. Like most foreigners who know the Chinese people, he loved them, for they are the glory of China. From long experience Stilwell had great confidence in the capacities of the Chinese soldiers, who even then were fighting on nothing.

In November, 1941, the Magruder Military Mission had already made an agreement with the generalissimo to train and equip the Chinese Army on the theory that it would then become unnecessary to ship thousands of doughboys to fight on Chinese soil. The war in China was initially handicapped by the decision to fight Germany first and Japan second. General Stilwell was never able to get 1 per cent of the American Army for use in his C-B-I theatre and was never able to get all the equipment he has wanted, because it has always been needed elsewhere.

On March 3, 1942, less than a month after he had arrived in China, General Stilwell was plunged into the calamitous Burma campaign without notice. He had to return to Chungking to induce the generalissimo to come to the front to vest him with sufficient authority to command the troops.

Even then the command was never secure or efficient. There were other troubles. At a time when the troops needed transport, most of China's trucks were hauling civilian loot out of Burma up the road into Chnia, where goods were worth huge sums of money.

When at last Stilwell got out of Burma into India he did persuade the generalissimo to let him feed, train and equip the Chinese soldiers who finally arrived. After training of a year and a half, those soldiers were the backbone of the Chinese divisions who got Myitkyina back last August and are now pushing toward Bhamo to free the Burma road. Inside China everything Stilwell has tried to do has been obstructed and delayed.

The generalissimo and his staff like the United States Air Force, which they get free and which asks for nothing except food and airfields, which we equip with buildings and installations. But the Chinese Government hedges and hesitates over anything involving the use of its armies. Foreigners can only conclude that the Chinese Government wants to save its armies to secure its political power after the war.

A nervous and driving field officer who is impatient with administrative details and political tangles, General Stilwell is no diplomat. He goes straight to the point in his dealings with anybody. He is plain and salty. He is per-

sonally incapable of assuming a reverential mood toward the generalissimo and he is impatient with incompetent meddling in military command. Although General Stilwell is anything but arrogant, the generalissimo complained that the American was trying to subjugate him.

But with the situation in China as it is, no diplomatic genius could have overcome the generalissimo's basic unwillingness to risk his armies in battle with the Japanese. Amid the intrigue and corruption of China's political and military administration, General Stilwell has been a lone man trying to follow orders, improve the combat efficiency of the Chinese Army, force open the Burma Road and get China back into the war.

Now he has been forced out of China by the political system that has been consistently blocking him and America is acquiescing in a system that is undemocratic in spirit as well as fact and is also unrepresentative of the Chinese people, who are good allies.

October 31, 1944

U. S. FORCED PLEDGE BY CHIANG ON WAR

By PRESTON GROVER
Associated Press Correspondent

NEW DELHI, India, Oct. 31—The removal of Gen. Joseph W. Stilwell as commander in the China-Burma-India theatre, it can be reported today, resulted from a combination of strategy and diplomacy such as could arise only in the Orient.

The abrupt new shaping of the whole American position in this part of the World War front began with the arrival in Chungking two months ago of Maj. Gen. Patrick J. Hurley and Donald M. Nelson, both carrying vast powers designed to get from China solid commitments for increased cooperation with the United States in the war against Japan.

The Associated Press is informed that the commitments were given virtually under threat of American withdrawal of her support of Chiang Kai-shek's government.

In turn, The Associated Press was informed under circumstances leaving no doubt of its accuracy, a last-minute softening in the American attitude resulted in an agreement for the withdrawal of General Stilwell as supreme commander in the C-B-I theatre as a face-saving and pacifying gesture demanded by the Generalissimo.

Story "Leaked" Through

So large are official "leaks" in Chungking and other Chinese political and military circles that major portions of the story of this strange shake-up in the war against Japan were known within hours after the events occurred.

As it was related to The Associated Press, General Hurley and Mr. Nelson explained to Generalissimo Chiang that there was much disappointment over the failure of the Central Government to come to an agreement with the Communists in the North so both they and the Central Government troops now blockading them could be brought against the Japanese in China.

Among the requests were:

First, that Chiang reorganize his Cabinet and eliminate reactionary obstructionists and anti-foreign members.

Second, that an American general be placed in command of Chinese operations not only in Burma but elsewhere in major operations against the Japanese.

During early conversations it evidently was assumed on both sides that General Stilwell was to be American commander.

The terms were put forcefully to Chiang, in some instances backed by specific messages from President Roosevelt. Stormy scenes followed. Chiang, as was expected, refused to dissolve or reorganize his Cabinet, although he accepted other conditions with the tacit admission that some of his commanders on the major fighting fronts in central China were not effective.

Then came an odd change in the proceedings.

Chiang became stubborn and it was discovered that H. H. Kung, his Finance Minister, visiting in the United States, was telegraphing him that the President was not supporting the stern position taken by his two representatives in Chungking.

Usually well-informed sources, whose reports The Associated Press believes reliable, stated that Mr. Kung telegraphed the Generalissimo that Harry Hopkins had informed him there was no cause for alarm in the American attitude and that if Chiang would hold out determinedly he would win all points.

Learning of these reports, the American negotiators evidently obtained a flat statement from the President in a message that he was not fooling and backed the negotiators at that point fully.

As their part in the bargaining, the Americans had the power to withhold lend-lease supplies and to withdraw Maj. Gen. Claire L. Chennault and his United States Fourteenth Air Force from China.

Finally an agreement was reached that included the term that an American would get command of Chinese field forces. It was a large pill to swallow, but in the interests of harmony Chiang evidently agreed at one stage to take it and keep the war going at top speed. He agreed to give General Stilwell command of Chinese field forces with the comment that he would "give him my full confidence."

Then, to the amazement of all the negotiators, Chiang declared that General Stilwell must go. He cited charges. For security reasons, the nature of the charges cannot be disclosed.

Charges Are Rejected

The Generalissimo was adamant and the United States representatives were faced with capitulation on this point or a break in the policy of supporting Chiang's Government. A few days ago General Stilwell was relieved of his command and left for America. Chiang was specifically informed, however, that the United States did not accept his charges against General Stilwell.

In China Chiang evidently gained "face" by the maneuver, which is looked upon in many Chinese and American quarters as capitulation.

Generally it is recognized that much time has been lost through the disagreements and that the American hope of close and harmonious relationship with the Chinese Central Government has been greatly shaken.

Around Chungking and at air bases there is much discussion of who is to blame for the defeats in central China. Many Chinese complain that General Stilwell and the United States have failed in the delivery of adequate supplies. The old bitterness between Generals Stilwell and Chennault is endlessly reviewed.

Critics of General Stilwell insist

that if he had turned over to General Chennault all the capacity of the "hump" airline, General Chennault's air force could have kept the Japanese from advanced American bases in central China, which have recently fallen to the enemy.

Supporters of General Stilwell and some within General Chennault's official family have argued that an air force alone cannot protect bases and that the weak Chinese performance last summer tested the Chennault contention and found it wanting.

China in Dictator's Grip

By THOBURN WIANT
Associated Press Correspondent

LONDON, Oct. 31.—The Kuomintang régime, headed by Generalissimo Chiang, has been—and is—more concerned with the inevitable civil war against the 80,-000,000 Chinese Communists than in the struggle against Japan.

After nearly two years in the China-Burma-India theatre as a war correspondent, I am convinced the Generalissimo and his party leaders are primarily—and mostly —interested in perpetuating themselves.

Democracy does not exist in China. There probably is no more effective dictatorship than that of the Kuomintang. There is no freedom of speech, or of press, or of much of anything else.

There are secret police, concentration camps and firing squads for those who dare to speak, or write, or act out of turn. There also are ingenious means of applying "do-it-or-else" pressure.

For years China has been on the verge of falling apart.

All this may sound strange to Americans, who had thought the Chinese had been fighting heroic battles against the Japanese for the last seven years.

Why hasn't the American public been kept informed? First, because of Chinese censorship. Second, because Washington held out hope that the mess could be cleaned up. Washington, through General Stilwell, gave Chiang every assistance possible under the circumstances.

The mess became so bad, however, that General Stilwell was finally recalled to Washington.

Stilwell Eager to Fight

I have just come to London after a leave in the United States and have excellent reason to believe that General Stilwell was always eager to fight the Japanese in China, without delay. On the other hand, the Generalissimo apparently reckoned the Americans would do the job for him eventually and that he could hoard most of his resources for the civil war.

General Stilwell did everything humanly possible. Some uninformed persons hastily interpreted his recall as a rebuke. Now they are beginning to see that he deserves not only a pat on the back but unique recognition for his long-suffering, conscientious, loyal, skillful service.

Few fighters have had to absorb so many blows—legal and otherwise—as 62-year-old Uncle Joe. He took them like the champion he is, and kept slugging.

For the last two years, and before, American military and civilian observers have left China for Washington with astonishing reports on conditions under the Generalissimo.

Early in 1943 an observer from China told me:

"I had to see it to believe it. Only Stilwell could keep going against such obstacles, political and otherwise."

He asserted that lend-lease materials were being saved for the civil war; that approximately 1,000,000 of the Generalissimo's troops were in northern China,

watching and sparring with the Communists.

He said that Chinese in many sectors were resisting only on a token basis; that goods were passing freely in many areas, from the Japanese to the Chinese and vice versa; that money and letters could easily be sent into and out of Japanese-occupied centers such as Shanghai and Hong Kong; that the money market seemed to be maneuvered for the benefit of those in power.

Correspondents knew all this but we could not write it then.

There remained hope for a change for the better. It was hard to see how it could become worse.

November 1, 1944

CHIANG GIVES SOONG DUTIES OF PREMIER

CHUNGKING, China, Dec. 4— Foreign Minister T. V. Soong, brother of Mme. Chiang Kai-shek, assumed the duties of Premier of China today in a popular move apparently paving the way for a working agreement between the Central Government and the Communists of North China.

Mr. Soong's attitude toward the Communists is known to be moderate, and his accession to greater influence comes coincidentally with unconfirmed reports of an agreement in principle between the two parties to wage a common war against Japan.

Mr. Soong, who stepped into his new post with his appointment as Acting President of the Executive Yuan in succession to his brother-in-law, H. H. Kung, is regarded in Washington and London as possibly's China's most capable diplomat and statesman.

Mr. Kung previously had resigned as Finance Minister and had been succeeded by O. K. Yui, for-

mer Mayor of Shanghai. Mr. Kung retains his post as head of four Chinese Government banks.

[Mr. Kung, who is on a mission in the United States, remains as Vice President of the Executive Yuan, the Chinese News Service reported.]

Although Generalissimo Chiang Kai-shek remains President of the Executive Yuan and, therefore, actually the country's Premier, it was felt that the appointment of Mr. Soong as his "right-hand man" would enable the commander in chief to concentrate more fully on his military tasks.

Mr. Soong is popular throughout the country, and his appointment will strengthen the Central Government immeasurably in the present critical military situation.

A report — possibly inspired— said that the Communist leader, Gen. Chou En-lai, had in his possession the draft of an agreement between the Central Government and the Communists, and that it awaited only the approval of other Communist leaders to become effective.

Donald M. Nelson, economic adviser to the Chiang Government, now is en route to Washington to report to President Roosevelt on the progress he has made toward getting Chinese industry geared up for an all-out war effort.

December 5, 1944

HURLEY APPOINTED AS ENVOY TO CHINA

WASHINGTON, Nov. 27—President Roosevelt announced today the appointment of Maj. Gen. Patrick Jay Hurley to be Ambassador to China.

General Hurley, who has accomplished many confidential missions for the President, is now in Chungking, where he went in company with Donald Nelson nearly three months ago, and is actively discharging the diplomatic duties of the office, which does not become official until approved by the Senate. This is expected to be done within the week.

In taking charge of American diplomatic relations in China at this time, General Hurley faces a delicate situation, involving the whole future of Sino-American relations, which has been brought to public notice through the removal of Gen. Joseph W. Stilwell and the recent Chinese Cabinet shakeup. It will be his task to contribute toward the strengthening of Chinese unity and to the development of Chinese action in the war against Japan.

Maj. Gen. Patrick J. Hurley
Associated Press, 1942.

Treated With Chiang Kai-shek

General Hurley, as representative of President Roosevelt in China, was closely associated with negotiations which led to these developments and the reported promise of Generalissimo Chiang Kai-shek to take strong measures to increase the Chinese war effort.

In dealings of a similar nature General Hurley has repeatedly distinguished himself in missions both in this country and abroad. It was on such a mission to the Soviet Union, where he spent two months late in the summer of 1942, that General Hurley brought back data on the Russian armies and their conduct of operations in the field, which he obtained by personal investigation and which brought invaluable first-hand knowledge of the Russian war effort to our Government.

General Hurley was decorated as the result of his work in the Far East, where he went on another assignment connected with our running of the Japanese blockade of the Philippines in 1942.

As Minister to New Zealand he performed a signal service early in the war and while in the Far East Theatre of Operations was wounded at Port Darwin in Australia in one of the first Japanese air attacks.

Born in Indian Territory

General Hurley was born in 1883 in the Choctaw Nation, Indian Territory, before Oklahoma was admitted to the Union. His early work was as national attorney for the Choctaw Indians, before serving in the first World War. In France he saw action in the Aisne-Marne, Meuse-Argonne and St. Mihiel offensives, rising from the rank of major to that of colonel at the end of the war. He was named a brigadier general in January, 1942, and was returned to active duty in April of that year. In December, 1943, he became a major general.

He had served as Assistant Secretary of War for a few months before becoming Secretary of War from 1929 to 1933 in the Hoover Cabinet.

General Hurley has taken an important role in various civilian activities, among which was assisting in the organizing of the United States Chamber of Commerce in 1912. He was chairman of the Republican State Convention in Oklahoma in 1926, and is credited with concluding the agreement with Mexico which indemnified the private owners of oil properties seized by the Mexican Government.

November 28, 1944

Chinese Burma Push Wins Bhamo; British Gain 17 Miles in Arakan

BHAMO, Burma, Dec. 15— Troops of the Chinese Thirty-eighth Division captured Bhamo unexpectedly at 2 P. M. today after the trapped Japanese garrison made a desperate attempt to fight its way south along the Irrawaddy River last night.

Chinese guns cut down the fleeing Japanese and their bodies dotted the Irrawaddy beach when Chinese troops entered the town this afternoon. Vultures already surrounding the dead Japanese flapped off as they passed.

[Smashing forward in the Arakan district, British forces pushed to within forty miles of the port of Akyab, on the west Burma coast. They also cleared Buthedaung, sixty miles north of Akyab, of Japanese, The Associated Press reported.]

The entire Japanese defense of Bhamo collapsed when the breakthrough failed and troops of Maj. Gen. Li Hung's Thirty-eighth Division, who had been steadily tightening the ring around the town for twenty-eight days, moved in to mop up the intricate network of trenches and bunkers where the enemy had held out.

A few Japanese were believed to be still hiding under some building foundations, but except for an occasional rifle shot the town was quiet for the first time in nearly a month.

Some of the bunkers in the enemy's defense fortifications were covered with six layers of teakwood logs.

Bhamo is at the end of the Irrawaddy River supply line, navigable by 300-foot steamers from Rangoon.

It's capture increases to approximately 400 miles the length of the new Burma-China supply route along the Ledo Road that has been cleared of Japanese.

[At last reports the Chinese in western Yunnan were within twelve miles of Wanting on the north and eleven miles on the east.]

CHINA COMMUNIST ASSAILS CHUNGKING

Mao, Party Chairman, Urges Suppression of Reactionaries, Parleys Having Failed

Mao Tse-tung, chairman of the Chinese Communist party, was quoted yesterday by the Chinese Communist radio at Yenan as saying that negotiations between the Communists and the Chungking Government had not "attained the least result." The dispatch was recorded by the Federal Communications Commission.

Mr. Mao said that there was little prospect of accomplishing the desired unity in China by negotiation. He accused the Chungking regime of "defeatism" and "obstinacy in holding to a one-party dictatorship."

The result of Chungking's policy, he said, was a China "artificially" split by a "reactionary group" and incapable of effective action against the Japanese invaders.

Remarking on American landings on Leyte and other military successes of the United Nations, the Communist leader warned against further Japanese gains in a divided China.

"The Japanese invaders will certainly resort to stratagems to induce capitulation of the Chinese Government through China's capitulators," he said.

Mr. Mao claimed that the Yenan regime alone had carried out the principles advocated by Dr. Sun Yat-sen in the revolution of 1911 for the creation of a "new democracy" and had been able to unite people "of all walks of life" into a "heroic army" that had "shattered all enemy offensives" and was about to launch a counter-offensive "to recover vast lost territory."

He called on the people of China to support "democratic patriotic movements" in the area under Chungking's control in their efforts to "suppress any reactionary authorities," to be vigilant against the activities of capitulators and to mobilize all forces to resist further Japanese advances.

"Our sole task is to cooperate with the Allies to overthrow the Japanese invaders," he went on.

CHINA COMMUNISTS REJECT 4 OFFERS

Gen. Chou Returns to Yenan With New Proposals—Hurley Aids in Negotiations

CHUNGKING, China, Feb. 14 (Æ)—China's Communists and the Chungking Government, whose long-standing differences have been declared a hindrance to China's war effort, have been negotiating for two weeks with the assistance of the United States Ambassador, Maj. Gen. Patrick J. Hurley, Information Minister Wang Shih-chieh disclosed today.

The Communists, after the two weeks of discussion, rejected a four-point settlement offered by the Chungking Government. Then the Government made new proposals which the Communist delegate, Gen. Chou En-lai, has taken back to Yenan, Mr. Wang declared.

The Government made a number of "important concessions" in the negotiations, according to Mr. Wang, who was one of the negotiators. Among them, he said, were these:

(1) A readiness to recognize the Chinese Communist party as a lawful political party.

(2) Inclusion of a high-ranking Communist official in the national military council.

(3) Inclusion of Communist representatives and representatives of other political parties in the Executive Yuan, with a view of forming a sort of wartime cabinet.

(4) Establishment of a committee of three to consider a reorganization of the Communist army and the question of supplies for it, with Government and Communist representatives on the committee having equal status and with possibly an American army officer presiding.

"The Communists considered these proposals unacceptable," Mr. Wang said, "and rejected them, although they brought forth a proposal to convene a conference of all political parties."

The Chungking government, "in compliance with the general idea of this request," has offered to convoke a conference of the Kuomintang [Government party], the Chinese Communist party and other parties, as well as some non-partisan independent leaders, to consider interim measures of military and political unification pending the convoking of a national congress, Mr. Wang said.

The Communists' Version

CHUNGKING, China, Feb. 14 (U.P.)—The Communist version of the break in the negotiations with the Government is that the discussions were snagged by the "refusal" of the Chungking government to grant to the Communists any real measure of power or voice in the Government. The chief Communist demand is for a curtailment of the personal power of Generalissimo Chiang Kai-shek in favor of an organization similar to the United States Congress, which would be the nation's highest authority.

Neutral observers were inclined to think that there was only a bare possibility of agreement between the two groups.

December 16, 1944

December 18, 1944

February 15, 1945

SOVIET DECLARES WAR ON JAPAN

RUSSIA AIDS ALLIES

Joins Pacific Struggle After Spurning Foe's Mediation Plea

SEEKS EARLY PEACE

Molotoff Reveals Move Three Months After Victory in Europe

By BROOKS ATKINSON
By Wireless to THE NEW YORK TIMES.

MOSCOW, Aug. 8 — Russia declared war on Japan tonight. In a dramatic press conference held at 8:30 P. M., Foreign Commissar Vyacheslaff M. Molotoff read the declaration, which was announced to the public at 10 P. M., Moscow time [3 P. M. New York time].

In view of Japan's refusal of the Allies' demand for unconditional surrender, Mr. Molotoff said, the Allies proposed that the Soviet Union "join the war against Japanese aggression and thus shorten the duration of the war, reduce the number of victims and facilitate the speedy restoration of universal peace.

"Loyal to its Allied duty," the Foreign Commissar continued, "the Soviet Government has accepted the proposal of the Allies and has joined in the declaration of the Allied Powers of July 26. The Soviet Government considers that this policy is the only means able to bring peace nearer, free the people from further sacrifice and suffering and give the Japanese people the possibility of avoiding the dangers and destruction suffered by Germany after her refusal to capitulate unconditionally."

Closing his concise statement, Mr. Molotoff declared:

"In view of the above, the Soviet Government declares that from tomorrow, that is Aug. 9, the Soviet Union will consider itself to be at war with Japan."

The Soviet Government's declaration comes three months after the victory over Germany, supporting rumors that some months ago the Soviet Government intimated it would join in the war against Japan three months after victory was won in Europe.

For the first time Mr. Molotoff revealed that the Japanese Government had asked the Soviet Union to mediate for a cessation of hostilities about the middle of June. Japanese Ambassador Naotaka Sato delivered the message, and also a special message from the Japanese Emperor, to Mr. Molotoff.

[A Moscow broadcast recorded in London said Japan's request was made in mid-July, the press services reported.]

"I can add," Mr. Molotoff said, "that President Truman, Prime Minister Churchill and Prime Minister Attlee were informed."

The Japanese Government refused the demand of the United States, Great Britain and China for unconditional surrender, made on July 26 "and mediation by the Soviet Government became absolutely groundless," Mr. Molotoff said.

After reading the statement, Mr. Molotoff said that he had communicated the Soviet Union's momentous decision to the Japanese Ambassador at 5 P. M. today. He told him that an identical statement would be made by the Soviet Ambassador in Tokyo.

After that he informed the Ambassadors of the United States, Great Britain and China, who, he said, had "expressed great satisfaction."

According to Mr. Molotoff, "Mr. Sato gave very careful study to the text of the declaration of war." He gave the Japanese Ambassador permission to send his last messages, after which communication was cut off. Mr. Sato's permission to return to Japan will be contingent upon similar facilities given to the Soviet Ambassador in Tokyo [Jacob A. Malik]. All Japanese in Moscow will enter the Japanese embassy.

In closing the press conference, which took less than a half hour, Mr. Molotoff said it was possible that there would be a new treaty with China. "The question is now under consideration," he said. Premier T. V. Soong and Minister of Foreign Affairs Wang Shih-chiek of China arrived in Moscow yesterday.

Although people all over the world had been speculating on the possibilities of the Soviet Union's joining the war against Japan ever since Pearl Harbor, and especially since the victory in Europe, this evening's declaration of war came as a complete surprise. At 7:30 correspondents were notified individually that an "important announcement" would be made in the press section of the Foreign Office.

Leaving the Hotel Metropole, correspondents noticed that the baggage of Japanese correspondents and other Japanese living there was being piled in the lobbies and loaded in automobiles outside. At the conference it was noticed that none of them was present. So when the party was conducted into Mr. Molotoff's conference room in an adjacent building, everyone suspected what the announcement was going to be.

Promptly at 8:30 Mr. Molotoff briskly entered the room, wearing a blue suit instead of the official State Department uniform. He seemed to be in high spirits. Without ceremony he sat at a desk and asked the correspondents to join him. He read his statement, which was translated into English sentence by sentence.

At 10 o'clock loudspeakers throughout Moscow played the national anthem and repeated the declaration of war, adding further information about the notification of the Allied Governments.

When the radio announcement was heard, people who were waiting in front of the metro station in the Square of the Revolution crossed the street to hear what was said. They received the announcement in thoughtful silence. Having been at peace for three months, the Russian people are at war again, with full understanding of what that means. About a half hour after the announcement formations of soldiers began marching through the square with dramatically heavy tread, singing war songs.

On the whole Moscow seemed to take the news of the resumption of war quietly—perhaps having expected something of the sort would happen.

Although nothing specific is known about the Russian Armies available for the Japanese war, it is generally believed tht adequate troops and supplies have been ready for some time. Troop movements across the vast stretches of Russia to the east have been observed recently. American lend-lease supplies have been arriving in Vladivostok without interruption in Russian ships.

JAPAN SURRENDERS

By ARTHUR KROCK

Special to THE NEW YORK TIMES.

WASHINGTON, Aug. 14—Japan today unconditionally surrendered the hemispheric empire taken by force and held almost intact for more than two years against the rising power of the United States and its Allies in the Pacific war.

The bloody dream of the Japanese military caste vanished in the text of a note to the Four Powers accepting the terms of the Potsdam Declaration of July 26, 1945, which amplified the Cairo Declaration of 1943.

Like the previous items in the surrender correspondence, today's Japanese document was forwarded through the Swiss Foreign Office at Berne and the Swiss Legation in Washington. The note of total capitulation was delivered to the State Department by the Legation Charge d'Affaires at 6:10 P. M., after the third and most anxious day of waiting on Tokyo, the anxiety intensified by several premature or false reports of the finale of World War II.

Orders Given to the Japanese

The Department responded with a note to Tokyo through the same channel, ordering the immediate end of hostilities by the Japanese, requiring that the Supreme Allied Commander —who, the President announced, will be Gen. Douglas Mac-Arthur—be notified of the date and hour of the order, and instructing that emissaries of Japan be sent to him at once --at the time and place selected by him—"with full information of the disposition of the Japanese forces and commanders."

President Truman summoned a special press conference in the Executive offices at 7 P. M. He handed to the reporters three texts.

The first—the only one he read aloud—was that he had received the Japanese note and deemed it full acceptance of the Potsdam Declaration, containing no qualification whatsoever; that arrangements for the formal signing of the peace would be made for the "earliest possible moment;" that the Japanese surrender would be made to General Mac-Arthur in his capacity as Supreme Allied Commander in Chief; that Allied military commanders had been instructed to cease hostilities, but that the formal proclamation of V-J Day must await the formal signing.

The text ended with the Japanese note, in which the Four Powers (the United States, Great Britain, China and Russia) were officially informed that the Emperor of Japan had issued an imperial rescript of surrender, was prepared to guarantee the necessary signatures to the terms as prescribed by the Allies, and had instructed all his commanders to cease active operations, to surrender all arms and to disband all forces under their control and within their reach.

The President's second announcement was that he had instructed the Selective Service to reduce the monthly military draft from 80,000 to 50,000 men, permitting a constant flow of replacements for the occupation forces and other necessary military units, with the draft held to low-age groups and first discharges given on the basis of long, arduous and faithful war service. He said he hoped to release 5,000,000 to 5,500,000 men in the subsequent year or eighteen months, the ratio governed in some degree by transportation facilities and the world situation.

The President's final announcement was to decree holidays tomorrow and Thursday for all Federal workers, who, he said, were the "hardest working and perhaps the least appreciated" by the public of all who had helped to wage the war.

Mr. Truman spoke calmly to the reporters, but when he had finished reading his face broke into a smile. Also present were Secretary of State James F. Byrnes and Admiral William D. Leahy, the President's personal Chief of Staff, and two other members of the Cabinet—Henry A. Wallace, Secretary of Commerce, and James V. Forrestal, Secretary of the Navy—managed to respond to a hurry call in time to be there. The agreement to issue the statements simultaneously in all the Allied capitals, and the brief period between the call to the Cabinet and the announcement, were responsible. Later the chief war administrators and Cordell Hull, former Secretary of State, arrived to congratulate the President.

President Addresses Crowd

After the press conference, while usually bored Washington launched upon a noisy victory demonstration, the President with Mrs. Truman walked out to the fountain in the White House grounds that face on Pennsylvania Avenue and made the V sign to the shouting crowds.

But this did not satisfy the growing assemblage, or probably the President either, for, in response to clamor, he came back and made a speech from the north portico, in which he said that the present emergency was as great as that of Pearl Harbor Day and must and would be met in the same spirit. Later in the evening he appeared to the crowds and spoke again.

He then returned to the executive mansion to begin work at once on problems of peace, including domestic ones affecting reconversion, unemployment, wage-and-hour scales and industrial cut-backs, which are more complex and difficult than any he has faced and call for plans and measures that were necessarily held in abeyance by the exacting fact of war.

But certain immediate steps to deal with these problems and restore peacetime conditions were taken or announced as follows:

1. The War Manpower Commission abolished all controls, effective immediately, creating a free labor market for the first time in three years. The commission also set up a plan to help displaced workers and veterans find jobs.

2. The Navy canceled nearly $6,000,000,000 of prime contracts.

The Japanese offer to surrender, confirmed by the note received through Switzerland today, came in the week after the United States Air Forces obliterated Hiroshima with the first atomic bomb in history and the Union of Soviet Socialist Republics declared war on Japan. At the time the document was received in Washington Russian armies were pushing back the Japanese armies in Asia and on Sakhalin Island, and the Army and Navy of the United States with their air forces—aided by the British—were relentlessly bombarding the home islands.

When the President made his announcements tonight it was three years and 250 days after the bombing of Pearl Harbor, which put the United States at war with Japan. This was followed immediately by the declarations of war on this country by Germany and Italy, the other Axis partners, which engaged the United States in the global conflict that now, in its military phases, is wholly won.

If the note had not come today the President was ready, though reluctant, to give the order that would have spread throughout Japan the hideous death and destruction that are the toll of the atomic bomb.

Officially the Japanese note was a response to the communication to Tokyo, written on behalf of the Allies Aug. 11 by Secretary Byrnes, which was itself a reply to a Japanese offer on Aug. 10 to surrender on the understanding of the Japanese Government that the Potsdam Declaration did not "prejudice the prerogatives" of the Emperor of Japan as its "sovereign ruler."

Plan on the Emperor

Mr. Byrnes wrote, in effect, that the Japanese might keep their Emperor if they chose to do so of their own free-will, but that he would be placed under the authority of the Allied Commander-in-Chief in Tokyo and would be responsible to that commander for his official and public activities.

Relief rather than jubilation that the grim and costly task of conquering the Axis is done was the emotion of officials, from the President down, who have traversed the long and agonizing road to victory since Dec. 7, 1941, when the Japanese attacked Pearl Harbor while Tokyo's "peace" envoys—Admiral Kichisahura Nomura and Ambassador Saburo Kurusu— were still continuing their negotiations with Secretary of State Hull. The road is piled high with the bodies of American soldiers, sailors, airmen and civilians who gave their lives that the victory might be attained.

And, in a solemn hour of triumph, the men in Washington that were their military and civilian commanders could not be jubilant in the lasting memory of these human sacrifices. On the contrary, they seemed more than ever resolved to produce a system of world security which for a long time would obviate the necessity of such sacrifices to dictators and aggressive nations; and to impress on the Japanese—as on the Germans— their crimes, nor relax their punishments, until they learn to follow the ways of peace.

Though the victory over the Japanese as well as the Nazis had always seemed assured to the American authorities, it did not become a certainty until the Allies — through United States invention and production, Allied military and scientific skills and the fortitude of the British, Chinese, Russian and American populations — were able to change from defense to attack. This change, so far as the Pacific was concerned, came after the Battle of Midway gathered force after the actions of the Coral Sea and the Philippines and came to crescendo with the captures of Saipan, Iwo Island and Okinawa, the perfection of radar and the discovery and use of the atomic bomb. But before these successes the story was very different.

The Japanese attack on Pearl Harbor found the Pacific Fleet divided, half of it crowded in the roadstead, the other half dispatched for Atlantic service for reasons of policy. These reasons grew out of President Roosevelt's decision that the Nazi menace required the fleet diversion to the Atlantic for immediate national defense, and out of his belief that, as he expressed it, he could "baby along Japan." This latter view was the foundation of the underlying policy by which the United States continued to furnish Japan with scrap iron, petrol and other materials transferable to war uses long after Japan by many officials was conceded to be bent on hemispheric and eventual world-wide aggression.

There followed the loss of the Philippines and Malaya, the death march of Bataan, the shelling of the coast of California, the desperate, costly invasion and divided struggle of Guadalcanal, the defense of the Antipodes and the slow process by which General MacArthur— necessarily long held to small resources — built up the force that won back the Philippines and whose commander will be the military ruler, civil supervisor and warden of the Japanese nation.

These are a few highlights in the violent chapter of unprecedented war that ended today with the receipt of the note from Tokyo. It is not strange that, remembering all these things, the President and high officials were under a strain as acute as any mother, father or wife of a man in the Pacific combat could have been while waiting for the words that would bring the chapter to a present close.

The alternative for the Japanese would, of course, have been national suicide. But there are many in Washington, students of this strange race or baffled by the ways of the Orient, who have predicted that such would be the decision of the Japanese military leaders to which the people would submit. The Japanese, they contended, would commit mass suicide before they would yield their god, the Emperor, to an alien enemy as his overlord.

But now this god, in the person of an ordinary human being, representative of other human beings who were vanquished with him, is to take his orders from a mortal man who, above all others, symbolizes the spirit of the alien enemy that was foremost in crushing the myth of divinity and shattering the imperial dream. And the Emperor, with his Ministers and commanders, has been obliged to accept the condition that disproves the fanatical concept used by the militarists of Japan to produce unquestioned obedience to orders issued in the Emperor's name, however much or little he may have had to do with them.

REDS WARN CHIANG TO AVERT CIVIL WAR

CHUNGKING, China, Aug. 19—The Chinese Communist commander, Gen. Chu Teh, told Generalissimo Chiang Kai-shek today that he must act immediately to avert the "grave threat" of civil war between Communist and Government forces in China.

His defiant note, asserting that 260,000,000 Chinese were "dissatisfied" with General Chiang's regime, coincided with foreign reports reaching Chungking that 20,-000 to 30,000 Communist guerrillas were converging on the Yangtze River port of Wuhu in possible preparation for a sixty-mile drive downstream to Nanking, which is to be the new seat of Chiang's Government. The Chungking Government did not confirm this report.

Telegraphing a series of six demands to General Chiang, the Communist general warned the Government leader to heed them, and he also insisted on full Communist participation in the surrender of Japanese forces in China.

General Chu demanded that the Communists take part in the Allied acceptance of Japan's formal surrender and in the peace conference. On internal issues, he demanded the abolition of what he called the Government's "one-party dictatorship" and called for an all-party conference to establish a "democratic coalition government."

There was no comment from General Chiang, who sent instructions by radio to the Japanese commander in China, Gen. Ysauji Okamura, detailing the flight routes for the enemy surrender envoys who are due Tuesday.

General Chu, contending that the Communists had borne the brunt of the war against Japan and accusing General Chiang of having met it "with folded arms," sent his six demands in answer to the Government leader's call for talks to discuss differences. The points were:

(1) Chungking should consult and reach an agreement with Yenan on the acceptance of Japanese and puppet troop surrenders and on any pacts and treaties concluded after the surrender.

(2) Communists should receive the right to accept the surrender of Japanese and puppet troops in those areas under Communist control, in "accordance with the terms of the Potsdam Declaration." In this connection, General Chu said that General Chiang's "extremely unreasonable" order that the Communists should remain at their posts and take no action in disarming the Japanese was a pretext for Chungking to take over the enemy's arms and create the "unprecedently grave threat of civil war."

(3) Communists should be allowed to send their own representatives to the Allied acceptance of Japan's surrender and should be permitted to participate in the post-war control of Japan.

(4) Communists should have the right to take part in the peace conference and in future conferences of the United Nations.

(5) The present "one-party dictatorship" should be abolished, an all-party conference called, and Government troops around Communist areas should be withdrawn and democratic reforms instituted throughout China.

(6) General Chiang should take steps to avoid civil war, and "on this point," General Chu said, "I now seriously warn you not to consider this unimportant."

General Chu went on to tell General Chiang that "the Chinese people are dissatisfied with you and your Government, which cannot represent the broad masses."

He said that his own order to Japanese General Okamura to lead his troops to surrender in Communist areas was "exceedingly just and greatly conforms with the common interest of China and her allies."

Finally, he reiterated that he resolutely and thoroughly opposed General Chiang's order that the Communists should not take independent action, and he called on the Generalissimo "publicly to admit your mistake and publicly to retract your order."

Meanwhile, General Chiang ordered General Okamura to fly his surrender envoys to Chihkiang in Hunan Province to capitulate to Gen. Ho Ying-chin, commander of China's field forces. The radiogram said the number of Japanese representatives should not exceed five, among whom should be a pilot familiar with airfields at Nanking and Shanghai.

General Okamura's deputy chief of staff, General Kiyoshi, will be one representative, it was disclosed. He was ordered to carry maps showing the order and deployment of troops of all Japanese forces in China, Formosa and Indo-China. In the event of bad weather, the mission was ordered to be carried out Wednesday.

In Chungking, meantime, all officials worked overtime on plans to take over Japanese-occupied areas. The Generalissimo appointed representatives of the National Military Council at Shanghai and Peiping and special commissioners who will take over communications.

Chinese Reds Report New Gains

Chinese Communist armies, operating in North and East China, captured six county towns from the Japanese during the period of Aug. 12-16, the Chinese Communist New China News Agency said yesterday in a dispatch transmitted by the Yenan wireless station.

The dispatch, recorded by the Federal Communications Commission, said that the Eighth Route Army had captured Taolin county town, sixty miles northwest of Kweisui, capital of Suiyuan Province, and Tunga county town, fifty miles southwest of Tsinan.

In the central Anhwei liberated area, units of the new Fourth Army's Seventh Division captured Wuwei County town, twenty miles west of Wuhu, while units of the Second Division captured Tingyuan County town, seventy miles northwest of Nanking; Chuyi County town, seventy miles north of Nanking and Laian County town, forty miles northwest of Nanking.

August 20, 1945

SOVIET-CHINA PACT REBUFFS REDS

By TILLMAN DURDIN
By Wireless to THE NEW YORK TIMES.

CHUNGKING, China, Monday. Aug. 27—The Chinese Communists can expect no aid or comfort from the Soviet Union in the threatened civil war in China. This, on first consideration, seems to be the implication of the Sino-Soviet treaty. The meaning of the treaty here last night.

Once in the main body of the treaty and once in a reply to a Chinese note, the Soviet Union pledges itself to respect the sovereignty and territorial integrity of China and not to interfere in the internal affairs of the country. In this note is a paragraph dealing with Soviet moral and material aid to China that emphasizes that this aid is to be given entirely to the "National Government as the Central Government of China."

The Sino-Soviet treaty and the related agreements clearly deal with China as represented by the present Chungking Government, and it is difficult to see how Russia now could render any material support to Yenan without violating the spirit and the letter of the treaty. The meaning of the treaty seems to be that Premier Joseph Stalin has conceded the prospect of a China dominated by Generalissimo Chiang Kai-shek's regime, strongly supported by the United States, and has exacted in return what he feels he needs in Asia to make the Soviet Union secure and to establish Russian power in the Pacific.

China has had to pay a price for the Soviet "non-interference" pledge. The price amounts to the re-establishment of the position Russia held in Manchuria before the Russo-Japanese war in 1905, plus the exclusion of the Chinese from Outer Mongolia. Yet the initial reaction of Chinese and foreign observers here is that the price is lower than it might have been, than many had expected and than rumor had reported.

Preliminary reports of the contents of the treaty here had it that the compact gave Russia joint management of Manchuria's industries and mines and conceded Soviet domination of Korea. A review of the text of the treaty actually has caused relief in some quarters and there were sighs of "it might have been worse." Premier T. V. Soong receives credit for close, astute bargaining with Premier Stalin.

It is too early yet for considered reactions, and nothing has been vouchsafed from Communist quarters. At present there is no ranking Communist representative in Chungking and really authoritative comment would have to come from Yenan. It is known, however, that the local Communist representatives have showed nervousness over the outlook ever since Premier Soong went to Moscow the first time. Russian policy being as devious and hidden as it is, few would choose to be categorical over whether the Chinese Communists ever would receive material Soviet support in the future. On the face of it, however, it looked as if they were on their own. And thus they were confronting formidable power in the strength of Generalissimo Chiang's armies plus United States support for these armies in the way of air and ground transportation and in equipment. There still may be civil war in China, but the prospect is less that such a war would be a camouflaged struggle between the Soviet Union and the United States.

Russia receives joint ownership and management with China of the main railways of Manchuria and joint use with China of Port Arthur as a naval base under the terms of the treaty of friendship and alliance and related agreements as concluded in Moscow on Aug. 14. The text of the treaty and agreements were released last night following their ratification Friday by the Chinese and Soviet Governments.

In a note appended to the treaty, China agrees to recognize the independence of Outer Mongolia if after the defeat of Japan a plebiscite of the people should confirm their desire for independence. In reply, Russia agrees to respect the "political independence and territorial integrity of the Peoples Government of Outer Mongolia." [The area has been operating since 1924 under a constitution drafted along Soviet lines.]

In another exchange of notes, Russia agreed to give China moral support and aid in military supplies and other material resources, this aid and support to be given entirely to the National Government as the Central Government of China. Russia reaffirms her respect for China's full sovereignty over the three eastern provinces of Manchuria and recognizes their territorial administrative integrity.

Article V of the treaty provides that the contracting parties will act "according to mutual respect for their sovereignty and territorial integrity and of non-interference in the internal affairs of the other contracting party." In a note, Russia agrees to the spe-cific application of this article to Sinkiang [the Central Asian province where Chinese and Moslem tribes have engaged in civil war since 1932]. The treaty and agreements are to remain in effect for thirty years.

Appended to the treaty is an agreement in which China declares Dairen a free port, agrees that the harbor master shall be a Russian and leases to Russia free of charge half of all port installations and equipment. The railways affected by the treaty are the Chinese Eastern and the South Manchuria, as well as auxiliary lines.

A minute appended to the treaty records that Premier Stalin stated that Russian troops would begin withdrawing from Manchuria three weeks after the capitulation of Japan, the withdrawal to be completed in a maximum of three months. The agreement regarding the railways provides that "except during such time when joint military operations are carried on by the two countries against Japan the railway shall not be used for transportation of Soviet troops."

The names of the two railways involved are to be dropped and hereafter are to be called by the one name, Chinese Changchun Railway.

The agreement provides that the general manager shall be a Russian but the president of the board of directors a Chinese. An agreement for the war period ment for the period of hostilities in Manchuria—which the Japanese took over in 1931-2 —provides that the supreme authority and responsibility in all matters relating to the prosecution of the war will be vested in the zone of operations, for the time required for the operations, in the Commander in Chief of Soviet forces. The Chinese National Government representative and his staff will be appointed to administer recovered territory and insure Chinese civil cooperation with the Russians. A Chinese military mission will be named to the Soviet commander to insure the active cooperation of the Chinese Administration, "being guided by the requirements and wishes" of the Soviet commander.

The agreement on Port Arthur provides for an area around the port in which the Russians have the right to maintain an army, navy and air force. The civil administration of Port Arthur and its surrounding area will be Chinese, but in the city the leading posts will be filled in agreement with the Soviet military commander and in the whole area the posts will be filled "taking into account Soviet interests in the area." The agreement says Soviet proposals in the area "will be fulfilled" by the Chinese Administration. The Soviet Government is entrusted by China with the defense of the naval base.

In case of war with Japan, Dairen shall be subject to the military supervision and control obtaining in the Port Arthur naval base. All properties jointly shared with Russia or installations made by Russia in Manchuria after thirty years will revert to China without compensation. The Russians receive the right to transport over the Chinese Changchun Railway military goods in sealed cars without customs inspection, but the guarding of such goods will be done by Chinese railway police. The agreement says the Chinese Changchun Railway will be operated as a "purely commercial transportation enterprise, with profits divided between China and Russia."

One of the provisions of the treaty binds each of the countries not to conclude any alliance and not to take any part in any coalition directed against the other.

Nothing in the treaty is to be construed as affecting the rights or obligations of the United Nations organization.

August 27, 1945

HURLEY ASSAILS OUR POLICY IN CHINA; RESIGNS AS ENVOY; MARSHALL NAMED

By BERTRAM D. HULEN

WASHINGTON, Nov. 27—President Truman today appointed Gen. George C. Marshall, retiring Army Chief of Staff, as his special envoy to China with the rank of Ambassador and accepted the resignation as Ambassador of Patrick J. Hurley, who earlier had resigned and issued a blistering denunciation of the administration of American foreign policy by "professional diplomats," especially the career diplomats of the lower levels.

The selection of General Marshall, who plans to leave promptly for his post, is regarded as attesting to the importance Mr. Truman attaches to the Chinese situation.

Ambassador Hurley said that he had had no difficulties with the White House or the Secretaries of State, and that he agreed with President Truman's Navy Day ad-dress, but that in effect he had been double-crossed by his subordinates among the professionals in the Chungking Embassy and in the State Department. That had led to a failure of our diplomatic policy in Asia, as he estimated it, for even though he had certain officials transferred from the embassy they appeared in the State Department as his "supervisors."

"America has been excluded economically from every part of the world controlled by colonial imperialism and Communist imperialism," he declared. "America's economic strength has been used all over the world to defeat American policies and interests. This is chargeable to a weak foreign service."

He said he saw a third world war in the making.

The resignation of Mr. Hurley apparently came as a surprise to officials, for it had been announced soon after he arrived here for a rest last month that he would return to his post. When he talked over the matter yesterday with James F. Byrnes, Secretary of State, he was prevailed upon not to press his resignation, according to Michael J. McDermott, special assistant to the Secretary of State, who made a statement for the State Department. Mr. Byrnes is expected to discuss it at his press conference tomorrow.

When Mr. Hurley issued his statement he seemed to assume that he would be returning to Chungking, for a time, at least. But the President acted quickly when he heard of the Ambassador's statement. He had before him the resignation that Mr. Hurley gave yesterday to Secretary Byrnes and later recalled, according to the explanation at the State Department.

The Ambassador is expected to elaborate his side of the case frankly in a speech before the National Press Club tomorrow.

President Truman pressed General Marshall back into service shortly after having received confirmation of a news-ticker flash that Mr. Hurley had resigned, the first intimation he had received of this intention. An hour before the announcement of General Marshall's appointment the White House said Mr. Truman had not yet received formal notice of General Hurley's action.

Calling General Marshall on the telephone at Leesburg, Va., where he has his home, the President asked him if he would go to China as his special envoy "to handle a particular job that needs to be done." He told the President that he would go and that he would report to him at the White House tomorrow for a conference with the Chief Executive and Secretary Byrnes.

Earlier in the day the President had conferred with Dr. Wei Tao-ming, the Chinese Ambassador, who in a discussion with reporters on leaving the White House sought to minimize the seriousness of the Chinese internal situation. He said there was "more shouting than shooting" going on between the Government and the Communists over the occupation of Manchuria.

"The Chinese Government has concluded a treaty with the Government of Soviet Russia by which our troops are to take over the occupation of Manchuria as soon as the Soviet troops withdraw," said Dr. Wei. "And the Soviet Government has undertaken to disarm all persons not authorized by my Government to bear arms. It is regrettable that the Communists have had to resort to armed force because China already has had eight years of war. But we cannot permit anything to interfere with our transportation and communication systems."

TEXT OF TRUMAN LETTER

The resignation of Ambassador Hurley was accepted in the following letter from the President:

Dear Mr. Ambassador:

I have your letter of Nov. 26 tendering your resignation as Ambassador to China, which you forwarded to me through the Secretary of State. I am grateful to you for the service you have rendered in this important and difficult post.

I regret that you feel unable to continue and therefore in accordance with your desires accept your resignation.

Very sincerely yours,
HARRY S. TRUMAN.

At the Capitol Senators refused to comment, saying Mr. Hurley's statement was "too confusing." Republicans as well as Democrats remarked that various parts of the statement seemed to conflict.

The selection of General Marshall, however, brought expressions of confidence.

State Department's Version

The State Department reaction was given by Mr. McDermott in the following statement:

"The Secretary was surprised at the news release by Ambassador Hurley that he had submitted a letter of resignation.

"When the Ambassador arrived from China he told the Secretary that because of his health he wished to resign, but later advised the President and the Secretary that he would return to China after taking a rest. That was on Oct. 9.

"Monday morning, Ambassador Hurley called to see the Secretary and presented a letter of resignation addressed to the President, setting forth the statements contained in the news release. The Secretary advised him of the serious situation existing in China and urged him, instead of resigning, to promptly return to China.

"The Ambassador returned in the afternoon and, after again discussing the situation in China, agreed to return to his post. He said, however, that he had an engagement on Wednesday to make a speech before the National Press Club and would prefer not to leave before that time.

"The Secretary told the Ambassador that would be entirely satisfactory. The Secretary then advised the President that the Ambassador would promptly return to his post."

Had Trouble in Unity Moves

He had carried out the late President Roosevelt's instructions to keep China in the war but his troubles developed when he next moved to carry out orders from the top and facilitate the bringing about of harmony in China.

He explained that he was making a public statement because he felt that "at this particular juncture in our history an informed public opinion would do much to give intelligent direction to our international objectives." This was the time, he declared, for "a complete reorganization of our policy-making machinery, beginning at the lower official levels."

Turning to the "professional foreign service men," he asserted that they "continuously advised the Communists that my efforts in preventing the collapse of the National Government did not represent the policy of the United States." They, he added, "openly advised the Communist armed party to decline unification of the Chinese Communist Army with the National Army unless the Chinese Communists were given control."

He stated that "the chief opposition" to his efforts to bring out unification in China "came from the American career diplomats in the embassy at Chungking and in the Chinese and Far Eastern divisions of the State Department."

While Mr. Hurley named no names in his indictment of the career diplomats, the State Department said that, according to its records, only three officials who were attached to our embassy in Chungking when he took over the post are now there. They were listed as J. Hall Paxton, Harry E. Stevens and Charles S. Millet, all second secretaries.

George Acheson Jr., who was counselor of the Embassy, is now in Tokyo as political adviser to Gen. Douglas MacArthur. His place has been taken in Chungking by Robert Lacy Smyth, another foreign service officer.

The State Department said its records showed that the others in the Embassy when Mr. Hurley took over, but who are not now there, were:

Arthur R. Ringwalt, second secretary, now assistant chief of the Chinese Division in the State Department; Horace H. Smith, second secretary, now first secretary in our embassy in Moscow; John D. Davies, second secretary, now second secretary in Moscow; John S. Service, second secretary, now assistant to Mr. Acheson in Tokyo; Raymond T. Ludden, second secretary, now consul to Kunming, temporarily in this country; Edward E. Rice, second secretary, now in the State Department; Philip D. Sprouse, second secretary, now consul in Kunming; Fulton Freeman, third secretary, now in the Chinese division in the State Department, and Hungerford B. Howard, third secretary, now consul in Shanghai.

Everett F. Drumright, who was technically second secretary of the Chungking Embassy, was said to have been in this country during the tenure of Ambassador Hurley. He is now chief of the Chinese Division in the State Department.

Chennault Praises Hurley

FORT WORTH, Texas, Nov. 27 (P)—Maj. Gen. Claire L. Chennault, former commander of the "Flying Tigers" and the Fourteenth Air Force in China, tonight praised Maj. Gen. Patrick J. Hurley for his stand, "in placing the issue of American foreign policy in China squarely before the American people."

"I was glad to see he [General Hurley] has placed the issue squarely before the American people with his release of the reasons for his resignation," General Chennault told the Star-Telegram.

"The issue I refer to is whether the policies of our President and our Congress will be implemented out there [in China] or whether they will be nullified by a few individuals in the State and War Departments," he declared.

"Now is the time when we must decide what our policy will be in the Far East and, having made that decision, we must implement it 100 per cent with all our efforts and force," the General said.

CHUNGKING RIVALS GREET MARSHALL

By TILLMAN DURDIN
By Wireless to THE NEW YORK TIMES.

CHUNGKING, Dec. 22 — Gen. George C. Marshall arrived in Chungking at noon today, marking by his presence here the beginning of a mission that promises to determine peace and unity in strife-torn China.

General Marshall flew from Nanking, where he had spent the night and where yesterday he had met and had a talk with President Chiang Kai-shek. He was welcomed by Premier T. V. Soong and Gen. Chou En-lai, chief of the Communist delegation here. After motoring into the city from the airport with Premier Soong, President Truman's special envoy was shown into his official residence, by the Premier. After lunch he relaxed in his apartment to recuperate from the arduous weeklong air journey from the United States.

The general's aides said he had no fixed program for the immediate future except for a Christmas dinner date with the Generalissimo and Mme. Chiang and several other social engagements. He is anxious to begin an immediate study of the situation here and is likely to start tomorrow by seeing callers and scanning reports. He has expressed a desire to keep social commitments to the minimum.

General Marshall did not meet newspaper men today but is expected to grant a press interview tomorrow.

General Marshall will have his main office in the United States Embassy. Rooms have been arranged for him at Army headquarters and he will probably spend some time there. He will probably settle down next week to receiving Kuomintang and Communist representatives and getting a thorough knowledge of all viewpoints.

General Marshall shook hands warmly as he was introduced to each official at the airport. There was a moment's hesitation in the making of introductions when he came to General Chou and the Communist leader stepped up and introduced himself. General Marshall smiled and said, "I am very glad to meet you." Then he was introduced by General Chou to other Communist representatives.

A band saluted his arrival with the American and Chinese national anthems and an honor guard of Chinese troops stood at attention as he walked to his automobile.

It is apparent, however, that, despite the reluctance of Communist leaders to comment, that the new Washington directive regarding the movement of Central Government troops to Manchuria and North China by American facilities has disturbed the Communists.

The Yenan Emancipation Daily News says:

"The problem of whether the sending of troops to North China and Manchuria is still necessary and whether American help shall be needed for this purpose should first be submitted to the People's Consultative Council for discussion before any action is taken. Otherwise the movement would be contravening President Truman's statement that United States support will not extend to United States military intervention to influence the course of Chinese internal strife."

The newspaper charged that "the large-scale transportation of Kuomintang troops undertaken by United States forces by sea and air has long constituted a factor i

promoting an denlarging the Chinese civil war."

The local Communist spokesman today endorsed the Yenan newspaper's views and indicated that the Truman directive, issued on the eve of General Marshall's arrival and Consultative Council talks, had caused some concern in Communist quarters.

The Communist press and Communist leaders continued today to stress their proposal for an unconditional cessation of fighting by both sides. They are awaiting a reply to their proposal from the Kuomintang.

The military aspect was marked today by a charge in the Kuomintang Central News Agency that fighting was going on at Chungyang in western Shansi, where Communists were said to be besieging the city. The agency reported that National troops had reoccupied Tsaoyang, near the Hupeh-Honan border.

Communists were said to be mining the railways into Jehol and Chahar from Peiping and digging an extensive network of tunnel defenses near Shihkiachwang in southern Hopeh.

The Communists continued to charge further Kuomintang concentrations of troops around their north China areas.

The United States Information Service mixed Russian and American diplomats and journalists and Chinese Kuomintang and Communist leaders and newspaper men together in a Christmas party tonight with such success that before the party was over women Communists were dancing with Kuomintang Ministers. Russians and Americans were pledging boundless friendship over glasses of Chungking gin fizz.

A radio broadcast tonight said the Communists in Shantung had "rejected" an American marine proposal to send a platoon of marines to Weihaiwei as an escort to repairmen who were to recondition a marine plane that crashed recently twenty miles from Weihaiwei. The Communists say the repairmen would be welcome, but that they did not want American troops in Weihaiwei.

Forty-five minutes after General Marshall passed one point on the road into the city a unit of Chinese troops, not knowing of his arrival, cleared areas near the road and started firing mortars and rifles across the highway in a practice battle. The maneuvers for a short time barred the way into Chungking for some cars of the welcoming group.

Arriving with General Marshall were James Shepley, State Department attaché, and Col. Henry A. Byroade, new United States military attaché in China.

Generalissimo Chung did not come to Chungking with General Marshall but is expected tomorrow. Lieut. Gen. Albert C. Wedemeyer, United States commander in China, is expected to reach Chungking in a day or two.

General Marshall's arrival finds Chungking keyed to a high pitch of expectation. The fervent welcome in the press this morning indicated hopefulness. The Communist press joined with the Kuomintang papers in hailing the American envoy.

December 23, 1945

CHIANG PROCLAIMS TRUCE AND REFORM

By TILLMAN DURDIN

By Wireless to THE NEW YORK TIMES.

CHUNGKING, Jan. 10—Only a few moments before President Chiang Kai-shek proclaimed a sweeping series of political and democratic reforms in China, a formal truce order, hammered out by Gen. George C. Marshall and representatives of the Chinese Government and the Chinese Communist party, brought a cease-fire order to the civil war fronts.

The agreement provided for an immediate halt to hostilities, full restoration of all war-blocked communications and the establishment of a control organization, with American participation, to supervise the carrying out of the armistice compact. The continued movement of Government forces in Manchuria and south of the Yangtze River is not prejudiced under the terms of the agreement.

This agreement highlighted a day of historic happenings in Chungking, all tied together, with dramatic timing and with close political relationship.

The Political Consultation Conference, an assemblage of party leaders and non-party persons, dedicated to working out a program of political unity and democratization for China, met in its

first session. The truce accord was reached after an emergency early morning meeting of the three negotiators just in time for President Chiang to reveal the agreement in his opening address to the conference.

In his speech President Chiang announced these far-reaching Government measures in the field of civil rights:

Steps to insure freedom of person, of conscience, of publication and of assembly.

Abrogation of secret police activity in assuring that rulings were being made under which only proper judicial and police authorities would be permitted to arrest, try or punish individuals.

Equality of "all legal parties before the law" and their right to open activity "within the law."

Release of all political prisoners "except traitors and those found to have committed definite acts injurious to the Republic."

Promotion of local self-government everywhere, with popular election to be held "according to law" and from "the lowest strata upward."

The supreme achievement of bringing at least an armistice and perhaps permanent peace to China came to fruition after a hitch in the discussion yesterday threatened to prolong if not seriously to endanger the negotiations. It is clear that the masterly mediation of General Marshall was a major factor in producing the final success.

Last night the three-man conference brought up a disagreement

and it was announced that the next meeting would not be held until 5 P. M. today, so as to give time for the two Chinese plenipotentiaries to seek instructions.

Gen. Chang Chun, the Government representative, told newsmen that difficulties had been encountered.

After attending a dinner party, General Marshall went to see President Chiang and remained in conference with him until midnight. At 12:30 General Chou received a telephone call asking him to attend a meeting at General Marshall's house at 8 o'clock this morning. At that time General Chou General Marshall and General Chang convened and in an hour's discussion had ironed out the differences.

The truce draft was worked out, typed and was ready for the press at 10 o'clock. A special messenger hurried with news of the success and the details to President Chiang. The President had kept the Consultation Council waiting for twenty minutes beyond the announced opening time of 10 o'clock. Then he stepped onto the platform of the conference hall and announced to an applauding house that peace had come to China.

The truce pact, as finally agreed upon, freezes the troops on both sides in their present positions everywhere, including Jehol. The Government forces that launched an invasion of that Communist-controlled province ten days ago will stay where they are.

The truce agreement excepts Manchuria and the areas south of the Yangtze River from the troop "freezing." It states that the cease fire order "does not prejudice military movements of forces of the National army into or within Man-

churia, which are for the purpose of restoring Chinese sovereignty."

The agreement provides for the immediate establishment of an Executive Headquarters in Peiping to direct the execution of the cessation of hostilities. This headquarters will consist of three commissioners, one representing the Chinese Government, one the Communists and one the United States. The Communist commissioner will be Lieut. Gen. Yeh Chien-ying, Chief of Staff of the Communist armies; the Government commissioner will be Gen. Cheng Chienmin, head of the Chinese Intelligence Department of the Board of Military Operations; the American commissioner will be Walter G. Robertson, United States Chargé d'Affaires in China.

Each of the Chinese commissioners will have a contingent of about a hundred officers and men under the Headquarters. Mr. Robertson will be aided by about twenty-five American service personnel, headed by Col. Henry A. Byroade, military attaché in China, who will be Mr. Robertson's executive officer.

General Marshall smiled broadly when the text of the joint agreement was presented to the press this morning, but he made no comment for publication except to praise the "earnest desire manifested by both sides to find a practical solution to the difficulties" during the negotiations.

Both Communist and Government spokesmen today said that the cease-fire order had already been issued. It was thought it might take at least three days for the order to reach some isolated units and for the fighting to stop. The Communists thought even longer would be necessary for the Communist guerrillas on Hainan Island since they have no radio.

The Political Consultation Conference met with thirty-six of the thirty-eight members present.

In addition to announcing the truce and the Government's intentions in respect to civil liberties, President Chiang red a prepared speech reviewing the responsibilities and the program of the conference.

"What we have to consider here," he said, "is a fundamental plan that will lead from war to peace, from resistance to reconstruction."

He urged the conference to see to it that the National Assembly was convened according to schedule, and said that, before the Assembly meeting, "we must try to eliminate by means of consultation and concerted endeavors all the factors that are likely to impair the unity of the national will, exert an influence adverse to social peace and stability or delay the work of national revival."

President Chiang then said:

"I am ready to accept all the decisions of the Conference if they are beneficial to national reconstruction and tend to promote the popular welfare and can help the democratization of the country."

January 11, 1946

CLASHES IN MANCHURIA MENACE CHINESE PEACE

Kuomintang Held Responsible for Failure to Fulfill Agreement

By TILLMAN DURDIN
By Wireless to THE NEW YORK TIMES.

CHUNGKING, April 13—Kuomintang - Communist relationships were again bordering on complete rupture in China this week. Armed clashes in Manchuria and embittered contacts between the two parties brought the country nearer to a renewal of far-ranging civil strike than at any time since the armistice of last January.

The picture today is in marked contrast with the brighter outlook of two months ago or even a month ago, when Gen. George C Marshall removed his direct personal influence from China and departed for Washington.

Aside from the constant fundamental factors of distrust and incompatability, there are two immediate causes of the present state of affairs—the inability of the two factions to agree on principles for over-all political cooperation and the arrival of the crucial stage in the struggle for power in Manchuria. The second really hinges on the first, since if the parties could achieve a workable basis for nation-wide political cooperation, a peaceful adjustment of the relationships in Manchuria would be possible.

At the end of January the leaders of the two parties, along with representatives of other parties and non-partisans, signed a comprehensive program for political cooperation and Government reorganization. The Kuomintang has been largely responsible for the fact that this program has not been implemented.

The January program provided that the Kuomintang would abdicate one-party dictatorship and hand over a minor share of its power in the Central Government to other political groups. Opposition to this program within the Kuomintang developed immediately and crystallized in the March session of the Central Executive Committee.

Although the Central Executive Committee adopted a general resolution approving the January program of the Political Consultation Conference, other resolutions and widespread sentiments among Rightist Kuomintang elements made manifest strong opposition to the PCC agreements.

The Kuomintang has sought to revise the constitutional principles approved by the PCC—which provided for a Cabinet system of government responsible to a popularly elected Legislature—in such a way as to centralize power in the hands of President Chiang Kai-shek and his party.

Efforts have been made to limit the representation of the Communists and the Democratic League in the policy-making State Council of the planned new interim government to less than one-third of the membership, thus eliminating the possibility of a veto on contentious questions. The Kuomintang has tried to allow the Communists' league only a nominal share of Ministries in the Executive Yuan and has demanded that the new regime operate on a basis of one-party tutelage laws, by which the Kuomintang has ruled the country since 1931.

The Kuomintang has attempted to pare down provincial autonomy and engineer a mission to the forthcoming Kuomintang-dominated Constituent Assembly so it could adopt whatever permanent Constitution it wished instead of one agreed on by the parties beforehand.

Political Prisoners Kept

The Government has only partly made good on Chiang Kai-shek's Bill of Rights promises, proclaimed at the opening of the PCC; still keeps political prisoners jailed and has arrested others, continues to utilize the secret political police to counteract opposition and still denies fundamental civil liberties in many parts of the country.

In a series of tedious and often acrimonious discussions with Communists and other political representatives, the Kuomintang delegation has modified some of its earlier post-CEC claims, and agreements have again been reached on all but a few vital points of difference.

However, the Communists and he Democratic League consider the differences still too wide to permit them to enter the new Government and they charge the Kuomintang has not displayed a genuine intention to give an effective share of its control of the Government to the Opposition elements.

No Political Settlement

Meanwhile, the spreading hostilities in Manchuria do nothing to promote a political settlement at the center.

In Manchuria the Government has a good juridical position for its present line of action. Under the Sino-Soviet treaty, forces of the Government's choosing are privileged to take back Chinese sovereignty in the northeast as the Russians withdraw. By the terms of the Jan. 10 truce agreement, signed by the Communists, Nationalist forces have the right to move in and within Manchuria for purposes of restoring sovereignty.

The present clashes in Manchuria are a result of Communist attempts to block and harass the advances of the Government armies.

Obviously, the Communists' aim is to force a recognition of their claim for a share in the political and military control of Manchuria.

"A. BAD CASE OF NERVES"

Messner in The Rochester Times-Union

In the process they are indulging in wholesale violations of the truce agreement. They have moved forces from North China to Manchuria, have expanded and moved their troops in Manchuria, have taken over many points since the armistice was signed and have torn up communications.

The Communists protest that they do not object to the Central Government's "taking over sovereignty" in Manchuria; but they want to be consulted about the process and they ask the fight be stopped—that is, that Government advances cease—while the discussions take place.

Such consultations with the Communists could only involve a territorial settlement of some kind. This would involve delay in the Nationalist advance, during which time the Russians would complete their withdrawal and Communists probably would assume control of the areas that the Red Army evacuated.

The Kuomintang insists a political and military settlement with the Communists in Manchuria can come after the "taking over" is completed; that the fighting is caused by Communist obstruction to the "taking over" and is not "hostilities" under the armistice pact.

The Communists, who fear that the "taking over" may mean a clean-up campaign against Communists in Manchuria, have a tenable position when they ask for a general political settlement there. They say the settlement should be now; the Central Government says later.

If political and military cooperation under the PCC agreement is to be nation-wide, there must sooner or later be recognition of the position of Manchuria to some degree or other.

With the Russians now rapidly pulling out of Manchuria, the climactic stage of the Kuomintang-Communist power struggle has been reached in this richest and most highly developed part of China.

Relations between the Kuomintang and the Communists recently entered a very bitter propaganda phase. Name-calling on the part of the Communists this week extended to Generalissimo Chiang, and the Yenan Emancipation Daily News made a strong personal attack on the Chinese war leader, charging he was once sympathetic to fascism and had, from 1932 and throughout the war, been willing to settle with the Japanese by giving up Manchuria. This sort of attack, passionately resented in Kuomintang circles, does not help toward a final agreement.

Both sides are now awaiting General Marshall's return. Unless the Communists, particularly in their stand on the Manchurian problem, have direct Russian backing, he may not find the situation that has developed insoluble. On the other hand, if the Communists' actions are the result of some new manifestation of Soviet foreign policy, things will be tougher and a settlement will devolve on Soviet-American relations.

General Marshall will still have potent weapons in the form of his personality and prestige and the weight of American economic and political power.

April 14, 1946

TRUCE IN SHANTUNG HALTS LONG FIGHT

NANKING, May 11 (Æ)—A truce in Shantung Province was announced officially today. The official Chinese Government Central News Agency said the truce was signed in Tsinan, capital of the province where Communist forces had been reported mounting new attacks earlier this week.

Yesterday Government and Communist negotiators arranged a cease-fire agreement for Honan and Hupeh in central China.

The Central News Agency reported that the Shantung agreement called for the immediate cessation of fighting and troop movements. The Government said three of its regiments had suffered heavy casualties in three months of fighting.

Fighting in the three provinces had sidetracked efforts to halt the trouble in Manchuria. Manchurian discussions presumably will be resumed, with Gen. George C. Marshall, special United States envoy, as mediator.

An official Government statement asserted that the Government lost 7,000 men in killed, wounded and missing in the battle of Changchun, when strong Communist forces captured the Manchurian capital April 18. It admitted the Communists had won a powerful position in Manchuria, saying they also had occupied forty-three other cities in the northeast territory, including Harbin.

May 12, 1946

Marshall Report on China Calls Liberals Only Hope

By BERTRAM D. HULEN
Special to THE NEW YORK TIMES.

WASHINGTON, Jan. 7—Gen. George C. Marshall, special envoy to China, whose appointment as Secretary of State was announced tonight, declared in a statement issued through the State Department today that the salvation of China "would be the assumption of leadership by the liberals in the Government and in the minority parties."

His statement, which called these liberals "a splendid group of men, but who as yet lack the political power to exercise a controlling influence," was in the form of a review of the situation before his departure for the United States to succeed Secretary of State James F. Byrnes. The statement was regarded as an appeal for a genuinely liberal movement to save China from the extremists of the Nationalists and Communists.

Whether General Marshall's report, buttressed by his new official stature, would result in jarring the Chinese into the adoption of a sane, democratic and constitutional program was a matter of conjecture.

The statement was in the nature of a report to the American people. General Marshall went candidly into the many phases of the Chinese problem.

The special envoy declared that efforts to bring about peace in China had been frustrated by "extremist elements of both sides." He spared neither the Communists who, he said, would not hesitate to wreck China to gain their own political ends, nor a "dominant group of reactionaries" in the Kuomintang, which he described as the first among "the most important factors" responsible for the breakdown of the negotiations between the Communists and the Nationalist Government.

Further, he deplored the "dominating influence of the military" upon the civil government.

He also condemned the propaganda of both sides with its "deliberate misrepresentation and abuse" of the United States, tactics about which he had found it difficult to remain silent. He described the Communist propaganda as "vicious," that of the Nationalist Government only as having contained "numerous misrepresentations."

Yet he refused to be completely discouraged, instead suggesting that "now that the form for a democratic government has been laid down by the newly adopted Constitution, political measures will be the best."

Between the dominant reactionary groups in the Government and the irreconcilable Communists, he maintained, "lies the problem of how peace and well-being are to be brought to the long suffering and presently inarticulate mass of the people of China."

In describing his efforts to get both sides together, he expressed the hope that the Government would offer a "genuine welcome" to all groups, including the Communists in the proposed reorganization.

January 8, 1947

U.S. ENDS MEDIATION IN CHINA; TROOPS WILL BE WITHDRAWN; FIERCER CIVIL WAR FORESEEN

YEAR'S WORK HALTS

U. S. Cuts Its Ties With Committee of Three and Truce Body

MOST OF 12,000 MEN TO GO

Admission of Failure of Our Efforts Seen—$500,000,000 Loan Still in Abeyance

By BERTRAM D. HULEN
Special to THE NEW YORK TIMES.

WASHINGTON, Jan. 29—The way was paved today for withdrawal of virtually all American forces from China as the State Department announced abandonment of the American effort to mediate between the Chinese Nationalist and Communist forces.

This country, it was announced, will end its connection with the Committee of Three. The committee, representing the United States, Chinese Nationalists and Chinese Communists, was set up at the instance of Secretary of State Marshall when he was President Truman's special envoy to China. It was the agency through which efforts were made during the past year to promote domestic peace and national unity.

The decision also involves ending United States connection with Executive Headquarters in Peiping, the organization representing the three groups that was designed to oversee the carrying out of the agreement of the Chinese factions for a truce and national unity.

Many Marines Likely to Go

Of 12,000 American Army, Navy and Marine Corps personnel in China, more than 9,000 are Marines, most of them occupied in supporting Executive Headquarters. The termination of that organization, therefore, is expected to result in the withdrawal of those Marines.

There will then remain in China 1,000 to 2,000 Marines at the training base at Tsingtao, the American Military Group of 750 officers and men at Nanking, which is engaged in training Chinese personnel at military schools in the use of latest weapons, and Army units stationed at various places to dispose of surplus property.

China is now expected to lose interest in the Committee of Three and Executive Headquarters and dissolve them.

Whether the United States decision will lead to an intensification of civil war or give impetus to the establishment of a coalition Government on liberal lines can only be surmised here for the present. It is regarded as a virtual admission of the inability of General Marshall to bring about peace in China. It was foreshadowed by his return to the United States and his personal statement on China of Jan. 7.

Action Not Punitive

The decision, it was emphasized in informed quarters, was in no sense punitive. Dr. John Leighton Stuart will remain as American Ambassador to China. If he resigns, a new Ambassador will be appointed, it was said. Dr. Stuart is accredited to the Government of Generalissimo Chiang Kai-shek, from which it was stressed the United States was not withdrawing recognition.

Ambassador Stuart is expected to facilitate the effort for unification and peace in China as opportunities arise but it was predicted that his role would not be as important as General Marshall's was.

The tendency appears to be to await the full Chinese reaction to General Marshall's statement of Jan. 7, in which he denounced the extremists in the Nationalist and Communist parties and called for the establishment of a Government that would utilize the services of liberals.

Officials insisted that the cessation of the organized peace effort did not end the American interest in promoting unity in China. They said the objective remained the same, the creation of a unified, strong China, friendly to the United States and a bulwark of peace and security in Asia.

"We are hopeful but not particularly optimistic regarding the situation," was the view of some.

An announcement of the creation of a coalition Government in China is expected soon. This will be scrutinized closely here for its implications.

The decision to terminate our connection with the Committee of Three and the Executive Headquarters was made by the State Department early today. Simultaneously Ambassador Stuart communicated it to Generalissimo Chiang. An hour later he informed Wang Ping-nan, the Communist representative in Nanking.

It caused diverse comment in Congress where the undertone was one of confidence in the judgment of Secretary Marshall.

The State Department announcement said:

"The United States Government has decided to terminate its connection with the Committee of Three, which was established in Chungking for the purpose of terminating hostilities in China and of which General Marshall was chairman.

"The United States Government also has decided to terminate its connection with Executive Headquarters, which was established in Peiping by the Committee of Three for the purpose of supervising in the field the execution of the agreements for the cessation of hostilities and the demobilization and reorganization of the armed forces in China.

"The American personnel involved in Executive Headquarters will be withdrawn as soon as possible."

In giving out the announcement, Michael J. McDermott, the State Department's press relations officer, said:

"Instructions regarding the withdrawal of Marines will be given later in conformity with the approved plans for the termination of American participation in Executive Headquarters."

The Committee of Three was set up more than a year ago at the instance of General Marshall to cooperate in bringing about peace and unity. General Marshall was the United States member and chairman. The Chinese Nationalists have been represented on it by Gen. Chang Chun and other generals. The Chinese Communist member throughout has been Gen. Chou En-lai.

The Executive Headquarters has been an agency for applying policies of the Committee of Three through sending teams of officers into many areas to bring about adherence to the program. Field teams and liaison groups were scattered over north China and Manchuria.

Nearly 2,000 Marines, Army personnel and civilian employes are directly connected with Executive Headquarters. They are to be withdrawn promptly, probably in a month. The great majority of the rest of the Marines in north China, who are on lines of communication and in other ways indirectly supporting the work of Executive Headquarters, are expected to follow.

The presence of United States military forces in China has been attacked by the Soviet Union and by Chinese Communists but there was no indication today that our decision was influenced by either.

Byrnes Promised Withdrawal

Our Marines in China reached a peak strength of 50,000 during the war but the number has been steadily reduced since. Former Secretary of State Byrnes said last month that those left in north China were required for Executive Headquarters and when that organization was no longer needed they would be withdrawn.

The status of the American loan of $500,000,000 that has been earmarked for China appeared to be not influenced by the developments. It has been immobile for a year, no allocations having been made from it by the Export-Import Bank because of the uncertain peace prospects in China.

There is no other economic program in behalf of China here but she is expected to receive some post-UNRRA relief from Congress this Spring.

January 30, 1947

Chiang's Forces Seize Yenan, Capital of the Chinese Reds

By TILLMAN DURDIN
Special to THE NEW YORK TIMES.

NANKING, March 19—Chinese Government troops bivouacked today in Yenan, sprawling, dusty, one-time capital of Communist China. The remote little city that for eleven years has served as the headquarters of Chinese communism was captured this morning after a week's drive by a Government column thrusting northward from Lochwan, fifty miles away on the border of the Yenan area.

Reports of what the Government forces found in Yenan are lacking here but it is certain that they occupied an almost empty town. Convinced that a Government attack was coming the Communists began the evacuation of Yenan almost a month ago. When this writer visited there by American plane from Nanking early in March the Communist center was half deserted. All official personnel and establishments had been moved away except what were needed for the bare essentials of a military and political headquarters.

Last Americans Leave

The Government's assault stepped off the day after two United States Army officers who had been serving as liaison men for the Peiping Executive Headquarters left Yenan, March 12, by plane. The Red capital was bombed and strafed for two days as land forces rolled up the winding road through the bare loess hills against light opposition.

The Communists evidently staged no concerted opposition to the Government drive and, in keeping with statements of Communist leaders two weeks ago, made no determined defense of the capital.

Government sources here tonight, however, asserted that 10,000 Communists had been killed and 2,000 captured in the drive on Yenan.

The Yenan leaders made it plain that the Communists would not offer frontal opposition to the Government's motorized and better equipped divisions, but would pull off to the flanks to harass supply lines, pick off small units and make extensive use of home-made land mines.

Became Capital in 1936

Yenan became the Communist capital in 1936 after the Communists had evacuated their old base in southern Kiangsi and had fought their way for thousands of miles through southwest and northwest China to the district embracing parts of northern Shensi, southern Ninghsia and eastern Kansu. During the Japanese war Yenan became a mecca for Left Wing partisans of Free China and was an educational and political center with a peak population of 50,000.

The old walled city was bombed out by the Japanese and most of the inhabitants moved into caves dug into the sides of the Yen River gorge, into which Yenan nestles. Primitive board or brick huts sprang up to form the nucleus of a new city on both sides of the old walls in the bottom of the river valley.

The Communists have not disclosed where their new headquarters will be established. One high Government source said here tonight that Gen. Mao Tse-tung and his colleagues had moved to Hinghsien, about a hundred miles northwest of Taiyuan, in Shansi. Other sources said that the Communist leaders were bound for Manchuria.

Seek Refuge in Villages

Families of the leaders and minor officials of northern Shensi are seeking refuge in numerous small villages and isolated farmhouses.

The Yenan radio was picked up here this morning. One news item broadcast was an account of the Government's advance toward the city.

The capture of Yenan will not prove of much military advantage to the Government; indeed, it may be a serious liability. Yenan is in the center of a sparsely inhabited and relatively poor area on the fringe of the more thickly peopled and productive Communist territory stretching through Shansi, Hopeh and Shantung.

Likewise, the occupation of Yenan will be no economic gain for the Government. Maintaining an overland supply route from Sian to Yenan may prove costly.

The Young Marshal, Chang Hsueh-liang, occupied Yenan before the Japanese war but had to evacuate it because of the difficulty of supplying his forces in the face of constant Communist guerrilla attacks. Recently the Communists have carefully denuded the countryside of food to intensify the supply problem of the Government.

However, the capture of Yenan is a psychological gain for the Government. The administrative difficulties of the Communists will be increased and their contact with the outside world, so necessary for propaganda, will be hampered.

The Yenan radio may continue to operate, since the Communists have a portable station, which can be erected and put into operation in a short time.

Called Turning Point

NANKING, March 19 (AP)—Shortly before the capture of Yenan was announced, Pong Hsueh-pei, Minister of Information, said that the city's fall might possibly effect a change of heart among Communist leaders, presumably sick of continued military losses.

He also said that the Government would consider the occupation of Yenan th turning point in the civil war.

"After the fall of Yenan the military situation in China will hinge on Communist policy, which up to the present has been to place implicit faith in armed forces," Mr. Peng said.

March 20, 1947

COMMUNISTS GAIN IN CENTRAL CHINA

By HENRY R. LIEBERMAN
Special to THE NEW YORK TIMES.

HANKOW, China, Dec. 21—Recent developments in central China, where the Communists have established three major bases, support the findings of Gen. George C. Marshall and Lieut. Gen. Albert C. Wedemeyer that it would be difficult to defeat the Chinese Communists by military means alone.

Despite Nationalist superiority in manpower and equipment, the Communists have extended their areas of control by the expert use of guerrilla military tactics, tight political organization and effective propaganda geared to the poverty existing in the Chinese countryside.

"Regular Communist troops are well trained and well behaved," said Dr. John I. Benson, Lutheran missionary from Minneapolis, who had to leave his station at Kiahsien in Honan Province. "When they first enter a village they give food to the hungry people. When they leave they are followed by nondescript Communist soldiers who take rice and clothing. These represent themselves as Chinese Nationalists and arouse the enmity of the people."

Although the Nationalist military command here has publicly recognized the need of winning mass support of the peasants to combat the Communists, the Government has found it difficult to lighten the burden on the peasantry in the midst of civil war and inflation. Taxation in kind has increased.

CAPITAL OF CHINESE COMMUNISTS FALLS

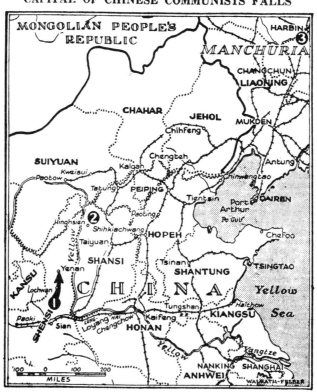

March 20. 1947

In the culmination of a northward advance from Lochwan, Nationalist troops entered Yenan (1). The Reds had for the most part evacuated the cave city. It was speculated that they might be bound for Hingshien (2) or might try to reach Harbin (3).

Some Burdens Unnecessary

Unnecessary burdens have been imposed on the masses by military maladministration, widespread corruption and the practice of permitting Nationalist officers to take their entire families with them to civil war areas. This practice appears to force underpaid officers to engage in constant graft in military areas to feed, house and clothe the families accompanying them.

Asked why the practice was allowed to continue, Lieut. Gen. Chang Chen, Nationalist commander at Sinyang, replied:

"Many officers come from Communist-held areas. If they left their families behind, the Communists would persecute them."

In the Communist armies officers and men share the same conditions. Nationalist officers enjoy far more comforts than their soldiers. Nationalist troops in this area get two bowls of rice daily, not much food for men who are expected to hunt Communists in the Tapieh mountains in bitt. cold.

Communist prisoners at the re indoctrination camp here seem to have been much better fed.

Wealthy Merchants Seized

Military headquarters here has begun to arrest merchants who refuse to make "voluntary contributions" to the Hankow Rebellion Suppression Committee, which is raising funds for the People's Militia.

While in Sinyang I visited a community of German Catholic missionaries, many of whom have lived in China for fifteen years or more. They stressed the need of American aid to Nanking to defeat the Communists.

"What kind of aid is needed most?" I asked Father Brockmueller, who recently had to evacuate his station in Honan.

"It would be necessary to send an American army," he replied.

Mukden Checks Communists

NANKING, Dec. 21 (UP)—Dispatches from Manchuria said tonight that Nationalist troops had stopped Communist drives upon Mukden from the north and south but that fighting was still intense west of the city.

Fighter planes and light bombers were reported to have been thrown into the defense of Mukden. If the Communists capture it, the whole Nationalist position in Manchuria probably would collapse.

Communists Report Gains

San FRANCISCO, Dec. 21 (P)—The Chinese Communist radio said today that Gen. Chen Yi and Gen. Chen Keng had "destroyed" more than 15,000 Government troops and captured more than twenty Honan towns in operations in Central China in the week ending Friday.

December 22, 1947

China's Reds Form North Regime As Forerunner for All of Country

NANKING, China, Sept. 1—The Communist North Shensi radio tonight announced the formation of a "North China People's Government," calling it the forerunner of a future "people's government" for all of China. Officers were elected and laws passed by a representative assembly, the radio reported.

The broadcast asserted that the 528 delegates to the assembly included representatives of Government-held areas and members of the Democratic League, a Leftist liberal group which was outlawed by Nanking last Oct. 28, as well as Communist party members.

The assembly met from Aug. 7 to Aug. 19 and elected thirty-nine North China Government commissioners by secret ballot on Aug. 17, reserving twelve seats for representatives from areas "that will be liberated in the future."

One of the elected commissioners is Tung Pi-wu, who was a Communist party representative in Nanking during the Marshall negotiations. He was also a Communist party representative in the Chinese delegation to the San Francisco conference in 1945.

Another is Communist Gen Nieh Jung-chung, whose armies have been pitted against government troops under Gen. Fu Tso-yi in North China recently.

The broadcast named as one of the assembly delegates the widow of Prof. Wen I-to who was assassinated in Kunming in 1946.

Workers, farmers, women, liberals, the "revolutionary army"—all are reported to have been represented.

In his opening speech to the assembly Tung Pi-wu called the meeting an "epoch-making event in the history of the Chinese revolution," and stated it was the prelude to a future "All China People's Government." He said that the assembly had been called at this time because the land reform program was completed, feudalism eliminated and production improved. The Communists took a vital step toward establishing a North China regime in June when they merged two large administrative regions into one military and political unit. At the time of the merger they announced that they would call a "People's Representative Assembly" to enact laws and complete the formation of a government.

The merger places 44,000,000 persons under the jurisdiction of the newly formed Government, according to Communist claims. This is a larger population than that in any other Communist administrative unit in China.

They live in an area stretching over parts of five provinces from Shantung through Honan Hopeh Shansi and Chahar. The area is to have its own army and its own branch of the Communist party in which, it claims, there are a million registered party members.

The North China administrative merger was followed at the end of July with a Communist announcement that the party would call a people's consultative council before next July to lay the foundation for a new nation-wide coalition government.

At that time Communist field commanders were instructed to prepare for "city warfare."

September 2, 1948

MANCHURIA IS LOST BY CHIANG REGIME; MUKDEN FALL NEAR

DEBACLE INDICATED

Last Government Aides Flee as Reds Advance on Beleaguered City

SEA ONLY ESCAPE ROUTE

By HENRY R. LIEBERMAN
Special to THE NEW YORK TIMES.

NANKING, Oct. 30—The loss to the Chinese Communists of all Manchuria, a rich industrial area and a leading incubator for World War II, became a recognized fact tonight as President Chiang Kai-shek returned unexpectedly from North China and marked his sixty-second birthday while Mukden lay prostrate before the advancing Communist columns.

A reliable but unofficial report from Mukden said that the last group of high officials left the city at 3 P. M. today by automobile, apparently trying to head south to Yingkow, the Government-held escape port on the Gulf of Liaotung.

Another unconfirmed report said that the Communists already had entered Mukden, which is now believed to be without a functioning Nationalist authority.

The Communist radio said that Gen. Lin Piao's "Northeast Liberation Army" was marching on the former Manchurian industrial hub and had passed its old defense anchors. The broadcast announced capture of Sinmin, forty miles west of Mukden, and asserted that another Nationalist division had been "annihilated" in the capture of Tiehling, forty miles northeast of Mukden.

9 Divisions Bottled Up

Earlier, Fushun, site of the famous open pit coal mines, twenty-five miles east of Mukden, was reported evacuated by Government troops. So far as is known here the Nationalists have left nine divisions bottled up on the Hulutao beachhead, one army that marched south to be evacuated from Yingkow and whatever miscellaneous troops remain in the Mukden area.

None of these forces is regarded as powerful enough for conducting any major military operation. The question in Nanking tonight is just how many can still be evacuated by sea. The number, it is felt,

111

will not come anywhere near comparing with the 300,000 to 350,000 that the Government had in south Manchuria.

This is the second time within a generation that the Central Government has had to write finis in Manchuria, which the Japanese gobbled up following the "Mukden Incident" on Sept. 18, 1931.

"The Young Marshal," Chiang Hsueh Liang, then a war lord in Manchuria, is now interned in Formosa for his part in the kidnapping of the Generalissimo at Sian in December, 1936.

Communist control of Manchuria, as was also the case under the Japanese, has raised a serious threat for the Nationalist troops commanded by Gen. Fu Tso-yi in North China. General Fu holds isolated territory that is becoming fully exposed to 400,000 Reds who are now consolidating their hold on Manchuria.

The Government here remained officially silent regarding developments in Mukden, whose two main airfields were evacuated yesterday while frantic civilians, officials and even military personnel tried to board the last commercial and Chinese air force planes.

The Generalissimo's return from Peiping, where he had been personally directing the Manchurian strategy, was interpreted, however, as a sign that he had given up the attempt to evacuate the bulk of his northeastern troops and to re-seal the Liaoning corridor leading into North China.

Accompanied by Madame Chiang, the Generalissimo arrived here by plans at 5 P. M. on the date coinciding with his birthday anniversary, as calculated by the Western calendar. His return is said to have been urged by Government officials who held that the President should be in the capital during the present military, economic and psychological crisis.

Besides the grave military picture, Premier Wong Wen-Hao's Cabinet is confronted by a complex of serious economic problems involving worsening commodity shortages and increasing budgetary stringency. Banking sources said that Government revenues had declined to a point where they were now covering only 10 per cent.

There is a growing disposition to place credence in the Communist claim that twelve Nationalist divi-

COMMUNIST VICTORY

The New York Times   Oct. 31, 1948

The Chinese Government lost control of Mukden (1) and nine of its divisions were bottled up at Hulutao (2). An American task force is at Tsingtao (3) a United States naval base.

sions were eliminated west of Mukden in a battle that disrupted Generalissimo Chiang's plan for evacuating Manchuria. It is difficult to comprehend how that many troops could have been eliminated in such a short time, however, unless they laid down their arms.

The Generalissimo's original intention to recover Chinhsien, pivotal point in the west Liaoning corridor, was frustrated, it was learned, when five divisions dispatched from the Hulutao-Chinhsi area either failed to make headway against the Communists in the corridor or turned back for some other reason.

Following this development a new phase of the plan is said to have called for the troops moving west from Mukden to maintain pressure on the Communists to cover a retreat down the corridor through Yingkow on the northeast shore of the Gulf of Liaotung.

According to information available here, the Fifty-second Army was dispatched to Yingkow. This army, it was said, was later ordered to return to Mukden. Whether it actually returned is unknown.

COMMUNISTS WIN ALL OF TIENTSIN; U. S. CITIZENS SAFE

Broadcast Reports Capture of Garrison Chief—Peiping Is Held Next Target

VICTORS' CONDUCT PRAISED

American Consul Terms It 'Exemplary'—Chiang and Aides Study Mao Terms

By HENRY R. LIEBERMAN
Special to THE NEW YORK TIMES.

NANKING, Jan. 15—The Communist radio today announced the complete occupation of Tientsin, North China's leading industrial center, by Gen. Liu Ya-lou's attacking Communist columns. According to the broadcast the city, which has a population of 2,000,000 and ranks second only to Shanghai as a commercial mart, was taken at 1:30 P. M. today after a final assault lasting twenty-seven and one-half hours.

The capture of Tientsin by the Communists was confirmed by a reliable independent report that indicated all United States nationals in the city were safe.

The report said that the Tientsin radio had broadcast a message from the garrison commander, Gen. Chen Chang-chieh, early this morning in which he informed the Communists that his troops were laying down their arms.

Soon thereafter it was stated that Communist troops marched down Tientsin's main street past the United States consulate firing rifle shots in the air.

The Communist radio said that the Tientsin garrison commander had been captured. It also reported the "annihilation" of the seven divisions that had been defending Tientsin. It would probably be more accurate to say, however, that the Nationalist forces there had withered away, just as a number of other Government concentrations had done before them.

Britain and the United States have turned down the Nanking Government's request soliciting the members of the Big Four to provide their good offices in an attempt to bring the Nationalists and Communists together for the purpose of ending China's civil war, it was learned today.

As far as could be determined, France and the Soviet Union have not yet replied. But little hope is held here that either power would undertake the job of a go-between, especially in view of Communist leader Mao Tze-tung's statement yesterday in which he virtually called for the Kuomintang's unconditional surrender.

The contents of the British and American notes were not disclosed.

Communist Terms Studied

Although there was no official reaction to the statement made by Mr. Mao, Government leaders gave the closest attention to the Communist leader's eight-point counterproposal for ending the civil war.

For Generalissimo Chiang Kaishek, who had indicated earlier his willingness to step down if peace with the Communists could be obtained, there seemed little room for political maneuvering.

A flurry of consultations at Generalissimo Chiang's official residence began today at 4 P. M. and lasted until 11 P. M., with the Generalissimo calling in party and Government officials for separate talks on Mr. Mao's statement. The Generalissimo's conferees included Huang Shao-ku, Kuomintang Minister of Information, and Chen Po-sheng, chief editor of the Central News Agency.

A special meeting of Premier Sun Fo's Cabinet is scheduled for tomorrow morning, and a separate meeting of the Kuomintang's Central Political Council is on the calendar for Monday.

It was also reported that the Generalissimo had summoned Dr. Carson Chang, head of the Democratic Socialists, and Tso Shunsheng, a leading member of the Young China party, for conferences tomorrow.

Meanwhile the official Central News Agency reported that "dispersal trains" would go into operation again on the Shanghai-Nanking railway tomorrow to remove "public personnel, official documents and property" from the capital.

A Ministry of Communications source also disclosed that the 2,500-ton vessel Hai Kang was due to arrive in Nanking soon to transport Government files and documents to Canton and Formosa.

October 31, 1948

January 16, 1949

PEIPING SURRENDERS TO REDS AS NANKING REGIME OFFERS TO CONFER ON FOES' TERMS

WAR IN NORTH ENDS

Transitional Coalition Is Arranged — Safety Assured Foreigners

By JEAN LYON
Special to THE NEW YORK TIMES.

PEIPING, Jan. 22—Peiping fell to Communists today—quietly, politely and in accordance with her traditions—a feat possible only in China. The Nationalists are bowing their way out while the Communists bow their way in under a complicated and somewhat unfathomable agreement.

The agreement, which was formally announced to the press tonight by Gen. Fu Tso-yi's official spokesman Gen. Yen Yu-wen who has reportedly been one of the main peace negotiators, in effect, establishes a separate peace for North China.

[The Associated Press said that the surrender terms included the removal of General Fu's name from the Communists' "war criminal" list.]

Broader Compact to Follow

The agreement provides for a transition coalition committee, made up of both Nationalists and Communists, to effect the takeover. Credit, thereby, goes to General Fu for negotiating the peace that the people of the city and North China have long been demanding. Credit goes at the same time to the Communists for the setting up of the long-promised coalition. What comes after the transition is not stated but reference is made to an "overall agreement" that will be drawn up by the coalition group.

The cease-fire order went into effect at 10 o'clock this morning and Nationalist troops were to begin moving out of the city at once

for "reorganization" at designated points and the coalition committee was to be formed to take over all military and political affairs of the city at an unspecified time.

There are thirteen points in the agreement, all applicable only to the transition period. The safety of the lives and property of foreigners is assured, continued functioning of telegraphic and postal communications is promised, the freedom of worship and the protection of religious property is agreed upon, and all the present Government and private organizations, including the Provincial Government, are to continue without change for the present.

Nanking Speeds Talks

By HENRY R. LIEBERMAN
Special to THE NEW YORK TIMES

NANKING, Jan. 22—A separate peace settlement for the Communist-besieged city of Peiping was concluded today as Premier Sun Fo's Cabinet prepared to negotiate for a general peace on the basis of the Communists' terms.

The arrangement under which Peiping is being yielded was made with the Communists by Gen. Fu Tso-yi, Nationalist commander in North China. Peiping has been encircled for more than a month.

Here, five delegates were named by the Cabinet to negotiate for peace as acting President Li Tsung-jen announced that his caretaker Government was ready to talk terms on the basis of the eight conditions laid down by the Communist leader Mao Tze-tung.

Mr. Mao's conditions, which were broadcast by the North Shensi radio on Jan. 14 called for the virtual surrender of the Kuomintang [Government party] and the punishment of "war criminals."

"The five Government delegates are ready to start negotiations with the delegates of the Chinese Communist party at a suitable place to be agreed upon by both sides," an official Cabinet statement said.

The Kuomintang representatives named to talk peace are:

Shao Li-tze, a long time peace advocate, chairman. Mr. Shao, 67,

is a former newspaper man who has held two provincial governorships. He served as a Minister of Information and represented China as Ambassador to Moscow from 1939 to 1942. He has negotiated with the Communists before.

Gen. Chang Chih-chung, another consistent peace advocate who served as director of the Generalissimo's headquarters in Northwest China before becoming Minister Without Portfolio in the present Government. He has also negotiated for the Kuomintang with the Communists in the past.

Peng Chao-hsien, a native of Shantung. He was educated in Moscow and once served as Consul General at Khabarovsk.

Chung Tien-hsieng, Minister of Water Conservancy, who is closely identified with Dr. Sun Fo's group in the Kuomintang.

Gen. Huang Shao-hsiung, a Kwangsi man who is a member of the clique led by General Li and General Pai Chung-hsi. He has been Governor of several provinces, including Kwangsi, and was once Minister of Interior.

None of the delegates, who appear to have been selected with the greatest care, is on the Communists' "war criminal" list.

It was reported tonight that the chairman, Mr. Shao, already had sought contact with the Communists through the broadcasting of a telegram seeking the good offices of Marshal Li Chi-sen, leader of the rump "Revolutionary Committee of the Kuomintang," and Shen Chun-ju, a member of the left-wing Democratic League. Both men are now somewhere in North China holding talks with the Communist leaders on the future shape of the projected coalition government.

At the same time Premier Sun was said to be planning moves aimed at releasing political prisoners and reopening mail and telegraph services with Communist-held areas. The Government seems to be sparing no efforts to convince the Communists that it really wants to make peace.

General Li declared tonight that his regime was acting with the "highest degree of sincerity and greatest efforts" to bring about a settlement.

He said he appreciated the difficulties of making peace and, like Generalissimo Chiang Kai-shek before him, asserted that he was prepared to withdraw from the Government if peace could be achieved.

"I believe that one day peace will certainly be restored," he added.

The appointment of the Kuomintang delegates, combined with the news that General Fu already had negotiated a separate peace settlement for Peiping, spurred the hopes of the man in the street that the long civil war was drawing closer to an end for the Yangtze Valley as well as North China.

Meanwhile Generalissimo Chiang, whose departure created little public excitement in the capital, arrived at his native home, Fenghwa, Chekiang Province, to observe the

The home in Fenghwa in Chekiang Province, southwest of Shanghai, to which the leader of China retired. Associated Press

Chinese spring festival holiday in "retirement" with the members of his family.

The first Communist reaction to the Generalissimo's retirement came tonight in a North Shensi broadcast asserting that General Li's elevation to the "bogus presidency" was a plot engineered by the United States Government. The broadcast, which ascribed this reaction to Communist "newspapers," maintained that the United States had supported his election to the

Vice Presidency last April "with this very purpose in mind."

"The fact is also noted that Chiang has placed notorious reactionary warlords such as Chen Cheng, Hsueh Yueh, Chu Shao-liang Yu Han-mou and Chang Chun in various southern provinces before his 'retirement,' the broadcast said.

"All indications are that the Kuomintang's reactionary Nanking Government has no sincere desire

for a genuine democratic peace."

A distinction is being made here, possibly on the basis of wishful thinking, between official statements of the Communist party and "propaganda" statements broadcast by the North Shensi radio without official attribution.

At least the Kuomintang officials, anxious to make peace, are hoping that the radio statements are only propaganda pressures that can be modified by proof of

"sincerity," a word that is recurring more and more in the Government's pronouncements.

According to reports from major Yangtze Valley cities, newspaper readers displayed the keenest interest in Generalissimo Chiang's retirement, and food prices started to drop immediately.

New hope for peace was apparent here, but here was little public excitement as a result of the Generalissimo's departure.

January 23, 1949

U. S. PUTS SOLE BLAME ON CHIANG REGIME FOR COLLAPSE, HOLDS MORE AID FUTILE; ACHESON BIDS REDS AVOID AGGRESSION

WHITE PAPER BLUNT

Stresses That Chinese Nationalists Failed to Utilize Past Help

ACHESON BARS DEFEATISM

Warns Communists to Shun Imperialism From Moscow— Wedemeyer Report Issued

By HAROLD B. HINTON
Special to The New York Times.

WASHINGTON, Aug. 5 — The Chinese National Government is on the verge of collapse solely because of the military, political and economic incapacity of the Kuomintang's leaders, the State Department found in a China White Paper made public today.

Secretary of State Dean Acheson, both in transmitting the report to President Truman and in oral comment on the document, rejected the theory that greater aid

from the United States could have enabled Generalissimo Chiang Kaishek and his lieutenants to defeat the Chinese Communists by force.

Mr. Acheson declared in his letter of transmittal to Mr. Truman that if the Chinese Communist regime should lend itself "to the aims of Soviet Russian imperialism and attempt to engage in aggression against China's neighbors, we and the other members of the United Nations would be confronted by a situation violative of the principles of the United Nations Charter and threatening international peace and security."

U. S. Assistance Is Cited

In a prepared statement after release of the White Paper, Mr. Acheson said that the National Government of China "has been unable to rally its people and has been driven out of extensive and important portions of the country, despite very extensive assistance from the United States and advice from eminent American representatives which subsequent events proved to be sound."

The White Paper included the controversial report on China made to President Truman by Lieut. Gen. Albert C. Wedemeyer in 1947. In his report General Wedemeyer recommended that Manchuria be placed under a guardianship or United Nations trusteeship of the United States, China, the Soviet Union, France and Britain, that this country continue economic aid to China under certain controls and that China reform her military

establishment and accept supervision of her field forces.

Secretary Acheson said that the voluminous record (more than 1,000 pages) with the official title, "United States Relations with China," had been made public at this time so that the public of the United States could understand fully the background of "the situation in China, which will test to the full our unity of purpose, our ingenuity and our adherence to the basic principles which have, for half a century, governed our policy toward China."

U. S. to Review Policy

The Secretary repeated that a complete review of United States policy in the Far East would be undertaken immediately, with the cooperation of the National Security Council, the National Military Establishment, the Treasury, the Economic Cooperation Administration, the Senate Foreign Relations Committee and the House Foreign Affairs Committee.

Raymond B. Fosdick, former president of the Rockefeller Foundation, who has been retained as a consultant for this review, along with Dr. Everett Case, president of Colgate University, will report to the State Department on Monday to begin the study, Mr. Acheson said. Other outside assistance may be sought, he added, in an effort "to bring to bear the united wisdom and resourcefulness of our Government in meeting the present situation and by future developments in Asia and the Far East."

Pending adoption of a long-range national policy toward that area of the world, Mr. Acheson said in a statement issued at a press conference, the State Department would be guided by the following basic principles, which he considers still valid:

1. Encouragement of the development of China as an independent and stable nation "able to play a role in world affairs suitable for a great and free people."
2. Support of the creation in China of economic and political conditions to safeguard basic rights and liberties, and to progressively develop the economic and social well-being of its people.
3. Opposition to the subjection of China to any foreign power or to a regime acting in the interest of a foreign power, as well as the dismemberment of China by a foreign power, openly or clandestinely.
4. Consultation with other interested powers on measures contributing to the security and welfare of the peoples of the Far East as a whole.
5. Support of efforts by the United Nations to maintain peace and security in the Far East.

Bars Defeatist Attitude

Mr. Acheson described the Chinese Communists as serving the imperialist interests of a foreign power, but conceded they had been able to persuade large numbers of Chinese that they had been acting in their interest. He indicated his belief that they would ultimately fail, saying that he did not "share the defeatist attitude which some current comments reflect."

"The United States, for its part," he said, "will be prepared to work with the people of China and of every other country in Asia to preserve and to promote their true interest, developed as they choose and not as dictated by any foreign imperialism."

Most of the information contained in the White Paper had been communicated in confidence to the Senate Foreign Relations Committee and the House Foreign Affairs Committee by Secretary of State George C. Marshall in February, 1948, Mr. Acheson said.

The bulk of the book is taken up by documents dealing with developments since V-J Day, although there is an introductory chapter giving the highlights of Sino-American relations from 1844 to 1943—from the signature of the Treaty of Wanghai through the open-door policy of Secretary of State John Hay and the support of China against Japanese aggression to the repeal of the Chinese exclusion acts.

As early as Sept. 22, 1944, Gen. Joseph W. Stilwell was complaining to General Marshall, the Chief of Staff, that Generalissimo Chiang believed that the war in the Pacific was nearly over and would be won without great Chinese expenditure of effort.

General Stilwell described the Generalissimo's policy as one of "grabbing for loans and post-war aid, for the purpose of maintaining his present position, based on one-party government, a reactionary policy, or the suppression of democratic ideas with the active aid of his 'gestapo.'"

Reports from a number of foreign service officers in the field, before and after General Stilwell's complaint, tended to confirm his estimate of the situation.

Maj. Gen. Patrick J. Hurley arrived in China about this time as President Roosevelt's personal representative, with the rank of ambassador. His mission was to get the National armies and the Communists to unite in fighting against the Japanese, instead of immobilizing large portions of their combat troops to watch each other.

"The defeat of Japan is, of course, the primary objective," he reported in December, "but we should all understand that if an agreement is not reached between the two great military establishments of China, civil war will in all probability ensue."

General Hurley undertook, on instruction from President Roosevelt, to act as intermediary between Generalissimo Chiang and the Communist leaders in Yenan, including Mao Tse-tung and Gen. Chou En-lai, who stayed part of the time in Chungking as Communist representative. As fast as he could get one side to agree to a plan for unification, the other would impose new reservations, and he resigned the mission, in the belief it was hopeless, on Nov. 26, 1945.

Meanwhile, a secret agreement had been reached between Premier Stalin, President Roosevelt and Prime Minister Winston Churchill at the Yalta conference in February, 1945. The White Paper devotes a chapter to this meeting, at which Mr. Stalin agreed to throw the Soviet Union into the war against Japan, in return for extensive concessions in Manchuria.

PRESENTS REPORT ON CHINA

Secretary of State Dean Acheson in his office with an open volume of the White Paper.

The New York Times (by George Tames)

"In general the Russian conditions were conceded," the White Paper comments. "It should be remembered that at this time the atomic bomb was anything but an assured reality; the potentialities of the Japanese Kwantung Army in Manchuria seemed large; and the price in American lives in the military campaign up the island ladder to the Japanese home islands was assuming ghastly proportions.

"Obviously, military necessity dictated that Russia enter the war against Japan prior to the mounting of Operation Olympic (the planned assault upon Kyushu) roughly scheduled for Nov. 1, 1945, in order to contain Japanese forces in Manchuria and prevent their transfer to the Japanese home islands."

The commentary conceded that it was unfortunate the commitments undertaken in the name of China were not made known to the Chinese Government.

"President Roosevelt and Marshal Stalin, however, based this reticence on the already well known and growing danger of 'leaks' to the Japanese from Chinese sources due to the debilitating and suppurative effects of the war," it is explained. "Here again military exigency was the governing consideration. At no point did President Roosevelt consider that he was compromising vital Chinese interests."

After V-J day, President Truman sent General Marshall to China in another effort to unify the country and avoid civil war. By that time, General Wedemeyer, who had succeeded General Stilwell in command of U. S. forces in the China theater, was reporting that Generalissimo Chiang intended to defeat the Chinese Communists in Manchuria before he consolidated his own position in North China—an operation that General Wedemeyer considered impossible.

General Marshall found China's economic and financial condition becoming rapidly weaker through inflation, administrative inefficiency and corruption, despite the fact the Government came out of the war with official reserves in excess of $400,000,000, with as much held in foreign exchange assets by Chinese citizens.

Cease-Fire Obtained

By January, 1946, he had obtained a cease-fire agreement from both the National armies and the Communist forces, and had sent out field teams to supervise execution of the agreement. Distrust on both sides fanned by breaches of the truce by both sides gradually led to a resumption of active hostilities, and General Marshall was recalled to the United States at the end of 1946 to become Secretary of State in a few weeks.

"There was a point beyond which American mediation could not go," the White Paper says. "Peace and stability in China must, in the final analysis, be achieved by the efforts of the Chinese themselves."

Before he left China, General Marshall recommended that Dr. John Leighton Stuart, president of Yenching University, be named as United States Ambassador to China. Dr. Stuart is now en route to the United States for consultations, after having been detained in Nanking for several weeks by the Chinese Communist forces.

Ambassador Stuart's reports continued to record inability of the National Government to deal with the worsening situation. After Generalissimo Chiang withdrew in favor of Vice President Li Tsung-jen, he reported that the Generalissimo still was interfering in governmental affairs to the embarrassment of his successor.

At home, Secretary Marshall advised President Truman, in the summer of 1947, to send General Wedemeyer on a fact-finding mission to China and Korea. In his final report, the General found his previous estimates of the military incapacity of the National Government's strategists still valid, and recommended that Manchuria be placed under a guardianship or United Nations trusteeship of the Soviet Union, Great Britain, China, France and the United States until the government was strong enough to establish control.

Because of this recommendation, the report was suppressed in Washington. It was considered that a proposal smacking of dismemberment would be fatal to Chinese morale at that period. The report is published for the first time as an annex to the White Paper.

General Wedemeyer recommended, in addition, that United States aid to China be continued, but under certain stipulations. These included political and military reforms, effective use of Chinese resources in a program of economic reconstruction and acceptance of American advisers in military and economic fields to assure that the United States aid was employed effectively.

In the military field, he urged that the National Government reduce its military budget and increase the efficiency of its military establishment through urgently required reforms; that it develop, with United States advice, a sound supply and maintenance program.

Role in Japan Ruled Out

He also recommended that it be permitted to buy military supplies and equipment from the United States; that it obtain ammunition immediately; that it complete quickly its plan for eight and one-third air groups and expanded air transport service; that it drop plans to participate in the occupation of Japan; and that it accept advice and supervision in its field forces, training centers and logistical agencies.

Before leaving China, General Wedemeyer was invited to address on Aug. 22, 1947, a joint meeting of the State Council and the Ministers of the National Government. He was highly critical of the Government and apparently aroused sharp resentment among many of his listeners.

The tragic sequence of events related by the documents in the White Paper concludes on a note consistent with its general theme. A report of April 23, 1949, from the United States Embassy in Nanking is quoted as follows:

"The ridiculously easy Communist crossing of the Yangtze was made possible by defections at key points, disagreements in the high command, and the failure of the air force to give effective support."

U. S. GIVES ACCOUNT OF TOTAL CHINA AID

Grants, Credits Since V-J Day Listed at $2,007,700,000 Apart From War Surplus

Special to THE NEW YORK TIMES.

WASHINGTON, Aug. 5 — The State Department, in the China White Paper released today, sought to cast up a balance sheet of the military and financial assistance extended since V-J Day to the Chinese National Government by the United States. Congressional critics frequently have asserted that it was insufficient.

Total grants and credits by the United States Government since V-J Day were listed as $2,007,700,-000. Grants and credits from the United Nations Relief and Rehabilitation Administration and from the Canadian Government brought the total to $2,263,500,000.

In addition, the White Paper listed surplus property originally costing $1,078,100,000 that was transferred to the Chinese Government for $232,000,000.

On the military side, the following judgment of Maj. Gen. David Barr, head of the joint United States military advisory group in China, given on Nov. 16, 1948, was quoted:

"No battle has been lost since my arrival due to lack of ammunition or equipment. Their military debacles, in my opinion, can all be attributed to the world's worst leadership and many other morale-destroying factors that lead to a complete loss of will to fight."

Military Leaders Inept

"The complete ineptness of high military leaders and the widespread corruption and dishonesty throughout the armed forces could, in some measure, have been controlled and directed had the above authority and facilities been available. Chinese leaders completely lack the moral courage to issue and enforce an unpopular decision."

An inescapable though unstated conclusion of the report was this:

So high a percentage of the arms provided by the United States have fallen into the hands of the Communists without ever inflicting serious battle damage on them that this country has been inadvertently arming enemies of the Nationalist Government.

The economic analysis took into account the difficult situation in China as a result of eight years of large-scale fighting. On the credit side it placed gold and dollar reserves in the hands of the Nationalist Government on V-J Day at $400,000,000, with an equal amount in foreign exchange values in the hands of private Chinese citizens.

"The Lend-Lease 'pipe line' credit from the United States of $51,700,000, and the Canadian credit of $60,000,000, had been only partially drawn upon by January, 1947," the account said. "Surplus property under the 1946 bulk sale agreement was just beginning to arrive in China.

Credits Not Drawn

"Of authorized Export-Import Bank credits for China, $54,600,-000 had not been drawn. In April, 1947, the United States Maritime Commission authorized the sale to China of surplus war-built merchant vessels on terms involving credits of $16,500,000.

"All these programs made available a continuing flow of usable and salable resources into the Chinese economy."

It was on Feb. 4, 1947, after a violent upheaval in the Shanghai money market, that Prime Minister T. V. Soong sought from Ambassador John Leighton Stuart an immediate credit of $150,000,000. It was wanted for the purchase of wheat and cotton and was to run for ten years.

"Politically, it will encourage the wavering elements in the minor parties to join the Government," Mr. Soong said in an aide-memoire he left at the embassy, "and it would encourage the progressive members of the Government to press forward for a speedy reorganization. A smaller sum than the figure mentioned will not have the effect necessary in this emergency."

Late in 1947, Congress appropriated $45,700,000 for the purchase of rice, wheat, flour and medical supplies. In 1948, a grant of $125,-000,000 was voted, along with $275,000,000 under the Economic Cooperation Administration's program.

The White Paper reported that, in a series of battles in Manchuria in November, 1948, the Nationalist forces had lost eight divisions, 85 per cent of whose equipment came from the United States. The losses included 100,000 American rifles and 130,000 rifles of other origin.

By December, 1948, the military attaché at Nanking reported that seventeen American-equipped divisions had been lost. After the fall of Manchuria a high Chinese officer told him that 80 per cent of all American equipment had been lost by capture or attrition.

CHINESE NATIONALISTS MOVE THEIR CAPITAL TO FORMOSA; NOW PLAN A GUERRILLA WAR

YUNNAN TOTTERING

Turn-Over to Reds Seen –Effective Opposition on Mainland Ceases

RESISTANCE HEADS NAMED

Headquarters Are Set Up in Sichang for 'Land, Sea, Air' Raids on Communists

By TILLMAN DURDIN
Special to THE NEW YORK TIMES.

HONG KONG, Dec. 8—The capital of the depleted Nationalist Government of China shifted for the fourth time today, this time to the island of Formosa, 110 miles off the mainland.

Premier Gen. Yen Hsi-shan arrived at the new capital city of Taipei this afternoon and announced his Cabinet would begin functioning there tomorrow.

The Nationalist move, signalizing virtual termination of effective resistance to Communists on the mainland, it is believed here, will clear the way to early recognition of the Peiping Government as the Government of China by many foreign powers.

An extraordinary session of the Executive Yuan in Chengtu last night decided to evacuate the Government to Formosa and proclaimed that Sichang, in Sikang Province bordering Tibet, would be

DISPERSAL OF CHINESE NATIONALISTS

The New York Times — Dec. 9, 1949

The Nationalist Government shifted its capital to Taipei on Formosa (1) after evacuating Chengtu (2). The military command transferred its headquarters to Sichang (3). The defection of Yunnan Province (4) to the Communists was believed under way. Communist forces have reached the Indo-China border at Tunghing (5). The Reds' radio said they had sealed all Kwangtung ports except Paksha (6) against further Nationalist evacuations from the mainland to Hainan Island.

the military headquarters for continued "land, sea and air" activities on the China mainland. Appointments of leaders to carry on guerrilla warfare were made.

Reds Nearing Chengtu

Generalissimo Chiang Kai-shek was due in Tapei late today or tomorrow. Planes are in the process of shifting from Chengtu to Taipei roughly one hundred persons of the thousand-odd staff members of the Government still remaining together from the Chungking evacuatio.

The Communists today were driving rapidly on toward Chengtu and were last reported only fifty miles away. Nationalist troops under Gen. Hu Tsung-nan were falling back southwestward in an effort to get into Sikang.

Premier Yen revealed in Taipei that he did not land at Kunming en route to Formosa because he had been warned of danger there. The turnover of Yunnan Province to the Communists was believed in process. Gen. Lung Yun, one-time warlord Governor of the province who has joined the Communists, is now in Hong Kong and has sent agents to Kunming to see his half-brother Gov. Lu Han.

Governor Lu is understood to advocate that Yunnan merely proclaim independence from the Chiang regime at this stage,

whereas General Lung is urging the announcement of full allegiance to the Communists. Most of the Yunnan Provincial Government has moved to Tali but Governor Lu still is in Kunming. Communist guerrilla units are increasingly active around Kunming.

New Leaders Named

Before it left Chengtu the Nationalist Government accepted the resignation of Gen. Chang Chun as director of the Southwest Command Headquarters. General Chang, one-time Premier and Foreign Minister, presumably will remain in his native province of Szechwan for the coming of the Communists.

Gen. Ku Chu-tung was named to General Chang's post. Generals Hu Tsung-nan and Yang Sen were appointed General Ku's deputies. General Wang Tsang-hsu and Tang Shih-tsun, Szechwanese who are both closely linked with Szechwan's powerful, secret Elder Brother Society (Ko Lao Hui), were appointed to lead the guerrilla armies. Gen. Huo Kuo-kuang was named to head the Sichang garrison headquarters.

A Taipei report quoted Premier Yen as having said Generalissimo Chiang was not resuming the Presidency for the time being, but that he would concentrate on military affairs. It is reported the Generalissimo's advisers have counseled him to hold off at least a month before taking his old post in order to see what Acting President Li Tsung-jen accomplishes on his mission to the United States.

It is doubted if the Nationalist seat at Taipei will have much to do with Hainan, the other island refuge for Nationalist generals and troops once engaged against the Communists on the mainland. There General Pai Chung-hsi of Kwangsi, Chen Chi-tang of Kwangtung and a number of other Kwangtung and Kwangsi generals have concentrated the remnant of the forces, numbering an estimated 150,000, in an effort to hold out against the Communists. Some Kwangsi and Kwangtung troops still are fighting in the hills of Southwest Kwangtung, but the Communist radio announces that all Kwangtung ports except Paksha at the tip of the Luichow Peninsula, which still is in Nationalist hands, have been blocked against further evacuations of Nationalist troops from the mainland.

U. S. AIDES FOUGHT CHIANG, SAYS JUDD

Special to THE NEW YORK TIMES.

WASHINGTON, Oct. 19—Charges of "conniving" against the recognized Government of China by United States officials while World War II was still in progress were made on the floor of the House today, just before the adjournment of Congress, by Representative Walter H. Judd, Republican, of Minnesota.

He supported his charges by placing in the Congressional Record a copy of a secret memorandum dated Oct. 10, 1944, from John S. Service, State Department observer stationed with the Chinese Communist forces at Yenan, to Gen. Joseph W. Stilwell, then commanding United States forces in China, Burma and India.

"We cannot hope to deal successfully with Chiang [Generalissimo Chiang Kai-shek] without being hard-boiled," Mr. Service wrote. "Second, we cannot hope to solve China's problems (which are now our problems) without consideration of the opposition forces —Communist, provincial and liberal."

Mr. Service recommended that Maj. Gen. Patrick J. Hurley, then in China as President Roosevelt's personal representative, visit the Communist capital at Yenan.

"The effect would be great," he added, "even if it were only a demonstration with no real consultation. But it should be more than a mere demonstration. He must, for instance, plan on eventual use of the Communist armies and this cannot be purely on Kuomintang terms."

The writer estimated that Chinese resistance would not cease with the collapse of the Kuomintang Government.

Mr. Judd told the House that he was making public Mr. Service's report because the State Department had omitted it from the China White Paper.

"After Mr. Service was transferred from China at the insistence of our Ambassador, General Hurley, he was involved in the Amerasia case," Mr. Judd said.

[In June, 1945, six persons were arrested and accused of participation in the removal of hundreds of secret documents from State Department military and naval files. Two of the defendants were co-editors of the magazine Amerasia, which had printed information contained in many of the documents. Three of the six escaped indictment.]

"The case was hushed up under circumstances never yet disclosed or explained," Mr. Judd charged. "Since then, he has been promoted several times and is now chairman of the committee within the State Department which makes recommendations for all promotions."

By way of contrast, Mr. Judd also filed a copy of a speech made by Lieut. Gen. Albert C. Wedemeyer in New York City, on Oct. 10, 1946. General Wedemeyer succeeded General Stilwell in command of United States forces in the China-Burma-India theatre.

"During the past twelve months," General Wedemeyer said, "the Generalissimo has worked selflessly and energetically to achieve economic stability and to create national unity through democratic procedures."

October 20, 1949

DEWEY FAVORS AID FOR FREE PEOPLES

Governor Dewey declared here yesterday that the Communist Iron Curtain could be "moved back a little" if the United States remained economically and militarily strong and helped the free democracies to become "sound enough not to follow the Communist roots down to destruction."

Taking time out from his campaigning for the election of Senator John Foster Dulles, Mr. Dewey told 800 delegates at the closing session of the Lithuanian American Congress that "it is entirely possible that economic warfare has made military warfare out of date." The meeting was held at the New Yorker Hotel.

Governor Dewey, calling Stalin the "greatest Czar of them all," said that the Soviet Union controlled 200,000,000 Russians and 200,000,000 Europeans from the Baltic to the Mediterranean. He added that "it is a matter of the deepest regret to me that my Government has allowed 400,000,000 more in China to be conquered by Soviet agents."

The United States should stop thinking that the end of the war brought peace to the world, he said. Many nations, like Lithuania, are suffering greatly under the Russians who, he declared, are trying to enslave the rest of the world by "traitors such as were recently convicted at Foley Square," by propaganda, and by economic pressures.

Declaring that the "cold war" could be won by peaceful means, Mr. Dewey said it was necessary to unite the free nations of the world, keep this nation strong, and "encourage the free peoples of Asia to start rolling back the Iron Curtain in China."

Kipras Bielinis, representing the Supreme Lithuanian Committee of Liberation, with headquarters in Western Germany, said that Lithuanians in their homeland were resisting collectivization, which he called "one form of genocide." Although thousands are being sent to Siberia, he said, Lithuanians are showing passive resistance by refusing to vote.

Mr. Bielinis said that although the Russians sent out trucks to round up voters, they could not get more than 75 per cent of the people in the cities to go to the polls.

November 6, 1949

AUSTIN DISCUSSES CHINA'S U. N. STATUS

U. S. Will Stress in Assembly, He Says, Right of Her People to Choose Own Government

Special to THE NEW YORK TIMES.

BUFFALO, N. Y., Oct. 22— Warren R. Austin, permanent United States delegate to the United Nations, indicated here tonight that the United States would stress in United Nations General Assembly debate the right of the Chinese people to choose their own government. He held out little hope that any Assembly decision would change the picture in China.

Commenting on Nationalist China's charges in the General Assembly that Soviet intervention in China was endangering peace, Mr. Austin told a conference sponsored by the United Nations Committee of the Buffalo Conference on World Affairs:

"We consider the case which the Chinese delegation has presented to the Assembly to be of great importance. It must be recognized, however, that, in view of the current course of events in China, this will be a most difficult matter for the Assembly to deal with. We cannot expect that the course of events will be reversed or halted merely by a pronouncement of the Assembly."

Then, in what some circles viewed as a preview of the United States stand on the Chinese issue, Mr. Austin added:

"What might perhaps emerge from the consideration of this case would be a reaffirmation by the United Nations of certain basic principles of the Charter as they apply to China's independence from foreign domination. Such a statement by the Assembly could have a significant long-term effect in demonstrating to the Chinese people that the United Nations has a vital concern in their welfare and their destiny."

In his address to the meeting, held in connection with the observance of United Nations week, Mr. Austin also said that "within a few days" he would summon representatives of the other four Big Powers to further consultations on the use of the veto in the Security Council. He noted that the Soviet Union had agreed that the five Big Powers — who hold the right of veto—should consult together before important votes were taken.

The new sessions would be an effort to find a way to put the agreement into practice. So far the Soviet Union has used the veto forty-one times.

Mr. Austin said that the United States and Britain would oppose Russia's major proposal before the 1949 Assembly, which stresses the Soviet plan of atomic energy control and a Five-Power peace pact. Instead, he said, the two Western powers would "introduce an independent resolution which trul, represents the firm determination of their peoples to save succeeding generations from the scourge of war."

October 23, 1949

GROUP HERE FIGHTS AID TO CHINA'S REDS

Committee to Defend America Hears Congress Members Urge Help for Nationalists

Four members of Congress last night urged renewed aid to Nationalist China and no recognition of the Chinese Reds under any circumstances. They spoke at a Carnegie Hall meeting of the newly formed Committee to Defend America by Aiding Anti-Communist China. One thousand persons attended.

Senator Herbert R. O'Conor, Democrat, of Maryland, said he was unalterably opposed to recognition of Communist China.

"It is wishful thinking to suppose we could do business with them," he said. "Recognition would only further expand their undemocratic and destructive forces."

He urged additional financial and material support for a "non-Communist unified regime," with strict adherence to yesterday's announcement by the State Department of its determination to disavow domination of any Chinese government by a foreign power, and stern resistance to the Russian efforts to unseat the present Chinese delegation to the United Nations.

By these means Nationalist China, he said, may retain faith in the United Nations as the recognized legitimate government of that land. Russia, he said, "had been exploiting the miseries of the Chinese people and the weaknesses of the Nationalist Government."

Other speakers were Representatives Earl T. Wagner, Democrat, of Ohio; John David Lodge, Republican, of Connecticut, and James Fulton, Republican, of Pennsylvania.

Mr. Wagner, in an interview at the Park-Sheraton Hotel before the meeting, declared that if Great Britain showed an eagerness to recognize the Chinese Communists, "we should seriously consider the question of aid to Britain."

He suggested we might go further and check whether some of the "so-called friendly" nations that seemed so anxious to recognize Communist regimes "are worthy of further United States support."

"Too long have the Reds ridden roughshod over the State Department, and done all in their power to bring this country into bad repute," he concluded.

Lieut. Gen. Albert C. Wedemeyer, in a message to the meeting, said his "faith in the Chinese people remains unshaken. Personally, I have never questioned Chiang Kai-shek's sincerity of purpose. I am convinced of his desire to establish true democracy in China. He has always been a symbol of China's consistent opposition to the forces of aggression."

November 29, 1949

KNOWLAND AND CABOT DIFFER ON CHIANG AID

Special to The New York Times.

PACIFIC GROVE, Calif., Dec. 11—Vigorous demands for aid to the Chinese Nationalists by Senator William F. Knowland, Republican, of California, and equally emphatic opposition to it by John M. Cabot, former United States Consul General in Shanghai, marked a three-day "China conference" at near-by Asilomar this week-end.

Senator Knowland accused this country of "trying to keep 240,-000,000 in Western Europe from going behind the iron curtain when 450,000,000 in China are being taken behind that curtain."

Mr. Cabot asserted that "In our battle with communism for the minds of men, it is one thing for us to uphold the free peoples of the world against the imposition of an aggressive tyranny, but it is a very different thing to uphold every rotten reactionary regime merely because it happens to be anti-Communist."

Former Mayor Roger D. Lapham of San Francisco, who headed the Economic Cooperation Administration's mission to China, called for recognition of the Communist Government as "the de facto Government in such areas of China as the Communists control." He pressed for this as "the only practical way to keep the door open as well as listen to what goes on behind the bamboo curtain."

A fourth major speaker, Representative Helen Gahagan Douglas, Democrat, of California, said she wanted more facts.

JESSUP DENOUNCES M'CARTHY CHARGES AS DANGER TO U. S.

Foreign Relations Are Harmed by 'False and Irresponsible' Accusations, He Asserts

FOUGHT REDS, ENVOY SAYS

Marshall, Eisenhower Letters Strongly Supporting Him Are Read at Senate Hearing

By WILLIAM S. WHITE
Special to The New York Times.

WASHINGTON, March 20—Ambassador at Large Philip C. Jessup accused Senator Joseph R. McCarthy today of making "false and irresponsible" charges that harmed this country's foreign relations and showed a "shocking disregard" for its national interest.

Dr. Jessup, who had been accused by Senator McCarthy, a Wisconsin Republican, of "an unusual affinity with Communist causes," swore before Senate investigators that he had no sympathy for communism and its objectives and never had. He offered past statements and other data to show that in the United Nations and elsewhere he had fought the Communists.

Mr. McCarthy's "innuendoes," the Ambassador asserted, were such as to shake the faith of foreign officials in the representatives of this Government abroad and to raise doubts that this country was really united in combating international communism.

As Dr. Jessup made his counterattack on Senator McCarthy, he had the support of Generals George C. Marshall and Dwight D. Eisenhower.

Both Strongly Back Jessup

Senator Millard E. Tydings, Democrat of Maryland, chairman of the Senate Foreign Relations subcommittee that is investigating the McCarthy charges of Communist infiltration of the State Department, read into the record letters from both generals backing Ambassador Jessup in the strongest terms.

General Marshall wrote as follows:

"My Dear Jessup:

"I am shocked and distressed by the attack on your integrity as a public servant.

"Throughout your entire service with me while I was Secretary of State you were clearly outstanding as a representative of the Government both as to your masterful presentations and the firmness of your opposition to all Soviet or Communist attacks or pressures.

"This was conspicuously the case during your handling on the [United Nations] Security Council of the Berlin blockade issue.

"Both the Under-Secretary, Mr. [Robert A.] Lovett, and I counted on you as a great source of strength to the State Department during those critical days."

Eisenhower Decries Charges

As president of Columbia University, from which Dr. Jessup is on leave, General Eisenhower said in his letter:

"My Dear Jessup:

"I am writing to tell you how much your university deplores the association of your name with the current loyalty investigation in the United States Senate.

"Your long and distinguished record as a scholar and a public servant has won for you the respect of your colleagues and of the American people as well. No one who has known you can for a moment question the depth of sincerity of your devotion to the principles of Americanism.

"Your university associates and I are confident that any impression to the contrary will be quickly dispelled as the facts become known."

When Senator Bourke B. Hickenlooper, Republican of Iowa, asked Dr. Jessup whether he had any objection to a "full examination by this committee" of the Government's loyalty files on him, the Ambassador replied:

"So far as I am concerned, everything in my record can be made public. Whether the Executive Department as a matter of policy should turn over such papers is not in my province. I have no objection to any information about me being made public at any time."

Early in the session, Mr. Tydings asserted that the names of eighty-one persons whose investigation Mr. McCarthy had asked had not reached him.

Subsequently Mr. McCarthy produced a registered mail slip showing that a communication including the names had been mailed to Senator Tydings Saturday night. Mr. Tydings, accepting a copy, said:

"I now gladly receive these names one month exactly after Mr.

McCarthy accused these persons on the Senate floor."

Senator McCarthy for his part had prepared a fresh attack on Dr. Jessup before the Ambassador took the stand.

In a letter to Senator Tydings, which was not put in evidence, Mr. McCarthy asserted that Dr. Jessup had a "very close association" with a "group of 'untouchables'" in the State Department "who have delivered China to communism."

For an adequate examination of Ambassador Jessup, Senator McCarthy argued, the subcommittee should have obtained the complete State Department, Civil Service Commission and Federal Bureau of Investigation files of Dr. Jessup and of Prof. Owen Lattimore of Johns Hopkins University, described by the Senator as a State Department consultant on Far Eastern affairs.

"In my opinion," Mr. McCarthy's letter said, "the issue is not whether Mr. Jessup is well-intentioned, nor whether he has made anti-Communist speeches, nor whether his friends will testify that his is a fine man.

"The issues are (1) will he continue running with the same pack that has to date done everything in the Far East that Russia wants? and (2) will he continue to be the 'voice of Lattimore'?

"While the files may convince the committee that Jessup is well-intentioned, I am sure the files will prove to them beyond a doubt that Jessup is a dangerously efficient Lattimore-front."

Senator McCarthy in a second letter and through the only Republican member of the investigating panel present, Senator Hickenlooper, demanded to be allowed to cross-examine Dr. Jessup.

Senator Tydings rejected this. In the first place, he asserted, Dr. Jessup was not present to cross-examine Senator McCarthy when the original accusations were made and had no warning that such charges were to be made.

In the second place, Mr. Tydings said, he was not going to try to "run" the subcommittee and would take up such a question as permitting Mr. McCarthy to cross-examine only when the full membership was present. Senator Henry Cabot Lodge Jr., Republican of Massachusetts, was absent, as he had been for most of the time since the hearings began.

Senator Hickenlooper renewed Republican demands that Mr. Tydings proceed forthwith to subpoena the State Department and other files dealing with the nine persons Senator McCarthy thus far has mentioned publicly in the inquiry.

Senator Tydings retorted, reading a long list of legal precedents, that Presidents including and since George Washington had refused to give Executive Department papers to Congress.

President Truman, Mr. Tydings said, certainly would refuse if the subcommittee presented him with a subpoena, whereas if a "gentlemanly" approach of request was continued, the State Department

119

was ready to let the subcommittee see the files as soon as a "cautious" approach could be worked out.

This "caution," he added, was believed to be essential by the State Department, lest the surrender of Administrative data in the present case set a precedent by which "unlimited" demands might later be made on the President by Congress.

Senator Brien McMahon, Democrat of Connecticut, then said that the Republicans did not really want the files. "What they really want," he added, "is a refusal by the Administration of those files."

At all events, Senator Tydings replied, he himself wanted to obtain the files; "assumed" that all the subcommittee members did, too, and he was going to go on using "the one" method to get them—by requests rather than by demands.

Senator Hickenlooper said that this position was one in which the subcommittee was apparently going to be allowed to investigate the files "at the convenience" of the State Department, and under its "restrictions and surveillance."

Defends Testifying for Hiss

Dr. Jessup conceded, under cross-examination by Senator Hickenlooper, that he had testified as a character witness for Alger Hiss, the former State Department official now under conviction for perjury.

"My understanding," he added, "is that there is a very simple part of our American system under which a person accused is entitled to have testimony regarding his reputation."

"Are you of the same opinion now about Hiss?" Mr. Hickenlooper asked.

"The testimony I gave," Dr. Jessup replied, "was as to his reputation. I see no reason to alter the statement I made at that time. It seems to me that this line of questioning, perhaps unconsciously, is designed to involve me in comments on the charges against Mr. Hiss.

"It is a very important part of our system that comments about matters before a court—and especially by lawyers—are not appropriate. I will not engage in such discussion of such matters. Let the courts pass on these things."

Dr. Jessup had been charged by Senator McCarthy with acting as a sponsor of the American-Russian Institute, an organization, said the Senator, which had "pro-Communist" members.

Dealing with this accusation, the only concrete one originally made by Mr. McCarthy, except the matter of alleged "affinity for Communist causes," the Ambassador testified that his name had been used as a sponsor not of the institute but of a dinner given by it on May 7, 1946, to make a posthumous award to Franklin D. Roosevelt.

To the best of his recollection, Dr. Jessup said, he had not attended the dinner, since from February to June of 1946 he had been "seriously ill in a hospital in New York City."

A HUDDLE AT THE COMMUNIST HEARING IN CAPITAL

Senators Bourke B. Hickenlooper (left) and Joseph R. McCarthy in a whispered conference yesterday. On the right is Senator Millard E. Tydings.   Associated Press Wirephoto

Pressed on the matter by Senator Hickenlooper, the Ambassador replied:

"I have told you I was ill in a hospital. When I have said that I did not recall attending the dinner, it was perhaps an understatement."

At all events, he testified, the whole business of sponsoring such a dinner was "wholly irrelevant" then to any question of loyalty, for the Attorney General had "expressly excluded" the institute from his first lists of subversive organizations and did not include it until April, 1949.

Senator Hickenlooper several times accused the Democratic majority of the subcommittee of "inexcusable delay" in subpoenaeing the files of Dr. Jessup and of others and thus leaving him with little information on which to conduct cross-examination.

Deferring to Dr. Jessup's denunciation of the theory of "guilt by association," Mr. Hickenlooper asked whether there was not "something to the doctrine of risk by association."

What he was protesting, Dr. Jessup answered, was a "tendency" to select two names on a list, "in some undefined context," then "to assume that the coexistence of these two names reflects a coexistence of attitudes between these two persons."

"By this theory," he added, "the wartime photographs of American G. I.'s shaking hands with Russian troops in Germany would mean that the G. I.'s were guilty of communism by association."

Jessup Stands by Principle

Senator Hickenlooper inquired whether a man who belonged to one organization declared subversive could be considered a subject requiring investigation.

"The important thing, Dr. Jessup replied, "is whether he knowingly belonged to an organization with Communist objectives."

"Would an association with two or three such organizations strengthen a suspicion?" Senator Hickenlooper asked.

"Not necessarily," replied the Ambassador.

"Fifteen such organizations?"

"Obviously, that would be cumulative," Dr. Jessup said, "but it would not affect the principle. It doesn't matter whether it was five, twenty-five or fifty-six organizations. The things that are important are whether at the time of a man's association the organization was known to be subversive, and the exact nature of the individual's association with it."

He read an extract from a recent letter by Peyton Ford, chief assistant to the Attorney General, which

said that many "front organizations" were designed to appeal to "loyal Americans," and that sometimes "a small minority subverts an organization."

This demonstrated, the Ambassador argued, that "mere association is not a sound basis for condemning an individual."

Senator Hickenlooper brought up an organization called the American Law Students Association and asked Dr. Jessup whether he had been an adviser to it.

"I have a slight recollection of it," said the witness. "What was the year?"

"I don't have the date," the Senator replied.

"The best I could do on recollection," Dr. Jessup said, "was to recall that about ten years ago some students at Columbia asked me to serve on the advisory board of some such organization. The last contact I had with it was in 1940."

"I believe," Senator Hickenlooper said, "that it (the Law Students Association) was an affiliate of the American Youth Congress, which (latter) was cited by the Attorney General as subversive."

"What date was the affiliation?" asked Dr. Jessup.

"I don't have the date," replied the Senator, who then said that the New York Communist newspaper, The Daily Worker, in 1937 had listed "the Law Students Association" as an affiliate of the American League Against War and Fascism, and the league had been cited as subversive later.

"I don't read that paper," Dr. Jessup said, "so I was unaware of that."

"Are you," Mr. Hickenlooper asked, "in complete agreement with the present China policy— that is, with the withdrawal of support from Chiang Kai-shek?"

"That is not pertinent to this inquiry," Senator Tydings interrupted.

"I am in complete accord," Dr. Jessup then answered, "with the policy of the United States."

"You were in accord," asked Mr. Hickenlooper, "with the policies by which General Marshall was sent to China—for the inclusion of some Communists in the Chinese Government?"

This, the Ambassador asserted, was "a misleading question" in assuming as fact the nature of the mission of General Marshall as described by Senator Hickenlooper.

Mr. Hickenlooper then brought out that Dr. Jessup knew Owen Lattimore and had seen him at the State Department in a group of about thirty persons some time before leaving on last Dec. 20 on a Far East mission.

The group, Dr. Jessup said, included Harold E. Stassen, a 1948 candidate for the Republican Presidential nomination, and was made up of men who hoped to "offer some ideas about the Far East."

"Did you later have a phone conversation in which you asked Lattimore to accompany you to China?" asked Senator Hickenlooper.

"At no time," replied the Ambassador.

Dr. Jessup conceded that in 1946 he had, along with other Columbia University professors, sent to THE NEW YORK TIMES a letter that proposed, as Mr. Hickenlooper summarized it, that the United States stop producing atomic bombs in hopes of an agreement for international control with the Russians.

"Do you still feel," asked Senator Hickenlooper, "that we should stop producing bombs?"

"I do not, sir," replied Dr. Jessup. "The 1946 statement was made without benefit of hindsight, and before the Baruch plan (for international control) had come forth, the policy of the United States then was to submit proposals. We have since found out that the Soviet Union is not ready to cooperate."

Senator Tom Connally, Democrat of Texas, chairman of the full Foreign Relations Committee who was sitting as a spectator, referred at one point to "the so-called charges, or whatever they are," against Ambassador Jessup. He did so in saying that the full committee hoped to have Dr. Jessup report on his recent Far East mission.

Senator Theodore Francis Green, Democrat of Rhode Island, told the Ambassador when he had finished:

"I congratulate you on the way you have so thoroughly cleared these so-called charges made against you. You are an established man, and you have friends who have come forward.

"But what would have happened to you had these charges been made when you were young and unknown? It is an appalling harm that might have been done—and may yet be done to young men now in the service. It has a terrible effect on our foreign policy when confidence in the State Department has been shattered."

Dr. Jessup said that "when you have representatives of the United States making official statements to other governments—especially as between this country and the Soviet Union—it is of the utmost importance that these other officials should have confidence in the official spokesmen of the United States."

"You are entitled to the thanks of all our people for the magnificent job you have done," Senator McMahon told the Ambassador. "I join with Generals Marshall and Eisenhower in paying tribute to you."

Row Over Files Continues

Tonight, the dispute between the Democrats and Republicans as to when and how the loyalty files should be made available was unresolved. Mr. Tydings told reporters that the State Department would be in touch with President Truman at Key West, Fla., and was trying to "evolve different alternatives to put up to the President."

He repeated a statement made earlier that Senator McCarthy, who had originally said that "at least fifty-seven Communists" were or recently had been in the State Department, had not yet "accused a single person by name of being a Communist."

Senators McCarthy and Hickenlooper, for their part, were still arguing that there was "plenty" of evidence already in the record to require Mr. Tydings to move at once for the loyalty files—not simply of the State Department, but of the Civil Service Commission and of the Federal Bureau of Investigation.

Senator Tydings told reporters that he understood that Seth W. Richardson, chairman of the Civil Service Commission's Loyalty Review Board, and J. Edgar Hoover, head of the Federal Bureau of Investigation, were personally opposed to the disclosure of the files in their possession.

March 21, 1950

U. S. CHINA POLICY CALLED CONFUSING

Americans Also Are Disturbed by Government Procedure, Opinion Poll Finds

An opinion poll taken by the Council on Foreign Relations among 720 "intelligent, well-informed Americans" shows that they "are confused and disturbed about the policy of their Government in China," the council reported yesterday.

Viewing the recent past "with a sense of frustration," disliking the way things have turned out but not knowing what the State Department could have done about it, "they register hesitation and uncertainty," when asked to outline a future course, the report said. On military cooperation with Europe, less than 7 per cent on the average were uncertain a year ago; on China 24 per cent were, it added.

The participants "frankly and somewhat unhappily admit that they didn't have the necessary information on which to base judgments," the council declared. Many of them blame "the failure" of the State Department to make known currently the course of events in China as the cause of their inability to form judgments with respect to American policy, the report asserted.

American Access Favored

A United States policy toward Communist-dominated China which would provide for American access to the Soviet ally, even on a limited basis, is supported by a majority of the participants, the council announced. The 720, members of affiliated committees in twenty-three cities, were asked to express agreement, disagreement or uncertainty regarding twenty-nine declarative statements on United States-Chinese relations.

One of the statements was: "American access to China, even on a limited basis, is so important to the American interest in Asia as to warrant American initiative in seeking some degree of mutual toleration between the United States and the Chinese Communist regime."

Sixty-four per cent agreed, thinking the United States had little to lose by such an initiative. Seventeen per cent were uncertain. Nineteen per cent disagreed, some pointing to Russian experience, others to Munich.

On American diplomatic recognition of the Communist regime, 39 per cent agreed that it was inadvisable because its effect would be to encourage communism in Asia, 27 per cent were uncertain and 34 per cent disagreed. In the event of recognition, 11 per cent favored United States Government loans to promote internal economic development by the Communist regime, 35 per cent were uncertain and 54 per cent were opposed; 18 per cent held that private investment should be encouraged, 37 per cent were uncertain and 45 per cent were opposed.

Summary of Findings

In a report on the inquiry edited by Joseph Barber, summarized general findings were said to reflect majority opinion among the group of persons. The summary asserts that "it is too late now for the United States to think of increasing its cooperation with the Chinese Nationalist Government" and holds that "the result of the civil war in China was largely the product of internal Chinese forces," although it notes that "both Soviet Russia and the United States brought their influence to bear."

The summary declares further that deviation from the Soviet line by the Chinese Communists is "highly uncertain" but would be likelier in domestic rather than in foreign policy. The larger the role of the United States in China's economic and cultural affairs, the likelier the prospect for deviation, it says.

March 30, 1950

121

CHAPTER 3

Rehabilitation and Consolidation
1949–53

*Mothers and children gesture with
empty rice bowls in plea for food
as they throng a street in Chiyang, 1946.*

COMMUNISTS FACE PITFALLS IN CHINA

Mao's Regime Must Solve Tough Economic Problems in Order to Maintain Rule

By HENRY R. LIEBERMAN

For the time being there is little that the United States can do actively to halt the revolutionary momentum that is now leading to the full-scale military conquest of China by 4,000,000 Communist troops. But as the world's leading economic power, the United States still seems to be in a position to affect future developments in China.

Despite the pro-Soviet hosannahs being sung in Peiping and the congratulatory telegrams that have been exchanged by world Communist leaders on developments in China, the Chinese revolution has not yet run its full course.

Thus far, there is not the slightest sign that Mao Tze-tung, the "Oriental Lenin," will turn out to be a Tito in establishing an independent Communist China operating outside the Soviet orbit. Nevertheless, the economic and political factors making for Titoism in China continue to exist.

Consolidation More Difficult

Some months ago, in a speech to his own Central Committee, Mr. Mao noted that the problem of consolidating power was far more difficult than the problem of acquiring power. As the Communists switched from their emphasis on the landless peasant (who got land and provided the manpower for Red military successes) to the urban worker (a more orthodox symbol of Marxist revolution), he told the committee in effect that the Communists would be able to continue ruling only if they succeeded in raising the national standard of living by industrializing the country.

It will undoubtedly be a long time—possibly twenty-five years—before anyone can gauge accurately the success or failure of Communist rule. Recent developments indicate, however, that present-day Communist China has not just one Achilles heel, but many.

The first problem to be solved is widespread economic distress, caused by disastrous floods in the Yangtze Valley, a North China drought that threatens to cut crop yields by an estimated 50 to 60 per cent, a Nationalist coastal blockade that proved more effective than originally expected and the disappearance of Economic Cooperation Administration aid to the major cities.

Since the end of the war, China's modern skeletal economy — superimposed on the old agricultural structure mainly along the coast—existed on the margin of fat provided by United States aid. Today, with ECA aid cut off and the blockade barring the entry of such raw materials as the Communists might otherwise be able to acquire with their limited exchange, the factories of Shanghai — China's largest industrial city—are operating at 25 to 50 per cent of capacity.

There is considerable unemployment, and the labor situation would be even worse if it were possible for employers to shut down their factories without first having to get permission from the government to do so. Shortly after the blockade was established, the Communists talked of moving factories to the interior and evacuating one-third to one-half of Shanghai's 5,000,000 to 6,000,000 inhabitants.

Lack of sufficient power facilities in the interior, however, has made the removal of factories difficult. Furthermore, a number of Shanghai residents who left the metropolis for the farm areas have returned to the city because they found conditions in the countryside bad, too.

Over the long haul, consolidation of Communist rule under Mr. Mao's industrialization program involves the tremendous task of lifting up by their own bootstraps a backward nation of 450,000,000 people. Aside from the factor of sheer mass, this predominantly agricultural population has traditionally been a net importer of food, let alone a producer of surplus food for export. China's tung oil and hog bristles, her ing exports, offer a far smaller margin for industrialization than did Russian wheat in the early days of the Bolsheviki.

Although China has not yet begun the process of industrialization, the peasants—who provided the manpower core for the Communist armies—already are being taxed heavily, under conditions of drought and flood, to feed 4,000,000 Communist troops and make it possible for the government to keep the price of foodstuffs reasonably low in cities that formerly enjoyed ECA food rations.

Unrest Laid to Taxation

The Communists have acknowledged the outbreak of a number of isolated peasant uprisings in Honan, Anhwei, Kiangsu and Manchuria. These they have attributed to "Kuomintang agents" and benighted secret societies. There is reason to believe, however, that much of this unrest is attributable to heavy taxation in kind and extra "food borrowing."

In discussing future aid from abroad, the Communists have told the Chinese people that they have the support of the Soviet Union, the Soviet bloc regimes of Eastern Europe and "democratic groups" elsewhere. But up to the present the Soviet Union has displayed a special interest only in Chinese territories bordering on the Soviet Union—Manchuria and Sinkiang. And even in Manchuria, where the Communists now hold power, the Russians have not yet returned the machines stripped from Manchurian factories.

From all indications, the dictates of the cold war—in so far as they have made necessary a closer affinity with Russia than common ideology would normally require—are apt to prove embarrassing to the Communists both politically and economically.

Despite the establishment of such institutions as a nation-wide "Sino-Soviet Friendship Association," neither the Russians nor the Communists themselves have been able to fill the economic void created by shrinking trade with the West and the elimination of United States aid.

Furthermore, the Communist press has found it necessary to provide answers to nationalistic Chinese sending in letter-box queries about the continuing presence of Russian troops in Port Arthur and Dairen and the logic of the Russo-Communist barter agreement for Manchuria.

Why, a number of Chinese have asked, has it been necessary to send Russia food from Manchuria when Shanghai itself needs food?

The Peiping radio, which has radiated persistent confidence in Communist China's future, has shown itself especially sensitive to any hint that the Red Revolution there may eventually be diluted. Of all the documents or statements ever issued by a United States organ or official, the Communists have reacted most strongly and most lengthily to the State Department White Paper. The anti-White Paper barrage continued for weeks.

The phrase that excited the bitterest and steadiest comment was Secretary of State Acheson's reference to "democratic individualism," a quality he said he hoped would eventually re-exert itself in China.

Mao Heads Peiping Regime; Program Supports Moscow

Red Government Launched —Chou's Name Is Linked to Office of Premier

By WALTER SULLIVAN
Special to THE NEW YORK TIMES.

SHANGHAI, Sept. 30—Mao Tze-tung, chairman of the Central Committee of the Chinese Communist party, was elected chairman of the new Central Government of the People's Republic of China today as the Chinese People's Political Consultative Council completed its job of launching the new government of Communist China.

Three other leading Communists and three non-Communists were named vice chairmen. The Communists are Gen. Chu Teh, Commander in Chief; Liu Shao-chi, a member of the Political Bureau and usually rated the highest ranking member of the party under Mr Mao, and Kao Kang, chairman of the Northeast People's Government.

The three non-Communist vice chairmen are Mme. Sun Yat-sen, widow of the founder of the Chinese Republic; Chang Lan, aged chairman of the Democratic League, and Li Chi-shen, chairman of the Kuomintang Revolutionary Committee.

The organ headed by Mr. Mao and the six vice chairmen is the Central People's Government Council which wields the supreme power of the Central Government.

The remaining fifty-six members of this Council were also elected today. Likewise 180 members of the National Committee were named.

Today's meeting, the first plenary session of the Chinese People's Political Consultative Council was adjourned. Normally it will meet henceforth only once every three years.

All the elections today were unanimous, according to a report of the official New China News Agency.

Notably absent from the list of those elected was Gen. Chou En-lai, leading Communist who played a major role in the formulation of the new government. However still unfilled is the post of Premier.

The latter will be head of the Administrative Council, which is one of the four organs that come directly under the Central People's Government Council, headed by Mr. Mao. The other three organs on this level are the People's Revolutionary Military Council, which will presumably still be headed by Gen. Chu Teh; the Supreme People's Court and the People's Office of Procurator General.

All the functions of government not covered by these three come under the Administrative Council, including the Foreign Affairs Ministry.

In a declaration passed today the Political Consultative Council repeated an earlier statement that the new regime would unite with "all peace and freedom loving countries, nations and people, first of all the Soviet Union and the new democratic countries, as allies to oppose jointly the imperialist plots for provoking war and to strive for lasting world peace."

Sunday has been named chief day for celebrating the formation of the new government and elaborate preparations are being made in Shanghai and, presumably elsewhere, for parades and other festivities on that date. A three-day holiday, beginning tomorrow has been proclaimed.

The text of the "common program" of China's new People's Democratic Republic was made public today detailing what are to be basic policies concerning the functioning of the Central Government, foreign relations, education, industrialization, the treatment of national minorities and many other fundamental issues.

Only an unofficial translation, issued by the New China News Agency is available so far.

The program guarantees that the people of the new republic have freedom of thought, speech, publication, assembly, association, correspondence, domicile, religion and the right to hold processions and demonstrations.

As indicated by earlier statements, these rights of the "people" will not apply to bureaucratic capitalists or "landlords."

The above freedoms are embodied in Article 5.

Article 49 adds that of "reporting true news." Utilization of the press for slander, the undermining of the state or inciting world war, will be prohibited, the program says.

The all-China People's Congress, which will be the supreme organ of the state over the continuing administrative structure when it is in session, will be elected by universal suffrage, according to the program. Likewise the "lower levels" of the People's Congress will be named by universal suffrage.

Jurisdiction Questions

Elections will not be held in any locality until the military government phase is terminated. The elections are also linked to the completion of agrarian reform.

Jurisdiction of the central and local governments will be determined by a decree of the central government so as to benefit "both national unification and local expediency," says Article 16.

The convening of the all-China People's Congress will be some time hence in view of the conditions set for holding local elections. In the meanwhile the Chinese People's Political Consultative Council will exercise the functions of that body.

The foreign policy provisions of the program state that the new Central Government will examine the treaties and agreements concluded by the Kuomintang Government with other nations and "recognize, abrogate, or revise or renew them, according to their respective contents."

Previously announced conditions for the establishment of diplomatic relations are reiterated. One of these is that a foreign state that established relations with the new regime would have to sever relations with the Kuomintang. The sixtieth and last article of the program provides that foreign nationals will receive asylum in China if "they are oppressed by their own Governments for supporting the people's interests and taking part in the struggle for peace and 'democracy.'"

In education, "the scientific, historical viewpoint" shall be applied to the study and interpretation of history, economics, politics, culture and international affairs, it was said.

The method of education will be "unity of theory and practice," with emphasis on technical education.

"In the realm of military affairs there will be a system of people's militia to maintain local order, lay the foundation for national mobilization and prepare for the enforcement of an obligatory military service system at the appropriate moment."

It is also provided that in peace the armed forces will "systematically assist in agriculture and industry so far as does not hinder military tasks."

In the field of economy, the program provides that the state shall "coordinate and regulate" state-owned enterprises, cooperatives, private capitalist enterprises and peasant and handicraft enterprises.

"All enterprises vital to the economic life of the country and to the people's livelihood shall come under unified operation by the state," Article 28 says.

Cooperatives are generally to receive preferential treatment. Private enterprises that are "beneficial to the national welfare will be fostered."

October 1, 1949

Mao Tze-tung
The New York Times

Reds Proclaim a Republic In China; Chou Is Premier

By WALTER SULLIVAN
Special to THE NEW YORK TIMES.

SHANGHAI, Oct. 1—Chou En-lai was today named in Peiping as Premier and concurrently Foreign Minister of China's new People's (Communist) Republic. At the same time the new regime declared itself the sole legal Government of China and invited recognition by other nations.

This was announced in a proclamation read by Mao Tze-tung, head of the Chinese Communist party, before a crowd officially estimated at 200,000 that gathered in the newly cleared Square of the Gate of Heavenly Peace, Peking's equivalent of Red Square in Moscow.

According to accounts by the official New China news agency, Mr. Mao said the Central People's Government Council, which was elected yesterday with Mr. Mao as chairman and which took office today, had selected General Chou to be head of the Administrative Council, the post carrying the title of Premier, and also to head the Foreign Ministry.

Chou En-lai has often represented the Chinese Communists in their negotiations, both with foreigners and with the Nationalists. He was chief delegate to the mediation talks sponsored by Gen. George C. Marshall during General Marshall's 1946-47 efforts to promote a coalition peace in China.

Educated in France, General Chou founded a French branch of the Chinese Communist party that included many important figures. Now 51, he has in recent years been regarded by outsiders as one of the top four leaders—the other three being Mr. Mao, Gen Chu Teh and Liu Shao-chi.

General Chou in recent weeks has apparently played a principal role in organizing the structure of the new Government.

The old top-level military administration seems to have been moved bodily into the new Government. Mr. Mao still heads the Central Revolutionary Military Council, now called the People's Revolutionary Military Council of the Central People's Government. Chu Teh still is commander in chief of the Army. This military structure now comes directly beneath the Central People's Government Council instead of the central committee of the Communist party.

The Council also named Shen Chun-ju as Chief Justice of the Supreme People's Court and Lo Jung-huan as Procurator General Shen Chun-ju is a 74-year-old jurist who recently was president of the Shanghai Law College before siding with the Communists Lin Po-chu, a member of the Communist party Politburo and one of the senior Communists, was named Secretary General of the Central People's Government Council.

Mr. Mao, in his proclamation on the establishment of the new Government, concluded by saying that the new regime had decided "to declare to the Governments of all other countries that this Government is the sole legal Government representing all the people of the People's Republic of China. This Government is willing to establish diplomatic relations with any foreign Government which is willing to observe the principles of equality, mutual benefit and mutual respect of territorial integrity and sovereignty."

The composition of the National Committee, one of the two top governement organs elected in Peiping yesterday, was announced here during the day. During the three-year intervals between the plenary sessions of the Chinese People's Consultative Council, the National Committee will perform much of its functions.

The National Committee is re-

NAMED AS PREMIER

Chou En-lai
The New York Times

quired to meet semi-annually, subject to modification by its own standing committee. The National Committee must elect this standing committee under which a Secretariat will be established.

Functions Defined

The functions of the National Committee, as set forth in the organizational statute of the Consultative Council are as follows:

1. Insure fulfillment of the resolutions of the Consultative Council and of the National Committee.
2. Debate and submit proposals to the Central People's Government Council.
3. Assist the Government in mobilizing the people for participation in "the People's Democratic Revolution" and national reconstruction.
4. Consult and submit joint lists of candidates for elections of delegates to the All-China People's Congress among the participating units of the Consultative Council.
5. Consult and determine the units, number and election of delegates for the next plenary session of the Consultative Council and convene that session.
6. Guide local united front activities.
7. Consult and settle other affairs relevant to the internal cooperation within the Consultative Council.

Eighteen vacancies to the committee were left for delegates from areas not yet under the control of the new regime. The organizational statute provides for the formation of local committees of the Consultative Council in principal cities, important regions and provincial capitals if the Council so decides.

CHINA'S REDS ADOPT OUTLINE OF REGIME

Peiping, Renamed Peking, Will Be Capital—Flag, National Anthem Are Chosen

By WALTER SULLIVAN
Special to The New York Times.

SHANGHAI, Sept. 27—The Chinese People's Consultative Council in Peiping today approved, without a dissenting voice. Organization statutes establishing the framework of Communist China's new Government that is expected to be formally proclaimed within the next two weeks.

Peiping was selected as the new Government's permanent capital and the name changed to Peking. A flag was selected and a provisional national anthem chosen. The flag will be red with a gold star in the upper left corner surrounded by an arc of four smaller stars. According to the Shanghai press, the large star represents the "leadership of the Communist party and the People's Liberation Army," while the smaller stars represent the four classes composing the new state: workers, peasants, petty bourgeoisie and national capitalists.

The Council also decided that the official calendar henceforth should be the generally used Christian calendar rather than one based on the anniversary of the Chinese revolution. The latter has been used for official purposes by the Kuomintang. The provisional anthem will be the "March of the Volunteers," described by the local press as popular during the war of resistance.

The Consultative Council has voted itself the top political organ of Communist China. Its next step is to elect a Central People's Government Council, which in turn will organize the new central regime.

The Government Council will represent the Central Government internationally and will rule domestically. The new central regime is described in the first article of its organizational statute passed today thus:

"The People's Republic of China is a state of the people's democratic dictatorship led by the working class, based on the alliance of workers and peasants rallying all democratic classes and various nationalities within the country."

Chou En-lai, top Communist party representative in framing the new government, told the delegates yesterday that while there would be a "congress system" akin to that of the Soviet Union, it would not be identical with the Soviet state.

He said the Chinese state would be a union of four "revolutionary classes", whereas the Soviet state is classless. The four classes are the workers, who are the leading class; peasants, petty bourgeoisie and national capitalists. He also discussed the frequently used term, "centralized democracy," which apparently refers to the subordination of elements in the government, including the judicial and executive, to the legislative in the form of the All-China People's Congress. The concept of checks and balances and a multi-party government is rejected in favor of unity of all elements.

Proclamation of China's Communist Government

HONG KONG, Oct. 2 (UP)—Text of the statement by Mao Tze-tung, Chairman of the Communist People's Republic of China proclaiming his new regime as broadcast by the Peiping radio:

People all over China have been plunged into bitter suffering and tribulation since Chiang-Kai-shek's Koumintang reactionary government betrayed the fatherland, conspired with the imperialists and launched a counter-revolutionary war.

However, the People's Liberation Army, supported by the people all over the country, fighting heroically and selflessly to defend the territorial sovereignty of the fatherland and protect the people's lives and property and relieve the people's suffering and struggle for their rights has eliminated the reactionary troops and overthrown the reactionary rule of the National Government.

Now the people's liberation war has been fundamentally won and a majority of the people has been liberated.

Enacted Organic Law

On this foundation the first session of the Chinese People's Political Consultative Conference composed of delegates of all democratic parties, groups, people's organizations, the People's Liberation Army in various regions, overseas Chinese and patriotic democratic elements of the whole country has been convened.

Representing the will of the people, this session of Chinese peoples:

Enacted the organic law of the Central People's Government of the peoples of the Republic of China;

Elected Mao Tze-tung chairman of the Central People's Government and Chu Teh, Liu Shao-chi, Soong Ching-ling (Mme. Sun Yat-sen), Li Chi-shen; Chang Lan and Kao Kang vice chairmen;

Also elected Chen Yi, Ho Lung, Li Li-san, Lin Po-chu, Yeh Chien-ying, Ho Hsiang-ning, Lin Piao, Peng Teh-huai, Liu Po-cheng, Wu Yu-chang, Hsu Hsiang-chien, Peng Chen, Po Yi-po, Nieh Jung-chen, Chou En-lai, Tung Pi-wu, Sai Fun-din, Jao Shu-shih, Tan Kah-kee, Lo Jung-huan, Teng Tsu-hui, Yu Lan-fu, Hsu Teh-li, Tsai Chang, Liu Ke-ping, Ma Yin-chu, Chen Yun, Kang Sheng, Lin Feng, Ma Hsu-lun, Kuo Mo-jo, Chang Yun-yi, Teng Hsiao-ping, Kao Chung-min, Sheng Kun-ju, Shen Yan-ping, Chen Shu-tung, Seto Mai-tong, Li Hsi-chiu, Huang Yen-pei, Tsai Ting-kai, Hsi Chung-hsun, Peng Tse-min, Chang Chih-chung, Fa Tso-yi, Li Chu-chen, Li Chang-ta, Po Chung-chang, Cheng Chien, Chang Hsi-jo, Cheng Min-shu, Tang Ping-shan, Chang Nan-hsien, Li Ya-tsu, Chang Tung-sun and Lung Yun as council members to form the Central People's Government Council;

Proclaimed the founding of the People's Republic of China, and, Decided Peking should be the capital of the People's Republic of China.

Council Decisions Listed

The Central People's Government Council of the People's Republic of China took office today in this capital and unanimously made the following decisions:

Proclamation for the formation of the Central People's Government, People's Republic of China.

Adoption of a common program for the Chinese People's Political Consultative Conference as a policy of the Government.

Election of Lin Po-chu from among the Council members as secretary-general of the Central People's Government Council.

Appointment of Chou En-lai as Premier of the State Administration Council and concurrently-minister of the Ministry of Foreign Affairs.

Mao Tze-tung as chairman of the People's Revolutionary Military Council of the Central People's Government.

Chu Teh as commander-in-chief of the People's Liberation Army.

Shen Chun-ju as chief justice of the Supreme People's Court.

Lo Hung-huan as procurator general, and,

Entrusted them with the task of the early formation of the various organs of Government to carry out the work of the Government.

At the same time the Central People's Government Council decided:

To declare to the governments of all other countries that this is the sole legal Government representing all the people of the People's Republic of China.

This Government is willing to establish diplomatic relations with any foreign government that is willing to observe the principles of equality, mutual benefit, mutual respect of territorial integrity and sovereignty.

October 3, 1949

Canton Orders Mme. Sun's Arrest; Nationalists' Action Called Futile

Special to The New York Times

HONG KONG, Oct. 8—The National Government's Executive Yuan, or Cabinet, meeting in Canton today, passed an order calling for the arrest of Mme. Sun Yat-sen, widow of the founder of the Chinese Republic. Along with Mme. Sun, the Canton order called for the arrest of eighty-three top Communists and their collaborators.

The Canton act is a futile gesture but in the case of Mme. Sun it represents a drastic step. So highly has she been esteemed by the Kuomintang, which was created by Dr. Sun, and which has been the governing party of the National Government since 1927, that heretofore no action has been taken against her despite her known anti-Government views of long duration. She is a sister of Mme. Chiang Kai-shek, Mme. H. H. Kung and Dr. T. V. Soong, all now in the United States.

Mme. Sun was recently named one of the Vice Presidents of the new Communist-dominated People's Republican Government at Peiping. She has also just been elected an official of the new Sino-Soviet Friendship Association. In a speech to the Sino-Soviet group in Peiping she declared that the "New Democracy" of the Communists had put flesh on to the skeleton of her husband's Three People's Principles. She also called Russia China's truest and most selfless friend.

A detailed defense of Communist China's action in aligning itself with Russia was voiced Thursday in Peiping by Liu Shao-chi, usually regarded as one of the strongest advocates among the Communist party leaders of the closest Chinese-Soviet relations. Mr. Liu, who had just been elected head of the new national Sino-Soviet Friendship Association, revealed officially for the first time the extent of the technical assistance that is being given by Russian experts to Communist China.

Russians Aid Rehabilitation

He declared that the Russians had aided the Communists in the rehabilitating of iron and steel plants in Anshan in Manchuria

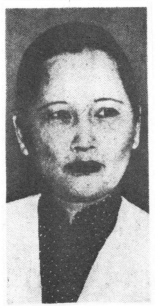

HER ARREST ORDERED

Mme. Sun Yat-sen
Associated Press

and Shihchingshan, west of Peiping and in reconditioning railways. He said that 200 Soviet specialists were now at work in Manchuria and other parts of China. The Russians had told him, he said, that they had come to China under the instructions of Premier Stalin to impart all their knowledge and technique to the Chinese people and that when the Chinese people had mastered what the Russians knew so that the latter were no longer needed the Russians had promised that they would return to the Soviet Union.

Mr. Liu asserted that Soviet engineers acted only as advisers and that their pay was the same as that of Chinese engineers of the same grade. Declaring that American and British engineers had always demanded very high pay in China, Mr. Liu stated that "never before in China have foreign engineers worked under such conditions as the Russians."

Mr. Liu contended that it was greatly to China's advantage to co-operate with Russia since China could study the experience of the Russians in their development of Communism with a view soon to taking the Russian path. He stated that Russia now had scientific knowledge that was entirely new and unknown to the rest of the world and that she possessed advanced theories of economics, banking, public finance, commerce and education that other countries did not have.

October 9, 1949

ONLY 4 CHINA REDS WIN A CLEAN BILL

HONG KONG, July 25—At a convention of the Central Committee of the Chinese Communist party in Peiping at the beginning of this month an intensive session of "criticism and self-criticism" was held, as a result of which only four Communist leaders were found to be without blemish.

These leaders were Mao Tze-tung, Liu Shao-chi, Lin Piao and Jao Shu-shih. The report came from a usually reliable source.

Notably absent from those who got "perfect scores" was Chou En-lai, Premier and Foreign Minister. While Army Commander in Chief Chu Teh likewise was not cited. This was regarded as less noteworthy since he has been active politically. The nature of the criticism leveled at Mr. Chou, however, was not known.

The choice of the four leaders as most faithful to the party notably had no relation to alleged right and left or pro-Russian or anti-Russian elements in the party. Thus less substance is given to flimsy rumors of a serious split in the Chinese Communist party.

Only one of the four had ever been to Russia before this year. He was Lin Piao, who went to Moscow for treatment of wounds in 1938. The only studying he is known to have done in Russia was of medical subjects while recovering in the hospital.

General Lin now is political head of the Central-South region and commander of the Fourth Field Army which, in the past two years, he led in the victorious march from Manchuria to the borders of Indo-China. He is only 42.

Mr. Liu has been described as "heir apparent" to Mr. Mao. In 1945, when Mr. Mao was in Chungking, he served as chairman of the Communist party. Mr. Liu heads the Sino-Soviet Friendship Association, which symbolizes his alleged position as leader of the international group among the Chinese Communists.

Mr. Jao is the least known of the four. At present he is secretary of the East China Bureau of the party's Central Committee. Whereas Gen. Chen Yi is political and military chief in East China, Mr. Jao is believed to be his superior in party matters. His influence has been strong during the past year on political developments in one of China's most populous areas. He has visited the United States and France.

The program of criticism and self-criticism was reportedly carried out by members of the Central Committee at their plenary session on June 6 to 9 in the presence of thirty-five members of the committee plus twenty-seven candidate members, forty-three secretaries of party committees in various provinces and cities and other party workers.

CHINESE REDS SPUR PROLETARIAN BIDS

Party Wants More Laborers as Members to Bolster Ties With Masses

By HENRY R. LIEBERMAN
Special to THE NEW YORK TIMES.

HONG KONG, Aug. 15 — An increasing number of laborers are being inducted into the Chinese Communist party as part of a multiphased drive designed to increase the party's proletarian element, correct "authoritarian methods of work" and strengthen relations between the party and Chinese masses on a united front basis.

According to pro-Communist dispatches and other reports reaching here, the proletarian infusion appears to be marked especially in Manchuria, where the Communists have instituted planned production in an attempt to establish a primary industrial base.

The Peiping People's Daily, official Communist newspaper, says that the party hopes to absorb one-third of all the industrial workers in China within the next three to five years. On the other hand, it has been said that the party has decided not to accept any more rural members in "old liberated areas" above the Yangtze, or novitiates in "new liberated areas" of South China until the land reform is completed there.

Membership Over 5,000,000

As of July 1, membership in the Chinese Communist party exceeded 5,000,000. Official statistics disclosed that at the beginning of this year, proletarian and semi-proletar-ian elements—that is, "urban workers, farm laborers, poor peasants and urban poor"—already constituted 62 per cent of the local branch membership.

The Communists began to stress the need for attracting more laborers into the party after the Central Committee's conference at Shihchichuang, in Hopeh Province, in March, 1949. It was at this conference that Mao Tze-tung, who previously had based the Chinese revolution primarily in the countryside, sounded the call for switching the party's center of gravity to the cities.

However, the substantial new influx of proletarians into the party has had to await the Communist seizure and reorganization of factories and urban areas.

Although the Chinese Communists always spoke of their theoretical proletarian base, even in the days when their activity was concentrated in rural areas, there is an overriding emphasis now on Marxist proletarian orthodoxy. The party is supposed to be a "party of the working class," leading the present coalition of laborers, peasants, "national capitalists" and urban shopkeepers to a higher Socialist phase of the revolution.

Many From Middle Class

Taking the party membership as a whole, the majority actually are of peasant origin. Many young political workers, however, come from the urban middle class, but recent party literature contends that they have attained the proletarian cast by virtue of their "political struggles."

It also is pointed out that 1,000,000 members have been steeled in the "military communism" of the "supply system." Under this system, Communists receive no wages and the party looks after their basic needs.

The requirements for membership in the Chinese Communist party favor aspirants with a proletarian background. A probationary period of only six months is said to be required for urban workers, coolies, laborers, poor peasants, urban poor and revolutionary soldiers. Probationary periods up to two years are said to be required for others, with graduated lengths of probation depending on specific backgrounds.

The party has had a phenomenal growth since its foundation in 1921. According to official figures, the membership has increased as follows: 50 in 1921, 300,000 in 1927, 1,200,000 in 1945, 3,000,000 in 1949 and 5,000,000 in July, 1950.

Mao Tze-tung assumed formal leadership of the party at the Tsunyi conference held in January, 1935, but the present Central Committee of thirty-three member dates to the elections held in Yenan in April, 1945. Four basic bureaus are said to operate under the Committee—the Politbureau, Organization Bureau, Propaganda Bureau and United Front Bureau.

Last March, instructions were reported to have been issued to all party members to strengthen their links with the Chinese masses and "non-party Democrats." According to the Peiping newspaper, members were told to study two speeches by Premier Stalin and Mao on the need for humility. The newspaper said that some Reds, especially those in the leadership, had been "guilty of putting on airs."

This campaign has been followed by a general "discipline readjustment campaign," marked by an expanded required reading list and nation-wide "self-criticism sessions."

A major problem is the "education" of the large number of new members who have entered the party in the last two years. Regional administrators still are complaining that they lack enough trained political workers.

Peiping Enlarges Gen. Lin's Role In Region Bordering on Indo-China

Veteran General Is Appointed to Fourth Key Position in South-Central Zone

By HENRY R. LIEBERMAN
Special to THE NEW YORK TIMES.

HONG KONG, Jan. 8—Gen. Lin Piao, whose Fourth Field Army troops are fighting United Nations forces in Korea, has just been given another appointment in an area far removed from the Korean battlefields. It is in Communist China's Central South Zone, whose territory extends down to Indo-China and includes the coast of Kwangtung Province.

Headquarters liaison between the Chinese Reds and Ho Chi Minh's Vietminh insurgents is believed to be centered in this zone at Nanning in Kwangsi Province, north of the Indo-China border. The Chinese Communists also have been harassed by sporadic guerilla activity in Central South China, where they have accelerated land redistribution and intensified the purge of dissidents and suspected dissidents.

A list of official Peiping appointments published here today by the Communist-supervised Ta Kung Pao disclosed that the 42-year-old General Lin, one of the ablest Chinese Red field commanders, had been appointed to a concurrent post as Chairman of Central South China's Financial and Economic Commission. He already held three top posts in this zone as Chairman of the Military and Administrative Council, Commander of Army Headquarters at Hankow and Secretary of the regional Communist party bureau.

No other Chinese Communist regional official, with the exception of Kao Kang in Manchuria, has been entrusted by the Peiping regime with such a concentration of power. General Lin's additional job makes him economic as well as military and political boss in Central-South China, which is ruled from Hankow and embraces the provinces of Honan, Hupeh, Hunan, Kiangsi, Kwangsi and Kwangtung.

His new appointment, actually

announced in Peiping on Saturday, was cited incidentally in a long list of promotions. This was the first official mention of General Lin in months. It stimulated new speculation about his recent whereabouts.

The young but veteran general, who has been fighting as a Red officer since the age of 19, first took up the regional command at Hankow after having led the Fourth Field Army from Manchuria all the way down into South China in the civil war battles with the Nationalists. He disappeared from official news when his troops started moving back to Manchuria about the time the Korean war broke out last June.

According to a number of reports received here, a joint Soviet-Chinese-North Korean staff headquarters was established at Changchun in Manchuria on Oct. 1. It was considered possible that General Lin's reorganized Fourth Field Army units came under the command of this headquarters, thus freeing him again for duty in a zone that has become increasingly important.

A former member of the Chinese Communist Politburo noted some time ago that General Lin and Kao Kang, chairman of the Manchurian Regional Government, were especially trusted by Mao Tse-tung and also respected by the Communist leader as "effective down-to-earth pragmatists."

General Lin is a native of Hupeh Province, where his father once operated a felt factory. He received his first military training at the Kuomintang's Whampoa Academy, participated in the Communist 1927 uprising at Nanchang and later rose rapidly to the top ranks of the Chinese Red Army. He headed the Red Army Academy at Yenan, fought the Japanese in North China and on the termination of the Japanese war went to Manchuria to command the "United Democratic Army" that eventually wrested the Northeastern Provinces from the Nationalists.

When General Lin's troops drove down through North and Central South China to the Indo-China border, an estimated 30,000 retreating Nationalists crossed the border from Kwangsi and were interned in Indo-China by the French. It was reported today that Gen. Huang Chieh, deputy commander of these troops, had passed through Hong Kong recently en route to Formosa for talks regarding their possible use against the Chinese Communist-Vietminh coalition.

January 9, 1951

REDS 'BEAT DRUMS' FOR PEIPING PURGE

HONG KONG, April 3—An official signal for widening and deepening the Peiping regimes terroristic drive to stamp out the "enemies of the state" in China's urban centers was given today by The People's Daily, leading Chinese Communist organ, in an editorial entitled "Beat a Drum and Wave a Flag for the Suppression of Counter-Revolutionaries."

Firing squads have been working overtime on the mainland in liquidating alleged counter-revolutionaries. On the heels of yesterday's official disclosures that ninety-one had been shot in Shanghai and at least thirty-one more in Canton, new official reports today revealed that another "large group" had been put to death in Tientsin March 31 and that twenty-three others had been executed in Swatow March 25.

Far from calling a halt to the increasing number of arrests and executions throughout the country, The People's Daily, which is published in Peiping, demanded the intensification of the counter-revolutionary crackdown by "bold and decisive action." In passages disclosing that some party members had expressed reservations about stepping up the urban purges, the editorial criticized such elements for "paralysis" in thinking that the liquidation process had gone far enough and "some softness and lack of decision" in thinking it would have unsatisfactory repercussions.

"This is a sign that they have underestimated the righteousness of suppressing counter-revolutionaries," The People's Daily asserted. Its editorial was broadcast domestically in Chinese by The New China News Agency.

Later, with regard to those party members concerned about the effects of blood-letting in heavily populated centers, the Peiping newspaper added:

"They do not realize that today there are also nests of counter-revolutionary elements. Large batches of reactionary party members, secret service men, disorganized reactionary military officers, big racketeers, big rascals, leaders of reactionary secret societies and religious sects have remained in the cities from Kuomintang days. Some have even infiltrated economic and cultural agencies of our Government."

Maintaining that "various classes" in Peiping and Tientsin had "warmly welcomed" the recent political executions there, The People's Daily held there was no need to fear internal repercussions so long as the masses were mobilized to participate in the suppression. It suggested that the "sentiment and wisdom of the masses" be employed in some phases of the "detection work" and called for more mass rallies and "accusation meetings," public trials and publicity.

April 4, 1951

CHINESE RED PARTY FACING HUGE PURGE

By C. L. SULZBERGER
Special to THE NEW YORK TIMES.

PARIS, April 28—What is expected to be the most numerically extensive Communist party purge in history is now being prepared in the Chinese People's Republic.

According to official Peiping statistics, 5,800,000 members are listed on the Communist party rolls. This entire register is to be re-examined to weed out those who are considered untrustworthy from the viewpoint of ideology, profession and family antecedents.

The implications are that the one principal criterion of loyalty that will be scrutinized is the degree of anti-Americanism displayed by the individual.

The Chinese party includes an extremely large proportion of farmers and "bourgeoisie," in addition to the orthodox Marxist category of the "working class." It would appear that the first two elements are especially likely to suffer during the forthcoming purge.

Leader of Purge Named

While it has not been confirmed yet, there are hints that this massive "purifying" process will be directed by P'eng Chen, a member of the party's Politburo, the Central Executive Committee and the Secretariat, as well as chairman of the Northeast Politburo in Manchuria—the area especially sensitive in Communist China today because of the Korean war.

Mr. P'eng was born in Shansi Province in 1899, was a former member of the Kuomintang and joined the Communists in 1926. He once directed the party school at Yenan during the days when that was Mao Tse-tung's stronghold, and has been one of the principal political commissars in Mr. Mao's army during recent years.

Judging by the initial purges in other Communist countries, it is not to be excluded that as many as 2,000,000 members may be stricken from the party rolls. Massive "purifications" on a similar proportional scale have been taking place during the last two years in the Soviet satellite states of Eastern Europe.

According to Mr. P'eng, the basic purpose of the forthcoming purge is, in the wake of the Communist conquest of the Chinese mainland, to prepare "for an all-out and systematic overhaul of the party organization."

The Politburo, following the usual Communist doctrine, which recognizes that a "people's democracy" is only the first stage of development toward the "Socialist" state in the Moscow parlance, acknowledges that "political power in China today is the political power of the new democratic type," but, it is recognized, this "is not yet the political power exercised by the dictatorship of the proletariat."

"Inasmuch as it is the revolutionary alliance of the working class, the peasants and petty bourgeoisie, the national bourgeoisie, and other patriotic and democratic individuals, it belongs neither to the type of parliamentary government nor to the Soviet type," according to the Politburo.

Thus, Mr. Mao inclines to relegate the Chinese governmental system even one step behind the usual phraseology, during the initial phases of a "people's democracy" as evolved in Europe.

It is evident that the forthcoming purge will be only the first of a series.

Mr. P'eng himself wrote in the Cominform's journal that "we are preparing once more to conduct an over-all rectification in the style of work of the party in order to strengthen the leadership for future revolutionary struggles and national construction, and to preserve and enhance the political, ideological and organizational purity of the party." He added:

"The systematic overhaul of the party organizations will once again be conducted in serious and careful fashion in a well-planned and prepared manner.

"Education will be carried on among all members to teach them how to be Communists.

"Leadership in the branches will be strengthened and their organizational life improved.

"Thus all party members will learn what is the criterion for a Communist and will be able to judge themselves from the standpoint of the ideological principles of communism.

"All good party members will continue to improve and further develop their enthusiasm and initiative.

"And all party members who have shortcomings and who have committed mistakes will be able quickly to deepen their consciousness and eliminate shortcomings and mistakes.

"Backward elements who are beyond reform, as well as undesirable elements who wormed their way into the party, will be expelled."

The Peiping Politburo apparently has decided that the party organization and distribution of party membership are out of balance. As a result, membership recruiting in relatively recently conquered areas (mainly South China) is ceasing for the present. It is indicated that the only new members who will be welcomed during the current purge process will be industrial workers.

In other words, the Chinese party seems to be openly adopting the pattern of orthodoxy as laid down by Moscow and, concurrently, reducing the last remote chances of a Titoist heresy's developing in China within the predictable future.

The Peiping Politburo openly backs now the proposition that "the Communist party of China is the political party of the Chinese working class."

The significance of these principles cannot be overstressed. China is basically an agrarian land filled with millions of farming households. Her merchant class, under precepts now recognized, becomes suspect as "bourgeois." The proportion of "industrial workers" in China is extremely small.

April 29, 1951

PEIPING QUALIFIES DEATH SENTENCES

Suspends Penalty for 2 Years in Some Cases but Executions Continue on Mass Scale

By TILLMAN DURDIN
Special to The New York Times.

HONG KONG, July 19—One of the innovations of Communist justice in connection with the current China mainland campaign to eliminate "counter revolutionaries" is the death sentence suspended for two years.

Persons receiving this penalty are put at hard labor and may at any time during two years be executed, but if they display what Communist spokesmen describe as "reformation repentance" their sentences may be commuted to further imprisonment.

Explaining this sentence in a column called "People's Letter Box" the official Peiping People's Daily termed the suspended death penalty a manifestation of Government magnanimity.

The People's Daily sought to lull possible objections that the Government was being over magnanimous by arguing that culprits would be forever deprived of any opportunity to harm others and would not waste the people's millet since they would be made to grow more than they consumed.

Meanwhile, copies of the People's Daily dated July 12, reaching here today, chronicled the mass execution on July 10 of 277 "counter-revolutionaries." The number is one of the highest ever recorded in Communist China for a single mass killing.

The paper reported that fifty-six had been sentenced to death with suspension for two years. Fifty-two others were sentenced to life terms and 178 to various terms of imprisonment.

The daily said that a huge crowd had turned up for a public denunciation meeting directed against the accused.

One was charged with being a spy for the Nationalists and causing the death of "800 Liberation troops." Another was alleged to have engineered an armed revolt as head of a Buddhist association.

The Shanghai Liberation Daily reported that fifty-eight "counter-revolutionaries" had been executed there on July 11. One of the persons executed was reported to be the manager of a British egg factory.

The Shanghai Liberation Daily of last Monday reported the execution in Shanghai last Saturday of fifty-seven persons, with twenty-two others getting suspended death sentences.

The Yangtze Daily News of Hankow reported that twenty-five "counter-revolutionaries had been executed at Kaifeng on June 26 before 10,000 onlookers.

Other executions were reported in various parts of the country, including the disposal of 165 former Nationalist officers in Swatow who had been charged with "falsely pretending to be progressives while planning to overthrow the Government.'

July 20, 1951

CHINA REDS MARK FOES AS PARIAHS

By HENRY R. LIEBERMAN
Special to The New York Times.

HONG KONG, Jan. 1—"Released under supervision of the masses!"

This penalty, which seems to be coming into increasing vogue on the mainland, applies to a special group of arrested "counter-revolutionaries" whose cases are now being disposed of by people's courts, military control commissions and people's representative bodies in Communist China.

They have escaped three sterner penalties prescribed for alleged enemies of the state: summary execution, indefinite imprisonment for "reform by labor" with a two-year reprieve from a firing squad subject to "good behavior" and specific terms of imprisonment for one year to life at forced labor. But they are not free.

Once they reach home their dwelling becomes a "special household." Divested of all rights as citizens and subject to supervision of both the local public security bureaus and the neighborhood "citizens security committees," these "controlled persons" are marked men and social pariahs under Mao Tse-tung's "people's democratic dictatorship."

Lose Freedom of Movement

"Persons listed as counter-revolutionaries and placed under surveillance in various districts of Kwangtung have lost most of their freedom of movement," the Hong Kong journal Sing Tao Jih Pao reported in a dispatch from Canton. "They are greatly discriminated against and their friends and relatives would not dare communicate with them. They can best be described as 'untouchables.' "

According to Chinese Communist reports, "controlled persons" must ask for permission to leave their house, "cancel their leaves" by reporting again when they return and provide authorities with detailed information on all their visitors and the subjects discussed. They cannot move from the house they are occupying, travel outside the locality or "engage in rumor-mongering."

Legally, the mainland report stated, such persons lose the right to elect or be elected, the right to hold any Government job, the right to join the army or any "people's organization" and the right to accept state honors. They are also divested of such rights as exist to "freedoms of speech, publication, assembly and domicile, removal, travel, demonstration and parade."

Furthermore, they must submit to reindoctrination, report activities of "other counter-revolutionaries," "protect Government property and avoid waste" and "strive positively for production." The term of supervision is officially said to be one to three years "in general" with provision made for shortening or canceling supervision if the person so controlled is credited with "great and meritorious achievements."

January 2, 1952

CHINESE REDS SPUR 'FREEING' OF WOMEN

Service Unit Set Up to Mediate Marital Rows—'Decadent' Females 'Re-educated'

By HENRY R. LIEBERMAN
Special to The New York Times.

SHANGHAI, Aug. 27—The Communist drive to "liberate" the women of China and make them more conscious of their political role in Mao Tze-tung's "New Democracy" was reflected today on two new fronts.

Married women employes of the Chinese customs service appealed to authorities to let them use their maiden names without adding the husbands' surname in signing official papers. "It is expected authorities will approve the request," said the newspaper Wen Wei Pao, which declared the Communist Government had "real respect" for the "independent character of women."

A women's service department, it was announced, has been set up under the newly organized Housewives Union to mediate family and marital disputes. The organization is similar to others already established in older Communist areas where politically conscious women have waged a fight on tyrannical fathers, wife beating, abuses of daughters-in-law by mothers-in-law and subjection of women in general.

Before the Women's Service Department was created, mediation of family disputes had been handled here by the Chinese Women's Association, which had heard cases twice weekly. Since the first of this month, it was reported today, the association has disposed of more than 130 disputes, mainly marital. According to Wen Wei Pao, reconciliations were effected in about 70 per cent of the cases, with 10 per cent resulting in divorce by mutual consent and 20 per cent being referred to the People's Court because of continuing differences.

Although the informal domestic court is concerned primarily with women's rights, it is also considering complaints of husbands who accuse their wives of leading a "decadent life" or being governed by "backward ideology." In reporting on such complaints, Wen Wei Pao stated:

"Educational and instructional work was carried out with regard to such women and active guidance was given them. The result has been that they have returned to the path of virtue and participated in production in several instances."

One of the disputes settled at yesterday's session involved a complaint by a cotton merchant that his wife was a habitual gambler. She has apparently promised reform.

Another case involved a complaint by a woman worker that her husband manhandled her after she had participated in a dramatic production staged during the Communist "troop-comforting campaign" here. "Due to the sincere repentance of her husband, Hu Hung-ching, and his promise that such an incident would not recur again, a peaceful agreement has been reached," Wen Wei Pao said.

The third case was an ordinary alimony case involving a husband and wife who had been separated ten years. Upon mediation the husband made a lump sum payment of 35 piculs of rice [a picul equals 133 1/3 pounds] and their separation was converted into a legal divorce.

August 28, 1949

China Reds Outlaw Polygamy

SAN FRANCISCO, May 3 (AP)—Red China put into effect its new marriage law, which outlaws polygamy and the sale of women, the Peiping radio announced today. Both practices have been condoned in China for thousands of years.

May 4, 1950

Chinese Reds Reported Scoring Big Success In Winning and Employing Support of Youth

By TILLMAN DURDIN
Special to THE NEW YORK TIMES.

HONG KONG, Aug. 29—Chinese communism has scored an important success in winning and utilizing the support of a large proportion of the young people of China.

Foreign diplomats, Roman Catholic and Protestant missionaries, foreign business man and Chinese who arrive here from the China mainland uniformly testify to the influence of the Communists on Chinese youth and estimate the majority of the younger Chinese are earnest partisans of the Communist regime.

The hold that the Communists have gained over the youth and the fact that the younger generation of Chinese now is virtually isolated from any but Communist influences are regarded as one of the most disturbing aspects of the Communist acquisition of power in China.

Millions of young persons are participating in the administration and communization of the country.

For years many things in Chinese communism have appealed to China's youth. It is bold and revolutionary. It is super-nationalist and gratifies the urge of Chinese youth to reassert China's greatness after generations of humiliation at the hands of foreigners and foreign nations.

It taps youthful idealism and youthful desires to serve the people and nation and at the same time offers satisfying ceremonial dances, parades, demonstrations, uniforms and travel.

In Communist China young men and women, 15 to 25, hold key posts everywhere. Even those who remain in school play vital political roles through constant participation individually and in groups in whatever cause or campaign the Communists want to push at any given time.

In the rural areas the Mayor of a small city may be a 21-year-old lad. Girls of 18 often are found commanding units of the police or helping to manage clean-ups of "counter-revolutionaries." Political cadres everywhere are often made up of individuals under 25, who frequently have the power of life and death over the inhabitants of an area.

August 30, 1951

CANTON BUSINESS MEN FACE RED REPRESSION

Special to THE NEW YORK TIMES.

HONG KONG, Feb. 1—Gen. Yeh Chien-ying, Communist Governor of Kwangtung Province, called on the people of Canton yesterday to "rise up and strike a strong counter-blow against the capitalists" in a speech that brought the Peiping regime's rapidly developing "quadruple opposition" campaign all the way down to China's southern borders.

The "quadruple opposition" campaign is based on four slogans, "anti-bribery, anti-fraud, anti-profiteering and anti-tax evasion." It is directed against private shopkeepers and industrialists, who have been charged with corrupting a number of backsliding Communists through bribery and obstructing the Government's economic policies.

"Law-breaking industrialists and business men in Canton have corroded revolutionary cadres like a plague, with the result that many wavering but pure-hearted cadres have become their victims, General Yeh said.

Addressing 600 delegates attending a People's Representatives Conference, the Communist Governor said publicly that they would get "special encouragement" in denouncing business men on "quadruple opposition."

PEIPING DEADLINE SET FOR 'CORRUPT' TO TALK

Special to THE NEW YORK TIMES.

HONG KONG, Feb. 9—Communist leaders in Peiping have fixed Feb. 15 as the final deadline for the "corrupt elements" in Red China's central Government to come forward and confess their transgressions voluntarily under an expiring policy of "leniency."

Finance Minister Po Yi-po, chairman of the National Austerity Inspection Committee, has announced that those exposed after this date would be confronted with the prospect of execution or imprisonment.

"All major culprits of corruption should choose their own path between death, imprisonment and absolution from punishment," he said. He declared that this was the last chance for wayward functionaries and added that he hoped they would not lose it.

Meanwhile, official dispatches reaching here from the mainland continue to chronicle the arrests of private business men accused of being insufficiently "candid" in making their confessions under the "quadruple opposition" movement.

This movement, which is being directed against middle class urban groups as part of the general swing to the Left in Communist policy, takes its label from its four main slogans: anti-bribery, anti-fraud, anti-profiteering and anti-tax evasion.

7 IN RED CHINA SHOT FOR CHEATING STATE

Special to THE NEW YORK TIMES.

HONG KONG, Feb. 18—Seven private contractors were sentenced to death and forty-seven others to jail terms on charges of defrauding the state in construction work on the Tienshui-Lanchow Railway in Northwest China. A Communist dispatch disclosed today they were tried before a mass meeting of 10,000 persons at Tienshui, Kansu Province, Jan. 21. Of those imprisoned, three received life terms.

Those turned over to the firing squad were accused of "swindling the state of property, oppressing and squeezing laborers, corroding political workers, sabotaging railway construction and refusing to repent." They also were charged with doing defective work on tunnels.

Meanwhile the purge of "corrupt" and "undisciplined" elements in the party and government is also continuing. Among those recently reported to have been dismissed in Manchuria are Yang Mien, chief of the foreign trade bureau, Chu Hua, chief of the Dairen Bureau of Commerce, and Tang Yun Chao, director of the Northeast Labor Bureau. In the Northwest, Wu Wen Lin, Vice Director for Cultural Affairs, has received "public warning" from the party.

In the Southeast eight more officials have been turned out, with Yang Ching Tien, president of the Yunnam Peoples Court, being "suspended to enagage in self-reflection."

BUSINESS IS TARGET OF PEIPING TERROR

Drive on 'Decadent Bourgeois' Nets Huge Revenues From 'Law-Breaking Capitalists'

By HENRY R. LIEBERMAN
Special to THE NEW YORK TIMES.

HONG KONG, March 6—Red China's war on "law-breaking" merchants, shopkeepers and industrialists, which began as a campaign to remold their "decadent bourgeois thought" is now reported to have taken on the aspect of a new terror in which the state is collecting large sums of extra revenue from harassed middle-class groups.

Recent arrivals from Shanghai and Tientsin said the atmosphere had again become thick with fear after the lull that followed last year's nation-wide purge of "counter-revolutionaries." According to these sources, suicides are increasing amid confessions, mutual "criticism" and anonymous denunciations of "law-breaking capitalists."

The arrivals from the mainland drew a picture of loaded police vans rumbling through the streets with sirens screaming and families waiting anxiously for the return of alleged "lawbreakers" whose names are being bawled out over public loudspeakers with instructions directing them to specific confession centers.

Hundreds of investigation teams are said to be poring over books of private enterprises, probing for fraud, and shop assistants are reported organized in cities throughout the country to reveal the economic transgressions of their employers.

The Chinese Industrial and Commercial news reported here today that local authorities in Kongmoon, Kwangtung Province, had ordered a number of drinking wells sealed for the duration of the "Wu Fan" campaign following three suicides by well drowning. The Wu Fan or "Five Anti" drive, which was originally labeled the "Quadruple Opposition" movement when it was launched in January, is now officially represented as being directed against five cardinal sins ascribed to Chinese business men.

These are listed as including "bribery, tax evasion, fraud, stealing state property and theft of state economic secrets."

A number of business men have been accused of profiteering and manipulating markets on the basis of information leaked by "corrupt officials" in state trading companies.

In Peiping investigation teams are officially reported to have found 40,000 out of 50,000 private enterprises "guilty" of breaking the law in some form.

The Hsinhua News Agency said these "law breakers" had been divided into "minor offenders," "half law abiding and half law breaking" and "habitual law breakers."

The agency said all except the "minor offenders" were being required to make up tax deficiencies. It added that the "serious offend-

February 2, 1952

February 10, 1952

February 19, 1952

ers" faced penalties ranging up to capital punishment for the "most serious offenders."

Mainland reports said the Peiping Government was deriving financial windfalls bu such means as:

¶Collection of "back taxes."

¶Deposits in Government banks of gold and silver dollars and United States currency by hoarders fearful of being exposed.

¶"Refunds" from business men accused of "stealing state property," reaping profits through leakage of "economic secrets," jacking up prices, delivering inferior goods or otherwise causing loss to the state on Government contracts.

¶Imposition of heavy fines on "serious offenders."

March 7, 1952

PEIPING DECREES NEW GRAFT LAWS

By HENRY R. LIEBERMAN
Special to THE NEW YORK TIMES.

HONG KONG, March 14—With political workers still processing tens of thousands of confessions and accusations in Red China, the Peiping Government has promulgated a new decree prescribing graduated penalties for all the big medium and little "tigers" bagged by the state in its double-barreled drive against "corruption." The decree, which was drawn up last Tuesday exempts "minor culprits" from penalties, provided they "confess frankly" and promise not to err again. "Big tigers" are confronted, however, with administrative and criminal penalties ranging up to death. Degrees of mitigation were provided for those who were "rank" and handed over their "graft proceeds" to the state.

The Chinese Communists apply the term "tiger" to relatively important culprits winnowed from the ranks of Government workers and private business men who have been exposed en masse to rounds of confessions, secret denunciations and public accusations.

The twin campaign involves a purge of corrupt, wasteful and bureaucratic elements in the Government and a collateral class war against middle-class economic groups in the cities.

Administrative punishment prescribed for Government workers includes a warning, demerit, demotion, suspension or dismissal. Criminal penalties include "control by supervision" for a one or two year period, "reform by labor," prison sentences ranging from short terms to life and execution by firing squads.

According to the Hsinhua News Agency, the decree defines a minor culprit in Government as on accused of graft amounting to less than one million People's dollars (about $50 United States money). Major culprits in Government are subdivided into the following categories:

"Little tigers"—those accused of graft amounting to between one million and ten million People's dollars. The penalty is administrative punishment.

"Medium tigers" — those accused of graft amounting to between 10,000,000 and 100,000,000 People's dollars. The penalty is administrative or criminal punishment depending on the "frankness of confession" and refund to the state of the graft proceeds.

"Big tigers" — those accused of graft exceeding 100,000,000 People's dollars. The penalty is criminal punishment, with the proviso that those who "recant voluntarily" and turn in their illegal proceeds may be exempt from criminal punishment.

Graduated penalties also are set down for private shopkeepers, merchants and industrialists. They have been subdivided into five categories — law abiding; basically law abiding; semi law abiding; serious offenders and most serious offenders.

Although official reports received in Hong Kong already have produced a list of "big tigers" running into the hundreds, the widest field for "tiger hunting" lies among harassed private business men in China's urban centers.

March 15, 1952

CHINESE EMPLOYES DENOUNCE BOSSES

By HENRY R. LIEBERMAN
Special to THE NEW YORK TIMES.

HONG KONG, April 7 — Fifty thousand persons jammed the Peoples Stadium in near-by Canton today and shouted pro-Government rally slogans as shop assistants and workers denounced their employers for alleged economic immorality.

It was a continuation of Red China's Wu Fan (Five Anti) movement, officially represented by a purge of the "five vices" attributed by the Peiping regime to the Chinese urban middle class. Deadly sins are listed as "bribery, tax evasion, fraud, theft of state property, and theft of state economic secrets."

According to the Canton radio, which broadcast the proceedings, Communist authorities in the Kwantung capital are now disposing of 44,000 Wu Fan confessions and denunciations. By this process, private shopkeepers, merchants and industrialists are being put through a wringer that is netting the Government considerable extra revenue in the form of "back tax" payments, refunds of "graft proceeds" and fines.

Special courts have been set up to try "major offenders" under both the Wu Fan and the collateral San Fan (Three Anti) movements. The latter is directed against "corruption, waste and bureaucraticism" in government. It was becoming increasingly clear, however, that the two movements were not merely fund raising drives.

Aside from charges of outright graft and thievery, the whole middle class is being accused of "vices" involving traditional business methods regarded by the Communists as obstacles to centralized economic control.

In a decree promulgated by Peiping on March 11, Premier Chou En-lai declared that the present movements were intended to liquidate the "dirt and poison of the old social order" and introduce a new code of "integrity and thrift." He said that anyone "undermining the state's economic and financial system" would henceforth be severely punished "without leniency."

Once the Wu Fan movement is completed, according to Communist reports, private business men are scheduled to be harnessed by economic groups into an All China Federation of Industry and Commerce paralleling the existing All China Federation of Labor.

As part of the centralization process, the Peiping Cabinet has ordered all military units and government bodies to register their subsidiary economic enterprises for absorption by the "proper central agencies."

During the Chinese civil war, while the Communists were fighting in scattered areas, many military units, political organs and even newspapers operated their own special factories and shops to help finance themselves. The Government now takes the stand that such decentralized operations are no longer necessary and have become inimical to overall economic efficiency.

Meanwhile, the Peiping regime has been cracking down on provincial governments for camouflaging accounts and setting aside unbudgeted funds to finance necessary projects for which central appropriations might not be forthcoming.

April 8, 1952

CHINA REDS PURGING LOWER PARTY RANK

Urban Bolsheviks Are Gaining at Expense of Members of Peasant Background

By HENRY R. LIEBERMAN
Special to THE NEW YORK TIMES.

HONG KONG, May 17—While the top leadership of the Chinese Communist party remains basically the same, with the reins of power still held by the men of Yenan, the Communist capital in wartime days, and by the civil war generals, some key changes have been taking place in the party's middle and lower ranks.

With the emphasis now on urban industrialization instead of on the "peasant war," the continuing revolution is consuming those who have been unable to make the necessary adjustments. The number of new urban Bolsheviks is increasing and the party press has been hurling the charge of "meritism" at those party veterans who have complained of having been poorly rewarded for their civil war hardships.

During the past few months a mass of domestic Communist dispatches have revealed that thousands of administrative cadres have been displaced in a "purification" process that has accompanied the Peiping regime's "Three Anti Movement." This movement, which was started in December, is directed against "corruption, waste and bureaucratism." At the same time, however, it also has involved a general ideological re-examination of party members as part of an over-all shift to the left in the party line.

"Right-Wing Sentiments"

Aside from "corrupt elements" sentenced to jail and in some cases executed, those accused of harboring "right-wing sentiments" and being "unable to distinguish friend from foe" are either being re-educated, assigned to "self-reflection," suspended or dismissed from the party.

Among those hit by the "purification" drive in rural areas are un-reconstructed local toughs who were hastily recruited as local administrators to assist in taking over "new liberated areas." They and back-sliding cadres of longer party standing are being displaced as "counter-revolutionaries, elements of the enemy class, renegades, spies and degenerates."

In the cities many jaded civil war veterans accused of having lost their revolutionary steam and succumbed to "sugar-coated capitalist bullets" are being succeeded by more enthusiastic new Bolsheviks. Party leaders have instructed subordinate publications not to let considerations of seniority interfere with the purge of "corrupt and decadent elements."

"Bold Promotion" Called For

The Peiping People's Daily, leading party organ, called last month for "bold promotion" of new cadres to replace those purged. Since then mainland dispatches have listed the promotions of large groups of new urban "activists" to fill vacancies created in Government offices, enterprises and trade unions by the "Three Anti Movement."

As a classic revolutionary prototype, the urban hsin kanpu (new cadre) "proletarian" origin has acquired an increasing edge over the average lao kanpu (old cadre) of peasant origin. The term cadre is applied in China, individually and collectively, to all Government and party functionaries and political workers.

The infusion of new urban "proletarian" blood into the party has been going on steadily since the establishment of the Peiping regime Oct. 1, 1949. Of 5,800,000 members claimed by the party last July, 2,700,000—almost one-half—were listed as having been enrolled as recently as 1949-50.

Indications, however, are that the party cadres have developed an increasing reluctance to make independent decisions. An East China official complained publicly about the reluctance of "some leading cadres" to shoulder their responsibilities for fear of committing errors. He said this tendency had become known in East China as "three shirks and one delay."

May 18, 1952

PEIPING CALLS OFF PURGE

No Reason Given for Ending Drive on Business Men

HONG KONG, June 15 (Reuters)—Communist China is calling off the country's biggest purge in modern times, the Peiping radio announced today.

Officially called the "five anti" movement, the purge was directed against private traders and business men. The five "anti," were listed as: tax evasion, bribery, theft of state property, theft of state economic secrets and cheating in carrying out Government contracts.

The Peiping radio said Premier Chou En-lai had instructed all provincial and local governments to wind up the purge he launched early this year. No reason was given. No deadline for the finish was given.

June 16, 1952

PEIPING PLANS NEW CHECKS

'People's' Agents Will Survey Work of Bureaucrats

Special to THE NEW YORK TIMES.

HONG KONG, Aug. 3—Communist China's supervisory agencies have been authorized to appoint "people's supervisory correspondents" in government organs, civic bodies and neighborhood associations to check on "all delinquencies, violations on law and trespassing on the rights of the people or the state."

The rules governing the appointment of the "supervisory correspondents" were promulgated in Peiping July 30, the Hsinhua News Agency said today.

The "correspondents" will function as on-the-spot representatives of the supervisory bodies that already exist at various administrative levels. These agencies, which operate under the National Committee on People's Supervision, have power to investigate and indict wayward bureaucrats.

The "correspondents" also will be required to evaluate local public opinion and report to higher official echelons on the attitudes of the "common people about government" policy, decrees and activities.

August 4, 1953

RED CHINA CALLING PEOPLE'S CONGRESS

Peiping Broadcasts the Plans for 1953 Sessions to Draft a National Constitution

By HENRY R. LIEBERMAN
Special to THE NEW YORK TIMES.

HONG KONG, Monday, Dec. 29—The Communists' Peiping Government announced today that an All-China People's Congress would be convened in 1953.

As provided earlier in the regime's projected political blueprint, the Congress is scheduled to assume a constitutional role as the "supreme organ for exercising state power" in Red China.

Plans were also announced for the election of local People's Congresses in a developing pyramid of "people's power." A basis for such local bodies already has been created in the form of "representatives conferences" that are now operating at village, district, county and city levels in many areas.

Decision to convene the national People's Congress involves regularization of the Peiping Government's structure after a three-year transition period. It has been accompanied by domestic broadcasts stressing three major tasks for 1953—the "Resist America—Aid Korea" movement, the start of "large-scale construction" and the strengthening of "national solidarity."

Electoral Law Indicated

Among the first duties of the coming All-China People's Congress, said the announcement broadcast by Peiping, will be the adoption of a constitution and passage of an electoral law. The means by which the Congress will be elected were not clear.

Since Oct. 1, 1949, when it came into being, the Peiping regime has operated under a blueprint called the "common program." The program was adopted by a Chinese People's Political Consultative Conference, which was convoked by the Communist party of China to establish the Communist-led Peiping coalition.

It was the 1949 Conference that named the present central government council headed by Mao Tse-tung. Under the "common program" the Conference, acting through a National Committee, is empowered to exercise the functions of an All-China People's Congress pending election of the Congress by "universal franchise."

According to the statement of the Reds' official Hsinhua news agency, the National Committee voted in Peiping on Dec. 24 to convoke the People's Congress.

The committee acted on a proposal by Premier Chou En-lai, who said the advent of large scale economic construction required changes "so that the people can play their full part in industrialization."

Advent of Five-Year-Plan

"Our country will put into effect its first five-year construction plan in 1953," Mr. Chou noted

Li Chi-shen, chief of what is called the Revolutionary Committee of the Kuomintang, and one of the Peiping regime's six Vice Chairmen, presided over the Dec. 24 meeting.

Mr. Chou, according to Hsinhua, said the convocation of the national People's Congress was made possible by a successful three-year recovery period, in which he claimed "great victories on all fronts." He asserted that the whole country had been "liberated" except for Formosa, that land reform had been "basically completed," that guerrillas and counter-revolutionaries had been "basically eliminated."

National defense had been strengthened, the people had been undergoing "patriotic education" and the "workers' leadership" was now firm, he added.

Mr. Chou said the Korean war had spurred rather than hampered Red China's economic and reform programs. He declared Communist China was in a position to carry on modern war and economic construction at the same time.

December 29, 1952

PEIPING PUTS BRAKE ON RED REVOLUTION

Dispatch of The Times, London.

HONG KONG, Sept. 20—Meetings of the Central People's Government Executive Council (Cabinet), which lasted all last week in Peiping, have emphasized a new trend in Chinese policy that the truce in Korea has reinforced.

The slowing down of the domestic revolution was underlined in a report on political and legal affairs by Peng Chen, member of the Political Bureau of the Communist party and vice chairman of the Commission for Political and Legal Affairs.

The campaign for suppression of counter-revolutionaries, he said, has been "fundamentally accomplished within the national frontiers," although vigilance will have to be maintained. He said those counter-revolutionaries and criminal landlords sentenced to surveillance and "reform through labor" had done well and were becoming useful citizens.

Mr. Peng acknowledged that the last few years had seen "feuds" between the old school of jurisprudence and the new, but said this was being overcome rapidly.

Many sentences promulgated during the land reform and other campaigns have been revised, and some decisions reversed. Some social reforms such as the new marriage law have not been fully adopted, but it was evident from the summary of his speech given by the Hsinhua (New China) news agency that no new changes were to be introduced for some time.

The Executive Council also approved a reshuffle of ministerial posts, which saw the first fall from office of a leading Communist since the Government came to power, the dismissal of Po I-po as Minister of Finance and his replacement by Teng Hsiao-ping, one of five deputy premiers under Chou En-lai.

The reshuffle includes the transfer of one Deputy Minister for Finance and the appointment of two new deputy ministers of this department and three new deputy directors of the official People's Bank.

Although there was no known cause to dramatize the departure of Mr. Po as a "purge" or split of any kind in the Government—he was a late recruit to the Government ranks from service of a war lord, Gen. Yen Hsi-shan—the development did make a break in an interesting sideline of Chinese traditions.

For centuries, the Province of Shansi has been the home of Chinese banking, and even the introduction of Western-style banks at the end of the nineteenth century did not end the dominance of the Shansi banking families. This dominance has survived all changes of government in China in the last half century.

Mr. Po was a Shansi man. Indeed, his fall may be partly explained by a conflict of loyalties that his provincial origins promoted.

September 21, 1953

MAO TAKING OVER GENERALS' POWERS

By DREW MIDDLETON
Special to The New York Times,

LONDON, June 29—The drastic concentration of power in the lands of Mao Tse-tung and a few Communist party officials at the expense of the local authority of military commanders impresses officials here as one of the most important developments in Communist China.

The process of reducing the prestige and influence of the generals began in November, 1952. Apparently it was completed by the Draft Constitution of the People's Republic of China made public in Peiping June 15.

The centralization of government is dictated, these sources said, by the enormous economic problems facing the Communist party. For, in working out the industrial and agricultural plans, it was found that the military leaders did not have the necessary training and background.

There is urgent need for economic progress. Steel production lingers under 2,000,000 tons a year. One estimate of Chinese economic conditions is that the Communist regime has not restored industrial production, agriculture and trade to the level of 1931, the year in which Japan launched her invasion.

In these circumstances, it is said, centralization of power accompanied by the introduction of trained administrators in regional governments was inevitable. Already centralization has progressed beyond the point

forecast in the program of the Chinese People's Political Consultative Conference at the end of 1949.

A central regime such as envisaged in the Draft Constitution should be more efficient than autonomous local officials each working toward a general goal. Under the new constitution there will be constant supervision and direction of local officials by the Central Government.

But China has an area of approximately 3,800,000 square miles and a population, according to the last government census, of 602,000,000.

Under those physical circumstances, it is pointed out, even the most carefully planned supervision of local government is likely to break down.

After the Communist victory, the Central Government, ruling in a land where communications were almost nonexistent, placed generals at the heads of various geographical districts that were larger than old provinces.

Almost immediately, sources there said, it was found that the generals and their subordinates were unable to cope with the purely economic problems that faced them. Gradually their autonomy was whittled away. By November, 1952, they had become representatives of the Central Government. Shortly thereafter most of the military commanders were replaced by civil officials.

The next step was the reconstitution of local government on something approaching the old provincial basis with authority exercised by the Central Government through its appointees.

The two highest governmental

organs under the old organization, the Central People's Government Council and the State Administrative Council, are now amalgamated into the State Council.

The National People's Congress, according to the Constitution, is the "sole organ exercising legislative power" in the state.

Election Procedure

The Congress is to be elected by the armed forces, provincial congresses and "Chinese residents abroad." It will meet once a year to adopt a budget and approve economic plans. Its functions are very similar to those of the Supreme Soviet in Moscow.

What little power is allowed the Congress will be exercised by its Standing Committee which can enact decrees, supervise the State Council, which has some of the functions of a government, and appoint or remove individual ministers.

At the top is the real seat of power, the Chairman of the Chinese People's Republic.

Article 40 of the Constitution says the Chairman, who will be Mr. Mao, "promulgates laws and degrees, appoints or removes the premier, vice premiers, ministers, chairmen of commissions and the Secretary General of the State Council, appoints or removes the vice chairmen and members of the National Defense Council, awards orders and medals and titles of honor of the state, proclaims general amnesties and pardons, proclaims martial law, declares a state of war and orders mobilization."

June 30, 1954

CHINA'S BASIC LAW HELD TEMPORARY

By HARRY SCHWARTZ

Communist China's first Constitution, adopted last week, provides for a political and economic system similar to that of the Soviet Union in many respects, but also differing sharply in some ways.

The English text of the Constitution, which was unanimously adopted in Peiping Sept. 20 by the National People's Congress, became available in New York yesterday in the latest issue of the Cominform newspaper. The document consists of a preamble and four major chapters, the latter divided into 106 specific articles.

In the official commentary on the Constitution, the Chinese Communist theoretician Liu Shao-chi declared that the document was intended to cover the period of transition to socialism "and cannot therefore fail to differ

from a constitution for a period when Socialist society has already been built."

The preamble defines Communist China as a "people's democratic dictatorship" during the transition to socialism. The state's central task during this period "is to bring about step by step, the Socialist industrialization of the country and * * * the Socialist transformation of agriculture, handicrafts and capitalist industry and commerce."

Preamble Mentions Soviet

The preamble contains the document's only two references to the "leadership of the Communist party of China" as well as mention of the "indestructible friendship with the great Union of Soviet Socialist Republics and the People's Democracies." The specific role of the Communist party or of the Soviet Union is not further mentioned.

Chapter I, General Principles, sets down the basic political and economic aspects of the Chinese Communist state. It provides for the equality of all nationalities but, unlike the Soviet Constitution, excludes any possibility of secession by any minority nationality concentrated in a particular area.

This chapter recognizes state ownership, cooperative ownership, individual ownership and capitalist ownership. Article 10 pledges the state to protect capitalists and their ownership of capital, but lays down the principle that capitalist industry will be used, restricted and then finally transformed "into various forms of state-controlled economy."

Economic planning by the state is to direct economic life. The state is to protect citizens' ownership of incomes, savings, houses and "the means of life" as well as their right of inheritance. Unlike in the Soviet Union, all land is not now nationalized—though it may be nationalized—and peasants may own land and other production means. The state will seek the "restriction and gradual elimination" of rich peasant economy.

The state structure set forth by Chapter II requires more than half the articles in the Constitution to define it. It provides for legislative, executive and judicial branches of government, both resembling and differing from Soviet and Western models.

A one-house legislature, the National People's Congress elected for four years, is declared "the highest organ of state power." It is elected by all citizens over 18 years old as well as by the votes of "Chinese residents abroad." "Should exceptional circumstances arise, making elections impossible," the term of office of a Congress may be prolonged indefinitely.

The Congress is to meet normally only once a year, unless convened ofter er by its Standing Committee, which exercises legislative powers between Congress sessions. The Congress is to pass laws, approve the state budget, elect the highest officials of the executive and judicial branches and "exercise all other functions and powers which the National People's Congress considers necessary"

The Standing Committee of the National People's Congress thus apparently is the Chinese counterpart of the Presidium of the Supreme Soviet in the Soviet Union, which normally issues de-

crees and makes appointments, all of which have up to now been automatically ratified by the Supreme Soviet, the nation's legislature, in its brief and infrequent meetings.

The chief executive officer is the chairman of the People's Republic of China, now Mao Tsetung. Working with the Standing Committee of the Congress, he can, under the Constitution, promulgate laws and decrees, remove even the highest subordinate officials, declare war and proclaim martial law. He is commander of the armed forces and head of the National Defense Council. He "represents the People's Republic of China in relation with foreign states," appoints or recalls foreign envoys and ratifies treaties.

For policy-making purposes, the chairman may convoke a Supreme State Conference attended by the vice-chairman of the People's Republic, the chairman of the Standing Committee of the

People's Congress, the Premier of the State Council "and others concerned."

The "highest administrative organ of the state" is the State Council, or Cabinet, headed by a Premier, now Chou En-lai, consisting of the vice premiers, heads of ministries and commissions, and the secretary general of the State Council.

This body is actually to carry out the daily work of Government. Its duties include the carrying out of the economic plan, controlling foreign and domestic trade, directing work concerning Chinese resident abroad, directing foreign relations and building up the armed forces.

The judicial branch of the Government consists of the Supreme People's Court, local people's courts at every level, and special courts established by law. A Procurator General supervises "all the departments subordinate

to the State Council." Trials are to be held in public unless otherwise specified by law and those accused have the "right to defense."

For purposes of local government, the country is divided into provinces, autonomous regions and municipalities directly subordinate to the central authority. Local legislative and administrative authorities are subject to the superior authority of higher organs up to the State Council and the National People's Congress.

Chapter III on the fundamental rights and duties of the citizen says all citizens are equal before the law, declares citizens "have freedom of speech, the press, assembly, association, procession and demonstration" and "freedom of religious belief."

Citizens may not be arrested except by order of a court or of a people's procurator. Their homes "are inviolable."

September 28, 1954

CHINA RED LEADER PURGED BY PARTY; COMMITS SUICIDE

By HENRY R. LIEBERMAN
Special to The New York Times.

HONG KONG, April 4—Kao Kang, former Communist regional boss in Manchuria and one of Red China's original Vice Chairmen, was officially reported tonight to have committed suicide.

He had been accused by the Chinese Communist Central Committee of "conspiratorial activities" aimed at seeking the leadership of the party and state by overthrowing Mao Tse-tung's Politburo.

Mr. Kao's death was disclosed in a series of communiqués issued by the Central Committee on a recent national party conference. The committee said this conference unanimously decided to expel him and Jao Shu-shih, the party's former organizational chief, from Chinese Communist ranks.

Although the Chinese Reds have been steadily purging their party in the lower and middle echelons, this is the first publicly announced purge of men near the top of the party hierarchy. When the present Central Committee was elected in 1945 Mr.

Kao held the No. 9 and Mr. Jao the No. 11 position.

The party conference, which was held from March 21 to 31, also took disciplinary action against seven lesser figures in the alleged "Kao Kang-Jao Shu-shih anti-party alliance." They are: Hsiang Ming, Chang Hsiu-shan, Chang Ming-yuan, Chao Teh-tsun, Ma Hung, Kuo Feng and Chen Po-tsun.

Official observers here were not wholly surprised by the announced downfall of Messrs. Kao and Jao. A prolonged Communist press blackout on their activities combined with criticism of "certain" top-level party members had produced intense speculation on their whereabouts.

Mr. Kao, once a rising star in Red China as onetime Politburo member and head of the State Planning Commission, had not been mentioned in mainland news reports for more than a year.

The Central Committee made only passing mention of his death in communiqués broadcast tonight by the Peiping radio.

Heaping public disgrace upon him posthumously, the party's governing board said he "even committed suicide as an expression of his ultimate betrayal of the party." No details were given on when, where or how he died.

The committee said his suicide followed a party "warning" issued to him after its fourth plenary session. At this session, held in Peiping February, 1954, Kao held the No. 9 and Mr. Jao the No. 11 position.

the party Secretary General, Liu Shao-chi, declared some "high-ranking cadres" had set up "independent kingdoms" and become too "arrogant."

In one of tonight's communiqués, the Central Committee charged the former Manchurian regional boss had sought to become General Secretary or Vice Chairman of the party committee and head of the State Council. Such alleged ambitions undoubtedly would have brought him into conflict with Premier Chou En-lai as well as Mr. Liu.

Mr. Kao, a Shensi man who was in his early fifties when he died, formed an alliance with Mr. Mao in Northwest China after the Communist "long march" from east-central China. As late as 1952 his pronouncements from Manchuria got top nation-wide play in the Communist press.

Among charges leveled at him now are those of having sowed "dissension," having created "dissatisfaction," having spread "rumors," and having "slandered" the Central Committee. Maintaining he had set up an "antiparty faction," the Central Committee asserted:

"For this purpose he raised the utterly absurd 'theory' that our party consisted of two parties—one, the so-called 'Party of the Revolutionary Bases and the Army,' the other the so-called 'Party of the White Areas'—and that the party was created by the Army."

The committee said Mr. Kao maintained he should hold "the major authority" with the argument he was the representative of the "Party of the Revolutionary Bases and the Army."

The 53-year-old Mr. Jao, veteran Communist from Kiang-

si Province, was accused of conspiring with Mr. Kao and using his position as organizational chief to the "party." According to the Central Committee, he thought Mr. Kao was "on the point of success" in 1953.

Mr. Jao also was accused of having adopted a "rightist policy of surrender" while serving as the party's regional political boss in East China from 1949 to 1953. In the fall of 1952 he was one of six high-ranking Chinese Communists who went to Moscow to attend the Nineteenth Congress of the Bolshevik party.

The Central Committee declared that party unity had been strengthened now that the "Kao Kang-Jao Shu-Shih antiparty alliance" had been "crushed."

It stated, however, there was still danger that hostile groups would try to sway "unstable and unreliable elements" inside the party.

Emphasis was placed on the need for constant vigilance to protect party unity in the midst of the alleged "imperialist" threat and social revolution on the home front. The committee called for continuing the party fight against the "tendency toward personal dictatorship and fragmentation."

Four statements were issued by the Central Committee on the national party conference, convened under a resolution adopted by party leaders in February, 1954. Sixty-two members and alternate members of the Central Committee and 257 representatives of party organizations throughout the country attended the conference.

The conference heard an opening-day speech by Mr. Mao and also listened to reports by other members of the party Politburo.

Besides deciding to expel those accused of "antiparty" activities the meeting was reported to have transacted the following additional business:

¶Approved a new draft of the present five-year plan, now in its third year, and called on the country to "work with care and industry to overcome difficulties and increase production."

¶Established a new Central Control Committee and a network of local control committees to strengthen ideological work, combat "subversive activities" and deal with "unwholesome trends within the party." Tung Pi-wu, head of the Supreme Court, was made head of the Central Committee.

¶Elected Gen. Lin Piao and Deputy Premier Teng Hsiao-ping as new members of the Politburo.

Other members of the present Politburo were listed as follows:

Mao Tse-tung, Liu Shao-chi, Chou En-lai, Chu Teh, Chen Yun, Kang Sheng, Peng Chen, Tung Pi-wu, Lin Cho-chu, Chang Wen-tien and Gen. Peng Teh-huai.

Chen Yun, a Deputy Premier, was said to have reported to the conference on the five-year plan.

April 5, 1955

PEIPING PURGE REVEALS RIVALRIES AT THE TOP

Signs of Unrest Focus Attention On How Communist Party Rules

By HENRY R. LIEBERMAN
Special to The New York Times.

HONG KONG, April 9 — As practitioners of the grim business of revolution by "struggle" for more than three decades, the Chinese Communists are not exactly unfamiliar with purge and violence.

They achieved national power by an all-out civil war as well as by the subtler techniques of propaganda, intrigue and political maneuver. In their time, they have liquidated countless nonparty Chinese tagged as "counter-revolutionaries."

Inside the Chinese Communist ranks there was some purging of party members before the Peiping Government was established in 1949.

A number of lower and middle echelon party members were among those imprisoned and executed during a "purification" drive in 1951 and 1952.

Top Men Were Safe

At least one alternate member of the party's Central Committee was expelled then. But by and large the top-ranking men around Mao Tse-tung seemed to be relatively immune, even though the revolution again began "eating" some of its "smaller" children.

It was not until the party's seventh Central Committee held its fourth plenary session in February, 1954, that the first of Mr. Mao's close "comrades in arms" met his downfall as a member of the Peiping regime.

The outcome of the fourth plenary session was disclosed this week by the Central Committee in an announcement that a recent national party conference had endorsed a decision to expel Kao Kang and Jao Shu-shih from the Chinese Communist party.

In passing, almost as a by-the-way, the committee statement said Mr. Kao had "committed suicide" after having received a "serious warning" at the 1954 meeting and having refused to admit his guilt."

Disciplinary action was also taken against seven other party men, according to the announcement. But the important persons purged were Messrs. Kao and Jao. The present condition of Mr. Jao was not disclosed.

Leading Figures

Neither was an ordinary Communist. Both were members of the party's Central Committee, and more.

Both were accused of having tried to "split the party." More to the point, they were accused by hearing conducted a "conspiracy" to reorganize Mr. Mao's Central Committee and make Mr. Kao the No. 2 man in the party and Premier of the State Council.

Mr. Kao was said to have argued that the army had created the party and that he represented "the party of the revolutionary bases and the army" as opposed to those representing "the party of the white areas." The latter reference may have been to party men who supervised underground work and conducted negotiations in the Nationalist cities eventually seized by the Red Army.

There is testimony from only one side as to whether Mr. Kao actually tried to supersede the party Secretary General, Liu Shao-chi (the underground specialist), and succeed Premier Chou En-lai (the negotiator) in a move threatening Mr. Mao himself. But there is no question he lost favor with the men who, after his purge, continue to run Communist China.

As Communist China is now organized politically, the sovereign power resides theoretically in the National People's Congress. This body functions under a constitution that was adopted by the first National Congress of 1,226 delegates last September.

The National Congress is chosen by indirect and controlled elections, mainly on the basis of geographical representation, for a four-year term. It elects, or more exactly, endorses, the top executive officers of the state.

These are the Chairman of the Republic, Vice Chairman, Chairman of the People's Congress Standing Committee, Premier of the State Council, President of the Supreme Court and chief procurator (prosecutor).

At the national executive level, the Chairman is the chief of state, commander in chief of the armed forces and head of the National Defense Council.

Day-to-day Government administration is in the hands of the swollen State Council, with its Premier, ten Deputy Premiers, eight general offices and thirty-five ministries and commissions. But the People's Congress Standing Committee, with the Communist party Secretary General as its present chairman, supervises the work of the State Council, Supreme Court and procurator.

Fundamental and decisive power in this over-all set-up is wielded by the leaders of the Chinese Communist party.

The Real Chiefs

Although the Chinese Communist Central Committee is supposed to be the party's "leading body," the real party power is wielded by Mr. Mao and his present twelve associates on the Politbureau. The power becomes even more concentrated in the party's five-man Secretariat, which consists of the five leading members of the Politiburo—an inner circle within an inner circle.

The Secretariat consists of Mr. Mao, Chairman of the state and party; Mr. Liu, chairman of the People's Congress Standing Committee and Secretary General of the party; Mr. Chou, Premier and Foreign Minister in the State Council; Gen. Chu Teh, Vice Chairman of the state and council and former commander of the Communist Army, and Chen Yun, an economic specialist now concerning himself primarily with the five-year plan while holding a concurrent Government post as a Deputy Premier.

The leader of the party since 1935, the shrewd, lumbering Mr. Mao—with an impressive record and enormous prestige—is still Number 1 man in Communist China. If it is true, as reported, that Mr. Chen is "Chou En-lai's man," then there may well be a fairly fine balance in the Secretariat.

Mr. Liu, a stolid, methodical man who comes from Hunan, the same province as Mr. Mao, could hardly have remained as Secretary General of a party headed by the latter if he were not fully trusted. Thus it is possible that 68-year-old General Chu, a weatherbeaten old warhorse and constitutional heir apparent on the Government side, is the balance wheel in the party Secretariat.

If anything should happen to Mr. Mao, now 61 and sometimes ailing, Messrs. Liu and Chou could become the leading contenders for party power. Although General Chu is in line for direct succession to the state chairmanship, Messrs. Liu and Chou are at present Communist China's outstanding figures, after Mr. Mao.

No Basic Disruption

It is not believed likely here that the Kao-Jao purge has basically disrupted the party or essentially affected Peiping's relations with Moscow. But the incident highlights the continu-

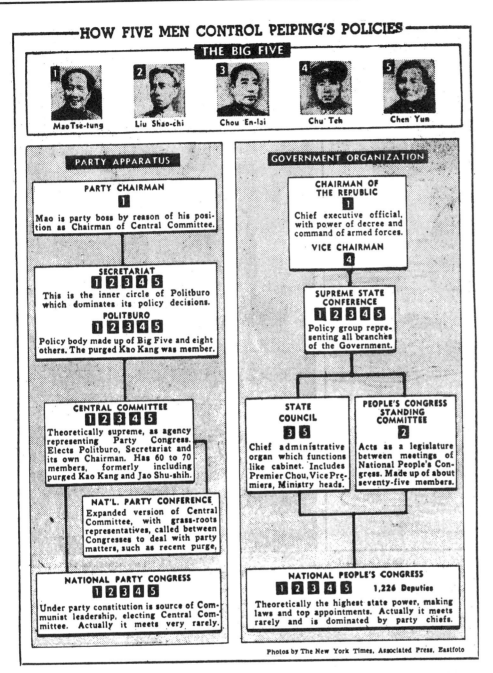

HOW FIVE MEN CONTROL PEIPING'S POLICIES

THE BIG FIVE

1 Mao Tse-tung 2 Liu Shao-chi 3 Chou En-lai 4 Chu Teh 5 Chen Yun

PARTY APPARATUS

PARTY CHAIRMAN 1
Mao is party boss by reason of his position as Chairman of Central Committee.

SECRETARIAT 1 2 3 4 5
This is the inner circle of Politburo which dominates its policy decisions.

POLITBURO 1 2 3 4 5
Policy body made up of Big Five and eight others. The purged Kao Kang was member.

CENTRAL COMMITTEE 1 2 3 4 5
Theoretically supreme, as agency representing Party Congress. Elects Politburo, Secretariat and its own Chairman. Has 60 to 70 members, formerly including purged Kao Kang and Jao Shu-shih.

NAT'L PARTY CONFERENCE
Expanded version of Central Committee, with grass-roots representatives, called between Congresses to deal with party matters, such as recent purge.

NATIONAL PARTY CONGRESS 1 2 3 4 5
Under party constitution is source of Communist leadership, electing Central Committee. Actually it meets very rarely.

GOVERNMENT ORGANIZATION

CHAIRMAN OF THE REPUBLIC 1
Chief executive official, with power of decree and command of armed forces.

VICE CHAIRMAN 4

SUPREME STATE CONFERENCE 1 2 3 4 5
Policy group representing all branches of the Government.

STATE COUNCIL 3 5
Chief administrative organ which functions like cabinet. Includes Premier Chou, Vice Premiers, Ministry heads.

PEOPLE'S CONGRESS STANDING COMMITTEE 2
Acts as a legislature between meetings of National People's Congress. Made up of about seventy-five members.

NATIONAL PEOPLE'S CONGRESS 1 2 3 4 5   1,226 Deputies
Theoretically the highest state power, making laws and top appointments. Actually it meets rarely and is dominated by party chiefs.

Photos by The New York Times, Associated Press, Eastfoto

ing possibilities of friction within a jungle of Communist politics that extends beyond the confines of the party's Secretariat.

Not all Chinese Communists may take the Central Committee at its word that Mr. Kao "committed suicide." If nothing else, this purge has probably intensified the suspicions and thickened the atmosphere of fear within the party.

Discipline Tightened

The Central Committee says the party is unified as never before now that the Kao-Jao "conspiracy" has been "crushed."

Nevertheless, it has set up a new system of control committees to tighten party discipline from the top down.

In pursuing an aggressive foreign policy while carrying out a program of forced industrialization and rural collectivization, the Chinese Communists do not seem to be making things easy on themselves.

The Peiping regime expects lagging farm production to be increased by means of the growing number of land-pooling cooperatives. But what if, despite Peiping's hopes, the cooperatives

—lacking sufficient incentive—do not provide enough farm produce to keep up with the industrialization program?

Amid the economic stringency, the rate of socialization and the foreign policy could become explosive issues in the party unless the official policy brings results.

While cracking down on Messrs. Kao and Jao at its February, 1954, meeting the Central Committee adopted a resolution that foresaw a "complex and acute struggle" during industrialization. The "struggle" is apt to go on inside the party ranks as well as in China's massive population.

April 10, 1955

By The Associated Press.
SAN FRANCISCO, Sept. 2—The Chinese Communists vowed today to "liberate" Tibet.

Noting that Tibet's priestly rulers had expelled the Chinese Nationalist mission July 9, the Communist radio charged that this was at "the instigation of British and American imperialists and their stooge, the Indian Nehru Government."

It was all right to kick out the Nationalists, said the Peiping broadcast, heard in San Francisco by The Associated Press, but it was the Communists' privilege to do so.

Insisting that Tibet was an integral part of China, the Communists said they intended to "liberate all Chinese territory, including Tibet, Sinkiang, Hainan Island and Taiwan (Formosa) and will not permit a single inch of territory to remain outside the rule of the Chinese Peoples Republic."

September 3, 1949

ADVANCE ON TIBET ORDERED BY PEIPING

Red Chinese Broadcast Quotes a Mobilization Directive Issued to Army Units

TOKYO, Wednesday, Oct. 25 (Æ)—The Peiping radio today said Chinese Communist troops were "advancing toward Tibet."

The broadcast, monitored in Tokyo, quoted "salutes" to the "People's Army advancing toward Tibet" issued jointly by the Southwest China bureau of the Communist Party in China, the Southwest military area, and the headquarters of the Second Field Army.

The Communist radio said a political mobilization directive had been issued to "People's Army units which have been ordered to advance into Tibet to free 3,000,000 Tibetans from imperialist oppression and to consolidate national defenses of the western borders of China."

[In Washington, Defense Department and other Government officials said no word had been received here of such an invasion move as was reported by the Peiping broadcast.]

The radio said the directive had told the Chinese Communist Army that the building up of Tibet would be a long-term project. It said soldiers "must make up their minds accordingly. They must economize in manpower and material during the advance and speedily build bridges to develop communications."

The broadcast continued:

"Every effort must be made to enhance the economic and cultural development of Tibet as soon as hostilities come to an end."

Tibetan Group to Go to Peiping

Special to THE NEW YORK TIMES.

NEW DELHI, India, Oct. 24—Fateful negotiations on the future relationship of Tibet to Communist China will be held in Peiping shortly between representatives of two governments.

The Tibetan delegation of seven that came here to meet the new Chinese Ambassador to India, Gen. Yuan Chung-hsien will leave for Kalimpong tomorrow and then proceed to Peiping via Hong Kong, a spokesman said tonight. The British will grant facilities for the Tibetans to pass through Hong Kong after having denied visas to the group last summer.

The Indian Government had hoped that the status of Tibet would be settled here, but General Yuan merely recommended that the Lhasa representatives go to Peiping. Permission for the journey has now been obtained from Lhasa.

Under the convention initiated at Simla, India, in 1914 but later repudiated by the Chinese Government of that day, Chinese suzerainty over all of Tibet had been recognized, but China had engaged not to attempt to convert the Trans-Himalayan state into a Chinese province. India still recognizes China's suzerainty—as distinct from sovereignty—and has suggested to the Peiping Government that Tibet's internal autonomy be respected.

As a result of China's failure to ratify the Simla Convention, Tibet

has never conceded any Chinese claim and has continued to assert her complete independence. Rumors of a Communist Chinese invasion of the country have been authoritatively denied here on the basis of first-hand reports from both Lhasa and Peiping, although minor border incidents have been acknowledged.

The visit of the Tibetans to Peiping is a development that Britain took great pains to avoid when the tripartite meeting of Chinese, Tibetans and British Indian Government representatives was arranged at Simla thirty-seven years ago. At that time, Britain regarded the high Tibetan plateau as an essential insulation between India and expanding China.

The British were determined not to allow the inexperienced Tibetans to venture into the "lion's den" by attending a conference that China had proposed should be held in Peking and they arranged that the meeting be held in British India instead.

The Indian Government is understood to be worried about the Tibet talks. Their outcome may be an expansion of Chinese power on the borders of India.

This would expose India to a new juxtaposition of spheres of influence that had previously been prevented by the intervention of buffer states, such as autonomous Tibet, sovereign Nepal and the semi-independent principalities of Sikkim and Bhutan.

In the context of today's political alignments, the extension of Chinese power to the Himalayan range might be tantamount to placing the Soviet Union cheek to cheek with India, although India's Prime Minister Jawaharlal Nehru takes the position that China will never submit to Soviet domination.

October 25, 1950

CHINESE REDS PUSH NEARER TIBET'S CAPITAL

The New York Times
Nov. 7, 1950

Communist soldiers were reported at Reting (A) in their drive on Lhasa and were said to be advancing on Gartok (B).

supply has continued until lately.

It is believed Peiping may make this fact the basis for a complaint against India of intervention of the Chinese sphere. India recognizes China's suzerainty over Tibet, while insisting that the internal autonomy of the Dalai Lama's realm be honored in accordance with the 1914 agreement between China, Tibet and British India.

In the second note to Peiping, India specified that the present Indian garrisons would remain at Gyantse and Yatung. Firm rejection of this proposal would be in keeping with the character of the Chinese Communist Government, as revealed in its surprisingly curt previous démarche to New Delhi

It is understood that India has about 300 soldiers garrisoned in Tibet in accordance with the agreement of 1906 to protect caravan routes, and maintain post and telegraph offices. India maintains a political officer at Lhasa and trade missions at Yatung and Gyantse, and it is proposed that these also remain.

There is speculation also that Indian trade agencies will be ordered out and that India's future connection with a conquered Tibet will be through a consular office.

The India News Agency, reporting a broadcast heard in Kalimpong, near the border of Tibet, said Peiping had asserted that the presence of Indian troops no longer was necessary as Tibet had become the "sole concern and responsibility of China."

The same agency, on the basis of reports in Kalimpong's Tibetan colony, put the invading Communist forces at Reting, sixty miles

northeast of Lhasa. Traveling over hard-packed and relatively level roads they were expected to reach the forbidden capital of the Living Buddha in three days, the agency said.

The advancing forces were said to be composed of the Chinese Second Field Army under one-eyed Gen. Liu Po-cheng and the Tibetan "People's Liberation Army" led nominally by the 13-year-old Panchen Lama, the "incarnate Buddha" whose religious standing seriously competes with that of Dalai Lama, priest-king of Tibet.

Trade Mission Leaves

Correspondents in the rumor factory of Kalimpong said that after the fall of Lho Dzong to the Chinese, the Tibetan defenders had withdrawn to Pembargo, also called Pemba Dzong, leaving the town of Shobando undefended.

Kalimpong also heard that Chinese from Sinkiang Province were advancing on Gartok in Western Tibet. It is understood that the Indian trade mission in Gartok has left. This, coupled with the departure of the Indian consul from Kashgar, in Sinkiang, China, is held as indicating at least a partial Indian withdrawal from territories acknowledged to be Soviet-controlled.

It also was reported in Kalimpong that two Britons, believed to be missionaries, had been captured by the Chinese forces.

Intelligence available here indicates that the masses of Tibetans, having known only exploitation by the Lamaistic Government, are willing, without reservation, to aid the Communists, since from their viewpoint no change can be worse than the present regime.

November 7, 1950

PEIPING ASKS INDIA TO END TIBET GUARD

By ROBERT TRUMBULL

Special to THE NEW YORK TIMES.

NEW DELHI, India, Nov. 6 — With invading Chinese Communist troops and pro-Communist Tibetan forces reported sixty miles, or seventy-two hours, from Lhasa, the Peiping Government has demanded that India withdraw troops stationed in Tibet to protect trade routes and maintain communications. This was reported in a Peiping radio broadcast heard in Kalimpong.

Indian sources had no comment

tonight on the broadcast and declined to confirm reports that a new note had been received from China. But it is said that such a demand was an obvious one for Peiping to make. It would be in line with the tone taken in the stiff rejection by Chou En-lai, Chinese Communist Foreign Minister, of India's first note objecting to the Chinese invasion of the autonomous Himalayan state.

This demand also would be the expected reply to India's second note, to which no reply had been announced here up to tonight.

Reports circulating in New Delhi said that China had accused India of supplying arms to Tibet's weak army of 10,000. Tibet obtained rifles and ammunition from India in the past by agreement and this

U.N. GROUP SHELVES DISCUSSION OF TIBET

Action Taken After India Says She Is Convinced Peaceful Settlement May Come

By A. M. ROSENTHAL
Special to THE NEW YORK TIMES.

LAKE SUCCESS, Nov. 24—United Nations action on the Tibet case was postponed indefinitely today after delegates heard India say she was convinced that a peaceful settlement could be reached between the Chinese Communists and the Tibetan Government.

The General or Steering Committee of the General Assembly decided unanimously to put off a decision on whether or not to recommend that the Assembly itself take up the Chinese Communists' march into Tibet. The request for debate had been put forward by El Salvador.

The United States, which always has voted in favor of full debate of every item put before the Assembly, went along with the move for postponement. Ernest Gross, United States delegate, made it plain that his country was taking the position that India, as the country most directly involved, should be allowed to take the lead.

India's delegate to the committee is the president of the Administrative and Budgetary Committee and is listed in protocol books as Lieut. Gen. His Highness the Maharajah Jam Saheb of Nawanagar, Rajpramukh of Saurashtra.

The Maharajah told the committee his country was more inter-ested in a friendly settlement of the dispute over Tibet than any other country. He went on:

"In the Peiping Government's latest note to India the People's Republic of China said that it had not given up hope of a peaceful settlement."

The Indian delegate said that the Chinese Communist march into Tibet apparently had come to a halt some 300 miles from the capital city of Lhasa. India, he declared, was convinced even now of the possibility of a peaceful settlement that would protect the autonomy of Tibet and take into consideration the country's traditional relations with China.

Dr. Hector David Castro, who had presented the case for Assembly debate on behalf of El Salvador, said the fact of a Chinese Communist invasion had been reported in the press of the world.

The Chinese delegate, Liu Chieh, did not object to postponement, but said the Tibet case was another facet of the "Soviet design on China," and should be studied in the Interim Committee, or Little Assembly, as part of Nationalist China's complaint that the Soviet Union had violated its treaties with China and was threatening Far Eastern peace.

For the Soviet Union, Jacob A. Malik insisted that Tibet was an integral part of China. He said the whole case involved Chinese domestic jurisdiction and was none of the United Nations' business.

In a move to speed the work of the Assembly the Steering Committee removed two items from the agenda of the Special Political Committee and shifted them to the work load of the Political and Security Committee. The items are the internationalization of Jerusalem and the Soviet Union's charge that United States planes have violated Chinese air space.

November 25, 1950

4-Month Tibet War Ended By Chinese Red Assurance

Apathy of the Dalai Lama's People Held Factor in Peiping's Victory

By ROBERT TRUMBULL
Special to THE NEW YORK TIMES

NEW DELHI, India, March 8—A simple promise by the Mao Tsetung Government to the Dalai Lama of internal autonomy in Tibet while the Chinese Communists take over the frontier patrol of the Himalayan state apparently has ended the four-and-a-half-month-old war in the realm of the Living Buddha with victory for Communist China without a single real battle, according to authoritative Tibetan sources in Kalimpong, Indian town on the Tibetan border.

They said a letter brought to the Dalai Lama's provisional capital at Yatung, near the Indian border, by a Tibetan courier from the Red Chinese Embassy in New Delhi last month "regretted the misunderstanding" between China and Tibet, and assured the Living Buddha that all Peiping wanted was "to secure the Tibetan frontier in order to protect Chinese territorial integrity."

The letter was said to have congratulated the 15-year-old Dalai Lama upon his assumption of full ruling powers two years before his legal majority and to have assured him that his authority in Tibet would be undiminished. He was invited to send representatives to Peiping immediately at the Mao Government's expense.

The letter was said to have been carried to Yatung from New Delhi by Dzasa Surkhang, who had been appointed to head Tibet's delegation to the United Nations protesting the Chinese Communist invasion in October.

On basis of the letter, the Dalai Lama is said to have reached a decision to send his Army commander in chief, Kunsang Sey, and a high-ranking monk to Peiping for negotiations. At the same time, it was reported that another Tibetan peace delegation, sent from Chamdo in Eastern Tibet and led by Rimshi Samdophotang, had reached Tatsienlu in Szechwan, China, and was proceeding by air to Peiping.

The two delegations are to meet in Peiping and conclude a Chinese-Tibetan pact conceding defense and foreign affairs to Communist China, while guaranteeing the integrity of the ancient monkish rule inside the country, the sources said. The probability of such an eventuality is confirmed by other reports that the previous Tibetan delegation to Peiping was being returned to Lhasa under the Dalai Lama's terrifying displeasure for not having completed its mission before the invasion took place.

To observers of Tibetan affairs, it appears likely that the Chinese Communist guarantee of the monks' absolute authority and privileges of taxation over 5,000,-000 devout subjects would be sufficient to wring from them the concessions that Peiping wants. It is improbable that the unsophisticated Tibetan officials will be inclined to question Red China's good faith in the face of such powerful and immediate inducement, especially since Tibet has virtually no military resources for resistance, and the population is apathetic.

Travelers from Tibet have been reporting for a long time that the rulers of the sparsely populated Himalayan state could place no dependence upon their people to stand by the ancient and oppressive theocratic rule against promises that Communists could make.

Significantly, the mission sent to Peiping from Chamdo, an important Tibetan fortress captured by the Reds in the initial onslaught, was said before proceeding to Tachienly to have made contact with the Tibetan chieftain of Eastern Tibet, who had gone over to the Communists. This personage is the father-in-law of the leader of the delegation.

It is important to realize that these worldly political maneuverings are distinctly interwoven with the strange Eastern religion in Tibet. Immediately upon making these momentous decisions, the Dalai Lama and his two leading tutors, Lingtu Tsang and Trichang Rimpoche, entered upon sacred rites of guidance and hope involving thousands of inhabitants of the beautiful Chumbi Valley, site of the Living Buddha's provisional capital.

March 9, 1951

TIBET MERGED IN RED CHINA

By HENRY R. LIEBERMAN
Special to THE NEW YORK TIMES.

HONG KONG, May 27—The Chinese Communists announced tonight they had achieved the "peaceful liberation" of Tibet through a political settlement that plants the five-starred Red flag of the Chinese People's Republic on the "roof of the world" overlooking India and Pakistan.

According to the Peiping radio, Tibetan authorities have finally agreed to end resistance and incorporate the theocratic Tibetan state into the structure of Communist China. This completes the Communists' conquest of the Chinese mainland, leaving the island of Formosa the only major Chinese territorial unit still outside their hands.

Tibet, with a population of 3,-000,000 or more, was brought under Chinese Communist control in a seventeen-point agreement signed in Peiping on May 23. Representatives of three Tibetan camps negotiated in Peiping late last month.

These included the Dalai Lama's group at Lhasa, the rival Chinese-sponsored clique of the Panchen Lama at Kumbum Lamasery in Tsinghai Province and the Communist-sponsored People's Government for the Autonomous Tibetan area, which was established at Kangting in Sikang Province last November. Although the Tibetan people were assured the right to rule themselves under the National Government's leadership, the Lhasa regime relinquished its power under the provisions specifying that Tibet must:

1. Unite with Communist China to oust "imperialist influence."
2. Permit the "People's Liberation Army" to enter to "strengthen national defense."
3. Yield control over its foreign relations to the Central Government.
4. Make its own troops available for gradual reorganization and absorption by the People's Liberation Army.
5. Allow the Central Government to establish a military command and a political and military affairs commission in Tibet to implement the settlement.

On the other hand, the Peiping regime promised to preserve Tibet's political institutions, maintain the present position of the young Dalai Lama, protect religious freedom, refrain from altering receipts of the temples, undertake a development program and permit the local rather than the Central Government to carry out "reforms." It promised further to let the old officials carry on provided they severed "pro-imperialist and pro-Kuomintang" ties and refrained from "sabotage and counter-revolution."

At the same time, it called for a return to Tibet of the Panchen Lama, who had been living under Chinese protection at the Kumbum Lamasery in northwest China. The reincarnate form of the Panchen Lama has been absent from Tibet since the early Nineteen Twenties as a consequence of a long-standing feud between the rival Lama cliques. The present incumbent, a boy of about fourteen, has never been in Tibet.

The Dalai Lama often has been represented as the temporal and the Panchen Lama as the spiritual ruler of the Tibetans. But the theoretical line of division has been obliterated by the power struggle of the Lama cliques clustered around them. The preceding Panchen Lama who died in China in 1937 left Tibet in 1923 in a dispute that involved the extent of his temporal control over the estates of the Tashilunpo Lamasery and financial contributions to Lhasa.

According to the Peiping radio, the present young Panchen Lama who is now in Peiping, celebrated his restoration by presenting gifts to high ranking government officials. Chairman Mao Tse-tung was said to have received a solid gold shield bearing his portrait.

The Lhasa regime was represented in the Peiping talk by Dzasak Khemeypa, a former Commander-in-Chief of the Tibetan Army, and Khentiung Thupten Tenthar, secretary to the Dalai Lama. The official head of the mixed Tibetan delegation, however, was Sawang Ngabo, who commanded the Tibetan troops that yielded after a brief encounter with the Chinese Communists at Chamdo last October.

Five Tibetans were said to have signed the Peiping agreement. The four negotiators who signed for the Chinese Central Government were headed by Li Wei-han, Cabinet Secretary General and chairman of the Minority Affairs Commission

May 28, 1951

RULE OF MINORITIES CHARTED IN PEIPING

Autonomous Regions' Planned for 40,000,000 'Non-Hans' With Some Self-Rule

By HENRY R. LIEBERMAN
Special to THE NEW YORK TIMES.

HONG KONG, Aug. 14—An outline for the establishment of three types of "autonomous regions" has been adopted by the Peiping Government as a blueprint for governing the basic concentrations of the 40,000,000 persons classified in China as belonging to the "non-Han" national minorities.

The official Hsinhua News Agency said today the outline was promulgated by Mao Tse-tung, chairman of the Central People's Government of the People's Republic of China, Aug. 9, following its approval by the Central People's Government Council. It authorized the creation of minority "autonomous regions" from the village level up, depending on the number of people and size of the area involved.

Based on the principles of the Common Program, Red China's fundamental law, the outline guarantees minorities the use of their national language, gives them certain powers of self-rule subject to central state policy and forbids "racial discrimination and oppression."

Based on Soviet Program

The minorities program is an adaptation of that introduced by Premier Stalin in the Soviet Union. Tibet, Sinkiang and Inner Mongolia are regarded as providing a basis for the eventual establishment of Soviet-style national republics. However, the nationality program has not yet been carried to that point in China.

The three types of "autonomous regions" specified in the blueprint include: (1) Those restricted to one minority group, (2) Those dominated by one group but also including other minorities, and (3) Those set up jointly by two or more minorities.

Culturally, more than 90 per cent of China's population consists of Han Chinese. National minorities, who live mainly along the periphery of China proper, embrace Mohammedans of various racial origins, Mongols, Tibetans, Koreans and such tribal groups as Yaos, Yis, Miaos, and Lolos.

May Include Chinese

The minorities outline, which includes forty articles, provides that various "autonomous regions" may encompass the Chinese section "in accordance with local, economic and political needs and historic conditions." Where the Chinese are numerous, however, it was stipulated that a "democratic united government" should be set up.

As is the case throughout China, the "People's Representatives Conference" was defined as the basic grass roots assembly for the "autonomous regions." Such conferences, whose members are sometimes elected, sometimes appointed, are normally convoked to establish an "autonomous government" and select its chairman and commissioners.

The "autonomous regions" are authorized by outline to develop their indigenous culture, administer their own finances, promote their own enterprises and organize their own security and militia units. All these activities, however, must conform with Central State policies and planning.

Subject to Higher Bodies

The "autonomous governments" are empowered to enact "unilateral regulations" for their areas but these must be submitted to superior organs for approval. Meanwhile, the superior organs have been urged to promote attitudes of "racial equality, friendship, solidarity and mutual aid" and to combat "inclinations toward jingoistic nationalism."

Thus far, according to Chinese Communist figures, 130 "autonomous regions" have been set up in areas inhabited by 4,500,000 people. The largest is the "Inner Mongolia Autonomous Area."

August 15, 1952

PEIPING PROMISES TIBET 'AUTONOMY'

Special to The New York Times.

HONG KONG, March 12—The Dalai Lama has been named head of a preparatory committee for establishing an expanded "Tibet autonomous region" within Red China's national framework.

The Panchen Lama, the co-ruler, has been appointed first vice chairman of the committee. The second vice chairman is Gen. Chang Kuo-hua, Chinese commander of the Tibet military district.

Formation of the committee was announced by the Hsinhua (New China) News Agency tonight as the young high Lamas, 20 and 17 years old, respectively, left Peiping on their way back to Tibet. The former political rivals for the religious leadership have been away from Tibet for six months. They arrived in Peiping last September as delegates to the National People's Congress.

While in Red China's capital they paid tribute to Mao Tse-tung and his Communist-ruled Central Government. They also made various statements endorsing Mr. Mao's policy of "unity" among China's "fraternal nationalities."

According to the Chinese Communist news agency, the preparatory committee for setting up the "Tibet autonomous region" will have the status of a state organ subordinate to the Central State Council headed by Premier Chou En-lai. The regional committee, it was said, consists of fifty-one members.

The committee's "main task," the dispatch said, will be to "prepare for regional autonomy in Tibet."

Meanwhile, the agency disclosed that rival groups backing the Dalai Lama and the Panchen Lama reached an agreement Jan. 19 on their "historic and unsettled problems."

The late predecessor of the present Panchen Lama left Tibet in the early Twenties following a series of internal feuds there. It was not until June, 1952, that the present Panchen returned to Shigatse, the center of the Panchen Lama's traditional stronghold in Tibet. Before then the young Panchen and his entourage had lived under Chinese sponsorship at the Kumbum Monastery in Tsinghai Province.

The Hsinhua agency said the State Council in Peiping had approved the agreement between the Dalai Lama and Panchen Lama groups.

In addition, the agency reported, the State Council decided to:

¶Extend the Tsinghai-Tibet highway to Shigatse, the second largest town of Tibet, and build a road from Shigatse southeast to Gyangtse.

¶Establish a Tibet transport bureau at Lhasa with subadministrative units for the Sikang-Tibet and Tsinghai-Tibet highways.

¶Build a hydroelectric station in Lhasa, set up a smaller thermopower plant at Shigatse and dispatch technicians to study conditions for building a hydroelectric plant at the latter place.

¶Establish a leather works and small iron works at Lhasa.

¶Repair and build dikes and dams to protect Lhasa and Shigatse from floods, expand the school systems at both places and improve an experimental farm at Lhasa.

Earlier 'Autonomous Region'

It was announced that the new preparatory committee for establishing a "Tibet autonomous region" would have two subcommittees for financial-economic affairs and religious affairs and ten departments. The departments will deal with: civil affairs, finance, construction, culture and education, health, public security, agriculture and afforestation, animal husbandry, industry and commerce and communications.

This is not the first "Tibet autonomous region" created by the Peiping regime. On Nov. 24 1950, a "Tibetan autonomous region government" was established at Kangting in China's Sikang Province.

The arrangements for setting up the new regional state organ for Tibet were officially said to encompass the "local government of Tibet, the Panchen Kanpo Lija and the People's Liberation Committee of the Chamdo area." An earlier Chinese Communist dispatch from Lhasa referred to the Panchen Kanpo Lija as the Panchen Lama's "former ecclesiastical and secular institution." Chamdo (Changtu) is about 380 miles northeast of Lhasa.

The Peiping announcement said the fifty-one members of the prepatory committee would include fifteen representatives of the "Tibet local government," ten of the Panchen Kanpo Lija, ten of the "People's Liberation Committee in the Chamdo area" five from among the Central Government personnel in Tibet and eleven from "major monasteries, religious sects and people's organizations."

The Peiping radio said 800 persons, including three Vice Premiers, were at the railway station to see the Tibetan Lamas off today.

The broadcast said the Dalai Lama and his party would visit in northwest and southwest China en route to Lhasa. It added the Panchen Lama's entourage would visit east and south China before returning to Tibet.

March 13, 1955

SINKIANG PROVINCE JOINS RED CHINA

By TILLMAN DURDIN
Special to The New York Times.

HONG KONG, Sept. 28—The Sinkiang Provincial Government has formally announced Sinkiang's adherence to the Communist Chinese regime.

More than thirty Sinkiang leaders were reported to have signed a manifesto proclaiming their support of the Chinese People's Consultative Council now in session in Peiping and their opposition to the Kuomintang.

All Nationalist officials were said to have been ordered to leave Sinkiang. Martial law was reported to have been declared in Urumchi, the provincial capital. Reports say there has been no bloodshed so far in Sinkiang and that two Nationalist armies that have been garrisoning parts of the province have withdrawn to the eastern borders.

Actually, Sinkiang has been virtually written off ever since the Communists captured Lanchow and Sining.

The Central Government's hold on the province has been shaky ever since Gen. Sheng Shih-tsai subordinated his regime to the Chungking Government in 1943 and enabled China to resume her sovereign status over Sinkiang. General Sheng for years had been a tyrannical, pro-Soviet dictator.

A succession of Governors followed General Sheng's removal by Chungking, with each regime proving unable to stem elements in the province that wanted to shake off Nationalist rule and establish an autonomous status oriented toward the Soviet Union. A rebellion by the Turki faction centered in the three northwestern districts of the province set up a regime virtually independent of the National Government in 1947, despite extensive concessions to provincial separatism conceded by Gen. Chang Chin-chung, the Central Government's plenipotentiary.

This so-called Ili regime, led by pro-Soviet Turkis, has maintained a close political and economic connection with the Soviet Union.

Less than 5 per cent of the population of Sinkiang is Chinese. Various Turki tribes of the province have been strongly anti-Chinese since the days of the original bloody conquests in that area by imperial China. Some observers here with a special knowledge of Sinkiang affairs still believe the Sinkiang people will not welcome even Communist Chinese rule and that the province may eventually attain a status of special autonomy closely oriented toward the Soviet Union where the racial kinfolk of the Sinkiang Turkis live.

September 29, 1949

PEIPING DEMANDS NEW PARTY PURGE

Struggle Against 'Decadent Elements' Is Asked in Official Newspaper

By HENRY R. LIEBERMAN
Special to The New York Times.

HONG KONG, May 12—A drive to purge "decadent elements" is developing among the rank and file of the Chinese Communist party.

The Peiping People's Daily, the party's leading newspaper, has called editorially for a "struggle" against such elements to "purify the ranks of the party."

Its editorial was circulated domestically yesterday by the Hsinhua (New China) news agency.

The Chinese Communist newspaper declared some party members had been "completely overcome by bourgeois concepts." It said the party had to be "ready to expose and criticize the effects of the bourgeois ways of life."

All party organizations were instructed to realize the significance of the drive against those who had headed for "deterioration and decadence." Party organizers were told to impose discipline on wayward members who refused to recant their mistakes.

The announced drive follows the March purge of the late Kao Kang, once regional boss in Manchuria, and Lieut. Gen. Jao Shu-shih, the party's former organizational chief. It was foreshadowed by the establishment of a new control committee at the national party conference that expelled the two along with seven lesser figures.

The Chinese Communists created the new control committees for the stated purpose of strengthening party discipline and combating "unwholesome trends." Their central control committee is headed by Tung Pi-wu, a politbureau member who is also president of Red China's Supreme Court.

As of February, 1954, the Chinese Communist party had a claimed membership of 6,500,000. In its latest "struggle" editorial, the People's Daily said the party could not prevent a few from going astray despite its indoctrination efforts on "Communist morality."

"There are some Communist party members who think the revolution is for their own personal happiness and so they wantonly demand enjoyment," the party newspaper declared.

"They must have the best houses, the newest cars and submit a huge account when they take a trip or call a meeting.

"Whether there is a need or not, they constantly welcome and send people off, entertain guests and spend lavishly, there being no sense of public or private affairs. They even spend state construction funds for outlays on personal welfare."

The Communist newspaper said some errant party members also tended to treat women as "playthings," resorting to "desertion, "beating" and "ignominious persecution." Such members were accused too of having been "tainted by bourgeois concepts.

May 13, 1955

PEIPING CUTS NUMBER OF PROVINCES TO 26

TOKYO, Monday, June 21 (AP) —Communist China is further centralizing her government "to suit the country's planned economic construction," the Peiping radio reported today.

Four provincial governments were eliminated and a regional level of government was abolished at the thirty-second session of the Government Council Saturday. As a result of the changes China lists twenty-six instead of thirty provinces, including Nationalist-held Formosa.

Abolished entirely were the administrative regions known as North, Northeast, Northwest, East, Central-South and Southwest China. Provinces formerly under them go directly under the Central Government.

In Northeast China, Liaotung and Liaosi Provinces will be merged into newly reconstituted Liaoning Province. Heilungkiang Province will absorb Sungkiang. In Northwest China, Kansu Province will take over Ningsia. Autonomous Inner Mongolia will absorb Suiyuan Province.

Eleven cities now administered by the Central Government were transferred to provincial administration, leaving only Peiping, Tientsin and Shanghai directly under national control.

China's Communists Set Up Regime North of the Yangtze

By The United Press

SHANGHAI, Monday, March 14—The Chinese Communists have established a regional Government for a three-Province area north of the Yangtze River, the Communist radio announced today. The area contains 50,000,000 persons.

The broadcast referred to the new set-up as the "Central Plains Provisional People's Government." It was believed that it might set the pattern for similar administrations over other territory under Communist control from the Yangtze to Manchuria.

The announcement said that the Government was formally set up on March 7 under a Government of twenty-one council members, elected by a "Provisional People's Congress" of eighty-one delegates at a four-day meeting.

The administrative area includes sections of Kiangsu, Anhwei and Honan provinces, large parts of which were overrun by the Reds in their two-month campaign now halted at the Yangtze River. The area lies between the Yangtze River and the east-west Lung-Hai Railroad.

The broadcast said that one of the twenty-one council members was Communist Gen. Liu Po-cheng.

Russian technicians are now overseeing the rehabilitation and production of the Fushun coal mines in southern Manchuria and are active in administration of the Chinese Changchun Railway (the former Chinese Eastern and South Manchurian Railways), a former Nationalist official in Mukden reported yesterday.

[Under the Chinese - Russian treaty of 1945, the Chinese Changchun rail system became the joint property of the Soviet Union and China, to be "jointly exploited by them." The Chinese agreed to supply the system with coal.]

The official, Chow Ching-shih, was secretary of the Northeast Commodity Regulation Bureau at Mukden under the Nationalist regime. He left Mukden on Feb. 7, reaching Shanghai after three weeks of traveling through Communist-held areas.

Mr. Chow said the Russians had made the Mukden Railway Hotel their residential headquarters. He could not give a detailed estimate of how many Soviet technicians were employed, but said a "great number" were helping to rebuild Manchurian industrial economy.

Mr. Chow confirmed earlier reports that the American consulate in Mukden under Consul General Angus Ward was virtually isolated under guard and that staff members of the British consulate had more freedom. He said there was no Soviet consulate at Mukden, only a commercial attache.

Reds Apply Pressure

NANKING, March 13 (UP)—New Premier Ho Ying-chin prepared to come here tomorrow from Hangchow to form a new Cabinet as ominous Communist troop movements north of the Yangtze River indicated that the Reds were ready to apply more pressure to force an early Government surrender.

Chinese reports today said that from three to five columns (from 60,000 to 100,000) of Communist Manchurian Commander Lin Piao's troops had arrived at the Suchow rail hub, 250 miles north of Nanking, where the main Government forces defending Nanking were defeated early this year.

Gen. Chang Chih-chung meanwhile told the Army organ Peace Daily today that President Chiang Kai-shek had no intention of leaving Chikow in the near future.

[Reuters reported from Nanking that President Chiang had left his home of Chikow, near Fenghwa, Chekiang, to live in retirement on the South China island of Kulangsu, according to authoritative but unconfirmed reports. These reports said that he left Chikow four days ago for Kulangsu, a former British possession off the port of Amoy.]

Peace Daily said that President Chiang had told General Chang that he was quitting politics for the next five years to give Acting President Li Tsung-jen a free hand.

It said that President Chiang talked "apologetically" of his previous political failures as result of which he did not intend to participate in politics again.

It said that President Chiang, as a member of the Revolutionary Government party, would continue to lead the Kuomintang in its revolutionary efforts and that he was paying close attention to party reforms strengthening party organization and reviving the party's revolutionary spirit.

The newspaper quoted General Chang as having said that President Chiang had gained eight pounds since his retirement and that his weight had increased from 118 to 126 pounds.

COMMUNISTS SET UP EAST CHINA REGIME

Regional Government Covers 5 Provinces and Formosa —Shanghai Is Capital

SAN FRANCISCO, Feb. 4 (AP)— The creation of a regional government embracing six East China provinces that include Shanghai and many other large cities was announced today by the Chinese Communists.

Included in the list was Formosa, Nationalist island stronghold which the Communists say they intend to capture this year.

Manchuria and Inner Mongolia have similar set-ups. And a northwest regional government was created Jan. 19 for the provinces of Shensi, Kansu, Ningsia, Tsinghai and Sinkiang.

Today's announcement by the Peiping radio was heard in San Francisco by The Associated Press. It said the new "East China People's Government" would "direct the work of the people's provincial governments of Shantung, Kiangsu, Anhwei, Chekiang, Fukien and Taiwan [Formosa]."

The population of the area was estimated by the Communists at 130,000,000. The area includes Shanghai, Nanking, Tsingtao, Foochow and other large centers.

The regional regime was said to have been set up in Shanghai Jan. 27, with Jao Shu-shih as chairman. He was political commissar of the Communist army that conquered much of the sphere he now rules.

TAIPEI, Formosa, Feb. 4 (AP)— China's Nationalists said today that the Communists had taken Fenghu Island, near the mainland seaport of Swatow, a possible base for an expected Communist invasion attempt against Formosa.

Fenghu is west of Namoa, a larger island used by the Nationalists to hamper the Communists' use of Swatow, opposite Formosa.

Continued Nationalist ground and air action was reported against Communist guerrillas on Hainan Island, which expects a Communist invasion attempt from the south mainland coast.

The Defense Ministry said that an attempt by the Hainan guerrillas to break out of the northwestern mountains to the coast had been thwarted. Total guerrilla strength in the area was put at 10,000.

On the mainland, the Ministry said, the Communists scored further advances in southern Yunnan, border province fronting Indo-China and Burma. It said that Nationalist forces had retreated into the mountains to carry on guerrilla warfare. This type of operation is the only one left to the Nationalists on the mainland.

February 5, 1950

CHINA TODAY OPENS POPULATION COUNT

Her First Census Since 1742 to Provide Data for Election of 'People's Congress'

By HENRY R. LIEBERMAN
Special to The New York Times.

HONG KONG, June 30—One of the most elusive basic statistics in the Far East—the exact size of China's tremendous population— may be established in the first comprehensive modern census taken in that country. The counting of heads in China is scheduled to begin tomorrow with all vital statistics being frozen for tabulation purposes as of midnight tonight.

The starting census date coincides with the thirty-second anniversary of the Chinese Communist party, which was organized in Shanghai July 1, 1921. Local statistical returns must be sent to Peiping, Red China's capital, before the end of October, a deadline that follows the fourth anniversary of the Communist-controlled Chinese People's Republic on Oct. 1.

No one knows just how many people there are in China. Judging by most past estimates and recent "land reform" figures, however, it would not be surprising if the new census revealed the Chinese Communists were now ruling 500,000,000 people—possibly more.

Census Needed for Election

As explained earlier by the Peiping radio, the census is being taken in preparation for the projected election of the "People's Congress" and also to provide the Government accurate population data for purposes of "economic and cultural construction." The elections, which are scheduled to be held on a national scale under the principle of universal suffrage, involve the establishment of an "All-China People's Congress" and a network of local "People's Congresses."

A National Census and Registration Office has been set up by the Ministry of the Interior to supervise collection of population statistics by a host of provincial, municipal, county and subcounty administrative units. The regulations require the head of every household to come to the election stations for registration purposes but also provide for house-to-house visits by a census taker wherever necessary.

The census workers have been instructed to watch out for "duplication or omission." A population count actually made on this basis would help to resolve many conflicting estimates on China's total population.

Figure Based on Estimates

Although China is generally acknowledged to have the largest population in the world, the 450,000,000 figure usually cited is based on an authoritative consensus rather than on ironclad statistical data. Population estimates in the last twenty years or so have ranged from 323,000,000 to 480,000,000 and even these disparate figures are outdated.

It has been estimated that China's population at the dawn of the Christian Era was about 55,000,000. The first recorded census taken during the reign of Emperor Chien Lung in 1742 provided a population figure of 143,411,559.

By 1945 the population was listed in the China Handbook [Nationalist] as 454,928,992 with the average size of family being 5.40 and males outnumbering females by 14.47 per cent. The 1952 "People's Handbook," which was published by the Shanghai newspaper Ta Kung Pao, cites a population figure of 486,571,237.

July 1, 1953

POPULATION OF CHINA PUT AT 582,603,000

Special to The New York Times.

HONG KONG, Nov. 1—After rechecking last year's census the National Bureau of Statistics in Peiping declared today mainland China's population, largest in the world, was 582,603,417, as of June 30, 1953.

A communiqué broadcast by the Peiping radio gave the total Chinese population as 601,938,035. This total includes 7,592,298 for Formosa and also 11,743,320 overseas Chinese.

The communiqué said 574,205,940 of the mainland population were counted in a census during last year's People's Congress elections. Local governments, it added, reported another 8,397,477 from remote places where no elections were held.

Of those counted by direct census, 51.82 per cent were said to be males. By age group, 58.92 per cent, the communiqué continued, were 18 and older.

The census takers were reported to have found 3,384 Chinese aged 100 or older. The communiqué listed 93.94 per cent of mainland population as Han (Chinese). The rest were classified as members of "national minority" groups.

The population figures given for the provinces of Liaoning, Kirin, and Hoilungkiang in Manchuria totaled 41,732,529. The Inner Mongolian autonomous area, the communiqué said, has a population of 6,100,104, and Jehol a population of 5,160,822. Szechwan, said to be inhabited by 62,303,999 persons, remains the most heavily populated province.

Urban population figures included 6,204,417 for Shanghai and 2,768,149 for Peiping.

November 2, 1954

MR. LOW ON THE CHINA RECOGNITION QUESTION

January 15, 1950

SOVIET RECOGNIZES CHINA RED REGIME; DROPS CHIANG LINK

By The Associated Press.

MOSCOW, Oct. 2—Russia today recognized the Central People's [Communist] Government of China.

The recognition was announced in a note to the Minister of Foreign Affairs of the new Chinese Communist Government from Soviet Deputy Foreign Minister Andrei A. Gromyko.

Russia also served formal notice that diplomatic relations had ceased to exist between Russia and the Chinese Government in Canton.

The Chinese Chargé d'Affaires said he had transmitted Mr. Gromyko's statement to Canton. "In the meantime," he said, "we are staying on here awaiting instructions."

The Chargé d'Affaires said he had been asked earlier in the day to come to the Soviet Foreign Ministry, where he received the Soviet declaration.

Diplomatic Colony Gets News

News of the recognition reached Moscow's diplomatic colony when most of its members were assembled at Spasso House, the home of United States Ambassador Alan G. Kirk, attending a movie. The picture was forgotten in the face of the news.

The next formal step in recognition by the Soviet Union is the exchange of ambassadors between the Central People's Government and the U. S. S. R. Each country must submit the name of an ambassador-designate to the other before the envoys are accepted.

Other countries may recognize the Central People's Government. It is assumed in diplomatic circles here that when this has been done, the Communist Government will ask the United Nations to recognize it as the Government of China

Soviet Press Hails Regime

By HARRISON E. SALISBURY

Special to THE NEW YORK TIMES.

MOSCOW, Oct. 2—The Soviet press today editorially greeted the formation of the new Central Chinese Government.

Almost half of the Soviet press was dedicated to the news of the establishment of the new Chinese Republic, which was hailed by Soviet Historian Eugene Tarle in Izvestia as one of the two "stupendous events" of the year—the other being the "world failure of United States calculations upon atomic monopoly."

The first page of Soviet central newspapers usually is confined largely to domestic news. Today, however, the Soviet press published on its first page the text of the declaration by Mao Tze-tung, in which he said the Central People's Government was the only legitimate government representing all of the Chinese people and asserted that "this government is ready to establish diplomatic relations with any foreign government which is prepared to observe the principles of equality, mutual benefit and mutual respect of territorial integrity and sovereignty."

To Mr. Mao's declaration was appended the text of a brief note from Foreign Minister Chou En-lai to Soviet Consul General S. Tikvinsky at Peiping, forwarding Mr. Mao's declaration.

"American Bosses" Hit

The leading Tadjik poet, Mirzo Tursunsade, wrote in Izvestia: "Now in the East there is not a single country where the banner of struggle will not gleam red, where toilers will not be inspired by the example of the peoples of the Soviet Union. The struggle for independence and national sovereignty, for reorganization of the world has begun to burn brightly over the whole East."

He recalled the words of the famous Indian poet, Rabindranath Tagore, who said, "The tighter are the chains, the quicker they will fall off," and added that "the victory of the Chinese people over the Kuomintang regime and its American bosses is the victory of all peoples in the struggle for peace."

The newspaper Bolshevik declared that "many millions of masses in the colonies and dependent countries are drawn into the movement for peace. The majestic success of the Chinese people, which under the guidance of the Communist party conducts the heroic struggle for the complete rout of the Kuomintang reaction, breaks down the plans of the warmongers in the East and weakens the general front of imperialism."

The editorial noted that the basic principle of the new Chinese state was the support of a stable peace, friendly collaboration and the struggle against imperialism, aggression and war.

Izvestia noted that the will for freedom and independence of the Indonesian, Malayan and Viet Namese people was "indestructible" and that the peace front was receiving more and more reinforcements as a result of "the widening national liberation movement."

Pravda declared that the victory of the Chinese people was of "tremendous importance" for the cause of peace and dealt a "cruel blow to the aggressive plans of imperialists in the Pacific region."

October 3, 1949

Red China Sets Relations As Price of News Activity

New York headquarters of Press Wireless, which transmits news dispatches, said last night the Chinese Communist Government had ordered correspondents in its territory from countries "without diplomatic relations" with the new Red regime to stop sending dispatches.

The information was received from Press Wireless' Shanghai office. It quoted the following proclamation of the Shanghai Military Control Commission:

"Effective today [Oct. 6], correspondents, including Chinese or foreigners representing foreign newspapers, press associations or radio broadcasting stations without diplomatic relations with the Chinese People's Republic [Communist] Government, should discontinue news activity, including the dispatch of press messages."

This automatically clamps the lid on all United States and other Western power news services and newspapers. Russia and her satellites and Yugoslavia have recognized the Communist regime at Peiping.

The prohibition on correspondents apparently already is in effect.

October 7, 1949

U.S., BRITISH DIFFER IN APPROACH TO MAO

By HENRY R. LIEBERMAN

The questions of recognizing the Communist-dominated Peiping regime and dealing with the Nationalist blockade, which has cut off Shanghai from vital sources of raw materials, have become the focus for distinct differences of opinion between the British and Americans on what to do about Red China.

The reference here is to the attitudes of foreign business men and officials in China. But there are clear-cut signs that the differences in approach are also matched in Washington and London, with the United States State Department—apparently still trying to resolve China policy with domestic political considerations—less certain than the British Foreign Office on what line to take.

As a case in point, the State Department was reliably reported to have frowned for weeks on attempts by the Pan American and the Northwest Airlines—the two American air carriers formerly operating in and out of Shanghai—to re-establish either regular service or set up a series of special flights. The projects were approved originally by the Communists. By the time the State Department acquiescence had been obtained, however, the Reds had changed their minds.

In Shanghai, where both foreign and Chinese business men have experienced the exasperations of nonexistent business, unimaginable labor difficulties (including "lock-in" detentions by workers seeking to enforce demands for exorbitant severance pay), heavy taxation and trying red tape, the prevailing American attitude is based primarily on a "let-me-out-of-here" feeling. On the other hand, the average British business man is determined to stick it out as long as he can and adjust himself to new conditions.

Stuart Strove for Unity

Although the United States Ambassador, Dr. J. Leighton Stuart, bent every effort in Nanking toward maintaining a united diplomatic front among the Atlantic pact nations and members of the British Commonwealth, it was apparent there that the British, Indian and French representatives were more eagerly disposed than the Americans to end the blockade and recognize the Communists with the greatest possible dispatch.

The British seemed primarily concerned about the British economic stake in China and Hong Kong, the French about Indo-China and the Indians about developments in Yunnan and the effect of the Chinese Communists on Southeast Asia.

One explanation for the difference in the British and American attitudes, perhaps the fundamental explanation, is the difference in size of British and American investments in China. Accurate figures on the present value of foreign investments in China are lacking, but the British stake is generally reckoned at about ten times ($1,500,000,000) that of the United States ($150,000,000). Moreover, the British also have a substantial economic stake in their free port of Hong Kong.

There is also an important difference in the general complexion of British and American investments in China, which explains—to some extent, at any rate—the difference in attitude of British and American business men. The British, with their closed-circuit China companies, trade "in" China; the Americans, with the notable exceptions of the Shanghai Power Company and the Shanghai Telephone Company, trade "with" China.

Divergent Opinions

Aside from economic self-interest, however, one is inclined to hear different and equally sincere arguments from British and American diplomats on the political pro's and con's of ending the blockade and recognizing the Communist-dominated regime.

One anti-Communist American argument may be summarized in these terms:

"Communists are Communists the world over, so let us do nothing to give aid and comfort to the Chinese Communists. Furthermore, they need us more than we need them. We have more to gain by sitting tight and making them come to us."

The typical and lengthier British argument tends to run about as follows:

"For economic and international political reasons, we must end the blockade as soon as possible. Although Manchuria and Sinkiang are now Russian spheres of influence, nowhere else in the world does the West have the economic foothold in a Communist country that it has in the Yangtze Valley. Countenancing the Nationalist blockade threatens this foothold and hurts Britain economically when she most needs foreign trade.

"It also endangers private Chinese enterprise, by forcing a decentralizing of what the West has built up in Shanghai and by accelerating the trend toward a State-controlled economy. It enables the Communists to blame the West for their economic woes. Furthermore, it forces the Communists to veer toward Russia at a faster clip and deprives the Nationalist elements inside the party of cards to play against the intense pro-Russian elements."

Any policy, based on either of the aforementioned arguments, involves a gamble. But now that the Russians have recognized the Peiping regime, which promises to bring the whole question of China recognition into the United Nations before too long, the United States is going to have to make up its mind.

October 8, 1949

INDIANS RECOGNIZE COMMUNIST CHINA

New Delhi Is First in British Commonwealth—Withdraws Bond With Nationalists

VIEWS PEIPING AS FIRM

In the U. N. Security Council Soviet Challenges Right of Tsiang to Retain Seat

NEW DELHI, India, Dec. 30 (Æ)—India today announced recognition of the Communist Chinese Government in Peiping.

The Indian Government said relations with the Nationalist Government of China would cease immediately.

India thus became the first member of the British Commonwealth to recognize Mao Tze-tung's regime. [Britain's recognition of the Peiping Government is said to be likely in January, and London reports say Pakistan, Ceylon, Australia and New Zealand may act simultaneously.]

Informed sources here said India decided to recognize Communist China for these reasons:

The Communist Government controlled practically the whole of the country; there was no evidence that the mass of the Chinese people opposed the Communist regime; the new Communist Government had agreed to abide by China's international obligations.

The whole relationship of the Commonwealth nations to China is to be discussed at the British conference in Colombo, Ceylon, opening Jan. 9.

December 30, 1949

BRITAIN ANNOUNCES HER RECOGNITION OF PEIPING REGIME

By RAYMOND DANIELL
Special to THE NEW YORK TIMES.

LONDON, Jan. 6—The Foreign Office announced this morning that Britain had offered de jure recognition to the Chinese Communist regime of Mao Tze-tung. One hour later Dr. Cheng Tien-hsi, Ambassador of Nationalist China, told the press that he believed his tory would show that in doing so the British Government had acted against Britain's "real and higher interests."

Foreign Secretary Bevin fixed the date for recognition of the Central People's Government of China before leaving on Dec. 27 for the Conference of Commonwealth Foreign Ministers at Colombo, Ceylon. Ceylon acted simultaneously with Britain in according recognition to Peiping.

[A Reuters report from Oslo said that Norway had decided to extend recognition to the Chinese Communist Government and an Associated Press dispatch from Copenhagen said that Denmark had decided on a similar step.

[Congress responded to the British move with mingled expressions of disapproval and acceptance. While the White House remained silent, the State Department said the action did not imply disagreement with Washington on a long-range objective on China.]

India, Pakistan, Burma, the Soviet Union and its satellites and Yugoslavia had previously recognized Communist China. Australia, New Zealand and Canada are expected to defer recognition.

Washington Kept Informed

Although the British Foreign Office made no secret of its intention to establish diplomatic relations with the new Chinese Government, which it does not like any better than does Washington, and kept the United States as well as the Dominions fully informed, it was expected here that its action would arouse a storm of protest in Congress and among some sections of the American press.

It was emphasized that recognition did not imply approval of communism or friendship for the Communists but merely faced the fact that the Chinese Communist Government now controlled most of China and was able to fulfill its international obligations.

Informed circles gave four principal reasons for Britain's action. These were:

1. That it was the legally correct thing to do.
2. That the practical necessity of diplomatic contact with the Chinese Government to protect Britain's great financial interests in China.
3. That the British Ambassador in China, and the colonial governors in Far Eastern territories with large Chinese populations, had been pressing for recognition at the earliest possible moment.
4. That the Singapore conference of British diplomats and colonial representatives in the Far East was unanimously in favor of recognition.

Commercial Stake Heavy

Britain's commercial stake in China is probably greater than that of any other nation in the world. A representative of the Chinese Association in London estimated that British capital investment in China amounted to more than £300,000,000, and it may be taken for granted that the representatives of these interests have been agitating strongly for recognition.

Further, it was said that although Mr. Mao is in Moscow now, apparently negotiating a new Sino-Russian alliance, the Chinese dislike of all foreigners, including the Russians, is expected to act as a barrier to any ideas that the Kremlin may entertain about making China a Soviet satellite according to the Eastern European pattern.

The whole problem of China and the effects of the Communist victory there and throughout the rest of Southeast Asia will be studied at the Colombo conference, opening Monday, with a view to finding some means of containing communism within its present limits.

The decision of the British Government to recognize the Communist regime was conveyed by the British consul general to that government's Minister of Foreign Affairs, Chou En-lai, this morning. Notice that Britain was terminating relations with Nationalist China had been conveyed to Dr. Cheng, the Ambassador of that government, at the Foreign Office last night by Hector McNeil, Minister of State.

The present British Ambassador to Nationalist China is now in Britain and probably will not return. It was expected that E. M. Dening, head of the Far Eastern Department of the Foreign Office who is now on his way to Colombo, would become the first British Ambassador to Mr. Mao's Government. Pending his acceptance, John Colville Hutchison, a career diplomat with long Far Eastern experience, will serve as chargé d'affaires.

It is not clear yet whether Britain intends to maintain contact with the Nationalist regime in Formosa but should she wish to do so, E. T. Biggs, British consul in Tansui, could be the means of effecting it. It was expected that Britain would soon follow her recognition of Mr. Mao's regime as the government of China in law as well as in fact by granting de facto recognition to Bao Dai's regime in Viet Nam, French Indo-China.

In his embassy in Portland Place, Dr. Cheng, who, upon Britain's recognition of the Mao Government, became just another private citizen, was shown a copy of the text of a message broadcast to Nationalist diplomats offering them service under the Communists. He merely said that he did not think many would want to work for the Communists.

He meticulously refused to make any other comment until 12 o'clock because he had promised Mr. McNeil that he would wait until he heard Big Ben strike noon before issuing his statement. It was six minutes past twelve when he read his statement.

"It has been the repeatedly declared policy of the British Government," he said, "not to intervene in the war in China, but what greater intervention could there be than giving recognition to the Communist regime at this moment?

"It is equivalent to burying us while we are still very much alive and history will say that China has received her knockout blow, not from her foes, but from her friends and former allies.

"Homage to force and violence is very dangerous in view of the present world situation, for if you worship Caesar you will have Caesars, and what is worse, the bad imitators.

"In spite of what has happened, you may be sure that one day you will need us again, as the history of the closing of the Burma Road has shown, and you may well count on us."

The Ambassador made his statement in a room hung with Chinese tapestries. The Foreign Office had informed him that he could have three months' grace in winding up the affairs of the embassy. After that it will be taken over by a new Communist ambassador.

Dr. Cheng, who is a former lawyer and speaks English with fluency, plans to remain here indefinitely. He said he did not think it would take three months to vacate the embassy. He could not afford, as a private citizen, to keep up so large a place, he said.

January 7, 1950

Report on China That General Wedemeyer Submitted to the President in 1947 After Survey

Report to the President

CHINA

Part I—General Statement

China's history is replete with examples of encroachment, arbitrary action, special privilege, exploitation, and usurpation of territory on the part of foreign powers. Continued foreign infiltration, penetration or efforts to obtain spheres of influence in China, including Manchuria and Taiwan (Formosa), could be interpreted only as a direct infringement and violation of China's sovereignty and a contravention of the principles of the Charter of the United Nations.

It is mandatory that the United States and those other nations subscribing to the principles of the Charter of the United Nations should combine their efforts to insure the unimpeded march of all peoples toward goals that recognize the dignity of man and his civil rights and, further, definitely provide the opportunity to express freely how and by whom they will be governed.

Those goals and the lofty aims of freedom-loving peoples are jeopardized today by forces as sinister as those that operated in Europe and Asia during the ten years leading to World War II.

The pattern is familiar—employment of subversive agents; infiltration tactics; incitement of disorder and chaos to disrupt normal economy and thereby to undermine popular confidence in government and leaders; seizure of authority without reference to the will of the people—all the techniques skillfully designed and ruthlessly implemented in order to create favorable conditions for the imposition of totalitarian ideologies. This pattern is present in the Far East, particularly in the areas contiguous to Siberia.

If the United Nations is to have real effect in establishing economic stability and in maintaining world peace, these developments merit high priority on the United Nations' agenda for study and action. Events of the past two years demonstrate the futility of appeasement based on the hope that the strongly consolidated forces of the Soviet Union will adopt either a conciliatory or a cooperative attitude, except as tactical expedients. Soviet practice in the countries already occupied or dominated completes the mosaic of aggressive expansion through ruthless secret police methods and through an increasing political and economic enslavement of peoples.

Soviet Writing Shows Expansion Plans

Soviet literature, confirmed repeatedly by Communist leaders, reveals a definite plan for expansion far exceeding that of nazism in its ambitious scope and dangerous implications. Therefore in attempting a solution to the problem presented in the Far East, as well as in other troubled areas of the world, every possible opportunity must be used to seize the initiative in order to create and maintain bulwarks of freedom.

Notwithstanding all the corruption and incompetence that one notes in China, it is a certainty that the bulk of the people are not disposed to a Communist political and economic structure. Some have become affiliated with communism in indignant protest against oppressive police measures, corrupt practices and maladministration of National Government officials. Some have lost all hope for China under existing leadership and turn to the Communists in despair. Some accept a new leadership by mere inertia.

Indirectly, the United States facilitated the Soviet program in the Far East by agreeing at the Yalta Conference to Russian re-entry into Manchuria, and later by withholding aid from the National Government. There were justifiable reasons for these policies. In the one case we were concentrating maximum Allied strength against Japanese in order to accelerate crushing defeat and thus save Allied lives. In the other, we were withholding unqualified support from a government within which corruption and incompetence were so prevalent that it was losing the support of its own people.

Further, the United States had not yet realized that the Soviet Union would fail to cooperate in the accomplishment of world-wide plans for post-war rehabilitation. Our own participation in those plans has already afforded assistance to other nations and peoples, friends and former foes alike, to a degree unparalleled in humanitarian history.

Gradually it has become apparent that the World War II objectives for which we and others made tremendous sacrifices are not being fully attained, and that there remains in the world a force presenting even greater dangers to world peace than did the Nazi militarists and the Japanese jingoists. Consequently the United States made the decision in the spring of 1947 to assist Greece and Turkey with a view to protecting their sovereignties, which were threatened by the direct or inspired activities of the Soviet Union.

U. S. Declares Intent To Call on the U. N.

Charges of unilateral action and circumvention of the United Nations were made by members of that organization. In the light of its purposes and principles such criticisms seemed plausible. The United States promptly declared its intention of referring the matter to the United Nations when that organization would be ready to assume responsibility.

It follows that the United Nations should be informed of contemplated action with regard to China. If the recommendations of this report are approved, the United States should suggest to China that she inform the United Nations officially of her request to the United States for material assistance and advisory aid in order to facilitate China's post-war rehabilitation and economic recovery. This will demonstrate that the United Nations is not being circumvented, and that the United States is not infringing upon China's sovereignty, but contrariwise is cooperating constructively in the interest of peace and stability in the Far East, concomitantly in the world.

The situation in Manchuria has deteriorated to such a degree that prompt action is necessary to prevent that area from becoming a Soviet satellite. The Chinese Communists may soon gain military control of Manchuria and announce the establishment of a government.

Outer Mongolia, already a Soviet satellite, may then recognize Manchuria and conclude a "mutual support agreement" with a de facto Manchurian government of the Chinese Communists. In that event, the Soviet Union might accomplish a mutual support agreement with Communist-dominated Manchuria, because of her current similar agreement with Outer Mongolia. This would create a difficult situation for China, the United States and the United Nations. Ultimately it could lead to a Communist-dominated China.

Five-Power Guardianship Offered as Answer

The United Nations might take immediate action to bring about cessation of hostilities in Manchuria as a prelude to the establishment of a guardianship or trusteeship. The guardianship might consist of China, Soviet Russia, the United States, Great Britain and France. This should be attempted promptly and could be initiated only by China. Should one of the nations refuse to participate in Manchurian guardianship, China might then request the General Assembly of the United Nations to establish a trusteeship, under the provisions of the Charter.

Initially China might interpret guardianship or trusteeship as an infringement upon her sovereignty. But the urgency of the matter should encourage a realistic view of the situation. If these steps are not taken by China, Manchuria may be drawn into the Soviet orbit, despite United States aid, and lost, perhaps permanently, to China.

The economic deterioration and the incompetence and corruption in the political and military organizations in China should be considered against an all-inclusive background lest there be disproportionate emphasis upon defects. Comity requires that cognizance be taken of the following:

Unlike other powers since V-J Day, China has never been free to devote full attention to internal problems that were greatly confounded by eight years of war. The current civil war has imposed an overwhelming financial and economic burden at a time when resources and energies have been dissipated and when, in any event, they would have been strained to the utmost to meet the problems of recovery.

The National Government has consistently, since 1927, opposed communism. Today the same political leader and same civil and military officials are determined to prevent their country from becoming a Communist-dominated state or Soviet satellite.

Although the Japanese offered increasingly favorable surrender terms during the course of the war, China elected to remain steadfast with her Allies. If China had accepted surrender terms, approximately a million Japanese would have been released for employment against American forces in the Pacific.

Assurances Are Given By the Generalissimo

I was assured by the Generalissimo that China would support to the limit of her ability an American program for the stabilization of the Far East. He stated categorically that, regardless of moral encouragement or material aid received from the United States, he is determined to oppose communism and to create a democratic form of government in consonance with Doctor Sun Yat-sen's principles. He stated further than he plans to make sweeping reforms in the government including the removal of incompetent and corrupt officials. He stated, that some progress has been made along these lines but, with spiraling inflation, economic distress and civil war, it has been difficult to accomplish fully these objectives. He emphasized that, when the Communist problem is solved, he could drastically reduce the Army and concentrate upon political and economic reforms.

I retain the conviction that the Generalissimo is sincere in his desire to attain these objectives. I am not certain that he has today sufficient determination to do so if this requires absolute overruling of the political and military cliques surrounding him. Yet, if realistic United States aid is to prove effective in stabilizing the situation in China and in coping with the dangerous expansion of communism, that determination must be established.

Adoption by the United States of a policy motivated solely toward stopping the expansion of communism without regard to the continued existence of an unpopular repressive government would render any aid ineffective. Further, United States prestige in the Far East would suffer heavily, and wavering elements might turn away from the existing government to communism.

In China [and Korea], the political, economic and psychological problems are inextricably mingled. All of them are complex and are becoming increasingly difficult of solution. Each has been studied assiduously in compliance with your directive. Each will be discussed in the course of this report. However, it is recognized that a continued global appraisal is mandatory in order to preclude disproportionate or untimely assistance to any specific area.

The following three postulates of United States foreign policy are pertinent to indicate the background of my investigations, analyses and report:

The United States will continue support of the United Nations in the attainment of its lofty aims, accepting the possible development that the Soviet Union or other nations may not actively participate.

Moral support will be given to nations and peoples that have established political and economic structures compatible with our own, or that give convincing evidence of their desire to do so.

Material aid may be given to those same nations and peoples in order to accelerate post-war rehabilitation and to develop economic stability, provided:

That such aid shall be used for the purposes intended.

That there is continuing evidence that they are taking effective steps to help themselves, or are firmly committed to do so.

That such aid shall not jeopardize American economy and shall conform to an integrated program that involves other international commitments and contributes to the attainment of political, economic and psychological objectives of the United States.

Part II—China

POLITICAL

Although the Chinese people are unanimous in their desire for peace at almost any cost, there seems to be no possibility of its realization under existing circumstances. On one side is the Kuomintang, whose reactionary leadership, repression and corruption have caused a loss of popular faith in the Government. On the other side, bound ideologically to the Soviet Union, are the Chinese Communists, whose eventual aim is admittedly a Communist state in China.

Some reports indicate that Communist measures of land reform have gained for them the support of the majority of peasants in

areas under their control, while others indicate that their ruthless tactics of land distribution and terrorism have alienated the majority of such peasants. They have, however, successfully organized many rural areas against the National Government.

Moderate groups are caught between Kuomintang misrule and repression and ruthless Communist totalitarianism. Minority parties lack dynamic leadership and sizable following. Neither the moderates, many of whom are in the Kuomintang, nor the minority parties are able to make their influence felt because of National Government repression. Existing provincial opposition leading to possible separatist movements would probably crystallize only if collapse of the Government were imminent.

Soviet actions, contrary to the letter and spirit of the Sino-Soviet Treaty of 1945 and its related documents, have strengthened the Chinese Communist position in Manchuria, with political, economic and military repercussions on the National Government's position both in Manchuria and in China proper, and have made more difficult peace and stability in China. The present trend points toward a gradual disintegration of the National Government's control, with the ultimate possibility of a Communist-dominated China.

Steps taken by the Chinese Government toward governmental reorganization in mid-April 1947 aroused hopes of improvement in the political situation. However, the reorganization resulted in little change. Reactionary influences continue to mold important policies even though the Generalissimo remains the principal determinative force in the government. Since the April reorganization, the most significant change has been the appointment of General Chen Cheng to head the civil and military administration in Manchuria. Projected steps include elections in the Fall for the formation of a constitutional government, but, under present conditions, they are not expected to result in a government more representative than the present regime.

ECONOMIC

Under the impact of civil strife and inflation, the Chinese economy is disintegrating. The most probable outcome of present trends would be, not sudden collapse, but a continued and creeping paralysis and consequent decline in the authority and power of the National Government.

The past ten years of war have caused serious deterioration of transportation and communication facilities, mines, utilities and industries. Notwithstanding some commendable efforts and large amounts of economic aid, their over-all capabilities are scarcely half those of the pre-war period. With disruption of transportation facilities and the loss of much of North China and Manchuria, important resources of those rich areas are no longer available for the rehabilitation and support of China's economy.

Inflation in China has been diffused slowly through an enormous population without causing the immediate dislocation which would

have occurred in a highly industrialized economy. The rural people, 80 per cent of the total Chinese population of 450,000,000, barter foodstuffs for local handicraft products without suffering a drastic cut in living standards. Thus, local economies exist in many parts of China, largely insulated from the disruption of urban industry. Some local economies are under the control of Communists, and some are loosely under the control of provincial authorities.

The principal cause of the hyperinflation is the long-continued deficit in the national budget. Present revenue collections, plus the profits of nationalized enterprises, cover only one-third of governmental expenditures, which are approximately 70 per cent military, and an increasing proportion of the budget is financed by the issuance of new currency. In the first six months of 1947 note-issue was tripled but rice prices increased seven-fold. Thus prices and governmental expenditures spiral upward, with price increases occurring faster than new currency can be printed.

Need Is Seen to Cut Military Budget

With further price increases, budget revisions will undoubtedly be necessary. The most urgent economic need of Nationalist China is a reduction of the military budget.

China's external official assets amounted to $327,000,000 on July 30, 1947. Privately-held foreign exchange assets are at least $600,-000,000 and may total $1,500,-000, but no serious attempt has been made to mobilize these private resources for rehabilitation purposes. Private Chinese assets located in China include probably $200,000,000 in gold, and about $75,000,000 in United States currency notes. Although China has not exhausted her foreign official assets, and probably will not do so at the present rates of imports and exports until early 1949, the continuing deficit in her external balance of payments is a serious problem.

Disparity between the prices of export goods in China and in world markets at unrealistic official exchange rates has greatly penalized exports, as have disproportionate increases in wages and other costs. Despite rigorous trade and exchange controls, imports have greatly exceeded exports, and there consistently has been a heavy adverse trade balance.

China's food harvests this year are expected to be significantly larger than last year's fairly good returns. This moderately encouraging situation with regard to crops is among the few favorable factors which can be found in China's current economic situation.

Under inflationary conditions, long-term investment is unattractive for both Chinese and foreign capital. Private Chinese funds tend to go into short-term advances, hoarding of commodities, and capital flight. The entire psychology is speculative and inflationary, preventing ordinary business planning and handicapping industrial recovery.

Foreign business enterprises in China are adversely affected by the inefficient and corrupt administration of exchange and import controls, discriminatory application of tax laws, the increasing role of government trading agencies and the trend towards state ownership of industries. The Chinese Government has taken some steps toward improvement but generally has been apathetic in its efforts. Between 1944 and 1947, the anti-inflationary measure on which the Chinese Government placed most reliance was the public sale of gold borrowed from the United States. The intention was to absorb paper currency, and thus reduce the effective demand for goods. Under the circumstance of continued large deficits, however, the only effect of the gold sales program was to retard slightly the price inflation and dissipate dollar assets.

A program to stabilize the economic situation was undertaken in February 1947. The measures included a wage freeze, a system of limited rationing to essential workers in a few cities, and the sale of government bonds. The effect of this program has been slight, and the wage freeze has been abandoned. In August 1947, the unrealistic official rate of exchange was replaced, for proceeds of exports and remittances, by a free market in foreign exchange. This step is expected to stimulate exports, but it is too early to determine whether it will be effective.

New Silver Currency Proposed as Check

The issuance of a new silver currency has been proposed as a future measure to combat inflation. If the government continued to finance budgetary deficits by unbacked note issue, the silver would probably go into hoards and the price inflation would continue. The effect would be no more than that of the gold sales in 1944-1947, namely, a slight and temporary retardation of the inflationary spiral. The proposal could be carried out, moreover, only through a loan from the United States of at least $200,000,000 in silver.

In the construction field, China has prepared expansive plans for reconstruction of communications, mines and industries. Some progress has been made in implementing them, notably in the partial rehabilitation of certain railroads and in the textile industry. Constructive results have been handicapped by a lack of funds, equipment and experienced management, supervisory and technical personnel.

On August 1, 1947, the State Council approved a "Plan for Economic Reform." This appears to be an omnibus of plans covering all phases of Chinese economic reconstruction but its effectiveness cannot yet be determined.

SOCIAL—CULTURAL

Public education has been one of the chief victims of war and social and economic disruption. Schoolhouses, textbooks and other equipment have been destroyed and the cost of replacing any considerable portion cannot now be met. Teachers, like other public servants, have seen the purchasing power of a month's salary shrink to the market value of a few days' rice ration. This applies to the entire educational system, from primary schools, which provide a medium to combat the nation's grievous illiteracy, to universities, from which must come the nation's professional men, technicians and administrators.

The universities have suffered in an additional and no less serious respect—traditional academic freedom. Students participating in protest demonstrations have been severely and at times brutally punished by National Government agents without pretense of trial or public evidence of the sedition charged. Faculty members have often been dismissed or refused employment with no evidence of professional unfitness, patently because they were politically objectionable to government officials. Somewhat similarly, periodicals have been closed down "for reasons of military security" without stated charges, and permitted to reopen only after new managements have been imposed. Resumption of educational and other public welfare activities on anything like the desired scale can be accomplished only by restraint of officialdom's abuses, and when the nation's economy is stabilized sufficiently to defray the cost of such vital activities.

MILITARY

The overall military position of the National Government has deteriorated in the past several months and the current military situation favors Communist forces. The Generalissimo has never wavered in his contention that he is fighting for national independence against forces of an armed rebellion nor has he been completely convinced that the Communist problem can be resolved except by force of arms.

Although the Nationalist Army has a preponderance of force, the tactical initiative rests with the Communists. Their hit-and-run tactics, adapted to their mission of destruction at points or in areas of their own selection, give them a decided advantage over Nationalists, who must defend many critical areas including connecting lines of communication. Obviously large numbers of Nationalist troops involved in such defensive roles are immobilized whereas Communist tactics permit almost complete freedom of action.

The Nationalists' position is precarious in Manchuria, where they occupy only a slender finger of territory. Their control is strongly disputed in Shantung and Hopeh Provinces where the Communists make frequent dislocating attacks against isolated garrisons.

In order to improve materially the current military situation, the Nationalist forces must first stabilize the fronts and then regain the initiative. Further, since the Government is supporting the civil war with approximately 70 per cent of its national budget, it is evident that steps taken to alleviate the situation must point toward an improvement in the effectiveness of the armed forces with a concomitant program of social, political and economic reforms, including a decrease in the size of the military establishment.

Whereas some rather ineffective steps have been taken to reor-

ganize and revitalize the command structure, and more sweeping reforms are projected, the effectiveness of the Nationalist Army requires a sound program of equipment and improved logistical support.

The present industrial potential of China is inadequate to support military forces effectively. Chinese forces under present conditions cannot cope successfully with internal strife or fulfill China's obligations as a member of the family of nations. Hence outside aid, in the form of munitions (most urgently ammunition) and technical assistance, is essential before any plan of operations can be undertaken with a reasonable prospect of success.

Military advice is now available to the Nationalists on a General Staff level through American military advisory groups. The Generalissimo expressed to me repeatedly a strong desire to have this advice and supervision extended in scope to include field forces, training centers and particularly logistical agencies.

Extension of military aid by the United States to the National Government might possibly be followed by similar aid from the Soviet Union to the Chinese Communists, either openly or covertly — the latter course seems more likely. An arena of conflicting ideologies might be created, as in 1935 in Spain. There is always the possibility that such developments in this area, as in Europe and in the Middle East, might precipitate a third world war.

[Part III of General Wedemeyer's report, which concerned Korea, was not included in the White Paper.]

Part IV—Conclusions

The peaceful aims of freedom-loving peoples in the world are jeopardized today by developments as portentous as those leading to World War II.

The Soviet Union and her satellites give no evidence of a conciliatory or cooperative attitude in these developments. The United States is compelled, therefore, to initiate realistic lines of action in order to create and maintain bulwarks of freedom, and to protect United States strategic interests.

The bulk of the Chinese are not disposed to communism and they are not concerned with ideologies. They desire food, shelter and the opportunity ot live in peace.

CHINA

The spreading internecine struggle within China threatens world peace. Repeated American efforts to mediate have proved unavailing. It is apparent that positive steps are required to end hostilities immediately. The most logical approach to this very complex and ominous situation would be to refer the matter to the United Nations.

A China dominated by Chinese Communists would be inimical to the interests of the United States, in view of their openly expressed hostility and active opposition to those principles which the United States regards as vital to the peace of the world.

The Communists have the tactical initiative in the overall mili-

tary situation. The Nationalist position in Manchuria is precarious, and in Shantung and Hopeh Provinces strongly disputed. Continued deterioration of the situation may result in the early establishment of a Soviet satellite government in Manchuria and ultimately in the evolution of a Communist-dominated China.

China is suffering increasingly from disintegration. Her requirements for rehabilitation are large. Her most urgent needs include governmental reorganization and reforms, reduction of the military budget and external assistance.

A program of aid, if effectively employed, would bolster opposition to Communist expansion, and would contribute to gradual development of stability in China.

Due to excesses and oppressions by government police agencies basic freedoms of the people are being jeopardized. Maladministration and corruption cause a loss of confidence in the Government. Until drastic political and economic reforms are undertaken United States aid cannot accomplish its purpose.

Even so, criticism of the results achieved by the National Government in its efforts for improvement should be tempered by a recognition of the handicaps imposed on China by eight years of war, the burden of her opposition to communism, and her sacrifices for the Allied cause.

A United States program of assistance could best be implemented under the supervision of American advisers in specified economic and military fields. Such a program can be undertaken only if China requests advisory aid as well as material assistance.

Part V—Recommendations

It is recommended:

That the United States Government provide as early as practicable moral, advisory, and material support to China in order to contribute to the early establishment of peace in the world in consonance with the enunciated principles of the United Nations, and concomitantly to protect United States strategic interests against militant forces which now threaten them.

That United States policies and actions suggested in this report be thoroughly integrated by appropriate government agencies with other international commitments. It is recognized that any foreign assistance extended must avoid jeopardizing the American economy.

CHINA

That China be advised that the United States is favorably disposed to continue aid designed to protect China's territorial integrity and to facilitate her recovery, under agreements to be negotiated by representatives of the two governments, with the following stipulations:

That China inform the United Nations promptly of her request to the United States for increased material and advisory assistance.

That China request the United Nations to take immediate action to bring about a cessation of hostilities in Manchuria and request that Manchuria be placed under a Five-Power Guardianship or, failing that, under a Trusteeship in accordance with the United Nations Charter.

That China make effective use of her own resources in a program for economic reconstruction and initiate sound fiscal policies leading to a reduction in budgetary deficits.

That China give continuing evidence that the urgently required political and military reforms are being implemented.

That China accept American advisers as responsible representatives of the United States Government in specified military and economic fields to assist China in utilizing United States aid in the manner for which it is intended.

APPENDIX A

[The following consists of excerpts from the appendix.]

The Chinese Government's position in Manchuria has been seriously weakened by Soviet actions. In spite of the Sino-Soviet Treaty of 1945 and its related documents, the Soviet Union has hindered the efforts of the Chinese Government to restore its control over Manchuria, has not given the "moral support and aid in military supplies and other material resources" provided for in these documents and has not permitted the Chinese Government freely to take over the civil administration of Dairen and the Port Arthur area. Rather, the Soviet Union has assisted the Chinese Communists in Manchuria by the timing of the withdrawal of Soviet troops and by making available, either directly or indirectly, large quantities of surrendered Japanese military equipment. Soviet machinations in western Sinkiang and among the Mongols have further embarrassed the Chinese Government. In brief, the Soviet Union has given no indication of any effort to assist the Chinese Government and has, instead, taken action which has aided the Chinese Communists in Manchuria. The result has been to strengthen the Chinese Communist position in Manchuria, with political, economic and military repercussions on the National Government's position both in Manchuria and China proper, and to make more difficult the attainment of peace and stability in China.

To advise at this time a policy of "no assistance" to China would suggest the withdrawal of the United States Military and Naval Advisory Groups from China and it would be equivalent to cutting the ground from under the feet of the Chinese Government. Removal of American assistance, without removal of Soviet assistance, would certainly lay the country open to eventual Communist domination. It would have repercussions in other parts of Asia, would lower American prestige in the Far East and would make easier the spread of Soviet influence and Soviet political expansion not only in Asia but in other areas of the world.

It is possible that the adoption of a "wait and see" policy would lead to the Generalissimo's finally carrying out genuine reforms which in turn would enable the United States to extend effective aid and which themselves would furnish the best answer to the challenge of communism. Because of an inevitable time lag in its results, however, such a policy would permit for an appreciable time the continuation of the process of National Government disintegration. At some stage of the disintegration the authority and control of the National Government m ght become so weak and restricted that separatist movements would occur in various areas now under Government control. At this point conceivably there might emerge a middle group which would be able to establish a modicum of stability in the areas under its control. It would then be possible for the United States to extend support, both moral and material, to any such group or combination of groups which give indication of ability to consolidate control over sizable portions of the country and whose policies would be compatible with our own. This, however, represents conjecture regarding a possible future course of events in China. There is the further possibility that such a policy would result at some point in the Generalissimo's seeking a compromise with the Chinese Communists, although it is likely that he would not do so until his position became so weak that the Communists would accept a settlement only on terms assuring them a dominant position in the government. At worst, under a process of continued National Government disintegration, it may be expected that there would be a long period of disturbance verging on chaos, at the end of which the Chinese Communists would

emerge as the dominant group oriented toward the Soviet Union.

List of Reform Steps Stress Aid to People

Reforms to improve the internal political situation should, in general, include measures which would (a) make for efficient government, (b) protect the basic freedoms of the people from arbitrary acts of repression, (c) remove civil administration from military control, and (d) contribute to the welfare of the people. These measures might include, *inter alia*, reforms such as the following: Complete separation of the Kuomintang from the Government and the emergence of the Generalissimo as the leader of the nation rather than of the party; reorganization of the National Government, including both the Executive Yuan and the State Council, to insure participation by responsible Chinese without regard to party affiliations; a clear-cut delegation of responsibility in the Government to increase efficiency, foster initiative, prevent the domination of governmental affairs and policies by one person and encourage entry into Government service of capable and progressive Chinese now unwilling to serve in the Government; the strengthening of the Control Yuan to ensure the removal and punishment of corrupt officials; the abolition of the existing secret police system; the cessation of arrests of civilians by military organs; the prompt and public trial of persons arrested and the full exercise of the right of habeas corpus; the cessation of the use of force and intimi-

dation against teachers and students and the reinstatment of university professors and students dismissed solely for their political views; the carrying out of a land reform program which would lighten the burdens of usury and taxation on the peasant as well as provide him land; decentralization of governmental power to permit more local autonomy and local participation in administration; removal of military officers from posts in civil government while on active status; and publication of complete information regarding fiscal policies and their implementation and of detailed data covering Government revenues and expenditures, including national, provincial and municipal budgets.

[Appendix B discusses economic matters. and Appendix C deals with social and cultural questions.]

APPENDIX D

[The following consists of excerpts from the appendix.]

It is recommended:

That the United States provide as early as practicable moral, advisory and material support to China in order to prevent Manchuria from becoming a Soviet satellite, to bolster opposition to Communist expansion and to contribute to the gradual development of stability in China.

That China be advised to request the United Nations to take immediate steps to bring about a cessation of hostilities in Manchuria and request that Manchuria be placed under a Five-Power Guardianship

or, failing that, under a Trusteeship in accordance with the United Nations Charter.

That China be advised to take steps to reduce its military expenditures in the national budget and at the same time increase the effectiveness and efficiency of the military establishment.

That China give continuing evidence that urgently required military reforms are being implemented.

That China, with the advice and support of the United States, develop and implement a sound program of equipment and improved logistical support.

That arrangements be made whereby China can purchase military equipment and supplies (particularly motor maintenance parts) from the United States.

That China be assisted in her efforts to obtain ammunition immediately.

That the 8½ Air Group Program be completed promptly and that consideration be given to expansion of its air transport.

That the China Mapping Program be extended in scope where practicable.

That the program for transfer of ships to China be completed as rapidly as China is able to utilize them effectively.

That the occupation of Japan program be dropped, but only with the concurrence of the National Government of China.

The military advice and supervision be extended in scope to include field forces; training centers and particularly logistical agencies.

U.S. PLAN ON CHINA BIDS NATIONS HONOR HER INDEPENDENCE

Jessup Introduces Resolution That Ignores Nationalist Plea for Boycott of Peiping

AMERICAN SHIP IS SHELLED

Second Isbrandtsen Vessel Hit Was En Route to Shanghai, State Department Hears

By THOMAS J. HAMILTON
Special to THE NEW YORK TIMES.

LAKE SUCCESS, Nov. 28—The United States turned a cold shoulder today toward a resolution offered by the Chinese Nationalist Government under which the General Assembly would call on all members of the United Nations not to recognize the Chinese Communist regime. A counter-proposal, introduced this morning by Dr. Philip C. Jessup, United States representative, in the Assembly's Political and Security Committee, would call on all nations:

"(1) To respect the political independence of China and to be guided by the principles of the Charter in their relations with China;

"(2) To respect the right of the people of China now and in the future to choose freely their political institutions and to maintain a Government independent of foreign control;

"(3) To respect existing treaties relating to China;

"(4) To refrain from (a) seeking to acquire spheres of influence or to create foreign-controlled regimes within the territory of China, (b) seeking to obtain special rights or privileges within the territory of China."

In his speech, Dr. Jessup said that some evidence and reports in the hands of the United States

"create grave cause for concern that groundwork is in fact once again being laid for a further Russian attempt to dismember China."

[The United States Consul General at Shanghai, Walter P. McConaughty, informed the State Department that the steamship Sir John Franklin of the Isbrandtsen Lines had been shelled and hit twelve times on the Yangtze River. A message from the ship's captain attributed the attack to two Chinese warships. The State Department will protest to Chinese Nationalist authorities.]

"The United Nations must be alert to see that the domination of China by one totalitarian power has not been displaced only to make way for the subjugation of that country to any other imperialism," Dr. Jessup said. "The common efforts of the United Nations in rescuing China and Japan from the grasp of imperialist and militarist power must not be nullified by acquiescence in new imperialist conquest by more subtle devices than outright war.

"Our purpose in submitting the joint draft resolution is to show the specific application of certain basic principles of the United Nations Charter to the existing situation in China. If the United Nations can through this resolution help all the nations to follow and give effect to those accepted principles in relation to China, the organization will have made a notable contribution to the maintenance of general peace and to the efforts of the Chinese people to promote in China the growth of free institutions, social progress, and better standards of life in larger freedom."

Dr. T. F. Tsiang, Chinese Nationalist representative, complained after Dr. Jessup had spoken that the new resolution, which has Australia, Mexico, Pakistan and the Philippines as co-sponsors, amounted to only an expanded version of the final point of his four-point resolution. This would call on all member nations "to refrain from taking advantage of the present situation in China for any purpose that is incompatible with the political independence and territorial and administrative integrity of China."

Dr. Tsiang then announced that he would continue to press for action on the three other points in his resolution: Non-recognition of the Chinese Communist regime, no

military or economic aid to the Chinese Communists and a finding by the General Assembly that the Soviet Union, "by obstructing the National Government of China and by giving aid to the Chinese Communists," had violated the United Nations Charter and the Sino-Soviet treaty of 1945.

Majority Held Doubtful

The omission of these provisions from the joint resolution resulted among other reasons, from the prevailing belief here that they would not get anything like the necessary two-thirds majority in the General Assembly, and that many member nations planned to recognize the Chinese Communist regime within a few weeks or months.

The United States found considerable difficulty in obtaining co-sponsors, even though the resolution, like that sponsored by the United States and Britain as a reply to the Soviet proposal for a Big Five non-aggression pact, amounts to little more than a restatement of the principles that are supposed to control the actions of all nations that have signed the United Nations Charter.

However, it is understood that the British Government, which apparently has refrained thus far from recognizing the Chinese Communists only as a result of pleas from the United States, would not agree to vote for the resolution until the United States delegation, at the last minute, inserted the sentence regarding respect for "existing treaties relating to China."

This would give the backing of the Assembly to the retention of Hong Kong, which was ceded to Britain under the Treaty of Nanking in 1842. However, Dr. Jessup referred in his speech only to the Nine-Power treaty of 1922, guaranteeing the territorial integrity of China, and the Sino-Soviet treaty of 1945. It had been the original intention of the United States delegation to base the entire resolution on the Nine-Power treaty, but this idea was dropped because of the fact that the Soviet Union was not a party to it.

Dr. Jessup said Dr. Tsiang's charges against the Soviet Union "indicate a continuation in the post-war period of previous Russian attempts against the integrity of that country," but made it clear that the problem before the Assembly was to "set standards" for applying the principles of the Charter to China, rather than "how governments individually may propose to meet the problems created by the civil strife in China."

Intended as Explanation

This apparently was intended as an explanation of the refusal of the United States to support the Chinese Nationalist proposal against

recognition of the Chinese Communist regime and in favor of a ban on military and economic help. However, Dr. Jessup suggested that the International Court of Justice decide on the question of the violation of the Sino-Soviet treaty.

Summarizing the charge that the United Nations Charter had been violated, he said that "the complaint is of an attempt at foreign domination of China, made through the Soviet-controlled world Communist movement and masked behind the facade of a national crusade to improve the life of China and its people."

"It will be for the people of China to make a final judgment as to the correctness of this interpretation of the Communist movement in China over the last thirty years," said Dr. Jessup, emphasizing that the Chinese Communist movement dates back beyond the acts of intervention charged to the Soviet Union.

Dr. Tsiang's speech to the committee had accused the Soviet Union of establishing regimes under its control in the Manchurian, Inner Mongolian and Northwestern provinces of China, although the Chinese resolution mentions only the Northeastern provinces (Manchuria). Dr. Jessup said that the Yalta agreement granted the Soviet Union only certain limited rights at Dairen and on the Chinese Eastern and South Manchurian Railways, which would not have impaired the sovereignty of China.

Informed sources indicated that the United States, for the time being, would abstain on the three controversial points in the Chinese resolution.

James Plimsoll of Australia said his delegation, as a co-sponsor, agreed with the United States delegation that it would not be appropriate at the present time to adopt the Chinese resolution.

Comment from other delegates was sparse. Alexis Kyrou of Greece said the experience of his country would lead her to favor protecting a member nation threatened with armed aggression from outside. Fernand van Langenhove of Belgium said the possibilities for United Nations action were "very limited" but that it was necessary to face the facts squarely.

Dr. Joao Carlos Muniz of Brazil said that delegates needed time to receive instructions, and proposed that the debate be adjourned until the General Assembly had completed its discussion of the British-United States resolution on compliance with the United Nations Charter. This suggestion was approved 36 to 2, the other countries, including the five members of the Soviet bloc, abstaining.

TRUMAN BARS MILITARY HELP FOR DEFENSE OF FORMOSA

President Cites Cairo, Potsdam Agreements on China Territory

U. S. DESIGNS DISAVOWED

Acheson Attributes Decision to Principles—Americans on Island Advised to Leave

By WALTER H. WAGGONER
Special to THE NEW YORK TIMES.

WASHINGTON, Jan. 5—President Truman set forth today a sharply restrictive policy toward Formosa, held by the Chinese Nationalists. He barred United States military intervention, aid or advice to the island bastion and limited assistance to current economic recovery efforts.

The President said this program conformed to the traditions of United States foreign policy in China, to a recent United Nations resolution against any nation's seeking influence or imperial aggrandizement in China, and to the Cairo and Potsdam agreements of 1943 and 1945.

At the Cairo conference in 1943 the United States, Britain and China agreed that Formosa had been stolen from China by Japan and that it should go back to China. The statement was incorporated into the Potsdam Declaration in 1945 and was made one of the terms of Japan's surrender.

Mr. Truman said the United States "has always stood for good faith in international relations," and that it had no intention of using its armed force for protecting the island from falling into the hands of the Communists in the course of a war he described as "the civil conflict in China."

Seeks no Special Rights

"The United States has no preda-tory designs on Formosa or on any other Chinese territory," the Chief Executive declared. "The United States has no desire to obtain special rights or privileges or to establish military bases on Formosa at this time. Nor does it have any intention of utilizing its armed force to interfere in the present situation. The United States Government will not pursue a course which will lead to involvement in the civil conflict in China."

This pronouncement of a policy, the subject of widely divergent speculation and predictions for the past several weeks, was made public at the President's news conference. It brought immediate and sharp reaction from Congress, where pressure has been strong for the use of United States military aid to defend Formosa.

Reaction spread swiftly also to the threatened area itself. United States officials were reported to be advising Americans to leave the island unless they had especially urgent reasons to stay.

There was no general evacuation warning, but advice on an individual basis. The precautions appeared, however, to have been taken in fear not only of a Communist attack but of a possible uprising by the Formosan natives against the weakening Chinese Nationalist forces. Many United States officials feel that order is maintained in Formosa only because of the approximately 250,000 Nationalist troops.

Acheson Elaborates

It is believed that between 100 and 200 Americans are on the island, including officials, missionaries and a few business and professional people, including employes of a construction concern working on Economic Cooperation Administration projects.

Secretary of State Dean Acheson, holding a news conference this afternoon at the President's request, elaborated on what Mr. Truman had said about United States tradition and added that the "underlying factors" of the decision on Formosa were matters of principle and not of military strategy.

These factors, he said, "have to do with the fundamental integrity of the United States and with maintaining in the world the belief that when the United States takes a position it sticks to that position and does not change it by reason of transitory expediency or advantage on its part."

"If we are going to maintain the free nations of the world as a great unit opposed to the encroachment of communism and other sorts of totalitarian aggression," he continued. "The world must believe that we stand for principle and that we are honorable and decent people and that we do not put forward words, as propagandists do in other countries, to serve their advantage, only to throw them overboard when some change in events makes the position difficult for us.

"We believe in integrity in our foreign relations. We believe also in respect of the integrity of other countries. That is a view not held by some other countries with respect to China.

"It is important that our position in regard to China should never be subject to the slightest doubt or the slightest question."

U. S. Integrity Paramount

Mr. Acheson said further that legalism and "lawyers' words" were not going to stand in the way of the integrity of the United States, and that there would be no "quibbling" about the legal situation, whatever it might be.

The Secretary of State asserted in defense of withholding military force from the Chinese Nationalists now on Formosa, that he had never heard a responsible military man say that the United States "should involve our forces in the island."

Like the President, Mr. Acheson emphasized that there was no lack of funds held by the Nationalists on Formosa. Mr. Truman's statement noted that "resources on Formosa are adequate to enable them to obtain the items which they might consider necessary for the defense of the island."

The Secretary of State observed that the Chinese Nationalists had used and could continue to use the funds to buy United States matériel and equipment.

In response to a question about the possible desirability of a military mission of advisers, Mr. Acheson declared that United States military advisers had been on the mainland of China for a long time, that their advice was not taken, and that in no way was any substantial use made of the mission by the Chinese Nationalists.

That mistake was made once, but the same mistake will not be made again, at least not in the same place, said the Secretary.

Denies Rift With Johnson

Mr. Acheson also denied that there had been important differences between him and Secretary of Defense Louis Johnson on the question of aiding Formosa. He said there had been minor differences, but they were confined to the degree of weight that should be given to the political and military factors in the situation.

He insisted that he and the Defense Secretary were not at cross-purposes.

Mr. Acheson also explained why the policy statement had been revised at the last minute to put "at this time" at the end of the sentence. "the United States has no desire to obtain special rights or privileges or to establish military bases on Formosa at this time."

"That phrase," said Mr. Acheson, "does not qualify or modify or weaken the fundamental policies stated in this declaration by the President in any respect. It is a recognition of the fact that in the unlikely and unhappy event that our forces might be attacked in the Far East the United States must be completely free to take whatever action in whatever area is necessary for its own security."

Possibly in anticipation of criticism that was to descend from Capitol Hill, the Secretary said that the policy statement was issued "at this particular time" to clear the air of confusion, both here and abroad, about United States intentions in Formosa.

Clarification Was Aim

Discussions that have ranged from gossip to contributions by "distinguished statesmen" have, according to Mr. Acheson, "stirred up a good deal of speculation, all of which, if allowed to continue would be highly prejudicial to the interest of the United States of America."

"Therefore," he continued, "it was the President's desire to clarify the situation."

It was learned, meanwhile, that the first statement on the Formosan situation had been asked of the Joint Chiefs of Staff by the State Department about eighteen months ago. Since that time, the policy based on that and other appraisals had been kept up to date by continuing evaluations.

January 6, 1950

Text of the Wallace Report on China

Following is the text of the hitherto unpublished report on China made by Vice President Henry A. Wallace to President Roosevelt in 1944:

Our first stop in China was at Tihua (Urumchi), capital of Sinkiang Province. The Governor, General Sheng Shih-tsai, is a typical war-lord. The Government is personal and carried out by thorough police surveillance. Ninety per cent (90%) of the population is non-Chinese, mostly Uighur (Turki). Tension between Chinese and non-Chinese is growing with little or no evidence of ability to deal effectively with the problem. General Sheng, two years ago pro-Soviet, is now anti-Soviet, making life extremely difficult for the Soviet Consul General and Soviet citizens in Sinkiang.

There seems little reason to doubt that the difficulties in the early spring on the Sinkiang-Outer Mongolia border were caused by Chinese attempts to resettle Kazak nomads who fled into Outer Mongolia, were followed by Chinese troops who were driven back by Mongols. The Soviet Minister in Outer Mongolia stated that Mongolian planes bombed points in Sinkiang in retaliation for Chinese bombings in Outer Mongolia. He did not appear concerned regarding the situation now.

Area Will Bear Watching

Soviet officials placed primary responsibility on General Sheng for their difficulties in Sinkiang, but our Consul at Tihua and our Embassy officials felt that Sheng was acting as a front for Chungking, willingly or unwittingly. Sinkiang is an area which will bear close watching.

Due to bad weather at Chungking, we stopped for two hours at the large 20th Bomber Command (B-29) airfield near Chengtu. The first bombing of Japan had taken place only a few days before. We found morale good but complaint was freely made of inability to obtain intelligence regarding weather and Japanese positions in North China and leak of intelligence to the Japanese.

Summary of conversations with President Chiang Kai-shek is contained in a separate memorandum. Principal topics discussed were: (1) Adverse military situation, which Chiang attributed to low morale due to economic difficulties and to failure to start an all-out Burma offensive in the spring as promised at Cairo; (2) Relations with the Soviet Union and need for their betterment in order to avoid possibility of conflict (Chiang, obviously motivated by necessity rather than conviction, admitted the desirability of understanding with U.S.S.R., and requested our good offices in arranging for conference); (3) Chinese Government-Communist relations, in regard to which Chiang showed himself so prejudiced against the Communists that there seemed little prospect of satisfactory or enduring settlement as a result of the negotiations now under way in Chungking; (4) Dispatch of the United

States Army Intelligence Group to North China, including Communist areas, to which Chiang was initially opposed but on last day agreed reluctantly but with apparent sincerity; (5) Need for reform in China, particularly agrarian reform, to which Chiang agreed without much indication of personal interest.

Soong Concerned

It was significant that T. V. Soong took no part in the discussions except as an interpreter. However, in subsequent conversations during visits outside of Chungking he was quite outspoken, saying that it was essential that something "dramatic" be done to save the situation in China, that it was "five minutes to midnight" for the Chungking Government. Without being specific he spoke of need for greatly increased United States Army air activity in China and for reformation of Chungking Government. He said that Chiang was bewildered and that there were already signs of disintegration of his authority. (Soong is greatly embittered by the treatment received from Chiang during the past half year.)

Conversations with Ambassador [Clarence E.] Gauss and other Americans indicated discouragement regarding the situation and need for positive American leadership in China.

Mr. Wallace and Mr. Vincent [John Carter Vincent, director of Far Eastern Office of the State Department] called on Dr. Sun Fo and Madame Sun Yat-sen. Dr. Sun had little to contribute. He was obviously on guard. Madame Sun was outspoken. She described undemocratic conditions to which she ascribed lack of popular support for government; said that Dr. Sun Fo should be spokesman for liberals who could unite under his leadership; advised Mr. Wallace to speak frankly to President Chiang who was not informed of conditions in China. Madame Sun's depth and sincerity of feeling is more impressive than her political acumen but she is significant as an inspiration to Chinese liberals. Dr. Sun Fo does not impress one as having strength of character required for leadership but the fact that he is the son of Sun Yat-sen makes him a potential front for liberals.

Mr. Vincent talked with Dr. Quo Tai-chi, former Foreign Minister and for many years Ambassador in London, and to K. P. Chen, leading banker. They see little hope in Chiang's leadership. Dr. Quo spoke in support of Sun Fo under whom he thought a liberal coalition was possible. Quo is an intelligent but not a strong character. K. P. Chen said that economic situation had resolved itself into a race against time; that new hope and help before the end of the year might be effective in holding things together.

Conversations with other Chinese officials in Chungking developed little of new interest. The Minister of Agriculture (Shen Hunglieh, who incidentally knows little about agriculture) showed himself an outspoken anti-Communist. General Ho Ying-chin, Chief of Staff and Minister of War, also an anti-Communist, is influential as a political rather than a military general. Dr. Chen Li-fu, Minister of Education, a leading reactionary party politician, also had little to say. Ironically, he took Mr. Wallace to visit the Chinese Industrial Co-operatives, which he is endeavoring to bring under his control to prevent their becoming a liberalizing social influence.

Conversations with provincial government officials were also without much significance. As an indication of political trends, there were unconfirmed reports that the provincial officials in Yunnan, Kwangsi, and Kwangtung Provinces were planning a coalition to meet the situation in the event of disintegration of Central Government control. In Szechwan Province the Governor, Chang Chun, is a strong and loyal friend of President Chiang. The loyalty of military factions, however, is uncertain. In Kansu Province the Governor, Ku Chenglun, is a mild-appearing reactionary who, during his days as Police Commissioner in Nanking, earned the title of "bloody Ku."

Developments subsequent to conversations with General [Claire L.] Chennault and Vincent in Kunming and Kweilin have confirmed their pessimism with regard to the military situation in East China. There was almost uniform agreement among our military officers that unification of the American military effort in China, and better coordination of our effort with that of the Chinese, was absolutely essential. It was also the general belief that, the Japanese having during recent months made China an active theatre of war, it was highly advisable to take more aggressive air action against such Japanese bases as Hankow, Canton, Nanking and Shanghai. However, the factor of loss of Chinese life at those places was recognized as an important consideration. It was the consensus that Chinese troops, when well fed, well equipped, and well led, can be effectively used. A number of Chinese generals were mentioned as potentially good leaders. Among them were Generals Chen Cheng, Chang Fa-kwei and Pai Chunghai.

Mongols in Control

In Outer Mongolia there is considerable evidence of healthy progress, military preparedness, and nationalist spirit. Soviet influence is without doubt strong but political and administrative control appear to be in the hands of capable Mongols. Any thought of resumption of effective Chinese sovereignty would be un-

realistic. On the contrary, it is well to anticipate considerable agitation in Inner Mongolia for union with Outer Mongolia after the war.

Specific conclusions and recommendations regarding the situation in China were incorporated in telegrams dispatched from New Delhi on June 28.

We should bear constantly in mind that the Chinese, a non-fighting people, have resisted the Japanese for seven years. Economic hardship and uninspiring leadership have induced something akin to physical and spiritual anemia. There is widespread popular dislike for the Kuomintang Government. But there is also strong popular dislike for the Japanese and confidence in victory.

Chiang, a man with an Oriental military mind, sees his authority threatened by economic deterioration, which he does not understand, and by social unrest symbolized in communism, which he thoroughly distrusts; and neither of which he can control by military commands. He hoped that aid from foreign allies would pull him out of the hole into which an unenlightened administration (supported by landlords, warlords and bankers) has sunk him and China.

Chiang is thoroughly "Eastern" in thought and outlook. He is surrounded by a group of party stalwarts who are similar in character. He has also, reluctantly, placed confidence in westernized Chinese advisers (his wife and T. V. Soong are outstanding examples) with regard to foreign relations. Now he feels that foreign allies have failed him and seeks in that and the "Communist menace" a scapegoat for his Government's failure. His hatred of Chinese Communists and distrust of the U. S. S. R. cause him to shy away from liberals. The failure of foreign aid has caused him to turn away from his uncongenial "Western" advisers and draw closer to the group of "Eastern" advisers for whom he has a natural affinity and for whom he has been for years more a focal point and activating agent of policy than an actual leader.

At this time, there seems to be no alternative to support of Chiang. There is no Chinese leader or group now apparent of sufficient strength to take over the Government. We can, however, while supporting Chiang, influence him in every possible way to adopt policies with the guidance of progressive Chinese, which will inspire popular support and instill new vitality into China's war effort. At the same time, our attitude should be flexible enough to permit utilization of any other leader or group that might come forward offering greater promise.

Chiang, at best, is a short-term investment. It is not believed that he has the intelligence or political strength to run post-war China. The leaders of post-war China will be brought forward by evolution or revolution, and it now seems more likely the latter.

POSSIBLE POLICY LINE RELATIVE TO LIBERAL ELEMENTS IN CHINA

Our policy at the present time should not be limited to support of Chiang. It is essential to remember that we have in fact not simply been supporting Chiang, but a coalition, headed by Chiang and supported by the landlords, the warlord group most closely associated with the landlords, and the Kung group of bankers.

We can, as an alternative, support those elements which are capable of forming a new coalition, better able to carry the war to a conclusion and better qualified for the post-war needs of China. Such a coalition could include progressive banking and commercial leaders, of the K. P. Chen type, with a competent understanding both of their own country and of the contemporary Western world; the large group of Western-trained men whose outlook is not limited to perpetuation of the old, landlord-dominated rural society of China; and the considerable group of generals and other officers who are neither subservient to the landlords nor afraid of the peasantry.

The emergence of such a coalition could be aided by the manner of alloting both American military aid and economic aid, and by the formulation and statement of American political aims and sympathies, both in China and in regions adjacent to China.

The future of Chiang would then be determined by Chiang himself. If he retains the political sensitivity and the ability to call the turn which originally brought him to power, he will swing over to the new coalition and head it. If not, the new coalition will in the natural course of events produce its own leader.

January 19, 1950

U. S. RECALLS AIDES IN CHINA AS PEIPING SEIZES OFFICES

PACTS HELD BROKEN

Communists Bar Face-Saving Device in Culmination of Long Series of Abuses

By HAROLD B. HINTON
Special to THE NEW YORK TIMES.

WASHINGTON, Jan. 14—Dean Acheson, Secretary of State, ordered today the withdrawal of consular personnel from the entire mainland of Communist-occupied China. The step had the specific approval of President Truman.

The action followed the seizure yesterday of the United States consular offices in Peiping in disregard of treaties of 1901 and 1943, and over the repeated formal protests of O. Edmund Clubb, Consul General in Peiping. The seizure, described by Chinese Communist officials as a "requisition," was effected by four civilian officials supported by the police.

The seized building was in one of four United States compounds in Peiping, and had been used prior to 1943 as barracks for the Marine Legation Guard. In 1943 the United States surrendered its extraterritorial rights under the Boxer Protocol of 1901. China guaranteed possession of this and other official United States buildings in perpetuity.

Connally Calls for "Amends"

Senator Tom Connally, chairman of the Senate Foreign Relations Committee, said tonight that the Chinese Communist Government must "make amends" for its disregard of international obligations in seizing the Peiping consulate.

This incident, the latest in a series of humiliations and harassments the Chinese Communists have visited on United States officials in several parts of China, has been building up since Jan. 6. The State Department had withheld any public announcement or discussion of it in the hope that higher Communist authorities would appreciate the gravity of the contemplated step and would find a way to overrule the action without "losing face."

Announcement was held up until it was certain the seizure had taken place and that there would be no official reconsideration. It was also delayed until Mr. Acheson's withdrawal orders had been dispatched to the 135 consular representatives and their families in Peiping, Tientsin, Shanghai, Nanking and Tsingtao. The consulate at Tsingtao has been closed for business for some time and its personnel is awaiting transportation.

W. Walton Butterworth, Assistant Secretary of State for Far Eastern Affairs, was the departmental spokesman in explaining the background of the incident.

"It is completely unprecedented," he said. "That is why we take such grave exception to it. It is more in the nature of application of tribal law than international law."

Recognition Made Remote

A high Administration official made it clear that the complete break of contact with the Chinese Communists would have no effect on President Truman's declared policy of non-intervention on behalf of the Nationalist Government in Formosa. What is left of the United States Embassy to China is with Generalissimo Chiang Kai-shek's Government, because that is the only Chinese Government officially recognized by Washington.

The Peiping incident, in Administration opinion, has pushed even further into the future the nebulous possibility of United States recognition of the Chinese Communist Government. In all the annoying actions against United States officials, the Peiping Government has never once apologized or undone unauthorized actions.

It has not only manifested no desire for United States recognition, but it has demonstrated it will not live up to the obligations that are a sine qua non, under international law, of recognition of a new government, in the opinion of officials here.

Such obligations include respect of property rights, recognition of American personnel, mutual respect for sovereignty and territorial integrity.

Mr. Butterworth said today that if the Chinese Communist Government was serious about seeking China's seat on the Security Council of the United Nations, it would have to accept the obligations of membership in the United Nations.

The Peiping seizure was carried out without any show of military force, and no United States representatives were arrested. The building from which they were ousted adjoins another principal building, and they simply moved codes and records, such as were not destroyed, into the second.

The movement started on Jan. 6, when the Chinese military authorities in Peiping issued a proclamation stating that land formerly occupied by foreign countries, under "unequal treaties," for the purpose of stationing troops would be recovered. The following day, they sent a communication to the Consul General "requisitioning" the building that was seized yesterday, as the proclamation had said that military exigencies would require immediate requisition of the foreign barracks.

At that point the State Department instructed Mr. Clubb to make known to Chou En-lai, Foreign Minister of the Communist Government, that the land and building in question were occupied as a result of the treaties of 1901 and 1943 and had not been used for quartering soldiers since 1943. They now house the offices of the Consulate General.

Mr. Clubb's communication to General Chou, as well as subsequent formal notes, was returned to him, although it was evident it had been opened and read. Some of the notes were sent back by the messenger who delivered them, and others were returned by registered mail. None of them, however, elicited any reply.

Move Made Through Britain

In Washington the State Department had notified the British Embassy of the developing situation, and on Jan. 10 it requested the British Foreign Office to have its officer in charge in Peiping convey a note of protest on behalf of the United States to General Chou or to the highest Communist official available. This was done.

In this communication an effort was made to give the Communists a face-saving device. It was stated that the United States Government had no objection to turning over to the Peiping authorities a plot of ground west of the consular compound, on which a United States building had been erected.

Mr. Butterworth explained today that the withdrawal of United States consular staffs would be done in an orderly manner, stretched over considerable time, and that "there won't be any one big dramatic exit." He said the officials would proceed to inventory Government property, pack their records and personal effects, and then await transportation.

The State Department will seek to supplement available commercial transportation, so that the diplomats may get out of China reasonably soon. Whatever means are provided for the officials will also be made available to about 3,000 United States citizens who are still in China, despite repeated warnings issued by the State Department as the Communist armies swept southward.

In his statement tonight Senator Connally said:

"The Department of State of the United States very properly has lodged aggressive protests with the Chinese Communists. It has also directed the closing of all of our consulates in China. Such action was entirely warranted, and I heartily approve of the same. The Chinese Communist Government is seeking diplomatic recognition. No nation is entitled to such recognition that does not respect international law and does not respect the representatives of other Governments and the rights of their citizens."

January 15, 1950

CHOU BRANDS U. S. CHINA'S WORST FOE

By HENRY R. LIEBERMAN

Special to THE NEW YORK TIMES.

HONG KONG, Sept. 30 — Chou En-lai, Premier and Foreign Minister of the Chinese People's Republic, denounced the United States today as his Government's "most dangerous enemy."

In a major speech delivered on the eve of Communist China's first anniversary as a state, he declared that the "United States Government has stood all along on the side of the enemy of the Chinese people in our war of liberation, using all its might to help the Kuomintang reactionaries in attacking the Chinese people."

"Since the establishment of the People's Republic of China, the hostile attitude of the American Government toward the Chinese people has become intensified," he said.

The address, which dealt with both foreign and domestic issues, was made to the National Committee of the People's Political Consultative Conference in Peiping and broadcast over a nation-wide hook-up on the China mainland. It was an unusually lengthy speech with the official Chinese text released here by New China News Agency running to 11,500 characters.

Refers to "Liberation" Plans

Without mentioning the Security Council's decision to permit the Peiping regime to participate in discussion of the Formosa problem at Lake Success, Premier Chou declared the Chinese Communists were still determined to "liberate" the island. He listed Tibet, too, as an area remaining on the Communists' "liberation" schedule.

Praising the "bravery and determination" of the forces of Kim Il Sung, the North Korean Premier, the Chinese Communist Premier also expressed confidence that the North Koreans would overcome "many difficulties for final victory" in Korea by means of "continued resistance."

Mr. Chou, who was the leading Communist negotiator in the abortive peace talks with the Kuomintang during General Marshall's mediation mission, hailed the "close military, economic and cultural alliance" established between the Peiping regime and the Soviet Union.

He pointed out that Communist China had also signed trade agreements with three countries of the Soviet bloc — Poland, Czechoslovakia and North Korea and was now negotiating similar trade pacts with East Germany and Hungary.

According to Mr. Chou, the Chinese People's Republic already has established full-fledged diplomatic relations with seventeen governments, including Burma, India, Denmark, Sweden, Switzerland and Indonesia as well as eleven members of the Soviet bloc. He said eight others had "signified willingness" to establish such relations — Britain, Pakistan, the Netherlands, Norway, Israel, Finland, Afghanistan and Ceylon.

Finding fault with the past British attitude toward Communist China notwithstanding Britain's offer of diplomatic recognition, Mr. Chou declared:

"The question of establishing relations with an imperialistic nation is more complicated than the question of establishing trade relations.

"Here I may especially mention the long but fruitless negotiations with Great Britain. The reason for failure to reach any results in the negotiations is because the British Government on the one hand signified its recognition of the People's Republic of China and on the other agreed to continued illegal occupation of China's seat in the United Nations by 'delegates' of the Chinese Kuomintang."

Scores British on Hong Kong

He added that the Peiping government also was "gravely concerned" over Britain's alleged "unfriendly attitude" toward "Chinese residents in Hong Kong and other places." The Communists have criticized the British immigration restrictions in Hong Kong and Singapore and the crackdown on some Communist organs under emergency regulations.

Mr. Chou reserved his bitterest attacks, however, for the United States. He accused the United States of "plotting" to bar Communist China from the United Nations and exclude her along with the Soviet Union from the signing of a Japanese peace treaty. He also complained about United States' support of Syngman Rhee's South Korean regime, declared the United States was rearming Japan and reiterated earlier charges about alleged bombing and strafing of Manchurian territory by American planes from Korea.

"The United States Government because of its frenzied and ruthless imperialistic aggression has been proved the most dangerous enemy of the People's Republic of China," he said.

ALL GOODS TO CHINA EMBARGOED BY U. S.

Non-Strategic Cargoes Placed Under Ban as Well as Vital Material for Communists

Special to THE NEW YORK TIMES.

WASHINGTON, Dec. 6—A virtual embargo on all shipments of any kind to Red China and to Manchuria was announced tonight by the Department of Commerce. In a tightening of regulations covering the movement of non-strategic as well as strategic materials, the agency called upon customs collectors to have goods unloaded from vessels on which they had been put under general licenses previously issued.

Tonight's action followed by less than three days the imposition of new restrictions on the shipment of goods to Red China, Hong Kong and Macao. The regulations, effective last Monday, had tightened previous curbs on the export of goods to those destinations.

Tonight's order, dealing with the export of goods of American origin, specified that all ships that have loaded cargo for Red China, Hong Kong and Macao under previous general export licenses must be stopped and their cargoes held if they come into any United States port before clearing the country.

Licenses to Be Required

Under the order, validated licenses will be required for each shipment to the specified Far East destinations if the vessel has not been cleared at its final port of departure in the United States or if it passes through the Panama Canal after having been cleared. These licenses, it was conceded, will be extremely difficult to obtain from the Office of International Trade. Under today's order non-licensed cargoes routed through the Panama Canal will be unloaded there.

The Commerce Department's action came a few hours after Senator Herbert R. O'Conor, Democrat of Maryland, had demanded in a Senate speech that the Government stop eight ships of American registry which, he said, were at sea with cargoes of strategic materials destined for China.

He said the ships had cleared the Port of New York after Nov. 2, but that it might still be possible to intercept some at the Canal Zone.

Today's order on cargoes excepted only perishable foods, not including frozen foods.

It was explained that many vessels clearing from New York for the Far East make final United States stops at San Francisco or other West Coast ports, where their cargoes can be inspected. Customs regulations, it was added, require that a ship call at the port her master has designated as his last port of call in this country.

The new licensing provisions provide penalties for ships that are diverted at sea to avoid touching at an American port where their cargoes could be inspected.

Order Includes Manchuria

Tonight's order covering foreign goods in transit through this country en route to China includes Manchuria, as well as Hong Kong and Macao, applies to merchandise whether or not it is of strategic value, and requires a validated export license for each individual shipment.

All commodities that are of strategic value have been under export license requirements for a long time. Non-listed goods have been granted a general license, which meant that they could be exported freely without special permission. Revocation of the general license now means that nothing whatever may be shipped to Chinese areas without special permission.

No licenses for the export of strategic material to China have been granted since the invasion of Korea and very few before that time, Commerce officials said tonight.

The British Crown Colony of Hong Kong and the Portuguese-controlled port of Macao are included in the destinations requiring special license because of the volume of goods that have been transshipped there to Red China in recent months.

Representatives of foreign traders here tonight said that the orders amounted to an embargo in everything but name. They predicted a speedy drying up of the currently small volume of goods moving to Red China and foresaw probable retaliation on the part of the Chinese in the form of a refusal by Communist China to ship tin, tungsten, tung oil and other strategic materials that have been imported here in growing volume over recent months.

RED CHINA PRESSES HATE U.S. CAMPAIGN

By ARTHUR MOORE

Copyright 1951 by the New York Times Company and North American Newspaper Alliance, Inc.

AT SEA, Off the China Coast, Feb. 5—Communist China's main immediate grievance against the United States lies in its firm belief that Washington still is supplying Chiang Kai-shek with war material and dreams of helping him to reconquer the mainland and to become an American puppet pillaging his countrymen while conceding to Americans a dominant position in foreign trade and the exploitation of China's resources.

The second grievance is a belief that the United States intends to make similar use of President Syngman Rhee in Korea. General of the Army Douglas MacArthur, who appears to have regarded these two men as former wartime allies to whom he owed some personal loyalty, gave some ground for suspicion by his visit to Formosa and his eulogy of Chiang.

The Chinese are not well informed about American internal politics and the fact that President Truman publicly rebuked General MacArthur for an unauthorized message published in the United States passed unnoticed as did much else, including the fact that there are no American troops in Formosa.

The Chinese believe Generalissimo Chiang and President Rhee, who cling to General MacArthur, are on America's back and they see little difference between Senator Joseph McCarthy and President Truman or Secretary of State Dean Acheson.

Walls in Peiping and Tientsin display posters and papers publish cartoons representing Americans as imperialists and brutal tyrants performing unspeakable outrages and dripping with the blood of their victims.

Recently there was a "hate week" and the whole nation is being taught—and this in time of peace—to hate another nation.

Sunday, Jan. 28, was a day of women's processions in protest against the United States. At half past nine in the morning I drove out to see the Summer Palace. I met long files of women marching to the Forbidden City with bands and banners and songs and slogans.

When I returned in the afternoon the processions still were going on. In late afternoon I went shopping in Morrison Street and covered the market and again met thousands on my way. As a method of preaching world peace the inculcation of hate seemed to me of doubtful efficacy. But there also were jolly children dancing the Yang-Ke, the popular peasant dance that the Army has brought from the country to the towns.

The whole parade was a day's outing and fun and probably when Chinese-American friendship is renewed, as it is bound to be sooner or later, the seeds of hatred will prove to have taken no deep root. Public opinion can shift quickly. The Yankees may be invited to dance the Yang-Ke.

U. S. Trips Are Shunned

At present the United States is pictured as a kind of inferno. For a Chinese merchant to go there on business or a student to study is impossible and to reveal that the thought of such madness could enter his head would be social suicide. No sane man would go to hell voluntarily.

The saying that every people gets the government it deserves does not commend itself. There are "good people" in America—those for example who read The Daily Worker—but they are bound in the chains of the capitalist oppressors and can assert themselves only by revolution.

How has this conception of the United States arisen? It has been suggested to me that a low type of American who haunted Shanghai has some responsibility. Shanghai had the reputation of being one of the most vicious cities in the world and among its gangsters engaged in dope traffic and the white slave market no doubt Americans were to be found. But I don't believe the Chinese judged Americans by these crooks or the latter could nullify the impression produced by devoted educationists and missionaries.

Latin America a Target

It is, however, true to say that whereas the Chinese do not accuse big British companies of meddling in politics in the present century American business gets no such acquittal. But the glaring example produced is not in China but in Latin America. The Chinese accuse Americans of making and unmaking dictators there to suit their business interests and of financing their partisans. In the Chinese view the Monroe Doctrine, originally designed to stop the spread of European colonization (and exploitation) in Central and South America, has become a charter for exploiters who under its cover monopolize control.

The dominant position in which the United States found itself at the end of World War II when Europe, including Britain, lay stricken has led it to set up a kind of perverted Monroe Doctrine in Asia, it is charged; in short, instead of the New World redressing the balance of the old, as the British statesman Canning hoped, the United States wants to upset the balance of the Old World.

This view of Latin America as a mere appendage of the United States leads to anger at the number of Latin "stooges" with voting powers in the United Nations and with their interference in the affairs of Korea and now in the affairs of China since they have supported the American resolution naming China an aggressor.

Had I had the opportunity I could have told Premier and Foreign Minister Chou En-lai on the basis of my experience in Korea that several things are not as they seem to him.

When General MacArthur returned from his interview with President Truman at Wake Island he spoke some winged words to Syngman Rhee, who then had to drop his plan of appointing governors for reoccupied provinces of North Korea.

I could have told Mr. Chou also that an American administrator appointed to assist in setting up interim civil authorities told me that he would have nothing to do with Syngman Rhee's nominees; that neither the members of the former United Nations commission nor of the new commission had the slightest use for Syngman Rhee; that the South Korean Assembly (which he is able to defy because like an American President he is elected for a term of years) has no use for him and ordered him to abolish martial law and to stop daily executions; that the American correspondents in Korea were as disgusted as the rest of us at these executions; that Brigadier Brodie, commanding the Twenty-ninth Commonwealth Brigade, forbade executions from taking place in his area and forced President Rhee's police to release their victims lest they be shot themselves; that the executions and burying alive of prisoners by North Koreans is equally savage and that for cruelty there is not a pin to choose between the North and South.

Any idea that President Rhee will politically survive the war may be dismissed. The intention of the Korean commission is that the South Korean and North Korean Governments both will disappear when free elections throughout the whole country have produced a constituent assembly, which will install a provisional government while it devises a constitution. But this knowledge does not penetrate to Peiping.

February 24, 1951

U. S. BARS RED CHINA IN TALKS ON JAPAN

Special to THE NEW YORK TIMES.

WASHINGTON, April 13—The United States rejected in full today British suggestions that Communist China take part in the negotiations for a Japanese peace treaty.

The brusque dismissal of proposals made by Britain about a fortnight ago was based on the fact that the United States recognizes Nationalist China and already has, in fact, given that Government a copy of the proposed peace settlement for its consideration.

Obviously stung by charges that the United States intended or was likely to meet the British requests, the State Department authorized Michael J. McDermott, its press officer, to make the following statement at a news conference:

"The United States recognizes the National Government of China and has not and does not contemplate discussions with the Peiping regime regarding the Japanese peace settlement.

"We have discussed the treaty with the Republic of China and have provided the National Government with a copy of the draft treaty. The United States has vigorously opposed the admission of the Peiping regime to the United Nations. We shall continue to follow that policy."

The admission of the Communist Peiping regime to the United Nations was not one of the points raised by the British in their aide memoire suggesting discussions with the Chinese Communists. The State Department's reference to that issue, therefore, could be designed only to answer that question in advance.

The British did propose, however, that Formosa be returned to "China"—by which they meant Communist China—and that the treaty make that clear as an ultimate, if not an immediate, objective.

Surrender Terms Noted

The State Department also had a response to that suggestion, but as a rejection it was less clearcut than that to the proposal that Communist China be brought into the treaty talks.

"Japan renounced all rights to Formosa at the surrender," Mr. McDermott said. "United States policy toward Formosa remains as repeatedly stated since the outbreak of aggression in Korea."

Asked to restate that policy once again, Mr. McDermott said that it called for the neutralization of the island by the Seventh United States Fleet, with the hope that its disposition could be settled by "peaceful means" in the future.

The Japanese treaty proposed by this Government does not specify that the Formosa issue will be settled, and states only the fact of Japan's renunciation of rights to the island. Originally, however, it was contemplated that the Big Four of the Pacific — the United States, Britain, China and the Soviet Union—try to negotiate the disposition of Formosa, and that if these powers failed within a year, the question would go before the United Nations General Assembly.

Ambassador-at-Large John Foster Dulles, who has led the settlement talks for this Government, meanwhile left for Japan today for another series of conversations with the Japanese and the initiation of Lieut. Gen. Matthew B. Ridgway to the subject.

General of the Army Douglas MacArthur has played an active part in the discussions of the treaty with the Japanese and he was being warmly praised today for his success in that role.

Before leaving this afternoon, Mr. Dulles made public a telegram he had sent General MacArthur on Wednesday shortly after he had been relieved of his commands.

Emphasizing that "both political parties" had agreed on a Japanese peace "along the lines you and I have discussed," Ambassador Dulles continued:

"As I said to you last February, the progress already made along the road to peace has been due to the foundation you have laid and the wise counsel you have given. I want to draw further on that counsel and look forward eagerly to seeing you again next week."

Brief Talk May Be Held

The general's response that he planned to leave Tokyo on Monday eliminated the possibility of extended talks, but both Mr. Dulles and State Department officials hoped that a brief exchange might be held between the two men.

The bipartisan character of the proposed peace settlement was underlined by a "best of luck" telegram to Mr. Dulles from Governor Dewey.

The Governor also paid his respects to the General's accomplishments in the treaty negotiations, and, by inference, to his policies in the Far East, the public expression of which cost the General his commands.

April 14, 1951

RED CHINA'S ASSETS IN U. S. ARE FROZEN

By WALTER H. WAGGONER
Special to THE NEW YORK TIMES.

WASHINGTON, Dec. 16—The United States, in actions believed to have fallen just short of a war declaration, froze Chinese Communist funds in United States territory tonight and prohibited United States ships from calling at Chinese ports.

These steps, taken less than twelve hours after President Truman had proclaimed a national emergency, completed an economic embargo characteristic of a state of war.

The State, Treasury and Commerce Departments acted in concert on the moves.

The United States took this action alone. That the Government had consulted other friendly powers was not denied, and the fact that the United States acted unilaterally indicated disapproval by the other nations.

The State Department said that the freezing of Communist China's assets and the barring of United States ships from her ports had been "forced upon us" by the intervention of the Chinese Communists in Korea.

"In view of the commitment of Chinese resources in this unprovoked aggressive activity," the Department continued, "this Government cannot permit the Chinese Communists to have access to United States supplies or assets in the United States, the use of which under present circumstances clearly runs counter to the interests and objectives of the United Nations in the Far Eastern crisis."

The Treasury Department said that the purpose of the controls was to "prevent financial transactions with these areas, which would be inimical to the interests of the United States."

The control of assets also was applied to those held by the North Koreans, but these were said to be "negligible."

The prohibition against calls by United States ships at Chinese Communist ports in effect merely tightened the Commerce Department order of Dec. 3 that barred all exports to Communist China.

Both actions were likely to have an adverse effect on such trading centers as British Hong Kong and Portuguese Macao. Chinese Communist funds had been used for purchasing supplies sent to those ports and then transshipped to embargoed China.

Although both orders go into effect immediately, they are not retroactive and do not invalidate transactions already completed.

The regulation blocking the use of Chinese Communist and North Korean assets applied to the continental United States and its territories. The effect of the ruling was to forbid transactions involving bank accounts or other such assets held by either the Communist regime or by its nationals.

The State Department said it was not the desire of the United States that the restrictions be permanent. But it added:

"So long as a willful group of Chinese Communist leaders are willing to subvert their national interests and the welfare of the Chinese people to the designs of international Communist imperialism, it is impossible for this Government to act otherwise.

"If the Chinese Communists choose to withdraw their forces of aggression and act in conformity with United Nations principles, this Government will be prepared promptly to consider removing restrictions and restoring normal trade relations."

To determine the extent and location of the assets to be blocked, the Treasury Department will make a census of Chinese and Korean property in the United States, beginning Monday morning.

December 17, 1950

RED CHINA SEIZES AMERICAN ASSETS

By HENRY R. LIEBERMAN
Special to THE NEW YORK TIMES.

HONG KONG, Dec. 28—The Peiping regime issued a decree today ordering the seizure of all United States property and freezing all United States public and private bank deposits in Red China as an act of retaliation against the "economic sanctions" applied by Washington.

[In Washington, according to The Associated Press, a top Commerce Department official estimated that all the American property newly seized in Red China would total "considerably less than $100,000,000." This official, who asked not to be named, said that most United States property in China had been seized when the Communist regime took over and that little was left to be "liquidated" under the new order by the Communist Government.]

Under the provisions of the decree promulgated by Premier Chou En-lai, United States nationals remaining in China will be able to draw on their accounts for living expenses only, with the permission of the local authorities.

The New China News Agency said that the Finance and Economic Commission of the State Council would issue a separate order regulating the amounts that could be withdrawn for such purposes.

The order affects diplomatic, missionary and commercial property of considerable value. This includes the imposing Embassy in Nanking, various consulates and a large number of houses acquired under the surplus property agreement with the Chinese Nationalists. It also includes mission schools and universities, privately owned real estate, the installations of the American oil companies, and the holdings of two American-owned utilities in Shanghai. The utilities are the Shanghai Power Company, which is owned by the Electric Bond and Share Company through the American and Foreign Power Company, and the Shanghai Telephone Company.

The Shanghai Power Company represents an estimated investment of $60,000,000, while the book value of the Shanghai Telephone Company was reckoned at about $17,000,000 after the Communists captured Shanghai in May, 1949.

According to the New China News Agency, Premier Chou's order was issued in retaliation against the "economic sanctions" announced by the United States on Dec. 16. This was a reference to

Washington's decision to freeze Red China's assets in the United States and prohibit American ships from calling at ports on the China mainland.

It was the second reprisal taken by the Communist-dominated Peiping regime against economic crackdowns by the United States. After Washington had applied blanket licensing restrictions on all American goods destined for Communist China, Hong Kong and Macao, Peiping responded with an embargo on shipments of China products to the United States and Japan. The Bank of China in Shanghai also suspended transactions in United States dollars, Canadian dollars and Filipino pesos.

"The American Government is trying to follow up armed aggression against Taiwan [Formosa], the bombing of the northeast [Manchuria] and the shelling of merchantmen with an attempt to loot the Chinese people of their property," the Communist news agency charged in a Chinese-language dispatch announcing Premier Chou's order.

The agency added that the Peiping Government was determined to "counter aggression and hostile action and prevent economic sabotage by Americans within the territory of the People's Republic of China."

It remains to be seen how the Peiping regime and the local governments will deal with the question of living allowances for the Americans remaining in China. The bitter anti-American campaign now being waged on the mainland already has made living conditions more difficult for American missionaries and educators who are unwilling to fall in completely with Communist propaganda lines.

The New China News Agency summarized Premier Chou's order on two points. Following is the unofficial translation of the Chinese-language text on these points:

"1. Local People's Governments shall control and make inventories of all property of American government and American enterprises. These properties may not be transferred or disposed of without authorization of the military and administrative commissions. In cases of provinces and municipalities that are under the direct jurisdiction of the Central People's Government such transfers and disposals should be authorized only by the Finance and Economic Commission of the State Council. Owners and those in charge of these properties shall be responsible for the protection of the properties.

"2. American public and private deposits within the territory of the People's Republic of China shall be frozen. Necessary expenses to maintain lawful merchants and the living of individuals may be withdrawn only upon approval by the local People's Governments. The amounts are to be regulated by the Finance and Economic Commission of the State Council in a separate order."

December 29, 1950

157

RUSK HINTS U. S. AID TO REVOLT IN CHINA

Assistant Secretary Promises More Help to Nationalists— Dulles Calls Mao Puppet

By RUSSELL PORTER

Dean Rusk, Assistant Secretary of State for Far Eastern Affairs, in a speech here last night promised continued aid to the Chinese Nationalists and, by implication, offered to help the Chinese people if they revolted against their Communist masters.

He pledged the United States also not to recognize the Communist regime in China, saying that it might be "a colonial Russian government" but was not Chinese and was not "the Government of China." The United States recognizes the Nationalist Government as more "authentically" representing the people of China, he added.

Mr. Rusk spoke at the Waldorf-Astoria Hotel, at the twenty-fiftn anniversary dinner of the China Institute in America, a non-profit educational group for better understanding between the Chinese and American peoples. The 800 guests included supporters and opponents of past State Department policy.

The Assistant Secretary's address seemed to confirm the apparent hardening of this country's attitude toward Communist China since the recall of General of the Army Douglas MacArthur last month revived the "great debate" on foreign policy. The Rusk statement represented the firmest support given by the United States Government to the Chinese Nationalists since they were dealt with adversely in the State Department's White Paper of 1949.

Speaking from the same platform as Mr. Rusk last night, Ambassador-at-Large John Foster Dulles, President Truman's special envoy to negotiate a peace treaty with Japan, strongly backed up Mr. Rusk's position. Mr. Dulles put into specific words Mr. Rusk's theme that the Communist Government of China was merely a "puppet" regime.

In the same veiled, diplomatic way as Mr. Rusk, Mr. Dulles joined in the appeal to the Chinese to rise against foreign domination. Mr. Dulles gave assurances that Communist China would not be recognized as "the voice of China." He also called for quick action by this country to aid friends of the United States, while they still existed, both in Formosa and on the mainland of China.

Senator Paul H. Douglas, Democrat of Illinois, and Charles Edison, former Secretary of the Navy, also spoke at the dinner. They pointed up the need for quick action by asserting that, in recent months, hundreds of thousands of Chinese had been killed by the Communists.

Senator Douglas, who has been mentioned as a possible Presidential candidate next year, urged the Government to adopt a world-wide anti-Communist program.

For the Far East, he advocated the use of the veto to keep Communist China out of the United Nations, keeping Formosa out of Red hands, extension of the Marshall Plan and land reform to Asia, a Korean peace settlement providing for occupation of North Korea for 100 miles above the Thirty-eighth Parallel, an economic blockade of Communist China, and aid from Nationalist commando raids and guerrilla action on the Chinese mainland.

Urges Propaganda Drive

He proposed also a mammoth campaign of propaganda and subversion in all countries behind the Iron Curtain and a new alliance in the Near East to include Turkey, Greece, Israel and as many Arab states as would come in.

The speakers were interrupted repeatedly by applause when they proposed stronger steps in support of the Chinese Nationalists and opposed the Chinese Communists.

Henry R. Luce, editor-in-chief of Time, Life and Fortune magazine, presided at the dinner as toastmaster.

Mr. Luce, in introducing Mr. Rusk, commented that his publications had been opposed to the State Department policy on China in many instances. Later Mr. Luce commended the speaker on his "strong and vigorous statement."

Mr. Rusk said in his address:

"It is not my purpose, in these few moments this evening, to go into specific elements of our own national policy in the present situatin. But we can tell our friends in China that the United States will not acquiesce in the degradation that is being forced upon them.

"We do not recognize the authorities in Peiping for what they pretend to be. The Peiping regime may be a colonial Russian government—a Slavic Manchukuo on a larger scale. It is not the government of China. It does not pass the first test. It is not Chinese.

"It is not entitled to speak for China in the community of nations. It is entitled only to the fruits of its own conduct—the fruits of aggression upon which it is now willfully, openly and senselessly embarked.

Calls Decision Up to Chinese

"We recognize the National Government of the Republic of China, even though the territory under its control is severely restricted. We believe it more authentically represents the views of the great body of the people of China, particularly their historic demand for independence from foreign control.

"That Government will continue to receive important aid and assistance from the United States. Under the circumstances, however, such aid in itself cannot be decisive in the future of China. The decision and the effort are for the Chinese people, pooling their efforts, wherever they are, in behalf of China.

"If the Chinese people decide for freedom, they shall find friends among all the peoples of the earth who have known and love freedom. They shall find added strength from those who refuse to believe that China is fated to become a land of tyranny and aggression, and who expect China to fulfill the promise of its great past."

Mr. Rusk charged that Russia was seizing North China and was driving the Chinese into foreign aggression, against the interests of China herself, to serve the aims of the "Communist conspiracy."

He appealed to Chinese all over the world, not merely in China and Formosa, to aid the Chinese people at home to "assert their freedom."

Dulles Cites 'Abuse' by Reds

Mr. Dulles said the people and Government of the United States should not be "fooled," but should "treat the Mao Tse-tung regime for what it is—a puppet regime." This could change, he added, because "the Chinese people are abused to a degree that is causing many Chinese Communist leaders to feel rebellious against the subserviency to Moscow."

"But, unless and until actual conduct gives clear proof of change, our national self-interest, our friendship for China, and the historical dedication of our nation to the cause of human freedom combine to require that no act of ours shall contribute to a Mao Tse-tung 'success' which could fasten the yoke of Moscow on the Chinese people," he added.

"My own official concern today is the Japanese peace treaty. I can assure you that, in negotiating that treaty, we shall not consider that the voice of Mao Tse-tung is the voice of China.

"While we thus adopt a negative attitude toward Mao Tse-tung and all his ilk, we should adopt a positive attitude toward the many Chinese who remain loyal to the welfare of China and to the friendship between China and the United States which in the past served China so well."

Senator Douglas repeated the Rusk-Dulles theme that the Chinese Communist Government was merely a "puppet" regime.

The Senator said it was obvious that the United States should not permit Red China to be seated in the United Nations unless it abandoned aggression and suppression.

"The United Nations should not reward aggression by admitting the aggressor to membership," he went on. "Naturally, we hope that the awakening consciousness of the British and French people, as well as other nations, will cause their Governments to join us in opposing such action.

Would Use Veto in U. N.

"But, if necessary, we should be prepared to exercise the veto. For it is surely improper to place a government whose hands are bloody with aggression upon a tribunal to keep the peace.

"Nor should we allow Formosa, whatever may be our views concerning the strategic importance of that island, to be taken over by the Chinese Reds. To do so would again be a reward for aggression and the loss of Chiang Kai-shek's army and countless political refugees to the Chinese Communists.

"In the third place, it would be fatal to admit Red China to the discussion of the Japanese peace treaty. That would be an invitation to futility and further conflict. It is wiser instead to proceed without them.

"I believe that American public opinion has crystallized in support of the three propositions which I have just stated and, from the testimony of General Marshall before the Joint Senate Committee, I had inferred that the Administration had adopted all of them. Secretary Acheson's press interview of Wednesday, however, raises some doubt in my mind whether he is willing to use the veto."

Mr. Edison said there were "countless" Chinese who had proved over the years their stanch friendship and loyalty to the United States. He said these Chinese were willing and ready "to buy time" for the United States to rearm against the common enemy, and added: "They are entitled to the same loyalty from us."

ACHESON DEFENDS YALTA AS NECESSITY; SAYS CHIANG BACKED GRANTS TO SOVIET; DENIES PRO-RED INFLUENCE ON POLICY

UPHOLDS SECRECY

Testifies U. S. at Yalta Did Not Know Atom Bomb Would Work

CALLS M'ARTHUR IDEA RISK

Secretary Asserts Plan Would Give Russia Cause for War—Takes Stand Again Today

By WILLIAM S. WHITE
Special to THE NEW YORK TIMES.

WASHINGTON, June 4—Secretary of State Dean Acheson declared today that the attacks General of the Army Douglas MacArthur wanted to make by bombers on Communist China would have given the Russians a legal basis to enter the Korean war.

This country's world allies, he said, even before General MacArthur's recommendations for harder action in Korea, had lived in "omnipresent" fear that the conflict would spread into a third world war.

The allies had in mind, the secretary indicated, the existence of a Soviet-Communist China treaty of alliance.

Testifying for a third day before Senate committees investigating President Truman's recall of General MacArthur from his Far East command, Secretary Acheson counter-attacked the Administration's Republican foreign policy critics on a scope running far beyond the MacArthur issue.

Back on Stand Today

He left the stand at 5:10 P. M. and will return at 10 A. M. tomorrow before the panel of inquiry, which is made up of the Senate Armed Services and Foreign Relations Committees sitting jointly in closed session.

He strongly defended the Yalta agreement of 1945, which secretly gave important concessions to the Russians as vital at the time to bring the Soviet Union into the war with Japan, which the military authorities then believed would be long and bloody. The United States, he said, did not know then whether the atomic bomb would work.

He asserted that in giving the Russians the southern half of Sakhalin Island, the Kurile Islands and rights in Manchuria, including the right to accept the Japanese surrender, President Roosevelt and his associates at Yalta acted only from the necessities of the case.

The Russians, he declared, could have got a great deal more by direct action, from which nobody could have stopped them, than they got in the effort to obtain their help in the war with Japan.

He asserted that the Chinese Nationalist leaders, including Generalissimo Chiang Kai-shek, not only had accepted the Yalta arrangement thankfully at the time but two years later still were in fear that the Russians might not go through with the Yalta plan.

The Chiang forces were proceeding on the assumption that they were going to get concessions in Manchuria and the diplomatic recognition of Moscow — two events that did not occur.

Leak in Secret Feared

The Secretary testified that the Chiang regime could not be told of the secret agreements at Yalta because these involved Russia's entry against Japan at a stated date and experience had shown that military secrets could not be kept by the Chinese.

He asserted that the United States could have saved China from the Communists only by a full and dangerous intervention there, which a Democratic Administration, a Republican Congress, the Eightieth, and the American people all had rejected as "abhorrent."

The year 1948, he said, was the last year in which any decision here could have maintained the Chinese Republic of Generalissimo Chiang. The Eightieth Congress of that year, he declared, cut even the relatively small aid proposed by the Administration, and perhaps rightly so.

He said there had not been in the State Department, in 1945 or any time since, that "pro-Communist" influence that some Republicans had charged had softened United States policy toward the Communists in China.

Mr. Acheson, in a comprehensive oral statement in defense of United States policy in China, gave what appeared to be materially different testimony from that of Secretary of Defense George C. Marshall on one point.

General Marshall had testified that in going to China in 1945 for President Truman, on an internal peace mission that ultimately produced efforts to bring the Communists into the Chiang Government, he had carried a policy directive largely or exclusively made by others.

Secretary Acheson on the contrary told the inquiry that General Marshall "assisted by some of his associates" had not accepted a proposed directive handed to him by the then Secretary of State, James F. Byrnes, but prepared a draft of his own.

Truman Approved Changes

This directive, Mr. Acheson continued, was then taken back to Mr. Byrnes, who made some changes of his own, which General Marshall approved. The end product was then taken up with President Truman at a meeting in which General Marshall was present, Secretary Acheson testified.

"It was ascertained by the President at that meeting," said Mr. Acheson, "that these papers were unanimously approved and agreeable to all concerned, and to himself."

On May 10, General Marshall had testified that "the drafting of the policy [for the China mission] was taking place in the State Department" while he himself was before Congressional committees investigating the Pearl Harbor attack.

"On one or two days during the lunch period," General Marshall had said, "I had a chance to talk to Mr. Byrnes briefly in regard to it" and finally one morning—whether it was a Saturday morning or not I don't recall—I met with Mr. Byrnes, my own advisers that I have mentioned, Mr. Acheson and Mr. [John Carter] Vincent.

"When the document was read through which had been drafted and which the men that were looking after my interests though was all right, but [sic] I spent my time up here and when I finished up here I was engaged, as you would understand, each day in trying to find what was the position I was to take against the questioning around this table, so my preparation for going to China was largely a matter in this room of the investigation regarding Pearl Harbor."

Secretary Acheson himself mentioned that General Marshall had had officer associates in drafting the directive.

Some months ago, in other testimony before a Senate committee, General Marshall had in substance disclaimed responsibility for the policy of the mission, with the explanation that he was at the time involved in the Pearl Harbor inquiry.

Hurley "Established Basis"

Secretary Acheson made these among many other assertions and points to his interrogators:

1. That a Republican, Patrick J. Hurley, "established the basis" for the subsequent mission by General Marshall that ultimately produced an effort, aided by the United States, to put the Chinese Communists into the Chinese Government.
2. That Generalissimo Chiang himself had wanted to settle the Communist problem "by political means."
3. That what the United States wanted during World War II and afterward was, first, to bring all Chinese factions together to fight the Japanese rather than each other and, second, to still a civil war that would have made evacuation of the Japanese difficult if not impossible.
4. That this country faced a far different Communist problem in China than in the European countries because in China the Communists were not scattered about but held a large area and controlled 116,000,000 people. This was in answer to a point persistently raised by the Republicans that the United States after giving up on the Chiang regime had gone on supporting other anti-Communist regimes in European lands.
5. That at the time of Yalta it was thought of "the utmost importance" for the Russians to come into World War II.
6. That in this "a price" had to be paid and the Secretary doubted that any present critic would have rejected the price at the time and not in hindsight.
7. That the United States had put 50,000 Marines into North China to enlarge Generalissimo Chiang's hold and had airlifted "whole Chinese armies" into areas being evacuated by the Japanese to aid the security of his regime.
8. That this country had removed 3,000,000 Japanese from China to Japan.
9. That General Marshall himself had no "direct hand" in any of the confused China negotiations immediately after the war's end

except to try for a cessation of hostilities.

10. That the plan that did emerge for a coalition China Government would in any case have given Generalissimo Chaing a veto over the Communists and that he would have held under his command fifty anti-Communist divisions to ten Communist divisions.

11. That General Marshall had repeatedly and without success pointed out to Generalissimo Chiang that he was overextending himself politically and militarily in his struggle with the Communists.

12. That at the end of 1946 Generalissimo Chiang's forces were 2,600,000 against 1,100,000 Communist regulars and that he had a superiority in firepower of three or four to one.

13. That among those who had said, in the summer of 1947, that the Generalissimo had to make "drastic and far-reaching political and economic reforms" to hold the loyalty of the anti-Communist people was Lieut. Gen. Albert C. Wedemeyer, an officer often quoted by the Republicans in their attacks on China policy.

14. That a United States army intelligence review in January of 1949 had reported that while Generalissimo Chiang had entered the year 1948 with a numerical superiority of almost three to one over the Communists they had ended the year with greater forces and a superiority in combat effectiveness.

15. That Maj. Gen. David Barr, head of a United States military mission to China, had stated that the Nationalists had never lost a battle for lack of ammunition or equipment but had suffered under "the world's worst leadership."

16. That 80 per cent of the American war material given to the Nationalists had been lost by them and that 75 per cent of it had ended in the hands of the Communists.

17. That from the end of World War II to early 1949, the United States had given grants and credits to Generalissimo Chiang of about $2,000,000,000 divided about equally between economic aid and military aid. The value of the military aid has been challenged by many Republicans.

Mr. Acheson's presentation of his case for the China policy was termed by the chairman of the investigating panel, Senator Richard B. Russell, Democrat of Georgia, "quite a performance."

Senator Alexander Wiley, Republican of Wisconsin, called it "a pretty clear statement as to the facts that heretofore were not brought to our attention."

Hiss Is Brought In

Among those who sharply cross-examined Secretary Acheson, Senator William F. Knowland, Republican of California, for the first time brought directly into the hearing the secretary's past relationship with Alger Hiss, who is under conviction for perjury for denying aid to Communist espionage.

Mr. Knowland pointed out that Hiss was in the American delegation to Yalta and asked Mr. Acheson what part he had in that designation.

"What I had to do with," the Secretary replied, "was to sign his travel orders, which I did, as I signed the travel orders of all members of that delegation."

"You made no recommendation of any kind that he [Hiss] be included on the mission to anyone, directly or indirectly?"

"No, sir," said Mr. Acheson.

He described the quoted views of former Vice President Henry A. Wallace on the nature of Chinese communism as "quite contrary" to those held in the State and Defense Departments in the year 1945.

In those departments, he said "there was no illusion about the character of the Chinese Communists or the fact that they were Moscow-inspired."

Secretary Acheson testified that the files of the State Department had not disclosed that any of this country's allies had been personally critical of General MacArthur.

The anxieties of the allies, he said, had long antedated General MacArthur's recommendations for bombing the China mainland and using Chinese Nationalist troops, which had come from the general "rather late in the game, and then rather in a rush."

Their concern, he said, had been manifest as far back as the Inchon landing, by which General MacArthur put forces behind the enemy.

At that time, the Secretary declared, the late Ernest Bevin, the British Foreign Minister, and Robert Schuman, then French Foreign Minister, had "wanted to be very clear that this whole effort was directed toward ending this aggression in Korea and that it was not going to go any further."

Mr. Acheson testified that "nowhere" could he see forces strong enough to threaten the hold of the Communists on China. This applied to the Nationalist Chinese guerrillas at work on the mainland, he said.

He agreed with some of his Republican questioners that some of the things done at Yalta were "arguable," but he asserted over and over that what was done there had to be done in the light of the information then at hand.

He denied a suggestion from Senator H. Alexander Smith, Republican fo New Jersey, that Yalta had "undercut" Generalissimo Chiang.

The Generalissimo's troops, he said, then were in the extreme southwest of China, whereas Manchuria lay in the northeast, and they could not have gone up to receive the Japanese surrender.

REDS PUT SQUEEZE ON CHINESE IN U. S.

Millions Being Extorted for Ransom and to Avert Death or Torture of Relatives

A systematic and apparently effective plot to extort millions of dollars from a majority of the 80,000 Chinese in this country for the benefit of the Chinese Communist Government is causing great concern in Chinatown settlements.

The shakedown racket, predicated on the Chinese-American's ties to his family still in Red China, is cutting deeply into the livelihood of Chinese merchants here. In hopes of halting the flow of currency to the Far East, allegedly to pay fines imposed by the Chinese Communists, the business men of Chinatown here and in other cities have warned their gullible countrymen that to send the funds is like pouring money down a drain.

Most outspoken is Chang Chung Hai, president of the Chinese Consolidated Benevolent Association, the arbiter of family-association disputes. In the last four months 60 per cent of the Chinese in New York, Boston, Washington, Chicago and San Francisco have received letters and follow-up cablegrams from their families in small villages or through agents in Hong Kong that follow one of two patterns, he said.

The letters tell of desperate family need and ask that United States gold be sent to protect their lives. They say that property has been confiscated and that the alternative to death and torture is cash—American cash. The missives from Hong Kong generally tell of the arrest of a relative and mention ransom demands varying from $500 to $1,000 for younger people and $1,000 for older persons, according to Mr. Chang.

Although the victims have been furtive about showing the extortion notes, the subject is the most discussed in Chinatown and enough of the messages have been collected for the Chinese Journal, a local paper, to plan a full page presentation.

Mr. Chang, who for American purposes uses the first name Woodrow, reported that many of the 15,000 Chinese in this city "foolishly" sent small sums when the first threatening missives arrived. As a result they have received follow-up letters asking for more —the standard pattern of extortionists the world over.

Most of the Chinese solicited here came from the Toishan district, now a Red stronghold, and while they nod agreement when responsible merchants emphasize the futility of sending currency back home, those who handle the communications report that the money still is traveling to the Far East.

Total Put In Millions

There is no accurate estimate of how much has been extorted from the Chinese in this country. Mr. Chang places it at "a few millions". The business men shrug but say "trade is slow". The few Chinese Communists in Chinatown call the extortion racket Kuo min tang (Chinese Nationalist) propaganda.

Reports from Hong Kong show that huge sums of foreign currency are pouring into Red China. There is no way of stopping the flow, American officials told The Associated Press, except by freezing dollar remittances to all foreign countries "and that obviously is impossible."

The ransom letters are a small part of the 1,500,000 letters a week from Red China to the United States, the official added, and it is a violation of the International Postal Union Agreement to open the mail.

While there is a Hong Kong law against "demanding money with menaces" it is not applicable as the missives are inter-family communications. Officially the Communist Government does not enter the plot.

ISLANDS OUTPOSTS FOR WAR ON PEIPING

Anti-Red Chinese Commandos Raid Mainland From Chain Not 'Neutralized' by U. S.

By HENRY R. LIEBERMAN
Special to THE NEW YORK TIMES.

HONG KONG, Nov. 24—Beyond the range of the Formosa-Pescadores "neutralization" zone, where the presence of the United States Seventh Fleet has frozen Communist and Nationalist combat operations, lie two little-publicized chains of Nationalist islands that extend almost 500 miles along the Southeast China coast.

The Chinese civil war continues in this non-"neutralized" sector.

While tying down numerically superior Communist forces and partly blocking such ports as Swatow, Amoy, Foochow and Wenchow, the Nationalists actually have seized the tactical initiative with small-scale commando forays that are increasing in size.

The militarized Nationalist archipelago is held by an estimated 75,000 regular troops, commandos and guerrillas, with the regulars constituting the bulk of the force and holding the main defense positions. Confronting them are more than 300,000 Communist troops in South Kiangsu, Chekiang and Fukien Provinces on the mainland.

Separated from the mainland by two to thirty-five miles of the choppy East China Sea, the Nationalist-held islands stretch from Nanpengchun, off the coast of northern Kwangtung, to Peiyushan, northeast of Taichow Bay off the coast of Chekiang. Projected northward from Formosa, the island bases give the Nationalists a commando reach that extends 265 miles above their capital in Taipei to within 160 miles of Shanghai.

Operating from about thirty-five islands off the coast of Fukien and Chekiang, the Nationalists have been disrupting coastal shipping, conducting political warfare against the mainland and launching periodic raids against weakly defended Communist positions. With their armed junks making frequent night landings, they are also gathering intelligence by means of infiltration and seizure of Communist prisoners.

This correspondent returned recently from a tour of the major Nationalist island bases, traveling on the 1,400-ton Chinese Navy destroyer Hsinyang. Thus far

Nationalist commando operations have been limited in scope. They may well assume greater importance in the future, especially if the Korean war continues.

811 Communists Captured

Although most of the Nationalist raids have involved small groups ranging from ten to 200 men, about 4,000 Nationalists attacked Communist-held Nanchi Island, off the Fukien coast, on Oct. 11, in a three-day operation. They took 811 Communist prisoners and left an unknown number of dead on the island.

"There will be more raids," said Wang Tiao-hsun, 39, tough-looking Fukienese who commands one of the Nationalist operational headquarters on an island off the coast of his native province. Wang Tiao-hsun, a former major general who now prefers to be called "Mister," said his group had conducted fifty-three operations against the Communists from June 1 to Oct. 14 of this year.

He discussed the Fukien military situation in an operations room whose walls were covered with military maps and captured Communist trophies, including flags, posters, Communist party membership cards and medals. Among the captured Communist equipment were two deflated hot-water bags with valve attachments. These are used as life preservers by amphibious Communist troops.

Stalin on Chinese Medal

Wang handed me one of the Communist medals.

"Look," he said with contempt. "A picture of Stalin on a Chinese medal."

Of the thirty-five islands held by the Nationalists, seventeen are off Chekiang, seventeen off Fukien and one is off northern Kwangtung. They range in size from about one square mile to fifty-one square miles.

The main Nationalist island bases off Fukien include Big and Little Quemoy, which are within artillery range of Communist-held Amoy; Matsu, forty miles northeast of Foochow, and the Paichuan Islands (Hsichuan and Tungchuan), about fifteen miles southeast of Matsu. Among the major Chekiang bases are the Yüshan Islands, about 160 miles southeast of Shanghai; the Tachen Islands, about thirty miles southeast of Haimen on Taichow Bay, and Peishan about forty miles northeast of Wenchow.

The top Nationalist commands are held in the Fukien group by Lieut. Gen. Hu Lien and in the Chekiang group by Lieut. Gen. Hu Tsung-nan.

"Defensively, these islands are outposts for the protection of Taiwan [Formosa]," the 45-year-old General Hu declared at his headquarters on Big Quemoy Island. "Offensively, they offer a springboard for attack."

The Communists tried to capture Quemoy in October, 1949, but failed. General Hu expressed confidence that he could continue to hold Quemoy.

"They have no sea or air power in this area," he said. "I have more."

The New York Times   Dec. 7, 1952

JABS BY NATIONALISTS: Forces of Chiang Kai-shek have been harassing the Communists along an island arc from Nanpengchun (1) to Peiyushan (2). They recently raided Nanchi (3).

The Chinese Nationalist Navy includes destroyer escorts, minesweepers, gunboats and such landing craft as LCT's, LCM's and LCI's. In addition, armed motorized junks are operating under the various commando headquarters.

Men like Comdr. Chow Fei, 36-year-old skipper of the destroyer Hsianyang, have been on patrol, blockade and ferrying missions. Outside the Formosa Strait, which is being patrolled by the United States Seventh Fleet, the Chinese Navy is on its own.

Most of the Nationalist islands off Chekiang and Fukien are mountainous humps that would be difficult to attack from the surface. New military roads and fortifications have been built.

Aside from the troops on the islands, the small local populations have been organized politically for purposes of security, indoctrination and active support of military operations. The people live mainly by fishing, raising sweet potatoes and peanuts and carrying on some interisland trade.

Poor as they are, however, they work with a spirit of camaraderie and zest. The Nationalists are giving economic aid to the fish-

ermen. New primary schools and adult education classes also have been established.

Occasionally, the interception of a blockade-running coastal ship provides such extras as oranges for Matsu, bicycles for Quemoy and steel for a roof for the stadium in Taipei. At one island I saw guerrillas and sampan men unloading 800 tons of board lumber from the Helikon, a 1,200-ton freighter that had a British flag painted on its hull. The Helikon had been operating along the China coast.

One of the islands I visited is Shangtachen. It is a small, octopus-shaped island that rises out of the sea off Chekiang, about 230 miles north of Taipei.

This small island has an area of only three square miles. Yet it is one of the most important bases in the entire chain held by the Nationalists. Two miles to the south is the island of Hsiatachen, which has a population of 10,000.

A short distance from the Tachen islands is the island of Chouyu, where the Nationalists permit mainland junks to make commercial calls. But the Tachen islands are sealed off for reasons of security.

Shangtachen is the headquarters of a Chekiang-Kiangsu anti-Communist National Salvation Army commanded by a Nationalist general with the pseudonym of "Mr. Ching."

All Are Volunteers

Planted on the sides of Shangtachen's reddish-brown hills are three Nationalist slogans that have been written out in white pebbles: "Combat Communism, Resist Russia," "Long Live President Chiang," and "Obey the Leader."

Along the slopes one of a new series of reorganized commando groups is now undergoing seventy-two days of training. Many of the men have fought as guerrillas before.

Each of the volunteers has taken the following oath:

"With the utmost sincerity, I swear to participate in the revolutionary struggle of anti-communism and national salvation; to wipe out our humiliation and avenge our woes. I swear to fight for our principles, to be a disciple of the father of our country [Dr. Sun Yat-sen] and to follow our leader [Chiang Kai-shek] unto the death.

"Under the leadership of Mr. Ching, I shall struggle to the last with the resolution that as long as I live, there can be no place for the Communist bandits. Where the bandit exists, I shall be no more. If I do not succeed, I would prefer to be a martyr."

It does not seem to be an empty oath, for the volunteers include former local officials, landowners, merchants and the sons of Chinese killed under Communist rule on the mainland. Such phrases as ching suan (liquidation"), tou cheng ("struggle dispute") and pao chou ("revenge") recurred frequently as various trainees told their stories.

Among those seeking pao chou is Little Kuo Yi-hsun, 16, who joined the guerrillas two and a half years ago after his mother and father were "taken away" by the Communists. Another is Yu Chung, 26, who was formerly a Buddhist monk.

"The Communist policy is poison —kill, kill, kill." he said. "Buddhists do not believe in killing. But I am no longer a monk. I am now a soldier because this way I can do things that are best for my country."

There are three basic kinds of Nationalist troops on the islands: regulars, who perform defensive duties; uniformed commandos, who go on raids in organized detachments, and non-uniformed guerrillas, who assist the commandos and engage in undercover work.

On top of their daily military training, commandos on this island get four hours of political training a week. They get a rice ration of twenty-seven ounces a day and are paid the equivalent of about ten United States cents each month. In addition, they receive an allowance of about one United States dollar a month to buy food extras.

The raid detachments consist of about 1,000 men each. The commandos rely heavily on automatic weapons. They also use carbines, bazookas and mortars.

Aside from the amphibious infantry groups, there is also a special artillery group using 75 mm. mountain guns, 57 mm. anti-tank guns and heavy mortars. For transport, the commandos rely on the Chinese Navy and on raid columns consisting of armed motorized junks.

One of the transport columns is commanded by Mme. Chiang Hsi-min, a veteran guerrilla. Heading the Women's Corps on Hsiatachen is Mme. Wang Pai-mei, a motherly looking woman who was also active in Chekiang as a guerrilla during the Japanese war.

All of the men, women and children between the ages of 8 and 35 are being organized in support of the Nationalist military effort in the Tachen islands. Organizational activity is intense, camaraderie is close, and the spirit seems to be high.

December 7, 1952

EISENHOWER TO FREE CHIANG TO ATTACK CHINA BY ENDING 'NEUTRALIZING' BY 7TH FLEET

By ANTHONY LEVIERO
Special to The New York Times.

WASHINGTON, Jan. 30—President Eisenhower has decided to end the "neutralizing" role of the Seventh Fleet in the Strait of Formosa to permit the Chinese Nationalists to attack the mainland as their improved capabilities permit.

The fleet, however, will continue to patrol the troubled Far Eastern water to prevent any Chinese Communist attacks on the strategic island of Formosa, on which the beleaguered Nationalist Government under Generalissimo Chiang Kai-shek has been situated ever since the Chinese Reds swept across all of China.

This major strategic decision, the first move by the President in his effort to end the Korean stalemate, was vouched for by Capitol Hill sources.

President Eisenhower is expected to announce it soon. His forthcoming message on the State of the Union, to be delivered before a joint session of Congress on Monday, would be the likely vehicle for the historic turn in foreign and military policy, but the place for the move could not be confirmed.

No Comment on Decision

Neither White House nor State Department spokesmen would comment on the decision, which was reported to have been reached by the President and John Foster Dulles, the Secretary of State. The Joint Chiefs of Staff were then said to have been called in and directed to carry out the decision and make whatever other dispositions would be necessary.

Two main reasons were advanced in justification for changing the neutralizing role that originally had been intended at the start of the Korean war in June, 1950, to localize the war on the Korean peninsula:

1. The intransigence of the Communist negotiators at Panmunjom, who have rejected every reasonable proposal for ending the war.

2. The viewpoint of the new Administration that in performing merely a neutralizing role, the Seventh Fleet was in effect protecting the Chinese Communist hold on the mainland.

In the first historic conference at Blair House right after the outbreak of the Korean war, the decision was taken to send the Seventh Fleet from its anchorage at Cavite, in the Philippines, to patrol the Strait of Formosa. Its mission was to keep the Nationalists from making attacks on the mainland, and at the same time to keep the Communists from seizing Formosa. In other words, the United States Naval force was to keep both sides from fighting each other.

The Chinese Communists had not yet entered the Korean war at least not overtly, and the Truman Administration felt that in taking this position the Chinese Communists would not be tempted to join the conflict at a time when United States forces were fighting against overwhelming odds.

Even after the Chinese Red armies surged into Korea, the Truman Administration insisted on maintaining the fleet in the neutralizing role, contending that to do otherwise would risk a world conflict. Communist China has a mutual assistance treaty with the Soviet Union, and it was feared that any action against the mainland might provide a pretext for Moscow's entry into the war.

The fact that the Nationalist Government is now to extend its naval raids from Red-held islands to the mainland does not mean that any large offensive action is likely or even possible, it was believed. Nevertheless, the strength and potential of all the forces led by General Chiang has been considerably increased through United States aid and training during the last two years, and aggressive use of the pent-up Nationalist forces is now expected.

Little Change for Fleet

The pending decision will mean little if any change in the disposition of the Seventh Fleet. The point is that the Chiang Government will be notified that Seventh Fleet fighting units will not impede Chinese naval units making forays against the mainland.

It was realized, of course, that the decision might also provoke Communist attacks on Formosa, which lies athwart the United Nations lifeline to Korea, and therefore that special alertness would now be necessary on and around the strategic island, which also has great significance in the protection of Japan.

Action by the President will be by executive order. It was in the same manner that former President Truman, after conferring with the highest military and civilian leaders, decided not only on the neutralizing role but put United States ground, naval and air forces directly into the conflict without consulting Congress in advance.

President Eisehonwer, however, probably will notify Congress either in the forthcoming message or by calling in its leaders, who are due for their usual weekly conference with him early Monday morning.

First Fruits of Trip

The action would be the first fruits of President Eisenhower's trip to Korea to study the difficult, stalemated war on the ground. During the Presidential political campaign he electrified the nation by announcing he would go there to see what could be done to hasten the end of the war.

The announcement stirred up a great controversy. At the time President Truman declared the solution of the war was not in Korea but in Moscow, and that if General Eisenhower had any new plan for ending the conflict he should come forward and present it immediately to save lives.

General Eisenhower kept his own counsel and made the trip with leading members of his Cabinet-to-be. Later Mr. Truman, in a news conference, said that General Eisenhower's announcement of the trip had been a piece of demagoguery. However, at the suggestion of his press secretary, Roger Tubby, he acknowledged that some good might come of it.

Administration sources have said no miracles should be expected as a result of the General's trip. One major proposal made by General Eisenhower was that the training of South Korean forces be speeded up so that many more of them could move into the front lines.

Meanwhile, it became known here that Admiral Arthur W. Radford, Commander in Chief of the Pacific Fleet, was due to arrive here Monday. Navy spokesmen said his visit was for a series of conferences on Navy matters.

January 31, 1953

Hoover Group Urges Ban
Special to THE NEW YORK TIMES.

UNITED NATIONS, N. Y., Oct. 8—Former President Herbert Hoover and six other prominent Americans announced today that they were circulating a petition, to be presented to President Eisenhower, opposing the admission of the "so-called Chinese People's Republic" to the United Nations.

Sponsors of the petition include Senator H. Alexander Smith of New Jersey and Representative Walter H. Judd, both Republicans; Senator John J. Sparkman, Democratic candidate for Vice President last year; Representative John W. McCormack of Massachusetts, the House Democratic leader; former Governor Charles Edison of New Jersey and Joseph C. Grew, former Ambassador to Japan.

The petition, which other prominent citizens are being asked to sign, lists eight reasons against the admission of Communist China:

1. Communist China is "constitutionally" unable to fulfill the Charter requirement that the admission of new members is dependent upon their ability and willingness to carry out the Charter.

2. The admission of Communist China would mean the expulsion of the Nationalist Chinese Government from the United Nations, which would be "an unthinkable outrage against human decency and international justice."

3. Communist China has "systematically" disregarded every human right and violated every freedom.

4. Communist China, by "aiding" in the aggression upon South Korea, "has proved itself an aggressor state."

5. The admission of Communist China would destroy the prestige and the position of the United States and of the free world in Asia.

6. Communist China violated the laws of war by torturing and murdering United Nations prisoners of war.

7. At a time when Communist dictatorship seems to be badly shaken in the Soviet Union and in the satellite states, the admission of Communist China "would restore the prestige and authority of the Soviet Government."

8. Communist China's admission "would encourage subversive totalitarian movements in the free nations of the world in the expectation that their success would be sanctioned by the free nations which still survive."

October 9, 1953

DULLES PROCLAIMS M'CARTHY IS WRONG ON FOREIGN POLICY

Hard Posture to Allies Decried by Secretary at News Parley

By JAMES RESTON
Special to THE NEW YORK TIMES.

WASHINGTON, Dec. 1—The Eisenhower Administration today proclaimed a fundamental split with Senator Joseph R. McCarthy of Wisconsin on the conduct of the nation's foreign policy.

In a formal statement approved by President Eisenhower at 8:30 this morning, John Foster Dulles, Secretary of State, rejected out of hand the foreign policy proposals made by Senator McCarthy in his nation-wide television broadcast last Tuesday.

Mr. Dulles did not mention Senator McCarthy by name, but he left no doubt about his target when he walked into his weekly news conference this morning and read a statement that started:

"Since I met with you last week there has been a widely publicized criticism of this Administration's foreign policy.

"The burden of that criticism was that we spoke too kindly to our Allies and sent them 'perfumed' notes, instead of using threats and intimidation to compel them to do our bidding.

"I welcome constructive criticism. But the criticism I refer to attacks the very heart of United States foreign policy."

Proposal by McCarthy

Senator McCarthy last Tuesday proposed that the United States tell its Allies:

"If you continue to ship to Red China, while they are imprisoning and torturing American men, you will get not one cent of American money."

In that same speech, the Wisconsin Senator noted that the United States Army recently had said that some 900 Americans taken prisoner by Red China still were unaccounted for. And he asked:

"Now what are we going to do about it? Are we going to con-

The New York Times
John Foster Dulles

tinue to send perfumed notes, following the style of the Truman-Acheson regime?"

Later in the day, Senator McCarthy flew into the Capital from Wisconsin and told reporters who met him at the airport that he had not read Mr. Dulles' statement. A reporter handed him a copy, and the Senator took it and asked "Do you think he could have been referring to me?"

Later, his office said he would hold a press conference tomorrow or Thursday.

Davies Issue Raised

Mr. Dulles also was asked to comment on the retention in the Government service of John Paton Davies Jr., a Foreign Service officer who is now United States Chargé d'Affaires in Peru. Mr. McCarthy had demanded to know last week why Mr. Davies still was in the Government service when the Senate Internal Security Committee had unanimously agreed to ask the Justice Department to consider indicting him for perjury.

Mr. Dulles said that two investigations of Mr. Davies were now in process, one by the State Department and one by the Justice

Department. He added that, after Mr. McCarthy's criticism of Mr. Davies last week, the latter had requested a new investigation.

Senator McCarthy's comment on Mr. Davies was:

"He was unanimously referred by the McCarran committee to the Justice Department in connection with a proposed indictment because he lied under oath about his activities in trying to put—listen to this—in trying to put Communists and espionage agents in key spots in the Central Intelligence Agency."

Mr. Dulles read his statement deliberately but with an occasional show of strong feeling. He refused to depart from the text, which had been discussed with President Eisenhower yesterday and checked by the President this morning.

The President is expected to make clear his support for Mr. Dulles' statement at his news conference tomorrow morning. It is understood that the President was urged by some of his advisers to let the Dulles statement stand alone and to skip tomorrow's news conference in view of the sharp questioning the split with Senator McCarthy was almost certain to arouse. The President, however, insisted that the conference be held.

The Secretary of State directed his criticism to Senator McCarthy's suggestion that the United States should force its Allies to follow a much sterner policy against Red China or cut them off without any aid if they refused. Mr. Dulles said that the United States would be firm and persistent in trying to obtain agreements with the Allies on what we believed to be right. He added that we would expect a fair sharing of efforts and burdens.

TEXT OF STATEMENT

Following is the text of the statement by Secretary Dulles:

Since I met with you last week there has been a widely publicized criticism of this Administration's foreign policy.

The burden of that criticism was that we spoke too kindly to our Allies and sent them "perfumed" notes, instead of using threats and intimidation to compel them to do our bidding.

I welcome constructive criticism. But the criticism I refer to attacks the very heart of United States foreign policy.

It is the clear and firm purpose of this Administration to treat other free nations as sovereign equals—whether they be large or small, strong or weak. My grandfather, John W. Foster of Indiana, himself a Secretary of State, said of American foreign policy that from the beginning it had been marked by "a spirit of justice, forbearance and magnanimity." I do not intend myself to mar that record.

The tide of recent events has made our nation more powerful but I believe that it should not make us less loyal to our great American traditions; and that it should not blur our dedication to the truths, expressed in our Declaration of Independence, that we owe a respect to the opinions of others.

Today it is to our interest to assist certain countries. But that does not give us the right to try to take them over, to dictate their trade policies and to make them our satellites.

Indeed, we do not want weak or subservient Allies. Our friends and Allies are dependable just because they are unwilling to be anyone's satellites. They will freely sacrifice much in a common effort. But they will no more be subservient to the United States than they will be subservient to Soviet Russia.

Determination to Be Free

Let us be thankful that they are that way, and that there still survives so much rugged determination to be free. If that were not so, we would be isolated in the world and in mortal peril.

Never in all our history was there a time when good friends and Allies meant so much to us.

Today the Soviet Union, with rapidly mounting atomic power, is deterred from attacking by the fact that we could retaliate with a devastating blow against the vitals of Russia. But that possibility exists only because we share the well-located bases of other friendly countries.

Also, we gain security because of an early warning system which permits of interception and civil defense. But this requires facilities in the friendly countries which are nearer the Soviet Union. Without that, such great industrial centers as Detroit, Cleveland, Chicago and Milwaukee would be "sitting ducks" for atomic bombs.

In addition to being dependent upon our Allies for prevention and defense against atomic attack, we look to their large industrial strength to keep the balance of world power in the free world favor. If their resources and facilities fell into the Soviet bloc, it would have the advantage over us, not only in the possibility of an initial knock-out blow, but also in terms of capacity to win a long, drawn-out war.

Mutual Respect Vital

Thus there is need, as never before, of cooperation between the free nations. Others recognize that. So do we. To maintain a cooperation of the free is a difficult and delicate process. Without mutual respect and friendship, it would be impossible. We do not propose to throw away those precious assets by blustering and domineering methods.

We shall be firm and persistent in trying to secure agreement on what we believe to be right. We shall expect a fair sharing of efforts and burdens. But we shall not try to be arrogant, or to demand of others what we ourselves, if circumstances were reversed, would reject.

In this way, we retain friendship and we usually reach agreement. The fact that some marginal disagreements persist is no reason for sacrificing friendship by attempting to coerce; the more so because the attempt would be fruitless.

These fundamentals of our foreign policy were agreed on by President Eisenhower and me before I took my present office. These principles still stand.

WASHINGTON, July 15 (AP) —The House went on record unanimously today as opposed to admission of Communist China to the United Nations.

By a roll-call vote of 381-0, it adopted a resolution reiterating its previously expressed position and supporting the President "in his expressed determination to use all means to prevent such representation."

The resolution does not require Senate action, being simply a demonstration of how the House feels about the situation. The Senate Foreign Relations Committee has added to the foreign aid bill a provision putting the Senate on record as against Communist China's entry.

December 2, 1953

July 16, 1954

SHANGHAI REDS URGE RETURN TO VILLAGES

Special to THE NEW YORK TIMES.

SHANGHAI, Aug. 5—With the exception of those held accountable for "major offenses," all landlords and rich farmers who had fled to Shanghai from Communist-held rural areas are now being invited to join the "Back to the Village" movement and participate in the drive to boost agricultural production.

Liberation Daily, the official Communist organ, said today that the party had decided to conduct a widespread propaganda campaign to "remove the fears that might be held by returning refugees."

Reporting on a list of new measures adopted by the East China branch of the Communist party it said that returning landlords and rich farmers would be allotted their "deserved share" of land and houses and given an opportunity for productive work and "self reform." Other farm workers who previously had deserted the turbulent war-ridden countryside also are invited to return to the villages.

"It is necessary to explain to them the policy of our party and welcome them to return home to join in production work," the newspaper said.

The "back to the village" movement here appears to have the double purpose of increasing agricultural output, especially in food and cotton, and of reducing the economic burdens imposed by conditions now prevalent in Shanghai. Shanghai's light industries are largely dependent on imported raw materials now cut off by blockade. The overflowing population of 6,000,000 also exerts a heavy drain on food supplies in this area in which crops have been seriously affected by floods.

August 6, 1949

CHINESE REDS HINT AT FOOD SHORTAGE

Crops in Manchuria and North Reported Below Normal, but Prices Are Stable

Special to THE NEW YORK TIMES.

HONG KONG, Oct. 31—Figures reported by the Peiping radio on food production this year in Manchuria and North China support the prediction made here last summer that a food shortage is certain this winter for a large part of Communist China.

A recent item from the Peiping radio said crops in Manchuria were only 70 per cent of normal, while a broadcast by the Communist New China News Agency here today said the average agricultural yield for the fall harvest in North China was 65 per cent of normal.

No over-all report has been made for Communist areas in the Yangtze Valley, but a recent dispatch said the fall harvest in Hupeh was satisfactory "except for flood areas," with extraordinarily good yields where crops were gathered. It is believed the general output in the Yangtze Valley is considerably below normal because of widespread floods and the civil war.

Today's Peiping report said 10,000,000 peasants in North China had been affected by drought, storms, floods and pests, with 500,000 needing urgent relief. About 11,000 tons of seed wheat and 1,500 tons of food rice were said to have been allotted for aid to farmers, many of whom additionally have been employed on work projects.

Normally a grain deficit area, North China on 65 per cent of its normal crops must necessarily have very thin resources this winter. Manchuria in a normal year has a food surplus and may have enough with 70 per cent of normal to feed the population if too much is not drained off under the trade agreement with the Russians signed this summer, giving the Soviet Union food in exchange for machinery.

Despite real and potential food shortages in North China and the Yangtze Valley, the Communists have managed to keep prices relatively stable and cities such as Shanghai, Tientsin, Peiping comparatively well supplied. Arrivals from Communist China say one reason for this is that the Communists have prevented the usual hoarding and speculation in food grains that thrived under the Nationalists and have forced onto the market food stocks held since before the Communist take-over. Operations of the State food trading companies in dumping supplies on the market at strategic times are said to have helped keep prices down.

November 1, 1949

Chinese Communists See Merit in Profit System

Special to THE NEW YORK TIMES.

SHANGHAI, May 14—The Communist radio in Peiping tonight expounded the merits of the profit system and capitalism as regards China's immediate future.

The broadcast was presented as a condensation of an article by Li Li-san, vice chairman of the All-China Federation of Labor.

It said that during the period of the "new democracy" capitalism would be necessary to develop the country. The broadcast said that Mr. Li believed the Communist party stood for communism but that since China was too backward economically—with only about 10 per cent of industry in her national economy—it would be quite a long time before communism could be realized.

A special point was made of the fact that labor would be unable to profit unless production increased and that that depended on adequate profit being assured to the owner.

May 15, 1949

CHINA'S REDS SEEK TRADE WITH WEST

Despite Tie to Soviet, Economic Factors Foster Attempts at Business With U. S., Britain

By HENRY R. LIEBERMAN

Under Mao Tze-tung's principle of "leaning to one side," the Chinese Communists have established themselves on the record and by their recent actions as the most devoted followers of Moscow's world Communist line.

Nevertheless, within the limits left open to them in foreign policy, there have been signs that the Communists are trying to ride two different kinds of horses. While continuing with their own revolution domestically and recognizing a Russian monopoly of interest in Manchuria and Sinkiang, the Communists have displayed a keen interest in continuing trade with the United States and Britain.

This does not mean that the Communists are ready to cut themselves loose from Russia or sacrifice any fundamental principle now governing the consolidation of tight Communist control throughout the country. It does seem to mean, however, that—for the time being, at least—the Communists are prepared to permit foreign business men and missionaries to operate in areas not closed to the West by the predominance of Soviet interest.

Factors in Sino-Soviet Ties

Among the apparent factors that have carried the Communists into the Soviet orbit are common ideology, the Communist conviction that United States democratic-capitalism is doomed and Russia's manifest strategic and economic interests in China's richest industrial areas — Manchuria, Sinkiang and North China. The Chinese Communists propose to raise living standards by industrialization, and China's coal and iron are concentrated in the north, in areas either adjacent or relatively close to the Soviet Union.

Almost as important, from all indications, are the United States' anti-Communist policy and the outbreak of Titoism as a major nationalist heresy in the world Communist front. On the basis of Chairman Mao's previous unorthodox revolutionary methods, including his accent on the peasantry and his program of cooperation with "middle capitalist" groups, Titoism certainly must have made Mr. Mao more suspect in the eyes of Moscow. Perhaps this explains why the Chinese Communists were among the first to denounce Premier Marshal Tito of Yugoslavia.

Despite their reliance on Manchuria as an industrial base that can be developed with Russian aid, the Chinese Communists are still responsible for economic conditions in China Proper as well as Manchuria—and the traditional lines of trade from China Proper extend toward the Western Powers and not toward the Soviet Union. Even in the North China port of Tientsin, which is beyond the effective blockading range of Nationalist ships and planes, the major trade is still with the United States and British-held Hong Kong.

Fared Worse at Soviet Hands

Furthermore, in Manchuria, where the Russians have immediate interests, the Chinese Communists have fared far worse as an ally of the Soviet Union than the Nationalists did as an ally of the United States. Where the Nationalists received United States aid unconditionally, the Communists now have to obtain machinery for Manchuria from the Russians by bartering away surplus Manchurian food, including soybeans—a crop most likely to produce foreign exchange.

Notwithstanding the pressures of ideology and alliance, the Communists, as the dominant force in a responsible government, cannot be unmindful of economic facts involving their own political future. They are clearly interested in diplomatic recognition by the West and continuing trade with the West—for machines, machine tools, such gasoline as Russia cannot supply and necessary raw materials, especially cotton for Shanghai's hard-hit mills.

There have been a few Communist excesses against foreigners such as when United States Vice Consul William M. Olive was brutally beaten after being arrested for an alleged traffic violation.

By and large, however, the Communists have adopted what they regard as a "correct" attitude toward foreigners—aloof and cold, but not hostile. After the Olive incident conditions improved noticeably.

Talked of U. S. Loan

On April 25, shortly after the Communists entered Nanking, twelve Communist soldiers broke into the home of United States Ambassador John Leighton Stuart. A few days later a Communist named Huang Hua, a former student of Dr. Stuart in Yenching University in Peiping, took over the handling of foreign relations in Nanking. In a subsequent talk with Dr. Stuart, it was learned, his former student sounded him out on the prospect of a United States loan for Communist China.

The establishment of the Nationalist blockade, for which the Communists have held the United States responsible, caused a toughening of the Communist attitude towards Americans.

Despite the Communist policy of having nothing to do with foreigners pending recognition of Communist China, however, Gen. Chen Yi, Mayor of Shanghai, received the ranking British business man there, John Keswick, head of the Jardine, Matheson Company, to discuss trade prospects.

Chairman Mao and other Communist leaders are already on record as favoring trade with the West and inviting foreign capital to operate there subject to the laws of the land. Just as the Communists are looking for means to continue trade for their own benefit, so the United States and Britain are looking for ways to cope with Communist China. On that problem there are clear-cut differences of opinion between the British and Americans—at least in China.

October 7, 1949

RUSSIAN ADVISERS FLOCK TO PEIPING

HONG KONK, Nov. 18—Reports here from foreign sources in North China estimate that there are now about 200 to 300 Russian advisers working in and out of Peiping and about 100 in Tientsin. There are known to be numerous Soviet experts in Manchuria but the North China sources do not know how many or what they are doing.

The newly arrived Russians are now said to be numerous enough in both Peiping and Tientsin to be noticeable. Other foreigners have become adept at spotting the new arrivals from their clothes and general demeanor. The newcomers are reported to be usually poorly dressed and many of them visit Peiping tailors soon after their arrival for new suits and new fur coats.

The Hotel du Nord on Hatamen Street in Peiping has been taken over by the Communist Government for accommodating the Russians. The hotel formerly was a hostel for United States Army personnel.

Russian experts are making their appearance in factories, power plants, mines, hospitals, agricultural experiment stations and on the railway. It is reported that Chinese, trained in American schools, are discovering that they often know more than the Russian expert assigned to help them. At a Tientsin hospital containing the latest American equipment, supplied through the United Nations Relief and Rehabilitation Administration, a Russian doctor said he had never had such improved materials to work with.

At a Tientsin power plant, which has been operating with outstanding efficiency under Chinese engineers, a number of whom are graduates of the Massachusetts Institute of Technology, a newly assigned Russian expert has nothing to do. However, the Chinese manager has found it necessary to move out of his house and turn it over to the Russian.

The influx of Russian advisers has not yet reached Shanghai to a marked degree, according to arrivals from there on blockade-running ships that reached here today. It is said, however, that popular report has it that many are due to arrive within a matter of weeks.

The North China sources say that a number of German technicians long resident in Tientsin have received tentative offers to go to Manchuria to help put back into operation the factories there from which the Russian army took the machinery in 1945.

The Germans are involved because many of the machines in the Manchurian factories installed under the Japanese are of German make or pattern.

November 19, 1949

CHINESE REDS FACE CRISIS IN FINANCES

Peiping Announces Issue of 'People's Victory' Bonds to Combat Inflation

By TILLMAN DURDIN
Special to THE NEW YORK TIMES.

HONG KONG, Dec. 3—The Communist Peiping Government today officially recognized a critical financial situation in Communist China and announced an issue of "peoples' victory bonds" in an effort to cope with it.

A Chinese language broadcast received here tonight reported the decision to float the national bond issue had been reached at a meeting of the Committee on Finance and Economies of the State Administration Council attended by President Mao Tze-tung. The amount of the bond issue or how or when it would be marketed was not mentioned but the broadcast stated the bonds would be redeemable on the basis of the commodity index, so that purchasers would be protected against loss of monetary value resulting from currency inflation.

Deputy Premier Chen Yun, who presided over the Administrative Yuan meeting, in an explanation of the necessity for the bond issue, cited the serious financial situation that had developed for the Peiping regime since the middle of October.

He pointed to the rapid increase in prices and the accelerated inflation of banknotes that had come about with the conquest of vast new territories and asserted the result had been a great increase in government expenditure without a corresponding expansion of revenues.

New Notes Held in Vain

Implying that the printing press methods of meeting government costs employed by the Nationalist regime when it was in Nanking were being resorted to by the Communists he emphasized his government "could not rely on covering expenses with new notes."

He said the new bonds would cover part of the Government deficits.

Mr. Chen promised retrenchment in Government outlays and said this should be possible now that the military campaign was drawing to a close. He stated efforts also would be made to collect more revenues, but acknowledged that even so the Government would continue to operate in the red.

President Mao was reported as stating his new government would face difficulties for a year or two

but that the rate of economic recovery in the "liberated" areas convinced him the country soon would be prosperous.

Minister of Finance Po Yi-po told the committee meeting the military and administrative expenses of the new government would take 60 per cent of the 1950 budget, with 23.9 per cent being devoted to the restoration of production and investment in economic reconstruction. He declared:

"We cannot but take over all former Nationalist troops and civil servants and feed them so they may be reformed and gradually diverted to productive activities."

The Finance Minister estimated the government soon would have on its payroll 9,000,000 persons performing military and administrative functions.

Military Outlay Low

Gen. Li Chi-sen, Kuomintang member and one of the six Vice Presidents of the Peiping regime pointed out the Nationalist Government had spent 80 per cent and more of the national budget for military purposes, while the Peiping Government was devoting only 38.8 per cent.

The Peiping broadcast gave no figures to show the new regime's actual financial condition. Obviously what is happening is that the facts of economic life in a China made destitute by years of civil and international war, overpopulation, maladministration, backwardness and foreign exploitation have caught up with the Communists—now that they have taken over responsibility for most of the country—just as these facts played a big part in destroying the Kuomintang.

Hong Kong business men and observers who follow developments in China have been aware of growing financial economic difficulties in Communist areas for some weeks. Information brought here in publications from China coast cities and bolstered by arrivals from Shanghai and North China shows a crisis cycle similar to those that jarred the Nanking Government every few months has hit Communist China.

Within a month the international exchange value of Communist currency has slid from 5,000 on the Shanghai black market, against the United States dollar, to 30,000. Between Nov. 1 and 15 the price of rice in Shanghai increased by four times.

State agencies have been dumping what basic commodities they could obtain on the markets in an effort to soak up banknotes and keep prices down, but with confidence in Communist currencies disappearing the people have staged a buying rush on staples in an effort to get rid of their banknotes. Several smaller banks in Shanghai have failed.

December 4, 1949

REDS REBUILDING MANCHURIA FIRST

HONG KONG, Dec. 26—Information from Communist China emphasizes the fact that Manchuria is receiving first priority in the national program of industrialization and rehabilitation.

The movement to recruit technicians and skilled workers from China proper for employment in Manchuria has just been concluded. During the recruitment period of several months the importance of building up Manchuria as the basic developed area of China was underlined.

Communist newspapers report that 3,000 persons are to go to Manchuria, a considerable total in view of the scarcity of trained individuals in China. It is stated that 60 per cent of the technical personnel have been assigned to duties in industrial enterprises. The remainder will work in railways and financial and economic organizations.

Evidencing official concern with promoting Manchurian development, one Shanghai newspaper recently gave prominence to reports of two groups of Shanghai business men who have been on investigation tours in Manchuria. Hu Chuen-wen, leader of one group, emphasized that favorable circumstances, such as natural resources already developed, industries, electricity supplies and communications, gave Manchuria advantages that must be further utilized in intensifying economic progress there. "Efforts must be exerted to mobilize all manpower and financial resources and send them to the Northeast," he said.

Asserting that Shanghai's industry must integrate itself with Manchurian production, he declared:

"The Northeast will become a region where heavy industry and state-operated enterprises will be the most fully developed, while Shanghai will become the area where light industry and privately owned enterprises will play a dominant role."

One member of this group stated that despite the growth of state enterprises in Manchuria private industry there still had a chance. He asserted there were now more than 70,000 private industrial concerns in Manchuria employing more than 200,000 workers. Machinery and iron industries are the most prosperous, he said. Another representative reported that in state enterprises sliding scales of pay for workers in accordance with output had been useful in promoting better production.

December 27, 1949

CHINA FAMINE BRINGS 'RETREAT' IN RED PLAN

Special to THE NEW YORK TIMES.

HONG KONG, March 16—The Peiping radio announced last night two more steps the Chinese Communist Government was taking against the spreading famine.

It has issued a directive on the spring sowing. It has given top transport priority to the moving of grain surpluses into areas of acute shortage.

The broadcast said 60,000 tons of grain, or three months meager rations for about 3,000,000 persons, and what the announcement called "two-thirds of the Inner Mongolian surplus," had reached Hopeh Province (Peiping). Moreover "great quantities" of rice from Manchuria and the Yangtze Valley were flowing into Shanghai.

Virtually every organization in Communist China had been ordered to join in the spring plowing and planting campaign. Because the land seizures and exactions against landlords last year probably were factors in the shortened crop, the new regulations pointed up a general retreat from the offensive against the landowners.

Generally, the directive provided that land must not be allowed to lie fallow. Government workers must mobilize the people to farm all available land; Government loans to farmers would be made only in tools, seeds and fertilizers, not in money, and deforestation was banned.

March 17, 1950

SHANGHAI 'DYING,' REFUGEES DECLARE

SAN FRANCISCO, May 23—Seven hundred persons, evacuated from Shanghai after long negotiations with the Chinese Communist Government, arrived in port today aboard the American President liner General Gordon. Among them were 257 refugees who had fled from Nazi Germany in the late 1930's, more than 100 of whom are going back to Europe.

United States and British business men, missionaries, educators and doctors joined in picturing the Chinese as disillusioned but helpless under the People's Government after having welcomed it during its early stages. Some industries, they said, were in the process of being expropriated; business houses were closing and Shanghai was "a dying city." There were, however, no food shortages in the cities, they added.

Harold G. B. Perry, who had engaged in industrial and consulting engineering in Shanghai after his retirement as chief engineer and technical adviser of the Standard Vacuum Oil Company, said he had lost his business. Chinese were closing up shops because of taxation and lack of business, he added.

"The Government has gone monopolistic and is trying to bypass the three major oil companies to extinction," Mr. Perry asserted.

"The Chase Bank is liquidating, the National City is going the same way and British banks in Shanghai are feeling the strain. Business is dead. The communists have a stranglehold on the country. Unionism in China is tied in with the Communist machine and the utilities are practically all run by the unions. There is an ominous sense of insecurity everywhere."

A. B. Wilkinson, technical director of the Shanghai Telephone Company, said the Communists were in China to stay unless they were dislodged from the outside. He said the authorities were exercising so much control over the phone company that it was "practically tantamount to taking control."

He credited the Communist Government, nevertheless, with being "a damned sight more honest than the Kuomintang post-war government." Post-war Shanghai, he said, had been running "chiefly on U. N. R. R. A. (the United Nations Relief and Rehabilitation Administration) gifts."

Instruction to Doctors

According to Dr. George J. Ulrich of Baltimore, who had practiced medicine in Shanghai since getting his Navy discharge in 1945, the Communists have "a tremendous health program" under way, including laboratories and medical schools, "with Russian equipment."

He said that Chinese doctors were being told: "You must learn Soviet ways and learn to use Soviet equipment."

"Coolies, labor union members and college students, who were all for the Communists during the first few months, now are 80 per cent on the fence or against them," he went on. "But it's a passive thing. They can't rise; that takes guns."

He said that Mao Tze-tung, the Chinese Communist leader, had formerly been pictured alone but that since his trip to Moscow his face and that of Premier Stalin had appeared together on posters everywhere.

May 24, 1950

CHINA REDS MODIFY REFORMS OF FARMS

New Law Drafted to Let Rich Peasants Keep Holdings and Landlords Retain Funds

By WALTER SULLIVAN
Special to THE NEW YORK TIMES.

HONG KONG, June 17—A new land reform law that is a radical departure from the Chinese Communists' traditional policy of equal distribution has been drafted by Peiping and is due to be applied this winter in an area inhabited by 100,000,000 peasants.

Rich peasants are to keep their land intact, confiscation being applied only to landlords. Likewise, landlords will be allowed to keep their hidden wealth in the hope they will invest their funds in industry or commerce.

Such a fundamental change in Communist policy indicates the seriousness of the situation facing the Peiping regime. The primary purpose of coddling rich peasants, Mao Tze-tung, chief of the Peiping regime, told the Communist party June 6, is to speed the restoration of agricultural production. He explained that with the war virtually over the Government now was able to help poor peasants with loans to compensate for "the disadvantage of having less land."

The implication is that despite the Communist efforts to forestall such a result the process of equal distribution of land in the past two years has slowed the recovery of rural production. Two reasons have been suggested for this. One is the confusion resulting in each community from the wholesale juggling of land and farmers and the other the weakening of farmers' morale by the belief that the Communists frown on wealth.

167

Top Body Studying Draft

The recently drafted land reform law is now being discussed in Peiping by the National Committee of the People's Political Consultative Conference, the highest political organ of the new Government. However, the drafting of the law appears to have been going on several weeks.

Land reform plans were presented Communist party by Liu Shao-chi ed to the Central Committee of the early this month and he then explained it to the National Committee. While the text of the draft has not been made public as yet its main points are evident in the directives already issued and in recent statements by Mr. Mao and Mr. Liu.

The policy of sparing landlords' property other than the means of production needed by the peasants is in complete contrast to past practice. Until this year the peasants were permitted to split up among themselves everything a landlord owned, leaving the landlord a share equal to what each peasant received.

For example, during the three months ending February, 1948, 12,000 carts were mobilized in Northern Manchuria to pass around the landlords' wealth. In addition to thirty-one tons of silver and 780 pounds of gold there were distributed 5,200,000 pieces of landlords' clothing.

Policy Foreshadowed

The new policy was foreshadowed by a directive for suburban land reform issued by Peiping in January of this year. This directive said it was forbidden "without exception" to search for the hidden wealth of landlords who were to be "allowed" to invest it. Spared from requisition were the lands of rich peasants being farmed by hired hands.

Presumably this directive applied to the distribution due next winter. It was echoed in a directive for Honan Province a month later that said: "Gold and silver treasures buried by landowners and old style rich farmers shall not be investigated but shall be allowed to be invested in industrial and commercial enterprises."

Throughout the past winter, however, the rich peasants' surplus lands have been requisitioned wherever land reform has been carried out. In North China the rich were allowed to keep about one-third of their "buried treasure" for investment.

In recent speeches Mr. Mao announced 160,000,000 already had experienced land reform and 100,000,000 were due for it next wintr, leaving 210,000,000 for the following winter or later. According to Mr. Liu the program is due to be "basically completed" within two or three years.

Mr. Mao on June 6 listed the land reform program as the first of eight requirements for an economic program. The Communists regard it not only as gaining them popular support but as a means of increasing greatly the purchasing power of the peasants and hence stimulating industrial expansion.

As evidence of this Mr. Liu said on May Day 800,000 bolts of cloth had been sold in Manchuria in 1947, 1,200,000 in 1948, 3,200,000 in 1949 and an estimated 9,000,000 this year.

According to Mr. Mao 100,000 political workers are waiting to study the new agrarian law prior to fanning out into the countryside to enforce it. Meanwhile, the organization of Peasants' Associations has been proceeding on a vast scale.

In the newly won area of Central China, with 43,000,000 inhabitants, 6,500,000 peasants already are enrolled, according to the latest official count. The administration of the land reform program will be in their hands.

June 18, 1950

CHINESE REDS EASE LAND REFORM LAWS

By WALTER SULLIVAN
Special to THE NEW YORK TIMES.

HONG KONG, June 30—The Agrarian Reform Law, which will affect the livelihood of 100,000,000 Chinese peasants this winter and probably even a greater number the following year, was promulgated in Peiping today.

As had been anticipated from earlier directives, the new law is a radical departure from established Communist policies. The full text received here enlarges the scope of the changes even beyond what had been expcted. Not only are the rich peasants to be spared land requisition but many who rent out their land will also be left alone.

The edge has been taken off the drastic measures embodied in earlier Communist land laws. Under the new law, those who rent out small plots of land to augment their incomes in non-agricultural pursuits will be allowed to keep their holdings.

Fundamentally, the most radical development — or concession — in the Communists' new agrarian law is the omission of the Communists' traditional principle of leveling rural wealth. The new law frankly states that those who were landless and poor will still be below average in wealth after the law is put into effect. The rich will still be rich.

Ordinary Tiller Gets More

The landholdings of the ordinary tiller who has some land and gets more in the course of reform will be "slightly and suitably more" than those of the peasants who at the start had little or no land.

The reason for the policy change is to try to raise food and industrial crop production at maximum speed. Earlier, the more drastic land distribution plans won for the Communists the intense loyalty of the poorer peasant masses. This was one of the pillars of Communist strength during the war years, but now the Communists consider maximum agricultural and industrial production the primary goal.

The purpose of the new law, as stated in its first article, is to end "feudal exploitation by the landlord class" so that three goals may be achieved: (1) "set free the rural productive forces"; (2) "develop agricultural production"; (3) "pave the way for industrialization."

The general principle is laid down that if a man is farming a piece of land, he is to keep right on farming it no matter how much of it he owns. Those who earn their living other than by farming but augment their income by renting out their land can keep a part equal to double the average per capita land holding of the community. Families none of whose members are capable of earning a living may rent out more than double the average local holding. The same applies "if the land proves to have been purchased with the earnings of the owner's own labor."

Lands of Rich Peasants

The lands of the rich peasants tilled by hired hands are to remain untouched, and in most areas these peasants can also retain rented out lots if these lots do not exceed the land they themselves are working. Full-fledged landlords, however, are to lose all their land except a share equal to what the landless peasants receive.

However, contrary to all previous Communist land laws, landlords' non-agricultural wealth is to be left strictly alone in the hope that they will invest it in industry and commerce.

Likewise, their urban and rural industrial holdings are to be untouched. Only their land, farm tools, draught animals and "surplus" grains are to be seized. Before, Communists even carted off landlords' clothes, and in the earliest Kiangsi distributions the landlords were ridden out of the town in a full-fledged class war.

While the agricultural lands of religious organizations and government institutions are to be requisitioned, "appropriate measures should be worked out by the local people's Government to solve the financial problems of such schools, orphanages, homes for the aged, hospitals, etc., as are dependent upon the income from the above land."

Modernized farms with mechanical implements are to be nationalized if rented out, but left alone if tilled by the owners. Redistributed lands may be sold or rented by a new owner. People's courts are to be set up in every country to move about trying "hated despots" and those who resist the agrarian law.

July 1, 1950

CHINESE REDS TAKE RICE OF LANDLORDS

By HENRY R. LIEBERMAN
Special to THE NEW YORK TIMES.

HONG KONG, Aug. 30—Landlords in the six provinces of the Central-South China military area have been forced to disgorge more than 500,000 tons of rice to hard-pressed tenant peasants under the "land rent reduction and rent refund" campaign being waged in this restive zone by Chinese Communists.

The campaign, which is serving as a preliminary to full-fledged land redistribution, is being carried out with the purpose of combating guerrilla activity and diverting the attention of the impoverished peasants from the bulging state barns. The proceeds of taxes levied in kind on agricultural production are stored in these public granaries.

A similar "rent refund" drive is scheduled to begin after the autumn harvest in Southwest China where the Communists also have had trouble with guerrillas. As an example of the political feasibility of such an approach, the Communists estimate that 80 per cent of the population of Southwest China consists of "poor peasants and tenants." It is noteworthy, however, that the Communists have announced they do not intend to carry out a campaign in the southwest areas inhabited by national minorities, notably the Lama-governed Tibetans.

80 Per Cent of Area Affected

In a dispatch from Hankow, headquarters of the Central-South China military area, the pro-Communist newspaper Ta Kung Pao said the "rent reduction and rent refund" campaign had already been applied in 80 per cent of the regional zone formed by the provinces of Honan, Hupeh, Hunan, Kiangsi, Kwangsi and Kwangtung.

The dispatch said membership in the Communist-sponsored "peasants associations," a prime means of organizing landless rural masses and "overturning society," had reached 18,910,000.

The Central-South campaign was instituted March 1 in the midst of the spring famine throughout the area. Current Communist literature declares that at that time while the peasants were hungry and lacking seed for spring cultivation, the necessity for transporting large quantities of public grain out of the area to other places enabled landlords and "special agents" to organize guerrilla raids on state barns.

The decision to turn the wrath of the hungry Central-South China peasants on the landlords was contained in the March 1 directive to party workers by regional party headquarters at Hankow. The directive stated:

"The present problem is whether

we will lead the peasants to demand rent repayment from the landlords so as to solve food difficulties, tide over the famine and carry on production, or allow local despots and special agents to dupe the peasants into plundering public grain, thus resulting in confusion and negligence in production."

Retroactive Refund

The rent refund campaign, which has been hitched to a collateral campaign directed at "local despots" or "village bullies" disrupting social order is being carried out on a retroactive basis. Landlords who are being charged with concealing and burying surplus grain are turning over rice to peasants, in addition to the 50 to 80 per cent tax in kind imposed on their lands' output by the state.

The squeeze is in keeping with Article 1 of the new National Agrarian Law, which calls for abolition of the "land ownership system of feudal exploitation by the landlord class."

Full fledged land redistribution involving an estimated agricultural population of 50,000,000 is scheduled to begin in Central-South China this winter. Meanwhile, a large number of peasants associations are being organized to pave the way for this land revolution and create the administrative apparatus for incorporating organized peasantry into the political system of the "New Democracy." Under the national regulations covering the formation of these associations, they are to consist of "tenant farmers, poor peasants, middle-class peasants, handicraft workers and poor revolutionary-educated elements in rural areas."

September 2, 1950

RED COOPERATIVES EXPAND IN CHINA

By HENRY R. LIEBERMAN
Special to THE NEW YORK TIMES.

HONG KONG, Oct. 7—An expanding network of cooperatives is being established in Communist China to provide a link between the state companies and organized groups of small private farmers and handicraftsmen. Consumer cooperatives are also reported being set up in factories, schools, government offices and army units.

More than 20,000,000 persons already have been organized into 34,000 rural and 3,000 urban cooperatives, according to the Communists.

The present drive has its roots in the cooperatives that were established by Communists in the hinterlands of Northwest China long before they achieved power. The system is now being extended on a national basis as a fundamental pillar of the overall economic structure.

As in the case of other social changes being wrought by Mao Tse-tung's "New Democracy" Manchuria is taking the lead in this instance. Kao Kang, chairman of the Northeast Regional Government, declared in a report released here today that 24 per cent of Manchuria's total population belonged to state-supervised cooperatives.

Published estimates hold that the Manchurian cooperatives are likely to handle one-fourth of the region's total retail business this year, their allotted share being projected at the monetary equivalent of 2,900,000 tons of grain. The cooperatives are said to have been organized in 159 of Manchuria's 167 counties, 318 of North China's 336 counties and 239 of East China's 428.

Peiping's People's official daily Communist organ reported recently that the membership of the Manchurian cooperatives was 8,740,000. It listed 6,166,000 members for North China, 4,060,000 for East China and 1,200,000 for the administrative regions of Northwest, Central-South China and Inner Mongolia. To some extent these figures are regarded as an indication of the Communists' administrative consolidation in various regions. For example, it is noteworthy that Southwest China is not listed and that Central-South China is lumped with Northwest China and inner Mongolia.

According to Communist cooperative literature, members do not share in the profits but are legally free to withdraw their capital shares. The inducements that are being offered to farmers and handicraftsmen include preferential prices on state goods, wider credit and cheaper marketing facilities.

Nevertheless there have been a number of reports, including an official statement by one provincial Governor, that many peasants have resisted attempts by zealous Communist political workers to organize them into "labor mutual-aid teams."

Communist writers have discussed the cooperative movement in terms of five types: Small production cooperative teams, supply and marketing cooperatives, consumers cooperatives, credit cooperatives and producers cooperatives. With regard to the producers' cooperatives one writer said in an article appearing some time ago in the Shanghai newspaper Wen Wei Pao:

"Such cooperatives will carry out collective production with abandonment of the economy of the individual producer. They can be universally introduced only after nationalization of the land and mechanization of production. At the present moment these can not yet be considered."

October 8, 1950

China Reds Plan Two State Farms On 38,000-Acre Wasteland Tract

By HENRY R. LIEBERMAN
Special to THE NEW YORK TIMES.

HONG KONG, Sept. 11—Two large mechanized state farms are being established by the Chinese Communists along the upper bank of the Yellow River near Paotou, in Suiyuan Province.

The New China News Agency said that reclamation workers equipped with thirty-three tractors, sixteen combine harvesters and other farm machinery were now clearing the first sections of 38,000 acres of wasteland scheduled to form the two state collectives.

According to the official Communist agency, the plan calls for clearing 42 per cent of the designated area in 1950 and bringing in crops on this portion next year. It added that work already had started on digging irrigation canals, building bridges and erecting farm buildings.

The two new farms will bring to thirteen the number of Soviet collective-type farms created by the Communists in the five provinces of North China. An undisclosed number of such state farms were previously established in Manchuria.

Plans in Manchuria

With technical assistance from Soviet advisers, Communist officials are carrying out high-tempo reconstruction and planned industrialization programs in Manchuria, which is operated as a separate regional unit of the Chinese People's Republic. Besides being a primary base for industrialization, Manchuria is also serving as a laboratory for social experimentation whose results the Communists apparently intend to extend southward below the Great Wall into China proper.

In addition to the state farms established in Manchuria, the People's Government in the northeast has set up a number of "public farms." These are believed to be similar to collective farms in the Soviet Union.

Kao Kang, chairman of the Manchurian regional government and secretary of the Chinese Communist party bureau there, revealed in a speech at Mukden last March that "each province and hsien [county]" had several or at least one "public farm." He said that even some of the county chus [subdistricts] had public farms but he added that the subdistrict farms were on a small scale.

The gradations of agricultural reorganization in Communist-dominated China now range from simple rent reduction in the "new liberated" areas of the south, southwest and west, through land redistribution above the Yangtze, to collectives in parts of North China and Manchuria. As an example of the mixed agricultural economy even in Manchuria, the Communists have singled out five different categories making up the rural economy of the northeast provinces:

Five Different Categories

1. Private peasant holdings worked by farm families.
2. Village consumers cooperatives and "labor mutual aid" organizations based on private property but with the peasants pooling labor, tools and plow horses on a cooperative basis.
3. A newly rising and developing "rice farmers" economy.
4. State and "public" farms.
5. Land rented out by widows, widowers, the aged and revolutionary soldiers unable to till the land received in the land redistribution process, and some idle land leased from the Government by "capitalists" to increase farm output.

Despite the organization of collectives, the Chinese Communists are emphasizing the need to maintain a private farm economy as its main agricultural base. With regard to rural areas, the official policy calls for the tightest political alliance with the "poor peasants" and substantial cooperation with the "middle peasants." Party workers also have been instructed not to go too hard on the "rich peasants," whose efforts are necessary to increase production.

At the same time, however, the party is conducting a drive to extend the cooperative and "labor mutual aid" movements.

In Manchuria, according to Communist dispatches, state farms have been settled by "surplus Government personnel." Kao Kang stated in his Mukden speech last March that this personnel had done enough to introduce scientific farming or popularize their experiments.

September 12, 1950

Chinese Reds Press Their Fight On Landlords in Reform Program

Special Tribunals Are Set Up to Punish Recalcitrants—Peiping Issues Guide Defining Rural Social Classes

By HENRY R. LIEBERMAN
Special to THE NEW YORK TIMES.

HONG KONG, Oct. 23—A general offensive has been launched by the Communist Peiping regime against landlords engaged in widespread sabotage of its land reform program.

With organized land redistribution about to begin in large parts of Northwest, East and South and Central China, the New China News Agency said today punishment reaching up to the death sentence would be imposed on recalcitrants opposing this social revolution.

Declaring the Government was paying very close attention to the present situation at various levels, the news agency stated that landlords had been resisting the redistribution process by such means as dispersing their property, giving away grain, butchering livestock, destroying farm implements, damaging houses and burning trees.

Landlords were also said to be offering large bribes to Communist political workers to obtain exemption, including, in some cases, their wives and daughters. The agency added there were "extreme cases," too, in which landlords were conspiring with Nationalist agents in spreading "malicious rumors" and "instigating uprisings."

Besides these forms of sabotage, land redistribution, scheduled to begin this winter in the "new liberated areas," has been preceded by a peasant stampede to market the fall harvest before it can be tapped either by tax collectors or land reform officials. Urban warehouses are reported to be bulging and grain prices have dropped as a consequence of this rush to dispose of the harvest.

Special Courts Set Up

Special "people's tribunals," distinct from the People's Courts, already have been established to police the land reform program at the hsien (county) level. Under the national regulations promulgated last July 20, the tribunals are authorized to sit in final judgment on class status and mete out penalties to those found guilty of disturbing the "revolutionary order."

Armed with power to "arrest, try and sentence," these courts may legally dispose of cases as follows: Death, prison terms, confiscation of property, hard labor, public apology and repentance, acquittal. The tribunals are supposed to consist of one chief judge, a deputy chief judge and several other judges, with the chief judge and half of the other judges selected by the Government and the remainder by "people's representative conferences."

Under the law, the accused is entitled to an advocate but the latter must be approved by the court. All sentences are legally subject to review by provincial governments and the governor must approve death sentences. No appeal is permitted in the cases of those found guilty as bandits, special agents and counter-revolutionaries.

According to the Shanghai Sin Wen Pao, the East China regional administration has buttressed the national law in its area with a more detailed law of its own. The Shanghai newspaper said the regional regime regarded individual sabotage, including intentional non-cultivation of land, as a lighter offense than armed opposition, which is punishable either by long-term imprisonment or death.

In detailing the kinds of sabotage with which the East China regime has had to cope, Sin Wen Pao listed the falsification of mortgages and other documents, sale of land, furniture and farm implements at low prices, dismantling of houses and destruction of forests. It mentioned a number of bribery attempts and noted that in Tunglu County of Chekiang Province, one landlord had worked his farm livestock unceasingly announcing he would rather have the livestock dead than give them away under the land reform.

Rural Classes Are Defined

As a guide for the "people's tribunals" to follow in carrying out the land reform the Peiping cabinet issued a statement Aug. 4 defining rural social classes in terms of five categories: landlords, "rich farmers," middle-class peasants, poor peasants and urban proletariat. A Chinese landlord was defined as follows:

"Landlords are those who own land, who do little or no labor and who rely on exploitation for their living. Landlords' methods of exploitation consist principally in exploiting the peasants in the form of land rent. In addition they are apt to make loans or employ farm hands or engage in industrial and commercial enterprises. The administration of public halls and collection of school rent also belong to category of land rent exploitation.

"Although some landlords are bankrupt, after bankruptcy they still refrain from doing labor in spite of the fact that they have labor power and their living conditions are still above those of ordinary middle-class peasants. Under these conditions they are still considered as landlords.

"Warlords, bureaucrats and rural riffraff are political representatives of the landlord class. They are the most vicious among the landlords. There are also small riffraff among the rich peasants." Meanwhile, the Chinese Communists are continuing with their campaign to root out guerrillas and "special agents." The New China News Agency announced today that twenty-five "nationalist spies," who had been landed on the Shantung Peninsula last May by two Kuomintang gunboats, had been executed Oct. 12 and 15. At the same time the pro-Communist Ta Kung Pao reported from Canton that seven persons had been executed by a firing squad there yesterday also for espionage.

October 24, 1950

Reds Seize Shanghai Power

SAN FRANCISCO, Dec. 31 (AP) —The Chinese Communist radio at Peiping announced today that the $75,000,000 United States-owned Shanghai Power and Telephone Companies had been placed under military control yesterday. The action followed Red China's order freezing United States assets and bank accounts and seizing missionary, medical, relief and cultural organizations.

January 1, 1951

American Properties Seized

HONG KONG, Jan. 1 (U.P.)—Reports from Shanghai said today the Chinese Communists had seized more than eighty American properties there but ordered all to continue operating, some under separate military control.

January 2, 1951

RED CHINA'S RAIL MEN TO GO ON PIECEWORK

Special to THE NEW YORK TIMES.

HONG KONG, July 23—All of Communist China's 530,000 railway workers are to be put on a piecework wage system, according to a Communist news dispatch from Peiping.

The dispatch said the new system would improve efficiency, raise output and increase the workers' wages. Standards are now being set for various railway jobs and one-fifth of the railway organizations in the country have introduced the new wage method already, the dispatch added.

The Communist reports say that, in a typical example of the effects of the new wage system, workers at shops near Peiping took three-fourths less time than before to manufacture spare parts and tripled production in June.

Meanwhile, other Communist reports indicate considerable concern with labor problems. An article in The Northeast Daily News in Mukden says that performance of most labor unions in Manchuria is unsatisfactory. The complaint is made that the unions still tend to concentrate on trying to raise wages and get better living conditions without linking these demands with increased production.

July 24, 1951

Model Worker in China Worn Out: He Toils, Talks, Meets, Loses Sleep

By TILLMAN DURDIN
Special to THE NEW YORK TIMES.

HONG KONG, July 26—The heavy strain being put on model workers in Communist China is causing grave concern to officials there. The Liberation Daily, official Communist organ of Shanghai, in its issue of July 15, just received here, voices anxiety over the situation and insists that "steps must be taken to end it."

The circumstances, as explained by the paper, indicate that model workers not only are hard pressed to maintain the high production levels that they have set for themselves and their team-mates, but more especially are being burdened virtually beyond endurance by the social and political demands put upon them as a result of their new positions of prominence.

To make its point, the Liberation Daily tells what has happened to one model worker, Yuan Kai-li, of the Second Steel Mill of Shanghai since he returned from the national congress of "model worker combat heroes" in Peiping last year.

Hero's Duties Almost Unending

According to incomplete statistics, says the paper, Yuan heads his group at the shop and has the following concurrent duties: He is a member of the executive committee of the factory's trade union, a member of the production committee, member of the factory management committee, propaganda officer for the party, vice director of a committee for the elimination of counter-revolutionaries, workers' representative at the Peoples Representative Conference of All Circles of Shanghai, Peoples Representative of the New Municipal Center, district vice chairman of the Consultative Council of the New Municipal Center and district peoples representative of his residential district of Yangtzepoo.

The paper reports that his many appointments required him to attend many meetings every week, most of which lasted two or three hours and in some instances more than ten hours. In addition, he was constantly sought for all production and administrative meetings as well as forums called as each new movement was launched.

Moreover, continues the paper, Yuan had to speak at mass meetings convened by the metal workers' trade union, the Shanghai trade union council and other bodies on such subjects as propaganda on current affairs, enlistment of young workers in institutions for the military cadres movement against United States rearming of Japan, suppression of counter-revolutionaries, and the significance of important labor anniversaries. These meetings "usurped one-third of his regular working hours," states the paper. It reveals that in May, Yuan once sat at meetings for four full days, and often he has had to participate right after his twelve-hour night shift and without having had any sleep in the series of meetings until his next shift in the evening.

Yuan Needed Glucose 'Shots'

Because he frequently went out to attend meetings, the Liberation Daily says, his fellow workers began to criticize Yuan, calling him a "model attending-meetings worker." Moreover, says the paper, Yuan's health began to be affected as well as his production, and quotes him as saying "from last December until May of this year I slept only three hours a day, sometimes five hours, and sometimes not a wink except a nap over the desk."

The paper states finally that Yuan had to have "at least five injections of glucose each month to keep him going," but even so he complained of dizziness and inability to work because he had to "think all the time what to say at the meetings."

The Liberation Daily declares that the record of Yuan's team is now down to Grade C and the "glory of a model worker has been tarnished." The journal says that the same phenomenon is prevalent among other model workers and concludes that "the trade unions and management should make an immediate correction of this deviation."

July 27, 1951

NORTH CHINA CROPS SEVERELY INJURED

Special to THE NEW YORK TIMES.

HONG KONG, Sept. 22— Seventy million mou (11,600,000 acres) of autumn crops have been affected by drought, floods and insects in North China, according to recent domestic Chinese Communist dispatches.

This includes cotton crops reported damaged by destructive aphids in Hopeh, Shansi and Pingyuan Provinces. The rate of damage by these plant lice is said to have ranged from 80 per cent in seriously hit districts to 20 per cent in districts affected moderately.

Meanwhile it was disclosed that the Communist party's North China bureau has issued a "famine relief" directive ordering regional political workers to undertake "self-salvation" production in the stricken areas as an "urgent task."

Agricultural analysts here expressed the view that with North China's autumn harvest either being or about to be gathered the situation probably was not immediately critical for the region as a whole. They suggested the directive might reflect the Peiping Government's concern over the prospect of a larger famine in the winter or next spring as the result of natural calamities.

Party Workers Told of Urgency

As paraphrased by the official Hsinhua News Agency, the North China directive, issued in Peiping Aug. 28, told party workers the matter of "self-salvation" production was urgent because "some famine stricken people have been given over to pessimism and disappointment." The directive added "counter-revolutionaries" were also exploiting the situation by "fabricating rumors and carrying out sabotage."

"All districts must see to it that not even one person is starved," the party order said. Declaring production campaigns would have an important bearing on next year's farm output, it called for mobilization of the peasants to exterminate insects, drain away flood water, collect substitute food, organize sideline work and draw up a plan for winter "production relief."

While the north China provinces of Hopeh, Shansi and Chahar have been hit by drought, Pingyuan is reported to have suffered floods that submerged 11,000,000 mou of farmland as the result of heavy rains in July and August. The drought is described as having been especially bad in Chahar where Communist political workers are conducting a "self-salvation" drive under the slogan, "Strive for 50 per cent of a crop."

Some Bumper Yields Reported

The Peiping Radio has made over-all claims of bumper harvests for a number of other areas, especially the rich rice granaries of Szechwan in the West and Hunan in central China. However, the claim for Hunan has been accompanied by a domestic press report that 15 per cent of the entire rice acreage of this province was affected by summer drought this year.

The reports of natural calamities in north China follow other domestic dispatches dealing with famine conditions in Kwangsi Pronvince and floods in West Liaoning (Manchuria) and East China whose coastal area from Shantung to Chekiang was swept by a typhoon between Aug. 18 and 22. As a consequence heavy rains following summer dry spell all flood control agencies on the Yangtze River have been put on an emergency alert.

According to experts here it is still too early to make a final judgment on the fall crop yields.

September 23, 1951

Chinese Resist Peiping Reform

SAN FRANCISCO, Nov. 22 (AP) —The Peiping radio today indicated that the Communist land redistribution system is meeting fierce resistance in Southern China. A Red broadcast, heard by The Associated Press here, declared that "an all out battle to uproot feudalism is raging in the southern half of China where land distribution is being effected in a region with over 90,000,000 population."

November 23, 1951

CHINESE REDS SEEK TRADE TIES ABROAD

By HENRY R. LIEBERMAN

Special to THE NEW YORK TIMES.

HONG KONG, Nov. 2—Premier and Foreign Minister Chou En-lai has renewed Communist China's offer to establish diplomatic and trade relations with non-recognizing powers on the basis of "equality, mutual benefit and mutual respect for territorial sovereignty."

The offer was made in a lengthy political report released tonight by the Peiping Government.

Mr. Chou held forth the prospect of blossoming Chinese trade for such powers in combination with a warning to "certain countries" that they would have to bear the consequences of cooperating with the United States in "unfriendly and even hostile" actions against the Peiping regime.

Earlier, Indian cultural delegates returning from a tour of China had dropped hints here that Communist China probably would be interested in renewing its trade ties with Britain, but was suspicious of the Western countries that had no "independent policy apart from the United States."

Although Britain has recognized the Peiping Government, the Chinese Communists have not yet followed through on establishment of full-fledged diplomatic relations.

"Everyone knows the people of our country, after liberating our entire territory, need to restore and develop our industrial and agricultural production and our cultural and educational work in peaceful surroundings free from menace," Mr. Chou said.

"Everyone is aware that the people of our country consider that countries of diverse social systems all over the world can exist peacefully side by side."

Mr. Chou actually made his political report eleven days ago, at the opening session of a meeting held by the National Committee of the Chinese People's Political Consultative Conference. Its delayed release by the official Hsinhua News Agency suggested that the Chinese Communists might have adjusted the timing with an air to achieving a maximum propaganda effect in connection with the approaching United Nations Assembly meeting in Paris.

The Premier made it clear that Communist China was interested in a number of other Far Eastern questions besides Korea. He denounced the Japanese peace treaty, asserted the Peiping Government would "never relax" in its efforts to "liberate" Nationalist-held Formosa, and said the United States had no right to "interfere in the internal affairs of Vietnam and other Asian countries."

November 3, 1951

REFORMS RECEDE IN RED CHINA ZONE

Special to THE NEW YORK TIMES.

HONG KONG, Dec. 14—After five years of the Communists' revolutionary agrarian reform in a group of North China villages, class distinctions have re-emerged, some recipients of land have again become improverished and large numbers of peasants—shunning the officially sponsored Labor Mutual Aid Teams—still "yearn for the capitalist way of getting rich."

These observations were made by Wang Chien, Communist party district secretary for Shansi in a recent report on that province. The report discussed conditions that followed the local liquidation of landlords and redistribution of land in 1946. It was published in the Peiping People's Daily of Nov. 11.

Mr. Wang said production had been increased by 15 to 25 per cent over pre-war levels; the standard of living had been raised; 82 per cent of school-age children were in school; the sales of rural cooperatives were up, and women enjoyed a new freedom. He drew a picture of the emancipated peasant woman attending literacy classes, becoming more interested in scented soap and refusing to be browbeaten by her husband.

"It is now gradually considered acceptable for a fiancée to wash her bethrothed's clothing or for a prospective mother-in-law to feed her prospective son-in-law dumplings," Mr. Wang wrote. He said "husband-wife models" had emerged and cases of infanticide had decreased.

In the cultural field, while the basic love for the traditional Chinese opera remained, such new recreational pursuits as table tennis and gymnastics had replaced the old forms of gambling.

At the same time he noted that some peasants still did not have enough to eat, that the practice of usury had reappeared and that it was difficult to maintain general political enthusiasm. Mr. Wang said only 20 per cent of the peasant families had "voluntarily" joined the Mutual Aid Teams, in which farmers pool labor, tools and livestock.

An additional 37.7 per cent of rural families had joined the teams because of "current difficulties in production." But 42.3 per cent still preferred to "work by themselves" along capitalist lines. Mr. Wang did not give the population of the five villages upon which he was reporting—Hsiachaung, Hsiachun, Hungchin, Chuanti and Suko.

"In Suko village, since 20 per cent of the families have amassed money and purchased land, the price of land is now double the price in pre-war years," Mr. Wang went on. "When it is impossible to buy land, the peasants make money by practicing usury, collecting interest in kind at rates that sometimes reach as high as 60 to 180 per cent a year. Such practice, while not universal, is worthy of our attention.

"Prominence of middle peasants and gradual emergence of new rich peasants are now characteristics of class relations in the countryside today.

"Since the land reform, ninety-six peasant families in the five villages have sold a total of 284.11 mow (about forty-seven acres) of land to pay for wedding and funeral expenses and the like. Ninety-nine peasant families have bought land."

December 16, 1951

CHIANG TO ACCEPT RED LAND REFORM

By HENRY R. LIEBERMAN
Special to THE NEW YORK TIMES.

TAIPEI, Formosa, May 6—Generalissimo Chiang Kai-shek declared in an interview here today that the Chinese Nationalist Government would recognize the Communist redistribution of land in the mainland of China under the principle of "land to the tiller."

While accepting the present stage of the Communist land revolution, however, he said his Government intended to reimburse the landlords for their confiscated land if the general succeeded in re-establishing himself on the mainland.

Alert, energetic and younger looking than his 65 years might suggest, General Chiang said the basis of the Nationalist political philosophy was still represented by the "Three People's Principles" of Dr. Sun Yat-sen. Dr. Sun's slogans were "Nationalism, Democracy and People's Livelihood."

Emphasizing that fundamental attention had to be paid to the principle of "People's Livelihood," General Chiang said:

"This is our first step. We have put into effect here the concept of a land-rent ceiling amounting to 37.5 per cent of the crop. Those who till the land will keep it, but there must also be compensation for the landowners."

In outlining some of the steps his Government would take if it succeeded in returning to the mainland, General Chiang denounced the Communist drive against the urban middle class in China.

"From our point of view it is contrary to the principle of livelihood to displace the middle class," he said. He noted that the Kuomintang believed in a government-regulated economy, but added that it also believed in wide opportunities for private entrepreneurs in agriculture, commerce and industry.

The general, who is President of the Republic of China and still the bulwark of the Chinese Nationalist regime, spoke bitterly of the actions taken by the Communists to destroy the Chinese family system.

Like other Nationalist officials here, General Chiang has one objective constantly before him—Hui Chia, meaning the return home. He is not unaware, however, of the difficulties that would be involved in re-establishing the Nationalist Government on the China mainland.

"We are not fully prepared to return to the mainland," he said. "It is hard to say when. It depends on many factors."

General Chiang said he was convinced that the Chinese intellectuals well as the Lao Pai Hsing (Old Hundred Names, the Chinese peasant) would rally to the support of the Nationalists in the event of a landing on the mainland.

"If we can seize one or two districts on the mainland and hold them three to six months I am sure the people would come to our aid," he said.

May 7, 1952

Chinese Villagers Revolt, Fight Reds 2 Days; 'Reform' Area Rising Disturbs Communists

Special to THE NEW YORK TIMES.

HONG KONG, April 3.—A local peasant revolt that broke out in Hupeh Province under China's new "agrarian reform" structure has produced the Chinese Communist observation that "feelings of enmity" are "still strong," even in rural areas where the landlords have been eliminated and the land has been redistributed.

The Hankow Yangtze Daily, an official Communist organ, made the observation in a March 15 dispatch that became available here today. It was appended to an account of a two-day village uprising in which 280 peasants engaged in hand-to-hand fighting with both militiamen and regular troops in Chishui County, about sixty miles east of Hankow.

According to the Communist newspaper, the uprising began Feb. 21 when the peasants, armed with swords and other weapons, stormed a village party office and assassinated the local party secretary. Two villagers were killed and one militiaman was wounded in the first battle, the dispatch said.

Fifteen more peasants were killed and wounded when the fighting was resumed the following day, the account continued. By 4 P. M., it said, regular troops had arrived from Huangkang, about twenty-five miles northwest of Chishui, and subdued a hard core of about fifty peasants who refused to surrender.

The Yangtze Daily said that twenty-three peasants were "captured alive," but it did not give the over-all casualty figure. Nor was there any explanation of the concrete issues involved in the uprising.

The editor of the Communist organ, after expressing surprise at the Chishui outbreak, said:

"If this sort of serious incident can occur in such an area, it serves to prove that even in areas where agrarian reform has been implemented feelings of enmity are still strong."

April 4, 1952

RED CHINA TO PUSH RISING PRODUCTION

By HENRY R. LIEBERMAN
Special to THE NEW YORK TIMES.

HONG KONG, July 14—With its third anniversary ten weeks away, the Peiping Government has announced a "new tide of construction," apparently destined to follow an initial three-year program aimed at rehabilitating China's war-damaged economy.

Chinese Communist reports from both China proper and Manchuria have emphasized the "basic completion" of reconstruction tasks and the establishment of conditions for expanding production beyond previous peak figures.

Past statements by Chinese Communist leaders have indicated that the Peiping regime's first three-year goal was the achievement of pre-war production levels by the end of 1952. Judging by official references to the comparative industrial output in Manchuria, the three-year target in these Northeast Provinces has been the Japanese production levels of 1943.

Some Pre-War Levels Reached

Vice Premier Chen Yun, chairman of the Committee for Economic and Financial Affairs in Peiping, asserted June 24 that Communist China had "generally restored and in some cases exceeded" pre-war production levels. He said food production was expected to approach the pre-war output this year and that cotton production already had broken the previous record.

Agricultural experts here feel that Communist China may well be approaching the pre-war level of grain production, which they estimate at an annual average of about 140,000,000 tons for both China proper and Manchuria from 1931 to 1937. Paring a substantially larger Communist figure, however, they reckon China's 1951 cotton crop at about 700,000 tons compared with the pre-war annual average of 550,000 to 600,000 tons.

Vice Premier Chen Yun also said China was producing more coal, iron and steel ingots than ever before but he did not make it clear whether this assertion took cognizance of Japanese production in Manchuria while the Northeast Provinces were severed from China. His statement was followed by a Communist report from Mukden declaring that "the main work" of restoring damaged Manchurian industry had been completed and that the Northeast regional government had devoted 90 per cent of its industrial investment to "new construction."

Japanese Output High

Notwithstanding a new railway project initiated by the Peiping Government in West China, it was considered doubtful here that the Chinese Communists were approaching the 1943 Japanese production levels in Manchuria. According to Japanese figures, heavy industrial output in Manchuria during that year included 5,400,000 tons of iron ore, 1,700,000 tons of pig iron, 840,000 tons of ingot steel and 485,000 tons of rolled steel.

The battered Manchurian electrical power grid is believed to provide limitations on immediate large-scale industrial expansion in the Northeast. This grid embraces the Sungari River Hydroelectric station near Kirin, where the Russians removed a number of generators after the Japanese war, and Supung (Sohio) station on the Yalu River, which was also stripped of some equipment and which has become a bombing target in the Korean war.

Peiping's preparations for industrial development have included by a tightening of state control over urban economy, the establishment new industrial training programs for young party cadres and by apparent efforts to provide extra incentives in the private economic sphere. Peiping also announced the abolition of the 20 per cent local surtax on the national public grain tax.

At the same time, however, the Hsinhua News Agency disclosed recently that government food companies and cooperatives had been buying wheat from peasants at prices "slightly lower" than last year.

July 15, 1952

CHINESE ADVANCE KEY RAIL PROJECT

Work on Kansu-Sinkiang Line to Feed Vast Industrial Area Is Described by American

Special to THE NEW YORK TIMES.

HONG KONG, Aug. 16 — An American traveler has reported the opening of advance engineering offices above Lanchow for the construction of the projected northwest Chinese railway that is scheduled to lead into Sinkiang Province and be linked eventually with the Soviet Union's Turkestan-Siberian railway in central Asia.

The report came from Walter Illsley, a technician associated with the Baillie Industrial School at Shantan, Kansu Province. He still is in China. Writing in the August issue of the China Monthly Review, which is published in Shanghai, he said the offices had been opened at Yungteng and Wuwei, about fifty and 140 miles north of Lanchow, respectively.

Mr. Illsley wrote that Northwest China—which includes the Provinces of Sinkiang, Kansu, Ningsia, Tsinghai and Shensi—had sufficient coal, mineral and petroleum resources to become an important industrial region. He noted that transportation was a key obstacle, but said this was being overcome with the construction of the northwest railway.

The American, discussing the projected railway in recording his observations on a truck trip from Shantan to Lanchow, said he saw railway surveying parties strung out at "frequent intervals" for some 240 miles beyond the farthest point of actual railway construction. He did not disclose how far construction had gone.

Fork in Railroad Shown

A map accompanying the article showed the proposed railway route, extending northward from Lanchow to Wuwei and then veering northwestward via the Yumen oil field district of Kansu to Urumchi (Tihwa), capital of Sinkiang. West of Urumchi, at a point somewhere near Manas, on the Manas River, the map showed the railway forking out, with one prong leading westward to Alma Ata via Ining and the other leading northwestward to Sergiopol via Tacheng.

There had been a number of earlier reports here on the railway. So far as is known, however, this is the first time the project has been discussed in a mainland publication.

The Chinese Communists already have completed a railway from Chungking to Chengtu in West China and now are engaged in extending this line northeastward toward Tienshui, in Kansu, whence the lateral Lung-Hai railway also is being extended to Lanchow. The Tienshui-Lanchow line is scheduled to be completed this year, but the entire northwest railway net is regarded by Western observers here as a long and difficult project that will take years to finish.

August 17, 1952

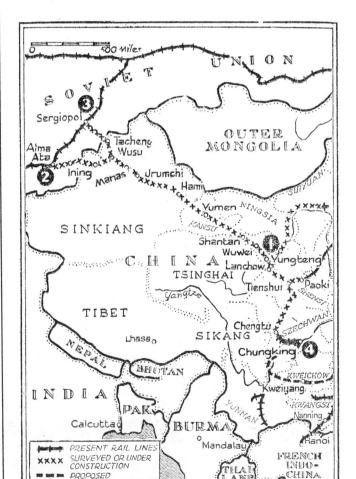

The New York Times   Aug. 17, 1952

CHINESE PROGRESS IN EXTENDING RAILROADS: Installations have been set up at Yungteng and Wuwei (1) for work on the projected line from near-by Lanchow to Alma Ata (2) and Sergiopol (3). Another route, from Chungking to Chengtu (4), has been completed.

PEIPING AIRS DESIRE TO TRADE WITH WORLD

Special to THE NEW YORK TIMES.

HONG KONG, July 20—Deputy Foreign Minister Chang Han-fu declared in a statement broadcast from Peiping today that Red China wanted to trade with all countries on terms of "equality and mutual benefit" as a means of developing her economy.

He maintained that the difficulties of British trade in China were caused by Britain's following the United States in adopting a "hostile attitude" and applying an "embargo policy" against the Peiping Government.

British companies in China would be permitted to deal with Chinese economic enterprises and would get Government protection if they obeyed the laws of the land, the broadcast said. If, however, the British concerns decided to shut down they could apply to local Government organs and would receive exit facilities "according to law," the broadcast added.

The broadcast said Mr. Chang made his statement July 5 in commenting on two British notes delivered to the Foreign Ministry in Peiping April 18 and May 19. In the latter note the British Chargé d'affaires, Leo H. Lamb, informed Peiping that the hard-pressed British concerns in China had decided to shut their enterprises and leave.

A British Foreign Office spokesman disclosed recently in London that a formal Chinese reply was received July 7, but refused to divulge its contents.

July 21, 1952

COMMUNISTS TIGHTEN CHINA TRADE CONTROL

Special to THE NEW YORK TIMES.

HONG KONG, Aug. 19—Regulations for the establishment of the projected All-China Federation of Industry and Commerce have been released by Peiping. This body which parallels the All-China Federation of Trade Unions, is organized to fit all types of urban economic enterprises into a tighter mold for purposes of more efficient government planning and control

The four "basic tasks" of the organization are listed as follows:
1. To lead industrialists and other businessmen in observing government laws and policies.
2. To direct them in developing production and improving their efficiency "under the general economic planning of the state."
3. To represent them in passing on their views to the Government and in consulting with trade unions on questions of labor-capital relations.
4. To organize them for "pursuit of studies, remodeling of ideology and participation in various patriotic movements."

The charter sets up three organizational tiers at the local, provincial and national levels.

August 20, 1952

Chinese Begin New Rail Line

Special to THE NEW YORK TIMES.

HONG KONG, Oct. 4—Wang Shih Tsai, the Vice Minister of Railways, has announced the start of construction work on a newly projected railway line extending from Lanchow, the capital of Kansu Province to Urumchi (Tihwa), the capital of Sinkiang Province. Sinkiang adjoins the Soviet frontier in central Asia. The statement was the first official mention of the Peiping regime's intention to push its railway building program into Sinkiang. It had been reported earlier, however, that Peiping was planning to link China's new northwest line with the Soviet Turksib railway via Sinkiang.

October 5, 1952

SOVIET BLOC GAINS RED CHINA'S TRADE

U. N. Survey Shows Change in Flow of Commerce—Far East Suffers a Slump

Special to THE NEW YORK TIMES.

UNITED NATIONS, N. Y., Nov. 23—The foreign trade of the mainland of China has undergone significant changes to the advantage of the Soviet sphere since the Communist regime of Mao Tsetung came to power there, according to the 1951 survey of the economies of the countries of Asia and the Far East, released today in Bangkok by the United Nations Commission for that region.

Exports and imports of mainland China reached three times the level of 1950, the commission's report said. The share of the Soviet Union and the countries of Eastern Europe within the Soviet sphere, which formerly held a minor position in the Chinese trade, increased from 21 per cent to 70 per cent of the imports and from 30 per cent to 77 per cent of the exports of mainland China, the commission estimated.

The figures indicated the extent to which the Soviet bloc, with closed economies engaging in international trade through state trading agencies on the basis of barter agreements, had succeeded in monopolizing the trade of the Soviet Union's newest satellite.

These agreements are coordinated by the Council for Economic Mutual Aid in Moscow.

The Economic Commission for Asia and the Far East warned that "if this change in the trade pattern of the mainland of China becomes permanent, among other effects, the entrepot trade of Hong Kong is likely to be seriously affected."

The economies of the countries of Asia and the Far East underwent a radical change during 1951, the commission's report said. The world slump in commodity prices in that year brought to a sudden end the preceding export boom caused by the outbreak of Communist aggression in Korea. As downward adjustments became necessary, unemployment rose, it stated.

The Asian farmer still produces less than he did before the war, although population has increased 10 per cent, the report said.

A large trade surplus of $1,130,000,000 in the first half of 1951 gave way to a trade deficit of $350,000,000 in the second half.

The countries in the region include Brunei, Burma, Cambodia, Ceylon, China, Hong Kong, India, Indonesia, Japan, Korea, Laos, Malaya, Nepal, North Borneo, Pakistan, Philippines, Sarawak, Singapore, Thailand and Vietnam.

November 24, 1952

China, Bulgaria in Trade Pact

Special to THE NEW YORK TIMES.

HONG KONG, Dec. 7—A 1953 barter agreement between China and Bulgaria, increasing this year's trade between the two countries by 70 per cent, was signed in Peiping Dec. 3, the Peiping radio reported tonight. The broadcast said the new agreement called for export to Bulgaria of Chinese nonferrous metals, cotton and "other imported materials." China is scheduled to receive Bulgarian machinery, electrical appliances, chemicals and other unlisted products.

December 8, 1952

Chinese Communists Enforce Their Land-Reform Program

Last July a Communist land-reform tribunal moved into Kwantung Province to enforce the Government's program, using executions as its main weapon. These farmers at Fukang, huddled together and bound, wait for tribunal's verdict. Ten were convicted of unspecified "violations."

Associated Press from Life Magazine

And here, on a sandy patch of soil, one rifle shot closes the case of Huang Chin-chi and liquidates his holdings for distribution to others more amenable to Communist regulation. These pictures were taken by a Chinese photographer who fled to Hong Kong and refused to reveal his name.

January 17, 1953

PEIPING DEMANDS LESS 'PAPERWORK'

Finance Minister Says Too Few Agency Heads Check Costs, Strive for Efficiency

By HENRY R. LIEBERMAN
Special to THE NEW YORK TIMES.

HONG KONG, Jan. 22—An intensified campaign against "bureaucratism" and "paper-workism" is being unfolded in Communist China with the dual objective of making Government economic organs more efficient and accumulating larger capital surpluses for the state's industrialization program.

Advent of the Peiping Government's first Five-Year Plan has been accompanied by heavy emphasis in the Chinese Communist press on a need for tighter "cost accounting" and larger returns from state-managed enterprises.

Financial and economic functionaries who are lagging behind in their "business study" have been warned officially that their future is "precarious."

"It is now time for us to remove some of them from their posts and replace them with new men," Finance Minister Po Yi-po declared early this month. Besides being finance minister he is party secretary in North China and vice chairman of the National Committee on Financial and Economic Affairs.

He issued the warning Jan. 6 in addressing a financial-economic ministers conference in Peiping according to the New China News agency.

Attacking "formalism," "self centralism" and lingering traces of the civil war "supply system" mentality, he demanded less paper pushing and better production leadership.

"The remnant of the 'supply system' concept in enterprise management means the fulfillment of a task without calculating the production cost and without considering the results," he said. "Persons retaining such a concept show an indifference to and assume no responsibility in accumulating capital for the state."

He called on ministers to promote a "viewpoint of business accounting," and added: "That is to say we must make meticulous calculations, increase output, raise quality, lower production costs, reduce outlays for non-productive purposes, cut administrative expenses and so on."

Meanwhile, in accordance with standard practice on national campaigns, the press has begun to follow that warning with local examples of bureaucratism and paperworkism. Instances already cited include granary food spoilages, reckless buying by state companies and pigeonholing of complaints from the public.

January 23, 1953

PEIPING BIDS REDS CURB LAND REFORM

'Reckless Expansion' of Farms Said to Be Irking Peasants and Cutting Production

By HENRY R. LIEBERMAN
Special to THE NEW YORK TIMES.

HONG KONG, July 1—The Peiping People's Daily, primary organ of the Chinese Communist party has criticized party workers in Honan and Chekiang Provinces for having engaged in "reckless expansion" of state farms in the face of opposition by private land-holding peasants.

The newspaper said "grave discontent" had been created among those peasants who had been required to move and exchange "good land for bad land" to make way for state farms. It said such practices had to be checked because they infringed on the interests of peasants, affected production and served to "alienate" the party from the masses.

"Apprehensive of the forcible exchange of land, some peasants lost their productive zeal and some refused to work for the state farms," The People's Daily declared editorially. "Consequently, about 80 per cent of the paddy on the Yiwu state farm [a county-operated farm in Chekiang] was allowed to rot."

The editorial, which was published June 19, said the Yiwu farm had requisitioned about twenty acres of land and required 195 peasant families to exchange fifty-four more acres under such circumstances that a number of peasants later produced less on the poorer land they had received. Listing similar examples in Honan, the newspaper noted that the Hsiayi county farm had demanded land occupied by 2,000 families and that considerable opposition had been aroused when the Loyang district farm decided to take land scattered in fourteen villages.

Other Criticisms Noted

The directors of the Nanyang state farm were criticized also for having forced peasants to "exchange their houses and land," while cadres at the Yushih county farm were criticized for failing to operate the 300-odd acres at their disposal following expansion of this enterprise. According to The People's Daily, farm cadres in Honan and Chekiang already had started "to rectify their errors."

The Communist organ declared that the state farms had been set up to serve as demonstration centers for peasants, to train cadres for scientific farm management and to lay the groundwork for converting "petty farming" to "mammoth agriculture." Its editorial noted, however, that the task of increasing agricultural output during the next few years depended on the "production zeal" of the whole farm population.

The warning against "reckless expansion" of state farms conforms with earlier strictures against "reckless pushing ahead" in the organization of "labor mutual-aid teams." The warnings follow an amended directive, adopted last February by the Communist party's Central Committee, that called for a halt in two "deviationist" trends in farm policy.

Rightist and Leftist Trends

The committee criticized the "rightist trend" of adopting "a passive attitude toward the movement for mutual aid and cooperation." At the same time, however, it criticized the "leftist trend" of "precipitate haste" in forming Socialist-type rural organizations.

As of last August, about a fourth of the peasant families in China were officially reported to have been organized into 6,000,000 "mutual-aid teams" and more than 3,000,000 "producers' cooperatives." About forty-five "state farms of a Socialist nature" and hundreds of smaller publicly operated farms also are reported to be in existence, along with a small number of collectives modeled on the Soviet kolhoz pattern. But the "small peasants' economy" still dominates the agricultural picture.

The People's Daily pointed out March 26 that only 0.02 per cent of peasant households had been organized into "semi-Socialist agricultural producers' cooperatives." It said state farms, including non-mechanized farms operated by provincial and county administrative units, now were working less than 0.3 per cent of China's total cultivated land.

July 2, 1953

Chinese Reds Fear Spring Famine; State Buying and Taxes Cut Output

By TILLMAN DURDIN
Special to The New York Times.

HONG KONG, Nov. 27—A serious food shortage is expected in Communist China by next spring. Informed sources here foresee the possibility of famine conditions in some regions.

Crop yields have been below expectations this year. An ill-timed frost hit winter wheat and later crops also have been affected by unfavorable weather as well as by other factors.

Despite the lower yield of some staples this year's over-all food production may turn out to be as high as that of 1952, but the program called for a 7.2 per cent increase and state food purchases and farm taxes were fixed accordingly.

In view of Peiping's need to export food along with other products to finance the capital goods required for Red China's new five-year plan, experts here believe the Government has proceeded to take its cut of farm products according to its original plans. The result is food scarcity.

Communist China exports grain, meats and other foods to Russia. This year Peiping is fulfilling a contract to supply Ceylon with 270,000 tons of rice in return for 50,000 tons of rubber.

Arrivals here from the China mainland reported that Shanghai and a number of other cities already were short of certain foods. Limited rationing is being enforced through the curtailment of the amount of rice, wheat, meat and a number of other foods that can be bought at one time. The rationing is expected to be severe as the winter progresses.

Besides natural factors, experts here think the Communist agrarian policies and the shortage of fertilizers and implements are also responsible for lagging farm output.

November 29, 1953

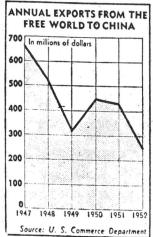

ANNUAL EXPORTS FROM THE FREE WORLD TO CHINA

Source: U. S. Commerce Department

The New York Times   Dec. 14, 1953

DOWN TREND: Free world exports to Communist China are now declining, after a pronounced bulge in 1950-51.

December 14, 1953

PEIPING TIGHTENS SCREWS ON FARMS

Press and Radio Bid Peasants Turn In Grains—Campaign Against Hoarding Is On

By TILLMAN DURDIN
Special to The New York Times.

HONG KONG, Dec. 11—Information reaching here indicates that the Chinese Communist regime is making the most intense effort since it was established to collect food grains from farmers.

Peasants in Red China not only pay a part of their cereal crops to the state for taxes but are also asked to sell to the Government at fixed prices all they have produced above their actual needs.

Peiping is trying to extract the utmost from the farmers in a food purchasing drive. Over the radio and in the press, farmers are exhorted to turn their surplus produce over to state agencies. Communist cadres in rural areas are using pressure, mass meetings, denunciations of hoarders and appeals to patriotic duty to induce the peasants to part with their cereals.

In a special phase of the campaign, directed at preventing farmers from selling surreptitiously to private merchants, speculators are being denounced for circumventing the policy of state grain purchasing. The Communist regime this winter obviously wants to acquire the maximum amount of food grains and other agricultural products. Several reasons are seen here.

Stocks are needed to fulfill Red China's export commitments to the Soviet Union and other Communist nations and to non-Communist countries such as Ceylon, with which Peiping has an agreement to exchange rice for rubber. Supplies are required also for provisioning of cities and in particular of workers employed on five-year projects in both rural and urban areas.

Experts here regard the high-pitched food collection campaign as additional evidence of heavy sacrifices the peasantry is having to make toward providing means for industrialization under the five-year program. Collections from farms are seen as part of a new effort to squeeze the utmost out of Red China's backward economy in the interest of creating an industrialized nation on the Soviet pattern.

Peiping's new issue of bonds, scheduled for next year, is another aspect of the construction drive. It was revealed yesterday in a Peiping broadcast that the bond issue would total 6,000,000,000 yuan or approximately $250,000,-000.

In view of the tribute from the Chinese economy that the Peiping regime has already taken in collections, fines, confiscations and a $100,000,000 bond issue in 1950, the new securities will tax the absorptive capacities of the Chinese people to the limit. In informed quarters here it is considered unlikely that the new bonds can be sold without forceful methods.

The bonds are viewed as a device not only to raise more capital for five-year plan construction but also to curb inflationary tendencies produced by extensive five-year plan expenditures. It is believed certain that the bonds and other means of raising capital for new construction will further lower living standards.

December 12, 1953

Red China Appeals for Trade

TOKYO, Monday, March 22 (Æ)—Communist China broadcast a new appeal to capitalist countries last night for "wide prospects for trade" if they ignored Allied embargoes applied after Red China entered the Korean war. Such dealings would benefit non-Communist countries, Peiping radio said, even though "the most reliable and solid foundation for China's trade" was with Russia and other "peoples' democracies." The broadcast quoted an article by Lei Jen-Min, retiring Vice Minister for Foreign Trade.

March 22, 1954

U.S. URGED TO KEEP CHINA TRADE BARS

The West must not let down its bars on trade with Communist China or any Soviet area if there is to be effective resistance to Red aggression in Asia, a Republican Congressman with long experience in the Far East warned yesterday.

Representative William H. Judd of Minnesota declared that American policy in Asia must be aimed at weakening the Communists, while also strengthening the free nations of that continent. The immediate objective, he said, should be prevention of any more Kremlin victories there, economic, diplomatic or political.

The Congressman, who for ten years was a medical missionary in the Far East, added that "we must recognize that what is at stake in Asia is the peace and possible survival of the free world, not just its trade." In addition, he said, short-sighted desire for trade would aid the Communists in exerting economic pressures to divide and weaken Western nations.

Addresses Trade Luncheon

Representative Judd was the main speaker at the World Trade Luncheon in the Waldorf-Astoria Hotel. The affair, sponsored by leading trade and civic groups, was part of New York observance of World Trade Week.

Mr. Judd cited "illusions" in the recurrent lure of trade offered by the Communists. One of these, he said, was that "by expanding trade with the Communist bloc, we can convert Communists into capitalists."

Others, he noted, held that increased trade would split Red China from Russia.

Declaring also that admission of Red China to the United Nations would be viewed as a Communist victory by free Asiatic nations, Mr. Judd added:

"Mao [head of the Chinese Communist government] conceivably might pull away from Moscow if he were compelled to in order to get absolutely essential goods, that is, if he began to lose in China. The first aim of our policy should be to make him lose. The way to do that is to make him fail, not help him to win. The best hope of creating friction between China and the Soviet Union is to keep the Chinese Reds locked, preferably smothered, in the arms of the Russian bear."

Congressman Judd termed the potentialities of Western-Communist trade greatly exaggerated. The best possibilities for more trade in Asia lie outside Red China in those free countries of the Far East, he asserted. These, he said, must be strengthened in every way, including an alliance of Southeast Asia and Pacific countries.

May 20, 1954

CHINA TRADE BAN SAID TO HURT REDS

British Official, Back From 4-Week Visit, Says Growth of Industry Is Retarded

LONDON, Nov. 9 (AP)—A British Government official who returned this week from a tour of Communist China's industrial centers said today that country unquestionably was being hurt by Western trade restrictions.

"It was a subject which came up everywhere I went, each time I talked with Government or industrial leaders," said Frederick J. Erroll, Parliamentary Secretary to the Board of Trade.

Mr. Erroll, whose four-week tour was the first visit to China by a British minister since the Communists took control there, said he had found a mixture of defiance and resentment toward the West's embargo on strategic materials.

"On one hand, the Chinese said the restrictions had been good for the country because they had forced China to become more self-sufficient," Mr. Erroll said in an interview. "But on the other hand they would demand: 'Why are you here to talk about trade when there is so much you will not trade?'"

Effects of Embargo Noted

During a tour that included all the major Chinese industrial cities, Mr. Erroll said, he saw much evidence that the nation's industrial expansion had been held back by the lack of Western trade, particularly in petroleum, ships and precision machinery.

The British official went to China on what he described as a ground-paving mission aimed at expanding British-Chinese trade in non-strategic materials. Britain eased her restrictions on such trade last May despite the United States' objections, but still prohibits the shipment of goods that might contribute to China's war potential.

Mr. Erroll's other main impressions gained during his tour included these points:

¶The Chinese are eager to check the price and performance of Western products against present equipment that has been obtained almost solely from the Soviet Union.

¶In the long run, Communist China's goal is economic self-sufficiency. The Chinese would like to be economically independent of both the Soviet Union and the West.

¶China, although still backward, has made great strides during her first five-year plan and may be expected to develop industrially as quickly as the Soviet Union.

¶Chinese industrial products, particularly the "liberation lorry," a four-ton truck, compare reasonably well with Western products. Chinese workmen have talent, brains and natural mechanical ability.

Although a twenty-man Chinese Communist trade mission is now on a month-long shopping tour in Britain, Mr. Erroll does not look for any sudden surge in British-Chinese trade.

"The Chinese are very price-conscious," he said. "That is why they want to compare our prices with those of Russia. And like all good bargainers, they are apt to be slow to buy."

The Board of Trade official predicted a gradual long-range expansion in British exports to Communist China, applying particularly to machine tools and industrial and chemical products.

The ban on petroleum products has been by far the most sorely felt of the Allied trade restrictions, Mr. Erroll found. The ban includes prospecting and drilling equipment. That is the main reason for the failure of China's petroleum industry to approach its goals, he reported.

November 10, 1957

RED CHINA AIMS AT CUT IN BIRTHS

Economic Troubles Linked to Excess Population by Party Newspaper

PEIPING, March 5 (Reuters)—The Chinese Communist party newspaper, People's Daily, said in an editorial on birth control today that economic development, however fast, could not yet catch up with China's rapid rate of population increase.

The editorial was the first carried on birth control by the party newspaper, and it was the first time that the current economic campaign had been linked officially with population problems.

The paper said that China's population of more than 600,000,000 was increasing at a yearly rate of 2.2 per cent (more than 13,000,000 a year, or roughly twenty-five a minute).

These 600,000,000, the newspaper said, are doing wonderful things under the leadership of the Communist party, and density of population is not in itself a bad thing. It added, however, that it would take several decades to bring the country from its backward position and many difficulties remained, especially for those with many children.

The editorial said that in August, 1953, the State Council instructed the health department to give instruction in birth control to the public.

No forcible orders should be given on birth control, the paper said. It suggested that Chinese should change their custom of early marriage and that propaganda should be directed toward encouraging youths not to marry until they were 25.

Contraceptives should be sold at cheap prices and all methods of birth control should be investigated and those that are safe should be widely practiced, the newspaper said.

Intensive propaganda has been going on throughout the country recently on birth control; contraceptives are now on display in drug stores, and next Friday a birth-control exhibition will open in Peiping.

March 6, 1957

CHAPTER 4

Revolutionary Foreign Affairs
1950–55

National Day in Peking, 1951.

Courtesy Eastfoto

MAO AIDE GIVES ASIA 'LIBERATION' PATTERN

Special to THE NEW YORK TIMES.

HONG KONG, Nov. 24—The development of "national liberation armies" on the pattern of the Chinese Communist armies was declared essential to the success of the struggles in Asian and Australasian countries for "national independence and a people's democracy" by Liu Shao-chi in a Peiping speech last week.

Mr. Liu, who is one of the vice presidents of the Communist-dominated Peiping Government, was addressing a conference of Asian and Australasian trade union delegates. The text of his address was released here today by the Communist New China News Agency.

Mr. Liu, who often acts as spokesman for Mao Tze-tung, Chairman of the Central People's Government in Peiping, asserted that liberation armies in Asiatic countries must be led by the Communist party and must establish bases from which activities can be launched and coordinated with the mass struggles in capitalist-controlled areas.

Mr. Liu declared:

"Armed struggle is the main form of the struggle for the national liberation of many colonies."

The Chinese Communist leader advised union delegates that the Communist parties must be the center of liberation efforts and that these must be built up through long struggles and coordinated with activities of the working class and "all other classes, political parties, groups, organizations and individuals who are willing to oppose the oppression of imperialism."

November 25, 1949

Burma Army Fights Chinese Nationalists

By Reuters.

RANGOON, Burma, Jan. 28—Burmese Army units have launched a campaign against a strong force of Chinese Nationalist troops in the mountainous frontier country of northern Burma, the Government announced tonight.

The statement charged that the Nationalist troops had "trespassed into Burmese territory" and were moving about from place to place without any permanent base.

The Chiang Kai-shek forces, under the command of Gen. Li Mi, retreated across the Yunnan frontier at the end of the Chinese civil war in 1950.

Their presence in Burma has brought repeated charges from the Chinese Communists, who have asserted they were plotting attacks on southern China with the aid of the United States.

[Previous reports have placed the Chinese Nationalist units in the Kengtong area of Northeast Burma.]

Henry B. Day, United States interim Chargé d'Affaires here, disclosed today that the United States asked the Nationalists to withdraw their troops from the Burmese border area at the request of the Burmese Government.

Had Promised to Withdraw

Mr. Day said that despite Nationalist promises to cooperate, their forces remained in this country.

The Burmese fear that the Communists may cross Burma's frontier to wipe out these troops.

Mr. Day said that it was up to the Burmese Government to bring up the question of Nationalist troops in its territory before the United Nations.

Recent reports reaching here from the Chinese frontier said that Nationalists reinforcements armed with United States weapons were moving daily from Formosa through Thailand to join General Li's army, now believed preparing for an April offensive.

Burma's new ambassador to Peiping, Hla Aung, said recently in Hong Kong that they were being led by United States officers.

Secretary of State Dean Acheson denied this charge in Washington Jan. 23, stating that the United States was not aiding the Chiang forces in Burma.

Mr. Day also said that to the best knowledge of the United States Government there were no Americans with the Nationalist troops.

January 29, 1952

U. N. Adjourns on Hopeful Note

By THOMAS J. HAMILTON
Special to THE NEW YORK TIMES.

UNITED NATIONS, N. Y., April 23 — The United Nations General Assembly wound up its agenda today by adopting resolutions calling for an impartial investigation of Communist charges that the United States had used germ warfare in Korea and for the withdrawal or internment of Chinese Nationalist troops operating in Burma.

With its agenda out of the way, the Assembly went into a recess that will last until there is an armistice in Korea or "other developments"—meaning a new breakdown in the Panmunjom negotiations—require consideration of the Korean question by the United Nations.

Sir Gladwyn Jebb of Britain, an Assembly vice president, who was presiding in the absence of Lester B. Pearson of Canada, the president, said that the second part of the session, which convened on Feb. 24, had been happy and satisfactory "on the whole," and that he hoped that it would not be long before the Assembly reconvened after a Korean armistice.

However, Ernest A. Gross, in his farewell appearance as a United States delegate, told the Assembly that "the campaign of lies charging United Nations forces in Korea with waging germ warfare continues," and said that Soviet opposition to a United Nations investigation "compounds two crimes—speaking evil and concealing evil" and "is utterly and completely iniquitous."

Today the Soviet Union continued to employ its new-found moderation of language and joined all the member states except Nationalist China in voting for a compromise Mexican resolution on the presence of 12,000 Chinese Nationalist troops on Burmese territory.

The resolution urges all states on the request of Burma to provide all the assistance in their power in facilitating the peaceful evacuation of the troops and also to refrain from helping them "continue their hostile actions against Burma."

The basic request is addressed primarily to the United States, which, at the request of Burma, has for some time been trying to persuade the Chinese Nationalist Government either to evacuate the troops or to order them to disarm and submit to internment.

Only China Abstained

The vote on the Mexican resolution was 59 to 0, with Nationalist China abstaining. Burma decided to vote for it today in recognition of "the solid moral backing of the United Nations given her complaint," despite the fact that the resolution did not condemn Nationalist China as an aggressor or, in fact, identify the "foreign forces."

By a vote of 51 to 5, with four abstentions, the Assembly adopted a resolution calling for a United Nations investigation of Communist charges that the United Nations forces in Korea—meaning the United States—had employed bacteriological warfare. The five members of the Soviet bloc voted against it, and Burma, India, Indonesia and Saudi Arabia abstained.

The opposition of the Soviet bloc is taken to mean that neither Communist China nor North Korea will admit the proposed commission, and since the resolution provides that the investigation will not take place unless both sides agree to cooperate, it is expected that the resolution will have no practical result.

Gross Attack Unanswered

Andrei Y. Vishinsky, the Soviet representative, who has so often decried the real and fancied actions of American "war-mongers," did not reply in kind to the attack made by Mr. Gross, and in fact avoided any approach to provocative language. On the other hand, the substance of what he said was exactly the same as what he used to say before the death of Stalin and the start of the Soviet peace offensive.

Mr. Vishinsky did not actually say that the United Nations commission would not be admitted, but that was the universal interpretation of his remarks. The lack of change in the Soviet position caused no surprise or alarm, but a number of delegates are concerned by the fact that in the last few days the Communists have handed over so many United Nations prisoners who do not belong in the "sick and wounded" classification, while holding on to others who clearly do.

This has aroused concern for fear that when the armistice negotiations are resumed at Panmunjom it will develop that the ambiguities in Communist China's recent offer regarding the repatriation of prisoners of war were inserted to produce another breakdown.

The offer stated that those unwilling to go back should be placed in the custody of a "neutral state," but said nothing about their ultimate status, while a subsequent statement by the Peiping Government seemed to indicate that the Communists would continue to demand the eventual repatriation of all prisoners as the price of an armistice.

The situation in the Assembly is that if there is an armistice, the Assembly will have to meet to call the political conference that is to be held within three months after the armistice to discuss the unification of Korea and other issues. This paragraph of the draft armistice agreement—which has been accepted by both sides—is so ambiguous that a prolonged debate here is expected on what states should attend and what items should be discussed.

If the armistice negotiations result in another deadlock, the Assembly does not have to meet again—it would do so only if a majority of its members so desired—until the 1953 session convenes on Sept. 15. However, most delegates believe that if hopes of an armistice are again dashed, the reaction in the United States will be so strong that an Assembly meeting might be needed for some of the actions the United States would then take to bring the war to a decisive end.

Accordingly, the general feeling of most delegates was, in the words of Brig. Gen. Carlos P. Romulo of the Philippines, that this had been a "Cross-Your-Fingers" Assembly. General Romulo said that "a splendid effort" had been made to recapture the spirit of San Francisco, where the Charter was drafted, but added that "it is well to keep your eyes and ears open."

April 24, 1953

U. N. ASKED TO OUST CHINESE IN BURMA

Special to THE NEW YORK TIMES.

UNITED NATIONS, N. Y., March 26—Burma submitted a complaint to the United Nations General Assembly today accusing the Chinese Nationalist Government of having committed aggression by refusing to require 12,000 Nationalist troops on Burmese territory "to submit to disarmament and internment in accordance with international law."

The long-threatened Burmese appeal to the Assembly also contained a draft resolution under which the Assembly would recommend that the Security Council "condemn the Kuomintang Government of Formosa for the said acts of aggression," and "take all necessary steps" to put a stop to them.

The resolution would also provide for an Assembly appeal "to all states to respect the territorial integrity and the political independence of the Union of Burma and to be guided by the principles of the Charter in their relations with Burma.

Aggressive Acts Cited

The complaint charged that 12,000 "Kuomintang troops" were now on Burmese territory, and that their "aggression" had been demonstrated "by their acts of hostilities against the forces of the Government of the Union of Burma and by their depredations against the civilian population."

"It is clear that in engaging in these illegal activities the Kuomintang troops are being directed and supported by the Government of Formosa," it declared. Nationalist troops were accused of carrying on "a veritable reign of terror looting, pillaging, raping and murdering, including the murdering of civilian officials of the Government."

In support of its charge that the Nationalist Government was responsible, the complaint asserted that Gen. Li Mi, the original commander of the Nationalist troops, had been moving between Formosa

and Monghsat, in the area where the troops were, and that "this and other evidence establishes that there is a direct link between the Kuomintang troops in Burma and the Kuomintang Government of Formosa."

The Nationalist forces, according to the complaint, retreated into Burma from Yunan Province of China after the victory of the Chinese Communists and remained in the frontier area. Later, however, some moved into an area near the Burma-Thailand border.

The Burmese complaint pointed out that she no longer recognized the Nationalist Chinese Government, and said that she had appealed to the United States, among other "friendly countries," to use their good offices to bring about the withdrawal of the Nationalist troops or their disarmament and internment, but that these efforts had been unsuccessful.

U. S. Position Delicate One

So far as is known, Burma's complaint is the first time in which the Assembly has been requested to recommend that the Security Council take action. The Assembly's steering, or general, committee is expected to meet Monday to decide whether to recommend the inclusion of the item on the agenda of the present session. If, as expected, the Assembly does so, the session will not end before the second half of April.

A United States spokesman declined to comment on the Burmese complaint, which, to the extent that it makes difficulties for the Chinese Nationalists, also will make difficulties for the United States. The Soviet Union, which has been unaccountably restrained in discussing President Eisenhower's order permitting the Nationalists to conduct military operations against the mainland, may use Burma's complaint as a basis for an attack on that policy.

A Chinese Nationalist spokesman said tonight that the Nationalist Government "does not as a matter of fact exercise control" over the Nationalist forces, which he described as guerrillas. The spokesman said this was all he could say at present.

March 27, 1953

BURMA WARNS U.N. ON CHINESE ISSUE

Delegate Says Force Will Be Used to Expel 6,000 Guerrillas if Necessary

Special to The New York Times.

UNITED NATIONS, N. Y., Oct. 11—Burma served notice today that she would use military force if necessary to deal with 6,000 Nationalist Chinese Guerrillas along her northern border.

The warning came from James Barrington, Burmese delegate. He told the General Assembly's Special Political Committee that Burma was gratified that about 5,600 Chinese troops already had been removed but that the situation was "intolerable." The remaining troops, he declared, still have a peaceful alternative: to get out "under their own steam" or submit to disarmament and internment.

The recurrent Burmese complaint against Chinese "aggression" goes back to 1950, when Gen. Li Mi's Nationalist troops fled across the Burmese frontier after Communist forces occupied the mainland. At one time it was contended that the guerrillas' jungle camps would serve as a foothold for attacks against Red China.

Since 1953, evacuation of roughly half of the guerrilla army has been carried out under the supervision of a three-nation military committee made up of Thailand, the United States and Nationalist China. The committee ended its work Sept. 1, reporting it had helped all those wishing to leave.

Formosa Shuns Responsibility

In reply to the Burmese protest, Dr. Chih-mai Chen reiterated his Government's stand that it had no control over the "irregulars" except the power of persuasion, that it had done its

best to induce the troops to leave finally and that it gave no help to the guerrillas and maintained no relations with the remnants in Burma.

The termination of the evacuation operation, Mr. Barrington told the committee, left it to Burma to work out a solution and he declared Burma still hoped the problem could be solved peacefully.

"We do not want to embark on large-scale military measures to solve this problem unless we have to," he said. "However, we cannot afford to leave thousands of alien troops on the loose in our countryside, plundering and pillaging and making a good thing out of the opium trade."

The Burmese delegate also called on United Nations help to bar foreign financial and other aid to the guerrillas. Burma's written report to the Assembly said that the Government had received "alarming" news that anti-Communist Chinese abroad planned to give $600,000 to support the Nationalist troops in Burma. Mr. Barrington called on the Assembly "to speak out in unmistakable terms" against the resumption of aid in any form.

Others Reported in Ranks

Dr. Chen contended that the guerrillas' ranks were not solely Chinese but also included considerable numbers of Karens, Kachins, Chins, Shans and dissident Burmese elements. "They certainly are not fifth columnists sent into Burma by the Chinese Government," he observed.

The Nationalist Chinese spokesman also complained to the United Nations members that Burma had obstructed the evacuation operation on several occasions and had violated the cease-fire arrangements made to speed the withdrawal.

Khenjati Punyaratabhan of Thailand, the only other speaker, said he had "misgivings" that Burma's report mentioned that troops were returning from Thailand to Burma and assured the committee that the joint frontier was "strictly supervised."

October 12, 1954

Nehru Said to Sway Peiping Toward Moderate Policies

By ROBERT TRUMBULL
Special to The New York Times.

NEW DELHI, India, Oct. 30—Prime Minister Jawaharlal Nehru is believed here to have sought to encourage the Chinese Communist regime toward courses of action aimed at lessening East-West tensions over Asian sore spots.

Red China's rulers are expected to accept Mr. Nehru's recommendations for reopening the Korean unification talks suspended in Geneva. Some declaration to clarify the anomalous status of large "overseas Chinese" populations in Southeast Asia is seen as another eventual outcome of the Peiping conversations.

It is felt here that Mr. Nehru's counsel of moderation on the Formosa question has already had some effect on the Chinese Communist leaders. The Indian Prime Minister was evidently unswayed from his conciliatory course by continual impassioned references by Peiping officials to Nationalist-held Formosa.

Detailed dispatches from Indian correspondents accompanying Mr. Nehru, taken together with reports from other sources, indicate the Indian Prime Minister has tried hard to moderate the attitude of the Red Chinese toward the United States.

Mr. Nehru's firm refusal to be drawn into an Asian pact with anti-United States implications is believed here to be the key to one of the "differences of approach" to which the Indian leader has made repeated reference in his public statements.

While Mr. Nehru has emphatically denied that these differences are as "sharp" as described in some reports in the Western press, it appears that the degree of disagreement may be a matter of individual interpretation. Mr. Nehru and most of the Indian commentators prefer to dwell on the more numerous amicable aspects of the talks.

Mr. Nehru is said to have found the Chinese leaders "sensitive" and "oversuspicious" of the West and to be living in some respects "behind a mental wall." And Mao Tse-tung is reported to have accused India of being "too anxious not to offend the West."

The Chinese were apparently pressing Mr. Nehru to join with Peiping in sponsoring an "Asian peace bloc" to counter the United States-sponsored Manila pact for collective security in Southeast Asia. They may have run up against the type of neutralist thinking in Mr. Nehru that has often baffled and irritated the West.

While Mr. Nehru has himself from time to time pleaded for a "third area of peace" in Asia and adjacent areas, he is reported to have declined to go along with Peiping's idea that such a grouping must involve more than merely an expression of sentiment.

The Chinese Communists, according to authoritative reports, wanted Mr. Nehru's concurrence in a policy of taking steps, whose nature was not specified, to counteract the activities of the Western powers to cement the Asian states against Red encroachments.

But Mr. Nehru stood on his argument that one "cannot counter war blocs with peace blocs," as one authoritative account of his conversations put it. One of the severest critics of the Manila pact, he was apparently no more amenable to joining an opposed grouping under Red China's sponsorship.

Sidestepped African-Asian Talk

The Indian Prime Minister was also reported to have expressed the opinion that the Chinese Communists "use words that are too strong" and that under the stresses that they now feel they "are not acting normally."

Mr. Nehru appears to have sidestepped Red Chinese overtures' toward participation in the projected African-Asian conference set for Bandung, Indonesia, in February.

The Indian Prime Minister, who has never been keen on the intercontinental gathering proposed by Indonesian Premier Ali Sastroamidjojo, is reported to have told his Chinese Communist hosts that the Colombo conference powers—India, Pakistan, Ceylon, Burma and Indonesa—that have called the African-Asian conference would decide who should be invited.

Mr. Nehru was wary of Premier Chou En-lai's suggestion that the states of Indochina—Communist North Vietnam, South Vietnam, Laos and Cambodia—should be included. The Indian leader evidently felt that Indochina's own situation should be ironed out first on the lines of the Geneva agreement.

Incidentally, there is a feeling in diplomatic quarters here that Mr. Nehru's Government may be on the point of recognizing the non-Communist Indochinese kingdoms of Laos and Cambodia.

Policy on Overseas Chinese

From the Western point of view it has been encouraging that when he was in Hanoi, capital of North Vietnam, Mr. Nehru obtained assurances from Communist President Ho Chi Minh that he would respect the integrity of the two small, weak, neighboring kingdoms.

It is generally agreed here that one of the topics uppermost in Mr. Nehru's mind when he went to Peiping was the status of the millions of Chinese in Burma, Thailand, Malaya, Indonesia and other Asiatic countries.

He is understood to have pressed the Communist Chinese to adopt India's policy in relation to her overseas nationals. That policy is that they must decide whether to retain their identity with their ancestral country and thereby forfeit rights to participate in political activities in the foreign nation, or become citizens of the adopted land.

Indian observers believe the Peiping rulers were somewhat persuaded toward Mr. Nehru's advice.

Indian correspondents who reached Red China ahead of Mr. Nehru reported a perceptible decline in fervor over Formosa since the Indian leader brought his conciliatory powers to bear on Communist leaders.

Diplomatic circles here conceive Mr. Nehru to have been greatly disturbed by the Communist attacks on the island of Quemoy. He is reported to have urged Peiping to rely on conciliatory measures and the passage of time for solution of the Formosa problem.

However, the Indian leader left no doubt of his sympathy with Peiping's claim to Chiang Kai-shek's island bastion when he remarked that, since India recognized the Communist regime as the only Government of China, "the Formosa question does not arise" in New Delhi.

Regarding Korea, Mr. Chou is reported to have given Mr. Nehru a strong hint that Peiping will soon make some move toward reopening the negotiations interrupted in Geneva. Mr. Nehru was said to have urged a policy of "keeping the door open" on the Korea question.

Western diplomats here have been encouraged by the fact that the Peiping meetings failed to produce the expected joint communiqué by Messrs. Chou and Nehru affirming Indian-Chinese solidarity. But Indian analysts caution against putting too much importance on this, as they say there is no doubt that Mr. Nehru's talks with the Red Chinese leaders produced greater "understanding" between the two countries.

It is believed in some authoritative quarters that as a result of the Peiping sessions Mr. Nehru has made a bid to become the official interpreter of the West to Communist China, no less than he has till now held the role of interpreter of Red China to the West.

A civil air pact between New Delhi and Peiping was concluded before Mr. Nehru left China. The opening of diplomatic relations between Red China and Nepal, the independent Himalayan kingdom in which India takes a virtually controlling interest, is expected shortly.

October 31, 1954

INDIAN LABOR MEN REBUFF RED CHINA

Peiping's Bid to Take Over Asian Trade Unions Gets Stinging Public Setback

By A. M. ROSENTHAL
Special to The New York Times.

NEW DELHI, India, May 21—Communist China's campaign to take over Asian trade union movements has received a major setback.

For the first time Peiping's ardent political wooing of important Indians has been rebuffed publicly and stingingly.

The story of Peiping's failure goes back a couple of years when Communist strategists decided to set up a new Asian labor organization.

The plan apparently had at least two aims. One was to capitalize on Asian labor movements on Communist China's political successes. Another was to try to wreck any Asian influence of the anti-Communist International Confederation of Free Trade Unions.

The impetus came from the Communists, but they were eager to have non-Communist labor leaders march in the front.

From Peiping went invitations to Asian labor leaders to come to China to take part in May Day celebrations and to see a bit of the country on a guided tour.

According to labor sources in New Delhi, Peiping's open-handed hospitality to labor is paid for by a 2 per cent tax on the monthly wages of all Chinese workers. The Indian National Trade Union Congress, the labor arm of Prime Minister Jawaharlal Nehru's Congress party, politely declined to take part officially in the Peiping celebrations. But some labor leaders from unions affiliated with the Congress went to Peiping in a private capacity.

Indian Visitors Irked in China

This week nine of thirty-two Indians who made the voyage cut short their trip and came home. They were angry and their statements showed it.

Charges were made by the In-

dians that the Chinese were trying to indoctrinate them and use them as tools in the formation of a Communist-dominated "Asian-African trade union movement."

Bikash Mazumdar, a seafarers' union executive, said the Japanese delegation in China had made a proposal for an Asian trade union organization to coordinate labor movements throughout the continent. Mr. Mazumdar said some Indians still in China supported the idea. He said it was opposed by nine Indians and Pakistani leaders.

Mr. Mazumdar said the Japanese proposal seemed aimed at starting "an Asian secretariat of the Comiform, and they wanted all the delegates to agree to this plan."

In labor circles in the Indian capital it was said the nine who walked out represented railroad, bank, seamen's and other unions and were among the most important men in the Indian delegation. Those who remained were described as having been generally associated with Communist-backed labor movements or Marxist societies.

Maps Showed Kashmir in China

The Indians who returned made it clear they saw many things they did not like. One of them hung on a wall in an office in Shanghai. It was a map that reportedly included Kashmir as part of China. Kashmir is under dispute between India and Pakistan. The map also showed as part of China the independent Hindu Kingdom of Nepal and the Indian protectorate of Bhutan.

The Indian labor leaders' stand was symptomatic of the double attitude many important elements in India take toward Communist China. In India Communist China is recognized as an important and growing Asian power one that will be in the international picture permanently. There is respect for China's political accomplishments. There is also a kind of glee at the sight of an Asian power pushing non-Asian powers around politically and presenting a strong military front.

But, at the same time, many Indian leaders are determined not to allow Communist China's influence to grow domestically in India.

In the border areas looking toward Communist China's protectorate of Tibet the security vigil is constant. As one Indian military man once said: "We are not looking for Americans up there in the northeast."

May 22, 1955

PEIPING TIGHTENS TIES TO INDONESIA

By ROBERT ALDEN
Special to The New York Times.

JAKARTA, Indonesia, April 28—Communist China today tightened its political, cultural and economic ties with Indonesia, the largest country in Southeast Asia.

A joint statement was signed by Communist Premier Chou En-lai and Indonesian Premier Ali Sastroamidjojo. It contained a passage in which, at least by implication, the Indonesian official expressed sympathy and support for Communist China's right to Formosa.

Before Mr. Chou's departure this morning after a two-day state visit, he and Dr. Ali signed a declaration. It placed Indonesia on record as subscribing to the five principles of peaceful coexistence as drawn up by Mr. Chou and Prime Minister Jawaharlal of India.

'Inalienable Right'

"The two Prime Ministers declare that it is the inalienable right of the people of any country to safeguard their own sovereignty and territorial integrity," the statement said. "They express sympathy and support to the efforts of either of the two countries in safeguarding its own sovereignty and territorial integrity.

Diplomatic observers here feel that this paragraph alludes to Communist China's claim to the Nationalist-held island as well as to the Indonesian claim to Netherlands New Guinea, or West Irian as it is called here.

Mr. Chou and Dr. Ali expressed hope that the two countries would develop an extensive mutual assistance program in the economic and cultural fields "on the basis of mutual respect, equality and mutual benefit."

Rich in Resources

Indonesia, rich in oil, rubber and tin, is able to provide more of the sinews of war than any other country in Southeast Asia.

The "peaceful coexistence" plank in the joint statement reads:

"The two Prime Ministers express satisfaction over the fact that Indonesia and China are living peacefully together as good neighbors on the basis of the principles of mutual respect for sovereignty and territorial integrity, nonaggression, noninterference in each other's internal affairs, equality and mutual benefit."

Mr. Chou and Dr. Ali expressed satisfaction over the conclusion of an agreement on citizens of dual Chinese and Indonesian nationality living in Indonesia.

They said that this agreement, which provides that such dual citizens must choose a single citizenship within two years, "is a good example of settling complicated and difficult international problems by means of friendly negotiations."

April 29, 1955

CHINA'S REDS SEEK TOKYO TREATY ROLE

By LINDESAY PARROTT
Special to The New York Times.

TOKYO, June 23—The Chinese Communists now are demanding a controlling voice in writing an eventual peace treaty between Japan and the Allied Pacific powers. In this they now are informing the Japanese people they will insist on reversal of the occupation's actions over the last three years—such as termination of war crimes trials, revision of reparations schedules and United States plans for general rehabilitation of the Japanese economy.

This story is now being told to the Japanese through Chinese broadcasts from Shanghai and Peiping, which are regularly received here. Today the Communists' official journal Akahata urges Japanese to "quickly prepare for a peace treaty on this basis."

The Peiping broadcast as headlined by Akahata asserts the "Chinese people who have sacrificed most and suffered most at the hands of the Japanese invaders" have every right to intervene in writing the treaty and stresses that the Chinese Communists rather than the Nationalist Government represent the "Chinese people."

U. S. Actions Are Assailed

Akahata, quoting the Peiping broadcast, informs the Japanese that the "conference should be participated in by delegates with full powers from the people of new democratic China." At the same time it asserts that the "new Chinese people have every right to declare illegal unilateral actions of the United States" regarding Japan, which generally include major occupation policies here.

"The great victory of the Chinese people in their liberation war in China has entirely changed the face of Asia," says Akahata's version of the Peiping broadcast.

The Communist claim to represent the Chinese people in place of the Chiang Kai-shek Government is a somewhat new note in Communist propaganda, and as far as can be learned here it has been introduced for the first time with the broadcast now covered by Akahata. For a long time the Communists have been charging that the United States has been violating the Potsdam agreement and "menacing peace and security in the Far East" by its policies toward Japan.

Recently Chinese broadcasts accused Secretary of State Dean Acheson of "finding pretexts" to postpone the Japanese treaty because he insisted that this must be settled by the eleven Allied Pacific powers rather than the Big Four, under the Russian veto. As far as is known, however, this is the first time the Chinese Communists have officially told Japan that they consider themselves the Chinese member of the Big Four for treaty writing purposes.

Some sources here regard the Chinese broadcast and Akahata's prominent display as an interesting trial balloon designed to test how far either the Western Allies or Japanese will go in conceding the Chinese Communist claims. It is pointed out that there is no reference to the fact that the Allies still recognize Generalissimo Chiang's Government as the legal regime in China.

However, many Japanese also are inclined to disregard this, taking the typical Oriental attitude that since the Communists apparently triumphed on the Asiatic mainland they must ipso facto be the legal administration.

In any case the broadcasts were well timed since for the last few weeks the Japanese have been agog over the prospect of an early peace treaty. This attitude apparently has been stimulated by the partial approach to the subject at the Paris conference—few Japanese understanding that this left the subject approximately where it was before.

June 24, 1949

PEIPING STEPS UP PROPAGANDA WAR

Radio Daily Accuses U. S. of Rearming Japan and Seeking to Set Up Bases There

Special to THE NEW YORK TIMES.

HONG KONG, July 8—Peiping is intensifying its propaganda against allied policies in dealing with Japan. Radio broadcasts from the Communist Chinese capital lately have had daily blasts against what the Communists alleged to be the rearming of Japan, plans to have United States bases in Japan and the drafting of a Japanese peace treaty without the participation of the Peiping regime.

This latest protest over the Japanese situation was carried in the Reds' New China News Agency dispatch broadcast this morning from Peiping. It quotes the Chinese labor leader, Liu Ning-yi as denouncing "the remilitarization of Japan" at a meeting of the executive committee of the Soviet-dominated World Federation of Trade Unions in the Red China capital July 4. Peiping is Asian headquarters of the W. F. T. U. and the center there is believed to be the chief directing point for Communist revolutionary activity in Asia.

Mr. Liu called on the "working class" of Asian countries to develop "an immediate, profound, widespread movement among the vast masses against the conclusion of a unilateral peace treaty with Japan and the rearming of Japan by the United States.

He urged active support for the idea of a conference of Asian and Australasian peoples "against American aggression and Japanese remilitarization."

"If we take action," Mr. Liu went on, "we will be able to smash the plan of the United States to draft a unilateral peace treaty to rearm the aggressive Japanese Government."

The publicity given to Mr. Liu's speech follows a vehement editorial on the Japanese situation transmitted yesterday by the Peiping radio from the newspaper Kwangming, organ of the Democratic League, a political group that now follows the Communist lead. The paper reaffirmed Peiping's right to help determine the settlement for Japan and said the Chinese Communist party had led the people to victory over Japan, with the moral assistance of the Soviet Union.

The Soviet Army "annihilated the Japanese Kwangtung Army and forced Japan to surrender," said the paper.

The United States moves for peace with Japan, it charged, represented the Americans' desire "to repeat the slaughter in China and all Asia with Japan as their military base, with Japanese war criminals as their tools of aggression and with the Japanese people as their cannon fodder."

"The Sino-Soviet alliance and the unity of the people of Asia are capable of defeating any aggressive forces," it concluded.

July 9, 1951

RED CHINA ASSAILS JAPAN PEACE PACT

Special to THE NEW YORK TIMES.

TOKYO, May 6 — Communist China issued a bitter denunciation against the new sovereignty of Japan today in a broadcast special statement over the Peiping radio by Chou En-lai, the Minister for Foreign Affairs. He described the Tokyo leaders as "lackeys" of the United States Government and made the open charge that the Japanese Government is planning to invade the Chinese mainland in an attempt to revive Japan's imperialist rule over Asia.

Hurling insults and invectives at what he called the "illegal" fruition of the treaty negotiations between Japan and the United States and other signatory nations, the Communist Chinese Foreign Minister accused the Japanese of "menacingly preparing for a new aggressive war."

There were several targets of Mr. Chou's anger starting with Japanese sovereignty itself and going through the dissolution of the Far Eastern Commission in Washington, the end of the Allied Council for Japan in Tokyo and finally the completion of the treaty between Premier Shigeru Yoshida's Government and Generalissimo Chiang Kai-shek. All these, the Foreign Minister said, were "serious, flagrant acts of provocation" that aroused "insurmountable indignation" among the people of China and for this reason the Chinese Communist Government had authorized him to issue a formal statement.

Accuses U. S. of Violating Pacts

Mr. Chou said the United States had played a "truculent and shameful" part in all these developments and he added that the United States Government had taken an "extreme step" in helping to carry out a separate peace treaty with Japan in what he said was a defiance of several agreements including specifically those made at Cairo, Yalta and at Potsdam.

Peiping's top foreign affairs official told radio listeners that "obviously" the United States did not hesitate to infringe the rights of other states because it was bent on intensified preparations itself for a "new aggressive war directed against the people of China and the Soviet Union and menacing all Asia."

Premier Yoshida came under particularly vehement attacks for concluding a treaty with the Chinese Nationalists on Formosa which, he said, proved that the Yoshida Government was simply carrying out the orders of its "United States masters." Mr. Chou said that the treaty with the Chiang Government had the aim of creating a military menace to the People's Republic of China just as the separate peace treaty for Japan was hostile to both the Soviet Union and China.

Treaty With Chiang Assailed

What was particularly "audacious and shameless," according to Mr. Chou, was that the treaty with Formosa was said to apply not only to all territory now under the Chiang regime, but to territory that might come under its control in the future. It was this future provision apparently that struck deepest in the Chinese Communist command at Peiping.

The Foreign Minister went on to say that immediately after the conclusion of the Japanese Peace Treaty, the Yoshida Government had released eighty-eight of the "most vicious Japanese war criminals," whose hands, he said, were stained with the blood of the Chinese people.

Mr. Chou concluded by saying the Chinese Communist Government felt it was necessary now to repeat earlier demands that all "occupation troops" be withdrawn from Japan, by which he meant the American troops who are now in Japan by agreement with the Japanese Government and no longer are occupation forces.

May 7, 1952

CHINA-MONGOLIA PACT LINKS RED CULTURES

Special to THE NEW YORK TIMES.

HONG KONG, Oct. 5—Communist China has concluded a ten-year economic and cultural agreement with Outer Mongolia, the Peiping radio announced today.

The agreement was signed yesterday by Chinese Communist Premier Chou En-lai and Outer Mongolian Premier Yumzhagiyn Tsedenbal, who is now visiting Peiping. Both were in Moscow at the same time recently while a Chinese Communist mission headed by Mr. Chou was negotiating with the Russians.

The Peiping radio said the Chinese-Mongolian pact contained two basic articles:

¶The contracting parties agreed to "establish, develop and consolidate cooperation in the economic, cultural and educational fields.

¶Concrete agreements are to be signed separately by the two countries' respective Departments of Economics, Trade, Culture and Education.

Premier Tsedenbal, 36-year-old financial expert who once headed the State Economic Planning Commission in Outer Mongolia, arrived in Peiping from Ulan Bator Sept. 28. He was accompanied by Foreign Minister N. Lhamsurun and Minister of Education B. Shirendyb.

October 6, 1952

OUTER MONGOLIA'S STATUS

Outer Mongolia—the country whose bid for admission to the United Nations has threatened to balk the "package deal" to enlarge the U. N. membership—is a 600,000-square-mile area in central Asia, sparsely populated by 900,000 people, of whom only 15 per cent live in cities. It is bounded on the north by Soviet Siberia and on the south by China.

The country occupies the northern part of the vast central Asiatic plateau, an area of gravel and sandy deserts criss-crossed by mountain chains and grassy steppes. Through the centuries its nomadic population has herded cattle, goats, sheep, camels and horses. The soil and climate are both poor for farming but some grain—wheat, oats, millet, rye and barley—and vegetables are grown.

Border Disputes

At the end of the seventeenth century Outer Mongolia came under nominal Chinese control. As long ago as the eighteenth century its borders were in dispute between Russia and the Chinese Empire; later Japan joined in the attempt to control or take over the weakly governed country.

In 1920 a Japanese-White Russian expedition seized the capital, now called Ulan Bator, and set up a puppet government. The next year a Soviet-inspired revolution overthrew the regime and in 1924 the Mongolian People's Republic was proclaimed.

Soviet-Style Government

The republic's constitution, adopted in 1940 and much-amended since, vests power in a "Great People's Khural" (parliament). Elections to parliament are conducted Soviet-style, with a single list of candidates. In the 1951 elections the list got 99.1 per cent of the votes cast. The executive power is vested in a seven-member Presidium, which actually runs the country.

In 1946 a treaty of friendship and mutual aid was signed between the Republic and the Soviet Union. Even before that the Soviet Union had taken a close interest in Mongolia, and many of its efforts have tended to tie the country tightly to Russia. Although communications are still chiefly by caravan route, railroads have been constructed. Russia and Communist China have cooperated recently to push through a railroad from Ulan Bator to connect with the Trans-Siberian Railway, thus providing an important new lifeline for China in the event of a coastal blockade.

Russians have helped develop industry and have improved communications in Mongolia. Moreover, there are close cultural and educational ties. The Mongolian alphabet was dropped in 1946 for one based on Russian, and many Russians have been sent to teach in the schools and colleges.

The treaty of 1950 between Communist China and the Soviet Union recognized the "independence" of the Republic. But Communist China has its own treaty of friendship and economic aid with Mongolia, and has made efforts to strengthen its influence there. In view of the fact that Mongolia was for so many centuries Chinese, there is the possibility of some tension between the two great Communist powers over Outer Mongolia in the future.

November 20, 1955

CHINESE REDS SIGN 30-YEAR ALLIANCE WITH SOVIET UNION

By HARRISON E. SALISBURY
Special to THE NEW YORK TIMES.

MOSCOW, Wednesday, Feb. 15—Signature of a thirty-year Soviet-Chinese Communist alliance of friendship and mutual assistance, with a provision of $300,000,000 in credits by the Soviet Union to Communist China and an agreement for the return of the Changchun railroad, Port Arthur and Dairen to China was announced early today in Moscow.

The announcement culminated a two-month visit of Mao Tze-tung in Moscow, during the latter stages of which he was joined by Chou En-lai. The negotiators on the Soviet side were Premier Stalin and Andrei Y. Vishinsky, Soviet Foreign Minister.

The agreement included a joint Soviet-Chinese expression that the peace treaty with Japan be concluded "in the shortest possible time." Both parties expressed the firmest adherence to the cause of "universal peace and the security of peoples."

The new alliance replaced that of 1945 (between the Soviet Union and Nationalist China) and includes broader security provisions. Under the new agreement both parties pledge mutual aid in the event of aggression, not only by Japan but also in the event of aggression by "any other state directly or indirectly associated" with Japan. Soviet-Chinese consultation is provided in all cases of important international questions affecting their interests.

The terms of the alliance state as its objective "to frustrate jointly any revival of Japanese militarism and repetition of aggression" by Japan.

The treaty affirms support by both parties of United Nations principles with which the alliance is specifically stated to be in accord.

The agreement on the Changchun railroad provides for the return of the line to China without payment upon signature of a Japanese peace treaty. At the same time the Soviet Union agreed to withdraw its troops from Port Arthur and turn over its facilities there to the Chinese with provision for mutual use in the event of war. Present Soviet facilities in Dairen would be similarly returned to the Chinese under arrangements to be negotiated later.

[The agreement provided that return of the railroad and the facilities in the two Manchurian cities would be effected no later than the end of 1952, regardless of whether a Japanese treaty had been signed.]

In addition to the alliance, the agreement on the Changchun railroad, Port Arthur and Dairen and the economic pact, the following notes were exchanged:

1. Suspending the 1945 treaty.
2. Confirming the complete independence of the Mongolian People's Republic.
3. Providing for transfer to China without compensation of property acquired by Soviet economic organizations from Japanese owners in Manchuria.
4. Transferring to China former military buildings in Peiping.

February 15, 1950

'THE FOSTER PARENT'

Green in The Providence Journal

August 1, 1954

MOSCOW SAYS STALIN FORESAW CHINA SHIFT

Special to THE NEW YORK TIMES.

MOSCOW, March 30—The foreign affairs journal New Times today published a significant analysis characterizing the victory of Mao Tze-tung in China as essentially an "agrarian revolution that has the basis and content of burgeois democratic revolution."

Basing its study squarely on the theories of the Chinese situation evolved by Premier Stalin in 1926 and 1927, the New Times differentiated between the present revolution of China and the Soviet revolution of 1917. It suggested that the present Chinese revolution more properly was to be compared with the Russian situation of 1905.

The New Times noted that Premier Stalin in 1926 had declared that the Chinese revolution would be in the nature of a bourgeois democratic revolution and quoted him as saying:

"I think that the future revolutionary power in China will, on the whole, remind one by its character of such a power as was spoken of here in 1905; that is, something like the democratic dictatorship of the proletariat and the peasantry with the difference, however, that it will be a predominantly anti-imperialist power. This will be a power transitional to non-capitalist or, more precisely, the Socialist development of China."

The New Times declared that Chinese events had fully justified the "brilliant" analysis by Premier Stalin nearly twenty-five years ago. It said that events in China had created the "possibility of limited participation in the revolution of national bourgeoisie" and asserted that Mr. Mao had won the victory through "creatively applying the concepts of Marxist-Leninist theory to Chinese conditions" and by following "unwaveringly" Premier Stalin's theory of the Chinese revolution.

March 31, 1950

SOVIET PROMISES PEIPING MORE AID

LONDON, Sept. 15—The Peiping radio said tonight that Communist China's leader Mao Tse-tung had announced his country and Moscow had negotiated "an unprecedented" new program of economic aid to the Chinese.

The radio quoted the Chinese Communist leader as having said in a message to Soviet Premier Georgi M. Malenkov:

"The two states have settled in one single negotiation the question of the construction of ninety-one enterprises and the question of long-term aid. This is unprecedented in history." The broadcast gave no details.

Mr. Mao's message said the "great Soviet Government has agreed to extend systematic economic and technical aid in the construction and renovation of ninety-one new enterprises in China and the fifty enterprises now being built or renovated."

The message added that the report on the new aid program was made today to the Administrative Council of the Central People's Government by Li Fun-chun, who was identified as member of a Chinese delegation to the Soviet Union.

The last indication that Chinese-Soviet talks were under way was in June, when it was announced in Moscow that a new Chinese delegation had arrived there.

In 1952, the Soviet Union agreed to lend China a sum equal to $300,000,000 as part of a general trade agreement between the two countries.

The Chinese leader said today that "the Soviet Government, on the basis of its rich experience in the great Socialist construction in more than thirty years, has put forward various proposals in principle and concretely concerning the task of China's five-year plan."

"These proposals will help us to avoid, as much as possible, committing errors and to reduce the twists and turns in the course of China's economic construction," it continued.

"On behalf of the Chinese Government and the Chinese people, I wish to express my heartfelt gratitude to the Soviet Government and people for this great, over-all, long-term and disinterested aid."

Mr. Mao said that because of the aid, the Chinese "will be able to build up step by step their own mighty heavy industry."

"This plays an extremely significant role in the industrialization of China, in helping her in her transition by stages to socialism and in strengthening the camp of peace and democracy headed by the Soviet Union," he added.

September 16, 1953

CHINESE REDS PROD SOVIET ON AID LAG

London Reports Request for Larger Shipments of Heavy Industrial Equipment

By DREW MIDDLETON

Special to THE NEW YORK TIMES.

LONDON, Jan. 8—The Chinese Communist Government is believed to have pressed the Soviet Union for larger shipments of heavy industrial equipment.

The occasion was the visit to Peiping of I. F. Tevosyan, First Deputy Chairman of the Council of Ministers and Minster of the Metallurgical Industry in the Soviet Government.

Mr. Tevosyan went to China to attend the opening of two steel mills and a blast furnace at Anshan, one of the new Chinese industrial areas. But it is believed here that he stayed to listen to his hosts' pleas for greater material economic aid from the Soviet Union.

Similar pleas will be made, it is predicted, by the Chinese trade delegation that has arrived in Moscow to discuss the trade agreement for 1954.

Those who watch economic and political developments in China for the British Government believe that there are increased indications of Chinese dissatisfaction with the type of economic aid now being sent to that country from the Soviet Union.

The chief complaint seems to be that China is not receiving the amount of machine tools, construction equipment and heavy industrial material that her planners require for their grandiose plans for industrialization.

The Soviet position appears to be that further large shipments of such equipment are unwise until China has trained the technicians to handle it. It is on the education and training of the Chinese industrial workers that the Russians seem to be concentrating.

There are no official figures here on the extent of the present interchange of personnel between the Soviet Union and China. One informed estimate of the number of Soviet industrial and agricultural experts working in China is half a million.

At any rate it is reported that Russians are running the Chinese steel industry, the expansion of the industrial area around Mukden and other enterprises and at the same time are training Chinese.

Meanwhile, there is a steady movement of Chinese workers to the Soviet Union for training in industrial plants and mines, on the railroads and in the technological colleges. It is believed that Chinese students now form the largest group of foreign nationals in Russian universities.

Soviet propaganda outlets, in both Moscow and in the Soviet Embassy at Peiping, are doing their best to make it appear that the Russian assistance program as it now stands is sufficient.

For example, the Moscow radio during the past week continued to emphasize in broadcasts to China the importance of Russian material aid. Praising the "enormous successes" of the industrial areas of northeast China, a commentator asserted that, in a large measure, these successes resulted from Soviet assistance, which "facilitates Chinese prosperity and power."

Dispersion or Concentration

Still, it is reported here, the Chinese do not think they are getting enough aid to enable them to carry out their plans for building new industrial areas.

It is believed that the planners of the Peiping Government want to disperse some of the nation's heavy industry, whereas the Russians prefer to keep it concentrated in northeast China.

But it is explained by experts of both countries that the sort of heavy industrial equipment that China seeks from the Soviet Union is exactly the type of material that Russia needs herself.

There is no prospect, it is emphasized, that the differences over the type of assistance given China by the Soviet Union has reached the stage where a serious break between the two Communist states can be expected.

But it was pointed out that, in the past, Chinese suspicions that China was being purposely relegated to the role of an industrial vassal of the great economic powers of the West was a source of indignation and enmity in China.

January 9, 1954

U. S. FOREIGN POLICY FOCUSES ON FAR EAST

The New York Times   Jan. 6, 1950

On the heels of President Truman's statement affirming a hands-off policy toward Formosa (3), main stronghold of the Chinese Nationalist Government, it became known that the Administration was seeking to set up a barrier against communism through aid programs, chiefly economic, for Japan (1), Korea (2), Indo-China (4), the Philippines (5) and Indonesia (6).

January 6, 1950

Division of Korea Started in 1945 As Part of War Plan to Beat Japan

By RICHARD J. H. JOHNSTON

Korea was divided into United States and Soviet zones of influence at the Thirty-eighth Parallel, north latitude, as a result of Allied military plans for the final assault on Japan.

While the precise details of this division, believed to have been agreed upon at Yalta in February, 1945, were never made public, authoritative military sources have indicated that the invasion of the Japanese home islands would have called for virtually all available Allied forces in the North Pacific, leaving lesser forces available for the conquest and occupation of Korea, where 178,000 Japanese troops were stationed.

These sources have said that it was planned for Soviet troops to push into the Korean peninsula from Manchuria and Siberia on the north while United States forces struck from the south. In this Allied pincers the untested Japanese Imperial Army of Lieut. Gen. Yashio Kozuki would have been smashed.

The sudden capitulation of Japan

on Aug. 15, 1945, made this plan unnecessary. Nevertheless, 72,000 United States troops, comprising the Twenty-fourth Corps, under the command of Lieut. Gen. John R. Hodge, landed in South Korea on Sept. 8, 1945, while an estimated 100,000 Siberian and Manchurian troops of the Soviet Army under the command of Col. Gen. I. M. Chistiakov occupied Korea north of the Thirty-eighth Parallel.

General Hodge then received instructions to disarm and evacuate Japanese forces in Korea in cooperation with the Russians. This action was to be followed immediately by combined United States-Soviet conferences on the scene, leading to the establishment of an all-Korean Government.

Soviet Spurned U. S. Efforts

Soviet military officials spurned all efforts of the United States commander to carry out these instructions. Japanese troops in the United States occupation zone were disarmed and removed to Japan by the end of November, 1945. These comprised more than three-quarters of General Kozuki's army. The fate of Japanese troops captured in the Soviet zone was never made clear.

Attempts to break the impasse were made at the Conference of Foreign Ministers in Moscow in December, 1945. There a decision on Korea was agreed to by the Soviet Union, the United States, Great Britain and France. The decision called for the establishment of a joint United States-Soviet military commission, appointed by the respective commanders in Korea. The commission met in Seoul early in 1946.

Its negotiations failed when Soviet representatives demanded all Koreans unsympathetic to communism or to the Soviet Union be barred from consultation or participation in the establishment of a government.

After lengthy exchange of notes between the two countries, the commission met again in Seoul early in 1947. It failed to reach agreement also over the question when the Russians revealed their original position unchanged. In November, 1947, over vigorous Soviet objections, the United States placed the Korea question before the United Nations.

During this period South Korea was governed by the United States Army under a military government regime. North Korea was at the same time being fashioned into a Communist-controlled satellite.

Temporary Commission Sent

The General Assembly, in 1947,

voted, over Soviet and Soviet satellite opposition, to take up the Korea question. A temporary commission was sent to Seoul in January, 1948. It reported to the United Nations Interim Committee the refusal of North Korean authorities to countenance its efforts at unification. The commission was instructed to proceed with plans to sponsor general elections, for the establishment of a Korean Government "in those areas open" to it.

On May 10, 1948, South Korea, where two-thirds of the country's 30,000,000 people live, went to the polls under United Nations auspices and elected 200 representatives to a National Assembly. Left open were 100 seats for representatives of North Korea when their election under U. N. observation could be arranged.

The Republic of Korea, based on the elections in South Korea, was inaugurated on Aug. 15, 1948. Simultaneously, the military government, which had more than a year before moved into an advisory capacity to the Koreans, ceased operations.

Almost simultaneously North Korea proclaimed itself the People's Democratic Republic of Korea, with a "temporary" capital in Pyongyang, North Korea, and claimed jurisdiction over the entire 85,000-square-mile peninsula. The Soviet Union and its satellites promptly granted recognition to this regime.

Both regimes then sought United Nations membership. The South Korean Government's application was rejected as the result of a Soviet veto in April, 1949. The Communist North Korean Government failed, despite Russia's efforts, to reach the Security Council for vote.

Moscow announced the completion of its troop withdrawal from Korea in December, 1948. Under terms of the United Nations resolution on Korea, withdrawal of troops from Korea was to have been observed and verified by United Nations representatives on the scene. Since the Russians refused the United Nations access to their zone, confirmation of the Soviet withdrawal announcement was not possible.

Withdrawal of United States troops was completed under the observation of the United Nations Korea Commission in June, 1949. The withdrawal was confirmed by the United Nations group and a report was forwarded to Lake Success by the commission. Remaining in Korea was the United States Military Advisory Group under agreement between the Korean and United States Governments.

June 26, 1950

HAINAN INVADERS AT ISLAND CAPITAL; ENTRY IS REPORTED

Top Nationalists Said to Have Fled Hoihow as 'Victory' Claim Proves to Be Unfounded

SOUTH REMAINS TO BE WON

But Success of Reds in North Is Held Precursor to New Blow at Chiang Prestige

By WALTER SULLIVAN
Special to THE NEW YORK TIMES.

HONG KONG, Sunday, April 23 —The Nationalist situation on Hainan deteriorated rapidly last night. Private reports from the island said that the top military and political leaders had fled Hoihow, the capital, by ship and plane during the afternoon.

By 6 P. M., with the shops boarded up, the inhabitants were said to be awaiting the entry of Chinese Communist troops, believed to be on the outskirts of Hoihow.

[A United Press report said a telephoned message to Hong Kong from Hainan Sunday morning told of Communist troops entering Hoihow and beginning to restore order. The Associated Press reported from Formosa that the Nationalists at Taipei had during the night lost contact with Hoihow.]

The echoes of a noisy "victory" celebration were still ringing in the ears of the residents, as was the case when Shanghai fell. It had been staged the previous day to celebrate the "annihilation" of the Communist army, which now may have cut the island in two.

Members of Gen. Lin Piao's Communist Fourth Field Army who had landed on the island early on Monday appear to have broken Nationalist resistance on the north coast. The seaborne Communist troops have been reinforced by units of the "Hainan column of the People's Liberation Army"—the large quasi-guerrilla force that controlled the interior of the island.

Communists Silent on Gains

According to the best available

ISLAND DRIVE GAINS

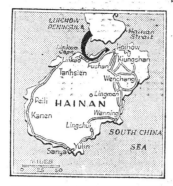

The New York Times   April 23, 1950

The Communist forces that had landed on Hainan in the area of Linkao were reported to have advanced along the coast to the outskirts of Hoihow (arrow on upper map).

figures, however, the total Communist forces on Hainan are fewer than half those of the Kuomintang troops.

Hampering a balanced estimate of the situation is the lack of reports from the Communist side. The Communists have not given their version of any of the military operations since the landing on Monday. Nor have they given any clue to the number of men they have ashore.

The prize is the largest habitable area remaining under Generalissimo Chiang Kai-shek. Formosa is slightly larger but it is crowded with lofty mountains.

Some persons here believe that the Generalissimo had not wanted to defend Hainan at the expense of weakening his final refuge on Formosa. Hence the best troops and the best weapons were kept on the latter island.

However, the amphibious conquest of Hainan, despite virtually unopposed sea and air attacks, is bound to have a serious effect on the morale of Formosa and the international position of the Nationalist Government.

The Communist conquest of Hainan is not yet complete. There are still probably one or two Kuomintang armies along the south coast between the guerrilla-held interior and the sea. However, the apparent conquest of the north coast of the island and the reported evacu-

ation of Hoihow airfield indicate that the dam has broken.

Attempts of the troops fleeing from the north coast to join the armies on the south side are imperiled by the guerrillas whose role now appears to be to prevent just such a movement.

Maj. Gen. Claire L. Chennault, retired, wartime commander of the United States Fourteenth Air Force, and now head of the Civil Air Transport airline, said he had lost contact with his airfield crew at Hoihow in midafternoon yesterday. Later it was learned that the airfield had been abandoned, with some of the planes flying to Sanya airfield on the south coast of the island. Some press reports said that ships in the harbor, including one British merchantman, had been seized to carry fleeing Nationalists.

The Nationalists' official Central News Agency came through early this morning with an explanation of why, after the great "victory" yesterday morning, the conquered troops suddenly appeared at the gates of the capital. It said that the announced surrender of 4,000 Communists had referred to their hoisting of white flags. Subsequently the Communists had pulled the flags down and attacked and drove twenty miles to the city, the Central News said.

Numerous dispatches and other reports from Hoihow described the near panic among the Kuomintang officials there. Hoihow had been the fugitive seat of the Kwangtung Provincial Government, which escaped from Canton when the Communists neared that city. The pro-Communist newspaper Wen Wei Pao yesterday morning reported that regulations had just been issued for the take over of the Hainan Government organs and for the garrisoning of the island.

The regulations were signed by the Hainan committee of the Communist party, the Hainan Provisional People's Government, headquarters of the army's Hainan column and the political department of that headquarters.

Other Canton press reports have told of the training of special cadres and teams among the Hainan natives on the mainland to take over the rule of the island.

Meanwhile the Nationalist report of having captured two "Russian advisers" seemed to have been lost in the shuffle. As it had been associated with the "victory" claim yesterday, there was increased skepticism here pending the sighting of the two prisoners by independent observers.

Still unknown is the price that the Chinese Communists had to pay for their gains on Hainan. Some United States visitors on Hainan had reported that the morale of the troops had been surprisingly high a few weeks ago. However, when they crowded ashore in flight from the mainland last November many of these soldiers represented a ragged and demoralized mob.

April 23, 1950

WAR IS DECLARED BY NORTH KOREANS; FIGHTING ON BORDER

By The United Press.

SEOUL, Korea, Sunday, June 25 — The Russian-sponsored North Korean Communists invaded the American-supported Republic of South Korea today and their radio followed it up by broadcasting a declaration of war.

The attacks started at dawn. The Northern Pyongyang radio broadcast a declaration of war at 11 A. M. (9 P. M. Eastern Daylight Time Saturday).

North Korean forces attacked generally along the border, but chiefly in the eastern and western areas, in heavy rain after mortar and artillery bombardments which started at 4 A. M. (2 P. M., Eastern Daylight Time Saturday). They were reported two and a half miles inside South Korea at some points.

[The State Department in Washington, receiving reports of the Korean fighting, was preparing to hold the Soviet Union responsible for the outbreak. The Associated Press quoted Korean Ambassador John Myun Chang as saying the Northern Korean attack was an aggressive action that could not have been carried out "without Soviet direction." Koreans indicated an appeal to the United Nations.]

Declaration Is Broadcast

Shortly after noon the Communists' radio at Pyongyang, the northern capital, said that war had been declared effective at 11 A. M.

A report received at 9:30 A. M. indicated that the North Koreans had captured the town of Kaesong, forty miles northwest of Seoul. Kaesong is headquarters of the First Division of the South Korean Army. It lies almost on the frontier.

It was believed here that eight American Methodist missionaries were in Kaesong—Lyman C. Brannon and his wife, Marian E. Bunds, Nellie Dyer, Mary H. Rosser, Bertha A. Smith, Lawrence A. Zellers and Christopher Jensen. Mrs. Zellers is in Seoul.

United States Ambassador John J. Muccio broadcast a statement to the 2,000 Americans in Korea—including a military mission—over the English-language radio station WVTP on the Communist attack. The North Korean forces were reported three to four kilometers (1¾ to 2½ miles) inside the frontier in the Ongjin Peninsula on the West Coast.

Advices said they were using tanks in the area of Chunchon, fifty miles northeast of Seoul.

Below Kangnung, on the East Coast, the invaders were reported to have landed from twenty small craft and to have cut the coastal highway.

Ambassador Muccio advised Americans to move about as little as possible. He promised to broadcast all new developments. He said:

"As yet it cannot be determined whether the northern Communists intend to precipitate all-out warfare."

Presumably the attacks mean a test of strength between the Russian-sponsored and United States-sponsored sections of this country, divided on the line of the Thirty-eighth parallel.

The North Korean attack came but a few days after John Foster Dulles, special State Department adviser, visited President Syngman Rhee of the Southern republic. Mr. Dulles is now in Tokyo with General MacArthur. Defense Secretary Louis Johnson and Gen. Omar N

Bradley, chairman of the United States Joint Chiefs of Staff Committee, returned to Washington yesterday from Tokyo, where they discussed the Korean and other Far Eastern situations.

There have been frequent guerrilla-scale clashes between forces of Soviet-sponsored North Korea and the South Korean forces, but none apparently have been as large as those reported today.

Threats have been made of an invasion of Southern Korea. One officer said here, on the basis of early reports: "This looks like the real thing." But there had been no intelligence reports of troop movements or concentration of supplies —such as would be needed for a real campaign—on the North Korean side. Also, the rainy season is just starting, and the season is the worst of the year for troop operations.

Military authorities emphasized that their reports were fragmentary and that the picture of the situation was vague.

Other sources said that South Korea's Army included about 93,-000 men with an additional 50,000 police and 6,000 or 7,000 coast guardsmen. The United States is uncertain about the exact size of the Soviet-trained North Korean forces but they are believed to be slightly larger.

The Soviet Union, with considerable fanfare, announced that all of its occupation forces had left left North Korea by the end of 1948. This was considerably earlier than the main body of United States troops left. United States officials, however, have said that Washington would hold the Soviet Union responsible for the actions of the North Korean Government under the Soviet puppet Kim Il Sung, a reasonably young man who came to ower using the name of a venerated Korean elder statesman.

Kaesong, reported captured, is the main town close to the parallel separating North and South Korea. Chun Chon, on the railroad in the northeastern section of the United States zone, is smaller but has valuable silk processing and silk textile manufacturing facilities that the United States has helped to develop as part of its campaign to revive South Korea's economy.

These towns, along with the Ongjin Peninsula, have been raided before—sometimes being the scenes of heavy fighting that killed fifty or more persons. Serious guerrilla raids began last year and no United States official has attempted to minimize the danger.

Virtually Stopped, U. S. Aides Say

SEOUL, Sunday, June 25 (Æ)— Communist troops from North Korea invaded South Korea at dawn today on a wide front, but United States military advisers said the invasion was virtually stopped by this afternoon.

Heavy artillery fire was continuing as the North Koreans attacked at least eleven points. Tanks supported the attacks on some fronts.

The advisers said the Northerners pushed three miles south of the border at one point before they ran into the first determined resistance from South Korean forces.

Strange planes droned over this uneasy capital of the Republic sponsored by the United States. No bombs were dropped.

There were no reports of aerial attacks anywhere. It was believed likely the Northerners would wait for skies to clear before sending planes over. They are known to have Russian-made fighters.

The attacks were spaced along the Thirty-eighth Parallel which divides this country at the forefront of the "cold war" between East and West.

Seaborne forces struck at two points along the east coast. The southernmost force hit forty miles south of the border.

June 25, 1950

U. N. CALLS FOR CEASE FIRE IN KOREA; DEMANDS NORTH WITHDRAW TROOPS

By A. M. ROSENTHAL
Special to THE NEW YORK TIMES.

LAKE SUCCESS, June 25—The United Nations Security Council found North Korea guilty today of breaking the peace, demanded that the Communist Government pull back its troops at once and called for an immediate cease-fire throughout Korea.

Ten members of the Council— the Soviet Union stayed away— rushed to Lake Success for an emergency meeting, requested by the United States, and acted swiftly on one of the bluntest resolutions e er presented in the United Nations.

Nine of those countries voted for the resolution handed in by the United States. There were no countries voting against it; Yugoslavia raised a hand in abstention.

The resolution carried with it the clear implication that the United Nations would move to take stronger measures if North Korea flouted the Council. United

States spokesmen said the motion was put forward under Chapter 7 of the United Nations Charter, the "last resort" charter, which permits the Security Council to invoke sanctions, blockade and even military action.

Question of Obedience

The key question debated in the delegates lounge after the meeting was: Would North Korea obey. Many delegates believed that the Northern Koreans would follow the Soviet line and announce that any action taken by the Security Council with the participation of the Nationalist Chinese was entirely illegal.

But even as the delegates were filing out of the Council chamber, the United Nations was taking steps to make sure the words of the resolution got through to authorities of North Korea and the Republic of Korea to the south.

Copies of the resolution were dispatched by commercial cable

and radio to North and South Korean capitals. And as backstop, the Voice of America, the British Broadcasting Corporation and All-India Radio were asked to broadcast the resolution, beamed to Korea.

The next phase for the United Nations is waiting—two days of waiting. The Security Council will meet again at 3 P. M. Tuesday; and it hopes to have a new report and possibly recommendations from its seven-member, on-the-spot Commission on Korea.

It was a report from that Commission that provided the basis for the action of the Council in denouncing the Northern Government and asking for withdrawal and cease-fire.

Trygve Lie Receives Dispatch

At 10:30 this morning, Secretary General Trygve Lie received a brief dispatch from the Commission telling of attacks from the North and warning that full-scale

war was shaping up. The Commission stated that there had been no confirmation of a published report that North Korea had formally declared war.

[President Truman said in Kansas City before his return to Washington on Sunday that he knew of no declaration of war. Press reports received over Saturday night from Seoul had said the North Korean radio broadcast such a declaration.]

By the time Mr. Lie received the dispatch, delegates were speeding back from week-ends in the country and were on their way to Lake Success for the extraordinary meeting of the Council. All through the night and the early morning, telephone calls had gone out to the delegates, summoning them.

The first step toward the meeting was taken by Ernest A. Gross, acting chief of the United States delegation. At 3 A. M., after hours of consultation with top-level State Department figures in

AT EMERGENCY MEETING TO DISCUSS KOREAN CRISIS

Dr. John M. Chang, Korean Ambassador to the United States, with Secretary General Trygve Lie of the U. N. at Lake Success yesterday.

The New York Times (by Patrick Burns)

Washington, Mr. Gross telephoned Mr. Lie, told him the United States judged North Korea to be an aggressor, and asked for the Security Council to be convened today.

From that point, the word went to Sir Benegal N. Rau of India, this month's chairman of the Council, who agreed to call the meeting. Secretariat workers were roused and got busy, phoning all delegations on the Security Council. The Soviet delegation got a call, of course.

The normal hush of Lake Success—most Sundays see just a few maintenance workers and skeleton-staff clerks on the job—was broken about 8 A. M. Five hours later the first diplomats showed up at the delegates' lounge.

When the Council came to order at 2:32 P. M., Sir Benegal gave the floor first to Mr. Lie. The Secretary General made a bluntly worded statement:

"The report received by me from States' case then. He told of the from other sources in Korea, make it plain that military actions have been undertaken by Northern Korean forces.

"The present situation is a serious one and is a threat to international peace. I consider it the clear duty of the Security Council to take the steps necessary to reestablish peace in that area."

Mr. Gross presented the United

States case then. He told of the news of the fighting in Korea, said the assault was launched by the North as an "unprovoked attack." It was a breach of the peace and and act of aggression, he said.

"This is clearly a threat to international peace and security," he added.

The United States delegate reviewed a few milestones in the United Nations activity in Korea —the establishment of the Commission, the holding of elections in South Korea, the General Assembly resolution declaring the Republic of Korea to be the lawful Government of the country.

Korean Envoy to U. S. Speaks

Mr. Gross presented his resolution. Sir Benegal invited Dr. John Myun Chang, Korean Ambassador to Washington, to speak. The Ambassador said that the invasion was an "all-out effort."

"Its objective is to destroy my Government and to bring my country under the domination of the Communist-supported puppet regime of the North," Dr. Chang went on. "However, the armed forces of our country are meeting the attack with fortitude and bravery.

"Our people are determined to resist the invaders and lay down their lives in order that a free and independent democratic Korea might survive."

Delegates from various member nations spoke up in favor of the United States resolution. One by one, the representatives of Britain, France, China, Ecuador, Cuba and Egypt echoed the same theme: The fighting in Korea was the fault of the Northern regime, it was an act of aggression, a breach of the peace and a threat to the rest of the world.

There was an hour-long time-out for delegates to assemble in an office provided by Mr. Lie and work out drafting changes in the resolution.

The Security Council convened again at 5:30 P. M. and Norway voiced support of the resolution as amended.

Attention turned at that point to Djuro Nincitch, the alternate delegate from Yugoslavia, who had been having a difficult day. He was in and out of the Council room during the afternoon, busy on the telephone with his chief, Dr. Ales Bebler, who was away in the country.

Mr. Nincitch told the Council that aggression from any side was untenable. But in Korea, he went on, there seemed to be lack of precise information that could enable the Council to pin responsibility.

The thing for the Council to do, said the delegate for Marshal Tito's Government, was to call for a cease fire, not blame anybody, not ask for withdrawal of the Northern troops and set out on an investigation that would bring in the facts needed for a final decision.

Mr. Nincitch presented a resolution to that effect and saw it defeated. Only Yugoslavia voted for her proposal. Norway, India and Egypt abstained. The United States, Britain, France, China, Ecuador and Cuba voted no.

Revision of Resolution

The delegates' amendment work on the United States resolution resulted in several changes. The United States had asked for a cease fire directed solely at North Korea. The amended version called for a general cease fire, but retained the accusation clause and the provision that North Korea retire its forces to the Thirty-eighth Parallel, the dividing line between North and South.

In the original version, the United States spoke of an armed invasion of the Republic. The amended resolution spoke of an armed attack on the Republic by forces from the North. In all cases, the United States accepted the amendments.

In addition to the immediate demands for cessation and withdrawal, the resolution called on all members of the United Nations to avoid giving assistance to North Korea. As one delegate said: "We are not talking there about assistance from Lower Slabodia."

As for the United Nations Commission on Korea, now in Seoul, the resolution directed it to observe the withdrawal of the North Korean forces—"if it can," was the mental reservation of most persons here—and to keep the Security Council informed.

Among after-the-meeting statements, Dr. Chang, the Korean Ambassador, said the resolution was a symbol of the feeling of the people of the world, but that he would have hoped for something stronger, more direct.

Mr. Gross said Warren R. Austin, chief United States delegate, was flying here from Vermont and would be in charge of the "next development department." Mr. Gross said any further steps that would be recommended by the United States in case of non-compliance would be decided on "at the highest level."

The resolution itself, Mr. Gross commmented, was a clear indication that the Security Council understood the gravity of the situation. A reassuring factor, he called that, and added:

"In the past it has not always been true that the United Nations has acted as quickly and as vigorously."

June 26, 1950

MOLOTOV-MAO TALKS REPORTED IN PEIPING

Special to THE NEW YORK TIMES.

HONG KONG, Aug. 16—The Hong Kong Wah Kiu Yat Po, a commercial newspaper with Chinese Nationalist leanings, reported today in an unconfirmed dispatch from Formosa that Soviet Vice Premier V. M. Molotov left Peiping Aug. 10 after reaching an understanding with Mao Tze-tung, Communist Premier, on Korea and Southeast Asia.

The paper gave no source, but the alleged information undoubtedly emanated from the Nationalists.

The paper reported that the Korean understanding provided that should United Nations forces in Korea launch a full-scale counter-offensive carrying them beyond the Thirty-Eighth Parallel the Chinese Communists would send 150,000 troops into Korea from Manchuria, with the Soviet Union supplying military equipment.

The paper reported that the Southeast Asian agreement provided that to avoid a third world war the Chinese Communists would not send armies into Southeast Asia, but would resort to infiltration tactics, with Chinese Communist Gen. Chen Keng in charge.

Wah Kiu Yat Po said that no decisions were reached regarding Formosa and Hong Kong, and added that Mr. Molotov was scheduled to return to Peiping after reporting to Prime Minister Stalin. Rumors like this are frequent in Hong Kong.

August 17, 1950

WE HOLD THE BEACHHEAD, BUT NOT THE INITIATIVE

By HANSON W. BALDWIN

Two armies, both growing in size and power, were still locked in an indecisive struggle last week as the Korean war ended its eleventh week.

The waxing and waning hopes of the U. N. defenders—who probably now number, including South Koreans, almost 150,000 men—changed by the hour during the week, as a definite defensive success was recorded, only to be succeeded by another enemy offensive threat. Surprise, the "necessary element of all military operations," altered the picture for the defense several times during the fighting, but nothing is ever certain in battle and there was always the possibility that the enemy might, in turn, be surprised.

Somber Pattern

But the ebb and flow of the Korean war—despite its daily inconsistencies — still presents the same somber pattern. The enemy still holds the strategic initiative; he is still attacking; he is still growing in strength and we are still fighting hard with limited means to hold a 120 to 130-mile front, which is too large for the defensive forces available but essential for the build-up necessary to a future offensive.

The week's fighting was a continuation of the determined enemy drive that started the last day of August. This drive, which opened in the south with a strong push toward Masan and Yongsan, gradually spread to the rest of the front, and has become a rather general offensive with more strong blows indicated. Its maximum objective undoubtedly was a clean break-through for the purpose of capturing the port of Pusan—vital to our supply—and destroying our armies. Its minimum objectives were the breaching of our Naktong River line, the capture of the "anchor" cities of Masan and Pohang, and of the communications "turntable" of Taegu.

Enemy Superiority Limited

So far, the enemy's offensive—which is still continuing — has failed completely in its maximum objective and has accomplished only part of its minimum objective —the capture of Pohang. But conditions on the northern front, where the enemy made substantial gains during the week, were far from secure; the general enemy attacks had forced the commitment of most of the U. S. reserves available in Korea, and our troops obviously were hard pressed. Yet, if our intelligence guesses were correct the enemy probably had no more than 170,000 men in or near the front line, which gave him only a limited numerical superiority over the combined U. S.-British-South Korean forces.

The conclusions that could be drawn from a week of some frustration in Korea were several:

The loss of Pohang, an auxiliary port which could be used for small-scale supply, though important, is not a major blow. The enemy had not captured the airfield six miles south of Pohang up to yesterday and until he controls the shores of the bay around Pohang his conquest is not secure.

Taegu, definitely threatened, as indicated by our evacuation of an airfield under construction there and of other facilities, would be a major loss. A communication hub, its capture by the enemy might force a major withdrawal of most of our line.

South Korean Weakness

The front in Korea cannot be considered adequately secure until the five divisions of tired South Koreans that have been holding the northern flank are replaced by, or stiffened with, sizable forces of U. S. or other troops. The enemy gains in the north started with a major break through the R. O. K. Capital Division, but there were apparently a number of inexplicable retreats, and even one report of a platoon-sized South Korean unit going over to the enemy.

The South Korean units have been holding shorter frontages than those held by U. S. divisions and their defense has been aided by the most difficult mountains, but nevertheless most of the enemy's advances were made through the South Korean portion of the front.

Soldier for soldier, the enemy in Korea seems to be outfighting us. This is a judgment subject to correction, and of course, part of the enemy's superiority is due to the weakness of the South Koreans, who still outnumber the U. S. forces. But the enemy's knowledge of the country, his better use of terrain, his infiltration tactics, superior intelligence, cross-country mobility and his tough and rugged foot troops, supplied by long lines of human porters, still gave him a man for man advantage, despite our air superiority.

Enemy Strength a Surprise

The strength of the enemy in his latest offensive has apparently surprised our forces in Korea. The volume of enemy artillery and mortar fire evidently was unexpectedly heavy, and, though the enemy showed in the south an inability to follow up rapidly initial gains, probably owing to our air superiority, he has displayed power in men, weapons and determination that was most unwelcome after the bloody casualties we had exacted from him and the attrition effects of our air power.

The results of the week's fighting and the conclusions that may be drawn from it invite speculation as to the future in Korea. When can we wrest the initiative from the enemy and go on the offensive?

To answer such a question the type of offensive has to be defined. We have already shown, for instance, that we are capable of a considerable offensive effort—on the scale of a divisional counter-attack or a spoiling offensive. Gen. Waldemar Erfurth's axiom that "only a mobile defender can surprise" is applicable to Korea. We have had road mobility, although sometimes our plethora of motor vehicles have clogged the limited network. But the North Koreans have had better cross-country — and particularly cross-mountain—mobility, and part of the surprising strength of their northern assault last week was due to their ability to sideslip their divisions to the eastward through the mountains.

Sea and Air Superiority

But we have mobility in two mediums which they cannot match without Russian help—the air and the sea. The sea flanks of Korea are vulnerable to determined amphibious assault at many places, as the small-scale landings made by South Korean Marines on offshore islands from Seoul to Masan show. When our troop strength in the Japan-Korea area permits—and it must be remembered that the build-up is constantly continuing—there would be no reason why we should not make a landing at one or several of many spots along the Korean coast.

But unless the landing was to be merely in the nature of a raid, it would have to be: (1) fairly close to our beachhead, for instance, at Pohang and coordinated perhaps with an offensive launched from the beachhead; or (2) limited to the seizure of a certain specific beachhead area, perhaps a peninsula, which could be held as Anzio was—though outside our main battle lines—as an independent operation.

Such offensive operations ob-

191

'ON READING THE NEWS FROM BACK HOME'

WHADDA THEY MEAN — "LITTLE WAR"?

Bimrose in The Portland Oregonian

viously would be limited, just as any that we can now contemplate from the beachhead itself probably must be limited. For our troop strength is not yet adequate —unless enemy morale collapses or his strength is much weaker than our intelligence estimates and the fighting picture indicates —to land with heavy forces deep in the enemy's rear areas, or to start a general offensive from our beachhead.

A Sea and Land Operation

For a sustained, large-scale offensive in mountainous country in Korea must entail a sizable superiority in firepower (which we possess, at least when our air is in action), in manpower (which we do not possess) and in supplies. To avoid the mountains a landing in the main coastal plain on the western part of the Korean peninsula—the main communications corridor north and south—would be logical, but again, until troops are available and supplies ready such a move, unless limited, would be pretty risky.

Clausewitz, the great advocate of ground power, put the pre-conditions for a strategic offensive succinctly in his "Principles of War" 130 years ago. They have not changed. The successful offensive requires, Clausewitz wrote, "con-

stant replacement of troops and arms."

'Easier for the Defender'

"This is easier for the defender [he continues] because of the proximity of his sources of supply. [Our air domination helps to offset this advantage, though not completely.] The aggressor, although he controls in most cases a larger state, must usually gather his forces from a distance and, therefore, with great difficulty. Lest he find himself short of effectives, he must organize the recruiting of troops and the transport of arms a long time before they are needed."

In summary, the time is approaching, or almost at hand, when U. S. forces, reinforced, should be able to undertake some limited offensive operations, either from the beachhead itself, and/or against enemy-held positions along the Korean coasts. But the timing of any such operations, and, indeed, their feasibility depend not only upon U. S. reinforcement but upon the enemy's strength. In any case, we should not expect unlimited assault, quick decision or rapid victory. Unless the enemy's will-to-fight fades away, or Russia withdraws her support, we do not yet have the strength to compel decision in Korea.

September 10, 1950

MacArthur Lands at Inchon; Heads in a Jeep for the Front

By The Associated Press.

INCHON, Korea, Sunday, Sept. 17—Gen. Douglas MacArthur came ashore at Inchon for the first time today. The United Nations commander went into the shattered port city for a front-line inspection of the west coast beachhead his landing forces had carved out of Communist-held Korea.

Inchon is now another Cherbourg, blackened and badly torn by the brief but sharp fighting that took place when the marines swept through it Friday night. Nevertheless, a high-ranking South Korean Navy officer said, "the people are happy."

General MacArthur was met upon landing at 9:35 A. M. (8:35 P. M., Saturday, Eastern daylight time) by Maj. Gen. Oliver P. Smith, commanding general of the First Marine Division. The division is part of the Tenth Corps which staged the amphibious operation here.

General MacArthur was accompanied by Vice Admiral Arthur D. Struble, commander of the United States Seventh Fleet, and Lieut. Gen. Lemuel C. Shepherd Jr., commanding the United States Fleet Marine Force in the Pacific.

The United Nations Commander started out in a motor caravan for the front line, about six miles from Kimpo. General MacArthur rode in the lead jeep.

Rear Admiral Sohn Wun Il, Chief of Naval Operations, said inhabitants were glad the Communists had been driven out. He is commanding the South Korean Marines who are policing the city and still flushing out snipers and rounding up enemy stragglers.

His command post is a battered shack near the waterfront. On either side are piles of debris, burned-out buildings and shell-torn docks.

The admiral said "the enemy is different now," and added, "they are not fighting—they fire a few times, then run away."

He said he did not believe the North Koreans had any organized army units this far north. But he added that they had forcibly recruited larger numbers of men from Inchon and surrounding areas, given them quick training and put them into the lines.

He said he did not think they would fight if they had a chance to surrender.

The people certainly do not look happy. If they are glad the war has finally passed them by, they do not show it. Perhaps that is just Oriental impassiveness. Today they were going about the sad business of trying to live in the midst of great devastation, to bury their dead, get a bowl of rice to eat.

All those things were taking place in Inchon today. The people were not so much as glancing at the marines and sailors pouring through or the masses of equipment and strange-looking machines coming ashore.

A woman sitting on the edge of a stone pier, motionless as the stones themselves, stared out across the harbor. It was littered with junks and half-sunken small craft. Perhaps one of them had been hers. Her eyes never shifted and her head never moved.

A Korean boy—he looked about 14 years old—made his way painfully down the street, holding his right leg stiff and straight. A blood-stained bandage was wrapped round his knee.

A fire still burned in the skeleton of a wrecked building. Close by the pier was a sagging, rickety shack that had been a soft-drink stand. The tiny structure itself was barely standing, but its bottles of cider and carbonated water were intact, though tilted sideways like tin soldiers in a child's game.

At an aid station in the open street United States soldiers and Koreans—South and North—lay side by side on litters. The medics were working over each as they came to them, without regard for nationality or political affiliations.

A few miles away, bright white and clean, a Navy hospital ship was riding at anchor. Many of these wounded would go there.

With the typical contrasts of war, boxes of ammunition were being unloaded from barges and manhandled into trucks right beside the rows of casualties on the dock.

A truckload of prisoners passed. The captives wore white clothing, not uniforms. They stood in the truck, packed tight and holding their hands over their heads. The marines said they had surrendered easily and "seemed anxious to be friendly."

Possibly this sudden change of heart was the explanation as well for the numerous flags of Nation-

U. N. COMMANDER AT THE INVASION SCENE

Gen. Douglas MacArthur (seated) and members of his staff on the bridge of the Mount McKinley off Inchon Friday. Left to right: Brig. Gen. Courtney Whitney, Brig. Gen. E. K. Wright, General MacArthur and Maj. Gen. E. M. Almond. U. S. Army Radiophoto via Associated Press Wirephoto

alist China that fluttered from scores of houses and shops.

Some of the symbols of the Communist regime were still lying around. They made interesting looking, if not reading material.

There was a whole sheaf of large photographs of Premier Stalin. Another poster showed a dead woman and a crying baby nestled against her breasts. United States planes were overhead. One was strafing a cow in the field near by.

Gen. Douglas MacArthur was the "star" of another Red poster. It was a poor likeness, recognizable mainly for the dark glasses and braided cap. He was brandishing an airplane with one blood-stained hand while heroic-looking North Koreans were pressing bayonets against his chest, causing a faint frown on the general's face.

September 17, 1950

He said that if a majority of United Nations members continued to support United States action in Korea and China "they shall not escape a share in the responsibility for lighting up war flames in the East."

Mr. Chou charged anew that American planes had violated Chinese territory on Sept. 22 and demanded that United States "invasion of Chinese territorial air by military airplanes" be placed immediately on the agenda of the United Nations General Assembly.

He demanded also that representatives of Communist China be admitted to the United Nations to take part in discussions of the charges against the United States.

3d "Invasion" Charged
Special to THE NEW YORK TIMES.

HONG KONG, Sept. 24—Chinese Communists charged today that American aircraft had crossed the Yalu River boundary separating Manchuria from North Korea on Friday and had "invaded" Chinese territory for the third time within one month.

An official New China News Agency dispatch asserted one plane had dropped twelve bombs on the northeast suburbs of An-'ung, injuring three persons and damaging houses within a 500-square meter area. The agency maintained a child was among the three wounded.

The Peiping People's Daily, organ of the Chinese Communist party, followed up the dispatch with an editorial terming the alleged incident "another act of naked aggression against China." The editorial called on the United Nations to take action against the United States.

"Since the fifth session of the United Nations General Assembly is being held we demand that the Assembly shall impose sanctions against further American acts of aggression in the People's Republic of China," the newspaper said.

"The Chinese people demand that the American Government be held responsible for all consequences of this new act of violence which the Chinese people will never forget."

Today's allegation follows the recent gratuitous admission by a Foreign Office spokesman in Peiping that Manchurian Koreans who had fought with the Chinese Communists in the civil war campaigns had moved across the border some time ago to fight with the North Koreans. This acknowledgement, which was accompanied by a statement that Communist China would "always stand on the side of the Korean people," has been interpreted here as a propaganda attempt to head off a possible United Nations drive across the Thirty-eighth Parallel in Korea.

Peiping Acknowledges Troops Aid North Korea

Special to THE NEW YORK TIMES.

HONG KONG, Sept. 22—The Chinese Communists admitted today that they had sent battle-trained Korean troops from Manchuria to participate in the Korean war.

In a dispatch published here by the left-wing press, the official New China News Agency quoted a Peiping Foreign Office spokesman as having declared:

"It is the proper right and sacred duty of Koreans in China to return to their fatherland to help in its defense and reconstruction."

The spokesman added, "We shall forever stand on the side of the Korean people."

September 23, 1950

PEIPING AIR FORCE WARNS U. S. FLIERS

Says It Will Smash Planes That 'Dare to Intrude'—Charge of New Raid Sent to U. N.

LONDON, Sept. 24 (Æ) — The Peiping radio said tonight the Chinese Communist Air Force would smash any United States warplanes "which dare to intrude over our territory again."

The warning was contained in a pledge of support to Communist President Mao Tze-tung from the People's Air Force of the East China military area, said the radio transmission monitored in London.

The message was one of many to Mr. Mao in connection with the approach of China's National Day, Oct. 1, the Peiping radio said.

This date indicated China's Communist rulers had abandoned the traditional Oct. 10 or "double tenth" holiday—the anniversary of the start of Dr. Sun Yat-sen's revolution against the Chinese monarchy. The Peiping message contained no explanation of the new date.

Peiping Warns U. N.

LONDON, Sept. 24 (UP)—Communist China charged today that the United States was determined 'to extend the aggressive war against Korea, to carry out armed aggression on Formosa and to extend further her aggression against China."

In a formal note to the United Nations, Foreign Minister Chou En-lai also declared that "the peace-loving peoples all over the world definitely will not stand in

September 25, 1950

ALLIED DRIVE HALTS AT 38TH PARALLEL; U. N. CHIEFS SAY M'ARTHUR CAN DECIDE ON CROSSING AND FIX SURRENDER TERMS

MAIN BATTLE OVER

Communist Forces End Organized Resistance as Allies Sweep On

FOES IN POCKETS FIGHT

Main North Korean Troops Make No Major Attempts to Break Allied Traps

By LINDESAY PARROTT

Special to THE NEW YORK TIMES.

TOKYO, Saturday, Sept. 30—Organized enemy resistance had virtually ceased today in South Korea as Allied columns thrust forward in all directions in sweeping unopposed advances.

On the east coast the South Korean Third Division reached the Thirty-eighth Parallel [United Press reports early Saturday said other South Korean forces had passed through Tanyang and were advancing toward Chechon. Still other South Koreans seized Chungju and moved toward Wonju.]

Thus far there was no announced decision here whether the United Nations troops would move across the boundary to attack the fortified line the Communists built years before the invasion of South Korea last June. South Korean shells were falling on a high ridge along the Parallel itself but no infantryman had crossed the line.

[As of early Saturday, the question of a crossing from a military standpoint appeared to have been undecided. An Eighth Army Information Officer denied early reports that Lieut. Gen. Walton H. Walker, commander of the United Nations forces in Korea, had ordered all troops to halt at the Thirty-eighth Parallel. Shortly after a spokesman for the South Korean forces said the Republican troops would not attempt to cross the Parallel unless ordered to do so by the United Nations.]

Troops Reach Yellow Sea

On the southwestern front motorized forces pushed to the shores of the Yellow Sea, drawing a new wedge between shattered Communist divisions already cut off from North Korea by the United Nations line from Taegu to recaptured Seoul.

The Eighth Army announced last night that friendly forces had taken Iri, on the main west coast railroad line north to Taejon and Seoul and about six miles inland from the coast where the Mangayong River empties into the Yellow Sea.

Iri is a key communications center of the "rice bowl" provinces of Soutswest Korea, from which the Communists had hoped to reap this autumn's harvest and move it up to the hungry north. The city's capture cut the last escape route by secondary roads along the west coast for the enemy penned in the southwest tip of Korea and yielded another small but usable advance airfield to the United Nations.

Allies Imperil Kunsan

Other United Nations forces drove west to Nonsan, north of the Kum River. Between them, they threatened Kunsan, the last important remaining west coast port and the largest city of the area still in Communist hands.

South of this area United States Twenty-fifth Division units neared Tamyang and to the north United States and South Korean forces joined at Chochiwon.

Where they could, the Communist invaders had pulled back behind the Thirty-eighth Parallel and elsewhere were fighting only when cornered or in small rearguards trying to hold positions until the larger bodies could retreat behind them.

Behind the United States and South Korean advance guards there was some sharp local fighting as isolated groups of North Koreans clung to their positions.

Near Hamyang in the southern area columns of the United States Twenty-fifth Infantry Division were fired on by one pocket of about 600 North Korean soldiers far behind the advance lines.

The enemy also had some workable artillery left between Kumjhon and Taegu and these guns were dropping shells along the main highway where convoys were bringing up supplies for the United States Twenty-fourth Division.

However, headquarters spokesmen said the enemy action in the south would have no effect on the general picture south of the Thirty-eighth Parallel.

In the Seoul region United States Marines slowly followed up Communist forces retreating northward to the boundary line along the Uijongbu road and paratroops of the 187th Regimental Combat Team pushed north along the Kimpo Peninsula between the Han River and the Yellow Sea.

The largest advances in the Seoul area, however, were made by infantrymen of the Seventh Division. They thrust to the east twenty-five miles from their positions around Suwon and patrols entered Ichon on a highway leading toward central Korea and a possible link-up with the South Korean advance troops there.

The Communists made no further attempts to break through the noose the United States troops had slipped around the enemy divisions in the south when United States Seventh Infantry Division troops from Inchon joined hands with a United States First Cavalry Division column from Taegu near Suwon.

Intelligence agents, however, identified stragglers from the North Korean Second and Third Divisions in the United States Seventh Division area. They said the Communists apparently had filtered up from the south in the hope of escaping across the Parallel.

As the fighting south of the boundary appeared to be drawing to a close, except for clearing out of pockets and mopping up of stragglers and guerrillas, the Allied Air Forces, which had been striking hard throughout the war, approached their maximum effort. Incomplete reports indicated that the planes would equal yesterday the record of 792 sorties established the day before.

In a single action near Taejon, the first temporary capital of the South Korean Republic after the fall of Seoul, pilots of F-80 jets and F-51 Mustangs said they had destroyed or damaged thirty-four tanks and had knocked out 140 trucks. It was at Taejon that the enemy had made the hardest resistance to the Allied advance in the last few days and the remnants of the Communist 100th Armored Division had been reported in this area. The tanks may have been their remaining Russian-made armor.

Superforts of the Far East Air Forces Bomber Command struck along the Korean east coast north of the Thirty-eighth Parallel and at rail and highway bridges in the neighborhood of the Communist capital at Pyongyang. Targets were rail lines and marshaling yards through which the enemy would have to move supplies and reinforcements to the fortified line along the border—near Singesan, Hamhung, Wonsan and Songjin.

September 30, 1950

KOREAN REDS HIT U. S. UNIT; NOW USE JETS

REGIMENT TRAPPED

Foe Employing Rockets Against First Cavalry Division at Unsan

U. N. TROOPS FORCED BACK

Only 24th Division Makes Gain and Then It Is Told to Halt Its Advance

By LINDESAY PARROTT
Special to THE NEW YORK TIMES.

TOKYO, Thursday, Nov. 2—North Korean Communists, reinforced by troops of the Chinese Red Army, savagely attacked today advance guards of the United States First Cavalry Division thrown into action near the west coast of Korea to reinforce the weakening South Korean troops.

The attack made north and west of Unsan, where the Communists had concentrated their strength during the last few days and had driven back South Korean spearheads by as much as thirty miles in some sectors. Using tanks, artillery and heavy mortar fire, the North Koreans cut off one regiment of the United States Cavalry Division. Other units of the division were reported to be attempting to fight their way through to reach the isolated troops.

The fighting was in progress between Unsan and Taechon, but a spokesman for the United States First Corps said the situation was too vague and confused to locate the positions to which the United States troops had been forced to retreat.

Admits Chinese Are Fighting

For the first time a corps spokesman officially admitted that "Chinese troops" were launching an assault.

"We don't know whether they represent the Chinese Government," he said, and added that it also was unknown whether or not Chinese reinforcements made up the bulk of the new strength that had enabled the shattered North Korean Army to take the offensive again—at least locally—against the United Nations move toward the Manchurian border.

The Communists launched their attack in the morning. According to reports from Korea, they used heavy rocket bombardment for the first time in the war. The latest accounts said the enemy had overrun several First Cavalry positions, capturing weapons and turning them against Americans who had been hurriedly brought up to the combat line after all but one United States division—the Twenty-fourth Infantry, farther to the west—had been out of the contact with the enemy and behind the Korean Republican spearheads driven in by the enemy counterattack.

This morning the North Koreans were reported to be within one half mile of Unsan.

Rockets Launched on Ground

The use of the rockets, fired from launchers on the ground, represented the second new weapon introduced on the North Korean side within the last two days. Yesterday for the first time the enemy flung jet-propelled fighter planes into combat.

Meanwhile, the ground advance of the Allied forces halted at Chongko, where the United States Twenty-fourth Infantry Division stood within eighteen miles of the border city of Sinuiju, reported to be the new capital of the North Korean Communist Government.

All along the rest of the front South Korean divisions were in retreat or on the defensive against enemy attacks strengthened by contingents of Chinese Communist soldiers trained in the Chinese Red Army.

Six enemy jet fighters made their appearance yesterday over Sonchon on the west coast, fought a brief dogfight with Mustangs of the United States Fifth Air Force and then flashed back toward the Manchurian border without casualties on either side. Observers said the jet-propelled planes resembled the Soviet model MIG-15, with swept back wings and a speed of 600 miles an hour. On the previous occasion jet planes were believed to have been seen over North Korea, but this was the first time they had appeared in combat.

Where the jets came from or where they went was not established. It is known, however, that the Chinese Communist Army has several airfields across the North Korean border where these aircraft might be based.

Though neither North Korea nor China is known to manufacture jet planes, in the operations around Shanghai during the Chinese civil war the Chinese Reds used jet-propelled fighters apparently of Russian design and manufacture.

Coupled with the intelligence reports yesterday that the North Koreans were receiving new supplies of tanks and self-propelled guns — also Russian-made — from across the frontier the appearance of the jet fighters was taken to indicate that the Communist Government of Mao Tse-tung also was committing part of its air force to battle to make good its assertion that it would not stand idly by while the Korean Red regime collapsed.

12 Other Enemy Planes Bagged

The sudden appearance of the enemy jet planes came during a day when the Communists, for the first time in a long period, were active in the air. Fighters and light bombers of the United States Fifth Air Force encountered a flight of enemy Yak fighters of the Soviet type east of Sinuiju yesterday—the first enemy planes sighted in weeks by Allied pilots. Three were reported to have been shot down and one was said to have escaped.

Reports from Korea said twenty-five enemy planes also had been sighted on the ground at an airfield near Sinuiju. A United Nations Air Force attack on the field destroyed nine — a total bag of twelve enemy planes for the day in the air and on the ground.

Speculation here previously had been that the North Koreans had received virtually no planes from their Communist neighbors because they lacked trained pilots and ground force crews and China and the Soviet Union had been reluctant to commit their own skilled technicians. There was no indication yet as to the nationality of the pilots of the jet planes that had gone into action.

The sole United Nations gains on the ground yesterday were made by the Twenty-fourth Division. One unit of the division advanced to Paegun north of Kusong To the south a second task force, in a march of forty miles in two days, thrust into Changko and was reported to have patrols as far forward as Namsi.

There the division halted. Reports from the front said orders to suspend the advance had come from headquarters of the United States Eighth Army, a statement that was not confirmed there, however.

The Twenty-fourth Division, far in advance of supporting units, might be considered to have outrun its communications or to have its flank endangered by the Communist counter-attacks on the weakening South Korean forces in the central sector, sources here said.

There were unconfirmed reports again today, however, that the United States forces would not thrust to the Chinese border, but would leave a "buffer" territory between them and the sensitive international frontier.

In a United States sector resistance was officially characterized as "light" to "moderate" but in the center and on the east coast the Communists were attacking savagely. The main fight was in the Unsan area where a communiqué issued by Gen. Douglas MacArthur said the enemy was "reacting strongly" to earlier United Nations advances.

On the east coast, where at least one regiment of the Chinese Communist Army and possibly as much as two divisions had been reported in action, the enemy drove to a point twelve miles from the large industrial city of Hamhung captured last month by South Korean forces.

[The Associated Press reported later that South Korean forces had advanced four miles north of Sudong in the region above Hamhung.]

The United States First Marine Division, which landed unopposed at Wonsan last month, was reported to be concentrating around Hamhung. So far as official reports were concerned, none of the United States force of 50,000 men that had landed on the east coast of Korea appeared to be in contact with the enemy in this area, but unofficial reports said the Marines were now moving to the front in the Hungnam-Hamhung area.

[Earlier The Associated Press reported that the Capital Division had pressed beyond captured Kilchu.]

In the air yesterday United States Superforts of the Far East Air Forces Bomber Command resumed ten attacks on North Korean communications after several days suspension. Beside the three Yaks shot down in the air, the fighter pilots report nine enemy planes destroyed and eight others damaged in sweeps on the Sinuiju airfield.

The Superforts hit railroad junction at Kanggye, flew along the railroad lines north of Sonjin on the east coast and again attacked the industrial city of Chongjin.

Light bombers attacked Huichon, hitting troops and supply areas and C-119 Flying Boxcars dropped food and ammunition to South Korean troops to the north now apparently cut off.

November 2, 1950

West Bids U. N. Ask Peiping To Withdraw Men in Korea

Six Nations Back Resolution Also Assuring Communist China Its Territory and Interests Would Be Protected

By THOMAS J. HAMILTON
Special to THE NEW YORK TIMES.

LAKE SUCCESS, Nov. 10—The Western powers introduced today in the United Nations Security Council a resolution calling on Communist China to withdraw its forces from Korea and at the same time assuring the Peiping Government that both its territory and its "legitimate" interests in the frontier zone would be protected.

The resolution did not specifically mention the hydro-electric installations in North Korea, which supply current for Manchurian factories. However, Sir Gladwyn Jebb of Britain, one of its co-sponsors, told the Council that the assurance regarding the frontier included "the great hydro-electric works which lie on the frontier and which should serve the peaceful industry and development of both countries."

Warren R. Austin, United States representative, said that the provisions of the resolution "should leave the authorities in Peiping in no doubt" and should "remove any foolish fears that the territory of China is endangered in any way by the presence of United Nations forces in Korea." He added:

"They should make clear that the means exist for the peaceful protection of all legitimate Chinese, Korean and Soviet interests along the Korean frontier. They should make clear that these interests are not protected by a thinly disguised invasion of Korea. They should make clear that the Chinese Communists' own interests will be served by an immediate withdrawal of their forces from Korea."

Discussion of the resolution was delayed by a two-hour wrangle with Jacob A. Malik, Soviet representative, who opposed consideration of the resolution because it was based on a special report by Gen. Douglas MacArthur, whom Mr. Malik called "the commanding general of the United States interventionist forces in Korea." The report, submitted Monday, charged that Chinese Communist forces had been stationed in the neighborhood of the most important Korean hydro-electric projects.

Mr. Malik also protested against discussion of the report pending the arrival of representatives of Communist China, who, it developed today, have not yet left Peiping because they were unwilling to set out until the United States promised to issue them visas.

Today's meeting originally had been scheduled to take up the Palestine question, and the Council, by a vote of 10 to 1, rejected Mr. Malik's motion to delete the Korean question (including the MacArthur report) from the agenda. It then adopted, by a vote of 9 to 0, with Egypt abstaining and the Soviet Union not participating in the vote, a French proposal to take up the Korean question as the first item on the agenda.

Although Cuba, Ecuador and Norway also were sponsors, the procedural wrangle left time only for Jean Chauvel of France, who introduced the resolution, Sir Gladwyn and Mr. Austin to speak before the Council adjourned at 6:25 without fixing the date of another meeting on the Korean question.

Vote Not Intended

Actually, as M. Chauvel and Sir Gladwyn made clear, there was no question of taking a vote today, and although the Council will take up the Palestine question Monday, it will not resume consideration of the new Korean resolution before Tuesday, if then.

Mr. Austin, it was understood, wanted another meeting tomorrow, but other delegates thought it would be better to wait and see how soon the Peiping delegation would get here. Some sources, in fact, pointed to the continued unexplained lull in activities of the Chinese Communist forces, and expressed the hope that the mere introduction of the resolution would be enough to calm the Peiping Government's fears, so that it might not be necessary to take a vote.

If a vote is taken, it is generally believed, Mr. Malik will use his veto, and the Western powers will then have to ask the General Assembly to adopt substantially the same resolution. Opinions are still divided on whether the Peiping Government's intervention was merely to protect its frontier and the hydro-electric installations, or carried a more sinister connotation, but in any event the resolution should provide adequate assurances on these points.

Mr. Austin departed from his prepared speech today to tell the Council that he had just received word that two United Nations B-29 bombers had been shot up by Russian-type planes seen coming across the border over the Korean city of Sinuiju across the Yalu River from Antung. He added that this state of affairs gravely prejudiced the successful completion of the United Nations mission in Korea.

A paragraph in the resolution, which called attention to "the grave danger which continued intervention by Chinese forces in Korea would entail" for the protection of legitimate Chinese and Korean interests in the frontier zone, reflected this sentiment in the United States delegation.

Both Sir Gladwyn and M. Chauvel emphasized the necessity of clearing up any possible misunderstanding regarding the purposes of United Nations action. They pointed out that the resolution for the most part merely repeats provisions of resolutions previously adopted by the Security Council and the General Assembly.

The resolution is, however, more specific on the protection of Chinese interests in Korea than the one adopted earlier this week by the Korean Interim Committee. M. Chauvel said that France attached special importance to this part, which asked the new United Nations Commission on the Unification and Rehabilitation of Korea to proceed to the frontier area as soon as possible to help settle any problems "in which states or authorities on the other side of the frontier have an interest."

Although the United States delegation is refusing to discuss any concessions to Communist China beyond the assurances contained in the resolution, other delegates are greatly concerned over the possibility that a war may develop from the present confused situation.

It is taken for granted that the Peiping delegation, whenever it arrives, will demand the admission of Communist China to the United Nations and the extension of its authority over Formosa.

No definite word on what Communist China wants is expected until the delegation arrives here. United Nations officials said today that the Peiping Government, in response to an invitation to take part in discussion of the Formosa question on Nov. 15, had replied by cablegram around Oct. 23 that its delegation would travel by way of Prague.

Secretary General Trygve Lie then asked the State Department to arrange for the visas to be issued in Prague, but it was not until Nov. 7—"Some say only after the voting booths had been closed," Mr. Malik observed today — that the instructions were issued to the United States Embassy in Prague.

However, a reliable source said today that a United Nations official had learned in a long-distance telephone conversation last night with the Foreign Minister of Communist China that the delegation had never left Peiping. United Nations officials denied that there had been such a telephone conversation, but in any event it is hoped that the delegation will arrive early next week.

November 11, 1950

U. S. TROOPS REACH FRONTIER OF MANCHURIA IN NORTHEAST; CHINESE HELD DEMORALIZED

By LINDESAY PARROTT
Special to THE NEW YORK TIMES.

TOKYO, Tuesday, Nov. 21—United States troops yesterday thrust to the Manchurian border on the Yalu River in the north-eastern section of Korea, brushing aside scant North Korean resistance.

Soldiers of the United States Seventh Division who took Kapsan Sunday had advanced eight miles to within five miles of the frontier before noon yesterday. By 4 P. M. they were within two miles and still moving north.

This morning, reports said, United States infantrymen were occupying hills overlooking the city of Hyesanjin, which straddles the Yalu River. Others were marching down into the river valley to occupy the city, which had been burned and battered by United Nations air strikes.

Reports here said troops of the Seventeenth Regiment of the Seventh Division were on the river bank before 11:30 A. M. today—the first United States unit to reach the frontier. [Maj. Gen. Edward M. Almond, Tenth Corps Commander, announced the capture of Hyesanjin, The United Press said.]

Resistance Fades

Some of the United States troops had fought stoutly at Kapsan until a tank attack had cleared the town and the Seventh Division's advance guards were under fire from the hills on the early stages of their march to the frontier. Late in the afternoon, however, resistance had dwindled to nothing. There were no signs of soldiers of the Chinese Communist army who earlier had been reported in the region. Gen. Douglas MacArthur's communiqué said sixty-five prisoners had been taken in the fighting in and around Kapsan but that all these were understood to be North Koreans.

The advance to the frontier was the second time United Nations troops had stood on the south bank of the Yalu River since the Korean war began. Last month South Korean Republican troops had reached the international boundary at Chosan, to the southwest on the Yalu, but had been compelled to retreat by the intervention of three Chinese armies that had cracked the United Nations lines in the west.

The Seventh Division advance represented a march of eighty miles from the east coast, where the division had landed amphibiously at Iwon, through some of the most rugged mountains in Korea and in temperatures that recently had fallen below zero.

Solid Line Set Up

Meanwhile, in other sectors of the front, United Nations troops continued slow, cautious advances, probing for the defense line the withdrawing Communists were reported to have built somewhere along their main lines of communication with Manchuria — the roads from Suichon north to the frontier near Sakchu and Kanggye. Increasing contacts with the enemy noted by offical reports during the past twenty-four hours seemed to indicate United Nations advance guards might be nearing such a defense position—if it existed.

A headquarters spokesman yesterday gave some clue to the rather mysterious movements of the Chinese Communist soldiers who had forced United Nations troops to make withdrawals of up to fifty miles in their counter-offensive last month, then had broken off the attack and had largely avoided contact with United States forces. From the questioning of about 150 Chinese prisoners the spokesman indicated it was learned that the Chinese had quickly become demoralized by the fire power of a modern army and the total United Nations control of the air.

The volume of fire that the Chinese had to face was far heavier than they had imagined or than even the veterans of the Chinese civil war had ever encountered. The low-level strafing by United States jets and Mustangs also was a new and nerve-shattering experience.

At least in the case of one division of the Chinese Communist Thirty-eighth Army which the spokesman was able to detail, soldiers received only ten days' supplies of hard bread and millet when they crossed the Manchurian border at Manpojin on Oct. 20. Thereafter they lived on parched corn obtained from the countryside. There was an attitude of mutual distrust between the Chinese of this outfit and North Korean soldiers and the Chinese were told by their officers they would be executed if they were captured by the United Nations.

None of these Chinese were volunteers, the prisoners said, and they knew of no volunteering in Manchuria for Korean service.

The men were loaded aboard trains at Mukden and warned not to speak Chinese, though few knew any other language, after crossing the border and to destroy all papers and letters linking them with China. Then they marched down from Manpojin at night over mountain paths off the main roads. They went into action at Kaechon near Ongju on the central front on Nov. 5 and three days later began to retreat.

Picture of the Front

From east to west along the front reports gave the following picture yesterday:

In the extreme east the South Korean Capital Division, with United States air support, reached Yongchon, north of the Orangchon River. They met heavy enemy resistance for a time and there were reports the enemy was moving some reinforcements south in truck columns to check the advance.

[An Associated Press dispatch from the northeast front said the South Korean Capital Division had captured Chuchonhujang and had penetrated to within twenty-five air miles of Chongjin.]

United States Marines patrolled the banks of the Changjin Reservoir with little or no contact with the enemy. Here and in the Kapsan region advanced troops were supplied by airdrop. Three C-119 transports dropped 32,000 pounds of rations and motor fuel yesterday to Seventh Division troops north of Kapsan, it was announced.

In the central sector of Korea, a spokesman said, United Nations troops were in contact with each other now right across the peninsula, though no continuous line exists linking the Eighth Army in the west and the United States Tenth Corps on the east coast.

Along the western perimeter the South Korean Eighth Division met "moderate" resistance north of Tokchon. Reports said they were about three and one-half miles north of the town, making "limited" gains. The Republican Seventh Division north of the Kunu-Tokchon road had thrust approximately 5,000 yards north and east of the town. After inflicting fifty casualties on an enemy delaying force estimated at two companies, they met little opposition.

[The Associated Press said the South Korean Third Division had clashed with a pocket of Communists twenty-two miles southeast of the Changjin reservoir, killing about forty-five of the enemy.]

The United States First Cavalry Division patrolled north of Won in the Changchon River valley and was reported in the vicinity of Kangjong. On the far bank of the Changchon other cavalry troopers entered Ipsok, about five miles north of the walled city of Yongbyon. They met mortar and machine-gun fire and there were reports of 2,000 Communists strongly dug in somewhere to the north in advance of what might be the new enemy defense line.

Stalled by Roadblock

Four miles west of the Taeryong River, patrols of the British Commonwealth Brigade ran into an enemy roadblock. They called for an air strike that apparently eliminated the position. Near Kumo yesterday a British combat patrol killed an entire enemy patrol of fifteen men.

In the guerrilla fighting behind the United Nations lines, the enemy was reported vacating some positions near Pyonggang in central Korea. The Turkish Brigade threw back a guerrilla attack in the Kaesong area, killing five Communists and taking thirty prisoners.

An attack against United States units south of Singye was repulsed and patrols of the United States Second Division killed thirty-one of the enemy and captured two near Songchon where planes in close support of ground patrols strafed a large body of Communists with "excellent results."

In the air cloudy weather caused suspension of attacks on Yalu River towns. An Air Force spokesman said a recent order demanded that pilots must make "complete visual runs" over targets on or close to the frontier in order to avoid international incidents. If clouds obscure either the target or the path over which the planes must travel to make their bomb runs, the attack is prohibited.

With visual pin-point bombing impossible along the Yalu, B-29's struck a secondary target at Nanam, on the east coast. One hundred and sixty tons of general purpose bombs hit a storage, supply and staging area for enemy troops. Fighters of the United States Fifth Air Force yesterday kept the Huichon road in the west under almost constant attack in close support of the United States First Cavalry Division and the Republican Seventh Division.

November 21, 1950

U. N. FORCES LAUNCH A GENERAL ASSAULT IN WEST KOREA TO CLOSE VISE ON REDS; M'ARTHUR AT FRONT, AIMS TO END WAR

7 DIVISIONS STRIKE

Attack on 60-Mile Front From Pakchon on West to Tokchon on East

GENERAL HOPES FOR PEACE

Headquarters Dubious on Foe's Return of 27 Captive G.I.'s —Drive in East Pressed

By LINDESAY PARROTT
Special to THE NEW YORK TIMES.

TOKYO, Friday, Nov. 24—Gen. Douglas MacArthur, who flew today to the Korean front, announced the launching of a "general assault" by the United Nations forces in the Western sector of the Korean front in a movement to close a vise on enemy positions south of the Yalu River.

"If successful, this should for all practical purposes end the war, restore peace and unity to Korea, enable the prompt withdrawal of United Nations military forces and permit the complete assumption by the Korean people and nation of full sovereignty and international equality," General MacArthur said.

General MacArthur's announcement was issued as he flew from Tokyo early in the morning to the Western sector in Korea north of the captured enemy capital of Pyongyang. The announcement said "General MacArthur personally is present on the Western sector of the battlefront."

[General MacArthur, at the front, was quoted by The Associated Press as saying: "I hope to keep my promise to the G. I.'s to have them home by Christmas."

[United States Eighth Army headquarters in Korea reported gains made by both United States and South Korean forces all along the front against no opposition.]

Final Stage of Battle Seen

General MacArthur pictured the newly begun assault in the west as the final stage of the campaign to crush the enemy made by ground troops advancing in the northeast, and planes hammering enemy communications down from the Manchurian border.

The new assault came after three weeks of cautious Allied advances in the west, in which improved positions were secured for the jump-off against the enemy.

The efforts of these air-ground operations, since the North Koreans and Chinese Communists broke off their surprise attack after forcing United Nations withdrawals up to fifty miles, has been a "massive compression and envelopment" of the Communist armies, General MacArthur said. This is "now approaching its decisive effort," he added.

The troops of the United States Seventh Infantry Division that advanced to the Yalu River at Hyesanjin cut the Communist armies in two, dividing the eastern and western sectors, General MacArthur asserted. The air attacks "sharply curtailed" further reinforcements from the Chinese Communist armies and "markedly limited" the arrival of essential supplies from north of the frontier, he declared.

Attack on 60-Mile Front

"This morning the Western sector of the pincer moves forward in a general assault in an effort to complete the compression and close the vise," General MacArthur said.

The United Nations' jump-off, made with seven divisions—United States and South Korean—was along a sixty-mile line running roughly from near Pakchon on the right to Tokchon on the extreme left flank.

On the left the line had been held by the South Korean First Division, the British Commonwealth Twenty-seventh Brigade and the United States Twenty-fourth Infantry and the First Cavalry Divisions and on the right by three South Korean divisions—the Sixth, Seventh and Eighth.

Unofficial reports said these United Nations forces were faced by approximately 100,000 Communists who had been hastily preparing defense lines farther north.

These reports would indicate the contesting forces were approximately equal as the United Nations assault was launched. The United Nations Command, however, had available two United States divisions previously reported engaged largely in guerrilla fighting—the Twenty-fifth and Second Infantry Division—the 127th Regimental Combat Team, the British Twenty-ninth Brigade, armed with heavy Centurion tanks and the South Korean Third Corps.

As the Communist troops continued limited withdrawals · all along the front, apparently reluctant to bring on a major engagement, there was much speculation here regarding the lull in the fighting since the enemy broke off his

AMERICANS CROSSING A FROZEN STREAM IN NORTH KOREA

Infantrymen of the U. S. Seventh Division in the Kapsan area enroute to the Manchurian border

surprise attack three weeks ago. Attention also was being called to what seemed a conciliatory gesture of the Chinese of the return of twenty-seven wounded United States prisoners from a Yalu River internment camp Tuesday.

Skeptical on Captives' Return

The reason for the return of twenty-seven United States prisoners is still obscure. The men themselves indicated there were still several hundred more in the camp at Pyongatek on the Yalu River, where they had been held. The inclination here is to ask if the Communists wish to be conciliatory what they have done with the hundreds of Americans herded north from Seoul and other prisons and who have not returned.

The beginning of the new assault was announced after the typical United Nations patrol probing had been continued on the west against only local resistance and United States and South Korean forces had pressed their drive in the northeastern sector.

United Nations soldiers made gains of several miles in the east and central sectors, while fighters and light bombers of the United States Fifth Air Force flew in close support, strafing and rocketing enemy troop concentrations, and B-29 Superforts hit Kanggye, Sakchu and Kusong, three main supply points close to the Chinese frontier.

Again the largest advances were made by the South Korean troops operating in the frozen northeastern sector, where Communist forces had been cut off from the rest of Korea by the United States Seventh Division's drive to the Yalu River at Hyesanjin.

South Koreans Closer to Border

On the coast elements of the South Korean Capital Division reached the vicinity of Sodong, five miles below Nanam and about eight miles from the important and heavily bombed industrial center of Chongjin.

One column of the South Korean Third Division took the town of

Hapsu and stood about thirty-five miles from the border at an important crossroads from which one highway runs northwest to Hyesanjin and a second northward toward Musan on the Yalu River where the Chinese Communists had been reported concentrating.

On the Yalu River United States infantrymen of the Seventh Division fanned out west of captured Hyesanjin.

There was no report from other troops of the Seventh Division last reported moving up a road toward Samsu—another reported Communist concentration point—toward the Yalu River below Hyesanjin.

In the central sector the strongest enemy resistance came along the west side of the Changjin reservoir where troops of the United States First Marine Division thrust patrols forward as far as Yudam, where the big lake and its power dams are fed by the waters of the Kum River.

Farther south, South Korean forces made additional advances into the central region, where only

light forces had plugged the gap between the United States Eighth Army on the west and the Tenth Corps operating from east coast bases. South Korean troops thrust about eight miles from Hukshu to the vicinity of Sackang and advance guards were about twenty miles from a junction with the South Korean Eighth Division in the neighborhood of Yongwon, moving eastward.

The B-29 attacks on Kanggye, Sakchu and Kosong were made with 500 pounds general purpose bombs and were aimed particularly at storage centers and rail lines running south to the front in a resumption of the interdiction campaign against the enemy's supply lines. The only opposition the big bombers met was some anti-aircraft fire between Kanggye and the Manchurian border.

Fighters, limited by cloudy weather in the morning to 115 sorties, plastered Unsan where between twenty-five and thirty buildings were destroyed including two tanks that had been hidden under one of them.

November 24, 1950

ALLIED FORCES CONTINUE RETREAT AS ENEMY MENACES SUPPLY ROAD;

By LINDESAY PARROTT
Special to THE NEW YORK TIMES

TOKYO, Thursday, Nov. 30— The United Nations forces fell back yesterday under a heavy Communist attack to seek defensive positions in the western sector of Korea.

At the same time reports indicated that Chinese cavalry troops, pouring around the imperiled right flank in the central sector, had driven a deep wedge between the United States Eighth Army and the Tenth Corps on the east and might have linked up with strong North Korean guerrilla forces northeast of the former Red capital of Pyongyang.

Official reports and spokesmen at Gen. Douglas MacArthur's headquarters abandoned the previously expressed view that the United Nations "general assault" announced by General MacArthur last week had been only temporarily halted.

Retreat Began Tuesday

A communiqué issued by the United Nations commander said "withdrawals" to a designated line of defense had begun as early as 6 P. M. Tuesday. The enemy developed a general counter-offensive

in the west that hit United States and South Korean divisions in massive strength after they had been deployed for an attack north to the Manchurian frontier on the Yalu River, a headquarters spokesman said.

[While The Associated Press quoted an Eighth Army spokesman in Korea as having indicated the Chinese pressure was easing on the northwestern front, a United Press dispatch said that seven Chinese regiments were attacking in the central area near the Changjin Reservoir, threatening the United Nations communications lines there.]

Four United Nations divisions— the United States Twenty-fourth, Twenty-fifth and Second, and the South Korean First — completed their retreats to the south bank of the Chongchon River under a heavy attack. At last reports they were holding positions with their backs to the Yellow Sea along a narrow perimeter at some points only fifteen miles from the coastal road through Sianju and Anju, main supply route from Pyongyang.

The United Nations soldiers were plodding back in bitter cold

along roads choked with traffic while the Eighth Army spokesman said the enemy apparently was bringing up tanks west of the river at critical points near Kunu, to which the United States Second Division withdrew in hard fighting.

Reds Thrust Through Gap

The Eighth Army said one Chinese column sweeping around the right flank was within thirty miles of Pyongyang.

Three others were reported to be thrusting through a wide gap in central Korea between the United Nations forces on the west and east coasts.

The enemy had pushed through the walled city of Yongbyon and, the Chongchon River valley village of Won. Heavy confused fighting here reported in the neighborhood of Kunu, fifteen miles from the main advance base at Sinanju. The Reds had pushed down from Yongbyon to threaten Kunu. An Eighth Army spokesman said last night there was no indication as to which forces held the key village.

On the right, where the South Korean Second Corps had made withdrawals up to twenty miles from north of the wrecked city of

Tokchon, the Chinese Communists pushed into Pukchang and Taepyong approximately fifty miles northeast of Pyongyang. Intelligence reports said United Nations troops coming up to reinforce the right flank had found enemy roadblocks and ambushes along the road from Sunchon where the Communists apparently infiltrated deep behind the South Korean lines in an attempt to block communications with Pyongyang.

There is a "possiblity" that a South Korean regiment still is holding out at Maengsan on the extreme right, nine miles northeast of Pukchang where it had been surrounded since noon Monday by Communists who swung wide around the Allied flank in the center of the peninsula between the Eighth Army and the independent United States Tenth Corps, the headquarters spokesman said.

[United States First Cavalry Division elements were hit before midnight near Kujong, sixteen miles east of Sunchon, The Associated Press reported. Under Chinese pressure the United States troops fell back four miles to blocking positions near Sinchang. At the same time two reassembled regiments of the South Korean Sixth Division were fighting alongside First Cavalry troops fifteen miles east of Sunchon.]

In this area more than 10,000 North Korean troops cut off in the United Nations advances earlier in the fall had been reported operating. They are under the command of North Korean Gen. Kim Chaik and some reports said their orders were to drive back to the old Communist capital. Whether or not this could be accomplished was doubtful but a link with the advancing Chinese would release the North Korean guerrilla forces from the trap in which they were caught in September.

Along the right and center the Communist attacks were made in force. The Eighth Army spokesman said elements of six Chinese armies now had been identified in the western sector—a force of 180,000 men at full strength.

Only on the extreme left, where the enemy had offered little resistance to earlier United Nations' advances along the west coast, lesser pressure was reported. The United States Twenty-fourth Infantry Division, which pulled out of Chongju for the second time, reported no contact with the enemy yesterday. However, the communiqué said one United Nations regiment had been compelled to retire after an enemy push on the division's front and flanks ten miles north-northeast of Naechongjong.

In other attacks the Communists had forced the complete retirement of the South Korean First Division south of Taechon.

Most Withdrawals 'Successful'

Generally, the United Nations withdrawals to "planned" positions were made successfully and in some areas United Nations troops broke contact with the foe and were able to form new lines undisturbed, Allied headquarters accounts said. At other points there was violent fighting, with retreating units cut off by enemy infiltration.

A Turkish battalion that had fought its way out of a trap in the general neighborhood of Kunu was holding its new position.

[The United States Second Division sent a regiment five miles southeast of the Kunu sector to aid the Turkish brigade near Kaechon. Two United States battalions were reported overrun, The Associated Press said. The Turks had cut their way out of a trap near Wawon and later the Brigade was reported pulling back from Kaechon.]

In the northeastern sector of Korea enemy resistance was hardening on the front of the United States First Marine Division near the Changjin Reservoir and the United States Seventh Infantry on the Yalu River in the Hyesanjin-Samsu area. The Marines fought off more enemy attacks west of Yudam, but their thrust to the west to relieve the pressure on the critical western front appeared to have been halted. Headquarters said there was "increasing pressure" against the Marines.

The attacks on two regiments of marines were made by two enemy forces with an estimated strength of three regiments each. The infiltrating Communists had built roadblocks behind the marines along the Yudam road and farther south on the mountain highway from the coast to Hagaru at the reservoir's southern tip.

Intelligence reports said the marines' supply line had been cut between Hagaru and Yudam. Yesterday two C-119 transports of the Far East Air Forces dropped 30,000 pounds of rations and ammunition to the encircled Leathernecks.

There was minor fighting up and down the Hagaru-Hamhung road, the marines' one link with their coastal base after their thrust fifty miles inland to the snow-covered mountain spine of northeastern Korea.

[The United Press reported that new Communist attacks against Koto, south of Hagaru, had cut the United States supply route in that area. In all the enemy was said to have established at least twenty-four road-blocks in the Koto-Hagaru Sinhung-Yudam area.]

A large enemy concentration also was reported east of the reservoir, where one tank-led Communist force attacked yesterday. It appeared that the Marines might yet have to cut their way out from their advanced position beyond Yudam.

The enemy also used tanks against the United States Seventh Division, which had thrust to the Yalu River in a 100-mile march from its coastal bases. The Communists launched a "heavy" counter-attack against the Seventh Division with no results as yet officially reported.

Here also some elements of the United States force were attempting to clear out enemy roadblocks in their rear along their long communication lines through the mountains.

The South Korean Capital Division scored the sole United Nations advance in Korea, thrusting forward some miles north of Chongjin on the east coast as the enemy, had driven them back slightly earlier this week, folded under the fire of United States naval ships off shore.

Flying through overcast weather and snow flurries yesterday, United Nations fighter planes concentrated on close support for the hard-pressed United Nations ground troops. Fighters with napalm bombs, rockets and 50-caliber machine-gun fire hit enemy observation posts and troop concentrations south of Tokchon and reported 150 enemy casualties.

South of the same city fighters hit the hills and ridges where the enemy was believed to be concealed and killed 50 Communists caught in the open between Tokchon and Chongju. North of Pakchon on the other flank of the United Nations line, the Air Force reported the hills "covered with Communists." These were attacked by Fifth Air Force Mustangs with undetermined results.

Royal Australian Air Force pilots attacked enemy forces hiding during the daylight near Taechon on the United Nations left, and other fighters struck at concentrations near Yongpyong. B-26 light bombers made night close-support attacks on the front of the United States First Corps, dropping bombs only 1,000 yards in advance of the United States lines.

B-29 Superforts struck again at Chongsongjin, where an international bridge across the Yalu River already had been knocked out. This time the city was plastered with incendiaries by eight B-29's. Pilots reported that "smoking" fires had been seen as the Superforts turned for home.

Fighter bombers hit the Communist base at Kanggye with bombs, rockets and incendiaries. There was light anti-aircraft fire along the Yalu River, but no indications of further crossings by troops or supply convoys, the Air Force said. Again, as for the last fortnight, there was no intervention by enemy planes.

A spokesman said the enemy's supply task had become easier since the lines of communication had been shortened and the task of interdiction had become more difficult, with the Manchurian end of the line protected from attack.

U.S. Prestige Ebbs on Korea, Europe-Asia Survey Shows

By C. L. SULZBERGER
Special to THE NEW YORK TIMES.

PARIS, Dec. 6—The disastrous dénouement in Korea of the first United Nations effort to block aggression by military force has resulted in a tremendous blow to the prestige of that body, and it has been accompanied by an equally serious loss of confidence in the United States position in international leadership.

This has been true particularly among the larger nations of Western Europe, the weak Middle East and India. In some countries, anti-American feeling is becoming more vocal. There is a mounting fear that the prospects of another world war are being brought closer daily to the doorsteps of lands geographically far removed from the Asiatic battlefields.

Despite the atmosphere of pessimism and anxiety developing in worried Europe and Asia, a surprising sturdiness of spirit seems evident in Western Germany and many Continental nations, including Yugoslavia, Greece, Belgium, the Netherlands and Scandinavia.

This general impression of the impact of the Chinese Communist intervention and the resulting military rout on various political and psychological horizons is garnered from a survey conducted by correspondents of THE NEW YORK TIMES in many capitals of Europe, the Middle East and Asia.

It is difficult, of course, to appraise public thought or to evaluate the shifting views of governmental leaders. Even in the areas where gloom appears preponderant, sizable bodies of opinion remain calm and determined.

Of particular importance to the United States is the attitude prevailing among the larger powers of Western Europe and in India. In boiling down the reports from the capitals of those lands, one finds the following convictions:

BRITAIN

United States prestige has suffered a serious blow, and Anglo-American relations have been hurt. Many Britons would regard British involvement in a war with China as inexcusable. Privately, scores of Members of Parliament have been denouncing United States policy and Gen. Douglas MacArthur's strategy, although, except for left-wing labor elements, pressure by the leaders of both parties has muffled the expressions of that attitude. While a strong pacifist sentiment exists in the Labor party, "neutralism" so far has been repressed.

Should a formal war with China ensue, it is believed that the British Government, after hesitation would have to support the United States.

The United Nations has neither gained nor lost prestige. When the Korean incident broke out this summer it was felt that the United Nations had finally become an effective force. The United States got the credit when things were going well; now it receives the discredit.

FRANCE

The decline in American prestige has been little short of disastrous. The spell of General MacArthur's generalship is questioned. Washington's policy of firmness and toughness is viewed skeptically in the light of its results. There is a deep-seated fear that the Republican party's influence in favor of Generalissimo Chiang Kai-shek has diverted United States policy too much toward Asia and simultaneously has prevented recognition of the Peiping Government.

It is impossible to measure the growth of "neutralism" or anti-American sentiment. Both feed on a distrust of the United States, a distrust that has risen sharply since the Korean setback.

In the event of war with Communist China, France realizes that she could not keep out, even if she abandoned Indo-China.

Officially, United States prestige always has been sustained, as France sees her only hope in collective security. Popular faith in that body shifted with the course of the Korean venture. Today, for many, the United Nations has become a medium for restraining the United States.

ITALY

The 30 per cent of the Italian population that is sympathetic to communism already had such a low opinion of the United States that it could not grow worse. But even among the pro-American majority United State prestige, politically and militarily, has been severely damaged. Fears are reviving that the United States would not be able to prevent the occupation of Western Europe if the Soviet Union should march. Many persons now charge Washington with political incompetence and with "landing us in a mess."

Nevertheless, the majority feels that it must sink or swim with the Western world. The Government endorses President Truman's attitude of firmness. American prestige is still high enough to prevent any dangerous hesitation by the national leadership when the outlook is black.

The prestige of the United Nations has sunk to the extent that the prestige of the United States has sunk. Italy's confidence in the United Nations' ability to protect her against invasion or to handle a ticklish international situation has dropped almost to zero.

INDIA

United States prestige has suffered immensely. There is a deep feeling in Government circles that the trouble could have been averted had the Peiping regime been admitted to the United Nations. The damaging military reverses in Korea and Mr. Truman's mere mention of the atomic bomb have had disastrous repercussions.

New Delhi Communists have been trying to rally Leftist groups to storm the United States Embassy if the atomic bomb should be used in Korea. Certain other groups are secretly pleased to see the Westerners trounced by Asians. There is also resentment that New Delhi's advice against crossing the Thirty-eighth Parallel went unheeded.

The prestige of the United Nations has diminished. The Indians feel that it is of scant use when one party to a dispute is excluded from membership. Nevertheless, India still sees in that body the best remaining hope for peace.

The mood of other countries both European and non-European is reported as follows:

WESTERN GERMANY

Advices from Frankfort say that there has been no marked deterioration in American prestige. A nation of soldiers appreciates the impact of mass formations and remembers vividly its own experiences on the Eastern front in World War II. There still remains a belief that the United Nations will not be expelled from Korea. A Government spokesman said two days ago that "war is not all victories."

AUSTRIA

There is no doubt that the United States has lost great prestige. One Cabinet Minister considers privately that this may be the severest reverse that the United States has ever suffered, and "it will be interesting to see how the American people react." Another official reflects: "It is another Pearl Harbor, but apparently democracy begins to really stir only after it has been kicked in the pants."

YUGOSLAVIA

United States prestige is unaffected, either with the government or the people, according to reports from Belgrade, which stress an awareness of the logistical problem and the physical handicaps facing the United Nations forces. There is a realization that the United States rearmament program only now has got under way and a feeling that the United States is carrying almost the entire burden of fighting in Korea while most Western European governments are not playing their part.

GREECE

While the United States is criticized for having permitted its armed forces to dwindle after the war, Washington's strong stand on Korea is admired. Some persons have been made susceptible to Communist propaganda about American "recklessness" as a danger to peace, but the overwhelming sentiment in Greece favors the United States and the United Nations.

BELGIUM

United States prestige is intact, and neither neutralism nor anti-Americanism is growing. There is a belief that the United Nations is being proved ineffective when all its members are not peace-loving. Belgium would probably support the United States in a Chinese war, but she would keep her troops at home for the protection of Europe.

THE NETHERLANDS

A growing concern with American ability to cope with the international crisis is noted, and there is no hope that Britain can stabilize the "emotional' character of United States politics. Despite the worry about American "impulsiveness," there are no signs of a waxing neutralism.

SCANDINAVIA

United States prestige has not suffered, but General MacArthur's judgment is widely questioned. The Swedes recognize that the "United States has been playing in a 'stacked' card game." There is no anti-American feeling, but United Nations prestige has suffered severely. One newspaper said: "If the United Nations was a stock company, its stock would probably be quoted around zero at this moment."

THE MIDDLE EAST

It is reported from Cairo that a conviction exists in the Arab world that the United States has blundered in Korea. American prestige has never been high since Washington's policy on Palestine was formulated. It is still lower now and General MacArthur's famous "Home by Christmas" remark is cited as a typical example of unwarranted American overconfidence.

December 7, 1950

TRUMAN AND ATTLEE URGE PEIPING TO NEGOTIATE FOR PEACE IN KOREA

By JAMES RESTON
Special to THE NEW YORK TIMES.

WASHINGTON, Dec. 8 — President Truman and Prime Minister Attlee of Britain ended their weeklong conference today with an appeal to Communist China to negotiate a peaceful solution of the Far Eastern war on the basis of "a free and independent Korea."

In a communiqué issued at the White House the two leaders said they were in "complete agreement" on a lot of things, including the principle that there could be no thought of appeasement in Korea. They emphasized however, that on the basis of the principles of the United Nations they were willing to talk.

"Every effort must be made to achieve the purposes of the United Nations in Korea by peaceful means and to find a solution to the Korean problem on the basis of a free and independent Korea, * * *" the communiqué said.

Chinese Stand Awaited

"If the Chinese on their side display any evidence of a similar attitude we are hopeful that the cause of peace can be upheld. If they do not, then it will be for the peoples of the world, acting through the United Nations, to decide how the principles of the Charter can best be maintained. * * *"

Though the conference ended on this note it provided little tangible evidence that the President and the Prime Minister had been able to reach agreement on fundamental and specific points that would almost certainly come up in any negotiations with the Communists.

On the question of (1) the future of Formosa, (2) whether Chiang Kai-shek or Mao Tse-tung should be recognized, and (3) whether the Chinese Nationalists or the Chinese Communists should represent China in the United Nations—all basic conditions of peace in the eyes of the Peiping regime—Mr. Truman and Mr. Attlee were unable to agree.

The communiqué said that Mr. Attlee still recognized the Communist regime and considered that it should represent China in the United Nations. It added that the United States was still opposed to seating the Communists in the United Nations, and while it didn't say so directly, it is known that Mr. Truman and Mr. Attlee disagreed fundamentally on the future of Formosa.

Moreover, they disagreed to the end over the United States proposal that if Communist China did not negotiate a just settlement, she should be subjected to economic sanctions and a limited blockade.

Negotiated Settlement Doubted

In practical terms, therefore, there was little reason to believe that any real basis for a negotiated settlement of the Korean war came out of the White House talks. The hope tonight in this regard lay rather in the improved news from Gen. J. Lawton Collins, Army Chief of Staff, who had just returned: the situation is far from hopeless, and it could be improved, if the Allies would just stop wringing their hands about it.

For a conference arranged on an hour's notice—the hour after Mr. Truman terrified the British with the announcement that he was considering using the atomic bomb in the Korean war—this one had some tangible progress to report. In specific terms, the communiqué announced that the President and the Prime Minister had agreed on these things:

1. The United States would inform the British if world conditions changed to a point where it was seriously thinking about dropping the atomic bomb. Under the Quebec agreement in World War II, Britain and Canada had a veto on dropping the bomb. Mr. Truman did not make any such offer this time, but Mr. Attlee's associates said, nevertheless, that the Prime Minister was "satisfied."

2. No appeasement and no thought of rewarding aggression in the Far East or anywhere else.

3. Both countries would increase their military capabilities as rapidly as possible and expand the production of arms to be used by other free nations allied to them.

4. Plans for the pooled defense of the North Atlantic must be rushed and a supreme commander (Gen. Dwight D. Eisenhower, though they did not say so) should be appointed "soon." This was expected to be done in a week or ten days.

5. Both countries would work together and with other countries to increase the production of strategic raw materials and see that such materials did not get into the hands of potential enemies, but were allocated instead to the free countries that needed them. This was a particularly important point for the British, who feared that, as a result of large United States rearmament and stockpiling purchases, Britain was going to start running out of such commodities as sulphur and zinc in the next few months and find herself with considerable unemployment.

6. The free nations of Asia, now in greater danger as a result of the Communist successes in Korea, would continue to receive as much assistance from the two countries as possible.

7. The United States and Britain would do everything possible, through whatever channels were open, to impress upon Communist Russia and Communist China that the policy of the West was peace, and to "seek a peaceful solution of existing issues."

Several parts of the communiqué were worthy of special attention. For example, in the passage offering peace negotiations to the Chinese Communists, it referred to a "free and independent Korea."

Cairo Declaration Cited

This language was taken from the 1943 Cairo Declaration, under which the United States, Britain, the Republic of China and (later) the Soviet Union promised not only the eventual creation of a "free and independent Korea," but the return of Formosa to the Republic of China.

British officials, after today's meeting at the White House, said that Britain backed the Cairo Declaration "as a whole," and implied that if the Chinese Communists agreed to the creation of a "free and independent Korea," maybe it would be possible to throw in Formosa as a basis for peace negotiations.

United States officials, however, state that the United States Government places no such construction upon this language. The State Department is willing to have the United Nations discuss the Formosa question. It wants to settle that question peacefully, but as the communiqué said, it wants the issue of Formosa to be settled in such a way that (1) the interests of the people of Formosa and (2) the maintenance of peace and security in the Pacific are safeguarded.

The background to that is this: Mr. Attlee wanted Mr. Truman to agree to discuss Formosa, recognition of the Chinese Communists, and the seating of the Chinese Communists in the United Nations as part of a Korean settlement. Mr. Truman, however, declined to tie these things together. He was supported by Secretary of State Acheson, Gen. George C. Marshall, Secretary of Defense, and Gen. Omar N. Bradley, chairman of the Joint Chiefs of Staff, on the proposition that Formosa should not be permitted to get into Communist hands so long as there was danger of war in the Pacific.

When Mr. Attlee arrived here last Monday, he said: "My aim in these talks is to align our policies in the new and troubled situation in the world and to find the means of upholding what we know to be right."

Box Score of Conference

When he left here this afternoon for New York, and Ottawa, the general feeling among well-informed men was that the box score looked about as follows:

Policies aligned: Fight together "in Korea." Appeasement (which is never officially defined) is out. Europe is the decisive theatre of the conflict with Russian imperialism. Production of arms and raw materials must be increased and distributed fairly within the noncommunist coalition. General Eisenhower is wonderful.

Policies unaligned: Formosa. Recognition of what Chinese government? Who should represent China in the United States? Who should decide whether to drop the atomic bomb in Korea? Mr. Truman says he should; Mr. Attlee, while "satsified," thinks the decision should be made only with agreement of all those nations that have troops fighting for the United Nations in Korea.)

"There is no difference between us as to the nature of the threat which our countries face or the basic policies which must be pursued to overcome it," the Prime Minister and the President said.

The general conclusion here tonight was that the first half of this statement was correct.

December 9, 1950

PEIPING BARS KOREA CEASE-FIRE PARLEY

By A. M. ROSENTHAL
Special to THE NEW YORK TIMES.

LAKE SUCCESS, Dec. 22— Communist China today denounced the United Nations Korean truce team as illegal, announced that it would not negotiate with the committee, and once again named its price for peace in Korea.

The price was set by Foreign Minister Chou En-lai. It was:
1. Removal of the United States Seventh Fleet from Formosan waters.
2. Withdrawal of "foreign troops" from Korea.
3. A seat in the United Nations for Communist China.

The Chou statement, broadcast by the Peiping radio, apparently ended any hopes that the Chinese Communists would dicker with the three-man truce committee set up by the General Assembly to try to bring about a cease-fire in Korea. As of tonight there were no signs that a formal message was on the way from Peiping to Lake Success.

Parallel Held "Obliterated"

The statement by Mr. Chou was broadcast in Chinese and English by the Peiping radio. Monitored versions became available here and in Tokyo. From the Japanese capital, the Associated Press quoted Mr. Chou as having said that the crossing of the Thirty-eighth Parallel by United Nations forces—he called them American forces—had "obliterated forever this demarcation line of political geography."

The cease-fire committee refused to comment on the statement broadcast by Peiping and said it was still waiting official response to the cablegrams it had sent to Communist China. But, if no reply

202

is sent directly to the United Nations within the next few days, the cease-fire group will begin work on its report to the Assembly.

The next phase after the report is made will be played out in the Assembly's Political and Security Committee, which has several options. It can take up a six-power resolution demanding a Chinese Communist withdrawal from Korea or, less likely, it can start debate on an Asian-Arab resolution for a parley on the Far East.

Speculation at U. N.

There was only speculation here as to what the United Nations would do when the Chinese Communists rebuffed a withdrawal demand. But "thinking out loud," one informed source said that the possibility of applying diplomatic and economic sanctions against Peiping would be considered.

The announcement from Peiping included a repetition of the charges last week by Communist China's special envoy to the United Nations that the cease-fire plan was a "trap." The idea of a cease-fire committee was presented by a group of Asian and Arab nations, which also put forward the resolution suggesting a conference on Far Eastern affairs has not yet been debated.

Mr. Chou's statement started with an attack on the truce committee. He said it had been set up without the participation or approval of Peiping and therefore was illegal. His regime, Mr. Chou went on, will "carry on no negotiations with the illegal" committee.

Several times in his statement, Mr. Chou said that the Chinese people wanted peace in Korea. He attributed the war to the "aggressive war plan" of the United States.

The Foreign Minister of Communist China declared that when United States troops were victorious Washington was "not agreeable" to stopping the war.

"Only when the United States aggressive forces suffered defeat did they propose negotiations and want a cease-fire," he said.

Mr. Chou charged that the United Nations itself was being "manipulated" by the "Anglo-American bloc." The organization, he said, has violated its own Charter and is "not defending but destroying world peace." Mr. Chou summed up Peiping's position in these words:

"The Central People's Government of the People's Republic of China again emphatically declares that the Chinese people still hope for a peaceful settlement of the Korean question. However, the only acceptable basis for negotiation is that all foreign troops must withdraw from Korea and let the Korean people settle their own domestic affairs.

"The United States aggressive forces must withdraw from Taiwan [Formosa] and representatives of the People's Republic of China should occupy their legal seat in the United Nations. This is what the Chinese people want. The righteous people of the world hope for a peaceful settlement of the Korean question."

Mr. Chou's statement of conditions contained nothing new, and the rejection of the cease-fire-first idea had been made plain by Wu Hsiu-chuan, Peiping's representative here, who left for home on Tuesday. But, until the Peiping radio's broadcast, some delegates had continued to hope that the Chinese Communists would not finish the job of slamming the door in the face of the truce committee.

Most of the delegates to the Political and Security Committee are reported to be ready for a meeting at short notice. But the plans of the truce committee to wait until next week before writing a report made it likely that the Political Committee would not be summoned until late next week or after New Year's Day.

Chou Charges Illegality

TOKYO, Dec. 22 (U.P.)—Mr. Chou started his statement with a denunciation of the cease-fire committee.

"The United Nations General Assembly resolution on the so-called cease-fire three-man committee did not have the participation of or consent of the Chinese People's Government's delegates," he said. "As the Chinese People's Government has stated time and again, this type of important resolution, passed without participation of China's formal representatives, and especially an important resolution concerning Asia, is illegal and invalid.

"Therefore neither the Chinese Government nor its representatives are prepared to have any contact with this illegal three-man committee." He continued:

"The Chinese Government has advocated the Korean war be settled quickly and proposed again that all foreign troops be withdrawn from Korea for settlement of the Korean problem.

"However, not only did the United States Government reject this type of proposal, it even rejected negotiations for a peaceful settlement. Invading troops of the United States arrogantly crossed the Thirty-eighth Parallel at the beginning of October. The United States Government, recklessly ignoring warnings from all quarters and following the provocative crossings of the border by Syngman Rhee in June, thoroughly destroyed and hence obliterated forever this demarcation line of political geography."

"I can understand that delegations of thirteen Asian and Arab countries proposed the Korean peace settlement plan from their desire for peace. However, they could not defeat United States strategy to first obtain a cease-fire and later negotiate." He added:

"If the Asian and Arab nations really want peace they should escape from United States pressure and abandon the evil method of a three-man cease-fire committee."

December 23, 1950

SEOUL ABANDONED TO RED ARMIES; CITY AFIRE; U. N. RETREAT ORDERLY

By LINDESAY PARROTT
Special to THE NEW YORK TIMES.

TOKYO, Thursday, Jan. 4 — United Nations forces early this morning abandoned Seoul, and the capital of the South Korean Republic for the second time fell into the hands of invading Communist armies.

[The Associated Press reported Thursday morning that Chinese troops took Seoul after United Nations troops had blown the last bridge across the Han River and the last Allied plane had left Kimpo Airfield, ten miles northwest of the city.

[General MacArthur said that four, and possibly as many as seven Chinese armies (corps), numbering about 120,000 men, plus two North Korean Communist corps, were driving toward Wonju, fifty-five miles southeast of Seoul.]

The announcement of Seoul's evacuation was made by a spokesman for the United States Eighth Army. Earlier eyewitness reports said the city was blazing with more than 200 fires as some citizens destroyed their homes before fleeing to the south.

The Chinese, in the strength of at least two divisions with stronger forces echeloned behind them, flung final attacks against the barbed-wire entanglements the United Nations defenders had built in the outskirts of the city. Observers in Seoul last night could see trip flares go up in bursts of color as the Chinese forced their way through the wire.

Packed With Convoys

Roads leading south from Seoul were packed with heavy convoys while guns of the United Nations fleet off Inchon and United States and British rear guards covered the retreat. President Syngman Rhee and the remaining members of his Cabinet had left the city yesterday to establish again a provisional capital somewhere to the south, as they did last summer.

Official announcement identified the United States heavy cruiser Rochester and cruisers and destroyers of Britain, Canada, Australia and the Netherlands as standing by off the coast. The Rochester, the first ship to bring her 8-inch guns into play, opened fire on enemy positions last night.

Rear Admiral L. A. Thackery, commanding the United Nations naval forces in the Yellow Sea, said transports and chartered merchant ships were in position in case the ground forces should move by sea. The Navy said "thousands" of civilian refugees were being removed from the Communist-threatened area. Carrier-based planes armed with rockets and napalm were flying protective cover over the United Nations ground troops.

Refugees Mingle With Troops

Streams of refugees mingled with the retreat. Some of the refugees had previously moved out of the city, then returned, hoping the capital could be held.

Electric power and telephonic communication with Seoul were cut off last night and the last convoys moved through pitch-dark streets. Gunfire could be heard within three miles of the city's center, where the enemy apparently was laying down a mortar barrage on entanglements.

President Rhee and the Cabinet members left the city yesterday on a special plane. Last night, the last employes of the Republican Government, whose fate might be execution at Communist hands if they were left behind, were begging rides on trucks. Others were plodding down the roads on foot.

The Chinese attack on the city came from two directions: down the main coastal highway from Munsan and the inland road directly south from Uijongbu. Reports said the United States Twenty-fourth Division and the British brigades had been in contact throughout the day in the final defense of Seoul. Navy guns began firing on the enemy yesterday as the Chinese moved into range.

Reports were lacking this morning on the weight of the fighting that had preceded the fall of Seoul, although previous official accounts had said the Chinese were making their major assault regardless of casualties. Correspondents who left the city last night to make their reports from an air base in southern Japan, said there was some volume of rifle and machine-gun fire in the outskirts — apparently a rear-guard engagement.

Eyewitness accounts said some of the city's best known buildings were in flames, among them the Banto Hotel, where the United States Embassy has offices. It was a far bitterer day for the city than its fall last summer.

At that time little damage was done to Seoul. Since then, however, the city was pounded first by United Nations planes, then by the guns of both sides in its recapture after the Allied amphibious landings at Inchon. Some of its finest structures, such as the Central Government Building, had been under repair up to the last. Now they were being destroyed again.

The United Nations Command's "scorched earth" policy has been to leave no facility standing which the enemy might use, no building standing where Communist troops might conceal themselves from the ever-present Allied air strikes.

The evacuation of Seoul came after daylong attacks yesterday during which the Chinese pushed their way through the United Nations lines north of the capital. The assault was made first in battalion strength. Then the enemy built up his forces to an estimated two divisions.

Front-line observers said the Communists attacked in waves with automatic weapons and mortar support but without artillery or tanks. The infantry came on, sometimes under point-blank fire of United Nations guns and more than 300 air strikes during the day.

The fighting dwindled somewhat last evening after days of hard combat. The Eighth Army spokesman said front reports indicated the enemy, having launched a major attack and driven deeply into the United Nations lines, was massing for an all-out punch to take the capital.

The final attack had been expected early this morning. By 8:30 A. M., however, observers on the scene said all United Nations troops had been withdrawn and were safely across the Han River. Three United States divisions and a heavily armed British brigade were included in the retreat.

Reports said the heaviest fighting came south of Uijongbu, where Chinese attacked in waves to storm the ridges overlooking the main north-south highway and the railroad line.

The fighting apparently was less severe on the extreme United Nations left, where the enemy faced crossing the wide tidal estuary of the Han River. An Air Force spokesman acknowledged, however, that installations of the Kimpo Airfield between Seoul and Inchon on the river's west bank were being destroyed last night. [According to The United Press, a Far East Air Force spokesman said United States fighters and light bombers "are no longer in operation" at Kimpo Airfield.]

From across the river observers this morning described the enemy as "at the edge" of the city and apparently moving into the streets. Some of them were mounted, apparently Mongol horsemen, two divisions of whom had been reported with the Chinese Communist forces in Korea. Up to this morning, however, the enemy made no attempt to cross the stream and engineers still were standing by to blow the bridges after the last refugees had crossed.

Some of the most successful fighting in the battle that preceded the fall of Seoul was done by United States tanks which came into action before the enemy was able to move up the armor that he had been massing near the Thirty-eighth Parallel. The tanks, backed by British, United States and Australian troops, made two counter-attacks on the Uijongbu road yesterday covering the infantry withdrawal.

The intelligence section here said air sightings showed the enemy had at least thirty-five tanks south of the boundary Dec. 31. But because of air attacks, difficulties in transporting fuel or other reasons they evidently had not come up fast enough to oppose the United States armor, for no tank-to-tank engagements were reported.

The same seemed true of the enemy's heavy artillery. Headquarters said that during the past few days the Communists had brought up big 122 mm. and self-propelled guns on the roads from Yonchon and Chajang to Uijongbu. But front reports said the enemy attacks yesterday were launched with little if any artillery support, the Chinese relying on mortar barrages followed by an infantry onrush regardless of casualties.

While the Chinese moved into Seoul, official reports indicated the Communists might be planning a blow in force to the east down the center of the peninsula—the same maneuver used last summer in the initial invasion of South Korea. Gen. Douglas MacArthur's communiqué reported United Nations troops were "heavily engaged" with the enemy west of Communist-held Chunchon, about thirty-five miles northeast of Seoul.

[Communist troops also have overrun Kapyong, southwest of Chunchon, The United Press reported.]

Using familiar infiltration tactics, the Communists are setting up road blocks behind United Nations lines in the central area, the communiqué said. These were "successfully eliminated," according to official accounts. Observers noted, however, it has been a frequent Communist tactic to attempt to establish themselves in the rear just before launching a frontal assault.

Enemy forces also were reported near Yongpo, not far inland from the coast of the Sea of Japan, which United Nations forces are defending against "heavy enemy opposition."

[A later report by The United Press placed Communist forces at a point twenty-six miles due east of Hongchon, which is on the Chunchon-Wonju highway. That point is approximately fourteen miles south of Yongpo.]

General MacArthur's communiqué said four Chinese army corps and two North Korean corps were moving west and south from their original positions opposite the abandoned United Nations beachhead at Hungnam on the Sea of Japan.

The Chinese apparently are troops of Gen. Chen Yi's Third Field Army, which had been reported in the eastern region. Headquarters suggested their objective might be the important communications center of Wonju, about fifty miles south of the Thirty-eighth Parallel in the middle of Korea.

For the second successive day "flying boxcars" of the Far East Air Force's Combat Cargo Command were dropping supplies of gasoline and ammunition to United Nations troops in Central Korea. More than 150 tons were sent in by air.

Fighter planes were up again this morning in what the Air Force called a "massive assault" to slow the Chinese-North Korean advance. In yesterday's operations Fifth Air Force fliers reported 2,000 enemy killed and wounded from air strikes and destruction or damage of 1,500 buildings housing troops or supplies. During the first three days of the New Year, the Air Force said, an estimated 5,500 enemy casualties were inflicted by planes and 4,100 buildings damaged or destroyed.

Last night and early today, B-26 light bombers flew and hit a large supply dump north of Yonchon, blasted railroad trackage near Hwachon in Central Korea and dropped bombs and jellied gasoline on storage buildings.

About half the fighters of the Fifth Air Force, Maj. Gen. Earle E. Partridge said, were assigned yesterday to close-support missions. Attacks were made on large concentrations south of Yonchon and Kaesong and near Koyang and Munsan. The communiqué said planes again were hitting Hamhung, the badly battered industrial city on the east coast from which the United States Tenth Corps had withdrawn, and which, apparently, now is being used as a supply base by the Communists.

January 4, 1951

Red China's Reply to U. N. on Truce Plan

Special to THE NEW YORK TIMES.

LAKE SUCCESS, Jan. 17—The text of Peiping's reply signed by Foreign Minister Chou En-lai to the United Nations cease-fire plan for Korea follows:

(Official translation from the Chinese)
I have the honor to acknowledge receipt of the cablegram dated 13 January 1951, transmitted by Mr. Owen [David Owen, Acting Secretary General] at the request of the First Committee of the General Assembly, on the principles concerning the Korean and other Far Eastern problems. In the name of the Central People's Government of the People's Republic of China I wish to reply as follows:

[1]

The Central People's Government of the People's Republic of China has always maintained and still maintains that a rapid termination of the hostilities in Korea has been sought by negotiations among the various countries concerned with a view to the peaceful settlement of the

Korean question on the basis of the withdrawal of all foreign troops from Korea and the settlement of Korean domestic affairs by the Koreans themselves; that United States armed forces must be withdrawn from Taiwan (Formosa); and that the representatives of the People's Republic of China must assume their rightful place in the United Nations. These principles were also mentioned in my statement of 22 December 1950, transmitted by cable to Mr. Entezam, President of the General Assembly, on the same day, and are now well known to the whole world.

[2]

On 13 January 1951, the First Committee of the United Nations General Assembly adopted without the participation of the representative of the People's Republic of China various principles concerning the Korean and other Far Eastern problems, the basic points of which are still the arrangement of a cease-fire in Korea first and the conducting of negotiations among the various countries concerned afterwards. The purpose of arranging a cease-fire first is merely to give the United States troops a breathing space. Therefore, regardless of what the agenda and subject-matter of the negotiations may be, if a cease-fire comes into effect without first conducting negotiations to fix the conditions therefor, negotiations after the cease-fire may entail endless discussions without solving any problems.

Besides this fundamental point, the other principles are also not clearly defined. It is not clearly stated whether the so-called existing international obligations refer to the Cairo and Potsdam declarations, and this may easily be utilized to defend the position of aggression maintained by the United States in Korea, Taiwan and other parts of the Far East. We understand that many countries in the First Committee agreed to the principles adopted on 13 January, 1951, because of their desire for peace. It must be pointed out, however, that the principle of a cease-fire first and negotiations afterward would only help the United States to maintain and extend its aggression, and could never lead to genuine peace. Therefore, the Central People's Government of the People's Republic of China cannot agree to this principle.

[3]

With a view to a genuine and peaceful solution of the Korean problem and other important Asian problems, I hereby submit, in the name of the Central People's Government of the People's Republic of China, the following proposals to the United Nations:

A. Negotiations should be held among the countries concerned on the basis of agreement to the withdrawal of all foreign troops from Korea and the settlement of Korean domestic affairs by the Korean people themselves, in order to put an end to the hostilities in Korea at an early date;

B. The subject-matter of the negotiations must include the withdrawal of United States armed forces from Taiwan and the Taiwan Strait, and Far Eastern related problems;

C. The countries to participate in the negotiations should be the following seven countries: the People's Republic of China, the Soviet Union, the United Kingdom, the United States of America, France, India and Egypt, and the rightful place of the Central People's Government of the People's Republic of China in the United Nations should be established as from the beginning of the seven-nation conference;

D. The seven-nation conference should be held in China, at a place to be selected.

[4]

If the above-mentioned proposals are agreed to by the countries concerned and by the United Nations, we believe that it will be conducive to the prompt termination of the hostilities in Korea and to the peaceful settlement of Asian problems to hold negotiations as soon as possible.

January 18, 1951

SOVIET CALLS FOR TRUCE PARLEY, BOTH SIDES TO QUIT PARALLEL; OMITS PREVIOUS KOREA DEMANDS

By A. M. ROSENTHAL

Special to THE NEW YORK TIMES.

UNITED NATIONS, N. Y., June 23—The Soviet Union called today for talks to set a cease-fire in Korea and write an armistice providing for withdrawal of both sides from the Thirty-eighth Parallel.

Moscow's overture was made public by Jacob A. Malik and contained no reference to any of the Korean peace conditions previously set by the Soviet bloc at one time or another: a deal on Formosa, admission of Communist China to the United Nations and withdrawal of foreign troops from Korea. It was the first time in more than five months that the Soviet Union had come through on the record with a peace proposal.

Mr. Malik, speaking on a United Nations radio program that was broadcast in the United States today and will be broadcast internationally beginning tomorrow, said that the "Soviet peoples" believed the Korean war could be settled. As a "first step," he went on, talks should be started between the belligerents—he did not name them— for a cessation of hostilities and withdrawal from the parallel.

Holds Peace Attainable

"Can such a step be taken?" he asked, and then gave this answer:

"I think it can, provided there is a sincere desire to put an end to the bloody fighting in Korea. I think that, surely, is not too great a price to pay in order to achieve peace in Korea."

If the United Nations or the Western powers decide on a follow-up to the Malik statement, it can come in one of several ways: Direct talks with the Soviet delegation, an approach by the President of the General Assembly, a Security Council meeting, or face to face meetings between the commanders in the field.

Mr. Malik's reference to a cease-fire conference among the "belligerents" was taken by some observers as possibly meaning that the Soviet Union would not insist on sitting in since it has contended all along it has had nothing to do with the war. The Chinese Communists also have not admitted direct intervention and have been speaking of Chinese "volunteers" in Korea, so it was believed possible that Mr. Malik was talking about a conference between the United Nations and the North Koreans.

Step Toward Solution Seen

United Nations official circles, in first informal reaction, said that the Malik statement seemed to go a long way toward meeting peace conditions set by the United States and the peace appeal made in Ottawa on June 1 by Secretary General Trygve Lie.

In his Ottawa speech, Mr. Lie said that if a cease-fire could be arranged "approximately along the Thirty-eighth Parallel, then the main purpose of the Security Council resolutions of June 25 and June 27 and July 7 will be fulfilled, provided that the cease-fire is followed by the restoration of peace and security in the area."

The first resolution Mr. Lie mentioned denounced the North Koreans for attacking and called on them to withdraw, the second asked member states to come to the aid of the Republic of Korea and the July 7 motion set up the unified command under the United States.

Mr. Lie said in Ottawa that the military objectives of the United Nations were to repel the aggression and he has indicated several times he believes those objectives have been met.

As for the United States, the last formal views of this country on the conditions for a cease-fire were set before a United Nations truce committee on Dec. 15, 1950. They were: A cease-fire throughout Korea, a demilitarized zone of twenty miles starting at the parallel and running north, withdrawal of guerillas, and strict United Nations supervision throughout the country to prevent violation of the cease-fire.

Despite the belief that the new Soviet statement was a substantial lowering of the Kremlin's price for peace, it was pointed out here that some differences still existed between the announced United States conditions and Mr. Malik's suggestions. Among the differences were:

1. The United States has made a point of insisting that safe-

guards be provided through United Nations supervision to make sure there was no build-up for a new attack. Mr. Malik did not specifically include that point.

2. The United States envisaged a buffer zone running north from the parallel into North Korea. Mr. Malik spoke of a withdrawal from the parallel, which might include the possibility of a buffer zone, but which would mean that the southern boundary of any "no man's land" would be in South Korea.

Peiping's Reaction Not Known

There was speculation—but no answer here—as to whether the Soviet Union had cleared the Malik statement with Peiping, or was acting on its own. One observer commented that if the Soviet Union had not had advance consent from Peiping, that would be an even bigger story than the Malik statement itself because it could mean a split between the two largest Communist powers.

Mr. Malik's statement was made on a program of the United Nations radio division called "The Price of Peace," and each week featuring a different chief delegate. The Soviet delegate had been approached several times to take part but only a couple of weeks ago gave his consent. It was the first time a Soviet delegate had

appeared on a United Nations program since Andrei A. Gromyko voiced a brief anniversary message about four years ago.

Normally "The Price of Peace" broadcasts are recorded a week or ten days in advance and distributed textually immediately on the condition they be held for release until broadcast time. But Mr. Malik, apparently waiting for final word from the Moscow Foreign Ministry, did not agree to begin recording until last night, when United Nations paraphernalia was moved to his delegation headquarters, 680 Park Avenue.

Mr. Malik recorded English and Russian versions of his speech. The English disks were broadcast in this country by the Columbia Broadcasting System and will be rebroadcast tomorrow over WQXR at 7:45 P. M.

The speech will also be carried in Canada, Australia, India, New Zealand, Pakistan, South Africa, the Philippines, the Near East, Iran, Liberia, West Africa and Latin America. The Russian version will be beamed toward the Soviet Union by United Nations radio facilities, perhaps on Monday, the first anniversary of the start of the Korean war.

Mr. Malik's text took about seventeen minutes to read and as he had only about fourteen minutes of air time, not all of it was recorded.

In the first part of his address the Soviet delegate made the usual charges against the "ruling circles" of the United States, the North Atlantic Pact and the foreign policies of the Western nations.

He gave star billing to the North Atlantic Pact as the "chief reason" for the East-West split, contending that it was directed against the Soviet Union and its supporters. He also attacked the establishment of United States military bases abroad, the "remilitarization of Western Germany" the "revival of Japanese militarism," and the "mad armaments race."

Once again the Soviet delegate blamed the United States for the Korean war, attacked the "seizure" of Formosa and the "bombing" of Chinese territory. All these acts, he said, showed that the United States was trying to extend war in the Far East.

But the Soviet Union, Mr. Malik declared, had no aggressive plans at all and was interested only in peace. He went back to 1932 to quote Premier Joseph Stalin as declaring that the Soviet Union and its people were "anxious" that war between the Soviet Union and the United States never take place.

As for Communist China, Peiping has refused to answer any of the overtures of the United Nations since the adoption on Feb. 1 of the resolution condemning her

for aggression in Korea. On Jan. 22, the Chinese Communists told the Asian-Arab bloc that they would agree to a limited-period cease-fire set up at the first meeting of a seven-nation conference that would then proceed to discuss withdrawal of foreign troops from Korea and Formosa. The Chinese Communists also demanded "definite affirmation" of their right to sit in the United Nations.

In the past few weeks, there have been rumors that the Soviet Union was putting out "peace feelers." It was reported that the Soviet Union was using Swedish channels to suggest a cease-fire on the Thirty-eighth Parallel, but Mr. Malik denied the story.

The Soviet delegate charged that the "ruling circles" of the United States were transforming the United Nations into an instrument of war. He hit at the branding of Communist China as a guilty party in Korea and denounced the failure to admit Peiping to the United Nations.

"The Soviet Union will continue its struggle to strengthen peace and avert a new world war," he went on. "The peoples of the Soviet Union believe that it is possible to defend the cause of peace. The Soviet peoples further believe that the most acute problem of the present day—the problem of the armed conflict in Korea—could also be settled."

June 24, 1951

TRUCE IS SIGNED, ENDING THE FIGHTING IN KOREA

By LINDESAY PARROTT

Special to The New York Times.

TOKYO, Monday, July 27—Communist and United Nations delegates in Panmunjom signed an armistice at 10:01 A. M. today [9:01 P. M., Sunday, Eastern daylight time]. Under the truce terms, hostilities in the three-year-old Korean war are to cease at 10 o'clock tonight [9 A. M., Monday, Eastern daylight time].

[President Syngman Rhee of South Korea promised in a statement at Seoul Monday to observe the armistice "for a limited time" while a political conference tried to unify Korea by peaceful means, The United Press said.]

The historic document was signed in a roadside hall the Communists built specially for the occasion. The ceremony, attended by representatives of sixteen members of

the United Nations, took precisely eleven minutes. Then the respective delegations walked from the meeting place without a word or handshake between them.

The matter-of-fact procedure underlined what spokesmen of both sides emphasized: That though the shooting would cease within twelve hours after the signing, only an uneasy armed truce and political difficulties, perhaps even greater than those of the armistice negotiations, were ahead.

Signers Are Expressionless

The representatives of the two sides were expressionless as they put their names to a pile of documents, providing for an exchange of prisoners, establishment of a neutral zone for the cease-fire and a later political conference that would attempt to settle the tragic

Korean questions, unsolved by three years of fighting that caused hundreds of thousands of casualties.

According to the latest figures, revealed July 21 by the Department of Defense, the United States has suffered a total of 139,272 casualties. This included 24,965 dead, 101,368 wounded, 2,938 captured, 8,476 missing and 1,525 previously reported captured or missing, but since returned to military control.

Early this afternoon the Allied part in conclusion of the armistice agreement was completed at advance headquarters near Munsan, where Gen. Mark W. Clark, United Nations commander, put his name to the documents previously signed at Panmunjom.

General Clark signed in the presence of some of his high-ranking officers, Vice Admiral Robert

P. Briscoe, commander of the naval forces in the Far East; Gen. Otto P. Weyland, head of the Far East Air Forces; Gen. Maxwell D. Taylor, Eighth Army commander; Lieut. Gen. Samuel Anderson of the Fifth Air Force, and Vice Admiral J. J. Clark, heading the Seventh Fleet.

Also present at Munsan was Maj. Gen. Choi Duk Shin, former South Korean representative on General Choi, who walked out of the United Nations armistice team. the meetings at Panmunjom last May, also had boycotted the ceremony there this morning. As a result, no South Korean representative signed the truce, which South Korea will observe, at least temporarily, but did not approve.

Almost simultaneously, General Clark's headquarters in Tokyo released a message the general had written in advance of the armistice

—a grim warning that the mere military armistice would not permit the United Nations to relax its vigilance against communism.

"I must tell you as emphatically as I can," said the statement, addressed to all members of the United Nations Command, "that this does not mean immediate or even early withdrawal from Korea. The conflict will not be over until the Governments concerned have reached a firm political settlement."

General Taylor, at Eighth Army heaquarters in Korea, echoed General Clark's views and warning.

"There is no strong feeling that our problems here are over, nor that the armistice is an occasion for unrestrained rejoicing," he said.

For the United Nations, the documents were signed at Panmunjom by Lieut. Gen. William K. Harrison Jr. For the Communists, the signer was Lieut. Gen. Nam Il of North Korea, a Russian-trained school teacher who donned a military uniform after the outbreak of the Korean war.

Each Signs Nine Times

Seated at separate tables, each put his name nine times to nine copies of the armistice agreement in English, Korean and Chinese.

On General Harrison's table stood a miniature flag of the United Nations. The North Korean flag decorated the Communists' place in the meeting house. On a central table lay piled copies of the agreement, bound in stiff blue cardboard covers. Aides passed them in turn to the two signers.

Pooled dispatches over Army communications from Panmunjom said General Harrison signed the first copy of the agreement at 10:01 A. M. General Nam put his signature to the final copy at 10:11 o'clock, ending the brief ceremony.

Because of what General Clark called unreasonable restrictions demanded by the Communists, the top military leaders of the opposing armies did not appear at the session. The enemy, it was revealed, had demanded that if Marshal Kim Il Sung, North Korean Premier and Commander in Chief, and Gen. Peng. Teh-huai, commander of the Chinese Communist troops in Korea, came to Panmunjom, all correspondents and all representatives of South Korea would be barred from the neutral zone. General Clark refused.

Following signing of the truce documents by General Clark, the agreement was scheduled to be sent to Marshal Kim and General Peng. Their names probably will be affixed in their secret headquarters near the bombed out North Korean capital of Pyongyang.

The United Nations delegation appeared on the scene at 9:30 o'clock this morning, alighting from helicopters that had brought them from Munsan, and filing past a guard of honor representing all units and services fighting on the peninsula.

Allied Observers Present

General Harrison was accompanied by his fellow American delegates, Rear Admiral John C. Daniel, Brig. Gen. R. N. Osborne and aides. The observers from the United Nations members lined the Allied section of the hall.

There were representatives of Turkey, Thailand, the Netherlands, France, the United Kingdom and the Commonwealth countries, Colombia, Belgium, Denmark, Luxembourg, Ethiopia, Philippines and Norway.

The Communists came to Panmunjom in a fleet of jeeps, thirty-five correspondents of Iron Curtain countries accompanying them. Altogether, it was calculated that there were 130 press and radio correspondents and photographers of many nations in the hall.

Outside the thin wooden walls there was the mutter of artillery fire—a grim reminder that even as the truce was being signed men were still dying on near-by hills and the fight would continue for twelve more hours.

As the delegates settled in seats, aides took the bound copies of the armistice agreement from the central table and passed them to their chiefs. Marine Col. James C. Murray, one of the few Americans present today who saw the start of the truce negotiations two years ago, handed the documents to General Harrison and pointed out to him the place where he should sign. Both General Harrison and General Nam used a single fountain pen.

Lieut. Col. H. M. Orden of the liaison officers group blotted General Harrison's signatures and returned the documents, one by one, to the central table, from where they were passed to General Nam by a North Korean colonel, You Ju.

At no point in the armistice negotiations have the delegates given each other greetings beyond a possible silent nod. The procedure was the same today.

At one point General Harrison whispered briefly to Colonel Orden and an interpreter, Lieut. Kenneth Wu. There was a click of cameras and the grinding of newsreels. Otherwise, only the distant artillery broke the silence.

At 10:10 A. M. General Harrison finished, and General Nam one minute later. The North Korean general glanced at his watch, rose and strode quickly from the hall, without a glance at the United Nations table.

General Harrison strolled out in more leisurely fashion. To correspondents who asked him for comment, he smiled and posed for pictures, saluted the honor guard and greeted some United Nations representatives before he climbed into a helicopter to fly back to Munsan at 10:27 A. M.

Inside the hall, the signed documents remained on the central table, watched by security guards and liaison officers, who remained for a brief meeting with interpreters. Presumably they were arranging the later signing of the armistice by the high commanders.

July 27, 1953

JAPANESE REPORT RED CHINA STRAIN

By LINDESAY PARROTT
Special to THE NEW YORK TIMES.

TOKYO, May 24—Communist China, after eighteen months of costly warfare in Korea, may be approaching exhaustion of its available military potential, some well-informed Japanese sources are inclined to believe.

This may be the background of Chinese willingness to resume armistice talks at Panmunjom, according to Japanese analysis, and if no truce results, because of Soviet demands that the price of a cease-fire be set higher, increased tension between China and its powerful Communist neighbor is likely to be the result.

Both Japanese and high United Nations authorities here believe that although the original proposal to renew negotiations was made by Chinese Premier Chou En-lai, the Soviet Union has been "calling the signals" at the conference table, where the principal Communist delegate is a former Soviet officer, Gen. Nam Il of North Korea. Such a duality of purpose might explain the Communists' apparent eagerness to reopen the talks and their subsequent refusal to agree to terms put forward by the United Nations.

In a recent survey, the conservative Tokyo monthly, Chuo Koron, attempted to assess the cost to China of the Korean war and the possible repercussions on future Communist policy in the Far East. The tentative conclusion was drawn that further adventures were not to be expected at least until after a settlement in Korea has provided a breathing spell for the hard-pressed Chinese.

Chinese Burden Stressed

Chuo Koron's writer, Shigeo Takahashi, suggested that with a two-front war in Korea and Indo-China and with the necessity for guarding the long China Sea coastline, now open to attack from Formosa after President Eisenhower's withdrawal of the United States' Seventh Fleet, China even with Soviet military supplies was carrying the maximum burden possible for its overstrained economy.

The Japanese monthly cited three factors. The first was Chinese losses in men and supplies in the Korean war. Until early this year, it was calculated, Chinese casualties in Korea were 840,000 men. The cost in matériel was estimated at the equivalent of $2,-400,000,000, a drain that the writer found had seriously hampered the fulfillment of the Chinese five-year plan.

The situation has been aggravated, the writer found, by failure of Czechoslovakia and Poland to provide construction materials contemplated under the Chinese economic rehabilitation plan. United States bombing of the big Yalu River power installation providing energy for the Mukden industrial complex and of lesser dams inside Korea was deemed to have placed an additional burden on the shaky war machine.

Recently Japanese repatriates returning from China have told of strict rationing of electric power in Manchuria after the bombing attacks.

A second factor cited as causing apprehension in China was the increasing reliance of the nation's war effort on Soviet assistance, while the United Nations in Korea is able continuously to replace foreign with Korean troops and increasingly to make use of Asian resources. The growing quantity of matériel now produced in Japan is a case in point.

As a result of the policy of the Republican Administration in the United States in strengthening Asia to combat aggression in Asia, Japanese observers suggest, the Communists have lost an advantage they possessed in the early days of Chinese intervention in Korea—pinning down Western manpower and straining Western resources without the commitment of Soviet industrial potential. The finding is at least in part corroborated by the observations of the military that all Chinese and North Korean weapons and supplies now are of Soviet origin. The captured Japanese and Chinese Nationalist resources with which Communist China began the war have apparently been exhausted.

A third element embarrassing Chinese military plans, the Japanese analyst found, consists of political differences between the Peiping regime and the Kremlin. This involves not only long-range questions of spheres of influence in Sinkiang, Inner and Outer Mongolia and Manchuria, but also Moscow's apparent determination to play the part of senior Communist partner in Asia.

Chuo Koron's analysis, which attracted considerable attention here, asserted that the Soviet Union "willfully" turned down the Indian proposal last year for settlement of the Korean war, although "the Soviet Union had been informed of the proposal by Red China beforehand."

May 24, 1953

Economic Aid Pact Signed By Peiping and North Korea

TOKYO, Tuesday, Nov. 24—Communist China's official radio announced today that the Chinese and North Korean Communist Governments signed a ten-year economic assistance agreement in Peiping yesterday.

Under the new accord the Chinese Communists agreed to write off "all supplies given and expenses incurred" in their program of aid to the North Koreans from the beginning of the Korean war to its end this year. In addition, the Chinese Communists promised to give North Korea a grant of "8,000,000,000,000 yuan" over the next four years to help the Koreans restore their shattered economy.

Japanese economic sources said 70 yuan are now worth about one Japanese yen. This means the Chinese grant is valued at about $317,000,000.

Two months ago the North Koreans negotiated a similar economic assistance pact with the Soviet Union. The latter promised to give its Korean satellite 1,000,-000,000 rubles ($250,000,000 at the nominal rate of exchange) in aid and also to ease the terms of the repayment of North Korea's debt to the Soviet Union.

[A statement by Secretary of State John Foster Dulles and President Syngman Rhee of South Korea, issued Aug. 7 upon their approval of a mutual defense treaty, described a program of three to four years to rehabilitate the Korean economy at a cost of about $1,000,000,000, subject to appropriations by the United States Congress. It noted that $200,000,000 had already been authorized, out of defense savings.]

The new Chinese-Korean accord was signed in Peiping by the Chinese and North Korean premiers, Chou En-lai and Kim Il Sung. The Peiping radio said the original lines of agreement were laid down in a talk between Premier Kim and Communist China's leader, Mao Tse-tung on Nov. 13. Negotiations of the new pact occupied nine days.

The official text of the pact broadcast by Peiping said the agreement had been reached by the two Communist states "to further strengthen the economic and cultural ties" between them.

It was significant that the Communists made no secret that the new Chinese-Korean aid agreement had been negotiated with the participation of the Soviet Union. The Peiping radio listed as one of the negotiators V. V. Vaskov, charge d'affaires of the Soviet embassy in Peiping.

The accord included three articles providing:
1. Communist China and North Korea "shall extend to each other all possible economic and technical aid, carry out the necessary economic and technical cooperation and endeavor to promote cultural exchange between the two countries."
2. Separate agreements are to be negotiated under the pact by "the economic, trade, communications, cultural and educational departments" of both sides.
3. The agreement is to be ratified "soon as possible" and unless abrogated by either side one year before its termination the agreement will automatically be extended for another ten years.

Political Discussion

In addition to economic problems, the representatives of the two Communist countries also discussed political matters. The communiqué said Premiers Chou and Kim "fully exchanged views on the convocation of the [Korean] political conference."

The Communists used the announcement to say they fully supported the unification of Korea by peaceful means. The two Communists nations promised to "cooperate with all countries concerned in the great cause of carrying out the peaceful unification of Korea."

But the emphasis of the announcement covering the Peiping negotiations was on economic matters. The Chinese said they had "particularly at heart the question of the economic restoration of the Democratic People's Republic of Korea as a result of war damage."

The Chinese promised to use the money grant to give Korea coal, cloth, cotton, grains, building material, communications equipment, metal products, machinery, agricultural tools, fishing boats, paper and stationery "and other daily necessities of the people."

The Chinese agreed to help the Koreans rehabilitate their devastated railway system and supply locomotives and passenger and freight cars. The Chinese also announced they had accepted the Korean proposal to extend the air route of the "Soviet-Korean jointly operated aviation company" over Chinese territory "in order to facilitate a quicker resumption of civil air transport between the Soviet Union and Korea."

PEIPING TO RECALL 7 KOREA DIVISIONS

Red Broadcast Says 70,000 Will Leave in Two Months— New Commander Named

Special to The New York Times.

TOKYO, Monday, Sept. 6—The Peiping radio announced last night that Communist China would withdraw seven divisions from North Korea this month and in October.

The announcement, in a Japanese-language broadcast, apparently was intended to inform the Japanese that China would match the withdrawal of United States forces from the peninsula announced recently.

During the Korean war Chinese "People's Volunteers" divisions usually numbered about 8,000 men. The Communist pullout, when completed, would number about 55,000 men.

Military sources here have estimated Chinese strength in North Korea at about 1,000,000. It is known also that the Chinese recently have been attempting to rebuild the North Korean armed forces, possibly in an effort to equal the twenty divisions equipped by the United States for South Korea.

Although the broadcast gave no hint whether the Chinese divisions would be replaced, it was assumed their role north of the Thirty-eighth Parallel might be undertaken by North Korean troops.

The Peiping radio also announced that Chinese Gen. Peng Teh-huai, who headed the "People's Volunteers," had now laid down his command. He was replaced by the former deputy commander, Gen. Teng Hua, Peiping said.

General Peng is generally understood to have exercised overall command of both the Chinese and North Korean armies during the fighting on the peninsula. He was one of the signers of the armistice agreement. The broadcast did not reveal whether General Peng had received a new post or where the seven divisions to be removed from Korea would be redeployed.

Some observers here are inclined to couple the unusual announcement of the troop movements with the recent Chinese "war of nerves" threatening invasion of the Chinese Nationalist stronghold on Formosa and recent attacks on Quemoy Island, off the mainland coast. When it was announced that United States divisions would be withdrawn from Korea, the Chinese radio asserted they were to be shifted elsewhere for "further aggression" in the Far East.

The possibility therefore appeared that the announcement was intended to indicate that China might be prepared to go ahead with the Formosa plans despite the United States troop movements.

November 24, 1953

September 6, 1954

Ho Chi Minh Said to Make Secret Arms Deal With Mao

By C. L. SULZBERGER
Special to THE NEW YORK TIMES

SAIGON, Indo-China, May 8—French intelligence has received information indicating that Ho Chi Minh's rebel Viet Minh "government" has concluded a secret military agreement with Mao Tzetung's Communist regime in China.

While all details of this suspected accord still are lacking it is believed it provides for accelerated arms deliveries by China to Viet Minh. It is known that Chinese Communists captured 60,000 rifles as well as other large stocks of equipment at Hainan, much of which might be more useful to the Communist cause in the Viet Nam war than to China.

As a result of this, plus further information of the arrival of large amounts of Soviet equipment in China—which might release additional arms to Ho Chi Minh, France has strongly urged the United States to speed up deliveries of material, especially of aircraft, to her forces in Viet Nam.

The French together with some Viet Nam troops have been ameliorating the military situation here during the last two months. But this improvement has depended to a large degree upon their complete control of the air.

This is true despite the fact that France and Bao Dai have no modern bombardment aircraft and astonishingly few fighters. However, to date Ho Chi Minh has had neither aircraft nor anti-aircraft artillery to help him.

The French are acutely worried about the possibility that this situation may change. They have urged the United States to make available immediately sizable quantities of the latest type of World War II fighters and fighter bombers.

Furthermore, it is understood France has pointed out to the United States the eventual possibility that even more up-to-date air equipment may be required if the Soviet Union, through China, intervenes directly on Ho Chi Minh's behalf.

The French have detailed reasons for believing that Mr. Mao and Ho Chi Minh have reached an understanding that includes delivery to Viet Minh of arms and munitions from China. Furthermore, suspiciously hostile preparations have been reported in South China. The capture of Hainan makes the job of aiding Viet Minh considerably easier since Ho Chi Minh controls much of the coast opposite that island.

Gen. Lin Piao, one of Mr. Mao's ablest military leaders, is reported both here and in Bangkok to have set up new headquarters in South China. He is organizing specially trained guerrilla bands there. Some fear that these units eventually may be turned over to Viet Minh.

Several Armies Built Up

In addition the Chinese have built up several large armies in the south. Although these still are understood to be concentrated about sixty miles from the Viet Nam frontier, it is believed that within four or five days a force of 50,000 could be assembled for an attack.

Likewise reliable information now has been received that increasing numbers of Soviet and Japanese type fighter planes are showing up in China from Soviet arsenals. While these aircraft are so far reported flying only in the vicinity of Shanghai and Nanking, numerous large shipping cases recently have been received in Canton and it is believed by some that they contain aircraft parts.

Soviet planes actually seen include MIG jets with sweptback wings and Japanese Zeros, presumably from those captured by the Soviet in Manchuria. It is understood that 2,000 Soviet technicians have been established in a special military mission near Hangchow.

Several hundred German specialists have been sent by the Russians to Wusih. The Soviet Union has built up an increasing number of radar stations manned by Soviet personnel. Loads of Soviet trucks and Bofors guns have arrived in Hangchow.

Formosa Attack Expected

While the French realize that most of this military preparation is probably linked first to the impending Chinese attack on Formosa and second to over-all tenseness occasioned by the "cold war," nevertheless it adds a point to pressure for more United States aid here.

The French feel they are the only fighting force on hand to oppose the extension of communism toward southeast Asiatic areas of vast interest to the entire North Atlantic community of nations. They argue they are protecting not just the French union in Indo-China but also Thailand, Malaya, Singapore, Indonesia and the Philippines. Therefore, they argue that the least Washington can do is make available more equipment and economic aid as speedily as possible.

French military leaders wish to be in a position to capitalize on recent gains brought about by victories in the Tonking area. They do not want to be restrained by lack of material from rapid progress. They fear the day when Ho Chi Minh receives not only more equipment but perhaps some kind of an air force from China and the Soviet Union. Viet Minh already has a serviceable airfield at Backan in Tonking. It could construct more strips or base planes in South China. Hainan could become the equivalent of a huge carrier.

The actual formula under which aid will be provided is not thought here to present any insuperable difficulties. Broadly speaking, a basic system already has been worked out. This provides that United States authorities should hand over military equipment here to a quadripartite board, including representatives from France and from each of the three Indo-Chinese states in the French Union—Viet Nam, Laos and Cambodia.

Control Issue Minimized

Previous arguments by certain Viet Nam leaders that this would allow France too much control of distribution recently have been toned down. The French feel they can work more easily with the new Tran Van Kuu Government than its predecessor under Nouyen Phan Long and that the new Cabinet will be more capable in all fields.

The basic formula covering American aid also would provide for deliveries of some small arms directly to the Indo-Chinese states for the purpose of equipping militia forces. This is considered urgently necessary. Some villages in the north are defending themselves against Viet Minh raiders with wooden spears.

Such militia equipment deliveries would be doled out gradually as required and would be checked carefully to prevent any of it from being smuggled to Ho Chi Minh's forces. In this respect the United States, remembering sad experiences in Kuomintang China, is especially sensitive.

Finally, economic aid would be handled on a more direct United States-Viet Nam basis than the military assistance program. However, efforts would be made to establish a quadripartite supervisory mechanism to prevent "Balkanizing" the area and to obtain maximum efficiency of coordination.

While a final accord on lines of this formula now is being reviewed in Paris, the main points have been more or less harmonized here after discussion with the Viet Namese by High Comissioner Leon Pignon and Edmund A. Gullion, energetic United States chargé d'affaires in Saigon. The emphasis of the French now appears to be even more upon speed and quantity of military assistance—above all, aircraft—than upon further argument about its means of distribution after arrival.

May 9, 1950

RED CHINA STEPS UP ARMS TO VIET MINH

By C. L. SULZBERGER
Special to THE NEW YORK TIMES

HONG KONG, May 15—Authoritative reports from Canton indicate that Communist China has stepped up the tempo of supplies being sent by land and sea to the Viet Minh rebels in Indo-China under an agreement between Mao Tse-tung and Ho Chi Minh. These reports have led to some conjecture about the possibility of a more formal military venture by the Chinese Communists in support of their ideological brother to the south.

Of course this type of speculation inevitably must remain in a vacuum until confirmed by events. It is hoped, but not necessarily believed, by observers here that the new and firmer United States attitude on Southeast Asia may influence the Communist leadership in Moscow and Peiping to avoid ventures that could lead to rapid deterioration in the already delicate world situation. Another strong United States declaration on Indo-China will shortly be made.

Since the Mao-Ho Chi Minh agreement dating from early this year, arms deliveries from China to the Viet Minh movement have been accelerated — especially this month. It is expected that the Communist capture of Hainan may facilitate this process. The existence of the Mao-Ho Chi Minh agreement was confirmed by the capture of some documents reporting decisions of an "Indo-Chinese Communist party" executive meeting that not only mentioned the accord but also expressed disagreement with Mao Tse-tung's "plan of operations."

Railway Being Constructed

It is reported that Soviet officers are now supervising Chinese deliveries to the Viet Minh. A railway is being constructed, believed under Soviet technical direction, from Luichow to Chen Nan Kuan, and will be completed by midsummer. Several South China airports, especially Kwangsi, are being modernized.

A large core of the Peiping Government's forces have been concentrated around Liuchow. The entire area south of there has been placed under highly restricted supervision. While the Chinese regime clearly needs troops to quell guerrillas in the Liuchow Peninsula and Pearl River areas (made up of remnants of Pai Chung-hsi's troops and bandits and pirates normal to the area), the assembled forces are too large for that purpose.

In addition to armies already disposed near Indo-China (army as a term is vague and exaggerated in China) the following forces could move south pretty quickly: the Fifty-second Army (Swatow), the Forty-fourth Army (Canton), the Forty-first Army, the Forty-second Army, the 123d Division, the 124th Division and the 125th Division.

There is no doubt that Mao Tse-tung's military position is becoming increasingly if gradually strong. It is believed that fifty Soviet LA-9 fighters and some Soviet jets have been received at Amoy Airport and that many of their pilots are Russian. As of the beginning of this month, it was known that at least fifty-five Soviet jets were in Shanghai and probably more were stored there in crates.

Gas From Western Sources

This Communist accretion of force comes not only from the Soviet bloc. Last month at least one shipment of aviation gas from Western sources was smuggled to Tientsin. A Philippine concern reportedly is offering for sale twenty-five United States fighters plus large quantities of rifles and ammunition to Peiping and guaranteeing delivery. United States citizens are said to be involved in these transactions. Spare parts for United States-type aircraft have been smuggled through both the Philippines and Hong Kong to China.

There is a slowly mounting fear among one segment of the Hong Kong's Chinese population, which had planned to sit out China's initial years of turmoil in this British colony. Many who fear this summer will produce the fall of Formosa and a more aggressive Communist drive into Southeast Asia now are planning to move to the Philippines or even farther abroad.

Various arguments exist con-

cerning the probability or improbability of Soviet-sponsored aggression in Southeast Asia—even despite stiffer United States support for that threatened area. It is said that th Japan and the Soviet Union have carried on large-scale campaigns in recent years under the guise of "incidents" instead of "wars," and perhaps they feel the same formula could be applied to attain their ends south of here.

Some military men believe the Soviet Union wishes to try out its jet aircraft operationally in the same fashion as various powers tested weapons on the proving ground of the Spanish Civil War.

Excessive Size of Missions

It is also argued by some that the excessive size of the Soviet military missions in Shanghai and Canton bodes ominously.

Other observers feel that the strains of internal revolution in China might make the focusing of attention on an external action a welcome political diversion. Much grumbling continues about the latest wave of profit taxes (payable in the equivalent of United States dollar value) on Canton shops and businesses, forcing a new series of closings.

Only 100 of Shanghai's 500 Chinese banks remain open as a result of taxation and forced subscription to victory loans. Half of that remainder are applying for permission to close. Peasant opposition to Communist fiscal policies—as is normal the world over—appears to be increasing in violence.

It is said that some Chinese Communist leaders of a Nationalistic hue like Tung Pi-wu and certain military chiefs like Chen Yi believe that the resolving of

China's deteriorating economic crisis should have priority over anything else in Peiping. Their arguments are said to be in favor of partial demobilization and attempts at some form of political accommodation with the West.

Favor Preparation for Action

However, the "internationalists" who appear to control the party are said to oppose this and to have favored preparation for military action to divert public attention from local difficulties. Judging from all signs to date, this theory is dominant.

Of course the campaign against Hainan and the expected attack on Formosa may be as far as it is intended to go. But arms shipments to the Viet Minh, the Mao-Ho Chi Minh agreement and the physical preparations in the south leave open other possibilities.

There are entirely unconfirmable reports that Moscow is preparing for large-scale Communist strikes and demonstrations during the late summer in Hong Kong and Japan to support demands for British and United States evacuation of those positions.

However, in properly gauging importance of the facts reported, one must always recollect that where opposed by force, as in Berlin, Greece and Yugoslavia, the Soviet Union has at least temporarily abandoned actions that could lead to another world war. It is therefore possible that the new and firmer United States policy in Southeast Asia may forestall "formal" action.

It is also always possible that deliberately hostile maneuvers are being staged in this region with the purpose of diverting the emphasis of United States attention from

Europe and inducing it to spread its forces too thinly over too large a geographical perimeter.

There are some who argue that Moscow is too realistic to embark on a more aggressive policy in Indo-China or to permit China to do so; that it will merely step up arms and other aid to the Viet Minh continually to tie down France for an indefinite period and prevent her European rearmament and that of the North Atlantic Treaty forces.

At the same time it is held that Moscow is far more intent on the development of North China and not vitally interested presently in what happens to the south and to the populous Yangtze Valley. It is known that some factories have been transported from the south to the north and some Chinese technicians "kidnapped" and sent to northern cities.

In this connection there are three theories:
1. That Moscow wants the industrial north to expand production as swiftly as possible and eventually support the south.
2. That eventually it would like to incorporate that northern economy with that of the Soviet Union's maritime province into a Far Eastern Ruhr.
3. That during the period of years required to bring this about, it does not matter particularly what "incidents" occur in south China that can serve as a buffer to the more valuable north.

If this line of over-all reasoning is correct, certain old China hands feel, Moscow will not allow Peiping to risk a real war over Indo-China but will, on the other hand, allow all sorts of adventurous policies to continue—judged, short of that fundamental risk.

May 16, 1950

French 'Invasions' of China Charged by Peiping Regime

HONG KONG, Nov. 23—Communist China charged officially tonight that French ground and air forces in Indo-China had carried out numerous "provocative invasions" of Chinese territory in the southern border provinces of Yunnan, Kwangsi and Kwangtung.

The Communist-dominated Peiping regime warned the French Government at the same time it would be held responsible for the consequences of alleged "shameless, barbaric behavior" of its troops. According to the New China News Agency, the Peiping regime has lodged a "stern protest" with the French.

The Chinese Communist news agency, in a Chinese-language broadcast received and translated here, attributed its dispatch on the Indo-China protest to an unnamed Foreign Office spokesman. He was said to have listed the alleged border violations dating from Dec. 14, 1949, to last Oct. 31.

"Our border defense troops have been instructed to hold the frontier firmly and to deliver counter-blows to the provocateurs," the agency said in reporting the spokesman's comments. The Communist news service said he added that the Chinese People's Republic reserved the right to "ask

for compensation for losses sustained by the Chinese people and present other demands."

The Peiping regime's new propaganda pressure on the French with regard to Red China's southern border follows a long series of Peiping blasts leveled against "American and British imperialists" in connection with Formosa, Manchuria and Tibet. In an English language broadcast tonight, the Peiping radio charged a total of 218 United States planes had crossed the Korea-Manchuria frontier and "intruded into Northeast China" thirty-three times in the five-day period from Nov. 15 to 19.

The Chinese Communists, who are still reported to be supplying and training Ho Chi Minh's Vietminh insurgents, charged that the alleged French air and land "encroachment" on Chinese territory over the eleven-month period had caused "heavy losses to Chinese

lives and property." Their Foreign Office spokesman said this had "exposed the French Government's imperialistic intention to be hostile to the Chinese people." He maintained that the Chinese people were "indignant" over what he termed the "bloodthirsty atrocities" involving "armed provocation," bombing and strafing.

Lists Alleged Incidents

The spokesman listed the following alleged incidents from Dec. 14, 1949 to Aug. 31, 1950:

Kwangtung—a ground force incursion resulting in the killing and wounding of twenty-two persons; Kwangsi—twenty-two air violations with casualties of one killed and one wounded; Yunnan—two ground force incursions and a March 24 civilian junk incident involving the death of two persons.

Asserting that the French ground and air invasions had become "more intensified" during September and October this year, the spokesman catalogued the following additional alleged incidents for this sixty-one-day period:

Kwangtung—two cases of air violation; Kwangsi—eighteen air violations and thirteen ground incursions involving bombing, strafing and ground fire, with claimed casualties of thirty-one killed, nineteen wounded and more than 120 houses and a bridge destroyed; Yunnan—thirty air violations and ten ground incursions, with casualties of two killed and one wounded.

The spokesman also said French troops twice had aided Yunnan guerrillas in attacks on the Chinese Communist Army.

November 24, 1950

RED CHINA WAR AID TO VIETMINH LARGE

By HENRY R. LIEBERMAN
Special to THE NEW YORK TIMES.

SAIGON, Indo-China, June 28—Although Korean War demands have strained the Chinese Communist supply capacities, the Peiping regime is reliably reported to be continuing supply of arms, ammunitions and military equipment to Ho Chi Minh's Vietminh Army in Indo-China.

This aid is reaching these Communist-led insurgents by sea from Hainan Island and by land from South China where the training of Vietminh troops is also said to be continuing.

In the multi-national military circles here, there are varying estimates on the current volume of Chinese Red assistance; some observers remark that the Korean War has obviously placed a premium on Chinese instructors as well as Chinese arms. It was suggested in these quarters that the Vietminh radio's recent emphasis on the prospects of a "long war" might be related to new supply difficulties.

Nevertheless there is general agreement that the military aid already delivered to Ho Chi Minh from Red China has given the Vietminh Army greater striking power since last fall. According to French sources, the Chinese Communist aid to the Vietminh Army up to June 1 has included:

1. Equipment for three divisions, some heavy equipment for two additional divisions and artillery, engineering and communications equipment for a number of non-divisional units.
2. Supplies of ammunition, food and clothing.
3. Training of troops, non-commissioned officers and officers at camps in Yunnan and Kwangsi Provinces, with some officers also being trained in Canton and Peiping.
4. Attachment of Chinese advisers, staff specialists, instructors, truck drivers and radio operators to various Vietminh Army echelons in Indo-China. This Chinese "complementary staff" has been estimated at 4,000 to 6,000 persons.

Such assistance has not given the Vietminh Army anything resembling the firepower of the French-Bao Dai forces, which are receiving American military aid.

At the same time Red China's help is credited with having enabled the insurgents to increase their officers corps, improve their supply organization and maintain five shock-troop divisions in the field for offensive operations. Besides being increasingly well equipped, the regular Vietminh Army in North Vietnam (Tongking) seems, as the result of more training and more expert staff work, also to be increasingly skillful in the deployment of its divisional formations.

The Vietminhese are largely dependent on outside sources for heavy equipment. Thus the material aid from China is evidently an important factor in the size and effectiveness of their regular forces.

French sources estimate there are now 125 regular Vietminh battalions totaling 138,000 men — eighty-four battalions in Tongking, twenty-one battalions in Central Vietnam and twenty battalions in South Vietnam.

The insurgents are believed to have had thirty-two regular battalions in the spring of 1949 and seventy-two in the spring of 1950.

June 29, 1951

DULLES WARNS RED CHINA NEARS OPEN AGGRESSION IN INDO-CHINA

PEIPING ROLE CITED

Secretary Reveals That Chinese Are in Action —Retaliation Hinted

By WILLIAM S. WHITE
Special to The New York Times.

WASHINGTON, April 5—The United States warned the Chinese Communists today that they were approaching a form of undisguised aggression in Indo-China that might bring major retaliation.

John Foster Dulles, Secretary of State, emphasized again and again the Administration's grave view concerning the position in Asia. He appeared before the House Foreign Affairs Committee to support the new Mutual Security Program.

Mr. Dulles made public a fresh, top-secret United States intelligence report that Chinese Communists had been identified in actual combat alongside the Communist-led Vietminh in Indo-China.

He made it plain that the United States was in urgent consultation with other free peoples in the Indo-China theatre in an effort to draw up, if need be, a free-nation front against the fall of Indo-China.

He spoke of "united action" and declared that, as of now, he could only "deprecate" suggestions that the United States would intervene, alone if all else failed, to hold Southeast Asia from Communist imperialism.

Nowhere did he totally and finally exclude such intervention if it came to that as the only way to save the free world's position in Asia.

Secretary Accuses Peiping

In a statement that combined a world review and an appeal for Congressional approval of continued military and economic aid to the free world, Mr. Dulles accused Communist China of "intensifying Communist aggression in Indo-China."

In the questioning period that followed he read off in support of this charge a document that, as he put it, told "an ominous story." The document presumably had just been cleared through this country's highest strategic body, the National Security Council, of which President Eisenhower is chairman. It follows:

"Most recent advices with respect to extent of Communist Chinese participation in the fighting at Dienbienphu [the presently vital position in Indo-China] indicate the following:

"1. A Chinese Communist general, Li Chen-hou, is stationed at the Diebienphu headquarters of General [Vo Nguyen] Giap, the Vietminh commander.

"2. Under him there are nearly a score of Chinese Communist technical military advisers at headquarters of General Giap. Also, there are numerous other Chinese Communist military advisers at division level.

"3. There are special telephone lines installed, maintained and operated by Chinese personnel.

"4. There are a considerable number of 37-mm. anti-aircraft guns radar-controlled at Dienbienphu, which are shooting through the clouds to bring down French aircraft. These guns are operated by Chinese.

"5. In support of the battle there are approximately 1,000 supply trucks, of which about one half have arrived since March 1, all driven by Chinese Army personnel.

"6. All the foregoing is, of course, in addition to the fact that the artillery, the ammunition and equipment generally comes from Communist China."

Mr. Dulles added parenthetically that some of the artillery had come from the Skoda Works in Communist - held Czechoslovakia.

Before the information on the Chinese Reds' assistance to the Vietminh, the United States had made no secret of the help it was sending to Vietnam, Laos and Cambodia.

This help included B-26 light bombers, C-119 transport planes, supply parachutes, napalm or jellied gasoline, landing ships for amphibious operations in the swampy delta country, ammunition, medical supplies and other matériel.

The United States also has provided, in response to French requests, technicians to instruct the French and Vietnamese in the use of equipment supplied under the military aid program.

Representative Albert P. Morano, Republican of Connecticut, demanded whether the evidence of direct Chinese Communist participation in the Indo-China aggression was not enough to bring into play the Administration's threat of instant and massive retaliation against major aggression.

Mr. Dulles was careful in his reply, but firm. He recalled that in a speech in St. Louis last September he had warned that the Chinese Communists could not undertake in Indo-China the kind of assault they had undertaken in Korea "without grave consequences which might not be confined to Indo-China."

This declaration was in substance that the Chinese might in these circumstances draw a counter-attack not on their position in Indo-China but on mainland China itself.

In the St. Louis speech Mr. Dulles had specifically mentioned the dispatch of Communist "armies" into Indo-China as the sort of act that might bring "grave consequences" outside Indo-China.

Recalling this address, Secretary Dulles told Representative Morano that while "technically" the Chinese Communists had not done precisely the thing he had warned them against, they were "coming awfully close to it."

He used much the same expression, again without elaboration, in a colloquy with Representative Walter H. Judd, Republican of Minnesota.

"What you have said about the active intervention of the Chinese Communists can only mean that they don't take you seriously," Dr. Judd said.

"About a year ago the President said that if the truce in Korea merely allowed the Communists to increase their fighting in Indo-China it would be a fraud. It seems they think the President was bluffing and that they are prepared to call his bluff and get away with it."

Mr. Dulles replied that the President had not said quite this, though he had warned against a new Chinese Communist aggression elsewhere. The Secretary then added: "I believe they are skirting very close to doing the kind of thing against which the President gave that warning. They are not perhaps openly and flagrantly committing aggression, but they save themselves from that charge only by technicalities.

"They, of course, claim that this is not aggression; that they are only aiding patriots in carrying on a civil war for their independence. * * * They are coming awfully close to the line the President laid down."

Dulles Prodded on U. S. Plans

Representatives James G. Fulton, Republican of Pennsylvania, suggested that Mr. Dulles really was saying about this: that if the menace in Southeast Asia "became serious enough, we will act —alone or with others."

"Not quite that," replied Mr. Dulles. "You say, 'alone.' This threat is to many countries. I would deprecate 'action of the United States alone.'"

"But," persisted Mr. Fulton, "does your statement rule it out?"

"It does not rule it out." said Mr. Dulles. "The only thing I am talking about now is united action."

After a subsequent, closed-door conference between Mr. Dulles and the committee, the acting chairman, Representative John

M. Vorys, Republican of Ohio, commented that "united action" could be taken inside or outside the United Nations.

Action outside the United Nations, of course, would imply a concert between the United States and the allied nations in Asia, of whom Australia and New Zealand are among those bound to this country in a defensive alliance.

Mr. Dulles declined to answer in public a committeeman's question as to whether he proposed to have the United States take the Indo-China crisis to the United Nations.

Mutual Aid Needs Stressed

The Secretary's prepared statement was built around the urgency, as the Administration saw it, of early Congressional action for a continued Mutual Security Program for the fiscal year beginning July 1.

No details of this request in terms of total money were given, but earlier Administration budget estimates had indicated that Congress would be asked for $2,500,-000,000 in new money, or what is called obligational authority, for military aid to friendly countries and approximately $1,000,000,000 for economic and technical assistance.

There remains unspent in this military-economic-technical fund more than $9,000,000,000.

Actual spending for the new fiscal year, that is, in new money and from money already in the till, is expected to run about $5,400,000,000 as against $5,500,-000,000 for the fiscal year now about to end.

It was not certain, however, that these figures, the latest officially given out, would remain unchanged. For one thing, Mr. Dulles spoke of a plan to spend in aid of the French in Indo-China about what is being spent in this fiscal year—approximately $785,000,000.

All that he said otherwise, however, suggested that spending in that critical theatre would not necessarily be measured by such things as budget estimates and that the United States was profoundly unlikely to "economize" there in the middle of a military crisis.

Special to The New York Times.

PARIS, April 5—Secretary of State Dulles' statement that Chinese Communists were participating in the Vietminh action against Dienbienphu received partial confirmation here today. Officials said it had been known that for a long time the Chinese had been present at all echelons of the Vietminh Army, including command headquarters.

Mr. Dulles' assertion that Chinese were manning Vietminh anti-aircraft batteries was neither confirmed nor denied. Sources did say, however, that there had been a considerable increase in the deliveries of Chinese war equipment to Vietminh in recent weeks and it was possible a number of "technicians" were provided along with it.

April 6, 1954

U. S. URGES ALLIES TO BACK WARNING TO CHINESE REDS

Asks Britain, France, Thailand, Australia, New Zealand and Philippines to Join in Move

DULLES TALKS TO ENVOYS

Diplomatic Circles in Paris Call Indo-China Step Good Gamble, Others Fear It

By WALTER H. WAGGONER
Special to The New York Times.

WASHINGTON, April 6—The first step toward possible "united action" against Chinese Communist intervention in Indo-China has been taken by the United States.

The State Department has suggested to six other allies, European and Asian, that they join in a common warning against further aggression by Communist China in any part of Southeast Asia.

April 6, 1954

212

The countries that have received this proposal, in talks here extending over the last several days, are Britain, France, Australia, New Zealand, the Philippines and Thailand.

The State Department answered "no comment" when asked about reports of the proposed joint declaration, but other diplomatic sources left no doubt that the suggestion had been made.

Henry Suydam, State Department news chief, declined to discuss reports of the proposed action, which have come from London, Paris and Canberra, Australia, but he confirmed that John Foster Dulles, Secretary of State, had consulted as recently as yesterday with diplomatic representatives of the six other governments "on the general situation confronting Southeast Asia."

[Diplomatic circles in Paris viewed the Dulles proposal on Indo-China as a justifiable gamble. Other quarters in France were alarmed. Only light action was reported from besieged Dienbienphu.]

Dulles Speech Here Cited

The proposal for a joint declaration followed Mr. Dulles' statement in New York March 29 that the "imposition" of the Communist political system on Southeast Asia "by whatever means, would be a grave threat to the whole free community."

"The United States feels that the possibility should not be passively accepted, but should be met by united action," the Secretary declared.

And yesterday, further setting the stage for some kind of joint effort, Mr. Dulles told the House Foreign Affairs Committee that the Chinese Communists were "coming awfully close" to a new aggression in Indo-China.

As indications mounted in support of Mr. Dulles' warning of "united action," diplomatic sources began to wonder whether United States policy might not have taken a new turn since last Feb. 10.

On that day, facing a news conference, President Eisenhower said that no one could be more bitterly opposed than he to United States involvement in a hot war in Indo-China. He said so far as it was humanly possible, he would make certain that it did not happen.

At the same meeting, the President later said he could not conceive of a greater tragedy for the United States than to get heavily involved, particularly with large units, in an all-out war in that region.

But on the basis of statements and communiqués going back more than two years, the United States and its Western Allies have long held the threat of counter-attack over Peiping should the Chinese Communists openly enter the Indo-China conflict.

The most recent was Mr. Dulles' speech of last Jan. 12, when he reiterated his warning in St. Louis last September that, "if there were open Red Chinese Army aggression [in Indo-China], that would have 'grave consequences which might not be confined to Indo-China.'"

There have also been these other suggestions that the Allies would act in unison against Chinese Communist intervention in Indo-China, or any other weak spot in Southeast Asia.

A Western Big Three foreign ministers' communiqué issued here last July 14, declared that "an armistice in Korea must not result in jeopardizing the restoration or the safeguarding of peace in any other patr of Asia," and that the fight of the three Associated States of Indo-China against "aggressive communism is essential to the free world."

In may, 1952, while the Truman Administration was still in power, Mr. Dulles asked an audience in Paris, in words very much like those he has used more positively since he became Secretary of State, whether it was not time for the Chinese Communists to know that if they sent their forces into Indo-China, "we will not be content to meet their armed forces at the point they select for their aggression but with retaliatory action of our own choosing."

And in January, 1952, during the United Nations General Assembly meeting in Paris, John Sherman Cooper, a United States delegate, served notice that any further Communist aggression in Southeast Asia "would, in the view of my Government, be a matter of grave concern which would require the most urgent and earnest consideration by the United Nations."

That statement of intentions promptly got the support of the British and French delegations.

April 7, 1954

The New York Times   *April 8, 1954*

EISENHOWER EXPLAINS DANGER TO STRATEGY: Loss of Indo-China to the Communists, the President told his news conference yesterday, would imperil the military position of the free world in the Far East (cross-hatching) and threaten its vital resources there.

April 8, 1954

FRANCE HOLDS UP REPLY TO U. S. BID

Cabinet Said to Prefer Action at Geneva on Warning to the Chinese Reds

By HAROLD CALLENDER

Special to The New York Times.

PARIS, April 7—The French Cabinet decided at a meeting today to postpone its reply to the United States proposal for a joint warning to Communist China against further intervention in the Indo-Chinese war.

The ministers seemed inclined to do everything possible to save besieged Dienbienphu and asked for more United States planes, tanks and artillery. But they appeared disinclined to join in the proposed diplomatic action pending the Geneva conference on Korea and Indo-China due to open April 26.

The Cabinet was reported to believe that if the Geneva talks failed to yield results France would then have to ask the United States to assume greater responsibilities for the defense of Indo-China and to agree to the "internationalization" of the war that the French so far have opposed.

Reluctance to anticipate this eventuality, even by a joint declaration of several nations, appeared reflected in a statement reported to have been made to the Cabinet by Marc Jacquet, Minister for the Associated States. He was quoted as having said that no French or French Union troops in Indo-China had yet come into contact with any Chinese soldiers.

This statement did not conflict with Secretary of State Dulles' assertion that Chinese troops were manning the anti-aircraft batteries of the Vietminh, but French officials have steadily shown reticence about the increasing Chinese participation that Mr. Dulles emphasized.

Press Silent on Dulles

The statements by Mr. Dulles about Chinese combatants at Dienbienphu were kept out of the Vietnamese press on order of the French High Commissioner, according to a dispatch from Hanoi by the French news agency France-Presse. The dispatch said the Vietnamese radio was forbidden to broadcast comments made in Europe and the United States on the Dulles statements.

It was understood that at today's Cabinet meeting the view was expressed that the declaration proposed by the United States had better be made at Geneva in the presence of the Russians and the Chinese than before that meeting. It was suggested that such a timing would be more effective and less dangerous than making the declaration now.

There were renewed indications that the French ministers were counting on negotiations over Indo-China at Geneva with the Russians, Chinese Communists and the United States on the assumption that an agreement would involve concessions on both sides. Mr. Dulles has ruled out recognition of Peiping as such a concession but the French have emphasized that he did not rule out, or indeed mention, concessions regarding trade with Communist China.

The French Foreign Office revealed yesterday morning that the United States had proposed a joint declaration, although official confirmation of it has not yet come from Washington. The reason for this French action was not wholly clear, but the result was to alarm many Frenchmen and this did not facilitate a favorable reply from the Paris Government.

April 8, 1954

EDEN ASKS DULLES TO DEFER WARNING TO PEIPING ON ASIA

By DREW MIDDLETON
Special to The New York Times.

LONDON, April 12—Britain urged Secretary of State Dulles today to accept Western unity of intention and action at the Geneva conference as an interim substitute for his proposal for an immediate warning to the Communist bloc against further aggression, in Southeast Asia.

Diplomatic circles, both United States and British, believe that Mr. Dulles has modified his original suggestion of a Western declaration of "united action" in advance of the Western powers' meeting with the Soviet Union and Communist China in Geneva two weeks from today.

Anthony Eden, British Foreign Secretary, stressed his Government's view that priority in Western planning for the time being must go to the preparation of a united front for the coming conference. But the United States delegation has been told emphatically that Britain is just as aware of the dangers of Communist success against the French in Indo-China as is the Administration in Washington.

Should the Communists block progress toward a peaceful settlement in Geneva, Britain would be willing to join in a warning declaration and discuss the form and extent of a defensive alliance in Southeast Asia, official sources assert.

[In Paris, where Mr. Dulles will go Tuesday to continue his Far East talks, a Cabinet crisis arose. Without Cabinet approval Georges Bidault, French Foreign Minister, signed an agreement with Britain on the European army, and several Ministers threatened to resign.]

Talks Are Expanded

The United States-British talks, which appear to have expanded well beyond their original scope, opened in the morning with a discussion of the border disputes between Israel and Jordan.

Mr. Eden and Mr. Dulles considered how best to bring representatives of Israel and Jordan together at a conference where their differences could be discussed in a calmer atmosphere than would be possible in public proceedings.

Both Mr. Dulles and Mr. Eden favor the establishment of a small working party of the United Nations Security Council to consider the dispute between two Middle East nations, it was reported. The quarrel already has reached the Security Council, which has before it complaints from both sides. Israel has been sensitive about cooperation with the Mixed Armistice Commission, a Foreign Office official said, and Jordan has rejected an Israeli request to attend a conference under the armistice agreement.

Under the Israeli-Jordanian agreement, attendance at an armistice review conference called by either side is mandatory, as is the United Nations Secretary General's obligation to summon it.

In the afternoon the United States delegation of Mr. Dulles, Douglas MacArthur 2d, Counselor of the State Department; Livingstone T. Merchant, Assistant Secretary for European Affairs, and Winthrop W. Aldrich, United States Ambassador to Britain, finally got to the meat of the present conference: the dispute about the approach to the Indo-Chinese question.

Mr. Eden headed the British group, which included the Foreign Office's two Ministers of State, Selwyn Lloyd and the Marquess of Reading, and W. D. Allen, Deputy Under Secretary for Far Eastern affairs.

There will be a third meeting tomorrow morning and there was an important but informal discussion tonight at Ten Downing Street, where Prime Minister Churchill entertained Mr. Dulles and Mr. Eden at dinner.

This is some distance from the original intention of the Secretary of State. But at the moment it appears to be the best he can get before the meeting in Geneva.

However, it is believed the Secretary of State and his lieutenants are satisfied by the British willingness to join in a defense organization for Southeast Asia and to use the British Government's influence with the two commonwealth nations — Australia and New Zealand—that are prospective members of the organization.

The only stipulation the British raise is that the establishment of this organization be preceded by close consultation among the nations involved.

Although Mr. Lloyd refused to indicate the policy the Government was advancing in the present talks, Labor members through the device of asking questions of intricate construction, were able to put their party's views before Parliament during the day.

Sir Richard Acland asked the Government to avoid any arrangements with Mr. Dulles "by which we threaten the Chinese" or joining the United States in the killing of "large numbers of people by hydrogen or atomic bombs."

Woodrow Wyatt asked the Government to make it clear to the Secretary of State that the issue in Indo-China was not between Communists and the West but between the "Nationalists who have been captured by the Communists and the French, who will not give their country independence."

214

Today's discussions of what the West could and could not do in Indo-China developed differences between the British and United States approaches to this problem but they also demonstrated to Mr. Dulles the extreme concern the British Government felt over the situation in Indo-China.

Mr. Eden insisted the British Government felt it would be playing into the hands of the Communist bloc to prejudice whatever slight chances of success there might be in Geneva by issuing such a declaration as Mr. Dulles had proposed. The British repeatedly made the point that in the opinion of the Conservative Government the immediate task for the West was the coordination of policy for the Geneva conference.

The details of a three-power approach to the conference are to be worked out at talks among representatives of the United States, France and Britain opening in Paris Wednesday.

It is expected that the London part of Mr. Dulles' visit will end with the issuance of a short statement emphasizing United States-British solidarity and referring firmly to the need to maintain freedom in Indo-China, something the British have never doubted.

April 13, 1954

CHOU WARNS U. S. AT GENEVA PARLEY TO GET OUT OF ASIA

Premier Says Peiping Won't Tolerate Violation of Its Territorial Integrity

DULLES BARS RED'S PLAN

Calls Proposal of Nam Il to Unify Korea a Move to Gain Control of the Peninsula

By C. L. SULZBERGER
Special to The New York Times.

GENEVA, April 28—Communist China accused the United States today of having violated China's territorial integrity and warned that this would not be "tolerated."

In his first speech before the Geneva conference and in the Western World, Peiping's Premier and Foreign Minister, Chou En-lai, assumed a role for his country of sharp belligerence. His words were angry even if they were read in a quiet, indeed monotonous, high-pitched voice.

Mr. Chou asserted that the United States had occupied Formosa in June, 1950, and that this was Chinese territory.

He proposed that "all foreign military bases in Asia be removed, foreign armed forces stationed in Asian countries be withdrawn, the remilitarization of Japan be prevented and all economic blockades and restrictions be abolished."

Later a spokesman from the Chinese Communist delegation clarified this implied demand in alleging that the United States had "more than several hundred military bases in Japan."

Deliberately Timed

The Chinese revolutionary's address clearly was deliberately timed to come as a direct and immediate rebuttal to Secretary of State Dulles and the United States position. Mr. Dulles and his Government have withheld diplomatic recognition from Peiping, kept it out of the United Nations and relegated it to a status here lower than that of the Big Four powers.

The Secretary of State had announced his intention yesterday of addressing the nineteen delegations now considering means of formalizing a peace in Korea. Mr. Chou gave no advance notice of his wish to speak, but he had obviously been saving a prepared text.

Mr. Dulles carefully reiterated the United States position on Korea. He called upon the conference to demonstrate the "strength of honorable and nonaggressive purpose" in order to force a just peace and to avoid the Communists' efforts to benefit from their attack against the Republic of South Korea and the will of the United Nations.

The Secretary of State laid great stress upon the fact that what was at stake in this issue was not merely Korea but "the authority of the United Nations."

Thus opened the great debate between the enemy powers. It was conducted with impassive diplomatic nicety. Neither statesman regarded the other as he read his manuscript into the microphone before his desk. During a brief interlude each ignored the other in the antechamber where refreshments were served. But the implications were strong and angry. Neither speaker sought to disguise deep-seated resentment.

Mr. Chou strayed from the subject of Asian peace to that of the European Defense Community and the hydrogen bomb—on each of which he echoed the Moscow position.

Mr. Dulles spoke first. He rejected the Communist proposals for a Korean unification solution as set forth yesterday by Gen. Nam Il, North Korea's Foreign Minister.

North Korea proposed all-Korean elections under the supervision of a commission composed of representatives chosen by the Parliaments of North and South Korea. South Korea asked that elections be held only in North Korea.

The Secretary said there was no need for a new peace plan since the United Nations General Assembly resolution, of Oct. 7, 1950, was still applicable. This provided for the holding of elections supervised by the United Nations in Korea.

Mr. Dulles said this resolution "established a commission to complete the unification of Korea by observing elections in that part of Korea where observed elections have not yet been held."

"That part of Korea," to which Mr. Dulles referred is North Korea.

Recalls Other Negotiations

The Secretary recalled that for seven years the Western Big Three had been seeking to negotiate German unification and Austrian liberation with the Soviet Union without success. From this, he observed, "nothing has been accomplished, but something has been learned."

What has been learned, he said, is what motivates Soviet Communist policy—"largely influenced by the fear of freedom. The Communist ruling class believes that a society is most peaceful and most productive if its members conform to a pattern which is prescribed by rulers possessed of absolute power. This inherently involves a suppression of freedom, for freedom implies diversity, not conformity."

"But it is not enough that freedom be suppressed within what is now the Soviet orbit," the Secretary added. "Freedom is contagious. Accordingly, freedom outside that orbit can not be acquiesced in. The area of suppression must be constantly expanded in order to preserve the existing area of suppression."

Fitting into this over-all political scheme the Communist aggression in Korea, Mr. Dulles warned that "Communist doctrine authorizes accommodation when the opposition is strong. It is our task here to show such strength of honorable and nonaggressive purpose that the Communists will find it acceptable to grant unity and freedom in Korea."

The Secretary described the North Korean plan as a scheme to gain control of all Korea similar to the Soviet attempt to gain control of all Germany by its proposals last February at the Berlin conference.

Reminding his audience of the heavy casualties suffered by United States soldiers defending the United Nations cause, he said, "the United States must reject that proposal because it does not meet the requirements of a free, unified and independent Korea, for which so much blood has been expended and suffering endured."

While Mr. Dulles was talking, two members of the Chinese delegation went forward to advise the day's chairman, Anthony Eden, Britain's Foreign Secretary, that Mr. Chou wished to speak. During the Secretary's address Mr. Chou busily took notes.

In his speech Mr. Chou noted that this was the first time his Government's Foreign Minister had met with those of the Big Four and he thought the very fact of the Geneva conference "signifies in itself the growing possibility of settling international disputes by the peaceful means of negotiations."

However, from that point on he unleashed a series of accusations against the United States as seeking to dominate Asia and obstruct the Asian peoples' movement for "national liberation."

He insisted that the United States and South Korea had "forcibly retained more than 48,000 Korean and Chinese war prisoners" and Peiping "in no way considers this question closed."

April 29, 1954

Troops Are Withdrawn by Chiang From All Blockade Bases but One

Special to THE NEW YORK TIMES.

HONG KONG, Wednesday, May 17—Chinese Nationalists have withdrawn from all except one of their blockading bases along the China coast, apparently for a last stand on Formosa.

Chiang Kai-shek's headquarters announced last night the withdrawal of 150,000 troops from the Chusan Islands in the past four days. These islands have been the Nationalists' naval and air base for blockading the mouth of the Yangtze River and the city of Shanghai.

Other reports said Mansan Island, guarding the approaches to Canton also had been evacuated. A broadcast from Peiping said Tungshan Island, opposite Formosa, had been captured by Communist amphibious forces last Thursday night.

Apart from Formosa and the neighboring Pescadores Islands, the only territory remaining to the Nationalists appears to be Quemoy Island, off Amoy. Last night the Nationalist Army headquarters on Formosa announced that Quemoy would be held and the blockade continued despite the mass withdrawals of the past few days.

The maneuver was made in conformity with the "needs of the over-all strategy in our anti-Communist war," the announcement by the Nationalist General Staff said. The retreat was effected to "deal a heavier blow to the enemy at the most favorable time and place," it was added.

Communists have been massing for an assault on both Chusan and Mansan Islands. The Nationalist withdrawal was made to "smash the scheme" of the attacking Communist armies, Formosa said. Coastal steamers arriving here reported sighting a heavily laden convoy of sixteen Liberty ships and other vessels leaving Chusan over the week-end.

In addition to the troops, part of the civilian population was evacuated from Chusan, the official Nationalist report said. This probably referred primarily to dependents and officials. Also abandoned was the air base at Tinghai on Chusan from which many devastating air raids had been launched against Shanghai.

The crew of the British coastal steamer Ethel Moller had previously told how their commandeered ship had been used for the evacuation of Tungshan Island. Apparently aware of the impending Communist assault, 2,000 troops boarded a Nationalist L. S. T (Landing Ship, Tank) last Thursday afternoon, they said. Another 150 boarded the Ethel Moller to escape the attackers.

According to Peiping, resistance on Tungshan collapsed in nine hours. The attacking troops were part of Gen. Chen Yi's Third Field Army, which is slated to make the assault on Formosa.

Irregular Troops Left

Press reports from Macao quoted travelers from Mansan Island in the Pearl River delta as saying that withdrawal from that Nationalist base began Sunday. Evacuation apparently was completed the next day, with only irregular troops left behind.

The British ship that sighted the convoy off Chusan said Nationalist gunboats still were patrolling the mouth of the Yangtze, with a British warship on watch just outside territorial waters.

The Nationalists' jitters on the remaining islands in their hands were highlighted with the announcement of new measures to try to entice the Communist underground to come into the open.

According to the official Central News Agency, the Generalissimo's son, Chiang Ching-kuo, as director of the Defense Ministry's political department, has given members of the underground two weeks to give up. If they send in by mail the names of their superiors and colleagues, as well as a pledge of their withdrawal from the Com-

NATIONALIST SETBACK

munist party, they will not be arrested and will be allowed to continue in present jobs, "other than spying for the Reds," the report asserted.

A large number of high ranking Nationalists are believed to have been executed recently as an aftermath to the mass arrests of men and women in all branches of the Nationalist Government and armed forces. Official figures are not available but those arrested are believed to number more than 1,000, including a number of assistants to American and other foreign correspondents.

May 17, 1950

FLEET GUARDS FORMOSA

By ANTHONY LEVIERO
Special to THE NEW YORK TIMES.

WASHINGTON, June 27—President Truman announced today that he had ordered United States air and naval forces to fight with South Korea's Army. He said this country took the action, as a member of the United Nations, to enforce the cease-fire order issued by the Security Council Sunday night.

Then acting independently of the United Nations, in a move to assure this country's security, the Chief Executive ordered Vice Admiral Arthur D. Struble to form a protective cordon around Formosa to prevent its invasion by Communist Chinese forces.

Along with these fateful decisions, Mr. Truman also ordered an increase of our forces based in the Philippine Republic, as well as more speedy military assistance to that country and to the French and Vietnam forces that are fighting Communist armies in Indo-China.

After he had started these moves that might mean a decided turn toward peace or a general war, the President sent Ambassador Alan G. Kirk to the Russian Foreign Office in Moscow to request the Soviet Union to use its good offices to end the hostilities. This was an obvious proffer of an opportunity for Russia to end the crisis before her own forces might get involved.

Door Opened for Russia

In the capital this was regarded as being at once a possible face-saving device for Russia in a showdown crisis and a feeler to determine her intentions.

The decisions amounted to a showdown in the "cold war" with Russia, in which this country has at last decided to begin shooting in a limited area. Yet all the decisions followed a carefully worked out formula of action within the framework of the United Nations, as well as unilateral moves that avoided any direct provocation of the Soviet Union.

Mr. Truman based the decision to fight for the South Koreans entirely on the Security Council resolution which called upon all members of the United Nations to help carry it out. And at the Pentagon it was explained that our air and naval forces would fight only below the Thirty-eighth Parallel line that divides South Korea from the Russian-sponsored North Korea.

"The Security Council called upon all members of the United Nations to render every assistance to the United Nations in the execution of this resolution," Mr. Truman stated. "In these circumstances I have ordered United States air and sea forces to give the Korean Government troops cover and support."

Russia Is Not Mentioned

Mr. Truman carefully avoided mentioning Russia in his statement. He pivoted today's great shift in United States foreign policy on a conclusion that the "cold war" had passed from an uneasy passive stage to "armed invasion and war." He blamed "communism."

"The attack upon Korea makes it plain beyond all doubt that communism has passed beyond the use of subversion to conquer independent nations and will now use armed invasion and war," he said. "It has defied the orders of the Security Council of the United Nations issued to preserve international peace and security. In these circumstances the occupation of Formosa by Communist forces would be a direct threat to the security of the Pacific area and to United States forces performing their lawful and necessary functions in that area."

President Truman took the unusual action of virtually ordering the Chinese National Government to cease its air and sea operations against the Chinese mainland. He tersely stated that the Seventh Fleet "will see that this is done," adding that the future status of Formosa would have to await peace in the Pacific, or a peace settlement with Japan, or United Nations action.

In many major speeches Mr. Truman has not hesitated to name Russia as the country that had obstructed peace efforts in the United Nations through her use of the veto or the boycotting of its meetings.

In military parlance, the term "cover and support" used by Mr. Truman as missions for our forces means that they would seek to destroy any North Korea air, ground or sea forces, as well as their installations, that are encountered below the Thirty-eighth Parallel. They would do the same in support of any counter-offensive that the South Korea forces might be able to mount.

Thus the complexion of the Korean situation was changed overnight. Yesterday officials were inclined to see South Korea, with her small, poorly equipped forces, as good as lost. It was acknowledged, as President Syngman Rhee of South Korea had complained, that aid in the form of munitions and supplies was "too little and too late."

Victory Is Seen for South

Today the view was that American air and naval forces could assure overwhelming superiority to South Korea and bring victory, unless, of course, Russia similarly aided North Korea.

The decisions were made last night in Blair House and before the night was over the coded action orders were being radioed to Gen. Douglas MacArthur in Tokyo and to other pertinent places. The formula encompassing all the action, it was learned authoritatively, began to take shape Sunday night in the first Blair House conference and it was custom-tailored for the resolution that the United States representative was directed to introduce in the Security Council meeting that night.

The correlated diplomatic action in Moscow was announced this afternoon by the State Department. Ambassador Kirk delivered a note, the text of which was not published.

Lincoln White, State Department press officer said:

"The Embassy asked that the Soviet Government use its influence with the North Korean authorities for the withdrawal of the invading forces and the cessation of hostilities."

President Truman was gratified with markedly good reaction that followed news of his decisions. There was typical bipartisan support as in other great emergencies that have faced the country, and Mr. Truman was particularly pleased with the message he received from Gov. Thomas E. Dewey of New York, his opponent in the Presidential race of 1948. He promptly sent a grateful reply. As one White House official expressed it, "there was a wonderful closing of ranks."

The unity on the political front was more than matched among the high civilian and military leaders of the nation who made the recommendations for action. Mr. Truman, before he even left his home in Independence, Mo., on Sunday to cope with the crisis, had formed a determination to do something drastic, something that would be neither appeasement nor merely passive. Both Defense and State Department officials, it was learned, worked with great harmony and easy agreement on the recommendations that were drawn up to meet his basic requirements.

Secretary of State Dean Acheson was said to have been a strong hand in working out the diplomatic requirements, both as to Moscow and the Security Council, and in urging the use of force. Those at the fateful council with the President in his home at Blair House last night were the same that met with him Sunday, after his hurried return from Independence.

They were Mr. Acheson, Philip C. Jessup, Ambassador at Large, John D. Hickerson, Assistant Secretary of State for United Nations Affairs, and Dean Rusk, Deputy Under Secretary of State; Louis Johnson, Secretary of Defense; Gen. Omar N. Bradley, chairman of the Joint Chiefs of Staff; Gen. J. Lawton Collins, Army Chief of Staff; Gen. Hoyt S. Vandenberg, Chief of Staff of the Air Force; Admiral Forrest P. Sherman, Chief of Naval Operations; Frank C. Pace Jr., Secretary of the Army; Thomas K. Finletter, Secretary of the Air Force; and Francis P. Matthews, Secretary of the Navy.

The proposed actions—air and naval support for South Korea to enforce the United Nations resolution and the decision on Formosa establishing unilaterally a line of

WHERE TRUMAN ORDERED ACTION IN FAR EAST

The New York Times — June 28, 1950

The President has directed United States planes and warships to go to the assistance of South Korea (1) and ordered the Seventh Fleet to prevent any Communist attack on Formosa (2). Reinforcement of United States forces in the Philippines (3) and speedier military aid to that country and to Indo-China (4) were also set in motion by the President. The Seventh Fleet has been reported in the area south of Okinawa (cross).

United States defense in the Western Pacific—were already familiar. Mr. Truman canvassed the situation once again from every possible angle and then made his decisions. That, in brief, was the story of the meeting as told by one familiar with it.

This morning Secretary Johnson, Stephen T. Early, the Deputy Secretary of Defense, and Generals Bradley and Collins went to the President's office before 10 A. M. and apparently reported that the orders had gone out,

Then in mid-morning, before the announcement was made to the world, Mr. Truman summoned Congressional leaders and members of the committees dealing with foreign affairs in the Senate and the

House. There were Republicans and Democrats, including Speaker Sam Rayburn, Senator W. Scott Lucas, the Senate Majority Leader, and Senator Tom Connally, chairman of the Senate Foreign Relations Committee, and John Kee, his opposite number in the House.

Secretary Johnson said, as the President's statement indicated, that none of our ground troops would be committee in the Korean conflict.

President Truman, as if to inspire confidence and calm in public, walked instead of drove to Blair House.

He lunched with his Cabinet. Eight were present, Maurice J. Tobin, Secretary of Labor, being out of town.

Fleet to Quit Formosa at End Of Korea War, Says Truman

By ANTHONY LEVIERO
Special to THE NEW YORK TIMES.

WASHINGTON, Aug. 31—President Truman expressed the hope today that Communist China would not intrude in the United Nations effort to establish peace in Korea and asserted the Seventh Fleet would be withdrawn from Formosa when the Korean conflict was settled.

Thus the Chief Executive enunciated in a new form this country's assurance that it has no territorial or other designs on Formosa.

The position on the delicate Formosa issue has been that the United States was merely neutralizing that strategic island until its legal status could be settled peaceably by the countries that would participate in a Japanese peace settlement. Then United States concern would end.

Today's assertion by Mr. Truman that the Seventh Fleet would be withdrawn at the end of the Korean war raised the possibility of restoring the status quo ante before a peace settlement, if the Korean war should end before the treaty is settled.

The President echoed Dean Acheson, the Secretary of State, in expressing the hope that Communist China would keep her armies out of the Korean conflict. In a news conference yesterday Mr. Acheson said this country was making it plain in every possible way that this country had no aggressive intentions toward China or any other country in the Far East.

The related questions of Korea and Formosa came up together in Mr. Truman's news conference today.

"Mr. President, how great do you regard the danger of Red China becoming involved in the action in Korea?" a reporter asked.

Mr. Truman replied that he hoped there was no great danger of such involvement in the United Nations action to establish peace in Korea.

The next question referred to the letter embodying Formosa policy that Mr. Truman wrote to Ambassador Warren R. Austin, United States representative in the United Nations, as a result of the contrary position suggested by Gen. Douglas MacArthur in a message to the Veterans of Foreign Wars. That message, withdrawn at the President's request, implied that this country should insist on holding Formosa as a United States base. The question follows:

"Mr. President, in your message on Sunday you gave as one of the reasons for neutralizing Formosa the fact that a conflict between the Chinese Communists and the Chinese Nationalists there might threaten the security of the United Nations forces operating in Korea or even might lead to an extension of the Korean war to the Pacific area. Does that mean that when peace and security are restored in Korea by the United Nations forces, the United States Seventh Fleet will be withdrawn from the Formosan Strait?"

The Formosan situation was set out in his several messages, the President replied, and it was one that would be settled in the Japanese peace treaty with the Allies who fought in the Japanese war and those nations that have occupation forces in Japan now.

Of course, he added, it would not be necessary to keep the Seventh Fleet in the Formosa Strait after the Korean conflict was over; its presence there was a flank protection on this country's part for the United Nations forces fighting in Korea.

In the Senate, Kenneth S. Wherry of Nebraska, Republican floor leader, declared that Mr. Truman was "engaging in wishful thinking" if he thought the Chinese Communists would not attack Formosa as soon as the American fleet was withdrawn. He also asked whether the President's statement meant this country would give the Nationalist forces no help if the Chinese Communists attacked.

Mr. Truman declined to say anything more about the MacArthur incident, reiterating that he considered it closed. In reply to a question whether the United Nations ground forces would not go beyond the Thirty-eighth Parallel in fighting the North Korean Communists, Mr. Truman said he could not answer the question.

He likewise said he was unable to say anything about the report brought to him from Tokyo by General J. Lawton Collins, Army Chief of Staff, and Admiral Forrest P. Sherman, Chief of Naval Operations.

Today Ambassador V. K. Wellington Koo, Chinese Nationalist Ambassador, conferred with Secretary Acheson reporting on the situation in Formosa.

He told reporters that the Formosan people would support the Chiang Kai-shek Government if the Communists invaded their island. Asked about a report that the Chiang Government would seek a $35,000,000 loan here, Dr. Koo said the report was not official but that such a request was being considered.

September 1, 1950

PESCADORES FORM FORMOSA BULWARK

By HENRY R. LIEBERMAN
Special to THE NEW YORK TIMES.

MAKUNG, the Pescadores Islands, Nov. 22—The Chinese Nationalists hold the Pescadores, the Chinese Communists want them and the United States Seventh Fleet is standing guard to preserve the status quo as part of Washington's "neutralization of Formosa" policy.

As measured in terms of their natural resources the sixty-four coral islands that make up the Pescadores group are hardly worth all this attention. The total area is no more than fifty square miles. A population of about 80,000 ekes out a poor existence by fishing and growing short kaoliang, sweet potatoes, and peanuts on the porous sandy soil.

Neither the Chinese Nationalists, the Communists nor the Seventh Fleet, however, is interested in these islands because of their intrinsic wealth. Their interest stems basically from the fact that the Pescadores—or Penghu Islands, as the Chinese call them—have considerable strategic importance.

Facilitate Reconnaissance

Lying in the Strait of Formosa about seventy-five miles off southern Formosa, the Pescadores stand athwart the Chinese Nationalists' last remaining lifeline. Besides their key significance for the defense of Formosa, these islands also facilitate reconnaissance along the China coast and help the Nationalists to interdict coastal shipping carrying priority cargoes of value to the Chinese Communists.

The Japanese, who held the Pescadores from 1895 to the end of the war with the Allied powers in 1945, developed a large naval base here at Makung. The base was capable of handling vessels up to 20,000 tons.

Like Formosa itself, the Pescadores are now under the protection of the Seventh Fleet's Task Force 72—a group of patrolling ships and planes commanded by Capt. John F. Greenslade. The Chinese Nationalist forces committed to the defense of the islands include a naval squadron and troops under the command of 46-year-old General Li Chen-ching, a Shantung man.

The Pescadores garrison, which consists of soldiers who arrived here from Tsingtao and Shanghai in the spring of 1949, is built around North China troops with a creditable battle record. According to military observers the fortifications and other defense preparations on the islands are also well above the average.

Living Standards Deteriorate

Maj. Gen. Wu Ching-yung, Chief of Staff of the Makung headquarters, said that United States aid of wheat and flour had been coming in from Formosa to provide the northern troops with the kind of basic food to which they are accustomed. Some Economic Cooperation Administration aid also has been given for health, construction and repair projects designed to improve the civilian standards of living.

Although the E. C. A. has helped to restore part of the old ice-storage facilities and concerned itself with the repair of the fishing equipment, the total fish catch is still far below the catch in Japanese times.

A number of motor fishing vessels have been commandeered by the military to ferry troops and supplies among the various islands. Furthermore, security measures limit the time that fishing vessels can spend at sea.

Overall efforts are now being made in Formosa and the Pescadores to increase the fish catch. For the island inhabitants here this would mean the restoration of lost income. For the Nationalist soldiers it would mean much needed improvement in their present diet.

STRATEGIC ISLANDS

November 23, 1951

U.S. SAID TO RAISE FORMOSA ARMS AID

Current Grants to Nationalists Will Total $400,000,000, 80% for the Military

By HENRY R. LIEBERMAN
Special to THE NEW YORK TIMES.

TAIPEI, Formosa, Jan. 30—United States military and economic assistance to Chinese Nationalist Formosa for the fiscal year 1953-54 is scheduled to total about $400,000,000, according to an authoritative estimate here.

While economic aid will remain roughly the same, the cost of this year's military aid program is unofficially estimated at about $80,000,000 more than last year's. An informed source said the higher figure was due largely to new shipments of jet aircraft and "certain other items."

The current program, administered here by the Mutual Security Mission of the Foreign Operations Administration, is said to involve an outlay of $106,800,000. Of this amount about $30,000,000 represents "common use" shipments of commodities, supplies and equipment allocated to the Nationalist military establishment.

Arms Aid Four-fifths of Total

Military aid accounts for about four-fifths of the total program. In addition, the Nationalist military establishment is drawing on counterpart funds, that is, local funds accruing from the sale of commodities for civilian use imported under the economic assistance program. It is estimated that about 45 per cent of the total counterpart funds will go this year of military projects.

The cost of supporting the Nationalist military establishment of between 550,000 and 600,000 men remains the dominant characteristic of the economic picture here. With large-scale imports of military aid requiring extra expenditures of local currency, the Central Government is borrowing money from the Bank of Taiwan (Formosa) to cover a budgetary deficit directly attributable to its own military outlays.

Wholesale prices rose by about 15 per cent last year. Notwithstanding inflationary pressure, United States officials here regard present economic conditions as being relatively good in relation to existing problems. The consensus is that there has been a steady trend toward increased stability.

Formosa produced bumper crops of 1,640,000 tons of rice and 880,000 tons of sugar last year, while industrial production was about 20 per cent higher than in 1952. The peak electric power load is said to be 280,900 kilowatts, compared with 230,000 kilowatts in 1952 and 152,000 kilowatts under Japanese rule, before 1945.

Textile Output Increasing

Although Formosa still requires raw cotton imports, a new, privately operated textile industry of 170,000 spindles is supplying most of the textile needs of the island's population. Priority also is being given to expanding plant capacity in the production of chemical fertilizers.

Sugar exports are serving as the leading producer of foreign exchange. Formosa's "ordinary" foreign trade amounted last year to the equivalent of $230,363,000, and there was a favorable trade balance of about $29,000,000.

Meanwhile, the Government has completed distribution of land under its reform program. Absentee landlords who were required to sell their holdings have been, or are being, compensated in bonds and stocks in Government corporations.

Despite its gains, it is generally acknowledged here that Nationalist Formosa is by no means in a position to do without United States aid while it continues to support its present military establishment. Last year there was considerable talk of a "four-year program" aimed at making the island relatively self-supporting, but the United States thus far has not underwritten the economic costs of such a program.

A basic question still remains unanswered with regard to the goals of United States aid. While United States officials tend to think in terms of building the economy to a point where the need for assistance will no longer exist—or at least virtually disappear—the Chinese Nationalists think in terms of eventually returning to the mainland. Specific long-range economic planning is difficult under such circumstances.

January 31, 1954

FORMOSA CAPTURE IS URGED BY CHOU

Chinese Red Leader Calls for Determined Action in Report Adopted by Top Council

By WILLIAM J. JORDEN
Special to The New York Times.

TOKYO, Aug. 13—Communist China's Government Council has approved unanimously a suggestion by Chou En-lai, Premier and Foreign Minister, that determined action be taken to "liberate" Formosa.

The Peiping radio announced this morning that Mr. Chou made his suggestion as part of a foreign policy report at a council meeting Wednesday. The Premier, who recently returned from the Geneva conference, spoke before the country's top leaders, including Mao Tse-tung, chief of state.

There has been an increasing volume of threats to Formosa in Red China's propaganda releases.

Mr. Chou said the "liberation of Taiwan" [Formosa] would be "an exercise of China's sovereignty, and it is China's own internal affair." He said the Government would not tolerate foreign interference in its attempts to capture the island off the mainland.

This was an obvious warning to the United States, which has assigned its Seventh Fleet to prevent attacks on the Nationalist China stronghold.

In a direct reference to reports that the United States was considering a mutual defense pact with Nationalist China, Mr. Chou warned:

"Any treaties concluded between the United States Government and the traitorous Chiang Kai-shek group entrenched on Taiwan would be illegal and without any validity whatever. If any foreign aggressors dare to prevent the Chinese people from liberating Taiwan, if they dare infringe upon our sovereignty and violate our territorial integrity, if they dare to interfere in our internal affairs, they must take upon themselves all the grave consequences of such acts of aggression."

It was recalled here that in 1950 Mr. Chou made a similar bristling speech in which he warned that Communist China would not sit by idly if "foreign aggressive forces" approached its borders. Soon afterward, when United Nations and South Korean troops crossed the Thirty-Eighth Parallel and moved toward the Yalu River, Chinese Communist "volunteers" went into action in Korea.

Much of Mr. Chou's report dealt with results of the Geneva conference and the Indochina settlement. Throughout, he repeatedly attacked the United States as the only major threat to peace.

He said the Peiping Government had four major tasks in the foreign policy field. They were:

1. To strive with other nations concerned to insure implementation of the Indochina peace settlement and to seek peaceful settlement of the Korean question.

2. To liberate Formosa.

3. To strengthen its relations of "peaceful cooperation" with other nations.

4. To "strive for the establishment of collective peace in Asia."

The Chinese leader declared that talks were going on in Washington and Taipei for a treaty of mutual security. He said the United States also was trying to "whip together a so-called Northeast Asia defense alliance composed of Japanese reactionaries, the Syngman Rhee clique and the traitorous Chiang Kai-shek."

Chou charged that United States naval and air forces had been assigned to "put up a continuous show of force and make provocations along the borders of our country." These are "desperate measures of perpetual enmity against the 600,000,000 people of our country," and are "clearly provocations of extreme gravity," he added.

August 14, 1954

U. S. AND FORMOSA SIGN DEFENSE PACT

Special to The New York Times.

WASHINGTON, Dec. 2—The United States and Nationalist China signed today a mutual defense treaty. The pact pledges their common efforts toward "the preservation of peace and security" in the Far East.

Each country declared that an armed attack on the other's territory would be regarded as "dangerous to its own peace and safety," and that each would "act to meet the common danger in accordance with its constitutional processes."

Seated before cameras and microphones in the State Department's fifth floor reception room, Secretary of State Dulles signed for the United States and George K. C. Yeh, Nationalist Chinese Foreign Minister, for the Formosa Government.

After the ceremony, Secretary Dulles said in a brief prepared statement that he concurred in a message sent yesterday by President Chiang Kai-shek stating that "a necessary link in the cnain of Far Eastern defense has now been forged."

'Sooner Than Expected'

"It is my hope," Mr. Dulles declared, "that the signing of this defense treaty will put to rest once and for all rumors and reports that the United States will in any manner agree to the abandonment of Formosa and the Pescadores to Communist control. The signing of this treaty is an expression not only of the good-will and friendship existing between the Governments of the United States and of Free China, but also of the abiding friendship of the people of the United States for the Chinese people."

Mr. Yeh replied:

"It has been my privilege and honor to be associated with Mr. Dulles in the making and signing of this treaty of mutual defense between my country and the United States of America. I am happy to recall that throughout the negotiations for this treaty, conducted at Taipei and Washington, we have been guided by the principle of mutuality and the spirit of friendly cooperation.

"It is the hope of my Government that this treaty will serve to promote the common cause of freedom, particularly at this juncture of the world situation."

Mr. Dulles then shook Mr. Yeh's hand and said:

"It is a very happy day."

"It comes sooner than we expected," the Foreign Minister replied.

The treaty will become effective when approved by the Senate. President Eisenhower is expected to submit the pact to the Senate early next session. Little or no opposition is expected.

December 3, 1954

Text of Mutual Defense Treaty

WASHINGTON, Dec. 2 (P)— Following is the text of the mutual security treaty signed today by the United States and Nationalist China:

The parties to this treaty,

Reaffirming their faith in the purposes and principles of the Charter of the United Nations and their desire to live in peace with all peoples and all governments, and desiring to strengthen the fabric of peace in the West Pacific area,

Recalling with mutual pride the relationship which brought their two peoples together in a common bond of sympathy and mutual ideals to fight side by side against imperialist aggression during the last war,

Desiring to declare publicly and formally their sense of unity and their common determination to defend themselves against external armed attack, so that no potential aggressor could be under the illusion that either of them stands alone in the West Pacific area, and

Desiring further to strengthen their present efforts for collective defense for the preservation of peace and security pending the development of a more comprehensive system of regional security in the West Pacific area,

Have agreed as follows:

ARTICLE I

The parties undertake, as set forth in the Charter of the United Nations, to settle any international dispute in which they may be involved by peaceful means in such a manner that international peace, security and justice are not endangered and to refrain in their international relations from the threat or use of force in any manner inconsistent with the purposes of the United Nations.

ARTICLE II

In order more effectively to achieve the objective of this treaty, the parties separately and jointly by self-help and mutual aid will maintain and develop their individual and collective capacity to resist armed attack and Communist subversive activities directed from without against their territorial integrity and political stability.

ARTICLE III

The parties undertake to strengthen their free institutions and to cooperate with each other in the development of economic progress and social well-being and to further their individual and collective efforts toward these ends.

ARTICLE IV

The parties, through their foreign ministers or their deputies, will consult together from time to time regarding the implementation of this treaty.

ARTICLE V

Each party recognizes that an armed attack in the West Pacific area directed against the territories of either of the parties would be dangerous to its own peace and safety and declares that it would act to meet the common danger in accordance with its constitutional processes.

Any such armed attack and all measures taken as a result thereof shall be immediately reported to the Security Council of the United Nations. Such measures shall be terminated when the Security Council has taken the measures necessary to restore and maintain international peace and security.

ARTICLE VI

For the purposes of Articles II and V, the terms "territorial" and "territories" shall mean in respect of the Republic of China, Taiwan and the Pescadores; and in respect of the United States of America, the island territories in the West Pacific under its jurisdiction. The provisions of Articles II and V will be applicable to such other territories as may be determined by mutual agreement.

ARTICLE VII

The Government of the Republic of China grants, and the Government of the United States of America accepts, the right to dispose such United States land, air and sea forces in and about Taiwan and the Pescadores as may be required for their defense, as determined by mutual agreement.

ARTICLE VIII

This treaty does not affect and shall not be interpreted as affecting in any way the rights and obligations of the parties under the Charter of the United Nations or the responsibility of the United Nations for the maintenance of international peace and security.

ARTICLE IX

This treaty shall be ratified by the United States of America and the Republic of China in accordance with their respective constitutional processes and will come into force when instruments of ratification thereof have been exchanged by them at Taipei.

ARTICLE X

This treaty shall remain in force indefinitely. Either party may terminate it one year after notice has been given to the other party.

In witness whereof the undersigned plenipotentiaries have signed this treaty.

Done in duplicate, in the English and Chinese languages, at Washington on this second day of December of the year one thousand nine hundred and fifty-four, corresponding to the second day of the twelfth month of the forty-third year of the Republic of China.

For the United States of America: JOHN FOSTER DULLES.

For the Republic of China: GEORGE K. C. YEH.

December 3, 1954

100 Communist Planes Raid Nationalist Isles Off China

By The Associated Press.

TAIPEI, Formosa, Jan. 10—At least 100 Communist Chinese planes pounded the Tachen Islands from dawn until late afternoon today in one of the biggest air raids of the civil war, the Defense Ministry announced.

Nationalist defenders on the outpost islands 200 miles north of Formosa threw up fierce anti-aircraft fire. The defenders reported that two attackers were destroyed and two damaged. There was no indication whether Nationalist planes were engaged.

The Communists threw into the attack propeller-driven light bombers and fighter-bombers, which were escorted by at least twenty-eight swift MIG jet fighters, a communiqué said.

[The Peiping radio said Monday that three formations of planes had attacked Tachen harbor. It said one landing craft and "another naval vessel" had been destroyed and one landing craft and a supply vessel damaged. Reuters said Nationalist planes bombed Communist-held Tienao Island, fourteen miles north of the Tachens, and Red "warships" near Sungmen, southwest of the Tachens, early Tuesday.]

The Nationalist Defense Ministry reported more than 300 Red bombs were dropped but said most of them fell into the sea. It conceded, however, that there were "considerable" civilian casualties and said more than ten houses were destroyed. Emergency relief measures were ordered.

Seven Waves of Planes

The Ministry said only that military losses were being investigated. The estimated 20,000 defenders of the Tachens, northern anchor of the Nationalist offshore islands, are well dug in.

The raiders, in seven waves, came from the big network of Communist bases in the Shanghai-Hangchow-Ningpo triangle, 100

to 200 miles north of the Tachens, the Ministry reported.

The communiqué said eight La-11 fighter-bombers, four Tu-2 twin-engine light bombers and twelve MIG jets were in the first wave, which attacked at 6:55 A. M. All three types of planes are manufactured in the Soviet Union.

In the second wave were four La-11's and four MIG's. The third wave consisted of twelve La-11's and eight MIG's. Then came three waves of a total of forty Tu-2's. Their MIG escort, if any, was not given.

The final wave of four LA-11's and four MIG's flew over the Tachens at 4:23 P. M. All the

time, other MIG's at a great height were seen over the Tachens apparently observing the progress of the attack.

The Ministry said one of the downed attackers crashed south of Sanmen Bay, which is north of the Tachens, and the other plummeted into the sea southwest of the Tachens.

The Tachen attack is expected to be a subject of close consultation between the United States and Nationalist China. It is possible the Nationalists might think the situation called for their Air Force to raid the air bases on the mainland.

Unofficial quarters were convinced the Communist attacks

were intended as a pointed challenge to the United States, whose Seventh Fleet guards Formosa and the near-by Pescadores from invasion.

Some circles thought it possible the Communists had already refused the request of Dag Hammarskjold, United Nations Secretary General, for the release of eleven jailed United States airmen and deliberately planned today's attacks to emphasize an uncompromising, get-tough policy.

January 11, 1955

CHINESE REDS TAKE ISLE NEAR TACHENS IN SEA-AIR ASSAULT

By HENRY R. LIEBERMAN
Special to The New York Times.

HONG KONG, Jan. 18—The Chinese Communists announced tonight they had captured Nationalist-held Yikiang Island in an amphibious assault.

They reported the seizure of this outpost seven and a half miles northwest of the Tachens, off the Chekiang coast, in a landing operation that followed a heavy air bombardment of Yikiang and the Tachens. A Nationalist Defense Ministry communiqué said sixty Red aircraft dropped more than 200 bombs on these islands between 7:58 and 8:20 A. M. today.

[Secretary of State Dulles said in Washington Tuesday that the loss of Yikiang, a mile-long island, was of no particular importance. However, Defense Department officials viewed the capture of the island as portending an eventual Communist attack on the Tachens. Both Yikiang and the Tachens are outside the scope of the recently concluded mutual defense treaty between the United States and Nationalist China.]

According to Nationalist sources in Taipei, Formosa, the Communists attacked Yikiang with an invasion fleet of about seventy vessels.

Radio contact between Yikiang and Upper Tachen Island was broken at 6 P. M. Large fires on Yikiang were reported to have been observed from the Tachens.

Communist warships shelled fortified Upper Tachen Island at 1 P. M.

A Nationalist force estimated to total 2,000 guerrillas had been holding Yikiang. A regular Nationalist division consisting of 10,000 men is dug in underground on hilly Upper Tachen.

No details were available on the size of the Communist landing force.

[More than 200 Chinese Communist planes rained several hundred bombs on the Tachen Islands shortly after noon Wednesday, the Defense Ministry reported, according to The Associated Press.]

The attack on Yikiang marked the first substantial amphibious effort by the Communists since they touched off the present intermittent flare-ups along the southeast coast of China last September. It developed within the framework of a continuing "liberate Taiwan [Formosa]" propaganda campaign in China.

Yikiang is about 230 miles north of Formosa. It is eighteen miles off the Chekiang coast, but only five miles southeast of Communist-held Toumen Island.

The Peiping radio said the Communist assault force landed on Yikiang at 2 P. M. under cover of air and naval gunfire. It added that the Red troops also had had artillery support. According to the Nationalists, the latter support came from Toumen.

A Nationalist announcement

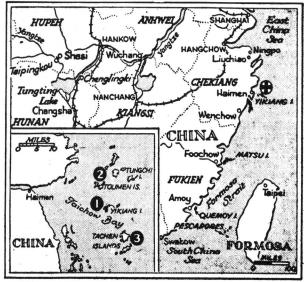

The New York Times   *Jan. 19, 1955*

Peiping announced the capture of Yikiang (cross on large map and 1 on inset) after a bombardment from Toumen (2). The Communists also shelled the Tachen Islands (3).

said ninety-six shells fell on Yikiang between 8:59 and 10:20 A. M. Later the Nationalist Defense Ministry said the guerrillas on the island were "fighting courageously" against the invaders. The Chinese Communists said the Yikiang battle ended "a little after 4 P. M."

In a short announcement on the Yikiang battle, the Peiping radio said "mixed formations" of planes participated in the morning air bombardment. The Nationalists asserted that the aircraft had included twenty-nine TU-2 bombers, twenty-three LA-11 and four Il-10 propeller driven fighters and four MIG-15 jet fighters.

These planes were said by the Nationalists to have come from Ningpo, ninety-five miles northwest of the Tachens. Two months ago, the Communists were reported building a closer air base at Liuchiao.

Today's Red air-force strike followed an air raid against the Tachens Jan. 10, the day Secretary General Dag Hammarskjold of the United Nations concluded his talks with Premier Chou En-lai in Peiping.

A dispatch from Taipei tonight said thirty ships had been spotted in the vicinity of Penshan Island, thirty-two miles southwest of the Tachens.

January 19, 1955

PRESIDENT SIGNS FORMOSA MEASURE; SEES PEACE GUARD

By ELIE ABEL
Special to The New York Times.

WASHINGTON, Jan. 29—President Eisenhower today signed the Congressional resolution endorsing his authority to defend Formosa at the risk of war.

The President's signature, at 8:42 A. M., gave the force of law to the joint measure passed last night, 85 to 3, by the Senate at his request. The House of Representatives had approved it on Tuesday, 409 to 3.

General Eisenhower hailed Congress' action as a step to preserve peace in the Formosa Strait by making it clear that the United States would fight, if need be, to help the Chinese Nationalists resist invasion from the Communist mainland.

"We are ready to support a United Nations effort to end the present hostilities in the area," he said, "but we also are united in our determination to defend an area vital to the security of the United States and the free world."

The President's emergency powers are to be invoked with orders to the Seventh Fleet to raise an air umbrella over the evacuation of Nationalist garrison troops from the Tachen Islands, 210 miles north of Formosa.

Islands Not Named

The Congressional resolution endorses the President's authority to secure and protect not only Formosa and the Pescadores Islands, which have been guarded by the Seventh Fleet since 1950, but also "such related positions and territories" as the Quemoy and Matsu Islands, off the Communist-held mainland.

These islands are not named in the resolution. They were omitted deliberately to leave the United States a measure of flexibility in any cease-fire talks, and to avoid entangling the United Nations Security Council in a jurisdictional squabble.

Although the Administration has never said so publicly, it recognizes that Quemoy and Matsu are unquestionably Chinese territory, unlike Formosa and the Pescadores, which belonged to Japan until the end of World War II.

Associated Press Wirephoto

FORMOSA RESOLUTION SIGNED: President Eisenhower signs resolution authorizing him to act in defense of Formosa. Standing are, from left, Senators Walter F. George and Styles Bridges; Secretary of State Dulles, and Senators William F. Knowland and Alexander Wiley.

High officials have indicated that the United States would not hesitate to end its protection of the offshore islands if the Communists, in return, would stop clamoring for Formosa and accept a cease-fire.

Senator William F. Knowland of California, Republican leader in the Senate, served notice today that the Administration—if it had some such barter arrangement in mind—could count on his determined opposition.

"I think it would be a sheer act of appeasement," he said.

Washington settled back for a week-end of watchful waiting after the President signed the Congressional authorization. He took off at 9:15 A. M. to play golf and rest in Augusta, Ga.

Secretary of State John Foster Dulles left about the same time for a week of fishing in the Bahamas. He had delayed his departure to witness the signing of the resolution.

The President's signature was needed to give the Congressional action force because it was a joint resolution of the House and Senate.

A joint resolution is commonly a legislative proposal involving a single matter that could not be considered a comprehensive law. The contents of some joint resolutions, however, are totally indistinguishable from the contents of bills. And, in practice, there is little distinction between a joint resolution and the usual bill.

Like a bill, a joint resolution becomes law when signed by the President or passed over his veto. An exception is a joint resolution proposing amendments to the Constitution. This does not require the President's signature.

A concurrent resolution, on the other hand, is not used to enact legislation and is not binding or of legal effect. It is passed in the form of a resolution of the chamber in which it originates with the other house concurring. It expresses only intent, purpose or sense. It is not submitted to the President for approval.

The decision whether a resolution is labeled "concurrent" or "joint" is made by the member of Congress who introduces it. As in the case of the Formosa resolution, some measures are drafted by the Administration for introduction.

The signature ceremony was attended by ten Congressional leaders and two Republican Governors, Paul Patterson of Oregon and Arthur B. Langlie of Washington, who had breakfast earlier with President Eisenhower.

The Congressional group included:

Senator Walter F. George, Democrat of Georgia and chairman of the Senate Foreign Relations Committee; Senator Knowland; Earle C. Clements, Kentucky Democrat and acting majority leader; Thomas C. Hennings Jr., Democrat of Missouri; Styles Bridges, Republican of New Hampshire; Alexander Wiley, Republican of Wisconsin, and Eugene D. Millikin, Republican of Colorado.

Also Representatives Joseph W. Martin Jr. of Massachusetts, Republican House leader; Carl Albert of Oklahoma, Democratic whip, and Carl Vinson, Democrat of Georgia, chairman of the House Armed Services Committee.

Twelve Pens Used

Seated at a round oak table with fifteen pens on it, the President used twelve to sign the resolution and distributed them to those present. He dipped a new pen in the ink bottle for each stroke. He put the three unused pens back in a box on his desk.

He wrote: "Approved: Dwight D. Eisenhower, Washington, D. C., 29 January, 1955."

Seeking to use one or two more pens, the President asked an aide, "What else can I put down here?"

Some one suggested he record the time. So the President added, "8:42 A. M." He went on to read this prepared statement:

"I am deeply gratified at the almost unanimous vote in the Congress on this joint resolution. To the members of the Congress and to their leaders here with me today I wish publicly to thank them for their great patriotic service.

"By their vote, the American people through their elected representatives have made it clear to the world that we are united here at home in our determination

to help a brave ally and to resist Communist armed aggression.

"By so asserting this belief we are taking a step to preserve the peace in the Formosa area. We are ready to support a United Nations effort to end the present hostilities in the area, but we also are united in our determination to defend an area vital to the security of the United States and the free world."

Opinion here is the next move should be left to the United Nations, now that the United States had made clear it would fight to hold Formosa and the Pescadores

Islands, even if this meant hitting the mainland or the offshore islands to break up an invasion force.

No official word has been received here so far of the Chinese Communist reaction to Britain's diplomatic campaign to win Premier Chou En-lai's cooperation.

The British efforts, however, aroused Senator Knowland's suspicions. Interpreting a speech yesterday by the British Foreign Secretary, Sir Anthony Eden, as part of the build-up for an agree-

ment with the Communists based on the surrender to them of the off-shore islands, Mr. Knowland said he was "deeply concerned," although the cease-fire move had his general approval.

He said he had discussed the matter with Mr. Dulles, but did not disclose the Secretary of State's position. In his own opinion, Mr. Knowland said, the time has come to stop thinking of cease-fire agreements "on terms that the Communists would lay down if they were victors."

January 30, 1955

FORMOSA HAS KEY ROLE IN U. S. PACIFIC STRATEGY

By HENRY R. LIEBERMAN
Special to The New York Times.

TAIPEI, Formosa, Jan. 29—There is general agreement between United States and Chinese Nationalist military men here on the strategic importance of Formosa and the Pescadores. But there is still a difference in the point of view on the matter of just how to deal with the over-all problem of China.

The Nationalists are not merely interested in defending Formosa and the Pescadores. They would also like to see these islands used as comeback bases for a United States-supported Nationalist counter-attack against the Chinese mainland.

While determined to defend Formosa and the Pescadores against Communist attack, the United States is eager to avoid war. At the same time, in all its tactical approaches to the Chinese problem, the United States—as a world power—must also be mindful of the attitudes of its various allies and the policies being pursued by them.

On the other hand, the basic aspiration of the Chinese Nationalists is an eventual return to the mainland of China. Although they must tailor their tactics in terms of the free world's urge to peace, it is plain that the Nationalists can now get back to the mainland only within the context of a larger Far Eastern conflict.

The Nationalists do not advocate war. They talk of "peace" too. But they are still betting that the East-West struggle is irreconcilable and that sooner or later the Communists will go too far.

In the meantime, they are determined to do all they can to

protect their seat in the United Nations and their claim to Chinese sovereignty as the Republic of China. Even if the Nationalists eventually have to accept a United Nations cease-fire effort, they will almost certainly resist any move to link a cease-fire with a "two-China" solution of the Chinese problem.

Life-or-Death Issue

Looked at from the Nationalist point of view, the defense of Formosa and the Pescadores is not merely a matter of strategy. It is a matter of life or death. Formosa is the Nationalists' last-ditch base. For them there is no other line on which to fall back.

Nor can the Nationalists look dispassionately or deal lightly with any proposal that they give up some of their offshore islands outside the primary Formosa-Pescadores defense complex. Some argue, for example, that if the United States is concerned with bases thousands of miles away it should not be difficult for the Americans to understand why the Nationalists are concerned with bases less than 250 miles away.

Having promised to "liberate" mainland China and defend what territory they now hold, the Nationalists are alive to the psychological as well as military implications of a retreat from the Tachen Islands, some 200 miles north of here. As for the present military argument, it was put this way by one of the leading figures in the Government here:

"Perhaps the Tachens are of little value in themselves. But if we abandon the Tachens, the

Communists will go next after Matsu Island—and so on."

No mention was made of either the Matsu or Quemoy Islands when President Eisenhower told Congress that defense of Formosa and Pescadores also made it necessary to take "account" of "closely related localities and actions." However, it is assumed here that these "localities" include Matsu, about 100 miles northwest, and Quemoy, about 120 miles west of Formosa.

Unless the Communists touch off a bigger war, it is highly unlikely that the United States would underwrite a Nationalist invasion of the mainland of China. But in the light of General Eisenhower's message to Congress, the United States is not about to turn Formosa and the Pescadores over to Red China.

President's Points

The President told Congress that the United States regarded it as "important" for Formosa and the Pescadores to remain in friendly hands. He summed up the strategic importance of these Nationalist-held positions as follows:

"In unfriendly hands, Formosa and the Pescadores would seriously dislocate the existing, even if unstable, balance of moral, economic and military forces on which the balance of the Pacific depends.

"It would create a breach in the island chain of the Western Pacific that constitutes for the United States and other free nations the geographical backbone of their security structure in that ocean.

"In addition this breach would interrupt north-south communications between other important elements of that barrier and damage the economic life of countries friendly to us."

Formosa and the Pescadores, then, are not being looked upon by the United States as an iso-

lated unit, but as part of a "balance" of strategic forces in the Pacific. The equation consists of a number of interrelated factors, and at this stage, the psychological factor is regarded by various observers here as no less basic than the purely military factor.

Whether the Korean war ended in a victory, a defeat or a draw, is a matter of debate. But the Indochina outcome in Vietnam was certainly no victory for the West, and whether it terminates in a stalemate seems to depend largely on the will of the South Vietnamese to resist communism.

When the United States signed an armistice in Korea, men who had fought the Communists longer in North Vietnam's Red River delta wondered why they should be expected to continue the fight there. If Formosa were turned over now to Red China, it is suggested here, the retrogression rate in Asia would be likely to develop in geometric rather than arithmetic proportions.

Psychologically, too, Formosa is ruled by a Chinese Government that represents the only Chinese obstacle, great or small as it may be, to a complete Communist sweep among the Chinese people. If the Communists displaced the Nationalists on Formosa, the question of whether Southeast Asia's "overseas Chinese" were for Generalissimo Chiang Kai-shek or Mao Tsetung would become virtually academic.

Militarily Formosa is part of a defensive chain that also includes the Philippines, Okinawa and Japan, with South Korea lying on the upper flank. How close the Philippines is to Formosa on the south, and Okinawa is to Formosa on the northeast was underlined in practical terms this week when United States jet fighter-bombers reached this island from both places in less than one hour's flying time.

January 30, 1955

EFFORTS TO HALT FORMOSA FIGHTING SUSPENDED BY U.N.

By THOMAS J. HAMILTON
Special to The New York Times.

UNITED NATIONS, N. Y. Feb. 14—The Security Council suspended today its efforts to stop the fighting between Nationalist and Communist China over the small islands off the China coast.

Communist China's rejection of the Council's invitation to send a representative to discuss the question was a principal reason for the Council's decision to adjourn without considering any form of resolution.

The Council did not fix a date for its next meeting. One can be called by Dr. Victor A. Belaunde of Peru, Council President for February, either on his own volition or at the request of any member.

Today's action leaves the way clear for what Henri Hoppenot of France called "traditional diplomacy" to take over, through either diplomatic exchanges or an international conference.

M. Hoppenot was the only Western member of the Council who said publicly that the Council should not go ahead with a discussion of the coastal island question in the absence of a Peiping representative.

A Bitter Soviet Attack

M. Hoppenot recalled that when the Council issued the invitation to Peiping two weeks ago it felt that "the situation could be examined appropriately only with the participation of all those who were most directly concerned in its peaceful settlement."

Arkady A. Sobolev of the Soviet Union was more explicit. After a bitter attack on United States "aggression" he told the Council, slowly and emphatically, that "it is impossible to solve international problems, especially in the Far East, without the participation of [Communist] China."

The only delegate who protested against the Council's failure to act was Dr. T. F. Tsiang of Nationalist China. He appealed to it to "muster enough courage to face the basic and monstrous fact of the aggression of international communism in the Far East."

Dr. Tsiang did not, however, introduce a resolution. Generalissimo Chiang Kai-shek said in Taipei, Formosa, today that the United Nations ought to impose sanctions against the Communists, but the mood of the Council was clearly against any kind of resolution that would irritate Peiping.

On the other hand, the Council voted down, 10 to 1, Mr. Sobolev's motion that it take up the Soviet demand for the ouster of United States and other "non-Chinese" forces from all the Chinese islands, Formosa included.

Two weeks ago the Council placed on its agenda both the coastal islands question and the Soviet proposal, which accused the United States of aggression, and invited Communist China to take part in the discussion of the coastal islands. At the same time, however, the Council decided that it would not take up the Soviet proposal until it had disposed of the coastal islands question.

Mr. Sobolev contended that the Council's failure to consider a resolution on the coastal islands meant that it had decided to do nothing. Therefore, he said it should immediately take up the Soviet proposal, which also called for the exclusion of Dr. Tsiang from the proceedings.

Mr. Sobolev's statement brought emphatic denials from Sir Leslie Knox Munro of New Zealand, who had submitted the question of the coastal islands to the Council as a situation threatening international peace and security, and from other western delegates.

Henry Cabot Lodge Jr. of the United States declared "it is clear that the Council has not completed its consideration of the New Zealand item."

"Indeed, it has hardly begun to do so," Mr. Lodge added.

From the outset most Council members had pinned their hopes of effecting an informal cease-fire on private talks with the representative to be sent by Communist China, rather than on a public debate.

The rejection of the invitation is generally interpreted as meaning that the Chinese Communists would not be satisfied with getting the coastal islands, which the Council majority was willing to hand over to them in return for a provisional agreement not to attack the Nationalists on Formosa and the Pescadores Islands.

In any event, most Council members felt that the Soviet Union would veto any resolution, even one expressing regret that the invitation had been rejected.

In effect, the Council is standing aside while Britain and India continue their efforts to arrange a settlement. One Western delegate said developments in London and New Delhi in the next two or three days would decide whether the Council would meet again.

In any event, the Council, at the suggestion of Sir Pierson Dixon, British representative, agreed without a vote to adjourn without taking any decision on the coastal islands.

February 15, 1955

EISENHOWER INSISTS U. S. WILL NOT HELP A CHIANG INVASION

By ELIE ABEL
Special to The New York Times.

WASHINGTON, March 2—President Eisenhower spoke out today against any claim by the Chinese Nationalists for United States help in invading the Communist mainland.

He also asserted that the West wanted peace in the Formosa Strait and could become embroiled in war only if the Communists forced it into war.

The President frowned when he was asked whether the United States had given Generalissimo Chiang Kai-shek any reason to expect moral and logistical support for a return to the mainland.

The Nationalist leader, in a filmed interview with Senator Margaret Chase Smith, Republican of Maine, televised last night, said he was preparing a "counter-attack" on the mainland and expected Washington to back him up.

"I thought that this whole thing had been discussed so thoroughly there could be no question of America's attitude in this matter," the President said.

"The United States is not going to be a party to an aggressive war," he added emphatically. "That is the best answer I can make."

The Nationalists, in fact, are bound by an exchange of notes that was appended to the recently ratified Formosa mutual defense treaty not to strike at the mainland without express approval from the United States and to refrain from the use of force except in self-defense.

The Administration, furthermore, has made clear its conviction that General Chiang could not mount a successful assault on the mainland out of his own resources on Formosa. The Generalissimo, nevertheless, keeps proclaiming his intention to recapture the mainland.

General Eisenhower's comment, which was made at his press conference this morning, did not appear to rule out aid to the Nationalists under any and all circumstances. Nor was he suggesting, officials here said, that any Nationalist attempt to invade the mainland would be an act of aggression.

His meaning, as interpreted by competent officials, was that only if the Nationalists made the attempt in response to, or as a consequence of, aggression from the Communist side would the United States consider helping them.

The President said earlier that he was not giving up on a cease-fire in the Formosa Strait. A reporter reminded him that a month had passed since Congress voted its endorsement of his authority to use United States air and sea power in defense of Formosa and that the cease-fire efforts had failed so far. He asked General Eisenhower if there was anything more the United States could do, or whether the decision of peace or war in the Far East lay with the Communists alone.

"You never give up in the pursuit of a legitimate and desirable objective merely because you are defeated the first time and discouraged," the President said.

He said Secretary of State Dulles was on Formosa meeting with General Chiang and that he might bring home to Washington "some new ideas or variations of ideas to put in our calculations."

But he acknowledged that the Communists would decide whether it was to be peace or war.

"The Western world wants peace in that area," he declared. "Therefore, the only way that we can be embroiled is through some action on the part of the opposing side."

March 3, 1955

DULLES WARNS RED CHINA FORCE WILL MEET FORCE

By ELIE ABEL
Special to The New York Times.

WASHINGTON, March 8 — Secretary of State Dulles warned Communist China tonight that the United States was no "paper tiger."

The tiger analogy is a favorite of Communist propagandists, who depict the United States as snarling bravely enough but in the end backing away from a fight. Mr. Dulles suggested that the American tiger still had powerful teeth and claws.

He put Peiping on notice that a resort to force might be countered by "the greater force that we possess."

The United States, he said, has "new and powerful weapons of precision, which can utterly destroy military targets without endangering unrelated civilian centers." The Secretary evidently was referring to tactical nuclear weapons that can be fired from cannon or dropped from fighter-bomber planes on the battlefield, rather than the city-destroying hydrogen bomb.

But Mr. Dulles, in a broadcast speech, again left shadowy the precise response of the United States to an attack on the Quemoy and Matsu Islands off the south China coast.

Essential Ingredients

President Eisenhower will decide that question, he said, "in the light of his judgment as to the over-all value of certain coastal positions to the defense of Formosa, and the cost of holding those positions."

The Secretary of Defense, Charles E. Wilson, also deferred to General Eisenhower when asked at his press conference whether the United States would fight to prevent Communist capture of the offshore islands. Mr. Wilson's reply was that the President would know whether or not to defend these positions.

Mr. Dulles took his radio and television audience on a tour of the troubled Asian horizon, retracing his two-week trip to seven countries, Burma, Cambodia, Formosa, Laos, the Philippines, Thailand and Vietnam.

Brave words and patriotism alone, he said, cannot preserve the freedom and independence of the small nations on Communist China's doorstep. The essential ingredients, Mr. Dulles added, are "the deterrent power of the United States and our willingness to use that power in reponse to a military challenge."

He said Peiping seemed determined to make such a challenge. The Communists at the same time were persistently trying to belittle the power of the United States and to cast doubt on its resolution, Mr. Dulles said.

Their propaganda portrayed the United States as a "paper tiger," one that "will always find reasons to fall back when faced by brutal and uncompromising power," Mr. Dulles said.

He cited Peiping's boasts of victory over the West in Korea and Indochina and in the bloodless evacuation of the Tachens by the Nationalist Chinese. While acknowledging that the United States had made great sacrifices and shown great restraint in the interests of peace, Mr. Dulles suggested that it might be unsafe for Peiping to assume "that our love of peace means peace at any price."

"We must, if occasion offers, make it clear that we are prepared to stand firm and, if necessary, meet hostile forces with the greater forces that we possess," he declared.

Congress' Action Praised

He described as a "big step in the right direction" the Congressional resolution that endorsed President Eisenhower's authority to defend Formosa and the Pescadores with the force of United States arms. Mr. Dulles said that that action, more than any other recent step, had inspired confidence among free Asians.

In the case of Formosa, he said, the question is not what to defend but how to defend it. He pointed out that by the terms of the recently ratified mutual defense treaty with Nationalist China, as well as the Congressional resolution, the United States was committed to defend Formosa and the outlying Pescadores Islands.

The resolution, however, permitted a flexible defense not necessarily confined to Formosa and the Pescadores themselves, Mr. Dulles said.

"How to implement this flexible defense of Formosa, the President will decide," he said, indicating that General Eisenhower would weigh the military and psychological value of the offshore islands such as Quemoy and Matsu against the cost of holding them.

He expressed the hope that Communist China's military activities were not the first stage of an attack against Formosa and that a cease-fire might be attained. Up to now, however, the efforts of the United Nations and of friendly nations to "find substance for these hopes" have been unrewarding, Mr. Dulles said.

Peiping seems determined to conquer Formosa, he declared, and the response of the United States to such a move "will have importance both to Formosa itself and to all the Southeast Asia and Pacific countries."

Appearing earlier in the day before the Senate Foreign Relations Committee, Mr. Dulles made these principal points about the outlook on Formosa:

¶The United States is not trying to use Quemoy and Matsu as bargaining counters for a cease-fire.

¶Apart from new gun emplacements on the mainland facing Quemoy, there are no signs of a Communist military build-up of the size that would be needed for an invasion attempt.

¶The pattern of the Communists' air operations up to now does not suggest an imminent invasion.

Mr. Dulles, in the closed door session, was pressed for details of his talks on Formosa last week with Generalissimo Chiang Kai-shek by Senators William F. Knowland, Republican of California, and Wayne Morse, Democrat of Oregon.

His Reply Is Guarded

His guarded reply evidently did not go much beyond his public statement at the end of the talks. Mr. Dulles also declined to go into detail about his discussions during the Bangkok conference of the Manila Treaty powers with Sir Anthony Eden, British Foreign Secretary, when questioned on this point by Senator Morse.

In his address tonight, Mr. Dulles said that subversion, rather than open aggression, was probably the greatest danger in Southeast Asia.

The Bangkok conference, he said, dealt with this problem as well as the related ones of improving economic and social conditions and strengthening the military defenses of the area.

To meet the military threat he declared, the eight signatory nations will rely mainly or mobile allied power to deter aggression rather than on large static forces. The United States contribution, he added, will be chiefly air and sea power.

March 9, 1955.

President Says Atom Bomb Would Be Used Like 'Bullet'

WASHINGTON, March 16—President Eisenhower disclosed today that atomic weapons would be used with "bullet" precision against military targets in the event of war. In any combat, "where these things are used on strictly military targets and for strictly military purposes, I see no reason why they shouldn't be used just exactly as you would use a bullet or anything else," he asserted.

Thus, he signaled the likelihood that any future conflict in which the country became engaged would be an atomic war with tactical atomic bombs and atomic artillery shells.

He emphasized use of the smaller atomic weapons on military targets only, as contrasted with such massive destruction weapons as the hydrogen bomb, which can wipe out whole cities.

According to Federal law only the President can make a decision on the use of atomic weapons.

His statement backed up the Secretary of State, John Foster Dulles, who yesterday outlined a pattern of using new atomic devices for pinpoint military retaliation anywhere in the world.

The twin statements by the President and Mr. Dulles were aimed at the Communists. Mr. Dulles indicated that it was up to Red China's leaders whether the tactical weapons would be used in the event of a Communist Chinese attack on Quemoy and Matsu Islands in the Pacific.

The President's response on the atomic weapons was based on a question at his news con-

225

'They Would Be Used'

He said he would not comment "in the sense that I would pretend to foresee the conditions of any particular conflict. * * *" But, he continued, the United States had been "active in producing various types of weapons ever since World War II.

"I believe the great question about these things comes when you begin to get into those areas where you cannot make sure that you are operating merely against military targets. But with that one qualification, I would say, yes, of course, they would be used."

Later he observed that the possibility of war was greater than in his younger days when "we were raised in an atmosphere of complete confidence." As a result greater time and effort must go into maintaining armed forces.

This, he said, was one of the reasons "that the great policies of any enlightened nation must be producing of conditions that will be more peaceful."

The President also viewed adequate defense as "one of the most serious problems facing us today." It is "all the more serious because it is one of those facts that human beings just rather recoil from looking squarely in the face," he said.

"I have one great belief: nobody in war or anywhere else can ever make a good decision if he were frightened to death.

"You have to look the facts in the face but you have to have the stamina to do it without just going hysterical."

Report Called Reassuring

He recalled the Atomic Energy Commission's report on lethal fall-out from a hydrogen bomb explosion and observed that "it was intended" to be reassuring and not terrifying.

The President appeared before newsmen in a chocolate brown suit with a double-breasted jacket and without a trace of the cold that has bothered him in recent days.

He referred a question on whether the hydrogen bomb exploded in the Pacific a year ago was a super H-bomb to Lewis L. Strauss, Chairman of the Atomic Energy Commission.

Mr. Strauss responded in a statement that A. E. C. comment on speculation about nuclear weapons "would provide a prime method whereby unfriendly powers could derive details of our weapons and our means of defending ourselves."

The A. E. C., he said, would adhere "to a policy of not commenting in reports and speculation regarding the composition of weapons" in the interest of national defense and security.

At the same time, he said, the commission was progressively making available to the public more information dealing with research and power reactors and other facts of atomic energy for peaceful uses.

March 17, 1955

PRESIDENT SHUNS STAND ON QUEMOY

By ANTHONY LEVIERO

WASHINGTON, March 23— President Eisenhower reiterated today this country would not use atomic weapons in a "police action" but declined to predict how he would characterize a fight over Quemoy and Matsu.

Again the President refused to disclose whether this country would fight for those Chinese offshore islands.

The guessing over Quemoy and Matsu was resumed in the President's news conference.

The evidence indicated that the Administration had added the term "measured retaliation" to "massive retaliation" as a concept of foreign policy discussion.

"Measured retaliation" appears to be the official title for the less-than-massive retaliation expounded last week by Secretary of State Dulles. The President followed up with a similar thesis.

Hope of Limiting War

Under this concept it is hoped to limit war by employing small or tactical atomic bombs, as Mr. Dulles said, against strictly military targets. It is being discussed with particular reference to the touchy Far Eastern situation. The "massive retaliation" strategy evidently would be reserved for a general or world war.

General Eisenhower was reminded that he said on Jan. 13 that atomic weapons would not be used in a "police action." He replied that a police action was not war but a restoring of order. He went on to say that war was a resort to force for reaching a decision in a particular area.

"And whether the war is big or not," the President said, "if you have the kind of a weapon that can be limited to military use, then I know of no reason why a large explosion shouldn't be used as freely as a small explosion."

He explained that was what he meant last week when he said small atomic weapons might be used exactly like bullets against strictly military targets.

Again the President spoke against indiscriminate use of atomic weapons, declaring: "I repeat, the concept of atomic war is too horrible for man to endure and to practice, and he must find some way out of it. That is all I think about this thing."

A reporter asked:

"If we got into an issue with the Chinese, say, over Matsu and Quemoy that we wanted to keep limited, do you conceive of using this specific kind of atomic weapon in that situation or not?"

"I must confess I cannot answer that question in advance," the President replied.

President Eisenhower went on to say there were two factors about war. The first was that the only unchanging factor in war was human nature.

"And the next thing is that every war is going to astonish you in the way it occurred, and in the way it is carried out," the President added.

Hence he said he would make no prediction, that the questioner would have to wait on the "kind of prayerful decision that may some day face a President."

"We are trying to establish conditions where he doesn't," he added.

The term "police action" was a source of political controversy a few years ago. Former President Truman used it about the Korean war in the sense that the United Nations collectively were seeking to restore order after the Communist aggression. In all but the political context the Korean conflict had been regarded as a war a "limited war" and President Eisenhower agreed today that "it became one [limited war], anyway."

President Eisenhower said again that "any just, reasonable solution of the difficulty in the Formosa strait would receive our most earnest and sympathetic consideration."

He said this in reply to a question whether any effort was being made either by the Administration or through the British to negotiate a cease-fire. The President explained that the British representative in Peiping had presented this country's viewpoint to Red China, "but there is no specific plan at the moment."

March 24, 1955

U. S. EXPECTS CHINESE REDS TO ATTACK ISLES IN APRIL; WEIGHS ALL-OUT DEFENSE

By ANTHONY LEVIERO
Special to The New York Times.

WASHINGTON, March 25—A significant change in policy and defense planning is under consideration here in the belief Red China will begin its campaign to capture Matsu and Quemoy about the middle of April.

The first intimations of an abrupt hardening of this country's position may come in the White House meetings that President Eisenhower has scheduled

with Congressional leaders on Wednesday and Thursday.

There is as yet no sign that President Eisenhower has decided to intervene militarily to prevent the capture of the islands. But military advisers are urging him to do so, and on an all-out basis. He is being urged, if this country is drawn into the conflict, to destroy Red China's industrial potential and thus end its expansionist tendencies.

On such a basis the United States would be committed to the use of atomic weapons in war for the second time. President Eisenhower recently explained that the United States would not hesitate to use precision atomic weapons against purely military targets even in a limited Far Eastern war.

Soviet's Position Weighed

The Soviet Union is expected to continue to provide Red China

226

with arms and supplies in such a conflict but not to intervene directly. The conviction is still strong in official quarters that Russia does not wish to risk a general war while the superiority of the United States Strategic Air Command is as great as it is.

Whether the Congressional leaders will be confronted with a made decision in this context remains to be seen. It is expected, however, that at least they will be briefed on the Formosa crisis as the military advisers now view it.

A reappraisal of the country's whole position with respect to Red China is under way. Collaterally the "new look" defense policy that resulted last fall in sharp reductions in Army, Navy and Marine manpower is being re-examined.

The view at the time was that this country should level off to a position of steady strength for a long "cold war," but that the policy would be re-examined if the international situation deteriorated in any material way. In the Pentagon it is deemed that the time to do this has arrived, but as yet it is believed the reappraisal has not gone far beyond the military level. It is believed, however, that Secretary of State John Foster Dulles has been supporting the new outlook.

Mr. Dulles returned from his recent tour of the Far East convinced that the United States must no longer retreat in that area, and moreover that it must convince Red China that it will not do so.

Chance of Strong Action

In the light of official estimates that the present sporadic artillery duels may soon develop into open hostilities for the off-shore islands, observers see a likelihood that the United States may soon take some strong action in the area. This might be a diplomatic move or a show of military force, or both.

That is the problem that the President is pondering, but always with a persistent hope that some honorable solution may be found without a resort to force.

A summary of the Far Eastern situation, as it is viewed here, follows:

Mao Tse-tung and Chou En-lai, the Chinese Communist leaders, have had a series of unbroken successes for three or four years and there is no reason to expect they will desist from their aggressive policies. From their point of view it would be a sound military tactic, in view of the vacillating United States policy, to continue to probe.

Hence on the basis of available information the Reds are expected to strike for Matsu Island the middle of April. This timetable could vary by a few weeks and to some extent it would be tied psychologically to the African-Asian conference that will open in Bandung, Indonesia, April 18.

The Reds are capable of capturing both the Matsu and Quemoy groups if they are opposed by the Nationalists alone.

An attack upon the bigger Quemoy group is looked for about the end of May or early June. No great build-up is yet apparent for such a two-phase operation, but United States forces learned in Korea that the Chinese Reds were clever at concealment.

Opposite Quemoy, it is estimated, the Communists have about 250 artillery positions, not all manned, and it is acknowledged they would have a tough problem to man them all and to bring up the great quantity of ammunition needed for such a concentration.

In addition to these positions, there is also a sizable number of anti-aircraft installations. Aerial reconnaissance indicates that some heavy equipment has been moved forward for action. While the Reds' logistics problem is tough, their great capability for piggy-back transportation as in Korea is being kept in mind.

It is believed possible for the Reds to capture Matsu, manned by a division of Nationalists, by the end of April or early May. Supporting the estimate of a drive in April is the build-up of an airbase near Kienow. The Reds would have to employ a sizable landing force to take Matsu because the beaches there are not favorable.

An operation against Quemoy, about five miles off the mainland and defended by about 50,000 Nationalists, would probably begin with artillery preparation, from the potentially great concentration of enemy guns, but the Communists could not reduce the island with artillery fire alone. It would not be too difficult a feat to throw Communist landing forces from the mainland across the narrow stretch of water.

To win the two island groups, however, the Reds would have to extend their air assaults to Formosa itself. Much of the Nationalist air and ground support of the defenders would have to come from there.

The vital question then is whether the conflict for the off-shore islands will be related to the defense of Formosa, to which the country has committed itself. That is the critical question that President Eisenhower must decide.

If the decision is made to intervene it should not be done on a localized basis, or with the "privileged sanctuaries" and other limitations of the Korean war, according to the President's advisers.

They say the United States should go in determined to win and to do so would require mobilization and a reversal of the retrenchments ordered in the ground forces under the new-look policy. It is their contention that the aim should be to destroy what industrial potential Red China has built up.

Red China has a potential for producing weapons, but is dependent on the Soviet Union for air power as well as for many other things. Support from Russia for a sustained war would be difficult across the rather primitive Trans-Siberian routes.

There is no evidence that Red China has received any atomic weapons from Russia, and the belief here is that Red China wishes to avoid involvement in a general war.

The offshore islands are the key to Nationalist morale. Although Formosa could not be taken by the Reds for a couple of years even if the islands were lost, that would shatter the Chiang Kai-shek regime. The end result, according to the appraisal here, would be a thorough defeat for the United States throughout Asia.

This is the picture before the officials who are making the "agonizing reappraisal."

March 26, 1955

EISENHOWER SEES NO WAR NOW OVER CHINESE ISLES

By W. H. LAWRENCE
Special to The New York Times

WASHINGTON, March 28— President Eisenhower does not share the view that war in the Formosa Strait is imminent.

He does not believe, as some military leaders do, that the Chinese Communists will begin a campaign to capture Matsu and Quemoy Islands about the middle of April.

The best political and military intelligence reaching the White House is that the Chinese Reds have not yet undertaken the kind of military and aviation build-up that would make an attack likely in the near future.

The President did not like stories published over the weekend that said his military advisers were satisfied that such attacks might begin by mid-April. They were said to be urging upon the President a definite declaration that he had decided that the United States would intervene militarily to prevent the capture of the Nationalist-held islands off the Chinese mainland.

The White House believes it is aware of the source of these stories, and treats them as "parochial," representing the view of only one man or one service.

Danger Not Discounted

It is the President's conviction that he has more information— both political and military—

available to him than the source of last week's scare headlines.

He does not discount the danger in the Formosa Strait, but he does not think the Chinese Communists are ready for the major attack that would be necessary if they were to attempt to dislodge the Chinese Nationalists from Quemoy and Matsu.

Politically the President thinks the Chinese Reds would not launch such an attack on the eve of the African-Asian conference, scheduled to begin April 18 in Bandung, Indonesia.

In these conclusions, the President has the backing of the National Security Council and Secretary of State Dulles.

The President is still unwilling to say flatly whether the United States would go to war for the defense of Quemoy and

227

Matsu under any and all circumstances.

He still sticks, in general, to the language of the resolution passed by Congress in February authorizing the defense of Formosa and "related areas." Whether Quemoy and Matsu would fall within the "related areas" is a decision that has not been finally made, but it has been considered in many alternative forms.

General Eisenhower may speak out on this subject at his news conference called for 10:30 A. M. Wednesday. He does not, as of this moment, feel it wise to blueprint for the Communists what the United States might or might not do under all circumstances.

The main factor in the President's unwillingness to accept the probability of a Chinese Communist attack by mid-April is that the signs of a major build-up have not appeared.

This is not to say there is not constant danger in the Formosa Strait. But it does suggest to the President and his top advisers that the Reds have not assembled the aircraft and troops, or completed the air bases and landing craft, for a sustained, major, continuing attack.

The President does not think that Quemoy and Matsu can be taken without a major attack. The President realizes that among his military advisers there are some who think the time has come for a showdown with the Chinese Communists.

Some of them think that a naval blockade alone would bring Peiping to its knees.

But the President does not share this conviction. He is fully away of his responsibilities, not alone as President, but also as Commander in Chief. He is determined to make such decisions himself, and not leave them to his military subordinates.

The President was not pleased that some news accounts published last week-end indicated an Administration decision that was not his decision. He does not question that the views published were given out in good faith and in complete honesty, but he is disturbed that an erroneous impression was given to the people of the United States and of the world.

Whether he has rebuked the officer he thinks was responsible for the stories could not be ascertained.

It is not likely that he has kept his displeasure to himself. Some of the statements made caused allies of the United States to lodge inquiries with this Government as to whether the stories represented United States policy. They were told they did not.

One statement published last week-end was that the President was being urged to use atomic weapons, if necessary, to destroy Red China's industrial potential and thus end its expansionist tendencies. This view did not please the President either.

March 29, 1955

PEIPING STEPS UP THE TENSION OVER TAIWAN

By HENRY LIEBERMAN

Special to The New York Times.

HONGKONG, Jan. 21—Communist China stoked up the "tension" pot in Taiwan (Formosa) Strait this week under more propaganda pressure. It added stronger words and a heavier than usual off shore island shelling to the brew of armed incidents, psychological tussling and military preparations which had continued to simmer over the small fire in that area.

The desultory ambassadorial-level talks between the United States and the Chinese Communists went on at Geneva. But after accusing the United States of "dragging out" the talks and hinting that it might pull out, Peiping announced bluntly that it would not accept a United States formula for renunciation of force in the Taiwan area subject to the "right of individual and collective self-defense" for both sides.

Reassert Claim

The Chinese Communists called again for a conference at the Foreign Ministers' level to relieve the "tensions." At the same time, however, they reasserted their claim to Taiwan and main-

tained that the United States had no right of defense in an area where the latter has undertaken to help defend Taiwan and the Penghu (Pescadores) Islands.

Meanwhile Peiping is again accusing the United States of "occupying" Taiwan, "stepping up" military activity there and sending planes to "intrude" into its "territorial air" in "provocative acts."

The Chinese Communists also have seized upon the Dulles "brink of war" interview. Their propagandists have represented this as a "renewed clamor for atomic war" against the China mainland and declared that the "Chinese people cannot be intimidated." Psychological and political warfare, including the "tension" aspects of the "brink" technique as practiced in Peiping, are regarded by various observers here as a major aspect of the present picture in Taiwan Strait. But those holding such a view do not minimize the military danger along the east coast.

Artillery Fire

It has not been just a matter of words in Taiwan Strait. A seven-hour artillery exchange occurred in the Quemoy Island

SITUATION ALONG TAIWAN STRAIT

East China Sea

Nanping
Foochow
MATSU
102 mi.
Keelung
Taipei
Railroad being built
Hsinchu
CHINA
Tsinkiang
New highway completed
Taiwan Strait
TAIWAN (FORMOSA)
117 mi.
Amoy
QUEMOY
29 mi.
PENGHU (Pescadores)
Tainan
Causeways under construction
Kaohsiung

AIR BASES: [X] Nationalist [X] Communist   0   50 Miles

sector Thursday. It was the heaviest gunfire there since Sept. 3, 1954 when Communists fired 6,000 shells at the Quemoy area in emphasizing the resumption of their Taiwan "liberation" campaign. On Thursday, Taipei announced, the Communists fired over 2,900 shells at Nationalist-held Quemoy and adjacent islands. The Nationalists slammed shells back at the Communists from their offshore positions.

Sporadic artillery exchanges of less intensity have been going on in the Quemoy sector for some time. Even at the height of the "Geneva Spirit" the Communists continued to develop their coastal military potential and the Nationalists their offshore island defenses both in the Quemoy sector and in the Matsu sector farther up the Fukien coast.

Nationalist planes have been making regular reconnaissance flights over Communist positions and occasionally attacking concentrations of Communist shipping. There has been relatively little aerial contact, however, and the Chinese Communists have not tangled thus far with the United States Seventh Fleet destroyers patrolling Taiwan Strait.

No Attack Indicated

On Quemoy last month Lieut. Gen. Liu Yu-chang, Nationalist commander there, said he had seen "no indications" that the Communists were planning an attack in that sector "in the near future." He added, however, that one could "not tell for sure" and that he was ready for an attack at any time.

According to other military sources there has been no dramatic numerical build-up in Communist troop strength along the East China coast in some time. But these sources point out that the Communists have long had enough troops for offshore-island operations and that continuing the "technical" build-up along the coast was now the important thing militarily.

The Chinese Communists have been developing their coastal strength in terms of such factors as communications, airfields and artillery potential. In an obvious attempt to improve their supply situation in the Quemoy sector the Chinese Communists have constructed a causeway from the mainland to Amoy Island facing Quemoy on the east and are constructing another from the mainland to Tateng Island four miles north of Quemoy.

Two-thirds of that Nationalist-held island is already within range of Communist artillery.

Building Railway

As part of the communications build-up the Chinese Communists have been constructing a railway leading from Yingtak on the existing Hangchow - Nanchang line southward into Fukien. The Nationalists believe that this supply route is to lead to Nanping with one branch extending from there to Foochow near Matsu and another continuing south to Amoy opposite Quemoy. A recent Peiping dispatch said the target date for completing this line had been advanced one year, indicating that the new target is sometime in 1956. Earlier reports had reached here that the Communists had built an improved coastal road between Foochow and Amoy along with feeder roads leading into this artery.

For some time now the Chinese Communists have been extending their coastal airfields southward. They have improved the field at Foochow and have been developing at least six new points twenty-five to 125 miles from Quemoy.

An airman in Taiwan said the staging bases would provide the Communists with advantages of "time, space and flexibility" by forcing a dispersal of opposing air strength in the event of major hostilities. The Chinese Communists clearly aim to win Taiwan eventually. But the question of whether they will attack the offshore islands in the foreseeable future, and if so in what way, has become a general guessing game marked by varying points of view.

Showdown Move

Some believe the Communists may possibly attack Quemoy and Matsu before long to force a showdown and strike at Taiwan by going after the substantial number of Nationalist troops on the offshore islands. More believe the Communists will not attack because they do not want to risk a war with the United States, because they do not want to jeopardize their infant industrialization program, because they want to maximize the effectiveness of "peaceful coexistence"—and because they are not ready for a showdown.

Between these poles there is another school here that holds that while the Communists may not attack Quemoy or Matsu they may risk limited military maneuvers to dramatize the "tension" in Taiwan Strait. This school suggests the possibility of an intensified artillery barrage, air attacks or an assault on one or more small islands in either the Matsu or Quemoy complex.

In this connection, however, there seems to be the tricky question of how close to the "brink" you can get.

REBUFFS TO REDS AND NEHRU BRING BANDUNG DISCORD

Asian-African Parley's Even Course Is Being Disrupted by Procedural Disputes

WEST RECEIVES SUPPORT

Iraqi Denounces Colonialism, Zionism and Communism—Cambodia Joins Neutrals

By TILLMAN DURDIN
Special to The New York Times.

BANDUNG, Indonesia, Tuesday, April 19—The Asian-African conference entered its second day with controversies and ruffled tempers threatening to disrupt and delay its progress.

The even course planned for the twenty-nine-nation conference was considerably disturbed by developments yesterday, and efforts to keep differences from growing were begun today.

A distinct breakaway from the leadership of Jawaharlal Nehru, Indian Prime Minister, has developed on a number of procedural matters.

In addition, yesterday's session heard a vigorous anti-Communist attack by Dr. Fadhil al-Jamali, Minister of State of Iraq and leader of his delegation, and expressions of affinity with the United States and the West by the acting Iranian delegate, Dr. Djalal Abdoh.

[Prince Wan Waithayakon, speaking for Thailand, called on the Communists Tuesday to prove their intention to live up to the spirit and letter of "peaceful organization because it was threatened by Red subversion and possible aggression," The United Press said. For that reason, he asserted, Thailand wants to know what the Reds mean by "coexistence." Reuters said Prime Minister Mohammed Ali of Pakistan defended the right of self-defense "exercised singly or collectively."]

Chou Plans Address

When the conference opened this morning for a public ses-sion, Chou En-lai, Premier of Communist China, told news men that he had come to the gathering to make friends, not to quarrel. However, he added that he was planning to make a speech at this afternoon's session.

It had been reported earlier that Mr. Chou would not make a public address. Autograph hunters and photographers crowded around the Chinese leader as he took his seat.

Competent sources reported this morning that Mr. Nehru tried after yesterday's speech by Dr. al-Jamali to mollify conference tempers and urge that indulgence in recriminatory speeches be avoided. Whether Mr. Chou's speech, which he announced this morning he would give, would observe this Nehru attitude is not known.

Dr. al-Jamali named colonialism, Zionism and communism as evils that disturbed world peace and harmony. He scored communism as a "subversive religion" that bred hatred among classes and peoples. He reviewed the history of Communist aggression in Eastern Europe and Central Asia and said the Communists "confront the world with a new form of colonialism much deadlier than the old."

An emphatic speaker, Dr. al-Jamali faced Mr. Chou when he said: "Today the Communist world has subject races in Asia and Eastern Europe on a much larger scale than any old colonial power."

He received more applause than any other speaker.

The Iraqi leader called Zionism, which fosters a Jewish national homeland in Palestine, "the worst offspring of imperialism." He said he hoped the conference would brand Israel an illegitimate state and an aggressor and see to it that "Arab rights in their own home in Palestine are recognized and restored."

He also made a bitter attack against French policy in Tunisia, Algeria and Morocco and against the segregationist course of the white minority in South Africa.

Mr. Chou sat impassively through Dr. al-Jamali's attack on communism. But last night it was reported that Mr. Nehru was apprehensive that the Chinese Communist Premier might feel impelled to speak in answer and thus possibly plunge the conference into disputes.

At preliminary talks Sunday, the viewpoint of Mr. Nehru; U Nu, Premier of Burma; Dr. Ali Sastroamidjojo, Premier of Indonesia, and a number of others had generally prevailed. It called for the conference to avoid specific controversial problems and develop as a friendly discussion

meeting. A seven-point agenda along these lines was adopted. There was majority concurrence in Mr. Nehru's view that speeches should not be delivered but merely circulated for reading.

Some Object to Plans

The plans were discussed without the presence of a number of delegation chiefs who arrived late. Yesterday Mr. Mohammed Ali led objections to plans made without him. He and other delegation chiefs opposed Mr. Nehru's view that speeches should not be delivered—to save time and avoid controversy—and to other procedural plans.

Tatsunosuke Takasaki, chief Japanese delegate, pictured Japan as a nation dedicated to peace in a speech he delivered at this morning's session. He said Japan was eager to contribute her share to the promotion of economic cooperation for the common prosperity of the Asian-African region.

The Japanese leader expressed regret over Japan's role in World War II, saying she had inflicted damages upon her neighbor nations, but ended by bring untold miseries upon herself.

At yesterday's plenary meetings that followed opening speeches and ceremonies, sentiment developed against Mr. Nehru on the question of public speeches. It was finally decided that delegates who wished to could give addresses at the public sessions.

The desire, particularly of anti-Communist delegations, not to let conference publicity fall to Mr. Nehru and the predominantly neutralist conference staff was shown in the adoption of a ruling that the conference would issue a daily communiqué and a final communiqué at the end. Mr. Mohammed Ali succeeded also in getting agreement to the keeping of a verbatim record of all conference statements.

As a result of the decision to hear addresses, a public session was held under the conference chairman.

Yesterday twenty-three delegation chiefs gave notice of their intention to speak. This morning it appeared that almost everybody had decided to deliver addresses, taking up conference time that Mr. Nehru had hoped would be devoted to committee work.

Prince Norodom Sihanouk, former King of Cambodia, announced in his speech that his country had definitely aligned itself with "the community of neutral nations, among them India and Burma." He endorsed the principles calling for non-aggression, noninterference in internal affairs and mutual respect and equality that form the basis of declarations of relations between India and Communist China.

Dr. Abdoh of Iran referred to "aggressors" who "reinvent colonialism" under such forms as

subversion and economic or political interference. Emphasizing that underdeveloped countries must build up their economies politically and economically, he praised the economic assistance received by Iran from the United States and cited it as "a fruitful way of reaching real economic and political independence, of combating colonialism under all its forms."

The Iranian said some politicians had misinterpreted the true intentions of the Bandung gathering by pretending it was directed against the white man and the West. He called this "ridiculous" and against "the principles of our cultures."

Lieut. Col. Gamal Abdel Nasser, Premier of Egypt, affirmed his country's faith in the United Nations but accused that organization of a failure to act in accordance with human rights with regard to North Africa and the Israel dispute.

"Brutal Violation"

He said the establishment of Israel "under the eyes of the United Nations and with her help and sanction" was a "brutal and immoral violation of human principles."

Sir John Kotelawala, Prime Minister of Ceylon, proposed that the Asian-African nations offer themselves as mediators between the Communist and anti-Communist blocs to work out a plan for peace and create machinery to implement it. He said the nations of the West, despite their science and weapons of mass destruction, were at a loss to find ways to rid themselves of the fear, hysteria and despair caused by the prospect of a new war that would annihilate mankind.

Ceylonese sources were responsible for a report today that Sir John, following up his speech of yesterday, might try to promote an eight-power conference on Formosa. The reports were that Brig. Gen. Carlos P. Romulo of the Philippines, Prince Wan and Mr. Chou would be invited, along with representatives of the Colombo powers, Ceylon, India, Pakistan, Burma and Indonesia. General Romulo said he had not been approached on the proposition.

As a result of yesterday's sessions, the agenda has been modified to incorporate only five main headings. These are economic cooperation, cultural cooperation, human rights, problems of dependent peoples and promotion of world peace and cooperation. The original proposal had included peaceful and military uses of nuclear energy as separate topics. These may be taken up under the present items.

Pakistani Lists Principles

BANDUNG, Tuesday, April 19 (Reuters)—Prime Minister Mohammed Ali of Pakistan advanced seven principles to the Asian-African conference here today. He listed the principles as:

1. Respect for the sovereignty and territorial integrity of all nations.
2. Recognition of the equality of every independent and sovereign nation.
3. Abstention from interference in the internal affairs of one country by another.
4. Non-aggression against the territorial integrity or political independence of any country.
5. The right of self-defense exercised singly or collectively.
6. The right of self-determination of all peoples and abhorrence of colonial exploitation in any shape or form.
7. The settlement of all international disputes by peaceful means, namely negotiation, mediation or arbitration.

Romulo Warns of Perils

BANDUNG, Tuesday, April 19 (Æ)—General Romulo, who had announced he would "take on all comers" if defense arrangements of Asian nations with the West were attacked, did not mention communism by name in his speech today. But he warned the Asian and African nations "not to surrender blindly to a new super-barbarianism, a new super-imperialism, a new super-power."

"There is one road to change which some countries have adopted and which offers itself to the rest of us as a possible choice," the Philippine delegate said.

"This is the road which proposes a total change through total power, through avowed dictatorship and forcible manipulation of men and means to achieve certain ends, rigid control of all thought and expression, ruthless suppression of all opposition, pervasive control of human life in all spheres by a tightly run, self-selected organization of elite individuals."

April 19, 1955

CHOU ASKS FOR U. S. TALKS ON EASING FORMOSA CRISIS

By TILLMAN DURDIN

Special to The New York Times.

BANDUNG, Indonesia, April 23—Chou En-lai announced here today that Communist China was prepared to negotiate directly with the United States over Formosa and Far East questions in general.

A statement to this effect was released by the Premier of Communist China at the headquarters of the Asian-African conference. It came as the climax of a week of talk by Mr. Chou of peace and nonaggression and caused a sensation in conference quarters.

Prior to his public announcement, Mr. Chou disclosed at a luncheon his intention to propose United States-Red China talks.

He attended the luncheon with Dr. Ali Sastroamidjojo, Premier of Indonesia; Sir John Kotelawala, Prime Minister of Ceylon; Jawaharlal Nehru, Prime Minister of India; Brig. Gen. Carlos P. Romulo, chief delegate of the Philippines; Prince Wan Waithayakon, Foreign Minister of Thailand; Mohammed Ali, Prime Minister of Pakistan, and U Nu, Premier of Burma.

The luncheon was the materialization of a plan of Sir John, made public earlier this week, for convening the eight Asian leaders to discuss the possibility of a Formosa peace settlement.

'Friendly' to U. S. People

The eight officials returned from the luncheon to the conference headquarters at 4 P. M. and would say only that Mr. Chou would have an announcement. They then entered a closed meeting of the conference's political committee.

Two hours later the Chinese Premier and Foreign Minister sent a member of his delegation out of the meeting into the conference hall to pass his statement to correspondents.

The statement said:

"The Chinese people are friendly to the American people. The Chinese people do not want to have war with the United States of America. The Chinese Government is willing to sit down and enter into negotiations with the United States Government to discuss the question of relaxing tension in the Far East and especially the question of relaxing tension in the Taiwan [Formosa] area."

The spokesman was reluctant to elaborate on the statement. However, he said the announcement meant "direct bilateral talks" and not a multipower conference of the type proposed for Formosa negotiations recently by the Soviet Union.

He said there was no plan to transmit the statement officially to Washington and added it would be circulated by the press and thus reach the United States Government.

General Romulo said the Chou statement was not the product of discussions and a joint decision at the luncheon. He said the luncheon was marked by light conversation and afterward, at a brief talk between the eight men, Mr. Chou had stated his intention to make the announcement.

The Philippines official said he had been noncommittal since he had not been empowered by his Government to discuss Formosa. Prince Wan reportedly manifested a similar reaction but the Premiers of the Colombo powers voiced approval. The Colombo powers, so named because of a meeting at that Ceylon city in 1954, are India, Pakistan, Burma, Indonesia and Ceylon.

The announcement immediately became the top subject in conference circles. Most delegations felt the Red Chinese offer was a good move and opened up the possibility of a peaceful settlement of the Formosa issue. There were, however, dissents from this view among officials wary of Communist maneuvers.

The statement brought Mr. Chou's peace campaign here to its high point. It won for the Chinese Communists and the neutralists, headed by India, the dominant position in the conference atmosphere that had been established by the anti-Communist delegations.

Mr. Chou had timed his announcement astutely to come as the conference, now scheduled to terminate tomorrow evening, entered its final phase. He drew support among delegates by creating the feeling that a Formosa settlement might after all come from an Asian-African move.

Move Is Assessed

Observers here asserted that Mr. Chou's move could be mainly propaganda designed to appeal to Asian sentiment favoring an Asian solution of Asian problems and aimed at putting the United States in the position of accepting or rejecting an Asian initiative.

The United States has had few supporters here for a policy of fighting over the offshore China islands of Quemoy and Matsu and to this added to the favorable impact of Mr. Chou's gesture.

A source close to the Chinese Communist delegation said Peiping might agree to having Nationalist Chinese officials attend a Formosa conference as observers. The source admitted prospects were slim for a final Formosa settlement, but that a Red China-United States meeting might at least reach some arrangement that would diminish the likelihood of war.

Meanwhile, subcommittees engaged in drafting declarations on such subjects as racialism, colonialism, promotion of peace, Indochina, destructive uses of atomic energy and disarmament advanced to a stage today that permitted plans for closing the conference tomorrow evening.

The day was marked by continued clashes over the colonialism issue between the neutralist and Communist powers that wanted no allusions to the colonialist aspects of communism and the anti-Communist states that insisted on phrasing encompassing Communist domination and methods of infiltration and subversion.

It was during sessions of the committee of chief delegates discussing world peace that Mr. Chou engaged in extensive elaboration of Communist China's peaceful and friendly intentions toward other nations. He stated that all the world's problems could be settled peacefully, including his country's differences with the United States.

He dwelt at length on Peiping's desire to live in peace with Asian neighbors and made particular mention of Japan, the Philippines, Thailand, Laos and Cambodia.

Mr. Chou assured Prince Wan of Thailand that he could be "absolutely certain" Communist China would not attack Thailand and said although Peiping had no relations with Thailand he was eager to negotiate an agreement with Bangkok settling the question of the dual nationality

231

of the 3,000,000 Thailand Chinese.

Similar Assurances Given

He gave similar assurances to Cambodia, Laos, the Philippines and Japan. He said at a dinner party last night he had emphasized Communist China's nonaggression aims to General Romulo and had asked him to transmit these promises to the Philippines President, Ramon Magsaysay.

The Communist Chinese Premier paid a tribute to Ichiro Hatoyama as the elected leader of the Japanese people and invited neighboring nations to send inspection teams to Communist China's borders to ascertain that no aggressive preparations were being made against them.

He said if neighboring peoples felt Communist China was not treating them correctly their complaints should be brought to him, and they would be settled.

Mr. Chou had a seven-point program for peace. The points covered respect for international boundaries, abstention from aggression and military threats, noninterference by one nation in the internal affairs of another, recognition of the equality of races and nations, respect for the rights of people to choose their own way of life and their own political and economic systems, a curb on nuclear and bacteriological weapons and an arms truce combined with peaceful use of atomic energy and the reduction of armaments by the great powers.

He offered the program as a change from his five principles of coexistence, but defended these by saying that Prime Minister Sir Anthony Eden of Britain, according to information given him by Mr. Nehru, had expressed approval of the principles. He said he would be delighted to join Sir Anthony in a statement on the principles.

The Five Principles

The five principles are respect for the national sovereignty and integrity of all nations, renunciation of intervention or interference in the territory or internal affairs of other nations, mutual cooperation for the promotion of mutual interest, recognition of the equality of races and nations, large and small, and nonaggression.

Mr. Chou denied charges of Communist aggression through infiltration and subversion.

He warned nations against joining regional groupings against Communist China. These, he said, would cause China to seek the support of likeminded nations and thus tensions would be increased.

April 24, 1955

BANDUNG PARLEY ENDS IN HARMONY; FOES OF REDS GAIN

By TILLMAN DURDIN
Special to The New York Times.

BANDUNG, Indonesia, Monday, April 25—The Asian-African conference closed last night, and pro-Western spokesmen saw substantial successes in its final decisions.

The twenty-nine-nation conference ended with a public session of speech-making and mutual congratulations after a week of intensive discussion.

A communiqué incorporating the declarations hammered out during the week recorded unanimously adopted statements on questions ranging from disarmament to the status of the small British protectorate of Aden.

Pro-Western leaders pointed with satisfaction to a clause in a declaration on the promotion of world peace and cooperation that justified the membership of Asian-African nations in alliances such as the North Atlantic Treaty Organization and the Southeast Asia Collective Defense Treaty Organization.

Anti-Communists cited as evidence of their strength at the conference numerous clauses in the communiqué. They were gratified by frequent expressions of support for the United Nations and its agencies, clauses approving foreign capital investments and economic cooperation with countries outside Asia and Africa. Particularly pleasing to them was the fact that declarations avoided backing Communist China for a United Nations seat.

Generalizations Adopted

It was recognized, on the other hand, that cooperating neutralist nations and Communist China also scored in conference proceedings. The communiqué did not carry mention of Communist imperialism and colonialism, as first proposed by anti-Communist leaders, and most declarations were of a general nature of the kind that did not bind Communist China in specific pledges.

The communiqué presented a façade of common views among the participating nations that is expected here to be used by Peiping as manifesting unity between Communist China and the nations of Asia and Africa. The moderation of Chou En-lai, Premier of Communist China, in frequently backing down in debates and agreeing to proposals of anti-Communist leaders won him considerable approval.

Mr. Chou concluded his display of mildness and friendliness with his offer to negotiate with the United States over Formosa. This move intensified the favorable impact he created and made the conference an over-all success. It also was a success in some ways for the anti-Communist nations that proved to be stronger and more assertive than had been expected.

The closing day of the conference yesterday was the most crowded of the week. Differences in committees over declarations on colonialism and statements of principles for peace lasted until 6 P. M., when agreement was finally reached and a joint communiqué was approved.

Only a half hour after the main political committee of delegation chiefs had ended its work the chiefs and other members of the delegations assembled in the conference auditorium for the final public plenary session.

Huge crowds massed around the hall and cheered the weary officials as their cars drove up in a drenching rain.

Under the chairmanship of Dr. Ali Sastroamidjojo of Indonesia the session gave formal assent to the communiqué. The document revealed that another Asian-African conference was planned and that time and place had been left to be fixed by the Colombo powers that called Bandung meeting — India, Burma, Indonesia, Pakistan and Ceylon. Conference quarters say the next meeting is likely to be in Cairo.

Speech-making at the session lasted for two hours. There was a general tribute to the job of organization and providing facilities done by Indonesia.

Dr. Ali was host at a reception immediately after the plenary meeting. Premier Chou and members of his delegation mingled freely with the guests and the Chinese Communist Premier seemed in good spirits.

He joined Prime Minister Jawaharlal Nehru, Premier U Nu of Burma and Premier Gamal Abdel Nasser of Egypt at a dinner following the reception.

Nonaggression Pledged

Under a declaration on world peace and cooperation the conference nations ratified a ten-point statement pledging nonaggression, settlement of disputes by peaceful means and friendly cooperation. The declaration mentioned respect for the right of each nation to defend itself "singly or collectively" in conformity with the charter of the United Nations.

This gave sanction to pacts such as that of the Atlantic and Manila defense groups. However, there was added the qualification that the conference members would not use arrangements of collective defense "to serve the particular interests of any of the big powers."

One statement in the declaration said all nations should have the right freely to choose their own political and economic systems and their own way of life in conformity with the purposes of the Charter of the United Nations. The declaration urged disarmament and prohibition of nuclear and thermonuclear weapons and appealed to the world powers concerned to reach agreement to suspend experiments with such weapons.

The declaration urged United Nations membership for Cambodia, Ceylon, Japan, Jordan, Laos, Libya, Nepal and a unified Vietnam but did not mention backing Communist China for a seat. The declaration asked that the Asian-African nations precluded from being elected to the Security Council under existing agreements should become eligible.

Another declaration supported the rights of the "Arab peoples of Palestine" and a peaceful settlement of the Palestine question. Indonesia's claim to West New Guinea was supported and the conference urged the Dutch to reopen negotiations.

The declaration supported the position of Yemen in claiming the British protectorate of Aden and the southern parts of Yemen known as the protectorates and urged the disputants to arrive at a peaceful settlement.

Another declaration denounced colonialism "in all its manifestations" and called for independence for all colonial peoples. The declaration had caused the most heated debate of the conference and the anti-Communist powers finally dropped references in a draft declaration to Communist colonialism, subversion and infiltration.

The declaration supported the rights of the people of Algeria, Morocco and Tunisia to self-determination and independence. The French Government was urged to bring about a peaceful settlement.

Another statement approved the human rights principles set forth by the United Nations and opposed racial segregation and discrimination, particularly in South Africa.

A declaration on culture called for cultural exchange between the conference countries on a bilateral basis, a qualification insisted on by anti-Communist spokesmen who did not want to be committed to a general cultural exchange with Communist China.

A declaration on economic cooperation recognized that foreign economic aid "had made a valuable contribution." Mutual technical assistance was pledged and the early establishment of the special United Nations fund for economic development was urged.

Text of Final Communique
of Asian-African Parley

It was recommended that the International Bank for Reconstruction and Development devote "a greater part of its resources" to Asian - African countries. Early establishment of an international finance corporation also was favored. Diversification in the economies of Asian-African countries was urged and collective action to stabilize the prices of raw materials produced on the two continents.

BANDUNG, Indonesia, April 24 (Reuters)—The final communiqué of the Asian-African conference follows:

The Asian - African conference, convened by the Governments of Burma, Ceylon, India, Indonesia and Pakistan, met in Bandung from the 18th to 24th of April, 1955.

In addition to the sponsoring countries, the following twenty-four countries participated in the conference:

Afghanistan, Cambodia, People's Republic of China, Egypt, Ethiopia, Gold Coast, Iran, Iraq, Japan, Jordan, Laos, Lebanon, Liberia, Libya, Nepal, the Philippines, Saudi Arabia, Sudan, Syria, Thailand, Turkey, Democratic Republic of [North] Vietnam, State of Vietnam and Yemen.

The Asian-African conference considered the position of Asia and Africa and discussed ways and means by which their peoples could achieve the fullest economic cultural and political cooperation.

A. Economic Cooperation:

1. The Asian-African conference recognized the urgency of promoting economic development in the Asian-African region. There was general desire for economic cooperation among the participating countries on the basis of mutual interest and respect for national sovereignty.

The proposals with regard to economic cooperation within the participating countries do not preclude either the desirability or the need for cooperation with countries outside the region, including the investment of foreign capital.

It was further recognized that assistance being received by certain participating countries from outside the region through international or under bilateral arrangements had made a valuable contribution to the implementation of their development programs.

2. The participating countries agree to provide technical assistance to one another, to the maximum extent practicable, in the form of:

Experts, trainees, pilot projects, and equipment for demonstration purposes;

Exchange of know-how, and establishment of national and—where possible—regional training and research institutes for imparting technical knowledge and skills in cooperation with the existing international agencies.

Development Fund Proposed

3. The Asian-African conference recommended:

The early establishment of a special United Nations fund for economic development;

The allocation by the International Bank for Reconstruction and Development of a greater part of its resources to Asian-African countries;

The early establishment of an international finance corporation, which should include in its activities the undertaking of equity investment; and

Encouragement of the promotion of joint ventures among Asian-African countries in so far as this will promote their common interest.

4. The Asian-African conference recognized the vital need for stabilizing commodity trade in the region.

The principle of enlarging the scope of multilateral trade and payments was accepted. However, it was recognized that some countries would have to take recourse to bilateral trade arrangeemnts in view of their prevailing economic conditions.

5. The Asian-African conference recommended that collective action be taken by participating countries for stabilizing international prices of and demand for primary commodities through bilateral and multilateral arrangements, and that as far as practicable and desirable they should adopt a unified approach on the subject in the United Nations Permanent Advisory Commission on International Commodity Trade and other international forums.

Diversification Favored

6. The Asian-African conference further recommended:

Asian-African countries should diversify their export trade by processing their raw materials whenever economically feasible before export; intra-regional trade fairs should be promoted and encouragement be given to the exchange of trade delegations and groups of businessmen; exchange of information and of samples should be encouraged with a view to promoting intra-regional trade; and normal facilities should be provided for the transit trade of landlocked countries.

7. The Asian-African conference attached considerable importance to shipping and expressed concern that shipping lines reviewed from time to time their freight rates often to the detriment of participating countries.

It recommended a study of this problem and collective action thereafter to put pressure on the shipping lines to adopt a more reasonable attitude.

8. The Asian-African conference agreed that encouragement should be given to the establishment of national and regional banks and insurance companies.

9. The Asian-African conference felt that exchange of information on matters relating to oil, such as remittance of profits and taxation, might finally lead to the formulation of a common policy.

Nuclear Energy Stressed

10. The Asian-African conference emphasized the particular significance of the development of nuclear energy for peaceful purposes for Asian-African countries.

The conference welcomed the initiative of the powers principally concerned in offering to make available information regarding the use of atomic energy for peaceful purposes;

Urged the speedy establishment of an international atomic energy agency which should provide for adequate representation of the Asian-African countries on the executive authority of the agency; and

Recommended that Asian and African governments take full advantage of the training and other facilities in the peaceful uses of atomic energy offered by the countries sponsoring such programs.

11. The Asian-African conference agreed to the appointment of liaison officers in participating countries, to be nominated by their respective national governments, for the exchange of information and matters of mutual interest.

It recommended that fuller use should be made of the existing international organizations, and participating countries who were not members of such international organizations but were eligible should secure membership.

12. The Asian-African conference recommended that there should be prior consultation of participating countries in international forums with a view, as far as possible, to furthering their mutual economic interest. It is, however, not intended to form a regional bloc.

B. Cultural Cooperation:

1. The Asian-African conference was convinced that among the most powerful means of promoting understanding among nations is the development of cultural cooperation. Asia and Africa have been the cradle of great religions and civilizations which have enriched other cultures and civilizations while themselves being enriched in the process.

Thus the cultures of Asia and Africa are based on spiritual and universal foundations. Unfortunately, cultural contacts among Asian and African countries were interrupted during the past centuries.

The people of Asia and Africa are now animated by a keen and sincere desire to renew their old cultural contacts and develop new ones in the context of the modern world. All participating governments at the conference reiterated their declaration to work for closer cultural cooperation.

The Asian-African conference took note of the fact that the existence of colonialism in many parts of Asia and Africa, in whatever form it may be, not only prevents cultural cooperation but also suppresses the national cultures of the peoples.

Basic Rights Found Denied

Some colonial powers have denied their dependent peoples basic rights in the sphere of education and culture, which hampers the development of their personality and also prevents cultural intercourse with other Asian and African peoples.

This is particularly true in the case of Tunisia, Algeria and Morocco, where the basic right of the people to study their own language and culture has been suppressed.

Similar discrimination has been practiced against African and Colored people in some parts of the Continent of Africa.

The conference felt that these policies amount to a denial of the fundamental rights of man, impede cultural advancement in this region and also hamper cultural cooperation on the wide international plan.

The conference condemned such a denial of fundamental rights in the sphere of education and culture in some parts of Asia and Africa by this and other forms of cultural suppression.

In particular, the conference condemned racialism as a means of cultural suppression.

3. It was not from any sense of exclusiveness or rivalry with other groups of nations and other civilizations and culture that the conference viewed the development of cultural cooperation among Asian and African countries.

For World Cultural Ties

True to the age-old tradition of tolerance and universality, the conference believed that Asian and African cultural cooperation should be developed in the larger context of world cooperation.

Side by side with the development of Asian-African cultural cooperation the countries of Asia and Africa desire to develop cultural contacts with others. This would enrich their own culture and would also help in the promotion of world peace and understanding.

4. There are many countries in Asia and Africa which have not yet been able to develop their educational, scientific and technical institutions.

The conference recommended that countries in Asia and Africa which are more fortunately placed in this respect should give facilities for the admission of students and trainees from such countries to their institutions.

Such facilities should also be made available to the Asian and African people in Africa, to whom opportunities for acquiring higher education are at present denied.

5. The Asian-African conference felt that the promotion of cultural cooperation among countries of Asia and Africa should be directed towards:

(A) The acquisition of knowledge of each other country;

(B) Mutual cultural exchange and,

(C) Exchange of information.

6. The Asian-African conference was of the opinion that at this stage the best results in cultural cooperation would be achieved by pursuing bilateral arrangements to implement its recommendations and by each country taking action on its own wherever possible and feasible.

C. Human Rights and Self-Determination:

1. The Asian-African conference declared its full support of the fundamental principles of human rights as set forth in the Charter of the United Nations and took note of the Universal Declaration of Human Rights as a common standard of achievement for all peoples and all nations.

The conference declared its full support of the principle of self-determination of peoples and nations as set forth in the Charter of the United Nations and took note of the United Nations resolutions on the right of peoples and nations to self-determination, which is a prerequisite of the full enjoyment of all fundamental human rights.

2. The Asian-African conference deplored the policies and practices of racial segregation and discrimination which form the basis of government and human relations in large regions of Africa and in other parts of the world.

Such conduct is not only a gross violation of human rights but also a denial of the fundamental values of civilization and the dignity of man.

The conference extended its warm sympathy and support for the courageous stand taken by the victims of racial discrimination, especially by the peoples of African and Indian and Pakistani origin in South Africa; applauded all those who sustained their cause; reaffirmed the determination of Asian-African peoples to eradicate every trace of racialism that might exist in their own countries; and pledged to use its full moral influence to guard against the danger of falling victims of the same evil in their struggle to eradicate it.

3. In view of the existing tension in the Middle East caused by the situation in Palestine and of the danger of that tension to world peace, the Asian-African conference declared its support of the rights of the Arab people of Palestine and called for the implementation of the United Nations resolutions on Palestine and of the peaceful settlement of the Palestine question.

D. Problems of Dependent People:

1. The Asian-African conference, in the context of its expressed attitude on the abolition of colonialism, supported the position of Indonesia in the case of West Irian [Dutch New Guinea] on the relevant agreements between Indonesia and the Netherlands.

The Asian-African conference urged the Netherlands Government to reopen negotiations as soon as possible to implement their obligations under the above-mentioned agreements and expressed the earnest hope that the United Nations could assist the parties concerned in finding a peaceful solution to the dispute.

2. In view of the unsettled situation in North Africa and of the persisting denial to the peoples of North Africa of their right to self-determination, the Asian-African conference declared its support of the rights of the people of Algeria, Morocco and Tunisia to self-determination and independence and urged the French Government to bring about a peaceful settlement of the issue without delay.

E. Promotion of World Peace and Cooperation:

1. The Asian-African conference, taking note of the fact that several states have still not been admitted to the United Nations, considered that for effective cooperation for world peace membership in the United Nations should be universal, called on the Security Council to support the admission of all those states which are qualified for membership in terms of the Charter.

In the opinion of the Asian-African conference the following countries which were represented in it—Cambodia, Ceylon, Japan, Jordan, Laos, Libya, Nepal and unified Vietnam —were so qualified.

The conference considered that the representation of the countries of the Asian-African region of the Security Council in relation to the principle of equitable geographical distribution was inadequate.

It expressed the view that as regards the distribution of the nonpermanent seats, the Asian-African countries which, under the arrangement arrived at in London in 1946, are precluded from being elected, should be enabled to serve on the Security Council so that they might make a more effective contribution to the maintenance of international peace and security.

2. The Asian-African conference having considered the dangerous situation of international tension existing and the risks confronting the whole human race from the outbreak of global war in which the destructive power of all types of armaments including nuclear and thermonuclear weapons would be employed, invited the attention of all nations to the terrible consequences that would follow if such a war were to break out.

Disarmament Proposed

The conference considered that disarmament and the prohibition of production, experimentation and use of nuclear and thermonuclear weapons of war are imperative to save mankind and civilization from the fear and prospect of wholesale destruction.

It considered that the nations of Asia and Africa assembled here have a duty toward humanity and civilization to proclaim their support for the prohibition of these weapons and to appeal to nations principally concerned and to world opinion to bring about such disarmament and prohibition.

The conference considered that effective international control should be established and maintained to implement such prohibition and that speedy and determined efforts should be made to this end. Pending the total prohibition of the manufacture of nuclear and thermonuclear weapons, this conference appealed to all the powers concerned to reach agreement to suspend experiments with such weapons.

The conference declared that universal disarmament is an absolute necessity for the preservation of peace and requested the United Nations to continue its efforts and appealed to all concerned speedily to bring about the regulation, limitation, control and reduction of all armed forces and armaments including the prohibition of the production, experimentation and use of all weapons of mass destruction and to establish effective international control to this end.

3. The Asian-African conference supported the position of the Yemen in the case of Aden and the southern parts of Yemen known as the protectorates and urged the parties concerned to arrive at a peaceful settlement of the dispute.

F. Declaration of Problems of Dependent Peoples:

The Asian-African conference discussed the problems of dependent peoples and colonialism and the evils arising from the subject to what is stated in the following paragraph, the conference is agreed:

1. In declaring that colonialism in all its manifestations is an evil which should speedily be brought to an end;

2. In affirming that the subjection of peoples to alien subjugation, domination and exploitation constitute a denial of fundamental human rights is

234

contrary to the Charter of the United Nations and is an impediment to the promotion of world peace and cooperation;

3. In declaring its support of the cause of freedom and independence for all such peoples; and

4. In calling upon the powers concerned to grant freedom and independence to such peoples.

G. Declaration of Promotion of World Peace and Cooperation:

The Asian-African conference gave anxious thought to the question of world peace and cooperation. It viewed with deep concern the present state of international tension with its danger of an atomic world war.

The problem of peace is correlative with the problem of international security. In this connection all states should cooperate especially through the United Nations in bringing about the reduction of armaments and the elimination of nuclear weapons under effective international control.

In this way international peace can be promoted and nuclear energy may be used exclusively for peaceful purpose. This would help answer the needs, particularly of Asia and Africa, for what they urgently require are social progress and better standards of life in larger freedom.

Freedom and peace are interdependent. The right of self-determination must be enjoyed by all peoples and freedom and independence must be granted with the least possible delay to those who are still dependent peoples.

Indeed all nations should have the right freely to choose their own political and economic systems and their own way of life in conformity with the purposes and principles of the Charter of the United Nations.

Free from distrust and fear and with confidence and good-will toward each other, nations should practice tolerance and live together in peace with one another as good neighbors and develop friendly cooperation on the basis of the following principles:

1. Respect for the fundamental human rights and for the purposes and principles of the charter of the United Nations.

2. Respect for the sovereignty and territorial integrity of all nations.

3. Recognition of the equality of all races and of the equality of all nations, large and small.

4. Abstention from intervention or interference in the internal affairs of another country.

5. Respect for the right of each nation to defend itself singly or collectively in conformity with the charter of the United Nations.

6A. Abstention from the use of arrangements of collective defense to serve the particular interests of any of the big powers.

6B. Abstention by any country from exerting pressures on other countries.

7. Refraining from acts or threats of aggression of the use of force against the territorial integrity or political independence of any country.

8. Settlement of all international disputes by peaceful means such as negotiation, conciliation, arbitration or judicial settlement, as well as other peaceful means of the parties' own choice in conformity with the Charter of the United Nations.

9. Promotion of mutual interest and cooperation.

10. Respect for justice and international obligations.

The Asian-African conference declares its conviction that friendly cooperation in accordance with these principles would effectively contribute to the maintenance and promotion of international peace and security while cooperation in the economic, social and cultural fields would help bring about the common prosperity and well-being of all.

The Asian-African conference recommended that the full sponsoring countries should consider the next meeting of the conference in consultation with other countries concerned.

April 25, 1955

SOVIET AND INDIA IN ACCORD

By CLIFTON DANIEL
Special to The New York Times.

MOSCOW, Thursday, June 23—India and the Soviet Union jointly called today for a complete ban on nuclear weapons and a substantial reduction of conventional armaments.

Their declaration, signed here last night by Prime Minister Jawaharlal Nehru and Premier Nikolai A. Bulganin, also expressed the "earnest hope" that the "legitimate rights" of Communist China on Formosa could be satisfied "by peaceful means."

The statement also reiterated the "conviction" of the Soviet Union and India that "the continued refusal to admit the Chinese People's Republic to the United Nations lies at the root of many troubles in the Far East and elsewhere."

They said the role and authority of the United Nations would be enhanced by admitting Communist China.

Indochina Truce Cited

The declaration, made public at 6 o'clock this morning, also exhorted all those concerned in the armistice agreement in Indochina to "do their utmost fully to discharge their obligations."

In particular the declaration urged that where elections were to be held as a preliminary to a political settlement efforts should be directed to the "full implementation" of the armistice agreement.

The joint declaration, the product of negotiations held here during a fifteen-day official visit by Mr. Nehru to the Soviet Union, proclaimed the joint support of the two countries for the five principles of peaceful coexistence worked out by Mr. Nehru and Chou En-lai, Chinese Communist Premier.

In addition to endorsing these principles the two Governments expressed their conviction that the principles were "capable of wider application." In the observance of these principles, the declaration said, "lies the main hope of vanishing fear and mistrust" and "lowering world tensions."

In the climate of peace that could be created by these principles, the declaration said, it would be possible to seek peaceful solutions of international questions.

This passage reflected the approach that Mr. Nehru in his public statements in Moscow had said should be applied to the problems of war and peace and international misunderstanding.

It was followed by a passage that even more clearly bore the personal stamp of the Indian Prime Minister. This passage said:

"Both Prime Ministers recognize that in various parts of the world there is on the part of the smaller and weaker states a vague and possibly unreasoning fear of bigger powers. They feel that it is essential to dispel this fear in all possible ways. Here again the best remedy is to adhere unflinchingly to the principles of coexistence enunciated above."

Those principles are: Mutual respect for each other's territory, nonaggression, noninterference in each other's internal affairs, equality and mutual benefits and peaceful coexistence.

Suspicion Still Found

It was noteworthy that the passage relating to the fears of smaller powers and all other passages made no reference to one group of great powers or another

and therefore were equally applicable to both.

However, they added that "fear and suspicion" still dominated in large areas and causes of tension still remained in the Far East. In that connection, they spoke out for Communist China's "legitimate rights" on Formosa and to a place in the United Nations.

They said it was also important that all qualified states should be admitted to the United Nations.

The two powers asserted they had given special consideration to the Indochinese situation because of their special responsibilities arising from the Geneva agreement on Indochina. While there have been difficulties, they said, "the implementation of the agreement has on the whole so far been satisfactory." There followed the exhortation to uphold the agreement.

Shortly after issuance of the joint declaration, Mr. Nehru was leaving Moscow this morning by plane for Warsaw, Vienna, Belgrade, Rome, London and Cairo. He will be in London for two days, July 9 and 10.

Mr. Nehru, who received in this country the most tremendous reception ever given to a foreign statesman, was being seen off by the entire Soviet leadership.

The joint declaration, which first appeared here in the morning newspapers, also acclaimed the results of the Asian-African conference held at Bandung, Indonesia, in April. The declaration said the meeting had been of

The Indian and Soviet Prime Ministers commended particularly the conference declaration on the promotion of peace and cooperation.

The declaration, reflecting statements made by both sides during Mr. Nehru's visit, recognized recent signs of improvement in the international situation and the "more general appreciation" of the dangers of atomic war.

The joint declaration was signed yesterday in the great Kremlin Palace at the end of another crowded day for Mr. Nehru, which included inspection of the Soviet Union's experimental atomic energy power plant.

Mr. Nehru had expressed a special wish to see the installation and so far as there has been any public announcement he is the first foreign visitor to observe it in operation.

Visit to Atomic Plant

Accompanied by Lazar M. Kaganovich and Anastas I. Mikoyan, two Soviet First Deputy Premiers, the Prime Minister and his party spent two hours at the plant seeing a documentary film about its operations and inspecting the installation itself The plant, which has a capacity of 5,000 kilowatts, is operated by the Soviet Academy of Sciences.

The brief announcement of the inspection trip issued by Tass, the Soviet news agency, did not indicate where the plant was situated.

In mid-afternoon Mr. Nehru returned to the Kremlin for final discussions with Premier Bulganin, Nikita S. Khrushchev, the Communist party chief, and Messrs. Kaganovich and Mikoyan. This was the third formal talk he had with the Soviet leaders.

After a farewell reception given by Mr. Nehru at the Sovetskaya Hotel, he and his Moscow hosts went back to the Kremlin for the signing of the declaration.

On his visit to the atomic plant Mr. Nehru was accompanied by his daughter, Mrs. Indira Gandhi, the secretary general of the Indian Foreign Office, N. R. Pillai; the chief of the European section of the Foreign Office, Azem Hussain, and the Indian Ambassador to Moscow, K. P. S. Menon.

The Indian journalists, who have accompanied Mr. Nehru everywhere else on his fifteen-day tour of the Soviet Union, were not permitted to see the atomic plant.

PRESIDENT REPORTS GAINS FOR PEACE, SAYS GENEVA PROVED ALL DESIRE IT; U. S. AND RED CHINA ENVOYS TO MEET

By DANA ADAMS SCHMIDT
Special to The New York Times.

WASHINGTON, July 25—The United States and Communist China announced plans today for direct conversations by Ambassadors.

The talks, dealing with the release of detained civilians and "other practical matters," will begin in Geneva next Monday.

Officials made it clear the conversations would also touch on the release of United States fliers now held as prisoners by the Chinese Communists. This was not mentioned in the simultaneous announcement, they said, because the matter was primarily in the jurisdiction of the United Nations.

The ambassadorial meeting grew out of an offer made by Chou En-lai, Communist Chinese Premier and Foreign Minister, at the Bandung conference last April to talk directly to the United States.

The conversations will be limited to matters directly at issue between the United States and Communist China and will not, at least at this stage, touch upon general Far Eastern problems. President Eisenhower emphasized this condition during his meeting with Congressional leaders this morning.

No Change Seen in Policy

After hearing a report from the President and Secretary of State Dulles at the White House, Senator William F. Knowland, Republican of California, said the agreement to talk with the Communist Chinese "does not indicate in the slightest any change in our announced policy that we would not negotiate on questions affecting the Republic of China without their presence."

This limitation would indicate that there would be no discussion of the two questions Mr. Chou is primarily interested in discussing—the future status of Formosa, seat of the Chinese Nationalist Government of President Chiang Kai-shek, and the admission of Communist China to the United Nations.

Officials declined to say whether a cease-fire in the Formosa Strait might or might not be discussed. Among diplomats, however, it was suggested that this subject might be dealt with if Communist China released all the United States civilians and military personnel now held in China and if an atmosphere of confidence was gradually built up.

State Department officials said that until the fifty-one Americans held in China were released it would be difficult to go on to discussion of any "other practical matters."

25 Civilians in Prison

In addition to eleven airmen serving prison sentences as "spies," twenty - five United States civilians are in prison, three are under house arrest and twelve have been refused exit permits.

The United States will be represented at the Geneva talks by U. Alexis Johnson, Ambassador to Czechoslovakia, who initiated negotiations a year ago for the release of detained United States civilians. Since then these talks have been carried on at fifteen meetings by Consul General Franklin C. Gowen and Chinese Consul Shen Ping. The Chinese freed twenty United States civilians and four aviators during the year.

Henry Suydam, State Department spokesman, said the department "knows of no cases of Chinese civilians who have applied to go to Red China who are not free to go." He added that if the Chinese Communists believed that was not true, "we are willing to listen to their cases and investigate."

Mediation by the British Chargé d'Affaires, Con D. W. O'Neill, in Peiping, and suggestions by the Indian and Burmese Governments brought about the United States-Communist China agreement to hold conversations, officials said.

"Practical matters" that might be negotiated in addition to the release of detained citizens, officials said, may include arrangements to prevent Chinese Communist interference with United States air patrols off the coast of Korea, and arrangements permitting transfer of funds by business men leaving Communist China.

If the Geneva talks lead to an improved atmosphere, the diplomats said, conversations between Washington and Peiping on the ambassadorial level might eventually lead to conversations by foreign ministers, as proposed by Senator Walter F. George, Democrat of Georgia, in a television broadcast last night.

Senator George said today there had been "some little discussion" of his proposal at this morning's White House conference. Asked whether he meant that there might be talks by foreign ministers, Senator George replied: "Oh, yes."

Senator George's thought, however, clearly went well beyond anything the State Department has in mind at present.

Announcement of Talks

The State Department announced the Geneva talks in the following statement:

"As a result of communication between the United States and the People's Republic of China through the diplomatic channels of the United Kingdom, it has been agreed that the talks held in the last year between consular representatives of both sides at Geneva should be conducted on ambassadorial level in order to aid in settling the matter of repatriation of civilians who desire to return to their respective countries and to facilitate further discussions and settlement of certain other practical matters now at issue between both sides. The first meeting of ambassadorial representatives of both sides will take place on Aug. 1, 1955, at Geneva."

Later the department issued a fuller statement. This told who would represent the United States and gave the background on the previous Geneva negotiations.

It told how, after Mr. Chou had said at the Asian-African Conference at Bandung in April that he was willing to have direct talks, several Governments looked into the possibilities of such meetings. The result, it said, was the "suggestion" that the Geneva talks be resumed on the ambassadorial level.

The statement said that it had been made clear that the talks do not involve diplomatic recognition of Communist China.

CHOU URGES PACT FOR PEACE IN ASIA INCLUDING THE U.S.

TAIPEI TALK ASKED

Chinese Red Optimistic on Settling Civilian Repatriation Issue

By HENRY R. LIEBERMAN
Special to The New York Times.

HONG KONG, July 30—Premier Chou En-lai of Communist China called today for the signing of a collective peace pact among countries of the Asian-Pacific region, including the United States.

Mr. Chou advocated a pact of this kind to replace what he termed "the antagonistic military blocs now existing in this part of the world."

He also said the Peiping Government was willing to negotiate with "the responsible local authorities" of Formosa for "peaceful liberation" of the island.

[The Chinese Nationalists rejected the suggestion as Communist "double-talk."]

Mr. Chou, who is also Foreign Minister, made both proposals in a foreign policy report to the closing session of the National People's Congress in Peiping. He spoke less than seventy-two hours before the scheduled start of the Ambassadors' talks between the United States and Red China in Geneva.

The talks are designed to assist in the repatriation of civilians who desire to return to their respective countries and also to facilitate further discussion of "certain other practical matters" at issue.

Understanding Is Urged

The Chinese Communist Premier said it was necessary for both sides to show sincerity in these talks and establish contacts to "increase mutual understanding and trust." He asserted:

"China for her part, in accordance with her consistent stand of striving for the relaxation of tension, will endeavor to make the forthcoming Sino-American talks at the ambassadorial level pave the way for further negotiations between China and the United States."

Mr. Chou, whose speech was reported by the Hsinhua (New China) News Agency, sounded fairly optimistic on the possibility of settling the civilian repatriation question.

He said "it should be possible" to reach a "reasonable settlement on this matter at the outset if both sides were "sincerely desirous of negotiation and conciliation."

Premier Chou made this proposal on the question of civilian repatriation:

"We are of the opinion that, since there are no diplomatic relations between China and the United States at the present time, each of them can entrust to a third country the task of looking after the affairs of its civilians in the other country and primarily the affairs concerning return of these civilians to their own country."

The repatriation question affects various Americans held in China and a number of Chinese students in the United States. But the use of the term "civilians" leaves unclear the question of the eleven imprisoned United States airmen and eleven other Navy and Coast Guard fliers now believed to be among about sixty Americans detained in China.

"The number of American civilians in China is small and their question can be easily settled," Mr. Chou said. He told the People's Congress there were, on the other hand, a "great many overseas Chinese" in the United States, including several thousand students.

In discussing "certain other practical matters," Premier Chou reasserted Peiping's claim to Formosa and insisted there was no cease-fire issue between the United States and Red China.

In his offer to negotiate with "the responsible local authorities" of Formosa, Mr. Chou was presumably referring to President Chiang Kai-shek's Nationalist Government.

In effect he seemed to be proposing that the Chinese Nationalists negotiate with Peiping for their surrender. He noted there were various precedents in the Chinese civil war for such a "peaceful liberation."

"It should be made clear that these would be negotiations between the Central Government and local authorities," Mr. Chou stated. "The Chinese people are firmly opposed to any ideas or plots of the so-called 'two Chinas'."

He charged the United States was interfering in China's internal affairs. In addition, he said it had created "tension" in the Formosa area through what he called the "occupation" of Formosa and "interference with the liberation of China's coastal islands."

Other Issues Mentioned

Mr. Chou also mentioned several other "practical matters" connected with Peiping's present relations with the United States. He listed these as follows:

¶Trade embargoes: Declaring Red China was "concerned about the extremely unjust policy of blockade and embargo," he called for removal of such barriers.

¶United States military activity in the Formosa area: He said Peiping would "like to see" the United States "withdraw its armed forces from Taiwan [Formosa] and Taiwan Strait, leaving Chinese territorial air free from further intrusions and China free from threat of demonstrative war maneuvers."

¶Alleged subversion and sabotage: He said Red China demanded that "foreign countries concerned" put an end to "subversive activities against China and to the dispatching of saboteurs into China."

After calling at this point for an Asian-Pacific collective peace pact, Mr. Chou added:

"We recognize that for the above wishes to be fulfilled it is necessary first of all that China and the United States should display sincerity in negotiation, that the two sides establish contacts to increase mutual understanding and trust."

While stating that Peiping would "continue to strive" for peace, Premier Chou warned that this should not be regarded as a "sign of weakness."

Early in his speech, Mr. Chou hailed the results of the Big Four talks in Geneva and said these would "positively contribute to the further easing of world tensions." He told the Peoples' Congress, however, that the Far Eastern situation remained "explosive."

He referred to the following tension centers in addition to Formosa:

¶Vietnam: Mr. Chou said the "most urgent task" now was for the authorities of both zones to get together to discuss the 1956 "unification" elections projected for partitioned Vietnam at last year's Geneva conference.

¶Laos and Cambodia: Mr. Chou charged the United States-Cambodia military assistance agreement of May 16, 1955, was "incompatible" with the Geneva accords. He also charged the Southeast Asia Collective Defense Treaty group was "attempting to interfere" in Laotian internal affairs by "making use of royal Laotian troops to attack the Communist-sponsored Pathet Lao units.

¶Korea: Mr. Chou declared the armistice there was "still unstable" and added the supervisory commission system was confronted with "danger of being wrecked." He declared countries concerned "should not sit idly by and allow this state of affairs to develop further."

The Communist Premier called for consultation among participants in the 1954 Geneva conference on alleged "threats to break" the Geneva agreements on Indochina. He said Peiping also favored an international Far Eastern conference and felt Asian countries "should be widely represented."

RED CHINA TO FREE ALL U. S. CIVILIANS; 29 DUE TO DEPART

By HARRISON E. SALISBURY

Special to The New York Times.

WASHINGTON, Sept. 10— Peiping has agreed to set free all United States civilians remaining in Communist China.

The first ten of those Americans known to be in China whose release had not been arranged previously will be freed through Hong Kong "within a few days," the others "expeditiously."

News of the Chinese decision was contained in an announcement made in Geneva by U. Alexis Johnson, the United States representative, and Wang Ping-nan, who represented Peiping. It was released simultaneously in Washington.

The timing of the Chinese Communist action was believed to be designed to assist in creating a favorable atmosphere for further talks with the United States and for United Nations deliberations on questions concerning China.

The United States reaffirmed today the right of any Chinese in the United States to return to mainland China should he so desire. The United States also agreed that if any Chinese felt his departure was being obstructed he might apply to the Indian Embassy for assistance.

Number Remains Uncertain

Henry Suydam, a State Department spokesman, said the United States was "delighted" to have obtained agreement at last on the release of American citizens long held in China.

The precise number of Americans still in China is uncertain. The Chinese announced Tuesday that they were prepared to give exit permits to twelve civilians. Presumably these twelve would be the first to leave via Hong Kong. However, the State Department has had no direct word as to when they are expected there.

Today the Chinese announced that ten more Americans who had been held in jail or under house arrest would be freed within a few days. This leaves nineteen American civilians known to be in China who will, in the terms of today's announcement, be set free "expeditiously."

Eighteen of this group are believed to be in custody.

The announcement on Tuesday marked the first time in the negotiations that the Chinese had agreed to release any of the detained civilians. Today's announcement had been expected since then.

Before agreement on the civilians was obtained the Chinese set free United States airmen detained since the Korean war.

There may be other United States citizens in China, but the State Department has no firm knowledge of them. A list of nearly 500 American personnel missing in the Korean war has been submitted to the Chinese, but no indication that any of these are alive or in Chinese hands has been forthcoming.

Mr. Suydam emphasized that "no side understandings or agreements" had been reached by Communist China and the United States in connection with the release of the civilians. He said that today's action did not constitute any form of recognition of the Peiping regime and that the announcement was not an agreement between China and the United States but was in the form of "agreed parallel unilateral statements."

Mr. Johnson, United States Ambassador to Czechoslovakia, and Mr. Wang, Red China's Ambassador to Poland, met fourteen times over a period of six weeks. On several occasions Red China threatened to break off the talks unless the United States changed its position.

The decision with respect to the release of civilians completes the Geneva discussions under the first point of a two-point agenda. The second point is listed simply as "other practical matters at issue," and it is under this heading that broader conversations between Communist China and the United States may take place.

Mr. Johnson and Mr. Wang will meet again Wednesday. Their first task will be to decide which questions they wish to discuss and the order in which they will be taken up.

On the Chinese side there is a broad range of subjects that the Communist Government probably would like to talk about. These include the establishment of diplomatic relations, lifting of the trade embargo, a seat in the United Nations and the broad subject of Far Eastern security.

The United States has indicated it feels that chief among the questions should be the establishing of a firm cease-fire in the Formosa Strait between Red China and the Nationalists.

Conversations on relations between the United States and China are not expected to get far unless the Chinese, by one means or another, offer a firm, public and official renunciation of the doctrine of the use of force in international relations.

Secretary of State Dulles has established this as the essential prerequisite to any move toward the entry of Communist China into the organized society of nations.

The State Department attitude was that the Chinese decision to release Americans was a step in the right direction but a somewhat belated one. However, there was no tendency to belittle the importance of establishing the right of American civilians to freedom, regardless of the status under which they are held. Of the civilians whose release is imminent twenty-eight have been detained by some form of judicial or quasi-judicial process and the twenty-ninth was held for a time in jail and lately freed.

Of the ten Americans who Mr. Wang said would be released through Hong Kong within a few days seven have been in jail and three under house arrest.

Those held in jail are: Lawrence Robert Buol, Stockton, Calif.; Dilmus T. Kanady, Houston, Texas; Levi A. Lovegren, Seattle; Dorothy Middleton, Cicero, Ill.; Sarah Perkins, 156 Fifth Avenue, New York; Walter A. Rickett, Seattle, and the Rev. Harold W. Rigney, Chicago.

The following are under house arrest: the Right Rev. Frederick D. Gordon, a native of Somerset, Ohio; the Rev. Joseph Eugene Hyde of Lowell, Mass., and the Rev. James Gerald Joyce of Clinton, Mass.

As far as Chinese in the United States are concerned, Mr. Suydam emphasized that they had always been free to go back to mainland China should they so desire. The only exception was the case of 129 students against whom temporary detainers were placed at the time of the Korean war.

Mr. Suydam estimated that these constituted not more than 3 per cent of the 4,000 to 4,500 Chinese students in the United States at that time. Those affected had a high degree of technical skill that might have aided the Chinese war effort.

The detainers against all 129 were removed before the Geneva discussions began, Mr. Suydam said. Under the terms of the United States announcement, they and all Chinese are free to invoke the aid of the Indian Embassy if they feel they are under any impediment from United States authorities. Peiping may ask the Indian Embassy to investigate the situation with respect to any case.

Mr. Suydam revealed that of the 129 students at least fifty had left the United States for mainland China. He said thirty-four left between May 26 and Aug. 27 and three more planned to leave Sept. 17. He added that 173 Chinese left the United States for the Far East between July 11 and Aug. 31, but he did not know how many were bound for the mainland.

September 11, 1955

PEIPING ASKS U. S. FOR BAN ON FORCE

Special to The New York Times.

WASHINGTON, Nov. 7— United States officials said today that Communist China had proposed to the United States a joint declaration renouncing the use of force as an instrument of national policy.

Wang Ping-Nan, Chinese Ambassador to Poland, was reported to have offered such a declaration at Geneva along with a pledge to respect foreign territorial interests on the Chinese mainland if the United States in return would make three concessions.

These would be: Withdrawal of the United States Seventh Fleet from the Formosa Strait, withdrawal of support from Generalissimo Chiang Kai-shek, President of National China, and elimination of the embargo on trade with Communist China.

The State Department declined all official comment on the ground that it had agreed to keep secret the Geneva conversation between U. Alexis Johnson, United States Ambassador to Czechoslovakia, and Ambassador Wang.

Formosa Is Crux

It was learned authoritatively, however, that the United States had no objection to declaring what officials said should be obvious, namely, that it did not believe in the use of force as an instrument of policy.

On the other hand, a similar declaration by Communist China would be unsatisfactory to the United States unless it said specifically that the Communists would not use force to "liberate" Formosa.

In their statements the Chinese Communists make a clear distinction between their willingness to renounce force in international affairs and their unwillingness to do so in the case of Formosa, which they regard as a domestic affair.

Ambassador Wang's proposals were reported to be the terms on which Communist China would like to enter into conversations on the foreign ministers' level, between Secretary of State Dulles and Premier Chou En-lai, who is also Foreign Minister.

United States officials said that a Communist pledge to respect foreign territorial interests on the Chinese mainland would be welcome, although the United States had none and these interests had not recently been at issue.

November 8, 1955

Text of U. S. Statement on Geneva Negotiations With Chinese Reds Over Taiwan

WASHINGTON, Jan. 21 (AP)— Following is the text of a State Department statement, with attached documents, issued today, in connection with the Geneva talks with Red China:

Ambassadorial Talks at Geneva

The Chinese Communists issued a misleading statement on Jan. 18 regarding the Geneva discussions which have been taking place between United States Ambassador [Alexis] Johnson and Chinese Communist Ambassador Wang [Pingnam]. It is thus necessary that the record be set straight.

These conferences were started last August to discuss the repatriation of civilians and other "practical matters at issue."

Agreement to Repatriation of Civilians

On Sept. 10, 1955 the representatives of both sides, by agreement, issued statements that civilians were entitled to return to their own countries (Annex A).

The Communist declaration stated:

"The People's Republic of China recognizes that Americans in the People's Republic of China who desire to return to the United States are entitled to do so, and declares that it has adopted and will further adopt appropriate measures so that they can expeditiously exercise their right to return."

As of today, four months after this declaration was made, only six out of the nineteen for whom representations were being made on Sept. 10 have been released. Thirteen Americans are still in Communist prisons.

As for the United States, any Chinese is free to leave the United States for any destination of his choosing, and not a single one has been refused exit. The Indian Embassy, which was designated to assist any Chinese who wished to leave, has not brought to the attention of this Government any case of a Chinese who claims he is being prevented from leaving, nor has it stated that it is impeded in any way in carrying out its functions under the terms of the Sept. 10 agreed announcement.

Discussion of Reunciation of Force

After this agreed announcement was made, the two sides proceeded to discuss "other practical matters at issue between them."

The Communists suggested the topics of the termination of the trade embargo against Communist China and the hold-ing of a meeting by the foreign ministers of both sides.

Ambassador Johnson at the Oct. 8, 1955 meeting, pointed out that progress in further discussions could not be expected in the face of continuing Communist threats to take Taiwan [Formosa] by military force, and suggested that both sides agree to announce that they renounced the use of force generally and particularly in the Taiwan area and agree to settle their differences by peaceful means. The United States representatives made clear that this renunciation of the use of force was not designed to commit the Communists to renounce pursuit of their policies by peaceful means with respect to Taiwan. These proposals were in the terms shown as Annex B.

Three weeks after the United States proposal to renounce the use of force, the Communists on Oct. 27 proposed a draft, a copy of which is shown on Annex C. In this proposal, the Communists pointedly omitted any reference to the Taiwan area, or to the recognition of the right of self-defense, and inserted a provision for an immediate meeting of foreign ministers.

This proposal was unacceptable because it would have made it possible for the Communists to claim that the proposal did not apply to the Taiwan area, which is the very place against which the Communist threats are directed, and to claim further that the United States had renounced the right to use force in self-defense. Ambassador Johnson further pointed out that consideration of higher level meetings was neither appropriate nor acceptable under existing circumstances.

On Nov. 10, 1955, Ambassador Johnson, in an attempt to reach an acceptable form of declaration, submitted a new draft declaration (Annex D). This made clear that the renunciation of the use of force was without prejudice to the peaceful pursuit of its policies by either side; that it had general application, but applied particularly to the Taiwan area; and that it did not deprive either side of the right of self-defense.

The United States proposal was rejected by the Communists, who, on Dec. 1, 1955, made a counter-proposal (Annex E). This represented an advance over their previous proposal in that it dropped the provision for talks on the Foreign Minister level in favor of the continuance of Ambassadorial talks, but still pointedly omitted any references to the Taiwan area and to recognition of the right of self-defense.

In a further effort to reach agreement, Ambassador Johnson. at the Jan. 12 meeting, suggested two simple amendments to the Communist counter-proposal. These were the insertion of the words "without prejudice to the inherent right of individual and collective self-defense" and of the words "in the Taiwan area or elsewhere." This United States revision of the Chinese counter-proposal is shown in Annex F.

The Communist Public Statement

This was the status of the discussions when the Communists released their public statement of Jan. 18.

The Communist statement apparently rejects the United States proposal. It states "Taiwan is Chinese territory: There can be no question of defense, as far as the United States is concerned * * * yet the United States has demanded the right of defense of the Taiwan area. Is this not precisely a demand that China accept continued occupation of Taiwan and that the tension in the Taiwan area be maintained forever?" And further, it states: "The American side continues to demand that our side accept that the United States has 'the inherent right of individual and collective self-defense' in China's Taiwan area. This is what our side absolutely cannot accept."

The U. S. Position

Two points must be made clear. First, the United States is not occupying Taiwan, and Taiwan has never been a part of Communist China. The claims of Communist China and the contentions of the United States with respect to this area are well known and constitute a major dispute between them. It is specifically with respect to this dispute that the United States has proposed the principle of renunciation of force and the settlement of differences by peaceful means. This is the principle which the Communists say they have accepted.

In this connection the United States has made completely clear that in renouncing the use of force neither side is relinquishing its objectives and policies, but only the use of force to attain them.

Secondly, the United States has rights and responsibilities in the Taiwan area; also it has a mutual defense treaty. Accordingly it is present in the Taiwan area. The Communist refusal to state that the renunciation of force is without prejudice to the right of self-defense against armed attack can only be interpreted as an attempt to induce the United States to agree that if attacked it will forego the right to defend its lawful presence in this area.

The right of individual and collective self-defense against armed attack is inherent; it is recognized in international law; it is specifically affirmed in the Charter of the United Nations. No country can be expected to forego this right. Indeed the Communists should be as anxious to preserve this right as is the United States.

Conclusion

The present exchange makes clear that:

1. Four months after the Communists announced that they would adopt measures to permit Americans in China to return to the United States, thirteen Americans are still held in Communist prisons.

2. The United States proposed that the parties renounce the use of force without prejudice to the right of individual and collective self-defense against armed attack, in order that the discussions might take place free from the threat of war.

3. The United States made clear that this renunciation would not prejudice either side in the pursuit of its objectives and policies by peaceful means.

4. The Communists, while stating that they accept the principle of the renunciation of force, have deprived such acceptance of its value by refusing to agree that it is without prejudice to the right of individual and collective self-defense against armed attack and that it is app :cable to the Taiwan area.

In short, the Communists so far seem willing to renounce force only if they are first conceded the goals for which they would use force.

The United States, for its part, intends to persist in the way of peace. We seek the now overdue fulfillment by the Chinese Communis 3 of their undertaking that the Americans now in China should be allowed expeditiously to return. We seek this not only for humanitarian reasons but because respect for international undertakings lies at the foundation of a stable international order. We shall also seek with perseverence a meaningful renunciation of force, particularly in the Taiwan area.

Annex A

Agreed Announcement of the Ambassadors of the United States of America and the People's Republic of China

The Ambassadors of the United States of America and the People's Republic of China have agreed to announce measures which their respective Governments have adopted concerning the return of civilians to their respective countries.

With respect to Chinese in the United States, Ambassador Johnson, on behalf of the United States, has informed Ambassador Wang that:

1. The United States recognizes that Chinese in the United States who desire to return to the People's Republic of China are entitled to do so and declared that it has adopted and will further adopt appropriate measures so that they can expeditiously exercise their right to return.

2. The Government of the Republic of India will be invited to assist in the return to the People's Republic of China of those who desire to do so as follows:

A. If any Chinese in the United States believes that contrary to the declared policy of the United States he is encountering obstruction in departure, he may so inform the Embassy of the Republic of India in the United States and request it to make representations on his behalf to the United States Government. If desired by the People's Republic of China, the Government of the Republic of India may also investigate the facts in any such case.

B. If any Chinese in the United States who desires to return to the People's Republic of China has difficulty in paying his return expenses, the Government of the Republic of India may render him financial assistance needed to permit his return.

3. The United States Government will give wide publicity to the foregoing arrangements and the Embassy of the Republic of India in the United States may also do so.

With respect to Americans in the People's Republic of China, Ambassador Wang Ping-nan, on behalf of the People's Republic of China, has informed Ambassador Johnson that:

1. The People's Republic of China recognizes that Americans in the People's Republic of China who desire to return to the United States are entitled to do so, and declares that it has adopted and will further adopt appropriate measures so that they can expeditiously exercise their right to return.

2. The Government of the United Kingdom will be invited to assist in the return to the United States of those Americans who desire to do so as follows:

A. If any American in the People's Republic of China believes that contrary to the declared policy of the People's Republic of China he is encountering obstruction in departure, he may so inform the office of the Chargé d'Affaires of the United Kingdom in the People's Republic of China and request it to make representations on his behalf to the Government of the People's Republic of China. If desired by the United States, the Government of the United Kingdom may

also investigate the facts in any such case.

B. If any American in the People's Republic of China who desires to return to the United States has difficulty in paying his return expenses, the Government of the United Kingdom may render him financial assistance needed to permit his return.

3. The Government of the People's Republic of China will give wide publicity to the foregoing arrangements and the office of the Chargé d'Affaires of the United Kingdom in the People's Republic of China may also do so.

Annex B
United States Statement and Proposal on Renunciation of Force, Oct. 8, 1955

One of the practical matters for discussion between us is that each of us should renounce the use of force to achieve our policies when they conflict. The United States and the People's Republic of China confront each other with policies which are in certain respects incompatible. This fact need not, however, mean armed conflict, and the most important single thing we can do is first of all to be sure that it will not lead to armed conflict.

Then and only then can other matters causing tension between the parties in the Taiwan area and the Far East be hopefully discussed.

It is not suggested that either of us should renounce any policy objectives which we consider we are legitimately entitled to achieve, but only that we renounce the use of force to implement these policies.

Neither of us wants to negotiate under the threat of force. The free discussion of differences, and their fair and equitable solution, become impossible under the overhanging threat that force may be resorted to when one party does not agree with the other.

The United States as a member of the United Nations has agreed to refrain in its international relations from the threat or use of force. This has been its policy for many years and is its guiding principle of conduct in the Far East, as throughout the world.

The use of force to achieve national objectives does not accord with accepted standards of conduct under international law.

The Covenant of the League of Nations, the Kellogg-Briand treaties, and the Charter of the United Nations reflect the universal view of the civilized community of nations that the use of force as an instrument of national policy violates international law, constitutes a threat to international peace, and prejudices the interests of the entire world community.

There are in the world today many situations which tempt those who have force to use it to achieve what they believe to be legitimate policy objectives. Many countries are abnormally divided or contain what some consider to be abnormal intrusions. Nevertheless, the responsible governments of the world have in each of these cases renounced the use of force to achieve what they believe to be legitimate and even urgent goals. It is an essential foundation and preliminary to the success of the discussions under Item 2 that it first be made clear that the parties to these discussions renounce the use of force to make the policies of either prevail over those of the other. That particularly applies to the Taiwan area.

The acceptance of this principle does not involve third parties, or the justice or injustice of conflicting claims. It only involves recognizing and agreeing to abide by accepted standards of international conduct.

We ask, therefore, as a first matter for discussion under Item 2, a declaration that your side will not resort to the use of force in the Taiwan area, except defensively. The United States would be prepared to make a corresponding declaration. These declarations will make it appropriate for us to pass on to the discussion of other matters with a better hope of coming to constructive conclusions.

Annex C
Chinese Communist Draft Declaration on Renunciation of Force, Oct. 27, 1955

Ambassador Johnson on behalf of the Government of the People's Republic of China and Ambassador Johnson on behalf of the Government of the United States of America jointly declare that,

2. In accordance with Article 2, Paragraph 3, of the Charter of the United Nations, "All members shall settle their international disputes by peaceful means in such a manner that international peace and security, and justice, are not endangered"; and

3. In accordance with Article 2, Paragraph 4 of the Charter of the United Nations, "All members shall refrain in their international relations from the threat or use of force against the territorial integrity or political independence of any state, or in any other manner inconsistent with the purposes of the United Nations";

4. The People's Republic of China and the United States of America agree that they should settle disputes between their two countries by peaceful means without resorting to the threat or use of force.

5. In order to realize their common desire, the People's Republic of China and the United States of America decide to hold a conference of foreign ministers to settle through negotiations the question of relaxing and eliminating the tension in the Taiwan area.

Annex D
United States Draft Declaration on Renunciation of Force, Nov. 10, 1955

1. The Ambassador of the United States of America and the Ambassador of the People's Republic of China during the course of the discussions of practical matters at issue have expressed the determination that the differences between the two sides shall not lead to armed conflict.

2. They recognize that the use of force to achieve national objectives does not accord with the principles and purposes of the United Nations Charter or with generally accepted standards of international conduct.

3. They furthermore recognize that the renunciation of the threat or use of force is essential to the just settlement of disputes or situations which might lead to a breach of the peace.

4. Therefore, without prejudice to the pursuit by each side of its policies by peaceful means they have agreed to announce the following declarations:

5. Ambassador Wang informed Ambassador Johnson that:

6. In general, and with particular reference to the Taiwan area, the People's Republic of China renounces the use of force, except in individual and collective self-defense.

7. Ambassador Johnson informed Ambassador Wang that:

8. In general, and with particular reference to the Taiwan area, the United States renounces the use of force, except in individual and collective self-defense.

Annex E
Chinese Communist Draft Counterproposal for an Agreed Announcement Dec. 1, 1955

1. Ambassador Wang, on behalf of the Government of the People's Republic of China, and Ambassador Johnson on behalf of the Government of the United States of America, agree to announce:

2. The People's Republic of China and the United States of America are determined that they should settle disputes between their two countries

through peaceful negotiations without resorting to the threat or use of force;

3. The two ambassadors should continue their talks to seek practical and feasible means for the realization of this common desire.

Annex F
United States Revision of Chinese Communist Dec. 1 Counterproposal

1. Ambassador Wang, on behalf of the Government of the People's Republic of China, and Ambassador Johnson, on behalf of the Government of the United States of America, agree to announce:

2. The People's Republic of China and the United States of America are determined that they will settle disputes between them through peaceful means and that, without prejudice to the inherent right of individual and collective self-defense, they will not resort to the threat or use of force in the Taiwan area or elsewhere.

3. The two ambassadors should continue their talks to seek practical and feasible means for the realization of this common desire.

U.S. AND COMMUNIST CHINA TALK ON BUT GET NOWHERE

Meetings Between Ambassadors in Geneva Fail to Bring Agreement on the Issues

By JOSEPH N. MORGENSTERN
Special to The New York Times.

GENEVA, April 27—In the past twenty-one months the United States and Communist China have faced each other across a conference table in sixty-six meetings here. They have been meetings of men, never of minds.

The men are Alexis Johnson, United States Ambassador to Czechoslovakia, and Wang Ping-nan, Communist Chinese Ambassador to Poland. Their agreed agenda in the marathon talks is beguilingly simple:

(1) "The return of civilians of both sides to their respective countries," and (2) "other practical matters at issue between the two sides."

In practice there is little agreement on what the agenda means.

For Ambassador Johnson it means the release of eight Americans still held in Chinese jails (there were forty-one when the talks began in 1955), and a Sino-American renunciation of force in the settlement of all disputes between the two nations, including the Taiwan (Formosa) area.

Chinese View

Ambassador Wang lends a broader interpretation to the agenda. For him its first point includes the release of an unspecified number of Chinese nationals said to be held prisoner in the United States, while the second point embraces:

Relaxation of the United States trade embargo against Communist China, a foreign ministers' meeting between John Foster Dulles and Chou En-lai, "people's contacts and cultural exchange," a protean term which usually means United States permission for reporters to visit China, and a joint renunciation of force alluding to the territorial rights of China over Taiwan.

For each meeting the two diplomats fly to Geneva from their respective posts, Mr. Johnson in Prague and Mr. Wang in Warsaw. Sometimes they share the same airplane, but rarely speak to each other at any length. Mr. Wang's English is not good, while Mr. Johnson speaks neither Chinese nor German, Mr. Wang's only European language.

Good Start

Each Ambassador brings two aides and an interpreter along. Progress is slow because each speech is followed by an interpretation. The meetings usually last two or three hours, and no stenographic records are kept of them.

The Geneva meetings had an auspicious beginning. On the first day, Aug. 1, 1955, China released eleven American airmen she had previously imprisoned as spies.

On Sept. 10, 1955, Mr. Wang promised that all Americans who wanted to leave China would be released "expeditiously." Since then thirty-five Americans have been released, and Ambassador Johnson considers this ample justification for the meetings and their continuation. Two more of the eight civilians who remain are due to be released in June after serving three-year terms. Two others are serving life sentences—John T. Downey

of New Britain, Conn., and Richard Fecteau of Lynn, Mass.

At the same time China has repeatedly charged that the United States is detaining thousands of Chinese nationals. Last February India announced that her embassy in Washington, which was invited to act as intermediary in assisting any Chinese who wanted to return either to Taiwan or the mainland, had reported no such cases of detention and that India considered the Chinese charges unsubstantiated.

The United Kingdom's chargé d'affaires in Peiping is supposed to act in the same third-party capacity, but the British there have not been granted sufficient freedom to visit or communicate with United States citizens in China.

Early in the negotiations the United States and China said that they would announce agreements promptly and keep disagreements private. Since Sept. 10, 1955, there have been no agreements to announce, but there has been noisy public debate on the meetings' progress, especially the variant texts produced by both sides on the proposed renunciation of force.

Countless drafts of the document have been devised. Most of Ambassador Johnson's versions have asserted that the renunciation would not prejudice either nation's pursuit of peaceful policies or either side's inherent right of individual and collective self-defense.

In his own drafts Ambassador Wang has included references to the necessity of a foreign ministers' meeting, and territorial integrity of the signatory nations.

No agreement on renunciation of force has been reached, although Ambassador Johnson is adamant in his refusal to negotiate other matters before it is achieved and before the eight civilians are released.

These are important, perhaps crucial, questions at the Geneva talks, and they are certain to be revived when the two Ambassadors meet again on May 15.

CHAPTER 5

Laying the Foundations of Socialism

A rural enterprise of wheelmaking aids the Great Leap Forward.

CHINESE PUBLICIZE FIRST 5-YEAR PLAN

Books, Posters and Press Tell People of Indus'.ialization Program to Start in '53

By HENRY R. LIEBERMAN
Special to THE NEW YORK TIMES.

HONG KONG, Dec. 12—Preparations in Peiping for the advent of Communist China's first five-year plan are being accompanied by a flood of posters, books, pamphlets and newspaper dispatches designed to make the process of industrialization come alive for the average Chinese.

There are color posters on how to lay a brick and how to attend a machine—Soviet style; magazine layouts of mechanized farms, slick books on a Huai River conservation project and press discussions on differences between "productive, consumptive and floating" fixed assets.

By this time almost every participant in a mainland "study group" must know that a "fixed asset" is officially regarded as a capital asset with an effective life of at least one year and a value of at least 1,000,000 Peoples dollars (approximately $42.68 in United States currency). If the domestic press is any guide, one of the key phrases in China today is "chi pen chien she" (basic construction).

With their usual flair for pinpointing a motif and sustaining a propaganda drive, the Communists appear to have made the dismal categories of economics dramatically new and meaningful for Chinese eager to see their country develop. As explained by the pro-Communist paper Ta Kung Pao here, "basic construction" is a "Russian term"—almost as if capital construction were non-existent outside the Soviet bloc.

The Peiping regime's projected five-year plan is scheduled to begin in 1953.

Besides establishing a new State Planning Commission and five new "industrialization" ministries, the Communists recently completed the reorganization of China's higher schools with the aim of turning out more technicians. The stated objective is to produce 150,000 extra technicians within the next five or six years.

Among the new technical schools are a college of geology, an iron and steel institute, an institute of metallurgy and an institute of aeronautics. In the regular colleges about 100 "specialized majors" have been introduced so graduates will emerge fitted for specific jobs to which they will be assigned by the state.

Sectional Bureaus Set Up

A total of 65,893 students are reported to have passed their college matriculation examinations in September under the new system of "centralized enrollment." A breakdown of students by courses of study was listed as follows:

Engineering, 33,632; education, 8,406; medicine, 6,500; science, 5,420; agriculture and forestry, 4,250; the arts, 3,760; finance and economics, 2,700; politics, 720, and fine arts, 435.

Meanwhile, "basic construction' bureaus are being established sectionally throughout the country.

Regional reports refer to intensified geological surveying, the mobilization of construction working corps, and increases in the number of state engineering companies.

According to the Peiping radio, plans for the construction of the ambitious and lengthy Lanchow-Sinkiang Railway in Northwest China are scheduled to be completed by the end of this year. In 1953, however, the reported communications development plan calls for the actual construction of 480 miles of railroads and 4,000 miles of highway.

December 13, 1952

PEIPING'S ECONOMY HELD TRUCE SPUR

First 5-Year Plan Is Designed to Industrialize Nation on Lines of Soviet Union

By HENRY R. LIEBERMAN
Special to THE NEW YORK TIMES.

HONG KONG, July 10—After three years of reconstruction, the Chinese Communists have launched their first five-year plan this year with the objective of industrializing agricultural China just as the Communists industrialized the Soviet Union. The plan is regarded as a major reason for the Peiping Government's desire to achieve a cessation of military hostilities in Korea.

According to Li Fu-chun, vice chairman of the Committee of Economic and Financial Affairs the Government plans to give primary emphasis to the development of heavy industry. He declared in a recent speech that such an approach was necessary to lay the foundations of industrialization, promote modernization of the armed forces and guarantee steady expansion of the "Socialist sector" of the economy.

With the Chinese population now believed to exceed 450,000,000 and the present "petty agrarian economy" admittedly producing relatively small capital surpluses, the industrialization of China is apt to be either slower or more violent than that of the Soviet Union.

Early this year, following the introduction of the five-year plan,

Chinese Communist spokesmen said China could handle Korea and industrialization simultaneously But there is a widespread feeling here that the expenses and preoccupations of the Korean war have imposed substantial limitations on Peiping's infant industrialization program.

Defense Costs Run High

Even if one discounts the possibility of unpublicized "supplementary military budgets," Communist China's acknowledged national defense expenditures for 1953, as announced last Feb. 12 by Finance Minister Po I-po, have been set at the equivalent of about U. S $2,200,000,000. This is more than twice as much as the Chinese Nationalists used to spend for all of their annual budget.

Last January Chia To-ru, another vice chairman of the Committee of Economic and Financial Affairs, disclosed that there had been a 30 per cent cutback in building plans because of inadequate working force and materials. Official reports since then have revealed shortages and delays in the delivery of materials and equipment in East China and Manchuria.

Red China, which is now carrying on the bulk of its foreign trade under barter deals with Soviet bloc countries, is being required to develop its industrial economy primarily out of surpluses derived from Chinese agriculture. Pointing out that China could not depend on foreign loans as a "principal method" of industrialization, The Peiping People's Daily declared last Nov. 20 that industrialization funds would have to be accumulated gradually out of production by state enterprises and budgetary savings.

But the published figures for the 1953 budget, which amounts to the equivalent of United States $9,864,700,000, revealed an uncovered gap approximating United $527,700,000 even before the Government disclosed the occurrence of a wheat blight in five provinces astride and above the Yangtze several months ago. According to Premier Chou En-lai, the task of increasing grain production this year promises to be "arduous."

Teng Tzu-hui, director of the Chinese Communist party's Rural-Village Work Department, stated recently that China hoped to increase her yearly agricultural output by 70 per cent during the next ten years. He said this goal called for a production of between 275,-000,000 and 300,000,000 tons of food annually by the end of the second five-year plan in 1962.

Meanwhile, the first five-year plan seems off to a fairly modest start.

The Government is continuing with its ambitious project of connecting the Chungking-Chengtu Railway with the Lanchow-Tien-shui Railway and extending the latter line into Sinkiang Province on the northwest Chinese-Soviet frontier. But only about 360 miles of new railway are scheduled to be opened to traffic this year.

With the capital investments of industrial departments set at 150 per cent above the planned figure for 1952, the state expects the value of industrial output to be about 23 per cent higher in 1953 than last year. Two sets of percentage goals announced in Peiping last Feb. 4 and later on May 7 show the following alterations in production goals for 1953, the first year of the first five-year plan (1952 = base of 100):

	Feb. 4 Pcts.	May 7 Pcts.
Grain	109	....
Tea	116	....
Cotton	116	....
Cotton Yarn	109	109.4
Cotton Piece Goods	116	110.5
Coal	100	....
Crude Oil	142	129.1
Electrical Power	127	118.3
Pig Iron	114	113.3
Steel Ingots	123	122.1
Rolled Steel	....	134.8
Machine Tools	134	....
Power Generators	....	290.9
Electric Motors (in KW)	....	141.2
Metal-Cutt'g Lathes (No.)	....	104.6
Copper Lathes	....	128.6
Caustic Soda	131	....
Nitric Acid	....	134.3
Ammonium Nitrate	....	132
Copper	139	....
Lead	149	134.6
Zinc	154	132
Cement	117	129.7
Paper	106	107.9
Timber	138	135

New Products Planned

Among the new products reported planned for 1953 are seamless steel tubes, silicon steel sheets 6,000-kw. steam turbines and generators, 20,000-kva. transformers 1,450-kw. electric motors and Soviet-type planers, lathes, three-meter shears and five-meter thread milling machines. The announced goal of a 15 per cent increase in labor productivity this year suggests, however, that most of the projected higher output for 1953 is expected to come from improved labor efficiency rather than new machinery.

Some Soviet machinery is apparently reaching China under the Chinese-Soviet credit agreement of Feb. 14, 1950, but there are no signs of any striking large-scale Soviet economic aid.

The Chinese Communists, who concede that they have much to learn about industrialization, have acknowledged early difficulties in the execution of their first five-year plan. Among some of the difficulties recently cited by the mainland press are:

Overambitious "adventurous plans," weakness of coordination as a result of "self-centralism," "wrong concept of design and shortage of designers," "poor quality and quantity of construction work," "alarming waste and irresponsibility," "violation of the financial control system" and "continuous occurrence of fatal accidents and damage to equipment."

Several basic steps already have been taken by the Peiping regime to create a foundation for planned industrialization. These include:

¶Administrative moves involving the establishment of a new State Planning Commission, a series of new industrialization ministries and more intra-ministry "Basic Construction Departments" and regional construction companies.

¶The start of a geological survey pegged primarily to the search for additional sources of non-ferrous minerals, "colored metals" and coal.

¶Reorganization of the education system to meet the need both for top level technicians and more skilled specialists to handle particular jobs as quickly as possible.

According to Chinese Communist spokesmen, the industrialization program will require 150,000 to 200,000 top-level technicians and about 500,000 "intermediate and junior technical personnel" during the next five or six years. "Specialized majors" have been established in the technical schools to qualify students for specific jobs, while short-course training classes have been started at factories and mines.

About 219,700 students are officially reported to be enrolled in institutions of higher education. Primary emphasis is being given to engineering training.

During the last three years the Communists have restored China's railway system and undertaken the construction of several new railways and a large-scale water conservation project on the Huai River. They also report that 1952 production exceeded virtually all previous peak levels for both agriculture and industry, except in the case of coal.

Peiping officials have stated that China produced 163,750,000 tons of food and 1,290,000 tons of cotton last year. Ecomic analysts here have doubted these figures and also are puzzled by the statement that Red China outproduced the Japanese in Manchuria with a much lesser amount of electrical capacity. These analysts estimate that China produced about 140,000,000 metric tons of grain and a little more than 6,000,000 tons of cotton in 1952.

RED CHINA IS FACING INDUSTRIAL TROUBLE

TOKYO, Saturday, Jan. 2 (P) —A review of 1953 and a look into 1954 today by the Peiping People's Daily, official organ of Red China's Government, hinted at troubles both past and present in changing over the nation's sprawling millions to communism.

The Peiping radio broadcast a long editorial on the workings of the first year of the Government's five-year construction plan and what to expect in the New Year.

"We are well aware that it will take a very long time for us to pass into socialism," the editorial noted.

Dealing with the speed of industrial development, the newspaper cautioned, "it would be wrong, of course, for us to raise our demands to too high a level nor should we expect industry to grow at the same ratio as before."

The editorial said the Red Government, needing money for industrial construction, will issue National Economic Construction bonds this year. The purpose, it stated, is "to draw the people into supporting national construction with surplus cash or funds that can be saved by practising economy."

YANGTZE FLOODS SLOWLY RECEDING

Traffic Is Resumed on Key Railway Line — Peiping Shuns Relief Offers

By HENRY R. LIEBERMAN
Special to The New York Times.

HONG KONG, Sept. 5—River levels in east central China were reported falling slowly tonight and traffic was resumed on some sections of the Peiping-Hankow railway after the biggest floods of the century in the Yangtze and Hwai River valleys.

Barring further heavy downpours as the rain belt shifts northward to the Yellow River basin, the worst was apparently over. But despite the subsiding flood waters the Peiping Government remains confronted by serious problems of famine relief and economic dislocation.

According to the Peiping People's Daily, official Chinese Communist organ, the recent floods inundated about 6 per cent of China's total "cultivated area." This figure indicates that more than 20,000 square miles of cropland were under water.

At the same time, however, the floods are officially described as having been worse than the record 1931 Yangtze and Hwai River disasters. In 1931, the Yangtze and the Hwai ran rampant in floods that inundated an area of 34,000 square miles and affected a farm population of 25,200,000.

With lagging agricultural output already imposing a drag on Peiping's industrialization program, these swollen rivers struck hard again in fertile rice lands around Tungting Lake, Poyang Lake and in south and central Anhwei Province. As reported by the People's Daily, "the early rice crop was submerged and the late rice crop could not be planted in good time."

Rice accounts for 41.6 per cent of China's total food output while millet, corn, kaoliang and potatoes account for 40 per cent and wheat for 10 per cent.

The recent rice land floods follow a wheat blight last year in north central China as a result of a series of calamities, including unseasonable frost, insects, pests and hailstorms.

In the opinion of political observers here, the floods will undoubtedly upset Peiping's 1954 economic plan and possibly also require re-examination of China's present barter position within the Soviet trading bloc. China's foreign trade pattern involves exchange of agricultural and mineral products for industrial goods.

After last year's wheat blight the Government tightened its control over the national grain market under a policy of accelerated agricultural "socialization." Observers here are now watching to see what effects the floods will have on this "socialization" program.

Substantial crop acreage is reported to have been flooded in Hunan, Hupei, Kiangsu, Anhwei and Chekiang provinces and the Government is sending food into rice-growing centers that normally export food to other parts of China.

One mainland report said the Ministry of Interior had appropriated 450,000,000,000 yuan since the end of June (about $19,000,000 at the official rate) for relief in the stricken areas.

Tens of thousands of Chinese, including troops, peasants, laborers and government workers, are reported to have been at work in the Yangtze and Hwai valleys fortifying dikes and strengthening embankments. In the tri-city area of Wuhan (Hankow, Wuchang, Hanyang), authorities provided thirty locomotives, 650 freight cars, more than 1,000 trucks, fifty-five ships, 300 barges and 500 boats to haul earth, stone and other repair materials.

Official mainland dispatches credit these flood fighters with having saved Hankow and Nanking from being submerged. Other reports state, however, there has been some flood seepage in both cities.

"There is almost a solid sheet of water between Changsha and Hankow with water spreading to about twenty miles north of Hankow," said a traveler who recently flew over this area. "Tungting Lake and the [Yangtze] river were one."

Rainfall in the lower and middle reaches of the Yangtze was two and a half times greater than normal between April and July, according to the New China (Hsinhua) news agency.

During the 1931 flood, the agency recalled, the Yangtze River level at Wuhan reached a record high of 92.76 feet. On Aug. 18 this year, it added, the Yangtze level at Wuhan was 97.51 feet.

The river level is said to have fallen somewhat at Wuhan, but is still regarded as being above danger level. Flood workers there have been warned to remain on the alert. An alert is also being maintained along the Yellow River where the flood season is said to be late this year.

RED CHINA ASKING CONTINUED PURGE

Peiping Newspaper Renews Demand for Elimination of 'Counter-Revolutionaries'

By HENRY R. LIEBERMAN
Special to The New York Times

HONG KONG, July 3—Communist China's leading newspaper re-emphasized today the theme of a purge of the "revolutionary ranks."

The new purge demand came as members of the National People's Congress began gathering in Peiping for a session scheduled to open Tuesday.

The Peiping People's Daily, official organ of the Communist party's Central Committee, called editorially for elimination of "all counter-revolutionaries who may have wormed their way into the ranks of the revolution."

This theme was blended with another attack on Hu Feng, a Marxist writer-critic and People's Congress delegate who has been under heavy criticism in the mainland press for several months.

The Chinese Communists have made him a key symbol in a developing crack-down that now appears to be threatening alleged "counter-revolutionaries" inside as well as outside their official ranks.

Session to Approve Plan

The national People's Congress is being called for the announced purposes of endorsing a revised draft of the 1953-1957 five-year plan and adopting a 1955 state budget. It is expected the Peiping regime may also ask this body to formalize Hu Feng's expulsion and underwrite a broader drive against "Hu Feng elements."

According to the Communist newspaper the Shanghai police arrested fifty-three members of the mystical I Kuan Tao society in April. They were accused of having carried out "subversion under the cloak of preaching taoism."

The People's Daily said thirty-two others had been tried on charges of belonging to "the secret liaison department of the Kuomintang" in Kiangsu, Anhwei and Shantung. It added that six had been ordered executed and twenty-six given

sentences ranging from police surveillance to life imprisonment.

Twelve more were reported to have been tried in Heilungkiang North Manchuria, on charges of belonging to an "underground Kuomintang organization" based in Mukden. The penalties were not revealed.

The People's Daily also reported the trial of eleven alleged members of a "Kuomintang northwest working team" at Tingsi, Kansu province March 24. It said six had been sentenced to death, two given life imprisonment and others sentenced to terms of five to twenty years.

July 4, 1955

CHINA'S RATIONING HELD TEMPORARY

Special to The New York Times.

HONG KONG, Sept. 21—The Chinese Communists' rationing of grain, edible oil and cotton cloth has been ascribed by an official to shortages that developed last year.

Deputy Premier Chen Yun in an address to the National People's Congress acknowledged that the controlled purchase and supply of these basic consumer items affected the daily lives of the Chinese people. But he declared the controls were necessary to meet their growing needs, prevent hoarding, stabilize prices and "successfully consummate the first five-year plan."

Mr. Chen, a high-ranking member of the Communist party's politburo as well as head of the aNtional Financial and Economic Affairs Committee, said the controls were "temporary." His speech was summarized by the Hsinhua (New China) News Agency.

The controlled supply and distribution of grain was introduced last November under a decree that outlawed private trade in

grain and required tne peasants to sell their "surplus grain" to the state at fixed prices. Provision was made for a rationing system under which consumers would buy their cereals against food purchase ertificates or census books.

Shortly afterward, the same system was applied to cooking oil. This was followed on Sept. 14, last, by two new decrees that extended the state's "planned purchase and planned supply" controls to raw cotton and cotton cloth.

Under the cotton decrees, cloth is to be distributed on the basis of "control figures" fixed for each administrative unit. An official announcement said cloth purchasing coupons would be issued for two six-month periods beginning this month.

Mr. Chen said the rationing controls were not caused by failing production or excessive exports but chiefly by a "phenomenal increase of the people's purchasing power."

Last year, he said, China produced 165,000 tons of food, compared with an annual average of 140,000,000 tons between 1931 and 1936. In 1953, he continued, the country also produced 1,175,-000 tons of cotton compared with a pre-war peak of 800,000 tons.

September 25, 1954

Communique on 7 Accords
Text of the Soviet-Chinese Communist

LONDON, Oct. 11 (Reuters)— Following is the text of the Soviet-Chinese Communist communiqué broadcast by the Moscow radio:

On the Soviet Government Delegation's Visit to the Chinese People's Republic

During the stay of the Soviet delegation in the Chinese People's Republic, talks were held on the question of Chinese-Soviet relations and the international situation between the members of the delegation on the one hand and the Premier of the State Council and Minister of Foreign Affairs of the Chinese People's Republic, Chou En-lai, and others.

The Chairman of the Chinese People's Republic, Mao Tsetung; the Deputy Chairman, Chu Teh; the Secretary of the Central Committee of the Communist party of China and Chairman of the Permanent Committee of the All-Chinese Assembly of People's Representatives, Liu Shao-chi, also took part in the negotiations.

The negotiations took place in an atmosphere of sincere friendship and mutual understanding.

The following are the joint declarations of the Governments of the Soviet Union and the Chinese People's Republic on questions of Chinese-Soviet relations, and the international situation and on the question of relations with Japan; their joint communiqué on the question of the Port Arthur naval base; on the question of the existing mixed Soviet-Chinese shareholding societies; on agreement relating to scientific-technical collaboration; and on the building of the Lanchow - Urumchi - Alma Ata railway.

In addition, agreements were signed on the question of the Soviet Government's provision to the Government of the Chinese People's Republic of a long-term credit amounting to 520,000,000 rubles and a protocol concerning the Soviet Government's rendering of assistance to the Government of the Chinese People's Republic.

For the construction of a further fifteen enterprises and increasing the volume of sup-

plies of equipment for 141 enterprises envisaged under a previously signed agreement, the total value of the additional supplies of equipment from the U.S.S.R. will amount to 400,-000,000 rubles.

JOINT DECLARATION OF THE GOVERNMENTS OF THE U. S. S. R. AND THE CHINESE PEOPLE'S REPUBLIC

The Government of the U.S.S.R. and the Government of the Chinese People's Republic establish the existence of complete unity of views both in the sphere of the growing multilateral cooperation between the two states and in questions relating to the international situation.

During the last five years, since the historic victory of the Chinese people and the creation of the Chinese People's Republic, relations between the Soviet Union and the Chinese People's Republic were established based on close cooperation, fully corresponding to the treaty of friendship, alliance and mutual aid of Feb. 14, 1950.

At the basis of this treaty lies

the sincere striving of the Chinese and Soviet people to render each other mutual aid, to help the economic and cultural progress of both countries, the further strengthening and development of fraternal friendship between them, and by that means to help in consolidating peace and security in the Far East and the whole world, in accordance with the aims and principles of the United Nations.

Experience has shown the great vital force of the cooperation established between the Soviet Union and the Chinese People's Republic, which is a reliable bulwark of peace and security in the Far East and an important factor in the cause of maintaining general peace.

The Governments of the Soviet Union and the Chinese People's Republic declare that the friendly relations that have been established between the U. S. S. R. and the Chinese People's Republic form the basis of further close collaboration between the

two states, in accordance with the principles of equality, mutual advantage, mutual respect of state sovereignty, and territorial integrity.

246

Both Governments are unanimous in their striving to continue to participate in all international actions aimed at strengthening peace and will consult each other every time questions touching upon the common interests of the Soviet Union and the Chinese People's Republic arise, with the aim of coordinating their actions aimed at insuring the security of both states, the maintenance of peace in the Far East and all over the world.

The Geneva conference, which led to cessation of military activities in Indochina and opened the possibility for a solution of the Indochinese situation in conformity with the legitimate national interests of the peoples of this area, showed the importance for the cause of peace of the participation of all the great powers in exchanging all the urgent international problems on which the United Nations charter places the main responsibility for the maintenance of international peace.

It has also shown the complete groundlessness of the policy of the ruling United States circles who are preventing the Chinese People's Republic from taking its lawful place in the United Nations Organization.

Such a policy, like the direct acts of aggression committed by the United States toward the Chinese People's Republic and the continued occupation by the United States of a part of the Chinese People's Republic's territory, in particular the island of Taiwan [Formosa], and the military and financial support to the Chiang Kai-shek clique which is hostile to the Chinese people, all these are incompatible with the tasks of maintaining peace in the Far East and lessening of international tension.

Both Governments consider abnormal the situation in which Korea continues to remain divided in two parts, despite the natural aspirations of the Korean people for national reunification into a united, peace-loving democratic Korean state.

One of the important problems, the solution of which would have a great importance for the consolidation of peace in the Far East, is the reunification of Korea. They consider as essential the convening in the nearest future of a conference on the Korean problem, with a broad participation of the states concerned.

The Soviet Union and the Chinese People's Republic resolutely condemn the setting up of an aggressive military bloc in Southeast Asia, for at the oasis of this bloc lie the imperialistic aims of its initiators directed first of all against the security and national independence of Asian countries as well as against the interests of peace in the area of Asia and the Pacific.

They deem it necessary to declare that the Soviet Union and the Chinese People's Republic will continue to build their relations with countries of Asia and the Pacific, as well as with other countries, on the basis of a strict observance of the principles of mutual respect for sovereignty and territorial integrity, of mutual nonaggression,

mutual noninterference in domestic affairs, equality and mutual advantage and peaceful coexistence which opens wide possibilities for the development of fruitful international cooperation.

Both Governments are deeply convinced that such a policy corresponds to the fundamental interests of all peoples, including those of Asia, the security and well-being of which can be guaranteed only on the basis of the mutual efforts of countries in defense of peace.

The Soviet Government and the Government of the Chinese People's Republic will, for their part, make all efforts to contribute to the unsolved international problems, including those pertaining to Asia.

JOINT DECLARATION OF THE GOVERNMENTS OF THE U. S. S. R. AND THE CHINESE PEOPLE'S REPUBLIC CONCERNING RELATIONS WITH JAPAN

After the end of World War II, Japan in accordance with the provisions of the Potsdam agreement was to be given full national independence, had to create her own democratic institutions and develop her independent peaceful economy and national culture.

The U. S. A., however, as the major occupying power in Japan charged with the main responsibility of implementing the Potsdam decisions, has grossly violated these decisions and, trampling underfoot the interests of the Japanese people foisted upon Japan the San Francisco "peace treaty" and other agreements that run contrary to the above-mentioned agreements of the states.

Nine years have elapsed since the end of the war and Japan has not been given independence. She continues to be in the state of a partly occupied country. Her territory is covered with numerous United States military bases, set up for purposes that have nothing in common with maintenance of peace and insuring the peaceful and independent development of Japan. Japan's industry and finance are dependent on American military orders. In foreign trade Japan is restricted, which has a pernicious effect on her economy, notably on the peaceful branches of industry.

All this cannot fail to insult the national sentiment of the Japanese people, creating an atmosphere of uncertainty among them and restricting the many abilities of the Japanese people.

The present position of Japan creates the justified anxiety among the peoples of Asia and the Far East that she might be used in aggressive plans alien both to the interests of the Japanese people and to the task of maintaining peace in the Far East.

The peoples of the Soviet Union and of the Chinese People's Republic express their deep sympathy for Japan and the Japanese people who have found themselves in a difficult position as a result of the above-mentioned treaty and agreements dictated by foreign interests.

They believe that the Japanese people would find enough strength in themselves to take the path of liberation from foreign dependence and that of the revival of their mother country, the path of establishing normal relations, broad economic cooperation and cultural ties with other states, in the first place with her neighbors.

The Governments of the Soviet Union and the Chinese People's Republic in their policy with regard to Japan, are moved by the principle of the peaceful coexistence of states, irrespective of their social systems, being confident that this is in accord with the vital interests of all peoples. They stand for the development of extensive trade relations with Japan on mutually profitable terms and the establishment of close cultural relations with her.

They also express their readiness to take steps to normalize their relations with Japan' and declare that Japan will meet full support in her striving to establish political and economic relations with the U. S. S. R. and the Chinese People's Republic and that all her steps to provide conditions for her peaceful and independent development will meet full support.

SOVIET-CHINESE COMMUNIQUE ON THE EVACUATION OF SOVIET MILITARY UNITS FROM THE JOINTLY USED CHINESE NAVAL BASE OF PORT ARTHUR AND THE TRANSFER OF THIS BASE TO THE COMPLETE DISPOSAL OF THE CHINESE PEOPLE'S RE-PUBLIC

Taking into consideration the change in the international situation in the Far East in connection with the ending of the war in Korea and the establishment of peace in Indo-

china, as well as taking into account the strengthening of the defense potential of the Chinese Peoples Republic, the Governments of the Soviet Union and the Chinese People's Republic, in accordance with the relations of friendship and collaboration that have become established and are strengthening increasingly between the two states, have agreed that Soviet military units are to be evacuated from the jointly used naval base of Port Arthur and the installations in that area are to be transferred without compensation to the Government of the Chinese People's Republic.

The implementation of the steps connected with the evacuation of Soviet military units and the transfer of installations in the Port Arthur Naval Base Area to the Government of the Chinese People's Republic, it has been decided by both sides, will be the responsibility of the Soviet-Chinese Joint Military Commission in Port Arthur, formed in accordance with the agreement of Feb. 14, 1950.

The evacuation of the Soviet troops and the transfer of the installations to the Government of the Chinese People's Republic in the Port Arthur Naval Base Area will be completed by May 31, 1955.

SOVIET-CHINESE COMMUNIQUE ON THE TRANSFER TO THE CHINESE PEOPLE'S REPUBLIC OF THE SOVIET SHARE OF PARTICIPATION IN MIXED COMPANIES

In 1950 and in 1951, according to an agreement between the Soviet and Chinese Governments, four mixed Soviet-Chinese companies were set upon a basis of parity; a company for the mining of non-ferrous and rare metals in Sinkiang Province of the Chinese People's Republic; a company for the extraction and refining of oil in this province; a company for

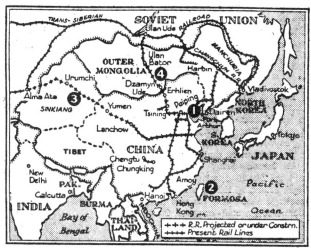

The New York Times   Oct. 12, 1954

SOVIET-CHINESE ACCORD: The Russians agreed to withdraw troops from Port Arthur (1) and joined the Communist Chinese in a demand that the United States end its "occupation" of Formosa (2). New railroad links across Sinkiang (3) and Outer Mongolia (4) are to be built.

the building and repair of ships in the town of Darien, and a company for the organization and exploitation of civil airlines.

This was at a time when the young Chinese People's Republic was facing the tasks of reconstructing its national economy. The formation of Soviet-Chinese companies made it possible to organize within a short time the work of enterprises which were part of these companies to widen considerably their production capacity to raise the general technical level by using advanced Soviet experience in economic building. Thus the mixed companies played their positive part and made a definite contribution to the reconstruction and development of Chinese economy.

At present, when the Chinese People's Republic, having reconstructed her economy, is successfully fulfilling the first five-year plan, Chinese economic organizations have accumulated the necessary experience and can themselves manage the activity of enterprises which are part of the mixed companies. The Governments of the U. S. S. R. and of the Chinese People's Republic have reached agreement that the Soviet share of participation in the mixed Soviet-Chinese companies will be transferred entirely to the Chinese People's Republic on Jan. 1, 1955. The value of this share will be compensated over a number of years by supplying to the Soviet Union goods which are items of usual export from the Chinese People's Republic.

Thus, those enterprises which are at present part of the mixed Soviet-Chinese societies will become entirely state enterprises.

Both Governments are of the unanimous opinion that this decision corresponds to the relations of friendship established between the Soviet Union and the Chinese People's Republic

and will contribute to a further strengthening of economic cooperation on the basis of equality, mutual aid and a respect for mutual interests.

SOVIET-CHINESE COMMUNIQUE ON THE SIGNING OF AN AGREEMENT ON SCIENTIFIC-TECHNICAL COOPERATION

Talks on Soviet-Chinese scientific-technical cooperation have been held in Moscow and Peiping between the Governments of the U. S. S. R. and the Chinese People's Republic. The talks, which were conducted in a sincere and friendly atmosphere, ended in the signing on Oct. 12 in Peiping of an agreement on scientific-technical cooperation between the U. S. S. R. and the Chinese People's Republic.

On behalf of the Government of the U. S. S. R. the agreement was signed by the Deputy Chairman of the Council of Ministers of the U. S. S. R. [Anastas I.] Mikoyan, and on behalf of the Government of the Chinese People's Republic by the Deputy Premier of the State Council of the Chinese People's Republic, Li Fu-chun.

In accordance with the agreement, the two Governments agree on the implementation of scientific-technical cooperation between both countries through the exchange of experience in all branches of national economy. Both sides will hand over to each other technical documents, will exchange appropriate information and will also commission specialists to give technical assistance and to acquaint themselves with the achievements of both countries in scientific-technical fields.

The transfer of technical documents will be carried out by both sides free of charge with the sole exception of payment

for the actual costs of preparing the copies of the documents.

To work out measures for carrying out cooperation and presenting to both Governments the necessary recommendations, a Soviet-Chinese commission of seven members from each country has been set up. The commission will meet not less frequently than twice annually, alternatively in Moscow and Peking [Peiping]. The agreement is signed for five years.

Unless one of the parties declares within one year before the date of expiry of the agreement its willingness to terminate the agreement, it will remain in force for a further period of five years.

The conclusion of the Chinese-Soviet agreement on scientific and technical cooperation is a new and important contribution to the cause of the further strengthening of cooperation between the U.S.S.R. and the Chinese People's Republic in the interests of both countries, as well as in the interests of strengthening peace.

JOINT SOVIET - CHINESE COMMUNIQUE ON THE BUILDING OF A RAILWAY BETWEEN LANCHOW, URUMCHI AND ALMA ATA AND ORGANIZATION OF DIRECT COMMUNICATION

With the purpose of strengthening mutual economic and cultural relations, the Governments of the U. S. S. R. and of the Chinese People's Republic have agreed that both sides, in the nearest future, should begin the building of a railway line from Lanchow through Urumchi, on Chinese territory, to Alma Ata on Soviet territory.

The Chinese Government takes upon itself the building of this railway line on Chinese territory. The Soviet Government takes upon itself the building

on the territory of the Soviet Union. During the building of the said railway line on Chinese territory, the Soviet Government will render every technical aid to the Chinese Government. The building of a sector of this railway, from Lanchow to Yumen on Chinese territory, has already been started, in 1953.

JOINT COMMUNIQUE OF GOVERNMENTS OF U. S. S. R., THE CHINESE PEOPLE'S REPUBLIC AND MONGOLIAN PEOPLE'S REPUBLIC ON THE BUILDING OF A RAILWAY FROM TSINING TO ULAN BATOR AND ORGANIZATION OF DIRECT COMMUNICATION

The Governments of the U. S. R., the Chinese People's Republic and the Mongolian People's Republic, with the aim of strengthening economic and cultural relations between them, concluded on Sept. 15, 1952, an agreement relating to the building of a railway between Tsining in the Chinese People's Republic, and Ulan Bator in the territory of the Mongolian People's Republic. The above-mentioned railway will be linked with the railway running from Ulan Bator to Soviet territory.

The building of the railway from Tsining through Erhlien the frontier of China is being undertaken by the Chinese Government. The building of the railway from Ulan Bator through Dzamyn Ude to the frontier of Mongolian People's Republic is being undertaken by the Government of the U. S. S. R. and the Government of the Mongolian People's Republic.

The three contracting governments have agreed to complete the building and the linking of the above-mentioned railway and to organize a direct connection in 1955.

October 12, 1954

PEIPING PLANNER URGES AUSTERITY

Goal Is Socialism in 15 Years, Full Industrializing in 50— Officials' Pay Still Cash

Special to The New York Times.

HONG KONG, June 21 — Li Fu-chun, head of Communist China's Planning Committee, has called for "stringent austerity" to help convert the nation to "socialism" within fifteen years and make it an "advanced" industrial country in half a century.

He said three five-year plans would be required to "build socialism." The Peiping regime's first one was begun in 1953.

The Hsinhua (New China) News Agency reported today that Mr. Li, a Deputy Premier, told a group of conferees June 13 that the "fragile foundations" of Communist China's industries restricted the present pace of capital accumulation. Nevertheless, he emphasized the need for greater savings to provide the "enormous capital" required by the state's industrialization program.

Mr. Li denounced "waste" on "nonproductive" projects and urged a 10-to-15 per cent cut in new building costs.

The Deputy Premier called for less architectural ornamentation, curtailed use of automobiles, no serving of refreshments or cigarettes at Government meetings, and no banquets except for the entertainment of foreign guests. He said official personnel living in dormitories would have to provide their own furniture after the projected switchover to the new wage system.

A Chinese monitor's misunderstanding of a domestic Peiping radio broadcast led to an erroneous report yesterday that Government workers in Communist China would be paid in kind rather than in money as of July 1.

According to a subsequent wireless dispatch from Peiping, the public functionaries now being compensated in the form of state-supplied "daily necessities" are scheduled to be shifted over to a money payment system of "real" [actual] wages effective July 1.

Beginning in August, the dispatch said, rents and utility charges will be collected from official personnel living in state-supplied dwellings.

June 23, 1955

New Railway in Red China
Special to The New York Times.

HONG KONG, Thursday, June 23—The Hsinhua (New China) News Agency reported this morning a new 190-mile railway had been completed in Communist China from Litang on the Hunan-Kwangsi line southeastward to Chankiang on the Luichow Peninsula above Hainan Island.

June 23, 1955

Peiping Completes Rail Link
Special to The New York Times.

HONG KONG, June 30—A new rail link, sixty-five miles long and with sixty-five tunnels accounting for one-fourth of its length, has been completed in the Peiping area from Fengtai northwest to Shacheng. Hsinhua (New China) news agency said construction work, begun in 1953, was completed today, six months ahead of schedule.

July 1, 1955

PEIPING REVISES ITS 5-YEAR PLAN

By HENRY R. LIEBERMAN

Special to The New York Times.

HONG KONG, Wednesday, July 6 — Communist China's revised Five-Year Plan was projected by its chief architect today in terms of a reduced grain target, somewhat slower agricultural collectivization and continued stress on heavy industry.

Vice Premier Li Fu-Chun, head of State Planning Commission, outlined the altered plan in a report to the opening session of National People's Congress in Peiping. According to the Peiping radio, 1,105 delegates gathered in the Huai Jen Tang (Hall of Benevolence) for the second annual meeting of the Congress.

Mao Tse-tung, and number of other top-ranking Communist officials were present as honored delegates while Ho Chi Minh, president of North Vietnam, who is still visiting in Peiping, attended as a guest. Liu Shao-chi, secretary general of the Chinese Communist party, presided as head of the People's Congress standing committee.

On the agenda, it was announced, are endorsement of a revised draft of the Five-Year Plan, adoption of a 1955 budget, enactment of a military conscription law and consideration of a project to tame the Yellow River. The 1953-57 Five-Year Plan has been changed in midcourse following approval of such action by a Communist party conference.

In his lengthy report on the plan, Mr. Li announced that the present blueprint called for increasing the 1952 grain output by 17.6 per cent to 192,800,000 tons in 1957.

Originally the Communists envisaged a 30 per cent increase in grain production by the end of their first Five-Year Plan.

Regarding industry, Mr. Li said the 156 construction and renovation projects that the Soviet Union was helping Red China to design remained the core of 694 "above norm" projects covered by the plan. The "norm" is understood to be about U. S. $1,265,000 for a light industrial project and $2,110,000 for a heavy industrial project.

Mr. Li said the value of the industrial production was scheduled to be increased 98.3 per cent during the plan. He said the Peiping regime intended to spend funds worth more than 700,000,000 ounces of gold (the current United States rate is $35 a fine ounce) for economic construction and cultural and educational development during the five-year period

Goals for Over-all Period

For the first time since the plan was started in 1953 concrete figures were revealed on goals set for the over-all period. Mr. Li listed the industrial goals for 1957 compared with 1952 as follows:

Steel: 4,120,000 tons compared with 1,350,000 tons (Peiping regime's 1954 estimate was 2,170,000 tons).

Electricity: 15,920,000,000 kilowatt hours compared with 7,260,000,000 kilowatt hours (1954 estimate 10,800,000,000 kilowatt hours).

Coal: 113,000,000 tons compared with 63,500,000 (1954 estimate 81,990,000).

Generators: 227,000 kilowatts compared with 30,000 kilowatts (no 1954 official estimate).

Electric motors: 1,050,000 kilowatts compared with 640,000 kilowatts. (No 1954 estimate.)

Cement: 6,000,000 tons compared with 2,860,000 (1954 estimate 4,730,000 tons).

Machine-processed paper: 650,000 tons compared with 370,000 tons (1954 estimate 480,000 tons).

Cotton piece goods: 163,720,000 bolts compared with 111,630,000 bolts. (No 1954 official estimate. Last year's official estimate was given in terms of 4,600,000 bales of cotton yarn.)

Machine-processed sugar: 686,000 tons compared with 249,000 tons. (No 1954 official estimate.)

Other 1957 goals are:

Cotton: 1,635,000 tons; jute and ambary hemp, 365,000 tons; tobacco, 390,000 tons; sugarcane, 13,150,000 tons, and sugar beets, 2,135,000 tons.

Mr. Li said that forty-eight major projects would be constructed or rebuilt at Anshan, Manchurian steel center, during the eight-year period ending in 1960. When these projects are completed, he said, Anshan is scheduled to produce 2,500,000 tons of pig iron, 3,220,000 tons of steel and 2,480,000 tons of rolled steel.

Mr. Li told the People's Congress that fifteen new steam power stations, each with a capacity of more than 50,000 kilowatts, would be built during the Five-Year Plan. He said the plan also embraced construction work on thirty-one coal-mining enterprises each with capacity more than 1,000,000 tons.

Mr. Li declared it would still take about fifteen years to carry out a "Socialist transformation" of Red China and forty to fifty years to achieve a "high degree of Socialist industrialization." Despite the apparent slowdown in the rate of agricultural collectivization, he made it clear the Communists would continue to follow the path of collectivization.

July 6, 1955

RED CHINA SPEEDS SOCIALIST CHANGE

Forms 'Joint' State-Private Companies and Lightens Its Grip on Farming

By HENRY R. LIEBERMAN

Special to The New York Times.

HONG KONG—A speed-up in the "Socialist transformation" of agriculture and privately owned urban business enterprises marked the third year of Red China's first five-year plan.

During the last half of 1955 the Chinese Communists just about doubled the number of land-pooling agricultural "producers' cooperatives." Toward the end of the year they also told private business men to make "mental preparations" now for nationalization of the "means of production."

Meanwhile, the Government has stepped up the formation of "joint" state-private companies. This intermediate process of nationalization involves reorganizing, consolidating and rationizing individual companies by trade groupings under unified state direction.

The Government, which has had a tight grip on the over-all economy for some time now, is in the midst of regrouping small economic units into larger and more rigidly controlled units. In Shanghai, for example, 187 "joint" enterprises in the heavy industrial field are being regrouped into fifty-three enterprises

While moving toward the "trustification" of the private urban economy, the Chinese Communists have announced their intention to "buy off the bourgeoisie." This procedure, Peiping has stated, is to involve the allocation of "part of the profit" or temporary interest payments to the "capitalists" while their enterprises are being nationalized during the course of "more than ten years."

No further compensation is contemplated.

The Land-Pooling Plan

The agricultural "producers' cooperative," which pools individual farm plots and brings private tillers into a collective farm unit, also pays temporary dividends to those contributing land. But the "producers' cooperative" regulations call for gradual elimination of these land dividends and step-by-step conversion to "communal property."

As of early November, there were more than 1,240,000 "producers' cooperatives" in China.

Last July Mao Tse-tung, the Chinese Communist leader, estimated that there were then an average of twenty-six families in each cooperative. If the average has remained constant, and counting four-and-a-half persons to a family, close to 30 per cent of farm population already has been "cooperativized."

The Peiping Government, following the trend of other nations that need cheap food for livestock and their people, has ordered an increase in corn production.

All of Red China's major domestic programs are being geared to the 1952-1957 industrialization plan. According to visitors arriving here from the mainland, a phenomenal amount of building is going on in China amid rigid regimentation and continuing crackdowns on alleged "counter-revolutionaries" and "economic saboteurs."

The mainland press still refers to problems and difficulties: lagging farm output and the need for more marketed grain, poverty in the countryside, shortages of technicians, waste and red tape, poor quality of various finished products. But still, the building program continues.

Vast Investment Planned

Although the present five-year-plan was instituted in 1952,

the plan was revamped by the Chinese Communist party last March and first made public when it was endorsed in July by the National People's Congress. According to Li Fu-chun, head of the State Planning Commission, it projects an outlay of 76,640,000,000 yuan (U. S. $32,-357,552,000) for "economic construction and cultural and educational development."

Of this total, he said, 42,740,-000,000 (U. S. $18,033,756,000) is earmarked for investment in capital construction. The remainder, he added, covers outlays in such categories as geological and engineering surveys, engineering planning, stockpiling, repairs, experimentation, acquisition of additional equipment, operational capital and training of technical personnel.

Altogether the plan embraces 1,600 major capital construction projects, of which 694 are in the industrial field. The core of the present industrial program is represented by 156 Soviet-sponsored construction and renovation projects for which the Soviet Union is supplying technical help and selling equipment to the Peiping regime.

Before the end of the plan in 1957, work is scheduled to begin on 145 of the 156 Soviet-sponsored projects. In 1955 work was due to begin on thirty-seven

of these projects and to be continued on fifty-four others.

One of the Soviet-sponsored projects involves the construction at Changchun, in Manchuria, of China's first automobile manufacturing plant. This plant, which has a projected annual capacity of 30,000 trucks, is scheduled to be completed during the present plan.

Work is also scheduled to begin before 1957 on a tractor plant with an annual capacity of 15,000 tractors of 54-horsepower each. In addition, the Soviet Union is assisting Peiping in the expansion of Red China's productive capacity in electrical power, coal, iron and steel, nonferrous metals and machine tools.

In the transportation field, construction work was completed last year on the Tsining-Ulan Bator Railway, which links North China with Soviet Siberia via Outer Mongolia. Red China is still pushing the construction of the Lanchow-Sinkiang Railway, which is eventually scheduled to link Northwest China by rail with Soviet Central Asia via Sinkiang.

Construction is also continuing in West China on the Chengtu-Pacchi line, which will feed into the existing Lunghai-Pacchi-Lanchow Railway. Another strategi-

cally important railway is being built in Southeast China from Yingtan, on the existing Chekiang-Kiangsi Railway, southeastward to Amoy opposite Nationalist-held Quemoy Island.

Work was begun last year, too, on the construction of a double-decker road and railway bridge spanning the Yangtze in the Hankow area. Peiping also has announced a dramatic long-range plan to harness the Yellow River in North China and develop its hydroelectric potential.

Red China's 1952--57 plan calls for an expansion of electrical power output from 7,260,000,000 to 15,900,000,000 kilowatt hours. In mid-1954 Premier Chou En-lai estimated that year's power output at 10,800,000,000 kilowatt hours, while the 1955 plan called for a 19.3 per cent increase over 1954 power output.

Data On Output And Goals

The following table indicates Peiping's production goals and interim production in various categories under the present five-year plan:

(In Tons—000 Omitted)

	1952 Output	1954(a) Output	1955(b) Goal	1957 Goal
Coal	63.530	81.990	94.043	113.000
Steel	1.359	2.170	2.567	4.120
Cement	2.860	4.730	5.756	6.000
Paper	370	480	523	650
Food crops	163.900	169.500	178.484	192.800
Rice	68.427			81.770
Wheat	18.125			23.725
Soya Beans	9.517			11.220
Raw cotton (c)	1.304	1.092	1.317	1.635

(a) 1954 industrial estimates by Premier Chou En-lai, Sept. 23, 1954.
(b) 1955 industrial goals compiled on basis of Mr. Chou's 1954 estimtes and officially announced percentage increases.
(c) Pre-1957 cotton figures interpolated from officially-announced percentages.

Ultimately the Chinese Communists intend to alter the geographical distribution of industrial enterprises to bring factories closer to sources of raw materials and develop the interior. New iron and steel combines are projected for the Hankow area in Central China and Pactow in North China.

At present, however, Manchuria is still China's primary industrial base.

While the five-year plan projects a 98.3 per cent increase in the value of gross industrial output, the value-increase tempo has slowed down with the beginning of heavy industrial construction. It is going to take time for the new factories now being built to produce.

During the 1949-52 "reconstruction" period, while the old economic machine was being restored, the value of industrial output is said to have increased at the average rate of 36.9 per cent a year. In 1955 the value of industrial output was scheduled to be increased by 7.7 per cent.

As before, Peiping's industrialization program is still largely dependent on the surpluses from Chinese agriculture —and these are admittedly small. The five-year plan calls for the reclamation of 6,367,660 acres of "arable wasteland," as well as the extension of the "cooperativization" movement to increase the amount of marketed grain.

All the indications are that the 1955 harvest was better than that in 1954, when there were disastrous floods.

Only scanty information is available here on just how much resistance Peiping is encountering in its collectivization drive. An article published in 1955 by the Chinese Communist periodical, Political Study, suggests that it is not all clear sailing.

"Since the winter of last year a very abnormal phenomenon has appeared in some areas," the article said. "That is, peasants slaughtered and sold livestock massively, felled trees and became inactive in making production investments."

Visitors arriving here from China report that the people in the cities and along the lines of transportation seem well dressed and reasonably well off. In a speech last July 31, however, Mr. Mao declared that "only 20 to 30 per cent" of the peasants were "prosperous or comparatively prosperous."

Red China's program for "Socialist transformation" of its economy is spread out over three five-year plans. With agriculture apparently still the weakest aspect of the picture the present outlook seems to be for continuing difficulties, continuing political repression and continuing industrial development.

Eastfoto

RED CHINA'S CORN CROP: Members of a farm cooperative study Indian corn harvested in Heilungkiang Province. Reports to Western sources say 1955 harvest was good.

January 4, 1956

RED CHINA SETS UP 10 NEW MINISTRIES

2 National Commissions Also Are Established in Seeming Industrialization Move

By HENRY R. LIEBERMAN
Special to The New York Times.

HONG KONG, May 12—Communist China set up ten new ministries and two more national commissions today in an apparent attempt to adjust administrative machinery to developing industrialization.

Po Yi-po, former head of the National Construction Commission, was named chairman of a new National Economic Commission. The Peiping Government also established a National Technological Commission headed by Huang Ching, who has been listed here as Minister of the First Machine Building Ministry.

The Hsinhua (New China) News Agency said administrative changes had been approved by the National Standing Committee of the People's Congress following a report by Premier Chou En-lai. In another dispatch from Peiping, the Chinese Communist agency reported that the National People's Congress would meet next month to adopt the 1956 state budget.

Mao Tse-tung, head of state, made twelve new appointments after the Congressional Standing Committee, headed by Liu Shao-chi, Secretary General of the Communist party, had approved the administrative changes. Among the new appointments was that of Lo Lung-chi, a Democratic League member known earlier by many Americans in China, to the post of Minister of Timber.

Other New Ministries

Others named to head new ministries were listed by Hsinhua as follows:

Minister of Metallurgical Industry and head of the National Construction Commission—Wang Ho-shou.
Minister of the Power Equipment Industry—Chang Lin-chih.
Minister of City Construction—Wan Li.
Minister of the Food Industry—Li Chu-chen.
Minister of Marine Products—Hsu Teh-seng.
Minister of Land Reclamation—Wang Chen.

The dispatch said a new City Services Ministry also had been established, but it was not clear who was named to head it. The report referred to Sha Chien-li as Minister of Light Industry, a post formerly held by Chia To-fu.

While making the changes, the Congressional Standing Committee decided to abolish the Ministry of Heavy Industries, the Third Ministry of Machine Building, the Ministry of Local Industry and the Municipal Construction Bureau, according to the Peiping dispatch. The report said the Standing Committee had set up a Municipal Bureau of Supplies and renamed the Experts Bureau the Bureau of Foreign Experts, with that agency coming directly under the State Council.

Red China has been getting substantial technical assistance from the Soviet bloc, especially the Soviet Union. Soviet experts have been helping the Peiping Government to draw up a twelve-year scientific-development program.

May 13, 1956

CHINA NOTES GAIN IN FIVE-YEAR PLAN

PEIPING, June 18 (Reuters)—Li Fu-chun, a Deputy Premier, told the National People's Congress, Communist China's Parliament, today that China was in a position to fulfill her current five-year plan ahead of schedule.

But he and other leaders said that, if certain problems were not solved, China's development would not be as speedy or as complete as hoped for.

Mr. Li, chairman of the State Planning Commission, said the related development of agriculture, light industry and heavy industry was one of three problems important for the national economy.

The second problem was the overconcentration of industrialization in the interior, to the partial neglect of coastal areas. The third, he said, was the relation between the state's accumulation of capital and the improvement of living standards.

Productivity at the end of 1955 was up 41.8 per cent over 1952, but real wages were up only 6.9 per cent, he said.

Mr. Li said some managements, "too intent on making a profit" for the state, had neglected workers' welfare.

The Minister of Public Health, Madame Feng Yu-hsiang, told the Congress that knowledge of birth control was necessary for both the health of mothers and the better upbringing of children.

She said that favorable conditions existed for the carrying out of the national policy of wiping out a dozen serious diseases, including malaria, in seven to twelve years.

June 19, 1956

CHINA REDS ADMIT UNJUST ARRESTS

Security Chiefs Note Errors in Drive—Cite Corrective Steps but Urge Vigilance

By HENRY R. LIEBERMAN
Special to The New York Times.

HONG KONG, June 22—Two leading security officials acknowledged in Peiping today that "mistakes" had been made in Communist China's drive against "counter-revolutionaries." Some "wrongful" arrests and sentences were admitted.

In speeches to the National Peoples Congress, the Public Security Minister, Lo Jui-ching, and the Procurator General, Chang Ting-cheng, said the "defects and mistakes" were being corrected.

"Some have already been rectified, others are in process of being corrected," Mr. Lo declared. He and Mr. Chang, whose job is to prosecute "enemies of the state," characterized Peiping's present policy on "counter-revolutionaries" as one of "leniency" combined with suppression.

They warned the Peoples Congress that "counter-revolutionaries" still existed in Communist China despite the successes both men said had been achieved in reducing the number.

'Complacency' Decried

The officials said there had been some "shortcomings" on the side of "complacency." Mr. Lo told the congressional delegates that public security organs had not prevented "all the acts of sabotage," that "some important cases" had not been unearthed in time, and that a number of "counter-revolutionaries" had not been brought to justice.

"On the other hand, we arrested some against whom warrants might well have been withheld rather than issued, and in a few cases we even arrested persons who should not have been arrested," the Security Minister added.

Mr. Chang said there also had been cases of erroneous sentencing. But cases of "wrongful arrest or sentencing" represented "only a very small fraction of all cases handled," he added.

No figures on the number of cases handled were given in the Hsinhua (New China) news agency account of the public security reports. The two officials ascribed the "defects" to failure of the top security organs to explain policy "fully and clearly" at lower levels. Mr. Lo said policy forbade the use of torture to "exact confessions" and added: "No arrests should be made unless absolutely necessary."

"Special importance must be placed on close leadership and strict supervision by the party and Government over the security organs," he declared. "This is decisive."

The chief procurator stated in his report that "counter-revolutionaries" had engaged in "unbridled sabotage" during the winter of 1954 and the first half of 1955. He told the congress this "sabotage" had been directed against land collectivization, state purchase and distribution of grain, and nationalization of industry and commerce. Mr. Chang said a "struggle" had been waged against such "counter-revolutionaries" and had achieved considerable success.

Cases Have Decreased

During the first three months of this year, he said, the number of cases in eleven provinces and municipalities, including Peiping, Tientsin and Shanghai, was one-third lower than during the same period last year.

Mr. Lo said there was "greater security" throughout the country than ever before. He told the delegates, however, that the number of "spies" sent in by "imperialist and Chiang Kai-shek [the Chinese Nationalist leader] secret agent organizations" had increased substantially this year.

The Public Security Minister said that because of this the struggle against "counter-revolutionaries" was still "acute and complicated." Mr. Lo called for "resolute blows" against "diehards," coupled with lenient treatment of repentants.

Both officials told the Congress that international developments and Communist China's achievements had caused those who had hoped for President Chiang's return to the mainland to become despondent. Mr. Lo urged "close attention" to the "tendency to division and disintegration" among "the remaining counter-revolutionaries."

June 23, 1956

PEIPING TO EASE TRADE CONTROLS

Local Units in Commercial Structure Will Get Some Freedom, Congress Told

By HENRY R. LIEBERMAN
Special to The New York Times.

HONG KONG, June 30 — A leading Chinese Communist official declared today that the Peiping Government was preparing to loosen some of its rigid controls over local units in the state-dominated trading system.

The official, Vice Premier Chen Yun, said the Government would continue its present controls over grain and cloth, both of which are now rationed. "Unified purchases and sales will also be continued for such commodities as oil and fats, sugar, paper, cigarettes and matches," he said.

But Mr. Chen told the National People's Congress (Parliament) in Peiping that state trading departments would henceforth be free to determine locally what goods they wanted to buy from factories for sale on local markets.

He said there were 30,000 items on the "free" list and cited towels, stockings, soap and enamelware as examples.

The deputy premier explained that factories would supply trading companies with those commodities left over after the departments had bought what they wanted. He said this would be on a credit and commission basis and he added that the factories themselves could market the goods remaining after the needs of the trading departments had been met.

Change in Companies' Status

Mr. Chen also called for a change in jurisdictional control over the "joint" state-private trading companies. He said these partnership companies should be managed not by commercial departments placing Government contracts but by specialized corporations organized by the "industrial departments."

Mr. Chen who is one of Communist China's "big five" as a member of the party Secretariat, addressed the closing session of the People's Congress. Complaints about state trading operations had been voiced at earlier sessions.

Before the 1,025 delegates adjourned, they also heard Premier Chou En-lai sum up developments at the two-week parliamentary meeting.

Mr. Chou said greater emphasis would be placed on "division of power between the central and local authorities" in future "state systems." He disclosed that a preliminary draft document on this division of power already had been circulated for discussion to provincial and city governments.

In his speech on domestic trade operations, Mr. Chen declared that the projected changes represented the development of a "free market within the framework of the planned economy." However, he told the delegates that the state was still determined to guard against inflation by controlling those commodities for which demand exceeded supply.

"There will be no currency inflation in our country" he was quoted as saying by the Hsinhua (New China) News Agency. "We are carrying out free sales and free purchases to a certain extent on a solid Socialist basis."

The emergence of the limited "free market" follows a "Socialist transformation" drive in which virtually the entire urban economy of Communist China has been brought under Government supervision through the formation of the "joint" state-private companies.

Private business men who once owned these units outright are officially said to be getting interest of 5 per cent on their share. It was announced earlier in Peiping that urban "Socialist transformation" involved a process of "buying off the bourgeoisie."

Replying to the criticisms regarding state trading operations, Mr. Chen acknowledged there had been various "mistakes and shortcomings." He said there had been "fluctuations in processing orders, improper supply of raw material, reductions in the varieties of certain products and failure of pattern and design of goods to meet popular demand."

But he told the delegates he felt that the results of the "socialist transformation" drive had 'in the main" been excellent.

The Vice Premier discounted assertions by some delegates that the joint companies would find it hard to provide the Government with the full amount of revenue planned for this year.

Mr. Chen said the average profits of 241 Shanghai joint companies surveyed in May, 1955, had been "20 per cent on capital" and ranged "up to over 100 per cent."

CHOU SAYS CHINA WILL GIVE PEOPLE MORE DEMOCRACY

Communist Premier Indicates Congress Will Meet Oftener and Vote May Be Widened

The following dispatch is by Reg B. Leonard, a correspondent for The Melbourne (Australia) Herald, who is visiting Communist China.

World & by Reg B. Leonard.
The Melbourne Herald.

PEIPING, Aug. 5—Important changes in Communist China's political structure are contemplated, Premier Chou En-lai said in a ninety-minute interview yesterday.

In a talk on China's policies, he discussed the progress of the nationalization program. He said it should be possible soon to "enlarge the democratic base of our system of government."

The Premier said achievement of a substantial measure of full socialism should make it possible to extend democratic political processes. Particularly there may be more frequent meetings of the National People's Congress and greater scope for criticism and self-criticism. The People's Congress now meets infrequently, but its Standing Committee meets several times monthly.

There is also the prospect of liberalization of the voting system, Mr. Chou said. Many former landlords have already received voting rights, and that privilege may be extended to other groups, including counter-revolutionaries, who have expiated their crimes, he said.

Policy Called Unchanged

Mr. Chou speaks English well but cautiously. He does not rely on his interpretation of questions, but has them repeated in Chinese by a Foreign Office expert. Then he replies in Chinese and checks while the translator repeats in English.

He is a dark, friendly man, handsome, in his mid-fifties. He is about 5 feet 8 inches tall, and his hair untouched by gray. He is reasonably trim for his years.

The Premier was relaxed as he ranged over world affairs, showing emotion only when referring to Taiwan (Formosa).

Premier Chou said there had

been no fundamental change in Communist China's internal policy in the last few years. The consistent aim has been to develop a form of socialism in which agriculture and the handicrafts are operated cooperatively and capitalism contained in joint state-private enterprises.

Mr. Chou was asked if he was certain China's economy was strong enough to carry the strain of the enormous projected industrial building expansion.

He replied China was backward economically and all of the nation's formidable manpower and other resources would have to be mobilized to insure success of the construction program.

Much will depend on the rate of production of essential goods, he said.

One thing can be said with certainty—all China wanted peace to build up the nation, he added.

Mr. Chou, who is also Foreign Minister, referred to the United States as ostrich-like for refusing to recognize Communist China. He was much more moderate in referring to Australia. He felt there could be a considerable increase in trade and cultural contacts between Australia and Red China and that this would be a positive step toward the establishment of diplomatic relations.

Mr. Chou rejected the proposition that the United States should be included in negotiations about the future of Taiwan. He said it was a province of China. How it should be "liberated" was none of the United States' business, but entirely a matter within China's sovereignty. Outside interference could not and would not be tolerated, he declared.

"China's attitude is clear," Mr. Chou said. Negotiations between China and the United States to ease Far East tensions and between China and Taiwan about the future of that offshore island are entirely different matters, he declared.

The first is international, while the second is exclusively domestic, he asserted.

Optimistic on Peace

He said he saw brighter hope for world peace, although some reactionary groups, notably American, were menacing it. He condemned all Western "military blocs," supported Indonesia's claim to West New Guinea, Cyprus' demand for self-determination, and backed Egypt's nationalization of the Suez Canal.

The Communist Premier said no progress could be reported from the Chinese-United States ambassadorial talks at Geneva because the United States wanted a one-sided declaration about renouncing force as an instrument of Far East policy.

Although at the National Congress in June Mr. Chou charged

powerful Americans in charge of foreign policy were obstructing the change from the "cold war," he said in the interview there were those who exceeded Secretary of State Dulles in this regard.

"There is a definite trend toward relaxation, and the 'cold war' is becoming increasingly unpopular," Premier Chou said. "Viewed in this light, the prospect of lasting peace is considerable, but there still are groups of adventurers who are threatening it."

Military blocs were a dangerous factor, Mr. Chou declared, because they divided nations that should be friendly. He said he did not believe such pacts were for defense only. Military blocs interfered with the freedom and sovereignty of participating countries and were resented by the mass of people who wanted international friendship, he asserted.

August 6, 1956

CHINESE STREAM INTO NORTHWEST

Men and Materials Being Poured Into Region to Exploit Its Minerals

The following dispatch is by David Chipp, a British correspondent of Reuters, who has just completed a 5,000-mile round trip from Peiping to the northwest of China.

LANCHOW, China.

China is opening up her northwestern territories with the speed and planning of a military operation and much of the fervor of a crusade.

After a two-week trip covering more than 3,000 miles in Kansu and Sinkiang Provinces the main impressions gained are of the importance and investment being placed by the Chinese Government in this area, which is rich in mineral wealth. Great material advances already have been made, and even greater progress is planned.

Throughout the region, which stretches up to the Soviet border, the direct control of the central Government on development plans and on political life is everywhere apparent.

There are Soviet advisers and experts and plenty of Soviet machinery, but no more than in other parts of China, and the overriding impression is that China is in complete charge.

Peiping's orders stretch into the remotest villages, where the ever-present cadres and party members are kept in constant touch with the capital through provincial committees. Nowhere is there any external evidence of Soviet influence outside the technical sphere.

A Land for the Young

The region is rapidly becoming a land for young people. Thousands, together with many older ones, are moving westward daily in huge groups for construction work on oilfields, roads and railroads and for building new towns and factories.

The movement may develop into the largest mass migration in history, as China fills up this sparsely populated border land of deserts and mountains under plans to turn it into one of her most important economic areas.

The migrants have come mostly from the eastern part of the country and if any of the thousands who stream through Lanchow daily are being forced to go against their will they give no sign of it.

The vast majority come after having been persuaded by party members and officials who are adept in mass psychology and who hold out the twin inducement of "patriotism" and rewards.

Chinese officials say that in an area as economically vital as this, unwilling labor would be a drawback rather than an asset.

And there are rewards. In the northwest wages are much higher than in other parts of China. Some workers earn almost double what they would get elsewhere, and welfare conditions are better.

During the National People's Congress (legislative meeting) in June, the Government was sharp-

ly criticized, and it acknowledged that it had neglected wages, housing and welfare in many places. But in this area the authorities are trying to insure the contentment of the settlers and so attract more with good living conditions, high wages and as many welfare facilities as possible.

Some English Spoken

Throughout the tour and in the most unlikely places I encountered a surprising number who spoke English but only a handful who knew Russian. Some gave a patriotic answer to questions on why they were going West. Others frankly admitted that they thought they would be better off and have better jobs.

A vast amount of equipment is being sent into the area.

In Lanchow, a rapidly growing railroad junction that serves as a base for the whole Northwest, there are acres of construction materials ranging from wicker baskets and shovels to oil drilling machinery.

The roads from the present railhead at Yumen, 500 miles to the northwest, to the new oilfields in the Tsaidam basin in Tsinghai province (bordering on Tibet) and in North Sinkiang (bordering on the Soviet Union) are continually busy with streams of heavily laden trucks.

The speed of construction leaves behind it an overall impression of untidiness. There is no time for the niceties of building or for appearance. Some of the work is slapdash.

If there is forced labor, then it is nowhere apparent either in attitude of the workers or in the pace at which they work.

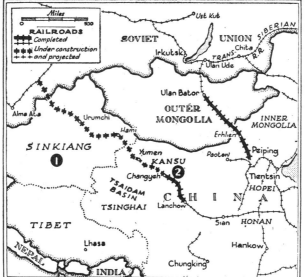

The New York Times   Aug. 13, 1956

RED CHINA OPENING NEW TERRITORY: A traveler in Sinkiang (1) and Kansu (2) found extensive development.

August 13, 1956

RED CHINA TREBLES COLLEGES' OUTPUT

But '56 University Crop of 64,000 Is Short of Needs in Economic Expansion

Following is the first of a number of dispatches by Reg Leonard, correspondent of The Melbourne Herald, who recently completed an extended trip through Communist China:

PEIPING, Aug. 9 — A few weeks ago, 64,000 young men and women graduated from China's universities. After the summer vacation they will start their tasks in the national construction program.

Since 1953, said the graduation day announcement, the annual output of graduates has trebled. But the Ministry of Higher Education is far from satisfied. More than three times 64,000 could have been placed this year, its spokesman said.

Probably this should be discounted as propaganda. But the year's graduation tally is on record, and perhaps it indicates as well as anything can the tempo of China's advance.

The great question is whether it can be continued and accelerated. There is a restless, impatient mood among the long-range planners, most of whom are young and imaginative. To many of them, today's progress is only a jog-trot. They would go faster but are held back by shortages of scientists, skilled technicians, engineers, economists, teachers—and general "knowhow".

This correspondent had the impression that there was an inclination in the national Long-Term Planning Office to allow enthusiasm for blue-prints to nudge realism aside.

This office prepares the five-year plans. Originally, it also supervised the work of carrying them out. It is significant that since last year this more detailed job has been done by the National Economic Commission.

Like every other Government authority, the commission encourages the never-ending campaigns to "beat the targets." But its economists know that there must be limits to the speed with which one of the world's most backward countries can be brought to the standard of nations that have advanced with the times.

Accent on Heavy Industry

In the present five-year program, the accent is on heavy industry. Its expansion rate is regulated by capacity to pay. Forty-eight per cent of the Government's funds come from state-owned enterprises, mainly light industries. Many of these, like textiles, for instance, depend on primary production for raw materials. A couple of cotton crop failures would seriously contract a major source of Government revenue.

Even in the most cautious assessment, it has to be agreed that great things are happening in China.

The achievements of the first five-year plan are impressive. Such heavy industry as has been established with massive Soviet aid is apparently operating efficiently and at high production levels.

Building construction is fast. New railroads are steadily opening up undeveloped country. New industries, notably steel and oil, are beginning to give the sinews that a growing nation needs. Light industry is expanding. Agriculture, in swift transition to complete socialization, is producing more.

All this in a few years is spectacular progress, but there is a hard and unbelievably long road to travel before China's living and industrial standards approach those of the leading powers.

Clearly, a country in which men still do the work of oxen, where commonplace amenities like refrigerators and electric cookers are unknown among the ordinary people, where a bathroom is a luxury and running water still a novelty, is not going to become an all-mechanized industrial power next year or the year after—or ten years after that.

It will take a long time and tremendous effort. But any objective survey of what is happening in China must concede that the Chinese people are attacking the task with determination and unbounded enthusiasm.

Young Chinese have been convinced that China will be the world's greatest industrial power within their lifetime. On paper, this belief seems reasonable.

At the present rate of population increase, China will have 1,000,000,000 people long before the end of the century. If all goes according to plan in the next twenty to twenty-five years, great rivers will be harnessed and agriculture will be booming. Oil will be pouring from rich new wells.

The ore deposits around Paotow in Inner Mongolia will have lifted steel production far above today's inadequate 3,000,000 metric tons a year, less than a thirtieth of the United States output. The population will have been redistributed. The country will have been completely industrialized.

Whether the country's economic resources can stand such intense development and rapid expansion may be questionable. Here is an analysis of the financial position this year, when the first five-year plan is supposed to reach its peak.

The national budget provides for total expenditure of 30,742,-770,000 yuan. Applying the Bank of China exchange rate of 2.3 yuan to the United States dollar, this means total expenditure of about $13,366,000,000.

According to Finance Minister Li Hsien-nien, 52 per cent of this total, or about $6,950,000,000, will be for economic construction, and rather more than half of this, or $3,500,000,000, for industrial development.

And of that $3,500,000,000, 85.5 per cent will be spent on heavy industry. That works out at about $2,925,000,000, or rather less than $5 a head for China's population of 600,000,000.

This would not seem an electrifying effort were it not for the fact that the labor component of any project in China costs only a fraction of what it would cost in any Western country. The monthly pay of the average Chinese worker is no more than a skilled Western worker could earn in a few days.

Even with this, one wonders where all the money is coming from for the second five-year plan beginning Jan. 1, 1958, and for the mammoth third plan that is scheduled to complete all basic industrial undertakings.

The Chinese are planning such things as doubling steel production every four years, bringing it to 36,000,000 tons a year by 1970; building nearly fifty great dams, laying thousands of miles of new railroad and tens of thousands of miles of new highway, developing oil fields, completing immense electrification projects, creating an Oriental Detroit in the Manchurian automobile city of Changchun, and completing the industrialization of China within twenty-five years.

As high an authority as Premier Chou En-lai said in an interview that the program would call for every ounce of effort and economic knowledge the nation can produce.

Rewards for "model workers" and "advanced workers," emulation campaigns, pep talks, piecework incentives are part of the acceleration process.

So productivity is increasing, spectacularly in some industries. New factories, training centers, housing blocks are going up swiftly behind grotesque tangles of bamboo scaffolding.

Substantial aid, men and machinery, is coming from the Soviet Union, but this correspondent saw no evidence whatever to support reports that Moscow was "running" China.

On the contrary, Soviet experts seemed to be treated with due regard for their knowledge and skill, but without deference. Nobody bends the knee in China these days.

August 21, 1956

PEIPING RETAINING SOME CAPITALISM

Private Businesses Operate in Partnership With State —But End Is Expected

Following is the second of a number of dispatches by Reg Leonard, correspondent of The Melbourne Herald, who recently completed an extended trip through Communist China.

PEIPING, Aug. 10—At this stage anyway, there is a fundamental difference between Soviet and Chinese communism.

In the Soviet Union, the state virtually owns all enterprise. In China, there is still a strange system of partly submerged but not yet suffocated private enterprise, and "capitalists," as the Communists call anyone with more than a wage, are given a place in the social structure.

No one has much doubt what the end will be. But there are certainly still plenty of people drawing fixed dividends from the investments of pre-Communist years. How long it will last is anyone's guess. The end could come swiftly, unexpectedly.

Until this year, private shareholders were getting 25 per cent of the net profit of businesses they once owned but in which the state is now senior partner. That was stopped abruptly and a fixed dividend of 5 per cent on the value of the "capitalist's" investment was decreed.

Some day, the 5 per cent plan will probably end just as swiftly and the socialization of industry and commerce will be complete.

The Chinese Communist party's policy toward private business has been to bring it to full socialization with as little pain as possible. In Peiping these days, senior officials even talk softly about businesses that were seized in the first frantic months of what they all call "liberation."

In Government and administrative quarters, you seldom hear a good word about the United States, but I was told that it was wrong to say United States enterprises in China had been declared forfeit.

They have only been taken in reprisal for the freezing of Chinese assets in the United States, it was said. At present, they are "under Chinese management," but the problem is to be resolved when diplomatic relations are established.

The argument about the death of many British enterprises was that most were in financial trouble and their owners were glad enough to see the state take over on the basis of debts paid and compensation granted.

The Communists admit straight-out seizure only of businesses "acquired corruptly and operated unfairly" by get-rich-quick officials in Generalissimo Chiang Kai-shek's administration.

In all the principal cities of China today, there is a vast industrial and commercial partnership between the state and private enterprise.

It is said that the "capitalists" joined voluntarily. Technically, that may be so. But had they not "played ball," unquestionably they would have been crushed.

In all these jointly run enterprises, the state is undisputed boss, but not necessarily in managerial control. In many cases, those who ran the businesses as private concerns continue to manage them.

At first, partnerships were negotiated business by business, but this process was far too slow for the Communist policy-makers. Early this year an express change-over, whole trades at a time, was decreed for all sizable towns.

The result was the establishment of tens of thousands of new partnerships covering all but small businesses. The State Statistical Bureau calculated that production from the few factories that remained wholly private concerns would almost reach the vanishing point by the end of this year.

In 1954, private enterprise was still chalking up 25 per cent of China's industrial output. Last year, the figure fell to 16 per cent. This year it will be 0.4 per cent. That is about the end.

This correspondent went to Shanghai, greatest commercial city in the country, to find out what the "capitalists" thought about this.

Their assessment of the new order has to be examined in the light of the fact that they had no choice anyway. Either they joined the partnerships or went bankrupt.

But all voted for the new fixed 5 per cent dividend plan. It gives some security, they said, and is an agreed figure reached at talks between Government representatives and the predominantly "capitalist" Federation of Commerce and Industry.

The Melbourne Herald

RIDICULE is employed by the Chinese Communists to make the people conscious of production goals. The girl's derisive drawing accuses a fellow-worker of not pulling his weight.

Following is the third of a number of dispatches by Reg Leonard, correspondent of The Melbourne Herald, who recently completed an extended trip through Communist China.

PEIPING, Aug. 11—China's formidable arms bill is preventing maximum industrial development.

Almost as much is being spent on the armed forces this year as on the expansion of heavy industry, which has top priority in the first five-year program.

A breakdown of budget figures shows that about $2,925,-000,000 will be spent on heavy industry. The defense program, although said to have been cut, will cost $2,670,000,000.

China, of course, has none of the manpower problems that some industrialized Western countries have. But the figures show what a great lift could be given to the development program if the armed forces were reduced and defense spending pruned.

The official justification for defense expenditure accounting for just under 20 per cent of the national budget is that "American imperialists" are threatening from Taiwan (Formosa), which is held by the Chinese Nationalists.

The Communist Government appears coolly confident of its ability to finance great projects of war and peace simultaneously. Certainly, its pay problems are not considerable. Details of the Chinese workers' earnings, in military or civilian occupations, come as a shock to the Western visitor.

Here are some examples of weekly pay in skilled industrial occupations: automobile plant worker, $7 to $10; textile worker, $7 to $12; flour mill worker, $7.50; oil field shift foreman, $13; Journalist, $10 to $15; bridge-builder on the Yangtze River, $7 to $15.

By most Western standards, this is poverty pay. But in China there are the compensations that rents are low and food is cheap.

Millions of Chinese live in squalor, but stories that they are starving are false. In half a dozen cities visited, food was plentiful. There were excellent supplies of fruit and vegetables and no evidence of shortages. Of course, in such a vast territory as China there might be local crises.

At most factories or construction projects, canteens provide a meal for the equivalent of about 10 cents.

The housing position is difficult for a Westerner to appreciate. Houses with gardens, as most of us know them, are only for the élite. Persons in privi-

---

One millionaire textile tycoon and his brother operate nine large textile plants, all in partnership with the Government. Their half-yearly dividend, just paid, was nearly $327,000.

Perhaps the "capitalists" are whistling in the dark. But it is surprising what unanimity there is in their declarations that they get fair treatment from state representatives in joint enterprises, that their suggestions are seldom rejected and that their complaints, even at the national level, are dealt with promptly and almost always effectively.

The visitor always runs the risk of being introduced only to the "right people," but this correspondent nominated several places where he wanted to go and no changes were suggested. On the surface, there was rea-

sonable satisfaction with the system of joint operation.

Change in Agriculture

While much industry and commerce have been semi-socialized by the partnership formula, agriculture is going through swift processes toward complete communization.

During the last few months there has been a brisk campaign to swing all farming into "advanced cooperatives," which appear to be more efficient and more rewarding than the private tilling of small plots.

There are two kinds of cooperative farms. In the lower group, partners retain a small measure of private ownership and are paid rent for cattle and implements they bring with them.

The Communists are trying to speed the rather reluctant

peasants to the "advanced cooperatives" stage, in which rental payments cease and livestock and implements become communal property.

The state handles sales through its marketing agencies. It keeps 12 per cent of the proceeds as its share and sends the rest for distribution among cooperative partners.

The Communists say 108,000,-000 peasant households, or 90.4 per cent of the total, have been brought into the co-operative network. About 73,000,000 families are in the higher cooperatives.

There are many indications in China of the probability that, having started cautiously to get as many people as possible on their side, the Communists now feel they are in a position to push ahead much more swiftly with the Socialist transformation.

August 22, 1956

leged callings — intellectuals, industrial experts, opera leaders—can get apartments.

But for the scores of millions in the industrial working force, there is amazing congestion and little privacy. The majority of city workers live in hovels. In the older parts of cities, especially Peiping, they are not much better than crumbling huts. Few have kitchens and bathrooms are virtually unknown.

In Shanghai, conditions for the mass of 6,000,000 persons may be rather better than in Peiping, but they are still inadequate.

Major Effort Made

Any survey of housing conditions would be lopsided if it did not recognize the work the Communist authorities are doing to correct a desperate situation. It is a noteworthy effort, but so far it is only scratching the surface.

Workers consider themselves lucky if they get a place in the dormitories built adjacent to most new factories, or in new villages on the outskirts of industrial cities.

Most dormitories would be substandard according to Western ideas of slum clearance. In some of them, families of seven or eight are packed into two small rooms. In single quarters, rooms are shared by four or five persons.

In some of the workers' settlements even small families get two rooms and a private toilet. There are no bathrooms, but public showers are provided. Three families share each kitchen and laundry.

As compensation for the crowding, rents are at absolute bedrock. In one housing settlement the only charge for families was 5 yuan a month for maintenance and 1 yuan for

water and electricity, the total equivalent of 60 cents a week. In Peiping, rents average 5 per cent of pay.

At some of the housing settlements, amenities and services were splendid even if housing standards were disappointing. One project on the outskirts of Shanghai had a nursery for children up to four years, five kindergartens, four primary schools, two secondary schools, a department store and a clinic, and a cultural hall for the 6,300 families living there.

There, briefly, is how the workers live. How they play is a humorless story. There is not much zip about entertainment and recreation in a Communist society.

Physical culture has become a fad in China. "Daily dozen" radio sessions are immensely popular. If you are talking to someone when these come on, you are likely to be left standing until your companion completes his exercises.

The Chinese engage in sports with frightening intensity and the Communists have built some fine stadiums in the larger cities.

Entertainment is mainly lofty, heavy drama, story-telling, cultural exhibitions, films with strong political flavor. There are no gambling sports and no night clubs, but week-end dances are held in many factory canteens and workers' clubs. No cheek-to-cheek though—It is definitely an arm's-length performance.

In some places, notably Shanghai, where the Western influence of many years is still felt, trumpets still blare, clarinets sigh and United States-type music is played for such utterly bourgeois dances as the fox trot and the tango.

August 23, 1956

RED CHINA PLANS A HUGE MIGRATION

Millions to Be Shifted West in Program to Develop New Areas, Raise Farm Output

Following is the sixth in a number of dispatches by Reg Leonard, correspondent of The Melbourne Herald, who recently made an extended trip through Communist China.

PEIPING, Aug. 14—Nothing in China is more spectacular than the Communist Government's plans to resettle millions of people.

They are part of a long-range program to increase agricultural production while strengthening vulnerable and thinly populated areas in the west and north.

If the program is carried through, it will involve one of the greatest mass migrations in history. A million families will participate in the first stage and many millions over ten or twelve years.

The Economic Planning Commission has been given the job of draining off the surplus populace from the overcrowded eastern central provinces and developing new agricultural lands in tracts from Sinkiang Province around to the extreme northwest.

Another reason why the Communists want a substantial population move to Sinkiang and beyond is that rich new oilfields have been found in the northwest close to the Soviet border

and Government policy makers want Chinese authority increased in this area of thirteen minority groups, including Uigurs, Kazakhs, Mongols and White and Red Russians.

Housing Problem Is Great

Like many other Chinese projects, the great population move is not yet beyond the planning stage. It will involve an immense accommodation problem, but this does not seem to worry the authorities. Chinese Communist pioneers are not expected to demand—and certainly do not get —even elementary comforts in accommodation.

Chinese administrators stoutly deny that direction of the populace will be necessary to make the migration plan practicable. They insist there will be no compulsion and maintain enough volunteers will appear when an "educational" campaign has been developed.

Some young Communists are fanatical enough to go anywhere, and a rosy propaganda picture will probably draw many older persons from among the country's uninformed and incredibly poor peasant population of nearly 500,000,000.

The population resettlement plan opens up the broader question of whether there is any forced labor in China today. Almost certainly there is for prisoners. Apparently they are used for manual labor wherever it may be needed in desolate areas. But Government officials deny that there is any direction or compulsion for ordinary workers.

This is an assertion that cannot readily be checked, but the fact that higher wages and bonuses are paid to workers on development projects far from settled areas suggests that cash inducements have a part in recruiting labor. On some jobs— for instance the Yangtze River bridge at Wohan—bonuses up to 25 per cent of the basic wages are paid. There is no shortage of labor on these terms.

Changing Jobs Is Difficult

Once a job has been accepted, it is not easy to change it. Labor exchanges need good reasons before they will approve a transfer.

No evidence of extensive forced labor could be found by this correspondent. If any such

practice exists, of course it would hardly be exposed to foreigners.

There is quite blatant "persuasion" of workers, however, and the trade unions that are nationally organized for all major secondary industries apply whatever pressure may be needed to get manpower for new projects. The "persuasion" takes the form of frequent pep talks on national duty, personal interviews by Communist party officials and propaganda through the state-controlled newspapers and radio services.

Thus, even if there is no forced labor in China for any but convicted persons, there certainly is not the same freedom of employment Western nations know.

Virtually all industry and commerce is now run either by the state itself or by partnerships with private business men in which the state is the boss, so there are no competitive wage salary offers to attract skilled personnel.

There has been a steady improvement in wages over the last few years. This year's increase for many grades of specialists and factory hands averages a little more than 14 per cent.

Wages Keyed to Output

Top Government officials have acknowledged the inadequacy of this rise and promised something better for next year. But in China wage increases depend entirely upon production. If output fails to rise, so does pay.

At this stage of China's industrialization, wage adjustments affect only about one sixth of the populace. For the other five-sixths toiling on the land there is never prosperity, and often privation.

For them everything depends upon the seasons.

Now floods are threatening devastation in other areas, particularly the north. Thus there is seldom a time where there is not an agricultural crisis somewhere in China's vast area. The peasants have become accustomed to reverses and poverty.

Even in what the Communists claim is a vastly improved cooperative farming society, the average peasant income for a seven-day work week is said to be not much more than the equivalent of $224 yearly. This, moreover, is the Communists' figure, probably inflated for propaganda purposes.

August 26, 1956

RED CHINA'S AIMS SERVED BY UNIONS

Workers' Federation Wields Vast Power in Carrying Out Nation's Policies

Following is the seventh of a number of articles by Reg Leonard, correspondent of The Melbourne Herald, who recently made an extended trip through Communist China.

MELBOURNE, Australia, Aug. 16—China's 12,600,000-strong Trade Union Federation is the Communist party's industrial whip-cracker.

Its members are shock troops when the party executive frames new policies for industry or defines new production targets.

The all-China Trade Union Federation is far more than an organization to safeguard workers' conditions. It is a political instrument of considerable power and influence.

It was started as a secretariat twenty-five years ago, when the Communists first planned control of the working class movement and ultimately of the nation. It had many reverses during the turmoil of the civil wars, but since 1950 it has been operating with solid Government backing under legislation granting it extensive rights.

No one can buck the unions in China now. This year the federation had a new charter, which will eventually bring under its control new classifications of manual workers and most professional men and women.

The unions have organized shrewdly. Their first aim has been to get firm control of key industries. Today the federation's word is law in all heavy and most light industries; in railway, road transport, postal and telecommunication services; in the electrical trades, education and the important petroleum and salt industries.

Now that building has so important a place in the national planning program, the union leaders are moving to bring the new labor force under party control.

There is activity, too, in the organization of agricultural workers. This is simple enough for the peasants on state farms. They are wage earners and can be marshaled like any other group of workers. But millions of peasants are in the cooperatives, and there are complications about drawing technically self-employed men and women into the union structure.

Nevertheless, a way will doubtless be found because there has been dissatisfaction in high places about the slowness of political education among the rural masses.

The federation is also going for bigger fish. The first moves will be made soon to form unions for doctors, geologists, bank employes, civil aviation personnel, supply marketing staffs and cultural workers.

When this program is completed, the federation will have immense power in almost every important civil activity in China.

The unions are not shy about acknowledging their political role. Their official publications say definitely that each union must be "a school of communism for workers to launch labor-stimulation drives, strengthen labor discipline, train activists and bring their enthusiasm into full play."

Membership, the fee for which is 1 per cent of wages, is not compulsory. On the contrary, there is rather stern selectivity in considering nominations because members are expected to be fervent Communists capable of enlightening "backward" workers. So applications are subject to a double check before acceptance.

Mao's Wishes Carried Out

When a directive comes from Mao Tse-tung, Chairman of the Central People's Government, or the top Communist Party Executive, the unions are expected to get busy among the workers. Here is an example entirely unrelated to politics but demonstrating how far union activity goes:

Mr. Mao instructed his party aides at all levels: "Develop physical culture. Improve the people's physique."

The unions jumped to it. Activists were told to move in smartly and organize rank-and-file workers into physical-development clubs, groups and squads.

That was only a couple of years ago. Today, under trade union direction, 80,000 organized teams are giving 1,000,000 workers regular exercise in basketball, volleyball and football competitions. A dozen national athletic organizations are the functioning center for hundreds of provincial associations.

The activists never let up. Their orders are to produce worker-athletes. They try to find champions and sometimes do.

During the last few months union-organized sports meetings have recorded new national records and put ten men and women athletes among certainties for Olympic Games selection.

Union "persuasion and encouragement" are responsible for the now familiar sight of training at dawn in the streets and parks of China's cities and, in some degree, for an almost fanatical enthusiasm for radio-directed physical culture sessions.

In Mr. Mao's education drive, too, the unions are playing their part. The first move has been to reduce illiteracy, so today there are more than 11,000 part-time union-controlled schools in factories and other industrial establishments.

Social Amenities Shown

These activities demonstrate that the unions in China have a wider role than negotiating over wage rates and industrial conditions. However, these activities make up their principal function.

The unions also interest themselves in housing. In fact, they have been showing their teeth about this lately. There has been strong criticism of low-gear progress in the building of new "dormitories," as apartment buildings are called, and the top Communist secretariat has taken notice. The ministries and other authorities responsible for rehousing have been ordered to revise and speed up their plans.

August 27, 1956

RED CHINA PLANT IS A VAST SCHOOL

CHANGCHUN, China, Aug. 16 (Reuters)—A major factor that may hold China back in her drive toward industrialization is the lack of trained engineers and technicians.

There is a solid core of skilled workers in the older plants, many of whom were employed during the long war-time Japanese occupation. There are others who have been trained by Soviet advisers in the last few years.

One of Communist China's tasks today is to train hundreds of thousands more.

Every factory seems overstaffed because of the presence of great numbers of apprentices who later will be sent to other factories. Technical schools and colleges are in abundance in every city in China, and many more are being built.

Lack of training and experience is very apparent in China's first motor truck factory at Changchun in Manchuria. Although it now is fully equipped with the latest Soviet machinery and is almost ready to start production of four-ton Liberation trucks, it will not be working at its full capacity of 30,000 trucks a year until 1958.

A Huge Technical School

The factory is now little more than a huge practical technical school, where young pupils, not yet used to the machinery they handle, are taught by a group of Soviet technicians.

Their inexperience is shown by their wages, which are low compared with other industrial workers in Manchuria, and their need for further training is shown by the number of instructions and cautionary notes written on blackboards all over the factory.

One poster called for gentleness in dealing with machines that were out of order. A series of drawings showed it was better to open a lock with a key than with a hammer.

But the factory is impressive and much of the machinery brand-new. In the gear-cutting shop, there were a number of United States and British machines, some of which were old and had been rebuilt, but a few of which looked new.

A few trucks, all of whose parts are made in China, already have come off the assembly line.

In spite of the lack of training and the mistakes by workers and management through their inexperience, the general impression given by Manchuria is one of a great potential. On the foundations laid by the Japanese during their occupation and intensive industrialization, the Chinese and Russians are building an even more massive structure.

Russians Rebuilding Area

Many of the Japanese factory buildings remain, but most of the equipment was either pillaged when supplies became short at the end of World War II, destroyed in the fighting, or carried off by the Russians as war booty.

Since the Communists came to power in China in 1949, the Russians have been pouring back aid into the area that they ravaged after the war. Much of the equipment is Soviet or from other East European countries and many of the 205 construction projects that the Soviet Union agreed to help design and provide equipment for are in Manchuria.

In contrast to the modern and well-kept machinery are many of the factory buildings, which, although they have an emphasis on production, appear to be neglected or put up in a hurried and haphazard fashion. Some are in a dreadful condition and others seem on the point of falling down.

Housing for the workers has been neglected for other construction work, though this is being hurriedly rectified following outspoken complaints in the National People's Congress. Now in every city a great deal of investment and building materials seem to be going into the building of large blocks of workers' apartments and dormitories.

Wages are being revised throughout Manchuria and the whole of China. Workers will get an average increase of about 14 per cent after bitter complaints that wages were lagging far behind the great increase in productivity.

Manchuria is a strange mixture of Japanese, Russian and modern Chinese architecture with the vast majority of the buildings of unsurpassed ugliness. The cities themselves are modern and well laid out and the Japanese built pleasant garden suburbs away from the smoke and noise of industry.

As one moves north, the Japanese influence declines and the Russian influence increases. In every town are huge war memorials commemorating the fact that the Soviet Union fought for five days against the Japanese in August, 1945.

There seem to be more Soviet technicians and experts, at least to be seen, than in other parts of China. In Harbin, the northernmost of the big industrial cities, there is still quite a large Russian emigre colony. Many of its members are now said to have taken Soviet citizenship.

Soviet influence does not appear to stretch beyond the technical field and the whole area appears to be firmly administered by the Chinese.

September 23, 1956

was a further proof of the general relaxation of restrictions and the willingness of officials to give statistics instead of percentages.

The director said that this year's production of crude oil was estimated at 1,200,000 tons, compared with 121,000 tons in 1949 and 308,000 tons in 1943. According to the second five-year plan, the production will reach between 5,000,000 tons and 6,000,000 tons ni 1962. This, the director said, would meet between 50 per cent and 60 per cent of total needs.

This means that China's yearly consumption during the second five-year plan will be about three times that at present, and during the period of the third five-year plan, with more mechanization, it will increase even more.

Vast Reserves Foreseen

But the director expressed confidence that the country's oil reserves were virtually unlimited and added that there were proven reserves of at least 100,000,000 tons. He said that a third of the country was over a sedimentary-basin and there was ample evidence of oil seepage.

At present, nearly half the production comesfr om the Yu-

men field in Kansu Province, in Northwest China. This year's production will be 520,000 tons, an increase of 135,000 tons over last year. Production at this field has been increasing steadily since 1950, when it sood at 96,000 tons. This year's big increase is due to the completion of the railroad, which means that the field can now be exploited to the full.

China's great hopes lie in the fields in the Tsaidam Basin, bordering Tibet, and at Karamai, in north Sinkiang. Though many wells already have been sunk, big production must await the completion of railroads.

The Government attaches the greatest importance to the rapid increase in oil production. This year, 728,000,000 yuan (about $290,000,000) is to be spent on capital investment in the oil industry.

There still are only a relatively few workers in the industry, and 42,000 of the total of 112,000 are at Yumen. Every day trucks are moving into Tsaiban and Karamai carrying equipment and workers.

A huge new refinery and a factory for making oil drilling equipment are being built at Lanchow, the railroad junction that is the gateway to the northwest.

November 11, 1956

CHINA PINS HOPES TO FARMS AND OIL

Major Export to Spur Output of Petroleum Is Linked to Mechanization Needs

PEIPING, Nov. 10 (Reuters) —Communist China's future development and the ambitious construction to be carried out in the first three five-year plans depend on agriculture, the age-old source of her wealth.

Speeches at the recent Communist party congress emphasized this. The Chinese leaders said again and again that the growth of heavy industry, the expansion of light industry and the necessary corresponding improvement in the people's livelihood depended on increased agricultural production.

The goals of this increase are large, and by the end of 1967 the Chinese hope to achieve two and a half times as much grain production as in 1955. This would mean a huge increase between 1962 and 1967 (the third five-year plan). Grain output last year was 184,000,000 tons, and the goal for 1962 is 250,000,000

tons—which would leave an increase of about 200,000,000 tons for the following five years.

Some of this increase, it is hoped, will come from greater production due to the collectivization of agriculture, the reclamation of virgin lands and better safeguards against natural disasters. Despite the efforts of the Communists in building better embankments along the major rivers and improving drainage and irrigation, floods, droughts and typhoons this year may have destroyed 7,000,000 tons of the harvest.

Mechanization the Key

If the increase is to be achieved, it will depend mainly on mechanization of agriculture and improved communications. Road and railroad building are among the priority tasks of the second five-year plan. Both will mean a considerable increase in China's consumption of oil.

In a recent interview, the director of the planning department of the Ministry of Petroleum, Yang Hai-Pung, said that China's own output at present met only a third of the country's requirements but that it was hoped that by the end of the third five-year plan she would be able to supply from her own wells all the oil she needs.

This interview, at which oil-production figures were given,

CHINA IS IN THROES OF ECONOMY DRIVE

Newspapers Lead Campaign to Reduce Waste of Public Funds and Manpower

PEIPING, Feb. 9 (Reuters)— Communist China is in the throes of an economy drive.

Newspapers have been attacking organizations that arrange lavish entertainment for little reason, those who use Government cars for pleasure and the high living of some minor officials.

The campaign, aimed not only at saving money and materials but also at preventing wastage of manpower through bureaucracy, was initiated at a meeting of the Central Committee last November.

It has been advertised by means of cartoons, posters and newspaper articles that have called on the people to exercise the strictest economy to prevent a slowdown in the country's progress and in improvement of the standard of living.

Cartoons Play Key Role

The cartoons, which play an important part in every Chinese drive, are often of a high artistic and entertainment value, though not a few are of such a bawdy nature that they would be unacceptable to Western newspapers.

The People's Daily, chief Communist organ, recently carried a cartoon attacking the high life of some officials, in which one panel was devoted to a banquet drawing depicting the more unpleasant results of overeating and overdrinking.

The second panel showed officials stripping a furniture store and carrying away their purchases in Government trucks, while the third showed their families arriving at the state department store in official cars, many of which were lined up outside.

Many of the attacks are aimed at local organizations that say "let's have a party" on public funds at the slightest excuse. Some of these may be following the example of the central authorities, who entertain foreign guests and delegations with huge banquets and lavish receptions.

Wastage Criticized

One example cited was the case of a district office in Hupeh Province that held a party when its chief went to Peiping for special studies. In the accounts, the report added, this party was entered as expenses connected with holding a meeting of local officials.

An article in one newspaper declared that a touring opera company was lavishly entertained wherever it went. The actors and actresses were "drowned in wine" to show the esteem in which they were held by their hosts, who usually charged the meal to "expenses," and were often so drunk they were unfit to act.

Other attacks have been made on local organizations that buy unessential things. Among the things bought by district offices and youth committees with their surplus funds and described by informants as "not necessary" were bicycles, phonographs, accordions, and cameras. The cameras, one group explained, were for "surveying work."

The drive is not against parties as such but merely against those that are paid for out of public funds. People are being encouraged to take life more lightly and to enjoy their leisure more. Meetings and study periods have been cut down so that people can relax more.

PEIPING BELIEVED RULED BY A TEAM

Observers Note Camaraderie Among 'Big 3' but Say Mao Acts as the Final Arbiter

PEIPING, March 16 (Reuters) —The majority of foreign observers here believe that there is a real collective leadership in Communist China and a striking identity of views on major subjects among leading Communists.

They discount reports of a long-standing struggle for power and disagreement on relationship with the Soviet Union between the two men who are ranked second and third to the chief of state, Mao Tse-tung. The two men are Liu Shao-chi, chairman of the Communist party's standing committee, and Chou En-lai, Premier and Foreign Minister.

Every indication given by their policies and their attitude when seen in public together lead observers here to believe that they are a team of friendly colleagues.

It is noted, however, that collective leadership in the realms of policy and Government in no way diminishes the position that Mr. Mao holds in China.

The affable Premier is the internationalist. Mr. Liu, whose demeanor on personal contact belies reports of his coldness and lack of humor, is responsible for much of the administrative planning and theoretical work. But the chief of state stands out above his colleagues as the undisputed leader.

Although Mr. Mao leaves much of the day-to-day running of the Government to others, his twenty years of leadership of the party makes him still the final arbiter on all major policy matters.

At 63, Mr. Mao looks remarkably healthy. Since passing 60 he has begun to learn English and also is reported to have been taught to swim.

Most observers agree that Mr. Liu, 51, is the chief of state's most likely successor as leader of the Communist party. Mr. Chou, 58, the better known of the two in the West, is said to rank third.

The two other members of the "big five" are 70-year-old Marshal Chu Teh and the country's leading economic expert, 51-year-old Chen Yun.

PRODUCTION RISE IN CHINA SLOWED

Figures Indicate 5.6% Gain, Smallest Since Communists Took Over in 1949

PEIPING, April 23 (Reuters) —Communist China's industrial production in 1957 will show the smallest rise since the regime came to power in 1949, according to official estimates.

This is symptomatic of the scaling-down of production goals, which was necessitated by raw material shortages and appraisal of agricultural possibilities, on which the whole economy rests.

The value of industrial production will be 5.6 per cent higher than last year, which would mean a rise from 55,800,000,000 yuan [$22,400,000,000] to 58,924,800,000 yuan. This is less than half the increases predicted by Premier Chou En-Lai when he addressed the eighth Communist party congress last September, and 0.4 per cent below the figure announced two months ago. However, the 1957 figure, if reached, will surpass the original target for the end of the first five-year plan by nearly 10 per cent.

Increases in the value of industrial production in the last five years' have fluctuated considerably, depending on the previous year's harvest and showing the important place occupied by agriculture in the economy.

Shortages in agricultural raw materials, particularly cotton, oil-seeds and sugar beets, which were damaged or destroyed by floods, typhoon or drought in 1956, will help to flatten the graph of increasing industrial value.

Peasants also are being allowed to keep more for their own use, as part of the Government's plan to improve living standards and prevent discontent.

While production of most items will increase this year, it is admitted that some, including cotton goods, may fall by comparison with 1956. The emphasis will be on greater production, and economy in the use of basic building materials, such as iron, steel, coal, lumber and crude oil.

These are expected to increase so as to exceed considerably the five-year goals. The only exception will be crude oil, which will show an increase of 29 per cent, although the planned production of 1,422,780 tons will be nearly 600,000 tons short of the original 1957 goal.

The shortage of raw materials, in spite of all increases, has been caused by building running ahead of supply.

In further effort to increase supplies, the Government has directed local administrative units to restore, improve and develop small coal and iron mines, iron foundries and brick kilns.

At the same time, manufacturers are being asked to use native products instead of industrial raw materials whenever possible. It is suggested, for instance, that bamboo instead of metal be used for the covers of flasks, and that more china or glass cups be made in place of tin mugs.

Experts from the Soviet Union and other Eastern European countries have been criticized for designing and supervising the construction of up-to-date factories that are unsuitable for Chinese conditions and have become little more than showplaces.

One is the motor car factory at Changchun, in the northeast, which is working at one-tenth capacity because of the shortage of raw materials.

Other steps taken to counteract shortages include more intensive bulk purchasing of industrial crops and a directive to the Foreign Trade Ministry to place orders in good time, thereby insuring more speedy delivery.

February 10, 1957   March 17, 1957   April 24, 1957

SHOPPER IN CHINA HAS A LONG WAIT

Time in Queue Often Futile, 2 Communist Reporters Learn in a Survey

By GREG MacGREGOR
Special to The New York Times.

HONG KONG, June 24—The shopper in Communist China suffers many a headache and aching feet, the Chinese press has disclosed.

There are long lines of weary customers, and a person "may not be able to get what he wants after having spent several days in these queues," two Chinese reporters wrote after a survey.

Using Taiyuan, 250 miles southwest of Peiping, as a test center, the Hsinhua (New China) News Agency assigned the two correspondents to investigate causes of consumer bottlenecks. Translations of their reports, which were published in Peiping May 25, reached here today.

Taiyuan may have been chosen by the news agency because of its rapid growth during the last five years as an important machine tool production center. Its population is approximately 1,000,000, compared with 500,000 in 1952. Taiyuan may also have been chosen as a typical progressive city of China under the Communist regime.

Neglect Is Indicated

A number of points in the report gave strong support to a long-held belief that many of China's internal troubles stemmed directly from neglect of or a lack of sufficient consideration for the needs of the people in favor of concentration on industrial expansion.

The correspondents suggested that, because state control of distribution had largely eliminated business competition, the authorities felt themselves under no pressure to improve public service.

The correspondents, Sha Yin and Kuo Chieh, said in their report, for example:

"In the case of grain the number of sales centers has been reduced to 102 this year, compared with 184 in 1954, when grain was placed under planned procurement and supply by the state.

"The number of retail sales clerks has also decreased from an original 750 to 716. As a result each sales clerk is obliged to receive an average of 1,590 customers [the period was not specified]. A customer is used to dividing his grain ration into several or even more than a dozen installments in procuring grain."

"According to regulations," the report went on, "a sales clerk is obliged to tell the customer the exchange rate among twelve different types of grain. This adds to the burden of work of the sales clerk in meeting the demands of their customers."

The report told of first impressions a stranger received upon entering the city.

"Upon entering Taiyuan city one is bound to see customers queueing up before grain stores, cake shops, bathhouses, barber shops, photo shops and food departments of department stores," it said. "Shorter queues may have about a dozen persons but the longer ones are made up of scores, even hundreds, of persons. In some cases a person may not be able to get what he wants after having spent several days in these queues."

The correspondents said that some persons naïvely attributed the troubles to shortage of sales personnel and the higher living standards of the masses. They said this explanation was without basis of fact.

Excuses Assailed

Another unsatisfactory explanation, they asserted, was one given by grain authorities, the increased population.

The two reporters noted that the people felt that, while it was quite true that living standards had improved, with a resulting increased demand for certain consumer goods, grain and many consumer goods were state-controlled and supplied to the people in a planned manner regardless of purchasing power.

The report said the people did not attribute the difficulties met in obtaining living essentials entirely to shortages, but largely to neglect of distribution and commercial business by the state.

June 25, 1957

RED CHINA DELAYS NEW 5-YEAR PLAN

PEIPING, Sept. 28 (Reuters)—China is to increase investments in agriculture, irrigation and the reclamation of waste land next year, according to Po I-po, one of the nation's leading economists.

In a recent speech on the economic plan for 1958, the first year of the second five-year plan, Po I-po, chairman of the National Economic Commission, stressed the importance that would be attached to the development of agriculture.

The fact that this important speech, the first indication of plans for next year, was made by Mr. Po I-po, led observers here to believe that a separate plan was being prepared for 1958 and that the over-all five-year plan would not be announced until later.

The National Economic Commission deals with short-term planning, while long-term, over-all plans are drafted by the State Planning Commission, a separate body.

China is at present experiencing economic difficulties and many observers here think that it will not be possible to agree upon final plans until the effects of this year's harvest are known, about the middle of next year.

A draft for the second plan was submitted to the Chinese Communist party's eighth congress in September, 1956, but since has been in the hands of experts for revision.

Its final form will depend on agriculture, which is the foundation of the whole Chinese economy. In the opinion of some observers, the planners have neglected agriculture in the rush for industrialization.

Appropriations for agriculture and related subjects, such as water conservancy and forestry, have been relatively small, representing only about 14 per cent of economic construction expenditure in 1956 and in the 1957 estimates.

Industry Is Dependent

The production of food and industrial crops must continue to increase if shortages are to be avoided, the peasants to be kept contended and industry to prosper. More than 50 per cent of China's industries use agricultural raw materials, the bulk going to light industries on which the planners rely for quick profits to invest elsewhere. Agricultural production, therefore, has a direct effect on industrial output and progress.

Grain production has gone up every year of the first five-year plan and this year's estimates are higher than the original figure given for 1957. But they are 5,000,000 tons less than a figure given earlier in the year.

It is estimated that production of all grains, including soybeans, will reach 201,000,000 tons this year, an increase of 35,000,000 tons over 1953.

In the next five years, greater annual increases will be needed if the target of 262,000,000 tons for the end of the second five-year plan is to be reached. This figure was set after the bumper harvest of 1955. Since then, the Chinese have experienced some of the natural disasters that can defeat all plans.

September 29, 1957

Peiping Reports Bridge Over Yangtze Finished

The New York Times   Sept. 26, 1957

Special to The New York Times.
HONG KONG, Sept. 25—The Yangtze bridge, biggest ever built in mainland China, was officially announced to have been completed today.

The Peiping radio reported that 200 automobiles and a train crossed the bridge for the first time this morning in a trial run from Wuchang, capital of Hupeh Province, to Hankow.

The bridge, one of the key projects of Red China's first Five-Year Plan, links the two river ports and thereby connects China's two main north-south rail lines.

Described by the radio as a double-decked span, the bridge has a total length of more than a mile.

September 26, 1957

Mao Is in Moscow; He Hails Soviet Tie

By MAX FRANKEL
Special to The New York Times.

MOSCOW, Nov. 2—Mao Tse-tung, leader of Communist China, arrived in Moscow today. He is probably the most important of the gathering here to show the unity and might of international communism.

Virtually all the reigning heads of Communist nations and parties, with the notable exception of President Tito of Yugoslavia, will make the pilgrimage here to join in next week's celebrations of the fortieth anniversary of the Bolshevik Revolution.

Expected in addition to Mr. Mao, who is the Chinese Communist chief of state and party chairman, are Poland's party leader, Wladyslaw Gomulka, and Premier Jozef Cyrankiewicz; Premier Janos Kadar of Hungary, Gheorghe Gheorghiu-Dej, First Secretary of the Rumanian party, and most other Eastern European leaders.

From Western Europe are coming such Communist party chiefs as Palmiro Togliatti of Italy and Maurice Thorez of France. Ho Chi Minh, President of North Vietnam, arrived in Moscow yesterday, and Yumzhagin Tsedenbal, Premier of Outer Mongolia, flew in this evening.

For the most part, their time in Moscow will be taken up with ceremonial assemblies and receptions. Key events will be a huge Kremlin reception, a rally to be addressed by an as yet unnamed Soviet keynoter and a monster military parade in Red Square next Thursday, the day of the anniversary.

But the serious business of relations among Communist nations will inevitably arise. It is thought, too, that Mr. Mao may visit Warsaw and that this, in turn, will promote other exchanges among Communist leaders.

Hosts to the visitors will be the Soviet Communist party and Government, which soon after Mr. Mao's arrival were announcing the expulsion of Marshal Georgi K. Zhukov from the party's ruling circles. All the visible signs were that Nikita S. Khrushchev, the Soviet party chief, had scored a major personal triumph and had greatly increased his public prestige.

Mr. Khrushchev, Premier Nikolai A. Bulganin and Marshal Kliment Y. Voroshilov, Soviet chief of state, headed a large delegation that greeted Mr. Mao at Moscow's Vnukovo Airport. Other members of the party Presidium were on hand, as were Marshal Ivan S. Konev, chief of the Warsaw Pact forces; Marshal K. S. Moskalenko, commander of the Moscow Military District; Air Marshal Pavel F. Zhigarev, and Gen. Ivan A. Serov, state security chief.

Mr. Mao's speech of greeting was short and general. He congratulated the Soviet party and his intention to make the trip until last week's notice that he would attend the anniversary celebrations.

The Chinese Communist chief last visited the Soviet Union at the end of 1949 and the beginning of 1950.

Marshal Tito, who also had been expected, announced last week that he would not be able to make the trip because of an attack of lumbago. Vice President Eduard Kardelj of Yugoslavia will head his country's delegation to Moscow.

Government on the anniversary and on Soviet scientific advances, in particular the successful launching of an artificial earth satellite.

The Chinese leader denounced what he described as United States "imperialism" against Syria and other Arab nations. As for the key issue of Moscow-Peiping relations, he declared:

"There are no forces that separate us. We will always be together and struggle for peace throughout the world."

Mr. Mao had been expected to come to Moscow sometime in July to return Marshal Voroshilov's visit to Peiping and to try to negotiate new Soviet aid for Communist China.

Associated Press Radiophoto

CHINESE COMMUNIST LEADER GREETED IN MOSCOW: Mao Tse-tung, left, the chief of state and Communist party chief, as he arrived yesterday at the capital airport. Welcoming him were Nikita S. Khrushchev, center, Soviet Communist chief, and Premier Nikolai A. Bulganin. Mr. Mao will take part in commemorating the Bolshevik Revolution.

November 3, 1957

PEIPING EXPANDS STATE CAPITALISM

Food Nationalization Decree Bars Private Grain Sales —Canton Controls Tight

By HENRY R. LIEBERMAN
Special to THE NEW YORK TIMES.

HONG KONG, March 13—A tightening of state economic control has been taking place in Communist China under what the Peiping Government calls the "general line of the state in its transition toward socialism."

A steady expansion in the operations of the state companies and the state-controlled rural cooperatives has been accompanied by a food nationalization decree banning private trade in grain.

In the cities consumers are now buying grain and cooking oil from state-designated dealers against "census cards" and "food-procurement certificates."

In addition to monopolizing the rural procurement and urban distribution of grain, the state is extending its control over other types of business in the cities. An official report from Canton disclosed today, for example, that more than 2,200 private concerns in that South China city already had entered the "orbit of state capitalism."

This orbit, in which the state exerts control, either by means of joint ownership or by designating private companies as its agents, is said to embrace eighteen lines of business in Canton.

In addition to various kinds of food enterprise, these lines include such fields as shipping, motor transport, telecommunications supplies, pharmaceuticals, chemicals, dyestuffs, pigments, bamboo wares, fuels, cigarettes and wine.

Of the 2,200-odd concerns now hitched to "state capitalism" in Canton only seven were listed as mixed enterprises, owned jointly by the state and private interests. These joint companies were described as being engaged primarily in foreign trade, communications and transport.

Few in number are, however, more than 1,300 private concerns were said to have entered the "state capitalist" sphere as purchasers of state-supplied wholesale goods and as retailers of these goods at prices, and under marketing rules, fixed by the state.

According to the Canton report, 130 commodities are being supplied to these middlemen on a basis of planned monthly allocations. The report said that the commodity exchange control office of the local Bureau of Industry and Commerce determined the "classes of people to whom goods are to be sold, the scope of merchandise to be handled by private merchants and the selling prices."

Merely Purchasing Agents

An additional 460 private concerns were said to be acting as purchasing agents for state companies, with 480 other private concerns acting as selling agents in the "marketing of special commodities on behalf of the state."

In January, the report added, eighty private commercial companies were organized to help the state-operated Canton municipal oils and fats corporation distribute edible oil.

The development of "state capitalism" in Canton is related to an overall urban economic program launched last fall with the organization of an All-China Federation of Industry and Commerce.

Private businessmen attending an organizational meeting of this body were told that their mission during the "transitional phase" of "state capitalism" was the "continued acceptance of Socialist reform."

March 14, 1954

COLLECTIVE FARMS DUE IN CHINA BY '60

Peiping Plans Gradual Shift Instead of Abrupt Change Along Soviet Lines

By HENRY R. LIEBERMAN
Special to The New York Times.

HONG KONG, Nov. 1—An answer to the question of how soon the Peiping Government intends to collectivize the land in China has been given by Teng Tzu-hui, head of the Chinese Communist party's Rural Work Department.

He envisages a gradual shift to full-fledged collective farms following "cooperativization" of Chinese agriculture during the first and early part of the second five-year plans.

This staging appears to project a general drive to hitch Chinese peasantry to Soviet-style collective farms in the midst of the 1958-62 plan.

The announced aim is to coordinate "collectivization" with a developing industrial capacity to produce modern farm equipment. According to Mr. Teng, the Peiping regime intends to "popularize" horse-drawn farm implements and introduce "partial technical reforms" between now and 1962.

He estimates it will take a third five-year plan before mechanization of agriculture can be carried out on a "comparatively more comprehensive scale."

Producer Cooperatives Stressed

Meanwhile, emphasis is on expanding the number of "producer cooperatives." Under this system, land plots are pooled and worked "cooperatively," with those contributing capital being reimbursed for their capital shares as well as for their labor.

In effect the system already involves the collectivizing of land units. The present timetable calls for increasing the number of "cooperatives" from 100,000 to 500,-000 by next year, to 1,500,000 by 1956 and to 3,000 000 by 1957.

Before spring plowing in 1957, the last year of the first five-year plan, the "cooperative" pools are scheduled to embrace about one half of the total peasant households and 60 per cent of China's farmland.

Mr. Teng says "cooperativization" may be "basically achieved" by 1958 in the principal agricultural regions. He reckons the average size of a "cooperative" at twenty families.

Departs from Soviet Lead

The Communist official discussed agricultural policy in a report published in the Sept. 1 issue of the China Youth Journal. The report, which was made earlier to a youth conference on rural work, is one of the most comprehensive outlines that has yet reached here on Peiping's present agricultural program.

Mr. Teng stated China's present low industrial level made it difficult to follow the lead of the Soviet Union by collectivizing and mechanizing simultaneously. He said a phased gradual approach was also necessary because the Chinese peasant is "steeped in the concept of private ownership," because Peiping's rural tasks were "exceedingly heavy" and because it lacked sufficient personnel.

The official declared the transitional "cooperative" could be "more readily accepted" by the peasants because it offered the prospect of capital dividends. He said the "land reward" could be gradually diminished as the "cooperatives" developed, but stressed the need for a simultaneous increase in the labor return and cautioned against abrupt changes.

November 2, 1954

RED CHINA PUSHES FARM COLLECTIVES

More Agricultural Exports Needed to Finance Plan for Industrialization

Special to The New York Times.

HONG KONG—In 1954 Communist China, which depends on agriculture for the surpluses needed to finance industrialization, experienced the worst floods of the last century in the rice land areas of the Yangtze and Huai River Valleys.

Although the Government acknowledged that 10 per cent of China's total cultivated land had been inundated, the Peiping radio reported later that the 1954 grain output would probably be 170,-000,000 tons for the year compared with 165,000,000 tons in 1953.

The explanation was that a greater wheat output had offset the drop in rice production.

Up to now industrial development has been marked by intensified building activity in Manchuria, some preliminary building in China proper and the continuing railway construction program. Track-laying has been completed on the Chinese section of Chining-Ulan Bator railway and work is continuing on the projected Chengtu-Paochi line in the west and on the Lanchow-Tihwa line in northwest China.

Industry's Output Rises

Industrial output increased fairly rapidly while the Communists were putting existing plants back into operation during the 1949-52 reconstruction period. But the rate has slowed down now that the Communists are undertaking new capital construction.

This construction has gotten off to a necessarily slow start in terms of building objectives for the whole Five-Year-Plan period.

According to the Peiping People's Daily, industrial capital construction in 1953 accounted for 12 per cent of the total projected volume. The Communist newspaper said 15 per cent more of the Five-Year-Plan volume would be completed in 1954 if all targets were met.

About 600 new industrial units are scheduled to be built during the first Five Year Plan. Of these the "sinews" are the original 141 Soviet-supported projects and the fifteen undisclosed projects added to this list in 1954.

Premier Chou En-lai has announced that most of these projects will be completed in 1958.

New Strains on Economy

The Chinese economy already is feeling the new demands exerted upon it by an industrialization program that is running parallel with large military expenditures. With its 1954 budget of $10,500,000,000, estimated here at about one-third of the national income, the Government has been squeezing off the capital surplus by means of profits from its state monopolies, heavy taxation and forced individual "patriotic savings."

Under its program of "planned purchase and supply" the state now monopolizes the grain and cotton markets on a nation-wide basis.

In an apparent effort to extract more surpluses from agriculture, the state has increased the organization of "producers cooperatives," which involve the retooling of small farm units into collectives. Last August there were 100,000 of these cooperatives; in 1955 the number is scheduled to reach 500,000.

This, however, is only the beginning.

The outlook is for a continuing process of farm collectivization and for more general belt-tightening as the Chinese people are asked to make further sacrifices to support the state's costly industrialization and national defense programs.

January 4, 1955

CHINA REDS SLATE A PARTY CONGRESS

Communists Also Decide to Step Up Land-Pooling by Private Farmers

By HENRY R. LIEBERMAN
Special to The New York Times.

HONG KONG, Oct. 15—The Chinese Communist party has decided to convoke its first national party congress in ten years. The party also decided to step up the rate of mobilizing private tillers into land-pooling "agricultural producers' cooperatives."

Separate resolutions on the party congress and expansion of producers' cooperatives were adopted by the Communist party Central Committee at a formal session held from Oct. 4 to 8 under the chairmanship of Mao Tse-tung, head of the Chinese Government.

A communiqué on the meeting was put out today by the Hsinhua (New China) News Agency.

The agency said the central committee also had adopted regulations on the number and election of delegates to the forthcoming eighth national party congress. No date was given for convocation of a new congress.

Party Last Met in 1945

The last party congress was held in 1945 at Yenan in the northwest loess lands of Shensi Province before the Communists came into power in Peiping. It was this congress that elected the party steering group that now rules the China mainland.

Much of the discussion at the recent Central Committee meeting was reported to have centered on the question of "developing agricultural producers' cooperatives." Hsinhua news agency said the discussion followed a report by Mr. Mao on July 31 calling for intensification of the land-pooling movement in the countryside.

This speech, which was not reported previously, was made to the secretaries of the provincial, municipal and special area committees. According to the Communist news agency, Mr. Mao declared that a "new upsurge" was in sight for "the Socialist mass movement in rural areas all over the country."

He was also said to have criticized what he called "the rightist error" in this regard. Mr. Mao's directive, the Peiping dispatch said, already has been "widely transmitted" to the rural areas. Today the official news agency reported that an "upsurge in the agricultural cooperative movement" already had started.

Dividends on Land

Under a revision, adopted three months ago, of the present five-year plan, one-third of China's 110,000,000 peasant households are scheduled to be mobilized into "producers cooperatives" by the end of the plan in 1957. At the end of 1954, according to the State Statistical Bureau, there were almost 500,000 such cooperatives embracing 11 per cent of the peasant households and cultivating 14 per cent of the land.

Land in these "pre-collectives" is farmed cooperatively. Those contributing land are officially said to draw dividends on their capital contributions in addition to "wage point" payments for labor.

In organizing producers cooperatives, the Government is giving interest-bearing loans to those in the "poor peasant" category to help them do their part. According to the Peiping magazine Current Events, the interest rate is 4 per cent monthly.

Today's announcement on the Chinese Communist Central Committee's recent meeting said thirty-eight committee members, including Mr. Mao and twenty-five alternate members were present. When the present Central Committee was elected at Yenan in 1945, it had forty-four members and thirty-three alternates.

The present steering group is the seventh in the party's history since 1921. Its recent meeting was its sixth plenary session since it was organized.

80 Speeches at Meeting

According to the Hsinhua news agency, 388 party stalwarts not on the Central Committee also attended the recent meeting. The agency said there were eighty speakers and added that the speeches of 167 others unable to get the floor because of lack of time were printed for distribution.

The communiqué on the meeting said "important speeches" had been made by the following politburo members:

Liu Shao-chi, Secretary General of the party; Chou En-lai, Premier and Foreign Minister; Marshal Chu Teh, Government Vice Chairman; Chen Yun, Deputy Premier; Marshal Peng Teh-huai, Defense Minister; Peng Chen, Mayor of Peiping; and Teng Hsiao-ping, Central Committee Secretary.

October 16, 1955

CHINA REDS PRESS POOLING OF LAND

Number of the Cooperatives, Doubled in Three Months, Is Now 1,240,000

By HENRY R. LIEBERMAN
Special to The New York Times.

HONG KONG, Nov. 21—The accelerated mobilization of private tillers into land-pooling producer cooperatives has been going full blast in Communist China.

With at least four months to go, the Chinese announced this morning they already had virtually attained the goal set by Mao Tse-tung, Communist leader, for 1,300,000 producer cooperatives by next year's spring sowing.

The "rich peasant," who is now excluded from the cooperatives, is the prime target in the drive to harness the "poor" and "middle" peasants into land-pooling units.

The campaign is being accompanied by continued denunciation of "rural counter revolutionaries." But the official story of the present upheaval is still emerging from China's rural areas in terms of statistics instead of human displacement.

The statistics underline the speed and scope of the collectivization movement.

According to the Hsinhua (New China) News Agency, the number of producer cooperatives reached 1,240,000 on Nov. 10. The agency said 590,000 cooperatives were set up in the last three months and ten days.

Plan to Be Exceeded

At the present pace, the agency said, the goal of 1,300,000 cooperatives by the spring sowing is likely to be exceeded. When the Chinese Communist leader last July 31 called for doubling the number of cooperatives he noted that the 650,000 units existing as of June embraced 16,900,000 peasant households. He said there was an average of twenty-six peasant households in each cooperative.

Mr. Mao said some units had seventy to eighty families, some more than 100 and a few as many as several hundred. He referred to a total rural population of 500,000,000, consisting of 110,000,000 peasant households.

It is not known what the present average is for the expanded number of cooperatives. If one assumes a constant average of twenty-six farm families to each unit, with four and a half persons to a family, today's Hsinhua News Agency figures suggest that:

¶Close to 30 per cent of China's farm families already have been mobilized into cooperatives, which the Peiping regime calls semi-socialist collectives.

¶About 69,000,000 peasants were organized into these units during a 102-day period up to Nov. 10.

Progress Held Impressive

The average may now be less than twenty-six households to a cooperative. But even allowing for a reduced average the collectivization rate seems impressive.

Land vested in producer cooperatives is farmed collectively with labor payments being made on basis of wage points. Under the present system those contributing land or other capital draw payments for these contributions but such dividends are scheduled to be eliminated eventually.

In his July 31 report on collectivization Mr. Mao declared China intended to achieve a basic Socialist transformation of agriculture over an eighteen-year period by the time of the completion of her third five-year plan in 1967. He compared this with the 17-year period required in the Soviet Union from 1921 to 1937.

Declaring that agricultural output was too low, Mr. Mao told the party there was contradiction between the lagging farm output and the growing demand for marketed grain and industrial raw materials. He said Socialist industrialization could not be achieved without the collectivization of agriculture.

Mr. Mao said only 20 to 30 per cent of the Chinese peasants were "prosperous or comparatively prosperous." He argued in fact that the 60 to 70 per cent who were having difficulties provided an important motive force for land pooling inasmuch as they wanted to "rid themselves of their poverty."

November 23, 1955

MORE NEWS FROM RED CHINA

A quarter of a century ago Soviet peasants struck back against enforced collectivization by slaughtering their livestock. For many who did so it was a reaction of blind, primitive rage. If their livestock were to be stolen from them by the collective farms, the peasants reasoned, the animals might as well be killed and eaten. The result was a massive reduction in Soviet livestock, the consequences of which are still apparent today.

Now from Communist China comes news of a new campaign of livestock slaughter. The Peiping regime has ordered that cattle can neither be sold nor slaughtered without Government permission. It is no mere coincidence that this same period of "wanton slaughter" of livestock has also been one of tremendous pressure on China's peasants to join collective farms. The pressure has been so great these past few months that it is now officially claimed that 40 per cent of the farmers have joined cooperative farms, the precursors of full-fledged Soviet-style collectives.

Like the Soviet peasants before them, Chinese peasants are obviously protesting against forced collectivization. Whether this method of protest will be any more effective now in China than it was in the early Nineteen Thirties in Russia remains to be seen. But we should not forget that Communist China today is even poorer than the Soviet Union was in 1930, and it can even less afford a tremendous loss of agricultural capital.

RED CHINA NEARS LAND POOL GOAL

Peiping Says 85% of Farm Families Are Collectivized in Accelerated Drive

By HENRY R. LIEBERMAN
Special to The New York Times.

HONG KONG, March 5— Eighty-five per cent of China's farm families were officially reported today to have been collectivized in the Peiping regime's amazingly rapid land-pooling drive.

With only two months of the year gone, Communist China says it already has reached the collective target set for 1956 under shifting timetables in which the fixed pace has become faster and faster.

The 85 per cent figure was cited by the Peiping People's Daily, the leading Chinese Communist newspaper, in reporting that 100,000,000 peasant households had been organized into land-pooling "producers' cooperatives" as of mid-February.

Forty-eight per cent of China's farmers, the newspaper added, are working on full-fledged Soviet-style collective farms. Those pooling their land in the "producers' cooperative" theoretically draw a dividend, but such dividends are quickly being eliminated.

The People's Daily percentage for "producers' cooperatives" is apparently based on a larger total of farm families than the 110,000,000 usually mentioned by the Chinese Communist organ.

Last December, when the cooperative percentage figure was said to have passed 60 per cent, the Chinese Communist leader Mao Tse-tung declared that more than 50,000,00 farm families had been collectivized in a "few months."

The indications are that at least another 25,000,000 peasant households have been brought into cooperative units since then. At this rate, the collectivization program is almost certain to be virtually completed at the end of this year.

In keeping track of this drive, official observers in Hong Kong have watched closely for signs of the kind of resistance that marked the collectivization drive in the Soviet Union.

Last December the Peiping government acknowledged in an order prohibiting "wanton slaughter" of cattle, that farmers had been killing off livestock at an unusual rate. The domestic Chinese Communist press also has referred to organizational problems and the need for being on the alert against "counter-revolutionaries" in the rural "struggle."

Last year, however, the Communist press referred to such problems as administrative snags, "sabotage" by "rich peasants" and "fluctuations in peasant thought." It commented that the problem of "overcoming the psychology of private property" was "not simple."

In a speech last July, Mr. Mao indicated there was some opposition inside the Communist party to a rapid collectivization rate. Since his criticism of those who were proceeding with "bound feet," security squads have been organized in the collectives to guard against the "rich peasants" and ferret out "counter-revolutionaries."

The big unanswered question is whether the system of quotas, bonuses and penalties on the collectives will provide the incentives needed to meet the state's increased production targets.

CHINA'S PEASANTS RECLAIMING LAND

Peiping Resettles Hundreds of Thousands in Virgin Areas Along Borders

By HENRY R. LIEBERMAN
Special to The New York Times.

HONG KONG, April 29—Hundreds of thousands of Chinese are being resettled in the country's border areas. The objective is to reclaim barren land, to increase the food output for industrialization.

Farmhands from surplus population centers are being shifted as permanent settlers to Heilungkiang in northern Manchuria, to Tsinghai, Kansu and Sinkiang in northwest China and to Inner Mongolia. Large numbers have migrated to those areas from Honan, Shantung, Hopei and Kiangsu.

By the middle of next month 120,000 persons from Shantung are scheduled to leave for Heilungkiang. Aside from volunteers, the settlers are believed to include former peasants who are required to leave overpopulated cities.

Literacy Drive Pressed

In a December speech on the literacy campaign in his province, a Heilungkiang deputy said 1,158,000 illiterates would be among the migrants to northern Manchuria "in the nearest future." This represents a substantial increase over the reported migration of 200,000 to Heilungkiang in 1935.

That Manchurian province, whose population in 1953 was 11,897,000, has a reclamation goal of 1,852,000 acres this year. More than 1,200 reclamation teams are said to have been organized.

At the same time teams led by youths are engaged in local reclamation projects. Such teams have been active in Hopei and the rice bowl province of Hunan.

But the accent seems to be on reclaiming untill land in the remoter border regions, this movement is bringing more Chinese into areas inhabited by national minority groups, confronting the Mongol shepherd with more farmers and increasing the number of ethnic Chinese in zones close to the Soviet frontier.

China is apparently counting heavily on its resettlement for reclamation program to increase food output.

The People's Daily, chief Chinese Communist newspaper, has acknowledged that the weak point of China's agricultural economy at present is that there is too little land for too many people. It estimates the amount of arable land at 273,000,000 acres, less than half an acre per person for a population of 600,-000,000.

The Government estimates that China has 250,000,000 acres of wasteland. The press holds that if one-third of it can be reclaimed over several five-year plans, the increased acreage could yield an extra 50,000,000 tons of food a year.

Industrial workers are also migrating to the borderland areas. According to a dispatch from Shanghai, more than 32,000 workers, 2,000 skilled metal workers and 1,000 construction workers have left there for northwest China to work on railway, oil and other development projects.

Meanwhile, work has been started in Northwest China on the construction of a new oil refinery at Lanchow to process crude oil from the Yumen Fields in Kansu. A railroad from Lanchow is expected to reach the oilfield this year.

COLLECTIVES' GAIN SURPRISES CHINA

Elimination of Private Farms Said to Surpass Goals — 56% of Peasants Enlisted

By Reuters

PEIPING, June 8—Communist China's rapid advance toward the complete collectivization of agriculture has outstripped even the most optimistic forecasts of its leaders and planners.

A Peiping Government agricultural expert said today that it was possible that China might this year have a "bumper harvest."

He said that winter wheat, which has been harvested in the area south of the Yangtze River, had shown a 10 to 20 per cent increase over last year. He added that reports from all over the country told of increased acreage sown and prospects of good harvests and higher yields.

But he emphasized that it was still too early to be certain or to make any sort of forecast, though the rain that had fallen so far was "just right."

Already 56 per cent of all peasant families are members of Soviet-style collective farms and it seems certain that this figure will rise to more than 90 per cent of the 120,000,000 peasant families in China by the spring of next year. This would be at least eighteen months ahead of plans published as late as last January.

Collectivization is an integral part of Red China's plan to increase its agricultural production two and a half times by 1967, the end of the third Five-Year Plan. It must be increased to serve the wants of the growing industrial society, to pay for imports and industrialization and to feed the rapidly expanding population.

Officials hope that collectivization will bring a more efficient use of land and facilitate the distribution and wider use of improved strains of seed and better fertilizers. Above all they expect that labor will be organized in a more economic and useful way.

Mechanization Planned

Thus peasants who formerly spent much of the winter in idleness can now be used on subsidiary tasks, such as digging irrigation canals and wells, doing flood prevention work, reafforestation or reclaiming land. These measures are part of the try-wide drive to help increase crease production by preventing the natural calamities that have so often ravaged China's agricultural lands in the past.

In addition, collectivization prepares the way for the mechanization of agriculture, which is planned for the future.

The spread of collectivization is a natural process in the socialization of the country for even with the accent on industrial development, agriculture remains the major factor in all Chinese life. It is the nation's immediate wealth and the daily occupation of about 80 per cent of its population of 600,000,000.

But the speed of its development in the last nine months has been nothing short of amazing.

Last July Mao Tse-tung, the Chief of State, laid down the plans and the party line on agricultural cooperation.

Mr. Mao's speech emphasized that collectivization must bring about a rise in agricultural yields and said socialization must not be hindered by those who wanted to "mark time" or those who wanted to go too fast and force collectivization on the countryside.

Rich Peasants Assailed

Mr. Mao said: "What still lingers in the countryside is capitalist ownership by the rich peasants and individual peasant ownership—an ocean of it. As everyone has noticed in recent years the spontaneous tendency in the countryside to develop toward capitalism is daily growing stronger and new rich peasants are springing up everywhere. Many well-to-do middle peasants are striving to become rich ones."

It was a striking indication that the Government was aware that the poorer peasants might accuse it—and perhaps were already doing so—of not completing the revolution.

The official classification of peasants is: poor peasants—those with no land or so little that they have to hire themselves out as laborers; middle peasants—those with enough land to live on and who do not hire labor; rich peasants—those who have more land than they can work themselves and who employ labor.

To give the peasants "correct leadership," the Government sent out a task force of young party propagandists into the countryside to "guide and assist" the peasants.

Speed Is Unexpected

These ideological commandos achieved a success the speed of which (or so it would appear from the figures he quoted) even Mr. Mao himself did not expect, though he was far more optimistic than many party members.

In many places the transformation has been gradual to allow the peasants to adjust themselves slowly, but of recent months the change has been much quicker.

The peasants have adjusted from mutual-aid teams, where peasants merely helped one another in busy seasons, to semi-Socialist cooperatives, where they received pay for work done and land owned, variously, in proportions of 70-30 or 60-40. Finally, they have formed advanced cooperatives (actual collective farms) where all land, animals and some implements are held under joint ownership and a peasant's income is reckoned only by work done.

When Mr. Mao made his speech last July, about 14 per cent of the peasant families throughout China were members of some sort of cooperative. By January the figure was 60 per cent and by the end of March 90 per cent, of which 56 per cent were members of actual collective farms.

All Communist edicts on cooperation say that peasants must not be forced to join but must be shown the advantages and persuaded by example.

Shortage of Experts Noted

The propagandists were expected to work on the poor peasants, who make up 60 to 70 per cent of the rural population. They were expected to stress the advantages of cooperative farming and explain that the peasants had everything to gain in higher incomes and joint ownership of land.

The success of the agricultural cooperative movement is expected to be demonstrated by a rise in farm production. But a continued increase of production will depend not only on better seeds and fertilizers and a large cultivated acreage but also on the efficient running of the collective farms.

There remains a serious problem in the lack of trained men to run these collectives and direct the work of in some cases as many as 2,000 families. Allied to this is the danger of too much centralization and of mistaken direction by party officials whose knowledge of Marxist theory often far exceeds their ability as agricultural experts.

These troubles, and the Communist Government's evident concern and determination to overcome them quickly, are borne out by almost daily articles, editorials and letters in the newspapers, criticizing some aspect of collectivization or the management of some particular farm.

Self-criticism is part of the creed of communism and the Chinese leaders and policy makers seem to be fully aware of the problems that attend collectivization.

The present aim for all collectives in the country can be seen in farms near Peiping that are presumably models of their kind.

In one of these, made up of more than 2,000 families, which supplies vegetables to Peiping, the planning was evident and it would be most strange if such an organization did not produce more than the earlier haphazard farming.

Collective Is Depicted

This full collective is made up of four cooperative farms that were until January only semi-Socialist. In one of these alone, the area of cultivated land has increased more than 2 per cent following the merging of land and the elimination of boundary ditches and banks.

Irrigation and drainage ditches and seven new wells were evidence of the work done through the winter. Travelers say the whole face of the country is being changed by this organized winter work.

In another small collective farm of about 900 families that has been in operation for about four years, the director said that last year the yield had risen nearly 20 per cent and that the incomes of peasants had risen accordingly and in some cases even more.

These collectives are run by a director and his deputy, assisted by small administrative staffs and responsible to a management committee that meets about every two weeks. This committee is elected by a conference of farm representatives that meets every three months and each of whose delegates represents eight to ten families. On smaller cooperatives all family groups send representatives.

Peasants are organized into work groups and the leaders of each group assign tasks. Work is done under the general supervision of the management committee, which decides what is to be planted each year.

June 10, 1956

RED CHINA REPORTS ON ECONOMY IN 1956

HONG KONG, Aug. 1. (AP)—Communist China has announced a virtual end to private ownership with the completion of the country's "Socialist transformation plan."

The economic report for 1956 issued by the State Statistical Bureau said the plan had been basically completed. The 6,000-word communiqué was broadcast by the Peiping radio today.

It said that by the end of 1956 more than 110,000,000 households, or 92 per cent of the total, had joined agricultural cooperatives.

Land worked collectively exceeds 100,000,000 hectares (250,000,000 acres), or 90 per cent of all cultivated land, the report said. Private industry is for the most part now under joint state-private management, it added.

Of the country's gross industrial output for 1956, private industry accounted for only 1.3 per cent, the report said.

August 2, 1957

PEIPING REVISES ITS FARM SYSTEM

Reduces Size of Collectives and Asks Higher Incomes for Needy Peasants

By TILLMAN DURDIN
Special to The New York Times.

HONG KONG, Sept. 16 — Sweeping changes were ordered today in Communist China's system of collective farms. The changes were prescribed by the Central Committee of the Chinese Communist party.

A Peiping radio report received here said three new directives called for smaller collectives, a revision in the system of incomes for members and a reorganization in administrative methods.

The new measures are evidence of serious shortcomings in the collective farm system and in China's food supply. Last year there were food shortages for some sections of the population and admitted difficulties in collecting food quotas from the countryside.

The directive dealing with the size of collectives says that from now on a village of "just over 100 households" should in general form one collective. This will mean a splitting up of many collectives that contain hundreds of households and take in several villages.

The need for limiting the size of collectives was ascribed to "the present characteristics of agriculture and the low level of technique and management."

The measures order the collectives to establish a system of unified management with control by groups at different levels. It is also directed that collectives institute a system of rewards "in proportion to the overfulfillment of production targets and deductions where production falls short of targets."

The new rulings note that some collective farm officials have committed errors in handling finances, in administering production or in dealing with personnel. The measures call for an improvement of management methods.

The measures order increased attention to the problem of the former upper middle peasants who have been a disgruntled element under collectivization. The rulings add it is necessary to unite with the former upper middle peasants and at the same time "criticize, persuade and educate them."

Collective farm officials were told that they must "in adjusting economic benefits of members place reliance particularly on former poor and lower middle peasants."

Measures were prescribed for increasing the incomes of collective members in economic difficulties, and it was stipulated that members should be permitted to own a certain number of domestic animals.

China's peasants went into the collective system last year with a surprising lack of resistance. Since then, however, it has become apparent that resistance to the system has developed and that large-scale mismanagement and the evasion of regulations have occurred.

To make the first year of collectivization especially attractive to the farmers, the Government allowed the peasants to keep more grain than ever before and made other concessions to the rural areas.

The sense of official statements is that collectivization has resulted in the state's getting proportionately less farm output.

September 17, 1957

herness (Communist-style)—This Peiping poster for a national savings scheme reflects the new Chinese family ideal, one freed from male domination and dedicated to the state.

Deep Challenge to China's Communists

**'or ages the family was the basic social and political unit in China. The Communists
ave gone far toward smashing it, but can they reshape it to their design?**

y PEGGY DURDIN

IGHT years ago, when the Communists were still settling into the ancient, gracious city of eiping, they announced a fundamental licy. Breaking the old Chinese fam-' system, they stated, was an absolute rerequisite to building the new Socialist society. At Mao Tse-tung's pernal insistence, even before they had inted down the last remnants of hiang Kai-shek's broken armies and ireaucracy, party and Government mmenced a full-scale attack on the lassic" family.

The Communist father-figure, who lotes Lenin and Confucius with equal cili:y, was well aware that erecting s brave new Marxist world depended first demolishing the old. No one iew better than this rebellious farm-

er's son, carried to triumph by men and women from the brown, green and golden rice and wheat fields, that for most of China's five hundred million peasants the male-dominated family was still the basic political and social unit, the source of ethics, the molder of personality, the framework for religious practices, the link to a long-fingered past, and the single most important focus of loyalty, far overshadowing that echo of an echo called a state.

THE old Chinese family still gripped Chinese rural life in the twentieth century because it had developed gradually and logically to meet man's basic need: survival. For millenniums this great stretch of landscape—a third larger than the United States—has been tirelessly punitive to the Sons of Han—through drought and famine, or through

flooding rivers that suddenly sweep homes, livestock, ruined crops and dead, bloated bodies down wide new channels to the sea.

The effort of any Chinese Government to reach, rule or help its people was balked by defiant mountains, treacherous water and sheer, stubborn space, spider-webbed faintly with little roads marked out by wooden wheels and trudging peasant feet. No ruler—neither Dragon Emperor demanding tribute from all of Southeast Asia nor Chiang Kai-shek receiving recognition from great Western powers—could protect the Middle Kingdom's own little clusters of farmers from foreign invaders, war lords, epidemics, earth exhaustion, venal officials, famine, and callous, thieving soldiers.

The tremendous circle of city wall (great stone lifted on great stone by decades of hoe-hardened hands) which

enclosed my North China childhood home protected the town from nothing: not from smoke-colored clouds of locusts, warring armies, cholera, leprosy, starvation; not, for centuries, from the Yellow River, petulant and greedy like a pampered, favorite concubine; not even from the endless swarms of bandits, one of whose heads sometimes hung, a bloody, ineffective warning, outside a wall already breached by bribe and treachery.

TO cope with this—the realities of China—the family simply took on the roles of government, school, insurance company, old people's home, orphanage, old-age pension and unemployment relief agency, social center, factory and business. It set standards of behavior and disciplined the wrong-doer. It organized religious rites and festivals.

Chiefly by

GGY DURDIN is a freelance writer who s reported on the Far East for many years.

HOUSEWIFE—She has new prestige, if only for economizing on food and consumer goods.

PEASANT—Housework is not enough; she must work outside as nearly full time as pos

word of mouth and example, the family passed down through generations China's technical skills (from patching crumbling dikes to creating matchless shapes and glazes in pottery), her fund of everyday wisdom, her protective armor of courtesy, her myths, her attitudes toward life and her code of Confucian-colored ethics. Infinitely multiplied in space and time, the Chinese family made possible for the world's second largest country, not nationhood, but the homogeneity and long survival of one of the finest civilizations man has experienced.

In theory, every Chinese found complete fulfillment in harmonious relationship with "all within the Four Seas." In fact, the connections of each self-sufficient kinship group to the world outside it were tenuous, like shadow writing; they dwindled, not with time, but with distance. Province and state were cloud images on some far horizon; family was real; ruler and ruled, only a reflection of the father-son relationship. "Civic sense" was an unimagined luxury; a man living honorably by precepts of long-dead ancestors need not even *try* to rescue a drowning stranger. But every relation inside the family was close, solid and as clearly outlined as good calligraphy. In a system offering little leeway for non-

conformity, but remarkable security, every person had his niche, rights, duties and prescribed attitudes—submission and devotion were *owed* by children to parents, wives to husbands, younger to elder brothers.

This family structure rested on several pillars. One was loyalty to the household or clan, overshadowing all other allegiances as Peiping's great gates overshadow men passing under them. Another was complete male supremacy.

"When a boy is born," the Chinese saying goes, "he is laid on a bed and given jade to play with. When a girl is born, she is put on the floor and given a tile to play with." If the family rice bowls were empty, she was not infrequently abandoned, alive, where hungry dogs roamed outside the walls of the city. She could be sold into prostitution or slavery.

AT best, a woman was a second-class citizen, married to produce male children for her husband's family, without status (until she became a mother-in-law or grandmother), without property rights, without redress against ill-treatment, whether beatings by her husband or the more subtle sadism practiced by many a mother-in-law to make her son's wife pay with formidable interest for the endless

slights, deprivations and brutalities she herself had suffered for so long a time.

When the Japanese captured my city, a middle-aged peasant woman literally caked in mud collapsed inside the gate of the American hospital. She had spent the night neck-deep in a slimy village pond to hide from raping soldiers and then stumbled the long miles to the city. Just before dying of a heart attack, she pulled off a ring of cheap jade—her only personal and private possession—and gave it to the doctor who had tended her. She spoke for generations of Chinese women when she said, "In all my life, you are the only person who ever loved me."

A third pillar of the family was filial piety—obedience to, care and support of, respect and affection for parents. A decade ago, this was still China's nearest approach to deep-felt, universal religion and its highest ranking virtue, embroidering Chinese myth and literature as clouds and dragons festooned the imperial garments.

"If one shows respect for his parents at home, he does not need to burn incense in a far-off temple," said the practical proverb. "Filial piety begins with serving parents, leads to serving the Emperor and ends in establishing character," said the great sage. A good son would, *ipso facto*, be a faithful friend and a loyal subject. Political re-

bellions, Chinese said, were never le by men who honored their parents Father-son was the apex of all huma relationships.

A Chinese owed filial piety, not only to his parents and to all the elderly but to his long line of ancestors, alive in a way beyond the experience of th most blue-blooded Westerner. Honor able Chinese worshiped before thei ancestors' tablets, tended their grave —those round mounds that ripple end lessly across the great face of China— and had many sons, indispensable for insuring the dead happy, continuing immortality.

THIS veneration for ancient authority and most of the other traits the Chines family fostered, are exactly those which Communists anywhere must obliterate The fundamental Communist technique of public denunciation and self-criticism collide with the family's regard fo "face." New Marxist worlds are no built by respect for the past. Nor ar they built by the cynical realism ex pressed in the universal Chinese phras "Mei yu fa tze"—"There's no help fo it"—with which generations shrugge off those vagaries of heaven and na ture the family was powerless to aver ("Man can *change* nature and *bea* Heaven," Peiping said again recently.

The irreverent scorn for governmen officialdom and armies—a scorn tha

INIST—She has equal rights with men, but the basic equality is equality in "production."

STUDENT—For her, the party has taken over the moral and social functions of the family.

e family system helped produce—is adly sin in China today. "Bourgeois" d near-criminal are the Chinese re-rd for manners, sense of humor and oportion, patience and tolerance to hich tight family living gave birth. asked how he kept nine generations ppy under one roof, a famous Prime inister replied by writing, one hun-ed times, the character for "forbear-ce," a nasty word in the Marxist dic-nary.)

In direct contrast to Communist phi-sophy, the Chinese family system en-uraged back-breaking industry—and e sacrifice of everything else, includ-g honesty—for the profit and ad-ncement of a single, blood-related oup. The resulting nepotism became —as the Kuomintang illustrated—a onstrous vice in China, fatally ob-ructing the conduct of business, war government.

In the cities, Western machines and eas, termite fashion, had begun to dermine the family by the time fe-ale Communist cadres—earnest and rtually desexed—marched toward the mato-colored walls of the Imperial ty, where perfumed concubines, incing on crippled "golden lily" feet, d waited on the pleasures of the ons of Heaven. By 1949 females were ual to males "in law"; young people ere rebelling against parental author-y and marrying "for love"; and

mixed dancing, coeducation, women in industry and the professions were no longer innovations. Both Mao Tse-tung and Chiang Kai-shek had dis-carded their old-fashioned wives for two varieties of "new" women.

With greatly increased communica-tions, education, industrialization—and socialization—the rural family also would have altered beyond recognition in this century. But Communists are revolutionaries, not reformers; they force change, not wait for it. So, clearing the way for the "new" family, the party leveled its guns at every vital part of the old kinship unit: masculine supremacy, filial piety; the cohesion, the loyalty, the economic basis and the social, moral and cultural functions of the family.

* * *

THE Communists' first salvo at the "old family basis" was the Mar-riage Law promulgated in May, 1950, based on Marx, Engels, Lenin, Stalin and Mao, and not too unlike earlier, largely unenforced Kuomintang legis-lation. It banned arranged and child marriage, sale of children, concubinage, polygamy, discrimination against ille-gitimacy and interference with the right of widows to remarry. It gave women equal rights with men to work (by Peiping's creed, equality in "pro-duction" is the basic equality), in status in and outside the home, in prop-

erty rights, in divorce and retention of name.

While eradicating real abuses, this legislation had motivations more cen-tral to Peiping's purposes than hu-manitarianism. Giving women half the family property, letting them break marriages, leave homes, husbands, par-ents, in-laws and ancestral tablets and perform men's jobs (locomotive driver, street chairman and busybody, coopera-tive head, petty official, Cabinet Min-ister, even general) demolished a key pillar of the family—masculine suprem-acy—and thereby weakened the en-tire family structure, as one would wreck a painting by blotting out its pivotal figure.

The importance of this legislation overturning the old male-female bal-ance can be measured by the fact that Peiping used all its apparatus of prop-aganda — probably never anywhere equaled and certainly never surpassed —to publicize and enforce it. In addi-tion to using such techniques as staging group marriages in front of Mao's portrait (not portraits of family an-cestors), enlivened by "speak bitter-ness" stories of ex-slaves or ex-prosti-tutes, Peiping sent hordes of cadres —one million for a single province—to put the new law into practice.

Radical changes directed by virtually untrained, often stupid and arrogant—

and, alas, even old-fashioned—cadres created a crescendo of dislocation. For instance, in Kwangsi, Communists re-ported, "Many women are marrying and divorcing at will and even become absolute romanticists! Cadres have in some cases married and divorced eight times within a year. The number of children born out of wedlock has great-ly increased * * *. Everywhere there are monstrous phenomena of the Three Plenties: plenty of divorce, plenty of infanticide and plenty of female sui-cide." Taking stock, the Communists since about 1953 have pushed the Mar-riage Law reforms steadily, but less hurriedly.

* * *

SYNCHRONIZED with the attack on female slavery and male su-premacy was Peiping's assault on filial piety through a daringly direct tech-nique: denunciation of the father by his children, particularly by sons. Ac-cording to centuries-old standards, this is an act of shame and degradation, the nearest a Chinese can come to defama-tion of an altar.

It is no accident that the Commu-nists allow not a single Chinese to complete the all-important, agonizing process of thought remolding without blackening his father. In each periodic national campaign—against graft and corruption, against rightists, etc.—children have had practice in libeling and rejecting male parents. During the campaign to remake intellectuals in 1952, one of Peiping's great university presidents was publicly arraigned by his daughter in a famous speech: "* * * Since you cheat all the people, why shouldn't you be cheating me? Even if the parental love between a father and daughter is true, it is completely insignificant compared with the love among the masses. Anyway, your love is only deceit. * * * Do you think a few drops of false tears can buy over my heart? * * *"

LAST fall, during their biggest heresy hunt to date, the Communists organized a two months' "struggle" against Dr. Li Tsung-en, the Glasgow-educated scientist, administrator, gentleman and scholar who, since 1947, had been president of the Peiping medical school and hospital that fathered modern medicine in China. No one knows whether misery flickered in any heart as each of Dr. Li's employes, colleagues and old, trusted friends vied to vilify him. But certainly no nerve twitched with surprise when Dr. Li's own son stood up to castigate his father.

Peiping has progressed as far against family loyalty as it has against masculine supremacy and filial piety. Putting "individualist" family interests before those of the state is "rightist," at the very least, and can be criminal. Communists say one must love the country, cooperative and family—the nouns always follow in that order. In exact reversal of the Confucian principle, Peiping explains that those who do not first love the state and cooperative cannot love the family. Motivation for work and sacrifice must be, not a kinship group, ancestors and descendants, but party, state, cooperative and the long-term welfare of 600,-000,000 members of the "Socialist family." Anyway, it is hard to be loyal to relatives when one may be judged guilty for living or associating with them, for failing to watch or betray' them or simply for *having* them.

THE Communists have also badly damaged family cohesion and solidarity. Privacy was always a luxury in China; outside interference, which was formerly spasmodic, is now continuous. Cadres, government officials, members of the party, street committees, cooperatives, study groups, labor unions, women's and young

Communists' organizations all have the privilege of prying into what any member of a household does, says, eats or believes. Group meals and group housing have increased. The state separates family members at will. It is sending city workers' families to the countryside; it may ship an only son thousands of miles away to one of China's far frontiers, so that he will never again see, much less tend, the ancestral graves the Communists have not yet dared destroy physically.

Nor is there any time or money for family activities. "Sunset workers"—people in towns or cities who leave their

--- REJECTION ---

All over China, during their first years of power, the Communists staged public trials of landlords and "counter-revolutionaries" by "the masses" in which sons dramatically slandered, betrayed and virtually condemned their own fathers to death or long imprisonment. In a famous propaganda story, a high Communist army officer visited his old home, just "liberated" from the Kuomintang. There, before his weeping family, an ugly crowd threatened, abused and unjustly accused his father of landlordism. Asked to speak, the officer refused, with tears, to interfere with "the People's justice." His old father got a brutal mob beating; the son got party praise, fame and a medal.

offices at the end of working hours—are scolded in print. For a peasant now to take a couple of days off for an old-fashioned family wedding would not only be politically dangerous and financially impossible; the free time simply is not available. Besides doing his regular farm work, he is "voluntarily" planting trees, building wells and irrigation ditches, killing "pests" (flies, mosquitos, sparrows, rats), collecting fertilizer, learning to read, writing Socialist songs, getting ideologically remolded and discussing politics ("Is capitalism or socialism better?" "Shall we quadruple our production?" "Should we work harder and eat less?"). Any crevice of empty minutes the party fills with meetings.

IN the past two years the Communists have wrecked the economic foundation of the family. More than 95 per cent of. China's peasants have joined cooperatives. Not the

household head, or family council, but the state, party and collective own the land and tools, decide when and what the family members sow and reap, when and how much they work, how much and what they have to wear and eat. A man has no precious bit of land or hoard of cash to leave his sons or give to help them "get ahead." Anyway, since a manual laborer is theoretically already at the peak of Communist society, the very idea of "getting ahead" is selfish, bourgeois, rightist and even counter-revolutionary.

The party is steadily taking over, too, the moral and social functions of the family. A barrage of Socialist indoctrination in and out of schools preaches Communist, not Confucian, theology: manual work is sacred and noble, the party is God, Marxist orthodoxy and labor records are the best criteria for judging character, feelings for the opposite sex should not be bourgeois—"hand-holding near the flowers in the moonlight" or "drowning in the muddy pit of love"—young people should postpone marriage in the interests of the state, etc.

Though its chief motivation is economic necessity, the Communists' intense effort to popularize birth control is another stroke against the "classic" Chinese family. Ancestor worship does not thrive on "family planning."

* * *

BUT the Communists have not waited to demolish all the old ways before spreading their concept of the "new Socialist family" in the rich rice valleys of Szechuan, the sandy plains of Sinkiang, the tribe-inhabited peaks of Kwangsi, the humid little towns of Kwantung, the factory-filled cities of Manchuria. The Marriage Law roughly sketched this kinship group: the family is to be a work unit dedicated to building socialism under party control, with the hearts and minds of its members as subservient to state and party as their muscles.

In the last year, the Communists have made an interesting zig, or zag, in putting this family, Humpty Dumpty fashion, together. "The family is an integral part of society," high Government dignitaries have announced with an air of discovery. Reminding women to evangelize for socialism, practice birth control and encourage "leaping upsurges" in production, Peiping has, at the same time, told them to leave the glamorous cities and lathes and go back to hearth and home. There

they must establish "a harmonious, democratic family" in which men and women are equal, elders and mothers-in-law love the young, youth and daughters-in-law respect the old "in accordance with Socialist ideas and principles" and children are reared with "exemplary, moral, Socialist characters."

But creating good Communists *inside* the home does not relieve women of the obligation to work as nearly full time as possible *outside* it. On this point, the All-China Women's Federation, in a directive issued this spring was explicit: "Women are required to take an active part in the industrial and farm production and other tasks of construction and at the same time to make a success of their housekeeping and various side occupations * * *. It must not be construed that in the past women were mobilized only for participating in production and now they are required only to do housekeeping * * *."

PEIPING explains, "It is completely *wrong* to despise housework * * *. Management of the home with diligence and thrift is of exceptionally great importance to state Socialist construction. It affects the productive capacity of every member of the family. It saves consumer goods for the state and industry. It trains children to become Socialists who love work and endure hardship. It provides a good home life."

The Communists clearly explain the principal reason for this emphasis on the new family at this particular moment. Unable yet adequately to feed or clothe its own people, China must export food and cotton in vast quantities to pay for its priority objective: heavy industrialization. The chief of Peiping's many 1958 mottoes is "Work and Economize as Never Before." Women are chiefly needed, not in official jobs and factories, but to work in fields and pinch on every last drop of cooking oil and grain of cereal. ("Watch the boiling pot so not a spoonful of food boils over. Measure each daily ration carefully. Eat less. Grind water chestnuts or chaff to mix with flour. Substitute potatoes and vegetables for bread and rice. Serve nice liquid foods in summer and periods of slackened work.") Housewives must save every scrap of cloth. ("Wear your old clothes. Alter and patch them. Cut down adult clothes for children, older children's clothes for the younger. Wear the cloth-saving old-style Chinese dress instead of the more wasteful Mao Tse-tung uniform.")

WITH the population firmly placed in cooperative and factory, the state apparatus of control restrengthened, the party purged, critics of the regime again hunted out and silenced and the biggest reindoctrination campaign so far under way, Peiping may feel it is sufficiently strong and women sufficiently "saved" to mold a Communist family even though evil fragments of the old remain.

Anyway, Peiping has discovered it simply has not the money yet to support, rear and educate the young and feed and keep the elderly. Too many people have deserted the old folks already to suit Government or cooperative budgets. Peiping said last fall that young people and adults must "support and respect their parents so that the aged who are incapable of working will receive reasonable care during their lives and enjoy mental ease." And, perhaps, getting no younger themselves and remembering last year's instances of downright student rebellion, the Communists may wish to reinstate at least a modest respect for age.

As Peiping points out, the toughest reforms are ideological. It is not hard physically to disintegrate the family; pulverizing ancient ties, attitudes and feelings to whose enduring strength millions of round brown graves still testify is more difficult. It is at least interesting to read the words which Hsu Mao-yung, a veteran Chinese Communist party member and famous essayist, mute for many years, wrote last year in the "thaw" period before he was again shunted into silence:

"A month ago now my mother died. She died in sorrow and I was the cause of that sorrow. I had not gone to see her for twenty years. I asked her to join me but she didn't want that. It would have been impossible for her to get used to life except that of her village, where she gossiped with other old women and prayed with them the Buddhist prayers.

"When I was 12 or 13 years old, she found me strange and silent, as she did to the end. In 1926, I became a follower of the Communist Revolution and fled to Shanghai to avoid arrest by the Kuomintang. When, two years later, I went back to the village, she asked me: 'Are you still doing "that thing"?'

"**I**N 1937, I returned for a visit. Mother was overjoyed.

But I never went back again. How happy she would have been to see me. She knew about the Communist party and knew I was a party member. But I always remained a stranger to her, a mystery * * *. True, I sent her money regularly, but that is nothing. My only consolation is that I did what she wished a few years ago by helping her to get a coffin and the other things needed for her funeral. Do I have to 'confess' that I 'compromised with superstition'?

"I have served 'the People' with my whole heart but I neglected one of the people who had worked hard all her life, my own mother."

Perhaps what Mr. Hsu, comrade, party member, said or wrote or felt does not matter. The party labeled him a "vicious Rightist." And anyone can see that his mother was never really one of "the People."

* * *

SO far, the Communists' formidable and many-pronged attack on the old family has certainly achieved considerable success; to just what degree no one outside China—and perhaps few inside the country—can measure with any certainty. Probably the best tentative conclusion is a paradox: Peiping's tough, shrewd and varied thrusts against the old kinship unit have modified and profoundly shaken it, while the fact that the attacks continue shows the job is far from finished.

The male dominance and female subjection so central to the old clan relations are certainly appreciably lessened. Women hold all kinds of jobs, keep their pay and walk out on marriages. On the other hand, Peiping complains that even cadres sometimes sneer at female "comrades" and in some cooperatives, "in spite of all that has happened since Liberation," menfolk discriminate against and look down on women. Weakened as they have been by the demands and commands of the state, even filial piety and family loyalty are not dead; in the "thaw" last year, Communists discovered considerable "unreasonable" resentment among people whose "counter-revolutionary" fathers and other relatives had been killed, jailed or somewhat more gently punished by the state.

* * *

BACK about the time of William the Conqueror, a Chinese craftsman engraved on a vase of fine, gray-green celadon his message to posterity: "I have baked this

fine, first-class urn, hoping that after a hundred years its owner will give it to my descendants; hoping, too, that I may have a thousand sons and ten thousand grandsons, who will all enjoy wealth, high position, long life, good fortune and unlimited happiness."

Like China's great art of porcelain-making, this ancient Chinese concept of the family has passed its zenith. The old mold has been cracking for a century; perhaps the Communists will shatter it completely. But there is no guarantee that Peiping can create a new one exactly to its pattern. People can and sometimes do resist certain kinds of shaping. The potter conceives the design; he does not create the clay, which may resist or influence his hand and purpose.

Who can tell, today, whether Peiping will find the two- and three-thousand-year-old clay of the Chinese countryside less malleable, in the end, than it expected?

June 15, 1958

'OLD LOOK' DRESS BACK IN RED CHINA

Drab 'People's Uniform' May Now Be Shed, but Peiping Draws Line at Lipstick

By HENRY R. LIEBERMAN
Special to The New York Times.

HONG KONG, Aug. 6—The "old look" is back in China, and women on the Communist ruled mainland are going to look like women again.

The official word is out that the drab, baggy trouser-and-tunic "people's uniforms" may be replaced by dresses. Thus, for those women who are interested, back comes the more flattering chi pao or chang san (long gown)—with colors, too.

But the Peiping regime has this reservation:

"The long gowns for women must not be too close fitting. They must be a little bit bigger than the body of the person who wears them."

This means there still will be a great difference between the loose fitting Peiping Chi Pao and the snug, shortened Hong Kong version with side slits.

Even so, Communist China is experiencing a kind of "revolution" in fashions, one that af-

fects men and children as well. For the word is also out that men may wear Western style suits if they like and that children should look "gay."

According to a report reaching here today from Peiping, women in the Chinese Communist capital are already crowding the cooperatives and buying up lengths of printed colored cloth. Many are also digging out the old Chi Paos that were hidden away when the communists came to power in 1949.

The signal for the fashion change has been given by Chang Chin-chiu, Vice Minister of the Textile Industry, a woman. Another key figure in the back-to-the-chi-pao movement seems to be Chiang Feng, an Academy of Arts official who has condemned the idea of sartorial uniformity.

Discussing the fashion situation in the June issue of the magazine New Observer, Miss Chang declared that, despite the present austerity campaign, dress styles had become "incompatible" with a "many-spendored life." She told New Observers readers:

"The pattern of dress displays not only a person's sense of beauty and prestige but also his mood of joyous living and his robust physique. Where there is genuine democracy and freedom and where everybody has employment and leads a life of contentment, the status of well-being is naturally reflected in the material color and pattern of dress."

But this does not mean, she warned, that Chinese women should put on powder or lipstick and devote too much time "making up."

When the Nationalists were defeated, the cities were taken over by men and women wearing mustard colored uniforms. Before long, the regimentation in dress was also extended to the city dwellers.

The vogue became the "peoples uniform," made of blue or gray cotton cloth, or the "Lenin uniform," a standardized variant with two rows of buttons. Women as well as men wore visored caps.

Later, the Communists began encouraging urban dwellers to put on their "best" for such special occasions as national celebrations and visits of important foreign delegations. But the day-to-day dress remained regimented and dismal.

August 7, 1955

271

Peiping Again Warns Youths To Inform Against Families

By GREG MacGREGOR

HONG KONG, Feb. 26—Communist China has renewed efforts to make Chinese youth inform on their friends and relatives, according to reports received here from Peiping.

In a plea based on allegiance to the Communist party, Red leaders told the younger generation through an article in Chung Kuo Ching Nien (China Youth) that they must not hesitate to inform security police of suspicious actions of their own parents.

Sons and daughters of upper-class families and former landlords were cautioned against breaking all ties with relatives prematurely when a chance remained to win anti-Communists over to the party line.

But, while urging youths to carry on missionary work for the Communist party in their own families, Peiping also warned them against absorbing "counter-revolutionary ideas from close family association." Such tendencies will be punished severely, Peiping said.

"For youths who were brought up in landlord families or whose direct relatives were counter-revolutionaries," Peiping continued, "they should abide by the policy of the party and clearly demarcate ideological boundaries with landlords and counter-revolutionaries, stand on the side of the party and people in fighting against their reactionary acts, ideology and viewpoints."

The renewal of the campaign to turn children against their parents in the interests of communism was regarded here as an indication of new concern in Peiping over the state of security. Other reflections of this concern were the recent shifts in Canton of thousands of Government workers to remote farming areas, increased directives to security police to exercise vigilance and increased pleas to anti-Communists in China to surrender and repent.

In Red China, much the same as most other Communist or fascist states, special attention is paid to indoctrination of the young generations as future leaders. Last year alone, for example, 10,000,000 primary and middle school children donned the red scarves of the Young Pioneers to raise national membership to 30,000,000. The principles of the Young Pioneer leadership are based on Communist party ideologies.

The Red leaders are also quick to act against an outbreak of any dangerous anti-party line views in the higher institutions of learning. This was evident recently in the firm stand taken by Peiping against sympathy by college students for the Hungarian masses.

The present effort to cast young people in the role of informers for the Communist party carried this message:

"They [youths] must resolutely expose and sever relations with those landlords who committed serious crimes and refused to repent, and counter-revolutionaries who committed grave crimes in the past and refuse to confess now or who are still carrying on sabotage activities."

February 27, 1957

'Model' Chinese Youths Report Sister as Spy

Special to The New York Times.

HONG KONG, Oct. 5—There was every reason for the brothers Li to be tempted. About all they had in life was their membership in the Young Communist League.

Li Yung-ming, 20 years old, and Li Yung-chuan, 19, were students in the same Canton middle school. Their parents were too old to work. Li Yung-ming's job as plastics factory apprentice made him the sole support of a family, the Peiping radio said tonight.

Elder Sister Li Chiung visited Hong Kong twice this summer and returned with a possible way out. "Join me as underground agent of Chiang Kai-shek and we can all be rich," she urged the older boy. He told his brother and they reported her.

The other day 1,500 schoolmates cheered at an assembly as the brothers Li were proclaimed "model league members" and given "material rewards."

Sister Li Chiung was not present. She was in prison.

October 6, 1958

REDS RE-EDUCATE CHINESE MASSES

'Study Group' Found Most Effective Means to Spread Idea of 'New Democracy'

By HENRY R. LIEBERMAN
Special to The New York Times.

NANKING, June 19—An intensive process aimed at eliminating "reactionary Kuomintang thought" and inculcating the masses with the ideas and disciplines of Mao Tze-tung's "New Democracy" is now taking place in China. The process is operating through a mushrooming complex of party-sponsored schools, "universities," "reindoctrination courses" and study groups.

The study group is the most pervasive means of re-education. This method is used as a technique in extra-curricular political discussions held in schools and also reaches down to the larger mass of people in the factories, craft guilds, Government offices, newspapers and almost every other type of organized social group.

Just how the study group functions is reflected in a typical meeting held by staff members of the Nanking power plant which has its offices in an old building off Hsin Chieh K'ou, Nanking's main circle. Forty members, including ten women and an office boy, attended. Also present as advisers were two uniformed representatives of the Nanking Military Control Commission and a labor union delegate from the powerhouse, a Mr. Kung.

The study group meeting, held after working hours, actually was the third conducted by the plant's business office. Two previous sessions had taken up Mao Tze-tung's book, "New Democracy," on a theoretical basis. In the chair this time was Chang Hung-kao, head of the plant's General Affairs Bureau, and the subject under discussion was an editorial entitled "Reconstruction of New Nanking," recently published by the official New China Daily News.

After all attending the meeting had signed their names in the recording book, individual copies of the editorial were distributed in pamphlet form. Chairman Chang, a thin middle-aged man in Western clothes, explained that the subject had been changed, after consultation with the union delegate and other "active participants," from a theoretical discussion to a discussion of problems confronting Nanking.

"The best way is to stimulate interest at the start with practical problems and come to doctrines and principles of the 'New Democracy' later," Mr. Chang said. "Theories are not easy to understand for beginners."

Union delegate Kung then spoke. "Now that we are liberated we are masters," he said. "But to be masters is not an easy thing. We must qualify ourselves for our new position. We must study to improve our technical knowledge for the construction and industrialization of China, to clear out the evil influence of the Kuomintang regime and to indoctrinate ourselves in the principles of the 'New Democracy.'"

It was decided to convene each Thursday. Then one of the "active participants," a Mr. Sun, raised the question of why staff members had to study and why they should study in groups. Exploiting the negative side of the argument to stimulate debate, he said:

"In the past we have been able to hold our jobs without studying and we can carry on work now, too, without studying. Also, even if we want to enlarge and improve our knowledge we can read books individually in our spare time. So why should we have meetings?"

Need Seen to Learn 'New Things'

"In the past we were working for the four rich families (Chiang, Soong, Kung, Chen) and an alliance of bureaucratic capital with foreign imperialism," Chairman Chang observed. "Rich became richer and poor and even middle class became poorer. Now it's different. So we must learn new things to prepare ourselves to participate in the reconstruction of the new China."

"I am a man over fifty and have studied abroad," said Chang Lanko, Deputy Chief Engineer, a graduate of Cornell. "Due to polite flattery by younger people, I considered myself sufficiently educated. I even read books sometimes, but this was motivated by the prospect of personal advancement. Now I study for a different purpose. I realize now that only through the advancement of the whole society is there a chance for individual advancement. It was individualism among other things that led to bribes, corruption and private influence in the Kuomintang regime."

"Because I had no personal connections, I was put to work here as an accountant, even though I studied civil engineering," said another man. "I was so discouraged at fumbling with ten digits that I made no effort to study. Now I want to learn new things and use my skill for the benefit of the people."

"As we are only newly liberated, there is still an evil influence on our way of life," one of the girls said. "The purpose of this study group must be to learn new principles so that we will change our conceptions about society and adapt ourselves to catch up with the advancing times."

Group Study Preferred

As to why study should take place in groups instead of individually, virtually all who spoke expressed the view that group study was preferable because individual mental capacity was limited and because it was possible to learn more by exchanging views.

Union Delegate Kung, asked to explain how study groups functioned in older "liberated areas," said small groups of eight to ten persons were formed as nuclei with a number of these groups being merged into a larger body. Key persons, he said, were appointed to collect material, outline discussion and make conclusions. Other individual members of the group, he added, then studied the materials in their spare time and brought their opinions back to a small meeting with the chairman consolidating the ideas for discussion again at a larger group meeting.

Throughout the meeting, the two representatives of the Military Control Commission remained silent. Despite the effort of several enthusiastic participants to stir up interest there seemed to be a trace of caution and the majority of those attending did not speak.

The general impression here is that the study group technique is a more effective means of indoctrination than the long, dry lectures used by the Kuomintang. From all indications, however, the new technique still has a long way to go before it achieves the desired result.

'Liberated' Women in Red China Constitute Backbone of Regime

Emancipation Decree After Civil War Won Millions of Fanatic Supporters— Feminine Influence Now Widespread

CANTON, China, Aug. 13—Women are the backbone of Chinese communism. They are Mao Tse-tung's most fanatical supporters.

The Chinese leader won them with a master stroke when dramatic reforms were necessary to consolidate his revolutionary victory.

Mr. Mao turned from the violent aftermath of war to make two decrees. One granted complete equality to all women. The other freed young people from the obligation to heed the "wisdom" of their elders. Immediately, scores of millions of emancipated women and teen-age girls were on his side.

Before what the Communists insist on calling "liberation," there was a measure of freedom and tardily recognized equality for the few women who had won places in the professions and business. But among the masses, the male remained distinctly the superior animal and women were expected to respect and obey.

The Communists changed that with a stroke of the pen. It was a brilliant tactical move because it brought millions to their side at a time of uncertainty and instability.

Since then, women have gone ahead boldly in China. Today, they are independent, hardworking, apparently quite capable when they have the opportunities.

Equality Is Stressed

They miss no chance to stress their equality with men. They are the standard-bearers for Mr. Mao's socialism, the shock troops against doubters, the "pep talkers" in industry, the militant, hero-worshipping disciples of the men who snapped their chains.

Here is Chinese communism's most formidable force, because it carries with it millions of men. Chinese men are no different from other men the world over. They never admit it, but they are swayed by feminine influence.

So today, vast numbers of husbands, sweethearts and boy friends are tagging along with the women as crusaders for Mr. Mao.

Before his blood-drenched revolution succeeded, a handful of Chinese women had smashed through prejudice and won a place in the professions. Others had succeeded in business, particularly in Shanghai where Western influence was strongest. Today, the field has widened and women are prominent everywhere.

In every farming co-operative a woman is either director or deputy director. They have responsible positions in industry and commerce. They have equal voting rights with men, and 148 of them are members of the National People's Congress, the nearest thing China has to a deliberative Parliament.

Watchdog over their interests is the powerful, militant All-China Women's Federation, which has a force of 300 feminists seeing that the equality rule is obeyed.

All physically fit Chinese women are expected to work. Even if the job is only tending the pigs on a cooperative farm, it is recognized as part of the national effort. In industry and commerce, in schools, offices, banks and ministries, women get equal pay for equal work.

In all the new factories this correspondent saw, there were clinics and rest rooms for pregnant women. Management said mothers had fifty-six days off with pay after the birth of a child. Women workers confirmed this.

China's new marriage law has helped women by providing freedom of choice and abolishing "arranged" unions. It makes marriage simple and divorce by consent little more than a matter of registration. This is the procedure:

When girl meets boy and they decide to marry, they go to the office of their local Government and register their names. If there is no bar like lineal relationship or medical defect, marriage certificates are issued immediately.

Should a marriage go on the rocks and both parties decide that divorce is the way out, they go again to their local Government office, provide proof that any children of the marriage are provided for, and the union is dissolved on the spot.

Clothing Is Drab

Despite their emancipation, Chinese women now are among the world's drabbest.

Few of them bother about make-up, although the "better classes" use a little lipstick on important social occasions. Hair is outrageously neglected and nearly all women wear untidy cotton jackets and creased "Sloppy Joes." Not one in a thousand wears the smart, high-necked gown that is Oriental fashion.

The justification is that women found slacks and jackets more convenient during the war against the Japanese and in later civil turmoils, so most of them discarded frocks as normal wear. Now they are all members of the labor force, and trousers are again more convenient for factory work.

The decline to shabbiness started with the hysteria of war and has now become a habit difficult to correct. Gay cotton textiles are on sale, but few women buy them.

Some venturesome girls who think clothing should be brightened up become so shy when they wear brightly colored blouses that they hide them beneath their drab, shapeless jackets.

All this makes the Chinese woman one of the most inelegant in the world. Publicists are trying to organize a reform movement, but it is heavy going.

Strangely enough, the men do not seem to mind the depressing shabbiness of the women. They are no fashionplates themselves, so their standards of dress-consciousness are not particularly high.

Still, China's women are generally happy in their new life of equality. In fact, they seem to prefer today's status to the restraints and inferiority that might come with restoration of the old order.

Mr. Mao thinks so, too. That is why he is doing everything he can to consolidate the support of the world's largest army of militant feminists.

BIG RADIO NET AIRS CHINA PROPAGANDA

Manchuria and Northern Area Hear Voice of Peiping—Aim Is to Cover Entire Country

Special to THE NEW YORK TIMES.

HONG KONG, Jan. 21—According to the Peiping radio, Chinese Communists have built up a vast propaganda network through which the voice of Peiping will be heard by virtually half of China's vast population.

In North China and Manchuria, the Communists assert, the propaganda network already is showing results. Unofficial reports said branches of the gigantic network were being set up in other parts of the country.

When the nation-wide network is in full operation the Communists will be able to make their line of thought known to the country's 450,000,000 inhabitants within twenty-four hours.

Peiping will be the nerve center of this propaganda network. From there the Chinese Communist policymakers will be able to transmit their speeches and the influential People's Daily in Peiping will be able to broadcast its editorials to even the smallest villages in China. This is the first time in Chinese history that rural districts have received such special attention.

Special Training

The Communist New China News Agency disclosed that 8,000 party members in North China recently were mobilized to undergo special training in propaganda work. They form the nucleus of the propaganda network.

They were assigned to handle political indoctrination and supervise the "learning of current affairs" among 2,000,000 People's Militiamen in North China.

In Hopei Province alone more than 40,000 primary teachers were trained to mold students and lead local political activities in rural districts. The province also trained 30,000 "winter school" teachers to conduct adult classes among farmers. The network also has 6,000 full time propagandists to distribute material received from Peiping.

In the neighboring province of Shansi "winter schools" for farmers have special "newspaper reading classes."

In conducting propaganda, the Communists employ various forms, mostly vocal and visual. There are street-corner theatrical performances. "Yanko" songs and dances, singing storytellers, lantern slides, movies, cartoons, blackboard newspapers and housetop loudspeakers to relay Communist broadcasts.

Newscasts Copied

In Hopei as well as Shansi Province copyists in every county listen to Communist newscasts from Peiping and distribute mimeographed sheets which are used as "textbooks" for various winter schools.

In North China, according to the New China News Agency, the propaganda network handled the recent "anti-American Korean aid movement so successfully that farmers whose minds previously were paralyzed now are responding warmly to the call of resisting Americans and defending the fatherland." "Many have put down names to join the people's volunteers" in Korea or to serve as stretcher bearers," the news agency added. "They have also shown a high degree of enthusiasm in turning in grains to state granaries."

In Manchuria the Communist propaganda network is built on workers' schools where laborers attend classes after working hours. In the North Manchurian province of Heilungkiang alone there are more than 34,000 authorized propagandists. In Antung City, which is across the Yalu River from the North Korean city of Sinuiju, 1,400 propagandists drum up feeling against the United States.

In the western Manchurian province of Jehol 360 laborers attend workers' schools and 200,000 peasants attend winter schools where propaganda also is intensively conducted both in basic party lines and as current affairs.

January 22, 1951

SCIENCE IS FETISH OF CHINESE YOUTH

Peiping Stressing Research and Technology in Drive to Overtake the West

This is the last of four articles on Communist China by Walton A. Cole, the editor of Reuters, who recently returned from a visit to that country.

LONDON, Feb. 26—Traditionally it has been the role of youth to rebel against old ways.

In Communist China I found youthful executive administrators who, though in their late twenties or early thirties, had been in their jobs for nearly ten years. It is they who are challenging and sweeping away the concepts of centuries and are establishing new traditions.

To them everything must be subjugated to the task of creating a new and great China. No sacrifice or personal discomfort is too great for this end.

Learning is no longer the prerogative of the limited few. Universities are crammed to their limits. They turn out young men and women burning to place China on an equal technological footing with the Western world. Science is their fetish.

An Outlook on Science

"Science will make people more and more independent in their thinking," one prominent Chinese leader, still in his thirties, assured me during my visit. "Christianity is the cult of a slave society, the capitalist society that recognizes some should be poor and some should be millionaires and invests power in one individual over thousands of his fellows.

"Science will make it clear to those people that there is nothing man cannot explain, and there is no need to rely for comfort on some supernatural spirit, which is how we understand religion.

"How does the earth go round? How does the moon go round the earth? These were strange questions to primitive people. They could only be answered by the supernatural.

"But they are answered now, among other things, by the Soviet sputnik orbiting round the world."

Peking University is one of sixteen in China that have been reorganized since the Communists took over. This is its sixtieth anniversary, an occasion that will be marked by the opening of one of the biggest libraries in the world, a new physics laboratory and a new laboratory for dynamic mechanics, the first of its kind in China.

Specialists Being Trained

The university has an enrollment of 8,434 students that will reach 10,000 by the end of the year. It concentrates on training specialists for research and teaching work in the fields of theoretical and basic science. The number of laboratories has increased in eight years from twenty to 210.

Departments at Peking University include a School of Journalism, where 350 students are now being trained for jobs in the newspapers, news agency and radios that are the eyes, ears and lungs of the state and workers' organizations. Their starting salary will be $28 a month on an eight-hours-a-day, six-days-a-week work schedule. There is no overtime and no vacations, although compassionate leave is granted.

The head of the department outlined to me the Communist approach to journalism.

"In the West the conception of journalism is that merely of a medium of mass communication of ideas," he said. "In our conception press and news work generally is part of the political struggle in the class society. The press of a given class shall serve its own interests and that is why in China there are newspapers serving the trade unions, youth, women and the party. We think that the press is one of the superstructures of the state and has a given economic objective."

Peking University is situated, among other places, on the grounds of the old Yenching University, which once had American missionary support. Twenty-one per cent of the students are women, and most of them are in their early twenties. Among the students are peasants and workers who are given an intensive, telescoped advance course, often at night schools, before they take their university entrance examinations. Students undergo a medical examination before admission and, like workers in organized industry, an annual X-ray as a check-up for tuberculosis.

Failures are usually advised to go into factories or to work on the farm, not always a popular suggestion. One Western observer suggested to me that this would become an increasing problem, as there were many who, having gone part way in their search for education, would be loath to turn back to a life of manual labor.

As everywhere in China, political education is a constant preoccupation. Most students devote two four-hour periods each week to political discussion and exposition of Communist party policies.

Science is seen as communism's handmaiden, and the impact of this belief is felt far outside the walls of the universities. Bookstalls are filled with books and magazines devoted to rocket and planetary travel, and the Soviet sputnik is a favorite cartoon topic.

In Shanghai the former home of a British tycoon has been taken over for use as a Youth Palace and now houses a number of hobby clubs for young people.

Shanghai also has a Cultural Palace, where adults can pursue similar hobbies and studies and which boasts an attendance of 10,000 persons a day. The Cultural Palace was once a hotel, and its present use is typical of what has happened to many former landmarks.

With gambling illegal, the Shanghai Racecourse is now an arena for ceremonial parades. The Turf Club is a museum and the dog-racing track has been transformed into a theatre seating more than 14,000. Though social traditions have been swept aside, the Government has intervened to preserve national treasures and monuments such as Peiping's Forbidden City, the Ming Tombs and the Great Wall of China.

There are no dance halls in Shanghai. Movie theatres draw capacity audiences, but the film fare is almost always devoted to some theme demonstrating the virtues of Communist society. Live theatre is much the same, though traditional Chinese opera still has its stanch following.

Drinking in excess is frowned on, but a quart of cheap beer can be had for the equivalent of about 15 cents, whisky of 60 per cent alcohol content for 75 cents and sorghum wine in a crockery bottle for $2.

People laugh and love and have fun in China, just as they do everywhere else in the world. But no one in China is ever very far from the pressure and surveillance of a giant political machine, which not only supplies most of the individual's material needs from the cradle to the grave but also directly influences his thoughts. The goal is: China a great world power soon, and equal footing with any nation in the world now.

SHANGHAI REDS CURB WEDDING PRESENTS

Special to The New York Times.

SHANGHAI, Aug. 24—Under the heading "Private Life of Employes Comes Under Control," the newspaper Ta Kung Pao today told of the code of austerity regulations governing employes in the state-owned Central Electrical Equipment Factory here.

The rules embrace many facets of life ranging from a ban on birthday parties to limitation of the number of dances and moving pictures attended. The code conforms to the nation-wide austerity program outlined in Peiping recently by Chou En-lai, vice chairman of the Communist party. He urged his countrymen to forego celebrations and the exchange of gifts.

The program is designed to help offset the Kuomintang blockade and the stringencies of an economy that seeks to be independent of Western support.

According to Ta Kung Pao, the rules decided upon by the electrical factory are in part as follows:

No gifts shall be exchanged on national holidays. Wedding presents or funeral gifts can be given only by "very close" friends and should not cost more than the equivalent of about thirty-five cents. Unnecessary feasts such as farewell banquets should be eliminated and dining should be on a Dutch treat. Taxi dancing is forbidden and other forms of amusement such as movies or regular dancing are limited to once a week.

REDS COMMUNIZE SCHOOLS IN CHINA

Many of Parents Object to Herding Children Into Boarding Institutes

By TILLMAN DURDIN
Special to The New York Times

HONG KONG, Jan. 5—An increasing number of children in Communist China are being put into boarding schools established as part of the country's new system of communes.

Communist newspapers reaching here contain much evidence that many parents have objected strongly to their youngsters' leaving home to live at school. However, the boarding school system seems to be spreading despite the parental misgivings.

The Nov. 6 issue of The Kwang Ming Daily reported that boarding schools for a system of merged primary middle schools had been established in forty counties of Honan with a population of more than 10,000,000.

Other reports from Kirin, Anhwei, Hopei, Shantung and Kiangsu describing the establishment of boarding schools provide evidence that millions of children in Communist China, mostly in primary schools, are studying away from home.

The reports also make it clear that children, even of primary-chool age in the new boarding schools, not only are being incorporated into a disciplined system of living and study, but also have become a work force of considerable importance. In accordance with recent Communist party res-

olutions on the communes, youngsters from the age of 9 upward do regular work, while reports indicate that primary-school children of 7 or 8 do light "subsidiary" tasks.

The Kwang Ming Daily said that in the Honan schools younger primary school children "do not take part in major forms of labor, while older ones spend from one to two hours daily in labor." The paper said junior middle-school students spent half their time in study and half in labor.

In the Kirin boarding schools, The Kwang Ming Daily reported, children work in factories and cultivate farm plots. Third and fourth-grade students give six hours a week to labor, those of he fifth and sixth grades eight hours a week.

The newspaper articles cite parents' fears that the children will not be well fed and otherwise looked after, but dispose of these fears with reports that teachers have become competent nurses and guardians and that the children thrive under the boarding-school systems. The China Youth Daily of Peiping, in its Oct. 25 issue, chided parents who thought their children would suffer from being deprived of mother love.

"Parents should understand that their children are going to live in a Communist state, where the old and young will both be properly taken care of," the paper said, and "that it is for society to raise and educate the young into a new generation and give the kind of love that no maternal love can ever hope to compare with."

Newspaper editorials say the boarding-school system has the advantage of removing children from what in some cases are the bad ideological environment of homes and surrounding them with the influence of good Communist training.

Mao Tse-tung as Poet

Poet Mao.

It's an old Chinese custom for politicians and rulers to be famous as poets. Mao Tse-tung, the boss of Communist China, is no exception. For years a number of his poems, although unpublished, were quoted widely—by his fellow students at the Changsha First Normal School in the Twenties, by his comrades in exile on the "long march" to the caves of Yenan in the Thirties, by the bureaucrats who now administer his regime.

Recently, the editor of a new Peiping magazine, Poetry, asked permission to publish some of the leader's compositions. Mao obliged, and added a letter of apology and admonition:

"I have never wished for these to be published formally, because they represent an antique style of expression and I am afraid of sowing a wrong seed which might influence our youth incorrectly. Also, there is very little poetic inspiration in my work and nothing out of the ordinary * * *. With regard to the whole question of poetry, the new style should of course be the trend to follow. * * *

All of my remarks I offer you only as advice." The "new style" Mao recommends requires the use of the colloquial language, pai-hua, which since 1920 has been taught in Chinese schools. His poems are written in the ancient Chinese literary language, in use for at least 2,000 years and as archaic as Elizabethan English.

In form also they are old-fashioned. They are written in the stylized patterns of ancient Chinese verse, according to rules set down more than eight centuries ago. Some contain outright propaganda— praise of Communist troops, disparagement of past glories. But the mood of most is retrospective and meditative, filled with elegiac personal emotions evoked by nature rather than with precepts for the "new Socialist man." If they had not been published at a time when Mao seemed to be relaxing artistic controls—and if the poet's identity had not been known—party critics might have called them counter-revolutionary.

Here is a selection of Mao's poems.

SNOW

THE Northern scene:
a thousand miles
sealed with ice,
ten thousand miles snowflakes floating,
seeing before and beyond the Great Wall
one wide white space,
the great river
above, below,
stops fast.

Silver snakes dancing,
hills.
Slow, snow, elephant,
plateau.
Both envy heaven's height.

So, on a clear day
you see a red clothed girl
all wrapped in white,
enchanting.

Rivers, mountains
with charm bewitching
lure countless heroes to contest
in bowing for their favours.

I regret that the King of Ch'in
and the King of Han
lacked a little
in their gentleness;
that the King of T'ang and the King of Sung
were wanting somewhat
in awareness.
Genghis Khan
blessed by heaven
knew only
how to bend the bow
and shoot the great eagle.

All these, departed.
Would you find the true heroes?
Look around you today.

CHANGSHA

STANDING alone in the cold autumn,
the Shiang River flowing northward
on Orange Isle;
hills all red;
forests thick stained;
the river full with transparent greenness,
boats wrestling in the flow.

The eagle beats the open sky,
the fish fly

in shallow water.
In sharp weather
all things strive against their bonds.

I, forlorn in vastness,
ask the great ageless earth,
"Who rules the rise and fall?"

Here for pleasure I have brought
a hundred friends;
and I remember those were years of mark.
As fellow students
we were young,
our brilliance then beginning,
spoke out our thoughts
obeying our ideals.
Seeing our country strengthened our words,
thinking the old time dukes
as dust.

Do you remember
in the middle of the river,
beating the water,
the wave stopped the flying boat?

SWIMMING

AT Changsha drinking water,
at Wuchan eating fish,
ten thousand miles long.
I cross the long river

with sky spreading far.

I care not if the wind blows and the waves beat,
to swim is as sweet
as wander in a quiet court
and today I have leisure.

Confucius stood by the water saying,
"What has passed cannot return."
The wind swings the sails
the Snake and Tortoise Hills
are still.
A great feat accomplished,
a bridge flies north to south
turning heaven's obstacles
to a broad highway.
We shall change the river's stony walls
and Wushan's clouds and rain
quite intercept
until a full smooth lake appears
within the gorge.
And if the Spirit in these hills still lives,
startled will she turn and see
how the world has changed.

LONG MARCH

THE Red Army
is not afraid
of the hardships
of a long and difficult journey.
A thousand mountains
and ten thousand rivers
mean nothing to them.

The Wulieng Mountains twist and surge and fall
and Oomung Range lies wide and huge
with paths too hard.

The waters of the Jinshia River
beat against the cloud-touched cliff warm.
The iron chain of Dadu Bridge
Stretches across the chasm cold.

Especially I like the snow
Spreading a thousand li
Over the Min Mountains.

The whole army comes through
all laughing.

THE PAVILION OF THE YELLOW CRANE

ENDLESS
sourceless
river
flowing through China

and the heavy railroad
piercing
north to south,
rain mist shrouds,
Snake and Tortoise Hills
grip the great river.

Where has the yellow crane flown?
All that is left is the traveler's haunt.

With my winecup
I make an offering
to the ever flowing waters.
My heart is as full as the rising river

ON SEEING CHINESE OPERA ON NATIONAL DAY, 1950

THE long night
with difficulty
ends over China.
A hundred years
the devils danced with long sleeves.
Five hundred million
could not come together.

The cock crows;
day breaks over the world
and music swells from here
to far off Sinkiang.
Never before.

April 28, 1957

PEIPING LAUNCHES CHRISTIAN REFORM

Drive Is On to Unify Religious Sects, Eliminate Overseas Support and Influence

HONG KONG, Sept. 24 (UP)— The Peiping radio in the capital of Communist China announced today that the reformation of Christianity in China was under way, including unification of various religious sects and the end of financial support from abroad.

The broadcast gave the text of a state-church declaration, outlining the future course of the Christian religion in China, which, it said, had been composed last July. It said that 1,527 pastors, students, theologians and leaders, including representatives of the Y. M. C. A., the Y. W. C. A. and Chao Chi-chen, Dean of Theology at Yenching University, already had signed the declaration.

The conditions under which churches and missionaries will be permitted to carry on their work in China include:

1. Purge of imperialist influence.
2. A halt to accepting support from abroad.
3. Education of followers against the evils of "imperialism, feudalism, bureaucratic capitalism."
4. The recommendation that the churches should "unify various sects."

Imperialist Ties Noted

The statement, said to be the work of forty representatives of "various Christian churches in China" and issued with Government approval, complained that during the last 140 years there had been a close relation between Christianity and imperialism in China, largely because missionaries had come from imperialist countries.

Because of the Chinese Communist victory, the imperialists "will attempt to make use of Christianity to carry out provocative agitational activities and develop reactionary power," it warned. Therefore it continued, Christian churches and Christian institutions throughout China must "rid themselves of all imperialist influence" and guard against imperialist intrigues, especially from the United States.

Churches and institutions now receiving support from abroad must prepare to become self-supporting in the near future, the statement said. They must instruct the masses of Christians to "recognize clearly the crimes committed by the imperialists in China" and "encourage Christians to take part in the movement for peace and educate them to support the Government's land reform policy," it went on. Churches also must practice self-criticism, the declaration warned.

The broadcast also included an editorial from the official Peiping People's Daily News, which stressed that the Communist regime wanted freedom of religion, but added that "pure religious belief must be detached from foreign aggressive and reactionary activities."

Many Catholics and Protestants are "good citizens," supporting the Government's political and social reforms, the newspaper said, but asserted that the Government could not tolerate "subversive activities."

Satellite Pattern Seen

Protestant mission officials said yesterday that the Chinese Communist church-state declaration closely followed a pattern set by Communists in other satellite territories.

The Rev. Dr. John A. Mackay, president of Princeton Theological Seminary and president of the Board of Foreign Missions of the Presbyterian Church in the U. S. A., reported that a number of Protestant denominations already had adopted a policy of placing their mission interests in the hands of Christian nationals.

The Chinese Communists in all likelihood will permit missionaries to function as long as they bring in such benefits as medical or welfare assistance, he declared.

According to Dr. Mackay, the Presbyterian Church is one of the few Protestant bodies to permit missionaries to remain in China. To date, he said, there are more than 100 Presbyterian missionaries in China. Before the Communist drive there were 500.

September 25, 1950

U.S. MISSION WORK BANNED BY PEIPING

All Chinese Churches Ordered by Reds to Suspend Ties With Americans at Once

By TILLMAN DURDIN
Special to THE NEW YORK TIMES.

HONG KONG, July 27—Regulations announced in a Peiping radio dispatch received here tonight appear to represent the finishing blow for American missionary activity in Communist China. The regulations order all American church missions that have been financing church educational, cultural and charity work in Communist China to "suspend their activities immediately."

The new rules, which were signed by Chou En-lai, Communist Premier and Foreign Minister, and came into force last Tuesday, stipulate that all Chinese churches must immediately sever their relations with the American missions and other missions financed largely with United States funds.

The Peiping move obviously was another step in the move to eliminate foreign, particularly American, influence among the Chinese Christians, and making Chinese Christian churches independent of United States and other Western connections.

The new regulations make no mention of Catholic and Protestant missions conducted by other nationalities than American.

The Tuesday decree provides for an early departure of the dwindling number of American church workers who still remain in China, with the exception of those whom the Communists wish to detain. With regard to "American personnel working in Chinese institutions and organizations," the new regulations contain the following points:

1. "Those who have spoken or acted against the People's Government should be immediately dismissed, and those who have committed crimes should be reported to the Government for punishment according to the law."
2. "Those who wish to leave should be given permission to return to their country."
3. "Those who have not spoken or acted against the People's Government and are considered necessary to be left behind at the expense of Chinese institutions and organizations may remain. However, they may not take up executive or administrative offices in said institutions and organizations."

The regulations further provide that medical or welfare institutions operated by Chinese Christian churches or organizations that are self-supporting may continue to operate, but boards of directors must be set up to insure carrying out of the Government decrees. Those Chinese Christian churches or organizations whose funds are insufficient may apply to the government for subsidies or to be taken over.

Tax Exemption Offered

However, universities, middle or primary schools, except religious schools, operated by the churches or Christian organizations must be disassociated from the churches.

Buildings used as churches or offices by self-supporting Chinese Christian churches, and the Young Men's and Young Women's Christian Association will be exempt from real estate taxes.

Most foreign church workers of all nationalities in Communist China have found their work severely circumscribed or made virtually impossible in the last year. Americans in particular have been largely barred from their activities as a result of anti-United States moves by the Government or Government-inspired popular hostility.

Most American Christian workers in Communist China for a long time have been leaving China or attempting to leave.

A number of American missionaries have been imprisoned or subjected to mass "trials." Many suffered not only the expropriation of the mission properties, but their personal belongings as well.

Under the conditions of the present high pressure anti-American and anti-Western feeling being inspired and organized by the Communists, most Americans and other foreign mission workers, except for a few teaching in universities, have concluded that the possibilities of their useful service in China has finished.

July 28, 1951

A TALE OF EXODUS FROM RED CHINA

Special to The New York Times.

HONG KONG, May 13—The Roman Catholic parish of Father Ambrose Poletti covers about 250 square miles of Hong Kong's New Territories adjoining the Kwangtung frontier of Red China.

Father Poletti, a bearded missionary from the Italian side of Lake Como, is priest, friend and counsellor to about 700 Chinese Catholics in his parish. The lean priest, who is 51 years old, is a many-sided man of multiple tongues, including Cantonese, Hakka and even some Fukienese.

Before coming to the New Territories seven years ago, Father

Poletti spent nineteen years trying to bring religion to the Bias Bay pirates on the Chinese side of the border.

Since 1950, however, Father Poletti's main job has been the reception of thousands of missionaries flowing out of Red China in a depressing exodus over the Lowu Bridge on the Hong-Kong-Kwangtung frontier, Up to last July, when the stream began drying up, he sped to the border daily on an unecclesiastical motorcycle.

"I missed only two days—once when I had malaria and the other time when I went to the funeral of my former bishop," he said at his mission. "In the last four years I've met 3,400 Catholic missionaries and also a few hundred Protestant missionaries.

"I've seen every kind. Some looked all right. Others couldn't even walk or stand after the torture [in prison] of segregation, starvation, having their hands tied behind their backs and, most important, questioning, questioning, questioning—day and night."

Less Than a Trickle Now

Father Poletti now has more time to spend with his parishioners at a new church in Fanling because the flow of missionaries from the China mainland has become less than a trickle. The Communists have virtually completed the liquidation of a century and a half and more of foreign missionary work in China.

Protestant and Catholic missionaries from all parts of the West had been active in China. China, in fact, was long a favorite field for missionary endeavor. This included education, medicine and public health, orphan care, youth activity and relief as well as religion.

Protestant groups in the United States contributed generously to education and relief in China. American contributions were also a major support for 320 Catholic orphanages and a number of Catholic educational institutions on the mainland.

In 1951 the Chinese Communist press listed thirteen American-supported Christian universities in China along with 203 mission hospitals as well as the orphanages. It was estimated somewhat earlier than one-eighth of China's college graduates and 250,000 lower-school graduates had been educated at American-supported institutions.

As of late 1950, the Communists reported that there were 5,500 foreign Catholic and 1,700 Protestant missionary workers among 3,000,000 Chinese Catholics and 700,000 Chinese Protestants. Mission sources here estimate there were about 2,000 Protestant missionaries and about 900,000 Chinese Protestants when the Communists came to power.

Americans Reported in Jail

At any rate few Western mis-

sionaries are left in China. Of the twenty-seven Catholic missionaries still remaining, twelve including eight Americans, are reported to be in jail. An American Protestant Missionary, Paul Mackinson, a Lutheran, is also listed by the United States consulate here as being in jail.

One other American Protestant missionary is said to be in Communist China. She is Ella Wilcox, 83, a Presbyterian believed to be living in semi-retirement at Yeungkong, Kwangtung.

The Chinese Communists declared all-out war on the foreign missions in late 1950, charging that the missions were the "cultural wing" of Western "imperialism."

This campaign gathered steam after Peiping's intervention in the Korean war. It was coupled in 1950 and 1951 with a general "hate America" drive marked by an increasing number of missionary arrests.

Three American missionaries died as prisoners in 1951. They were Bishop Francis X. Ford, a Catholic, and Drs. William L. Wallace and Warren L. Winter, Protestants.

May 14, 1956

Two in Red China to Die For War of Paper Arms

HONG KONG, Sept. 26 (Æ) —Communist China has condemned to death two Taoist religious leaders accused of trying to equip an army of the spirit world with paper weapons to attack the Communist party.

The strange story of Li Kwei-ying and Chiang Chang-en was told in the Sept. 9 issue of Kwang Ming Jih Pao, Peiping organ of the fellow-traveling Democratic League, just received here.

Mr. Li and Mr. Chiang were caught an dtried in the Province of Hunan.

The paper said their crime was "preparing paper-made robes, swords, warships, banners, bows and arrows in a vicious attempt to equip an army of the other world and attack the Communist party."

Apparently a people's court in Hunan did not take the charge too seriously. It let off Li and Mr. Chiang with eight-year sentences. But the masses questioned the light sentences the paper said, the case was reviewed and the two were condemned to die.

September 27, 1957

PEIPING PROMOTES OLD HERB THERAPY

Red Chinese Seeking to Fuse 'Legacy' of Ancient Arts and Modern Medical Theory

By HENRY R. LIEBERMAN
Special to The New York Times.

HONG KONG, Nov. 13—A Government-sponsored movement is under way in Communist China to promote Chinese herb medicine and integrate the country's old national "legacy" with modern, Western medical techniques.

The legacy includes acupuncture (pricking with a needle) and cauterization, or "toasting."

New stress apparently is being placed on this special branch of Chinese medicine. Physicians in Canton are officially said to have been "exchanging experiences" in classes designed to link Western research on the nervous system and the conditioned reflex with the Chinese art of the nerve needle and the searing moxa stick, made from leaves of the Chinese wormwood.

The Communist press called on Western-trained physicians to make a "serious study" of Chinese medicine. Meanwhile, Chinese "herb doctors," whose traditional diagnostic approach embraces "observation, smell, questioning and pulse feeling," are being taught to use the thermometer, stethoscope and blood-pressure gauge.

A fusion between old and new is envisaged in the drive to "standardize the theories of Chinese medicine, summarize its clinical experience, absorb its essence and discard its residue." In the process practitioners have been added to various hospital staffs as advisers and greeted at "welcome rallies."

Scoffers Are Criticized

Western-trained Chinese doctors have been criticized for sneering at the herb and acupuncture practitioners. On Oct. 20 the People's Daily, official Communist organ, charged that the Government policy on Chinese medicine had not been carried out because public health leaders had been "poisoned by bourgeois ideology" and opposed to "the motherland's medical legacy."

The party newspaper declared that the promotion of traditional medicine would further the "progress of modern medicine." It added that health leaders had failed to realize that the "broad masses are in need of herb medicine" and that the "herb doctors" must play their role.

About 80 per cent of the Chinese people continue to rely on traditional medicine, the People's Daily said in another article on Nov. 2. It added that the "efficacy of Chinese medicines not

only has been proved by prolonged clinical experience but also has been corroborated by modern scientific conclusions."

In tracing the long history of Chinese medicine, the Peiping Kwangming Daily noted that the first Chinese "book of herbs" "most probably" had been written in the first century B. C. Plans have been announced for republishing twenty-two medical classics.

A recent dispatch from Shanghai said physicians there were testing 154 prescriptions and remedies on the basis of material gathered by the Health Ministry. These were reported to include fifty-five prescriptions for general, women's and children's diseases and ailments, forty-six for surgical cases, twenty-six for injuries and wounds, nineteen acupuncture and massage techniques, and eight in a category covering the throat, the eye and others.

The Kwangming Daily reported Oct. 29 that a 70-year-old Szechwanese had developed an "efficacious and aromatic" medical powder for treating malaria by inhalation. The ingredients were said to include four Chinese medicines.

According to the newspaper, more than ten persons suffering from malaria had recovered after inhaling the mixture's aroma and clinical tests also had produced evidence of a cure.

November 14, 1954

PEIPING IN A DRIVE ON ECONOMIC FOES

Workers' Courts Established for Minor Cases as All Prosecutions Increase

By HENRY R. LIEBERMAN
Special to The New York Times.

HONG KONG, April 1—Communist China's Committee on Political and Legal Affairs has called for tightening of the "people's democratic dictatorship" in 1954. It is reported to have decided to intensify the prosecution of cases related to Government economic policies marked by increasingly rigid state controls.

The committee on political and Legal Affairs functions as part of the Cabinet structure in Peiping and is headed by Tung Pi-wu, a member of the Chinese Communist Politburo. Its statement was distributed domestically by the official Hsinhu (New China) News Agency March 29.

Declaring the Government's present economic programs involved a "complex class struggle" amidst an alleged threat of "American imperialism," the statement said:

"We must effectively protect economic construction, especially in the factories, mines, communications and in financial economic and trade departments. Generally apart from continuing severely to suppress counter-revolutionary sabotage we must also apply the necessary legal sanctions to criminal elements undermining national construction and the people's democratic order."

Crackdown Has Begun

In fact, the Peiping regime already has started cracking down on merchants, peasants and grain dealers accused of "sabotaging" the Government's economic programs. These programs include state monopolization of the grain market, the speed-up in the organization of agricultural "producers' cooperatives" and "mutual aid teams" and the drive to steer private concerns into a controlled "state capitalist" sector.

In the midst of this drive a merchant was recently executed and ten others, including a government employe, were sentenced to prison in Tientsin on charges of defrauding the state in business deals and either giving or accepting bribes.

One dispatch said a high percentage of food dealers had committed "illegal acts" in some communities and added:

"The people's governments in various areas have properly dealt with these law-defying merchants in accordance with the seriousness of their offenses."

With private trade in grain now banned, many urban food dealers have been designated to act as agents to sell grain for the state.

Apparently expecting more crowded dockets in the regular "People's Courts," the Peiping regime has decided to establish a system of local "Mediation Committees" to handle minor civil disputes and "light or trivial criminal cases."

The Peiping People's Daily said editorially March 22 this system would enable judicial organs to concentrate on "major or serious cases."

A system of "Production Enterprises Comrades Tribunals" also has been set up to enforce "labor discipline" in various state factories and mines.

SPEED OF CHINESE IMPRESSES INDIANS

1,200,000 Peasants Built 100-Mile Canal in 80 Days, Mission Says

Special to The New York Times.

NEW DELHI, India, July 16— An official Indian delegation has returned from China impressed with the Communist regime's methods of flood control.

What struck the Indians most was the employment of "human labor" on almost every kind of work. They said that little of machinery was to be seen in the course of the 7,500-mile tour that took them deep into the country.

Another aspect that struck the delegation as remarkable was the speed with which some of the longest irrigation canals had been completed. They gave as an instance the North Kiangsu Canal in the Hwai basin. This canal, 420 feet wide and 100 miles long, was completed in eighty days by more than 1,200,000 peasant laborers, the delegates said.

The Indian delegation was composed of two top-ranking engineering experts, Kanwar Sain, chairman of the Central Water and Power Commission, and Dr. K. L. Rao, director of designs in the same organization. They were sent to China particularly to study flood control methods with a view to adapting them in harnessing erratic Kosi River in eastern India. Called the "river of sorrow," the Kosi is said to present the same difficulties as the Chinese rivers of carrying a tremendous quantity of silt, thus making dam construction impossible.

In its two months' stay in China the delegation studied all the major projects on the Yellow, Hwai, Yangtze, Yungting and Pearl Rivers.

A report giving the impressions of the delegation was released today by the Ministry of Irrigation and Power. It said the Chinese Government had evolved an integrated plan for flood control of all major rivers, resulting in an efficient system of dike protection to lands.

The delegation observed that the Chinese Government laid emphasis on acquainting the workers with the purpose of every project to obtain their fullest cooperation.

Every work site provided numerous amenities such as libraries, theatres, music, photo displays and medical and educational facilities, the report said. It added that every worker was paid according to his work and was assured of a minimum wage.

Chinese Reds Report New 'Cure' For Burns: Communist Theory

Case History of a Shanghai Steelworker Notes 'Struggle Between Proletarian and Bourgeois' Treatments

By HAROLD M. SCHMECK Jr.

An impassioned case history purporting to show how illness can be cured by Marxism-Leninism has been printed in an American medical journal.

It is carried in Industrial Medicine and Surgery for June, and is identified as a reprint from The Chinese Medical Journal in November, 1958.

The article begins:

"The process leading to the saving of the life of Ch'iu Ts'ai-K'ang, steelworker of the Shanghai Third Steel Mill, who was burnt by molten steel, was a process of grave and intense struggle between proletarian and bourgeois therapeutic methods."

Mr. Ch'iu had suffered burns covering 89.3 per cent of his body surface, according to the article, and this produced "a feeling of hopelessness" among the attending physicians. They quoted an American authority as having said a case was always fatal if more than 70 per cent of the body area was seriously burned.

The doctors were moved to vigorous action, however, by an encouraging message from the Communist party committee of the steel mill. This "correctly pointed out that what could not be done in capitalist countries we could do."

Literature Is Checked

Thus inspired, forty physicians at the Shanghai Second Medical College checked all the available literature on burns in a single morning and decided on fifteen methods of treatment, the article said.

Later, sixty medical students were sent out to search the countryside for specimens of bacteriophage, a virus that infects bacteria, to treat leg infections from a germ called Bacillus pyocyaneus. A blood infection from the same organism was treated with the antibiotic polymyxin in doses larger than

those considered safe in Western practice, the report said.

At the suggestion of party officials skin grafts were done earlier than is customary in the West. A dietitian conferred daily with the patient to find foods that would stimulate his appetite. Hospital staff members vied in giving skin grafts and transfusions.

The patient was quoted as telling the doctors:

"Cure me, I'm needed in production. I can leave my wife and child, but not my furnaces."

To his wife he said, "You have brought my pay, did you pay my party dues?"

Physicians' Comment

After the two-month fight to save Mr. Ch'iu, the article observed, the senior doctors commented:

"It's true that disease can be treated by Marxism-Leninism . . . Without the party, intellectuals like us could not possibly have broken out from the established rules of bourgeois experts."

In New York yesterday an expert on treatment of burns said the description of the case made it seem highly unlikely that more than half of the patient's body had been seriously burned. The treatment as described included no real innovations, he observed.

A bacteriologist noted that the treatment of infections was compatible with Western procedure except for use of bacteriophage. This, he said, went out of style as ineffective in the Nineteen Twenties.

Industrial Medicine and Surgery commented that the article "illustrates how industrial medicine is practiced (and dictated to) in a Communist nation. The article should be an effective argument to those who believe * * * medical science can always remain aloof from politics."

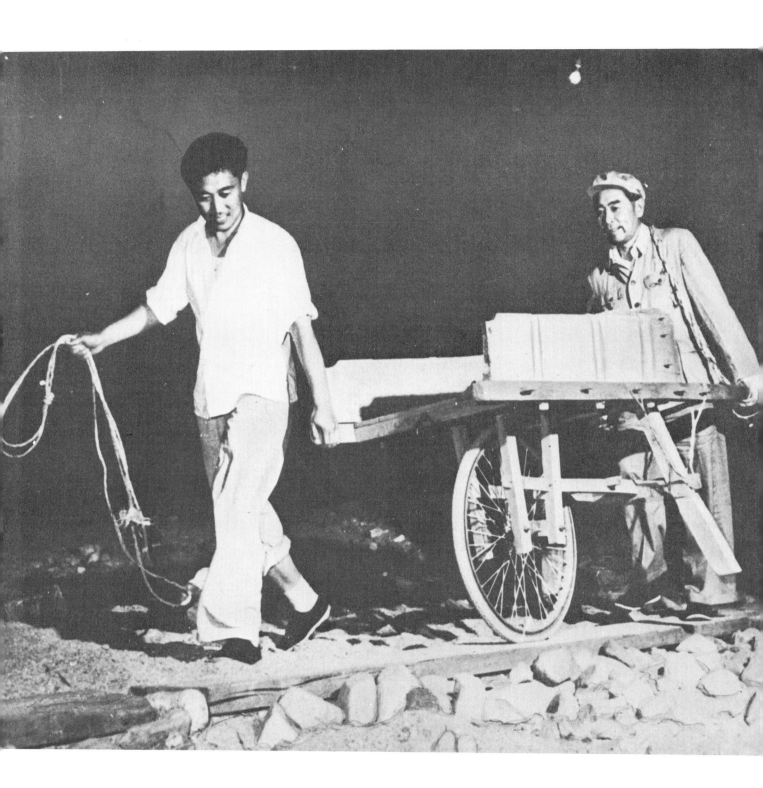

CHAPTER 6

"Let Politics Take Command!"
1957–59

*Chou En-lai trundles a wheelbarrow
as an industrious example to workers
building a dam near Peking, 1958.*

Courtesy Gilloon Agency

CHINA REDS ENLIST LEADING THINKERS

Party Improving Conditions for Professional Classes in Membership Drive

By HENRY R. LIEBERMAN
Special to The New York Times.

HONG KONG, April 14—Hundreds of "higher-level intellectuals" in China are being inducted as members of the Chinese Communist party.

Official reports have been reaching here from cities throughout the country on this party membership drive for professors, engineers, physicians and scientific research specialists.

Among the new party members are such persons as Cheng Minteh, a professor in the Department of Mathematics and Dynamics at Peiping University; 62-year-old Ching Pao-shan, a wheat expert in Nanking, and Ma Kuo-min, a mining engineer in Chungking.

The Peiping Government is also improving conditions of life for the upper-level intelligentsia in terms of prestige, improved work facilities and greater material rewards.

Among the fringe benefits now being enjoyed by various professors, according to the press, are "more spacious quarters, additional furniture and bathrooms."

Special Tables Reserved

At the Northeast Institute of Pharmacology in Manchuria, special mess hall tables have been reserved for professors so they do not have to queue up for meals. At the Steel Industry Institute in Peiping as well as elsewhere, "preferential treatment cards" have been issued to academicians for use in the barber shop, clinic and consumers' cooperative.

The Yungli-Chiuta chemical plant in North China has reportedly started to provide motorcar transportation for older technicians who had trouble getting to and from the plant. In Shanghai, 130 old writers, painters, historians and other intellectuals are now enrolled in an institution that gives them 50 to 100 yuan ($20 to $40) a month so they can continue their work.

Both the membership drive and the improved treatment for intellectuals are related to Peiping's industrialization program. The stated goal is to bring Red China's "most urgently needed" scientific, technical and cultural capacities to within sight of "advanced world levels" by 1967.

Peiping esimates that China has 3,840,000 intellectuals engaged in scientific research, education and the arts. But of these only about 100,000 are listed as "strong intellectuals of the higher level."

According to Chou En-lai, Chinese Communist Premier, about one-third of those in the "higher-level" category were trained after establishment of the Peiping regime in 1949.

Mr. Chou set the stage for the present treatment of intellectuals in a report to the Chinese Communist Central Committee last Jan. 14. In calling for fuller use of the existing intellectual resources, he advocated a party attitude of more "confidence" in intellectuals, greater incentives for them and intensified educational efforts to increase the number of "full Socialist intellectuals."

The Premier proposed a "suitable adjustment" of salaries for intellectuals, extended services and a rationalized system of promotions. At the same time, he called for conferment of degrees, titles and other rewards for accomplishment.

Since then the Peiping Government also has recognized complaints by professors that they had to attend too many meetings, that they were harassed by too many visitors and that they needed more assistance in their work, according to the domestic press. Reports and meetings are being restricted, visiting hours limited to stated periods and the number of assistants increased.

Steps are also being taken to expand library facilities and increase the number of available foreign technical publications.

Premier Chou is officially reported to have told the Central Committee in January that 45 per cent of China's intellectuals were "progressive." He said 40 per cent were "middle-of-the-road elements," while a "little over 10 per cent" were "backward elements."

April 15, 1956

PEIPING RELAXES CURB ON DEBATE

More 'Crowing' Is Urged on a Factual Basis' to Help End Backward Technology

Special to The New York Times.

HONG KONG, May 26—Communist China's intensified "March on Science" — a campaign aimed at catching up with the technologically advanced powers — has been accompanied by a move to permit somewhat freer academic debate.

The Chinese Communists have called for this relaxation—within the bounds of Marxism-Leninism and Maoism—under a new slogan derived from the classics: "Let hundreds of schools crow in competition."

The slogan is based on an allusion to philosophical debates during the latter part of the Chou Dynasty (1122-255 B. C.). This was the period in which Confucius (551-479 B. C.) lived.

Chien Chun-jui, deputy chief of the State Councils Office on Culture and Education, urged different "schools" to "crow," in a speech reported May 11 by the Peoples Daily in Peiping.

He told an "advanced workers conference" Communist China needed more debate on a "factual basis" to advance academic learning, improve its body of knowledge and overcome its scientific and technological "backwardness."

In a passage indicating a confident attitude among the Chinese Communists, Mr. Chien said Peiping did not have to be "afraid" in allowing more latitude in discussions of "technical and academic questions."

Willing to Learn From West

He declared that Communist China would continue to "learn first" from the Soviet Union. But he added that it was also prepared to learn the "advanced science" of the "capitalist" countries—especially the United States, Britain and France.

"We shall thoroughly implement the policy of free debate on academic questions," Mr. Chien was quoted by the People's Daily as having said. Just what comes under the heading of "academic questions," however is not yet clear.

The Chinese Communists have clearly not abandoned their basic theories or their political "thought control." In a May 7 Peiping article stressing the need for more research on the history of Chinese philosophy Prof. Feng Yu-lang declared such research should be threaded "through the Marxist viewpoint stand and method."

Measured against an earlier blanket dogmatism, however, the new policy appears to mean relatively more leeway for Chinese academicians, scientists and technologists.

During the 1951-52 intellectual "ideological remolding" campaign, the author of a book on "railway statistics" was denounced in the mainland press for having devoted 60 per cent of the book to "peddling American and British railway statistical methods."

Intellectuals Favored

With developing industrialization exerting a greater demand for highly trained people, the Peiping Government is now giving Chinese intellectuals favored treatment.

The mainland press has acknowledged that Communist China's ney young teachers are still not so good as the "old teachers." An article in China Youth, published in Peiping, commented that the young ones "knew what but not why."

Primary emphasis now being given to a "March on Science" calls for catching up with "advanced" countries in the "most urgent" technical fields in the next twelve years.

According to Premier Chou En-lai, Peiping intends to separate the "urgent" from the "non-urgent" and "systematically utilize the latest achievements of Soviet science" as quickly as possible in the "urgent" fields.

Greater attention is also being given to historical research. In his May 7 article, Professor Feng quoted Mao Tse-tung, Chief of State, as having said:

"China today represents another course of development for historical China. As Marxist historicists, we should not sever ourselves from history. We should sum up the history from Confucius to Sun Yat-sen and inherit this treasured part of history."

May 27, 1956

PERSUADE FOES, CHINA REDS TOLD

By HENRY R. LIEBERMAN
Special to The New York Times.

HONG KONG, June 25—The Chinese Communist Parliament was told today that "persuasion" would replace harsher methods in the class struggle.

Li Wei-han, head of the Communist party's United Front Department, enunciated before the National People's Congress (Parliament) in Peiping a policy of domestic "peaceful coexistence." He declared:

"The Central Committee of the Chinese Communist party has put forward the policy that the Chinese Communist party should coexist with democratic parties over a long period of time, and that there should be mutual supervision and first of all supervision over the Chinese Communist party. This is a momentous policy."

Other developments at today's parliamentary session, according to the Hsinhau (New China) News Agency, included the following.

¶After similar admissions by the Public Security Minister and the Procurator General, the President of the Supreme People's Court, Tung Pi-wu, a Politburo member, conceded again that some "counter-revolutionaries" had been handled too harshly.

Mr. Tung said the courts spent considerable time last year dealing with "sabotage" cases during the "crucial stages of Socialist transformation." He said that while the death penalty had been imposed in very few cases, it was now necessary and possible to treat "counter-revolutionaries" with "even greater leniency."

¶A Deputy Minister of Commerce, Yao Yi-lin, acknowledged again that criticism of the ministry for supplying "unacceptable goods' and piling goods up in one place while running short in another was justified. He said that selling centers would henceforth be given freedom to accept the commodities they wanted instead of being required to take allocations.

¶Eight Shanghai business partners of the state in "joint companies" critcized the State Trading Administration and complained that the Government was not paying enough on orders given to the companies.

In a statement circulated at the congressional session they said that state trading organizations had not operated efficiently and called for transferring the "joint companies" from state supervision to trusts run by various trades.

In his "united front" report, Mr. Li declared that the "transformed" Chinese capitalists had "definite abilities and experience." He urged party members to learn from them as well as from other nonparty members who had useful knowledge to impart.

Though Mr. Li asked better treatment for the "capitalists," he also told the congress this group still needed more reforming.

In observing that the situation was more favorable for the "method of persuasion" he explained that the method was that of "reasoning, emulation, criticism and self-criticism, and encouragement coupled with criticism."

MAO TELLS PARTY TENSION IS EASING

But Chinese Reds' Congress Is Warned That Suez and Taiwan Are Trouble Spots

By Reuters.

PEIPING, Sept. 15—Mao Tse-tung, Communist China's Chief of State, told representatives of the Chinese Communist party today that there had been a "trend toward relaxation of tension in the international situation."

Opening the first Congress of the party in eleven years, he declared: "The only ones who crave war and do not want peace are certain monopoly capitalistic circles in a handful of imperialist countries who look to aggression for their profits."

However, both Mr. Mao and Liu Shao-chi, who is generally considered the second-ranking man in the party, saw a threat to peace in the current Suez dispute.

Taiwan (Formosa) also was singled out as a trouble spot. Mr. Liu, who spoke after Mr. Mao, said Taiwan continued to be occupied by "American imperialists" and this "is the greatest threat to our security."

Negotiation Favored

He said the Peiping Government was willing to use peaceful negotiation to avoid the use of armed force. If China has to use armed force, Mr. Liu added, it will be when there is no longer any possibility for peaceful negotiation, or when peaceful negotiation has failed.

Mr. Mao, who is chairman of the party, said China firmly supported Egypt's action in nationalizing the Suez Canal Company and "resolutely" opposed any attempt at armed intervention against Egypt.

"We must completely frustrate the schemes of imperialists to create tension and prepare for war," he told 1,022 delegates representing more than 10,700,000 members in the Chinese Communist party.

China must give active support to national independence and liberation movements in Asia, Africa and Latin America, he added.

The congress, the eighth held by the Chinese Communist party, is the first since 1945. In the interval the Communists have advanced from being a party in opposition, often underground, to become the rulers of a country of more than 600,000,-000 people.

In 1921, when the party was founded in Shanghai, there were twelve members at a congress representing a party of about 100. Three men present today who attended that first meeting are Mr. Mao, Tung Pi-wu, president of the Supreme People's Court, and Li Ta, now a professor at Wuhan University.

Strict security precautions were taken around the conference hall today and no non Communist journalist was allowed to attend the meetings or even to approach the building. Some of the delegates are believed to be members of outlawed parties from other countries.

Mr. Mao and other Chinese leaders received a standing ovation as they mounted the rostrum and stood while the Communist Internationale was played.

Mr. Mao said in his twenty-minute speech that Communist China was not isolated and that she must further develop friendship and cooperation with the "camp of socialism."

"We must endeavor to establish diplomatic relations based on territorial integrity and sovereignty and equality and mutual benefit with all countries willing to live peacefully with us," he added.

The task of the Congress, he said, is to sum up the experience gained since 1945, to unite the whole party and to join with all those from home and abroad who can be united "to build a great Socialist China."

He made no direct reference to Stalin or the "cult of personality" [a Communist euphemism for one-man rule], but said the tasks confronting China were in general similar to those that faced the Soviet Union in the early period following its foundation.

"In transforming China from a backward agricultural country into an advanced industrial nation, we are confronted with many heavy tasks and our experience is far from being adequate," he declared.

Mr. Mao said the Chinese Communist party now was more united and consolidated than at any time. "We have achieved great success in every field of work but we have also made some mistakes," he said. Among shortcomings that he said were contrary to Marxist-Leninism, he cited subjectivism in thinking, bureaucracy in work, and "secretarianism" in organizational questions.

Mr. Liu declared that to defend China "we must continue to strengthen our national defense forces." In a speech that lasted four hours, he attacked "United States imperialism" and said: "United States monopoly capitalists are taking advantage of the favored position it gained as a result of the wealth amassed during the second world war."

The United States "has organized military blocs, established military bases, created international tension and prepared for a new war," he asserted. He said that Britain and France to some extent expressed a desire for peaceful coexistence but were still trying to cling to their privileges as colonial powers.

Mr. Liu warned that any attempt to reverse the nationalization of the Suez Canal Company by force not only would meet with resistance from Egypt but would be condemned by the whole world.

The Chinese party congress has emphasized the policy of peaceful coexistence that all "Socialist" countries follow, he said. "But on the other hand, United States imperialism continues with its arms drive, opposes the development of East-West relations, and fears peaceful coexistence as it does the day of doom."

PEIPING COUNTERS HOSTILITY TO ARMY

Orders Propaganda to Ease Soldier-Civilian Tension— Aid to Veterans Stressed

By GREG MacGREGOR
Special to The New York Times.

HONG KONG, Feb. 12—Communist China has ordered the immediate start of a propaganda campaign to ease tension between the armed forces and civilians.

The original order, dated Jan. 16, was said by the State Council to be of "important significance." Copies were reported to be in channels of distribution to people's councils and Army units in all provinces, autonomous districts and municipalities.

The document emphasized the importance of eliminating all tension groups without delay and stated that Army personnel responsible for "violations of laws and discipline and estrangement from the masses should be criticized and properly dealt with."

It added that civilians who do not support the Army and who "exclude and persecute" veterans must also be dealt with sternly.

The order said that immediately upon its receipt responsible persons should "proceed with concrete arrangements and report respectively to the Minister of Interior and the Political Department of the People's Liberation Army on the progress of their work."

The propaganda campaign is officially known as "Support the Army, Honor Its Dependents— Support the Government and Love the People."

In the State Council's order, an explanation was made that "some" Army units had not attached "due importance" to relations with the civilian masses.

Admissions that "some" veterans were discontented and that many dependents were in difficulties and had not received proper care also were included in the order.

It also cautioned officers and men stationed in frontier areas or among minority groups to exercise particular care in respecting local customs and in dealing with the people in surrounding communities.

February 13, 1957

Party Stresses Ideology
By HARRY SCHWARTZ

Ideological weakness within the Chinese Communist party is causing anxiety among that party's leaders, according to a Peiping radio broadcast as monitored in the United States.

A new campaign to re-educate Chinese Communists has been announced by Lu Ting-i, chief of the Propaganda Department of the Central Committee of the Communist party. The campaign is needed, Mr. Lu adds, because many Communists have "petty bourgeois" ideas and are not yet "proletarians ideologically."

The ideological weakening of the Communists is apparently linked with the rapid rise in the party's membership. Mr. Lu reveals that there are now 12,-000,000 members in the Communist party, three-fifths of whom joined the party after it had conquered the mainland of China.

The re-education campaign is apparently not intended to be a mass purge. Mr. Lu calls for "prudence" toward erring members and says that "erroneous ideas should not be dealt with crudely." He attacks those who would treat ideologically incorrect "comrades as they do the enemy."

But Mr. Lu makes clear that Communists will be purged if they resist the re-education campaign. He declares that "a resolute struggle, even to the point of expulsion from the party, should be waged against those who obstinately refuse to correct their mistakes and who carry out activities detrimental to the party."

Mr. Lu indicates that the need for the re-education campaign has arisen because of heretical ideas now being backed by some Communist party members. He declares that "some people, in the name of anti-doctrinarianism, want in fact to oppose Marxism-Leninism or to 'revise' the basic principles of Marxism-Leninism."

Mr. Lu's report that the Communist party now has 12,000,000 members indicates a sharp growth during the last six months. Last September, the Chinese Communist party congress heard a report that its membership at that time was 10,730,000.

March 17 1957

Favorite Red Theory Is Exploded by Reds

By WILLIAM J. JORDEN
Special to The New York Times.

MOSCOW, April 15—A devastating attack appeared in Moscow today on one of the favorite theories of many Communists: that there is complete unanimity of views between the broad masses of people and the Communist party and the Government officials who speak and act for them.

This unusual and surprisingly frank discussion of one of the least mentioned but most serious problems for Communist theoreticians appeared originally as an editorial in Communist China's leading newspaper, the Peiping People's Daily. It was reprinted in full today in Pravda, obviously with the approval of the leadership of the Soviet Communist party.

The tone of the article and the fact that it was given such prominent display here made it clear that conflict between the masses and the party and governmental bureaucrats was not exclusively a problem for China but for all states that call themselves Socialist, including the Soviet Union.

Frankness Counseled

The most interesting aspect of this exposé of one of the most serious administrative problems in the Communist world was not that excessive bureaucratism was criticized. That has been done before. The unusual aspect was that differences between the average man in a Socialist state and party and the government officials who control his destiny should be described frankly as one of the numerous "contradictions" that plague this kind of society.

"Contradictions" is a word usually reserved to describe conflicts of interests between classes in a capitalist society and the differences that separate capitalist and Socialist societies. It is a strong word, indeed, to apply to the situation prevailing between the broad masses of the people in a communist country and the bureaucrats who run machinery of government and party.

The Chinese analysis of the problem said there were many reasons why sharp differences could arise between the people and officialdom in a communist country. It said that the masses directly participated in production, were primarily engaged in physical labor and "find it difficult to exercise directly their right to administer." The officials, on the other hand, are seldom engaged in physical labor and exercised directly their right to run affairs in a socialist state.

The masses concentrate on things here and now the editorial said, while officials devote most of their energies to long-range and general problems. The people pay more attention to immediate interests and requirements of a limited character while the officials "can ignore with relative ease" the present situation and the vital needs of the people, the report said.

The People's Daily added that, however serious these contradictions might be, they were not in the same class with the differences that separate "us and our enemies." It said they arose more from misunderstanding and poor ideological training than "conflict of fundamental interests."

Bureaucrats Blamed

Most of the blame for the prevailing situation was placed on the party and government bureaucrats. Many of them were said to be ignorant of the situation prevailing among the people, of failing to understand public opinion. They are "slow in doing many things that can and must be done" for the people, the paper said.

"They even rudely suppress and ignore the opinion of the masses, rudely violate the people's rights and interests" the report said.

The people's daily said that public and party officials who acted in this manner were "only a minority" in Communist society. But it said their actions had aroused the "righteous dissatisfaction" of the people and had to be overcome "with all seriousness."

The article in the Soviet Union leading newspaper called on the party and government officials to meet and really get down to close contact with the people. It said there should be regular discussions of the matter between factory managers and workers, between teachers and students, between directors and members of cooperations.

"An atmosphere should be created at all these meetings in which the people can really express freely their views, and in which they will really want to express their views," it said.

This was an unusually strong criticism of the carefully planned and staged gatherings that occur so often.

Officials were admonished to hear the people's opinion and wherever possible to carry their ideas into action. Where it was not feasible to carry out the people's wishes, it was the official's responsibility to give a full and satisfying explanation, the paper said.

April 16, 1957

CHINA REDS TASTE WORK OF MASSES

PEIPING, May 5 (Reuters)—Government officials, intellectuals and army officers in some parts of Communist China did a little laboring work today alongside peasants and workers.

They were the vanguard of what was expected to become a country-wide movement. Recent directives from the Communist party's Central Committee called on leaders to overcome bureaucracy by keeping in close touch with the masses.

Bureaucracy, which is gaining a stranglehold on some Chinese organizations, is one of the main targets in a "rectification campaign" that is just beginning.

The campaign is an ideological way of fostering what is called "right Marxist thinking," especially in regard to "contradictions between leadership and people." It will last about a year and will permeate all levels of official and party life.

Many Government organizations in Peiping and other parts of the country were holding meetings over the weekend to discuss how the campaign could best be carried out.

Drive to Widen Later

It will not go beyond the level of county organizations, large factories and universities until September, but it will spread to basic administrative units and throughout the party during the fall.

Much of the education work of the campaign will involve digesting a four-hour speech by Mao Tse-Tung, head of the state, to a Supreme State Conference Feb. 27.

This speech, containing a twelve-point directive, was called "On Correctly Handling Contradictions Within Ranks of the People." It has been studied by higher level groups throughout the country for the last few weeks. Ideological teams briefed by Mr. Mao himself have been spreading the word.

The rectification campaign, which was started officially by a party directive this week, was a continuation of this study. According to the directive, no force of any sort will be used and the whole campaign will rest upon persuasion and self-help.

Observers here believe the campaign will not limit the trend toward liberalization and relaxation of internal tensions, which has been apparent over the last year.

The directive specifically states that the rectification campaign should strengthen the policies of "long-term co-existence" with regard to non-Communists in China and "let 100 flowers blossom and 100 schools of thought contend" in the spheres of intellectual endeavor and creative art.

CHINA REDS FACE 'BRAIN WASHING'

Party Group's Re-education by Persuasion Expected to End Dissension

PEIPING, May 7 (Reuters)—Communist party members in China will be "brainwashed" in a campaign to solve "contradictions" within the party, a spokesman said today.

Chou Yang, deputy director of party propaganda, outlined the campaign at a news conference attended by foreign newsmen. He emphasized that the brainwashing would be done through persuasion and argument and not by force or intimidation.

"Some people think ideological remolding not very pleasant words and 'brainwashing' worse," Mr. Chou said. But people need to wash their faces in this changing world, he added.

He said the main efforts in the campaign to improve relations between party leaders and the people would be directed against the bureaucracy. As the link between leaders and the rank and file, the bureaucracy is likely to be a source of danger to the party and its relations with the people, he added.

If the bureaucracy develops into little dictatorships, Mr. Chou said, "our policy is to permit such unfortunate ways of overcoming it as strikes or disturbances."

He added that the right to strike was the same as the right to free speech and other freedoms. Strike leaders will not be punished, he said.

Mr. Chou indicated the party still had no hard and fast rule to determine whether or not criticism of the Communist leadership was counter-revolutionary. He said: "We do not have yet any definite way of distinguishing always between antagonistic and non-antagonistic contradictions within the ranks of the people."

The Chinese official said some intellectuals, both inside and outside the party, were reluctant to make the best use of more intellectual freedom.

Some doctrinaires held that such freedom was dangerous and that "weeds might overcome the flowers if all were permitted to bloom together." Some non-party intellectuals are apprehensive that if they put forward contrary ideas "they would be criticized in the same way as before," Mr. Chou explained.

Although there have been achievements in uniting the party and intellectuals since 1949, Mr. Chou said, the policy at times has been a "little too rough" and too generalized.

He said these apprehensions would be overcome little by little and that the party would not again use the policy of "many people criticizing one person."

Mr. Chou was asked about the Chinese writer Hu Feng, whose arrest nearly two years ago caused a stir among intellectuals in China.

Mr. Chou said that he was aware many foreigners were worried about this case but that Mr. Hu had contacts over many years with "the enemy" and counter-revolutionaries. His case "was not in essence a contradiction within the ranks of the people," the official added.

PEIPING CHANGING OFFICIALS' DUTIES

Reds Seek More Efficiency Through 'Rectification of the Styles of Work'

PEIPING, June 8 (Reuters)—Chinese Communist leaders are attempting a thorough overhaul of the work of government and organization of all levels through a nation-wide "rectification" campaign.

The campaign, which is aimed at the "rectification of the styles of work" of all officials, has been launched by the central committee of the Communist party. It will consist of the "ideological remolding," or, as one official put it, the "brainwashing" of every member of the Communist party.

Non-party officials have been told that they can join in on a voluntary basis.

The campaign will be thorough and will stretch into the remotest parts of the country, affecting the most distant Communist party members. But it seems certain that this one will lack the physical ruthlessness and force that have been features of earlier campaigns since the present Government came to power in 1949.

Harsh Methods Ruled Out

It has been specifically promised that only argument and persuasion will be used and that the campaign must eschew force or indoctrination.

Improvements will be achieved by criticism and self-criticism, and it is said that past methods of mass criticism, with unfortunates bearing the brunt of savage attacks in mass meetings and in newspaper campaigns, will not be used again.

Observers here think these promises will be carried out and that the campaign will continue the present trend of some internal relaxation and easing of tensions. The chairman of the People's Republic of China, Mao Tse-tung, has insisted that the present policies of long-term co-operation with non-Communist party people and freedom for intellectuals shall continue.

It is thought unlikely, at least in the foreseeable future, that the present policies, which are based on the central theme of the "unity" of the Chinese people, will be changed or endangered by a return to old pressures.

The main purpose of the campaign is to increase efficiency generally throughout the country and attempt to do away with some of the present discontent which, according to Marxist terminology, has been caused by "bureaucracy, sectarianism and subjectivism."

Bureaucracy A Target

Bureaucracy, which has the same definition in any language —even though the Chinese say that "Communist bueaucracy is a hard-working bureaucracy"—will be the main target in the campaign. For bureaucracy has become manifest, according to the leaders, to an alarming extent in many organizations, Government departments and in almost every facet of Chinese life.

The second "sin" to be combated in the campaign is that of subjectivism, which was defined recently by a Communist official as "divorcing oneself and one's thinking from actual conditions." This results in doctrinairism and a blind following of the Marxist "scriptures" without any thought for actual or practical conditions.

The third of the major targets in the rectification campaign is sectarianism, which has been found in the arrogance of some Communists, particularly among the young. These have taken a superior and dominating attitude and have caused great resentment among such people as scientists and writers and government officials who are not members of the Communist party.

June 9, 1957

Peiping Organ Publishes Letters Of Critics Scoring Red 'Perfidy'

By GREG MacGREGOR
Special to The New York Times.

HONG KONG, Saturday, June 22 — A public accusation of perfidy against the leaders of Communist China was published in the leading party organ in Peiping recently, according to translations available here.

In the latest of a number of outspoken criticisms against the Communist leadership, a professor of the People's University in the Chinese capital was quoted as having said in a letter to the People's Daily:

"To kill Communists and to overthrow you cannot be called unpatriotic because you Communists are no longer of service to the people.

"Even if the Communist party is destroyed, China will not perish. This is because we will not become traitors even if there is no guidance of the Communist party." The author of the letter was named as Professor Ko Pei-chi.

The unusual attack on the Communist leadership was the strongest to appear recently in a series of criticisms that has been permitted and publicized on the mainland since a policy of free criticism was adopted by the Communist party's Central Committee last year. The new policy was brought to the attention of the Western world recently following the publication of a speech made last February by the Chinese Communist leader Mao Tse-tung.

Under the slogan of, "Let a hundred flowers blossom and let a hundred schools of thought contend," open criticism of almost all branches of Red leadership in China have appeared in the Communist-sponsored press in an apparent effort to display the freedom of Chinse Red rule.

A heated criticism of the Government for restrictions against writers, artists and producers of public plays and moving pictures began in January, for example, and is still raging. Peiping was openly denounced for trying to force members of these groups to work for the good of the state at the expense of artistic creation.

University students openly defied Red authorities last fall after the Hungarian uprising, and again this year against political activities in the schools. Reports of these criticisms were duly reported in the Communist press.

Troubles in the armed forces between troops and officers also were described in print, and later, criticisms by civilians against members of the armed forces were published and broadcast over the Peiping short-wave radio.

In the first criticism from Professor Ko, which appeared in the May 31 issue of the People's Daily, he was quoted as saying: "I believe that the party masses' relationship of today is as different from the party masses' before the liberation as two poles apart."

He accused the party of contending that food and materials were plentiful when there actually was scarcity. He said party members and cadres were profiteering at the expense of the people and identified them as those "who before wore worn-out shoes and now ride in small sedan cars and wear woolen uniforms."

In a second letter to the same publication, also printed for public distribution, the professor said, "up to this moment the masses of people still harbor worries about airing their views. This completely shows that the masses dare not believe the word of the Communist party. The party should take particular notice of this point because the people cannot stand without faith."

June 22, 1957

RED CHINA URGED TO COMBAT CRITICS

Pravda Reprints Editorial From Peiping Assailing Attacks on Party

By MAX FRANKEL
Special to The New York Times.

MOSCOW, June 23 — Soviet readers were told today that powerful "bourgeois" elements in China were trying to exploit the new freedom of discussion granted by the Chinese Communist party to destroy the nation's Communist Government.

As a result, Pravda declared, the Chinese working class now must organize a "decisive counter-attack."

As in other reports of Chinese ideological developments in the last two months, the Soviet Communist party organ avoided all comment or interpretation. But Pravda devoted a half page to an extensive summary of an editorial that appeared yesterday in The People's Daily of Peiping under the same title used here, "Unusual Spring."

Czechs Cite Soviet Example

In another article today, Pravda presented a testimonial from Czechoslovak Communists declaring that, despite national differences, Prague had consistently found it best to follow the Soviet example in building communism.

The Chinese editorial, as summarized here, said that "right-wing elements" launched a "furious" attack on the party leadership last month, right after the Communist party began its campaign to eliminate "contradictions," or conflicts, between the governors and governed in China.

Included in the campaign was an invitation from Mao Tse-tung, Chinese chief of state, to non-Communists to help by expressing themselves freely or as he put it in an adaptation of an old Chinese proverb, to let different schools of thought contend in the field of ideas. But bourgeois forces, the editorial said, abused this slogan for their own ends and organized their own campaign to undermine socialism "under the cloak of giving the party aid."

Furthermore, the Pravda summary reported, these anti-regime forces were "actively gathering

286

followers among democratic parties and groups, intellectuals merchants, youth and students.'

Thus strengthened, the report continued, right-wing elements started to exaggerate mistakes of the Chinese Communist party and created an atmosphere in which there was discussion only of shortcomings, and never of the Communists' positive achievements. They also were said to have maintained that bureaucracy was inevitably the product of socialism and ever synonymous with it, that "sectarianism," or a refusal of party leaders to mingle with the masses, was the usual product of proletarian dictatorship and that "subjectivism" was the product of Marxism.

The Peiping Government "at first" decided to let the people recognize enemies themselves, the editorial said, adding that they did. But it asserted that the political class struggle still existed in China "and will continue to exist for a long time."

The summary carried by the Soviet news agency Tass did not indicate Moscow's attitude toward the debate in China.

The traditional Soviet view has been that "contradictions" are a phenomena of decadent capitalist societies. It is maintained that, since the Soviet Union is the oldest and the most successful of the Communist states, its organizational and ideological example should serve as an inspiration and a model for other "Socialist" countries.

Lack of Coalition Scored

HONG KONG, June 23 (AP)—Mao Tse-tung, Chinese Communist chief of state, and Premier Chou En-lai have been criticized by a leading non-Communist Chinese editor for their failure to establish a coalition Government.

The critic, Chu An-ping, is ditor-in-chief of the Kuang Ming Jih Pao, organ of all eight non-Communist parties tolerated by the Chinese Reds.

Mr. Chu made his criticism June 1, during the second of a series of fortnightly forums in Peiping between the Communists and the non-Communist parties. A copy of the Communist People's Daily, which printed his remarks, has just reached this British colony.

"Recently people have raised many opinions against the junior monks," Mr. Chu said, "but no one has yet said anything about the old monks. I now put forward an example and ask Chairman Mao and Premier Chou to give me some information.

"Before the liberation we heard that Chairman Mao advocated the formation of a coalition Government together with non-party members.

"After the founding of the regime in 1949, in the Central People's Government of that period three of the six deputy chairmen and two of the four deputy premiers were non-party members. That looked like a coalition Government anyway.

"Later, however, after the Government was reorganized and the number of deputy chairmen was reduced to only one, the chairs of all the former non-party deputy premiers were removed to the standing committee of the National People's Congress [highest legislative body]. That was still all right.

"But at this moment there are twelve deputy premiers in the State Council and not even one of them is a non-party member."

June 24, 1957

MAO'S POLICY SEEN AS TRAP FOR FOES

Special to The New York Times.

HONG KONG, Tuesday, June 25—Indications of an impending policy re-examination in Communist China and a nationwide purge are seen in the Peiping People's Daily, organ of the mainland regime.

A copy of the paper that reached here today contained an editorial saying that the new freedom of thought and expression called for by Mao Tse-tung Chief of State, in his February speech, helped to expose shortcomings in the party but also unmasked "capitalistic rightists."

"The masses can now distinguish the faces of the different people," the editorial stated.

The implication was that the relaxation of curbs on speech and various forms of expression had been designed to smoke out dangerous elements.

The editorial suggested that internal fears which arose after the Hungarian anti-Soviet uprising, brought about a more liberal interpretation of the policy voiced in Mr. Mao's slogan, "Let a hundred flowers bloom, let a hundred schools of thought contend."

The Hungarian developments wrongly encouraged many capitalistic rightists in a mistaken belief that Communist governments could be overthrown and changed easily, the editorial said.

Chou Tells Non-Reds Persistent Criticism May Bring Reprisal

By Reuters.

PEIPING, June 26—Chou En-lai, Premier of Communist China, warned the nation's non-Communist representatives today that they might be classed as "enemies of the people" if they persisted in criticism of the regime.

Mr. Chou's statement was the first reply by a senior Communist to recent attacks on the Communist party made by some "democrats," including three Cabinet ministers. The People's Daily, official party newspaper, already has condemned these "Rightists."

The Premier delivered a 20,000-word speech at the opening session of the National People's Congress (Parliament). He was reporting to the 1,042 delegates on the work of the Government in the last year.

Mr. Chou said he hoped the critics of the Government, "profiting by their own experience and increased awareness, will repent and accept opportunities of remolding themselves."

Although his speech dealt mainly with domestic problems, Mr. Chou included a strong attack on the world-wide policies of the United States, declaring that "the new colonialism will end up no better than the old colonialism." It is possible, he said, for Communist nations to "force the imperialist war bloc to accept the principle of peaceful coexistence provided we can unite with all possible forces internationally and persist in our struggle."

Mr. Chou did not indicate that there would be any purge or other drastic action because of the recent criticisms here. In a speech published here last week, Mao Tse-tung, the Chinese Chief of State, described "contradictions" that were permissible within the ranks of the people and called for the "unity of all patriotic Chinese." Although Mr. Mao recommended freedom of speech for differing views, he urged dictatorial methods against "the enemy."

The Premier emphasized today that the Communist party would "allow no wavering on the basic state system of our country." He rejected such "bourgeois tricks" as direct elections and two-party or multi-party systems of government.

In his discussion of foreign affairs, he said the "unity of the camp of socialism" was strengthened, not weakened,

June 25, 1957

after the anti-Communist revolt in Hungary.

'Proletarian Equality' Upheld

"Facts have proved that international Socialist unity based on proletarian internationalism and equality could not be destroyed by provocation," he declared.

In general the Premier was optimistic about the domestic outlook for China. He revealed that there was a budget deficit of 1,800,000,000 yuan last year, but he said "achievements in 1956 were tremendous." [The yuan is worth about 40 cents at the official rate.]

This is the first announced budget deficit since the Communists came to power in 1949. But Mr. Chou said that over-all expenditure and revenue for the first five-year plan, which ends in December, would be balanced.

Warning to Non-Communists

HONG KONG, June 26 (AP)—Mr. Chou, in his speech today, warned members of China's non-Communist parties that they would be excluded from the present "united front" if criticism of the regime became excessive. About one-fourth of the positions in the Chinese Government are filled by non-Communists and non-party-members.

The Premier disclosed that a purge of "counter-revolutionaries" after the Communists seized power in 1949 brought execution to 16.2 per cent, or about one in six, of the accused by 1952.

Because last year's crop was "not so good" and because food reserves were down, the Premier said, it has been necessary to slow down the tempo of construction this year. He declared that because of the predominance of agriculture and the frequency of natural disasters, "it is unrealistic to expect the national economy to develop at a uniform and even pace every year."

The Communist Premier declared that "remnant counter-revolutionary forces" remained in China. He announced that the purge had sentenced 42.3 per cent of those captured to "reform through labor," placed 32 per cent under surveillance, and eventually freed 48.9 per cent "after some re-education."

Mr. Chou did not specify how many had been arrested, imprisoned or executed. A statement attributed previously to Mr. Mao put the executions at 800,000.

[Mr. Mao's statement appeared in excerpts, made public in Warsaw, of an address to Chinese Communist leaders Feb. 27. When an edited version of the text was published last week in Peiping, the reference did not appear.]

June 27, 1957

6 Anti-Reds Seized After Fight in China

By The Associated Press.

HONG KONG, Friday, June 28—Communist China has reported the seizure of six "counter-revolutionary assassins" in a gun battle in which a Government political worker was killed and two soldiers were wounded.

It was the second instance of Government action against dissident groups to become known here within a few hours.

The official Hsinhua (New China) news agency, in a report that was dated two weeks ago but reached Hong Kong only yesterday, said Army security forces arrested the six "hard-core elements" June 5 at Pucheng, on the coast opposite Nationalist-held Taiwan (Formosa).

The reported break-up of this ring took place five days before the arrest in Nanking of the leaders of another organization said to have been bent on overthrowing the Communist Government. This action by security forces was announced by the Peiping radio last night.

The men involved in the Pucheng gunfight belonged to a group that called itself the "Fan Chun," or "Anti-Army," according to the Communist news agency. Hsinhua said they had tried to kill Yeh Ho-chin, leader of a militia team, and Huang Ho-sen, secretary of the New Democratic Youth League. Mr. Yeh was said to have been wounded.

Those arrested included Chen Shih-sheng, a ringleader of the "counter-revolutionaries," the agency said. It continued:

"These counter-revolutionaries had held five secret meetings during the period from the latter part of February to the early part of this year, formulated operational plans and appointed 'army, division and battalion' commanders in an attempt steadily to expand their organization, to assassinate Government personnel and to loot cooperative supply depots, as well as to perpetrate other kinds of criminal activities."

Group Long Under Scrutiny

The leaders of the Nanking "counter-revolutionary" organization were arrested after a long investigation, the Peiping radio said. It indicated that the seizures might have been one development of the current "rectification" campaign initiated by Mao Tse-tung, the chief of state, in which individuals were encouraged to voice criticisms of the Communist regime.

"During the recent high tide of the rectification campaign," the Peiping radio said, "they [the counter-revolutionary organization] pasted up written slogans to wage their propaganda."

The broadcast said the organization called itself Chung Hua Chien Kuo Tang, which means Party of the Foundation of the State.

The organization was discovered June 10 in a Nanking textile plant after it had remained relatively inactive for a long period, according to Peiping. The announcement indicated that the group had been in existence long before the Communists came to power in 1949 and had committed many crimes.

Last year, the broadcast said the organization began a campaign to recruit followers and enrolled many, but no figure for the size of the group was given.

'Right-Wing' Students Cited
Special to The New York Times.

HONG KONG, June 27—The National University of Peiping has been used as a center for disseminating anti-Communist views and a base of "rumor mongering," Kiang Lung-chi, the institution's vice chancellor, has told a subcommittee of the National People's Congress (Parliament), according an official dispatch received here today.

The report by the Hsinhua (New China) news agency from Peiping said Mr. Kiang described a number of "extremely fanatical right-wing" students in the university as being "overtly against the leadership of the Chinese Communist party and the people's democratic dictatorship."

Criticisms of the Chinese Communist leadership, originating mostly with lower echelon executives, educators and public officials, continued to filter into Hong Kong today, but reports from Peiping indicated that the publication of attacks on the regime would be drastically curtailed.

RED CHINA OFFICIAL IN PUBLIC APOLOGY

Special to The New York Times.

HONG KONG, Saturday, June 29—A high-ranking public official in Peiping made the first major public apology for his recent outburst of criticism against the Red leadership of China in the copy of the People's Daily that reached here yesterday.

An apology and self-renunciation for his words was made by Chang Po-chun, the Minister of Communications. His act was interpreted here as an indication that the experiment of allowing free criticism of the Communist regime from high sources had just about run its course. The criticisms were too numerous and too sharp for comfort and safety, it is believed.

The Communications Minister's criticisms were publicized on May 22. He proposed, in effect, that a political planning board be created that would give the eight minor political parties strength equal to, or greater than the Communist party.

Mr. Chang said repentently: "I have failed to live up to the expectations of the Communist party and Chairman Mao [Tse-tung], who has guided me and trusted me these past years. I committed a serious mistake ideologically."

Nowhere in the apology was there a concrete explanation as to why the official had recanted.

The People's Daily said earlier in the week that the campaign of open criticism had brought the enemies of the state out into the open. The newspaper said, in effect, that the campaign had served its purpose.

ALL MAO FLOWERS NOW BLOOM ALIKE

End of His 'Rectification' Finds the Critics Banished and Regime Shaken Up

By TILLMAN DURDIN
Special to The New York Times.

HONG KONG, Jan. 11 — In Communist China, rectification, which Chief of State Mao Tsetung has said will become a permanent fixture, has had its effect.

The country is beginning the New Year in an atmosphere of enforced conformity in marked contrast with the climate of criticism and dissension that marked 1957. The discontented have had their say and have been cowed into silence. Their strictures against the regime have produced some reforms, but the right to oppose or even to question the basic tenets of the system is not among them.

Eight months have now passed since the rectification campaign began last May. Its start marked a sharp repudiation of a policy promulgated earlier in the year by Mao in two now famous speeches. Mao bade the nation engage in free criticism in the interest of resolving contradictions in society and bringing to light defects in the Communist party and Government. He said: "Let a hundred flowers bloom, let a hundred schools of thought contend." The objective of "free criticism" was to purge and reinvigorate the party, but the response quickly broadened into a movement that involved the whole population and the regime at all levels.

It seems clear that Mr. Mao and his colleagues were impelled by the realization that their vast, oppressive, bureaucratic system needed shaking up.

June 28, 1957

June 29, 1957

January 12, 1958

PEIPING CONGRESS BANS 57 DEPUTIES

Credential Chief Announces 'Parliament' Will Dismiss All 'Rightist' Members

PEIPING, Feb. 1 (Reuters)— The National People's Congress, Communist China's "parliament," banned fifty-seven deputies from its opening session today for straying from the rigid party line.

Ma Ming-fan, chairman of the credentials committee of the 1,226-member body, said all the "rightists" deputies would be dismissed from the Congress. They include three Cabinet ministers ejected from the Government yesterday.

Mr. Ma said that sixteen of the deputies already had been dismissed by local Congresses and that thirty-eight others had been ordered to stay away from the session here. He indicated the latter would be formally dismissed later.

Among the thirty-eight "rightsts" ordered to stay away were ten members of Congress committees and the National Defense Council. The Congress, whose opening session was attended by Mao Tse-tung, chief of state, and Premier Chou En-lai, adopted a resolution stripping all ten of their committee posts.

The expelled officials include Lung Yun, a former Nationalist general and governor of Yunnan Province, and Madame Hsieh Hsueh-hung, once hailed in Communist China as the heroine of the abortive revolt against the Chinese Nationalists in Taiwan (Formosa) in 1949.

Had Criticized Regime

The charges against the expelled deputies date back to last June, when there was outspoken criticism of the Communist party.

Finance Minister Li Hsien-nien declared at today's session of the Congress that defense expenditure would be cut 830,000,- 000 yuan (about $336,000,000) in 1958.

He termed this a "noteworthy feature of the budget and maintained it was "in radical contrast to the budgets for arms expansion" of the United States and other Western countries.

Mr. Li said the budget was aimed at expanding production and announced there would be a 40 per cent increase in financial aid to agriculture. There will be more farm loans and higher advance payments for the purchase of produce by state commercial enterprises, he said.

The budget speech was marked by cautious optimism. Mr. Li urged the Chinese people to be "hard-working and thrifty," a statement in marked contrast with the Government's buoyant enthusiasm of two years ago.

Mr. Li said that China was still "economically and culturally backward," but that the country was striving to equal or surpass British industrial production within fifteen years or slightly longer.

Observers felt this reference to a "slightly longer" period indicated that Government predictions were becoming more cautious in the wake of past agricultural and industrial setbacks.

CHOU QUITS POST AS FOREIGN CHIEF

By Reuters.

PEIPING, Feb. 11—Premier Chou En-lai gave up his job as Foreign Minister today to a long-time friend.

His successor is 57-year-old Marshal Chen Yi, French-educated Communist. Mr. Chou, 60, has been Premier and Foreign Minister since the Communists gained power in China in 1949. He retained the Premiership.

The shift, urged by the Premier himself, was approved at the closing session here of the National People's Congress (Parliament) as part of a shake-up that involved the abolition or merging of several ministries.

Twelve Ministers were removed from their posts and six of them were among nine new appointments made.

Three men appointed today replace three non-Communist Ministers ousted for Rightist activity twelve days ago. Six Communists who lost their jobs in today's shuffle were not named to new posts.

The new Foreign Minister, a Communist party member for thirty-five years, is one of China's ten Deputy Premiers, a member of the Central Committee of the Communist party, a Deputy Chairman of the National Defense Council and Mayor of Shanghai.

He studied in France in the early Nineteen Twenties. He joined forces with Mr. Chou to form a branch of the Chinese Communist party in France.

On his return home, Mr. Chen served successively as adjutant to a Chinese warlord, as newspaper editor and magistrate until 1927, when he joined the political branch of the Chinese Army.

Led a Communist Army

He played a prominent part in Communist military campaigns, leading an Army that fought the Japanese in East China during World War II. He headed the forces that took Nanking and Shanghai from the Nationalist forces in 1949.

Premier Chou told the Congress today that the reorganization of ministries would strengthen efficiency in China's long-term planning.

The Congress approved the following changes and successors to the purged Rightist ministers, all three of whom were members of small non-Communist parties tolerated by the Communists:

¶The Timber Ministry, headed by Lo Lung-chi, who was ousted, has been absorbed by the Forestry Ministry, headed by Liang Hsi.

¶Chang Nai-chi has been succeeded as Food Minister by Sha Chien-li, Minister of Light Industry and, like Mr. Chang, a leading member of the small China Democratic National Construction party.

¶Chang Po-chun's former post as Communications Minister has been filled by Wang Shou-tao, a member of the Central Committee of the Communist party.

Observers here believe that there is no suggestion of disgrace for the six Communists who lost their ministerial posts in the shuffle.

Six Ministers Removed

The six Communists who lost their posts are:

Wang Ho-shou, whose National Construction Commission was abolished.

Li Chu-kuei, replaced as Minister of the Petroleum Industry by Yu Chiu-li.

Lai Chi-fa, whose Ministry of the Building Materials Industry was merged with the Ministry of Construction, headed by Liu Hsiu-feng.

Wan Li, whose Ministry of Urban Construction also was merged with the Ministry of Construction.

Huang Ching, relieved as head of the First Ministry of Machine Building, which absorbed the Second Ministry of Machine Building. Chao Erh-lu, head of the dissolved ministry, was put in charge of the combined First Ministry of Machine Building. The Third Ministry of Machine Building was made the Second Ministry.

Liu Lan-po, whose Ministry of Electric Power was merged with the Ministry of Water Conservancy. The combined ministry was placed under Fu Tso-yi, former Minister of Water Conservancy.

The following other ministry changes were made:

The Ministry of Urban Services, headed by Yang Yi-chen, was renamed the Second Ministry of Trade.

Li Chu-chen, former Food Industry Minister, was appointed to the Ministry of Light Industry, which absorbed Food Industry.

Chang Hsi-jo, former Education Minister, was appointed chairman of a new Commission of Cultural Relations with Foreign Countries.

Yang Hsiu-feng, former Minister of Higher Education, was appointed head of a merged Education Ministry.

The congress approved the 1958 budget and a twenty-six letter alphabet, which it is hoped will simplify the problem of learning Chinese.

REDS BEGIN PURGE IN 2 CHINESE AREAS

By TILLMAN DURDIN
Special to The New York Times.

HONG KONG, Nov. 14—The Governor of Shantung has been dismissed in a sweeping crackdown by the Peiping regime on officials in that North China province.

The Governor and subordinate officials of Liaoning Province in Manchuria are believed to be involved in a similar purge.

Reports of the purges carried out by the Chinese Communists in Shantung and Liaoning were contained in recent copies of Jenmin Jihpao (People's Daily) of Peiping and other publications in China that have just arrived here.

These reports indicate that officials of the two provinces are under fire because they have been ineffective and non-cooperative in carrying out in their provinces Peiping's 1958 "big leap forward" program of economic expansion.

The Liaoning Governor under attack is Tu Che-heng, who has also been holding the post of first secretary of the Liaoning provincial Communist party committee.

The Shantung Governor in disgrace is Chao Chien-min, who has held the position as first secretary of the provincial party in Shantung.

Mr. Chao is also an alternate member of the Central Executive Committee of the Chinese Communist party. He was listed as Vice Minister of Railways at the time he took over the Shantung Governorship in 1955.

The Tsingtao Daily, which is published in the main port city of Shantung, said on Oct. 29 that Mr. Chao had been dismissed and replaced by Tan Chi-lung, a subordinate member of the Shantung provincial administration.

Named along with Mr. Chao in the crackdown on the Shantung officials is Wang Cho-ju, the Vice Governor; Tse Yang-yuan, chairman of the Provincial Planning Commission; Kuo Shi-hyi and Tsao Yung, vice chairmen of the commission, and Hsu Chung-yi, director of the Finance Department.

Whether all these officials have lost their posts was not clear, but this appears to be true. Jenmin Jihpao has reported that in the counties and districts of Shantung, which has 50,000,000 people, 40,000 cadres (local officials) were involved in the purge, which presumably means they have been dismissed.

That many Shantung officials have been in trouble has been public knowledge for some time. Jenmin Jihpao and other Chinese Communist publications have printed a number of reports during the last year of the failings and negative attitudes of Shantung functionaries, and Mr. Wang, the vice governor, has been singled out for attack.

However, there have been few definite indications that a shake-up was brewing in Liaoning, and details of what has happened are lacking here. But positive evidence that a purge has occurred was contained in the Nov. 5 edition of Jenmin Jihpao, which included an advertisement for a new Liaoning magazine called Theoretical Study.

The advertisement indicated that the current issue of the magazine was devoted almost entirely to articles described as dealing with the "thorough purging of the anti-party factionist clique" and on "evil influences" in agriculture and industry.

The Governor has been in charge of the province's agricultural program. Wang Cheng, second secretary of the provincial party committee has been in charge of the industrial program.

A Hsinhua (New China) News Agency dispatch printed in Chinese Communist paper Oct. 30 reported a meeting under way in Shenyang (Mukden), the Liaoning capital, of top party cadres from all over the province "to eliminate nonrevolutionary elements."

This coupled with the fact that the Hsinhua agency has reported that the posts of both the first and second secretaries of the Liaoning party committee are now filled by new men, is taken here as good evidence that Messrs. Tu and Wang have been ousted.

Liaoning, which has a population of 20,000,000, contains the industrial centers of Shenyang and Anshan, and was cited recently as a province with one of the poorest "leap forward" agricultural records in the country this year. Its grain production was reported to have increased only 30 per cent, whereas the output in most other provinces is up 100 per cent, and in some even more.

November 15, 1958

TOP PEIPING TALKS ON POLICY HINTED

Leaders Are Thought Having Secret Parley as Regime Is Beset by Problems

By GREG MacGREGOR
Special to The New York Times.

HONG KONG, Aug. 1—Reports of a closely guarded conference of Chinese Communist leaders reached here through usually reliable sources this week.

The reports were supported by the unexplained absence of Mao Tse-tung, head of the Chinese Communist party; Liu Shao-chi, chief of state of Communist China; Premier Chou En-lai, Marshal Chu-teh and others from recent state and social functions.

The Peiping radio, normally a source of Chinese Communist policy announcements and propaganda directives, has been unusually moderate in tone in the last month, a change from its threats, accusations and denunciations. This was interpreted as another indication that a top-level policy review might be in progress or just ended.

High-ranking dignitaries who have visited Peiping in the last few weeks have been met by lower officials than usual. Requests for audiences with Chinese Communist leaders have been politely denied.

Refusals have been accompanied by such explanations as "he is at the mountain top," according to diplomats and trade leaders passing through Hong Kong.

The Chinese Communists have admitted at least three major problems:

1. A nation-wide food shortage, particularly in cities.
2. Major trouble with the commune system in at least some areas.
3. Serious damage from floods, droughts, locust plagues and hailstorms.

Although Peiping has tended to attribute all three problems to natural disasters, critics of Chinese communism pointed out that food shortages were known to exist before heavy floods struck this spring and commune troubles were disclosed by refugees last winter.

Chinese circles here have accused Peiping of maladministration and lack of consideration for the people.

Food shortages developed about the same time that record gains in food production were being announced from Peiping, critics said. Hong Kong became aware of the shortages from refugee disclosures and an increasing number of written pleas from relatives and friends in China for food.

The critics said much of Peiping's troubles had resulted from indiscriminate demands on producers.

According to statistics compiled here from various Chinese Communist reports, it was estimated that 77,187,500 long tons of foodstuffs had been taken from farmers by the Government last year.

This tonnage included rice, wheat, millet and kaoliang (grain sorghums) collected as taxes and enforced Government purchases from producers. The official grain yield as reported by Peiping last year was 375,-000,000 long tons—a figure challenged strongly by anti-Communists. A long ton is 2,240 pounds.

Many observers believe Peiping actually took slightly more than one-third of the entire food production of mainland China—a percentage considered far too high to maintain adequate food supplies in the face of poor distribution and natural disasters.

Exports to the Soviet Union and Soviet-bloc states in Eastern Europe in exchange for raw materials and industrial products were known to consist of much of the agricultural production. Exports to neutralist nations in Asia and Africa also were known to drain China's food supplies substantially.

August 2, 1959

Chinese Reds Shift Top Military Men

By TILLMAN DURDIN
Special to The New York Times.

HONG KONG, Sept. 17—Communist China changed the top leadership of its armed forces today.

The Peiping Government announced that Marshal Lir Piao had been named to replace Marshal Peng Teh-huai as Minister of Defense.

Marshal Lo Jui-ching has been appointed to succeed Gen. Huang Ko-cheng as Army Chief of Staff.

Marshal Lo was shifted from the position of Minister of Public Security, which he had held for ten years. This post was given to Gen. Hsieh Fu-chih, former military commander of Yunnan and head of the Yunnan provincial Communist party.

No new appointment was announced for General Huang.

Marshal Lo once served as political commissar for Marshal Lin. His appointment may mean sterner attention to loyalty and discipline in the armed forces.

The military changes were made simultaneously with the granting of pardons on a wide scale to persons undergoing punishment for political and ordinary crimes and counter-revolutionary activities. The pardons were given in connection with the tenth anniversary of the Chinese Communist regime, to be celebrated Oct. 1.

There was no indication how many prisoners would be affected.

Stigma to Be Removed

These developments were revealed in a Peiping radio broadcast. It said the measures had been approved by the standing committee of the People's Congress (Parliament) and the State Council, or Cabinet.

The pardons were proposed by the Communist Central Committee in decisions signed by Mao Tse-tung, chairman, last Monday.

The broadcast also said the Central Committee had decided that "bourgeois rightist elements, who have shown both in expression and deeds that they have duly reformed and turned over a new leaf, will hereafter not be designated as rightist elements."

This means that many professors, minor party members and intellectuals who were branded as rightists during the big 1957-58 "rectification" movement will have the label removed.

Observers here were hesitant about assessing the significance of the military changes.

The shift in leadership brought into the defense post, at the age of 51, one of Communist China's youngest military men and relieved, at 58, one of its toughest fighters. Marshal Peng commanded Chinese forces during the Korean War.

Marshal Lin's appointment suggested a possible tightening of relations with the Soviet Union. For the last year he has headed a committee, under the Communist Politburo, charged with planning the modernization of the armed forces. The committee has worked with a Soviet military commission, including four generals.

It has been reliably reported that reorganization plans call for revamping the "human-wave" type of ground forces into streamlined divisions capable of using the most modern equipment, including nuclear weapons.

Divisions are reported to have been changed into the pentomic type being used by the United States. The armed forces are estimated to number 2,500,000 men.

A Bold Commander

Marshal Lin established a reputation as a bold, clever commander during the Japanese war and in the subsequent conflict between Communists and Nationalists for control of China.

He was a successful guerrilla leader against the Japanese. Wounded in March, 1939, he was sent to Moscow for treatment.

There he studied military science, and on his return to Communist wartime headquarters at Yenan, was made head of the military academy, called the Military Political University for Resisting Japan.

After the Japanese war, Marshal Lin organized Communist troops in Manchuria. They eventually conquered the entire northeast for the Reds. For a period after the Communist takeover of the mainland he was political and military head of the central-south region, with headquarters at Hankow.

He dropped out of sight in 1952 and was reported sick with tuberculosis or recuperating from wounds suffered in Korea. He began to reappear in public about a year ago.

He is a member of the Politburo's standing committee and a vice-chairman of the Central Committee. Since the early days of the Communist rebellion in Kiangsi, he has been a favorite of Mr. Mao and Marshal Chu Teh, former Commander in Chief.

Marshall Peng was also an effective commander during warfare against the Japanese and the Nationalists. He became deputy commander of Communist forces under Marshal Chu.

Unlike Marshal Lin, however, he has little formal education, having run away from his peasant home in Hunan when a boy to join the army.

Stocky and with graying, close-cropped hair he remains a Vice Premier of the regime and a member of the Politburo and the Central Committee.

The new Chief of Staff is a year older than Marshal Lin. One of the inner circle of leaders, Marshal Lo has been known chiefly as director of vast secret and regular police forces.

General Huang, 60, was Chief of Staff only eleven months. He was suddenly put into the job last fall after the cease-fire at Quemoy to replace Gen. Su Yu.

Little is known of General Ssieh, the new 61-year-old security chief. He has been in Yunnan for years where he has dealt with Burma border problems.

PEIPING ACCUSES 'RIGHTISTS' ANEW

Says They Seek to Damage Solidarity and Discipline of the Communist Party

PEIPING, Dec. 19 (Reuters)—Dissident "Rightist opportunists" among China's nearly 14,000,000 Communists, under fire for months for opposing basic party policies, were accused today of undermining party solidarity and discipline.

A long article in the party's theoretical journal, Red Flag, also charged them with having "anarchist views" and "sowing disagreement," carrying on "factional activities" and seeking freedom to indulge in "anti-party activities inside the party."

The article, which said their viewpoints were soaked with "bourgeois individualism and liberalism," repeated earlier accusations that they wanted to pave the way for the return of capitalism.

The article said the present struggle against the "Rightist opportunists"—whom it did not name but described as only a "handful"—concerned the fate of the country and people.

Though the opportunists have committed serious errors, the party still wants to win them over, the article continued, but "if they stick to their faults and are unwilling to correct them, then it is only themselves who should bear the responsibility."

All party members were urged to "carry on criticism and self-criticism, raise political consciousness, strengthen the training of their party spirit and overcome tendencies of bourgeois individualism, liberalism and anarchism so that the whole party will be even more closely united around the Central Committee and Comrade Mao Tse-tung."

Red Flag said the opportunists put forward "absurd" arguments that there was no democracy in the party because it would not let them speak.

CHOU SAYS CHINA PLANS TO DOUBLE BUILDING EFFORT

Maps Vast Rise in Spending in Second 5-Year Period— Promises Higher Pay

By Reuters.

PEIPING, Sept. 16—Premier Chou En-lai forecast today big increases in Communist China's revenue during the second Five-Year Plan, beginning in 1958. He also foresaw a doubling of expenditures on construction and substantial wage rises.

In a report to the Eighth Congress of the Chinese Communist party, Mr. Chou said it was possible for the total national income from 1958 through 1962 to increase by 50 per cent over the total for the previous five years.

On investment in capital construction, he said, proposals for the new plan estimate an increase from 35 per cent of the nation's over-all revenue to about 40 per cent.

Because of the increase in over-all revenue expected during the second Five-Year Plan, this will mean that the "actual amount of money spent on the second Five-Year Plan would be twice that spent on the first Five-Year Plan," Mr. Chou declared.

According to published figures (though this was not included in the part of the speech released to non-Communist foreign correspondents) the target for 1952-57 investment was equivalent to about $28,000,000,000.

Big Rise in Output Seen

Mr. Chou said the value of China's industrial production in 1962 would be double that originally planned for 1957, and the value of agricultural production would be 35 per cent higher than the 1957 goal. But he emphasized that most of the 1957 targets already had been exceeded.

The only concrete figure given to correspondents was that for grain production, which would total about 1,100,000,000 tons for the full period of the second Five-Year Plan.

Annual production in 1962 would be roughly 250,000,000 tons, according to the estimates. This would be about 60,000,000 tons above the target for 1957, which the Chinese hope will be exceeded this year despite floods, drought and typhoons. But observers felt the goal was not so ambitious as some earlier statements had indicated.

Mr. Chou said that if agricultural production went according to plan, peasants would be able to increase their earnings 25 to 30 per cent. He estimated that workers' wages also would show an average increase of 25 to 30 per cent.

On rough estimate, the Premier said, the amount of consumer goods available both in cities and in the country would increase by 50 per cent over the 1957 targets.

He said that commercial organizations should organize some free markets, under the leadership of the state, to meet the needs of the people. He predicted that market prices would continue to be stabilized, but warned that some adjustment would be made in prices that were unreasonable. He called the new plan "vigorous, stable and realistic."

The Premier asserted that industrial development, with stress on heavy industry, was the core of the country's Socialist transformation, but said all forms of development should be integrated to achieve a balanced economy.

He said that improvement of communications was one of the fundamental tasks of the second Five-Year Plan. Recently production and commerce in some areas of China have been brought virtually to a standstill by traffic congestion.

Both Mr. Chou and Teng Hsiao-Ping, who gave a report on "Revision of the party's Constitution," mentioned decentralization of authority and control, which has been one of the main themes of the Congress so far. The Premier said local authorities must undertake more and more responsibility for industrial production.

September 17, 1956

MILITIA IN CHINA HAS A CIVIL TASK

Movement Takes on Aspect of a Disciplined Force for Work Program

By TILLMAN DURDIN

Special to The New York Times.

HONG KONG, Oct. 17—The "everyone-a-soldier movement" in Communist China looks to observers here more like a work program than anything else.

The movement is described in publicity from Peiping as an effort to enroll every able-bodied man and woman in the country in the militia. This home defense force, Peiping statements say, is being formed to prepare the entire nation gainst possible invasion by "American Imperialists."

If all the figures that have appeared in Peiping newspapers recently for militia enrollments in individual provinces are added up, the total approaches 100,000,000. Everyone physically fit between the ages of 16 and 50 is subject to enlistment. On this basis the total could eventually mount to the vicinity of 300,000,000.

Militiamen and women do elementary drilling practice with rifles, but it is believed that only key personnel, mostly former soldiers, get permanent possession of weapons.

The militia members primarily work in the fields, factories and offices. Their militia training and discipline facilitates control of their activities.

Creation of the militia formations was made one of the primary tasks of the new communes that have been formed from the merger of collective farms. The commune directors will have charge not only of growing and marketing crops but of factories, transportation, sports, schools, stores—in fact every phase of life in the communal area, including the militia.

In decreeing the formation of the communes, the Communist authorities have emphasized that life in them is to be in a military pattern, with the militia providing the organizational framework. Dispatches from Communist China speak of militia groups marching to work, with the inevitable songs celebrating the joys of farm work, and going about their tasks in general as organized units.

Peiping has used the war tensions growing out of the Taiwan Strait situation to push the new militia force, which appears to be a wholesale enlargement of the more genuinely military and much smaller pre-1958 militia. By using patriotic appeals and generating fears of invasion by the United States, the Communists have been able

to form the communes, with their militarized system of organization, much more quickly than would otherwise have been the case.

Some experts here on China believe the militia movement is to some extent taking the place of the nation-wide rectification, or ideological remolding, campaign that has now lasted more than a year and has run its course. The militia movement seems to be used, like the rectification drive, as another method of indoctrination and control and of producing a disciplined work force. Its relation to defense of the country is regarded as largely coincidental.

October 19, 1957

BIG-POWER STATUS HELD PEIPING GOAL

China Reds Are Working Tirelessly to That End, Visiting Editor Says

This is the second of four articles on Communist China by Walton A. Cole, the editor of Reuters, who recently returned from a visit to that country.

LONDON, Feb. 24—Determination to fulfill what they believe to be China's destiny as a leading world power, if not the leading power, is the motive that drives political chiefs and department officials charged with modernizing that nation of 650,-000,000 people.

They do not spare themselves, and so set an example to all. It is commonplace for an official appointment to be fixed in a time range of 7 A. M. to 10 P. M. Not infrequently the chief of a diplomatic mission in Peiping is summoned for consultation at 4 A. M. and finds that senior officials who wish to talk to him have been in continuous study session on some subject since dinner time.

Like all workers except those on the land, the officials ostensibly have an eight-hour day and a six-day week, exclusive of meal hours. But such is the fervor for work that no one I met appeared to give the slightest thought to adhering to such duty schedules.

Superficially, it might seem that the Chinese Communist

leaders must be in a vacuum regarding the day-to-day occurrences in the outside world. These occurrences have little or no place in the Chinese press or on the radio. But by means of intelligently compiled news digests, based in the main on the monitoring of all available radio and news sources, and by scrutinizing the world's daily and periodical press, they are among the best informed individuals on current affairs that I have met.

U. S. Denounced by Press

The world outside, as seen through these digests, cannot appear other than topsy-turvy when compared with the accounts in the Chinese press of the always-"correct" and "unified" Communist bloc. Capitalism and its "handmaiden, imperialism" are condemned. The condemnation is directed against the Government of the United States or the "ruling capitalist clique"—never the American people as such.

Bitter things are said and written about the United States. The United States is accused of trying to encircle the Communist countries, of stimulating war fear so that its armament industries will buoy up its economy and of giving aid to underdeveloped countries only to create markets for its own goods.

Peiping's leaders frankly admit that China is short of foreign currency and is a "backward country." They advocate barter deals as the basis of foreign trade, but assert that in no circumstances would they accept any outside aid to which strings were attached.

Struggling to build up their own industries through a series of ambitious five-year plans, they have selected Britain as the industrial nation whose output must be surpassed by 1972. By then China's population will be sixteen times that of Britain.

Workers are exhorted toward the goal of surpassing Britain by posters prominently displayed in factories.

One poster read: "The 1972 goal for China is 40,000,000 tons of steel [eight times current output], equaling estimated British production." (Current British steel production is at an annual rate of 21,000,000 tons.) Another poster read: "Workers of this factory shall resolutely accomplish their avowed task in the first quarter of 1958, during which, in 144,000 working hours, we shall produce three medium-size turbines, two large turbines and one high-powered specialized turbine."

Two Races Are Depicted

Wall cartoons have the same theme: a tweed-jacketed John Bull astride a snorting ox over which leaps a Chinese steeplechaser on a magnificent horse; or Soviet and Chinese athletes outstripping in individual races a fat, bespectacled American with cigars draped round his running kit and a barrel-waisted

Englishman in a top hat and a garishly checked tweed vest.

Zeal for building the new China is propagated everywhere. Giant billboards portray the features of "model workers" who have excelled at their jobs: Sung Ta-chen, a bridge worker with 500 rivets a day to his credit, or Ten Yu-hou, a successful pig farmer with a national record for not losing piglets.

A Scottish sea captain from Alexandria, Dumbartonshire, who was staying at the same hotel at Canton, told me that never in thirty years' experience of all the ports of the world had he had a 7,000-ton general cargo unloaded so quickly as that week in Shanghai. Working day and night in relays, the dockers unloaded his vessel in slightly less than one-third of the fastest turn-around time he had ever had before.

In a turbine factory I visited near Shanghai, a drum beat at noon and bells rang while workers dashed to hear the latest production statistics. They greeted the statistics with excited cheers, as though they were hearing football results.

Monthly Wage Is About $23

The factory operates on three eight-hour shifts, with free meals for night workers. Most city factory workers appear to have an average income of about $23 a month, although the national average for China is more like $23 a year—the peasant, of course, living in the main off the land.

Chung Ming, chairman of the Shanghai Trade Union Council, told me there were 16,000,000 trade union members in China. In any plant or factory there is only one trade union. Dues are paid by the members themselves and amount to about 1.5 per cent of a man's wage, which in most factories would be in the $23-to-$25-a-month range. Of this, the worker may pay $2 a month for a three-room apartment. Union membership is said to be optional, but there appear to be few abstainers.

"The trade unions are organized to enable the workers to accomplish the state plans and observe the laws promulgated by the state," Mr. Chung said. "A function of the trade union is to insure that the executives of all enterprises carry out the state plans fully and discharge all tasks that have been set.

"When individual executives violate the state laws and so harm the interests of the state, the trade union is responsible for protecting the interests of the working class by intervention.

"There is a democratic system in all factories enabling workers' councils to discuss plans of the enterprise together with the executives and express their opinions. Where executives make mistakes or have obvious shortcomings, the workers are at liberty openly to criticize through meetings and wall newspapers.

"The management has to answer openly and frankly all these criticisms and to make self-criticism before the workers. Where mistakes are serious and there is no attempt to eradicate them, the workers' council may decide to recommend that the executive should be removed."

Union Officials Criticized

Trade union officials themselves are subject to "self-criticism and discipline," which, in Mr. Chung's words, are the "watchwords of trade unionism in China."

"We are criticized as officials for not making a sufficiently efficient organization for the workers to achieve full production, and for a tendency not to go to factories and spend time with the workers, and indeed work there," he said. "Now all the officials in the trade union movement spend at least one day a week working on the benches in factories with the workers."

Mr. Chung said many troubles were settled by the workers themselves. One man was habitually late for work. Solution: all chip in and buy him an alarm clock. Another was depressed and careless. He had wife trouble. Fellow workers reconciled them and the man is now said to be a "model worker."

This criticism is a vital part of the much-publicized "rectification" campaign aimed at increasing efficiency and, incidentally, exposing those who hold "rightist" ideas.

February 25, 1958

CHINA ORGANIZING A PEASANT FORCE

By HARRY SCHWARTZ

The organization into communes of Communist China's 500,000,000 rural population has been depicted by the Peiping radio in military as well as economic terms.

The communes are being pushed at a frantic pace throughout the Chinese countryside.

The Peiping radio reported Tuesday that in Honan Province 99.98 per cent of the peasant population had already been organized in such communes.

In the new Chinese communes there are being combined agricultural, trade, industrial and military personnel and facilities over entire counties or townships. In many of them, the

Peiping broadcasts indicate, all significant vestiges of private property are being wiped out, including even the peasants' right to farm their own small garden plots or to raise their own pig or other livestock.

In essence, the aim of the communes, as given by the Peiping broadcasts, is "to organize along military lines, to do things the way battle duties are carried out, and to live collective lives." The radio added:

"The broad masses of the peasants, who have gone through the long years of the armed struggles of the people's revolution know perfectly well that military lines are not a thing to be feared. On the contrary, it is only natural to them that the whole population should be citizen soldiers ready to cope with the imperialist aggressors and their lackeys.

"Although the organization of agricultural labor along military lines at present is for waging battles against nature and not human enemies, it is nonetheless not difficult to transform one kind of struggle into another. If and when external enemies dare to attack us, the entire armed population will be mobilized to wipe out the enemies resolutely, thoroughly and completely."

Exceeds Soviet Aims

The new communes being formed throughout China apparently go far beyond anything now existing in the Soviet Union, and even beyond the recommendations of Premier Nikita S. Khrushchev. Early last month Western experts thought the new Chinese communes were simply the application to Communist China of Premier Khrushchev's program for amalgamating small collective farms and for creating "agrogorodi," or farm, cities.

Even private family households are apparently destined to disappear in the new communes, where the "collective way of life" is to be the rule. The communes are said to be forming large numbers of public canteens, nurseries, kindergartens, tailoring teams and the like, so as "to make full use of labor power, to enable women to play full part in field work, and to insure that there is no waste of the labor time of men and women."

The organization of the farm communes appears to have a close connection with Communist China's present effort to make a "great leap forward" in all spheres of economic activity. Presumably the program for the "great leap forward" envisages the building of major new factories, irrigation works, canals, and other similar extensive capital improvements that will require large numbers of workers, such as will be provided by the militarized organization of Chinese peasants under the new commune system.

September 7, 1958

NEHRU IS PUZZLED BY NEWS OF CHINA

India 'Trying to Get Facts' on Reds' Latest Activities, but Is Unafraid, He Says

By ELIE ABEL
Special to The New York Times.

NEW DELHI, India, Nov. 17 —The Prime Minister of India puffed gratefully on a cigarette at the end of a long, wearing day and talked of Communist China as of a neighbor down the street whose ways might be odd but whom there was no reason to fear.

Jawaharlal Nehru talked of what Peiping likes to call the great "leap forward" campaign —of millions of people being herded into communes, of steel furnaces sprouting in everyone's backyard, of peasants being marched to the fields like soldiers to the parade ground.

"It certainly makes people think," Mr. Nehru said. "We are intrigued by it. We are trying to get the facts. But we are not afraid of China in military terms, not at all. It is wrong to say that India keeps silent out of fear."

In hope of getting the facts on the sensational successes that Peiping proclaims almost daily, Mr. Nehru said, the Indian Government will soon be sending a small team of specialists into China. These experts hope to gauge Peiping's assertions against its achievements in the fields of agriculture, fertilizer production and village industries.

But the Prime Minister left no room for belief that China's way could ever be India's way.

"The Chinese more than any other people have a capacity for inner discipline," he said. "We Indians don't have it at all."

India, in fact, is moving in the opposite direction. Instead of regimenting the villagers and telling them what to do, India is trying "to get millions of people on the move" by giving the peasants the widest possible autonomy to manage their own affairs, Mr. Nehru said.

"In the old days it was the landlord and the villagers who looked after the wells, tanks and irrigation channels," he went on. "Now the landlord is gone and the village must do it. Too often there is a feeling that the Government should do everything for them.

"That's why we must encourage self-reliance. It fits in to some extent with the old Indian tradition of village self-government."

The Prime Minister, in a reflective mood, received this correspondent in the study of his official residence last night.

The interview, which lasted ninety minutes, touched on many topics: the views of the late Mohandas K. Gandhi on the use of electricity in cottage industries, the problem of succession in a democratic government, last month's military coup in Pakistan and Mr. Nehru's frustrated desire to walk among the people of his country unrecognized.

He acknowledged that the Indian peasant was often conservative, that it was difficult to "pull him out of the old rut of habit." But the peasant can be moved, Mr. Nehru insisted, so long as he is made to see the goal ahead.

The Prime Minister made no exaggerated claims for India's community development program, designed to teach the peasants to help themselves, which has now spread to half the villages in this nation of villages. The results, Mr. Nehru said, are spotty: "both energy and passivity are present."

But in the 300,000 villages where the community development idea is at work, it has "made a difference to them," he said.

Mr. Nehru was asked whether he proposed to share part of his leadership burden with younger men, now that he was entering his seventieth year.

"How do you go about building someone to take your place?" he replied. "I don't understand all this talk about choosing a successor. Perhaps it is easier in a dictatorial regime; there you deal with smaller groups."

In a parliamentary democracy, Mr. Nehru seemed to suggest, the choice of a new leader cannot be preordained.

November 18, 1958

FULL COMMUNISM IS SEEN FOR CHINA

General Chu Predicts Red Goal Will Be Achieved in This Generation

By TILLMAN DURDIN
Special to The New York Times.

HONG KONG, Nov. 21—Gen. Chu Teh, Communist China's deputy chief of state, told a youth conference in Peiping today that "the Communist society that Communists have striven to achieve for more than a hundred years" would be realized in this generation.

He said the peopie of Communist China were pressing ahead through the organization of communes and the high speed development of industry and agriculture with the building of socialism and preparing of conditions "for the future transition from socialism to communism."

He said the Communist aim was to industrialize the entire country and run agriculture like a factory industry to "attain the highest world levels in the spheres of science and culture."

Greater Efforts Urged

General Chu, who is also vice chairman of the Central Committee of the Chinese Communist party, called on the 5,000 young men and women gathered for the second National Conference of Active Young Builders of Socialism to exert their utmost efforts, "together with the remainder of the people of the whole country, to achieve ever greater victories." He said 1959 would be decisive as the second year of the three-year term Peiping has laid down for a maximum national effort to create a modernized prosperous country.

General Chu was the principal speaker at the opening of the youth meeting, which Peiping radio reports received here described as the occasion of festive enthusiasm. Gathering in Peiping's biggest stadium, the delegates sang songs and cheered the rostrum of top personalities, which included Premier Chou En-lai, Lin Po-chu, Gen. Ho Lung and leaders of the Communist party.

West Held Declining

Banners proclaiming "we must liberate Taiwan, Penghu, Quemoy and Matsu" were among those on display. General Chu also touched on this theme, although he did not give it prominence. The general hailed the advances of Communist China and other Communist countries and maintained that "day by day the camp of imperialism headed by the United States is declining."

The conference includes peasants, industrial workers, fisher-men, physicians, nurses, artists, teachers, truck drivers and servicemen.

The opening of the conference coincided with the announcement of several outstanding events in the construction field. The Peiping radio reported that the second of the world's two biggest open-hearth furnaces at the Anshan iron and steel works had gone into operation. The first began producing last month.

The Anshan plant is scheduled to produce 4,500,000 tons of steel this year, almost half of the plan for 10,700,000 tons.

It also was announced that tens of thousands of workers had begun the construction of a 190-mile irrigation canal at the bend of the Yellow River in Inner Mongolia. It is designed to irrigate 920,000 hectares (2,266,320 acres) of land and generate 70,000 kilowatts of electricity.

November 22, 1958

PEIPING ADMITS ERRORS

Communes Cause Discontent —Complaints Rectified

PEIPING, Dec. 13 (Reuters) —Chinese Communist newspapers have conceded mistakes in the running of the more than 26,000 communes set up in the last six months.

There also have been official reports of dissatisfaction, misgivings and even opposition to some aspects of mass life in the military-style social units.

Communist leaders have sent out thousands of inspection teams with the job of "reorganizing, consolidating and improving" the communes. The teams investigated peasant complaints about food and ordered improvements in the service in the public mess halls.

Criticism also was leveled at commune leaders who overemphasized military operations —a system under which the people are grouped in production brigades for greater discipline and efficiency.

A number of provinces reported new measures to make sure commune members got enough rest and to improve nurseries for workers' children.

Observers said the officialdom also appeared to be trying to eliminate fears that the commune system would destroy family life.

December 14, 1958

MAO RESIGNS POST AS CHIEF OF STATE; KEEPS PARTY JOB

Reason for Move by Chinese Red Leader Is Obscure— Communes Held Factor

SOVIET ROLE IS ASSAYED

Western Envoys in Warsaw Feel Khrushchev May Have Had a Hand in Decision

Dispatch of The Times, London.

HONG KONG, Dec. 16— Foreign Minister Chen Yi announced today that the Central Committee of the Communist party decided Dec. 10 to approve a suggestion by Mao Tse-tung that he give up his job as Chairman of the Chinese People's Republic.

Mr. Mao, who is 65 years old, will retain the leadership of the party and the people, the committee said.

No reason was given for the step, which means Mr. Mao will not ask the National People's Congress for a renewal of his mandate. There has been no indication from Peiping of Soviet influence despite suggestions to this effect abroad.

Diplomats Informed

Mr. Chen read a statement to the diplomatic corps. It said:

"The decision was taken by Mao Tse-tung in the interest of the party and the Chinese people. Mao will remain head of the party and of the people. If the situation demanded that Mao should again become President of the Republic, he can be re-elected to that office in accordance with a decision of the party."

Despite his well-known distaste for formalities and administration, Mr. Mao's decision may well be regarded as having more positive causes than weariness. It is almost certain that the long emergency session of the Central Committee in Wuhan produced some explosive speeches and reproaches on the consequences of the headlong pace represented by the commune program.

Constitutional Role

There is another aspect. It was carefully explained when the present Constitution was adopted in 1955 that the supreme governorship of the state was "vested in the standing Committee of the National People's Congress and the Chairman of the Republic.

"The Chairman of the Republic takes no part in the sessions of the Standing Committee, nor does he guide the work of the State Council, but he may convene the Supreme State Conference," it was further explained. Being elected by the National People's Congress and responsible to it, he cannot be opposed to the people; therefore he needs and has no veto."

Actually there has been increasing insistence on the party dictatorship that, in the last resort, has been wielded by Mr. Mao and increasing subordination of State Council, or cabinet, and all state organs both in the capital and in the provinces.

This was almost certainly a factor in the present crisis, since severe criticisms of state organs and bureaucracy were a prelude to the assumption of both party and administrative powers by party officials at all levels.

December 17, 1958

RED CHINA SLOWS COMMUNE DRIVE; PUSHES REFORMS

Party Delays Plans to Adopt New System in Big Cities— Cites Individual's Needs

By Reuters.

PEIPING, Dec. 18 — The Chinese Communist have slowed their dash toward communal living. A party resolution published here tonight calls a temporary halt to plans to set up large-scale communes in the big cities.

The 10,000-word document said the slowdown had been ordered because of the complex-ities of the sweeping social changes involved.

At the same time, it demanded improvements in the running of some of the 26,000 communes already established throughout China's rural areas.

The party called for great consideration for the individual well-being of an estimated total of 500,000,000 peasants being organized in these social units for communal life on military lines.

The resolution warned "over-eager" party members that the ultimate goal of communism was not so near nor so easily attained as some seemed to think. It advised them not to be in too big a hurry to complete the program.

Central Committee's Decision

The resolution was passed by the party's Central Committee at its twelve-day session that ended last week. At that time the committee also approved Mao Tse-tung's suggestion that he retire from his post as chairman of the Government.

Observers said the decisions on communes seemed to be the result of a pause for sober reflection after the exhilarating gallop of the last six months to increase industrial and agricultural production.

The party resolution apparently represented a shift of emphasis in party thinking from future prospects to present problems. It warned against getting "dizzy with success."

Wage incentives are still necessary to encourage "labor enthusiasm," the resolution said. The communes, in addition to being self-supporting, should seek to produce sufficient commodities to exchange for cash to meet the members' needs.

8 Hours' Sleep Prescribed

Fears that all private property such as houses, clothing, furniture and bank deposits would have to be surrendered to the communes must be dispelled, it went on.

In their enthusiasm for the production drive, the resolution said, party members should not neglect the well-being of the masses. The people should never have less than eight hours' sleep and four hours for meals and recreation daily, according to the document.

"In building residential quarters," it said, "attention must be paid to housing suited to the living together of men and women and the aged and young of each family."

December 19, 1958

PEIPING REPORTS HUGE GAINS IN '58

Reds Say Output of Major Farm and Industrial Goods Was Double 1957 Level

By TILLMAN DURDIN
Special to The New York Times.

HONG KONG, Dec. 31—A picture of great economic growth is given in a year-end review of accomplishments in Communist China for 1958 issued in Peiping today.

Hailing the overfulfillment of the 1958 economic plan, a Hsin-hua (New China) news agency dispatch broadcast from Peiping said the State Statistical Bureau estimated that the output of major industrial and agricultural products in Communist China for the last year had doubled or more than doubled the 1957 output.

Gross industrial output was reported to have been 60 per cent above 1957 in value.

The combined total of industrial and agricultural output was said to have increased 70 per cent. Living standards were said to have risen, but no figures were given.

Big Increase in Steel

The Statistical Bureau gave the following figures for major products:

Steel — 11,000,000 tons, more than double last year's output.

Machine Tools—More than 90,-000 in number, or more than three times 1957 output.

Coal—270,000,000 tons, more than double the 1957 output.

Electric Power — 27,500,000,000 kilowatt-hours, or 42 per cent above 1957.

Petroleum — 2,250,000 tons, 54 per cent more than 1957.

Cotton Yarn—6,660,000 bales, 43 per cent more than last year.

Cotton Cloth — 6,400,000,000 meters, 27 per cent more than 1957.

Investment in capital construction was estimated at the equivalent of $9,680,000,000, more than 87 per cent above last year and equal to approximately half the total investment for Communist China's First Five-Year Plan, which ended last year.

New Factories and Mines

Almost 700 large factories and mines were reported to have begun part or full operation. Thousands of small industrial enterprises, making steel, cement, fertilizer, machinery and other products, were installed.

The final figure on output of grains (including potatoes) was given as 375,000,000 tons, compared with 185,000,000 tons for last year. Cotton output was estimated at 3,500,000 tons, compared with 1,640,000 in 1957.

Output of soybeans, peanuts, rapeseed, sesame, hemp, jute, silk cocoons, tea and fruit was reported to have increased greatly. Output of tobacco, sugar cane and sugar beets was said to have been double or more than double 1957 levels.

Hsinhua said Communist China "has basically solved the problem of grain with a yield per capita amounting to 600 kilograms [1,322 pounds]. The agency asserted that "this has torn to pieces the imperialist reactionary assertion that China could not solve the contradiction between the rapid increase in its big population and the 'very slow increase in agricultural output.'"

Irrigation Extended

The report said the bumper harvests this year were made possible through construction of irrigation facilities for 32,000,000 hectares of farmland, renovation of low-lying waterlogged areas totaling 14,000,000 hectares, and effective control of soil erosion on 116,000 square miles of land. A hectare is 2.471 acres.

Improved farm techniques permitting huge per-hectare increases in yields was given as another reason for big harvests.

More than 1,300 miles of new railway tracks were reported laid, bringing the total mileage of railways open to traffic to approximately 20,000.

Domestic prices were reported to have been stable during the year, with a slight drop in retail prices of manufactured goods and a slight increase in purchasing prices for agricultural products bought from peasants by the state. The retail price index for twenty-nine major cities was said to have dropped .9 per cent compared with last year.

CHINA MIXES REWARDS TO SPUR ITS WORKERS

Although Materialism Is Attacked, Its Incentives Are Recognized

By PEGGY DURDIN
Special to The New York Times.

HONG KONG, Jan. 17—The recent remarks by Soviet Premier Khrushchev and First Deputy Premier Anastas Mikoyan on China's communes seem to have created a widespread impression that Communist China has abolished the system of using material incentives for labor. In fact, since the Chinese Communists came to power nine years ago, they have used wages and material rewards in one form or another as work incentives. It is true that this subject been recently debated in China's official press, and Peiping certainly wishes and endeavors to spread and strengthen the Communist "one for all" morality while gradually weakening any "selfish bourgeois" motivation.

There may be inner party differences on how fast this "education" can be accomplished. But Peiping has even been using the piecework system in factories and today it is paying wages and bonuses in the communes. Rebuking scattered overzealous and impetuous comrades in the communes who emphasized the principle of "everyone according to his need" at the expense of "everyone according to his work," the Communist party's Central Committee in December stated with the utmost clarity that material incentives in and outside the communes must operate now and continue to operate for a long time to come.

Vital Question

The question of incentive was a particularly vital one in 1958, the first year of the ambitious second five-year plan for China's 650,000,000 people.

Through 1958 virtually everyone — children, aged, blind, crippled, the faceless hordes of prisoners being "reformed through labor, nomads, primitive tribespeople and mothers of small children—worked to and beyond capacity. Eventually health and efficiency were so seriously affected that the party issued the dictum—after the steel quotas were reached and the crops gathered — that

everyone must get eight hours of sleep except in special rush periods.

Among the inducements Peiping used to increase production, material incentives figured largely. Like Americans, Chinese worked for food, clothes, housing, higher pay and promotion.

The urban population generally received wages without overtime. The Communists report, however, that those factory employes on a piece-work basis who increased their income 30 to 100 per cent made farmers and less fortunate workers jealous, sacrificed thoroughness to speed, avoided tough jobs and—worst of all—in an evil bourgeois manner "struggled for leather shoes, watches and woollen clothes" as one worker "brokenheartedly" admitted. After prolonged "education" Peiping says most of China's piecework laborers "voluntarily" demanded abolition of the system so they could "work for socialism, not money." They even reported refunding some of their extra earnings.

'Voluntary' Work

In rural areas, through most of 1958, each family in an agricultural collective received pay in proportion to the work points earned by family members in regular farm work, excluding a great range of "voluntary" activities. Further to increase production Peiping allowed peasants to tend small individual vegetable plots and keep a few pigs and fowl.

When almost all of China's 550,000,000 peasants had joined communes by the late summer and fall, the work-point system was replaced by fixed wages on the principle of "everyone according to his work" and by "free" benefits on the principle of "everyone according to his need."

While the party press indignantly was denying that "free services" would create "lazy-bones," evidently some poorer, less ambitious peasants slack-

ened efforts. Meanwhile formerly hardworking farmers, resentful of "eating the same dish" as their more shiftless neighbors, lost labor enthusiasm—particularly in communes where "good-hearted but impetuous" cadres announced that communism, waiting in the wings, forbade individual ownership of fowls and pigs and promised everyone all or most of the "ten guarantees"—free food, clothes, housing, schooling, medical care, burial, haircuts, theatre, heating and weddings.

Wage Decree

So the party's central committee firmly ruled in December that funds for wages would be larger and would increase faster than free benefits.

The party emphasized that material incentives would last a very long time, in fact until the far-off day when all goods were abundant, culture and selfless morality prevalent, and differences obliterated between the town and country worker and the manual and intellectual laborer.

The Communists admit the better the livelihood the better the work enthusiasm. But modernizing the country overnight has easy priority over individual benefits. In any case, material incentives alone could not make people who were long famous for their industry shoulder a labor load possibly now heavier than any in their history.

Certainly some Chinese are spurred on by political desire as well as job promotion—first they are named "model workers" then "activists" spearheading the party's campaigns and finally members of the sanctum sanctorum, the party, with the accompanying power prerequisites and the Mao-Marx version of Chinese "face."

Feverish Campaign

The Communists utilize cleverly the constant promises of future pie in the sky, hate, and xenophobia as well as national pride, patriotism and today's widespread Asian determination to be as strong and powerful as the West. Hence the exaggeration of achievements, the constant use of the phrase "miracles never before seen in history of world" which boasts that China achieved in twelve months an increase in coal production which took Britain thirty-two years. As the Chinese farm workers are plunged into one tense, fevered campaign after another they are almost mesmerized by statements that everyone loves selfless labor, by competition among groups, by repetition of goals like surpassing Britain in less than fifteen years, by constant "shock" and superhuman efforts followed by further upgrading of production targets.

Insulated from other worlds, they are bombarded with work propaganda via officials, activists, banners, wall murals, newspapers, cartoon books, magazines, radio, movies, plays, loudspeakers at work sites and even New Year posters. Additionally the Chinese appear to be subject to a kind of fatigued self-hypnotism through constant meetings where people must voice doubts on loaded queries like "will increased production help our motherland" and finally express complete conviction. There is also a clever element of self-hypnosis in the insistence that every Chinese write poetry and stories about love for the party and for the backbreaking "great leap forward."

Fear Used

Among the work incentives fear must also be mentioned. With security officials everywhere, it is unsafe to strike or refuse labor and to express anger or despair at overwork even to members of one's family and closest friends, who can "gain merit" by tattling. For venting disgust or complaints one can be ostracized and worked over around the clock by the party activists and groups in terrifying sessions of public criticism. Expressions of discontent may be labelled as such dark crimes as "fabricating rumors" or "sabotaging construction," for which punishment may be banishment to border areas, reform through labor or the more severe penalties as a counterrevolutionary, landlord or rich peasant.

Perhaps it is safe to conclude that outside the party most Chinese work bitterly hard because they must and some, particularly among the young, because they want power, approval or prestige status for China. It is certainly safe to say that the Chinese Communist party has been and is clever enough to see that none of these factors singly or combined would suffice without the basic "bourgeois" material incentive.

FUGITIVE CHINESE DECRY COMMUNES

Special to The New York Times.

HONG KONG, Jan. 29—Seven Chinese fishermen who escaped with 906 others from the mainland in recent months said today they had fled because of intolerable conditions in the communes.

"We had to work eighteen hours each day for the commune and all our catches of fish went to the Government," they said. "We were forcibly separated from our families."

The seven men were Chung Sung, Tsui Tam-shing, Tsui Ng, Lee Mar-lai, Chung Fan, Lee Tam and So He. They told their stories in the offices of the Hong Kong Fishing Industry and Commercial General Association.

They said they were forced to join communes last August and immediately put on work shifts of 6 A. M. until midnight, seven days a week.

Their wives and children were ordered ashore for manual labor and forbidden to return to their men.

They were forced into the labor production movement, Tsui Ng, a weather-beaten man in his mid-thirties, said.

"Women and children between the ages of 13 and 55 were put to work at the hardest labor, earth-carrying and construction," he continued. "Women over 55 were each given twenty-five children to care for."

The fishermen said that during the first month in the commune they were given $6 Chinese currency (about $2.40 United States currency) to support their families ashore and 30 cents a day Chinese money for their own labor and food.

But in mid-September, they said, the $6 payment was stopped and they were paid $1.50 Chinese money every eight days.

They said that in their area, near Swabue, there were no physicians to attend the sick, and that bodies of the dead were made into fertilizer.

They escaped, they said, by pleading sick and getting permission to go ashore in search of medicinal herbs. During the night they stealthily collected their families, reboarded their junks and unfurled their sails. They reached Hong Kong waters in twelve hours, they said, after eluding two armed patrol junks.

RED CHINA COURTS GO TO COMMUNES

Campaign Enforced in Field by Mobile Judicial Units That Do Farm Work

By TILLMAN DURDIN
Special to The New York Times.

HONG KONG, Feb. 10—The courts last year operated as an integral part of Communist China's high-pressure production drive. They were also powerful instruments in enforcing acceptance of the country's new system of communes.

Judges, procurators and security men often went as teams into the fields and factories and dealt out summary judgments on the spot. Public trials were frequent and in many instances the persons on trial were accused and denounced at organized mass meetings.

Mainland China's regional newspapers for the last few months, now available here, provide a record of these judicial activities through a series of reports of operations during 1958 of the provincial courts.

Murder and Arson Alleged

For example, The Hopei Daily News of Tientsin dated Oct. 29 revealed a new outcropping of "nefarious activity" in Hopei last September shortly after the establishment of the communes and simultaneously with the start of a campaign for making iron and steel in small rural furnaces.

A report on the Higher People's Court of Hopei said former landlords, former rich peasants, "counter-revolutionaries and bad elements" had "manufactured rumors to disturb the people" and "carried out large-scale poisoning and committed arson and murder."

The Higher Court report said

courts in all parts of the province "promptly sent cadres deep into the front lines and in cooperation with public security procuratorial agencies took measures for preventing sabotage by the enemy." Crimes were dealt with "openly on the spot so that the work of the courts was combined with the party's central tasks and with the production work of the broad masses."

One former rich peasant was reported to have put arsenic in food being prepared for the members of a commune. "An anti-Socialist element" in the Tangshan steel works was caught trying to blow up blast furnaces by putting old cannon shells in coke.

The sentences imposed on these persons were not specified. The Higher Court report, however, made clear that the courts operated among the workers and peasants and dealt with laggards, malcontents and the opposition in drumhead fashion.

Punishments were meted out by judicial personnel who simultaneously were doing manual labor, according to the Kiangsi Higher Court report in The Kiangsi Daily News of Nanchang. The report told of seven judges in Shangjao County who disposed of sixty-three cases while they worked for sixteen days collecting manure and destroying sparrows, mosquitos, rats and flies.

The provincial court reports make clear that no objective rules were applied in the rough-and-ready judicial proceedings that have now become commonplace in Communist China. The sentences were prescribed in accordance with the political and economic requirements of the time and place and to serve the supremacy of the Communist party and its program. The Shansi report said that during the half-year period 11,352 counter-revolutionaries were "ferreted out," and 12,898 criminals found "among persons who roved about and elements whose background was not clear."

RED CHINESE TROOPS AID GROWTH PROJECT

Special to The New York Times.

HONG KONG, Feb. 25—The military services in Communist China are becoming increasingly important as a work force in the country's campaign for economic development.

Gen. Fu Chung, deputy director general of the political department of the Chinese Communist Army was quoted recently in the Communist press as having said the manpower assigned by the army to "Socialist construction" in 1958 was almost triple that of 1957.

No figures were given but from separate items in Chinese Communist newspapers in recent months it is evident that hundreds of thousands of army men are spending a large part of their time at building irrigation dams, helping farmers with collecting crops, transporting goods for civilian use, dredging rivers and assisting in operating workshops.

In addition, army, navy and air force men grow a large part of their own food in plots cultivated wherever they are stationed.

RED LAND REFORM IN CHINA TRACED

This article comes from Dr. Sripati Chandrasekhar, prominent Indian social scientist, who recently returned from extensive travel in Communist China.

© 1959 by The Associated Press.

It is natural that in any underdeveloped country the problem of agriculture and food supply should assume paramount importance. This is particularly true in China, where famine has stalked the land from time immemorial.

During the last 100 years, what with a series of wars with Western nations, Japanese aggression after 1931, a thirty-year civil war and World War II, there has been a constant state of political unrest, economic dislocation and recurring famine. China has not known peace for even two consecutive years during the last century.

About twenty-five years ago, when China, in the throes of widespread famine, appealed to the International Red Cross, the Red Cross declined help on the ground that it was designed to meet national emergencies but that famine in China was not an emergency but a chronic state of affairs.

No One Starves Now

The situation between 1946 and 1949 was so desperate that the price of a measure of rice, because of rocketing inflation, soared and kept changing from hour to hour.

What have the Communists done to solve the food problem?

While there was some shortage of food and famine three years ago, the problem has been solved today from the quantitative point of view. No one starves in China now. Though the common man does not have meat or fruit, everybody gets at least a bowl of rice and some cabbage.

This is saying a great deal when you remember that China's population today is about 650,000,000.

Any satisfactory solution of the food problem in Asian countries implies revolutionary changes in land ownership and methods of cultivation. The Chinese Communists have effected, by and large successfully, such drastic changes. Their agrarian reforms have passed through four distinct changes between 1949 and 1958.

Four Changes Listed

The first stage witnessed the public trials of landlords. And when the long-suffering peasantry knew that the new regime meant business, they accused the landlords of all the crimes known to man—from harsh treatment, withholding grain from a starving peasant's family, raping the peasant's daughter or taking his women as concubines, down to brutal murder.

It is possible that some landlords were guilty of these crimes, but there were no lawyers to defend them. Most landlords pleaded guilty for the simple reason that they knew their end was near no matter what their defense. It is estimated that about 2,000,000 landlords were executed.

The second stage involved the distribution of land to landless peasants. The average peasant received a few mou of land. (A mou equals about a sixth of an acre.)

Within two years the third stage was launched. It was said that private ownership of land was neither socialism nor communism, that it was both a serious economic barrier to greater production, so desperately needed, and a theoretical obstacle to Socialist reconstruction. Thus collectivization was ushered in.

The peasants were made to see the need for collective ownership, for intensive cultivation, use of abundant fertilizers and mechanization were impossible on tiny plots.

From a modest beginning of 300 cooperatives in 1952 the number rose to 14,000 in 1953 and to 600,000 in 1954. By the spring of 1956, China had 1,300,000 cooperatives. This meant that only a small number of the 500,000,000 peasants were outside the cooperatives.

But China was not yet out of the woods from the point of view of food supply.

Therefore the fourth and present stage—the people's communes, which were causing such heart-searching when I was in China.

February 19, 1959

Associated Press

MECHANIZATION IN COMMUNIST CHINA: Workers use harvesting machine in a rice paddy. Increased use of such equipment has been stressed in raising production.

OVERSEAS CHINESE CUT REMITTANCES

HONG KONG, Feb. 25 (AP) — The Chinese Communists' establishment of people's communes has led to a drastic drop in remittances from overseas Chinese.

According to a survey throughout Southeast Asia the drop amounts to several million dollars.

Estimates of the normal flow of funds through Hong Kong, the biggest funnel for remittances to Communist China, range from $3,000,000 to $8,000,000 a month. This has been cut 40 to 80 per cent since the communes were established, according to unofficial estimates.

The Foreign Exchange Control Bureau in Singapore reports that remittances dropped about 50 per cent in November and December, to the equivalent of $380,000 a month from $670,000.

A spokesman for 500,000 Chinese in the Philippines says remittances from that area have been reduced to a trickle. Saigon reports that Chinese in South Vietnam have virtually given up trying to send money home.

The Overseas Chinese are afraid the money will not reach their relatives. And if it does they are afraid the relatives will not be able to use it or, if they do, that it will be held against them.

February 26, 1959

Red China Reports Drought

PEIPING, June 3 (Reuters) —The Communist party newspaper People's Daily said thousands of acres of farmland in northeast, north and southwest China were suffering from a serious drought.

June 4, 1959

RED CHINESE MET MAIN 1958 GOALS

Grain, Steel and Coal Plans Exceeded, Peiping Reports —Cotton Output Short

PEIPING, April 15 (Reuters) —Communist China met its main production goals last year but fell short in its output of raw cotton and cotton textiles, according to official statistics published here today.

Harvests of two other staple crops, peanuts and rapeseed, both used for the production of vegetable oil, also appeared below earlier estimates, as did the total of pigs.

But in her 1958 "great leap forward" China achieved her ambitious production goals in three vital areas—steel, coal and grain.

The Hsinhua (New China) News Agency said the country's industrial and agricultural production had doubled and unemployment had been eliminated.

Steel production reached 11,-080,000 tons, more than double the 1957 figure. Pig iron production reached 13,690,000 tons, which was 2.3 times as much as in 1957. Grain output was 375,-000,000 tons, or double that of 1957. Coal was listed among items in which production more than doubled in 1958.

Nearly All in Communes

More than 99 per cent of the rural households by the end of 1958 were organized into people's communes.

About 1,000 large industrial and mining projects were listed as being under construction in 1958 and 700 were reported as having being put into full or partial operation, including fifty-four built with Soviet help.

Also listed were the irrigation of nearly 80,000,000 acres and the reforestation of about 66,000,000 acres, six times the area covered in 1957. About 6,200 miles have been added to inland shipping routes and work has begun on dredging and enlarging the Grand Canal, silted up for more than 100 years.

The figures were given in a communiqué issued by the State Statistical Bureau.

On the production of cotton yarn and cloth, it said textile mills turned out 6,100,000 bales of cotton yarn and about 6,175,-000,000 yards of cotton cloth in 1958. This was less than earlier official estimates by 560,000 bales of cotton yarn and 758,-333,000 yards of cotton cloth.

Observers also noted that the figure established today for the 1958 cotton crop, 3,319,000 tons,

was 31,000 tons less than the preliminary estimate announced at the end of last year.

The cotton goal originally was set at 3,500,000 tons last year. Observers recalled earlier Chinese press reports that the picking of last year's cotton harvest had been slowed because farm workers were diverted to steel making last fall.

April 16, 1959

Liu Succeeds Mao As Chief of State Of Peiping Regime

By Reuters.

PEIPING, April 27—Liu Shao-chi, a leading theoretician of the Chinese Communist party, was elected today to succeed Mao Tse-tung as Communist China's chief of state.

But Mr. Mao, the most revered figure in the Chinese Communist hierarchy, retains the all-important role of Communist party chairman. He announced in December that he would step out as Chairman of the Chinese People's Republic, a post corresponding to that of head of state.

Mr. Liu was elected to succeed Mr. Mao by the National People's Congress, which is meeting here. The 72-year-old Marshal Chu Teh, formerly Deputy Chairman of the republic, was elected chairman of the Standing Committee of the People's Congress, a post formerly held by Mr. Liu.

Chou Renamed Premier

Chou En-lai was re-elected Premier, a post he has held since the founding of the Communist regime in 1949.

Mr. Liu was elected chairman by a vote of 1,156 to 1. The one vote was cast for Tung Pi-wu, 73-year-old former Chief Justice of the Supreme Court.

Mr. Tung was elected one of the two deputy chairmen of the republic at today's Congress session. The other deputy chairman chosen was Mme. Sun Yat-sen. She is the 68-year-old widow of the founder of modern China and a sister of Mme. Chiang Kai-shek, wife of the Chinese Nationalist leader.

Mme. Sun had been one of six deputy chairmen in the first Government formed by the Communists when they came to power in 1949.

When news of Mr. Liu's election was announced, thousands of demonstrators, beating gongs, flying red banners and exploding firecrackers, poured into Peiping's Square of Heavenly Peace.

Girls in vivid green, blue and red silk dresses, waving colored scarves, danced to drums and the clash of gongs and cymbals while loudspeakers blared out a Chinese folk dance.

Peiping's main streets, usually dimly lighted, were aglow tonight. Hundreds of bulbs strung out along the curving roofs and eaves of main buildings illuminated their outlines against the night sky and red stars and neon signs shone from housetops.

Big, pumpkin-shaped red lanterns dangled from the Gate of Heavenly Peace at the entrance to the Imperial City. Processions beating drums marched past the gate carrying huge portraits of Mr. Liu and Mr. Mao.

Mr. Liu was regarded as one of the likely candidates to succeed Mr. Mao, but no word of his choice leaked out publicly before today. Mr. Liu remains a member of the policy-making Politburo and a deputy chairman of the Central Committee, and his new job seems to enhance his power.

Tall and slim, with an oval face usually set in a solemn, impassive expression and a crop of bushy hair brushed straight back, Mr. Liu is easy to pick out among the party leaders. Though physically striking, he has been out of the limelight shed on other Chinese Communist rulers.

An energetic organizer, Mr. Liu as a chief theorist in the Chinese party has been an important figure among those guiding the formation and building of the Communist state.

Observers do not expect any change in China's domestic or foreign policy to result from today's changes.

Some thought Mr. Liu's election might be an indication that Mr. Mao is beginning to move quietly into the background of the Chinese Communist scene.

It is thought likely that Mr. Mao now will devote more time to theoretical writing, perhaps summarizing and explaining the practical experience and achievements of the Chinese in own way.

It was Mr. Mao and Marshal Chu who, in 1928 in a South China mountain stronghold, formed the nucleus of the Communist army that was to attain power twenty years later.

They were still together in 1954 when Mr. Mao was elected Chairman of the Communist republic and Marshal Chu deputy chairman, the posts they left today.

In other congress business today, sixteen deputy chairmen

of the Congress Standing Committee were elected, including both the Panchen Lama and the Dalai Lama of Tibet.

The Panchen Lama, installed by the Chinese as ruler of Tibet after last month's revolt, got 1,152 votes. The Dalai Lama, who fled into exile in India during the revolt, polled the fewest of the sixteen, with 1,108.

The Dailai Lama, who the Chinese say went into exile "under duress," was a deputy chairman of the old committee, but the Panchen Lama was only an ordinary member.

More than 2,000 persons, including Central Asian tribesmen in bright costumes and Buddhist monks in saffron robes, gave Mr. Mao a standing ovation when he walked into the meeting hall for today's Congress session.

They rose again to applaud Mr. Liu when his nomination was approved.

Nominations of the new leaders were approved by delegates of the Congress, which opened here ten days ago, in a closed session on Sunday in preparation for today's formal nomination and election.

Unanimity Is Doubted

TOKYO, April 27 (AP)—An indication that the Chinese Communist leaders had not been unanimous in the nomination of Mr. Liu earlier this month came from the Peiping radio. Implying that there was some opposition to Mr. Liu's elevation, it said cryptically that he "had the support of a large segment of party members." There has been speculation that Mr. Chou and Mr. Liu are rivals for Mr. Mao's mantle of power.

Chief Justice Tung was replaced in the Supreme Court by Hsien Chueh-tsai, who has been Interior Minister. The Chief Prosecutor, Chang Ting-cheng, was re-electted.

April 28, 1959

RED CHINA URGES 'REALISTIC' GOALS

By GREG MacGREGOR
Special to The New York Times.

HONG KONG, June 14—Indications that Communist China might fail this year in achieving certain announced production goals appeared recently in an official party publication.

Calling for establishment of production targets on a "more realistic" basis, Hongqi (Red Flag) stated in an editorial.

"These targets should not be formulated in the imagination of a handful of persons behind closed doors."

"In fixing production targets,

we should refrain from wishful thinking, from replacing reality with imagination and from thinking that the higher the targets the better," the editorial stated bluntly, in what appeared to be an indirect admission of some production failures.

It then went on to point out the futility of setting production goals such as those in agriculture at two to three times the maximum yield for purposes of submitting impressive figures.

"We should first carry out practical inspections and analyses on the volumes of production on the various pieces of land in 1958, the possible increase that may be brought about this year, dependable measures for increasing production and other realistic conditions," the editorial continued.

"The planned targets should be fixed most realistically, considering local manpower, material and financial resources, the extent to which the men may develop their subjective enthusiasm, various other favorable conditions, realistic difficulties, and measures to be taken to solve such difficulties."

The editorial stated that the practice of setting production targets 10 to 20 per cent below the highest output levels was commendable. It said such a system would not only be reasonable but would also leave room for certain teams and individuals to stand out by exceeding production goals.

"We emphasize that production targets must be set on a realistic basis because we want to keep our two feet on the ground," the editorial said.

It added that if targets were more realistic workers would become more determined and enthusiastic. It also said that impossible targets destroyed worker initiative and, consequently, failed to achieve the very objective of the entire "leap forward" program.

June 15, 1959

RED CHINA ADMITS '59 FARM SETBACK

By GREG MacGREGOR
Special to The New York Times.

HONG KONG, June 20—The Chinese Communists have reported that agricultural goals will not be met this year.

"This year some communes have scored an increase in unit area yield, but total sowing areas were much less than last year," an official said last week. "Thus there was actually no increase and in some cases

there were even decreases reported."

Grain production in Communist China last year totaled 375,000,000 tons, according to the annual production report issued early this year from Peiping. The grain production goal set for this year was 525,-000,000 tons.

"We cannot carry out immediately the new system of reaping more while planting less because our country's agricultural production is still not high-yielding generally," the Peiping newspaper Hsinmin Jihpao (People's Daily) which is generally regarded as the official spokesman for the Chinese communist party, said in an editorial.

"In order to be high-yielding we need tractors, large amounts of chemical fertilizer, modern agricultural machinery and effective insecticide devices," the publication explained.

"At present our country does not have the above-mentioned prerequisites."

The tone of the editorial was different from boasts earlier this year that great advances had been made. At that time the paper said that Chinese Communist ideology "has seized the mandate of heaven and man at last can defy nature and defeat it in its most vicious moods."

Floods that have hit almost every province in China this year were responsible for the huge agricultural losses. However, Peiping said that "more realistic" goals should be set in the future.

"The agricultural production of our country is highly dependent on natural changes," the editorial in Hsinmin Jinpao continued in a subdued tone. "Sometimes we can have a bumper harvest one year and sometimes a poor harvest in another.

"Under such circumstances the system of reaping more while planting less is unsafe—it can even be dangerous and harmful."

The most damaging flood in the history of Kwantung Province struck June 11 and it was reported yesterday that millions of peasants were fighting the flood waters.

North of the Yellow River drought took its annual toll, while hailstorms flattened wheatfields in Shantung Province on the northeast coast, damaging houses and creating a need for emergency rations.

The rapid transition to communes last year was believed by many observers to have been the basic cause of the distribution bottlenecks and confusion in production areas.

Workers were shifted and problems arose from the revolutionary change-over that have been felt severely this year. Acute food shortages in the cities have been among the most serious recent results.

June 21, 1959

FACTORIES REPORTED CLOSING IN RED CHINA

BELGRADE, Yugoslavia, July 19 (UPI)—The Peiping correspondent of the Yugoslav Communist newspaper Borba reported today that thousands of Chinese industrial enterprises founded this year were being closed, and that "millions" of workers were being transferred from industry to agriculture.

"Return to the village again" is the latest slogan of the Red Chinese Government, the correspondent, Djordje Bogojevic, reported.

"The workers were originally simple peasants who were transferred in millions from their land to steel production, industry, mines, transport and capital construction," he wrote.

But now, he said, "tremendous masses of new workers have nothing to do in the new factories and are now encouraged by Peiping to return to their villages and fields."

The report added that shortages of raw materials had caused many enterprises to operate only a few hours a day, making hundreds of thousands of workers virtually idle.

July 20, 1959

CRITICISM ON RISE AGAIN IN RED CHINA

Curbs on Discussion Eased —Commune Rules Altered to Let Families Cook

By GREG MacGREGOR
Special to The New York Times.

HONG KONG, July 26—Reports are increasing here of open criticism in Communist China of that country's leadership. In addition, there are many recent indications of changes in major mainland policies.

These changes include a retreat from rigid commune principles, revision of farming methods, de-emphasis of "back-

yard" steel production and revision of urban food-production systems.

Since the curtailment two years ago of the campaign to "let a hundred flowers bloom, let a hundred schools of thought contend," criticism has been discouraged. It was generally believed that the Chinese Communists sensed serious problems ahead if an unexpected surge of criticism was allowed to continue.

The ensuing period of virtually unopposed party dominance led to a leadership in Peiping of unprecedented dictatorial powers, political observers have reported.

However, an increasing number of setbacks and failures of mainland projects this year are believed to have led Peiping toward encouraging more freedom of thought and constructive criticism.

As early as last April, for example, Premier Chou En-lai cautioned party members that they must "not blame the ones who speak but take every criticism as a warning."

Last month Tao Chu, head of Communist party in Kwangtung Province, moved even further back toward the abandoned "blooming flowers" campaign of the national party leader, Mao Tse-tung, Mr. Tao said:

"We should allow everyone to air his views freely as long as the views are based on the spirit of promoting Socialist construction. Some comrades have feared that discussions on shortcomings might be taken advantage of by the reactionaries, but even if we do not talk about them the reactionaries will trump up harmful rumors."

Mainland publications quickly fell into line to point out that "even the sun has spots" that detract from its perfection.

"To hear both sides makes one clever; to hear one makes one stupid," Jenmin Jihpao (People's Daily) said. "Opinions antagonistic to our own are not necessarily wrong. The majority need not be right; once Chairman Mao himself was in the minority."

Whether the new policy of encouraging criticism would be accepted by Chinese intellectuals was a matter of considerable doubt here. The sharp policy revision of 1957 with its resulting suppression of free thought and open criticism was undoubtedly still clear in the memories of the Chinese people, observers here said.

The evidence of a retreat from rigid commune principles has aroused interest here recently.

The most convincing evidence came recently in a directive from a top-ranking Chinese Communist leader, Vice Premier Teng Tzi-hui. It said that families or family groups could henceforth cook their own food and eat in privacy in the company of their own choice.

Vice Premier Teng went so

fas as to say that individuals, families or groups who did not want to eat at regulated times with large groups, could request rations and revert partially to the traditional Chinese family system of eating together.

After outlining idealistic advantages of mess halls and absolute communal existence under the mess hall system, Vice Premier Teng admitted the failures of collective feeding.

Urges Voluntary System

"Some mess halls had long queues of diners waiting for their turn and it wasted a lot of their time and they didn't have satisfying meals there," the Communist leader said in an uncharacteristic burst of candor for a Chinese official.

Mr. Teng said that "the future development of socialization of rural housekeeping" would have to be based on a "voluntary principle."

Vice Premier Teng made it clear, however, that the Chinese Communists did not intend to become lenient in commune operation, regardless of what immediate problems had to be faced.

July 27, 1959

VISITOR REPORTS COMMUNE CHANGE

He Says He Found Easing of Rigid Control Over Red China Villagers

By GREG MacGREGOR
Special to The New York Times.

HONG KONG, July 31—More evidence of the easing of restrictions in Red China's commune system emerged today in an interview with a merchant just back from a visit to his former home.

The business man, who asked that his name be withheld, visited Kong-mei, in South China's Pearl River delta.

He said the town of about 5,000 population had been organized early under the commune system introduced two years ago. He outlined some of the changes he noticed in the system during his visit last week.

He reported workers were no longer "under the lash" of dictatorial Chinese Communist political cadres. Although all village residents of working age had to maintain a daily quota, compulsory working hours, which had begun at 4 A. M., were no longer enforced.

Women Given Consideration

Women workers were given consideration of four to five days off monthly, he said. Adult males still had to work every day to fill their quotas, but no longer worked under a threat, he added.

"In general, the people still had to work from morning till night to fulfill their work, but there were no more compulsory working hours, no minute-to-minute supervision," the merchant explained.

The commune mess halls, where all village residents had been forced to eat at hours prescribed by the cadres, were closed down at the end of May, he said. Individual rations had been resumed.

The returned traveler reported that the existing monthly ration per person was about an ounce and a quarter of edible oil and about thirty pounds of rice for each working adult, with various adjustments for others. Tobacco was not on the ration list, but was expected to be limited later, he said.

Restaurants were beginning to reopen on modest scales, he reported.

Difficulties Reported

Plots of land were granted for cultivation. Food-ration leftovers were being used to feed scattered groups of livestock almost mysteriously acquired by villagers, he said.

The merchant said the people seemed happy with their newly acquired "freedom." At least they could eat at home, work when they liked, rest when they felt necessary and enjoy some family life—all denied under the former system of communes, he added.

"But I should not say the scene in my village has changed into a bright one," he continued, saying that the villagers had less resistance to disease because of chronic weakness, mainly from malnutrition and overwork.

"Medical supplies have gone," he said. "Medical care is supposed to be free, but little is actually done."

The returned visitor said the residents of his village felt their conditions were better than those of city dwellers.

He said they had managed to butcher two water buffalos last month to provide their first beef in two years. They talked of endless lines in Canton for bread and meager portions of rice during recent months.

Food price reports from Canton this week indicated chicken was selling at the equivalent of about $3 a pound, when available in the black market. Eggs were 12 cents each and dog meat, a Cantonese delicacy, $1.20 a pound.

The merchant said money had little value in the communes because nothing could be purchased with it under the commune government.

August 1, 1959

PEIPING DEFENDS OUTPUT FIGURES

Minimizes Its Confession of Inflated Totals—Stresses New Economic Drive

By TILLMAN DURDIN
Special to The New York Times

HONG KONG, Aug. 27—Communist China put the best face possible today on its admission yesterday of inflated production claims and lowered output targets.

Peiping propaganda minimized the importance of the confession that 1958 output figures for farm products and steel had been greatly overestimated.

The publicity concentrated on the fact that, despite the reduced 1959 targets, expected production this year would attain the goals set for the second five-year plan (1958-62) in the plan's first two years.

The Peiping radio reported tonight that yesterday's call of the Chinese Communist party for "pre-schedule fulfillment of the second plan evoked rejoicing throughout the country." The broadcast said mass rallies in cities and people's communes had hailed the party's call and pledged redoubled efforts to meet production aims.

Organizations Mobilized

According to information here, meetings have been held by provincial Communist party branches and other organizations to mobilize for a new economic drive. Appeals to workers and local officials to redouble their efforts are combined with denunciations of "Rightist opportunists," who are said to have doubted the feasibility of achieving production goals.

Observers here characterized the more moderate 1959 production targets announced in Peiping yesterday as high but nearer a realistic level than the previous figures.

There was a general feeling in informed quarters here that even the scaled-down farm figures for 1958 were in many cases probably higher than actual production. From refugees coming here it has been evident all year that food shortages in China have been acute.

The admission on exaggerated production figures aroused speculation here over whether the whole process of falsification of figures last year and the subsequent reassessment had involved a split in top Chinese leadership. It was believed that the inflated statistics of last year and the hasty initial development of communes were so closely associated with Mao Tse-tung that if anyone is subject to criticism it is the chairman of the Communist party.

No Evidence of Disfavor

However, there is no definite evidence that Mr. Mao is in disfavor with his colleagues. On the contrary, the Central Committee resolution on economic reassessment pays tribute to his leadership and lays down the new policies in his name.

The resolution emphasizes that there has been nothing incorrect about the Communist party's economic policies and that the miscalculations of production were simply due to inaccurate estimates by lower officials.

Observers here point out that political pressures in connection with last year's "rectification" drive and super-production program virtually made it a test of loyalty for lower officials to report huge outputs.

August 28, 1959

PEIPING STRESSES DOCTRINE OF WORK

People Constantly Exhorted to Intensive Efforts— Final Goal Is Vague

The following dispatch was written by Frederick Nossal, correspondent of The Globe and Mail, Toronto.

PEIPING, Nov. 1—The main religion of new China is work. Only through hard work can a good Communist reach his paradise.

It may be some decades off, but the people of China are constantly being reminded just how much work can achieve.

What the end result will be nobody is quite prepared to say, but somewhere in the future lies the final goal—a vague and golden dream, an elusive yet dazzling mirage on the horizon.

In the past, primitive men worshiped the sun and the rain because these brought water and warmth and light and life. Today, the Communists of China worship work because work brings bigger and better machines, more dams and railways, higher production and swifter progress.

It is an all-embracing religion that has swept the world's

largest population into its fold and has created the most massive working bee in history.

Not everyone of China's 650,-000,000 is a true follower of this creed, but even the unbelievers can see the results and join in the work because China is their land.

China's leaders preach about work in newspapers, magazines, over the radio and loudspeakers, in motion pictures and now on television.

It takes a little time for a Westerner to understand the sermons, for some of the terms are quite strange to our ears.

Competition Fostered

Under the headline of "Emulations for High Wheat Yield Among Young Chinese Peasants," the Hsinhua (New China) news agency recently distributed a report about keen competition among tens of millions of young peasants.

The contestants were trying for faster sowing, better quality wheat and deeper plowing.

The same day it was announced that coastal Fukien Province had carried off the Red Banner in an inter-provincial rivalry for more salt output.

One issue of the China Youth Daily devoted a page of photographs and reports on overfulfillment of this year's goals ahead of schedule by Chinese workers who have already started on next year's targets.

Each day there are reports that somewhere in China more workers have pledged themselves to fulfill their work quotas ahead of schedule. Explaining the work drive, the Communist party talks about the "full mobilization of the masses," about "the liberation of China's social productive forces" and about "simultaneous development of industry and agriculture and simultaneous development of heavy and light industry, with priority going to heavy industry."

Shift to Communes Praised

The party demands greater, faster, better and more economical results, and hails the transformation of more than 110,000,000 individual peasant households into more than 24,000 communes as a "glorious victory."

Its leaders praise "the inexhaustible power and wisdom of the industrious and courageous Chinese people," speaking of the past with pride and of the future with hope.

Premier Chou En-lai has written that adoption of the mass line of work has enabled China's Socialist cause to advance swiftly and smoothly and has insured the country's growth "by leaps and bounds in the last ten years, and especially in the last year and this."

"Thanks to the big leap forward in these two years," he adds, "the major targets originally set for 1962 in the Second Five-Year Plan will be overfulfilled. We shall thus be able in the next three years to make bigger progress in industry and agriculture and devote more efforts to strengthening certain weak links.

"It can be anticipated that the Second Five-Year Plan will be five years of a big leap forward. Since such tremendous changes have taken place in China's national economy in the past decade, the changes in the next decade will certainly be even more spectacular. By that time, China will have exceeded Britain in the output of most of the major industrial products."

Premier Urges Speed

But the Premier stresses that China must continue to work and study hard, to work energetically so as to improve agriculture, to strive for higher targets "at a speed which the Western bourgeoisie dare not even dream of."

To understand the Communist party's worship of work properly, one must live in Communist China. One must stand in a street of Peiping and watch workmen tear down an ancient city wall—higher than a three-story city building, about fifty feet thick, filled with tens of thousands of tons of earth and rock and several miles in length.

To understand why this religion has so many converts among the young people of China, you must sit next to a Chinese, and you must hear him say in cheerful tones, and yet in a voice just tinged with anguish at the injustice of it all:

"You have a car at home, of course! In the United States of America many people have two cars. My wife and I haven't got a car. In twenty years maybe we will have a car, and a television, too. But 670,000,000 people can't all have cars and television sets all at once.

"First, we must work!"

November 9, 1959

RED CHINA TRADE WITH WEST GROWS

European Business Men In Peiping Face Long Delays but Negotiate Big Deals

Dispatch of The Globe and Mail, Toronto.

PEIPING, Dec. 2—Western business men who come to Peiping to talk in the headquarters of the Ministry of Foreign Trade often have an endless and infuriating wait. They have reported that negotiations that might take two weeks in any other country can last two to three months in Peiping.

"The Chinese try to wear you down by these delaying methods," a man from Oslo said.

"They may be Communists, but they're also excellent business people who can bargain as well as any capitalist."

There are big deals awaiting any Westerner prepared to adapt himself to the wearying trading methods of the Chinese Communists.

To date, Peiping has established trade relations with ninety-three countries and regions. It has concluded trade treaties or agreements with twenty-seven of these, including Finland, Sweden, Denmark, Norway, India, Ceylon, Indonesia, Burma, Afghanistan, Cambodia, Yemen, Tunisia, Morocco, Iraq and the United Arab Republic.

China has also signed private agreements or contracts with business concerns in France, Britain, West Germany, Austria, Switzerland, Belgium, Italy and the Netherlands. Now Peiping is trying to step up trade with Latin America.

The official Communist line is that you cannot separate economics from politics. The Ministry of Foreign Trade has said that good trade relations depend largely on a friendly political atmosphere.

But in fact this is not always true. West Germany is a typical example. Peiping loathes Bonn and looks on Chancellor Konrad Adenauer as a nuclear war-monger.

Business, however, is business, and if West Germany can supply something China needs, whether it be metals, machines, or anything else, at a cheaper price than another country, Peiping will buy.

China will either barter or pay cash. It seems to have a vast reserve of sterling funds through the great volume of trade it does via Hong Kong.

Gen. Morris A. Cohen, the old China hand from Canada who was aide-de-camp to Sun Yat-sen, founder of the Chinese Republic, reported that some years ago the Chinese gave him £100,-000,000 ($280,000,000) with which to buy tractors from Britain. At that time, he said, United States pressure was so great Britain was forced to refuse the order.

Business executives from Hamburg, Zurich, Helsinki, Oslo and Copenhagen, from London and Brussels and Paris, see in China the vast market of the future. They realize that here are more than 650,000 people working to achieve the material living standards and the industrial development that the West has enjoyed for decades.

The Western traders sell chemicals, pharmaceuticals, ferrous metals and steel products, vehicles, farm implements and automobiles, machine tools and power generators, scientific instruments, microscopes and photographic apparatus.

And they buy agricultural produce, silks, laces and ivory, jade and pearls, hand-made paper and earthenware. In fact, today China can export almost anything from a complete factory to bed sheets and medicinal herbs.

Exports of capital equipment are still very small, but sometimes Peiping sells or gives machinery to an under-developed African or Asian nation for reasons of prestige and propaganda.

China tries to trade as much as possible with other Communist-bloc countries. Of imports between 1950 and 1958, Communist countries supplied 96.6 per cent of petroleum, 99.5 per cent of locomotives and 92.1 per cent of trucks.

December 13, 1959

The 'Human Inflation' of Red China

The billion mark is within sight for China's population, and the resulting pressures on the country's resources pose a problem for both her rulers and her neighbors.

By SRIPATI CHANDRASEKHAR

MADRAS, India.

BABIES are now arriving in Communist China at the rate of some 55,000 a day. At this rate, China's population soon will be increasing each year by more than two Australias, and in a dozen years may have added the population of a United States of America.

In the past, a serious analysis of China's population was hazardous, if not impossible, because no one knew for certain its size and composition. Since China had never had regular scientific censuses or complete and continuous vital statistics, there were as many estimates and "guesstimates" of China's total population and birth and death rates as there were writers on China.

This guessing game came to an end when the Communist Government conducted China's first modern, nation-wide, scientific census in 1953-54, revealing a total mainland population, as of June 15, 1953, of some 583 million. The figure was surprising even to the Communist Government. It meant that all previous analyses of China's economic and demographic positions were misleading, since they had assumed a population of about 450 million.

How valid is this Chinese Communist figure? Statistics under communism have definite strategic value; they are not readily divulged, nor abundant when given out. This does not mean that the Government does not have them, for large-scale economic or social planning is impossible without dependable statistics. But the Government does not always choose to release them, and when it does there is always the suspicion that they may not reflect the true state of affairs.

A major objective of my rather extensive travels in China at the end of 1958 was to study China's population problems and policies and evaluate her population statistics. I met numerous economists, statisticians, medical workers and other officials connected with the census, the Statistical Bureau and the Ministry of Health. I inquired into the operation of the Vital Registration Law, passed in January, 1952, in every city, town and village I visited. Despite Peiping's recent confession of falsified statistics in certain sectors of China's economy, I believe that the 1953 census figures, by and large, are correct.

What is the demographic picture of China today? Projection backward on the basis of the 1953 census placed the 1949 population at 540 million. Today the number has increased to about 680 million. The annual rate of increase has risen from 2 per cent in 1950 to 3.5 per cent last year.

The birth rate per 1,000 has fallen slightly, from 37 in 1952 to 34 in 1959. The death rate per 1,000 has registered an impressive decline, from 18 in 1952 to 11 in 1959. Barring major war or internal revolt, famine or epidemic, China could reach the billion mark within about three decades.

Regional food shortages and floods in 1955 sharpened the Government's awareness of China's population problem. Excessive and ill-spaced births also were clearly depriving the country of real wealth in terms of womanpower for fields and factories. A number of

planners argued that a breathing spell was imperative to give the economy time to catch up.

As a result, the Government decided to adopt a policy of population control. In 1956, a "great debate" on birth control was launched—one of those official debates whose outcome is determined in advance.

To silence orthodox Marxist critics, no less a man than Liu Shao-chi, the party theoretician and pamphleteer, now Chief of the State, convened a birth-control conference. When Premier Chou En-lai visited India in November, 1956, one of his first requests in New Delhi was for information on India's experience with family planning. Throughout 1957, the Government waged a determined campaign.

"An ideal family," every newspaper, poster, journal, and loudspeaker affirmed, "should have three or four children in a planned manner."

Family-planning exhibitions and technical guidance centers were opened in many Chinese towns and villages to explain the official policy of population control. Newspapers and magazine articles, radio talks, films, traveling exhibits, official instructors and singing guides were utilized all over the country to hammer away on the need for limiting family size, the advantages of doing so and the means of doing it.

THE realism of the approach startled many visitors to China during this period. Complete details were shown in what amounted to animated diagrams, and anything which was not clear was explained by formidable women guides without prudery or squeamishness. The authorities were leaving nothing to chance: the most illiterate peasant left an exhibit knowing exactly what to do to prevent a large family.

However, when I visited China late in 1958, the birth-control policy had been reversed, the exhibits closed down and the films withdrawn. This remains the present state of affairs. Everybody assured me that the outside world had misunderstood the birth-control campaign, that it had not been designed to reduce the population but to protect the health of China's mothers.

ALL over the country, everyone I met insisted that China was not only not over-populated, but actually under-populated and facing an acute labor shortage! There is no greater wealth—so went the

new party line—than that represented by human beings, all of whom are primarily producers and only secondarily consumers, and there is nothing the Chinese people under communism cannot achieve; in view of the work to be done and the targets to be achieved, 650 million people are not nearly enough. However, I was assured that all this did not mean that birth-control advice and contraceptives were no longer available.

I received the most authoritative statement of the new policy from the Vice Minister for Health, Mr. Wu Yun-fu. "There seems to have been some misunderstanding on this question abroad ever since the campaign was called off at the beginning of the year," he said. "We don't call it family planning or birth control or planned parenthood. These terms as used in capitalist countries have an entirely different connotation. We call it in China *planned births.*"

Peiping parade—China alone accounts for one-quarter of the human race. Here massed Chinese, some bearing dismantled mortars, march

"This looks to me like a distinction without a difference," I said.

"No, no. There is a difference. Planned births are for the sake of the mother's health. Too many births have a bad effect on work, production and study."

MR. WU went on to explain that too many pregnancies meant a woman's frequent absence from factory or farm, which interfered with production. Besides, too many children would leave no leisure for the mother, or the father, for that matter. Since Communist China wants everyone to study intensively during leisure hours, a large family can be a handicap.

"We don't encourage contraceptives, for contraception is not the end of our policy," he continued. "Two births may be considered too few and six children may not be considered too many. The Government has not laid any restriction on the number of children a couple can have. They may and should have as many children as they can, so long as the health of the mother is not impaired."

"Can a mother resort to contraception on economic grounds —that is, for reasons of poverty?" I asked.

"But there is no poverty today, thanks to our cooperatives and communes. All children are taken care of. So there is no question of poverty being a reason for controlling the size of the family."

Since visiting China I have tried to disentangle the complex reasons why the birth-control campaign was called off. One was undoubtedly the deep-rooted Chinese tradition and sentiment in favor of large families, a tradition which many doctors—mostly gynecologists and obstetricians in city hospitals—believed would take at least a generation to overcome. As might be expected, this sentiment is stronger among peasants than among industrial workers.

I also gathered indirectly that the family-planning campaign had been launched at an inauspicious time—that is, during the collectivization of farms and on the eve of introducing communes, when the Government was relatively unpopular in the countryside. The peasants apparently suspected some devious motive and therefore did not take to family planning. Had the movement been launched in the wake of the early and popular, but short-lived, land-redistribution program, the peasants might have accepted the innovation.

CHILD CARE—Youngsters of working mothers are cared for in a Communist nursery. Some 55,000 babies are born in China every day.

SUSTENANCE—Women serve as farm laborers in Communist China to help the nation feed its huge—and rapidly growing—population

ANOTHER, and perhaps more important reason for abandoning the birth-control campaign was ideological. All Chinese discussions of population are prefaced by an ardent rebuttal of the "bourgeois and reactionary" Malthusian doctrine that improvident fertility and over-population are the causes of poverty.

According to Marx, over-population is impossible under socialism, for the poverty of the peasant and worker grows from feudalism and class exploitation, underproduction and maldistribution, and quickly vanishes under communism when the nation's resources are fully exploited. Malthusianism and its modern variant, neo-Malthusianism, or birth control, were devised by the capitalists to delude the workers into believing that they were responsible for their own poverty.

THIS view has been dinned so thoroughly into the population that everyone, from the Government guide and rural school mistress up to responsible officials, recites it at the mere mention of China's population problems. Even while the family-planning campaign was in full swing sporadic articles upholding the traditional Marxist viewpoint continued to appear in Chinese journals. Thus the campaign was ideologically embarrassing.

Furthermore, Russia's view is that a big population is good in itself and, while China is not a satellite of the Soviet Union, there is obvious need for a united front on ideological questions from Peiping to Warsaw. When Russia honors mothers who bear many children, China can hardly deplore her own large population—especially when it also gives her a certain added importance in the Communist camp.

In fact, the Chinese Communists seemed to delight in the sheer immensity of their numbers. The fact that China alone accounted for one-quarter of the human race, and all the Communist countries for a third, was a matter of intense pride.

But the most important reason for scrapping the birth-control campaign was probably a local political one. The feeling gained ground that the birth-control drive would be interpreted as a confession of failure, an admission that Peiping was incapable of delivering the goods. And so, in typical Communist fashion, there was a sudden and complete reversal.

There may be yet another switch some day. The Chinese Communists are said to have told recent visitors that when their population reaches 800,000,000 they expect to reinstitute an intensive birth-control program.

What is the likely consequence of this meandering population policy? Extensive public-health programs, maternal and child-health services, free medical aid and similar measures are reducing the death rate in all age groups, while the ambivalent birth-control policy is not helping to reduce the present high birth rate. As a result, China's potential for future population growth is enormous.

IS China's huge population an asset or a liability? The answer cannot be a simple yes or no, for it depends on too many factors. For example, if the young (under 16) and old (over 60) age groups are disproportionately large, the working population will be hard put to it to support them; but the advantages of an ample working group are obvious. Also, if the people are healthy, trained in modern skills and have access to the needed resources, a large population will certainly be an asset. But a large, illiterate population, in poor health and without adequate resources, hampers a country's efforts to advance.

In underdeveloped countries with democratic governments a large and growing population is a liability. This is because any increase in output tends to be eaten up by population increases, leaving no surplus for capital formation or higher living standards. One has to run fast merely to stand still.

BUT that is not true in a totalitarian country like Communist China, where the Government has complete control of the nation's material and human resources. China's construction and production methods today are primitive, based almost entirely on human labor. The vast areas of China which the Communists propose to colonize are marginal land, mountainous and near-desert, requiring incredible amounts of human labor to become habitable. Thus, it seems to me, Peiping is encouraging the masses to multiply so that they can be harnessed to do the work of the beast and the machine.

China's huge population also can be a military asset for its rulers. The likely pattern of future war would deny the military value of mere numbers divorced from industrial potential and advanced technology, but for the present Communist China can at least hope to make up in quantity what she so obviously lacks in quality.

Despite these apparent advantages, however, China is bound sooner or later to face the old Malthusian dilemma. Already she finds the task of feeding, clothing, housing and educating her people one that strains all her resources. No matter how loud her reiterations of Marxism, as her millions increase the ghost of Malthus will continue to haunt China.

In this setting China's mounting numbers cannot but alarm her neighbors, especially in view of her lack of emigration outlets and her expansionist Communist ideology. It is in this sense that China is likely to become a demographic danger spot in Asia.

December 6, 1959

PEIPING TEMPERS ITS BID FOR TRADE

Special to The New York Times.

HONG KONG, Dec. 10—Communist China's approach to foreign trade has undergone a sober reappraisal.

This follows the fadeout of a great trade drive in non-Communist markets last year and Peiping's subsequent embarrassment at finding itself unable to fulfill contracts worth several million dollars.

Foreign business men returning from the autumn trade fair at Canton report that Communist officials exhibited considerably less enthusiasm than eighteen months ago when, in the year of the "great leap forward," China offered grain, textiles and light industrial products in great quantities and below market prices.

Each spring and autumn the Communists hold a fair at Canton, where they transact most of their business with non-Communist foreigners.

Prices Are Increased

At the latest fair, prices were closer to world market figures than in the past, and in many lines the Communists were not able to offer the quantities buyers were after.

Some business men said they felt the Communists were reluctant to sell, despite the display of goods.

The general impression of the business men was that the Communists deliberately kept up the prices of goods in short supply. They did not want to take orders they could not fulfill. At the same time, the emphasis was on prompt shipment rather than forward sales.

"They have learned a lesson from their past failures," said a British trader. "They know they overextended themselves and they are trying to avoid doing that again."

The spring trade fair of 1958 was the prelude to a drive that flooded Southeast Asia with textiles, steel bars, cement, foods and manufactured goods, ranging from pianos to fountain pens, at prices well below those of similar goods from other countries.

Meanwhile, however, the "leap forward" had produced an upheaval with the creation of communes and "backyard" blast furnaces throughout China. Even where these were able to produce exceptional results (and this was not widespread), the lack of adequate transportation canceled the gains.

The movement of men and materials in connection with the "leap forward" was more than the railways could cope with.

The Communist export corporations clamored for transport in vain.

Moreover, neither in 1958 nor in 1959 did agricultural or industrial production reach the levels originally forecast, and often where there was transportation there were not enough goods to fill the orders.

The results were most apparent at the beginning of this year. Communist China's exports to Hong Kong fell away from a peak of $30,000,000 in December to $15,000,000 in January. The decline has continued.

Exports from China to Singapore and Malaya were averaging $7,000,000 a month at the end of 1958, but in the first months of this year they were also down 50 per cent. Some deliveries were stopped so suddenly that the importers suffered financially.

Improvements Reported

Not surprisingly, fewer foreigners attended this year's fall fair. Those who did found that things had changed. They came away impressed by the marketing procedures, by the apparent earnestness of the officials on the subject of shipments, and by the improved finish to some manufactured items.

The Communists say transactions amounting to $200,000,000 were concluded at the fair. Observers here treat this figure with reserve.

Visitors say the main foreign buying was in light manufactured articles and building materials. The United Arab Republic is understood to have been a big buyer for these lines.

Although the first trade drive faltered, China is consolidating its economic forces for a new attack on the same markets, economic observers here believe. A nation-wide campaign to improve transportation facilities is reported.

China still represents a trade threat to other producing countries of Asia, particularly Japan.

December 13, 1959

CHINESE REFUGEES CROWD HONG KONG

Special to The New York Times.

HONG KONG, Jan. 9—The number of refugees arriving in Hong Kong from Communist China has increased with the onslaught of winter—a grim winter in China by all accounts.

Since the vast majority of the refugees enter this British colony illegally, it is impossible to count them. However, the police estimate that the numbers are increasing. Marine Division patrols are catching more this month.

Renewed Peiping pressure on peasants and factory workers to step up production with no corresponding improvement in conditions is a main factor behind the refugees' flight. They report that in the communes the peasants must work long hours with little more than rice gruel as their reward.

Every night junks slip by the Communist patrol boats and head for Hong Kong bearing men, women and children.

Refugees Dodge Patrols

Some are stopped by British patrol boats. Others are caught by immigration officers when they step on shore. They are escorted out of British waters and must either return to their point of departure or make another attempt to reach Hong Kong later in the night.

Those who arrive safely quickly melt into the community. Many disappear into the tenement areas, where wash hangs on bamboo poles above the streets and as many as fifty people live in one room. Dark narrow stairways smelling of incense and frying fish lead to the cramped quarters they will share with relatives or friends.

The rest find their way into the shanty towns that straggle up the bare, brown slopes of Hong Kong's harborside hills, where a home is a hut of tin sheets, cardboard and sacking and congestion is so great that people sleep in shifts.

More than 50,000 refugee children roam the streets and squatter areas without proper homes or families. Little bundles of rags in street doorways turn out to be sleeping infants.

Often before they can speak, the refugee children are vagrants and beggars or "runners" for narcotics peddlers and gangsters.

Yet still the refugees come. They come knowing the conditions under which they will have to live and despite the fact that escape from China is perilous. Death is sometimes the fate of those discovered attempting to leave.

The refugees constitute a permanent problem for Hong Kong's Government.

In a way the refugee has been Hong Kong's salvation. The exodus from China has given the colony a labor force that has enabled it to develop a remarkable growth in export industries.

However, Government efforts to absorb the refugees have not been able to keep pace with the stream of new arrivals.

In 1948 Hong Kong's population was about 1,700,000. Today the population is estimated at 3,000,000 and some welfare workers believe it is "well on the way" to 4,000,000.

100,000 Refugees a Year

Annually an estimated total of 100,000 refugees make their way into the colony. Annually, too, the natural increase of births over deaths is about 100,000.

This is a tremendous population pressure on a territory of Hong Kong's size, comprising, in effect, some 375 square miles of rocky islands and a strip of mainland, with only twelve square miles available for residential and commercial building.

In the tenements of Wanchai and Old Kowloon, the density of people to an acre is 2,500. This is sixteen times the population density of New York's most congested slums.

The majority of refugees are smuggled in here from Macao. It is easier to escape from China into Portuguese territory. Through 'travel agencies' they make contact with smugglers and arrange passage by junk to Hong Kong. The cost averages $5 for children and $25 for adults.

Since 1954 the Government has resettled 300,000 refugees at a cost of $15,000,000.

However, the Government program has aided only a minority of the refugees.

January 15, 1960

CHINESE WARN U.S. OF GENEVA BLAME

By HENRY R. LIEBERMAN
Special to The New York Times.

HONG KONG, Jan. 24—Communist China warned the United States tonight it must take responsibility for "all the consequences" if the ambassadorial talks at Geneva break down on the questions of Taiwan (Formosa) and civilian repatriation.

A Foreign Ministry spokesman in Peiping charged again the United States was "occupying" Taiwan and "interfering" in "China's internal affairs." He asserted again the United States was preventing Chinese from returning to mainland China.

The spokesman reiterated Communist China's opposition to the United States formula for renouncing the use of force in the Taiwan area subject to the mutual right of self-defense. He maintained the Peiping regime had "succeeded to China's entire territory" and the United States had no right of self-defense in this territory.

Meanwhile, the Peiping regime continued to press for a meeting with the United States at the foreign ministers level.

The spokesman said the Geneva talks had "proved incapable" of settling "such a major substantive question as relaxing and eliminating tension" in the Taiwan area. He added:

"The Chinese side holds that a Chinese - American conference of the foreign ministers must be held, as this is the practical and feasible means for settling this question."

Tonight's lengthy statement, which repeated many points made earlier by Peiping, was the third pronouncement on the Geneva talks issued this month by a Chinese Communist Foreign Ministry spokesman.

It was put out by the Hsinhua (New China) news agency shortly before Prime Minister Eden was scheduled to leave Britain for his talks with President Eisenhower in Washington.

Communist China's renewed agitation on the Taiwan [Formosa] question is expected here to make that question an important item for discussion at these talks.

Follows U. S. Statement

Tonight's Chinese Communist pronouncement followed a statement issued in Washington Saturday to correct what the State Department called a misleading version by Peiping on developments at Geneva.

The State Department said Communist China was still holding thirteen Americans in prison four months after it announced it would adopt measures permitting them to return home. Denying the Communist Chinese assertion that the United States is detaining Chinese, the State Department declared again any Chinese was free to leave for any destination of his choice.

As for renunciation of force, Washington said the United States had proposed this so discussions between the two sides could take place free from the threat of war. It said the formula would not prevent either side from pursuing its objectives and policies peacefully.

The State Department pointed out the United States was not occupying Taiwan and that Taiwan had never been part of Communist China. It said the United States had a mutual defense treaty with the Chinese Nationalists on Taiwan and that international law recognized the right of individual and collective self-defense against an attack. It added:

"In short the Communists so far seem willing to renounce force only if they are first conceded the goals for which they would use force."

Against this background Peiping asserted tonight that the "new China" had "succeeded to China's entire territory and sovereignty." Its Foreign Ministry spokesman said this was an "undisputable fact" that "no statement by the United States Department of State can alter."

The spokesman said the United States-Nationalist mutual defense treaty was an infringement on "China's sovereignty." He continued to contend that "tension" in the Taiwan Strait was international, while Taiwan itself was a domestic problem.

The spokesman also continued to make a distinction between "ordinary American residents" and alleged American "lawbreakers" in China. He said "all the sixteen American residents who applied" had been permitted to depart.

CHOU BIDS CHIANG CONFER ON WAYS TO 'FREE' TAIWAN

By Reuters.

PEIPING, June 28—Premier Chou En-lai of Communist China formally offered today to negotiate with Generalissimo Chiang Kai-shek's Nationalists on "steps and conditions for the peaceful liberation" of Taiwan (Formosa).

His speech, addressed to the National People's Congress (Parliament) here, represented another step in a policy launched at the Asian-African conference at Bandung, Indonesia, last year.

Its comparative restraint, even when referring to the United States, was seen here as part of a growing endeavor to relax both external and internal tension.

Mr. Chou made no concessions and reiterated all of Communist China's earlier demands. But the tone of his speech was far more restrained and less aggressive in content than those he gave to the two previous congresses.

Reviewing the world situation, he touched on colonialism, the "cold war," United States foreign policy and relations between East and West. He predicted that the "traditional friendships" of the Chinese and American peoples would eventually lead to diplomatic recognition of his Government by the United States.

First Formal Invitation

Mr. Chou repeated the remark he made in an interview last month that the prospect was increasing for "peaceful liberation" of Nationalist-held Taiwan.

Communist China had hinted at the possibility of negotiations for some time. Last July Mr. Chou offered to negotiate with the "local authorities" on Formosa rather than the Nationalist Government itself.

Today's offer was the first formal invitation for negotiations to the Chiang regime.

"On behalf of the Government, I formally declare: We are willing to discuss with the Taiwan authorities on specific steps and conditions for the peaceful liberation of Taiwan," Mr. Chou said, "and we hope that the Taiwan authorities will send their representatives to Peiping or some other appropriate places at a time when they consider proper to begin these talks with us."

The Premier's speech seemed to be aimed at Asian and Arab opinion and at those in the West who are calling for an end to the "cold war" and recognition of Communist China.

Mr. Chou conceded "certain legitimate interests . . . arising from long historical connections" of Britain and France in some areas of Asia and Africa. He also praised the wisdom of the British withdrawal of troops from the Suez Canal zone.

He supported India on Goa and Indonesia on Dutch New Guinea and emphasized Arab rights.

[India is demanding that Portugal cede the enclave of Goa, on the Indian west coast. The dispute over West New Guinea concerns Indonesian demands for cession of the territory by the Netherlands.]

Mr. Chou again put his case concerning the current Chinese-United States talks in Geneva [on American prisoners in Communist China]. Once again, he called for a meeting between himself and Secretary of State Dulles on Far East issues.

His speech fitted well, in its rejection of force as a solution, with current Chinese policy in internal affairs—emphasizing that persuasion and education rather than force are now the Government's weapons.

"The Chinese people are determined to liberate Taiwan," Mr. Chou declared. "Since we issued the slogan of striving to liberate Taiwan by peaceful means, many Kuomintang [Nationalist] military and political personnel in Taiwan and abroad have expressed their patriotic desires.

"We believe that those who wish to promote the peaceful liberation of Taiwan and the complete unification of our motherland will certainly grow in number from day to day. This is an inexorable trend.

"The dying gasp of the Taiwan authorities [who are] following the United States definitely cannot last for long."

Visits Are Proposed

The Premier assured all military and political personnel on Taiwan whose families were on the mainland that they could communicate with their relatives and friends and return to the mainland for short visits.

If responsible officials on Formosa had doubts, he promised, "they can also send people to the mainland to find out the situation."

"We guarantee the latter freedom of movement in coming and going," he added.

Mr. Chou said the United States, which has no diplomatic relations with Communist China, was "like an ostrich hiding its head in the sand, not daring to face the fact that the People's Republic of China exists."

He said the ruling circles in the United States were "in an acute dilemma, in which both peace and war are difficult alternatives."

January 25, 1956

"So far," he continued, "the advocates of continuing the 'cold war' still occupy the dominating position."

There are still some people who support the "evil intrigue" of two Chinas, Mr. Chou said, adding: "this kind of foolishness is absolutely hopeless."

"Even toward the United States, we have the same desire for friendly relations," the Premier declared. "We are deeply convinced that the day will come when the Chinese and American peoples, because of their traditional friendship, will resume their ties through their respective governments."

Mr. Chou repeated his attacks on the Western trade restrictions imposed on his country. He charged that the nations forced to pursue this policy were suffering more than Communist China from it.

June 29, 1956

Red Chinese Charge Aggression by U. S. On Taiwan Missiles

By Reuters.

HONG KONG, May 11—Communist China's Foreign Ministry issued a statement tonight describing the installation of United States guided missiles on Taiwan (Formosa) as "an act of aggression."

It was the first official comment from Peiping on the United States announcement that a United States Air Force unit equipped with Matador missiles was being moved to the Chinese Nationalist island.

The statement, broadcast by the New China News Agency, said:

"On May 7, 1957, the United States announced that a United States Air Force unit equipped with guided missiles would be stationed on the Chinese territory of Taiwan.

'Indignation' Expressed

"On May 8, military personnel of the United States forces of aggression in Taiwan announced that advanced elements of guided missiles units had arrived in Taiwan.

"This is another serious, provocative action of the United States Government in persistently pursuing its policy of carrying out aggression against China and aggravating tension in the Far East.

"The Chinese Government and people express their great indignation at this action and lodge a strong protest against it.

"People throughout the world desire relaxation of international tension and realization of the principle of peaceful co-existence in international relations. For a long time, United States encroachment of Taiwan has created tension in the Taiwan area.

"The Chinese Government has always stood for relaxing and eliminating tension in the Taiwan area through peaceful negotiations and has made repeated efforts in this direction.

"Taiwan is China's territory and the liberation of Taiwan is China's internal affair. On this question of internal affairs, the Chinese Government has also repeatedly raised the call for peaceful liberation of Taiwan.

"However, the United States Government not only has refused to hold serious talks on the question of tension in the Taiwan area but has resorted to all devices to tighten its grip on Taiwan and to obstruct and disrupt settlement by the Chinese themselves of their internal matter of liberating Taiwan.

"The United States' provocative action of stationing guided missile units in Taiwan not only exposes the aggressive and bellicose nature of its policy of installing guided missiles all over the world to create tension, but also shows more clearly its scheme of turning Taiwan entirely into a United States dependency and base for atomic war.

"The Chinese Government hereby solemnly declares: The determination of the Chinese people to liberate their own territory is unshakable; the United States must bear full responsibility for its action of aggression."

May 12, 1957

PEIPING RESENTS TOKYO'S '2 CHINAS'

Literature at Fair Mentions Red and Taiwan Regimes, Incensing the Former

By ROBERT TRUMBULL
Special to The New York Times.

TOKYO, Feb. 17—Chinese Communist officials have been showing extreme sensitivity lately over what they apparently regard as a growing Japanese tendency to accept "two Chinas," one under the Peiping regime on the mainland and another ruled by the Nationalists on Taiwan (Formosa).

Communist China's Premier Chou En-lai has assailed Japan's Prime Minister, Nobusuke Kishi, in recent statements for refusal to consider recognizing Communist China at this time, while Tokyo continues to maintain full diplomatic relations with the Chiang Kai-shek Government. Actually, Mr. Kishi has avoided directly mentioning the "two Chinas" concept brought out several years ago by one of his predecessors, Ichiro Hatoyama.

However, in recent days Peiping's irritation at Japan has been aggravated by two incidents. One was the visit of thirteen Japanese newspaper men to Taiwan, which the Communists' Hsinhua (New China) news agency described in angry terms as part of a United States "scheme" to "create two Chinas" with Japan's help.

Catalogues Cause Trouble

The other incident concerned some material distributed by Japanese exhibitors at the Japan Trade Fair in Canton. According to reports by Japanese sources, some catalogues given away by Japanese companies made references to shipments of their products to "Nationalist China" and "Communist China," differentiating between the two.

A catalogue for Japanese locomotives, apparently left over from stock printed for distribution in Taiwan, outraged Communist sensibilities by reproducing the flags of the United States and Nationalist China in full color.

Another catalogue, for Chinese aster seeds, stated that these flowers grow in "Communist China" and "Manchuria." These are geographical designations that the Peiping regime does not accept.

The effect was said to have been disastrous to the Japanese hopes for sales. When the Japanese discovered that their catalogues were offensive to their hosts, according to dispatches from Canton, they tore out the offending pages or crossed out the objectionable words.

This, it was said, only further incensed the Chinese, who declared indignantly that their injured feelings were not to be soothed in any such casual manner.

Japanese exhibitors ran into linguistic difficulty with Communist dialectics too. In a pamphlet extolling Japanese farm implements, tools were described as alleviating "painful labor."

A Japanese correspondent wrote that "this also angered the Chinese, who contend that work is divine and that to call it 'painful labor' is an insult to the workers."

According to the account given by the Canton correspondent of the big Japanese newspaper Asahi, the catalogues infuriated Sun Yueh-i, deputy mayor of Canton and vice chairman of the Canton branch of the China International Trade Promotion Committee.

Mr. Sun told Japanese newspaper men, the Asahi correspondent said, that "China will never tolerate 'any machinations to recognize two Chinas.'" The Chinese official then declared that the United States was "behind the intrigue to establish two Chinas," and that "the Japanese Government was following the United States' policy."

February 23, 1958

TRADE WITH JAPAN HALTED BY TAIWAN

Nationalist China Cancels Commercial Ties in Anger Over Peiping-Tokyo Pact

TAIPEI, Taiwan, March 19 (AP)—Nationalist China broke off commercial relations with Japan today as a protest against the private trade agreement concluded recently between a Japanese group and Communist China.

Existing contracts were canceled and negotiations for future contracts were suspended. Taipei newspapers reported strong support for the move from the communities of overseas Chinese that dominate much of the commerce of Southeast Asia and predicted that they would boycott Japanese goods.

It was doubtful, however, whether the Nationalist Government in Taiwan (Formosa) would go so far as to break off diplomatic relations with Tokyo. President Chiang Kai-shek's Government ordered the break

307

In an effort to force the Japanese Government to refuse approval of the agreement with Peiping. The Nationalists objected not to the commercial aspect of this pact but to subsidiary provisions that it felt implied a measure of diplomatic recognition of Peiping.

These included the stationing of permanent trade missions by Japan and Communist China in their respective capitals, and permission for Peiping's mission in Toyko to fly its flag and use secret codes. Premier Nobusuke Kishi has indicated that the flag provisions might prevent approval of the agreement of his Government.

Japan and Communist China have traded for several years under private agreements. The recent pact provides for $98,000,000 worth of commerce in the next year.

The Chinese Nationalists' resentment has been building up since the agreement was signed March 5. On March 14 Generalissimo Chiang's Government suspended a trade conference with Japan that opened in Taipei March 8.

Concern Voiced in Tokyo
Special to The New York Times.

TOKYO, March 19—Japanese Governmental and financial circles were badly shaken by reports from Taipei that Nationalist China had decided to break all trade relations with Japan.

The Chinese action threatens to have a serious political effect on the Government of Premier Kishi. Taiwan is a $98,000,000-a-year customer of Japan.

Disruption of Japan's trade with the Nationalist Chinese could cost one big Japanese company a pending $500,000 contract for electric generator parts.

Premier Kishi has not yet given official certification to the private agreement with Peiping, but such approval has been implied. The Chinese Nationalists contend that the trade missions to be set up in Tokyo and Peiping will in effect be the equivalent of consulates.

Mr. Kishi and Foreign Minister Aiichiro Fujiyama have sent the strongest assurances to Taipei that Japan contemplates no official relations with the Communist Chinese Government. Mr. Fujiyama announced in the Diet (parliament) today that Japan would refuse to negotiate a new fishing pact with Peiping, replacing the present private agreement that expires in June.

TOKYO APPROVES RED CHINA TRADE
Special to The New York Times

TOKYO, April 9—The Japanese Government approved today a private trade agreement between Japan and Communist China.

The pact was signed in Peiping March 5. It calls for the equivalent of $98,000,000 in trade each way during the next twelve months.

In a note to the three Japanese private organizations that negotiated the agreement, Premier Nobusuke Kishi emphasized that Japan would not recognize the Peiping Government.

Foreign Minister Aiichiro Fujiyama said that the flying of the national flag by the Chinese trade mission to be established in Tokyo "will not be recognized as a right, but will be protected under the domestic laws of Japan." This was interpreted to mean that Japan would not object to the flying of the red and gold Communist flag.

It was over the flag issue that Nationalist China recently severed commercial relations with Tokyo. The word from Taipei, Taiwan, tonight was that the Nationalist Government appeared to have been pacified temporarily by Japanese assurances that no de facto recognition of the Peiping regime was involved.

Informed Nationalist sources said their Government did not want to press the matter too hard in view of the coming Japanese elections. It does not want to embarrass Mr. Kishi and the Liberal - Democratic party in the election battle with the Socialists. However these Chinese doubt that the Premier's statement will satisfy the Peiping Government.

Japan has indicated that she would not consider it a serious violation of the law protecting foreign flags if some anti-Communist element were to tear down the Chinese Reds' flag.

An unofficial translation of Mr. Kishi's statement follows:

"The Government, in the light of the necessity for expanding Japanese-Red Chinese trade, will respect the spirit of the fourth private Japanese - Communist Chinese trade agreement. On the basis of its stand that it will not recognize the Peiping Government, and taking existing international relations into consideration, the Government will give its support and cooperation, within the limits of various internal laws, toward the attainment of the objectives to expand trade."

The trade mission will be permitted to use secret code in communicating with the mainland.

Red China Cuts Off Trade With Japan; Nullifies Contracts
By The Associated Press

TOKYO, May 10—Communist China notified Japan today it was suspending all business between the two nations "because of Premier Nobusuke Kishi's hostile attitude toward China."

The head of Communist China's trade delegation, which has been negotiating in Tokyo since March 30, issued a statement saying his Government had stopped issuing import and export licenses to Japan. Major Japanese trading concerns also were informed by cablegram from Shanghai that their contracts had been nullified.

The action followed a blistering attack on Mr. Kishi yesterday by Chen Yi, Chinese Communist Foreign Minister.

Attempt to Hurt Kishi

The Chinese action has been interpreted as an attempt to discredit Mr. Kishi's conservative Government in the May 22 Japanese elections.

Communist China last month nullified a $190,000,000 trade agreement with Japan when Tokyo refused to grant diplomatic recognition to the Chinese Communist flag here.

Li Chuo-chih, head of the Chinese delegation in Tokyo, told Japan today his delegation was discontinuing more than forty days of negotiations "because of Kishi's hostile attitude and obstruction."

Mr. Li's delegation has been negotiating for implementation of a steel agreement amounting to £200,000,000 ($560,000,000) over a five-year period. The agreement was signed last February in Peiping. A contract for 150,000 tons of Japanese steel and iron had been initialed.

In his press statement Mr. Li said "the Japanese Government imposed improper conditions for China's shipment of rice [in payment for the steel] and delayed our negotiations."

Meanwhile, major Japanese trading companies received cabled messages from Chinese trading concerns in Shanghai canceling all outstanding contracts. The messages specifically said the cancellation applied also to Chinese shipments to balance Communist China's trade debts to Japan. Such debts totaled £8,500,000 ($23,800,000) as of March 31.

Japan Charges Interference
Special to The New York Times.

TOKYO, May 10—An unofficial Foreign Ministry statement accused the Peiping Government today of interfering in the internal affairs of Japan in the midst of the Japanese national election campaign.

The Foreign Ministry took exception to Mr. Chen's attack on Mr. Kishi. Mr. Chen accused Mr. Kishi of sabotaging the private Tokyo-Peiping trade agreement, and declared the Japanese Premier had "the hallucinations of an idiot" if he thought Communist China must trade with Japan.

In harping on its right to fly its flag in Japan, Communist China is deliberately bringing up an issue that has no direct relation with trade, the Japanese Government said.

Chinese Communists Shell Quemoys in Record Attack

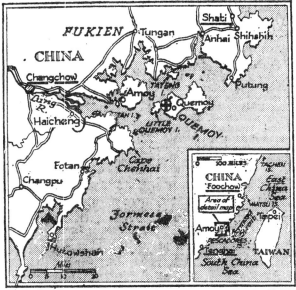

The New York Times   Aug. 24, 1958
Chinese Communist guns shelled Quemoys (cross) heavily. Underlined places are the sites of new Red air bases.

Taipei Reports 40,000 Enemy Shells Hit Offshore Islands — Taiwan Prepares for Possible Invasion Attempt

Special to The New York Times.

TAIPEI, Taiwan, Aug. 23 — Chinese Communist guns shelled Nationalist-held Quemoy and Little Quemoy tonight in what was officially described as the heaviest bombardment yet experienced by those offshore islands.

The Nationalist Defense Ministry here said the Communists fired more than 40,000 shells at the islands in a two-hour pounding from 6:30 to 8:30 P. M. local time. The shells came from the vicinity of Communist-held Amoy, a few miles west of the Quemoy Islands.

In tonight's bombardment, the Communists fired more than five times the number of shells that fell on the Quemoys during the previous record shelling of June 24, 1947. At that time they fired more than 9,000 rounds.

Tense For Several Weeks

The situation on the Nationalist-held offshore islands of Quemoy and Matsu has been tense for several weeks.

A Defense Ministry spokesman, Rear Admiral Liu Hoh-tu, said the shelling "might or might not be the prelude to a possible attack on Quemoy or a diversionary move for such a possibility on Matsu.

He also said that the Nationalist batteries retaliated against Communist positions but could not say to what extent.

An unspecified number and type of Communist planes circled Quemoy during the action, according to the official Nationalist Central News Agency, but did not bomb or strafe.

Responsible officials denied a report that the Nationalist commanders on Quemoy and about a score of United States Military Assistance Advisory Group personnel stationed there had evacuated the island. They said the bombardment caused no American casualties.

The casualties among the estimated total of the 50,000-man Nationalist garrison and 47,000 population of Quemoy was not made known here.

Tension in the Taiwan Strait area began when the Chinese Communists occupied the seaboard air bases facing Taiwan and, according to reports, reinforced their military positions around the offshore islands a month ago.

The announcement of the Quemoy bombardment came as Taipei correspondents were boarding a Nationalist destroyer escort for a visit to Matsu, on the other end of the Nationalist defense perimeter.

The trip was canceled and the ship was ordered to stand by for emergency action.

In the past week the Quemoy situation has been normally quiet, with periodic Communist shellings, mostly confined to propaganda leaflet projectiles. Matsu, in the same period, underwent one of its regular air alerts, with the occasional sighting of Communist jets and leaflet shelling.

The Nationalists, at a recent briefing in Quemoy, said the Communists now had at least one artillery division among their units opposite Quemoy. The biggest guns known to be among their artillery are of the 152-mm. caliber.

August 24, 1958

DULLES CAUTIONS PEIPING ON ISLES

Says Effort to Take Quemoy and Matsu Would Present a Threat to Peace

By JACK RAYMOND

Special to The New York Times.

WASHINGTON, Aug. 23 — Secretary of State Dulles warned Communist China today not to attempt seizure of the small offshore islands of Quemoy and Matsu in the Taiwan (Formosa) Strait.

He said any such effort would constitute a "threat to the peace" in that area.

These islands have remained in Nationalist Chinese hands since 1949 when Generalissimo Chiang Kai-shek's regime was driven off the mainland and settled in Taiwan.

Frequently the object of Communist Chinese seizure threats ever since, the islands were subjected to a powerful bombardment last night.

Invasion Move Weighed

Reports received here suggested the possibility that the bombardment, in the wake of a general military build-up on the mainland in that vicinity, would presage a Communist military invasion.

Secretary Dulles commented, as he departed today for a week's vacation, that the situation had eased somewhat in the Middle East but was worsening in the Far East.

His warning was contained in a letter to the acting chairman of the House Foreign Affairs Committee, written and made public today, as Washington became concerned over the bombardment of the Quemoy garrison. The acting chairman, Representative Thomas E. Morgan, Pennsylvania Democrat, had asked Mr. Dulles yesterday for comment on the situation.

Evidence of the Chinese Communist build-up in Fukien Province on the mainland opposite the fortified offshore islands has been noted for more than a week.

Soviet-made MIG-17 jet planes have been seen in the vicinity, apparently in replacement of the earlier MIG-13's. Communist here have been inclined to re-Chinese garrisons for ground forces have been increased by several divisions and auxiliary troops.

However, military experts gard the build-up, although notable, as insufficient for the type of amphibious invasion that would be required for an actual effort to capture the Nationalist-held islands.

It is believed possible that the arrived recently in the vicinity were part of the 200,000 men recently removed from North Korea and sent to the Quemoy area for normal garrison purposes.

In his reply to Representative Morgan, Mr. Dulles said the Communist military build-up "suggested that they might be tempted" to take the Nationalist-held islands by force.

It would be "highly hazardous" for anyone to assume that an attempt to attack and conquer the islands "could be a limited operation," Mr. Dulles added.

An invasion effort would "constitute a threat to the peace of the area," he went on. "Therefore, I hope and believe it will not happen."

On this premise presumably, Mr. Dulles took off on a week's sailing vacation in Lake Ontario. The Secretary said he planned to go with friends on a small boat in Lake Ontario, as he has done in the past.

Mrs. Dulles is not going with them, he explained, because she vacationing in Maine. The Air Force plane was to take Mr. Dulles and his aides to Watertown, N. Y.

"I hope to be out of contact with the world for a week," he said. He added jokingly, "I hope I don't have to come back prematurely."

Pentagon Concerned

While Mr. Dulles' opinion that last night's bombardment did not necessarily presage an invasion effort coincided with the views of military experts, there nevertheless was some concern at the Pentagon that intelligence reports may prove inadequate.

The possibility of a Chinese communist invasion of the offshore islands raised again the question of whether the United States would help defend these islands.

The United States is pledged, in accordance with a treaty with Nationalist China, to help defend Taiwan and the Pescadores Islands. Whether the defense of the Matsu and Quemoy Islands is included in that pledge has never been explicitly stated.

The purpose of keeping the treaty vague on this point has been to keep the Chinese communists guessing. On March 3, 1955 Mr. Dulles declared that President Eisenhower would decide "at the time" whether an attack on these islands constituted an attack aimed at Taiwan.

Mr. Dulles' statement was made in reference to the resolution passed by Congress earlier in the year, authorizing the President to use American forces, "as he deems necessary for the specific purpose of securing and protecting Formosa and the Pescadores against armed attack."

The United States has helped build up the military defense of Quemoy and Matsu. It has provided weapons and funds for military construction there. The United States Military Assistance Advisory Group in Formosa has a group of fifteen to twenty officers stationed on Quemoy Island.

The United States also has kept the Seventh Fleet alerted in the area.

August 24, 1958

EISENHOWER SEES INCREASED NEED TO GUARD QUEMOY

He Says Offshore Isles Hold Third of Taiwan's Force —7th Fleet Reinforced

By E. W. KENWORTHY
Special to The New York Times.

WASHINGTON, Aug. 27—The offshore islands of Quemoy and Matsu are more important to the defense of Taiwan (Formosa) than they were three years ago, President Eisenhower said today.

The President made this statement at his news conference a few hours before the Navy announced that the aircraft carrier Essex and four destroyers had been detached from the Sixth Fleet in the Mediterranean and were en route to join the Seventh Fleet in waters around the Formosa Strait.

The Navy said that the Essex and her escort had reached the northern end of the Suez Canal.

U. S. Forces at Stand-by

The Chinese Communists have put the Quemoy group under increasingly heavy artillery and air bombardment for the last week.

Washington has placed the Seventh Fleet and the Fifth Air Force on Okinawa on a precautionary alert. In the Philippines, Sangley Point and Cubi Point naval air stations, and the Air Force base at Clark Field have been put on a stand-by alert.

The Quemoy group is fifteen miles east of the Chinese port of Amoy. Matsu, 200 miles to the north, lies in the estuary of the Min River, off Foochow. Between Quemoy and Taiwan, 150 miles across the Formosa Strait, is the Penghu (Pescadores) group, thirty miles west of Taiwan.

Importance Explained

The reason for the increased importance of the offshore islands, the President said today, is that "the Nationalist Chinese have now deployed about a third of their forces to certain of these islands west of the Pescadores, and that makes a closer interlocking between the

defense systems of the islands with Formosa than was the case before that." [Question 6, Page 10.]

Prior to this build-up, the President said, the offshore islands were looked on as "outposts," even though they were "strongly held."

The over-all strength of the Chinese Nationalist forces is estimated here at 600,000 men. Of this total, 463,000 are in the army. The rest are divided between the navy and air force.

The air force has 420 planes, mostly fighters and fighter-bombers. The navy has four destroyers, thirty-one to forty patrol escorts, eleven mine-layers, and 105 to 115 amphibious craft.

The President's statement would mean that the Chinese Nationalists have about 200,000 men deployed on Quemoy, Matsu and the lesser islands.

The President refused to speculate on whether the changed situation would affect any decision he might have to make on the use of United States forces to defend the islands if the Chinese Communists launched an amphibious attack.

"You simply cannot make military decisions until after the event reaches you," he said. "Now, it might affect it if, under a whole series of circumstances—but there are all sorts of permutations and combinations of these factors, and I would say you couldn't make any arbitrary answer to that." [Question 6.]

However, the President emphasized that the United States was not going to "desert our responsibilities or the statements we have already made." [Question 12.]

The best thing that could be said at the moment about the uneasy situation in the Formosa Strait, the President added, was contained in the letter that Secretary of State Dulles wrote last Saturday to Representative Thomas E. Morgan, the acting chairman of the House Foreign Affairs Committee.

Two Key Documents Cited

Mr. Dulles told the Pennsylvania Democrat that it would be "highly hazardous" for any one to assume that an attack on the offshore islands "could be a limited operation."

It would, he said, "constitute a threat to the peace of the area."

The "responsibilities and statements" to which the President alluded are contained in two documents.

The first is the Mutual Defense Treaty between the Chinese Nationalist Government and the United States, which the Senate ratified in February, 1955.

In this, the United States pledged itself to come to the defense of Taiwan and the

Penghu group.

The offshore islands were not mentioned, although a clause of the treaty said that its provisions could be extended to "such other territories as may be determined by mutual agreement."

Mr. Dulles told the Senate Foreign Relations Committee then that the addition of other territories would amount to an amendment of the treaty requiring Senate consent.

Although the Government of Generalissimo Chiang Kai-shek would like the United States guarantee extended to the offshore islands, the Administration, for both military and political reasons, has not been willing to give an unqualified commitment to defend territory lying so close to the mainland.

The Formosa Resolution

The second document is the so-called Formosa Resolution, passed by the House and the Senate at the President's request in January, 1955, at a time when the Chinese Communists were heavily shelling the offshore islands.

In this resolution the President was authorized "to employ the armed forces of the United States as he deems necessary for the specific purpose of securing and protecting Formosa and the Pescadores against armed attack."

This authority included "the securing and protection of such related positions and territories of that area now in friendly hands."

The "related positions" plainly meant the offshore islands, and the intent of the resolution was to warn the Communists and keep them guessing.

On March 3, 1955, Secretary Dulles said that the President would decide "at the time" whether any attack on the offshore islands constituted an attack against Taiwan.

On the basis of the President's statement today and Mr. Dulles' letter Saturday, there is speculation here that the Administration has resolved to meet any attack on Quemoy and Matsu.

Officials here agree that the Chinese Nationalists, by deploying so much of their strength on the offshore islands, have limited the freedom of action of the United States. They also agree that this was probably the principal reason behind the build-up.

These officials note that the offshore islands have little economic value. They also agree that while the possession of the islands by the Nationalists makes it more difficult for the Communists to mount an attack on Taiwan, their military value is limited. But the prestige value of the islands is great, these officials say.

Seventh Fleet Has 71 Ships

The dispatch of the 33,000-ton Essex raises to five the number of carriers in the Seventh Fleet. The others are the attack carriers Hancock, Lexington and Shangri-La, and the anti-submarine carrier Princeton.

The destroyers escorting the Essex are the Sherman, Roan, Haile and Royal. The Seventh Fleet will now have a complement of seventy-one ships.

When the President was asked today what discretion a local commander had in the use of tactical atomic weapons, he replied: "It is not possible to use these weapons except with the specific authority of the President." [Question 7.]

There was, he thought, one possible exception—"that if the United States itself or any of its armed forces are under attack, that they can use any measures necessary for their defense." But he could not remember, he said, whether this directive specifically mentioned atomic weapons.

JAPAN WILL SEEK U. S. PACT CHANGE

Foreign Chief Pledges Step as Leftists Assail Use of Bases to Aid Taiwan

By ROBERT TRUMBULL
Special to The New York Times.

TOKYO, Aug. 30—With rising tension in Formosa Strait, the Leftists in Japan are increasing pressure on the Government to prevent the use of Japan as a base for United States support to the Chinese Nationalists.

Socialists in the House of Representatives Foreign Affairs Committee questioned Foreign Minister Aiichiro Fujiyama closely today on the implications of the controversial United States-Japanese security treaty in the context of current Communist Chinese invasion threats against the Nationalist-held offshore islands.

Without acknowledging outright agreement with the Socialist point of view on the United States bases here, Mr. Fujiyama promised that in his trip to Washington next month he would seek "some revisions of the pact so as to make it meet the existing situation."

The treaty cannot be revised or canceled without the consent of the United States. Mr. Fujiyama said that he was not optimistic that all of Japan's questions concerning the pact could be settled during his conversations with Secretary of State Dulles, scheduled for Sept. 11 and 12.

"Under the terms of the treaty," said Kei Hoashi, a Socialist member of the Foreign Affairs Committee, "Japan cannot make any protest to the United States even when her armed forces move out of their bases in Japan for the Formosa (Taiwan) front."

"This is a dangerous situation for Japan," the Socialist spokesman declared.

In answer, Mr. Fujiyama said merely that "we hope that the question of Formosa Strait will be settled peacefully."

The Foreign Minister added that Japan regarded the conflict between the Communist and Nationalist Chinese in the strait as "an internal affair of China."

The Japanese who desire closer relations with Communist China for the sake of trade are convinced that their ambitions are seriously imperiled by the continuing use of United States bases in Japan against the Chinese Communists.

In the view of many Japanese, the present routine use of United States bases here for reinforcement of the Seventh Fleet in Formosa Strait and for rotation of United States air units to Taiwan involves Japan in the China situation more directly than is desirable. A shooting conflict between the United States and Communist China, they feel, would make Japan's position even more delicate.

Under the terms of the United States-Japanese security treaty, the Tokyo Government has no control over deployment of United States forces in Japan. Many Japanese besides the Leftists feel strongly that this provision is a derogation of Japan's sovereignty, and they want Mr. Fujiyama to try to change it when he goes to Washington.

The boiling situation in Formosa Strait has given a topical point to these views that the Conservative Government of Premier Nobuske Kishi's Liberal-Democratic party cannot ignore.

"The United States-Japanese security pact should be revised in such a way as to meet the desire of the Japanese people and the existing situation in Japan," Mr. Fujiyama acknowledged to the Socialist critics in the Lower House committee today. "We have now self-defense forces and the feelings of the Japanese people now differ from those prevailing at the time the pact was concluded.

"Naturally, it should be my responsibility to effect some revisions of the pact so as to make it meet the existing situation.

"I think there are three ways to achieve this aim: First, to make a new treaty to replace the existing one; second, to effect partial revisions of the existing clauses of the teaty, and third, to retain the present treaty as it is and to adjust the pact through political methods."

Mr. Fujiyama stated in answer to another question that the present Japanese Government had "no intention" of recognizing Communist China.

"However, the Government desires to improve Japan's relations with Red China in trade and other fields," he added.

The Japanese Socialist party announced an official stand on the Taiwan situation today calling for the United States to "cease political and military intervention" and for Communist China to drop attempts to settle the Taiwan issue by force. The Communists, the Socialist statement said, should turn to "peaceful means" in their conflicts with the Nationalists.

Meanwhile Mr. Fujiyama rejected categorically a six-point demand by Communist China for settlement of the differences that caused the Peiping Government to break off all trade and other relations with Japan.

The crux of the Peiping demands concerned allegations that Japan was "intriguing" to create "two Chinas," one Nationalist and one Communist. Mr. Fujiyama denied this.

Peiping's key demand that Japan send a delegation to Peiping to "apologize" for the tearing down of the Communist Chinese flag in a Nagasaki department store—the immediate reason given for Red China's suspension of trade—was rejected by Mr. Fujiyama.

Text of Peiping Statement

HONG KONG, Sept. 4 (Reuters)—Following is the text of a statement by the Chinese Communist Government on China's territorial waters, as broadcast from Peiping:

The Government of the People's Republic of China declares as follows:

1. The breadth of the territorial sea of the People's Republic of China shall be twelve nautical miles. This provision applies to all the territories of the People's Republic of China, including the Chinese mainland and its coastal islands, as well as Taiwan and its surrounding islands, the Penghu Islands, the Tungsha Islands, the Hsisha Islands, the Chungsha Islands, the Nansha Islands and all other islands belonging to China which are separated from the mainland and its coastal islands by the high seas.

2. China's territorial sea along the mainland and its coastal islands takes as its baseline the line comprising straight lines connecting basepoints on the mainland coast and those on the coastal islands on the outer fringe, and the water area extending twelve nautical miles outward from the baseline is China's territorial sea. The water areas inside the baseline, including the Pohai Bay and the Chiungchow Strait, are Chinese inland waters. The islands inside the baseline, including the Tungyin Island, the Kaoteng Island, the Matsu Islands, the Paichuan Islands, the Wuchiu Island, the Greater and Lesser Quemoy Islands, the Tatan Island, the

311

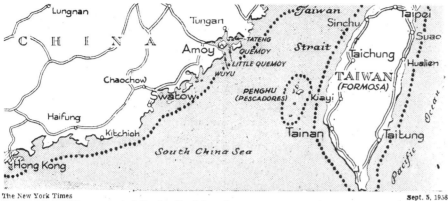

The New York Times   Sept. 5, 1958

Communist China asserted its territorial waters were now twelve miles from its shores and the shores of Taiwan, which it claims, as shown approximately by the dotted lines.

Erhtan Island and the Tungting Island, are islands of the Chinese inland waters.

3. No foreign vessels for military use and no foreign aircraft may enter the Chinese territorial sea and air space above it without the permission of the Government of the People's Republic of China.

Any foreign vessel while navigating the Chinese territorial sea must observe the relevant laws and regulations laid down by the Government of the People's Republic of China.

4. The principles provided in Paragraphs 2 and 3 likewise apply to Taiwan and its surrounding islands, the Penghu Islands, the Tunksha Islands, the Hsisha Islands, the Chungsha Islands, the Nansha Islands, and all other islands belonging to China.

The Taiwan and Penghu areas are still occupied by the United States by armed force. This is an unlawful encroachment on the territorial integrity and sovereignty of the People's Republic of China. Taiwan, Penghu and such other areas are yet to be recovered, and the Government of the People's Republic of China has the right to recover these areas by all suitable means at a suitable time. This is China's internal affair, in which no foreign interference is tolerated.

September 5, 1958

Far East Crisis

Over Taiwan Strait

The conflict between Chinese Communist and United States interests in the Far East was moving toward a showdown last week.

Communist military pressure against the Nationalist-held offshore islands brought from the United States the strongest commitment it has yet made to defend the islands. The U. S. served notice that a Communist attempt to invade the islands would be met with an American counter-attack, including bombardment of the Chinese mainland.

Thus a line was firmly drawn in the Far East and the big question now was: Would the Communists cross it? The consensus was that they would not. To do so might well precipitate a big war, and the belief is that Russia does not want its Chinese ally to push things that far.

Instead, the Communists appear to be building up military pressure as a prelude to pressing their diplomatic aims, including sovereignty over Taiwan, and thus once again raising among the allies the divisive issue of Washington's commitment to the Nationalist regime.

Yesterday, Chinese Premier Chou En-lai called for diplomatic talks for "the defense of peace" and Washington announced its willingness to negotiate.

Nonetheless, the prestige of both sides was heavily engaged in the Taiwan Strait and a point of no return—accidentally or deliberately—could easily be reached.

The Background

The Communist seizure and consolidation of power on the mainland of China a decade ago initiated an era of grave and almost continuous crisis in the Far East. Fundamentally, the crises were caused by the expansionist pressure of the Peiping regime in cooperation with Russia and the world Communist movement. The pressure was felt in Korea, in Indo-China and throughout Southeast Asia, and even in the far western reaches of the China land mass on the borders of India and Tibet.

Within that context, the conflict between the Chinese Communist regime and the Nationalist Government on Taiwan was at first largely symbolic. Generalissimo Chiang Kai-shek had fled to Taiwan and several of the smaller offshore islands with an army of about 600,000 after his Government collapsed on the mainland in 1949.

But his cause was clearly hopeless; his threats to reconquer China, hollow. Up to the summer of 1950 official United States policy was to deal gingerly with Chiang, discourage his notions of reconquest, and to accept the fact that Peiping would ultimate establish control over Taiwan and the smaller offshore islands.

Policy Changes

Communist aggression in Korea in 1950 changed that policy. Washington re-evaluated the strategic importance of Taiwan—a link in the great island chain formed by Japan to the north and the Philippines to the south—in the light of the clear evidence that the Communists were ready to pursue their Far East aims by force. President Truman ordered the U.S. Seventh Fleet to patrol the waters in the 100-mile wide stretch between Taiwan and the mainland and in 1953 President Eisenhower announced a policy generally described as "unleashing Chiang Kai-shek." In purely military terms, the "unleashing" was meaningless. Leashed, or unleashed, Chiang was in no position to launch a serious attack against the mainland unless backed to the hilt by U.S. military force. But the new policy created a certain amount of psychological pressure against the Peiping regime and it implicitly committed the United States to the fortunes of the Chiang Government and the territory it held, including a number of islands right on Communist China's doorstep. Chief among them were the Quemoys, which lie just off Amoy harbor three to five miles from the coast, and the Matsus, 150 miles to the north and about ten miles from the mainland.

Danger Points

The Quemoy and Matsu islands have since become the danger points in the conflict between Communist China and the U.S. in the Far East. The first major crisis over them occurred in 1955 when Peiping launched a series of raids and artillery attacks as an apparent prelude to invasion. The U.S. response was the Formosa Resolution of 1955, overwhelmingly passed by both Houses of Congress, which stated:

That the President of the United States be and he hereby is authorized to employ the armed forces of the United States as he deems necessary for the specific purpose of securing Formosa [Taiwan] and the Pescadores [a group of islets off the coast of Taiwan].

In terms of Quemoy and Matsu, the meaning of the resolution—deliberately ambiguous—was to leave to the President's discretion whether an attack on the islands might be a threat to the security of Taiwan. The Chiang Government, however, interpreted the resolution as encouragement to reinforce its garrisons on Quemoy and Matsu. A steady military build-up began.

The United States' allies were deeply disturbed by the Formosa Resolution and the potential commitment to Quemoy and Matsu. But Communist pressure against the islands eased after the Formosa Resolution and the issue receded.

Then last month, signs began to accumulate that new trouble was brewing. On July 31, Soviet Premier Nikita Khrushchev journeyed to Peiping for a four-day conference with Chinese Communist leader Mao Tse-tung. In the weeks immediately following the Peiping conference, the evidence pointed to a Mao-Khrushchev decision on new military moves in Taiwan Strait. Stepped up Communist artillery bombardment of Quemoy culminated on Aug. 23 in the heaviest shelling in the island's history.

The attacks produced warnings from Secretary of State John Foster Dulles and President Eisenhower, but the warnings had no marked effect on Communist military activity in the Strait. Once again the question came up as to whether the United States, under the terms of the Formosa Resolution, intended to defend the offshore islands. Thus the stage was set for the events of last week.

Week of Tension

The week began with concentrated efforts by the Communists to blockade the 100,000-man Quemoy garrison with fleets of torpedo boats. The Nationalists claimed to have sunk a number of torpedo boats, but the claims as well as the actual Communist naval strength in the area were matters of dispute. One thing seemed certain: the blockade was creating a serious problem for the Nationalists. A Nationalist spokesman said: "Our supply line to the offshore islands is threatened and there is a limit beyond which we alone will not be able to solve the problem."

In Washington Secretary of State John Foster Dulles engaged in an urgent round of conferences with top U. S. military and civilian officials and with representatives of the United States' allies. On Thursday he flew to President Eisenhower's vacation headquarters at Newport, R. I. He was closeted for an hour and forty-five minutes with the President in Mr. Eisenhower's office at the Coasters Harbor Island Naval Base while some seventy reporters waited outside. Then Mr. Dulles emerged to issue a prepared statement. It said:

* * * The President has not yet made any finding * * * that the employment of the armed forces of the United States is required or appropriate in insuring the defense of Formosa. The President would not, however, hesitate to make such a finding if he judged that the circumstances made this necessary * * *. In this connection we have recognized that the securing and protecting of Quemoy and Matsu have increasingly become related to the defense of Taiwan. * * * A Presidential determination, if made, would be followed by action both timely and effective.

Statement Clarified

What little ambiguity was left by the statement was dispelled in a subsequent briefing which the press was requested to attribute only to a "top Government official." The "official" made it clear that a decision had been reached to help defend Quemoy and Matsu if the Nationalist garrisons there proved unequal to the task. These were two of the exchanges:

Q. Would the bombing of concentrations on the mainland be a part of the defense of Formosa?

A. It might become so * * *.

Q. Is it fair to interpret this [statement] as a very stiff, blunt warning to Peiping not to try to make an attack against Quemoy?

A. If I were on the Chinese Communist side, I would certainly think very hard before I went ahead in the face of this statement.

The gravity of the situation was underscored by reports that the U. S. was considering escorting Nationalist vessels in running the Quemoy blockade. During the week the Communists proclaimed a twelve-mile territorial limit off the coast. The twelve-mile limit would include both Quemoy and Matsu and presumably provide the basis for Communist charges of "aggression" and invocation of the Sino-Soviet mutual defense treaty if U. S. craft helped break the Quemoy blockade.

It was in this explosive situation that Premier Chou yesterday made his bid for resumption of the ambassadorial talks between the United States and Communist China which broke up last December in Geneva. The talks, begun in 1955, dealt mainly with the question of Americans held prisoner by the Peiping regime, but eventually went on to other issues, including a demand made by the United States in 1955 for a renunciation of force by both sides in the Taiwan Strait. A few hours after issuing the demand for talks, Peiping announced a general mobilization of its 600,000,000 people for "the struggle against war provocations by American imperialists."

Yesterday President Eisenhower flew from Newport to Washington for a conference with Mr. Dulles, Secretary of Defense Neil H. McElroy, chairman of the Joint Chiefs of Staff Gen. Nathan F. Twining and other Government officials. At the conclusion of the meeting, the White House issued a statement saying that the United States "stands ready promptly to meet" with the Chinese Communists to resume the ambassadorial talks. The statement added:

Naturally * * * the United States will adhere to the negotiating position it originally took in 1955 — namely, that we will not * * * be a party to any arrangement which would prejudice the rights of our ally, The Republic of China.

September 7, 1958

KHRUSHCHEV LETTER ASKS U.S. TO RECOGNIZE PEIPING

U. N. ACTION URGED

Russians Would Curb Use of Naval Power to Enforce Policy

By WILLIAM J. JORDEN
Special to The New York Times

MOSCOW, Sept. 8—Premier Nikita S. Khrushchev has urged President Eisenhower in a lengthy letter to revise United States policy on China and to extend formal recognition to the Chinese Communist regime.

The Soviet Premier said that strained relations between Washington and Peiping were at the heart of the crisis in the Far East and that as a result the world faced the danger of war.

There was only one suggestion in the Premier's letter for talks of any kind. He said there had been too many instances of shifting naval and air fleets around the world to bring pressure on other countries. He proposed that this matter be taken up by the United Nations and that such military forces should be held "within their national frontiers."

Soviet View Outlined

The Soviet leader outlined Moscow's position regarding the Taiwan Strait as follows:

¶There is only one China and its Government is in Peiping.

¶That Government has every right to "take all necessary measures against the traitor Chiang Kai-shek" and to "liberate" all Chinese territory, including the offshore islands and Taiwan.

¶The United States has no right to interfere in what is clearly an internal Chinese affair.

¶Any attack on Communist China would be considered here as an attack on the Soviet Union. In that case the Soviet Government would do everything to "defend the security of both states."

Delivered on Sunday

Mr. Khrushchev's letter to President Eisenhower was delivered in Moscow Sunday evening to Richard H. Davis, United States Chargé d'Affaires. The text was made public tonight by the official press agency Tass.

Mr. Khrushchev's thesis was that the entire situation in the Far East and the threat of war could be attributed only to the United States and its policy in that area. It was therefore up to the United States to alter its basic position on China before the situation could be ameliorated.

Mr. Khrushchev accused the United States of following "a policy of war" in the Far East. He said the United States was trying to prevent the "liberation of Taiwan" and to "keep this Chinese island as its military base." He said transfers of United States naval units were coming to indicate areas that would be subjected to "blackmail and provocation."

"You will perhaps find what I said above too sharp," Mr. Khrushchev wrote. "I beg to differ. The only thing I want to do in this letter to you, just as on other occasions, is to speak my mind and to emphasize the full gravity of the situation which has developed in the area of Taiwan and China's offshore islands as a result of the United States actions.

"If we were to clothe our thought in outwardly courteous diplomatic wording, we would find it, I think, more difficult to see each other's point."

Mr. Khrushchev said he was anxious that President Eisenhower, the United States Government and the people of the United States, "with whom we desire only good relations," should understand correctly the consequences which United States actions in the Far East might have. He told President Eisenhower that "reservations and misunderstandings in such affairs are most dangerous."

"An attack on the Chinese People's Republic, which is a great friend, ally and neighbor of our country, is an attack on

313

the Soviet Union," Mr. Khrushchev wrote.

No Desire to Exaggerate

The Soviet Premier said he was stating this fact not to "exaggerate unnecessarily" or to "utter some kind of threat." He said he merely wanted to call to President Eisenhower's attention the situation that neither the Soviet Union nor the United States could avoid if war were to break out in the Far East.

Mr. Khrushchev's solution to the present crisis was a sharp reversal in United States policy as he had outlined it. He urged that there be an improvement in United States-Chinese relations. He conceded that recognition or nonrecognition of the Communist regime was an internal affair of the United States Government.

"But at present," he added, "the United States Government policy with regard to China has brought about a situation when the question of the United States attitude to China has transcended the boundaries of purely domestic affairs of the United States."

There is only one China, Mr. Khrushchev wrote, and that is on the mainland, not on Taiwan or other islands. Only the Chinese Communist Government should be representing China in the United Nations, he said.

"I believe that every person who is really alarmed for the fate of the world cannot but speak up for an end to the abnormal and dangerous situation which has developed as a result of the present political line of the United States Government in the Far East," Mr. Khrushchev wrote the President.

"The Soviet Government is convinced that it is necessary for this end to give up, above all the narrow-minded and absolutely unrealistic approach to the great historical changes which have taken place in China, it is necessary to recognize the lawful rights and interests of the People's Republic of China and to end once and for all the policy of provocations and blackmail against the Chinese people."

Mr. Khrushchev said there could be no stable peace until the United States Seventh Fleet withdrew from the Taiwan Strait and until United States troops left Taiwan. He told President Eisenhower that the alternative of peace or war in the Far East "will depend entirely on the further action of the Government of the United States."

Mr. Khrushchev said he was certain the American people wanted peace and hoped they would understand correctly the intent of his message.

Navies Termed Obsolete

MOSCOW, Sept. 8 (UPI) Mr. Khrushchev, in a reference to the United States Seventh Fleet in the Taiwan Strait, said navies were virtually obsolete in the nuclear age.

"In the age of nuclear and rocket weapons of unprecedented power and rapid action, these once formidable warships are fit, in fact, for nothing but courtesy visits and gun salutes, and can serve as targets for the right types of rockets," the Soviet Premier said.

September 9, 1958

U. S. OPENS TALKS WITH RED CHINESE IN 3-HOUR SESSION

By A. M. ROSENTHAL
Special to The New York Times.

WARSAW, Sept. 15—United States and Chinese Communist diplomats met for almost three hours here today to discuss the Far Eastern crisis. They then decided to take two days off to consult their governments on the next move in the negotiations.

Both sides had pledged to keep strict secrecy on what was said in the little Polish palace where the talks are taking place. Beyond a few hurried words of formal hopefulness uttered at the beginning and the announcement at the end that the next session would take place Thursday morning, the United States and Chinese negotiators would say nothing.

But the opinion of diplomats and political observers, Communist and non-Communist, in Warsaw was that the situation in the Far East was so dangerous that the talks would not be allowed to drag on indefinitely.

Bid to U. N. Held Likely

It was believed here that unless there developed some hope for real negotiation, rather than mere discussion, the United States would put the crisis before the United Nations.

Everyone here realized that the Warsaw talks were not taking place in a vacuum but were tied to what might happen concurrently thousands of miles away in the Taiwan Strait. The setting for the talks—a graceful park where mothers pushed baby carriages and a flute player practiced trills—was relaxed but inside the tan stone palace the mood was one of urgency.

The two negotiators are their government's Ambassadors in Warsaw. Jacob D. Beam of the United States and Wang Ping-nan of Communist China had seen each other many times at diplomatic receptions, but as is the custom with United States and Communist Chinese representatives all over the world, each had pretended the other did not exist.

Today they sat in an eighteenth century drawing room the Poles had changed into a conference chamber by taking out damask chairs and putting in some mahogany tables. Mr. Beam and Mr. Wang sat at separate tables facing each other and talked through interpreters. Each man had two other assistants.

It was felt here, however, that the instructions carried in the assistants' brief cases would allow little room for negotiation unless there was some withdrawal from positions emphasized again and again in Washington or Peiping.

Mr. Wang's superiors in Peiping have said repeatedly that a solution can lie only in recognition of Communist Chinese sovereignty over the small islands off the China coast. Mr. Beam's superiors in Washington, including President Eisenhower, have said that the Warsaw talks would not be allowed to damage the interests of Nationalist China, which holds the contested Matsu and Quemoy islands.

Objectives Differ

The two Ambassadors also seemed to have clearly different ideas of what the negotiations were supposed to accomplish.

The United States wants the talks to result in an end of hostilities in the Taiwan Strait and a declaration that force will not be used.

Just how much Mr. Beam will be permitted to offer in exchange is not known here, and quite probably will be determined by what the Communist Chinese themselves have to say.

Before he left Warsaw for talks in Peiping about ten days ago, Mr. Wang told other diplomats that his Government could not agree to any understanding that cast any doubt on Peiping's determination to gain control of Taiwan and the offshore islands. Nothing that has been said in Peiping since then has made any diplomat here believe Mr. Wang has received any drastic new instructions.

As for Mr. Beam, it is believed likely that he has been instructed to make proposals again for some sort of cease-fire arrangement, a step the Communist Chinese have indicated that they consider only a part of the whole problem.

The two diplomats and their assistants came to the place of meeting just before 3 P. M. The talks are being held in the Mysliwiecki Palace.

Built as a Hunting Lodge

It was built in 1775 as a hunting lodge—that is what its name means—by Stanislaw August Poniatowski, the last King of Poland.

It is a small palace as palaces go, having eighteen rooms, and is built in a gentle arc. Part of the building is baroque and part classical, but the styles do not clash.

Mr. Beam, when he arrived, made a hurried statement that he was happy the talks were starting so quickly and that he hoped they would achieve constructive results. Then he climbed the carpeted staircase into a reception room.

A few minutes later Mr. Wang said much the same thing, substituting "fruitful" for "constructive" and adding a few pleasant words about Warsaw.

Mr. Wang went into a different reception room and after a few minutes a Polish protocol officer brought the two delegations together in the conference room.

September 16, 1958

314

SOVIET WARNS JAPAN ON RED CHINA ROLE

Special to The New York Times.

TOKYO, Sept. 16 — The Soviet Union warned Japan today against allowing the United States to use her territory for "aggression" against Communist China.

In a note delivered to the Foreign Ministry, the Soviet Government urged the Japanese Government "to appraise the situation coolly and to take adequate measures to prevent the Japanese land from being used by American forces for aggressive acts."

Nikolai B. Adyrkhayev, counselor at the Soviet Embassy, announced the contents of the notes in a press conference.

The Japanese Foreign Ministry, in a brief statement issued tonight, rebutted the contention of the Soviet Government that Japan was participating in aggressive acts.

"Japan has pursued a foreign policy to settle all disputes peacefully," the statement said.

WASHINGTON, Sept. 16 (UPI)—The United States today branded as a smoke screen for Communist aggression the Soviet demand that Japan oust United States forces from Japanese bases.

The State Department said the Soviet Union "is trying to divert public attention from the support and encouragement it is giving the Chinese Communists" in their attacks on the Nationalist-held islands of Quemoy and Matsu.

WASHINGTON BARS CHINA COAST RAIDS

Stresses Diplomatic Efforts and Improved Convoys to Aid Quemoy Isles

Special to The New York Times.

WASHINGTON, Sept. 23— United States officials ruled out today any attempt in the foreseeable future to break the Quemoy blockade by aerial bombardment of Chinese Communist gun emplacements on the mainland.

Instead, they said, new efforts will be made in the diplomatic field to prevent a worsening of the conflict.

These officials emphatically rejected reports that the United States was preparing to tell the Communists that they would have to agree to a cease-fire or face aerial bombardment by Nationalist or United States planes.

The United States, the officials said, will continue to cooperate with the Chinese Nationalists to break the artillery blockade of Quemoy. But it will do this by trying to make the convoy system more effective, they added.

Negotiations Pressed

While this effort to supply the Nationalist defenders goes on, officials said, a parallel attempt will be made to convince the Communists that they have much to gain by negotiating peacefully in Warsaw for an easing of the tension over Taiwan and the lesser islands.

If this attempt fails, the alternative will be presentation of the whole issue to the United Nations.

Diplomats in the capital saw in all this some evidence that Secretary of State Dulles was being influenced by political and editorial criticism of the dangers of his Far Eastern policy.

Mr. Dulles, it was reported, is drafting plans for presentation of the Quemoy issue to the United Nations in case the Warsaw talks continue to prove fruitless. He was also said to be insisting that the Nationalists should refrain from aerial bombardment of the mainland.

U. N. Held Next Step

"Our policy," an official said tonight, "is to negotiate a cease-fire and go on from there to a peaceful settlement of the dispute. Obviously, threats of bombardment by us or the Nationalists would not be in accord with this policy. If the Warsaw talks do not produce a cease-fire, the next step is the United Nations."

Privately the Administration is understood to be taking a much more severe line with President Chiang Kai-shek than it is taking in public. He is said to have been left in no doubt that any new military attack on the mainland that would raise the possibility of involving the United States in direct military action against the Communists must be taken only with United States approval.

Washington is taking this line because any Nationalist aerial attack on the Communist gun emplacements might lead to Communist pursuit of the Nationalist bombers back to Taiwan and probably to Communist attacks on Taiwan itself.

Such attacks would presumably oblige the United States, under its treaty with Nationalist China, to enter the war. Accordingly, Washington is insisting on a veto of any Nationalist action that might provoke a counterattack on Taiwan.

Officials here are drawing a distinction between United States defensive measures to block an armed conquest of Quemoy and Matsu by the Communists and offensive measures by the United States or the Nationalists against the China mainland.

It is recognized that the distinction between defensive and offensive measures is getting narrower all the time. The Nationalists are using up more supplies every day than are getting through the Communist blockade.

Thus the day may come when the defense of the Nationalist garrisons on the offshore islands may require more effective offensive action against the Communist gun emplacements. But it is said here that this can probably be done short of aerial bombardment before the supply situation on Quemoy and Matsu becomes critical.

For example, more effective long-range guns can be sent to Quemoy and Matsu. The supply of arms and food to the Nationalist garrisons can be increased by more effective United States air and naval action. If absolutely necessary, United States naval vessels can convoy supplies inside the Nationalist three-mile limit. Such a course would be tried, even in tricky shallow water, before Washington would agree to any aerial bombardment of the mainland.

Intelligence reports from the Quemoy area note with satisfaction that there is still no invasion fleet in the vicinity. There has been a build-up of Communist arms and men on the Fukien coast opposite Quemoy, but no fleet of ships that could carry out the Communist invasion threats, it was said.

In Warsaw, where Ambassadors Jacob D. Beam and Wang Ping-nan have been negotiating, the talks thus far have not been encouraging. Reports of the third meeting yesterday recorded no progress toward a cease-fire.

September 17, 1958

September 24, 1958

315

State Department Transcript of Remarks Made by Dulles at News Conference

Special to The New York Times.

WASHINGTON, Sept. 30 — Following is the text of the State Department's transcript of Secretary Dulles' news conference today:

5 Q.—Mr. Secretary, in referring to the previous question on the renunciation of force, is it the position of this Government that the United States expects or supports the idea that the Nationalist Chinese Government is some day going to return to the mainland either by force or some other means?

A.—Well, that is a highly hypothetical matter. I think it all depends upon what happens on the mainland. I don't think that just by their own steam they are going to get there. If you had on the mainland a sort of unrest and revolt, like, for example, what broke out in Hungary, then the presence of a free China with considerable power a few miles away could be a very important element in the situation. I think that we would all feel that if there had been a free Government of Hungary in existence within a few miles of Hungary at the time when the revolt took place, that the situation might have developed in a different way from what it did.

So I wouldn't want to exclude any possibility of a situation developing on the mainland of China or on parts of the mainland of China which might not lead to reunification of some sort between mainland China, or that part of mainland China, and the free Government of China, the Republic of China now on Formosa. I do not exclude it

10 Q.—Mr. Secretary, you mentioned a few minutes ago an exchange of letters between yourself and Foreign Minister Yeh in December, 1954. In that exchange it was agreed that military elements which are the product of joint effort of the two countries would not be removed from the treaty area without mutual consent. Did we agree, as President Chiang said yesterday, to the fortification of the off-shore islands and their build-up?

A.—The United States did not feel that it was sound to make the major commitment of force to those areas that the Chinese Government wished to make. In view, however, of the very strong views of the Republic of China, we were acquiescent in that. We did not attempt to veto it. The result is, I might say, one of acquiescence on the part of the United States, not of approval. Nor did we attempt

to veto it after having used persuasion.

17 Q.—Mr. Secretary, inasmuch as you say you do not think it was sound for the Nationalist Chinese to have built up their forces on Quemoy and Matsu, I would like to ask you if you now think it would be sound to work out some arrangement for the withdrawal of those forces from those two islands?

A.—It all depends upon the circumstances under which they would be withdrawn. I think to withdraw as a retreat under fire would not be a wise step to take because of the probable impact of that upon other peoples, other countries and upon the morale, indeed, on Formosa itself.

18 Q.—Would you state, sir, the circumstances under which you think a withdrawal could be achieved?

A.—If there were a cease-fire in the area which seemed to be reasonably dependable, I think it would be foolish to keep these large forces on these islands. We thought that it was rather foolish to put them there and, as I say, if there were a cease-fire it would be our judgment, military judgment, even, that it would not be wise or prudent to keep them there.

19 Q.—Mr. Secretary, you seem to emphasize the need for a dependable cease-fire. Could you tell us how you can get a dependable cease-fire with the Communists whose promises you don't like to accept?

A.—That is certainly a fair question and a difficult one to answer. I believe that promises of the Communists are never dependable merely because they are promises. They are only dependable if there are unpleasant consequences in case the Communists break their promises. And I believe that circumstances could be created where it would be felt that the consequences of breaking this promise would be so undesirable to the Communists that we could assume that they would probably live up to their promise, not because of the sanctity of the given word—which they do not believe in—but because of expediency.

20 Q.—Mr. Secretary, would it be necessary for a cease-fire to be written or unwritten? Could it be a de facto cease-fire gained simply by the cessation of shooting without anything being written?

A.—I think it could be de facto.

21 Q.—Mr. Secretary, some Senators seem to believe

that the Administration is extending the area of the security treaty with the Republic of China and they are recalling that in February when you went before the Senate Foreign Relations Committee and said if you had any intention of extending the area you would return to the Senate. Is this a proper construction, you think, that is being put upon our activity there?

A.—No, I do not. The situation is that we do not have any legal commitment to defend the off-shore islands. We do not want to make any such commitment. We do not have it today.

What we are acting under is the authority of the Joint Resolution, which is equally the law of the land, which says that if the President believes that the defense of those off-shore islands is necessary or appropriate for the defense of the treaty area, then he can use the forces of the United States for that purpose. And that is the way it was understood and that is the way we want it.

I would say today, if the United States believed that these islands could be abandoned without its having any adverse impact upon the potential defense of Formosa and the treaty area, we would not be thinking of using forces there. It's because there is that relationship, under present conditions, conditions primarily of the Communist making, that there is the tie-in there.

They say this is a push which is designed not merely to push the Chinese Nationalists out of Quemoy and Matsu but to push the United States out of Formosa. And when you have the edge, the front edge, of a wedge that is driving in, and where they say they are not going to stop at the first obstacle but to go on, then you have to decide whether by allowing the wedge to gather momentum and go on you are strengthening or weakening the defense of the area you are committed to defend. That is the problem we have to think about.

22 Q.—Mr. Secretary, do you see any progress so far in a little more than two weeks of negotiation and crisis that now has gone on for more than a month; do you see any progress at all toward a peaceful settlement either on an agreed basis or on a de facto basis?

A.—I feel that there is a slight tendency toward a stabilization of the situation, and I feel on the whole that there is less likelihood of the hostilities intensifying and enlarging than I thought was the case a couple weeks ago.

23 Q.—Mr. Secretary, what do you have in mind when you say you think the circumstances could be created which would make breaking a cease-fire commitment by the Communists unpleasant? Were you talking about some joint Allied commitment for Formosa itself, or something else?

A.—I am thinking of sanctions that might be applied, perhaps by other nations in addition to the United States. For example, possible trade sanctions and the like.

26 Q.—Under Secretary Herter said in a speech yesterday that the Quemoy and Matsu Islands are "not defensible in the defense of Formosa" and that the Chinese Nationalists' very devotion to them is "almost pathological." Do you subscribe to those views?

A.—I didn't hear the first sentence that you read. Are not defensible?

Q.—Are not defensible in the defense of Formosa. It is phrased rather awkwardly, but it is a direct quote.

Q.—In The New York Times it says, "not strategically defensible in the defense of Formosa."

A.—Well, I don't like to comment on isolated quotations from a speech. I'd rather see what the full text said. I'm not familiar with it.

27 Q.—Mr. Secretary, you said twice at the outset this morning that the United States policy has not changed. Yet during the course of the news conference you have seemed to clarify at least two major points that, so far as I know, have not been publicly clarified by the department before, to wit: the reciprocal aspect of renunciation of force and the fact that the United States considered it foolish to build up military force on the islands and that under certain circumstances they should be withdrawn. If these two points are major and important, as they seem to be, why haven't they been expressed publicly before?

A.—Well, there is nothing really new in our attitude on either of those propositions. I think, if you will go back, for example, to study the record of our prior talks with the Chinese Communists, we have assumed that the renunciation of force should be reciprocal if it occurs and that it would be obviously quite impractical and quite wrong to ask the Chinese Communists to abandon use of force if they were being attacked by the Chinese Nationalists. I might say that when we speak about renunciation of force it has always been a renunciation of force except for purposes of self-defense. Perhaps I did not make that clear before. So that if anybody it attacked, then the renunciation of force would, of course, not apply.

28 Q.—Mr. Secretary, is it fair to say that while United States policy has not changed as of now, there is a possibility of some important changes provided there is some give on the Chinese Communist side?

A.—Yes, I would say so. Our policy in these respects is flexible and adapted to the situation that we have to meet. If the situation we have to meet changes, our policies change with it.

October 1, 1958

PRESSURES MOLD U.S. CHINA POLICY

Record Since Reds' Victory in 1949 Shows Response to Five Diverse Forces

By E. W. KENWORTHY

Special to The New York Times

WASHINGTON, Oct. 4 — United States policy concerning Taiwan and the offshore islands has been the product of five pressures: those exerted by the Chinese Communists, the Chinese Nationalists, partisan politics, public opinion and the United States' principal allies.

These pressures, as a record of events since the Chinese Communists won the mainland in 1949 reveals, have caused the policy to shift direction from time to time. The record also shows that the very existence of the Nationalist regime has confronted the United States with a constant series of dilemmas.

The following is a résumé of the main events and policy decisions from 1949 to the present day.

A Question of Defense

When Generalissimo Chiang Kai-shek retreated to Taiwan in December, 1949, the United States Government was confronted with the question of whether it should "defend Formosa," as Taiwan was then known.

On Dec. 29, the National Security Council decided that United States forces should not be used to defend the island and on Jan. 5, 1950, President Truman announced:

"The United States Government will not pursue a course which will lead to involvement in the civil conflict in China. Similarly, the United States Government will not provide military aid or advice to Chinese forces on Formosa."

This policy decision brought denunciations from a Republican group led by former President Herbert Hoover and Senators William F. Knowland of California and H. Alexander Smith of New Jersey.

Former Senator Tom Connally, Foreign Relations Committee chairman, replied:

"Whenever this subject is brought up again, I am going to want to know who the Senators are who want to plunge this country into war—not directly to do so but to risk doing so—in the name of bitter attacks on the President and the Secretary of State."

The late Senator Arthur H. Vandenberg, leader of the so-called moderate Republicans on the issue, complained of the Administration's failure to consult Congress but said he wished to avoid "active American military preparation" for the defense of Taiwan.

Generally the press and public opinion, based on samplings, showed the country behind the Administration's position and adverse to "adventures" in Asia.

On Jan. 12, 1950, Secretary of State Dean Acheson, in a speech, drew the United States Pacific defense line "from the Aleutians to Japan, thence to the Ryukyus and the Phillippines."

"So far as other areas of the Pacific are concerned," Mr. Acheson said, "it must be clear that no persons can guarantee these areas against attack."

This excluded China and Taiwan from the defensible area.

With the invasion of South Korea, in June, 1950, the "no defense" policy with regard to Taiwan collapsed. In view of the Communist attack, President Truman announced:

"The occupation of Formosa would be a direct threat to the security of the Pacific area and to the United States forces performing their lawful and necessary functions in that area."

He ordered the Seventh Fleet to patrol the Taiwan Strait with the double purpose of preventing a Chinese Communist attack and any aggressive action by General Chiang's forces against the mainland that would widen the scope of the Korean war.

This was the "leashing" of the Chinese Nationalists against which the Republicans inveighed in the 1952 campaign. In his State of the Union message on Feb. 2, 1953, President Eisenhower "unleashed" Generalissimo Chiang. He declared the "deneutralizing" of Taiwan by stating that the Seventh Fleet would no longer be "employed to shield Communist China."

Truman Orders Recalled

As a matter of fact, the situation was then quiet in the area and remained so for some time. Generalissimo Chiang did not have the amphibious equipment to attack the mainland. The Chinese Communists had their hands full in North Korea and in the supplying of Communist forces in the Indochina revolt against France.

By August, 1954, however, Peiping was free to turn the pressure on the offshore islands. Amid reports of a military build-up on the mainland, President Eisenhower was asked at his news conference on Aug. 17 what would happen if the Chinese Communists did attack Taiwan in force.

The President replied that he had reaffirmed Mr. Truman's orders when he assumed office.

"Any invasion of Formosa would have to run over the Seventh Fleet," he said.

On Sept. 3 Communist guns opened up on Quemoy, and the Nationalist returned the fire. The Pentagon gave Generalissimo Chiang the go-ahead to use his planes to destroy the Communist shore batteries and any concentration of troops and junks.

With the Communist bombardment continuing and Nationalist planes making daily raids on Amoy fortifications, three of the four members of the Joint Chiefs of Staff voted to recommend to the President that if the Communists tried to seize Quemoy, United States planes should join the Nationalist Air Force in bombing mainland communications. Secretary of State Dulles concurred.

The dissenting member of the Joint Chiefs was Gen. Matthew B. Ridgway, Army Chief of Staff. He was joined by Gen. Walter Bedell Smith, Under Secretary of State, who persuaded the President to call a National Security Council meeting. The meeting was held Sept. 12.

Admiral Arthur W. Radford, Chairman of the Joint Chiefs, argued for action against the Communists. Secretary Dulles, it was reported, supported him. Secretary of Defense Charles E. Wilson was said to have counseled action only after "provocation." Vice President Richard M. Nixon, who was campaigning on "peace," was reported to have opposed United States intervention. The President supported General Smith and General Ridgway.

The Communist barrage let up in mid-September, and the strait was quiet through October and early November. But the threats from Peiping continued.

Three questions confronted the Administration: What was to be the extent of the United States commitment to Generalissimo Chiang? How was he to be "released"? Could a cease-fire be obtained, and at what price?

Pressure on Chiang

The Administration decided that the first two tasks could be achieved through one instrument—a defense treaty with Taiwan, for which Generalissimo Chiang had been pressing—and which had been under discussion for months. It was decided he should get his defense treaty, but only with a firm undertaking that he would not engage in any provocative attacks.

Secret talks were begun with the British on how to obtain a cease-fire under United Nations auspices.

From briefings of reporters it became generally known that the decision to "re-leash" the Chinese Nationalists and to seek a cease-fire meant that the Administration had recognized the virtual impossibility of Generalissimo Chiang's return to the mainland and had, in effect, settled on a "two Chinas" solution.

By the same route it was understood that if the Communists would accept a cease-fire and observe it, the United States was prepared—with all the weight supplied by General Chiang's dependence on the United States—to induce him to abandon the offshore islands. But, it was said, the United States was not yet prepared to approve United Nations membership for Communist China—even on a "two Chinas" basis.

At the end of November, 1954, Peiping threw a wrench into these plans by launching an attack on Wuchiu Island and by announcing that eleven United States airmen and two civilians had been sentenced to long terms on charges of espionage.

General Chiang, seeing his opportunity, called on the United States to pledge defense of the offshore islands as well as Taiwan and the Pengkus (Pescadores). Senator Knowland called for a United States blockade of Communist China.

President Eisenhower refused to be stampeded. He said at his news conference:

"We must make certain that our efforts to promote peace are not interpreted as appeasement * * * but we must, on the other hand, be steady and refuse to be goaded into actions that would be unwise.

"It is possible that a blockade is conceivable without war. I have never heard of it historically. A blockade is an act in war intended to bring your adversary to your way of thinking or to his knees."

On Dec. 2, 1954, the treaty with Taiwan was signed. In a statement Mr. Dulles emphasized that it committed the

United States only to the defense of Taiwan and the Penghus.

As for the new "leash," the Chinese Nationalists agreed they would use force against the mainland only with the United States' consent, except for emergency action under the inherent right of self-defense.

On Jan. 17, 1955, the Communists launched air attacks against the Tachens, 200 miles north of Formosa. Two days later President Eisenhower said the Tachens were not essential to the defense of Taiwan. He added that he would like to see the United Nations "attempt to exercise its good offices" to secure a cease-fire. Taipei strongly objected to his remark about the cease-fire.

As the attacks continued, President Eisenhower on Jan. 24 laid the "Formosa Resolution" before Congress. Its principal clause empowered the President to employ United States armed forces "as he deems necessary for the specific purpose of securing and protecting Formosa and the Pescadores," including the protection of "related positions" —that is, the offshore islands.

A small group of Senators led by Herbert H. Lehman and Hubert H. Humphrey, tried to pull the offshore islands out from under the umbrella, but their amendment mustered only thirteen votes and the resolution was law four days after the President had submitted it.

On Jan. 31 the United Nations Security Council voted, with only Nationalist China opposed and the Soviet Union abstaining, to take up the question of a cease-fire and to invite Communist China to take part in the debate.

Chou En-lai, Chinese Communist Premier, rejected the idea of a cease-fire and said Peiping would not go to New York unless it was given China's seat at the Security Council.

On Feb. 7, 1955, Secretary Dulles, in testimony before the Foreign Relations Committee on the mutual defense treaty, assured the Senators that "an

agreement to extend the coverage of the China defense treaty to additional territories would, in practical terms, amount to an amendment of the treaty and should be submitted to the Senate for its advice and consent."

The treaty was voted readily.

Within a few days the United States evacuated Nationalist forces from the Tachens. In a speech in New York on Feb. 16, Mr. Dulles explained that the Tachens were "virtually unrelated" to the defense of Taiwan.

With the situation still critical, Adlai E. Stevenson proposed on April 11 that the United States ask its allies and the uncommitted nations "to join with us in an open declaration condemning the use of force in the Formosa Strait and agreeing to stand with us in the defense of Formosa."

"Fortified by such an international declaration," Mr. Stevenson said, "I should think that Quemoy and Matsu would have little further importance to the Nationalists, let alone to us."

Mr. Dulles' comment occasioned some surprise. He said that aside from attaching too little importance to Chinese Nationalist attitudes, "Mr. Stevenson has in fact endorsed the main features of this Administration's program."

Two weeks later came what many hoped would prove to be the turning point in the whole issue. On April 23, Mr. Chou said: "The Chinese Government is willing to sit down and enter into negotiations with the United States to discuss especially the question of relaxing tension in the Taiwan area."

Mr. Dulles was on a brief vacation and in his absence Under Secretary Herbert Hoover Jr. issued a statement: "Of course the United States would insist on Free China's participation as an equal in any discussion concerning the area."

An immediate cry of protest went up from allied and neutral nations. Returning to Washing-

ton two days later, Mr. Dulles quickly set matters straight.

Bilateral Talks Backed

He said that the presence of Nationalist China was not necessary for cease-fire negotiations, which could be conducted "bilaterally" between the United States and Communist China.

"If we could get assurances there was to be no attack against Formosa, we would accept those," he said.

But Mr. Dulles insisted the assurances on a cease fire must be public in order to have "adequate sanction" behind them.

Diplomatic meetings between the two nations began in August, 1955, and continued— there were seventy-three in all —until last December. Repeatedly the United States tried to get Peiping to agree to a renunciation of force, "particularly in the Taiwan area." Always the Communist delegate struck out that phrase.

Throughout this period there was a de facto cease-fire, which was broken only occasionally by desultory shelling. Taipei used the period to build up its strength on the offshore islands, until roughly a third of its force—about 100,000 men— was deployed on them.

Last Aug. 23, Communist guns began a large-scale barrage against Quemoy, Little Quemoy and two smaller islands near by. Peiping demanded that the United States withdraw its forces from the area. On Sept. 4, after a conference with the President at Newport, R. I., Secretary Dulles said:

"Any such naked use of force would pose an issue far transcending the offshore islands and even the security of Taiwan. It would forecast a widespread use of force in the Far East which would endanger free world positions and the security of the United States."

Mr. Dulles made it clear that, under the Formosa Resolution, the United States would come to the aid of the Nationalists to prevent the seizure of the offshore islands.

In a national broadcast, a week later, President Eisenhower stated the Administration's decision even more forcefully:

"I do not believe that the United States can be either lured or frightened into appeasement. I believe that, in taking the position of opposing aggression by force, I am taking the only position which is consistent with the vital interests of the United States and, indeed, with the peace of the world."

The Administration's decision set off a debate far more intense than that which took place when the resolution was adopted.

By and large, Republican legislators stood behind the President and Mr. Dulles. But influential Democratic Senators were highly critical.

Criticism Abroad

State Department officials conceded that they found little support for the Administration in the 100 newspapers used to test press opinion, or in the letters from private citizens coming into the department. Congressional mail was running heavily against the policy, according to many Senators.

There also was intense criticism of United States policy in allied and neutral countries.

At his news conference last Tuesday Mr. Dulles said that the United States had "acquiesced" in the build-up of military forces on the offshore islands although it believed it "was rather foolish to put them there." He said further that it would be "foolish" to keep them there "if there were a cease-fire" that was honored.

Finally, he said, that the cease fire could be a "de facto" one.

It is precisely here that many Washington observers believe the Secretary has indicated a marked departure from previous policy. In April, 1955, he had insisted that the cease-fire must be public.

PEIPING OFFERS CEASE-FIRE IN QUEMOY AREA FOR WEEK IF U. S. STOPS CONVOYING

Special to The New York Times

HONG KONG, Monday, Oct. 6 — The Chinese Communists ordered today a one-week suspension of their shelling of the Nationalist offshore islands "out of humanitarian considerations."

Defense Minister Peng Teh-huai said the Nationalists "will be fully free to ship in supplies on condition that there be no American escort."

He proposed immediate talks between the Communist and Nationalist Governments for peaceful settlement of what he called the "internal Chinese matter between you and us."

[United Press International reported from Taiwan that Communist guns fell silent Monday morning. According to The Associated Press, a Nationalist convoy with United States escort reached Quemoy after the hour set for the start of the cease-fire.]

Calls U. S. Joint Enemy

The message was broadcast by the Peiping radio early today and was addressed to "all compatriots, military and civilian, in Taiwan, Penghu [Pescadores], Quemoy and Matsu."

In bold, broad terms Marshal Peng described the thirty-year war between the Communists and the Nationalists as a useless struggle between brothers. He pictured the United States as "the common enemy."

"We all are Chinese," he said. "Of all choices, peace is the best."

Marshal Peng, who is also a Deputy Premier, said: "I have ordered the bombardment to be suspended on the Fukien front for seven days starting from Oct. 6."

Nationalist Raids Cited

Quemoy and, to a lesser extent, Matsu have been under Communist shellfire since Aug. 23.

The Defense Minister said Communist military action in the Quemoy area was of a "punitive character" designed "just to call your attention" to the "far too rampant leadership" of the Nationalist leaders, who in the past "ordered aircraft to carry out wanton raids on the mainland, dropping leaflets and secret agents, bombing Foochow and harassing Kiangsu and Chekiang, reaching as far as Yunnan, Kweichow and Szechwan.

He said: "Can this be tolerated? Hence this firing of a few shells just to call your attention."

Speaking in brotherly and sometimes even in fatherly fashion, Marshal Peng firmly implied that the peoples under Communist and Nationalist rule were in basic agreement and there was no problem between them that could not be settled by immediate United States withdrawal from the Asian scene.

Marshal Peng said: "Taiwan, Penghu, Quemoy and Matsu are Chinese territory. To this you agree, as proved by documents issued by your leaders, which confirm that they are indeed not territory of the Americans.

"Taiwan, Penghu, Quemoy and Matsu are part of China. They do not constitute another country. There is only one China, not two, in the world. To this you also agree as proved by documents issued by your leaders.

"The military agreement signed between your leaders and the Americans is unilateral; we do not recognize it. It should be abrogated.

"The day will certainly come when the Americans will abandon you. Do you not believe it? History will bear witness to it. The clue is already there in the statement made by Dulles on Sept. 30. In such circumstances, do you not feel wary?"

[In his news conference of Sept. 30, Secretary of State Dulles called a return to the mainland by the Nationalists "highly hypothetical." He said that in case of a revolt on the mainland it was "hypothetical and problematical" whether Generalissimo Chiang Kai-shek would return as head of government. Mr. Dulles also said the United States had no commitment to help the Nationalists return to the mainland.]

Expresses Sympathy

Expressing sympathy for the 130,000 "hungry, cold" troops and civilians on Quemoy, Marshal Ping promised that Communist forces would not interfere with supply convoys in the next seven days provided they were not escorted by United States forces.

Marshal Ping said: "The war between you and us has been going on thirty years. It is not good that it is not yet stopped. We propose that talks be held to effect a peaceful settlement. You were notified of this by Premier Chou En-lai several years ago. This is an internal Chinese matter between you and us, not a matter between China and the United States.

"The issue between China and the United States is United States invasion and occupation of Taiwan, Penghu and the Taiwan Strait, and this should be settled through negotiations between the two countries, which are now being held in Warsaw."

Marshal Peng pictured the ultimate departure of the United States not only from Taiwan but from the entire Western Pacific as inevitable.

Marshal Peng said only by such a withdrawal could the United States regain the initiative. "Otherwise, it [the United States] will be at a disadvantage because it will then be always on the defensive," he said.

"There is no war between the People's Republic of China and the United States," Marshal Peng said, "and so the question of a cease-fire does not arise."

CEASE-FIRE: COMMUNIST REASONS

By HARRY SCHWARTZ

Last week's developments in the Taiwan Strait crisis contributed much in the way of both clarity and hope with regard to that sensitive and potentially most dangerous situation.

Most of the world was caught by surprise last Sunday when Communist China's Defense Minister, Marshal Peng Teh-huai, announced a week's cease-fire by his forces opposing the Nationalists on Quemoy and the other offshore islands.

But much of that surprise, and the speculation it set off, was stilled last Friday when the background of that cease-fire became known. Two weeks ago, we now know, the Communist Chinese, using the Norwegians as intermediaries, proposed to the United States an interim end of hostilities around the offshore islands. It was in response to that offer that Secretary of State Dulles eleven days ago announced the United States favors reduction of Nationalist garrisons on Quemoy and Matsu if the Communist shelling of those islands stops.

Peiping's Reasoning

In the light of this new evidence there appears possible now a reconstruction of the Communist Chinese thinking and expectations when they decided last summer to try to subdue Quemoy by artillery bombardment plus air and sea blockade.

Peiping's key expectation apparently was that these tactics could induce the Nationalist defenders of Quemoy to surrender. Presumably behind this judgment were two mistaken Chinese Communist intelligence conclusions: First, a wrong estimate of the morale of the Nationalist troops on Quemoy and their ability to stand up under the ferocious fire rained down upon them from the mainland; second, a wrong judgment about how effectively Quemoy could be blockaded by Peiping's ships and planes.

In retrospect it seems likely now that it was on this estimate of a quick and relatively painless conquest of Quemoy that Mao Tse-tung won Premier Khrushchev's consent for the Quemoy adventure when the latter flew so secretly and suddenly to Peiping ten weeks ago.

Against this background the key reason for Communist

China's decision to institute the cease-fire last weekend was the simple disappointment of its hopes. The Nationalist defenders, whether on Quemoy or on the even more badly battered little islands off Quemoy, did not surrender, and the Communist blockade of Quemoy proved less than impenetrable.

Fear of War

A second factor that seems to have played a role in Peiping's decision to ease the tension in the Taiwan Strait is the fact that as the battle continued fear rose around the world that this crisis might finally touch off World War III. Although it received no public expression, that fear can hardly have been less in Eastern Europe, the Soviet Union and Communist China itself than it was in the free world, where such anxiety was widely voiced.

It seems significant in this regard that Marshal Peng's cease fire announcement was issued almost simultaneously with Premier Khrushchev's statement carefully limiting the Soviet Union's obligation to go to war for Communist China for any reason short of an American "attack" on the latter. On the face of it that statement would seem to suggest that Soviet pressure was exerted on Peiping to prevent the Taiwan Strait situation from leading to ultimate catastrophe for all.

Finally, both in Moscow and in Peiping it was well appreciated that the Eisenhower Administration was under substantial pressure both from American public opinion and from this country's allies to adopt a flexible policy.

Hopes Failed

If this reasoning is correct then in the last half of last month the Communist leaders, once they had realized their hopes of quick victory at Quemoy would not materialize, were faced with the problem of "extrication with honor" which was defined in that period as the key United States problem. In the pressure exerted on President Eisenhower and Secretary Dulles they presumably saw the opportunity for at least the beginning of such extrication and hence they took their secret initiative.

The immediate problem now is whether the Communist bombardment will be resumed or the cease-fire will be extended.

It seems fair to say that the weight of Western opinion this week-end is that the cease-fire will be continued. Whether that proves true or not will depend upon the relative weight Mao and his colleagues — and presumably Premier Khrushchev as well — give to the different factors on each side of the issue.

In favor of a cease-fire's continuance is the simple fact that last week's events have made Quemoy less vulnerable to military attack than at any time since the firing began. Supplies have been replenished on a generous scale. The morale of the defenders has been raised by the clear fact that their resistance brought them surcease from bombardment. Meanwhile resumption of the bombardment would renew the grave risks which the first stage of the effort brought.

Against this the Communist Chinese leaders know that Generalissimo Chiang has already claimed victory in the first stage of the latest battle of Quemoy and will almost certainly renew that claim if the cease-fire is continued. Improvement of the morale of the Nationalists is no part of present plans in Peiping or Moscow.

Yet whether or not the cease-fire is renewed, Marshal Peng's declaration last Sunday made clear the ultimate direction in which Peiping sees victory over Chiang, a victory it expects to achieve without precipitating World War III.

It seeks that ultimate victory through use of political and psychological weapons. Marshal Peng's announcement set the tone by appealing to the Nationalists to capitulate before the United States "abandons you." Peiping is obviously hoping that the Nationalists, seeing Secretary Dulles' willingness to compromise on the issue of the offshore islands will at least in part decide that their cause is hopeless and they will never return as victors to the mainland. Such a conclusion, Peiping hopes, will cause subversion on Taiwan, perhaps culminating in a coup d'etat by elements willing to make a deal with Mao.

Chinese Gains

Whether or not these Peiping expectations are realized, Mao and his colleagues can console themselves with the thought that the crisis they began last August has put their country at the center of the world stage. The talks between the ambassadors of the United States and Communist China have been resumed in Warsaw, after an interruption of months, and wide circles of American public opinion, as well as the White House, have been forced to take another look at this country's policy toward the Chinese Communist regime.

That these results alone fully satisfy Peiping seems dubious. But certainly this past week the probability seemed to grow that there will be a political settlement of the Taiwan Strait crisis, a settlement from which Communist China may expect some gains, even though those gains may not be all that Mao and Premier Khrushchev hoped for when they conferred two and a half months ago.

Shells Again Hit Quemoy

TAIPEI, Taiwan, Sunday, Oct. 26 (AP)—Communist guns fired on the Nationalist offshore islands today a few hours after Peiping announced it would withhold firing on an off-again-on-again basis. The defense ministry here reported. Today was the first of the even-numbered days.

The first shells hit Quemoy at 9 A. M., the ministry here said.

The odd-date-even-date shelling plan was viewed by the Nationalists as an attempt to crack the newly-reinforced unity between them and the United States.

There were indications the Nationalists intended to defy the Communist warning not to move in supplies on odd days.

"It doesn't matter whether the Communists shell or not; we shall continue carrying supplies to Quemoy as usual," said the chief military spokesman, Rear Admiral Liu Hoh-tu

Warsaw Talks Suspended

WARSAW, Oct. 25 (AP)— The United States and Communist China today suspended their deadlocked talks on the Taiwan crisis for two weeks to "think it over."

The next session between Jacob D. Beam of the United States and Wang Ping-Nan of Red China was set for Nov. 7.

They held their first meeting in ten days this afternoon. Informed sources said they found no points of agreement during their parley of an hour and 45 minutes.

October 11, 1958

October 26, 1958

Asia and the Pied Piper of Peiping

By C. L. SULZBERGER

PARIS, March 31—This may not be pleasant reading in Washington, but there is no doubt that on his recent tour of free Asia the ineffable Mr. Chou En-lai achieved a personal triumph comparable to that of the Pied Piper of Hamelin. His individual charm and political magic were apparently sufficient to lead an important number of non-Communist statesmen into a mental cavern similar to that reserved for children by the medieval tootler.

Nobody knows precisely what, if anything, Chou was selling besides goodwill and his own attractive personality. But there is no question about the success of that particular bit of salesmanship—not only in remote Ceylon but among China's somewhat suspicious neighbors: Burma, Nepal, India, Pakistan and Afghanistan.

Pakistan's Prime Minister Suhrawardy, who has in his drawing room a silver-framed, inscribed photograph of the smiling Chinese, considers him "delightful and remarkable." Nehru—not usually in Suhrawardy's corner — observes: "Chou is a brilliant man, one of the greatest I ever met. He seems tolerant and perhaps more conservative than the others. Of course he is obviously a sincere Communist. But he gives the impression of being very open-minded. Whether he is or not, he gives that feeling. This is important."

Prince Daud, Afghanistan's crafty Premier, confides enthusiastically: "Chou has great personality. I found him very moderate." Daud's brother and Foreign Minister, Prince Naim, adds: "He wanted nothing here but to improve relationships. He is undoubtedly able and charming. He makes an outstanding impression."

A 'Smart' Man

In Ceylon Sir John Kotelawala who tangled with Chou at the famous Bandung Conference, acknowledges: "That man is smart. He knows when to get angry and when to be nice. He speaks good English and French, but he talks through a interpreter in order to gain time to think. He is a very practical fellow —and full of charm."

Kotelawala's successor, Prime Minister Bandaranaike agrees: "He is a cultured man and able. Chou wants friendship with as many peoples as he can. He completely repudiates the feeling that China is expansionist. He told me the Chinese have an enormous task of reconstruction; that this will require all their attention for many years to come."

In Nepal, which can now sense China's breath blowing across the Himalayas, there is nothing but affection for the recent visitor. Prime Minister Acharya remembers: "He made a very good impression." Foreign Minister Sherma continues: "He showed his friendliness toward the common man." Opposition Leader K. M. Singh says: "Chou joked with people and shook hands even with ragged men." A British diplomat admits reluctantly: "He left an excellent memory. It helped build confidence in China."

As a traveling salesman Chou's technique is admirable. When he visited a dam being constructed in Afghanistan by West Germans he went up to Herr Eberlein, the hard-bitten project boss, and said: "You look like the kind of a man who smokes cigars. Have one." He produced a large Havana.

A Knowledgeable Talker

Then, Eberlein recalls with admiration: "Chou started a technical discussion on sedimentation. He showed great knowledge. He thought our problems might be useful for comparison with China's Yellow River scheme."

In Lahore, capital of West Pakistan, the Chinese statesman delighted white-haired Governor Gurmani, a princely Nawab landowner. Puffing his hubble-bubble pipe, this stanch old capitalist recalls: "Chou appeared irked with India's intransigence on Kashmir; an admirable man. He praised our factory techniques and asked my permission to send his experts here to study them."

Chou is all things to all men. In Kabul he made a point of being photographed with his arms around a grinning batch of children. In Katmandu the camera caught him heartily embracing beggars. All over India his smile was framed in flower wreaths. "A smooth and antiseptic touch," concluded one sardonic Englishman.

Chou's baggage was labeled peace, Buddhism and pan-Asiatic friendship. He implied that China, like ex-colonies he visited, had just been "liberated from Western imperialism." He sought to speak not as Communist but as Premier of Asia's largest nation.

Neither Burma, India nor Ceylon was allowed to forget that China is the biggest Buddhist country. There were no sinister hints of atheist ideology. On the contrary, Chou trotted the Dalai and Panchen Lamas into India while he was there. He donated $2,000 to Ceylon's Great Temple of Buddha's Tooth and distributed religious tracts in Burma.

Chou En-lai's was an infinitely affable tour. Humility and an eager desire to learn were keynote themes. No one mentioned Hungary. Following in the footsteps of Peiping's piper one cannot but remember how he once charmed our own stern General Marshall. One need not be surprised by his success with Asian hosts. How do we intend to offset this highly potent propaganda?

April 1, 1957

WIDE CHINESE AID TO ASIA REPORTED

Peiping's Outlay Said to Top Help It Gets From Soviet

By United Press International.

WASHINGTON, Aug. 16 — Despite its own great domestic problems, Communist China has been giving more aid to Southeast Asian countries than it has been receiving from the Soviet Union, according to a study made public today.

A report by the National Planning Association, a private research organization, said that during China's First Five-Year Plan, ended in 1957, foreign economic assistance extended by Peiping probably totaled the equivalent of $647,000,000, most of it in grants rather than credits or loans.

The report said the extent of the aid grants was particularly striking since Soviet financial aid to Peiping had been by loans rather than grants.

Entitled "Communist Economic Strategy: the Rise of Mainland China," the report was prepared by A. Doak Barnett on a Rockefeller Foundation Grant. "Contrary to a widely held assumption," it asserted, "the financial assistance to Communist China from the Soviet Union has been limited."

Mr. Barnett said the Chinese had "largely carried the financial burden of economic development themselves." It is "remarkable," the report commented, that Soviet financial aid has been so small, since Communist China is the largest and most important of the Soviet Union's allies.

Soviet Technicians Vital

While Soviet technicians and equipment are "indispensable," according to the report, "the Chinese Communists have had to pay their own way in relations with the Russians for the most part."

Mr. Barnett noted that Soviet aid to China during the five-year period was only $130,000,-000, in the form of a long-term loan.

The report said most of Communist China's foreign aid went to other Communist countries, including North Korea, North Vietnam, Outer Mongolia, Hungary and Albania. But it said there had been $55,000,000 in grants to non-Communist countries, including Ceylon, Egypt, Cambodia and Nepal.

In addition, Peiping offered long-term loans to Burma, Yemen and Indonesia.

China's first economic aid program to a non-Communist country started in mid-1956, Mr. Barnett reported, when Peiping agreed to grant Cambodia $22,-400,000 and to build a textile plant, a cement plant, a paper mill and a plywood factory in Cambodia.

The report said China's economic growth during the First Five-Year Plan was "very impressive." Developments there since early 1958 have been "so revolutionary and startling that it is impossible at this time to evaluate them with any sense of confidence," Mr. Barnett wrote.

The report referred to the establishment of communes and Peiping's "dramatic new program" for decentralization of industry as the "most radical political, economic, and social reorganization ever attempted in so short a time by a large nation."

Mr. Barnett said the communes posed major questions for the future.

"If they succeed, great opportunities for accelerated development may be opened up for the Peking regime," the report said.

"If the Chinese people refuse to accept them in the long run, the communes could prove to be a great mistake which could have a very adverse effect upon every aspect of the Chinese Communists' program."

August 17, 1959

CASTRO SAYS CUBA WILL RECOGNIZE COMMUNIST CHINA

Premier Tells Rally Havana Will Cut Ties to Taiwan— O. A. S. Action Scorned

U. S. PACT IS CANCELED

Thousands Cheer as Copy of 1952 Military Treaty Is Torn to Pieces

By R. HART PHILLIPS
Special to The New York Times.

HAVANA, Sept. 2—Premier Fidel Castro told a cheering crowd of hundreds of thousands of Cubans tonight that Cuba would recognize Communist China and break off relations with Nationalist China.

Cuba would be the first Latin-American country to recognize the Peiping regime.

At the demand of the Premier, the rally, called to protest the recent actions of the Organization of American States, "decided" to cancel a military pact between Cuba and the United States.

The pact, signed in 1952, provides that arms furnished by the United States shall not be used against another Western Hemisphere country.

Pact Based on Rio Treaty

The pact was made under the terms of the 1947 Treaty of Mutual Assistance and Defense, concluded at the Rio de Janeiro conference of the twenty-one American republics that year.

Premier Castro tore a copy of the Cuban-United States treaty into pieces as the crowd shouted its approval. He said the United States Embassy would be notified tomorrow of the cancellation "by the people" of the bilateral pact.

The pact does not affect the United States naval base at Guatanamo, but Premier Castro declared that if the United States continued its economic aggression against Cuba, he would ask the people to approve an order that would oust Americans from the base.

Nationalizing to Continue

He said also that American-owned companies in Cuba would continue to be nationalized "blow by blow" for every aggression of the United States against Cuba.

Cuba, the Premier said, will accept "rocket support of the Soviet Union in case of an invasion by the United States as well as aid from Red China."

Cuba's decision to accept a Soviet offer of rocket support against any United States attack led to the resolution of the San José meeting of the Organization of American States that, in effect, censured Havana's course.

The establishment of diplomatic relations between Cuba and Communist China has been expected since Havana signed a commercial treaty with Peiping several weeks ago. Under that agreement Peiping agreed to buy 500,000 tons of sugar a year for five years and Cuba will receive various products in exchange.

Reading the clauses of the Declaration of San José which was approved by the Organization of American States in Costa Rica this week, the Premier asked if the crowd thought it was acceptable. The crowd screamed "No!"

In denouncing the Organization of American States, Dr. Castro declared that the recent meeting of its foreign ministers at San José, Costa Rica, had "sharpened the knife that the hand of Yankee imperialism wants to drive into the heart of Cuba."

"It's too bad that when we meet here to discuss the questions that were discussed in Costa Rica, there are not seated here the twenty-one chancellors of the American nations," he declared.

"It's too bad they can't be here to compare the language of diplomats with the language of the people."

Premier Castro and his Government have long contended that the military pact with the United States had been violated by Washington when it sold arms and ammunition to the Batista regime "for use against the Castro rebels."

The Premier, dressed in olive army fatigues and wearing a cap, appeared in excellent health. His voice did not become hoarse during his three-hour speech.

Radio announcers put the crowd at between 800,000 and 1,000,000. Other observers said the figure was more like 300,000.

The Premier read from a long document that he announced as the "declaration of Havana of Sept. 2, 1960." This document, he said, was the "voice of the Cuban people in a general assembly" and was in reply to the Declaration of San José.

The Castro paper condemned "open and criminal aggressions against the Cuban economy by the United States." This was a reference to the United States reduction in Cuba's sugar quota.

It condemned the United States for taking "centers of strategy," such as the Panama Canal and Puerto Rico. The Premier declared that the Puerto Rican people were "greatly oppressed."

The document also condemned the United States for preventing the entrance of Communist China into the United Nations. "Cuba reaffirms her policy to establish relations with all Socialist countries of the world," the Premier declared.

The Premier then asked the public to raise their hands if they were in agreement. Thousands of hands went up, hats were thrown into the air, flags and banners and handkerchiefs were waved. The tumultuous approval lasted several minutes.

Cuba has long maintained relations with Nationalist China, which has an embassy here. The end of diplomatic relations will leave the 30,000 Chinese in Cuba, most of whom are loyal to the Nationalist Government, without representation. There is only a small colony of Chinese Communists.

Industry and commerce halted at noon today in Havana and Government offices closed. In the interior, work was halted yesterday in the eastern provinces. It was suspended today throughout the western provinces.

Last night and today trains, trucks and buses poured workers and peasants into Havana.

Meanwhile, the Government seized the American-owned Minamax supermarket chain in Havana. The chain, which has thirteen stores in the city and its suburbs, is valued at about $5,000,000. It is owned by Americans who have lived in Cuba for many years.

The Ministry of Labor ordered the seizure on the ground that the managements was displaying a "hostile" attitude and had threatened to close. The general manager of the Minamax supermarkets, Emmet H. Hyman, is in the United States.

PEIPING CAMPAIGN IN AFRICA GROWS

Special to The New York Times.

HONG KONG, Aug. 31—Communist China is bidding for the friendship of the newly independent nations of Africa with the vigor of a candidate running for office.

The campaign could pay off when Communist Chinese membership is considered by the United Nations General Assembly.

Last year the question was shelved by a vote of 44 to 28, with 9 abstentions. Among some smaller nations there is a growing feeling that Communist China should be admitted. In Asia, Communist China has antagonized India and Indonesia in the last year. But these two countries and other neutrals still favor Peiping's admission. The change of Government in Laos may mean another vote for the Chinese Communists.

Fourteen African nations have become independent this year. Two more are due for independence and if the Mali split between Senegal and Sudan becomes permanent, the new African states will total seventeen.

Pressure Would Grow

Even a narrowing of the margin against admission will increase the pressure on the major opponents to China's membership.

Not all the African states emerging from colonial status are likely to vote for Communist China's admission. But many may be influenced by Peiping's flattering attention.

China has quickly greeted the independence of every new African nation, often in advance of the official ceremony in order to be ahead of all competition.

A steady stream of African visitors has been feted in Peiping.

In effusive newspaper editorials and in the formal messages of congratulation, Peiping has sought to establish itself as the new states' most dependable ally. At the same time it has sought to discredit the United States by branding it as the Africans' enemy.

Peiping propaganda broadcasts to Africa have increased by 40 per cent in the last year.

Liao Cheng-chi, chairman of the Chinese Committee for African-Asian Solidarity, recently warned the new African nations to beware of United States "sweet talk of friendship and mutual benefit."

Guinea has come in for Peiping's special attention. A cultural cooperation program was concluded between the former French colony and Communist China in June.

GUINEA GETS LOAN FROM RED CHINA

Friendship and Trade Pacts Give Africans $25,000,000 for Three-Year Period

Special to The New York Times.

HONG KONG, Sept. 13—Communist China agreed today to make a three-year loan of 100,000,000 rubles ($25,000,000) to Guinea.

The two countries signed a treaty of friendship and agreements on economic and technical cooperation and on the last accord provided for annual volume of exports on each side amounting to 1,200,000,000 Guinean francs ($4,920,000).

The conclusion of the friendship treaty and the two economic agreements was the climax to the visit to Peiping of Guinea's President, Sékou Touré. The President arrived Saturday at the invitation of the Chinese Head of State, Liu Shao-chi.

Premier Signs Treaty

The official Chinese Communist press agency, Hsinhua, in a dispatch from Peiping tonight said that the treaty of friendship signed by President Touré and Premier Chou En-lai stated that the strengthening of friendly cooperation between China and Guinea conformed to the fundamental interests of the peoples of the two countries.

It also said that the treaty helps the "strengthening of friendship and solidarity of the peoples of China and Guinea as well as among the Asian and African peoples and is in the interest of world peace."

The agreement on economic and technical cooperation provides that "with a view to helping the Government of the Republic of Guinea develop its economy," China will in the period of Sept. 13, 1960, to June 30, 1963, extend a loan of 100,-000,000 rubles "free of interest and with no conditions and privileges attached."

China and Guinea also issued a joint communiqué, which was signed in Peiping today by Mr. Liu and President Touré. It said that the parties to the communiqué had conducted "friendly and sincere discussions on the current international situation in Asia and Africa the question of further developing relations of friendship and cooperation between China and Guinea and other questions and agreed the views were reached with satisfaction."

The two parties hold that world peace must be consolidated, that peaceful coexistence must be realized among nations with different social systems and that peace must be based on five principles of mutual respect for sovereignty and territorial integrity, mutual non-aggression, non-interference in each other's internal affairs, equality and mutual benefit and peaceful coexistence" the communiqué said.

The two leaders declared their support for the "just struggle for the national liberation of the peoples of Algeria, the Congo, South Africa and other countries."

The loan Guinea gets under the economic agreement is one of the biggest made by Communist China to a country outside the Communist bloc. It is seen here principally as a propaganda move designed to raise China's prestige in Africa and to attract other new African nations into the Chinese Communist orbit.

September 14, 1960

CHINA LENDS GHANA NEARLY 20 MILLION

Special to The New York Times.

HONG KONG, Aug. 21—Communist China has agreed to grant Ghana a loan of 7,000,000 Ghanaian pounds (about $19,-750,000) without interest over a period of six years, the Peiping radio announced today.

The loan agreement was concluded during the recent visit to Peiping of President Kwame Nkrumah of Ghana. Communist China and Ghana will also sign a treaty of friendship.

Reporting details of the accord, the Peiping radio said no conditions or privileges were attached to the loan, which was made "with the view of helping the Ghanaian Government develop its economy."

The loan agreement stipulates, Peiping reported, that the loan be repaid within a period of ten years from July 1, 1971, either with export goods of Ghana or with currency of a third country agreed to by Communist China.

The agreement also says that the Chinese Communist Government—in accordance with the scope of the loan, its capability and the requirements of Ghana — will supply technical assistance and complete sets of "equipment, machinery and materials, technical and other goods."

August 22, 1961

RED CHINA WOOS LATIN AMERICANS

By JACQUES NEVARD

Special to The New York Times.

HONG KONG, Oct. 28—A Chinese Communist campaign to win friends abroad is focusing increasingly on Latin America. At the moment, cultural and other delegations from twelve Latin-American nations are visiting Peiping as guests of the Communist regime. Their goings and comings are being extensively reported in newspapers in the Chinese capital.

Peiping papers ran front-page articles and photographs today about a reception given for the Latin-American visitors yesterday by the Communist party chairman, Mao Tse-tung, and Premier Chou En-lai.

It is no secret that the Chinese Communists would like to see more Latin-American nations follow the path of Premier Fidel Castro's Cuba.

Cuban Actions Hailed

Just to make sure that that point gets across to the visitors, the influential Peiping Ta Kung Pao said in a commentary today:

"The heroism of the Cuban people, their courage in waging a resolute struggle against United States imperialism, has won the admiration of the Chinese people who fully support their righteous action."

The newspaper praised the Castro Government for taking over United States enterprises in Cuba. It asserted that United States investments in Cuba had been used as a weapon for controlling the country and had been the "source of all the miseries of the Cuban people."

Ta Kung Pao said the Cuban example proved "that the Latin-American countries can attain genuine national liberation and march along the road of genuine independent development only by freeing themselves from the control of United States imperialism and by firmly resisting its aggression."

Mongolian Press Joins In

The press campaign on Cuba is not limited to Peiping. Hsinhua, the official Chinese Communist press agency, reports that even newspapers in Ulan Bator, Mongolia, are participating. The newspaper Unian in the Mongolian capital said today that the United States was stepping up its threat against "free revolutionary Cuba and the Cuban people."

The newspaper added that the Mongolian people had always sympathized with the Cuban revolutionaries and that "in the present situation the Mongolian people gave even more resolute support to them and firmly stood on the side of the Cuban people, who were fighting heroically and doggedly to maintain their independence and sovereignty."

October 30, 1960

RED CHINA SEEKING LINKS WITH BRAZIL

Program of Inviting Leaders of Professions to Visit Nation Helps Peiping

By TAD SZULC

Special to The New York Times.

RIO DE JANEIRO, Nov. 19 —Communist China played host last month to five outstanding Brazilian writers, nine Congressmen, six judges and lawyers, a few labor leaders, one peasant leader studying revolutionary ideas and one samba band.

They were among the contingent of about 120 Brazilian intellectuals, politicians, professors, newsmen, professionals and artists who have been traveling to China in growing numbers in recent years. They have been going as guests of the Peiping Government, which is speeding its campaign to win friends and influence in Brazil as well as throughout Latin America.

Most of the visitors received warm welcomes that included audiences with Mao Tse-tung, head of the Chinese Communist party, or Premier Chou En-lai. Banquets were offered to the larger groups by organizations such as the Foreign Relations Institute or the China-Latin-America Friendship Society. The visitors report that their hosts are extremely well informed on Brazil and Latin America.

Chinese Surpass Soviet

It appears that the Chinese are making a greater effort than the Soviet Union to invite Latin-American guests. As a result there is more interest here in the Chinese than in the Soviet situation.

Brazilian Leftists returning from Moscow and Peiping contend that China, with its dynamism is more interesting to them than is the Soviet Union. One Congressman said that the Soviet Union, "from our viewpoint, already has become a settled society that can teach us nothing."

All Latin America is a target for Chinese Communist propaganda, which also includes daily Spanish and Portuguese short wave broadcasts. Delegations and individuals from most of the Latin-American republics are turning up in Peiping with increasing frequency.

Brazil, as the largest and most developed nation, seems to be receiving the greatest Chinese attention, aside from Cuba. Cuba is the only Latin-American country with full relations with Red China and the two-way traffic between Havana and Peiping is booming.

Intelligence sources report that Havana is becoming center of distribution for Red China's

323

propaganda in the rest of Latin America.

The vast majority of the Brazilian visitors to China this year are not Communists. Some do not have Leftist sympathies.

However, their own statements in Peiping and the actions of earlier visitors indicate that upon returning they will publish articles or books, deliver lectures or speeches in Congress and in general spread the word of how favorably impressed they were with Communist China. They also will advocate that Brazil should establish diplomatic and trade relations with China.

This appears to be the goal of the Peiping regime in issuing invitations to important Brazilian and other hemispheric leaders. The Chinese hope that favorable public opinion can create sufficient pressure to force the Latin-American Governments to recognize Red China.

Pressure on Quadros

The pressure will be strong on President-elect Janio Quadros, who takes office at the end of January, to recognize Red China and the Soviet Union. Senhor Quadros said during the campaign that he would take such action, but he

has been vague on the subject lately.

Vice President Joâc Goulart, who was re-elected last month although he is a rival of Senhor Quadros, said in a magazine interview here last week his Brazilian Labor party expected the new Government to resume relations with the Soviet Union and "all countries of the world."

Peiping purposely avoids inviting known Communists. The Chinese prefer to attract well-known non-Communist figures. And a survey of travel in China by outstanding Brazilian personalities show that the program has been successful.

Among those who have visited China in the last twelve months were the Secretary General of the Brazilian Communist party, Luis Carlos Prestes, and Lidio Lunardi, president of the National Confederation of Industries. Erico Verissimo, a novelist, and Candido Portinari, a noted painter, also visited China.

When twenty-six Congressmen went to Tokyo this fall for sessions of the International Parliamentary Union, all received invitations to go to Peiping. Nine congressmen and their wives accepted.

November 20, 1960

ASIANS REACT TO NEW THREAT BY PEKING

By ROBERT TRUMBULL

MANILA, June 15—China's resurgence under the Communist rulers in Peking has stirred old fears throughout Asia. The attack on India last year has caused many Southeast Asian countries to take an apprehensive new look at their colossal northern neighbor.

Peking's gesture toward India's northern border appeared to foreshadow an ultimate design of China to achieve political hegemony over all Asia. In the case of many smaller nations this would be a reassertion of Chinese dominance in the past.

The conquest of Taiwan, seat of President Chiang Kai-shek's Nationalist Government, would be an important step toward this goal, extending the Chinese Communists' military power into the Pacific in the strategic salient between Japan and the Philippines.

Continental Advance

Peking is supporting Communist military forces against the established non-Communist regimes in South Vietnam and Laos. China has aided Communist insurgency in Burma, the Philippines and Malaya and presumably would be ready to do so again. The same threat hangs over any country possessing the seeds of militant Communist revolution.

China might gain political dominance peacefully in key countries such as Japan through satellite Communist parties taking orders from Peking. Such political overturn in one country after another could conceivably give the Communist rulers of China effective sway over the entire Asian continent and its strategic island fringes.

China's overpowering weight on other countries of the Far East was vividly illustrated in Manila this week by an agreement of three nations in the area to explore ways of joining forces against "subversion." Top diplomats of the three powers—the Philippines, Malaya and Indonesia—left a clear impression that the source of their common fear, unnamed in their communiqué, was Communist China.

Peking's Maps

This is the immediate background of the Manila conference. The smaller Asian countries paid tribute to the Chinese Emperors in the past and most of the present countries are included in maps distributed by Peking showing the boundaries of ancient Chinese hegemony. And to keep the uneasy consciousness of history alive, all of the weaker nations in Asia possess closely-knit and economically powerful Chinese ethnic minorities with strong sentimental ties to their ancestral land.

The recent tour of friendly Southeast Asian countries by Liu Shao-chi, Communist China's head of state, may have acted as a catalyst of anti-Chinese feelings in the region. What pressures Mr. Liu may

have attempted on non-aligned leaders like President Sukarno of Indonesia, Prince Norodom Sihanouk of Cambodia and Gen. Ne Win of Burma can only be guessed at.

But in North Vietnam, a Communist-ruled state, Mr. Liu showed his fangs in an open warning that Peking does not tolerate neutrality—in this case neutrality between Peking and Moscow.

One well-informed Indonesian attributed the recent outbreak of anti-Chinese riots in his country to the backlash from Mr. Liu's visit. A rumor is going around in diplomatic circles that the Chinese leader, who is Mr. Mao's heir apparent as head of the Peking hierarchy, expressed himself forcefully to Dr. Sukarno on the Indonesian President's cold-shouldering of local Communists and his encouragement of Western contacts such as the recent entry of the United States Peace Corps into Indonesia.

Tour Brings Shift

Whatever may have happened, Mr. Liu's Indonesian tour was followed by an astonishing flip-flop that has now placed neutral Indonesia in a budding alliance with two of the most pro-Western countries in Asia.

Malaya has a mutual security pact with Britain and the Philippine archipelago is an anchor of the United States defense line in the Pacific. Anxiety over the prospective grouping of leftist-inclined Chinese minorities in Malaya and the British dependencies of Singapore, North Borneo and Sarawak—soon to be merged probably with the British-protected Sultanate of Brunei also included in the prospective Federation of Malaysia — brought forth the historic Manila meeting and its surprising accord on a joint security program.

The Manila recommendations will be placed before a summit conference of Dr. Sukarno, Prince Abdul Rahmàn of Malaya and President Macapagal of the Philippines in another meeting to be held in Manila, probably in July. Details must be worked out to implement the broad principles enunciated this week. These developments are a new evidence of the general determination among China's neighbors to resist encroachment.

Heretofore, this determination has been manifest chiefly in racist attitudes in which Chinese minorities have been the victims. Sometimes, as in the Philippines and Indonesia, resentment and fear of the Chinese has produced repressive laws governing the commercial activities of aliens—most aliens being Chinese in these cases. It is noteworthy that in discussing the "Chinese problem," Communist comes in only incidentally as if it were just one more bad thing.

Basis for Fear

A detached observer is forced to conclude that sentiments toward China would be essentially the same, whatever government reigned in Peking, especially if that government were a strong one. The fear, in short, stems from the bigness of China, the industriousness and acumen of the Chinese people and the persistence of Chinese settled abroad in maintaining a separate identity with a marked affinity to the fatherland, no matter how long they and their forebears may have been away. It naturally follows that countries with influential chinese populations develop an awareness of dangerous potentialities for spying \and Fifth Column activities on behalf of an acquisitive China.

Spokesmen for the three states at the Manila conference dwelled upon the desirability of expanding their prospective association to include other countries of the region.

With these views curren there is no discernible bar to an eventual grouping of all the non-Communist states of the Asia region from this beginning, perhaps excluding South Korea, South Vietnam and the Nationalist Chinese on Taiwan for political reasons.

So far the plans of Indonesia, Malaya and the Philippines to block Chinese expansionism is confined to their own corner of Southeast Asia. Their military weakness limits their capability without outside aid in counter-intelligence and internal security arrangements. However, their efforts can at least hamper Communist subversion in a strategic part of the world.

June 16, 1963

Red China Eases Aggressive Tactics in Effort to Break Out of Isolation

By SEYMOUR TOPPING

Special to The New York Times

HONG KONG, Jan. 13 — Communist China, seeking to break out of its relative isolation in the world community, has become more flexible in the tactics of its international relations.

Western diplomatic analysts said this trend became discernible in the latter part of last year and has now taken more definite form.

A chief aim of the new tactics was said to have been expressed by Mao Tse-tung, chairman of the Chinese Community party, in his statement today on the dispute in the Panama Canal Zone. The Peking leader urged the "broadest united front" of nations against United States global policies.

One analyst summed up the conclusions of an official study of the new look in Peking's foreign policy by saying that the Chinese Communists were trying to enlist support by being "all things to all people."

The tactics have been as varied as urging the Panamanian Government to expel the United States from the Canal Zone, the fostering of trade and other ties with France, promises of economic aid to Algeria and the rendering of assistance to Communist Vietcong insurgents in South Vietnam.

The current goodwill tour of Africa being made by Premier Chou En-lai and Foreign Minister Chen Yi was seen here as a manifestation of the urgent need felt by Peking to acquire more friends and allies.

The analysts cited four major factors in Peking's growing sense of isolation.

These are the United States opposition to the diplomatic recognition of Communist China and to its entrance into the United Nations, Peking's ideological dispute with Moscow, the Chinese-Indian border dispute and the Chinese Communist denunciation of the treaty for a limited nuclear test ban signed in Moscow last August.

U. N. Vote Shocked Peking

The three latter factors tended to persuade many peoples of Asia, Africa and Latin America that Communist China was committed to a hard line in international relations.

There were indications that Peking was shocked in late October when the General Assembly voted by a larger margin than in 1962 to bar Communist China from the United Nations.

In his visits to the United Arab Republic and Algeria, Premier Chou spoke out in favor of holding a second Bandung conference of African and Asian nations to advance the "10 points of peaceful coexistence" set forth at the 1955 conference. Twenty-nine Asian and African countries took part in that conference, held in Bandung, Indonesia.

In 1955, Peking pursued a policy of "peaceful coexistence" that emphasized friendship with neutralist countries and relegated to the background its support for violent revolutionary action.

The line changed in the latter part of 1957, apparently because of the sharpening of Peking's ideological dispute with Moscow. The Chinese Communists became increasingly hostile toward India and this culminated in October, 1962, in large-scale clashes on the Chinese-Indian border.

The analysts here do not believe that Peking is returning to its 1955 policy of "peaceful coexistence." In their ideological quarrel with the Sovie Communist party, the Chinese Communists are continuing to insist on violent revolutionary struggle, as in South Vietnam.

Peking's policy has become more flexible only in the sense that a greater variety of means are to be used to further its national aims and to strengthen its bid for revolutionary leadership of Asia, Africa and Latin America.

It was noted here that Premier Chou, on his African tour, has been careful to solicit support by tailoring his appeals to local attitudes rather than any insistence on a hard revolutionary line.

China-South Africa Trade Up

Special to The New York Times

WASHINGTON, Jan. 13 — Communist China has more than tripled its trade with South Africa in the last year despite recent assertions by Peking in African capitals that its economic boycott of the Pretoria regime was "firm and unshakable."

As reported here, the South African figures showing the rise in trade are proving to be a source of acute embarrassment to China.

The question of relations with South Africa is an aspect of the running rivalry between Communist China and the Soviet Union for the allegiance of the new African nations.

It touches upon the particularly sensitive racial issue as Peking seeks to identify itself as the friend of the colored peoples and to portray the Soviet Union as pro-white.

The latest Soviet - Chinese clash on race matters involved relations with South Africa, whose racial segregation policies are strongly opposed by nonwhite Africans, and was made to coincide with the current goodwill trip to Africa by the Chinese Premier, Chou En-lai.

Soviet Reports Increase

According to diplomatic reports here, Soviet embassies in African capitals began circulating reports of China's growing trade relations with South Africa about the time Mr. Chou began his tour. The Chinese immediately began to issue denials of dealings with South Africa.

Thus on Jan. 2 the Conakry radio in Guinea broadcast what it described as a formal denial by the Chinese Embassy of the "slanderous statements" that Peking maintained a relationship with Pretoria.

"As of July 1, 1960," the denial said, "the Chinese Government broke all the economic and commercial bonds with the South African colonial authorities."

The statement applauded the African governments for their decision to boycott South Africa economically and diplomatically.

However, official South African trade figures show that in 1962 China bought $1.5 million worth of South Africa's goods and raised purchases there to $6 million in the period between January and August of 1963.

January 14, 1964

CHOU TRIP CALLED A GAIN FOR PEKING

Red China Getting Greater Role on World Stage

By SEYMOUR TOPPING
Special to The New York Times

HONG KONG, Feb. 6—Premier Chou En-lai completed this week a seven-week tour of Africa that projected Communist China into a more influinitial role in world affairs.

This was the assessment made here by Western analysts of the Chinese leader's visit to 10 African nations.

The balance sheet, which was drawn up on basis of reports on Premier Chou's conversations with African leaders and his public appearances, indicates that the tour was a substantial success despite some reverses.

Tunisia has been considering recognition of Peking but has stressed that she would not shun the Chinese Nationalist Government on Taiwan. The Ethiopians limited themselves to assuring Mr. Chou that they intended to "normalize relations." Ethiopia now recognizes neither China.

The Premier sought energetically in private talks and in public speeches to counter assertions that Peking's policies were aggressive or committed to eventual war. Before leaving Mogadiscio, capital of Somalia, Mr. Chou said at a rally that conditions were favorable for revolutionary struggle but that world war could be prevented.

Nasser Seemed Skeptical

In Cairo, President Gamal Abdel Nasser appeared skeptical about Premier Chou's attempt to justify the Chinese Communist attacks along the Indian border in the fall of 1962. Leaders of countries such as Tunisia and Ethiopia were critical of Peking's refusal to sign the treaty for a limited nuclear test ban concluded in Moscow last August.

From the Western standpoint, one of the chief gains from the Chou tour was said to have been the Premier's exposure to the strong desires among many Africans for peaceful development, good relations with Western Governments and respect for the United Nations.

Only nominal support was expressed by most African leaders for Peking's call for a second conference of African and Asian nations similar to that convened in Bandung, Indonesia, in 1955.

Most of the leaders were more favorable to a suggestion by President Tito of Yugoslavia and Prime Minister Jawaharlal Nehru of India for a conference of nonaligned nations, which by its nature would exclude Communist China.

However, reports received here indicated that Premier Chou, who is a highly articulate, adroit diplomat, managed to persuade many Africans that Communist China was a friendly nation that was concerned with their problems.

Mr. Chou pledged that small aid programs maintained by Peking for countries such as Somalia, Mali, Guinea and Ghana would be expanded in scope and quantity.

"We Asians and African people are brothers sharing the same life, breath and destiny," the Peking leader said. He stressed common interests of the peoples of Asia, Africa and Latin America in a joint struggle against the United States, which he described as the arch-imperialist nation.

Tactics More Flexible

Despite his emphasis on revolutionary struggle, Premier Chou did not hesitate to attempt to establish good relations with "bourgeois" leaders such as Emperor Haile Selassie of Ethiopia.

This new flexibility in tactics reflected a recent appeal by Mao Tse-tung, chairman of the Chinese Communist party, for a broad "united front" against the United States. Analysts said the aim of the policy appeared to be to break out of the isolation imposed on Communist China by its hostile relations with the United States and ideological dispute with the Soviet Union.

Mr. Chou's tour was the most ambitious public-relations trip abroad that has been undertaken by any Chinese Communist leader since the regime established its control of the mainland in 1949.

Premier Chou cut short his African tour by postponing visits to Uganda, Tanganyika and Kenya. He visited the United Arab Republic, Algeria, Morocco, Tunisia, Ghana, Mali, Guinea, the Sudan, Ethiopia and Somalia. He also went to Communist Albania.

February 7, 1964

RED CHINA REBUKES MOSCOW ON PARLEY

Special to The New York Times

HONG KONG, May 31—All the Peking newspapers carried today as their major front-page story a Government statement declaring in sharp language that the Soviet Union had no grounds for seeking representation at a conference of Asian and African countries in Africa next year.

The Chinese Communist party organ Jenmin Jih Pao accused the Russians of using "a blatant threat and blackmail" to obtain an invitation to the conference.

Analysts here said the statement, made public yesterday, and the Jenmin Jih Pao article constituted perhaps the severest public rebuke of Moscow by Peking since the two began bringing their differences into the open.

The analysts believed the Chinese Communists were seeking not only to keep the Soviet Union out of the conference but also to discredit it among the nations of Africa and Asia and eliminate it as a rival to Peking's bid for leadership.

Replying to the Soviet contention that it should be invited to the conference because two-thirds of Soviet territory was in the Asian continent the Chinese statement said that equally important was the fact that nearly three-quarters of the Soviet population lived in Europe.

June 1, 1964

CHINESE FALTER IN ECONOMIC AID

Inability to Fulfill Pledges Irks Asians and Africans

By SEYMOUR TOPPING
Special to The New York Times

HONG KONG, June 23 — Communist China is being severely handicapped by its economic difficulties in its contest with the Soviet Union for influence over the nations of Asia and Africa, according to a compilation of reports here.

Peking is lagging far behind Moscow in economic aid and technical assistance to the underdeveloped countries. There has been widespread dissatisfaction with the quality of Chinese Communist aid.

Specialists here believe that the inability of Communist China to compete economically has motivated Peking's current intensive propaganda campaign to discredit Soviet aid program by calling them a form of neo-colonialism.

Peking in its contacts with Asian and African officials has tried to convince them that they can best build independent national economies through mutual aid rather than by relying on the Soviet Union, Western countries or the United Nations.

Reports received here indicate that the Chinese Communist charges that white nations are attempting to reimpose colonialism through economic-aid programs has had some effect on Asians and Africans.

Chinese Pledges Doubted

However, Peking has been unable to exploit as it had hoped the disappointment experienced by Asian and African officials when they failed earlier this month to obtain desired aid commitments from industrialized countries at the United Nations Conference on Trade and Development, held in Geneva.

These officials have become increasingly doubtful of the reliability of Chinese Communist pledges of economic assistance.

A statesman of one Middle Eastern country recently confided to a United States official that he felt that his government had been hoodwinked by Peking. The government had agreed to favorable terms for the sale of cotton in gratitude for a low-interest, long-term line of credit extended by Peking. Later, it was discovered that the line of credit was virtually worthless bycause of the limited availability and poor quality of the products offered by Communist China.

Obstacles Illustrated

Two reports published in Peking newspapers this morning illustrate some of the obstacles that the Chinese have encountered in trying to play, in an economic sense, the role of a major world power.

Jenmin Jih Pao, the Communist party organ, denounced Moscow for "bare-faced lies" in criticizing trade between Communist China and South Africa.

The Soviet press agency Tass had published a report showing that Peking's trade with South Africa had increased despite Chinese denunciations of that country's race separation policies and declarations by Peking of solidarity with black African countries.

The Chinese Communist commentary said that the Tass report was full of loopholes and reaffirmed Peking's hostility to what was termed the "fascist rule in South Africa. But it did not deny the substance of the report.

According to official sources Peking's imports from South Africa in the first eight months of 1963 were valued at $6 million as against $1.5 million for all 1962.

Peking made its purchases from South Africa, the bulk of which was grain, through French intermediaries.

The details became known when South Africa published trade statistics. The Chinese Communists have since reassured irritated Negro leaders in Africa that they no longer would deal directly or indirectly with South Africa.

The Chinese Communists, plagued by shortages of foreign exchange and food, purchased South African grain simply because the Peking officials felt they could not afford to forgo economic advantages solely or political reasons.

Mali Official in Peking

The Peking press also published speeches made at a meeting yesterday in honor of Jean Marie Kone, the Economic Planning Minister of Mali, who is visiting Communist China at the head of a Government delegation. Mr. Kone is one of a number of African leaders who have gone to Peking recently to discuss economic aid.

Although the Chinese speakers dwelt on a need to achieve self-sufficiency through mutual help among the Asian and African states, the Mali official emphasized his Government's desire to have friendly relations with all countries.

Mali has been a testing ground for the growing competition in Africa between Moscow and Peking.

According to a compilation here the Soviet Union had extended Mali a total of about $55 million in aid of which $25 million has been drawn, compared with $20 million extended by Communist China with a little more than $1 million drawn.

The Soviet Union had nearly 300 technicians in the country in 1963, while China had 200. About 300 Malian students and 15 technicans were studying in the Soviet Union, while none approved by the Government were known to be in Communist China.

June 24, 1964

Central African Republic Recognizes Red Chinese

TOKYO, Oct. 2 (UPI)—The Central African Republic has transferred its diplomatic recognition from Nationalist to Communist China, the official Peking press agency Hsinhua announced today.

The Central African Republic was formed in 1960 from the French territory of Ubange-Shari in Equatorial Africa. It lies north of the two Congos.

According to a diplomatic note from Communist China, made public by Hsinhua, the move was agreed upon in August. The note said the Central African Republic had decided to recognize Communist China as "the sole legal government representing all the Chinese people."

October 3, 1964

PEKING LOSING HOLD ON AFRO-ASIANS

By SEYMOUR TOPPING

Special to The New York Times

HONG KONG, July 3—Leaving behind the shambles of the aborted Algiers Conference of African and Asian leaders, Premier Chou En-lai, the Chinese Communist Premier and number one diplomatic salesman, returned to Peking this week with unhappy tales to relate.

Disheartening indeed to the revolutionary mandarins had been the attitudes of underdeveloped nations as preparations for the cherished conference collapsed amid chaos engendered by the coup d'etat of Colonel Hourari Boumedienne. Obviously, postponement of the conference to November 5 had robbed Peking of a chance to rally at a critical juncture opposition to United States policy in Vietnam.

Yet there were even more fundamental and disturbing implications for Chinese Communist leadership in the performance of African and Asian leaders during the Algiers hulabaloo. Bickering and crossfires among would-be conferees revealed a large degree of diversity within what Peking liked to look upon as the Afro-Asian Bloc.

Diversity Accepted

Diversity is the characteristic of life in the nineteen-sixties which both the Communist world and the Western alliance had come however reluctantly to accept. The Sino-Soviet ideological dispute had fragmented the international Communist movement. The maverick activities of President Charles de Gaulle of France had loosened the ties of the Atlantic Alliance and the West European Community.

Now the African and Asian nations, originally bound together in an anticolonial front and against what they feared was neocolonial economic and political exploitation, were also going their independent ways.

Many of the factors which had motivated the drive to unity at the 1955 Bandung Conference had become more the concern of ideological sloganeers in Peking than politicians, economists and engineers who were preoccupied with the practical problems of nation-building.

For Communist China, this was a disillusionment that put in question the foundation of the ideological doctrine of world development enunciated by Mao Tse-tung, the party leader. Asia, Africa and Latin America had been dubbed the "storm centers of world revolution" and therefore made the principal targets of propaganda, aid programs—both military and economic—and clandestine subversion.

These underdeveloped regions were regarded as more susceptible to being organized into a bloc responsive to Chinese Communist leadership.

Left-wing parties in these regions were believed to be more restive and prone to accept Peking's strategy of armed revolution and therefore would be more attracted to Communist China than the Soviet Union in the ideological debate between the two.

According to Mao's *weltanschauung*, which is related to his basic concept of guerrilla tactics, Asia, Africa and Latin America eventually would serve. to outflank the great industrial powers and bend them to the will of a new order conceived in Peking.

The bloc concept was put to one of its most challenging tests when

Peking attempted to exclude the Soviet Union from the Afro-Asian conference. Peking counted heavily on an implied racial appeal. It sought to persuade Africans and Asians that the Soviet Union did not qualify because it was a European nation although most of the country lies in Asia.

Racial Bias Limited

Shortly before the conference was to begin, there were signs that a majority of member nations, following the lead of such countries as India, Japan, the United Arab Republic and most of the British Commonwealth participating, would vote to admit delegates from Soviet Asia.

The failure of Peking to rally a broad front against the Soviet Union showed that racial appeal, when couched in terms of the non-white against the white, had limited attraction.

After all, there were Africans who recalled that their students had encountered racial bias from the yellow men of the Middle Kingdom when studying in Peking. And not long ago, despite its protestations, Communist China,

327

for practical economic reasons, had been trading under the table with apartheid South Africa.

More important was the fact that the realistic and growingly sophisticated leaders of Asia and Africa understood that their developing countries need good relations with the great industrial powers which are the white nations of North America, Western and Eastern Europe.

Communist China remains the world's largest underdeveloped country and it will take decades before its embryo industry comes abreast of the industry of a country such as Britain.

Nevertheless, at considerable sacrifice to its own capital-short economy, the Chinese Communists have sought, through economic aid, to woo underdeveloped countries.

Since 1954 Peking has committed the equivalent of $700 million in economic aid, with 1964 a banner year for grants and loans. This compares to more than $4 billion committed by the Soviet Union, a figure in turn dwarfed by the United States programs which, in the current year alone, will allocate nearly $1,500,000,000 to development aid.

Moreover only about $150 million of $700 million earmarked by Peking has been drawn by underdeveloped countries, simply because there is so little to buy in Communist China with blocked funds. The Chinese Communists have some consumer goods, such as textiles, to export, but their relatively primitive machinery and other capital goods do not meet the equipment demands of the industrializing countries of Asia, Africa and Latin America.

The Chinese Communists have beat the propaganda drum in Asia, Africa and Latin America for regional "self-sufficiency" but this has been like telling a hungry beggar looking into a delicatessen window that he really does not like salami and roquefort cheese.

There have been reports that Chinese Communists have asked Africans to sign over lands as collateral for loans with the intention of eventually settling them, but Hong Kong specialists on Chinese Communist affairs are highly dubious of these reports.

Chinese Communists get high marks for the manner in which their technicians, who number about 2,000 in underdeveloped countries, adjust to their host population and surroundings.

The Soviet Union by comparison has about 10,000 aid technicians abroad and the number of Americans is probably twentyfold what Peking dispatches for good samaritan work.

The volume of Chinese Communist trade is also very modest compared to that of the United

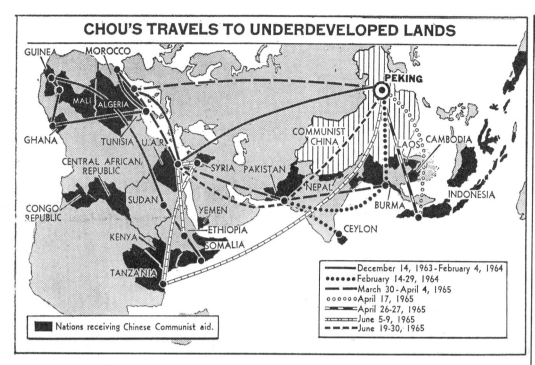

CHOU'S TRAVELS TO UNDERDEVELOPED LANDS

——— December 14, 1963 - February 4, 1964
●●●●● February 14-29, 1964
— — — March 30 - April 4, 1965
○○○○○○ April 17, 1965
=====April 26-27, 1965
⊢⊢⊢⊢⊢ June 5-9, 1965
– – – June 19-30, 1965

■ Nations receiving Chinese Communist aid.

Associated Press, United Press International

CHOU WOOS AFRICANS: The Chinese Premier (right) and an aide being greeted by Tanzania's President Julius Nyerere upon their arrival last month in that country on a goodwill visit.

States and the Soviet Union. In Africa where Peking has made a major effort, the total is less than five per cent of its world trade and about two per cent of international business done by Africans.

Cuban Example

Because of its economic limitations, it is most unlikely that Communist China will be able to take the place of the Soviet Union and the United States in underdeveloped countries. Cuba is a case in point. After a flirtation with Peking, whose militant revolutionary doctrine is more attractive to the Castro regime, Cuba

has been compelled to fall back on the economic largesse of the Soviet Union.

Competition from Peking has not allied the Soviet Union with the United States in development programs. No less than Peking, the Soviet Union aims to exclude United States influence and put the underdeveloped countries on the road to communism.

The Soviet Union is somewhat less likely in this competition to engage in such Chinese Communist shenanigans as shipping guns and guerrilla specialists from Burundi to the primitive man-hunting rebels of the Congo.

Although the Chinese Commu-

nists have now lost Burundi as a base since the government there expelled their embassy, Peking retains strong positions in Congo (Brazzaville), Mali and Tanzania. Peking Radio is the spokesman for dissident movements in Portuguese African colonies, South Africa and the Congo. About a third of Peking's 48 embassies abroad are posted in Africa and their staffs include many of the top Chinese Communist diplomats.

Despite their setback at Algiers, the Chinese Communists obviously intend to press their economic military, diplomatic and propaganda offensive in Asia, Africa and Latin America. Communis

China, by virtue of its size and will inevitably remain a leading and respected power among Asians and Africans.

Yet leaders of underdeveloped countries as a group display no tendency to accept the preachings of Mao Tse-tung as their gospel. More and more they seem to be dedicated to searching for stability rather than revolution now that the hates and fevers of the colonial period are fading.

To the peoples of the underdeveloped countries, Communist China symbolizes a credo of revolution. But the men in Peking have not yet provided them with a proven formula for creating prospering societies.

July 4, 1965

INDONESIA SAYS PLOT TO DEPOSE SUKARNO IS FOILED BY ARMY CHIEF;

REBEL CAPTURED

Radio Says Nasution Saved Regime—Some Clashes Reported

By SETH S. KING
Special to The New York Times.

KUALA LUMPUR, Malaysia, Oct. 1—An attempt to overthrow President Sukarno was foiled tonight by army units loyal to Gen. Abdul Haris Nasution, the Indonesian radio announced.

It said troops of the crack Siliwangi Division had captured Lieut. Col. Untang, a commander in Dr. Sukarno's palace guard.

[In Washington, a State Department spokesman said Friday the situation in Indonesia was "extremely fluid, even confused." Robert J McCloskey told a news conference the State Department was getting reports from the American Embassy at Jakarta, but "it is not presently possible to attempt any evaluation, explanation or comment."]

Late yesterday, a mysterious group calling itself the 30th of September Movement seized control of Jakarta.

Colonel Untang, who had announced over the Indonesian radio that he was the leader of the movement, said the group had seized control of the Government to prevent a "counter-revolutionary" coup by a Generals' Council.

General Backs Sukarno

General Nasution was quoted by the radio tonight as having denied that there had ever been a plan by the armed forces to depose President Sukarno.

With all communications with Indonesia cut except for the national radio, it was difficult for observers here to be certain what had happened in the confused 24-hour period beginning yesterday.

The Indonesian radio said tonight that units of the crack Siliwangi Division, which had been moved into Jakarta earlier this week to participate in an Armed Forces Day parade, had fought Colonel Untang's forces for control of strategic points in the capital.

In a special bulletin broadcast at 11 P.M., the Malaysia radio reported that Lieut. Gen. Ahmad Yani, the Indonesian Chief of Staff, had been killed by coup forces and that General Nasution had been wounded. The radio did not give its sources for this.

Struggle for Control

While it appeared that anti-Communist leaders of the army

The New York Times   Oct. 2, 1965
SCENE OF UPRISING: Indonesian territory is shaded

had regained control of Jakarta and that Dr. Sukarno had survived another attempt to remove him, the struggle for control of the floundering Government appeared to be continuing.

The Jakarta radio said at midnight that the Communist coup leader had inserted many names in his Cabinet list without knowledge of the individuals named. The radio said a number of lower-ranked military officers listed in the rebel Cabinet were actually loyal to the Nasution forces.

Radio monitors here later reported hearing a broadcast from Surabaya, the large seaport in East Java, which announced that a Col. Suhirman, commander of army units in Semarang,

Central Java, was supporting Colonel Untang.

Reds' Role Uncertain

There was still no indication of the role Indonesia's powerful Communist party played in the attempt to overthrow Dr. Sukarno.

The only mention of Communist officials was in a broadcast earlier today by the Untang group in which several minor members of the party were named in a 45-man Cabinet appointed by the 30th of September group.

If the Communists had accepted these posts, it would appear that they had supported the Untang movement. But there was no report here on the stand of D.N. Aidit, leader of the three-million-member

329

Keystone, Associated Press

TURMOIL IN INDONESIA: Armed forces loyal to Gen. Abdul Haris Nasution, right, are reported to have overthrown leaders of a plot directed against President Sukarno, left.

Communist party.

Observers here noted that Dr. Subandrio, Deputy Premier and Foreign Minister, was named as a member of the 30th of September Cabinet. If he is shown to have been with the rebels it will mean a drastic split in Dr. Sukarno's inner circle.

The Indonesian President has sought to preserve unity among Indonesia's divergent political factions through a "Nasakom" Government. The word is a contraction of the symbols for 60 nationalist, religious and Communist elements.

General Nasution has always been identified as a devout Moslem and anti-Communist. He led the Indonesian forces that put a bloody end to the Communist rebelion at Madiun in 1948. General Nasution tried in 1952 to force Dr. Sukarno to dissolve Parliament and check the drift of the Government to the left.

Sukarno's Health Cited

Observers here had been puzzled by the Indonesia radio's statement earlier today that the generals who allegedly planned the coup against Dr. Sukarno believed that the Indonesian leader had been in poor health since the first week in August.

After charging that these generals were sponsored by the United States Central Intelligence Agency, the broadcast said they had believed Dr. Sukarno would soon die.

"Their reasoning on this was not startling." the broadcast declared.

Yet President Sukarno has made many public appearances since Aug. 1. There have been no reports here to suggest that his health was any more fragile now than it had been in the past, when he was treated for a kidney ailment.

Dr. Sukarno apparently had not been seen publicly in the past two days. But on Monday night, he appeared with Dr. Subandrio at a Peasants' Day rally. In a speech he conceded that the Government could not force a halt in spiraling food prices.

INDONESIANS BURN A CHINESE SCHOOL

Special to The New York Times

SINGAPORE, Oct. 15 — A Chinese university was burned and one student was reported killed and more than 200 injured in Jakarta yesterday.

It was the worst violence in a wave of anti-Peking sentiment sweeping Indonesia since an attempted coup d'état two weeks ago.

Republika University was destroyed in a two-hour melee marked by hand-to-hand fighting between Moslem youths and Chinese students, according to reports received here.

Scores of policemen were unable to stop the brawl. The police fired into the two-story building with machine guns for 20 minutes. They said that Chinese students inside the building had started the shooting.

Campus Like Battlefield

About 60 students and 600 attackers fought with broken furniture, bottles, sticks and knives until the campus resembled a battle scene, with the flaming university in the background. One of the students was reported beaten to death.

Earlier young Moslems gathered outside Communist China's Embassy in Jakarta and screamed "Crush China!"

Anti-Chinese feeling has risen steadily in the last few days as the army-controlled press and radio have vigorously accused Peking and the pro-Chinese Indonesian Communist party of a role in the attempt at a coup against President Sukarno.

Fights between Moslems and Chinese have been reported in several parts of Indonesia, Chinese shops have been ransacked in villages and a Jakarta shopping district with many Chinese merchants has been closed to vehicular traffic for fear of bombings.

About three million of Indonesia's 105 million people are Chinese. Until the revolt, the Chinese were generally well-regarded in Indonesia and President Sukarno was cooperating closely with Peking.

October 2, 1965

October 16, 1965

Chinese Experts Leave

Special to The New York Times

JAKARTA, Indonesia, Nov. 19 — Chinese Communist technical experts helping to build the huge Conference of New Emerging Forces center here have been ordered home.

Their recall actually occurred two days after the abortive coup d'état of Oct. 1, Antara, the official press agency, reported. It was not disclosed until yesterday.

The vast complex of meeting halls and staff headquarters was to have been financed largely by Peking as the setting for a worldwide meeting of the New Emerging Forces next year. President Sukarno was pointing his foreign policy toward the meeting, at which he expected to reassert his claim to leadership of those countries he considers opponents of the Old Established Forces.

Peking had offered foreign credits of $16 million and was expected to supply a large share of the estimated cost of 60 billion Indonesian rupiahs.

Despite the withdrawal of the Chinese, local workmen were busy completing excavation for the main structure and starting to put up the steel frames of outbuildings.

November 21, 1965

Peking Protests Attack

Special to The New York Times

HONG KONG, Nov. 5 — Communist China has demanded a public apology from the Indonesian Government for an attack on the Chinese Consulate in Medan, North Sumatra, by anti-Chinese demonstrators.

In a note from the Chinese Embassy in Jakarta to the Indonesian Ministry of Foreign Affairs, Peking lodged the "strongest protest" and described the incident as an "extremely serious provocation."

November 6, 1965

Even Sukarno Can't Help Jakarta Communists Now

By SETH S. KING
Special to The New York Times

JAKARTA, Nov. 20 — It has been 10 years since President Sukarno first produced the word "nasakom" and despite all that's happened in Indonesia since then he is as determined as ever to pursue this concept.

Nasakom is one of many political contractions conceived by President Sukarno. It combines "nas" for nationalist, "a" for agama or religious and "kom" for Communist.

Until the abortive coup of Oct. 1 nationalist generally meant armed forces. Religious meant the Moslems, Catholics and Protestants. And Communist meant the Communist Party of Indonesia — the P.K.I.

The President for Life and Great Leader of the Revolution has been convinced for more than 10 years that the scattered and diverse people of Indonesia could not be held together unless these three elements are represented within the framework of his "guided democracy."

"You cannot ignore a party that polls 6 million votes in an election [in 1955, the last general election in Indonesia]" President Sukarno once declared. "I am not attempting to bring Indonesia to the far left but to achieve stability in this country."

Leftward Tilt

Actually, Indonesia was tilting steadily to the left and the P.K.I. was daily growing stronger through its influence with President Sukarno and the pressures it could exert through its 3 million members and the 10 million members of its front groups.

In effect, the nasakom principle was virtually nonexistent. Mr. Sukarno was following, or even initiating, policies that fitted the P.K.I. line quite comfortably. Nationalist and religious elements were present but largely ignored.

Then came the inept coup of Oct. 1 and in its aftermath President Sukarno is faced with balancing a problem far more difficult than any confronting him before.

Loyal elements of the armed forces overturned the coup group in 12 largely bloodless hours and restored the "Indonesian revolution" with President Sukarno still at its head.

But the coup plotters murdered six ranking generals and the Indonesian military leaders have been in full pursuit of the Communists ever since.

They have convinced the Indonesian people that the P.K.I. was the guiding force behind the coup and that the local Communists were aided by Peking.

Religious Pressure

Religious parties with the obvious backing of the army have been demanding that President Sukarno dissolve the P.K.I. and reconsider his alliance with Peking.

This past week non-Communist groups began showing their impatience at the President's delay.

Politically President Sukarno does not need the support of the Communists to continue as President for Life and Great Leader of the Revolution.

Evidence has been growing that the actual strength of P.K.I. was overrated. The party held its power and influence because President Sukarno supported them and followed their advice.

The President himself is not a Communist. But he is an avowed Marxist who believes Indonesia's hopes for prosperity lie in centrally directed Socialism.

His love affair with Peking was largely due, observers here believe, to his admiration for the organization and discipline of the Maoists. These attributes he knew were sadly lacking among his easygoing people, many of whom have acquired most of the basic necessities of life simply by picking them off the nearest tree.

But President Sukarno has known that Indonesia's exploding population, especially on the already dangerously crowded island of Java, could not tolerate this abundance much longer.

The spur that President Sukarno has used to prod his people has been a negative one. Indonesia's "revolution" has always been against something — against the Dutch, against Western imperialism, against Old Established Forces

who President Sukarno still claims are out to destroy Indonesia.

A Natural Ally

The Chinese Communists have been a natural ally in these attitudes. So have the Soviets, although lately in a much more qualified way.

President Sukarno is 64 and this is an advanced age for a Javanese. He knows he is not immortal and he wants, it is widely believed, to leave behind him a Communist element that would hold Indonesia to a path of disciplined Socialism.

But it was evident seven weeks after the coup that the President has not found an acceptable substitute for P.K.I. It is also evident that the army and religious groups are still determined to force him to ban P.K.I. and to prevent him from reconstituting a leftist party with any of the old P.K.I. elements in it.

Although none of the top P.K.I. leaders have been arrested, the party itself has been scattered and in many sections broken up entirely. What is left has gone into hiding.

Even if President Sukarno raises a leftist element that is acceptable to the other two parts of nasakom, the Communist party of Indonesia with its close links with Communist China appears finished for many months to come.

New Face to Peking

And a new face has been put on relations with Peking. The fact the army has gone on whacking Communists has made it impossible for the Chinese Communists to remain silent or to go on supporting Indonesia with unqualified enthusiasm.

Dr. Subandrio, the First Deputy Prime Minister and Foreign Minister, revealed earlier this week that trade relations with Peking had been briefly interrupted although they had, he said, been resumed.

Thursday it was disclosed for the first time that the Chinese Communist technicians working on the huge buildings for the Conference of New Emerging Forces had been called home last month. Peking had agreed to finance and help build this ambitious project with which President Sukarno hoped to regain his claim to leading the emerging countries of the world.

November 21, 1965

Peking's Undiplomatic Diplomacy

By SEYMOUR TOPPING
Special to The New York Times

SAIGON, Feb. 19—Once upon a time in Southeast Asia, it was the vogue to relate tales of naive, hapless American diplomats who were inevitably undone by their omniscient, infallible Communist counterparts. Nowadays, the wisecracks are about the fumbles of Chinese Communist diplomacy.

Most Southeast Asians are eager to be on good terms with the Communist goliath to the north, but they are finding it difficult to get on with the single-minded, seemingly humorless men in Peking.

After antagonizing the Indonesians, the Singaporeans, the Malaysians, the Thais and the Burmese, the Chinese Communists are beginning to crowd the North Vietnamese. Jealous of the recent expansion of the Soviet presence in Hanoi, the Peking leadership is pressuring the North Vietnamese to line up on its side in the ideological dispute against the Soviet Communist party.

Resentful as he may be of this elbowing, it is unlikely that President Ho Chi Minh will react violently, as did Premier Fidel Castro of Cuba, and denounce the Chinese Communists. The North Viet-namese need the support of their Communist neighbor in the struggle against the United States.

Hanoi's Position

It is possible to extrapolate from Hanoi's recent ideological statements what the North Vietnamese are telling the Chinese Communists to avoid getting trapped in the Peking-Moscow hassle. In pure ideological terms, they are saying that they are closer to the militant revolutionary creed of Peking than the Soviet strategy which allows for a peaceful transition to Communism. But the North Vietnamese are also insisting that they must remain neutral in the ideological polemics because North Vietnam must have Soviet aid to withstand the United States.

There are also unarticulated considerations underlying Hanoi's attitude. To retain their independence, the North Vietnamese must maintain a balance between Moscow and Peking. Someday, when the Vietnam war is over, they will also require Soviet economic assistance to reconstruct what they hope will be a united Communist country.

However, a crisis in relations between Hanoi and Peking may arise in connection with the convening next month in Moscow of the 23rd Congress of the Soviet Communist party. When Aleksandr Shelepin, a Soviet Presidium member, visited Hanoi last month, the North Vietnamese leaders agreed to send a delegation to the congress. Since then, the dispute between Peking and Moscow has worsened with the Chinese Communists referring to the Russians as "pimps of U.S. imperialism" and accusing them of joining with the United States in an encirclement of China. How Peking will view North Vietnamese participation in the Moscow doings, which are bound to have an anti-Chinese outcome, is a question that must be causing anxious handwringing among the Hanoi leaders.

Other governments of Southeast Asia, more removed from the shadow of Communist China, have been less tolerant of Peking's heavy handed diplomacy.

In Indonesia, President Sukarno seems to have lost out in the subtle struggle he waged to preserve good relations with Communist China. The army generals, who have been uprooting Peking's influence since the abortive Communist-supported coup of Sept. 30, have maneuvered the Government into recalling the Indonesian ambassador to Peking.

Across the Strait of Malacca, Peking has forfeited an opportunity to woo the predominantly Chinese city-state of Singapore. After the secession last August of Singapore from Malaysia as a consequence of a racial dispute between Chinese and Malay politicians, Prime Minister Lee Kuan Yew publicly flirted with the idea of improving relations with Peking. If the Singapore leader or the Malayan Government in Kuala Lumpur had any disposition to actually do business with Communist China, it has been discouraged.

The Chinese Communists recently sponsored the establishment in Peking of a Malayan National Liberation Front, a clandestine organization similar to the South Vietnam Liberation Front, dedicated to the overthrow of the Governments in Singapore and Kuala Lumpur.

It was the founding of a similar organization in Peking last year, the Thailand Patriotic Front, which galvanized the Bangkok Government into closer support of the United States military effort in Vietnam and the undertaking of a more vigorous internal anti-Communist campaign.

Burma Irritated

Closer to home, Peking has irritated the neutral Burmese, by alternating between overweening diplomatic courtship and ideological encouragement of the White Flag Communists who are trying to oust the Ne Win Government.

In all of Peking's scuffling with governments in Southeast Asia, there are two consistent factors. The primary cause of trouble is the insistence on the superiority of Chinese Communist ideology which, in its uncompromising arrogance, is similar to the ancient imperial view of China as the center of the universe and the repository of all wisdom. The other factor is the freedom of maneuver which Southeast Asian states have gained in withstanding Chinese Communist pressure either through the reassertion of Soviet influence in the region, or because of the power equilibrium created by American military firmness in Vietnam.

February 25, 1966

332

Sukarno Yields

"Bung Karno"—Brother Sukarno—has been President of Indonesia ever since he and other revolutionary leaders proclaimed the country a sovereign republic in August, 1945, two days after the Japanese surrender in World War II. He retained the title when the Netherlands, after a long struggle, finally recognized Indonesia's independence in 1949. Three years ago Mr. Sukarno—who regarded himself as the "eternal leader"—proclaimed himself President for life, and as late as this month he told followers, "I know my job. . . . Don't think that I will fall to any pressure from anywhere."

But last week the rule of the "eternal leader" seemed at an end. Although Mr. Sukarno still held the title of President, control of the country was in the hands of forces bent on reversing the pro-Communist drift that had marked the last years of the Sukarno regime. The man who flamboyantly dominated Indonesia while playing the roles of emperor, politician, supreme armed forces commander, and playboy—but now 64 years old and ailing—had been pushed into the background.

The power shift in Jakarta traced back to the abortive coup of last Oct. 1 and the purge of Communists that followed it. Whatever the precise ramifications of that never-fully-explained episode, one thing appeared clear: The delicate "nasakom" balance that had been the basis of President Sukarno's power over a nation of more than 100-million people stretched across the world's largest archipelago of 3,000 islands had been badly shaken.

"Nasakom" was President Sukarno's formula for deftly balancing rival groups under a policy of "guided democracy." The word is an acronym for a coalition of the military, the religious groups and the powerful Communist party, for years the largest outside Russia and China.

In world affairs, too, President Sukarno neatly balanced East against West in his reach for stature as an Asian leader. He was reported to have told President Kennedy in 1961 that, "I am the best bulwark in Indonesia against Communism," but he managed to obtain substantial aid from the Communist bloc as well as from the United States. Since 1963, the focus of Indonesia's foreign policy has been a campaign to "crush" Malaysia—which Mr. Sukarno has regarded as an extension of British influence in Southeast Asia.

Up to last September, the scales in Indonesia seemed to be tipping more and more toward the Communists. At home, President Sukarno increasingly heeded the requests of Communist leaders. Abroad, he more and more sided with Communist China and against the United States. Though his country's economy was drifting into chaos, he risked loss of American aid last year by saying in a statement directed at Washington "Go to hell with your aid if that aid is intended to make us retreat."

The crushing of the Communist-backed coup last October strengthened the army's position and caught President Sukarno in the middle. Military leaders stood by, or perhaps lent encouragement, as mobs and politicians throughout Indonesia carried out a wholesale slaughter of Communists. Estimates of the dead have ranged upwards of 100,000.

President Sukarno, however, continued to plead for the Communists on the theory that the guided democracy needed a leftist element to balance the right-wing military and Moslem organizations. In what appeared to be an effort to regain his previous "nasakom" balance, Mr. Sukarno last month fired Defense Minister Gen. Abdul Haris Nasution, one of the leaders of the anti-Communist movement. This set off a wave of unrest, student riots, and demands for an end to diplomatic relations with Peking. All this came at a time when the country was having mounting difficulties with inflation.

Yesterday events overtook Mr. Sukarno. With troops deployed throughout Jakarta, army leaders under Lieut. Gen. Suharto, the Army Minister and Chief of Staff, peacefully took over control and immediately banned the Communist party. Jakarta radio said President Sukarno had transferred his powers to General Suharto, although Mr. Sukarno retained the title as a figurehead. The general said in a statement he was taking control "for the sake of the integrity of the nation."

Though it was too early to make any long-term assessments, officials in Washington appeared to be pleased at the turn of events in Indonesia. While General Suharto said Indonesia would move neither to the right nor to the extreme left ("We are already left," he said), the feeling was that the trend would be away from Communist China's policies.

The military take-over—like the one in Ghana last month—clearly was a blow to Peking's prestige and may have been the final step in the destruction of Indonesia's Peking-oriented Communist party. As for President Sukarno himself, he appeared to be down, but nobody was forgetting that he has bounced back many times before.

March 13, 1966

Soviet-China Axis

An Analysis of Closer Tie Now Apparent

By TILLMAN DURDIN

The modifications of Communist theory and practice announced at the Soviet Communist Party Congress have brought about an ideological rapprochement between the Soviet Union and China.

In their Moscow statements the Russians have, in effect, moved into general conformity with the line proclaimed and followed for years by the Chinese Communist party.

Nikita S. Khrushchev, party chief, and other Soviet leaders said recently in Moscow that it was possible to bring about communism without violent revolutions. They explained that peaceful transitions from other systems to communism were possible and that non-Communist parties could assist in such transitions.

The Russians also declared a preference for collective leadership to the domination of individuals. In the international sphere, they proclaimed the possibility of co-existence and friendly relations between Communist and non-Communist states.

Views Long Held by Mao

These points of view have long been a part of the doctrines of the Chinese Communist party.

In his "new democracy" line of the Ninteen Forties, Mao Tse-tung, Chinese leader, elaborated the strategy of achieving revolution in China through a united front of workers, peasants and elements of the bourgeoisie favorable to political change.

Revolution was not achieved peacefully in China, but it did come about through the collaboration of groups and individuals in all classes of society and through the co-operation of a number of non-Communist political parties.

Since the formation of their Communist Government in 1949, Mr. Mao and his colleagues have further developed theories inherent in the "new democracy" line. They have affirmed a policy of collaboration of classes and parties for the period of transition to socialism and communism.

The Chinese modified the Leninist-Stalinist thesis that a period of proletarian dictatorship was necessary for the establishment of communism. They maintained the principle of coalition classes and political groups under what they described as the hegemony of the proletariat (the Communist party).

In practice the united front in China has been a facade. Power and administrative control have been kept in the hands of the Communist party. But non-Communist political leaders, intellectuals and managerial personnel have played a role.

At a Chinese Communist party conference in 1954, Liu Shao-chi, one of the chief party theoreticians, explained the party's policy of engineering a peaceful future transition to socialism and communism. But the Chinese maintain that groups and individuals not susceptible to re-education and assimilation must be liquidated.

The Chinese Communists emphasize that their program is particularly suited to Asian countries and they seek to inspire emulation elsewhere in Asia. The recent growth of the Indonesian Communist party is evidence of how effective the China program can be in another Asian nation.

The Chinese Communists also led in developing the thesis of peaceful co-existence between non-Communist and Communist nations They applied the possibilities of the peaceful co-existence line in China's relations with India.

The five principles of peaceful coexistence first enunciated by Chou En-lai, the Chinese Premier, and Jawaharlal Nehru of India have now been taken up by the Russians.

Just how much effect the Chinese views have had on bringing the Soviet leaders around to the new dogmas is difficult to say The Soviet Union and China have maintained an outward manifestation of unity and co-operation but below the surface it is likely there has been considerable debate.

The Russians may have been motivated in their changes of doctrine by a desire to increase Soviet influence, particularly in Asia. This could well result in an undercover clash with China's impact in the East.

February 25, 1956

Soviet-China Rift Charged to Stalin

By SYDNEY GRUSON
Special to The New York Times.

PRAGUE, Czechoslovakia, June 3—Nikita S. Khrushchev is reported to have told non-Soviet Communist leaders that Stalin almost caused a rupture in relations between the Soviet Union and Communist China.

Mr. Khrushchev, the Soviet ommunist party chief, spoke to party leaders when they gathered in Warsaw in March for the funeral of Boleslaw Bierut, First Secretary of the Polist United Workers (Communist) party, who died of a heart ailment in Moscow.

According to Communist sources, Mr. Khrushchev had a brief meeting with the party leaders at which he stressed the following points:

¶Stalin jeopardized China's alliance with the Soviet Union and thus endangered the solidarity of the Communist camp by demanding too much in return for aid to Red China.

¶Communist countries of Eastern Europe must work out their own internal problems without seeking Soviet advice on every detail. In this respect, Mr. Khrushchev is reported to have used the phrase "swim on your own."

Stalin Had Been Attacked

The funeral of M. Birut took place not long after the close of the Soviet party's Twentieth Congress. It was at a secret session of this Congress that Mr. Khrushchev made his now-famous speech downgrading Stalin and blaming the dead dictator for many evils in Soviet life.

The text of the speech, given to other Communist parties for study and distribution, makes no reference to international affairs except for the special case of Yugoslavia. Stalin was blamed for having banished Marshal Tito from the Communist family.

Mr. Khruschchev's remarks in Warsaw were in effect a broadening of his indictment against Stalin to include the former dictator's handling of relations with the Soviet Union's biggest and most powerful ally.

The Soviet party chief is reported to have spoken along these lines to the Warsaw gathering:

Stalin faced Mao Tse-tung, Red China's Chief of State, with a series of economic demands smacking of colonialism and insisted that he, Stalin, must have the same final word on the development of Communism within China as he had in other countries of the Soviet bloc.

Mr. Mao was extremely embittered by Stalin's insistence on jointly controlled companies and mining and industrial concessions, and he refused to submit to Stalin's authority over Chinese affairs.

Had it not been for the hardness of United States policy toward Red China, the Peiping Government might well have decided to break openly with Moscow as Marshal Tito did in 1948.

The situation was said to have been eased by Mr. Mao's visit to the Soviet Union at the end of 1949 and the beginning of 1950, but the tenseness in relations continued right up to the time of Stalin's death in March, 1953.

The main reason for the trip to China by Premier Nikolai A. Bulganin and Mr. Khruschchev after Stalin's death was to remove the causes of tension. This was done by the dissolution of jointly owned Chinese - Soviet compauies and the surrendering of concessions. Relations between the two countries now are reported to be close and cordial.

This is said to have been the essence of what Mr. Khrushchev reported on Stalin's relations with the Chinese leader.

Sources who have passed on this report said Mr. Khrushchev had asked permission to offer other Communist leaders one bit of advice on their internal affairs. He suggested that they all had the primary task of improving living conditions for their people as quickly as possible.

There is some evidence that the Russians have ceased trying to exert the same kind of overpowering control over the rest of their camp as had been practiced by Stalin.

Observers in Eastern Europe give as an indication of a developing trend in the relations between the Soviet Union and other Communist countries, the differing tempos of the liberalization process now under way throughout the area.

These observers believe that the Communist regimes in each of the Soviet bloc countries have been permitted to work out their own approaches to the problem of downgrading Stalin and readjusting to the lead given them by Moscow at the Twentieth Congress. The slavish copying of Soviet methods is at last being discouraged, the observers say.

Signs of Over-all Policy Seen

There is enough similarity in what is happening in each of the Eastern European countries to indicate the existence of an over-all policy. But there are basic differences in how the policy is being applied.

Hungary and Bulgaria, for example, have "rehabilitated" some executed Communist leaders without reservation. On the other hand, Czechoslovakia has upheld the execution in 1952 of Rudolf Slansky and other members of her party hierarchy although parts of the indictment charging them with Titoism have been withdrawn.

Mr. Slansky also was charged

with economic sabotage, Trotskyism and of having been an agent for Western imperialism.

Poland leads the rest of the Soviet bloc nations in permitting a greater measure of political and personal freedom for her people. Some loosening of the economic domination practiced under Stalin also has been indicated.

The Polish economic magazine Gospodarka Planowa recently conceded that the Russians had paid a special low price for Polish coal. The admission was an indirect one. The magazine said the Russians had agreed to pay the world price for future deliveries.

Soviet Tome Excises Repudiated Chinese

By HARRISON E. SALISBURY

The Great Soviet Encyclopedia has created a new "unperson." It has ordered the excision of the name of Kao Kang, a top Chinese Communist, said to have committed suicide two years ago under mysterious circumstances.

In apparent eagerness to fill the gap left by the elimination of Mr. Kao's biography, the encyclopedia editors included an article on a Tibetan town already listed under a different spelling in the multi-volume reference work.

The dropping of information on the Chinese Communist leader has revived speculation whether he might have been a key figure in the reported power maneuvering between Stalin and Mao Tse-tung, chief of state of Communist China. It also reopened the question whether Mr. Kao had actually committed suicide and if so, why.

The editors of the Soviet Encyclopedia have sent to their 300,000 subscribers do-it-yourself instructions designed to consign the name and existence of Mr. Kao to oblivion.

Following a technique conceived by the novelist George Orwell for creating an "unperson," the subscribers have been instructed to take scissors or razor blade and cut out the page bearing the biography and picture of Mr. Kao.

The encyclopedia began to appear, volume by volume, five years ago. About forty of an expected total of fifty volumes have been published thus far. Only once before have instructions to expunge data been issued.

The previous target of this technique was Lavrenti P. Beria, Soviet police chief, who was executed in December, 1953. Subscribers to the encyclopedia then received substitute pages containing an expanded article on the Bering Sea to be pasted in place of the Beria biography.

Now subscribers have been requested to paste in place of the biography of Mr. Kao in Volume 10 a page containing a twelve-line article and photo of Gyangtse, third largest town of Tibet, situated on the trade route from India to Lhasa. The new article gave the name of the town as Gantszy, in Russian transliteration.

But the intricacies of transcribing Chinese or Tibetan names into Russian being what they are, the editors apparently lost sight of the fact that there already was a four-line article on Gyangtse, in Volume 13, where it appears as Gyantze in

the Russian rendering.

The substitute page was mailed to subscribers with this note: "The State Scientific Publishing House of the Great Soviet Encyclopedia, recommends the removal from Volume 10 of Pages 213-214, instead of which you are being sent pages with a new text.

"Using scissors or razor blade, carefully cut out the indicated pages, preserving a strip to which the new pages are to be pasted."

The action of the Encyclopedia's editors directed attention to Mr. Kao's role in the Communist movement and raised the question as to why it was of importance to justify so radical an action.

The offending biography described him as a leading member of the Chinese Communist party. He was identified as a member of the Chinese Politburo, a Deputy Premier and chief of the Manchurian administrative region. There were no laudatory remarks, only official detail, all of which was accurate as of the time the biography was published in 1952.

In April 1955, the Peiping régime denounced Mr. Kao and Jao Shu-shih, another leading party figure, for "conspiratorial activities." The announcement said that Mr. Kao and Mr. Jao were exposed and denounced at

a plenary party session in February, 1954 after which Mr. Kao "committed suicide."

The time and place of the "suicide" were not revealed. Only fragmentary information has been published by Peiping as to the conspiracy. However, as leader of Manchuria Mr. Kao was in close relations with Soviet authorities, whose influence in the area continued strong even after the establishment of the Peiping regime.

Mr. Jao had been a Communist party leader in East China. He was one of the Chinese party's delegates to Moscow at the time of the nineteenth Communist party congress in October, 1952, a few months before Stalin's death.

Moscow's action in wiping clean the printed record of Mr. Kao's existence was taken as support of the seriousness with which the conspiracy was viewed both in Peiping and Moscow.

So far as a link between Mr. Kao and Stalin was concerned it was noted by State Department experts in Far Eastern affairs that the Manchurian leader would have occupied a strategic position in a struggle for power between Stalin and Mr. Mao. Mr. Kao's Manchurian area was for a time semi-independent and this was the basis of one of the charges Peiping lodged against him.

July 12, 1956

Red China Supports Poles Against Moscow Dictation

By SYDNEY GRUSON
Special to The New York Times.

WARSAW, Oct. 15—Communist China sides against the Soviet Union in the Communist world's ideological struggle over the number of roads to socialism.

Mao Tse-tung, leader of the Communist bloc's second mightiest power, has indicated to the Polish party his disapproval of the Soviet effort to re-establish a single Soviet road.

This correspondent has learned from reliable sources of a fragment of the discussion that recently took place in Peiping between the Chinese Communist chief and Edward Ochab, First Secretary of the Polish United Workers [Communist] party. M. Ochab was there for the Chinese party congress.

According to sources here, Mr. Mao told M. Ochab that the Poles should go ahead in

their efforts to obtain internal independence and develop their own Socialist system as the Yugoslavs have done.

The timing of the Ochab-Mao conversations was especially significant. They were held during the recent Yalta conference of Marshal Tito of Yugoslavia with Nikita S. Khrushhcev and other Soviet leaders.

The subject-matter of this conference and of the Khrushchev-Tito talks in Yugoslavia that preceded it now is well known. In effect, the Russians tried to convince President Tito of the dangers to the world's socialism of a too liberal interpretation of Moscow's promise of equality among all Communist parties.

A promise was given by the Russians in the Moscow declaration signed by Marshal Tito and Mr. Khrushchev last July 20.

June 4, 1956

335

This acknowledged "different roads of Socialist development in different countries."

During Mr. Khrushchev's recent stay in Belgrade he spoke at a dinner given for him by President Tito. The dinner was attended by Communists from other Eastern countries visiting Yugoslavia at the time. Mr. Krushchev spoke openly of the dangers to world communism as the Russians saw them and referred directly to evidences of unrest in Hungary and Poland.

Marshal Tito gave his answer in the form of a toast, pointedly reiterating the views he forced the Russians to concede in Moscow last summer. According to information available here, the Marshal did not budge from these views in the Yalta conferences that followed.

In the same fashion, the Polish party's liberal faction headed by Premier Josef Cyrankiewicz has not given way before the immense pressures being exerted to slow down the "democratization" of life here.

Situations Are Different

Inevitably a comparison is being drawn between the present Polish-Soviet situation and the Yugoslav-Soviet situation that existed in 1948 before Stalin had Yugoslavia expelled from the now-dissolved Cominform. However, the differences in the two situations are greater and more important than the similarities.

For one thing the geography is different and, as far as the Poles are concerned, compelling. For another there is no desire among Polish leaders to emulate the Yugoslav position as an independent force between East and West in international affairs.

One overriding concern unites the Polish leaders and the overwhelming mass of Poles as far as international affairs are concerned. This is the question of

the country's frontiers with Germany created on the Oder and Neisse Rivers after World War II. No matter their irritation or anger with the Poles, the Russians have never ceased supporting the Oder-Neisse line.

The importance of this in determining Poland's position in international affairs cannot be overestimated. The subject is raised in any discussion a Westerner has with Poles on the subject of Soviet-Polish relations.

Nevertheless, Poland's dependence on Soviet support of the Oder-Neisse frontier has not lessened the Cyrankiewicz-Ochab faction's drive for greater internal independence. The pending return to party leadership of Wladyslaw Gomulka, who had become a symbol of nationalism in Poland, will spur the drive.

M. Gomulka, former secretary general of the Polish party who served nearly four years in prison for Titoism, is due to be re-elected to the Politburo at a meeting of the eCntral Committee this week. It was learned today that he had attended a Politburo meeting Saturday, presumably to iron out final details of his formal resumption of power.

One of the Old Guard, which deposed M. Gomulka in 1948 at Stalin's bidding, has already fallen because of M. Gomulka's return. Hilary Minc "resigned" last week as Deputy Premier and member of the Politburo. Others who opposed M. Gomulka will be dropped. His authority and prestige are such that he can call virtually any tune he wants in Poland at this time.

It was expected that M. Gomulka would become the First Secretary at the party congress scheduled for next March. Now there is a rising demand for him to replace M. Ochab immediately, not only to strengthen the party in its relations with the Soviet Union but also for the vigor with which he is expected to attack Poland's serious economic situation.

PEIPING DISPUTES MOSCOW PRIMACY

Text of Its Recent Statement Called for Independence for Non-Soviet Red Parties

By HARRY SCHWARTZ

The text of a Chinese Communist statement last week asked for a measure of real independence for non-Soviet Communist parties.

Reports on the statement stressed its praise of Stalin and its condemnation of the allegedly behavior of President Tito of Yugoslavia. But the text, as printed in Pravda, calls on Moscow to refrain from interfering in the affairs of other Communist countries and to give other Communist parties a real voice in reaching common decisions.

Equality Is Stressed

A key passage in the 14,000-word Chinese statement printed in the Soviet party newspaper declares:

"Communist parties of all countries must be united, but at the same time must maintain their independence. Historic experience testifies that if these aspects are incorrectly joined and if either is neglected then errors are inevitable.

"Solidarity among Communist parties of all countries is strengthened when they maintain relations on a basis of equality and when they attain unity of views and of action by means of real, and not formal, consultation.

On the other hand, if in their mutual relations they forcibly impose their views on one another or replace comradely suggestion and criticism by interference in the internal affairs of one another, then their solidarity will be harmed."

Stalin Is Criticized

This demand for equality and mutual consultation is accompanied by an open attack on Stalin for his contempt of other Communist parties and his practice of ordering them to do as he wished. The Chinese statement declares:

"Stalin in his relations with fraternal parties and fraternal countries demonstrated a certain tendency toward great-power chauvinism. This consisted in ignoring the independent and equal position of Communist parties and socialist countries in the international alliance."

The declaration adds:

"Stalin demonstrated great-power chauvinism in the solution of specific problems and lacked the spirit of equality. He sometimes interfered incorrectly in the internal affairs of fraternal countries and fraternal parties, an interference that resulted in serious consequences."

Polish Reds Praised

The praise for the independence of Communist parties and countries indicates continued support for the Poles so long as they maintain their present pro-Soviet foreign policy. The Chinese statement specifically praises the present Polish Communist leadership headed by Wladyslaw Gomulka for its action against anti-Soviet elements in Poland.

The Chinese call for unity of all Communists on the ground that the "chief contradiction" in the world today is "the contradiction between us and our enemies (between the imperialist camp and the socialist camp). The statement thus contradicts a Yugoslav view that the world is not composed of two hostile ideological groups of nations.

This difference in approach leads the Chinese to declare: "Comrade Tito and other leaders of the Yugoslav Communist League maintained in their recent declarations concerning Stalin's errors and other related problems a position that in our view is not well rounded and is not objective."

The correct evaluation of Stalin, the Chinese statement declares, is this: "If Stalin's errors are compared with his achievements, then his errors appear to be only secondary in importance."

Chou Is in Moscow For Talks on Crises

Special to The New York Times.

MOSCOW, Jan. 7—Premier Chou En-lai of Communist China arrived today for important talks with Soviet leaders.

Experts here believed that the talks would be aimed at strengthening the unity of the Communist world and at working out plans for meeting some of its critical problems. Economic and ideological crises, especially in Hungary and Poland, are expected to head the list of matters Mr. Chou, Peiping's most influential spokesman in foreign affairs, will take up with the Soviet rulers.

Mr. Chou not only will hear the Kremlin's version of the current situation but also will get a first-hand look. A member of his party disclosed tonight that the Chinese Premier would visit both Warsaw and Budapest during his present tour. It was the first time that Hungary had been named as being on Mr. Chou's itinerary.

On his arrival at Moscow's Vnukovo Airport, Premier Chou stressed Communist China's friendship with the Soviet Union. He said strengthening those ties were "considered by us our highest international duty." He said comradely relations between the two countries were "eternal and unbreakable."

Premier Chou followed the Soviet line in denouncing the new United States policy on the Middle East. He said the fundamental fact of that policy was the United States' aim to replace Britain and France in Middle Eastern affairs.

He said the American policy also demonstrated that the "imperialists have not folded their arms."

The Communist Chinese Premier, speaking in a snowfall, again emphasized Peiping's position that the unity of the Communist countries was essential for their ultimate victory and that the main burden of forging that unity fell to the Soviet Union. He described the Soviet Union as the "most determined fighter against war and colonialism" and said the so-called Communist commonwealth was "led by the Soviet Union."

Party Dominance Emphasized

Mr. Chou also stressed the fundamental Leninist principle of the role of the Communist party in guiding the destiny of any "Socialist" state. This is an article of the Communist faith that has been under particularly strong fire recently in the Soviet Union's sphere, but especially in Hungary and Poland. This principle—the Communists' justification for one-party rule—was supported by the Chinese in their recent major policy statement published in the Peiping People's Daily and reprinted widely here.

Premier Chou probably will stress this point in his talks with Wladyslaw Gomulka, leader of the party in Poland, and Premier Janos Kadar in Hungary. The Kremlin leaders have made no secret of their distress over challenges to this doctrine in those countries.

So far as is known, there are no major outstanding differences between the Chinese and Russians that will have to be ironed out during Premier Chou's visit. Peiping's strong backing of the Kremlin position on terparty and intergovernmental relations has been made clear. One significant worry of the Chinese must be their anxiety as to how Soviet promise of economic assistance to Peiping will be affected by the recent disruption within the satellites and the Soviet Union's consequent assumption of heavy new economic burdens.

January 8, 1957

MOSCOW PRAISES MAO CAUTIOUSLY

Pravda Says Peiping View on 'Contradictions' Is Good, for Chinese at Least

By MAX FRANKEL

Special to The New York Times.

MOSCOW, July 16—The Soviet Communist party expressed cautious praise today for recent Chinese experimentation with Communist ideology.

Moscow's editorial writers noted that Peiping's assertions about "contradictions" between the governors and the governed were a good thing—for China. The Soviet press previously had restricted itself to reproductions of Chinese leaders' speeches and Chinese commentary on the ideological question.

Though it was restrained and carefully phrased, the first Soviet comment in the Communist party organ, Pravda, today left no doubt that Moscow approved of developments in Communist China. The Soviet newspaper even went so far as to suggest that "a number" of the principles raised in China were, of "great importance for the Marxist-Leninist theory in general." But it did not specify the principles or the nature of their importance.

What was widely regarded as ist doctrine was promulgated by Mao Tse-tung, leader of the Chinese Communists, in two speeches last February and March. He warned that even in a Communist society there were "contradictions" within the people that threatened to disrupt the unity of Government and party leaders with the masses.

This, in turn, Mr. Mao said, led to a triple evil of bureaucracy, sectarianism (isolation of the bureaucrats from the people) and subjectivism (failure to incorporate popular aspirations and "realities" into policy).

Peiping Drive Is Cited

Coincidentally, the Chinese Communist party began a campaign to permit what it called free and constructive discussion of the nation's problems and ordered its bureaucrats to get from behind their desks and work among people.

These developments had been reported here since mid-April and a version of Mr. Mao's first speech was reprinted in full when published last month.

But there was considerable curiosity about Moscow's attitude toward Peiping's new ideological position. It was recalled that Soviet theoreticians generally had looked upon "contradictions" as a phenomenon of capitalist society.

In his remarks to a United States television audience last month, Nikita S. Khrushchev, chief of the Soviet Communist party, said that Socialist (Communist) China was a young nation and that the Kremlin was watching its efforts with great interest. He expressed neither agreement nor disagreement with Mr. Mao's thesis.

[During the televised interview, Mr. Khrushchev was asked whether there were any contradictions between the leaders of the Soviet Union and the people. He said there were not. Both the question and the reply were omitted from the Soviet version of the interview.]

Moscow's views remained guarded throughout what the Chinese called their "unusual spring." The first public indictment of the ousted "anti-party" group of Gorgi M. Malenkov, Lazar M. Kaganovich and Vyacheslav M. Molotov included the charge that it had worked to obstruct good relations with other Communist nations.

Pravda said today that Mr. Mao's published speech "furnishes the Chinese people with a clear-cut orientation in the new situation [of socialism] and helps them to define lucidly which words and actions help the cause of socialism and which harm it."

Pravda characterized Mr. Mao's speech as "an outstanding event in China's political life," one reflecting "from a Marxist angle a number of fundamental issues that arose in China after the victory of the Socialist revolution." The article continued:

"The speech of Comrade Mao Tse-tung has multiplied the strength of the millions of supporters of socialism in China who have turned to a decisive offensive against the hostile sorties of Right-Wing bourgeios elements."

The publication said the "sweeping movement of criticism in China had led to revelations of shortcoming and mistakes and to "many valuable suggestions." It also called attention to what it termed successful isolation of "Right-Wing elements" during the campaign.

The Chinese Communists have charged that these elements tried to exploit criticism in order to seize leadership of the whole country.

The Soviet newspaper pointed proudly to the agreement between Moscow and Peiping on international affairs and the Chinese association in this respect with other Communist nations.

"Rooted as it is on the principles of Marxism-Leninism," Pravda said, "the People's China's foreign policy is a mighty factor for the further consolidation of the unity of the Socialist camp."

The occasion for the Pravda editorial, entitled "People's China on the Road to New Victories," was the conclusion of the session of the Chinese National People's Congress.

July 17, 1957

CHINESE EXODUS TO SOVIET IS SEEN

Experts of U.S. Agencies Say Population Pressure May Force Emigration

By DANA ADAMS SCHMIDT
Special to The New York Times.

WASHINGTON, Dec. 15— Chinese population pressures may lead to emigration into Southeast Asia in the near future and into the Soviet Union in the more distant future, according to United States Government experts.

While reporting friction between China and Burma over clandestine migration, the experts foresee much larger eventual population pressure upon Soviet territories.

This, they believe, may develop into a cause of conflict between the Soviet Union and Communist China.

A study completed by Washington agencies shows that China will probably have a population of 1,000,000,000 by 1980. At a conservative estimate it is calculated that the population of 583,000,000 as of July, 1953, is increasing at a rate of 2 per cent a year. This would double China's population every thirty-six years.

The Chinese Government has tackled this situation by ignoring its Marxist precepts and encouraging birth control. At the same time it is resettling Chinese in sparsely inhabited frontier areas.

On the basis of historical precedents the experts believe that frontier settlement may be the first stage in a process that could carry China's population well beyond her present borders.

On a small scale this is already happening in Burma, where the Chinese population now numbers about 500,000 compared with 300,000 before World War II. Since May, 1956, the Chinese no longer check emigration to Burma, which is proceeding at the rate of 1,000 a month.

The aim is believed to be to increase Chinese influence in Burma.

Much larger opportunities for settlement lie in the thinly populated regions of the Soviet Far East and Soviet Central Asia.

The studies made here indicate that resettlement within China's present borders is intended to shift population from the densely settled east to the sparsely inhabited west.

In a greatly accelerated colonization program the Chinese resettled about 700,000 persons in the western frontier regions in 1955, 700,000 more in 1956, and probably as many in 1957.

In Manchuria, people from near-by provinces of North China are being resettled along the lower Sungari River, not far from the Soviet frontier, and in other black-soil areas of Heilungkiang. There is a steady flow into the Paotow region of Inner Mongolia, where the Mongols are already heavily outnumbered by Chinese.

In Kansu, the area around the growing rail center and industrial city of Lanchow is receiving a stream of immigrants. Lanchow itself grew from 200,000 to 500,000 between 1949 and 1956.

In Sinkiang, with its huge area and undeveloped resources, large-scale resettlement is occurring along the Manass River (in Dzungaria) and around Urumchi.

Hainan Island in the extreme south, which can produce tropical products, including rubber, if properly developed, is to receive about 1,400,000 settlers.

December 16, 1957

Manning in The Phoenix Republic

"Which is the satellite?"

IS PEIPING CALLING THE SIGNALS FOR MOSCOW?
China's Wishes Must Be Considered
By Makers of Soviet Policy

By HARRY SCHWARTZ

There are few precedents in modern history for the abrupt change in the international diplomatic picture that took place last week following the Khrushchev-Mao talks in Peiping.

This week-end diplomats throughout the Western world are still debating the exact nature of the relationship between Mr. Khrushchev's Peiping visit and his turn-around on the summit meeting.

One school of thought holds that it was Mao Tse-tung's direct veto that caused Premier Khrushchev to retreat from his original position of last July 23, when he announced he was ready to go to New York City for a Security Council summit meeting. Another school of thought argues that Mao's role in the Khrushchev change was at most of secondary importance, and that Premier Khrushchev had had second thoughts about the matter even before he left Moscow.

Only the future can judge which of these views is correct. But the fact of the Soviet policy shift is clear, and it seems a certainty that this shift was one of the key topics discussed between the Soviet and Chinese leaders in Peiping.

The whole incident raises the broader question of the relationship between the foreign policies of Peiping and Moscow, and in particular of the changes Mao Tse-tung and his colleagues desire in Soviet foreign policy. It would seem most unlikely, after all, that the highest Soviet and Chinese Communist leaders would require four days of conferences only to resolve the issue of a Security Council summit meeting as against a General Assembly meeting for the Middle East.

Foreign Policy Discord

It has been known for some time that there was discord between Moscow and Peiping on foreign policy. There have been insistent reports from both Warsaw and Belgrade since last spring that the Communist Chinese wished to aggravate the international situation and felt Soviet policy was too cautious. The most official statement on this subject was made by Yugoslav President Tito last June when he implied in a public speech that Communist China was in favor of war. He quoted Chinese officials as having boasted that if another war came it could not be so terrible that it would not leave at least 300,000,000 Chinese alive.

The motive for Chinese warmongering, Tito indicated, was the belief that the higher the level of international tension the greater pressure Peiping could put on Moscow to give it additional military and economic aid. Other Eastern European sources have stressed the growing self-confidence of Peiping in its own strength, and the Peiping conviction that the West is now clearly defeated, a conviction expressed by the Chinese in the saying, "The East Wind has prevailed over the West Wind."

These reports plus the developments of last week suggest that the Chinese are pressing at least for the following changes in Soviet foreign policy:

(1) An all-out Soviet campaign aimed at getting for Communist China Nationalist China's place in all international bodies, including the Security Council. This implies an effort to force the United States to accept Communist China's admission into the United Na-

tions as well as an effort to force the United States to sit down with Communist China and the Soviet Union in a summit conference soon to discuss the most major international problems, such as disarmament and control of outer space.

(2) Peiping wants the Soviet Union to go all-out against Yugoslav "revisionism." It has not escaped Peiping's attention that, aside from verbal assaults directed at Belgrade, the Soviet Union and its Eastern European satellites have taken only one concrete action against Yugoslavia, the "postponement" of the Soviet-East German credit. It appears to be probable that Peiping finds it intolerable that trade and cultural relations between most countries in the Communist bloc and Yugoslavia have been relatively little affected by the renewal of ideological warfare.

(3) Peiping appears to want a much bolder policy by the Communist bloc in this period during which it believes the Communists hold a military advantage over the United States because of the Soviet Union's intercontinental ballistic missile. The military alert declared in Taiwan last week testifies to Generalissimo Chiang Kaishek's apprehensions that the Chinese Communists may strike at the Nationalists' off-shore islands or at Taiwan itself. That

kind of military adventure, or a similar one in Europe aimed at taking over West Berlin, fits in with the Chinese Communist notion the United States is a "paper tiger" that will not fight, but it conflicts sharply with Premier Khrushchev's effort to keep the world struggle in the realms of economics, politics and propaganda.

Communist China's ability to put pressure on the Soviet Union for its point of view, and, conversely, Moscow's need to pay at least some attention to Peiping's demands, derive from the levers Mr. Mao and his colleagues possess.

(1) Peiping knows that its adherence to the Communist bloc represents a major source of additional political, economic and military power for the Soviet Union vis-à-vis the free world, while Chinese acceptance of the Soviet Union as head of the Communist bloc sets an example that makes possible the cohesion of the bloc as a whole. In every dispute between Moscow and Peiping, Russia must always bear in mind the tremendous loss to its power and prestige that any break in this axis would bring. Moscow knows, of course, the advantages the alliance brings to the Chinese, but it must at all points be wary of the possibility that neglect of the Communist Chinese wishes may cause Peiping to conclude that the disadvantages of the alliance outweigh the advantages.

(2) The Soviet rulers know that hundreds of millions of people in Asia and Africa whom it is wooing—the people of the Asian-African nations that attended the Bandung Conference —are instinctively more sympathetic to Communist China than to the Soviet Union, whose ruling group, the Russians, are white. Therefore, it knows that its ability to get along with the Communist Chinese is necessary if communism is to make further progress in Asia and Africa. Moscow knows it must avoid giving the impression that it seeks to substitute the rule of white Communists for the former rule of the underdeveloped countries by white "capitalist imperialists."

(3) Finally, and not the least important, there is the position of Premier Khrushchev in the power struggle which is always at least latent in Moscow and which may at any time flare up again. There have been rumors for months, particularly from Poland, that Premier Khrushchev's dominance of the Soviet scene was threatened by an alliance between the Chinese Communist leaders and a Moscow faction headed by Mikhail

A. Suslov. Even if such an alliance has not existed, it is always a possibility. Knowing this, Premier Khrushchev must realize that his ability to preserve the Peiping-Moscow axis is a sina qua non not only for Communist strength in the world situation, but also for assuring his own personal primacy in Moscow. It is interesting to note that in his latest visit to Peiping, Premier Khrushchev thought it wisest not to bring along any of his fellow members of the party Presidium, and to associate himself publicly—and only himself— with the strengthening of the Chinese-Soviet alliance proclaimed in the communiqué he signed with Mao last week-end.

Danger of Conflict

The controls manipulated by Mao suggest that there is an area of policy-making in which both the Soviet Government and Premier Khrushchev must pay close attention to Chinese Communist wishes to to try to adapt Soviet desires and strategy thereto. But equally obvious there are limits beyond which neither Peiping nor Moscow can go without one becoming in effect the puppet of the other. It is when these limits are approached that the danger of conflict between the two powers arises.

Whether these limits were approached in the Peiping talks is conjectural. What the record of history suggests, however, is that as Communist China's power grows so too will its demands. Both Moscow and Peiping know that the latter, which claims a quarter of the human race, will not forever defer to the former. For the moment, a workable compromise seems to have been achieved in Peiping, though how long it will suffice not even Khrushchev or Mao Tse-tung can really predict.

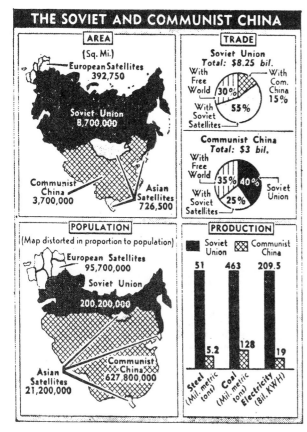

THE SOVIET AND COMMUNIST CHINA

AREA (Sq. Mi.)
European Satellites 392,750
Soviet Union 8,700,000
Communist China 3,700,000
Asian Satellites 726,500

TRADE
Soviet Union Total: $8.25 bil.
With Free World 30%
With Com. China 15%
With Soviet Satellites 55%

Communist China Total: $3 bil.
With Free World 35%
Soviet Union 40%
With Soviet Satellites 25%

POPULATION
(Map distorted in proportion to population)
European Satellites 95,700,000
Soviet Union 200,200,000
Communist China 627,800,000
Asian Satellites 21,200,000

PRODUCTION
Soviet Union / Communist China
Steel (Mil. metric tons): 51 / 5.2
Coal (Mil. metric tons): 463 / 128
Electricity (Bil. KWH): 209.5 / 19

August 10, 1958

KHRUSHCHEV, MAO MEET IN PEIPING, CHARGE WEST WITH WARLIKE MOVES

4-DAY TALKS HELD

Two Red Leaders Ask Session on Mideast, Troop Withdrawal

By WILLIAM J. JORDEN
Special to The New York Times.

MOSCOW, Aug. 3—Premier Nikita S. Khrushchev has spent the last four days in Peiping in consultation with Communist China's leader, Mao Tse-tung.

Messrs. Khrushchev and Mao jointly called in a communiqué for the immediate convening of a summit meeting to discuss the problem of the Middle East. They also demanded the prompt withdrawal of United States and British troops from Lebanon and Jordan, respectively.

They accused the Western powers of having moved the world to the brink of war. They warned that if those "imperialist war maniacs" caused a war all the peace-loving peoples would destroy them once and for all and establish "everlasting world peace."

Replies Believed Near

Amid the disclosure of the Khrushchev-Mao meeting, diplomatic circles in Moscow expected that the Soviet Premier's replies to the latest Western proposals on an East-West summit gathering on Middle East affairs would be delivered here tomorrow.

Leading military, diplomatic and Communist party officials of the Soviet Union and Communist China took part in the surprise meeting in Peiping.

Messrs. Khrushchev and Mao, the two leading figures in the Communist world, were said to have exchanged opinions on "a series of major questions confronting the two countries in Asia and Europe in the present international situation." The communiqué said they had reached "unanimous agreement" on measures for opposing "aggression" and preserving peace.

Full Accord Reported

The official report on the meeting exposed no new facets of the Moscow-Peiping relationship. It repeated the usual claims that the Soviet Union and Communist China were in full agreement on international problems, on the situation within the Communist orbit and on their own relations of "friendship, alliance and mutual assistance."

On Mr. Khrushchev's side of the table in the Peiping talks were Defense Minister Rodion Y. Malinovsky; Vasily V. Kuznetsov, Acting Foreign Minister while Minister Andrei A. Gromyko is on vacation, and Boris N. Ponomarev, a member of the Central Committee of the Communist party, who specializes in relations among Communist parties.

Joining Mr. Mao on the Chinese side were Premier Chou En-lai, Defense Minister Marshal Peng Teh-huai, Deputy Premier and Foreign Minister Chen Yi, and Wang Chia-hsiang, a member of the Secretariat of the Chinese Communist party's Central Committee and an expert on inter-party relations.

Tie to Summit Talks Seen

They were said to have met from Thursday to today. The communiqué carried today's date.

It was assumed by most observers here that Mr. Khrushchev's visit to Communist China, coming in the midst of preparations for a summit meeting on the Middle East situation, must have been related to that event.

But it also was recalled here that a visit by Mr. Khrushchev to Peiping had been freely predicted in Moscow some time ago, before the Middle East crisis developed. That was at a time when the question of relations among parties and governments in the Communist world, and especially the vexing problem of dealings with Yugoslavia, was receiving such widespread attention.

In this connection, the Soviet and Chinese leaders have again stressed that "revisionism"—efforts to alter fundamental Marxist-Leninist principles—was the "chief danger in the Communist movement." They added that revisionism had been "clearly manifested" in the latest program adopted by the Yugoslav Communists at their recent party congress in Belgrade.

World Affairs Stressed

But in their communiqué, Messrs Khrushchev and Mao concentrated largely on the international situation. They claimed "great success" in the pursuit of their foreign policy goals. They said that policy had found increasing favor in such countries as India, Indonesia, the United Arab Republic and other states in Asia, Africa, Europe and the Western Hemisphere.

In contrast with their program, they maintained, the "aggressive imperialist bloc," headed by the United States "monopoly groups," is opposing peaceful coexistence and stepping up "preparations for a new war."

Communist China joined the Soviet Union in the latter's call for a summit conference to discuss the Middle East situation. No distinction was made in the communiqué between such a gathering held within the framework of the United Nations and one held outside that body.

Friendship Stressed

It appeared here that the Peiping regime was putting its stamp of approval on a heads-of-government meeting even if it were organized through the United Nations Security Council, as the United States and Britain have proposed. If so, the Chinese Communists apparently thought the positive benefits of such a gathering would outweigh Peiping's reluctance to see anything done through a body on which the Chinese Nationalist regime of Generalissimo Chiang Kai-shek was represented.

Peiping's position on the United Nations is publicly supported here, though the Soviet Union has not hesitated to continue its activities in the Security Council despite the presence there of the Chinese Nationalists. Observers in Moscow thought it logical that Mr. Khrushchev, having expressed his willingness to attend a summit meeting under United Nations auspices, would want to go out of his way to reassert his close friendship for and cooperation with the Chinese Communists.

As a result of Mr. Khrushchev's visit, the Chinese had new assurances that they were not being left out in the cold in the matter of a summit meeting. The rest of the world, too, had new evidence that Peiping and Moscow were working closely together.

The Soviet Government realizes that any proposal to include Communist China in big power talks at this stage would destroy any chance of such talks' materializing. But it clearly does not want the world to forget about Communist China.

It was doubted here that any new military arrangements had been made between the two countries, though it was possible that joint action in case of necessity in the Middle East or elsewhere might have been considered.

August 4, 1958

Peiping Opens Nuclear Reactor; Warns U. S. on Atomic Arms

Special to The New York Times.

HONG KONG, Sept. 27—Communist China started operating its first atomic reactor and cyclotron today with a warning that atomic weapons were not the monopoly of "United States imperialists."

The 10,000-kilowatt heavy-water research reactor and 20,-000,000-electron-volt cyclotron were built with the assistance of Soviet specialists in the suburbs of Peiping.

At an inauguration ceremony attended by guests scientists and officials from the Soviet Union, North Korea, India and other countries, Vice Premier Nieh Jung-chen predicted speedy development from now on of atomic science in Communist China, the Hsinhua (New China) News Agency said.

He said Communist China's new atomic plant would be used for peaceful purposes. He nevertheless castigated the United States for opposing Communist China's bid to take over Quemoy, Matsu and Taiwan from the Chinese Nationalists. In this connection he stated that "United States imperialists should realize atomic weapons are not their monopoly."

'Blackmail Assailed'

The Vice Premier asserted that the "Chinese people absolutely will not tolerate" the use of "atomic blackmail" by the United States to interfere with the "recovery of our coastal islands and the liberation of Taiwan."

Dmitri V. Yefremov, deputy director of the Soviet Bureau for the Utilization of Atomic Energy, headed Moscow's delegation at the Peiping ceremony. He emphasized Soviet backing for Communist China in its dispute with the United States, but made no reference to Soviet atomic weapons as a factor in this support.

Mr. Yefremov said that if the "arrogant politicians and generals of the United States State Department and Pentagon dare infringe upon our great creative labors they will certainly receive the counter-blows that they deserve. He asserted that Communist China "has something to defend as well as the means to defend it with."

Solidarity Stressed

The Chinese and Soviet speakers hailed the new atomic plant as new evidence of solidarity between Moscow and Peiping. The installation had been rushed to completion as an achievement to mark next week's Oct. 1 national day of Communist China.

The new plant turned out its first radioactive isotopes for today's ceremony.

Another construction project finished this week as a triumph for the national day was the first big blast furnace of the new iron and steel complex being built at Wuhan. The furnace was erected with Soviet technical assistance. It is the largest in Communist China.

The furnace will turn out more than 2,000 tons of pig iron a day. More than 20,000 persons attended the ceremony opening the plant Thursday, including Soviet officials and specialists.

RED CHINA SPURS SINKIANG GROWTH

Ten-Year Industrialization Plan Revealed—Railroad to Russia Is Key

By TILLMAN DURDIN
Special to The New York Times.

HONG KONG, Oct. 15—The Chinese Communists have launched a ten-year program to turn Sinkiang Province into one of China's main industrial and agricultural bases.

The development plan, which has been put into operation, calls for the building of steel plants, textile mills, petroleum and sugar refineries and a large-scale electric power network in the remote Central Asian province.

Agricultural expansion will concentrate on making Sinkiang's vast semi-arid plains produce more cotton than any other part of China and contribute at the same time a large part of the country's wheat, fruit, sugar beets, grapes and livestock.

Details of the ten-year program were given in copies of the newspaper Sinkiang Jihpao that have just reached here. The papers are four months old but provide the most comprehensive information on the Sinkiang program to become available to the outside world.

Work on the plan coincides with inauguration of the first railway link from China proper into Sinkiang. Peiping announced yesterday that the new rail line had been pushed well into Sinkiang and that passenger traffic opened last Saturday from Lanchow to Hungliu, first station inside the Sinkiang border.

The 1,800-mile railway, which will connect Lanchow with Sinkiang's capital of Urumchi and link with the Soviet railway system at Aktogai, is already two-thirds finished and will be completed next year. The line from ports on the Yellow Sea, will permit through rail traffic 3,000 miles from Urumchi.

The railroad will provide the third rail link between China and the Soviet Union. The two others are the old Trans-Siberian connection in Manchuria and the Trans-Mongolian railroad, opened in 1955.

Three-fourths of Sinkiang's 6,000,000 people are Uighurs, a Moslem Turkic group. The proportion of Chinese has been growing steadily as a result of a state-sponsored movement of persons from China proper.

The province is called the Sinkiang Uighur Autonomous Region and an Uighur named Saifudin is Governor. Peiping's Communist control, however, is thorough-going and the most important man in the province is Wang En-mao, First Secretary of the provincial party.

The Communist rulers of Sinkiang have had trouble with the Moslems of the province and have had to suppress a movement to turn the province into an independent republic. One of the reasons for the new development plans may be to consolidate control and match the developments going on among Turkic peoples of the Soviet Union's Central Asian territories.

A copy of the June 8 edition of Sinkiang Jihpao says Mr. Wang described the Sinkiang development plan to a provincial party session as a program prescribed by the eighth national party congress earlier in the year.

Mr. Wang said Sinkiang would be required to build a heavy industry base by its own efforts. Sinkiang is a major petroleum region and its oil will facilitate industrialization plans.

Large-scale reclamation of wastelands, mainly for cotton planting, will call for the addition of 1,300,000 acres this year and similar areas in years to come. Educational plans call for the wiping out of illiteracy in the next three years.

Decline Expected in Soviet Role in Red China's Industrial Growth

By TILLMAN DURDIN
Special to The New York Times.

HONG KONG, Feb. 8—The Soviet role in the industrial growth of Communist China is expected to diminish but to continue of basic importance. This appeared here today to be a significant aspect of the 5,000,000,000-ruble economic agreement signed in Moscow yesterday between Premiers Nikita S. Khrushchev of the Soviet Union and Chou En-lai of Communist China. Experts on Chinese-Soviet relations here observed that the agreement provided for less Soviet participation in Chinese industrial construction than in the past. It is recognized, however, that there may be deals later for further Soviet materials and technical advice. The new agreement involves the equivalent of $1,250,000,000 over nine years at the official exchange rate. But total Soviet economic aid to the Chinese Communists in the first nine years of the Peiping regime is believed to have totaled more than 10,000,000,000 rubles ($2,-500,000,000).

The first Soviet economic support was a 1,200,000,000-ruble loan in 1950. A 5,600,-000,000-ruble agreement in 1954 called for Soviet participation in the construction of 156 major industrial projects, with repayment in Chinese exports.

In 1956, fifty-five new projects were added at a cost of 2,500,000,000 rubles. Last August it was announced that Moscow would assist forty-seven more projects, but no cost figure was given.

Most Soviet participation has been paid for concurrently by the shipment of Communist Chinese exports to Russia. Soviet materials and advice thus have been provided on what amounts to a barter basis.

There has been no major Soviet grant aid, such as that which the United States has given to other countries.

Little has been revealed on Moscow's military assistance to Peiping, but evidence indicates that Peiping has paid for it.

Communist China's exports to the Soviet Union last year have been estimated at 3,600,000,000 rubles and her imports from the Soviet Union at 2,400,000,000 rubles.

Communist China's exports to non-Communist countries in the last two months have dropped sharply. Food and other necessities are reported to be scarce in many parts of China.

One explanation advanced here is that China has stepped up exports to other Communist countries to pay for the Soviet industrial aid.

The Peiping radio said today that the new agreement provided that Communist China "will supply commodities to the Soviet Union in accordance with the existing Sino-Soviet trade agreement."

February 9, 1959

KHRUSHCHEV SEES NO CHINESE PERIL

Tells Russians Neighbor's Rapid Population Growth Is No Cause for Alarm

By HARRY SCHWARTZ

Premier Nikita S. Khrushchev has told the Soviet people that he has no fears about the possible consequences of rapid population growth in China.

In a speech printed late last month in Pravda, the Soviet leader said Communist China's population was growing by about 14,000,000 annually.

Recent American visitors to the Soviet Union, including Adlai E. Stevenson, have reported finding signs of concern among Soviet citizens and officials at the implications for their country of Chinese population growth. United Nations estimates have suggested that Chain many have about 1,000,-000,000 people by 1980 and 1,600,000,000 by the year 2,000, compared with the present 650,000,000.

Reply by Soviet Leader

Mr. Khrushchev declared that many foreign visitors had posed the question of Chinese population growth to him and suggested that Soviet leaders might be alarmed at this. Premier Khrushchev gave his answer in these words:

"Here you have an example of typical bourgeois psychology. Why should the quick growth of population in brotherly People's China or any other country frighten us? If all peoples will direct their creative efforts, their minds and their possibilities so as to increase the output of material goods and cultural values, then the needs of the peoples of the entire world will be satisfied abundantly and the so-called over-population problem on our planet will seem absurd."

Premier Khrushchev's remarks seem important because of a theoretical innovation he introduced into Communist doctrine at the Soviet party congress last January. He declared that Communist-ruled countries would reach the stage of utopian communism more or less simultaneously. Thus he reversed the earlier Soviet view that the Soviet Union and Eastern Europe would reach this stage before China.

Earlier Concern Noted

Soviet ideology assumes that a great abundance of all goods is an essential prerequisite for full communism. Thus the Premier's theoretical innovation last January implied that the Soviet Union would have to wait for full communism until the poverty stricken population of China had also achieved great abundance of goods.

There have been some signs in the past that Premier Khrushchev has been disturbed about China's growing population.

Diplomatic sources have reported that in the fall of 1955, when Chancellor Konrad Adenauer of West Germany visited Moscow, Premier Khrushchev expressed alarm privately about the implications of Chinese population growth, noting particularly, it is said, that the Chinese were able to work hard at a very low standard of living.

Less direct evidence of concern has been seen in Premier Khrushchev's emphasis in recent years on moving Soviet citizens into the Siberian area north of China and developing the resources and industrial potential of this region.

It has also been noted by foreign observers that several years ago Premier Khrushchev declared 200,000,000 people were not adequate for Soviet population and that it would be a good thing if that population were to rise by an additional 100,000,000.

The subject of rapid Chinese population growth is not normally discussed in the Soviet press. Nor have Soviet newspapers in recent years reported the variations in the Chinese Communist policy on this issue as reflected in the changing attitude toward birth control in recent years.

Anastas I. Mikoyan, Soviet First Deputy Premier, took the same position on Chinese population growth during his visit to the Unted States as Premier Khrushchev has now publicly taken. But Mr. Mikoyan does not speak with the authority of the Premier, nor were his remarks in this country publicized in the Soviet press on any scale comparable with the broad coverage normally given publication of Premier Khrushchev's speeches in the Soviet Union.

April 5, 1959

Soviet and Red China Compete For Power in Outer Mongolia

By HARRISON E. SALISBURY
Special to The New York Times.

ULAN BATOR, Outer Mongolia. The Soviet Union and Communist China are competing in classic great-power fashion for dominant influence in Outer Mongolia.

The competition is being carried on behind a camouflage of honeyed words and platitudes about collaboration and friendship among Communist states.

But neither camouflage nor verbiage can conceal the fact that here in Central Asia Soviet and Chinese policies are competitive and are directed toward divergent goals.

It may be that the Chinese-Soviet struggle for influence in Outer Mongolia is an isolated phenomenon stemming from peculiarities of geography and history. Outer Mongolia for 1,500 miles lies on the flanks of the two great Communist powers. Conflict between Czarist Russia and the old Chinese Empire arose in this area more than a hundred years ago.

There are indications that there are deeper divergencies in Outer Mongolia than either Moscow or Peiping would like to acknowledge. Diplomatic observers familiar with the situation in Peiping, Ulan Bator and Moscow believe that Mongolia may well prove the harbinger of future conflict between the two powers.

The importance of these developments to the United States is obvious. To even the most casual visitor it is apparent that Mongolia affords an unsurpassed laboratory for examination of divergent Soviet and Chinese policies.

Thus far, United States policy appears to have disregarded the opportunity. The United States has no diplomatic relations with Outer Mongolia.

The United States could easily play a considerable role here. The Outer Mongolian Government is eager to win recognition from the United States. It wishes to join the United Nations and to break out of its isolation.

No responsible official in Ulan Bator would think of saying anything publicly to offend Moscow or Peiping. But it is evident that Outer Mongolia is attempting to play the classic role of a weak country situated between two powerful neighbors, trying to balance one against the other. In this delicate game the ability to call in third powers is of major importance.

Outer Mongolia's ability to play the balancing game is handicapped by the fact that it is a member of the Communist bloc. For many years, Outer Mongolia was treated as a Soviet protectorate with no real voice in foreign relations.

Red China's Rise a Factor

The rise of Communist China has brought an end to Outer Mongolia's role as a quasi-vassal of Moscow. Today the Ulan Bator Government is seeking to establish non-Communist international relationships on a broad scale.

Thus far, the steps have been halting. Diplomatic ties have been obtained with several Asian nations. An effort is under way to extend these ties to Arab and African states.

What Ulan Bator really wants is recognition by Western great powers. A few Western correspondents have been permitted to come to Outer Mongolia. In September, an international congress of specialists in Mongol language and literature is scheduled. Mongolists from twenty-six countries have been invited. The participants will spend about ten days in Outer Mongolia, visiting historic sites.

An outstanding feature of the conflict between China and the Soviet Union is China's superior attractive force. Young Mongol intellectuals return from Peiping with a crusading spirit. No such emotional change seems to be produced by study or visits to the Soviet Union or Eastern Europe.

Peiping's Drive Noted

Diplomats stationed in Red China say a similar enthusiasm is instilled in many young Asians who view Peiping as the Mecca of their dreams.

These diplomats view China's efforts to influence Outer Mongolia within the framework of a diplomatic offensive to win wider influence, especially in Asian and African countries.

It is not easy for the Soviet Union to combat the ideological pull of Peiping. In the first place Moscow's record in Mongolia is hardly such as to inspire any enthusiasm.

True, the Communist regime was set up in 1921 with the support of the Red Army. But it is difficult to discover signs of any real Soviet assistance to or interest in Outer Mongolian problems from that time until about 1952, except for military questions.

Only a few small industrial enterprises were set up before 1952—a vodka factory, a small

The New York Times   Aug. 4, 1959

Soviet Union (1) and Communist China (2) are vying for the prize of dominant influence in Outer Mongolia (3).

packing plant, a little leather tannery and a coal mine. Traditional social patterns and the primitive nomadic life were hardly affected.

Moscow did display military interest in Outer Mongolia as a bridgehead against Japanese attack from Manchuria.

No Modern Army Built

Even this interest hardly extended to building up a modern army. Instead, Outer Mongolia was treated as a cavalry supply base. The Red Army drew on the country's fine horses. It requisitioned huge quantities of meat. It is probable that the Soviet Union deliberately held back the military development of Outer Mongolia lest the Japanese move in and take over any improvements installed by the Russians.

Not even the liquidation of the Japanese military threat with the Manchurian campaign of 1945 brought material change in Soviet policy.

Nor did the victory of the Chinese Communists in 1949 have any immediate effect. Only in 1952 and 1953, about the time of Stalin's death, did the Soviet Union begin to offer substantial assistance to Outer Mongolia's reforms. It was probably no coincidence that the adoption of a new Soviet aid policy coincided with the emergence of a vigorous Communist China on Outer Mongolia's southern and eastern borders.

The Soviet Union's ability to compete with China for Mongolian primacy should not be underestimated. The upper echelons of the Outer Mongolian Government and party bureaucracy are Moscow-trained men. There is no doubt that the So-

viet Union exercised an effective veto over Outer Mongolia's personnel and policy during most of the years from 1921 to 1952.

Premier Yumzhagiin Tsedenbal, an able, intelligent and vigorous chief executive, is a Moscow-oriented man.

Uniforms Are Similar

So are most of his assistants in the government apparatus and in the Foreign Ministry. Russian is the second language of most educated Mongols. English rather than Chinese is likely to be the third language. Uniforms worn by the Mongolian Army and police resemble those of their Soviet counterparts.

Mongols who have abandoned the national dress of brilliant silk gowns have adopted Russian-style clothing. They do not wear the blue uniforms and caps of the Chinese. The repertoires of the Ulan Bator theatres resemble those of Soviet provincial theatres, not Chinese.

And the vast and windy Sukhe Bator Square in the center of Ulan Bator, with its red stone mausoleum housing the remains of Sukhe Bator and Choibalsan, derives inspiration from Red Square and the Lenin-Stalin Mausoleum.

Cyrillic Script Used

Such contemporary art as Outer Mongolia has developed stems from Soviet Socialist realism. The architecture of the government and residential buildings rising in Ulan Bator is patterned after Soviet style. The chief Mongolian newspaper is called Unen, which means "truth" in Mongol, just as Pravda means "truth" in Russian.

Unen is printed in the Cyrillic

script used by the Russians. This is no accident. In 1946 Outer Mongolia at Soviet insistence replaced her ancient vertical script with a modified phonetic kind of Cyrillic.

This script is now taught in the schools and used in books and newspapers. But older Mongols still use the traditional script. Three weeks' close observation failed to uncover a single official who employed Cyrillic for writing notes of interviews or similar memoranda. Newspapers of Inner Mongolia, a part of China, are said to be popular in Outer Mongolia because they are printed in the old Mongol script.

The question of Mongol writing is closely associated with Soviet and Chinese maneuvering in the sphere of Mongol nationalism.

There are three principal areas of Mongol population. Independent Outer Mongolia has a population of about 1,000,000. The Chinese autonomous province of Inner Mongolia, inhabited by 1,500,000 Mongols and 7,000,000 Chinese, is an area of more advanced economy and culture than Outer Mongolia. Inner Mongolia is a Chinese base for exerting influence upon the Mongols of Outer Mongolia. It is probably no accident that easy population movements between the two areas are not permitted.

The third Mongol area, within the Soviet Union, was until about a year ago known as the Buryat-Mongol Autonomous Republic. The population of this area, just north of Outer Mongolia, is 671,000, of whom about half are Mongols.

Without explanation in July, 1958, the Soviet Union dropped the word "Mongol" from the designation of the autonomous area, which became simply the "Buryat Autonomous Republic." It is possible that this move was designed to weaken the cohesive ties of the Mongol populace and to set up a bulwark against any future "Greater Mongolia" concept advanced by the Chinese.

Great emphasis is placed by Outer Mongolia authorities on population growth. This seems to be related quite clearly to the fact that the population density of adjacent Chinese areas is sharply higher than that of Outer Mongolia. The demographic ability of Outer Mongolia to resist population pressures indefinitely is obviously limited.

These pressures are already being felt. The biggest element in China's aid program to Outer Mongolia is laborers, of whom there are said to be 20,000.

Chinese laborers are at work constructing roads, laying asphalt, digging sewer mains, erecting buildings, installing machinery. Every big project under way in Ulan Bator is being built with Chinese labor.

The contrast in appearance

between the Chinese and the Mongols is striking.

The Chinese are uniformly dressed in blue. They wear dark blue caps, except in rain, when they don broad straw hats and bright blue rain capes. They are strong, tall, fine-looking young men who move purposefully and confidently about the construction sites. The Mongols are smaller and diversely garbed.

The Chinese working force is not limited to Ulan Bator. Wherever there is a construction project, the Chinese are building it. A rush job to replace a bridge torn out by floods? The Chinese are working hard on it under arc lights at 2:30 A. M. A new irrigation project to turn a semi-desert into agricultural land? The Chinese, 500 strong, are carrying it out.

Soviet Aid Revised

Peiping is said to be pressing Ulan Bator to take more laborers often without charge. These are proposals that a small nation, struggling to lift itself by its economic bootstraps, finds hard to refuse.

Yet, the question that Outer Mongolia's Soviet-oriented officials must face is the ultimate outcome of the influx of vigorous young Chinese, highly skilled and culturally advanced. The danger of domination at the hands of the more vigorous, more advanced race is obvious.

Compared with the pervasive efforts of the Chinese, the Soviet Union's aid program seems conventional. The unbalanced economic arrangements of the Stalin era have been liquidated. Joint Soviet-Mongolian enterprises have been turned over to the Mongols. About 1,000,000,000 rubles of aid, much of it in the form of repayable loans, has been advanced.

More beneficent export-import relationships have been established. These, in effect, constitute a substantial subsidy to Outer Mongolia. The Soviet Union is now paying world market prices for meat. Chinese credits run about one-third of those offered by Moscow. But the Mongols say that the Russians drive a tough, hard bargain. Chinese credit, they say, is almost a gift.

Although for centuries the Mongols hated the Chinese for their overlordship and, thus, welcomed Russia's advance to their frontier in the nineteenth century, the position now seems to be reversed. The memories of Chinese rule are in the dim past. The Soviet Union is the more recent overlord.

"The momentum of the Chinese initiative is so great, the attractive force of Chinese dynamism is so overpowering," an Asian diplomat said, "that it is hard to see how, over the long run, Russia can maintain her position here. She is still the first power in Outer Mongolia. But five years from now this may well no longer be true."

The Western visitor to Outer Mongolia is struck by many unique impressions. Not the least of these is the immediate understanding that he feels with the Soviet community here.

In Geneva, New York or Moscow, Americans and Russians may find themselves on opposite sides of ideological and diplomatic barricades. But in Ulan Bator they seem part of the same European community.

"It is curious," a recent western visitor to Ulan Bator remarked, "how I feel toward the Russians. And, I must say, they are equally warm to me."

"I do not find that so strange," said an Asian diplomat who had just arrived from Peiping. "I think that you are merely experiencing a sensation which will be far more common in the future. To those

of us who watch the world from Peiping there seem to be far more grounds for accord than disaccord between America and Russia. What you and your Russian friends feel today in Outer Mongolia will tomorrow be experienced in Gorky Street, Moscow, and Pennsylvania Avenue, Washington."

And a Soviet official who has spent many years in Outer Mongolia said over a glass of vodka to an American visitor to Ulan Bator:

"Really now, standing here tonight can you think for any reason why we Russians and you Americans should fight? Is there anyone here to whom you feel closer?

"To peace!" the American proposed, raising his glass.

"To peace and the closest friendship of Russia and America," replied the Soviet official.

August 4, 1959

CHINA TIED TO SOVIET BY NEED FOR VAST AID

In Spite of Areas of Difference The Alliance Seems Firm Now

By TILLMAN DURDIN
Special to The New York Times.

HONG KONG, Sept. 26—It is a safe assumption that no officials in any world capital are following the course of Nikita Khrushchev's visit to the United States more closely than those in Peiping.

This interest is understandable. Russia and Communist China are not only neighbors but allies; they are bound together by military, political and economic ties of extraordinary tenacity. Important actions by one, especially in the sphere of international affairs, inevitably affect the other. As apparently the weaker of the two Communist giants, Mainland China is more dependent than is the Soviet Union on their special relationship, and Mao Tse-tung and his colleagues are consequently sharply aware of the fact that the outcome of the Soviet Premier's trip to the United States can have a far-reaching impact on their country and its policies.

Military Alliance

The interdependence of the Soviet Union and Communist

China is perhaps most importantly expressed in their military alliance. Together—Communist China with its vast manpower and Russia with her modernized nuclear-armed forces and industrial potential—the two states constitute the world's most formidable power bloc. Against their potential enemies, Communist China in the Far East represents an armed might that is a constant major preoccupation of the United States and its allies; in Europe, the Middle East and the Atlantic area, the Soviet Union is a still more powerful war machine and demands correspondingly greater Western counter-force.

The economic bonds between Russia and Mainland China have, after ten years of development, become extensive in scope. Since 1950 the Soviet Union has been supplying Communist China with capital goods and other essential imports at an average rate of about $200,-000,000 a year and recent agreements provide for continuation of these imports through 1967.

Industrial Imports

Imports include equipment for 291 of the largest and most basic new industrial enterprises in Mainland China, such as the big Wuhan and Paotow steel works, the Yellow River Sanmen Gorge hydroelectric installation and large chemical, automobile and machine-tool plants. In exchange for these imports, and in payment for Soviet military equipment, Communist China annually ships more than 50 per cent of its total exports to the Soviet Union. Communist China's economic development by now incorporates Russian types of equipment and Russian techniques in a basic fashion that would be difficult to change, while Chinese agricultural and mineral products have become integral parts of the Soviet economy.

Russia supplies Communist China's military forces with planes, submarines, guns and other weapons and has provided the experts and the organizational patterns with which Peiping is building up increasingly modernized and effective armed services.

The two countries have agreements covering extensive cooperation in scientific fields and providing for Soviet technical help in fields ranging from minerals and steel production to the development of atomic energy.

Since 1950, Communist China has added one new railway link with Russia, through Mongolia, to the Manchurian route that already existed and by the end of this year will have completed a third, through Sinkiang. Airlines and telephone circuits are additional aspects of the increasing physical ties between the two countries.

Russian is the most important second language of Mainland China and from Russia Communist China is continuously adopting art forms and other cultural attributes.

Despite the modification they have thought necessary for Chinese conditions, Communist Chinese officials base their developing political system, even their governmental organization, on Soviet models and Soviet experience. The two regimes in general give mutual support in their foreign policies

'ROOM FOR BOTH?'

Little in The Nashville Tennessean

and pursue common ideological lines.

Given their existing state of close collaboration, serious disagreement between Peiping and Moscow is difficult. Differences occur, however, and the rigid facade of absolute unity that leaders of the two countries attempt to present to the outside world makes the strains of any discord all the more severe.

Soviet Contribution

Russia is doubtless often irked by what appears to be a situation in which she gives more advantages than she receives. In the military sphere, for example, the Soviet contribution to their armed alliance is much greater than the Chinese. Despite the fact that Russia's participation in Communist China's economic development is not massive and incorporates little if any outright grant aid, Russia may well feel she provides, with her modern machines and techniques, in better fashion than she is recompensed. In payment, Russia takes many Chinese products that she cannot use and which, as world trade channels well know, often have to be dumped in the West and even back in Asia.

There has been disagreement over Peiping's system of communes. Moscow's aversion to the communes, probably based mainly on fear that they would not work and would endanger the whole prospect of communism in China, has been openly expressed by Mr. Khrushchev. Peiping modifications in the communes system, however, doubtless have diminished Soviet distaste and apprehensions.

There is certainly rivalry between the two powers in Outer Mongolia and possibly border tensions elsewhere as the Chinese push their millions of migrants and their economic development into Sinkiang, Chinghai and Tibet.

Discord surely crops up in the approach to other Asian countries. Peiping's abrupt termination of trade with Japan last year, with its resulting losses that Russia had to help make up, probably did not sit well with Moscow. Communist China's border squabble with India and its attacks on India over Tibet seem also to have

'READY FOR A FIGHT?'

Long in The Minneapolis Tribune

irritated Russia, and jeopardized Soviet wooing of India through economic aid and diplomatic support.

A very serious difference may be involved in Mr. Khrushchev's gestures toward the United States. If, indeed, the Soviet Premier is aiming for peaceful coexistence with the United States there is reason to believe that Peiping would consider this a wrong approach.

Communist China has a basic enmity toward the United States, not only over Taiwan but as a result of rivalry between Peiping and Washington for influence in the entire Far East. Communist Chinese leaders, moreover, appear to believe more emphatically than do Russia's that the capitalistic West is on the decline, and a natural corollary of this view would be a conviction that the Communist world should keep on the offensive and make no compromises with the West that would delay the capitalist collapse.

Communist China has outwardly manifested approval of the Khrushchev mission, but Peiping's many expressions of continued hostility to the United States and of doubt that "United States imperialist" elements would accept a genuine detente with the Communist world are evidence of anxiety and misgiving with regard to Soviet-United States relations.

No Serious Rifts

More certain assessment of Communist China's attitude in this respect must await the evolution of events. For the present, at least, in this matter, as in other aspects of Soviet-Chinese relations there are differences, but none that bars effective collaboration.

Differences over internal matters such as the communes are not likely to cause any serious rift unless the communes prove to be disastrous failures. At present they are being made to operate with reasonable effectiveness.

An over-all identity of interests far outweighs bickerings over domestic systems and tactics. Heavily dependent as it is on the Soviet Union, Communist China is in no position to break the bonds with Russia and for the time being shows no signs of doing so.

CHAPTER 7

The Trend toward Militancy
1960–65

Workers of a glass factory
in Amoy train as militiamen
during work break.

Courtesy Eastfoto

CHINA GROWS FASTER THAN RUSSIA

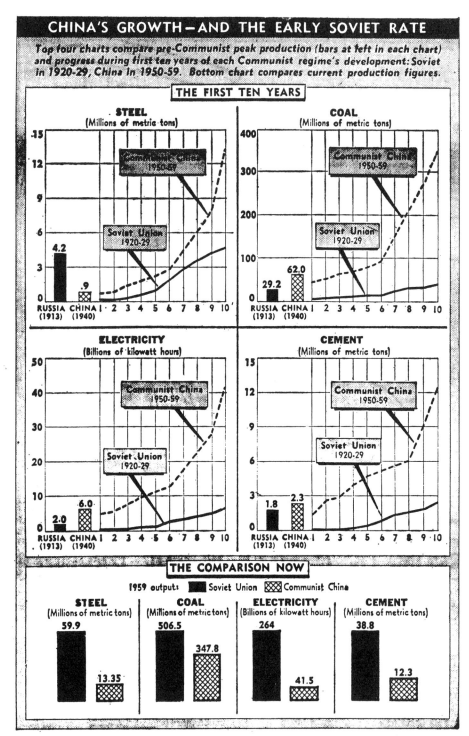

CHINA'S GROWTH—AND THE EARLY SOVIET RATE

Top four charts compare pre-Communist peak production (bars at left in each chart) and progress during first ten years of each Communist regime's development: Soviet in 1920-29, China in 1950-59. Bottom chart compares current production figures.

THE FIRST TEN YEARS

STEEL
(Millions of metric tons)

Communist China 1950-59
Soviet Union 1920-29

RUSSIA (1913) 4.2   CHINA (1940) .9

COAL
(Millions of metric tons)

Communist China 1950-59
Soviet Union 1920-29

RUSSIA (1913) 29.2   CHINA (1940) 62.0

ELECTRICITY
(Billions of kilowatt hours)

Communist China 1950-59
Soviet Union 1920-29

RUSSIA (1913) 2.0   CHINA (1940) 6.0

CEMENT
(Millions of metric tons)

Communist China 1950-59
Soviet Union 1920-29

RUSSIA (1913) 1.8   CHINA (1940) 2.3

THE COMPARISON NOW

1959 outputs ■ Soviet Union ⊠ Communist China

STEEL
(Millions of metric tons)
59.9   13.35

COAL
(Millions of metric tons)
506.5   347.8

ELECTRICITY
(Billions of kilowatt hours)
264   41.5

CEMENT
(Millions of metric tons)
38.8   12.3

Factors that have helped to give Communist China a faster rate of early growth than the Soviet Union include (1) help from other Communist regimes, (2) rapid imposition of tight discipline, (3) much larger work force and (4) development in an era of advanced technology.

By **HARRY SCHWARTZ**

Western analysts devoted much time last week to evaluation of the 1959 economic reports issued almost simultaneously last week-end in Moscow and Peiping.

One fact emerged clearly from the comparison of the two major Communist powers' economic progress: If the two nations' economic statistics can be trusted, Communist China's economic might now, at the end of the first decade of the regime's existence, is growing far more swiftly than that of the Soviet Union. Put another way, Communist China's advantage over the Soviet Union in rate of growth of industrial production now is roughly as great as the advantage of the Soviet Union over the United States.

The question of the reliability of the statistics is not a matter to be dismissed lightly.

Last year China admitted that its first astounding announcements about the magnitude of its "great leap forward" in 1958 had been grossly exaggerated, and that the actual gains made that year were smaller than claimed originally. But the gains Peiping says it made in 1959 do not appear so unreasonable as the claims it made a year earlier.

The Key Comparison

Assuming that the statistics of the two Communist nations are roughly comparable, the key comparison is this: Last year, Peiping asserts, its total industrial and agricultural output grew by 31 per cent over 1958; Moscow says that its 1959 national income rose 8 per cent in 1959.

What appears to be even more significant is the fact that the rates of growth of industrial production claimed by Peiping for the last two years are far greater than the rates of growth realized by the Soviet economy at the corresponding stage in the latter country's development. Put another way, Communist China now, at the end of its first decade of sustained economic development, appears to be moving ahead much more rapidly than was the Soviet Union at the end of the Nineteen Twenties. And the total volume of China's industrial output now—particularly heavy industrial output—is far ahead of the Soviet Union's at the beginning of the Nineteen Thirties.

Analysts trying to evaluate the significance of China's superiority over the Soviet Union in the rate of economic development point to four major factors which lie behind this phenomenon:

First is the existence of the Soviet Union and the other

Communist nations. From these allies China has received during the last decade a flood of help in the shape of technological information, training of specialists, modern machinery and the like. Besides, of course, the Chinese have benefited from the mistakes made earlier in the rest of the Communist bloc.

The Soviet Union, of course, also received foreign technological aid and capital equipment in the late Nineteen Twenties and early Thirties. But China has received much more of this help from its Communist allies than the Soviet Union did from capitalist countries in its comparable stage of development.

Second, the Chinese Communists succeeded in imposing tight discipline on their people much earlier and at much less cost than Lenin and Stalin were able to do three decades earlier. Collectivization of agriculture, for example, was not completed in the Soviet Union until about fifteen years after the Bolshevik Revolution. And before Soviet farms were collectivized, the regime had to win a battle against the peasantry in which roughly half of all Soviet agricultural capital was destroyed.

China, on the other hand, collectivized agriculture almost overnight barely half a decade after completing the conquest of the mainland. Two years ago Peiping set up the even more Draconian system of people's communes. All this was done in China without meeting anything like the stubborn resistance that Stalin encountered.

Third, in human terms, China had and has far more to work with than did or has the Soviet Union. Much of Peiping's suc-

cess in economic development to date has come simply from its ability to put its more than 600,000,000 people to work with an intensity exceeding anything ever known in Russia, while paying its people for their labor even less than Stalin paid his workers and peasants in the Twenties and Thirties. It may well be that never in history have so many people worked so hard for so little pay as in China this last decade.

'JUGGLER'

Fischetti, NEA Service

"A little less enthusiasm, dammit!"

Finally, the Chinese Communists have been the beneficiaries of the fact that they began their industrialization later than did the Russians, at a time

when the world level of technology is much higher than it was in the Twenties and Thirties. The large modern plants built in China in recent years are far more productive per unit of capital invested than plants built in Russia thirty or more years ago.

What of the future? The most obvious point to be made is that the factors enumerated above as operating in China's favor are still powerful. The possibility must be faced therefore that China's very rapid rate of economic development may continue for some years, even though there may be some slackening.

The prospect arises, for example, that some time in this decade China will be the third largest industrial power in the world, surpassing any of the Western European nations. This result is likely if China merely doubles its industrial output within the next decade. At the recent rate of growth, this would require only about three years or so.

Should anything like this rapid growth of Chinese economic power take place in the years immediately ahead, the balance of power will obviously be radically altered, with important consequences for the entire world.

For the Soviet Union the rapid growth of Chinese Communist economic power is likely to be particularly important. As it grows stronger, Peiping will probably become ever less dependent on the Soviet Union for economic assistance. Thus the most important lever Moscow has for influencing China

is likely to decline in effectiveness. At the same time, a steadily stronger China may well press more strongly than ever its demands for greater influence on the decisions of the Communist bloc.

For the United States and the rest of the non-Communist world the implications of a Communist China growing rapidly stronger can hardly be very attractive. A China bounding ahead in economic power is likely to exert strong influence promoting Communist strength in the under-developed lands of Asia, Africa and Latin America. The Chinese model, if these prospects are realized, is likely to be one increasingly regarded by the leaders of the under-developed countries as the magic solution for their problem of rapid industrialization.

Beyond that, of course, military power in the modern world grows hand in hand with economic power. The possibilities sketched above make it appear likely that well before the end of this decade China will be a modern military power with long-range rockets and nuclear weapons at its command.

All projections are speculative, of course. There is no guarantee that the Peiping regime will be able to hold its people down in the years ahead as successfully as it has in the decade gone by. Nevertheless, it cannot be ignored that China has already shown enough industrial dynamism in these last few years to cause the calculations for the future to be revised in many world capitals, including Washington and Moscow.

January 31, 1960

CHINESE MESSES FEED 400,000,000

73% of Rural Population Eats in Community Halls— Urban Units' Size Given

By TILLMAN DURDIN
Special to The New York Times.

HONG KONG, April 6—Four hundred million rural dwellers in Communist China now eat in community mess halls, Vice Premier Tan Chen-lin told the National People's Congress in Peiping today.

Mr. Tan said the vast rural network of community dining rooms now totaled 3,900,000

units and accommodated 73 per cent of the rural population. The latest figures give Communist China's total population as about 670,000,000.

The dining rooms operate as part of the system of communes, the basic social units for collective living in Communist China. The entire rural population of Communist China was incorporated into communes nearly two years ago and the system, which socializes every phase of life, is now being organized in the cities.

Mr. Tan, who is a member of the Secretariat of the Central Committee of the Chinese Communist party, stated that there were now 24,000 rural communes, each averaging 10,000 acres and comprising an average of 5,000 households and a labor force of 10,000 persons.

His address before the annual

meeting of Communist China's Government-controlled Parliament was reported here in a Peiping dispatch of Hsinhua, the official Chinese Communist press agency.

The Vice Premier's report on production, social and political aspects of the agricultural front today followed reviews at yesterday's Congress meeting of the new communes system in the cities.

Jen Chung-yi, Chinese Communist party secretary for Harbin, revealed that eight communes, incorporating 70 per cent of that Manchurian industrial city's population, had an average membership of 160,000 individuals.

Mr. Jen's information was the first indication to come from Communist China of the number of people being put into communes in the major cities of the country.

Mr. Tan lauded Communist China's leaps ahead in agricultural production and predicted that the country would fulfill two to three years in advance a twelve-year program for agricultural development adopted in 1956.

He said that the goal for pig-raising set for 1962 had already been reached and that the country produced 270,000,000 pigs last year.

The Vice Premier reported that the average annual income of the rural population in 1959 was the equivalent of $35, which was the goal for income set for attainment in 1962.

The average annual income of the rural population on the Nationalist Chinese-held island of Taiwan is about $140, according to Nationalist Government publications.

April 7, 1960

SHANGHAI KEEPS SPECIAL STATUS

Special to The New York Times.

HONG KONG, Aug. 3 — Shanghai has won a special status among the cities of Communist China and it is reflected in recent announcements that urban communes will be introduced there only when "conditions have ripened for their establishment."

Urban communes are being established at high speed in all other major cities.

The official explanation is that the situation in Shanghai is "complex." The real explanation seems to be that the Communists want to preserve Shanghai as a thriving center of commerce and industry.

However, communism has brought terror and tribulation to the city, China's largest and busiest metropolis.

During various campaigns against business men, intellectuals and "rightists," thousands have been exiled to distant villages and frontiers.

Gone are the gaudiness and cosmopolitan charm that once brightened the key commercial and industrial community. Only the serious pursuits remain.

Last year Shanghai produced 1,800,000 tons of steel, representing 13 per cent of the national total, and 2,200,000 bales of cotton yarn, 26 per cent of the national total.

This year Shanghai's steel goal is 2,500,000 tons, again 13 per cent of the country's goal. The city has become the second biggest steel-producing center on the China mainland, ranking next to Anshan, in Manchuria.

This year Shanghai plans to balance its budget at 11,442,-000,000 yuan ($4,767,000,000) for revenue and expenditure, and the Peiping regime will get 9,398,000,000 yuan ($3,915,000,-000) from Shanghai, about 13 per cent of the nation's income.

The population of the city was about 5,000,000 in 1949 when the Communists marched in. By 1957, more than 1,000,000 residents had been transferred to other parts of the country, most assigned to farms.

Despite this, the population of Shanghai continued to grow with a high birth rate and a steady influx of workers from the countryside (which the Communists initially tried to check but later encouraged.) Today the population is estimated at 7,000,000.

At first the Communists opposed development of coastal industries — partly as a defense measure and partly because they planned to develop the interior —and intended that the existing industries of Shanghai should be "maintained, used and transformed but not developed."

Development occurred, however, through the imagination and skill of Shanghai's surviving commercial and industrial leaders and workers.

Even allowing for inflation in the figures of Communist China's statisticians, Shanghai has made impressive progress. The total value of industrial output, according to Peiping, has increased sevenfold since 1949; the city's steel-producing capacity has increased more than thirty times; the output of machine tools has increased eighteen times; cotton yarn output has increased threefold.

August 11, 1960

Scientists Hear Red China Taps Vast Mineral Riches

By WALTER SULLIVAN

Intensive geological prospecting on the Chinese mainland in the last decade has disclosed mineral resources so extensive that they appear to make China one of the world's chief reservoirs of raw materials.

This was reported yesterday at a symposium on China sponsored by the Government's National Science Foundation and by ten leading scientific societies. The two-day symposium at the Commodore Hotel is designed to help fill large gaps in American knowledge of scientific and technological developments in Communist China.

It forms part of the annual meeting of the American Association for the Advancement of Science, which began here yesterday. The meeting will continue until Friday, with some 7,000 scientists participating.

The symposium was told that, in the last ten years, Communist China had jumped from twentieth place, in extent of weather observations, to rival Canada for third place. The United States and Soviet Union lead in this field.

Likewise, it was reported, the Chinese have made important advances in nuclear physics They now have four known nuclear reactors, all apparently designed for research, rather than for making atomic-bomb fuel. This report, of course, does not rule out the existence of secret fuel-producing reactors.

In this connection, one speaker noted that a number of Chinese nuclear physicists of wide repute had faded from the scientific literature. His interpretation was that they were too busy teaching and running institutes to do original work. He concluded that some of them might also be working on a secret project.

The discoveries of raw materials were described by Dr. Edward C. T. Chao of the United States Geological Survey. After World War II, he said, there were fewer than 200 active geologists in China, a fifth of whom had been trained in American and European universities.

21,000 Now in Field

Now, as a result of an intensive campaign during the last eight years, there are 21,000 "geological workers." Many of them, he said, are poorly trained by American standards, but the twenty-one high technical schools of geology are turning them out by the thousands every year. In addition, Dr. Chao said, more than 400 foreign geologists have been brought in, most of them from the Soviet Union and Eastern Europe.

Among the deposits found during the exploration of the hinterland, he said, was an unsuspected reserve of 7,000,000,-000 tons of iron ore in the Shansi area of central China. Another deposit, estimated at 3,000,000,000 tons, has been found in Honan province, he said. It assays at more than 50 per cent iron oxide.

One pillar of industrial growth in the United States has been the iron of the Mesabi Range in Minnesota. From 1892 to 1950 some 1,500,000,000 tons of ore were removed from it. The high grade ore is somewhat depleted now, but extensive lower grade ore remains and is usable.

The last few years have also brought to light two large molybdenum deposits in China giving that country a reserve of this important alloy metal larger than that of any other nation, according to Dr. Chao One of the sites is even richer than the well-known deposit now being mined at Climax Colo., he said.

No important deposits of uranium have been found, as far as he knows.

However, he said, a large deposit of ilmenite, an ore containing iron and titanium, has been found on the island of Hainan. Finally, he reported that an important deposit of nickel had been found.

Dr. Kung-ping Wang of the Department of Interior in Washington noted that the authenticity of this nickel deposit had yet to be verified. It would give China one of its most desperately needed metals.

He reported that China had plentiful coal deposits, including coking coal, but that the problem was to transport it, economically, to where it was needed.

He cited various instances of what the Government in China refers to as the policy of advancing on two legs. One leg is the highly sophisticated technology of modern industry; the other depends upon the primitive methods used in China for many generations.

Thus, Dr. Wang said, some mines in moist areas freeze the ground when sinking their shafts. Some diggings use continuous-mining equipment imported from the Soviet Union. China has one of the eight vertical zinc plants in the world. Yet everywhere there are plants and mines dependent primarily upon the hands and legs of thousands of men.

Chinese Inventions Cited

Among the speakers was Dr. J. Tuzo Wilson of the University of Toronto, who traveled through China and Taiwan two years ago as president of the International Union of Geodesy and Geophysics. He described recent developments on the mainland as a scientific "renaissance."

The science of geophysics, he noted, was "invented" in China. The seismometer was developed there in the second century and the compass and the clock, as well as printing, paper and explosives, all originated in China, he said. Rain gauges were set up in many Chinese areas long before such weather studies began in the Occident.

Now, Dr. Wilson said, the Chinese have traced their earthquake records back to 1139 B. C. after having put 150 historians to work examining ancient records. The result is a map of seismicity (or frequency of quakes) that is used in designing the new dams and other structures.

Dr. Wilson said that he had found morale low among the scientists on Taiwan. They received little support from the Nationalist Government, he said, and were still using antiquated equipment.

In contrast, he said, the Communist regime on the mainland is pouring money into science. Participants in the effort, he said, are fired by a passionate release of nationalistic energy, even though many are probably not sympathetic with communism.

The installation of four nuclear reactors in China was reported by T. C. Tsao of Columbia University. In view of China's rapid technological growth, he said, it would not be surprising if that country produced a nuclear explosion "in the near future."

Malcolm Rigby of the American Meteorological Society told of the increase in mainland weather stations from fewer than 100 a decade ago to more than 400. Sixty or seventy of them now release weather balloons daily for high-altitude observations. Upper air weather maps from China, he said, are on a par with those from the Soviet Union.

Specialists in physics, chemistry and mathematics all agreed that significant advances had been made on the mainland in the last decade, although the effort had been primarily in fields applicable to industrial expansion. Speaker after speaker named persons leading the Chinese effort who had been educated in the West.

Several had left posts at American universities to return to China.

The rapidity of developments in the last decade was attributed to such factors as: the existence, for the first time in many decades, of a strong central government; the allocation, by that Government, of extensive funds for science; and a sudden release of enthusiasm and interest in a scientifically minded population.

December 27, 1960

RED CHINA'S 'LEAP' SLOWED BY A LIMP

By TILLMAN DURDIN
Special to The New York Times.

BANGKOK, Thailand — Communist China's "Great Leap Forward" drive for economic expansion limped seriously in 1960, the third year of the Great Leap effort by Peiping.

Industrial output, upon which the Chinese Communists have always put chief emphasis, continued to grow impressively.

But agricultural production sagged, and as a result food rations during most of the year dropped to the barest subsistence level and exports and certain industrial enterprises were adversely affected.

Last month, the Chinese Communists reported that more than half of all their cultivated land in 1960 was subjected to the worst series of "natural calamities" in 100 years.

148,000,000 Acres Scourged

Authorities said 148,000,000 acres had been scourged by drought, floods, typhoons, hailstorms, frost, insects or plant diseases. From 49,000,000 to 64,000,000 acres were described as "seriously affected," and some of this land produced no crops at all.

This report was all the more significant because in 1959 natural disasters also affected some 100,000,000 acres of farmland in China. Official figures have not yet been issued on the actual crop output in 1960.

Western specialists in Chinese affairs believe unfavorable natural conditions are not a sufficient explanation for the poor agricultural record. They attribute part of Communist China's difficulties with farm production to the extreme collectivization of farming under the communes system.

In any case, last year's agricultural output undoubtedly fell below that of both 1959 and 1958. Grain output in 1959 was officially given as 270,000,000 metric tons and in 1958 as 250,000,000. The 1957 output was officially put at 185,000,000 metric tons.

Western observers regard the 1959 and 1958 figures as highly inflated. They believe Communist China's grain output in 1960 probably did not exceed that given in Peiping for 1957. The production of other key crops—cotton, soya beans, sugar cane and tobacco—is believed to have lagged with the trend in grain.

These results are in marked contrast with targets for the year that envisaged a 12 per cent increase in agricultural production above 1959 and 10 per cent increase in grain.

Shortage of cotton and other raw materials needed for manufactures certainly affected output of textiles and other light industries. The extent cannot yet be estimated, but reports from the Soviet Union and other countries receiving Chinese Communist exports indicate a decline in shipments both of raw and processed agricultural products in 1960.

The Peiping regime appears growing at a high rate despite the farm lag. Plans for 1960 called for a jump in steel production from 13,000,000 metric tons, as cited in 1959, to 18,400,000.

Year-end figures are not available, but it is believed that production of the main heavy industry categories showed increases, perhaps not up to the totals that will be announced, but to high levels nonetheless.

Communist China indisputably

is still forging rapidly ahead in developing its industry. It has already become an industrial power of great consequence, with a steel output exceeding that of France.

Peiping's plan for 1960 called for an increase in the value of industrial and agricultural output of 23 per cent, to a total value of $124,000,000,000. This target was certainly not attained in view of the poor agricultural yields and the fall short of goals in some industrial sectors.

In view of a growth in population of roughly 15,000,000 yearly (the total is now nearing 700,000,000) the agricultural output of 1960 is dangerously

near a pace just parallel with the population increase.

Peiping must do much better in the future if agricultural products are to be provided not only to feed the millions of new mouths but also to supply the needs of the export trade and the demands of industry for raw materials.

The means of reinvestment in economic expansion in Communist China are still being taken primarily from the agricultural sector.

At the same time only a minimum of investment is being put into this sector. Peiping has been attempting to bring farm output along mainly through exacting the utmost in physical labor from the farm population and conserving the maximum of farm output for industrial development by limiting the consumption of food and other daily needs in rural areas.

Despite the mixed record for 1960 Communist China plans to continue its all-out economic drive in 1961. Peiping confidently expects to achieve further expansion and to show a total gross national product equal to that of Britain by the end of 1962.

January 10, 1961

China Easing Communes; 'Leap Forward' Modified

Farm Failure the Cause

By HARRY SCHWARTZ

Communist China has substantially modified its system of "peoples' communes" and slowed down its "great leap forward" in industry in the wake of severe agricultural reverses last year.

Peiping radio broadcasts in recent weeks and other reports indicate that the commune system is being modified in a way that brings it closer to the Soviet collective-farm system. While the communes themselves are being retained, the new stress is on the production brigades, which in effect are the collective farms that existed before the communes were set up in 1958.

The production brigades are to have primary control of their own manpower, farm machinery and other resources and each brigade will have first claim on its net income, which means that better producers will benefit.

The emphasis on tying income to output provides incentives, which have been favored by Premier Khrushchev in the face of Chinese opposition. Heretofore the Chinese have advocated equalization of incomes and dependence on enthusiasm as a stimulus to production.

Reports from Peiping indicate also that Chinese farmers are to be permitted to have small private plots to grow part of their own food and that they are to be given more leisure than they have had under the rigorous communes.

The Chinese Communist party Central Committee has acknowledged that last year's farm production plan was not fulfilled. This is being attributed primarily to bad weather, said to have been the worst in a century. But the Chinese Communists are also accusing "landlord and bourgeois elements" of "sabotaging activities," and a purge of the party has been ordered.

Reports from Peiping said that Eastern European Communists there believed that much of Communist China's agricultural difficulties were a result of mismanagement in the communes. Newspapers in Red China's capital have been urging more efficient farming practices and hinting that there has been a substantial loss of enthusiasm and willingness to work among farmers.

Because of the bad harvest last year and the none-too-good harvest in 1959, inhabitants of Peiping, Shanghai and Tientsin are said to be primarily preoccupied with the problem of getting enough food. Their daily ration consists of only a small quantity of rice or grain, varied with a few vegetables.

High prices for meat and vegetables were reported in Shanghai's free markets. Similar markets in Peiping and Tientsin are reported to have been closed.

Shift in 1961 Plan Hinted

Statements by the party's Central Committee after its recent meeting have emphasized that all possible energies must be concentrated on agriculture. It has ordered that the 1961 economic plan be drawn up on this basis, suggesting to some observers that the original plan has had to be scrapped because of the agricultural difficulties.

A communiqué on the meeting of the Chinese Communist party's Central Committee last Jan. 14 to 18, as printed in Pravda, Soviet Communist party newspaper, ordered Government officials to "reduce capital construction measures" in heavy industry and to "concentrate our forces on the agricultural front."

It declared that the "tasks for the year 1961 are extraordinarily difficult" and referred to "temporary difficulties in market supplies" and "shortages of raw materials for light industry."

As originally formed in 1958, the people's communes combined the entire population and all the resources of the Chinese equivalent of a county. The notion was that all the manpower of the 50,000 to 100,000 in a typical commune would be available to work under military discipline wherever needed.

All private property was to be abolished and an attempt was made to approximate theoretical communist conditions by equalizing incomes, ending the use of money and making commune members' consumption independent of their contribution to production. A constant sore point has been the communal mess halls.

Directly and indirectly, Soviet spokesmen have criticized the commune system as too dogmatic an application of Marxist-Leninist theory.

The "great leap forward" is the term the Chinese Communists have used to described their intensive program of industrialization in recent years. This involved increasing production both in large modern plants built with Soviet help and in primitive shops.

January 29, 1961

PEIPING RETREATS IN ECONOMIC FIELD

Farm Crisis Forces Return to the Earlier Principle of Incentives for Peasants

Special to The New York Times.

HONG KONG, March 10—The Chinese Communist leadership has staged a massive retreat along the entire economic front of the "great leap forward."

Exceedingly short of food, raw materials and gold-earning exports, China has admitted to some "temporary difficulties." However, the present radical switch in policy is not acknowledged as such.

Local officials have failed to study party policy "sufficiently," a provincial party leader declared recently.

The biggest retreat has been on the agricultural front, where production last year failed to reach its goals and even started a slide due to a combination of bad weather and bad management.

Communist China, which claimed its disastrously poor harvests of the last two years primarily on drought and other natural calamities, reported today, however, it has had normal to heavy rain and snow in its main rice producing areas during the last ten days.

The precipitation came just as peasants in the Yangtze Valley rice bowl were making intensive spring sowing preparations, according to Peiping radio broadcasts monitored here.

According to the radio reports, preparations for spring planting are well under way.

In Hupeh Province, one of hardest hit by drought in 1959 and 1960, plowing of paddy fields was said to be nearly completed.

Communes Altered Radically

Although the weather outlook is better this year, the reorganization of the rural communes to counter the crop losses of the last two years has changed them radically from the original concept.

Some observers see in the agricultural retreat a return to the policies first advocated in 1956 and then abandoned in favor of the "great leap forward."

In 1956, stress was placed on the need for material incentive and some individual freedom for

the peasants to increase production.

These proposals barely had a chance to come into operation before they were swept aside in the economic upheaval of the "great leap forward."

Almost overnight the collectives were grouped into gigantic units of mass action — the people's communes; armies of men and women were moved about the countryside like pawns on a chessboard; peasants who should have been tilling the soil were ordered to make steel. The whole fabric of peasant life was so upset that the gains the Communists hoped to make by the mass movement of men and material were not realized.

Communes in Name Only

The communes exist now in name only. The peasant has been encouraged to engage in sideline occupations, such as handicraft work, raising livestock and breeding pigs and chickens. He has been given a small private plot on which to grow vegetables and other products.

Material incentives have been supplied in the policy of payment on the basis of work done and of giving rewards for overfulfillment of production targets.

Perhaps the most notable retreat has been in the return of the rural trade fairs, which the Communists acknowledge, have a tendency to encourage "capitalist ideas."

The rural trade fairs, said a recent article in a Peiping paper, "satisfy the requirements of commune members in production as well as in livelihood."

Industry Suffers Setback

On the industrial front, a retreat has been necessitated by the collapse of the country's agricultural program. Industry has had to give up manpower for the battle to raise agricultural production, while a shortage of raw materials has affected it adversely to a further extent.

The emphasis now is on "consolidation" rather than expansion; "quality" is stressed more than quantity.

Other newspaper articles have revealed that the advances in heavy industry over the last few years have been made at the expense of light industry. As a result, the Chinese people today cannot obtain the most common items such as pins, needles, paper, string and other consumer goods.

Accordingly, a new stress has been laid on overcoming these "temporary difficulties in market supplies" while the consolidation process goes on in heavy industry.

March 11, 1961

CHINA WIDENS RATIONING

Buyers Must Turn In Old Goods to Receive New

HONG KONG, June 2 (AP) —If one wants to buy a pair of socks in Communist China, he must turn in an old pair in exchange.

This rule, aimed at curtailing demand, applies also to underwear, mosquito nets, toothbrushes, brooms, light bulbs and a long list of other consumer items.

The system does not always work.

In Shanghai, for example, frying pans are in short supply. A person delivers his old frying pan to the store, collects a receipt for it and return weeks or months later when the store receives a new supply.

Refugees report the food rationing system has been expanded to the point where one needs special and separate cards to buy rice, sugar, vegetables, fish, flour and a score of other items.

June 3, 1961

CHINA STABILIZING NEW FARM POLICY

Reds See Decentralization as Spur to Production

Special to The New York Times.

HONG KONG, Sept. 12— Communist China's retreat this year from the unsuccessful agricultural policies of the "leap forward" period is to be followed by "a relatively long period of stabilization."

This is the message in two long articles in Hung Chi, authoritative journal of the Central Committee of the Chinese Communist party, on the "new relations of production" in the countryside.

Hung Chi sees the consolidation and stabilization of these new relations as the best means of insuring "the speedy development of production." It reaffirms the decentralization of management within the rural commune.

In effect, spectacular planning on a nationwide scale has given way to a degree of autonomy for the commune subdivisions "in the light of their own natural conditions."

Incentives Provided

The rural retreat assures for the peasant some material incentive and some individual freedom. He is encouraged to engage in side occupations such as handicraft work, raising livestock and breeding pigs and chickens.

Material incentives are provided in the policies of payment on the basis of work done and rewards for the overfulfillment of production targets.

He is permitted some measure of freedom to trade as part of a group or as an individual at the free markets.

This situation represents in some degree a return to the policies first advocated in 1956 and then abandoned in 1958 in favor of the "great leap forward" and the establishment of the communes, with a consequent uprooting of the peasants for participation in projects involving the use of mass manpower.

Roles Are Defined

The Hung Chi articles are especially concerned with defining the fixed roles of the commune subdivisions and establishing the new importance of the production team, a unit of "several dozen" households.

Several production teams, "100 or more families," constitute a production brigade, which corresponds roughly to the former "agricultural producers' cooperative" or collective farm.

"The production brigade in itself is an independent operational unit," Hung Chi declares.

But, the journal adds, it "must acknowledge the fact that the production teams have a certain autonomy in production management. Production teams know best the characteristics of their own agricultural production, their own collective needs and the needs of the individual commune members in them."

The commune is a county-sized unit and the county authorities act as the "management committee" of the commune. They merely "make recommendations concerning production plans to production brigades in accordance with the latter's actual conditions and state plans."

The production brigade then sets preliminary requirements for its production teams.

Plans Are Discussed

"After this, production teams formulate production plans for themselves following full discussion by commune members," Hung Chi says.

The relationship between the production brigade and its production teams is governed by a set of rules protecting the peasants' newly-established rights. A system called "three guarantees and one reward" requires the production team to fulfill its production plan, provide required labor and not to exceed the allowed production cost, in return for which it receives a "reward" if its production plan is overfulfilled.

At the same time a system called "four things that are fixed" assures for the production team a fixed area of land, and fixed amounts of manpower, draft animals and farming implements.

"In some production brigades, all or part of the draft animals and farming implements are owned by production teams," Hung Chi notes.

September 17, 1961

RED CHINA GIVES FARMS PRIORITY

Industrial Goals Reduced to Spur Output of Food

Special to The New York Times.

HONG KONG, April 16—The National People's Congress of Communist China has adopted a program calling for "diligence, thrift and hard work" and continued economic emphasis on agriculture at the expense of industry.

Observers here saw the action as evidence that Communist China was still suffering from the disastrous effects of its attempt to develop industry and agriculture simultaneously in the "great leap forward."

Industry clearly has been relegated to a subordinate role and, in line with the trend of the last eighteen months, the national economic effort will be focused almost entirely on agriculture, with grain and cotton having priority.

The program was presented to the People's Congress, the country's nominal Parliament, by Premier Chou En-lai. The Peiping radio broadcast a summary of the program, approved by the Congress in a three-week closed session that ended today.

Premier Chou said the economic situation had "already begun to take a turn for the better." But there was nothing in his report to indicate that the Chinese people could expect any early improvement in the present stringent rationing of food and clothing.

There was no mention of any intention to launch a third Five-Year Plan in 1963, although this is the last year of the second Five-Year Plan.

Premier Chou defended the Communist regime's policies, including the establishment of rural communes.

"The people's communes, which are of great historic significance, were set up in China's vast rural areas and gradually embarked on the road of sound development," he said.

The Premier also hailed the "leap forward" in economic and cultural construction, but he noted the "serious natural calamities" suffered from 1959 to 1961.

The Peiping radio said Premier Chou had "described in detail the successes and shortcomings in the last few years."

The Premier put forward "ten tasks for the adjustment of the national economy in 1962:"

"1. Strive to increase agricultural production, first of all the production of grain, cotton and oil-bearing crops.

"2. Make rational arrangement of the production of light and heavy industry and increase the output of daily necessities as much as possible.

"3. Continue to retrench the front of capital construction and to use material, equipment and manpower where they are most urgently needed.

"4. Reduce the urban population and the number of workers and functionaries to an appropriate extent by persuading first of all those workers and functionaries who came from rural areas to return to rural productive work and strengthen the agricultural front.

"5. Make a stock of inventories and examine and fix the amount of funds for each enterprise so that unused material and funds will be used where they are most needed during the present adjustment.

"6. Insure that the purchase and supply of commodities are done well and market supply conditions are improved.

"7. Work energetically to fulfill foreign trade tasks.

"8. Adjust cultural, educational, scientific research and public health undertakings and improve the quality of their work.

"9. Carry out firmly and thoroughly the policy of building the country with diligence, thrift and hark work to reduce expenditures and increase revenue.

"10. Continue to improve the work of planning to insure an all-round balance between the branches of the national economy in the order of agriculture, light industry and heavy industry."

Observers here commented that the first and second tasks aimed at alleviating serious shortages of food, clothing and such daily necessities as pots, pans and even pins.

The third task represents a continuation of the policy introduced in January, 1961, when the regime announced that capital construction would be reduced.

The fifth and sixth tasks are seen as an attempt to reduce hoarding and improve marketing procedures.

Observers noted with interest the seventh task, which suggested that China might be hoping to improve its trade ties with the Soviet Union. Trade between the two countries has fallen off, partly as a result of China's economic difficulties and partly as a result of the Chinese-Soviet ideological rift.

A Soviet trade mission arrived in Peiping last week for talks on this year's trade.

April 17, 1962

RED CHINA WARNS WEST ON TENSION

Widely Printed Article Says Capitalists Foment War— Scores Coexistence

By TILLMAN DURDIN
Special to The New York Times.

HONG KONG, April 2—Peiping newspapers have displayed prominently a warning that war between the Communist and capitalist nations may be inevitable.

The warning was contained in an article that appeared originally in Hung-chi, semi-monthly organ of the Central Committee of the Chinese Communist party. The article was reproduced on the front pages of all daily newspapers in the Chinese capital.

The long, unsigned commentary seemed to be an expression of opposition to the idea of peaceful coexistence espoused by Premier Khrushchev of the Soviet Union. It follows a long series of skeptical Chinese Communist comments on the possibility of peace between the two world blocs, but it goes further than any of the others in its sharp disparagement of peace prospects.

Lenin's Birthday Marked

The main points of the article were quoted in a Peiping dispatch from Hsinhua, the Chinese Communist press agency, which reached here yesterday. The article was printed to mark the ninetieth anniversary, on April 10, of the birth of Lenin.

The article reaffirmed the official Chinese Communist thesis that the present relaxation of East-West tensions is more apparent than real. "While juggling with peace, Eisenhower

and his like are making active preparations for war," it said.

"It is absolutely impermissible for us to mistake certain tactical changes on the part of imperialism for changes in the nature of imperialism," the statement asserted.

It then quoted Lenin as having said that "whoever has thought it is so easy to attain peace that one has only to mention the word peace and the bourgeoisie who present it on a silver platter is a very naïve person."

"The Marxist-Leninist parties do not reject peaceful means for carrying out the Socialist revolution," the article continued. "But when the exploiting classes use violence against the people the possibility of employing other means has to be considered; namely, the transition to socialism by non-peaceful means.

"The historical experience of mankind shows that the ruling class will not give up the state power of its own accord."

"Contradictions within the capitalist camp and the probability of wars breaking between Western countries emphasize the necessity to develop unity among the Socialist nations, headed by the Soviet Union," the article went on.

The Hung-chi statement concluded by citing an oft-repeated assertion by Mao Tse-tung, the Chinese Communist party chairman, that a new war would benefit communism. Mr. Mao was quoted as having said: "If the imperialists insist on unleashing another war, we should not be afraid of it." Then, according to the article, he continued:

"The first World War was followed by the birth of the Soviet Union. The second World War was followed by the emergence of the Socialist camp with a total population of 900,000,000.

"If the imperialists should insist on launching a third world war, it is certain several hundred millions more will turn to socialism. Then there will not be much room left in the world for imperialists, while it is quite likely the whole structure of imperialism will utterly collapse."

April 3, 1960

PEIPING'S VICTORY ON IDEOLOGY SEEN

By HARRISON E. SALISBURY

A violent ideological dispute between the Soviet Union and Communist China was raging on the eve of the summit meeting and may now have been resolved in favor of Peiping.

That conclusion has been reached by some specialists in Soviet affairs after examining texts of an unusual exchange of ideological arguments between Moscow and Peiping. The exchange occurred on the ninetieth anniversary of Lenin's birth, April 22—nine days before the U-2 incident.

The text of the Chinese arguments has been published in the April 26 issue of the English-language Peking Review, which has reached New York. The Soviet presentation was contained in an address at the Lenin stadium in Moscow by Otto V. Kuusinen, member of the Communist party's Presidium. His speech was published by Pravda, Soviet party newspaper.

It seems probable that the controversy and the radically opposed views of the Soviet and Chinese Communist parties played a major role in the evolution of Premier Khrushchev's policy on the eve of the Paris meeting.

The documents make clear that as late as April 22 the Soviet and Chinese positions were far apart. The Chinese were insisting that little or nothing might be expected from negotiation with the "imperialist West." They said that President Eisenhower had continued to conduct a warlike, aggressive policy despite the Camp David discussions with Premier Khrushchev last September.

The public Soviet position hewed strictly to Premier Khrushchev's position that discussions with the West were possible. However, some Soviet specialists believed that privately some members of Mr. Khrushchev's entourage supported the Chinese view.

When the United States reconnaissance plane was shot down in the Soviet Union, the Soviet opponents of Mr. Khrushchev's philosophy, aided by the powerful arguments advanced by the Chinese, may have been able, according to this view, to persuade a majority of the Soviet Communist party's Central Committee and its Presidium to switch over to the Chinese line.

If, as some signs now indicate, Moscow has gone over in major part to Peiping's point of

view, this would mean, the specialists said, further changes in Soviet policy. It would probably signal a new era of tough foreign policy and possibly a turn toward Stalinism domestically.

The first Soviet echoes of the Chinese point of view were contained in Mr. Khrushchev's public statements in Paris. A stronger reflection of the Chinese ideological position was contained in an article published this week by the Soviet ideological journal Kommunist, which was ostensibly an attack on President Tito of Yugoslavia.

Peiping Statement Frank

The documents in Peking Review, setting forth the Chinese view, were couched in unusually frank terms. They did not criticize Mr. Khrushchev by name. But in veiled terms he was referred to as a "revisionist" and a "distorter" of Lenin's teachings. There were slurs against his alleged lack of knowledge of the theory of Marxism-Leninism.

The Moscow statement was briefer. It called the Chinese, by implication, "dogmatists" and restated the known viewpoint of Mr. Khrushchev on the present world situation.

The dispute between the Russians and the Chinese had been in progress since last autumn. It arose immediately after Mr. Khrushchev's trip to the United States. Mr. Khrushchev contended it was possible to deal with the United States and that President Eisenhower was, essentially, a man of peace.

The documents disclosed that the dispute increased rather than diminished in intensity as the summit neared.

The Chinese documents charged that the United States under President Eisenhower's "personal direction" had consistently pursued a warlike policy since and despite the Camp David talks.

The Chinese attacked efforts to "whitewash" or "prettify" the actions of the United States. They contended that any effort to establish real peace between the "imperialist" and the Communist world was illusory. Their statement bristled with violent revolutionary quotations, taken from Marx, Engels and Lenin.

The Soviet presentation supported Mr. Khrushchev's contention that a "new epoch" had arisen in which it was possible to establish peace between the two systems. It held that the new balance of forces in the world had made the old Marxist concept of "aggressive imperialism" outmoded.

The Chinese statement did not name the Russians as their ideological opponents. Nor did the Russian statement name the Chinese. But a comparison of the two sets of arguments brought out the dramatic contrast in positions.

In some passages in the Peking Review, the Chinese directed their fire against "certain people" or "modern revisionists" without specifying who they were. Some arguments ostensibly were directed against Marshal Tito, but he was criticized for points that applied with equal validity to Mr. Khrushchev.

Peiping placed at the center of its case the 1957 Moscow declaration of the Communist parties. Moscow, on the other hand, did not even mention the 1957 declaration.

The declaration, issued on the occasion of the fortieth anniversary of the Bolshevik Revolution, sought to establish a common viewpoint on the world situation on the part of the Communist parties participating in the Moscow anniversary.

Attacking "right-wing opportunism," the Chinese said:

"Some say that this judgment of the Moscow meeting no longer holds good under today's conditions.

"We hold this to be wrong • • • As pupils of Lenin and as Leninists we must utterly smash all attempts of the modern revisionists to distort and carve up the teachings of Lenin."

The Chinese implied that since the death of Stalin there had been a decline in Leninist thought, an argument that seemed clearly directed at Mr. Khrushchev.

The Chinese said "modern revisionists" were contending that "the peace movement is everything, the final aim is nothing."

This, Peiping said, would result in a peace that "may be acceptable to the imperialists under certain historical conditions" but that would "lower the revolutionary standards of the peoples of various countries and destroy their revolutionary will."

The Chinese said that while it would be "a fine thing" if peaceful co-existence could bring about prohibition of atomic and nuclear weapons, "even under those circumstances, as long as the imperialist system still exists, the most acute form of violence, namely war, has by no means ended in the world."

Good Intentions Seen

"There are some people," said the Chinese, "who are not revisionists but well-intentioned persons who sincerely want to be Marxists but get confused in the face of certain new historical phenomena and thus have some incorrect ideas.

"For example, some of them say that the failure of the United States imperialists' policy of atomic blackmail marks the end of violence. • • • We should help these well-intentioned people to correct their erroneous ideas."

Presumably the "well-intentioned people" were Mr. Khrushchev and his supporters.

"The Chinese people," Peiping said, "have made a timely exposure of the fact that the U. S. Government headed by Eisenhower is since the Camp David talks between Comrade Khrushchev and Eisenhower last summer still continuing to carry out actively arms expansion and war preparations and enlarging its aggression.

"How would it help the international situation if this should be concealed or even whitewashed, prettified and extolled?"

The Chinese then cited thirty-seven incidents that they alleged showed United States policy was wedded to warlike aggression.

"Can it be said that all this has been concocted by the Chinese Communists?" Peking Review said. "The fact is that even after the Camp David talks and even on the eve of the East-West summit conference we see no change at all in substance in U. S. imperialist war policy, in the policy carried out by the U. S. Government and by Eisenhower personally."

Peiping challenged one of the most basic of Mr. Khrushchev's assumptions — that there would be no victors in a nuclear war.

"The result will certainly not be the annihilation of mankind," said the Chinese.

"On the debris of a dead imperialism," said Peking Review, "the victorious people would create very swiftly a civilization thousands of times higher than the capitalist system and a truly beautiful future for themselves."

"In regard to the question of safeguarding world peace at the present time," said the Peiping publication, "there are also certain people who declare that ideological disputes are no longer necessary." This appeared to an allusion to Mr. Khrushchev.

Three Documents Offered

The Chinese arguments in Peking Review were presented in three lengthy documents — one by the editorial staff of the chief Chinese Communist ideological journal, Hung-chi; another by the staff of the Chinese party newspaper, Jenmin Jihpao, and the third a report by Lu Ting-yi, a member of the Chinese party's Politburo, at the Lenin anniversary meeting.

The Soviet rebuttal to the Chinese arguments by Mr. Kuusinen was briefer. There were no citations from Lenin or Marx.

Mr. Kuusinen recalled that Lenin had first stated the principle of co-existence of the two systems, communism and capitalism.

"The principle of peaceful co-existence, as it did then, still lies at the basis of all Soviet foreign policy," he said. "Our party in recent years has creatively developed this idea of Lenin. In this connection the conclusions of the Twentieth and Twenty-first party congresses concerning the absence of the fatal inevitability of war in our epoch and the possibility of avoiding war are decisive."

This contrasted with the Chinese insistence on the inevitability of war and violence. Mr. Kuusinen used the word "epoch." The Chinese said that talk about different epochs "is merely drivel, concocting and playing around with vague, ambiguous phrases."

"Of course, aggression is connected with the character of imperialism," they said. "But it is impossible dogmatically to examine only one side of the matter. It is impossible not to note the appearance of great forces antagonistic to war."

Mr. Kuusinen said imperialism no longer ruled the world, the Socialist system was growing more powerful and the colonial system had collapsed. Now, he said, there has appeared "a broad 'zone of peace'" and even in imperialist countries there are strong forces of peace and democracy.

None of these factors was touched upon in Peking Review. The magazine described the imperialists as holding sway over colonial countries and ridiculed those to whom, as it said, "the peace movement is everything."

"Really," Mr. Kuusinen said, "do not all these powerful factors have real significance for deciding questions of war and peace?

"To be true to Marxism-Leninism today, it is not enough to repeat the old truth that imperialism is aggression. The task is to utilize all the new factors to spare humanity from the catastrophe of a new war. The dogmatic position is the backward position."

Mr. Lu's report, as printed in Peking Review, said:

"According to modern revisionists, there seems to be no longer any difference between socialism and imperialism, and whoever persists in fighting against imperialism and in revolution would be hindering peace and peaceful co-existence and a 'rigid dogmatist.'"

His reference to "rigid dogmatist," the Chinese stenographic report indicated, drew laughter from his audience.

"Whichever way you look at it," the Peiping official concluded, "none of the new techniques like atomic energy, rocketry and so on has changed, as alleged by the modern revisionists, the basic characteristics of the epoch of imperialism and proletarian revolution."

"Even those who for the time being do not understand the real situation," he added, "will gradually come to understand it with the help of the advanced elements."

In this context the Chinese apparently cast themselves in the role of the "advanced elements" and Mr. Khrushchev as one of those who did not "understand the real situation."

May 26, 1960

CHINA REAFFIRMS MAO'S 'HARD' LINE

Special to The New York Times.

HONG KONG, Sept. 29— Communist China's "hard" ideological line has been laid down in strong terms in a new volume of selected works by Mao Tse-tung, chairman of the Chinese Communist party.

The volume contains a quotation by Mr. Mao in which he declares that the only course open to Communists is to organize their forces to fight "imperialists" and to overthrow them.

"Only then can we hope to deal with foreign imperialist countries on the basis of equality and mutual benefit," he said, according to Hsinhua, the official Communist Chinese press agency. The agency carried excerpts from the volume tonight in a long report from Peiping.

Ends Silence in Dispute

The publication of the volume at this time is seen here as a direct challenge to Premier Khrushchev and the softer line he has espoused. It is considered all the more significant as it comes after a period of relative silence from Peiping on the subject and accordingly carries greater impact.

Hsinhua declared that publication of the volume was an important event for the Chinese Communist party and the Chinese people, as well as for the "dissemination and scientific study of Marxism-Leninism in China."

"The volume is not only of great historical significance but also of tremendous significance for present reality," Hsinhua said.

"It will become a powerful ideological weapon for accelerating the Socialist revolution and Socialist construction in our country and for intensifying the struggle against imperialism and modern revisionism," the press agency said.

The volume contains seventy writings by Mr. Mao, thirty-five of which were made public for the first time, during the period from August, 1945, to September, 1949, "the period of the Chinese people's liberation war."

It contains five commentaries on a United States State Department White Paper on Chinese-United States relations and former Secretary of State Dean Acheson's "letter of transmittal" to former President Truman. The commentaries "exposed the aggressive nature of United States imperialist policy toward China and its deep-seated hatred of the Chinese people, criticized certain people for harboring unrealistic illusory ideas about imperialism and called on them to 'cast away illusions and get ready for the struggle,'" Hsinhua said.

Counters Moscow Views

The quotations from Mr. Mao contending that imperialism must be overcome by force run counter to the doctrine advocated by Moscow that there can be a peaceful transition from capitalism to socialism and communism. There is also an echo of the Peiping doctrine that war is inevitable as long as imperialism exists. Premier Khrushchev disputes this view.

Two of Chairman Mao's articles "expound the line of the party in regard to peace talks with the Kuomintang (the ruling party of Nationalist China)" during the early period after the Japanese surrender in 1945.

The Communist party should do everything possible to win peace, Chairman Mao wrote and in the talks certain concessions would be permissible so long as the principle of not damaging the basic interests of the people was observed.

In another article Mr. Mao "combated the Rightist view * * * of making a pessimistic estimate of the international situation and of overestimating the strength of the enemy and of underestimating that of the revolutionary forces," Hsinhva's report continued.

"Comrade Mao Tse-tung pointed out that it was possible to overcome the danger of a new world war provided the forces of the people throughout the world waged resolute and effective struggles against the world's reactionary forces," Hsinhva said.

Mr. U. Mao also wrote that it was possible for imperialist countries and Socialist countries to 'reach compromises Such compromises are "only a matter of relations between countries, which are different from and should not be confused with the class struggle inside a capitalist country." he said.

The volume contains an interview with an American writer, Anna Louise Strong, in which Mr. Mao analyzes the "nature of the aggressive policy of United States imperialism."

Hsinhua said that in this interview Mr. Mao put forward his "famous thesis" that imperialism and all reactionaries were "paper tigers."

September 30, 1960

LATIN RED PARTIES SAID TO SUPPORT PEIPING'S POSITION

By SEYMOUR TOPPING

MOSCOW, Nov. 24—Well-informed sources reported today that in the current Communist party discussions here Liu Shao-chi, the Chinese Communist chief of state, had found surprising support among Latin-American delegations, as well as North Korea, Indonesian and Albanian.

The leaders of about eighty-five Communist parties are conducting the discussions.

The Latin-American delegations have listened sympathetically to Chinese Communist arguments for a more militant international program for achieving world communism.

They include Argentina, Venezuela, Colombia, Uruguay and Chile.

Liu Speaks for 4 Hours

Mr. Liu spoke Tuesday for four hours and was critical of certain facets of Soviet policy that have been identified with Premier Khrushchev.

It is understood, however, that Mr. Khrushchev has retained majority support, especially among the European parties, for his policy of peaceful coexistence.

This is a program for establishing Communist world supremacy through political, economic and psychological attraction without resorting necessarily to the ignition of revolutionary or international war.

Some of the delegations have been divided in discussions within themselves. For example, it is known that the intellectual wing of the Argentine party led by Rodolfo Ghioldi has been more attentive to Mr. Liu while the trade unionist faction has leaned to peaceful coexistence.

The Mongolian and Japanese delegations have wavered.

East German's Viewpoint

Certain delegations have special problems that tend to make them favor a blend of the two opposing viewpoints. Walter Ulbricht, leader of the East German Communist party, while one of Premier Khrushchev's most articulate supporters, would like to see a tougher and more forceful policy on Berlin. In general, it can be stated

that those delegations that are more militant are those that feel that they can gain power or attain certain national objectives only by more direct revolutionary tactics.

It was within this context that Pravda, the official Soviet party organ, warned yesterday against "dogmatism and sectarianism, which can also be the main danger at certain stages in the development of one or another party."

Schism Apparently Avoided

It is stressed by persons close to the discussions that the ideological differences expressed at the conference do not represent a definitive split. The conference apparently would regard another schism similar to the breakaway of Marshal Tito of Yugoslavia as a catastrophe for the Communist movement.

It was suggested that in evaluating the differences at the conference the same mistake should not be made as is made by some Communist observers in interpreting differences within the Western alliance.

Both the Communist and Atlantic-Pact blocs are cemented respectively by common overriding interests, which tend to resolve differences over tactics and strategy.

Chinese dependence on Soviet economic assistance was regarded as one among the complex factors that would mitigate against an open break.

The conference is expected to end shortly. Although the Communists publicly decline to confirm the existence of a conference, a communiqué that will sound a keynote of ideological harmony is expected.

If the conferees agree on such a communiqué, it will not necessarily mean that the variations in their respective party and state interests will have been eradicated.

It is possible that the Chinese will defer in ideological phraseology to such Khrushchev theses as peaceful coexistence, the non-exportability of violent revolution and the necessity of supporting national liberation movements regardless of whether they have an immediate pro-Communist revolutionary orientation.

The publication yesterday in Pravda of a reaffirmation by Premier Khrushchev of his intention to seek a disarmament agreement was interpreted as an indication that he would persist in seeking a new summit meeting with the West.

The Russian leader is believed to have contended in the Communist discussions that he should be permitted to probe the intentions of the Kennedy Administration after January before giving up the hope of attaining certain Communist objectives through negotiated settlements.

Another plenary session was held today.

What the current meeting has revealed stands as a good indication that the Communist bloc will feel the necessity for more frequent consultations.

November 25, 1960

Khrushchev-Mao Clashes On Party Issues Revealed

By HARRY SCHWARTZ

Documents in the hands of Western Governments show that the ideological conflict between the Soviet Union and Communist China in the last year and a half has been far more bitter and violent than Western public opinion realized.

The documents and reports disclose that Premier Khrushchev and Mao Tse-tung, Chinese Communist leader, as well as their spokesmen, traded bitter accusations in private correspondence and also at Bucharest and Moscow international Communist conferences last year.

The Chinese Communists accused the Soviet Premier of having adopted a revisionist line that abandoned Marxism and Leninism.

Premier Khrushchev, at the Moscow meeting, termed Mr. Mao a "megalomaniac warmonger."

The documents show that the Chinese Communists accused the Soviet leaders of having sought to sell out Peiping's interests to make a deal with the United States.

The Russians, in turn, accused the Chinese Communists of having failed to understand the nature of modern war and of attempts to trample over Soviet leaders for their own ends.

Sharp Words Exchanged

Some of the language reported used against the Chinese at last November's meeting in Moscow by Premier Khrushchev was obscene.

The sharp Soviet-Chinese war of words took place not only at the Bucharest and Moscow international Communist meetings last year but also at the meeting in Peiping last summer of the World Federation of Trade Unions.

The most vivid public example of the Communist Chinese anger over the Soviet policy was given at the World Conference of Orientalists in Moscow last summer, where 500 Chinese scholars had been expected to participate but not a single one appeared.

Western governments apparently received full accounts of the Soviet-Chinese dispute through leaks by Communist parties in Western nations.

A particularly full report on the bitterness and violence of the dispute in Moscow last November was apparently given in a long report prepared by the French Communist representatives at that meeting and circulated among leaders of that party.

The available information on the bitterness of the dispute would appear to support the view that the statement adopted by eighty-one Communist parties in Moscow in November was only a fragile compromise.

In that statement the Soviet view that world war is not inevitable was approved, but the Chinese demand for more vigorous political warfare against the West in under developed countries was also approved. In addition, the statement called "American imperialism" the worst enemy of the world's people and the main source of war danger in the world.

Informed sources reported yesterday that the Western governments had kept secret the information on the behind-the-scenes exchanges between the two Communist sides for political reasons.

Some officials involved have feared that if the United States, for example, sought to capitalize on its knowledge of the bitterness among the Communists, this might backfire and help drive the two chief Communist powers together.

Dispute May Have Eased

An official warned, however, that it could not be assumed that the bitterness and violence of the Soviet-Chinese dispute still persisted. He said the arrival of a Soviet trade delegation in Peiping last week suggested that relations between the two countries might have improved to the point where normal state relations were being resumed.

Before the arrival of the Soviet trade mission several days ago, there had been evidence that the dispute had not been fully resolved at the international Communist meeting in Moscow last November.

It also was noted that Communist China was buying large amounts of grain from Canada and Australia to fight hunger, while thus far no announcement of Soviet food assistance to Communist China has been made.

Peiping Buys in West

Moreover, Communist China recently bought a significant quantity of oil from Shell Oil Company, a leading Western petroleum concern, although Soviet oil exports to Western countries have been mounting rapidly in the last two years.

Communist China would not have had to plunge so hurriedly into the Western grain market or buy oil from a Western company if its relations with the Soviet Union were really amicable, Western observers have speculated.

Publicly, the basic issue in last year's dispute centered on an ideological question: Is world war between Communist and capitalist states inevitable?

Before last November's meeting, Premier Khrushchev had identified himself with the idea that such a war was not inevitable, while the Chinese had indicated they believed such a war was inevitable.

The public dispute between the two sides was conducted through newspaper articles in which Soviet authors attacked unnamed "dogmatists" and "Left sectarians."

At the same time, Chinese Communist authors attacked "revisionists" who were said to be seeking a revision of the teachings of Marxism-Leninism. The Chinese named only the Yugoslavs as revisionists, but many of their attacks seemed aimed at Premier Khrushchev's position as well.

Peiping Official Hopes Soviet Will Increase Economic Help

Foreign Minister, Who Once Belittled Role of Moscow Assistance, Hails 'Unity' of Communist Nations

By HARRY SCHWARTZ

The Foreign Minister of Communist China has indicated confidence that the Soviet Union will extend to his country increased economic aid as a result of negotiations under way in Peiping.

The importance of the negotiations was underscored last week by Pravda, organ of the Soviet Communist party, which called the talks "preliminary" and said they would be concluded when a Chinese Communist delegation came to Moscow.

The fact that both trade and aid were involved in the negotiation was made clear by the Soviet delegation's make-up. It is headed by a Deputy Minister of Foreign Trade, Pavel N. Kumykin, and I. V. Arkhipov, a Deputy Chairman of the State Committee on Foreign Economic Relations. The latter organization supervises Soviet loans and other forms of economic aid to other nations.

More Aid Not Mentioned

Pravda's announcement said merely that the negotiations would concern "trade-economic relations between the two countries." It made no explicit mention of further Soviet economic aid to Communist China.

But Foreign Minister Chen Yi devoted major attention to Soviet economic assistance in a speech he delivered last week at a dinner for the Soviet delegation.

As broadcast by the Peiping radio, Marshal Chen paid glowing tribute to past Soviet economic aid, saying it "has played an important role toward consolidating the victory of the Chinese revolution, restoring our national economy and laying an industrial foundation for building socialism." The aid, he said, "highlights the great proletarian internationalist spirit" of the Soviet Communist party.

This was in marked contrast with the Foreign Minister's slighting comments about Soviet economic aid in an interview he gave last November to a group of Japanese journalists. He asserted then that Soviet aid had not been very important for Communist China's economic development and had only been about equal to the aid Communist China itself had given other countries.

Friendship Stressed

However, Marshal Chen said in his speech last week:

"Now the talks on the question of mutual assistance and cooperation between our two countries in the fields of economy and trade will soon begin. We sincerely believe that under conditions of further strengthened friendship and unity between the two parties and countries of China and the Soviet Union, these talks will most assuredly result, through friendly negotiations, in the successful conclusion of an agreement on the basis of proletarian internationalist principles, in an atmosphere of mutual assistance, sincerity, friendship, and full understanding."

The present Soviet-Chinese negotiations take on added interest because of persistent reports that a promise of Soviet economic aid played an important part in making possible agreement at the meeting of eighty-one Communist parties in Moscow last November. According to these reports, a bitter Soviet-Chinese struggle at the meeting was partly resolved by Premier Khrushchev's pledge to increase Soviet economic aid to Peiping.

February 12, 1961

February 19, 1961

SOVIET DISCLOSES BIG CHINESE DEBT

By HARRY SCHWARTZ

The Soviet Ministry of Foreign trade has revealed that Communsit China owes the Soviet Union more than $300,000,000 as a result of a failure by Peiping to meet export commitments to Moscow last year.

The information was disclosed in the Soviet foreign trade magazine Vneshnaya Torgovlya.

Last April a joint Chinese-Soviet economic statement said that agricultural difficulties had prevented Peiping from meeting its export obligations to the Soviet Union, although no indication was given of the amount involved.

The Soviet decision to publish this information unilaterally appears to add another bit of evidence to recent indications of increased tension and coolness in Moscow-Peiping relations. It also showed that Communist China last year in effect received more economic aid from the Soviet Union — through an unplanned loan required by a Peiping trade deficit—than any nation had ever received before in a single year from the Soviet Union.

According to Vneshnaya Torgovlya, the Chinese Communist debt on last year's trade amounted to 288,000,000 new rubles, or more than $320,000,000 at the present official Soviet dollar-ruble exchange rate. This is equivalent to the value of almost half of all Soviet exports to China in 1958 and about a third of all Soviet exports to China in 1959.

The Soviet trade journal also disclosed a five-year repayment agreement that indicated that it would take Communist China some time to recover enough economically to pay this debt. The agreement was reached this year.

Communist China will pay nothing on the debt this year. It will pay 8,000,000 rubles in 1962, 50,000,000 rubles in 1963 and 115,000,000 rubles each in 1964 and 1965.

Though no trade figures are given, the journal indicates clearly that the volume of Soviet-Chinese commerce will drop sharply this year in order to permit a balance to be reached between Soviet and Chinese Communist exports.

Under the 1961 Soviet-Chinese trade agreement, Communist China will ship none of the main food items that hitherto have constituted a large share of its exports to the Soviet Union. These include rice, meat, eggs, vegetable oils and soy beans.

July 5, 1961

CHOU CHALLENGES KHRUSHCHEV MOVE AGAINST ALBANIA

Chinese Leader's Rebuke Causes a Sensation at Soviet Party Rally

By SEYMOUR TOPPING
Special to The New York Times.

MOSCOW, Oct. 19 — Premier Chou En-lai of Communist China openly contested today Premier Khrushchev's decision to banish Albania from the Communist bloc.

The Chinese Communist leader challenged and, by implication, rebuked Mr. Khrushchev from the speakers' rostrum on the third day of the twenty-second congress of the Soviet Communist party.

In his speech opening the congress, Mr. Khrushchev denounced the Communist rulers of Albania, who are supporters of Peiping's militant interpretation of Communist philosophy.

The Albanians were not among the eighty Communist and worker parties invited to the congress.

Denunciation Scored

In an obvious reference to Mr. Khrushchev's castigation of the Albanians, the Chinese Premier said, according to observers in the congress hall:

"If there are quarrels in the Socialist camp we consider that they should be settled through bilateral contacts and that a public denunciation does not contribute to the cohesion of the Socialist camp."

[Mr. Chou appeared to be calling on the Soviet party to abide by the policy statement adopted last November by eighty-one Communist parties. That statement demanded "defense of the unity of the world Communist movement" and "avoidance of any actions which may undermine that unity."]

Premier Chou introduced his speech of greetings to the congress by stating that his country was a friend of the Soviet Union and "all other countries in the Socialist camp, which extends from North Korea to the German Democratic Republic and from Vietnam to Albania."

Talk Causes Sensation

There was a scattering of applause from the 5,000 delegates but it quickly died away when it was observed that Mr. Khrushchev and other members of the Soviet Presidium on the stage were not applauding.

The remarks of the chief of the Chinese delegation included the customary expressions of friendship and cohesion with the Soviet Union. When Premier Chou left the rostrum he shook hands with Mr. Khrushchev.

His public opposition to Mr. Khrushchev on the Albanian issue caused a sensation. It represented the most open manifestation of the ideological dispute that has been waged privately for years between Moscow and Peiping.

In party conclaves, the Chinese Communists, with the support of General of the Army Enver Hoxha, the Albanian Communist chief, have opposed Mr. Khrushchev's foreign policy as too soft toward the West. Mao Tse-tung, the chairman of the Chinese Communist party, and General Hoxha have resented Mr. Khrushchev's program and his condemnation of the "cult of personality."

Malenkov Denounced

In speeches during today's sessions Mr. Khrushchev's deputies followed the example set on Tuesday by the Soviet Premier in castigating Lazar M. Kaganovich and Georgi A. Malenkov, two of the anti-party group expelled from the Soviet Presidium in 1957 for Stalinist practices.

Kirill T. Mazurov, First Secretary of the Byelorussian party organization, declared that the continued membership of Mr. Malenkov in the party was "impossible." The former Soviet Premier was demoted to running a power station after his ouster but he retained party membership.

There were some specialists on Soviet affairs here who expressed the view that Mr. Khrushchev had attempted to reassert his authority over the Communist bloc by making an example of Albania. His criticism of Albania was regarded here as an implicit criticism of Communist China.

Mr. Khrushchev chose a moment for his attack on Albania when Communist China is in a weak economic position at home and more eager than ever for Soviet economic aid. Peiping's economy has received a severe setback because of the devastation of its agriculture by drought and flood.

Premier Chou indicated in his speech that Communist China was not seeking an open break with the Soviet Union. The Premier reaffirmed his adherence to the declaration of the eighty-one Communist parties that met in Moscow last November.

The November meeting resulted in a manifesto that represented a compromise between the Soviet and Chinese views of the strategy to be pursued in the attainment of world communism. Mr. Khrushchev's thesis of "peaceful coexistence" with the Western nations was affirmed but the parties also decided to press more militantly in support of "national liberation movements" in Asia, Africa and Latin America.

Tass, the Soviet press agency, which did not publish Premier Chou's remarks on Albania, quoted extensively from those passages in which he expressed support for the policy of "peaceful coexistence" and the November agreement.

U. S. Is Denounced

Premier Chou read a message of greetings from Chairman Mao. It said relations between the Soviet Union and Communist China "have been tried and tested and are eternal and inviolable."

Denouncing the United States as the "sworn enemy of peace," the Premier declared:

"We actively support the liberation struggle of oppressed nations and oppressed peoples, resolutely oppose the policy of aggression and war conducted by the imperialist circles headed by the United States."

Well-informed sources said that the Chinese leader might attempt to raise the Albanian question and other issues in a closed meeting of the party leaders after the end of the congress later this month.

The Chinese Communists would have an opportunity to press for firmer action by the Soviet Union in support of Peiping's ambitions in Asia and its efforts to replace Nationalist China in the United Nations.

Some observers here linked the renewal of the attack on the Soviet "anti-party group," which also included Vyacheslav M. Molotov and Nikolai A. Bulganin and others, to the Albanian controversy.

As a matter of course, the "anti-party" group would have been covered in Mr. Khrushchev's speech Tuesday. It is traditional to review the period of party activity dating back to the last congress.

In this case, the review went back to the twentieth party congress in 1956 since the twenty-first congress in 1959 was an extraordinary one called for the presentation of the seven-year plan.

However, the extent to which Soviet party officials are dwelling on the sins of the "anti-party group" raised suspicions that broader implications were involved, possibly on an international scale. Former President Klimenti Y. Voroshilov was implicated Tuesday by Mr. Khrushchev in the "anti-party group" although he was sitting on the forty-one member Presidium of the congress.

Nikolai V. Podgorny, the party chief of the Ukraine, today denounced Mr. Kaganovich as a "degenerate who long since has had nothing of a Communist left in him."

Mr. Podgorny indicated that Mr. Kaganovich might lose his party membership together with Mr. Malenkov when he declared: "We consider that Kaganovich's

actions were incompatible with the title of Communist party member."

Mr. Kaganovich, who is 68 years old, headed the Ukraine party organization from 1925 to 1928 and from 1946 to 1947. One of Stalin's chief deputies, he was instrumental in bringing Mr. Khrushchev into the Moscow hierarchy.

Mr. Kaganovich has been variously reported as working as a factory director and as living in Moscow in retirement.

Mr. Podgorny accused Mr. Kanagovich of surrounding himself with unprincipled persons and of the persecution of devoted party officials.

October 20, 1961

SOVIET INFLUENCE IN MONGOLIA RISES

By HARRISON E. SALISBURY
Special to The New York Times.

ULAN BATOR, Outer Mongolia, Dec. 11—The Soviet Union apparently has won the first round of a contest with Communist China for dominant influence in Outer Mongolia.

The Chinese bid to supplant the Soviet Union as Mongolia's closest associate in the Communist world, which was showing progress two years ago, appears to have become the stanchest Soviet campaign, according to evidence here. Mongolia appears to have become the staunchest Asian supporter of Moscow in its quarrel with Peiping.

Two years ago Chinese were to be seen at every hand in Ulan Bator, engaged in a wide variety of labor and construction projects. Today, although there are said to be 10,000 to 12,000 Chinese in Mongolia they are seen less often.

The Chinese are housed in three large camps that resemble, at least superficially, concentration camps. The camps are three or four miles outside Ulan Bator, the capital of Outer Mongolia.

Camps Are Guarded

The camps are surrounded by high wooden fences with tall watchtowers at the corners and guards with submachine guns

such as used to be seen around Siberian labor camps. Whether these measures were taken at the instance of the Mongolian or the Chinese was impossble to ascertain.

Two years the Chinese lived near the center of Ulan Bator in big barracks and camps and in semifinished apartment houses they were erecting for the Mongolians.

There are plenty of Chinese consumer goods to be seen in Ulan Bator stores, but the Mongolian economic system appears to have swung strongly to the Soviet side.

One reason is that the Soviet Union has pledged $350,000,000 to Mongolia's third five-year plan, including the deferment of $60,000,000 in Mongolian repayments for past aid. This aid is for the years 1961 to 1965. Soviet aid to Outer Mongolia since 1948 has totaled $625,000,000, bringing the total Soviet investment to $975,000,000.

Chinese Pledge Smaller

The Chinese pledge to the five-year plan is only $50,000,-000, bringing the Chinese contributions to $115,000,000. Whether this includes the cost of Chinese labor battalions is not known.

Higher-ranking Chinese are as isolated from the Mongolians as the rest. They live in a country house about eight miles from the city.

According to Mongolians, there is almost no mingling between them and the Chinese. Some Mongolians say this results from Chinese policy. Mongolian officials insist, however, that relations with the Chinese are still entirely correct.

December 17, 1961

SOVIET-CHINA RIFT LAID TO MEDDLING

Moscow's 1959 Interference With Peiping Is Cited

By HARRY SCHWARTZ

The current edition of the China Quarterly ascribes the bitterness of the Soviet-Chinese ideological dispute partly to Peiping's resentment against Soviet backing for an anti-Mao Tse-tung faction in the Chinese Communist Politburo.

An article in the China Quarterly by David A. Charles says that Premier Khrushchev has repeatedly refused to apologize for his intervention in Peiping's internal affairs in 1959. That intervention, the article reported, consisted of support for a Politburo faction headed by Marshal Peng Teh-haui.

Mr. Khrushchev's aim, it was said, was the abandonment of the "great leap forward" and the communes, the two chief innovations credited to Mr. Mao in recent Chinese Communist history.

The "great leap forward" was a mobilization of the people to increase industrial and agricultural production in China.

Britons Edit Quarterly

The China Quarterly, published in London by the Congress for Cultural Freedom, is edited by two prominent British experts on Communist China. The congress is an international organization of intellectuals.

Mr. Charles, a British specialist in Communist affairs, has recently been engaged in collating reports from Chinese refugees.

Marshal Peng's efforts to reverse the Maoist line were made at the August, 1959 meeting of the Chinese Communist Politburo, the article reports. The attempt raised the specter of a military revolt against the political leaders in Peiping.

Marshal Peng was then Communist China's Defense Minister. One of his reported key supporters, Gen. Huang Kochang, was then Chief of Staff. On Sept. 17, 1959, while Premier Khrushchev was beginning his first United States visit as President Dwight D. Eisenhower's guest, the removal of both men from their key posts was announced.

Mr. Mao is reported to have told the meeting that if the generals took power, he would recruit another army to overthrow them as he had overthrown the Chiang Kai-shek regime. The generals present at the meeting thereupon reportedly arose and pledged their loyalty to Mr.

Mao and the Central Committee.

Marshal Peng, who is still nominally a member of the Chinese Communist Politburo, won great popularity as commander of the Chinese armed forces in the Korean War a decade ago. He is reported to have written a letter stating his views to the Soviet Communist party without informing his colleagues.

The letter was reported to have indicated the Marshal's agreement with the Moscow's criticism of the Chinese Communist experiments in the late Nineteen Fifties. At the two major international Communist conferences in 1960, in Bucharest in June and in Moscow in November, Premier Khrushchev was reported to have defended the Soviet Communists' right to conduct private and secret discussions with important leaders of other parties.

Marshal Peng was reported to have been alarmed by Mr. Mao's emphasis on basing Chinese Communist armed strength upon a mass untrained militia. The marshal believed that in the nuclear era the country needed a professional army of full-time soldiers. His memorandum to the Central Committee in August, 1959, however, was reported to have centered on the economic and political weaknesses of the official course.

Chou Assures Albania

Premier Chou En-lai, in a speech broadcast by the Peiping radio last week-end, pledged Communist China's "everlasting and unbreakable friendship as well as mutual assistance and cooperation" to Albania and her rulers.

At the same time, the Peiping radio announced that five new economic and technical cooperation agreements had been signed with Albania.

The new Chinese Communist statement of position came at a time when Moscow had gone far beyond its original charges against the Albanian leaders last October. Now Albania is considered by the Soviet leaders an "enemy" country whose present leadership and activities aid the cause of world "imperialism."

Premier Chou, on the other hand, credited the Albanians with "important achievements in the building of socialism." He said they had "enhanced the strength of the Socialist camp and heightened the fighting will of the Socialist countries." The "achievements," he said, resulted from "the correct leadership of the Albanian Workers [Communist] party headed by its long-tested leader, Comrade Enver Hoxra."

Mr. Hoxha has been repeatedly denounced in Moscow in recent months as a Stalinist who rules only by the use of murder terror, lies and deception.

January 21, 1962

359

Indian Border Fight Said to Widen Rift Of China and Soviet

By SEYMOUR TOPPING
Special to The New York Times

MOSCOW, Oct. 21—Diplomatic officials said today that the fighting on the Chinese-Indian border evidently had placed an added strain on relations between Moscow and Peking.

The Russians have so far declined to suport charges by Communist China of Indian aggression. They have remained silent about the frontier quarrel.

The Soviet press and radio did not mention the eruption of severe fighting yesterday or the protest by Peking to the Indian Government. Pravda, the Communist party newspaper, confined its news from Peking to a front-page item about passenger train production.

Privately, Soviet officials have expressed annoyance with what they regard as a useless territorial dispute that has made it difficult for Moscow to maintain a balance in its relations with the two Asian countries.

Chinese Article Cited

Western observers here discerned oblique criticism of the Soviet Union in an article distributed by the Chinese Communist press agency, Hsinhua. The article asserted that India had obtained an increase in aid from the United States because of her "provocative" border policy.

The Soviet Union ranks second to the United States as a donor of economic aid to India.

It was understood that the border fighting had had no apparent effect on the Soviet attitude toward Indian's interest in purchasing military aircraft from the Soviet Union.

An Indian delegation visited Moscow in August and found the Soviet officials accommodating on the question of selling MIG fighter planes, transports

and helicopters. Soviet reluctance was encountered when the Indian delegation also sought permission to manufacture some types of Soviet aircraft in India.

The negotiations are pending while India compares Soviet terms with those obtainable elsewhere.

The friendly relations of the Soviet Union with India have been a sore point for a long time between Moscow and Peking.

While the Soviet Union has limited its aid to Communist China, it has maintained its program of economic aid and technical assistance to India.

This policy has been in keeping with Premier Khrushchev's policy of "peaceful coexistence," which seeks, by attracting nonaligned countries, to tilt the world balance of power in favor of the Communist bloc.

The Khrushchev approach has been opposed by the Chinese Communists, who favor more militant revolutionary tactics to obtain world communism.

The Communist party of India has adopted a critical attitude toward Peking on the border question, although there is a faction, notably the Bengal group centered in Calcutta, which has supported the Chinese Communists.

While Indian officials frankly have hoped that the Soviet Union would act to restrain Communist China, the New Delhi Government has avoided raising the border question directly with Moscow.

However, there are indications that the worsening of the conflict has led Indian officials to consider an approach to the Soviet Union to explain the Indian case. It is considered likely that New Delhi would welcome Moscow's good offices in the dispute.

Moscow evidently has been reluctant to intervene because of the difficulty it has experienced in persuading the Chinese Communists to alter other policies affecting Asia.

Diplomatic officials here believe that the Soviet Union would be embarrassed if the Chinese-Indian border dispute is put before the United Nations and Moscow is compelled to take sides.

PEKING CRITICIZES RUSSIANS ON CUBA

Party Warns Soviet Must Back It in India Dispute

By ROBERT TRUMBULL
Special to The New York Times

HONG KONG, Oct. 31—Communist China's hate campaign against the United States reached a peak today. Newspaper editorials and articles called for worldwide support of Cuba against "imperialist aggression" directed by President Kennedy.

An editorial on the front page of the Chinese Communist newspaper Jenmin Jih Pao indirectly criticized Premier Khrushchev for having agreed to remove missiles from Cuba.

[In Peking, most foreign obervers interpreted the editorial as a reflection of Chinese Communist displeasure with the Soviet Union's decision to withdraw missiles from Cuba, according to a Reuters dispatch from the Chinese capital. In an earlier editorial Jenmin Jih Pao implied a demand that the Soviet Union must support Peking fully in its border dispute with India.]

The Peking newspaper, which voices Chinese Communist policy, implied that Mr. Khrushchev had bowed to the "United States' imperialist attempt to browbeat the people of the world into retreat at the expense of Cuba."

The editorial was broadcast by Peking in its daily summary of Chinese Communist press material.

Alluding to the exchange of messages between President Kennedy and Premier Khrushchev that led to the Soviet decision to withdraw its missiles, the newspaper said that

"the so-called assurance that the United States will not invade Cuba is nothing but a hoax.

Mr. Khrushchev was mentioned by name only once in the editorial. This was in a brief reference to the Soviet decision to withdraw its missiles. This action was followed, the newspaper declared, by an intensification of United States "military preparations for invasion of that country."

Hsinhua, the Chinese Communist press agency, carried the text of a similar editorial that will appear in tomorrow's edition of Hung Chi, a fortnightly publication of the Chinese Communist party's Central Committee.

The Hung Chi editorial praised Premier Fidel Castro and implied a strong rebuke to the Soviet policy of competition with the West in "peaceful coexistence," which the Chinese Communists have frequently condemned as "revisionism."

"Fidel Castro and his comrades-in-arms carried out a correct revolutionary line, closely relied on the broad masses of the people, persisted in a policy of opposing counter revolutionary armed force with revolutionary armed force, united all forces at home and abroad that could be united and isolated enemies of the revolution to the maximum extent" the Chinese party organ declared.

When this editorial is compared with past accounts of ideological differences between the Chinese Communists and Mr. Khrushchev, every phrase of the passage quoted can be read as criticism of the Soviet Government. Such an oblique method of criticism is common in the Chinese Communist press.

The North Vietnamese Workers' [Communist] party newspaper Nhan Dah said that the "attitude of the Soviet Union has upset the war provocations of the U.S. and it has had a definite effect in easing world tension," the dispatch from Hanoi said.

Quotations from the same editorial carried later by Hsinhua omitted the favorable reference to the Soviet Union.

BERLIN CONGRESS BOOS RED CHINESE

Peking Delegate's Attack on Yugoslavia Causes Angry Demonstration

By SYDNEY GRUSON
Special to The New York Times.

BERLIN, Jan. 18 — Communist China's delegate touched off a noisy demonstration at the East German Communist party congress today when he attacked the "Tito group" of Yugoslav Communists.

The criticism of the Yugoslavs as "usurpers of the title of Communists" who had "surrendered to the imperialists" was the Chinese answer to Premier Khrushchev's appeal on Wednesday for an end to polemics in their fierce ideological dispute.

The stormy scene in Werner Seelenbinder Sports Hall in East Berlin was a display of internecine bitterness that the Communists have not afforded the West before.

A description of the scene was available from the only Western reporter still being allowed in the hall—Jack Altman of Reuters news agency, which maintains an office in East Berlin. Other Western reporters were accredited to the congress for the first two days only.

Delegate Interrupted

Mr. Altman reported that whistles, books, shouts and stamping of feet interrupted the Chinese delegate, Wu Hsiu-chuan. The East German chairman of today's session, Paul Werner, rebuked Mr. Wu, calling his criticism of the Yugoslav Communists "unqualified and provocative."

"Yugoslavia is faithfully serving the cause of socialism," Mr. Werner said. At first, Mr. Wu tried to talk over the outbursts of whistling and shouting but he gave up eventually until Mr. Werner restored silence.

The rebuke did not stop him from continuing to attack Yugoslav "revisionism," which the Chinese have publicly stated includes the current Soviet policy of peaceful coexistence with the West.

Khrushchev Absent

Mr. Khrushchev stayed away from the stormy session. Instead he visited an East Berlin electronics factory where, in a brief speech to the workers, he scoffed at United States efforts to match Soviet achievements in space.

West German capitalists, Mr. Khrushchev said, would wait as vainly for the collapse of East Germany as the West had waited for the collapse of the Soviet Union.

"During 45 years they could not throttle us," he went on. "Now it is out of the question. Anyone who thinks they can do so, possibly by military means, prepares his own funeral oration. We are strong militarily but we wish to achieve victory in economic competition."

At the congress, the Chinese delegate repeated his party's proposal, already rejected here by Mr. Khrushchev, for a meeting of all Communist leaders to debate the ideological dispute. Without such a conference, Mr. Wu said, there was a "danger of a split" in the Communist camp. Mr. Khrushchev had argued just the opposite—that a conference could only result in a formal split.

Mr. Wu retorted sharply to the criticism of Communist China's attack on India made by Walter Ulbricht, the East German leader.

"It is regrettable that [Prime Minister] Nehru has been supported by some self-styled Marxist-Leninists," Mr. Wu said in a reference that could have included Mr. Khrushchev himself. These Communists had "shut their eyes" to the Chinese explanations of the dispute with India, Mr. Wu added.

Against a rising murmur from the delegates, Mr. Wu said Peking had sought a "fair and peaceful solution through negotiation" and had fought only in self-defense — a "minimum measure that any sovereign state would take."

Moscow Party Proposes Meeting at Any Level to End Ideology Rift

By THEODORE SHABAD
Special to The New York Times.

MOSCOW, Feb. 10—The Soviet Communist Party declared today that it was prepared to meet with the Chinese Communists "at any level and at any time" to discuss ideological differences.

The party offer, contained in an editorial article of Pravda, the party newspaper, appeared to open the way for a confrontation of the two adversaries, whose public debate has virtually split the Communist camp.

Pravda's long statement made it clear that the proposed meeting would be designed to "create better conditions" for a general conference of all Communist parties on such issues as present-day political tactics toward the West and the parties' attitude toward distinctive Communist systems like Yugoslavia's.

Evidently a reply to a recent editorial in Jen Min Jih Pao, the Chinese Party organ, the Soviet statement represented a further conciliatory step in the debate between the two parties, in which each side has called for unity and accused the other of departing from "true" Marxism-Leninism.

Warning that it was "time to rein in at the brink of the precipice" a Chinese editorial of Jan. 27 said:

Take Initiative

"We sincerely hope that the fraternal party that launched the first attack, meaning the Soviet Union, will suit its action to its words, take the initiative and return to the path of inter-party consultation."

Though denying that the Communist movement had gone to "the brink of the precipice," the Soviet statement conceded that it was inadequate simply to stop polemics as Premier Khrushchev proposed last month at the East German Party Congress, and to let the air cool in preparation for a general conference.

The statement acknowledged that such a truce would encourage the parties "to freeze the existing disagreements and remain in the same positions" and went on:

"Our party considers it expedient to hold bilateral or broader meetings that would help create better conditions for a conference of all fraternal parties."

Clearly addressing the Chinese, it added:

"The Soviet Communist Party declares: "If, in reply to this initiative of ours, any party, regardless of how substantial

the differences betw[een] be, displays interest i[n] al meeting, our party to have such a meeting level and at any time ac ble to both sides."

No Retreat

Through inviting the conference to thresh out differences, the Pravda editorial gave no indication of a retreat from the Soviet positions in the ideological debate with the Chinese.

On Yugoslavia, it reiterated the view that, despite "differences on some ideological questions," President Tito's regime was "socialist" and entitled to be part of the World Communist movement. The Chinese have contended that the Yugoslavs have placed themselves outside the camp by their "revisionist" policies.

Among the differences with the Soviet view, the statement said, are "attempts by some Yugoslav party figures" to equate the Western military alliance with its Communist counterpart. The Russians called such an approach "a departure from Marxist-Leninist class positions."

Distinguishing between an essential unity in the Communist camp on strategy and greater flexibility between the parties on tactics, the Soviet statement suggested that a way must be found to accommodate the different points of view within a world Communist movement.

"We must look forward to a day when the road of socialism will be chosen by dozens of other countries in Europe, Asia, Africa, America and Australia, it said." They will undoubtedly introduce great diversity into the solution of problems relating to the construction of Socialism."

The statement asserted that there must be basic agreement on a "single strategy" in the fight against capitalism, for the victory of Communism, for the triumph of "national liberation movements" and in the struggle against "imperialist wars."

As for tactics, it added, though unity in that respect is also desirable, there can be "different forms and methods" to achieve a common aim.

The statement also warned the Communist parties against extending ideological differences "mechanically" into the economic, cultural and political fields. This was taken as an allusion to the suspension of diplomatic relations between Albania and the Soviet Union and to the sharp drop in Chinese-Soviet trade as a result of the ideological split.

Tito a Main Storm Center
Special to The New York Times.

NEW YORK.

Pravda's statement made it clear that the sharply different Moscow and Peking positions toward Yugoslavia now occupied the center of the stage in the Soviet-Chinese ideological

January 19, 1963

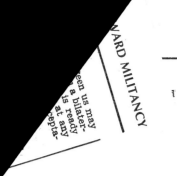

...es it
...ugoslavia
...rengthen the cen-
... planning principle in
...he management of the economy, to put foreign trade in order, to step up efforts for the
socialist reorganization of agriculture."

Yugoslavia differs from the
usual Communist society's organization in at least two major respects. It does not have
tight central economic planning, but instead has a market
economy in which publically
owned factories, stores and the
like compete for sales much as
do private companies in a capitalistic society. In addition, the
great bulk of Yugoslav agriculture consist of individual peasant farms and collective and
state farms play a small role.

Hanoi Reds Urge Parley

Special to The New York Times.

HONG KONG, Feb. 10—Com-
munist North Vietnam called
today for an international meeting of Communist parties to try
to heal the ideological rift between the Soviet Union and
Communist China.

Taking a compromise posi-
tion, the party's politburo said
"careful preparations" were
necessary but s h o u l d be
"speedy." The statement broadcast by the Hanoi radio and
monitored here, reflected North
Vietnam's continuing efforts to
act as a mediator.

February 11, 1963

MOSCOW ORDERS PEKING TO RECALL 5 AS UNDESIRABLE

Reprimands Embassy Aides for Distributing Copies of Criticism to Russians

By SEYMOUR TOPPING

Special to The New York Times

MOSCOW, June 29—The So-
viet Union has demanded the
immediate recall of three officials of the Chinese Embassy
in Moscow, it was disclosed today.

In a note delivered Thursday
to the Embassy, the Soviet
Foreign Ministry asserted that
the presence of the three officials and two other Chinese
Communist residents was no
longer desirable.

The five Chinese were repri-
manded for distributing in the
Soviet Union copies of Peking's
letter of June 14 to the Central
Committee of the Soviet Communist party.

The letter, which discussed
ideological differences, was denounced by the Soviet Central
Committee on June 18 as slanderous. Its publication was
banned in the Soviet Union.

Group Listed

The affected staff members
of the Chinese Embassy were
Mei Wen-kang, Lu Pei-hsin and
Wang Yao-tung. They were not
identified here by rank. The
others are Liu Tao-yu, a postgraduate student, and Yao Yi,
who was attached to an institute.

The expulsion order made
even more remote the prospects
of any reconciliation at the
ideological talks that are scheduled to open here next Friday.

East European sources here
said that the sharp increase in
Chinese-Soviet tensions in the
last two weeks made it possible
that a decision might be taken
to postpone the ideological talks
with the Chinese.

Ministry Raises Questions

Western analysts said that
Moscow and Peking now are
closer than ever before to a
formal ideological rupture of relations that would split the
world Communist movement
into two competing factions.

In Peking, a statement of the
Ministry of Foreign Affairs described the Soviet action as
"unreasonable and unfriendly."

The Chinese statement said
the expulsions raised the question of whether the Soviet Government "is deliberately trying
to undermine Sino-Soviet unity,
vitiate the relations between
the two states and create obstacles to the talks between the
Chinese and Soviet parties."

The Foreign Ministry said retaliatory measures would not
be taken against Soviet personnel stationed in Peking. "The
Chinese Government hopes that
the Soviet Government will not
take further rash steps detrimental to Sino-Soviet unity,"
the statement said.

There was no Soviet com-
ment on the statement. It was
transmitted here in Russian-
language broadcasts of Peking

radio. The expulsion order also
has not been published here.

Tonight, at the final session
of the Communist - sponsored
World Women's Congress, the
Soviet-bloc delegates and the
Chinese Communists supported
by their Albanian allies split in
the vote on the final resolution.
Angry shouts were exchanged
between the two factions during the open meeting.

Pravda, the Soviet party
newspaper, published this morning a speech by Premier Khrushchev in which he delivered his
first direct and public attack
on the leadership of Communist
China. The speech was made
on June 21 before a plenary
meeting of the Central Committee.

Mr. Khrushchev said "the
leaders of the Communist party
of China had exacerbated in the
extreme their differences with
the Communist party of the
Soviet Union and the entire
Communist movement."

Racialism Asserted

The Premier reaffirmed peaceful coexistence as the general
line of Soviet foreign policy.
He obliquely accused the Chinese Communists of adopting a
"national racial approach."

Premier Khrushchev's re-
marks about China were inserted
after the unexpected presentation here on June 15 of the
Chinese Communist letter. The
Soviet Central Committee contended that the letter had
violated an understanding to
avoid public polemics before the
opening of the ideological talks.

The long Chinese letter elaborated on Peking's contention
that Moscow has sacrificed the
interests of revolutionary struggles to pursue a policy of peaceful coexistence with the West.

Apart from differing with Mr.
Khrushchev on the tactics and
strategy for attaining world
Communism, the letter reflect-
ed the competition between
Moscow and Peking for the
leadership of the international
Communist movement.

East European sources here
said Premier Khrushchev would
discuss the tactics to be employed in the dispute with the
Chinese Communists in a top-
level conference in East Berlin.
He and other East European
Communist chiefs have gathered there ostensibly to celebrate on Sunday the 70th birthday of Walter Ulbricht, the East
German leader.

Delay May Be Sought

The sources said that the
sharp increase in Chinese-Soviet
tensions in the last two weeks
made it possible that a decision
might be taken to postpone the
ideological talks with the Chinese.

Soviet hopes for an understanding that would limit the
scope of the quarrel and maintain a facade of unity have been
shattered. Moscow has been resisting Chinese Communist in-

sistence on a showdown at a
general meeting of all the Communist parties.

The shock of the tough line
delineated in the Chinese letter
of June 14 has convinced Soviet officials that Peking believes it can gain adherents by
pressing the ideological debate.

Soviet exasperation boiled
over when the Chinese Em-
bassy here and Chinese students began handing out copies
of Peking's letters. Ignoring
the Soviet politicians, copies
went to Communist embassies
and journalists as well as to
some Soviet citizens.

Copies at Embassy

Western diplomats and newspapermen were able to obtain
Russian-language copies at the
embassy upon request. Earlier
statements attacking the Soviet ideological stand could be
picked up from display tables.

Peking radio has broadcast
the text of the June 14 letter
to Eastern Europe in several
languages.

The Foreign Ministry of East
Germany protested on June 21
to the Chinese Embassy there
against what it termed the illegal distribution of copies of
the June 14 letter.

Rumania, which has differed
recently with Moscow on Soviet
plans for the economic integration of Eastern Europe, was the
only Soviet-bloc country to publish a summary of the letter.

The statement of the Foreign
Ministry in Peking called the
Soviet explanation of the ex-
pulsion order "untenable."

It said that it was normal for
Chinese personnel in the Soviet
Union to distribute official
documents of the Chinese Central Committee.

The statement added that no
objection had been raised when
Soviet personnel in China had
distributed the Soviet letter of
March 30 to the Chinese Central Committee in advance of
its publication by Peking.

Tass, the Soviet press agency,
recently discontinued the distribution of its bulletin in
Peking.

The Soviet consulates in
Shanghai, Dairen-Port Arthur,
and Harbin were closed last
year. The official reason given
was that there were relatively
few Soviet citizens in China.

The Soviet Union suspended
diplomatic relations with Albania, Peking's ideological ally, in
December, 1961. Commercial
and diplomatic missions were
withdrawn from Albania in retaliation for Albanian propaganda attacks on the Soviet
leadership.

The other Soviet-bloc countries
have maintained curtailed diplomatic and commercial ties with
Albania. Only Rumania has
sent her ambassador back to
the Albanian capital.

June 30, 1963

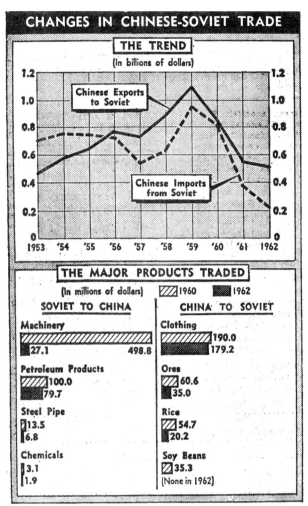

CHANGES IN CHINESE-SOVIET TRADE

THE TREND
(In billions of dollars)

Chinese Exports to Soviet

Chinese Imports from Soviet

1953 '54 '55 '56 '57 '58 '59 '60 '61 1962

THE MAJOR PRODUCTS TRADED
(In millions of dollars)   ▨ 1960   ■ 1962

SOVIET TO CHINA	CHINA TO SOVIET
Machinery 27.1 / 498.8	**Clothing** 190.0 / 179.2
Petroleum Products 100.0 / 79.7	**Ores** 60.6 / 35.0
Steel Pipe 13.5 / 6.8	**Rice** 54.7 / 20.2
Chemicals 3.1 / 1.9	**Soy Beans** 35.3 (None in 1962)

Charts are based on figures from official Soviet sources.

PEKING REPORTED BOLSTERING GUARD ON SOVIET BORDER

Indians Say Some Troops in Tibet Have Been Sent to Sinkiang Province

By SEYMOUR TOPPING
Special to The New York Times

NEW DELHI, Dec. 25—Communist China has shifted part of its Tibet military garrison into Sinkiang Province toward the border with the Soviet Union, according to information reaching official quarters here.

The Sinkiang border has been a source of tension between Peking and Moscow. In their exchanges of ideological recriminations, the two Communist powers have disclosed that thousands of border tribesmen fled into the Soviet Union from Sinkiang.

There have been persistent reports that the Soviet Union has reinforced its frontier military units.

Threat to India Eased

According to Indian estimates, elements of 15 Chinese Communist divisions remain in Tibet. However, the thinning out of the Chinese Communist concentrations has relieved some of the military pressure on India's northern frontier.

The reduction of Peking's forces in Tibet is one of principal reasons cited here for the Indian belief that the Chinese Communists will not attempt in the next months any incursion into India on a scale comparable with that of 1962.

It is also felt that Peking would not risk any military adventure that would invite criticism at a time when the Chinese Communist leadership

has embarked on major diplomatic and propaganda effort to gain adherents in Africa and the Middle East.

Sporadic Fighting Reported

This is the significance attached here to Premier Chou En-lai's current tour of Africa.

Peking was reported to be proceeding with its program for the political and economic consolidation of Tibet. In 1959, Chinese Communist troops occupied Tibet in force and ousted the theocratic government of the Dalai Lama after the Tibetans had rebelled against Chinese Communist encroachments on their autonomy.

The Chinese troops have been constructing permanent military installations in Tibet. Some of the troops have begun to cultivate their own land to augment food from Tibetan sources.

Reports filtering out of country through refugees and other sources say that sporadic fighting continues in the country. Fierce Khamba tribesmen, who rebelled against the Chinese Communists apparently occasionally stage raids on Chinese positions.

In recent weeks there has been an increase in the number of Tibetan refugees entering India through Sikkim. The movement is attributed to a shortage of food in Tibet and a relaxation of regulations imposed by Chinese Communist border garrisons.

Peking is attempting to introduce modern farming methods into Tibet. Machinery has been brought in and Tibetans are being organized for cooperative farming with the objective of eventually transforming their lands into collective or state farms.

Communist China has not succeeded in establishing a loyal Tibetan administration. Many Tibetans are believed to remain faithful to the Dalai Lama, who fled to India in 1959 when Chinese troops seized Lhasa, his capital.

The Dalai Lama is living quietly in India at Dharamsala, tending the needs of the estimated 20,000 to 40,000 Tibetan refugees in this country.

December 8, 1963

December 26, 1963

COMMUNIST PARTY ALIGNMENT AROUND THE WORLD

Soviet Union | Nations with Communist parties supporting Soviet Union
Communist China | Nations with Communist parties supporting Communist China
Nations with neutral Communist parties | Nations with divided Communist movement

September 6, 1964

KHRUSHCHEV SAYS PRIMARY RED AIM IS A BETTER LIFE

In Gibe at Peking, He Tells Hungary Goal Is Goulash, Not Just Revolution

By PAUL UNDERWOOD
Special to The New York Times

BUDAPEST, April 1 — Premier Khrushchev, in his first allusion to the Soviet Union's deepening ideological conflict with Communist China since Peking's attack on him yesterday, told workers at a factory here today:

"There are people in the world who call themselves Marxist-Leninists and at the same time say there is no need to strive for a better life. According to them, only one thing is important—revolution."

"What kind of Marxism is this?" he asked scornfully.

Communism will achieve little if it cannot give the people what they want, Mr. Khrushchev said, and he added:

"The important thing is that we should have more to eat— good goulash—schools, housing, and ballet. How much more do these things give to the enlargement of man's life? It is worth fighting and working for these things."

Electrification Stressed

Mr. Khrushchev made the remarks extemporaneously after he had delivered a prepared speech at a mass meeting of workers at Hungary's largest electrical equipment factory. Most of his remarks dealt with the necessity for greater electrification of the Soviet-bloc countries.

The Soviet Premier, who arrived in Budapest yesterday for an official visit, urged his audience to do their utmost to increase labor productivity.

"This is the only thing that will insure the victory of Communism," he said. "If the productivity of labor in the Socialist countries is lower than in the capitalist countries we shall not advance in our march to Communism and the conquest of capitalism."

Although no one spoke openly of the dispute between Moscow and Peking, Premier Janos Kadar confirmed what observers here had already assumed: that this was one of the principal topics of discussions under way between Mr. Khrushchev and the Hungarian Communist leaders.

In a brief speech at the factory meeting just before the Soviet Premier's half-hour address, Mr. Kadar said the talks between the Hungarian and Soviet delegations were concerned with relations between the two countries and "problems of the international working - class movement."

These talks began yesterday afternoon shortly after Mr. Khrushchev's arrival and continued this afternoon.

There were reports in Communist circles that Soviet and Hungarian party messages to the Chinese Communists would be published this week.

The Soviet-Chinese quarrel threw a meeting here of the International Association of Democratic Lawyers into chaos.

A series of shouting, stamping demonstrations, most of them against the Chinese, erupted repeatedly throughout an agenda debate until 6 A.M. today.

Mrs. Han Yu-tung, vice president of China's Supreme Court and the leader of the Chinese delegation, led off the attack last night by charging that "certain people" were pursuing an "erroneous line of not opposing imperialism, not supporting national independence movements and not relying on the peoples' mass struggle."

The chief Soviet delegate,

Lev Suvorin, accused Peking's representatives of trying to "undermine and falsify" the purpose of the meeting.

Mrs. Han retorted: "You speak with the voice of United States imperialism!" The rest of her tirade was drowned out by the demonstrations.

Chinese Accused of Racism

Special to The New York Times

PARIS, April 1—Communist China was accused today by a Soviet official of racial and chauvinist policies "no different from Nazism."

Bobodzhan G. Gafurov, deputy chairman of the Soviet Committee for African-Asian Solidarity, assailed the Chinese in an interview.

He came here from Algiers where he headed the Soviet delegation to the African-Asian Solidarity Conference last week.

Mr. Gafurov, in remarks to the French Press Agency, said: "The maddened anti-Communists of the United States want a war of the right and the maddened Chinese want a war of the left. There is no difference."

He charged that the Chinese wanted to unite the black and yellow races "against the whites."

"It is hate that they foment," Mr. Gafurov said.

He also accused the Chinese of carrying out a policy of "forced assimilation" in Inner Mongolia. Chinese, he said, are forced to marry Mongol women and Mongols to wed Chinese.

"In Sinkiang," Mr. Gafurov continued, "non-Chinese people are persecuted and take refuge in the Soviet Union, where they arrive naked, starved and destitute."

April 2, 1964

SHANGHAI YOUTHS SENT TO SINKIANG

China Settles Border Region With 100,000 in Year

By SEYMOUR TOPPING

Special to The New York Times

HONG KONG, Oct. 11 — Shanghai, the largest city in China, has sent more than 100,000 youths this year to the Central Asian province of Sinkiang, adjacent to the Soviet Union.

According to reports from Shanghai, the largest effort mainly involving recent graduates of junior and senior high schools, has been this fall.

Peking has accelerated the settlement of Sinkiang since border and territorial issues have been raised in its ideological dispute with Moscow. The Soviet Union has been accused of subversive activities and of enticing of tens of thousands of Moslems from the Uighur autonomous region of Sinkiang.

The Russians, who jointly exploited the mineral resources of Sinkiang until 1954, have contended that the Moslems who have come across the border are fleeing Peking's persecution of non-Chinese minorities.

The massive Chinese Communist settlement program in Sinkiang has served to shore up the defenses of the province and to displace the restive native peoples, mainly Turkic-

The New York Times   Oct. 12, 1964
Youths are being sent from Shanghai (1) to live in far-off Sinkiang Province (2).

speaking Moslems, with Chinese considered politically more reliable.

The Chinese have also been reported in recent months to be strengthening again their military garrisons in Sinkiang and the army-run state farms in the security zone along the frontier.

The transfer of the young Chinese to Sinkiang also helps the Chinese Government with its youth problem.

Millions of urban youngsters for whom no jobs can be found upon graduation from middle and technical schools have been sent to rural areas to work as farm laborers.

Much of this surplus resulted from the rapid expansion of the educational system during the "Great Leap Forward" from 1958 to 1960.

Too Many Were Trained

When the "Great Leap Forward" failed and industrial goals had to be cut back with priority reassigned to agriculture, many of the jobs that had been envisioned for recent graduates disappeared.

According to reports reaching here, when the youths arrive in Sinkiang, they are enlisted in the Sinkiang Construction Corps, a parliamentary labor organization run by former army officers.

Units of the corps are assigned tasks such as completion of irrigation projects. Recruits are given their clothing, food, housing and a monthly wage said to be worth little more than $1.

A few of the Shanghai youths have returned home to participate in rallies to encourage more boys and girls to volunteer for Sinkiang. However, most of those who leave apparently go on a permanent basis without any intention on the part of the authorities that they will ever return to Shanghai.

October 12, 1964

Chou Lauds Soviet Shifts, Hopes for Better Relations

Charles Taylor, The Globe and Mail
Chou En-lai

Khrushchev Fall a 'Good Thing,' Says Chinese Premier in Interview

This dispatch is by Maximo V. Soliven of The Manila Times, who has just completed a three-week visit to Communist China.

Special to The New York Times

HONG KONG, Oct. 28—Premier Chou En-lai of Communist China has expressed hope that relations between Peking and Moscow will improve following the downfall of Nikita S. Khrushchev. Mr. Chou said Mr. Khrushchev's replacement as Premier and party leader was a "good thing."

The Chinese Premier's comments were made in Peking Oct. 24 in an interview of an hour and a half's duration with four Filipino newsmen. He answered questions on a wide range of subjects.

The atomic bomb that China exploded on Oct. 16 was bigger than those dropped on Hiroshima and Nagasaki by the United States in 1945, he said.

He did not make the claim that the Chinese weapon was large by today's standards.

"Our atom bomb is small, but from the very first day of its birth it joined the struggle for peace," he said.

Peking's relations with the United States do not seem likely to improve in the near future, the Chinese leader remarked.

He had this comment on the removal of Mr. Khrushchev: "In one word, it is a good thing."

Asked whether he believed relations between Peking and Moscow would improve as a result of Mr. Khrushchev's downfall, he asserted:

"That is our hope. You can see this from the congratulatory message our party and state leaders sent to the new leaders of the Soviet party and state."

Looking fit at 67 years of age, the Premier emphasized his points with vigorous gestures, pausing only to sip from a white mug of tea on the table beside him. He wore the standard attire of the Chinese Communist hierarchy—a dark blue jacket and blue trousers. It has been reported that he was ill recently.

Translation from Harvard

Mr. Chou, although he speaks passable English and twice broke in to correct his interpreter's translation, spoke in Chinese. His remarks were rendered into English by Chi Chao-chu, a Harvard-trained Foreign Ministry interpreter.

Commenting on the first Chinese test of an atomic device, Mr. Chou said that Peking did not intend to "bargain with the nuclear powers" and that its purpose was "to break the nuclear monopoly and eliminate nuclear weapons."

He said that the Chinese proposal for a summit conference to discuss prohibitions on nuclear weapons had met with the approval of the "great majority" of heads of government of the countries with which China has diplomatic relations.

They consider that the proposal is reasonable, he said, "but also that it cannot be realized for the time being and that difficulties still exist." He said this was "because the United States is against such a proposal," an attitude expressed immediately after it was made.

Mr. Chou reiterated Peking's official declaration that it would "never under any circumstances be the first to use nuclear weapons." If the United States uses nuclear weapons against China it will resist, he added.

'Complete Prohibition'

The Chinese Government's proposal for a summit meeting on a "complete prohibition and thorough destruction of nuclear weapons" includes as a first step "an agreement that the nuclear powers and those countries which may soon become nuclear powers undertake not to use nuclear weapons—neither to use them against non-nuclear countries and nuclear-free zones, nor against each other," Premier Chou said.

Mr. Chou remarked that there were people who said that the Chinese atomic bomb was small and that no importance need be attached to it.

"It is true that, compared with the nuclear weapons now in the hands of the United States, our atom bomb is in-significant," he declared. "But we are, after all, now in possession of it and it is the fruit of our own efforts, of the efforts of Asians."

"Our purpose in acquiring atom bombs is not to threaten others," he added. "We are not like the United States."

Asked to comment on the prospects of Communist China's being admitted to the United Nations, the Premier said:

"That is a question which will come up even later because the United Nations is still controlled and manipulated by the United States and it is always thinking up all sorts of ways to obstruct restoration to the People's Republic of China of her position in the United Nations as the only legal representative of the Chinese people."

Discussing relations with Washington, he said:

"We have rich experience in dealing with the United States Government. The United States has held talks with the Ambassador of the People's Republic of China for more than nine years and yet it does not recognize the new China. It is at least quite an illogical state of affairs. Even the United States authorities admit this."

'Willing to Coexist'

China, he stated, is "willing to coexist peacefully with the United States on the basis of the five principles of peaceful coexistence between countries with different social systems. The five principles, enunciated as the basis of Chinese-Indian relations in 1954, are respect for territorial integrity and sovereignty, nonaggression, non-interference in the internal affairs of other states, equality and mutual benefit, and peaceful coexistence.

"The United States rejected this on many occasions, but it failed to state any reasons," Mr. Chou added.

With regard to relations with the Philippines, Mr. Chou said they "can and should be improved."

He said that Pakistan, although a member of the Southeast Asia Treaty Organization "which is under the leadership of the United States and which is used by it with hostile aims against China," had "become closer" to China.

"United States troops are still being stationed in Japan and part of Japanese territory is still being occupied by the United States, but Japan is still developing friendly relations with our country," Mr. Chou said.

Speaking of China's agricultural and industrial achievements, he said that "in view of China's large population, we are still a backward country just in the process of development."

The newsmen who interviewed Mr. Chou included Eliciano Magno of the Manila Daily Mirror, Agaton Santos of the Philippine News Service and Johnny Dayang of the Philippine National Press Club.

PEIPING SOFTENS HOSTILITY TO U. S.

Sees 'Gestures for Peace' in Kennedy Message, but Assails Most of Report

Special to The New York Times.

HONG KONG, Feb. 1—A tiny crack appeared today in the anti-United States facade that Communist China presents to the world.

Peiping found "some gestures for peace" in President Kennedy's State of the Union message to Congress. This was the first less-than-critical comment about a United States President to come out of China since the Communists came to power in 1949.

The remark was contained in a report on the message by Hsinhua, official Chinese Communist press agency. The report was printed prominently in all Peiping papers.

Aside from this, the report was condemnatory. Jenmin Jih Pao, official organ of the Chinese Communist party, carried it under the headline: "Olive Branch in His Right Hand and Bundle of Arrows in His Left."

Despite the generally antagonistic tone of the Hsinhua report, it concluded on a non-committal note, referring to the President's intention to explore promptly all possible areas of cooperation with the Soviet Union and other nations.

Charges War Preparations

Hsinhua said that the message showed that the keynote of United States foreign policy was "to step up arms expansion and war preparations and to intensify economic and cultural aggression."

The message also indicated that the United States was "bent on continuing to use the United Nations as a tool of its aggression against the Congo," the press agency asserted.

President Kennedy's message, Hsinhua continued, made an "unbridled attack" on the Soviet Union and Communist China and in particular lied about the "so-called Chinese 'menace' to Asia."

President Kennedy "also made it clear that the United States would never give up its subversive schemes against the East European Socialist countries," the agency declared.

However, even in its condemnatory passages, the Hsinhua report was considerably less vituperative than observers here have come to expect from Peiping in its comments on the United States.

A slight but perceptible softening of Peiping's attitude toward the United States has been observed in other articles. And a source in Hong Kong who is close to the Chinese Communists declares flatly that the local Communist newspapers have been ordered to tone down their anti-United States propaganda.

Despite this apparent restraint, the Chinese Communist press has lampooned or vilified all the major figures in the new Cabinet, including the President himself. The general propaganda line has been that the change in Administration does not mean any change in "imperialist" United States policies.

Western observers here speculate that Communist China's new line toward the United States may be a result of a Soviet request to give the Kennedy Administration a chance to prove itself. If so, they say, the Chinese Communists have given in to the request grudgingly and will be quick to tell the Soviet Union "We told you so" if President Kennedy and Premier Khrushchev do not hit it off.

February 2, 1961

Mauldin in The Chicago Sun-Times

"Chinese water torture."

April 21, 1963

Chinese Reds Offer Assistance To Left-Wing Regime in Laos

Foreign Minister Tells Rally Help Must Be Requested by Ousted Premier

Special to The New York Times.

HONG KONG, Feb. 2—Marshal Chen Yi, Foreign Minister of Communist China, said in Peiping today that the Chinese Communist Government would provide aid if it were requested by the "lawful Laotian Government of Prince Souvanna Phouma."

Speaking at a rally "in support of the Laotian people," he declared United States aid to the "illegal Government" of Prince Boun Oum was "unjust," while Soviet aid to the Souvanna Phouma regime was "just."

Marshal Chen charged that the aim of the United States was to intervene in all Southeast Asia and "directly threaten" Burma, Communist North Vietnam and Communist China.

He reiterated Peiping's support for an "enlarged" conference along the lines of the 1954 Geneva meeting on Indochina and for the reconstitution of the International Control Commission on Laos.

Both the conference and the commission can deal only with the regime or Prince Souvanna Phouma, he said, otherwise the situation would be "even more complicated, even more serious."

Ousted Premier to Return

Meanwhile, it was announced that Prince Souvanna Phouma, now in exile in Cambodia, would soon return to Laos to resume control of the country. The report was based on a communiqué issued by Ministers of his ousted Cabinet who have allied themselves with the pro-Communist Pathet Lao movement.

The communiqué was broadcast tonight by the Hanoi radio in North Vietnam, which quoted the Pathet Lao movement's radio. The communiqué was said to have been issued after a meeting of the Ministers.

Quinim Pholsena, Information Minister in the ousted Cabinet, advised the meeting of "decisions taken by Premier Souvanna Phouma on Jan. 25" designating himself and two others to "take charge of all Government affairs during the Prince's absence."

Quinim Pholsena said that Khamsouk Keola, Minister of Health under Prince Souvanna Phouma, had been appointed Acting Premier, and that Tiao Sisoumang Sisaleumsak, who was Deputy Minister of Rural Affairs in the ousted Cabinet, would head the Ministries of Social Welfare, Economy and Home Affairs.

February 3, 1961

TAYLOR'S MISSION IRKS RED VIETNAM

U.S. General's Saigon Plans Draw Communist Protest

SAIGON, Vietnam, Saturday, Oct. 14 (UPI) — Communist North Vietnam protested today to the International Control Commission for Vietnam against the scheduled visit of Gen. Maxwell D. Taylor, according to Hsinhua, the Chinese Communist press agency.

The report, monitored in Tokyo, said the protest "urged the International Control Commission to take measures in good time to prevent Taylor's arrival in South Vietnam."

General Taylor is being sent to South Vietnam by President Kennedy to survey that country's struggle against Communist guerrillas.

Trip Called Violation

North Vietnam called the trip "a most serious violation of the Geneva agreements," which ended the Indochina war and partitioned Vietnam into Communist and pro-Western states. The Control Commission was set up under the same agreements.

"This American general's mission is to intensify United States intervention in South Vietnam and prepare the way for introducing United States troops into that part of Vietnam," the Communist statement said.

Earlier, the Peiping radio disclosed that Chinese Communist and North Vietnamese leaders had held a strategy meeting in Peiping in advance of General Taylor's trip.

The broadcast reported that Mao Tse-tung, chief of the Chinese Communist party, and the North Vietnamese President, Ho Chi Minh, met last night in Peiping with other party and Government officials, including the Chinese Communist Defense Minister, Marshal Lin Piao.

The broadcast gave no information on the talks. But it was believed here that they dealt with the latest moves by President Kennedy to counter the increased Communist threat to South Vietnam.

October 14, 1961

Our New Stake in Vietnam

Fresh details are slowly emerging from reticent Administration sources about the expanded program of American participation in South Vietnam's anti-Communist struggle.

From now on Americans will be flying Vietnamese troops into battle and accompanying them in combat on the ground; Americans will help run the Vietnamese intelligence system, assist in military planning and have a voice in measures to improve social and economic conditions. If some of the more than 2,000 Americans now in South Vietnam get shot at in combat zones, they are authorized to shoot back.

These new arrangements, added to the many other steps the United States has taken to bolster South Vietnam, represent a very extensive American commitment. Americans certainly will be shot at; some will almost certainly be killed. Communist China has just sent to Hanoi a Chinese military mission headed by Marshal Yeh Chien-ying, Vice Chairman of the National Defense Council in Peiping. Marshal Yeh is a tough and capable soldier well known to many Americans as the Communist member of the truce agency set up by General Marshall during the latter's attempt fifteen years ago to halt warfare between the Nationalists and Communists in China. It can be assumed that Marshal Yeh will, with North Vietnam leaders, try to counter the stepped up American - Vietnamese effort in the South.

The extensive new American involvement in South Vietnam has been made on the basis of parallel commitments by President Ngo Dinh Diem to improve his regime. The effectiveness of what the United States is doing will largely depend on how far he proceeds in this respect. He has made commendable moves. Military pay is to be increased, command channels improved; he will consult frequently with his advisory National Council and take new steps against nepotism and corruption. We do not yet know whether these and other actions he contemplates will be sufficient to produce the governmental efficiency and popular morale required for the struggle ahead.

What is certain is that the increased American stake and American risk in South Vietnam now needs, more than ever, to be accompanied by a fresh, resilient and imaginative effort by President Ngo to mobilize resources for a fight that is certain to get harder before it gets easier. President Kennedy can only justify the new United States role to the American people on this basis.

December 22, 1961

AGAIN THE QUEMOY ISSUE

Peiping's Arms Build-Up Forces Kennedy to Reassert Ambiguous Warning Against the Use of Force

By MAX FRANKEL

Special to The New York Times.

WASHINGTON, June 30—Virtually every official of the Administration high enough to have an opinion on the subject, including President Kennedy, believes that the United States should never have done what it felt compelled to do again this week about Quemoy and Matsu: that is, ambiguously and vaguely to commit United States power to the defense by Nationalist China of two tiny groups of islands within shooting distance of the Chinese Communist mainland.

How and why this could happen offers a lesson not only in the vagaries of the cold war, but also in diplomatic intrigue and the constrictive nature of power, even Presidential power.

Quemoy and Matsu block the harbors of Amoy and Foochow, two relatively idle Communist ports in China's Fukien Province. The islands are about five miles from the mainland and about 100 miles from the Nationalists' main bases on Taiwan and the Penghu (Pescadores) isles.

To a struggling mainland China of 650,000,000, the offshore island groups can be little more than annoying pimples on the map; inherently, they are virtually useless. What is more, though physically close to the Communists, they have been and probably still are beyond Peiping's military reach.

Periodic Crises

And to the Nationalists who for all their talk have neither the military power nor diplomatic freedom to recapture the mainland from the Communists, the islands strategically are worthless and costly outposts that tie down about 70,000 troops.

Yet in 1954, again in 1958, and symmetrically, yet again in 1962, Quemoy and Matsu have become the foci of Communist military build-ups, stubborn Nationalist defenses and political and diplomatic crises for the United States.

For Peiping, assault of the islands seems to be a cheap way of kicking up an international storm, of making appear more real the alleged threat of Nationalist and United States attack.

For Taipei, defense of the islands has been about the only way of keeping alive the almost mystical dream of eventual return to the mainland, of dramatically demonstrating the military frailty of the Communists and the political power of the Nationalists over Washington.

And, for both Chinas, the islands have proved to be symbols of the civil war in which they claim still to be engaged, as well as hostages against a clear and logical demarcation of their respective holdings that would sooner or later lead a weary world to proclaim and recognize two separate and independent Chinas.

Prevent Conflict

Washington has tried to keep the two Chinas at least militarily apart since the day the Communists formed their mainland Government in 1949. Although the "leashing" and "unleashing" of President Chiang Kai-shek has been a favorite partisan issue here, the Administrations of Presidents Truman, Eisenhower and Kennedy have all tried to prevent conflict in the Taiwan Strait.

By treaty, the United States is committed to help defend Taiwan and the Penghus. By letter, it has also pledged the Nationalists against attacking the mainland without Washington's consent, and by ambiguous declaration of Congress and Executive, it has kept itself free to help defend Quemoy and Matsu if an attack on the islands were adjudged to be a threat to Taiwan.

How such a judgment might be made in the heat of battle or whether such a vague declaration was not an invitation to an avowedly "limited" Communist attack are legitimate questions—at least they have been raised by Senators, including John F. Kennedy of Massachusetts, and as recently as 1960 by Presidential Candidate Kennedy.

The islands are worthless, Mr. Kennedy then maintained, and should be excluded from the West's line of defense, because a fuzzy line, as in Korea, can only lead to adventurous probe by an aggressor. Later in the campaign Mr. Kennedy retreated somewhat from this view toward the more conventional and more ambiguous Eisenhower position.

In the eighteen months of the Kennedy Administration, however, a number of officials here have tried to take Candidate Kennedy at his original word and to do something about extricating the country from the commitment to the offshore islands. Whatever their hopes for ultimate success, they realized the policy could never be changed at a time of Communist threat, and just such a threat disrupted their plans about a month ago.

Piece by piece, intelligence analysts here assembled a picture of "very large" Chinese Communist troop movements in Fukien province opposite the offshore islands.

Is it a defensive build-up? Washington thinks that Peiping knows better than anyone its vulnerabilty to attack at this time of food crisis on the mainland. The Peiping regime might be truly frightened.

Offensive Ploy

Is it an offensive build-up? Washington thinks the size of the effort exceeds defensive needs, even though it would seem foolhardy for Peiping to believe that it could easily capture the offshore islands.

Or is it an offensive ploy with defensive purpose, a preemptive move prompted by fear? Or an effort finally to determine which Kennedy was the real Kennedy, the one that might defend the offshore islands or the one that had talked of giving them up as useless?

No one here could be sure. The only instruction of history was that whatever the Chinese Communists intended, they would reveal it only gradually and cautiously.

The Fukien build-up continued, and gradually analysts here lost their confidence that it was merely defensive. In a first move to deter attack, Washington let Peiping know that it knew of the military concentration.

Contact in Warsaw

Within forty-eight hours, Communist China replied. It issued a long and tendencious propaganda statement accusing the United States of plotting the infiltration and invasion of the mainland in the hope of embarrassing the Communists.

In Warsaw, the Chinese Communist Ambassador used his standing opportunity to call in the United States Ambassador to transmit a more direct warning against attack of the mainland. The United States diplomat, in turn, insisted that Washington had always opposed the use of force by either side and specifically denied plans to aid an attack on the mainland.

This assurance was apparently meant as much for Moscow as for Peiping, for the strategy of deterring Chinese Communist aggression logically calls on the one hand for a threat of United States involvement and on the other for a bid to persuade the Russians to restrain Peiping.

The Russians probably believe Mr. Kennedy's assurances as they believed General Eisenhower's. But the Nationalists, in their eagerness to bind the United States' diplomatic hand, let Peiping believe the worst, first by contradicting Washing-

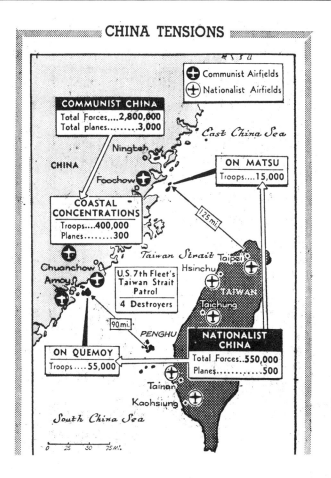

CHINA TENSIONS

Communist Airfields
Nationalist Airfields

COMMUNIST CHINA
Total Forces....2,800,000
Total planes.........3,000

CHINA

East China Sea

Ningteh

ON MATSU
Troops....15,000

Foochow

COASTAL CONCENTRATIONS
Troops....400,000
Planes........300

125 mi.

Chuanchow

Taiwan Strait   Taipei

Hsinchu

Amoy

U.S. 7th Fleet's Taiwan Strait Patrol
4 Destroyers

TAIWAN
Taichung

90 mi.

PENGHU

NATIONALIST CHINA
Total Forces..550,000
Planes...........500

ON QUEMOY
Troops....55,000

Tainan

Kaohsiung

South China Sea

0   25   50   75 M.

ton's reports about a mainland build-up and then by flagrantly reasserting their ambitions against the mainland.

Attack Suspected

The mainland build-up continued and the whole procedure was so remarkably like that of 1958 that a growing number of officials here expected at least another artillery attack on Quemoy. At mid-week therefore President Kennedy felt compelled to turn his back on Candidate Kennedy and to reassert the ambiguous Eisenhower

threat that Washington might or might not use force if Quemoy or Matsu were attacked.

Aware of Communist China's vested interest in proving the United States a "paper tiger" and aware of some ambitions on Taiwan to drag the United States into a war against the mainland, the President held to a narrow middle, saying he would decide what to do only as the situation developed.

The consensus here was that it would develop, but few would guess how far.

ANTIWHITE DRIVE BY PEKING IS SEEN

Chinese Blow at U.S. Held Move to Gain Worldwide Support of Colored

By TAD SZULC
Special to The New York Times

WASHINGTON, Aug. 12—A highly unusual but little-noticed formal statement by Mao Tse-tung last Thursday was regarded by officials here today as the opening of a major worldwide racial campaign by Communist China.

The 1,000-word statement by the chairman of the Chinese Communist party was primarily an attack on the United States and the Kennedy Administration for the "enslavement, oppression and discrimination" of the American Negro.

United States officials believed that the statement, one of the extremely rare pronouncements directly attributed to Mr. Mao, was, in fact, a formal bid by Peking for leadership of the world's colored people against the whites.

'Sharpening Class Struggle'

Mr. Mao said:

"I call upon the workers, peasants, revolutionary intellectuals, enlightened elements of the bourgeosie and other enlightened personages of all colors in the world — white, black, yellow, brown and so forth — to unite against the racial discrimination practiced by U.S. imperialism and to support the American Negroes in their struggle against racial discrimination."

"The speedy development of the struggle of American Negroes," he said, "is a manifestation of the sharpening of class struggle and national struggles within the United States."

"In the final analysis," he declared, "a national struggle is a question of class struggle."

The conclusion here was that Mr. Mao, in linking discrimination problems with the class struggle, was seeking to capture the sympathies of African and Asian populations in his growing contest with the Soviet Union.

Although the statement concentrated on the racial situation in the United States, the view

here was that the emerging anti-white policy of Communist China was also aimed at the Soviet Union.

It was recalled that during the conference of the Afro-Asian People's Solidarity Organization held last February in Moshi, Tanganyika, the Chinese delegation sought to expel the Soviet group on the ground that it was noncolored.

The open letter from the Central Committee of the Soviet Communist party, issued last July 14, pointedly mentioned this incident in detailing Moscow's charges against Peking.

It said that at Moshi "the leader of the Chinese delegation told the Soviet representatives that 'Whites have nothing to do here.'"

The Chinese, it continued, had taken the same position at a journalists conference in Jakarta, Indonesia.

The opinion here is that following the Soviet-Chinese split —and particularly after the signing of the limited nuclear test-ban treaty by the Soviet Union, the United States and Britain — Communist China has resolved to make the leadership of colored peoples in the world one of the mainstays of her foreign policy.m

The impression that Mr. Mao's statement was indeed the kickoff of a racial campaign seemed to be confirmed today by Peking broadcasts reporting that Jenmin Jih Pao, the official newspaper of the Chinese Communist party, carries an editorial based on his remarks and that a special mass rally devoted to the same theme was held in the Chinese Communist capital.

The broadcast said that one of the speakers at the rally was Frank Coe, who was described as "a friend from the United States."

Mr. Coe is a former secretary of the International Monetary Fund. After his resignation from the Fund in 1952, following charges that he had been a Soviet spy, Mr. Coe apparently went to live in China.

In his statement, distributed by Hsinhua news agency, Mr. Mao said that he was speaking out on the racial issue in the United States as a result of two requests from Robert F. Williams.

Mr. Williams is an extremist Negro leader now living in Cuba. He is under indictment in North Carolina on kidnapping charges.

The reason why such great importance is being attached to Mr. Mao's statement and why it is seen as the start of a major policy campaign lies in the special form of his pronouncement.

Experts in Chinese affairs here said that, as far as it was known, this was the first time that Mr. Mao had issued a formal statement over his signature.

In the past, they said, he has made public speeches, although the last recorded speech was in 1957. On rare occasions some of his remarks at receptions in Peking have been briefly quoted.

He was thus quoted six times in 1960, just before the abortive meeting between former President Eisenhower and Soviet Premier Khrushchev, which China opposed, and three times in October, 1961, when the Berlin crisis was in an acute stage.

Under the circumstances, therefore, the interpretation placed on Mr. Mao's statement, made before a group of obscure African visitors, was that Peking attached extreme importance to the racial matter.

Mr. Mao's rare public appearances seem to be restricted recently to Africans and Asians.

In his statement, Mr. Mao declared:

"The evil system of colonialism and imperialism grew up along with the enslavement of Negroes and the trade in Negroes; it will surely come to its end with the thorough emancipation of the black people."

"I am firmly convinced that, with the support of more than 90 per cent of the people of the world, the American Negro will be victorious in their just struggle," he said.

RED CHINA PLEDGES TO BACK CAMBODIA

Offers Support Against U.S. 'Imperialism' After Aid Is Canceled by Sihanouk

Special to The New York Times

HONG KONG, Nov. 20 — Marshal Chen Yi, Foreign Minister of Communist China, pledged "resolute support" for Cambodia today in what he called her "just and patriotic struggle against imperialism."

He declared that the Kingdom of Cambodia, which has "persevered in its policy of peace and neutrality," was now "seriously threatened."

"Instigated by United States imperialism and its lackeys, Cambodian traitors have organized a so-called Free Khmer movement and engaged in increasingly frantic attacks and subversive activities against the Kingdom of Cambodia," Marshal Chen said, according to a dispatch of Hsinhua, the Chinese Communist press agency.

U.S. Aid Ties Canceled

"In order to repel the threat of foreign forces and defend the independence and sovereignty of their country, Prince Sihanouk and the Cambodian Government are waging a courageous struggle and have taken a series of resolute measures.

"We greatly admire this dauntless spirit."

Yesterday Prince Norodom Sihanouk, Cambodian chief of state, announced in Pnompenh that he was canceling agreements under which the United States was granting military and economic aid.

He said the aid, amounting to about $24 million a year, was being used to undermine him. The United States has denied the allegation.

Prince Sihanouk charged that American equipment was in the hands of rebel Cambodians operating from neighboring South Vietnam.

Cambodia, the ancient Khmer empire, has followed a neutral course since becoming independent from France in 1954.

The Foreign Minister was speaking at a banquet in honor of Dr. Abdul Kayeum, Interior Minister of Afghanistan, who arrived in Peking today to sign a treaty relating to the boun-

August 13, 1963

dary between his country and Communist China.

Swing to Red Orbit Feared

PNOMPENH, Cambodia, Nov. 19 (AP) — Americans here are fearful that Cambodia's refusal to accept further United States assistance will swing her into Communist China's orbit.

The United States Ambassador, Philip D. Sprouse, was summoned to the Foreign Ministry, presumably to be told that United States assistance no longer was welcome. He has not seen Prince Norodom Sihanouk for several months.

Work on all United States projects halted Tuesday. The United States has been pouring in military and economic aid to try to keep Cambodia neutral.

Prince Sihanouk will ask the three million Cambodians to tighten their belts, will nationalize a number of businesses Dec. 31 and has announced that the Government will take over the banks next July.

There are about 300 Americans here. As soon as aid affairs are wound up, the total will drop to about 20, mostly embassy personnel.

Sixty-five United States soldiers are here, but actual training of the armed forces is done by 800 men of a French military mission. The French will remain, at least for the time being.

JOHNSON SCORED BY CHINESE REDS

By United Press International

TOKYO, Nov. 24—Communist China bitterly criticized President Johnson today and termed him a supporter of the late President Kennedy's "trickery policy."

"Since the emergence of the Kennedy regime," the Chinese Communist press agency Hsinhua said, "Johnson has positively supported various reactionary policies of the Kennedy Administration and participated in formulating and promoting such policies.

"Johnson has supported Kennedy's trickery policy and has called for the maintenance of such a policy in a series of his speeches."

The Chinese Communists reported the assassination of President Kennedy in a four-paragraph dispatch eight hours after it occurred. But they made no comment.

Hsinhua said Mr. Johnson "was one of the central figures in the Kennedy Government and has made frequent trips abroad."

The Chinese statement added that Mr. Johnson believed "the United States, in making two-faced antirevolutionary plots, must maintain a strong position on the basis of strong force."

"He also looks toward Cuba with animosity and has called for the elimination of the Cuban revolutionary Government," it said. "He once stated: 'We will never be satisfied until Communism is eliminated from Cuba and the Western Hemisphere.'"

Hsinhua asserted that President Johnson took "a strong position against the Chinese people" by his support of the Nationalists in Tawian.

"This was evident," the agency said, "when he visited Taiwan shortly after he became Vice President, and guaranteed a nonreduction of United States assistance to [President] Chiang Kai-shek and assured him the United States would take responsibility for defending Taiwan."

———

Peking Children Applaud

PEKING, Nov. 24 (Reuters)

—Chinese Communist newspapers published today 300-word identical inside-page reports on the assassination of President Kennedy.

They also published 600-word biographical sketches of President Johnson with caricatures and photographs showing him grim and unsmiling.

Authoritative sources said schoolchildren here applauded yesterday when they were told of the death of Mr. Kennedy, who had been represented to them in Peking propaganda as the world's wickedest man.

A diplomat from a neutral country reported that a Chinese member of the embassy staff commented when he heard of the assassination: "That's good news. He was a very wicked man."

The Chinese trade-union newspaper, Kungjen Jih Pao, printed a cartoon entitled "Kennedy Biting the Dust."

It depicted the late President lying face down after he had been shot.

The biographical sketch of Mr. Johnson contained a brief history of his political career and excerpts from his recent speeches.

It said he was a millionaire who "represents the interests of big oilmen and ranch owners in the South and big capitalists and industrialists in the North."

November 25, 1963

End of the 'Communist' World

By HARRISON E. SALISBURY

ON DEALING WITH THE COMMUNIST WORLD. By George F. Kennan. 57 pp. Harper & Row. $3.00

PERIODICALLY, George Frost Kennan, reins his fellow Americans up sharp and compels them to look squarely at one of those basic foreign policy issues that time, tradition, politics or equivocation has obscured or distorted. He first did this on a major scale in his famous Foreign Affairs articles of 1947, signed "X," in which he elaborated the policy of containment that, until very recent times, constituted the theoretical structure of American posture vis-a-vis the Communist world. He did it again with his Reith lectures in 1958 when he ruthlessly cut away the clichés of Western policy with respect to Germany and proposed a fresh effort at a settlement within the framework of the

Ulli Steltzer
George F. Kennan

real security issues involved. Unfortunately, despite Mr. Kennan's presentation, the German question has hardly budged.

Now, Mr. Kennan has thrust upon our attention another urgent demand—a demand that we strip from the Communist world the myth (in part of their creation, in part of ours) with which its reality lies concealed from our view. He asks that we formulate policies consistent with the actuality of a polycentric, not monolithic, Communism.

Decries 'Communist World'

Indeed, Mr. Kennan would prefer quietly to drop the concept of a "Communist world" overboard. There could be, he suggests, "no more useful innovation in the discussion, public and governmental, of the affairs of the 'Communist' orbit than a law which forbade all of us, including myself, to use the word 'Communist' at all, and forced us to treat the regimes and peoples of each of these countries, specifically, for what they are—which is something much more highly differentiated . . . than we commonly suppose."

And this, of course, is the crux of the matter. It is no longer one Communist world as it was, more or less, when Mr. Kennan evolved his containment theory. It is a world of many Communisms, of two great power systems, Russian and Chinese, of rapidly widening differences between smaller Com-

November 21, 1963

munist states and individual Communist parties—a "Communist world" in which differences are rapidly becoming as pronounced as within the so-called "free world."

It is a world in which the casual retort, "Well, they're Communists, aren't they?" becomes more and more meaningless as the concept is stretched to try to encompass at one and the same time Hoxha's antedeluvian Stalinists, Gomulka's free-thinking Poles, Togliatti's quasi-bourgeois party and Mao's blue ants.

To Mr. Kennan this astonishing metamorphosis is the single most important political fact of our time. He couples with this the commonsensical conclusion that unless we find a reasonable way to live and deal with these rapidly changing forces the alternative is nuclear mutual destruction. He sees a clear and present danger to the nation in the growth of the radical conservative approach which opposes to the many Communisms a single face and which stands for simple, across-the-board destruction of Communism, a program which Mr. Kennan equates with suicide.

Mr. Kennan has observed and studied Russia for a long time. He sees no future for "liberation" theories. He asks bluntly what the advocates of liberation proposed to substitute as a governmental system in Great Russia when, as and if they managed to tear away the surrounding national segments— the Baltic states, the Ukraine, the Caucasian lands, Central Asia. He finds no evidence that advocates of violent, short-term "solutions" of the Communist problem have begun to think through the catchwords they mouth.

Evolution Is Cited

And he draws quiet attention to the plain and obvious evolution of the Soviet state toward attitudes which makes it a much less difficult force with which to deal than it was 30 years ago.

He points repeatedly to the foolishness of trying to enforce uniform policy upon non-uniform states—of trying to straitjacket the Poles, the Yugoslavs, the Rumanians into the same kind of punitive measures that we think are appropriate for Castro's Cuba and Mao's China.

Like virtually every specialist in the field, he sees little but trouble ahead in the relations between Moscow and Peking, regardless of what each may do to try to patch matters up. He would not be surprised to see border hostilities between Russia and China (like those between Russia and Japan in 1938) but he expects them to halt short of full-fledged war.

Above all, he sees in the present situation one of opportunity for the West—a chance not only to influence the course of developments within the Communist world but to hasten processes favorable to our side, to tilt the balance not inconsiderably (although he concedes that the freeze between NATO and the Warsaw powers limits our field of maneuver), to strengthen the forces within Communist regimes that are tending toward relaxation and westernization and even perhaps to determine the ultimate outcome of the epic struggle between the two Communist centers, Moscow and Peking.

Once again, Mr. Kennan has served his countrymen well by forcing their attention upon a candid analysis of a central problem of our time.

May 6, 1964

wheat a eastern Europe, why Washington recognizes Moscow but not Peking, why Yugoslavia has been treated differently from her Communist neighbors, and why Washington signs agreements with a Government whose leader, Premier Khrushchev, boasts that he will "bury" the West.

Mr. Rusk's answer was that the United States had not one but three objectives in dealings with Communism:

¶To prevent the Communists from extending their domain and to make it increasingly costly, dangerous and futile for them to try to do so.

¶To work toward agreements or understandings that reduce the danger of war.

¶To encourage evolution within the Communist world toward national independence, peaceful cooperation and open societies.

The Secretary said the Administration needed no lectures on the dangers of Communist aggression, the arrest of which remained its principal concern.

Saigon Support Reaffirmed

He reaffirmed United States support for South Vietnam. He vowed not to abandon the Chinese Nationalist Government on Taiwan. He wondered, without naming names, why "any good American" would help Communist aggression by advocating United States retreat from commitments or cuts in the foreign aid program.

The containment of Communism is not enough, Mr. Rusk declared. He said the United States had to seek agreements that reduced the danger of a major war and had to respond appropriately to "an important new trend" in the evolution of some Communist societies.

"The Communist world is no longer a single flock of sheep following blindly behind one leader," Mr. Rusk said.

The Secretary drew distinctions between Communist countries, most broadly between those of East Europe and those of Asia.

The Soviet Union, he said, has refused to risk its national interests to promote world revolution, as the Chinese Communists wish. To that extent, he added, Soviet realism about the risks of aggression is preferable to Chinese militancy.

The United States has rightly helped to secure Yugoslav independence, Mr. Rusk asserted. It need not apologize to anyone, he added, for helping the Polish people to preserve their identity and aspirations.

Washington is responding to the independent attitudes of Rumania, encouraging the more permissive policies of Hungary,

Rusk Tells Why Policies Toward Red Lands Differ

By MAX FRANKEL
Special to The New York Times

WASHINGTON, Feb. 25 — Secretary of State Dean Rusk said today that the United States treated different Communist countries differently to encourage the evolution of some of them toward national independence and internal freedom.

Some Communist regimes, Mr. Rusk asserted, have become more responsive to their peoples' aspirations, and even the Soviet Union has begun to recognize some of the risks of promoting Communism by force.

For that reason, the Secretary said, Washington distinguishes in its policies between the Soviet Union and Communist China, or between Poland and Cuba. For that reason also, he said, it is consistent to sell wheat to the Soviet Union while enforcing an embargo against Cuba.

Acknowledging that he was perturbed by suggestions here and abroad that the United States' foreign policies had become confused and inconsistent, Mr. Rusk devoted a major address to the Administration's view of the Communist world. He spoke at the annual conference on full citizenship and

world affairs sponsored by the International Union of Electrical, Radio and Machine Workers (A.F.L.-C.I.O.).

The Secretary tried to cope with the criticism of foreign governments that the United States was applying a double standard by pressing for an embargo of Cuba while declaring itself free to trade with other Communist countries.

He addressed himself also to Republican charges that the United States was helping some of its enemies.

Some persons are deliberately sowing confusion for political or other reasons, Mr. Rusk asserted. Others are puzzled, he granted, "on more legitimate grounds."

Serious Questions Raised

Still, he said, the effect is to raise serious questions about why the United States has objected to other nations' trade with Cuba while it has sold

and watching signs of movement in Czechoslovakia and Bulgaria, he said.

The situation is quite different, Mr. Rusk continued, in Asia and in Cuba.

Chinese Attitude Disclosed

He said that contrary to "myth," the United States did not ignore Communist China. In fact, he said, direct exchanges with the Chinese in Warsaw have demonstrated their insistence on the surrender of Taiwan and have justified Washington's grave concern.

When China has a government prepared to renounce force and leave its neighbors alone, Mr. Rusk said, the United States will respond to it also.

Similarly, he added, there will be no change of policy toward the regime of Premier Fidel Castro in Cuba as long as it threatens other nations in the Western Hemisphere. He predicted the overthrow of the Castro Government by the Cuban people.

For these reasons, Mr. Rusk said, other non-Communist nations should take care not to encourage Communist militancy and not to interfere with the American Hemisphere's efforts to curb Cuba by embargo.

Chou Bids U.S. Pull Out

By JACQUES NEVARD
Special to The New York Times

DACCA, Pakistan, Feb. 25—Premier Chou En-lai called today for the removal of "United States forces of aggression and United States military personnel who are carrying out intervention in South Vietnam."

The Chinese Communist leader termed such a withdrawal the first requirement for peace in Southeast Asia. He also demanded that the United States halt its "armed intervention in Laos."

Mr. Chou's comments came in reply to a question at a news conference here on the eve of his departure from Pakistan after a week's visit.

Premier Chou also sharply criticized the United States as the "most vicious exponent at the present time of imperialist policies of war and aggression."

He said that "imperialists" of the United States "want to monopolize the world and have hegemony over the world—they want to meddle into everything —they want to interfere in the internal affairs of every single country."

The attack, delivered on the veranda of President Mohammad Ayub Khan's house in Dacca, was the first open reference to the United States the Chinese Premier had made in seven days in Pakistan.

The Premier, his Foreign Minister, Marshal Chen Yi, and their official party of 46 persons are scheduled to leave by air tomorrow en route to Ceylon, the last scheduled stage of their current tour.

Premier Chow flatly rejected the idea of a plebiscite by the people of Taiwan. Taiwan, he said, "is an internal affair of China and no outside interference is allowed."

During the current visit the Premier dropped China's previous "neutral" position on Pakistan's dispute with India over Kashmir and endorsed Pakistan's demand for a plebiscite among the Kashmiris.

Earlier in the only private interview he granted during his visit here, Premier Chou told a reporter for The Associated Press of Pakistan that China would welcome any peace-making efforts Pakistan might make between the United States and China.

Would 'Welcome' Efforts

"We would welcome the helpful efforts in this direction by our friends who are willing to offer their good offices between China and the United States," he said.

The Premier stressed that the United States would first have to "change its hostile policy toward China." That, he made plain later in his general press conference, depended entirely on the United States' withdrawal from Taiwan and the Taiwan Strait.

In answer to a question about the Chinese border dispute with India, Premier Chou said the dispute "can only be settled in a friendly and reasonable way." He added that even if the dispute "for a time cannot be settled, the day will surely come whne it will be settled in a peaceful way."

February 26, 1964

Peking Is Said to Adjust Economy for Possible War With Americans

By SEYMOUR TOPPING
Special to The New York Times

HONG KONG, Dec. 2—Communist China has made adjustments in its economic planning to take account of the possibility of war with the United States.

Reports reaching Hong Kong indicate that the measures are essentially of a defensive character and motivated by fears that the conflict in Vietnam may spread to mainland China.

Analysts say that Peking has avoided stirring up war hysteria within the country on a scale that would depress morale and affect production.

The precise precautionary steps taken to prepare the economy for a war emergency have not been reported in the principal Chinese Communist newspapers. Instructions have been communicated largely through Government and party organizations.

Plans have been discussed with cadres for the movement of factories from exposed cities to the interior. Defense construction, such as the building of new rail links, roads and an airfield in south China, has been given higher priority.

To furnish supplies to the Communist side in Vietnam, the manufacture and import of some items such as trucks has been increased beyond domestic needs.

Civil defense measures, such as the construction of air-raid trenches and shelters, have been taken in many cities, particularly in such southern centers as Canton and Foochow.

The nonessential population, particularly unemployed youths and elderly persons, has been asked to move from the cities to the countryside. This has been a long-standing policy of the Peking Government for purely economic and social reasons and the Vietnam crisis has provided a useful pretext to accelerate the process.

Analysts of Chinese affairs relate some of Peking's foreign buying programs in non-Communist countries to defense considerations.

Communist China will again import this year about six million metric tons of grain (a metric ton is about 2,200 pounds), and as in recent years part of the imports will go into reserves. In the event of a conflict with the United States, China's principal suppliers, Australia, Canada and Argentina, would cut off shipments.

Sterling Balances Reduced

Earlier this year Peking disposed of much of its sterling balances abroad and made large purchases of gold and platinum. The transactions may have been carried out because of doubts about the stability of sterling, but they also served to withdraw assets to mainland China that otherwise would be frozen in the event of war.

These precautionary moves over a period of months fall short of the economic mobilization that would be effected if the Chinese Communist Leadership felt that war with the United States was imminent. Nevertheless, the adjustments in the economy have been of a scope sufficient to upset national development planning at a critical juncture.

After a postponement of three years, Peking intends to initiate in 1966 its third five-year plan for national economic development. The Chinese Communist leadership is known to attach the highest importance to the successful launching of the plan.

Some of the caution exhibited by Peking in avoiding direct military entanglements in Vietnam and Laos can be attributed to economic considerations.

To promote a popular upsurge in production, the Chinese Communist party has undertaken two main lines of action.

It has expanded the number of "political departments," whose ideological indoctrination and control techniques are based on those utilized by the army, from the industrial and commercial sectors of the economy to some fields of agricul-

February 26, 1964

ture. An effort also has been made to curb abuses that have tended to discourage workers and peasants.

Instructions have been issued to factory managers to cut down on the number of meetings that their employes have been required to attend and to see to it that everyone has a chance to get eight hours' sleep a night.

The main drive in the economy as a whole remains directed at national development rather than preparation for war.

Peking Army Chief Urges A-War Plans

By MAX FRANKEL
Special to The New York Times

WASHINGTON, May 12—Officials here are studying what they regard as one of the most serious and systematic discussions of military doctrine to come from Communist China in many years.

It is a long article by Gen. Lo Jui-ching, Chief of Staff of the Chinese Army, that calls for "realistic" preparation for nuclear war, warns that China will attack non-Communist countries in case of war and expresses confidence that ground armies, not superior weapons, will prove decisive.

The article appears in the current issue of the ideological journal of the Chinese Communist party, Hung Chi (Red Flag), and is titled "Commemorate the Victory over German Fascism! Carry the Struggle against United States Imperialism to the End!"

General Lo's main points, according to analysts here, are the following:

¶The psychological preparation of the Chinese people for small-scale, medium-scale and large-scale war and even nuclear war must be given "first priority."

¶An "active defense is the only correct strategy" for the Communist countries against the United States.

¶After the appearance of atomic weapons, as before, "people and not things are the fundamental factor determining the outcome of war."

¶Although a war will "cause sacrifices, losses and destruction, it will also educate the people."

Complains About Soviet

On this last point, General Lo writes that China is "against the launching of wars by the imperialists, but we should not be afraid of war, still less should we oppose revolutionary wars out of fear of war."

This section reiterates Peking's complaints that former Soviet Premier Nikita S. Khrushchev and his successors are making "perverse" attempts to shrink from conflict and even to cooperate with the United States because of their fear of war and of modern weapons.

General Lo, in discussing psychological preparation of the populace, writes that to think of the possibility of nuclear war and to act according "is more realistic and more likely to win the initiative, so that, come what may, we shall be in a position to cope with the situation successfully."

This was said here to be the first public call for Chinese recognition of the risk of atomic attack. A similar theme was found in secret Chinese military documents acquired by the Administration in 1962.

In public, however, Peking has made only belittling comments about nuclear weapons, dismissing them as "paper tigers." General Lo repeats this theme, too, but his call for realism is thought to mark the start of a serious Chinese effort to "think about the unthinkable."

Space Traded for Time

In advocating "active defense" in contrast to "passive" or "pure" defense, General Lo defines it as a defense that trades space for time and prepares for a counterattack and offensive, comparable to Soviet strategy in World War II.

"Operationally," he writes, "the strategy of active defense should not have the holding or capturing of territory as its main objective. It should be to concentrate superior forces to destroy the enemy's effectiveness."

It also requires "pursuit to destroy the enemy at his starting point, to destroy him in his nest," the general says, citing such strategy as a reason for Stalin's success in establishing Communist regimes in Eastern Europe.

"In any future war against United States imperialist aggression, this is the only strategy for the Socialist countries to adopt," General Lo writes.

"We seriously warn the United States imperialists," he continues, "that they must not expect us to refrain from counterattacking once they have attacked us. Nothing comes so cheap."

In his section stressing "people and not things," General Lo writes that United States boasting of weapons superiority is meant to frighten and intimidate nations so that they can be defeated in a single battle or even without battle.

West, in Shift, Bids U. N. Put China Issue on Agenda

By THOMAS J. HAMILTON
Special to The New York Times.

UNITED NATIONS, N. Y., Sept. 17—The Western powers decided today to meet head on the question of Chinese representation in the United Nations. New Zealand, backed by the United States and Britain, proposed that the issue be listed on the agenda for the General Assembly, which will open its sixteenth session Tuesday.

The issue will be among the ninety-five items scheduled for the agenda, which is the longest in the Assembly's history.

The General Assembly was asked to consider whether the Nationalist Government on Taiwan or the Communist regime on the mainland should occupy China's seat in the United Nations. The Nationalist regime of Generalissimo Chiang Kai-shek now occupies the seat.

Keith J. Holyoke, Prime Minister and Minister of External Affairs of New Zealand, said in a memorandum that New Zealand's aim was to insure that the General Assembly faced up to "the many and complex elements" of the problem.

A spokesman said the United States would vote to include the item on the agenda. He emphasized, however, that the United States "strongly supports" the continued presence of Nationalist China in the United Nations and would maintain its opposition to the seating of Chinese Communists.

Every year since 1950 the United States, with the backing of Britain and other allies, has countered moves to seat the Chinese Communists by proposing that the General Assembly not take up the question. Every year the General Assembly has voted a year's moratorium on the issue.

However, Secretary of State Dean Rusk disclosed last summer that the United States no longer believed it could prevent the General Assembly from placing the issue on its agenda

this session. The United States, Britain and other Western powers have been consulting closely on what strategy to follow.

Soviet Move Expected

The surprise decision by the West resulted from the fear that the Soviet Union or India would raise the question in connection with the report of the Assembly's Credentials Committee. The Western governments think the Soviet Union may pose the issue Tuesday, immediately after the Assembly is called to order.

The Western governments believe that by themselves submitting the issue they have improved the chances for an Assembly decision that Chinese representation is an "important" question. If this happns, a two-thirds majority would be needed to transfer China's seat to the Communists.

Last fall the Assembly decided by simple majority to accept the credentials of a Congolese delegation headed by President Joseph Kasavubu. Backers of Communist China are expected to cite this precedent and to insist that Chinese representation is a matter of credentials.

Committee Study Proposed

Reliable sources have disclosed that the Western Governments, while not proposing a moratorium, will introduce a resolution to establish a special committee to study the problem of Chinese representation. The Assembly would not consider the question until after the committee had submitted its report.

Reliable sources said the idea of a committee originated with Britain, which has voted for a moratorium on the issue each year although she recognized the Peiping Government in 1950. It was understood that Britain informed the United States this year that she could not continue to vote for an outright moratorium and suggested the study group as an alternative.

The China Problem

Pitfalls Are Seen in Washington's Plan To Again Bar Peiping From U. N.

By THOMAS J. HAMILTON

Generalissimo Chiang Kai-shek's decision to acquiese in the admission of Outer Mongolia to the United Nations will almost certainly prolong Nationalist China's stay in the organization for another year, at least.

The Soviet Union had served notice that if the Nationalists vetoed Outer Mongolia's application, this would produce a Soviet veto of Mauritania. In turn this development would have cost the Nationalists the votes of perhaps a dozen French-speaking African states, which, although loyal to France and the West, were so determined to obtain the admission of Mauritania that they had threatened to vote for Communist China if the Chinese Nationalists used the veto.

Some of Communist China's supporters now concede that the Nationalists will not be expelled at the current session of the General Assembly.

The Major Problem

This year, instead of fighting to keep the issue off the agenda of the General Assembly, as they have before, the Western powers presented the item themselves before the Soviet Union got around to doing so. The new tactics reflected the declining strength of Nationalist China, as illustrated by the fact that a year ago less than half the membership voted in favor of postponing the issue.

This was confirmed when Nationalist China lost its seat on the Economic and Social Council despite the informal understanding in 1946 that all the great powers had what amounted to permanent membership.

Le Pelley in The Christian Science Monitor
"Well, well—Outer Mongolia, I believe?"

As a corollary, the United States has decided to back the appointment of a committee to study the Chinese representation issue and report back next year. Meanwhile, the Nationalists would continue to occupy China's seat in the General Assembly, whose decisions fix the membership of all United Nations organs except the Security Council, which makes its own decisions.

The projected study committee would also examine the question of expanding the Security Council and the Economic and Social Council to match the expansion of United Nations membership, which is now more than double what it was when the organization started operations in January, 1946.

Goal of Adjustment

This maneuver would be a

useful device because Britain and other countries that have recognized the Peiping Government are somewhat disenchanted with the results and are no longer willing to support a straight-out postponement. But the successful execution of the new tactics promises to be difficult.

For one thing, the plan to have the study committee examine both the Chinese representation issue and the expansion of the councils is an acceptance of the Soviet claim that the two issues are interconnected. For more than two years the delegates of the United States and other Western countries have insisted that there is absolutely no connection.

However, once the Western powers agree that there is such a relationship they may find the argument turned against

375

"I had to let him in to keep his uncle out."

Yardley in The Baltimore Sun

obvious in view of the fact that both North Korea and North Vietnam have sided with Peiping in the dispute over Albania.

Lesser of Evils

If the United States is to make any effort for a settlement with either the Russians or the Chinese Communists, the Russians are a better bet. Mr. Khrushchev, despite his shoe-pounding, certainly does not show the hatred for the United States that is apparent in declarations from Peiping. A "two Chinas" solution of the representation problem in the United Nations might well be one of the subjects discussed between Moscow and Washington if the Berlin situation should calm down to the point where such an effort at mutual understanding became possible.

October 29, 1961

General Assembly, for the firs time since the Communists gained control of the Chinese mainland in 1949, embarked upon a full-scale debate on who should represent China in the United Nations.

Until this year the United States had countered Soviet resolutions to seat the Communists with a proposal that the issue be postponed for a year.

Issue Faced by West

Last September, however, the Western powers decided to meet the question head on. New Zealand requested the inclusion of the issue on the Assembly agenda.

Valerian A. Zorin of the Soviet Union and the entire Soviet bloc walked out of the Assembly hall when Dr. Tingfu F. Tsiang, the chief representative of Nationalist China, took the floor to denounce the Chinese Communists as "even more bellicose than their Russian comrades, if that is possible."

Mr. Stevenson told the General Assembly that it was not a question of "bringing Communist China into the United Nations" but of doing the opposite.

"We must instead," he said "find a way to bring the United Nations — its law and spirit — back into the whole territory of China."

Invasion of Korea Cited

The United States representative attacked Communist China for having invaded Korea and for having sponsored the "communizing" of North Vietnam.

He also denounced Peiping for "war-like threats" against Taiwan, "armed conquest" in Tibet, and "pressing forward into new territory all along their southern borders. The last was a reference to Chinese occupation of Indian and Pakistani frontier areas.

Mr. Stevenson termed "wishful thoughts" the theory that Peiping's admission to the United Nations could bring "this unbridled power" under the influence of the community of nations.

Mr. Stevenson, emphasizing that "the Peiping authorities have shown nothing but contempt for the United Nations," remarked "they apparently don't even get along with the Soviet Union."

He quoted a statement by Chou En-lai, Premier of Communist China, that "the United Nations must expel the Chiang

---

them. The African and Asian members are extremely anxious to enlarge the Council this year, and may use the connection between the two issues as an additional reason for demanding a settlement of the Chinese representation question at this session.

As a further complication, the United States may have difficulty making good its claim that, while only a simple majority in the General Assembly is needed for the study committee, a two-thirds majority is required to expel the Nationalists and hand over China's seat to the Peiping Government.

If a decision can be postponed for a year, Washington will have time to re-study the problem of Chinese representation in the light of the bitter struggle which has come into the open, as the result of the debates in the twenty-second Soviet Communist party congress, between Mr. Khrushchev and Mao Tse tung, for leadership of the Communist world.

In 1950, when the Soviet Union walked out of the Security Council, it did so on the pretext that the proceedings were illegal in the absence of Communist China. The Soviet Union has continued to insist through the years upon the ad-

mission of the Peiping Government and of course it will do so again despite the party dispute with Peiping.

However, there are good grounds for the belief that the Russians have never wanted the Peiping Government in the United Nations, and still do not wish it to be admitted, because Chinese Communists would then have their own contacts with the West independent of Moscow. What is worse, a Chinese Communist delegation might then emerge as the principal spokesman for the Communist members of the United Nations.

Link to the Bomb

This belief has been strengthened by Moscow's failure in recent years to insist upon the participation of the Chinese Communists in either disarmament or nuclear test negotiations. Indeed it is clear that the principal reason for the Soviet Union's willingness to discuss halting nuclear tests was the hope that a prohibition of tests would deny the hydrogen bomb to Communist China as well as to West Germany and Japan.

The ideological breach between Moscow and Peiping seems to offer the West an opportunity to exploit these difficulties. It is all the more

STEVENSON TELLS U.N. NOT TO GRANT SEAT TO RED CHINA

Says Admission of Peiping Would Give Approval for Attack on Nationalists

SOVIET BLOC WALKS OUT

Zorin Leads Protest Against Tsiang's Talk as Debate on Representation Opens

By THOMAS J. HAMILTON
Special to The New York Times.

UNITED NATIONS, N. Y. Dec. 1 — Adlai E. Stevenson denounced Communist China today and said that its admission to the United Nations would give the organization's "seal of approval" to an attack on Taiwan by the Peiping Government.

Mr. Stevenson spoke as the

Kai-shek clique and restore China's legitimate rights, otherwise it would be impossible for China to have anything to do with the United Nations."

The United States representative said that it was "absurd and unthinkable" to expel Nationalist China. The reference to "legitimate rights," he said, could have only one meaning:

"That the United Nations should acquiesce in Communist China's design to conquer Taiwan and the 11,000,000 people who live there, and thereby to contribute to overthrow and abolish the independent Government of the Republic of China."

Apart from the question of United Nations acquiescence in an attack on Taiwan, Mr. Stevenson advanced the following arguments against seating Chinese Communist representatives:

¶Once admitted, a Peiping representative could not be expelled and "would stay—for better or for worse."

¶Peiping would exert "a most disruptive and demoralizing influence on the organization at this most critical moment in its history."

¶The admission of Peiping "could seriously shake public confidence in the United Nations" and, he said, "I can assure you it would do so among the people of the United States."

Debate Resumes Monday

The debate, which will be resumed Monday, is expected to continue for ten days or more.

Mr. Zorin insisted that the United Nations "cannot ignore a great state the population of which accounts for one-fourth of mankind."

Mr. Zorin attacked the nationalist Government as "a rotten political corpse" and "a miserable clique of apostates that was cast away by the Chinese people and that is alive by sops from the master's table of the power that guards it from the wrath of the Chinese people."

The Soviet representative charged that the United States "seized" Taiwan in 1950 and "turned it into a springboard for aggression against the People's Republic of China."

The Peiping Government alone has the right to decide whether it would use peaceful means or armed force for "the liquidation of the Chiang Kai-shek clique," he said.

Nationalist Scores Soviet

Dr. Tsiang attacked both the Soviet Union and the Peiping Government. He said it was clear "that the Communist regime on the mainland of China is the fruit of Soviet military intervention in my country."

He said that while "crocodile tears" had been shed over the "alleged lack of representation" of the Chinese people in the United Nations, delegates should shed tears of compassion "over the misery and the suffering of the 600,000,000 Chinese men and women on the mainland during the last twelve years."

Benoit Bindzi of Cameroon took the floor to reply to a statement by Mr. Stevenson that six young men from Cameroon were given guerrilla training in Communist China last summer.

Mr. Bindzi said that he had asked for information about this statement but regretted that the same solicitude had not been shown to Cameroon when it was being "dismembered and given to a neighboring country." This apparently was an allusion to the fact that the northern sector of the British Cameroons, in accordance with a United Nations-supervised plebiscite, was merged with Nigeria instead of with Cameroon.

Zorin Retorts to U. S.

Mr. Bindzi's statement gave an occasion to Mr. Zorin, who took the floor a second time to answer Mr. Stevenson, to charge that the American had failed in his attempt to "frighten small countries" into opposing the seating of Peiping.

Mr. Zorin ridiculed the idea that Communist China should be kept out of the United Nations because of "six miserable paratroopers." He declared that the Soviet Union, being "reasonable," had not proposed the expulsion of the United States for "organizing" the landings in Cuba last April because, he said Moscow realized that all of "the greatest powers" should be members of the organization.

The first round in the fight over Chinese representation will come when the General Assembly takes up the question whether a simple majority or a two-thirds vote would be necessary to seat Peiping.

The United States, Japan, Australia, Colombia and Italy introduced a draft resolution declaring that "any proposal to change the representation of China is an important question." Mr. Stevenson emphasized this point in his speech.

West Sees Victory

Under the charter, a two-thirds majority is required for "important" questions and a simple majority for others. The Assembly takes this decision by a simple majority. Western delegates are confident of victory.

Mr. Zorin did not mention this point. However, he issued a warning against any attempt to "confuse the issue" by proposing "an additional study" of the question. This was a reference to the original intention of the United States and other Western delegates to ask the Assembly to set up a committee to study the Chinese representation question and to report back next year.

A spokesman said, however, that the United States would not introduce such a proposal. It appears to have been dropped for lack of support.

December 2, 1961

RED CHINA DENIED SEAT IN U.N., 48-37; VICTORY FOR U. S.

Margin, Larger Than Last Year's, Is a Surprise— 19 Nations Abstain

By RICHARD EDER
Special to The New York Times.

UNITED NATIONS, N. Y., Dec. 15—The General Assembly rejected today a proposal to seat Communist China in the United Nations. The vote was 48 against the proposal and 37 for it. Nineteen nations abstained.

The failure to obtain a majority for admitting the Peiping Government made irrelevant a United States-backed resolution approved earlier. Introduced to meet the possibility of a slim voting edge for admission, it defined the question as an important one needing a two-thirds majority for passage.

The margin against admitting the Peiping Government, contrary to general expectation here, was slightly larger than it was last year. It amounted to a somewhat firmer United States victory — at least on a short-term basis — than the American delegation had expected.

History of Voting

While today's vote was on a proposal to seat Red China, voting in the previous ten years was on the issue of putting off consideration of Communist China's membership.

Following is a record of the voting:

	For.	Against.	Pct.	Abstain.
1951	37	11	77	4
1952	42	7	85	11
1953	44	10	81	2
1954	43	11	79	6
1955	42	12	77	6
1956	47	24	66	8
1957	47	27	63	7
1958	44	28	61	9
1959	44	29	60	4
1960	42	34	56	22

Today's vote defeated a Soviet-sponsored resolution calling for the immediate removal of "the representatives of the Chiang Kai-shek clique" of Nationalist China and the seating of the Chinese Communist Government.

Precedent Expected

Also defeated, by a vote of 45 to 30, with 29 abstentions, was an amendment offered by

Ceylon, Cambodia and Indonesia, which would have softened the wording of the Soviet resolution, although retaining its substance.

It was expected that the inclusion of the amendment would have picked up additional votes for the Soviet draft, though indications are that these would not have given it a majority.

A few minutes before the Soviet draft was defeated, the United States assured itself of a secondary line of defense against the possibility that the draft would win when a five-power resolution was approved, making passage of any substantive measure on China subject to a two-thirds majority. The vote was 61 to 34, with seven abstentions.

The approval is expected to give the United States a precedent to fall back on at the next General Assembly session, when the issue will come up again. The drift of sentiment here makes it likely that the United States may not again be able to muster a majority vote against the seating of Communist China.

This time, in the view of observers here, only vigorous campaigning and considerable pressure won for the United States. The Latin-American bloc, with the exception of Cuba, held firm, for example. Earlier Brazil and one or two others had indicated that they were wavering in their support of the American position.

The United States was also able to obtain abstentions or favorable votes from the so-called Brazzaville group—a group of African nations retaining close ties with France—in exchange for helping to secure the entrance of Mauritania into the United Nations in October.

By putting pressure on Nationalist China not to veto the candidacy of Outer Mongolia in the Security Council, the United States removed the possibility that the Soviet Union would veto Mauritania.

After today's vote, which followed two weeks of debate during which representatives of more than fifty nations spoke, the Soviet delegate, Valerian A. Zorin, said he was sure many nations that had been induced to oppose Communist China this year would change their minds at the next session.

Adlai E. Stevenson, the United States delegate, said that he was "gratified" by the results.

Britain Backs Admission

In addition to the Latin-American bloc, countries that opposed the Soviet resolution included most European nations, members of the Southeast Asia Treaty Organization, a number of African and Arab states, and the older members of the British Commonwealth.

Britain, however, voted for admission. So did Denmark, Norway and Sweden. All four recognize the Peiping Government. Except for the Brazzaville group, most of the new African nations supported the resolution, although Nigeria and Tunisia abstained.

Joseph B. Godber, the British delegate, said that his nation's vote did not imply that Britain wanted the Taiwan Government to be unseated. He also said that no General Assembly action that would admit Communist China would be binding on the membership of the Security Council.

First Time Since 1950

This is the first year since 1950 that the question of seating Communist China has reached the Assembly agenda. In 1950, when the Communist request for seating came, the Assembly set up a committee to study the matter, but it failed to come to any agreement. In the same year, the Security Council rejected a Soviet proposal to unseat Nationalist China.

Since then, the United States has fought the issue out in the General (Steering) Committee, where each year it has succeeded, by diminishing margins, in having discussion postponed and the question kept off the agenda.

Since the Assembly and the Council are equal, and each passes on the credentials of its own members, it would theoretically be possible to have one of the China Governments seated in one body and the other in the second body.

Several nations that voted against the Soviet resolution today had made it clear during the debate that they were not opposed to the entry of Communist China. What they could not accept, they stressed, was the unseating of the Taiwan Government.

December 16, 1961

U. N. Again Bars Peking; Assembly Vote Is 56 to 42

UNITED NATIONS, N. Y. Oct. 30—The General Assembly voted today to exclude Communist China from the United Nations for at least another year.

A Soviet draft resolution to seat Communist China in place of Nationalist China was rejected by a vote of 56 to 42. Twelve nations abstained. The vote represented a slight increase over last year in the margin of victory for the opponents of the plan to seat the Chinese Communists.

The United States, which has led the annual fight to keep the Peking Government out of the world organization, expressed "gratification" at the vote.

The official vote rejecting a similar Soviet proposal last year was 48 to 36 with 20 abstentions. But Norway, which was recorded as abstaining, announced later she wanted to be recorded in favor of the Soviet proposal.

In the most significant switch, eight African nations that abstained last year voted today against seating Communist China. Most of these votes came from the French-speaking countries.

Speaking for this group, Michel Gallin-Douathe of the Central African Republic explained that the members were opposed to expelling Nationalist China. But he implied that Communist China could be admitted as a new member in the future.

It was no longer possible to ignore Communist China, the African spokesman said, although members of his group had doubts about the "peaceful purposes" of the Peking Government. This was considered an allusion to the border fighting between India and Communist China.

The six countries admitted to the United Nations since last year's vote were divided on the plan to admit Communist China. Algeria, Burundi and Uganda voted for the seating of Peking. Jamaica and Rwanda voted against the resolution. The sixth, Trinidad and Tobago, abstained.

Laos and Tanganyika, which voted against the Soviet proposal last year, voted for it this year. Yemen switched its vote from yes to no.

Most members, however, adhered to their previous positions. Support for the proposal to seat Communist China continued to come from the Soviet bloc, Cuba, a number of nonaligned countries and few Western powers.

Britain and the Scandinavian countries, which recognize the Peking Government, voted for the Soviet draft resolution.

Joseph B. Godber of Britain explained that his Government profoundly deplored Communist China's "armed incursion" across India's northern frontiers, but he said this did not alter the British belief that Peking constituted the Government of China.

Border Fighting Is Issue

Speaking for the Soviet Union after today's vote, Valerian A. Zorin noted that a number of delegates had referred to what he termed "recent events on the Indian frontier" as a reason for excluding the Peking Government. He said Moscow was also concerned about the fighting between India and Communist China.

But Mr. Zorin insisted that the border conflict was an extraneous issue "dragged in here to prevent the seating of Peking. He maintained that the Chinese Communists had made "constructive proposals" designed to end the dispute.

The border conflict is against the interests of both countries, he added, and common sense requires a peaceful settlement as soon as possible.

The Soviet spokesman asserted that the United States was leading those who "closed their eyes to international reality" by rejecting United Nations membership for Communist China.

Expressing regret over the Assembly's decision, Mr. Zorin observed that the number of "positive votes" had increased from year to year.

The first speaker today in the Assembly was Liu Chien of Nationalist China. He presented a scating denunciation of both Peking and Moscow.

"World peace is now threatened by two international bullies," he asserted. "One is responsible for the grave situation in the Caribbean and the other for the situation on the Indian border."

The first of these, he went on, has the effrontery to demand that the second be seated in the United Nations.

Referring to V. K. Krishna Menon, the Indian Defense Minister, who was a leading advocate here in past years of seating the Peking Government, the Nationalist spokesman remarked:

"This year Mr. Krishna Menon is not with us. He is now in India directing the Indian Army in a war with the same Chinese Communists on whose 'peace-loving' qualities he had over the years lavished so much gratuitous praise."

India Backs Admission

India voted for Communist China's admission, but showed bitterness during the earlier debate by assailing Peking's flagrant, massive and premeditated aggression."

Just before the balloting, Tunisia suggested that the two paragraphs of the Soviet resolution be voted on separately. One paragraph called for admitting Communist China and the other for expelling Nationalist China.

The Soviet Union objected to this suggestion, however, and Tunisia withdrew it. The Soviet spokesman rejected the possibility of seating "two Chinas" in the United Nations.

Roll-Call Vote in U. N. On Seat for Red China

Special to The New York Times

UNITED NATIONS, N. Y., Oct. 30—Following is the roll-call vote by which the General Assembly rejected today a Soviet resolution to seat Communist China in the United Nations:

In Favor—42

Afghanistan	Laos
Albania	Mali
Algeria	Mongolia
Britain	Morocco
Bulgaria	Nepal
Burma	Norway
Burundi	Pakistan
Byelorussia	Poland
Cambodia	Rumania
Ceylon	Sierra Leone
Cuba	Somalia
Czechoslovakia	Soviet Union
Denmark	Sudan
Ethiopia	Sweden
Finland	Syria
Ghana	Tanganyika
Guinea	Tunisia
Hungary	Uganda
India	Ukraine
Indonesia	United Arab Republic
Iraq	Yugoslavia

Against—56

Argentina	Ivory Coast
Australia	Jamaica
Belgium	Japan
Bolivia	Jordan
Brazil	Liberia
Cameroon	Libya
Canada	Luxembourg
Central African Rep.	Madagascar
Chad	Mauritania
Chile	Mexico
China	New Zealand
Colombia	Nicaragua
Congo (Brazzaville)	Niger
Congo (Leopoldville)	Panama
Costa Rica	Paraguay
Dahomey	Peru
Dominican Republic	Philippines
Ecuador	Rwanda
El Salvador	Senegal
France	South Africa
Gabon	Spain
Greece	Thailand
Guatemala	Turkey
Haiti	United States
Honduras	Upper Volta
Iran	Uruguay
Ireland	Venezuela
Italy	Yemen

Abstentions—12

Austria	Netherlands
Cyprus	Nigeria
Iceland	Portugal
Israel	Saudi Arabia
Lebanon	Togo
Malaya	Trinidad and Tobago

October 31, 1962

De Gaulle Meeting With Johnson Still Subject of a Study

By DREW MIDDLETON
Special to The New York Times

PARIS, Jan. 9—A meeting between President Johnson and President de Gaulle in March is still being discussed through diplomatic channels, qualified sources said tonight.

Diplomatic sources indicated that General de Gaulle might find it possible after all to fly to Washington after his visits to the French Caribbean possions of Martinique and Guadelupe subsequent to his official visit to Mexico.

Other sources are sure that Mr. Johnson's disinclination to go to the Antilles to meet General de Gaulle has ended all prospect of a meeting in 1964.

The impression is growing among the diplomats that French moves toward diplomatic recognition of Communist China demand discussion between the two leaders.

French sources believe that recognition of Peking is essential to any settlement that will insure independence and neutrality in Southeast Asia. This, the sources said, is a major but not a compulsive factor in the Government's steady progress toward recognition of the Chinese Communist Government.

Another factor is France's feeling that in the current quarrel between the Soviet Union and China, it would be prudent and perhaps advantageous to open a Chinese window to the West. To do this France is apparently prepared to accept conditions of diplomatic recognition that, as in the case of Britain, will confine the missions in Peking and Paris to a chargé d'affaires and a small group of specialists.

The diplomats take it for granted that, should recognition be established, France would support Communist China's admission to the United Nations and that the French-speaking nations of Africa would follow suit.

The French are aware of United States disapproval of recognition. However, they insist that there has been no diplomatic intervention by Washington to dissuade them.

Decisions on whether to meet President Johnson in Washington, on diplomatic recognition of China and on the extent of France's next moves in the Indochinese Peninsula are being made by the general alone.

The campaign to reassert France's old position in Southeast Asia has been delayed to some extent by the failure thus far of the Government of South Vietnam to accept a new French Ambassador.

France has nominated Roger Robert du Gardier and has waited three weeks for his acceptance. Spokesmen said that a wait of a month was normal. They did not connect the delay with the failure of France to recognize the Government in Saigon right after the military Coup d'etat last November. Foreign diplomats do.

The French are open to suggestions from Laos and Vietnam about discussions of future economic aid. In the Indochinese Peninsula as in China and the Soviet Union, the French Government appears eager for new markets that will bolster political as well as economic interests.

DE GAULLE SETS UP TIE TO RED CHINA; KEEPS TAIPEI LINK

Act Is First Western Break From U.S. Aim of Isolating Peking in 14 Years

NATIONALISTS PROTEST

Call Move 'Most Unfriendly' but Do Not End Relations —Capital Voices Regret

By DREW MIDDLETON
Special to The New York Times

PARIS, Jan. 27—General de Gaulle's Government broke today with the United States policy of isolating Communist China and announced the establishment of diplomatic relations with Peking.

[The United States expressed regret over the action and said it was particularly unfortunate that it came at a time when the Chinese Communists were "promoting aggression and subversion." Observers in Hong Kong saw the recognition as a major triumph for Peking. The Chinese Nationalists assailed the Paris move as a "most unfriendly act."]

France's recognition of the Communist regime was the first by any major power since the Korean war began nearly 14 years ago. The step was hailed by Gaullists as an example of France's independence and as a move toward closer relations with another great independent power.

'Two Chinas' Policy

Government circles saw the recognition as a vital step in pursuit of President de Gaulle's policy of negotiating a settlement to secure the independence and unity of South Vietnam and other states of the Indo-Chinese peninsula.

For the moment the President has established a "two Chinas" policy. Kao Shih-ming, the Chinese Nationalist chargé d'affaires, after vehemently protesting the recognition at the French Foreign Ministry, made it known that there would be no immediate break in diplomatic relations between Taipei and Paris.

If this situation remains the same, France will become the only major Western power with full diplomatic representation in the Chinese Communist and Nationalist capitals.

Status of Britain

Britain, which granted recognition in January, 1950, has had a mission in Peking since before the Korean war, but her representation in Taiwan is limited to a consul and his small staff quartered outside Taipei.

The recognition was reported in a communiqué issued here and in Peking. It said:

"The Government of the French Republic and the Government of the People's Republic of China have decided, by mutual accord, to establish diplomatic relations.

"They have agreed, in this connection, to designate their ambassadors within three months."

A French official asserted that in negotiating the terms of recognition France made no commitment on China's representation in the United Nations.

This may have induced the Chinese Nationalists to continue relations with France, Western diplomats believed. They predicted that it would be difficult for France, after having recognized the Communist regime, to withhold support for Peking's claim to United Nations membership.

There have been a number of reports in diplomatic circles that France's former colonies in Africa, now independent states, would follow her example and recognize Peking. Of thirteen states, including Malagasy, only two, Senegal and Mali, now recognize the Communist Government.

French officials declared that the African Governments were "entirely free" in the matter and that France had not tried to influence them.

Diplomats believe that both Portugal and Mexico, which General de Gaulle will visit in March, are "on the road to Peking" and recognition.

France will select a chargé d'affaires to establish an embassy in Peking. The old French embassy has been requisitioned by the Chinese.

Dejean May Be Envoy

The newest candidate for the ambassadorship is Maurice Dejean, who has just left the embassy in Moscow. He has had Far Eastern experience.

One view of the United States protests on the recognition was that, since Washington was seeking a rapprochement with

379

the Soviet Union, criticism of the French action, which does not involve approval, was out of order.

The protest by Taipei was most vehement. Its embassy issued a statement denouncing "any settlement on the thesis of 'two Chinas'" and declaring that Taipei would not modify its policy of seeking to free mainland China from "the Communist yoke."

Thomas Cardinal Tien of Taiwan has sent a message to General de Gaulle asking him to reconsider his decision.

President Diosdado Macapagal of the Philippines has told the French President in a message that recognition would seriously weaken "the will to resist of the free nations of Asia which face a direct and proximate threat from neighboring Communist China."

French Foes Back Move

The recognition has received powerful support from French politicians, including many non-Gaullists. But a note of concern was sounded by some who endorsed the move. They feared that it would weaken ties with the United States and France's other allies in the North Atlantic alliance.

Senator Edgar Faure, who pioneered the recognition on a trip to China last year, declared that the French decision raised the principle of China's "reintegration in the international community."

Without this, Senator Faure said, none of the great questions of the time, peaceful coexistence or promotion of disarmament, could be resolved.

René Pleven, a former Premier, one of the critics of recoggnition, noted that the action had been advanced in the name of realism. Will the same criterion, he asked, be applied tomorrow for recognition of the Communist East German regime?

Maurice Faure, president of the radical party, found nothing to deplore in recognition. But he said he regretted that it might cause new dissension among the Atlantic allies and France's European partners.

Another former Premier, Paul Reynaud, warned that recognition would worsen the United States position in South Vietnam.

Waldeck Rochet, assistant secretary general of the French Communist party, hailed the establishment of relations.

January 28, 1964

U.N. BARS PEKING, BUT U.S. VICTORY IS CALLED HOLLOW

Assembly Rules That Action Needs Two-Thirds Vote— Final Tally Is 47-47

GOLDBERG SEES A GAIN

But Many Delegates Resent Pressure and Foresee Reversal Next Year

By DREW MIDDLETON
Special to The New York Times

UNITED NATIONS, N. Y., Nov. 17—Communist China was barred again today from admission to the United Nations. Diplomats suggested that the rejection amounted to a hollow victory for the United States, which had led the opposition to Peking's entry.

The vote was 47 to 47, with 20 abstentions and three delegations not voting, on a resolution calling for the seating of the Chinese Communists and the ouster of the Nationalists.

A prior resolution classified the admission of Peking as a "matter of importance" requiring a two-thirds vote for passage. This resolution was adopted 56 to 49, with 11 abstentions and one delegation not voting.

Goldberg Voices Pleasure

Arthur J. Goldberg, the chief United States representative, asserted that the vote had demonstrated "that it is not the United States alone" that kept Communist China out of the United Nations" but "a substantial vote of the membership."

The resolution on membership, he noted, failed to win even a simple majority.

Among diplomats, who compared the 1961 and 1963 balloting with today's, the prevailing opinion was that Communist China would be admitted next year.

A number of delegation heads, moreover, said they believed the cost to the United States of the victory would outweigh any advantage gained in barring the Communists for another year.

They suggested that American intransigence on admission had offended the nonaligned nations, the majority of which backed Peking's entry, and that the United States had given the impression of being more interested in keeping Peking out than in seeking a negotiated settlement of the war in Vietnam.

Tally Stirs Applause

The head of an Eastern European delegation declared gleefully: "The Americans are losing their grip. This is the last time they will boss the General Assembly."

There was a burst of applause from Peking's backers when the final score on the membership was shown on the big new indicator in the General Assembly hall. The applause was due, a delegate said, as much to the indications of waning United States authority in the voting pattern as to the narrowness of the outcome.

"Had the Americans not been able to push through the 'two-thirds rule,'" he said bitterly, "we would have won."

The issue of Peking's entry is dead in the General Assembly until at least next Autumn. But the Communists' sponsors intend to press for the inclusion of Peking in a world disarmament conference on the ground that the country possesses nuclear arms and impressive conventional forces.

Today's vote reflected significant changes since 1963, when Communist China's membership was last voted upon. In that year, admission was rejected by 57 to 41, with 12 abstentions, in a membership of 111 countries, compared with the present 117.

Three nations — France, the Central African republic and the former French Congo — have since switched from opposition to support. Eight others that voted then against Peking's admission, abstained today. They were Cameroon, Chile, Cyprus, Iran, Jamaica, Libya, Rwanda and Senegal.

Nigeria, which abstained in 1963, voted today in favor of admission, while Laos, which supported entry two years ago, did not vote this time.

The margin of victory for the United States and Peking's other opponents on the "important matter" resolution was appreciably smaller than in 1961, when the resolution was first adopted. The resolution was approved then by 61 votes to 34

380

with 7 abstentions, compared with today's result of 56 to 49 and 11 abstentions. The membership in 1961 was 104.

Six delegations that voted for the "important matter" resolution today abstained from the vote on membership. They were Chile, Iceland, Lebanon, Libya, the Netherlands and Trinidad and Tobago.

Vietnam Swayed Debate

From the start of the eight-day debate on seating Communist China, supporters of the Communists were influenced powerfully by a conviction that admission might enable the United Nations to negotiate a settlement of the war in Vietnam and bring stability to Southeast Asia.

"The United States kept the People's Republic out because it doesn't want a settlement," a non-Communist Asian diplomat said. "We do not care what Mr. Goldberg thinks the Chinese have said and done; we want peace, and we can make it only with their cooperation here."

Other backers of Peking's entry considered the United States attitude "reactionary and old fashioned."

The Administration, one backer said, "is still living in the fifties, when the United States could afford to override the wishes of a few African and Asian states. We nonaligned states are many now, and we will be heard again next year."

This year Peking's sponsors insisted that the seating of Communists must be accompanied by the expulsion of the Chinese Nationalists. This demand was regarded as a powerful argument for the defeat of the resolution. Another was the continued uncertainty about Peking's attitude toward admission. A diplomat from a country that had switched from opposition to support admitted after the voting that he still did not know whether the Communist Government desired admission.

Just before the voting, Ceylon and Mauditania tried to soften the language of the membership resolution. Cambodia, sponsor of the original resolution, asked the two delegations to withdraw their amendment.

An amended resolution, instead of calling for the expulsion of Nationalist China, would have said only that the General Assembly had decided that "the representatives of the People's Republic of China be seated in the United Nations and all its organs."

Members of the sponsoring delegations reporte dthat Peking had insisted on a resolution that specifically called for the Nationalists' expulsion.

Besides Cambodia, the sponsors of the membership resolution were Albania, Algeria, the former French Congo, Cuba, Ghana, Guinea, Mali, Pakistan, Rumania, Somalia and Syria.

The resolution imposing the requirement for a two-thirds majority was put forward by the United States, Australia, Brazil, Colombia, Gabon, Italy, Japan, Madagascar, Nicaragua, the Philippines and Thailand.

RED CHINA TO CUT ITS FORCE IN TIBET

Special to The New York Times.

HONG KONG, June 17—A tentative decision to withdraw an undisclosed number of Chinese Communist "cadres" from Tibet was announced by the Peiping radio today.

The move was seen here as a sign of a tactical retreat by the Chinese Reds from a remote and uneasy area they felt was difficult to control.

There was no official confirmation of a reported withdrawal of Chinese troops from Tibet, though earlier reports from New Delhi, India, suggested that a gradual withdrawal of troops might have begun.

The Chinese Communists moved into Tibet following a brief military action in 1950. They said then they planned to "liberate" Tibet, maintaining that the region was Chinese despite its previous independence, except for two brief periods of Chinese rule.

After the occupation, the Communists were reported to have sent 100,000 troops to Tibet and to have built roads and airports in the country.

No Sign of Eased Control

There was no sign of a relaxation of Chinese Communist control over Tibet. It was officially disclosed this week that a joint Chinese-Soviet surveying team was "stepping up" an air survey for a projected Tsinghai-Tibet railroad.

The decision to set up a "retrenchment committee" for a gradual reduction of overstaffed Chinese organizations in Tibet was believed to have come as a local stop-gap measure to soothe public sentiment there, as well as to ease a food shortage in that mountainous country.

Fragmentary reports of starvation in Tibet have reached here from time to time.

The food shortage, public dislike if not hatred for the Chinese, and Indian suspicion of the Communists' aims in Tibet were thought to be contributing factors to a Chinese tactical retreat from Tibet.

Such a tactical retreat was virtually decided upon last April, when Chang Kuo-hua, second vice chairman of the Preparatory Committee for the Autonomous Region of Tibet, announced at Lhasa that "democratic reform" for Tibet would not be carried out during Red China's second Five-Year Plan, which is scheduled to begin next year.

Observers here were not convinced that an announced withdrawal of Chinese cadres, military or otherwise, would help reduce a suspicion of Chinese Communist motives in Tibet harbored by Prime Minister Jawaharlal Nehru of India.

June 18, 1957

INDIANS CAUTION CHINA ON BORDER

New Delhi, Puzzled by Reds' Misleading Maps, Asserts Frontier Is Firmly Fixed

Special to The New York Times.

NEW DELHI, India, Dec. 2—India has firmly and repeatedly made known to Communist China that her international border is well known and that it will not be subject to negotiations.

At the same time, New Delhi has indicated that it will always be willing to settle any minor border adjustments through negotiations.

India's attitude toward the long-standing border differences with China was detailed today by authoritative sources.

There are two aspects to the frontier question. One involves the territory disputed between the two countries. The second is the persistent distribution by Peiping of maps showing large sections of Indian territory in the northeast and northwest as belonging to China.

On the first point, there has never been any major dispute between the two countries, which have 2,000 miles of common border. The only area claimed by both sides is at Bara Hoti, a two-square-mile strip of land 16,000 feet high in the Garhwal district of the state of Uttar Pradesh.

Neutralization Asked by China

Some Chinese soldiers crossed into the area in the winter of 1955 but withdrew subsequently. Communist China had wanted this area to be "neutralized," but India insisted that the territory was hers and in effect rejected the idea of neutralization.

Except for this incident, no part of India's territory has been disputed as such.

What has been causing concern to Prime Minister Jawaharlal Nehru and officials here, however, is the regularity with which China has been distributing maps showing large stretches of Indian territory as parts of China.

These maps show a large section of the North East Frontier Agency as Chinese territory. The area covered by this agency is about 30,000 square miles and lies north of the Brahmaputra River on the Tibetan border.

Before independence, this area was administered by the state of Assam. Subsequently the Ministry of External Affairs in New Delhi took over direct administration of the border area and constituted the

North East Frontier Agency in 1950, the year the Communist Chinese overran Tibet.

The Chinese maps also indicate Chinese jurisdiction in the eastern part of Ladakh, the Buddhist province of Indian-controlled Jammu and Kashmir.

While Indian officials are reluctant to question the motives of the Chinese regime, they appear to be puzzled as to why Peiping should continue to distribute these maps and assert that it has had no time to revise

them.

Mr. Nehru told Parliament some time ago that Communist China "has changed many things done by the Kuomintang [Nationalist] Government and I do not see any reason why they cannot change the map."

Peiping recently has assured New Delhi that it proposes to undertake surveys of China's border areas and will redraw the boundary lines in consultation with neighboring countries.

June 18, 1957

The New York Times

Dec. 6, 1958

AREAS OF CONTENTION: Chinese maps show eastern Ladakh (1) and part of the North East Frontier Agency (3) of India as Chinese territory. A 2-square-mile border area (2) of Uttar Pradesh is in fact disputed territory.

GUERRILLAS FIGHT RED RULE IN TIBET

Nomadic Khambas Reported Partly Successful Against Chinese Communists

By ELIE ABEL
Special to The New York Times.

NEW DELHI, India, Dec. 13—Tough Khamba guerrillas are reported to have won local successes in their stubborn struggle against the Chinese Communist rulers of Tibet.

The Khambas are a nomadic people of acknowledged bravery. The Chinese invasion eight years ago meant a threat to their old way of life. Never great respecters of authority, the Khambas had long resisted domination by the Tibetan Government at Lhasa.

Last June, according to reports reaching the Indian Government, they opened a new campaign of sabotage and

ambush in eastern Tibet. Without outside help, the Khambas set up their own local authorities in some parts of the interior.

The guerrillas, estimated at 30,000 to 40,000 men, also made it virtually impossible for the Chinese to use the new military road linking Lhasa with China proper through Chamdo.

Costly Highway

The road, built at great expense by Chinese Communist troops and Tibetan labor, follows the valley of the Brahmaputra River over some of the world's roughest terrain. At strategic points, where the road winds through Himalayan passes and gorges, Khambas have repeatedly blown bridges, started landslides and sniped at work parties.

All this is affirmed by Indian authorities, although there is no support here for reports of a popular uprising in Tibet comparable to the 1956 revolt in Hungary. Such reports are considered in New Delhi to be products of wishful thinking by Chinese Nationalists.

Of the Tibetan peoples, the Khambas have shown the most open and violent hostility to the Communist Army, Indian officials say. About three years ago tens of thousands of Khambas were displaced from traditional grazing lands by Chinese.

'Warlike Intent'

Many Khambas moved into Lhasa to seek the protection of the Dalai Lama, spiritual and temporal ruler of Tibet. Last summer they moved out "with obvious warlike intent," a New Delhi official said.

The Khambas are believed to have spread out into self-contained guerrilla formations and to have started to make trouble for the Chinese.

The general Tibetan public's resistance to Chinese Communist rule is said to take less violent forms. Indian travelers have told of new school buildings standing empty because parents in many districts refuse to send their children.

According to one report, the rigors of life in Tibet and the hostility of the people have caused many Chinese officials and army officers to grumble against being reassigned there. A special "rectification center" was set up this year to persuade recalcitrants to return to Tibet for additional duty, the report said.

December 14, 1958

TIBETANS BATTLE CHINESE IN LHASA

By ELIE ABEL
Special to The New York Times.

NEW DELHI, India, March 20 —Open warfare against the Chinese Communist overlords of Tibet has broken out in Lhasa, according to official information reaching New Delhi.

A spokesman for the Indian External Affairs Ministry confirmed reports that virtually the entire population of Lhasa had joined rebellious Khamba tribesmen in an unequal struggle against Chinese troops.

What apparently provoked the Lhasa uprising was an attempt by Chinese authorities to arrest the Dalai Lama, spiritual ruler of Tibet. His whereabouts has not been revealed publicly.

The Indian Consulate General in Lhasa was said to be in the center of the fighting between Potala, the Dalai Lama's winter residence, and his summer residence, called Norbulingka. The buildings are two miles apart.

The trouble started a few days ago, reports said, when the Dalai Lama was summoned to the headquarters of Gen. Chang Ching, the Peiping Government's representative in Tibet.

The young Buddhist leader did not obey the summons. A second message was then received from Chinese headquarters saying the Dalai Lama was to go there alone, without his abbots-in-waiting.

This news alarmed the Tibetan faithful and raced through the city. The women of Lhasa, including the Dalai Lama's mother, raised a cry of weeping.

Several thousand Lhasa residents gathered outside the winter residence and marched on the Indian Consulate General to appeal for help against the Chinese.

The last word from the Tibetan capital was that Chinese had started firing in a determined attempt to put down the uprising. The townspeople and the Khambas also were said to be using firearms.

Unofficial reports said fighting started three days ago. In view of the Indian Government's strenuous efforts in the past to play down reports of the Khamba uprising, confirmation of the Lhasa fighting came as a surprise.

It was only three days ago that Prime Minister Jawaharlal Nehru told the Indian Parliament:

"There may be some violence here and there; it is a difficult situation. But it is more a clash of wills at the present than a clash of arms or physical bodies."

The Khambas, a tough Nomadic people, rose in revolt against Tibet's Chinese overlords last summer. Their resistance took the form of sabotage, sniping and occasional skirmishes.

In some parts of southeastern Tibet along the Brahmaputra River Valley the Khambas managed to establish their own authority by forcing the Chinese to withdraw.

Indian officials have consistently cautioned reporters against making too much of the Khamba uprising. They took the line that the tribesmen had nothing but small arms and were no match for the well-equipped Chinese Army.

One of New Delhi's apparent fears was that in the event of an armed showdown the defeated Khambas would seek refuge in Indian territory.

In his statement to the lower house of Parliament Tuesday Mr. Nehru said it was always "embarrassing" to discuss events in a neighboring country on the basis of limited knowledge.

He acknowledged that the Dalai Lama, spiritual leader of the Tibetans, might have submitted to Peiping's authority under duress but went on to say that Chinese suzerainty over the isolated Himalayan country had been recognized in the past by all countries.

March 21, 1959

NEW TIBET RULE URGED

Chief Lamas Favor Autonomy Within Red China

Special to The New York Times.

HONG KONG, April 22—The early establishment of Tibet as an autonomous region in Communist China was urged today in statements from the Dalai Lama and Panchen Lama, chief temporal and spiritual leaders, respectively, of Tibet.

The two prelates presented messages at a ceremony in Lhasa marking the second anniversary of the formation of a preparatory committee charged with paving the way for the setting up of an autonomous region. They also sent similar messages to Mao Tse-tung, chief of state of Communist China.

The two chief Lamas noted in their statements that Peiping had decided not to carry out a communization program in Tibet for the period of the Second Five-Year Plan.

April 23, 1958

CHINESE REDS END DALAI LAMA RULE; RIVAL GETS POST

Special to The New York Times.

HONG KONG, March 28— Premier Chou En-lai of Communist China ordered today that the Dalai Lama's Local Government of Tibet be dissolved immediately because of a revolt against Chinese control.

The Chinese Communist Premier declared that the Preparatory Committee set up in 1956 for the proposed Tibetan Autonomous Region "shall exercise the functions and powers of the Tibet Local Government."

The order dictated that the 23-year-old Dalai Lama be replaced as head of the Preparatory Committee by the Panchen Lama, who is regarded as more amenable to Chinese Communist control. The 21-year-old Panchen Lama has been a rival of the Dalai Lama in Tibet's religious-dominated regime.

Dalai Lama 'Under Duress'

The whereabouts of the Dalai Lama was not given in the broadcast except for the statement that he was "under duress by the rebels."

A comment by an official press agency said that until further notice Chinese Communist troops would control all religious, social and governmental functions in Tibet.

This announcement was further substantiated by a military announcement signed by Chang Kuo-hua, Chinese military commander in Tibet.

In issuing the order, which was later broadcast over the Peiping radio, Premier Chou confirmed for the first time that a state of revolt had existed in Tibet since March 19.

Eighteen Aides Ousted

A later announcement by the official Hsinhua (New China) News Agency said a series of revolts against Chinese control had taken place since last summer in Tibet.

The official order also directed that eighteen advisers of the Dalai Lama be dismissed from the Preparatory Committee and replaced by sixteen supporters of the Panchen Lama.

The Panchen Lama was expected to be installed in the sacred Potala Palace of Lhasa, blanketed by clouds at its height of 11,830 feet above sea level.

The rebellion of March 19 was said to have been spearheaded by the fierce Khamba tribesmen, who rose up against Chinese troops to rescue the Dalai Lama from the Potala Palace.

At some time during the night, according to Chinese reports, the Dalai Lama was reached by the tribesmen and abducted from under the hands of the Chinese Communist guards.

The report did not say where the Dalai Lama was believed to have been taken, but observers here speculated that it would have been south of the Tibetan capital.

According to the Peiping report, Chinese forces in Lhasa were ordered into action against the Tibetans at 10 A.M. March 20 after a number of incidents. The report said the city was "controlled" after two days of fighting and that by March 23 about 4,000 Tibetan troops and large numbers of arms and ammunition had been taken.

March 29, 1959

PEIPING HAS HELD LAMA IN RESERVE

Panchen Under Red Control Since 1948—He and Dalai Rivals Since Boyhood

The Panchen Lama, the gentle, good-humored, 21-year-old monk who was named yesterday as nominal ruler of Tibet, has been a Chinese puppet in the play of power politics since 1948.

The Dalai Lamas and Panchen Lamas have been more or less rival popes in Tibetan Lamaism, a form of Buddhism, since 1925. The Dalai Lama, reigning at Lhasa, has been regarded as supported by the British, and by India since India's independence.

The Panchen Lama, reigning normally at Shigatse, 130 miles west of the capital, has been supported by China. This was true of the Kuomintang Government before the Communist revolution as it has been of the Red Government since.

The Chinese and Tibetans have been fighting each other since the seventh century A.D. The Chinese claimed Tibet at least as far back as the eighteenth century. Tibet declared her independence in 1911 after the Chinese revolution against the Manchu dynasty.

One's Temporal Ruler

Traditionally, the Dalai Lama is supposed to be the temporal leader of his 3,000,000 people, while the Panchen is the spiritual leader, but in contemporary times this distinction has been lost. Both live monastic lives surrounded by monks and are venerated as living Buddhas.

Both Lamas are chosen in the same way, among peasant boy babies determined to have been born at the exact instant the preceding lamas died. The baby who exhibits greatest curiosity about relics of the dead Lamas is considered by a committee of monks to be the one in whom the soul of the living Buddha is reincarnated.

There is an apparent discrepancy, however, in that the current Dalai Lama is believed to have been born June 6, 1935, although his predecessor died Dec. 17, 1933. Some authorities say that when a Dalai Lama dies, his spirit may roam in heaven before reincarnating itself in a newborn child.

On Nov. 30, 1937, Kum-bu-tze-den was born in Lihwa, Sikiang Province, China, near Tibet. When he was 6, holy men from Tibet declared him to be the Panchen Lama and took him out of the peasant's hut in which he was happily playing. In 1944, he was enthroned at Kumbum Lamasery, in Tsinghai Province, China, under the sponsorship of the Nationalists.

Meanwhile, the Dalai Lama, chosen in a similar manner and chosen in a similar manner, was reigning at Lhasa, capital of the remote, mysterious country walled up amid the highest mountains in the world. Regents were then acting for both boy Lamas. In 1947, armed bands of the regents fought inconclusive battles.

In December, 1950, the year following their seizure of power in China, the Chinese Communists invaded Tibet. Trailing them was a "Free Tibet Army" of 40,000 men under Geshye Sherap Gyamtso—and the Panchen Lama, then 13 years old.

The Dalai Lama, who had assumed his throne only the month previous, fled to Yatung, near the border of Sikkim. In 1951, the rule of Red China over Tibet was acknowledged in a treaty signed in Peiping. The titular leadership of the Dalai Lama was granted the Chinese Reds and he was reinstated at Lhasa. The Panchen Lama was immured in a monastic palace at Shigatse in case he should be needed later.

Both Lamas met in a public show of friendliness and unity at Lhasa in 1952. They visited Peiping together in 1954 and India in 1956 as tourists.

Industrialization Begun

Meanwhile, the Chinese Communists were attempting to modernize and industrialize Tibet by force and in a hurry. They tried to make the priests —a sixth of the male population—pray less and do more productive work. The Reds established secular schools, which were Communist and atheist.

In 1956 the hard-pressed Tibetans revolted, but were put down by bloodshed. The Chinese Reds then promised to soft-pedal their reforms until 1962. Still, protest riots, particularly in labor camps in Chinese provinces on the border of Tibet, continued.

A guerrilla force called the Miman began to ambush trade convoys on the new roads to China and India, using arms seized in raids on Chinese outposts. Three weeks ago, apparently widespread rebellion burst into flame.

The Dalai Lama was said to have torn up the treaty of 1951. The Chinese occupation forces moved to crush the revolt. The Dalai Lama fled. Peiping brought out the Panchen Lama, whom they had been holding in reserve for just such a moment, to take the throne at Lhasa.

Chinese Attack Kashmir Area; 17 Indians Are Killed in Clash

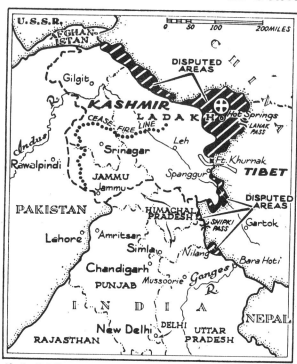

The New York Times   Oct. 24, 1959
Scene of clash between Indians and Chinese Reds (cross)

NEW DELHI, India, Oct. 23—The Government announced today that Chinese Communist troops had attacked an Indian force in Kashmir, killing seventeen Indians.

The clash occurred Wednesday in southern Ladakh at a point forty miles inside Indian territory. Three Indians were seriously wounded.

An Indian police party on border patrol, which had gone in search of two missing policemen, was fired on by Chinese troops entrenched on a hilltop, a communiqué said. It added that the Indians fired back in self-defense but were overwhelmed by the "superior strength" of the Chinese, who used grenades and mortar.

The incident took place approximately 100 miles east of Leh, the capital of Ladakh province. The site is about forty-five miles west of Lanak Pass which is the border in this sector between India and Communist-controlled Tibet.

The details of the incident were made public in a written statement by the Ministry of External Affairs. The Ministry said the Government had lodged a "strong protest" with the Peiping Government demanding the withdrawal of Chinese forces from the Ladakh area and the release of Indians in Chinese custody.

The protest note said also that New Delhi reserved the right to "claim adequate compensation" from Peiping when the precise extent of losses was known.

The Ministry said India had rejected a Chinese protest contained in a memorandum about the incident received yesterday. It said Peiping's version was "entirely contradicted" by Indian reports.

The communiqué added that New Delhi first heard of the incident Wednesday but was awaiting fuller details before taking up the matter with the Chinese. Therefore, the Ministry said, the Government was "surprised to receive the memorandum from Peiping giving its version of the clash and lodging a protest."

Officials described the incident as the "first major clash" between Indian and Chinese forces since the border dispute between the two countries took a serious turn last August.

Indian Outpost Seized

On Aug. 26 a strong detachment of Chinese troops entered about four miles into Indian territory in the North East Frontier Agency and occupied the Indian outpost of Longju.

Three Indians were killed in the encounter. The rest of the Indian personnel withdrew to a safer area a few miles south.

The Indian Army has since moved to within two miles of Longju and is waiting there pending a political settlement of the border disputes.

Addressing a news conference in Calcutta Wednesday, the day the Kashmir clash occurred, Prime Minister Jawaharlal Nehru said the desire for peace that existed in the Soviet Union was not to be found in Communist China.

He said the Soviet Union was "satisfied territorially" but that the Chinese had not yet "got over their first flush of revolutionary mentality."

Incident Described

The Government communiqué gave the following details of Wednesday's incident:

An Indian party was camping at a place called Hot Springs in southern Ladakh, about forty-five miles west of Lanak Pass. Two constables of the party who had gone out on patrol duty Tuesday in the neighborhood of Kong Ka Pass failed to return.

A section from the main party was dispatched to seek the missing policemen, but it failed to find them. Wednesday a detachment of the Indian party proceeded on patrol duty to continue the search. This party was "surprised by sudden and heavy fire" from Chinese troops entrenched on a hilltop.

The Indian party fired back in self-defense but was overwhelmed by the "superior strength and use of grenades and mortar."

The two policemen are still missing and are presumably in Chinese custody.

New Delhi has not yet received full information about how many were in the detachment, whether there were any more casualties and whether any more Indians have been taken prisoner.

The statement disclosed that India had not sent her Army into the Ladakh area and that "police parties" had been discharging their normal functions of patrol duty without hindrance.

The Government did not give any further reason why the Ladakh area continued to be under civilian police protection while the entire North East Frontier Agency had been placed under Army control.

CHOU-NEHRU TALK ENDS IN DEADLOCK

By PAUL GRIMES

Special to The New York Times.

NEW DELHI, India, Tuesday, April 26—Prime Minister Jawaharlal Nehru and Premier Chou En-lai issued a joint communiqué last night, indicating that their talks on the border dispute between India and Communist China had ended in a deadlock.

They agreed, however, that their aides would hold further meetings to study the details of the dispute over 51,000 square miles of frontier territory.

They said that "every effort should be made * * * to avoid friction and clashes in the border areas."

The communiqué was issued at the end of the six days of private talks. This morning Mr. Chou was to leave for three days in Nepal on his way back to Peiping.

Chow Denies Concessions

Premier Chou indicated in a news conference that he had made no concession whatever on Communist China's stand in the dispute which has gravely strained relations between the two countries. He insisted, however, that friendship between India and China was "immortal"

The news conference began after Mr. Chou had been host to Mr. Nehru at dinner at Chinese Communist Embassy. The meeting, with more than 100 newsmen present, lasted long after midnight.

The Chinese Premier used it to restate Peiping's territorial claims. He made clear that if any concessions were to be made, they had to come from India.

His major points were the following:

¶That the McMahon Line was "absolutely unacceptable to China" but that Chinese troops would not cross it. He added that this phase of the dispute had become "smaller" in his talks with Mr. Nehru.

¶That he had asked India to negotiate over territory in eastern Ladakh and meanwhile not to cross into the disputed thousands of miles that the Chinese have occupied there.

¶That Peiping did not have "any disputes" with the Himalayan states of Bhutan and Sikkim.

¶That only "individual areas" were disputed in the middle sector of the Indian-Chinese frontier — the stretch between the McMahon Line and Ladakh. Mr. Nehru has said that some of these areas could legitimately be subject to negotiation but not the entire frontier.

Mr. Chou indicated that the Chinese Communist troops had no intention of withdrawing from Longju, which India contends is in her North East Frontier Agency. The Chinese seized the outpost last August in clashes in which three Indian border policemen were killed.

Premier Chou insisted that, according to historical documents and even Indian maps, Longju is north of the McMahon Line and "not in the area that is under the jurisdiction of India." India contends it is just south of the line.

The line is named after Sir Arthur Henry McMahon, who negotiated it in 1914 as the representative of the then British Government of India. Peiping contends, as Mr. Chou repeated today, that the line was agreed upon in an exchange of secret notes with Tibetans to which China was not a party.

At the airport before Mr. Chou's departure, Mr. Nehru indicated to newsmen that India had clearly expressed to the Chinese Premier her feeling that Peiping had committed aggression. He said:

"If we think and I tell them they have come on our territory * * * it means they have committed aggression."

Mr. Nehru said that as a result of the talks the "high degree of tension lessens, naturally, for the moment." He added, however, that the "basic fact remains."

The Prime Minister said he did not think there would be further border clashes.

"If there is a definite desire to avoid clashes," he said, "they don't occur."

Mr. Nehru insisted there was "no question of barter" in the border dispute. He said India's and China's views were so "basically different" that naturally their conclusions were different.

Premier Chou stanchly denied that Communist China had committed aggression against India. He said that "we will never permit aggression against any country." He added that China had been a victim of aggression on Taiwan, which is held by the Nationalist Government of Generalissimo Chiang Kai-shek.

Calls Dispute Temporary

As in earlier statements since his arrival here last Tuesday, Mr. Chou referred to the dispute with India as "temporary." He said that if India assumed an "attitude of mutual accommodation"—as Communist China had—a settlement could be found.

At the start of the news conference, Mr. Chou read a statement that said:

"There is no basic conflict of interests between our two countries. Our two countries have every reason to remain friendly to each other for thousands and tens of thousands of years to come."

Premier Chou said Mr. Nehru had been invited to visit China "at a time convenient to him."

The agreement for continued talks on the official level was considered one of the few statements in the Nehru-Chou communiqué to indicate that the talks here had not failed completely. The communiqué said that Indian and Chinese Communist officials would meet from June to September 1 in Peiping and then in New Delhi. It said they would report to their Governments by the end of September.

India vs. China

During the eight years in which India and Communist China have quarreled about their borders, about 400 protest notes have passed between the two governments. One Indian observer remarked last week: "It is a war of protest notes; a never-ending one." The remark reflected a feeling that neither country was prepared to go beyond protests to the stage of serious fighting.

Mainly at issue is a 12,000-square-mile area of the Ladakh section of eastern Kashmir. India has long claimed the territory, but Chinese Communist maps published in the early 1950's showed it as Chinese territory. India protested mildly at first. China replied that India's maps had been drawn by "British imperialists," and by 1959 had moved troops into the Ladakh area to back up its claims. India then sent its own troops into the area. The dispute grew sharper in May, when India rejected a Chinese "ultimatum" demanding the removal of two Indian posts in the disputed area.

Last week China sent India a note declaring that an Indian patrol had infiltrated four miles into Sinkiang Province, adjoining the Ladakh area, in an effort to set up a "new base for aggression." The note said that a clash had been averted "only because the Chinese patrol exercised self-restraint."

India countered with a charge that 400 Chinese troops had encircled an Indian base in the area, and said it was a further example of China's "aggressive activities systematically pursued." A second Indian note on Friday cited more Chinese troop activity and said the Chinese "are increasing tension and . . . may create a clash at any moment."

Although tension thus increased as opposing troops came into closer contact in the Ladakh area, few observers felt that it would lead to serious conflict.

RED CHINA AGREES TO INDIAN PARLEY

Discussion of Disputed Area in Kashmir Would Be Based on Joint Report

Special to The New York Times.

NEW DELHI, India, Aug. 6—Communist China has "approved" India's suggestion that they settle their boundary dispute "peacefully through negotiations on the basis of a report of officials of the two countries."

China had been evasive earlier on India's suggestion to negotiate on the basis of this report. It was made by officials from both sides under an agreement between Prime Minister Jawaharlal Nehru and Premier Chou En-lai in April, 1960.

India had repeated the offer to negotiate in a note dated July 26. Mr. Nehru made the note public in Parliament today.

Note Cites Readiness

It said the Indian Government was prepared "as soon as current tensions have eased and the appropriate climate is created," to discuss the boundary question, on the basis of the report.

India published the 1,000-page report in February, 1961. It supported India's stand on the long border dispute over the Ladakh area of Kashmir and declared that Red China had made "unwarranted claims to about 50,000 square miles of Indian territory and was in unlawful occupation of 12,000 square miles" in Ladakh.

China did not officially acknowledge the existence of the report until last May 2, when excerpts from it were published to support the Chinese position. India denounced the publication as "a garbled and truncated version of the Chinese section of the report."

Although India has long claimed the disputed area in Eastern Kashmir, Chinese maps published in the early Nineteen Fifties showed it as Chinese territory.

In 1956, additional maps were published shifting the boundary. As a measure to ease tension, India has suggested that each side should withdraw beyond the boundary claimed by the other according to the 1956 maps.

However, China brought out still another new map in 1960 claiming an additional 3,000 square miles of the area. Peiping rejected India's proposal, saying it was "absurd to suggest withdrawal from one's own territory."

The Chinese reply to the Indian note disclosed by Mr. Nehru today said that "there need-not and should not be any preconditions" for discussion on the basis of the report on the area. The Chinese reply was not published, but Mr. Nehru said it was "disappointing" and added that the Indian Government would soon respond to it.

Informal Agreement

Observers here say that the sudden calm in the Ladakh area, after recent attacks on Indian troops by the Chinese, is a result of an informal cease-fire agreement between Defense Minister V. K. Krishna Menon of India and Foreign Minister Chen Yi of China.

They met in Geneva last month at the signing of the formal accords guaranteeing the neutrality of Laos. Marshal Chen is believed to have persuaded Mr. Menon that it was not necessary to set preconditions before opening negotiations.

Meanwhile Mr. Nehru was reported to have told his party members that India should on no account engage in any war with Communist China because it is now Pakistan's military strategy to attack Indian-held Kashmir if India and China become involved in a war.

CHINA-INDIA CLASH WORST IN 3 YEARS

Both Sides Rushing Troops to Tibet Border Area— 50 Casualties Reported

By The Associated Press.

NEW DELHI, Oct. 11—Indian and Chinese Communist troops have suffered 50 casualties in their most serious battle in three years along the disputed Tibetan border, it was reported today.

Both sides claimed a victory in the fighting, which broke out yesterday and appeared to be continuing in the high Himalayas. Communiqués in New Delhi and Peking said reinforcements were being rushed to the front.

A spokesman for the Indian Government said the Indians suffered 17 casualties and that the Communist losses were heavier.

Peking said 33 Communist soldiers were killed or wounded as the Indians "continued their reckless attacks." The broadcast said Chinese border guards stood firm and "aggressive Indian troops fled in confusion,

leaving six bodies and arms and ammunition behind."

Move by India Forecast

The Indians and Chinese both insisted that they were shooting only in self-defense

The firing broke out when as authoritative sources in New Delhi predicted that Indian forces were about to move in an effort to oust the Chinese from Himalayan territory.

The latest fighting centered north of the Kechilang river near Chihtung, along the northeastern frontier between India's Assam state and Chinese-occupied Tibet.

A Indian Government spokesman charged a Communist grenade hurled at an Indian outpost set the stage for a Chinese attack yesterday morning with two-inch motars and automatic weapons. The Communists accused the Indians of being the aggressors.

On the political front, Peking charged the Indian Government with stirring up "anti-Chinese waves" in India. The New China Press agency Hsinhua said a note was sent to New Delhi charging that "40 to 50 Indian ruffians" interfered with guests going to the Chinese Embassy in New Delhi Oct. 1 to celebrate the 13th anniversary of the Communist regime.

The note charged the disturbances was "a premeditated, planned and organized action connived at and sheltered by the Indian Government."

October 12, 1962

INDIA TELLS ARMY TO OUST CHINESE

Nehru Discloses Order to Expel Forces Near Tibet but Fixes No Deadline

Special to The New York Times

NEW DELHI, Oct. 12—Prime Minister Jawaharlal Nehru said today that the Indian Army had been ordered to oust Communist China's forces from Indian territory near the Tibetan border.

No deadline has been fixed for the task, he added. The Prime Minister noted that "wintry conditions have already set in there."

After twelve hours of severe fighting on the Tibetan border Wednesday, Indian and Chinese troops have ceased firing. However, the indications are that both sides are preparing to renew hostilities.

Area Reported Quiet

Officials listed Indian casualties as six killed, eleven injured and seven missing. A Foreign Ministry spokesman said Chinese casualties were estimated at nearly 100 dead or wounded. Peking has acknowledged 22 dead.

The spokesman said there was no firing yesterday and no report of any incident today.

Prime Minister Nehru said both sides were entrenched on the banks of a small river near an Indian post at Dhola, where the borders of India, Bhutan and Tibet meet.

He declared that the conflict had taken place "in spurts" and said the Indian troops there were under "definite instructions to free our territory."

He Assails 'Menace'

The Prime Minister was talking with newsmen before leaving for Ceylon on a three-day visit. He declared: "The Chinese are a menace to us."

In reply to a question, he added: "So long as this particular aggression continues, there appears to be no chance of any talks with the Chinese."

Both India and Communist China had proposed and agreed on a date for talks. However, following a Chinese advance in the eastern sector of their 2,500

mile-long disputed border, India refused to hold talks.

Indian officials said the Chinese were heavily reinforcing their positions. Nevertheless, they added, the Indian Army is prepared to face any situation.

Access Is Difficult

The Indian Army is reported to be well equipped and much superior in strength in the area of Wednesday's clash. The Dhola Post, at an altitude of 12,500 feet, is more easily accessible to the Indians than to the Chinese.

The Chinese are reported to be experiencing the same difficulties that the Indians are having in Ladakh, in the western sector of the frontier.

The Indians have access to the eastern sector of the border by land. The Chinese are reported to be airlifting all their equipment and men.

There is a land route from the Chinese side at Thang La, a pass near the Dhola post. This route was taken by the Dalai Lama, the Tibetan spiritual leader, in his flight to India in 1951 when the Chinese Communist Army entered Tibet. However, heavy snowfall in the Himalayas has blocked this route at present, according to reports.

It is also reported that the Chinese are want to entrench themselves on Indian territory before the severe winter, when operations would be impossible.

New Delhi is worried about a report that the Chinese have built two air fields fifty miles north of the Tibetan frontier with India. The Chinese are reported to have stationed bombers, jet fighters, transport planes and helicopters here.

There is apprehension here that Communist China may open an air offensive and cause a crisis not only in the eastern sector of the frontier but also in the western sector.

Politicians in New Delhi fear the possibility of a large-scale war with Communist China. In all official communications and protest notes to Communist China, India is carefully avoiding any phrase that would indicate such a possibility.

In the latest note, dated Oct. 10 and made public today, India declared that the trouble on the frontier stemmed from a Chinese misconception about the exact alignment of the border. This indicates that India hopes all will be well once the Chinese misconception is removed.

However, the Indian note asserted: "It is not India but the Chinese Government that is playing with fire." A Chinese note had warned that India was playing with fire and said: "He who plays with fire will burn himself."

October 13, 1962

THE M'MAHON LINE AT CRUX OF FIGHT

The Chinese-Indian border dispute involves 51,000 square miles of rugged mountains and dense jungles along a 2,000-mile common frontier.

The boundary has been called the McMahon Line since March 24, 1914, when it was negotiated with Tibet at Delhi by Sir Arthur Henry McMahon of the British regime. The Chinese Communists have refused to recognize it, but so had the preceding Imperial and Nationalist Governments.

The Chinese Communists said the line had been imposed on the Tibetan representative "behind the back" of the Chinese delegate. Communist opposition to the line—somewhat vague and never clearly demarcated—is based on its having been enforced by a colonial power.

Additionally both the Nationalists and also the Communists have insisted that their Government never ratified the agreement.

The Government of Prime Minister Jawaharlal Nehru has insisted, however, on the legitimacy of the boundary. Its stand is that the line had been officially negotiated by a previous regime—that of British India.

In 1959, Mr. Nehru, discussing the western sector of the disputed border, said that "this was the boundary of the old Kashmir state with Tibet and Chinese Turkestan [Sinkiang], nobody had marked it."

In the years following the drawing of the McMahon Line, Chinese troops guarded the traditional line there and did not encroach upon Indian territory. But on Sept. 8, 1959, Premier Chou En-lai said in a note to Mr. Nehru that the Chinese Government did not recognize the McMahon Line. "But Chinese troops have never crossed that line," he added.

Chinese Move In

Relations between the two countries were strained after Chinese troops occupied 12,000 square miles of the 15,000 that they claim in Ladakh province of Kashmir on the western end of the frontier and claimed 36,000 square miles in the east.

Mr. Nehru protested. He said maps showed the territory was clearly Indian. The Chinese replied that Indian troops had invaded Chinese territory.

Mr. Nehru contends that India's boundary runs from the region of Ladakh, in Kashmir, down to the boundary of Nepal, and again from Bhutan to the Irrawaddy-Salween River defile in Assam.

The McMahon Line, roughly defined, runs along the axis of the Himalaya from the northeast corner of Bhutan to the Isu Razi Pass on the northwest of Burma.

Talks between Mr. Nehru and and Premier Chou En-lai in April, 1960, failed to settle the dispute. Last year, however, the Chinese sent armed patrols into additional territory claimed by India. They also began a propaganda offensive against Sikkim and Bhutan.

In November, 1961, Mr. Nehru protested again to Peking, accusing it of 11 border violations since April, 1960. The note said "aggression has been added to aggression."

Chinese Asks Settlement

Last March, the Chinese appealed to India for an "early" negotiated settlement of the dispute. India responded to Peking's overture by reiterating that Chinese troops must withdraw before "favorable climate" for negotiations could be established.

There were, instead, further reports of border incidents. Fighting broke out last July in two disputed sectors of the Ladakh area of Kashmir. Both sides issued protests.

In August, India invited the Chinese Government to discuss preliminary measures for negotiations toward a peaceful settlement.

The note was in reply to the acceptance by Peking of an Indian offer for negotiations on the basis of a report made by officials of both sides after the meeting between Mr. Chou and Mr. Nehru.

Ten days ago, it was reported that troops on the border had engaged in their most serious clash in three years.

On the next day, Mr. Nehru said the Indian Army had been ordered to oust China's troops from Indian territory near the Tibetan border. No deadline was fixed for the task, but Mr. Nehru noted that "wintry conditions have already set in there."

Faced with increasing pressure, India was reported three days ago to be making quiet, unofficial approaches in Washington for military equipment.

Especially sought were high-altitude transport planes that could carry troops and supplies to remote Himalayan areas. Meanwhile it was reported from Peking that the Chinese had warned India in a note that its planes would immediately bring down any aircraft intruding into China's airspace."

India's interest in the transport planes was reported to have heightened greatly in recent months because of Delhi's dissatisfaction with the performance of AN-12 transport planes purchased from the Soviet Union in the last two years.

October 21, 1962

U. S. ARMS SPED AT NEHRU PLEA AS CHINA GAINS

By A. M. ROSENTHAL
Special to The New York Times

NEW DELHI, Oct. 29—Prime Minister Jawaharlal Nehru made an urgent request to the United States today for military assistance against the Chinese Communists. He received an immediate pledge that weapons would be rushed to India.

United States air transports loaded with guns and ammunition are expected to arrive by the end of this week. They will open a vital supply line to India in time of crisis and begin a historic new chapter in relations between the countries.

This was the first time in India's 15 troubled years of independence that she had made a direct appeal for military help. New Delhi had always feared that such an appeal might compromise her policy of nonalignment.

Appeal Has Ramifications

Mr. Nehru is not expected to abandon his policy of refusing alliance with blocs of the East or West. But the fact that in her hour of danger from Communist China India looked westward for succor and received it might turn out to be an emotional and political turning point for this country.

Mr. Nehru's decision has major political implications for the United States and the Soviet Union, which has offended India deeply by its sudden aloofness.

For India, facing an enemy superior in manpower and firepower, diplomacy and politics have become considerably less important at the moment than the need for modern rifles, machine guns and mortars.

Important Posts Lost

The fighting that began Oct. 20 has cost India 2,000 to 2,500 men dead and missing and the loss of important posts and strategic passes.

[Diplomatic sources in Washington said Monday that the Indian Army had lost "thousands" of men in the border fighting. The total of casualties was said to be well above the official New Delhi report of 2,500.]

Priority will go to the speeding of infantry weapons from the United States to bolster the poorly equipped Indian troops fighting the Chinese Communists along 1,600 miles of front on the mountain peaks and the jungle slopes of the northern frontiers. There was a lull in the fighting in the north today that could mean that the Chinese were regrouping. In Ladakh, 800 miles to the west, the Chinese captured two more posts.

Heavier weapons will be supplied to the Indians later if needed. Mr. Nehru did not ask for United States troops and there is no expectation that he will.

As far as can be seen from here, the United States has made up its mind to act with speed and political grace in answering India's plea for help. No political conditions were attached to the pledge of support and all questions of payment were put aside for the time being to open the supply line as swiftly as possible.

Financial experts from the United States and India will discuss such things as credits and deferred payments. However, the swiftness of the United States reply and the postponement of financial talks will make it quite clear to Indians that this is not a commercial transaction.

Mr. Nehru's request for aid was made to Ambassador John Kenneth Galbraith shortly after noon today. The foundation for the appeal was laid last week.

India Asks Sympathy

Six days after the Chinese attacked, Mr. Nehru sent a letter to all governments, except those of South Africa and Portugal, outlining India's position and asking for sympathy.

To Britain a few days earlier went a request for the purchase of automatic weapons. London assented immediately and two Britannias loaded with weapons and ammunition arrived at New Delhi airport this morning.

France and Canada were also approached for weapons and are reported to have agreed. Defense Minister V. K. Krishna Menon, who has built much of

his career on the theory that the Soviet Union would help India in case of an attack from Communist China, was reported to have made contact with the Soviet Ambassador here and to have been told no military aid from Moscow could be expected.

Many Indians, including Mr. Menon and, it is reported, Mr. Nehru, still hope that Moscow will be able to exert a restraining influence on Communist China. Westerners here do not believe that Moscow will give up its political struggle for India's friendship without more attempts to work out a formula for negotiation.

The Indian Government re-emphasized today that it would not negotiate until the Chinese withdrew in the northeast. If the Soviet Union can persuade the Chinese to withdraw, it will be able to present itself as the savior of peace.

Now the United States emerges as the most important friend in a time of emergency. What Indians appreciate most, one New Delhi editor said, is the fact that so far Americans have not been saying: "We told you so."

One obvious effect of Mr. Nehru's decision to appeal to the United States will be to weaken the prestige and influence of Mr. Menon. For years an important element in relations between the countries has been the strong mutual distaste between Mr. Nehru's chief aide and the United States Government.

Senior members of Mr. Nehru's Cabinet have been urging him to get rid of Mr. Menon. Many generals have been supporting the Cabinet members. Mr. Nehru's answer so far has been to keep Mr. Menon, but to take more and more direction of defense affairs into his own hands.

October 30, 1962

PEKING REBUTS INDIA ON FRONTIER ACCORD

PEKING, March 27 (Reuters) —Communist China told India in a polite note published here today that she should "learn honestly" from China and Pakistan how to settle border problems.

Indian objections to the recent Chinese-Pakistani border agreement were called "absurd and ridiculous" in the note, handed by Communist China to India last Monday. Peking said India's objections to the agreement with Pakistan were "absolutely inpermissible." The Chinese-Pakistani treaty affected the 300-mile border between Sinkiang and part of Kashmir, and the Chinese flatly rejected India's contention that Pakistan had no right to sign a treaty affecting Kashmir, which both India and Pakistan claims.

The Chinese notes repeated that the agreement was only provisional pending the settlement of the dispute over Kashmir and had no bearing on the ownership of Kashmir. It said Indian charges to the contrary were "fabrications and slander."

March 28, 1963

SOVIET MISSILES OFFERED TO INDIA

Moscow Believed to Pledge Rockets to Rebuff Peking

Special to The New York Times

NEW DELHI, Aug. 1—The Soviet Union has offered India missiles and other military equipment needed for India's defense against Communist China, qualified sources said today.

An Indian military mission to Moscow requested ground-to-

ground and ground-to-air missiles, transport planes and radar equipment. The mission, led by Subramanya Bhoothalingam, Secretary to the Ministry of Economic and Defense Coordination, went at the invitation of the Soviet Government.

The Indian mission is reported to have completed the major part of the discussion with Soviet authorities. The details of the transaction will be known here only after the Indians return. The mission has gone to Prague for a military deal with Czechoslovakia.

It is understood that the Soviet officials stipulated no restrictions on the use of the military supplies. The Indians have made clear that they wanted the supplies for use against a possible renewed attack from China.

Chinese Communist forces invaded India in the fall of 1962. On Nov. 22, Peking announced a cease-fire and the troops of both nations pulled back.

Although the Soviet Union has pledged to give India air-to-air missiles for the four MIG-21 jets already given to India, new military commitments by the Soviet Union would have far-reaching effects. Political observers believe Soviet military aid to India would have these effects:

¶It would prove India's position that her policy of non-alignment is realistic and that her acceptance of military aid from the West had not affected that policy.

¶It would demonstrate Soviet support for India in her dispute with China and would thereby strengthen India's position and influence in this part of the world.

¶It would widen the division between the two Communist powers to an extent that would make a rapprochement difficult.

¶The Soviet Union would move closer to the West in aiding India militarily against the Chinese.

However, these observers do not see an end of the cold war. The Soviet Union's main motive in aiding India, they believe, is to snub China and to strengthen the Indian Communists, who lost prestige after the massive Chinese attack last fall.

Although the Indian Government professes fears of a renewed Chinese attack, most Western observers do not share this view. The latest Chinese moves on the border, they believe, are mainly intended to consolidate China's gains of last year's fighting. The Chinese are reported to have sent reinforcements to the Indian border.

August 2, 1963

389

Mao Made a Political Exercise Of Swimming Yangtze 3 Times

Said After '56 Feat That 'Big Things' Such as U. S. Were Not to 'Be Feared'

By TILLMAN DURDIN
Special to The New York Times.

HONG KONG, Aug. 23—Mao Tse-tung, head of state and of the Communist party in Communist China, swam the Yangtze River in June last year not once but three times.

According to a June 13 copy of the Chang Chiang (Yangtze River) Daily News of Wuhan that has reached here, Mr. Mao covered approximately twenty-five miles in making the three crossings in a period of four days.

The newspaper devoted about 1,500 words to a feature article describing the Chinese Communist leader's feat.

Publicity was given several months ago to a Yangtze swim by Mr. Mao and pictures of the event have been printed in newspapers all over Communist China.

Heretofore the impression was that the 64-year-old Chinese Communist chief had made it across the swift, muddy Yangtze only once.

The Wuhan Daily emphasized there had been three crossings and reported that Mr. Mao felt well enough after the third trip to pooh-pooh the river's bigness and to say: "United States imperialism is very big but we have opposed it and nothing happened. So the big things in the world are not always to be feared."

The Wuhan daily (Wuhan is the name given to a metropolitan area on the Yangtze, in Central China, comprising Hankow Wuchang and Hanyang) said aides and party associates had tried hard to dissuade Mr. Mao from undertaking what they considered a risky venture but he refused to back down.

Protective younger swimmers and the Launch Yenan accompanied Mr. Mao on his crossings ready to come to his aid if he got into trouble. He wore white trunks and alternated between floating on his back, using a side stroke and a back

Associated Press
Mao Tse-tung

stroke, the newspaper said.

During the eight-mile crossing Mr. Mao sometimes dived into the water and sometimes put his hands behind his head and chatted with his companions while floating on his back, the newspaper went on.

The daily said that some of the men accompanying Mr. Mao in the water had become so cold their lips turned blue and that two had to give up in midstream and be hauled into the launch.

The first crossing took 2 hours and 4 minutes and covered a distance of eight miles. Mr. Mao was quoted as having said he could have swum for two more hours if he had something to eat.

He covered slightly more distance in his second crossing two days later and made the transit in the vicinity of the nearly finished Wuhan bridge, which will be the first to span the Yangtze. Despite the protests of friends he crossed again the next day.

August 24, 1957

Mao's Marxist Theories Spread To Masses in Peiping Campaign

Government and Party Aides Are Ordered to Study and Propagandize Writings

By TILLMAN DURDIN
Special to The New York Times.

HONG KONG, March 27 — Communist China is in the midst of a new campaign to progadandize the infallibility of Mao Tse-tung.

Communist party and Government officials throughout the country are being exhorted to rededicate themselves to the study of Mr. Mao's theories and at the same time to renew their efforts to spread the Communist leader's ideas among the masses.

A recent issue of Nanfang Jihpao, a daily newspaper in South China, announced that Kwangtung Province "has plunged itself into a movement for studying Mao Tse-tung's thought" with millions participating.

Peiping report recently said that in Heilungkiang Province the study of Mr. Mao's doctrines was being combined with a general Socialist re-education campaign conducted by a propaganda army of 1,460,000.

Effort Is Nation Wide

Reports from other provinces and cities show the nation-wide character of the campaign. Together with a general Socialist re-education effort, the campaign appears to be a successor in the sphere of thought-control to the dwindling drive against "Right opportunism" that flourished during the winter.

The propaganda asserts that the Communist leader's ideas provide an answer to every problem that arises in the development of communism in China. A recent issue of the China Youth News ignored any reference to any other present-day Marxist thinkers and called Mr. Mao "the world's greatest contemporary theoretician of Marxism-Leninism."

In Wuhan, according to Hupeh Jihpao, a daily, the teachers, students and staff of Wuhan University have set up a research institute on Mao writings. Headed by Li Ta, university president, the institute will compile histories and textbooks in philosophy, and political economy, based on Mao ideas. It will also conduct an intensive program of lectures and agitation regarding the Communist leader's thoughts in the university community.

In Shansi, the provincial daily has emphasized that Mr. Mao's ideas should not be a monopoly for just a few.

"The law of social development should not be mastered by a small number of people," the daily said, "but by millions."

Copies of Books Issued

The journal reported a province-wide drive to improve knowledge of Mr. Mao's writing and said that in a twenty-day period 300,000 copies of the leader's books had been distributed and that 1,520,000 more copies of his works in various forms had been ordered.

Reiterating this nationalist theme, a recent issue of the Shansi daily of Taiyuan said it was Mr. Mao's thinking that the masses must learn "because Mao Tse-tung thought is Chinese Marxism."

The paper added that "Mao Tse-tung thought is thought that unifies Marxist-Leninist theories with the practice of Chinese revolution."

According to Hsia Yen, vice minister of culture, "Comrade Mao Tse-tung has creatively developed the Marxist-Leninist theory of art and literature and solved problems that Marx, Lenin and Stalin failed to solve."

March 28, 1960

RED CHINA'S YOUTH TOLD TO AID FARMS

Special to The New York Times.

HONG KONG, Sept. 15 — Graduates of colleges in Communist China have been told to emulate the ox in toil to advance the interests of the peasants.

Mao Tse-tung, chairman of the Chinese Communist party, was quoted as the inspiration for this advice.

"All Communists, revolutionaries, revolutionary artists and writers should be oxen for the proletariat and the broad masses of the people, bending their backs to the task unto death," Mr. Mao is reported to have said, according to a recent article in the Kuangming daily, which is published in Peiping.

The article said that Mr. Mao's comment was directed at artists and writers but it could also serve as "a classical instruction" for this year's college graduates.

"An ox is a submissive tool for the peasants," the article said. "It works laboriously in agricultural production in the four seasons of the year. It can be led by the nose and made to do whatever work that is required. It serves the peasants year in and year out."

September 25, 1960

CHINESE REDS CUT RANK'S PRIVILEGES

Cadres Ordered to Do More Work and to Eat With Groups They Direct

By TILLMAN DURDIN
Special to The New York Times.

HONG KONG, July 28—The authorities in Communist China have recently made it more difficult for rank-and-file cadres (officials) to take things easy or permit the working masses to take things easy.

The harassed cadres, on whom falls the task of directing the country's millions of workers and peasants to produce more but to eat as little as possible, have now been told that they must spend at least half of their time in manual labor alongside the men and women they direct.

The cadres have been forbidden, moreover, to have separate messes. Hereafter they must take their meals with everyone else in the commune mess halls. The cadres are instructed to use the knowledge they gain to see that the communal restaurants function with maximum efficiency.

The new demands on the cadres have been reported in publications that have reached here in the last two months from the Chinese mainland.

Work Always Prescribed

Rank-and-file Chinese Communist officials—and top-rankers as well— have always had to do a certain amount of manual work. This has been prescribed to manifest the solidarity of officials with the working masses, dignify labor and eradicate the widely held attitude of pre-Communist Chinese that physical work is demeaning.

Manual labor for cadres was increased and put on a more systematized basis in 1958, when the "great leap" production drive got under way. It was made compulsory for officials, with few exceptions, to spend a month every year at farm or industrial labor, and it was decreed that rank-and-file white collar workers had to spend upward of a year living and working with people on farms and in factories.

The new directives, however, prescribe manual labor for cadres in addition to previous obligations in this regard. Cadres are being told they must cut down on the time they spend at their desks and increase the time they devote to physical work.

A recent issue of the Jenmin Jih Pao of Peiping revealed that in Swatow, Kwangtung Province, the district Communist party committee decided that district level cadres must devote enough days to total six months every year at productive farm labor. The directive

also said that the majority of county-level cadres must "move to rural areas and spend seven months a year in working in the people's communes and factories."

Hsinhua, the official Chinese Communist press agency, recently reported that "eating, living and working together with the masses has been turned into a system for all cadres at all levels in Sinkiang."

Many of the articles dealing with this new development in Communist China say that the cadres must take the opportunity, while working with the masses, to carry out inspections and investigations, assign production quotas and reform work methods.

August 4, 1960

CHINA EASES CURB ON INTELLECTUALS

Special to The New York Times.

HONG KONG, April 3—The Communist regime in China has turned to the much-maligned non-Communist · intellectuals and experts for aid and advice in its present time of economic crisis.

Recent articles in the mainland Chinese press show that efforts are being made to regain the confidence and cooperation of the "bourgeois" intelligentsia.

Subjected to interminable indoctrination or long periods of manual labor, an intellectual not in the Chinese Communist party was given little opportunity in the recent past to contribute to national planning.

In a turnabout resulting from the recognition in Peiping that bureaucratic muddling has had a lot to do with China's production slowdown, the regime is stressing now that even non-Marxists can be useful to the Government.

Since this represents a retreat from Peiping's former assertion that intellectuals must be both "Red" and expert, the Communist leadership has gone to great pains to explain the new tack to its regional officials.

A recent article in Jenmin Jih Pao, official Peiping organ of the Communist party, declared that it was not only in the "interest of the revolution" but was "in fact a long-standing class policy of the party" to invite a number of representatives of the national bourgeoisie to take part in the work of the Government.

An important feature of this cooperation, the paper said, is that the Government can in this way "hear opinions in time from the masses of all classes and strata and thus find it

easier to formulate and execute suitable policies and handle contradictions among the people correctly."

The article advocated caution in "helping non-party democrats to transform their bourgeois world outlook." It said the party should show "positive enthusiasm," but also patience.

In order to prepare China's intellectuals for this greater participation in national planning, the Communist leadership has in recent months been subjecting them to a new kind of "gentle" indoctrination.

Calling a group of intellectuals together, the party explains its policies, persuades the intellectuals to give their support and promises them rewards. At these "meetings of immortals"—the very name is designed to flatter the intellectuals—a pro-Communist leads the way.

April 9, 1961

ADULATION OF MAO SPURRED IN CHINA

By SEYMOUR TOPPING
Special to The New York Times

HONG KONG, Oct. 25—On a giant stage in Peking a portrait of Mao Tse-tung, the leader of the Chinese Communist party, was projected against the "heavens." Then a chorus of more than 2,000 voices praised him as the "sun in our hearts."

This theatrical spectacle, "The East Is Red," is one aspect of the party's campaign to exalt Mr. Mao as a Communist immortal, along with Marx, Engels, Lenin and Stalin.

According to word received here, Mr. Mao viewed the show Oct. 16, the day Communist China detonated its first nuclear device. It was also the day the world learned that Nikita S. Khrushchev, chief opponent of Mr. Mao for the ideological leadership of world Communism, had been removed from power in Moscow.

The adulation of the Chinese leader has been compared by Soviet Communists to the "cult of personality" that surrounded Stalin when he ruled the Soviet Union.

The Chinese party has spurred a national mass movement to study the writings of Mr. Mao. His thought is described as a guide to the solution of all human problems.

In factories, farms, schools and army barracks, under portraits of Mr. Mao, hundreds of thousands of groups assemble

to study his writings. The press has extolled such devotion as that of a family of seven that is said to have held political meetings within the family circle once a week for three years to study the leader's works.

The Peking radio broadcasts songs in his praise in conjunction with important announcements and news programs. "We praise the country, we praise the party, we praise Mao Tsetung: The world will be liberated," runs the refrain of one song.

The Chinese Communist party has rejected the Soviet epithet, "the cult of personality," used in the Russians' denunciation of Stalin and now in turn implied in Moscow in allusions to former Premier Khrushchev.

The Chinese Communist party sees no ideological sin in glorifying its chairman as its soul and symbol.

Analysts here have found an important difference between the "Mao cult" and the "Stalin cult." There is no evidence that the Chinese leader has taken advantage of his position to purge any political opponents.

The Chinese Communist attitude toward Stalin has been that his "merits outweighed his faults," but that among "some mistakes" he committed was excessive use of his power against "counterrevolutionaries."

With the removal of Mr. Khrushchev it is expected here that Chinese propagandists will be able to further the Mao prestige more effectively at home and abroad. Leonid I. Brezhnev, the new leader of the Soviet Communist · party, and Aleksei N. Kosygin, the new Premier, are not considered of sufficient personal stature to compete with Mr. Mao.

This will be of significance not only in the Chinese-Soviet contest within the international Communist movement, but also in the underdeveloped countries of Asia, Africa and Latin America. In those countries Mr. Mao is regarded as the man who successfully carried through a Communist revolution based on the peasantry rather than on the urban proletariat, as in Russia.

There is every indication that the next generation of Chinese Communist leaders intends to install Mr. Mao after his death as the Chinese counterpart of Lenin. The Chinese leader, who will be 71 years old Dec. 26, is believed to be in failing health, according to observers who have seen him in Peking recently.

Another possibility considered here is that Mr. Mao, because of his poor health or advanced age, may be given the post of honorary chairman of the party's Central Committee. The position was established in September, 1946, but has never been filled.

November 1, 1964

391

CHINA'S CHILDREN PARROT DOGMAS

Girl, 11, Echoes Peking Line on 'Modern Revisionism'

The following dispatch was written by Charles Taylor of The Globe and Mail of Toronto.

© 1964 by The Globe and Mail

SHANGHAI.

There was no doubt in the mind of Chen Li-hsao. Nikita S. Khrushchev was a bad man.

A pretty little girl, Li-hsao is 11 years old. A visitor touring Shanghai recently met her on a Sunday afternoon at the Children's Palace—a spacious mansion that was once the home of a British tycoon and is now a center where children come to sing, dance, work handicraft and learn about science. It is a showplace for foreigners.

Gao Ching, the secretary of the palace, was present during the tour. In a corridor there was a poster reading, "Don't Allow the United States Imperialists to Invade Vietnam!" She was asked whether it was healthy to indoctrinate children with such propaganda.

Her answer was, "We teach the children to hate the United States imperialists, but to love the United States people."

Asked about the Soviet Union, she replied, "The Soviet people are our friends, but the modern revisionists are our enemies."

All the time, Li-hsao sat still, with a shy and serious expression. Through an interpreter, she was asked what she knew about the modern revisionists.

At first, she hesitated. Then, after some encouragement from the interpreter and Mrs. Gao, she gave the answer: "The modern revisionists are in league with the imperialists against Marxism-Leninism. They are entirely against the revolution."

Asked who the modern revisionists were, she replied: "Khrushchev, who is the leader of the Soviet Union. They are against the will of the people, so they are doomed to failure."

How did she know this?

"The teachers tell me about world affairs. Also I know it from the children's newspapers."

The indoctrination of children is on an awesome scale in China. It starts in kindergartens, where 3-year-olds perform such ditties as "Sailing to [liberate] Taiwan." It continues through primary and middle schools and university, where students are required to digest the writings of Mao Tse-tung.

Through all five years at Hwa Tung University in Shanghai, students spend several hours a week on political education and "current affairs."

According to Chang Pao, the vice dean, some of the students are still obsessed with personal ambition and dreams of fame and wealth. Others have "tendencies toward intellectualism." But Mr. Chang was confident that these vices could be overcome by political education, especially the study of Chairman Mao's writings.

It was clear that only students with the proper political grounding would be allowed to teach the younger generation. Mr. Chang held that it was important for teachers to be "both Red and expert"—a favorite catch phrase—but he conceded that the basic criterion was "a correct political viewpoint."

Young people are shielded from dissenting opinions. Soviet polemics are printed, in order to be refuted. But with the press, radio and publishing houses all transmitting the party line, there is no chance for the young to study the basic viewpoints of other nations.

November 9, 1964

me he had 300 such youngsters; another had 90. The vice mayor of Taiyuan told me that last year his city shipped 6,000 young people out to the country. An official source said 320,000 secondary school students were sent to villages last year.

One purpose has been to use the schooled youngsters to lead rural China out of the Middle Ages. The young are required not only to work in fields but also to teach the illiterate, conduct propaganda and introduce more modern methods of agriculture and sanitation.

Yet every bit as important is the party's desire to toughen the young generation. This was made clear by the Communist party newspaper, Jenmin Jin Pao, which said recently, "The countryside is one of the best places where young people can be tempered."

Even more ambitious are plans for tomorrow. The top leaders decided last year that the young would never be allowed to look down on the countryside. Thus, by 1977 every student will be spending half his time at study and half at work, until he ceases to know whether he is an intellectual or a peasant. Even those studying medicine or nuclear physics will not be exempt.

It is difficult to know where this experiment will lead. It might create militant successors to the present generation of leaders. Yet it might also play havoc with the educational system at a time when China can hardly afford to tamper with it.

At the moment this system is one of China's proudest achievements. The Communists have poured into it vast effort, imagination and money. The visitor is constantly delighted by such experiences as finding 25 microscopes in a provincial secondary school.

However, this delight sometimes has to be moderated. One of China's leading educators, Huang Hsin-pai, said, "We haven't yet reached the point where all our children can enter primary school."

The number of secondary schools is even more inadequate. And of those who manage to enter high school, only one in 180 will be permitted to become a university student.

The explanation is both simple and incredible. The university will take in not all those equipped and willing, but only those needed by the current five-year plan.

Mr. Huang makes it clear that universities expect their students to develop the same steely revolutionary spirit that prevailed in wartime. Oddly, I heard the same notion advanced by a small, gray-haired principal of a secondary school in Peking.

"Our students assiduously study the works of Chairman Mao," he said. "We seek to bring students up in a spirit of class war, revolutionary tra-

Red China Today: Schools Mold Tough Revolutionaries

This is the fourth of a series of articles by Mark Gayn, author and editorial writer for The Toronto Daily Star, who has just completed a visit to Communist China.

© 1965 by The Toronto Star

CANTON, China—The other day a crowd gathered in Changsha, to the northeast of Canton, to watch children at play.

The youngsters, 9 to 12 years old, went at their game with the exuberance children display anywhere.

First, the children showed their skill at shooting, bayonet charging and military communication. Then the "signal corps" sent out such messages as "Destroy the invading warship" or "Support the Vietnamese people in their patriotic and just struggle against American aggression" and, inevitably, "Long live Chairman Mao."

Games Played by All

The final game could be called "Blow up the enemy fortress." In it the youngsters cut their way through simulated barbed wire, crossed imaginary trenches, climbed ropes and, at last, stormed the fortress.

The display was put on by children of six primary schools, but all youngsters in Canton are engaged in such pastimes as marching, camping, doing sentry duty and combating air and gas attacks.

These games are not confined to Changsha. In the last two months I observed them in schools and playgrounds wherever I went. I saw school girls plunge their bayonets into unseen American foes and boys toss "hand grenades." Everywhere, from kindergarten to university, I heard young voices raised in militant song.

Aim Is to Mold Minds

These games should not be misunderstood. Although the Communist party has spoken of the need to "make everybody a soldier," the real aim of all these games is not to march to war but to mold the minds of the young.

The storming of pillboxes by youngsters is only one small facet of a tremendous campaign to train a new and tough breed of revolutionaries.

Four out of five people in the Chinese Communist party are young men who joined it after it had triumphed. They are more literate and more sophisticated than the old leaders, and their gods are not always the same.

This caused the men who govern China to decide a couple of years ago to act. Though peace prevailed, the young would be made to feel as if battles still raged and sacrifices were still needed. Life would be made stern and demanding, militancy would become a way of life, total obedience to the party would be made the most important of all commandments.

Children Sent to Farms

One way to toughen the young has been to move them out of the cities into the countryside.

Wherever I went this spring, I found evidence of this migration. One commune officer told

dition."

"When our children go to communes they sometimes work so hard they drop with exhaustion," he went on. "But they rise again and resume workings, and through such labor the students begin to feel like working people."

Such zeal is common. The young drive themselves or are driven to sacrifice and exhaustion. Animal joy is subdued, frivolity is frowned on, sex is sublimated.

No Kisses in the Park

Boys do not meet girls at night. There are no stolen kisses in the park when the apricot and pear trees are in bloom. Girls wear shapeless trousers and scorn lipstick, ribbons, earrings and all those things that make girls girls.

Girls wait until they are 25 and boys 27 or 28 before they consider marriage.

There can be no doubt of the loyalty and devotion that the young have for the regime. They are the zealots, the mountain movers, the unquestioning followers. They storm sham fortresses, go to the countryside and study Chairman Mao's works to the point of numbness.

Yet the question is whether party leaders can freeze the thoughts and attitudes of the young forever, to make them immune to social change. One can also wonder what psychoses and maladjustments might result from suppressed sex urges.

Walking in Shanghai one warm night, however, I saw young couples sit close together, hold hands and even embrace. It was all dreadfully counterrevolutionary. But how reassuringly human it was.

June 10, 1965

TIDE OF REFUGEES FROM CHINA RISES

Young Men Fear Drafting for Service in Vietnam

Special to The New York Times

HONG KONG, June 9—The flow of refugees from Communist China has risen suddenly after a long period of quiet along the Chinese borders facing Hong Kong and Macao.

The number of refugees entering the Portuguese island of Macao exceeded 300 in April and 400 in May. Estimates are harder to make in Hong Kong because of the size of the community and the elusiveness of the refugees, but figures have been quoted ranging from a few hundred to more than 1,000 in May.

In the previous year the number of refugees reaching Hong Kong each month averaged about 100, and similarly low figures were recorded for Macao.

Many of the refugees now reaching Hong Kong are young men who were afraid they would be drafted for service in Vietnam, according to officials of refugee organizations here.

Other refugees said they had escaped from China because they were being subjected to intensified "socialist education," the current Peking phrase for indoctrination. Some complained that all their spare time was being taken up with militia training.

Food rationing in China is now described as "adequate" and this is no longer a key factor in the average refugee's decision to escape, although Hong Kong's abundance of foodstuffs and other consumer commodities in short supply in China provides him with an added incentive.

Thousands Fled in '62

Because of the improved food situation in China and tighter restrictions on travel, the present flow of refugees is not expected to come anywhere near the proportions of the 1962 exodus, when 80,000 people flooded into Hong Kong in one month and 60,000 more were turned back by the colony's police.

The 1962 exodus followed three years of severe hardship for the people of China and was partly precipitated by fear, which later proved groundless, that the food situation would worsen. The food situation has steadily improved since that time.

The size of the present influx is difficult to estimate because the refugees prefer to slip quietly into the colony without attracting attention. Most join relatives in crowded tenements or squalid shantytowns, perched on hillsides too steep for urban development, where new arrivals go purposely unnoticed.

Some make contact with private refugee organizations for help in finding work or for food handouts. Others are swallowed up in the community without anyone's being the wiser until a census count months or years later reveals their presence.

June 10, 1965

China Reveals Motive in a Purge

By SEYMOUR TOPPING
Special to The New York Times

HONG KONG, July 19—Chinese Communist newspapers in, an ideological denunciation of a recently shown film, have revealed the background of the dismissal of two senior Peking government officials.

The officials are Shen Yenping who was dropped as Minister of Culture at the National People's Congress in December, and his deputy, Hsia Yen, who removal was approved by the State Council on April, 30. No explanation was given when the two Communist party members were purged.

The film is "Lin's Shop," a somewhat sympathetic story of a small shopkeeper who is driven into bankruptcy by the corrupt practices of Chinese Nationalist officials during the nineteen-thirties.

"Lin's Shop" was first shown in 1959 and was warmly applauded both by Chinese Communist film critics and by ordinary moviegoers. It had been adapted by Hsia Thea, Deputy Minister of Culture, from a novel of the same name published in 1932 by Mao Tun. Mao Tun was the pen name of Mr. Shen, the Minister of Culture.

The film was screened publicly again after the dismissal of the two ministers in an obvious move to enable the press to tear it apart ideologically.

"Lin's Shop" is only one of the artistic and literary works being reviewed a second time to correct what are described as idological errors committed by Communist critics some years ago.

Explaining why this is being done, Jenmin Jih Pao, the Communist party newspaper, said editorially:

"We can teach the writers and artists a lesson and make them understand that only through integrating themselves with the workers, peasants and soldiers and by remolding their thoughts and establishing a proletarian world outlook can they create works favorable to Socialism."

The editorial conceded that the novel upon which the film "Lin's Shop" was based had some merit when it was published in that it represented a protest against the Chinese Nationalists.

But the production of the film in 1959, 27 years later, was castigated by the editorial as ideological heresy because it weakened the class struggle by generating sympathy for a shopkeeper, a petty capitalist. Scorning the humanitarian traits of Lin, the shopkeeper, the Communist newspaper declared:

"In a class society, no matter how warm is the superficial relationship of one man to another, it is still the class relationship which plays the most basic and decisive role."

Asserting that the function of literature was to arouse hatred for the bourgeoisie, the newspaper cited some of the dangers of exposing the Chinese people to a sympathetic portrait of Lin, the shopkeeper.

It said that children of capitalists might be led to "think that not all exploiting classes are bad and that their own bourgeois parents constituted a special case."

The party organ accused Hsia in producing the film of covering up a basic drive of the bourgeoise to restore capitalism. It warned that the appearance of what was termed "revisionism" in the Soviet Union and Yugoslavia illustrated that capitalism could be restored in a Communist society.

Jenmin Jih Pao declared that the struggle in Communist China against these tendencies would "last from five to 10 generations." "There will be a danger of the restoration of capitalism at times throughout this long period" the editorial concluded.

July 25, 1965

393

JOURNAL HINTS AT PEKING RIFT

Editorial Cites a Need for 'Struggle' Against Spread of Harmful Ideas

By IAN STEWART

Special to The New York Times.

HONG KONG, Sept. 30—Peking has hinted at the existence of internal dissension on the eve of celebrations marking the 16th year of Communist rule in China.

An editorial in Hung Chi, a theoretical journal published by the Central Committee of the Chinese Communist party, has called for a "struggle" against the spread of harmful ideas in the guise of Communist ideology.

The journal demanded a thorough break with "all obsolete ideas, notions, habits and conventions." It added that all old things that harmed people and Socialism should be "wiped out without mercy."

Subversive Siogans Cited

Old ideas, it said, "do not always reveal themselves nakedly but generally clothe themselves in Socialist and Marxist-Leninist terminology and slogans in order to survive and spread their influence."

Analysts said this appeared to be an indication that senior party officials had either fallen into disfavor or were actively questioning party policies. They said that the editorial provided the hierarchy with an ideological basis for combating officials waywardness.

Some analysts believed that the editorial showed that the hierarchy was dissatisfied with the way in which its policies were being implemented and was meant to serve merely as a warning to officials to produce better results and follow Peking's guidelines more closely.

In the economic field, two contradictory developments have emerged. On one hand, political controls have been tightened as a prelude to a production drive; on the other, directives have been issued cautioning against too much overtime or too many political metings for workers and peasants. This may be the issue on which there has been a dispute.

October 1, 1965

RED CHINA URGES A 'PEOPLE'S WAR'

Exhorts Vietnam and Others to Strike at U. S. Without Fear of Nuclear Reply

By SEYMOUR TOPPING

Special to The New York Times

HONG KONG, Sept. 3—Communist China urged the Vietnamese Communists and other leftist revolutionaries today to strike at United States forces without fear of nuclear retaliation.

Marshal Lin Piao, Defense Minister, asserted in a major doctrinal article that the American "colossus" could be defeated "piece by piece" by what he termed "people's wars" in Asia, Africa and Latin America. He said the United States would refrain from using its nuclear weapons because of a fear of international censure.

Peking newspapers devoted three-and-one-half pages this morning to the text of the article commemorating the 20th anniversary of the surrender of Japan. The article also was published by Hung Chi, journal of the Central Committee, and all municipal and provincial newspapers.

A summary of the statement was distributed yesterday by Hsinhua, the Chinese Communist press agency, and reported in today's issue of The New York Times.

Experts on Communist China said that the article, which was published with front-page photographs of Mao Tse-tung, head of the Communist party, was intended to elevate the Peking leader to the rank of principal architect of world revolution.

While the Vietnamese Communists and other revolutionaries are spurred to violent armed struggle against the United States and its allies, the article displays a great degree of caution in committing Communist China to direct involvement.

This is particularly apparent in references to the war in Vietnam. The article states that the Chinese people will do all in their power to aid the Vietnamese people in compelling the departure of the last American soldier. However, there is no specific commitment by the Peking Government, nor is there any allusion to an earlier offer to send "volunteers" and war matériel to Vietnam.

Propounding new dogma, the article by Marshal Lin held that the Maoist theory of revolutionary war should be applied as the basic strategy of achieving world Communism. It declared that so-called liberation wars in Asia, Africa and Latin America must be employed to encircle the industrial powers of North America and Western Europe.

This concept was described as growing from the tested Mao strategy of striking from rural bases at cities held by an enemy.

Russians Called Capitulators

The dogma implies that Peking would become at least the doctrinal center of an envisioned world order. Marshal Lin denounced Moscow, once the center of the international Communist movement, as now dominated by a heretical philosophy opposed to "people's wars" and dedicated to capitulation before United States power.

Specialists here said the article contained contradictions suggesting that Mr. Mao, who is 71 years old, had encountered frustrations in a practical attainment of his goals and was consoling himself by spinning out his theory to its ultimate extensions.

In doctrinal terms, the article warns revolutionaries that in people's wars "it is imperative to adhere to a policy of self-reliance." It declared that revolutionaries must "be prepared to carry on the fight independently even when all material aid from outside is cut off."

"If one does not operate by one's own efforts," it added, "does not independently ponder and solve problems of revolution in one's own country and does not rely on the strength of the masses but leans wholly on foreign aid—even though this be aid from Socialist countries that persist in revolution —no victory can be won or be consolidated even if it is won."

U.S. and Soviet Scorned

Marshal Lin expresses contempt of both the United States and the Soviet Union for their reliance on nuclear weapons and rockets.

In urging people's wars, the marshal assures revolutionaries that "in the final analysis the outcome of a war will be decided by the sustained fighting of the ground forces, by the fighting at close quarters on battlefields, by the political consciousness of the men, by their courage and spirit of sacrifice."

Vietnam is cited as an example where American power is being frustrated by a "people's war."

While expressing confidence in the ability of the Chinese Communist forces to defeat the "few million aggressor troops" of the United States, Marshal Lin makes it clear that Peking intends to fight with the United States only if war is imposed by Washington.

The article warns that, apart from the United States, there are others that possess nuclear weapons. But, oddly, the marshal does not directly repeat earlier assertions of Peking that it possessed nuclear arms. Communist China has carried out two nuclear tests.

The article asserted that the United States had been "condemned by the people of the whole world for its towering crime of dropping two atom bombs on Japan."

Peking Takes Victory Credit

At no point in the article of more than 50,000 words does Marshal Lin specifically give credit to the United States for the World War II victory over Japan. He assigns the role of the "main force" in the victory to Chinese Communist troops and asserts that it was only the Maoist theories that enabled a weak country to overcome such a powerful country as Japan.

Although the article repeatedly states that the peoples of Asia, Africa and Latin America are turning in growing numbers to the Mao theory of "People's war," analysts here have noted recently in statements by Peking manifestations of feelings of increased isolation.

The Chinese Communist leadership may have been disturbed by hints that North Vietnam is considering a negotiated settlement of the war.

The refusal of African and Asian leaders at the postponed conference in Algiers to follow Peking's lead may have stirred some doubts in the minds of the Chinese Communists about the effectiveness of their propaganda.

Premier Chou En-lai in a speech last night complained about the use being made of Asian and African countries by the United States and others to sound out North Vietnam on peace negotiations.

There have also been reports recently of a coolness in relations between Communist China and North Korea, which once was one of Peking's closest supporters in the ideological quarrel with Moscow.

September 4, 1965

PEIPING MINISTER TERMS AIR FORCE NO LONGER WEAK

Defense Head Asserts China Is Ready Against Attack, but Plans No Aggression

By Reuters.

PEIPING, Sept. 18—Marshal Peng Teh-huai, Defense Minister, announced today that Communist China was "no longer a country with a weak air force."

Speaking at the eighth Communist party congress here, Marshal Peng also said the country's armed forces now had 2,700,000 fewer men than at their peak in 1949.

[According to current estimates, Communist China's armed strength is 2,647,000 regulars. At the peak of the Korean war its forces probably totaled 4,000,000 men.

[The Soviet Union, giving wide publicity to the Chinese party congress, is making a strong bid for even closer ties with the Peiping regime.]

Marshal Peng, who is a member of the party's Politburo, said China agreed with the Soviet Union's proposals on disarmament. When an accord is reached, he added, China is willing to make further reductions.

The Defense Minister declared that although China was not up to the standard of countries with big air forces "we are no longer a country with a weak air force."

Disavows Aggressive Aim

"We have never considered and will never consider aggression against other countries," he said.

But, he added, although there is a tendency toward international relaxation of tension, "the imperialists are not willing to give up their policy of hostility toward the Chinese people."

Marshal Peng said the purpose of the Army was to defend China and her "Socialist construction" and to be "prepared to liberate Taiwan [Formosa] at any time."

Marshal Peng disclosed that 5,000,000 men had been fully demobilized since 1949 and a further thirty-one divisions and eight regiments had been transferred as a whole to construction work.

He said that in the past the armed forces were essentially made up of infantry. Now they are divided into five commands, Army, Navy, Air Force, Anti-Aircraft and Public Security, he added.

The Army, he said, is divided into infantry, artillery, armored troops, engineers, railway corps, signals and anti-chemical warfare corps. He made no mention of paratroopers.

Defense expenditures are down from 48 per cent in 1951 to 19.98 per cent of the national expenditures in 1956, the Defense Minister announced.

In another report, Po I-po, chairman of the State Planning Commission, told the congress the share of the national income devoted to accumulation funds had risen from 15.7 per cent in 1952 to 22.8 per cent in 1956.

Mr. Po, who is a member of the party's Central Committee, stressed the need for maintaining a proper relation between increases in accumulation and consumer goods to insure gradual improvement of the standard of living.

He said industrial production had risen by 204 per cent between 1952 and 1956. Agricultural production expanded by 19 per cent in the same period, Mr. Po reported.

Earlier, leaders of foreign Communist delegations, including Jacques Duclos of France and Mauro Soccimarro of Italy, made congratulatory addresses to the Congress.

September 19, 1956

Peiping Increases Arms Budget 16%

By Reuters.

PEIPING, April 21—Communist China announced today a 1959 budget calling for a 16 per cent increase in defense expenditure and a 40 per cent rise in the value of industrial and agricultural output.

More than 2,000 delegates at the National People's Congress (Parliament) heard the nation's planners list the new goals for another "great leap forward" in the economy.

The speakers said the goals were ambitious and entailed hard work.

Finance Minister Li Hsiennien, who submitted the budget, said:

"Our people are fully aware that they must be industrious and thrifty and put up with certain temporary difficulties to bring about a rapid change in the economic and cultural backwardness of their country."

Defense expenditure this year will total 5,800,000,000 yuan (about $2,300,000,000 at the official exchange rate), a rise of 16 per cent over the 1958 total. Increased spending also is allocated for administartion, education, social services and economic construction.

Revenue and expenditure for 1959 have been balanced at 52,000,000,000 yuan (about $20,800,000,000). This marks a 27 per cent increase in expenditure and 24 per cent increase in revenue over the 1958 figures.

Details of the economic plans were given by the Finance Minister and by Deputy Premier Li Fu-chun, who is chairman of the Planning Commission. Mr. Li Fu-chun said this year's plan would be "very hard" to fulfill.

The two planners also said that despite a 65 per cent gain in industrial and agricultural production last year, supplies of some non-staple foods and daily necessities were insufficient to meet growing demands.

Panchen Lama Attends

The Panchen Lama, 21-year-old Tibetan leader who has replaced the Dalai Lama as ruler in Lhasa, was one of the joint chairmen at today's session. Mao Tse-tung, chief of state, and Premier Chou En-lai attended the session.

Once again, the emphasis in the budget is on raising heavy industrial output, such as steel and coal. But the plans appear to offer some remedy for serious shortages last year in consumer goods.

The output of sugar, which has become scarce in the cities, is planned to go up 50 per cent. Crops of sugar cane and sugar beet are due to rise by 48 and 90 per cent respectively.

The plan calls for the growing of more vegetables, which also have been in short supply in towns, and the growing of non-staple foods near cities and industrial areas to save their being transported from other areas.

Another bid to ease the burden on the strained transport system was seen in plans to build more railroad freight cars and locomotives and lay more than 3,400 miles of new rail lines.

Some Statistics Given

Following are some of the production goals set by Communist China for 1959, with expected percentage increases over 1958:

	1959 Goal	Percentage Increase
Steel	18,000,000*	66.6
Coal	380,000,000*	40
Grain	525,000,000*	40
Raw cotton	5,000,000*	50
Draft animals	90,000,000	6
Railroad freight	520,000,000*	36
Producer goods	98,000,000,000†	46
Consumer goods	67,000,000,000†	34

In the following cases, only 1958 production figures were given, with the expected percentage increases in 1959:

	1958 Production	1959 Percentage Increase
Power generating equipment	800,000‡	350
Railroad locomotives	350	Over 50
Sugar	900,000*	Over 50

For certain items only volume of production for 1958 and 1959 was given, as follows:

	1958.	1959.
Pig iron	13,690,000*	23,000,000*
Electricity	27,500,000,000‡	40,000,000,000‡
Chem. fertilizer	811,000*	1,300,000 to 1,500,000
Pigs	180,000,000	280,000,000

*Tons. **Kilowatts. †Yuan. ‡Kilowatthours.

Defense Share Decreases

Special to The New York Times.

HONG KONG, April 21—Although the Chinese Communist defense budget for 1959 calls for a 16 per cent increase, the share of defense costs in the total budget is slightly smaller than in 1958 according to the Peiping radio.

Military outlays this year would be 11.2 per cent of the total budget compared with 12.5 per cent in 1958. The trend toward allocating a lesser share of national expenditures to military costs was established in 1956. Many expenditures in the defense sphere are believed budgeted under headings other than the national defense category.

Expenditures on economic construction, Mr. Li Hsien-nien said, would account for 61 per cent of total budget expenditures. Eleven per cent would be devoted to social services, culture and education.

In talking of the 1958 financial situation the Finance Minister conceded difficulties in supply transport in the latter part of the year.

He said the number of salaried workers in the country had increased by about 8,000,000. The Finance Minister said this and improved living standards of peasants had brought demands for nonstaple foods (meats and vegetables) and manufactured daily necessities that could not be met.

Mr. Li revealed a big expansion in Communist China's aid to foreign countries. He said the total cost would come to $250,000,000 and this would be 218 per cent of the allocation made last year.

April 22, 1959

PEIPING SAYS PARTY MUST RULE MILITARY

Special to The New York Times.

HONG KONG, Sept. 30—Political control must be supreme in Communist China's armed forces, Marshall Lin Piao, new Minister of National Defense, said in Peiping today.

He warned against bourgeois Rightist tendencies among military men and said the armed services must continue to be a labor force as well as a combat organization.

Marshal Lin's statement of his views in a 7,000-word newspaper article seemed to give fresh support to belief among Western observers here that discontent existed in Communist China's military services.

These observers think some servicemen are irked by the extent of Communist party domination of service activities and oppose extensive use of the armed forces for construction, factory and farm work.

Marshal Lin's article, printed today in Jenmin Jihpao (People's Daily), organ of the Chinest Communist party, dealt mainly with the political and production aspects of armed services activity.

It is considered possible here that Marshal Lin's recent appointment to replace Marshal Peng Teh-huai may mean that Marshal Peng shared dissatisfaction in the ranks of the military.

October 1, 1959

RED CHINA USING ARMY FOR LABOR

Soldiers Help to Spur Output —Marshal's Opposition Is Seen as Key to Ouster

Special to The New York Times.

HONG KONG, Jan. 26—The use of the army as a labor force has been given increasing publicity recently in the Communist Chinese press.

The Hsinhua (New China) News Agency said that officers and men of the army had contributed 40,000,000 man-days of "voluntary labor" last year to industry and agriculture.

This is the equivalent of sixteen days work for each of the soldiers in Communist China's Army, which is estimated to number 2,500,000.

The troops helped in the construction of 5,600 water conservation projects. They took part in building factories and workshops for iron and steel centers and other industrial enterprises.

Another Hsinhua report said that most army units had become self-sufficient in meat and vegetables by raising pigs and gardens "in their leisure hours."

Hsinhua said that it was a "time-honored tradition of the Chinese revolutionary army" to take part in production while defending the country.

Provincial papers have carried similar reports.

In the northeastern province of Liaoning, army units have made "brilliant contributions"

to construction, according to a Shenyang paper.

A Yunnan paper reported that soldiers in the province had contributed more than 9,000,000 man-hours to irrigation works and iron and steel works.

Hsinhua reported that the army had dispatched entire regiments to water conservation sites in Shantung to help the people's communes.

In Sinkiang the army was said to have created "an area of flourishing farms and orchards" out of a formerly desolate river basin.

Informed quarters here believe that there may be some relation between all these reports and the dismissal of Marshal Peng Teh-huai as Defense Minister last September.

Marshal Peng was replaced by Marshal Lin Piao, and Gen. Lo Jui-ching, Minister of Public Security, took over as Chief of Staff of the Army from Gen. Huang Ke-cheng.

Marshal Lin brought up the subject of opposition to army work programs immediately after his appointment. He wrote in the party's fortnightly Red Flag:

"Some years ago there were comrades who regarded it as an extra burden for the army to participate in mass movements and assist the people in production.

"They held that only drilling and lectures constituted training while participation in practical socialist struggles was not training but an obstruction to training which would bring 'more loss than gain.' Such a viewpoint is utterly wrong."

If opposition to army work programs was one of the reasons for Marshal Peng's dismissal, the recent articles could be interpreted as a justification for the regime's viewpoint.

February 3, 1960

Peking Confirms Program To Indoctrinate Troops

PEKING, March 6 (Reuters) —A 25-day conference of senior Chinese Army officers and commissars has drafted a blueprint for stepped-up political education in the army.

The Communist party's newspaper, the People's Daily, carried on its front page today a report on the conference, which ended a week ago, but gave few details of the proposed program.

A summary of the conference report referred to the necessity of speeding up modernization of the Army and said: "We must be prepared to stand much greater tests . . . and struggle for the safeguarding of our motherland, the liberating of Taiwan and defending peace in the Far East and the world."

March 7, 1963

Peiping Police to 'Love People'

HONG KONG, Jan. 16 (AP) —Communist China's secret police have been ordered to "love the people" next month. According to Ministry of Security statistics, the police performed 4,000,000 good deeds during a similar campaign last year— helping farmers sow seed, collecting fertilizer and aiding on road and water conservation projects.

January 17, 1968

Outline of Gains and Setbacks in China's Atom Plan

March 27, 1950 — Agreement was signed creating the Chinese-Soviet Nonferrous and Rare Metals Company to mine uranium and other ores in China's Sinkiang Province.

Oct. 11, 1954—Seven Chinese-Soviet agreements and declarations made public after visit to Peking by Premier Khrushchev. Soviet interest in the Sinkiang company was transferred to China, possibly with a provision for continued uranium deliveries to the Russians. Moscow pledged broad economic aid and the delivery of research reactors, atom smashers, radioactive isotopes,

specialists and operation manuals plus the training of Chinese at Soviet installations.

Also in 1954, a uranium ore-dressing plant was reported to have started operations in Sinkiang. It was powered by a new electric plant fueled by coal extracted from mines developed for that purpose. By 1955 there were said to be 11 mines in the Sinkiang complex extracting eight types of metal.

March, 1956 — Soviet-bloc atomic research center at Dubna, near Moscow, began operation with China paying 20 per cent of costs and supplying about a third of the researchers.

June, 1957 — Mr. Khrushchev survived attempt by Vyacheslav

M. Molotov and others to remove him as Communist party chief. His victory was attributed in some quarters to aid from Mao Tse-tung, the Chinese leader.

Oct. 15, 1957—Chinese-Soviet agreement concluded concerning "new defense technology" under terms of which Soviet Union was to help China develop atomic weapons.

March, 1958 — Military Scientific Institute created in Peking. Marshal Yeh Chien-ying was reported to be the officer in charge of military applications of nuclear energy.

May, 1958 — Foreign Minister Chen-yi said in Peking that China would build atomic

bombs. A similar statement was made by the head of the air force, Gen. Liu Ya-lou.

Aug. 23, 1958—Chinese began bombardment to capture Nationalist-held Quemoy and Matsu Islands.

Sept. 4, 1958 — United States put its military weight behind defense of Quemoy; said it might bomb the mainland if Taiwan were threatened.

Sept. 6, 1958 — Premier Chou En-lai said China was willing to negotiate with the United States on the crisis.

Sept. 7, 1958—Premier Khrushchev wrote to President Eisenhower asking that he refrain from military demonstrations and restating the Soviet position that an attack on China would be considered an attack on the Soviet Union. The timing of this statement, after the peak of the Quemoy crisis had passed, was taken as an indication that Moscow's commitment to use nuclear power to defend Communist China did not include such situations.

Also in September, 1958, a Soviet-built reactor in Peking went critical. Its announced characteristics suggested that it was used for research only; 1958, in addition, marked the opening in Peking of the Atomic Energy Research Institute.

In another 1958 development, the Soviet Union, according to a Peking statement last month, "put forward unreasonable demands designed to bring China under Soviet military control." This is presumed to have been a demand by Moscow for control over nuclear weapons furnished to China. The Peking statement implied that Chinese refusal to accept such control had led to the Soviet withdrawal of nuclear aid.

June 20, 1959 — The Soviet Union, according to a Peking statement of Aug. 15, 1963, abrogated the 1957 agreement on nuclear weapons development and "refused to supply China with atomic-bomb samples and technical materials for the manufacture of atomic bombs." The statement implied that a commitment to furnish bombs had been part of the treaty.

September, 1959 — Premier Khrushchev made a 13-day visit to the United States. According to the 1963 charges by Peking, he told President Eisenhower of the abrogation of the treaty with China.

July-August, 1960 — Soviet technicians were abruptly withdrawn from China, leaving many projects in chaos. The delivery of important industrial items, such as hydroelectric turbines, was reported to have been curtailed, with consequent damage to Peking's atomic program.

July 25, 1963—The treaty for a partial test ban was initialed in Moscow. Mr. Khrushchev told W. Averell Harriman, the United States negotiator, that Chinese nuclear capability was a long way off.

July 30, 1963—A trade-union delegate from Peking, Cha Kuo-chiang, told a Japanese Socialist newspaper that China would try to develop an atomic bomb within five or six years, despite the burden of such a project on the economy. His comment was later described by the Chinese as unauthorized.

Sept. 1, 1963—Hsinhua, the official Chinese Communist press agency, said that "even if we Chinese people are unable to produce an atom bomb for 100 years" the Chinese would not bow down to the nuclear powers.

Oct. 28, 1963—Foreign Minister Chen Yi said it would be several years before China could test a nuclear weapon.

October 29, 1963

CHINA TESTS ATOMIC BOMB, ASKS SUMMIT TALK ON BAN

By SEYMOUR TOPPING
Special to The New York Times

HONG KONG, Oct. 16 — Communist China announced tonight that it had exploded its first atom bomb. Peking pledged that it would never be the first to use nuclear weapons in the future.

A communiqué stated that a nuclear test was successfully conducted at 3 P.M. Peking time (3 A.M., Eastern daylight time) in the western region of China. No details were disclosed. [In Washington, the test site was reported to be in Sinkiang, a province bordering the Soviet Union.].

"The success of China's nuclear test is a major achievement of the Chinese people in the strengthening of their national defense and the safeguarding of their motherland as well as a major contribution by the Chinese people to the cause of the defense of world peace," the communiqué asserted.

An accompanying Government statement declared that the purpose of developing nuclear weapons was to protect the Chinese people "from the danger of the United States' launching a nuclear war."

Excesses Ruled Out

"On the question of nuclear weapons, China will commit neither the error of adventurism nor the error of capitulation," the statement said. "The Chinese people can be trusted."

The Peking statement formally proposed to the governments of the world that a universal summit conference be convened to discuss the question of a complete prohibition on and the thorough destruction of nuclear weapons.

It said that as a first step the summit conference "should reach agreement to the effect that the nuclear powers and those countries which will soon become nuclear powers undertake not to use nuclear weapons, neither to use them against nonnuclear countries and nuclear-free zones nor against each other."

The proposal was dismissed by Western observers here, as propaganda. The terms do not allow for practical negotiations with a view to reaching specific agreements, they commented.

Although Communist China became the world's fifth nuclear nation, following the United States, the Soviet Union, Britain and France, specialists here doubted that it had the capability of becoming a first-class military power during this decade.

The principal advantage accruing to it immediately is psychological and political. The entry of the first nonwhite nation into the exclusive "nuclear club" was regarded here as certain to have a strong impact on the peoples of Asia and Africa despite United States efforts to prepare them for Peking's accomplishment.

Western experts have estimated that it will take several years before the Chinese can build a delivery system. The withdrawal of Soviet military aid in 1960 disrupted Peking's program to develop ballistic missiles and left its air force largely obsolescent.

Altogether, this has been a triumphant day for Communist China.

The nuclear test was successfully carried out less than 12 hours after the announcement that Nikita S. Khrushchev, ideological arch-enemy of Peking, had been ousted from the leadership of the Soviet party and Government.

Greetings Sent to Brezhnev

Mao Tse-tung, chairman of the Chinese Communist party, and other top leaders, extended "warm greetings" in a message to Leonid I. Brezhnev, the new Soviet party leader; Aleksei N. Kosygin, the new Premier, and Anastas I. Mikoyan, President, who retained his office.

A cautiously worded Chinese message avoided mentioning Mr. Khrushchev or any outstanding issues. However, it concluded with a series of exhortations that analysts here viewed as an invitation to a new attempt at some kind of rapprochement. The message said:

"May the Chinese and Soviet parties and the two countries unite on the basis of Marxism-Leninism and proletarian internationalism!

"May the fraternal, unbreakable friendship between the Chinese and Soviet peoples continuously develop!

"May the Chinese and Soviet peoples win one victory after another in their common struggle against imperialism headed by the United States and for the defense of world peace!"

Wishes for Soviet Success

The message also expressed the hope that the Soviet party and Government "will achieve new successes in their construction work in all fields and in the struggle for the defense of world peace."

The signers of the message were Mr. Mao; Liu Shao-chi, President; Marshal Chu Teh, chairman of the Standing Committee of the National Peoples' Congress, and Chou En-lai, Premier.

Specialists on Soviet relations believe that the imminence of the detonation of the Chinese bomb was a factor in the decision by the Central Committee Wednesday to remove Mr. Khrushchev. A majority of the Soviet leadership evidently decided, for tactical reasons, at least, to adopt a more flexible attitude toward Communist China.

The Italian and Rumanian and many other parties have been opposed to any move to exclude the Chinese from the international movement. The imminent nuclear test was certain to give more weight to their views.

The analysts said that a formal split in the international Communist movement had been postponed and possibly averted by the ouster of Mr. Khrushchev.

The texts of the Moscow announcements were published this morning in Peking newspapers without comment. Jenmin Jih Pao, official organ, which carried the announcements under the headline "Kruschev Steps Down," subordinated them to a report on the cotton industry.

There was no expectation among analysts here that the change in Moscow would lead to any early settlement of the fundamental issues between Moscow and Peking. Divergencies of both ideological and national interests have become so profound that no quick solution is regarded as possible.

As part of the day's triumphs, the Labor victory in Britain was certain to please the Chinese Communists. Harold Wilson, the new British Prime Minister, has favored an improvement of relations with Peking and the detonation of its bomb was thought likely to reinforce his attitude.

The United States has opposed any disarmament agreement that would ban nuclear weapons without concurrent restrictions on conventional arms. Confronted by a Chinese Communist Army of two and a half million men, the United States, in defending Southeast Asia or Taiwan, would have to depend on its nuclear arsenal to curb aggression.

The Chinese statement obviously was intended to reassure the nonaligned nations, which have expressed misgivings about Peking's failure to adhere to the nuclear test ban treaty signed in Moscow last summer by the United States, Britain and the Soviet Union.

The statement described the treaty as a "big fraud" to fool the world about attempts by the signatories to consolidate their nuclear monopoly.

The statement reiterated the thesis of Mao Tse-tung, chairman of the Chinese Communist party, that the "atom bomb is a paper tiger" and that people, not weapons, decide wars. It said the aim of Communist China in developing nuclear weapons was "to break the nuclear monopoly of the nuclear powers and to eliminate nuclear weapons."

Hsinhua, the Chinese Communist press agency, reported that Mr. Mao and other leaders received more than a thousand young people, who sang and danced in a performance entitled "The East Glows Red."

China Is Reported Losing Soviet Arms

By SEYMOUR TOPPING
Special to The New York Times

HONOLULU, Dec. 3—A decline of the military striking power of Communist China is foreseen here as a result of the dispute between Peking and Moscow.

Military equipment, especially aircraft, obtained by Communist China from the Soviet Union is becoming obsolete. There is no evidence that it is being replaced by Moscow.

Senior United States military officials cite this development as a reason for their belief that Communist China will not undertake any overt military aggression in the near future.

Peking is expected to restrict its expansionist program to fomenting revolutionary activities in Southeast Asia, and to other subversion. United States officials believe that the Chinese Communists intend to give their primary attention to the support of the Vietcong guerrillas in South Vietnam, the pro-Communist Pathet Lao forces in Laos and subversive activities in Thailand.

Peking can continue indefinitely to provide the type of low-cost aid that is being channeled to the Pathet Lao and the Vietcong through the North Vietnamese Communists.

This is the view of top military officials in Hawaii, where the headquarters of the United States Pacific Command is situated. Adm. Harry D. Felt, the Commander in Chief, directs a unified command that supervises United States military activity in the Pacific, the Far East and Southeast Asia.

The estimate of officials that Communist China will not risk overt military aggression rests also upon three additional factors. These are the growing deterrent power of the United States forces and the strength of Chinese Nationalist troops on Taiwan and of Korean forces in South Korea.

The nuclear deterrent of the United States is scheduled to be enhanced with the assignment of the first Polaris-armed submarines to the Pacific at the end of next year. The tactical and strategic air forces in the Pacific are being backed by an increasing number of intercontinental ballistic missiles based in the United States. These have the capability of striking targets in mainland China.

Communist China's military power remains formidable in terms of the estimated total of 150 army divisions that it can deploy. Communist China is apparently producing enough light arms and equipment to maintain these forces.

But officials here discount the possibility that Communist China could mount an invasion of Southeast Asia like the invasion of South Korea. Southern China lacks the communications and industrial complex of north China and Manchuria, which supported the Korean operation.

The declining quality of the Chinese Communist Air Forces and Navy was regarded as a bar to any assault against Chinese Nationalist positions on the offshore islands or on Taiwan itself.

The Chinese Communist Air Force is believed to consist largely of 2,500 Soviet-built combat aircraft. These include 2,000 jet fighters, 300 medium jet bombers and some 200 piston-engine bombers.

By Soviet and United States standards, these aircraft are obsolete or soon will be. United States officials have not detected any of the newer Soviet aircraft in use by the Chinese force.

Large-scale Soviet military aid to the Chinese Communist armed forces apparently ended in the late nineteen-fifties when the dispute between Moscow and Peking took on serious proportions.

Officials here report that the Chinese Communist Navy is also showing signs of deterioration because of a lack of Soviet support.

Peking was estimated to have at its disposal 20 to 24 Soviet-built submarines. Some of these were shipped in prefabricated sections to Communist China in the middle nineteen-fifties.

The Chinese Communist submarines have been detected in operation so rarely that there are some doubts as to their combat capabilities.

United States officials say they would not be surprised if Peking exploded a nuclear test device within the next two or three years

PEKING TIGHTENS HOLD OVER ARMY

PEKING, May 25—Communist China is stripping its generals and other officers of their rank and insignia in a move to strengthen Communist control over the People's Liberation Army.

In a decree published in Peking newspapers today, the standing committee of the National People's Congress announced the decision.

Effective June 1, generals and other officers will no longer wear peaked caps, epaulets and special belts and service badges. Instead, all Chinese soldiers, sailors and airmen will wear a simple red star on their caps and a red badge on their collars.

About 150,000 officers, including 160 generals, are affected by the decree, according to Western estimates that place the total strength of China's armed forces at about 2.7 million.

Developed as a guerrilla force during the Chinese revolution, the People's Liberation Army adopted a system of ranks only in 1954. An editorial in today's Liberation Army Daily said: "Ten years of practice has proved that it is not in conformity with our army's glorious tradition, with the close relations between the officers and men, between the higher and lower levels and between the army and people."

There was no mention of graded pay scales, also introduced in 1954. It is thought that these may be retained.

Even without rank or insignia, there must still be men in command. As in earlier years, they will presumably have such titles as "comrade squad leader."

But observers said the decree had great political significance. It was in line with a key dictum of Mao Tse-tung: "The party will control the gun, and the gun will never be allowed to control the party."

In recent years, there have been signs that some officers opposed Government policies. In 1958, for example, there was apparent discontent among officers over China's failure to get modern weapons, including nuclear arms from the Soviet Union.

The Soviet Union, in the early days of the Bolshevik regime, attempted to democratize the army. Under the program commanders from platoon leaders to the commander in chief were to be elected by the soldiers or their committees.

A decree of Dec. 23, 1917, abolished all ranks, titles, decorations and insignia. These innovations helped to speed the demise of the old army, which was being rapidly demobilized, but they were not retained when the Red Army was reorganized early in 1918.

May 26, 1965

Peking Indicates Dissensi... Army's Political Comm...

Special to The New York Times

HONG KONG, Aug. 1—Peking indicated today that the control exercised by political commissars in the Chinese Army had been a continuing source of dissension.

It also revealed that Marshal Peng Teh-huai, the former Defense Minister who was purged in 1959, opposed political control of the army.

The subject of political control was discussed in a long article by Marshal Ho Lung, a member of the Political Bureau and a top commander with the Communist forces during China's civil war.

The article, which marked Army Day in the Peking ideological journal Hung Chi, stressed the superiority of the Chinese Army as a creator of "miracles." It appeared partly aimed at "bolstering" both military and civilian morale in the face of the threat of a war with the United States over Vietnam.

However, analysts believed the article was mainly aimed at emphasizing that the army must continue to adhere to the "indigenous method" that had proved successful in the past and to follow the maxim of the Chinese leader, Mao Tse-tung, that "the party commands the gun while the gun will never be allowed to command the party."

Peking has periodically taken steps to strengthen the control exercised by political commissars or "cadres" in the army. In 1961, regulations were issued calling on soldiers to "respect the cadres and obey their leadership." All insignia of rank were abolished in May, leaving officers as faceless as their men while the power of the already powerful cadres was enhanced.

Marshal Ho Lung's article did not name Marshal Peng, but it alluded to him, according to analysts.

It said that for a time following the Communist's accession to power in China "a few persons who stuck to bourgeois views on military affairs came to the fore again and created trouble."

The article continued: "In the name of building a modern, regular army, they advocated abolition of the party committee system in the army, which in reality meant abolishing leadership of the army by the party, weakening the political work and negating the democratic tradition and mass line of our army."

This "represented a vain attempt to push the People's Liberation Army on to the bourgeois road of army building," the article said.

The writer implied that the army still contained people with this same "bourgeois viewpoint," asserting: "The question of whether to preserve the democratic tradition and the mass line of our army and bring them into full play is an essential part of the struggle

...al Peopl...
...ber on "the struggle to imp... ment Mao Tse-tung's line for army building in opposition to the bourgeois military line." About the same time Marshal Ho Lung was reported to have 'scathingly denounced the revisionist military line."

The analysts said all this pointed to an element in the army that held a dissenting point of view on a number of issues. Apart from opposing political control, they are believed to want Peking's dispute with Moscow patched up so China's military forces can be modernized with Soviet help.

Jeifang Ribao, the armed forces publication, printed an editorial reflecting the official viewpoint, which dismisses China's inferiority in modern weapons.

The editorial said: "Armed with Mao Tse-tung's thinking and long tested in war," China's army was a "mighty force that no enemy in the world, with whatever weapons, can destroy."

It added: "No matter how ferocious U.S. imperialism is, no matter what means it adopts or what weapons it uses, no matter whether it forces us to fight a small or a big war, we are unafraid and are confident of winning."

August 2, 1965

399

CHAPTER 8

The Great Proletarian Cultural Revolution
1965–69

Red Guards storm the
Russian Embassy at Peking, 1967
(photo from inside the Embassy gates).

Courtesy David Oancia, The Globe
and Mail, Toronto.

PEKING EXHORTS KHRUSHCHEV FOES

Denunciation Termed Effort to Precipitate Overthrow

Special to The New York Times.

HONG KONG, July 14—The Chinese Communist leaders are preoccupied with a need to develop a group of young Communists who would be ready to take over from the old guard both in China and the Soviet Union, in the view of analysts of Chinese and Soviet affairs.

Peking's concern with this question is reflected in its latest attack on Premier Khrushchev for his "phony Communism," these experts say. The attack was published in Peking papers today in the form of an article by the editorial departments of Jenmin Jih Pao and Hung Chi, the principal Chinese Communist party organs.

'Fundamental Importance'

The article said that Mao Tse-tung, head of the Chinese Communist party, had affirmed that China must train and bring up millions of successors who would carry on the "cause of the proletarian revolution."

The succession question, it said, is a "matter of life and death for our party and our country."

The article declared that it was a "question of fundamental importance to the proletarian revolutionary cause for a hundred, a thousand, nay, ten thousand years."

"Basing themselves on changes in the Soviet Union, imperialist prophets are pinning their hopes of 'peaceful evolution' on the third or fourth generation of the Chinese party," the article continued.

"We must shatter these imperialist prophecies. From our highest organizations down to the grass roots we must everywhere give constant attention to the training and upbringing of successors to the revolutionary cause."

Similar stress on the need for the Chinese Communists to "win over the youth" was made at a recent Communist Youth League congress, which was attended by Mr. Mao and other leaders.

The analysts said the article was aimed at inciting Stalinists and other possible supporters of Peking to act to overthrow Mr. Khrushchev before he could succeed in his alleged "effort to restore capitalism."

It provided them with encouragement to act by asserting that Mr. Khrushchev was "betraying Socialism" and stood "diametrically opposed to 90 per cent of the total population."

Called 'Paper Tigers'

The article even called the Soviet leaders "paper tigers," a term previously directed at the United States.

The article also provided political ammunition for any potential opponents of Mr. Khrushchev by declaring that his "democracy of the whole people" was a "despotic dictatorship of the Khrushchev clique over the Soviet people." It charged that the Soviet leaders had "on more than one occasion bloodily suppressed striking workers and masses who put up resistance."

The Chinese described Mr. Khrushchev as an "incorrigible wastrel" who had "squandered grain reserves built up under Stalin and brought difficulties into the lives of the Soviet people.

Summing up, the article said that the issue confronting the Soviet people was "how to resist and oppose Khrushchev's effort to restore capitalism."

Liberal Leaders Foreseen

State Department experts on China have believed for a long time that a more liberal generation of leaders may follow the present regime in Peking. This policy was enunciated strongly in a speech last Dec. 14 by Roger Hilsman Jr., then Assistant Secretary of State for Far Eastern Affairs.

"We do not know what changes—I think there may be some changes—may occur in the attitudes of future Chinese leaders," he said. "But if I may paraphrase a classic canon of our past, we pursue a policy toward Communist China of the open door.

"We are determined to keep the door open to the possibility of change, and not to slam it shut against any developments which might advance our national good, serve the free world, and benefit the people of China."

London Hears Rumors Hinting That Mao Has Suffered a Stroke

But Peking, Quickly Replying to Report, Says That His Health Is Excellent

LONDON, May 30 (AP)—The British Government has received word from Peking that Mao Tse-tung, who has not been seen publicly for seven weeks, may have suffered a stroke. He is 71 years old.

British informants said, however, that there was no confirmation of the reports although there was speculation in several world capitals that the Chinese Communist party chairman was seriously ill. The British sources said their messages on Mr. Mao's health were strictly speculative and had been labeled as such.

In Moscow there have been reports that Mr. Mao's health is worsening. These rumors appeared to have originated with diplomats whose governments have diplomatic representatives in Peking. The British have a diplomatic mission there under a chargé d'affaires, Donald Charles Hopson.

The last time Mr. Mao appeared in public was on April 13.

On May 13, a deputy minister in Peking told a Western diplomat that Mr. Mao's health was good.

In London, Western diplomats suggested that the world might learn within the next few days whether the condition of China's leader was serious enough to have important political repercussions.

Premier Chou En-lai is to leave Peking shortly on a tour of Africa. The assumption among Western authorities is that if Mr. Mao's condition is serious, Mr. Chou will try to postpone his trip.

Chairman Mao is generally regarded as the strongman and principal theoretician of the Chinese Communist Government.

It was he who led the Communists to their victory over Chiang Kai-shek's Nationalists in 1949. Although he heads the party, he holds no governmental post. His position as the major source of Chinese Communist doctrine appears virtually unchallenged.

Peking Denies Rumors

PEKING, Monday, May 31 (Reuters)—A Foreign Ministry spokesman denied today rumors that Party Chairman Mao Tse-tung was ill.

"Chairman Mao is in excellent health," the spokesman said.

He did not say where the Communist leader is at present.

Many foreign diplomats believe he is away from the capital, resting or on tour.

Officials in London said yesterday that the British chargé d'affaires in Peking, Donald Hopson, had reported to the Foreign Office on speculation that Mr. Mao had suffered a serious deterioration in health, but Mr. Hopson was not able to say whether the rumors were true.

In Tokyo the Japanese news agency Kyodo quoted "authoritative sources" in Peking as saying that Mr. Mao attended a meeting in Peking yesterday of the Standing Committee of the People's Congress.

'Ready to See God'

Mao Tse-tung suggested early this year that he was "getting ready to see God very soon." His remark was reported by the American journalist Edgar Snow in The New Republic Feb. 27. Mr. Snow said it was made in a four-hour interview Jan. 9 in Peking.

Mr. Snow said Chairman Mao had seemed "in good condition," but he reported that Mr. Mao had smiled wryly and had said there seemed to be some doubt about his health. Asked whether he believed in God, Mr. Mao said that he did not but that some people, who professed to be well-informed, said there was a God.

One of the Chinese leader's physicians, Mr. Snow said, "informed me that Mao has no organic troubles and suffers from nothing beyond the normal fatigue of his age."

'Three Packs a Day'

The Snow interview took place some months after a talk of two and a half hours in Hangchow between Mr. Mao and a group of French politicians and industrialists. This was reported Nov. 14 by one participant, Edward Behr, director of a French television crew, in The Saturday Evening Post.

Mr. Behr said an attendant had guided Mr. Mao lightly by the elbow. Mr. Mao smoked incessantly, Mr. Behr said, and he appeared to be a "three-pack-a-day man," with "a bad case of smoker's cough; he breathed heavily and with a distinct wheeze."

"He also had some slight difficulty in coordinating his gestures," Mr. Behr wrote. "To light a cigarette, Mao (who is not left-handed) held the matchbox in his right hand and struck the match with his left. To get a better grip, he steadied himself by bearing down with both elbows on the arm rests of his chair."

2 Peking Writers Accused of Criticizing Regime

Special to The New York Times

HONG KONG, Feb. 15—Two prominent literary figures in Communist China have been subjected to an inquisition as severe as the legal prosecution that resulted in hard-labor sentences for two Russian writers

The consequences for the Chinese writers could be equally unpleasant, although their trial has been conducted in the press and no public pronouncement of sentence is expected.

Both men have given loyal service to the Peking regime in the past. One, Wu Han, is Deputy Mayor of Peking and a noted historian. The other, Tien Han, is a leading playwright who composed the words of Communist China's national anthem.

Attack Directed by Mao

Both wrote plays with a historical background that drew a moral for the present. Written in 1961, at a time when the country was in severe economic straits, their plays by inference criticized bureaucratic bumbling.

They have come under belated attack at the personal direction of Mao Tse-tung, chairman of the Central Committee of the Chinese Communist party. At the same time the Communist party has launched a general "rectification" drive

within the literary world. Hsinhua, the official press agency, reported that 160,000 literary and art workers had gone to factories, rural areas and armed forces to "remold their thinking."

Although Wu Han and Tien Han have not been arraigned before a judge, charges leveled against them in the controlled press carry the weight of a formal accusation. They include the allegation that the two men engaged in "antiparty" activities, a serious matter in a country where the word of the Communist party is law.

The Chinese writers are not likely to end up in jail, but they could find themselves just as effectively silenced and punished by a period of "socialist education" in a remote country area.

Similarities Observed

Observers here find marked similarities between the circumstances of writers in China today and the situation of writers in the Soviet Union 30 years ago. By comparison contemporary Soviet writers have considerably more freedom.

Wu Han, who is 56, has been Deputy Mayor of Peking since the Communists came to power in 1949. A specialist in the history of the Ming dynasty (1644-1912), he wrote about a

national hero of that period in a play that has been under official scrutiny.

The play, titled "Hai Jui Loses His Office," angered the regime because it suggested that traditional moral values could be taken over by contemporary society. The play was first criticized in a Shanghai newspaper, Wen Hui Pao, last November and has since been denounced in most major Chinese papers.

Wu Han has now conceded that he committed an "extremely grave error" in suggesting that traditional moral values could have any place in a Communist society. His views, he admits, were "basically capitalist and feudalist."

Anthem Appeals to People

Communist China's national anthem, "March of the Volunteers," addresses itself to the people:

Arise, all ye who refuse to be slaves!
With our flesh and blood.
Let us build our new great wall . . .
Braving the enemies' fire, march on!
March on! March on! March on!

Tien Han, who wrote these words, appears to have been making a more subtle appeal for social reform in the play that has resulted in his fall from grace.

He related the tale of an

imaginary heroine, Hsien Yao-huan, an official in the court of Empress Wu Tse-tien of the Tang dynasty (618-907).

Championing the rights of people against corrupt officials, the heroine petitioned the Empress for political reform. In the intrigues of the court, she was not a match for corrupt officials and was eventually killed. Tien Han implied that people like himself could not gain the ear of the government to criticize official shortcomings.

Jenmin Jih Pao, the organ of the Chinese Communist party, has accused him of distorting history and preaching an "idealistic historical viewpoint."

Tien Han, it said, "borrows historical characters and incidents to attack and decry current phenomena."

In the press attacks, Tien Han and Wu Han have been associated with "three reconciliations and one reduction," a slogan coined by Peking to package policies that it attributes to hostile forces. These elements are said to advocate reconciliation with United States "imperialists," Chinese "reactionaries" and Soviet "revisionists" as well as a reduction in Chinese aid to "liberation movements" abroad like that of the Vietcong in South Vietnam.

February 16, 1966

Peking Presses Cultural Purge; Army Joins in Call for Vigilance

By SEYMOUR TOPPING
Special to The New York Times

HONG KONG, May 4—A widespread cultural purge with clearly stated political overtones is under way within the Chinese Communist party.

The extent of the purge, and the seriousness with which it is being conducted, have been made clear in recent days by some of the most authoritative journals of the Chinese party.

The Army joined today in spreading the call for vigilance against "antiparty, anti-Socialist" intellectuals. An editorial in Jiefangjun Pao, the official army newspaper, asserted:

"Activities of these antiparty, anti-Socialist elements are not an accidental phenomenon. They are responding to the great international anti-

Chinese chorus of imperialists, modern revisionists and various reactionaries to revive the Chinese reactionary class, which has been struck down."

The army newspaper accused certain intellectuals, whom it did not name, of being linked to "right-wing opportunists" within the Communist party. The editorial asserted that the debate developing on the cultural front was not simply an academic dispute but a "struggle to the death" to eliminate bourgeois ideology.

[American analysts of Chinese affairs viewed the editorial's reference to "revisionists" as a thinly veiled charge that links had been established by Soviet Communists with some Chinese Communists. The Chinese

leadership has scorned the Soviet leadership as "revisionists" since their ideological break.]

The paper's view reflected the mounting intensity of the cultural purge in China, which is directed at compelling strict adherence to the dogmas of Mao Tse - tung, chairman of the Communist party, in literature, art, education and journalism. Political commissars have been accusing leading members of the intelligentsia of pretending to follow the party line while resisting the regime's efforts to "remold their thinking."

'Lordly Attitude' Condemned

Hung Chi, the ideological journal of the Central Committee, warned intellectuals that they would have to shed their "lordly attitude" and bow to the criticism of the masses.

"Workers, peasants and soldiers who are armed with Mao Tse-tung's thinking have a most acute sense for distinguishing flowers from poisonous weeds," the journal asserted.

Reports from China said that leading intellectuals had been jolted by the public humiliation of Kuo Mo-jo, the country's

most prominent scholar and the regime's spokesman on cultural affairs for many years.

The 78-year-old scholar has conceded that he failed in his voluminous published works to apply correctly the teachings of Mao Tse-tun C.

"Strictly speaking, according to the standards of today, all that I have written should be burned," Mr. Kuo said in a speech made on April 14 and published last week in the Peking press.

Intellectuals have interpreted the confession as a warning that no one in the cultural fields is safe from the party purge.

Mr. Kuo has been a literary and political collaborator of Chairman Mao. It was not known what part, if any, Mr. Mao took in impelling his old associate to make his unexpected speech of self-criticism. Mr. Kuo is president of the Chinese Academy of Sciences and chairman of the All-China Federation of Literary and Art Workers, and holds more than 20 other official positions.

Mr. Mao has been absent from public activities for five months and is believed to be

403

Kuo Mo-jo

Hsinhua

ill. However, today's Hung Chi article asserted: "Mao Tse-tung's ideas are the supreme directive for all our work."

Hsinhua, the Government press agency, reported that Mr. Kuo had spent May Day with factory workers in Chengtu, Szechuan, his native province. Mr. Kuo has been a prominent participant in national celebrations in Peking, particularly in his capacity as chairman of the China Peace Committee.

Observers said Mr. Kuo might have returned to Szechuan to undergo "molding of thinking among the masses." In his speech of self-criticism, he concluded by saying: "Now I must learn from the workers, peasants and soldiers."

The army newspaper asserted that a distinction should be made between antiparty intellectuals and those whose heart was with the party and Socialism and whose errors in writing poor works could be corrected.

There was no indication how Mr. Kuo or other prominent intellectuals known to be in trouble with the party were being catalogued.

There was an ominous tone in the attack of the army newspaper on intellectuals. The party's policy has been generally to remold disgraced intellectuals through persuasion rather than violent retaliation.

Hsinhua also distributed the text of a speech made Saturday in Peking by Premier Chou En-lai in which he stated: "A Socialist cultural revolution of great historic significance is being launched in our country. This is a fierce and protracted struggle as to who will win, the proletariat or bourgeoisie in the ideological field."

Calling for the eradication of bourgeois ideology from all cultural fields, the Premier declared: "This is a key question in the development in depth of our Socialist revolution at the present stage, a question concerning the situation as a whole and a matter of the first magnitude affecting the destiny and future of our party and country."

Bourgeois Bent Seen

Analysts said that the cultural purge was a manifestation of the sense of insecurity Mr. Mao and other leaders felt about the evolution of Chinese Communist society.

Despite lip service paid to Maoist philosophy by intellectuals, the party is complaining that many of them have failed to remold themselves inwardly and have retained bourgeois leanings that could endanger the revolution.

Many of the country's intellectuals are portrayed in reports from the Chinese mainland as "frightened men" who feel that they may be denounced at any time. Party ideologists are rereading literary and scholarly works that date from 1959 to find evidence of heresy.

May 5, 1966

Yugoslav Press Reports China Has Dismissed 2 Major Figures

BELGRADE, Yugoslavia, May 28 (AP)—The Yugoslav press agency Tanyug reported from Peking today that two top Chinese leaders had apparently lost their posts in an army campaign against persons who have differed with the Chinese party Chairman Mao Tse-tung.

It identified one of them as Peng Chen, Mayor of Peking. He was also listed as a member of the Politburo, a secretary of the Communist party's Central Committee and First Secretary of the municipal Communist party of Peking.

The other leader was identified as Lo Jui-ching, a secretary of the Communist party, Vice Premier, and chief of the army's general staff.

Tanyug said the dismissals would be made public within a few days.

If confirmed, they would involve the highest-ranking persons to fall in the purge that has wracked China in recent months.

Army Paper Attacks

Tanyug said these men were the targets of a newspaper campaign that began in the Chinese Army newspaper Jiefang-jun Pao, which was reprinted in the Peking-party paper, Peking Jih Pao. The Peking paper carried it under the headline "Let us unmask the so-called authorities and let us open fire upon the so-called authorities."

Yugoslavia, an independent Communist country, has both diplomats and newsmen in Communist China.

Tanyug said the internal struggle was apparently the cause of a postponement of premier Chou En-lai's planned trip to Cairo and Bucharest.

Mr. Lo dropped from public view last Nov. 26. He was the only military man among the nine members of the Communist party's Secretariat and was generally considered the operating head of the Defense Ministry.

Tanyug said it was considered significant that he did not appear at an important army political conference last January and noted that the campaign had been led by an army newspaper. This would indicate Mr. Lo no longer controlled the army. He held the rank of general before China eliminated military titles last year.

He got his high army post in September, 1959, when his predecessor, Peng Teh-Hua, was purged. Tanyug said one of his jobs was to rectify errors that had led to the dismissal of Mr. Peng. He may not have succeeded.

Mayor Peng of Peking did not appear at ceremonies honoring visiting Rumanian and Albanian delegations earlier this month. Observers of Chinese politics immediately speculated that he was in disgrace.

Mayor Peng, 67 years old, has not been mentioned in the Chinese press since March 27. One of his Deputy Mayors, Wu Han, and two newspapers under his general supervision have been criticized for their approach to Maoism.

May 29, 1966

Peking Charges 'Gangster Den' In Arts Is Backing Revisionists

Deputy Director of Party's Propaganda and 2 Opera Producers Attacked

PEKING—Newspaper editors and their political supervisors, continuing a campaign against "bourgeois" intellectuals, have attacked two Shanghai opera producers and the deputy director in the Propaganda Department of China's Central Committee of the Communist party.

The names of the producers and the party official have not been disclosed in print yet, but demands are being published that the "big boss" behind the "gangster den" be unmasked.

The two theatrical artists were assailed in a lengthy article on the operatic work, "Hai Jui Counsels the Emperor." The critic, Fang Tze-sheng, saw in this work an allegory on China during the period of disasters following the Great Leap Forward, China's attempt to speed agricultural and industrial production. The real intention of the producers, the critic said, was to urge party leaders to give up office and to let the revisionists take over.

The critic charged that backing for this effort was given not only by a "handful of persons" in Shanghai but also by a deputy head of the central committee's Propaganda Department who made suggestions, sent material and praised the production.

The Propaganda Department ranks in importance with the Organization Department in the Communist party. Its director, Liu Ting-yi, and four of its deputy directors are members of the party's central committee. A fifth deputy, Chou Yang, is an alternate member of the committee.

Responsible for All Art

The department is responsible for all cultural, scientific, literary and artistic and publishing work as well as for theoretical propaganda. Its importance is indicated by the fact that all men assigned to it have long party experience. Many are members of the top control body.

Tanyug, the Yugoslav news agency, reports that Peng Chen and Lo Jui-ching, respectively mayor of Peking and chief of the general staff, are rumored to have been dismissed from office.

Yao Hen-yuan, who wrote the initial criticism of Wu Han, the historian and vice mayor of Peking who has been denounced, wrote a lengthy article for Shanghai newspapers. It is reproduced in the Peking Review, an English-language weekly.

Implicated with Mr. Wu are Liao Mo-sha and Teng To, former editor in chief of the People's Daily and Front Line Magazine who, Mr. Yao said, "controlled and monopolized the leading posts in the ideological and cultural work of Peking."

The press now calls the case against the opera producers and the party official "The Gangster Den of the Village of Three Families."

The charges say:

¶Teng To asserted that the Communist party did not calculate the limits on labor power used in different kinds of capital construction, which could be construed as a charge that Communist rulers overworked the populace. "Had we followed this line not only would we have had no atom bombs but we would have been reduced to an imperialist colony," Mr. Yao said.

Teng To urged leaders to learn from and unite with stronger countries to facilitate development. The critic said this was the tune of rightist opportunists who were "slandering the party line for Socialist construction as forced and claimed China's only way out is to learn fom the Soviet revisionist clique and practice revisionism in China."

¶Wu Han, through plays using the material of history, was in reality defending those dismissed from office either for right opportunist tendencies or for a desire to maintain

amicable relations with the Soviet Union.

Among those dismissed were Peng Teh-huai, former defense minister. The author also saw in Mr. Wu's writing a denigration of Chinese leadership and a denunciation of party cadres at various levels.

University Chief Denounced
Special to The New York Times

HONG KONG, June 2 — The Chinese Communist party, in extension of its ideological purge of the country's cultural life, published today a denunciation of Lu Ping, president of Peking University.

Mr. Lu, a senior member of the party, and two other officials of the country's leading university were accused of having defied the leadership by shielding disgraced intellectuals who had been found guilty of bourgeois and Soviet revisionist activities.

Jenmin Jih Pao, the party organ, and other Peking newspapers published a statement denouncing the three officials. It had been drawn up by seven members of the philosophy department of the university.

The statement, which was posted on the campus, accused Mr. Lu of having suppressed the "strong revolutionary demand" of the university's teachers and students for a full role in the cultural revolution.

The broadening of the attack on the Peking party branch tended to support speculation that Peng Chen, a leading member of the Politburo, who is also general secretary of the branch and mayor of Peking, may be in serious trouble. He has not been seen publicly since the end of March.

Peking newspapers have been hinting that the identity of the prominent person who is charged with screening "anti-party activities" of the Peking branch may soon be disclosed.

January 3, 1966

PEKING RESHAPING HIGHER EDUCATION

Communists Find System Is Politically Unreliable — 2 Ministers May Be Out

By SEYMOUR TOPPING
Special to The New York Times

HONG KONG, June 24—Communist China is reshaping its 15-year-old system of higher education because the party has

found it to be politically unreliable.

Peking newspapers say that radical changes in student selection, grading and curriculums are being made in colleges and universities to eliminate "breeding grounds for counter-revolution" and to insure that the doctrine of Mao Tse-tung, the Communist party chairman, is passed from generation to generation.

There are hints that Ho Wei, Minister of Education, and Chiang Nan-hsiang, Minister of Higher Education, have been dismissed from their posts. Their names are no longer mentioned in the press.

The shake-up of the educational system is part of the "cultural revolution," or purge, that has been in progress for weeks.

Analysts believe that the cultural purge is related in some of its aspects to a struggle for power within the ruling hierarchy that already has toppled Peng Chen, a member of the Politburo and Mayor of Peking.

Marshal Lin Piao, the Defense Minister, and Teng Hsiaoping, Secretary General of the party, who are dominant figures in the Politburo, apparently succeeded in undercutting Mr. Peng by accusing his subordinates of deviating from the Maoist line.

In general, however, the "cultural revolution" is simply another phase in the recurring fight by the Maoists to curb a tendency within society to move toward revisionism or Communism of the Soviet type, in which attainment of material comforts is sometimes given priority over dedication to world revolution.

Experts in Hong Kong believe that academic standards in Communist China will deteriorate sharply over the next years as a consequence of the purge of numerous teachers who have been condemned as bourgeois or revisionist and of the shake-up of organization of college-level institutions.

The "cultural revolution," which hit Peking University last month, is reported to be disrupting institutions of higher education throughout the country.

Resistance by Professors

Party workers bringing the "cultural revolution" to school campuses evidently are encountering some resistance from professors and administrators. The Sian radio reported that Peking Kang, an experienced official who is secretary of the party committee at Sian Communica-

tions University, had been dismissed because he had attempted to oust agitators from the campus.

Denouncing "high and mighty" anti-party and anti-Socialist bourgeois "authorities who are occupying positions in the educational world," Jenmin Jih Pao, the party organ, warned:

"This struggle has only just begun and there are still many stubborn bourgeois strongholds that have not been breached."

The party's Central Committee and the State Council, meeting in Peking June 13, decreed abolition of the existing system of entrance examinations for higher educational institutions. The examinations were denounced as a tool utilized by anti-party elements to mold student bodies politically.

Hsinhua, the Government press agency, quoted Shih Chuan-hsiang, a Peking night-soil collector, as having said: "The bourgeois 'specialists' and 'professors' were daydreaming when they planned to prevent children of workers and peasants from attending school and from reading Chairman Mao's writings."

New Enrollment Method

A new method of enrollment, more favorable to children of workers and peasants, is being worked out "in which proletarian politics are right to the fore and the mass line is followed." Meanwhile, the Government has postponed the enrollment of new freshman classes for six months.

The party evidently intends to increase heavily the proportion of students of "proletarian background," who are regarded as most trustworthy politically.

According to information in Hong Kong, about 50 to 60 per cent of the students enrolled in higher institutions are children of workers or poor or lower-middle peasants, while the rest are from families said to have a bourgeois character. About 1.3 per cent of college-age youths in the country are attending higher educational institutions.

Jenmin Jih Pao said that grading methods and the content of curriculums would also be changed.

"New teaching materials must be compiled under the guidance of thought of Mao Tse-tung and the principle of placing proletarian politics in the forefront," the party paper said.

The changes having their first impact on departments of liberal arts and social sciences in colleges and universities. Technical faculties are to be reformed more gradually.

Eventually, the party plans to extend the changes to middle and junior schools.

June 25, 1966

Purges Show Red China Seeks To Widen Educational Upheaval

The following dispatch is by David Oancia of The Globe and Mail, Toronto.

© 1966 by The Globe and Mail

PEKING — When a sage in Confucianist China donned a long gown, it was a badge of learning that gave him position, privilege, influence and economic security that enabled him to turn his back on physical work for life.

A century of turmoil capped by the victory of the Communist revolution has resulted in many changes in the position of scholars. The gown has been discarded and rituals are vanishing and there has been unprecedented dedication to tasks, once considered beneath the dignity of Mandarin sages, to build China into a modern state.

But the Communist rulers are still dissatisfied. They have accused professors and university presidents of being "bourgeois" and "revisionist" and of not giving children of workers, peasants and soldiers an even break in institutions of higher learning.

Since early June the "cultural revolution" has been raging on campuses, a revolution characterized by students hurling accusations at fellow students, professors and administrators. The wholesale reorganization of the education system is now under way.

Admission System Altered

In mid-June the Communist party's Central Committee and the country's State Council (Government) announced that the old entrance-examination system for colleges was to be scrapped and enrollment was to be postponed until after the New Year to complete the "cultural revolution" and to work out a new admission system. One goal will be to absorb a greater number of "revolutionary young people from among workers, peasants and soldiers."

A hint of what is in store was provided recently when Jenmin Jih Pao, the party daily, gave prominence to a letter written by seven students urging the Central Committee and Chairman Mao Tse-tung to overhaul the arts colleges.

They called for the inclusion of Chairman Mao's works as a subject, the inclusion of the "class struggle" as a main course, the shortening of the school year, early graduation, and the dispatch of graduates to integrate with workers, peasants and soldiers, unconditionally and for a long time.

The students' proposal obviously has the approval of the leadership. An editor's note "warmly supported" what it described as their "revolutionary" suggestion.

Shorter Courses Urged

The students charged that the colleges neglected practical experience and were divorced from workers and peasants; that seventeen years of school took up too big a part of a youth's life; that too much emphasis was placed on book learning and scholasticism; that teachers tried to instill knowledge in much the same way as peasants fed Peking ducks, and that the length of courses wasted both teachers and manpower.

Perhaps the most telling criticism was about attitudes engendered.

The students proposed a cut in the length of university courses from five to two years. Part of each school year would be spent in productive labor in either industry or agriculture, in military training and in "class struggle."

They asked that colleges be made accessible to those with "revolutionary" experience and "progressive" thinking even if they had not finished senior middle school.

If, as seems likely, their proposal is accepted, yet another nail will be driven into the coffin of the ritual of the sages. The rulers seem determined to sweep them off the pedestal on which they once stood on and to put them to work in the army and factories and on farms.

The leaders know the history of their country and they apparently do not want intellectual Mandarins to assume power as they did after other dynastic changes in the past.

MAO BIDS PEOPLE UNITE WITH ARMY

Integration Order Is Called a Part of Peking Purge

HONG KONG, Aug. 2—Mao Tse-tung, Chairman of the Central Committee of the Chinese Communist party, has ordered greater integration between the armed forces and the Chinese people, with soldiers undertaking civilian tasks and civilians learning from the army.

His main aim is believed to be elimination of those professional characteristics of the army that might encourage new dissident elements.

Mr. Mao's "extremely important directions" on building the army were contained in a major editorial published yesterday in Chiefang Chun Pao, the armed forces publication. The editoral, marking Army Day, was reprinted in all Peking newspapers today with reports that the "mass movement to learn from the People's Liberation Army" had reached its climax.

By virtue of their closer contact, the army and civilian population will each act as the other's watchdog, according to the directive. At the same time, Mr. Mao apparently aims to invest civilian life with some of the "revolutionary spirit" Peking attributes to the army. Finally, the army will represent a disciplined labor force able to make an important contribution to the economy.

Lin Receives Praise

The editorial in Chiefang Chun Pao further bolstered the public image of Defense Minister Lin Piao by praising the way he had "most resolutely and thoroughly carried out Chairman Mao's ideas and line concerning army building." Mr. Lin has emerged as Mr. Mao's most likely successor.

Quoting Mr. Mao, the editorial said the army should be a great school in which soldiers should learn politics, military affairs and culture. Mr. Mao's proposals seem designed to keep soldiers busy.

Mr. Mao said: "They can also engage in agricultural production and side occupations, run some medium or small factories and manufacture a number of products to meet their own needs or exchange with the state at equal values. They can also do mass work and take part in the Socialist education movement in factories and villages."

The editorial said the third struggle took place "not very long ago." The editorial also referred to the current purge of party and Government figures that has been taking place in the name of the "proletarian cultural revolution."

The chief military victim of the purge, Lo Jui-ching, chief of the army's general staff, disappeared from public view last November, while civilian victims did not begin to fall until some months later.

Another possible purge victim is Hsiao Hua, chief of the army's General Political Department, who has not appeared at military functions for some time.

PEKING REDS BACK MAO AND AFFIRM MILITANT POLICY

By SEYMOUR TOPPING
Special to The New York Times

HONG KONG, Aug. 13—The Central Committee of the Chinese Communist party, meeting in plenary session for the first time since 1962, affirmed today that Peking would hold fast to its militant revolutionary policies at home and abroad.

The assembly endorsed the leadership of Mao Tse-tung, the party chairman, who presided over the session, and praised the ideological contributions of Lin Piao, the Defense Minister.

Mr. Lin, who is 58 and the youngest member of the Politburo, has emerged during the recent purge of the party hierarchy as the most influential deputy of the 72-year-old Chairman.

Support 'to the End'

In a communiqué issued after the meeting in Peking, the committee promised to support North Vietnam "in fighting to the end" against the United States, and it accused the Soviet Union of betraying the Vietnamese Communist cause.

The communiqué contained a hint that Peking intended to provide new assistance to the Vietnamese Communists.

"The plenary session fully agrees with all the measures already taken and all the actions to be taken as decided upon by the Central Committee of the party and the Government in consultation with the Vietnamese side concerning aid to Vietnam for resisting U.S. aggression," it said.

The communiqué declared that "an invigorating revolutionary atmosphere prevails in the whole country and the situation is one of a new all-around leap forward emerging."

Evocation of '58 'Leap'

The declaration evoked memories of Chairman Mao's 1958 "Great Leap Forward," a radical experiment in collectivization of farm and factory pro-

duction that ended disastrously and set the economy back by about five years.

The meeting, which was convened from Aug. 1 to 12 as the 11th plenary session of the eighth Central Committee, brought together senior party and Government leaders, regional, provincial and municipal party officials and representatives of Peking teachers and students.

It approved the principal decisions taken by the Politburo since the last plenary meeting, held Sept. 24 to 27, 1962.

At the last assembly, the Central Committee revealed the purge of Huang Ko-cheng, the Army Chief of Staff, and Tan Cheng, Vice Minister of Defense, who were deputies to Marshal Pen Teh-huai, the Defense Minister, who had been dismissed earlier.

The communiqué of the latest meeting, which was distributed abroad by Hsinhua, the Government press agency, made no mention of the most prominent victims of the current purge.

These are Peng Chen, a member of the Politburo and Mayor of Peking; Lo Jui-ching, chief of the Army General Staff, and Lu Ting-yi, Minister of Culture and head of the Central Committee's propaganda department.

The communiqué asserted that the purge, which has been dubbed by the party as the great cultural revolution, would be pressed against "the handful of antiparty, anti-Socialist rightists."

Apart from the dismissal of senior party officials, the purge has affected thousands of students and teachers in institutions of higher education who have been accused of failing to support Maoist revolutionary concepts.

The meeting urged party members "not to be afraid of disorder" in making revolution and in arousing the masses against the bourgeois rightists.

The communiqué also called for an international united front against the United States, which was denounced as "the most ferocious common enemy of the peoples of the whole world."

It asserted that the Kremlin leaders, who were condemned as "scabs", could not be included in this united front because the Soviet Union was collaborating with the United States in an attempt to attain world domination.

YOUTHS IN PEKING RUIN ART OBJECTS

Statues Are Called 'Demons of Old Ruling Classes'

By The Associated Press

TOKYO, Aug. 26—Communist China's rampaging young Red Guards have destroyed Greek, Roman and Chinese art pieces, including statues of the Venus de Milo and Apollo, the Peking radio said today.

The broadcast, monitored here, said students and instructors from the Peking Normal Academy had joined art students who dragged out the art objects, smashed them and set them afire Wednesday in front of the Peking Central Art Academy. The account said the youths had denounced the objects as "demons and monsters of the old ruling classes."

Peking's Hsinhua press agency said "the revolutionary rebel spirit" of Peking's young Red Guards had "sparked off a prairie fire that is sweeping the whole of China."

The agency said this fire was "burning down all the decadent influences of the bourgeois and feudal classes as well as all old ideas, old culture, old customs and old habits."

The broadcast, however, omitted mention of sacking homes of so-called "capitalists," breaking of windows, roughing up of citizens considered opposed to the ideology of the Chinese leader, Mao Tse-tung, and kangaroo courts in the streets by the teen-age, self-appointed defenders of Maoism, and acts of vandalism against religious institutions, as reported by foreign newsmen. Japanese reporters sai the adolescent hordes are, in effect, reimposing the bleak drabness of China's gloomiest economic days.

Any sign of a better life is attacked by the Red Guards as symbols of remaining or resurgent capitalist, bourgeois thinking, and denounced as anti-Socialist and anti-Maoist.

Western-style skirts and traditional Chinese women's costumes, which had begun to reappear in city streets, vanished when the Red Guards started their campaign, the reports said.

The better restaurants have been told to serve only cheap meals, tailors not to make fancy costumes, barbers not to give "bizarre" Hong Kong-style haircuts.

Meanwhile, speculation on the fate of President Liu Shao-chi increased as Hsinhu disclosed that Mr. Mao had received a Tanzanian goodwill mission in Peking. Mr. Liu was not present.

The 68-year-old President, generally believed to have been replaced by Defense Minister Lin Piao as No. 2 man in the Communist party, has not appeared in public since Aug. 18.

SOVIET IS REVILED BY PEKING THRONG IN ALL-DAY RALLY

By Reuters

PEKING, Aug. 29 — Thousands of demonstrators paraded today in a street near the Soviet Embassy in a rally against "revisionism" — China's name for Soviet Communism.

No incidents were reported and the well-disciplined marchers never went nearer than 100 yards from the embassy in a demonstration that lasted all day.

[Japanese reports from Peking said further demonstrations planned for Tuesday apparently had been canceled by the Chinese leadership to avoid a possible diplomatic break with the Soviet Union, The Associated Press reported from Tokyo.]

The embassy was guarded by about 200 Chinese troops and policemen. Foreign diplomats and correspondents, who received printed invitations to attend, moved freely among the marchers.

Compound's Gates Shut

The main gates of the walled embassy compound remained closed. Soldiers and policemen formed a double row to guard the gates. But the embassy was subjected to a din of amplified drumming and shouted slogans from the marchers.

The demonstration began with a formal ceremony changing the name of the Street of Growing Prestige to Anti-Revisionism Street.

The demonstration seemed to some observers to be partly a defiant reply from the militant Red Guards to a Soviet note last week complaining about their "hooligan pranks" outside the embassy.

The Red Guard, loose bands consisting mostly of teen-agers, are the vanguard of China's continuing "great proletarian cultural revolution" aimed at removing all old and foreign influences from Chinese life.

Restraint Is Urged

Although the youths have government approval for their activities, excesses in recent days have prompted official admonishment that reasoning, not violence, is the path to success.

In the demonstration, young Red Guards placed huge portraits of the party chairman, Mao Tse-tung, and of Marx, Engels, Lenin and Stalin a few paces in front of the green-domed embassy's gates. The spot is near where foreign diplomats and newsmen were taunted and threatened last week.

The portraits blocked the passage of any car that might try to leave or enter the embassy.

Most of the demonstrators crowding the streets around the embassy were Red Guards. Each demonstrator carried a red booklet of quotations from Chairman Mao's works, and shouted in unison slogans attacking Soviet "revisionism."

It was a well-organized rally and the demonstrators lined the neighboring streets in orderly fashion.

Reporting generally on the progress of the revolution, Hsinhua, the official press agency, said the young Red Guards had responded well to the call for more discipline and civility in pressing their crusade.

"They are determined to become model workers in applying mass discipline and carrying out the policies of the party and the state and to build the Red Guard into highly organized and disciplined ranks of revolutionary young people," it said.

The agency reported in another dispatch that the revolution had swept through every city in China.

During the ceremony in which the street was renamed, Red Guards gave a series of speeches denouncing Soviet revisionism at the top of their voices from a platform built on the boulevard on the opposite end of the street from the embassy. Then the demonstrators marched out of the street leading to the embassy, but continued to stream past the platform beating drums, gongs and cymbals and shouting slogans all day.

Every column of marchers was led by a big garlanded gilt-framed portrait of Chairman Mao, followed by a percussion band. Pairs of loudspeakers were placed every few yards along the embassy street, making it impossible to be heard except by shouting loudly.

Behind the embassy walls there was no sign of activity, but Soviet sources said a side gate was being used for embassy business.

Guards Seem Less Active

Meanwhile, the Red Guards continued their activities in the city center, but there appeared to be fewer than last week.

Diplomats and correspondents have seen several cases of rough treatment of Chinese adults, mostly in the night before the mass rally. Others involved young people, probably about the same age as some of the Red Guards.

In one case a girl, about 16, was seen being driven off in a Red Guard truck with older people, presumably members of her family. The girl wore a tall, pointed hat with inscriptions denouncing her. The adults wore placards around their necks.

There was still no word on what had become of about 16 Chinese nuns believed to have been in a convent occupied by the Red Guards last week.

Eight foreign nuns who were also in the convent when it was taken over have been expelled from China for "illegal espionage activities."

East Germans Abused

BELGRADE, Yugoslavia, Aug. 29 (Reuters)—Two East German diplomats and their families were attacked by Chinese demonstrators near the Soviet Embassy in Peking last night, the Yugoslav news agency Tanyug, reported from the Chinese capital today.

It said the East German Embassy in Peking was reported to have made an immediate sharp protest to the Chinese Foreign Ministry.

Tanyug said that in the attack, which occurred as the East Germans rode in a car, the 16-year-old son of the East German military attaché in Peking was knocked down and his leg was injured

TOKYO, Aug. 29—Japanese observer in Peking has reported that the juvenile violence now sweeping Communist China is seemingly under high-level direction to rid the populace of elements hostile to Chairman Mao and Defense Minister Lin Piao, Mr. Mao's heir apparent in the Peking hierarchy.

The movement "has a strong color of a coup" planned by supporters of Mr. Mao and Mr. Lin, Tadashi Nogami, Peking correspondent of Asahi Shimbun, said in a telephone dispatch to his Tokyo office. The report was published in the mass-circulation newspaper today.

"Behind the Red Guards there is a well-planned leadership," Mr. Nogami declared. "Some degree of order is being maintained and the movement is linked to the highest organ.

"The actions of the Red Guards are backed by strong powers and nobody can make any complaint against any action they take."

MOSCOW, Aug. 29 (Reuters) —The Soviet Union was silent today on the massive anti-Soviet demonstration being staged outside its embassy in Peking.

Asked if any response to the demonstration was planned, a Government spokesman declined to comment.

The newspapers Pravda and Izvestia ignored the demonstration.

Restrictions Ordered by China On Activities of the Red Guards

The following dispatch is by David Oancia of The Globe and Mail, Toronto.

© 1966 by The Globe and Mail

PEKING — China's paramilitary Red Guard movement, the chosen instrument of Chairman Mao Tse-tung and Defense Minister Lin Piao in the current purge, appears headed into a period of adjustment.

Pragmatism appears to have triumphed on the domestic front. To avoid disruption of economic activity the Red Guards have been ordered to stay out of factories, mines, farms, research institutes and service establishments.

They have also been told to keep out of the campaign against corruption, graft, embezzlement and maladministration.

The Communist party leadership has, in effect, established a division of labor between the cultural revolution and production.

Jenmin Jih Pao (People's Daily), the Communist party's newspaper, said in an editorial that "in building Socialism, there is a spiritual front and a material front. The former is for the remolding of old ideologies and the raising of Socialist revolutionary consciousness. The latter is for the transformation of nature and the development of a Socialist national economy."

The editorial, which had the tone of an edict from the Communist leadership, said separate staffs should be established to handle the cultural revolution and production. The production staff, it said, should devote its energies primarily to improving the quantity, variety and quality of output.

"If the original arrangements of our cleanup movement in cities and the countryside are considered proper by the masses and if the movement is being carried out effectively, then no change should be made," the paper added. "The Red Guards and revolutionary students should not interfere with arrangements and need not participate in debates.

"Since workers and the poor and lower-middle peasants are the main force in the revolution, they are entirely able to carry out the revolution in their own units. Outsiders who are blind to conditions are apt to hinder production if they interfere."

The Chinese press again flung harsh words at the Russians, whom it described as revisionist and "a scheming and sinister gang whose tactics are double-faced." Soviet leaders were accused of calling for united action on Vietnam while selling out the Vietnamese revolution.

"They are renegades of the international Communist movement, termites of the working class and scum in the revolutionary ranks," a Jenmin Jih Pao article said. "We will never take any 'united action' with them. We will thoroughly expose the renegade features of this bunch of scabs and wage a tit-for-tat struggle.

Wave of Suicides Reported

HONG KONG, Sept. 9 (UPI) —Communist China's Red Guard movement has caused a wave of suicides, according to reports today from refugees.

The refugees also said tightened security by Chinese border guards was making it more difficult to flee to Hong Kong or Macao.

Meanwhile, the Peking radio said today that Communist China had ordered its army "to heighten alertness and make all preparations for waging a war."

Mao Throat Cancer Reported

HONG KONG, Sept. 9 (AP) —A newspaper here said today that Mao Tse-tung had cancer of the throat and had lost part of his voice.

Quoting arrivals from Communist China, Hisn Sheng Wan Pao (New Life Evening Post) said:

"Mao improved slightly but he can no longer make a lengthy speech." The report could not be confirmed.

Meanwhile, a Japanese newsman in Peking reported that a student group apparently modeled on the Red Guards had encountered dissiouity in Sian, capital of the northern province of Shensi.

The correspondent reported that a wall newspaper posted in a Peking street said the student group had been refused recognition by the Sian Industrial Institute's committee and the cultural revolution committee. Instead they were beaten and refused meals at their school.

The students then sought recognition from the Shensi provincal party committee. When it was refused they began a hunger strike on Sept. 5, the account said. The students were joined in the hunger strike by 30,000 others from 200 schools.

The Japanese report said the leader of the party's northwest China bureau finally agreed to the students' demands.

September 10, 1966

MAO IS ACCLAIMED AT PEKING RALLY

Special to The New York Times

HONG KONG, Saturday, Oct. 1 —Mao Tse-tung, the Chinese Communist leader, was given a tumultuous reception when he appeared at a National Day in Peking's Tienamen Square today to celebrate Communist China's 17th anniversary.

His chief deputy, Defense Minister Lin Piao, spoke on behalf of Mr. Mao and the Communist party's Central Committee. It was the fourth time in less than two months, that the two men have appeared at a Peking rally and that Mr. Lin has spoken for Mr. Mao, who is chairman of the committee.

Mr. Lin's speech was full of praise for chairman Mao and stressed the importance of the current "proletarian cultural revolution," a widespread purge of people and ideas.

Mr. Lin said the cultural revolution was aimed at striking down those who were taking the capitalist road and at further strengthening the "proletarian dictatorship."

Thousands Shout Slogans

Cheerleaders led thousands of Red Guards, members of Communist China's new militant youth organization in shouting slogans in praise of Mr. Mao. Long before he appeared, massed Red Guards were whipped into a frenzy of enthusiasm by leaders of the movement.

The cheerleaders again and again stirred the huge crowd to chant, "Long live Chairman Mao!" The Peking radio, which broadcast the rally, described the cheers for Mao as "rolling thunder."

Jenim Jih Pao, the party newspaper, said in a National Day editorial broadcast by the Peking radio that the Red Guards together with the militia would provide backing for the Chinese army if the United States was rash enough to attack China. It described China's defenses as invincible.

Last night, Premier Chou En-lai delivered a favorable report on the state of the nation. In his speech he also showered praise on Chairman Mao and included glowing comments on the cultural revolution.

Premier Chou renewed Peking's pledge to continue supporting the Communists in Vietnam and said the United States was using the United Nations in collusion with the Soviet Union "to hatch new peace-talk plots." He said the United Nations had "no right whatsoever to meddle with the Vietnam question."

"The heroic Vietnamese people will never yield," Mr. Chou said. "All intrigues of United States imperialism and modern revisionism are doomed to failure."

Analysts said the Premier's speech was full of broad generalizations and contained little substance. In line with the present trend in China, it was more concerned with praising Mr. Mao and the cultural revolution than with providing any significant factual information.

October 1, 1966

China, Revamping Schools, Expels Alien Pupils

The following dispatch is by David Oancia of The Globe and Mail, Toronto.

© 1966 by The Globe and Mail, Toronto.

PEKING, Sept. 27 — About two weeks ago foreign students still in Peking joined the widespread ta tze bao (wallpaper) war by displaying posters complaining about their segregation from the main stream of student life.

The posters did not stem from anti-Chinese attitudes; rather, they reflected a desire to get a better first-hand look at the cataclysmic changes taking place, through closer contacts with Chinese students.

Their hopes were dashed about a week ago when the Government summoned representatives of the embassies concerned and told them the students would have to leave China as soon as possible. They were also told that no foreign students would be accepted for another year.

The decision was not surprising. Revamping the educational system according to the thoughts of the Communist party chairman, Mao Tse-tung, is one of the primary targets of the cultural revolution.

Few exceptions are being made in the application of this most recent order. About 500 Albanians and 200 North Vietnamese — both from countries having close ties with China—are apparently expected to go. Others

409

affected include 40 French, 15 Russians, two Bulgarians, 30 Mongolians, 30 Cambodians, a number of Nepalese and individual students or research workers from Switzerland, Sweden and Algeria and several other African countries.

Some Can't Return

Because of summer vacations, many of these students are in their own countries and thus will not be allowed to return.

The fate of some students who could in a sense be considered political refugees is still in doubt. Included among these are an unknown number of Africans and perhaps as many as 300 Indonesians who came to China when President Sukarno still spoke in terms of a Peking-Jakarta axis. These, some observers feel, would be in trouble with the governments of their countries if they had to return.

Another question is the future of Chinese students abroad under reciprocal exchange programs. Chinese students are known to be doing advanced work in Britain, France, Switzerland, the Soviet Union and several Eastern European countries. Diplomatic observers feel the Chinese will likely recall these, perhaps to join the Red Guards and take part in the currnt revolutionary drive.

With this most recent decision China has, in effect, served notice that it would prefer no complications from the presence of foreign students as the social structure is being thoroughly shaken up, purged and reorganized to conform with the ideas of Chairman Mao and his comrades.

All-Round Skills Planned

The nature of the effort can be seen in the embryonic plans for educational reform. The traditional systems of existing institutions are to be scrapped. Mr. Mao's works are to become the teaching material and the general aim will be to produce graduates with the all-round skills of farmers, industrial workers, soldiers and intellectual workers. Children of peasants, workers and soldiers evidently are to be given preference in the new admission system.

Published proposals for revamping the school system call for a general shortening of the educational period and abolition of the postgraduate system. Under the old system students spent six years in primary school, six in high school and another five or six years in universities or technical institutes.

If the new proposals are adopted, subjects considered as frills by some Chinese revolutionaries will be either curtailed or eliminated. Included among these are history, arts and philosophy. Technical courses ranging from agricultural subjects to engineering will be taught under a part-work, part-study system.

The Globe and Mail, Toronto (by David Oancia)

FOR CHINESE COMMUNIST ONLY: Signs like these, placed on a Peking bookstore by Red Guards, call for strict adherence to the ideas of Mao Tse-tung, Communist party chairman. Some foreign students posted signs of their own, deploring their exclusion from the mainstream of student life in the country. But they were rebuffed.

October 2, 1966

Chinese Reds Begin Drive to Glorify Lin Piao

Special to The New York Times

HONG KONG, Oct. 11—A campaign has been launched in China to glorify Lin Piao, the Defense Minister, and underline his new role as heir apparent to Mao Tse-tung, the Communist party's Chairman.

This represents a significant shift in emphasis on the part of Peking. Until recently Mr. Lin was content to stand in Mr. Mao's shadow and be acknowledged simply as the party leader's chief aide and spokesman. Today he is being praised in his own right and his name is appearing more frequently in the press as the authoritative voice of the hierarchy.

Mr. Lin increasingly appears to be taking on the mantle of China's strong man while the deification of Mr. Mao appears to be removing him from the mundane affairs of the state and party. Analysts say it has become difficult to tell just where Chairman Mao's authority ends and Mr. Lin's begins.

The task of praising Mr. Lin has fallen mainly on Chiehfang Chun Pao, the armed forces newspaper, and senior army officers, but other papers have reproduced their glowing words of praise. Mr. Lin has been lauded not only for "creatively applying" Chairman Mao's thought but also for introducing his own "important measures."

Lin Issued Directives

Hsinhua, the Chinese Communist press agency, earlier this week described new directives issued by Mr. Lin on the study of Chairman Mao's works as "extremely important." Hsiao Hua, director of the army's general political department, announced the new directives and described Mr. Lin as the "most intimate comrade in arms of Chairman Mao, his best student and best example in creatively and applying Chairman Mao's works."

This praise was echoed today by Chiehfang Chun Pao, which said Mr. Lin had always implemented Chairman Mao's thought and followed his correct line "most faithfully, firmly and thoroughly."

An officer formerly under Mr. Lin's command praised the Minister's military record in an article in Canton's Hung Wei Pao. He said Mr. Lin had done "great meritorious deeds for the liberation undertaking of the Chinese people in past revolutionary wars."

Mr. Lin is now openly acknowledged as chairman of the powerful military affairs committee of the party's Central Committee, a post formerly held by Mr. Mao, although no formal announcement of Mr. Lin's appointment has been made. He was previously one of three deputy chairmen.

The intensified adulation of Mr. Lin is believed to be aimed partly at increasing his stature in preparation for his eventual succession to Chairman Mao and partly at strengthening his hand for further purging of important party figures.

The Chinese press has continued to refer to the existence of "people in power who have taken the capitalist road" and has reported attacks on Mr. Lin. Accordingly, analysts believe that the violent political upheaval that has resulted in the downfall or demotion of a number of senior members of the Politburo, may soon have a resurgence.

An article in the Central Committee publication Hung Chi recently recalled that the Paris Commune, which Peking commemorates annually, required that "all persons elected to public offices must be service personnel serving people, not the bourgeois type of bureaucratic politicians oppressing the people."

The Paris Commune also stipulated that "electors could at any time recall and replace the elected," the magazine noted. The Commune was an insurrectionary government that ruled Paris briefly in May, 1871.

As Hung Chi is edited by Chen Po-ta, a protegé of Chairman Mao and the man in charge of the purge, analysts said the article was aimed at providing justification for the further dismissal of party officials. One top official considered a possible target is Liu Shao-chi, head of state, who has been demoted from second to eighth place in party rankings, but could still represent a threat to Mr. Lin because of his past prestige and influence.

Education Reform Is Aim

Special to The New York Times

TOKYO, Oct. 11—A contingent of the Red Guards said in Peking today that one of their major objectives was the creation of a new educational system capable of spearheading a worldwide revolution, dispatches to Japanese newspapers said.

In a three-hour interview with Japanese correspondents, the group of 30 students of a high school attached to Tsinghua University described the achievements of the Red Guard movement.

They declared that they had reduced their principal and eight other "reactionary" teachers to the status of school servants, forcing them to do "such chores as sweeping floors and growing vegetables."

It was at the Tsinghua University high school that the Red Guards were first organized May 29, the students said. They added that the movement spread across the country and was encouraged by Chairman Mao at a rally in Peking Aug. 18.

According to the students, the membership of their Red Guard unit rose from an original 40 members to 265 out of a total student body of 1,300. They said children of the "bourgeois class" still accounted for 40 per cent of the school's enrollment.

Interference Is Charged

The organization of the first Red Guard unit, the youngsters said, was "entirely voluntary," having resulted from an "explosion of our anger" when the principal "interfered with our endeavor to study the thought of Mao Tse-tung."

The teen-agers said 60 per cent of the student body represented the so-called "five Red classes"—peasants, lower-class farmers, workers, revolutionary leaders and armymen—that are eligible for membership in the Red Guard.

The Red Guards said that demands for dissolution of the minor fellow-traveling parties in China and for abolition of interest payments to former industrialists had been "entirely our voluntary actions." Neither demand has thus far been implemented by the authorities.

The Young Communist League and the Pioneers, the traditional Communist youth organizations that have been abolished in China, were "not good because they lost their class character," the youngsters told the Japanese correspondents.

October 12, 1966

RED GUARDS START A PEKING EXODUS

© 1966 by The Globe and Mail.

PEKING, Oct. 27—Icy winds out of the northwest swept through the streets of Communist China's capital Friday as a mass exodus of visiting Red Guards got under way.

The youths, from all parts of China, have been flooding Peking on a program to permit them "to exchange revolutionary experiences." At the weekend, some 1.5-million of them were in the capital.

With their belongings neatly wrapped up in colorful bedrolls and slung on their backs, teenage girls and boys formed block-long queues at railway stations and truck and bus pickup points today.

Some did not wait for motorized transport. In the Peking suburbs, columns could be seen streaming into the countryside, carrying portraits of Chairman Mao Tse-tung and scarlet banners. Some had marched hundred of miles in this way.

Discipline Is Goal

The exodus marks the beginning of a new attempt to bring greater order and discipline into Red Guard activities, a move presumably backed by Premier Chou En-lai and other cabinet members without at the same time calling off a struggle over policy that apparently still is unresolved.

The winds tugged at the posters around the square of Heavenly Peace in the heart of Peking. Some were torn to shreds but new ones were put up as the wave of criticism of those charged with taking capitalist or revisionist ways continued.

Two of China's top leaders—Chairman Liu Shao-chi, the country's chief of state, and the Communist party General Secretary, Teng Hsiao-ping, the man in charge of the Red Guard movement, were among those named in the latest posters, on Tatzebao.

Others again criticized included Li Hsueh-feng, chief of the party's Communist Peking municipal committee, and his deputy, Wu Teh. They took over the Peking branch following the purge last June of Peng Chen and his colleagues and an associated drive to reform Peking University.

A meeting has been scheduled to examine Mr. Li's stewardship. One of his deputy secretaries, Kuo Yin-chiu, has been dismissed.

In recent days the teen-agers staged a noisy sitdown in front of the Coal Mining Ministry Building. They attacked leaders of other technical and economic ministries and held demonstrations on the narrow street leading to the Soviet Embassy.

Many of the youths were poorly equipped to cope with Peking's relatively cool autumns. Some had come from tropical parts of China, with light cotton clothing and no shoes.

Concern grew about the numbers who were becoming ill while in Peking.

At 3 o'clock Monday morning, according to posters, that can be seen, a group from Red Guard headquarters went to the office of The People's Daily to express their concern.

One of the editors put them in touch with Premier Chou, who told them that the party central committee had studied he Red Guard question and was preparing new instructions.

The Premier said that in the interim, Peking students should not leave the capital.

October 28, 1966

CHINESE BRINGING FACTORY TO FARM

Special to The New York Times

HONG KONG, Oct. 27—Peking today lauded "a new type of state farm" engaging in both agriculture and industry. Its personnel also study and undergo military training.

The farm was established in an area reclaimed from wasteland in Kiangsi Province in East China, according to Hsinhua, the Chinese Communist press agency. More than 11,000 people take part in grain production, the raising of silkworms and silk weaving.

Hsinhua stated: "It is a state farm combined with a silk mill; a school for training of revolutionary workers and at the same time a military reserve unit training for the people's war; a town in the countryside and a rural district with urban conveniences."

This represents the application on a small scale of directives issued by the Chinese Communist leader, Mao Tse-tung, earlier this year designed to remove differences between people in the cities and those in the country and between intellectuals, industrial workers, peasants and soldiers.

Analysts believe Mr. Mao is seeking to create a classless community modeled on his guerrilla base at Yenan in 1935.

Expansion Seen as Aim

The state farm in question has been in operation for several years. Its success appears intended to serve as a stimulus for introduction of Mr. Mao's new economic concept on a nationwide scale.

There are indications that the concept has met with some opposition. The Communist leader's directives were issued in August when they were described in the press as "a call to turn all fields of work into great revolutionary schools where people take part in both industry and agriculture, and military as well as civilian affairs."

Since Mr. Mao's word is supposed to be virtually sacred in China, analysts find it strange that little has been heard of his call since it was first announced. It contains elements of radical economic measures adopted in 1958 as part of the "Great Leap Forward" expansion program and analysts believe it may have been opposed by moderate elements within the Chinese Communist party who recalled the chaos created by the ill-fated program.

These analysts believe it is one of the issues at stake in the power struggle within the hierarchy. While Mr. Mao and

411

his chief aide, Defense Minister Lin Piao, have undertaken a widespread purge of their opponents, Peking concedes that dissenting voices are still making themselves heard in the policy-making councils.

The Hsinhua article is expected to be the first shot in a propaganda campaign aimed at whipping up a national outburst of support for Mr. Mao's program under direction of his supporters.

The article stressed the importance of the success that had been achieved at the Kiangsi state farm.

Mixed Communities

"As time goes on," it said, "this combination of agriculture with industry increasingly reveals its great political and economic significance. By building factories within the farm, industry is set close to its source of raw material, food grain, and other farm byproducts and this cuts down cost."

By scattering urban districts about the countryside, it added, farms can enjoy the convenience of shopping centers, hospitals and other public services.

"Workers and farmers live together in mixed commuities," Hsinhua said. "This helps to consolidate the worker-peasant alliance."

October 30, 1966

Some Chinese Propagandists Purged

By CHARLES MOHR
Special to The New York Times

HONG KONG, Nov. 22—The purge of Communist party officials in China has fallen especially heavy on propaganda chiefs. At least 20 of the party officials known to have been purged, or more than a third of the total, were propaganda or literary officials.

Among them were Chou Yang, deputy director of propaganda of the party's Central Committee; Wang Kuang, propaganda chief for five provinces of central-south China, and Tseng Tun, a propaganda leader for Hupeh Province, in Mr. Wang's region. All had held their posts for many years.

The Chinese press has been denouncing these men and others like them for many weeks, asserting that for years they frustrated the will of Chairman Mao Tse-tung.

Some of the charges are built around published quotations from the officials, while others appear to be based on informers' accounts of private conversations.

Taken together they make up a catalogue of what constitutes heresy today, when Chairman Mao and his heir-apparent, Lin Piao, the Defense Minister, are carrying out a strong political offensive.

Said to Oppose Mao

Among the main charges against such men as Mr. Chou, Mr. Wang and Mr. Tseng are that they opposed and denigrated the idea of Mr. Mao's infallibility and that they opposed the Great Leap Forward—an attempt in 1958 to push industrialization and the development at the local level through such means as backyard iron smelters.

The men are also accused of opposing the establishment of rural communes, the absolute supremacy of politics over technique in art, education and the press, and the renewed class struggle throughout the country.

The propaganda chiefs are accused of protecting others. The press hints that other high officials, perhaps in the Politburo itself, have also tried to shield them.

A Hupeh Province broadcast said that one of the charges against Mr. Wang was that he had advanced the idea that the thought of Chairman Mao was only "a Chinese form of Marxism-Leninism" rather than a new peak of development of Marxist thought.

Mr. Wang is accused of having disapproved of a newspaper headline that said "Mao Tse-tung Is the Revolutionary teacher of the People of the World," and of having changed it to read "The People of the World Comment on the Thought of Mao Tse-tung."

Last January, the broadcast said, he opposed the newly intensified program, begun by Mr. Lin to popularize the study of Mr. Mao's thought and told a group of newspapermen that constant stories and pictures depicting the masses joyfully boning up on Mr. Mao's works were dull.

"Do you newspapermen read them?" he is said to have asked.

In an editorial Jenmin Jih Pao the party newspaper in Peking, accused Mr. Chou of having made a speech to a group of literary figures, urging them to dare express dissident views. This meant, the newspaper said, that "he encouraged people to rise against the party's leader."

The economic chaos brought on by the Great Leap Forward forced a political retreat in which less politically attuned experts regained favor.

November 23, 1966

RED GUARDS' TRAVEL IS CURBED BY PEKING

PEKING, Nov. 2—The heroes' welcome accorded 65 Chinese students who returned to Peking today after expulsion from the Soviet Union tended to overshadow a sweeping new measure aimed at minimizing dislocations caused by millions of teen-age Red Guards traveling around the country to "exchange revolutionary experiences."

The emergency order was posted on the wall of Peking's modern railway station before the arrival of the students in the coaches of the Trans-Siberian express from Moscow.

An edict issued by the State Council Monday ordered a five-day suspension of all travel by Red Guards beginning yesterday and put future movements of the paramilitary groups under control of the army.

The order complained that some groups had delayed schedules by surrounding trains to prevent their departure and even by climbing into locomotives to try to persuade the engineers to change their destinations.

November 3, 1966

Mao's Wife Assails Peking's City Party Leaders

HONG KONG, Dec. 4 (UPI)—The Peking radio reported today that the wife of Mao Tsetung had demanded that all opponents of the Chinese Communist leader "be wiped out once and for all."

The broadcast said Chairman Mao's wife, Chiang Ching, made the call in an attack on the Peking municipal party committee.

The broadcast, monitored here, disclosed that Miss Chiang had been appointed consultant to the General Political Department of the Chinese Army. She was identified previously as the deputy head of the group that is in charge of the current cultural revolution.

According to the broadcast, she accused the new Peking committee of being "as rotten as ever." The old committee, headed by Peng Chen, a former Politburo member, was one of the first targets of purges under the cultural revolution.

"The old Peking municipal party committee was collaborat-

Eastfoto
Chiang Ching

ing with reactionary powerholders," she was quoted as having said.

"They are antiparty, antirevolution and they must be completely wiped out so they can never come into power again.

"The new Peking municipal committee is also resisting revolution. It is the same old stuff as the old committee.

"They are reactionary, two-faced, they insult Chairman Mao. They attack us. They must be wiped out once and for all. For if we do not wipe them out, how can we carry on the revolution?"

She apparently held out the olive branch to those who wanted to repent.

"Those who are willing to change and reform can come to our side," she was quoted as having said. "But they must come without any old influence. And in the future, depending on their performance, they still have chances to become leaders."

December 5, 1966

MAO FOE'S ARREST IN CHINA REPORTED

Ex-Staff Chief of Army Is Named—Attacks on Other Leaders Are Intensified

By The Associated Press

BELGRADE, Yugoslavia, Dec. 23—A former army chief of staff in Communist China has been arrested, indicating that the dominant faction in the Communist party is about to deal decisive blows to its high-ranking foes, Tanyug said today.

An announcement said the former army chief, Lo Jui-ching, was "taken away" Tuesday, the Yugoslav press agency said in a dispatch from Peking. It added that this was taken to mean that he had been arrested. Japanese dispatches from Peking said the arrest had taken place.

The reports coincide with an intensifying campaign against two of the highest leaders in China, President Liu Shao-chi and Teng Hsiao-ping, Secretary General of the party.

Tanyug gave the following reasons for believing a showdown was near:

Mr. Lo was a member of a circle of high officials close to Mr. Liu and Mr. Teng, who have been denounced by the faction led by Chairman Mao Tse-tung and Defense Minister Lin Piao, Mr. Mao's heir apparent. They are accused of having followed a bourgeois and pro-Soviet line.

Rally Set Tomorrow

Another announcement in Peking said a rally against Mr. Liu and Mr. Teng would be held Sunday.

"With this announcement," Tanyug said, "the actions against the two high leaders enter their closing stage and their demotion from high functions is evidently forthcoming."

The Mao-Lin faction has been pictured in previous Communist dispatches as hesitant to strike at Mr. Liu and Mr. Teng because they enjoyed strong backing in the party at the highest level as well as on regional and provincial levels.

Now some of the regional, provincial and central organs of the party have come under attack, Tanyug said.

December 24, 1966

Red Guard Signs Denounce Peking's Foreign Minister

TOKYO, Thursday, Dec. 29 (Reuters)—The Red Guards denounced Foreign Minister Chen Yi in their wall posters in Peking yesterday, a Japanese correspondent reported from Peking today.

The correspondent of Asahi Shimbun, a leading national daily, said the Red Guards had attacked interference with mass movements by the Foreign Minister's wife, Madame Chang Chin, and the speeches and actions of Chen Yi himself.

He said Chen Yi's son, Chen Shao-lu, was also accused of "errors."

December 28, 1966

EX-DEFENSE CHIEF ARRESTED IN CHINA

Red Guards Report Seizure of Peng Teh-huai, Who Led Forces in Korean War

By Reuters

PEKING, Dec. 28 — Red Guards have arrested the former Defense Minister, Peng Teh-huai, who commanded Communist China's forces in the Korean war, a Red Guard newspaper reported here today.

The newspaper, Hung Chi (Red Flag), published by the Red Guards of the Aviation Institute in Peking, said a group of Guards from the institute seized Mr. Peng at 4 A.M., Saturday in Chengtu, the capital of Szechwan Province in Southwest China.

On Monday the Tanyug press agency of Yugoslavia reported that Lin Shao-chi, the chief of state and a principal victim of the cultural purge, faced arrest soon.

Mr. Peng, accused by the Red Guards of opposing the ideology and policies of Chairman Mao Tse-tung, served as Defense Minister and a Vice Premier for five years.

He was replaced in 1959 by Lin Piao, who emerged last summer as Mr. Mao's heir-apparent.

Mr. Peng, 64 years old, was believed to have opposed intensification of the dispute with the Soviet Union in the event that this should hamper modernization of the army.

He disappeared from the public scene a few weeks before the appointment of Lin Piao in his place was announced.

The latest edition of Hung-chi, which was circulated here today, was the first Chinese Communist newspaper to mention Mr. Peng's name since his dismissal. However, he has been denounced on Red Guard posters recently.

Peking observers believed his arrest and the publicity given to it, like similar actions earlier this month in the case of the former Peking Mayor, Peng Chen, were part of the steadily mounting campaign against Liu Shao-chi and the Communist party secretary general, Teng Hsiao-ping.

Both men have been accused in Red Guard posters of being leaders of a bourgeois line in the Communist party, which Peng Chen and Peng Teh-huai have also been accused of following.

Red Guard loudspeaker trucks have been touring the streets here this month quoting Chiang Ching, Mr. Mao's wife and deputy leader of the group directing the cultural revolution, as having said Red Guards were entitled to seize known "counterrevolutionaries."

New Red Guard posters today said Vice Premier Chen Yun and a former Vice Premier, Teng Tzu-hui, both out of the public scene for a long time, had been criticized at recent Red Guard meetings.

Red Guard newspapers also announced that the teen-age activists intended to "launch a struggle" during the winter against the science department of Lin Piao's Defense Ministry because some people in it were reactionaries.

The newspapers renewed calls for mass "struggle" meetings against Mr. Liu and against Teng Hsiao-ping. Some of these meetings were believed to have been held already.

Mrs. Liu Confession Reported

WASHINGTON, Dec. 28 (AP) —The wife of Liu Shao-chi, Communist China's chief of state, has made a written confession saying she has betrayed the teachings of Mao Tse-tung, The Washington Post said today.

"For Lady Bird Johnson to announce suddenly that she has been plotting to overthrow the U. S. Government is unimaginable," The Post said in a dispatch from Hong Kong by Stanley Karnow. "Yet an admission of that magnitude has been made [by Mrs. Liu] in one of the most remarkable documents to emerge from the convulsions currently shaking Communist China."

Peng Teh-huai

"I betrayed the [Communist] party and Chairman Mao's trust, solicitude and teachings," Mrs. Liu was quoted as having said. "This has greatly troubled me."

Mr. Karnow said the 3,000-word confession was written in October and that it had been made available by what Mr. Karnow called unimpeachable sources.

The 68-year-old Mr. Liu was denounced this week by the teen-aged Red Guards at a rally in Peking.

His wife, who is in her middle forties, said her errors had roots in the "poison of bourgeois education and capitalist influences." She said these left her with "many old ideas, old customs and old habits" that had come to the surface only as a result of recent events in China.

The Post said that according to a report from Hong Kong, Mrs. Liu's daughter was detained by the Red Guards earlier this month and was charged with sabotaging the so-called cultural revolution the Red Guards are carrying out.

Mr. Karnow said there had been reliable reports that Mrs. Liu was publicly denounced by her daughter for acting like an empress.

Mr. Karnow's dispatch said Mrs. Liu, "reputedly an intelligent woman who came from a well-to-do Peking family had studied English at Catholic University in Peking. Later she served as an interpreter with the Communist group that, under Gen. George Marshall's auspices, discussed peace with the Chinese Nationalists in the days after World War II."

December 29, 1966

PEKING REPORTS SHANGHAI STRIKE OVER MAO POLICY

Special to The New York Times

HONG KONG, Monday, Jan. 9—The Peking radio indicated today that many workers in Shanghai had gone on strike to protest Mao Tse-tung's "cultural revolution."

The official radio also hinted that disturbances and political resistance were widespread in China by saying that this was "not only the problem of Shanghai but also of the whole country."

[According to Japanese reports from Peking, thousands of farmers in the Chusan Islands southeast of Shanghai have joined uprisings against Red Guards supporting Mr. Mao, The Associated Press reported. Page 3].

Letter Made Public

Information about the events in Shanghai, China's largest manufacturing center, emerged in a letter that the Peking radio quoted from 11 pro-Mao organizations in the city. The letter said that "bourgeois reactionary elements" in Shanghai had "plotted" to cut off the city's water and electrical services and public transport in order to destroy the cultural revolution.

"A part or the great part of the Red forces in some factories have stopped production or left the factories," the letter said, according to a translation of the radio report made here.

The broadcast indicated that the strike was continuing when it addressed itself to workers and said, "We hope you can follow Chairman Mao's teachings and distinguish between right and wrong . . . and go back to your production positions and back to the road of the cultural revolution."

It said workers who did so "would not be scolded."

The letter quoted in the broadcast called on "all the revolutionary students and cadres" to unite with "revolutionary workers" to "smash the counterattack by bourgeois reactionaries and raise the cultural revolution to a new stage in the factories."

The letter was also printed in three major Chinese newspapers in Peking, including the party paper, Jenmin Jih Pao, the broadcast said.

It quoted an editorial note from Jenmin Jih Pao as having said that the letter was "very important" and "called for a general attack on the bourgeois reactionary line."

The letter was first published in a Shanghai newspaper on Jan. 5, indicating the trouble in the city had lasted for some time.

"Cultural revolution" is the term that the Chinese have applied to an attempt begun last year by Mr. Mao and Defense Minister Lin Piao to stamp out all habits of so-called bourgeois thought in China and wrest day-to-day control of the Communist party from officials accused of opposing Mr. Mao's ideas.

Movement Extended

A decision was announced in late December to expand the cultural revolution from schools and youth movements into factories and farms. Some political analysts believe that this has touched off the reported violence and disturbances.

In Peking, Red Guard wall posters in the streets reported violent clashes last week in the East China city of Nanking between forces supporting the cultural revolution and those opposing it.

Other Red Guard posters seen by Japanese journalists indicated there had been disturbances in Peking factories, too.

The crisis seemed to be caused by a determined effort by some Communist party officials to resist the formation of pro-Mao workers' committees in industrial enterprises to "supervise" and "criticize" the work of the party officials in charge of the enterprises.

The Chinese press called for the formation of such committees in late December.

Mr. Mao and Mr. Lin also want to "put politics in command" in industry, believing that ideological fervor can produce more goods than cautious management methods adopted by some old-time party bureaucrats.

The Peking radio broadcast today said that in Shanghai a "handful" of foes of the cultural revolution "have tried in every possible way to go against Mao's policy of taking hold of the revolution to stimulate production." It said they must be "severely punished."

China Counterrevolution

By CHARLES MOHR
Special to The New York Times

HONG KONG, Jan. 8 — Violence reported in Nanking may have been touched off by Mao Tse-tung's decision to spread his "cultural revolution," or purge, into China's factories and farms, some political analysts said today.

It also appeared possible to some observers that the cultural revolution had begun to devour its own children and that those directing the purge on behalf of Chairman Mao and Defense Minister Lin Piao were purging their own ranks. There was, however, a dismaying shortage of hard information with which to assess the turmoil.

News Analysis

Japanese and Eastern European correspondents in Peking reported seeing wall posters asserting that there had been fighting in Nanking between Maoist "revolutionary" groups and large numbers of people apparently supporting the local Communist party organization.

Some of the posters asserted that 54 people had died in Nanking and 900 had been wounded. The posters left an impression that anti-Mao elements were in control of the city and had cut transport and communications links to it.

None of this could be independently confirmed.

If such fighting took place, some analysts believe, it was probably caused by an attempt to carry out a decision recently made by the Mao-Lin faction to expand the "cultural revolution" into factories, mines and farms.

Supervision Urged

In two recent editorials the official publication Jenmin Jih Pao urged workers to elect revolutionary committees to "supervise" the work of cadres in the regular Communist party hierarchy, which controls all enterprises in China.

Such a move, especially if joined by fanatic young Red Guards could easily lead to conflict with party officials who deny having ideological shortcomings that might require correction by such hastily formed "mass" organizations.

The cultural revolution as a whole represents a struggle by the Maoist faction to wrest control of the party machinery from a large group of national and provincial party leaders, including the chief of state, Liu Shao-chi, and the party's general secretary, Teng Hsiao-ping.

The fate and the role of various Chinese personalities have become increasingly cloudy in recent days as the number of wall posters has increased.

Most of the Red Guard posters are believed to be "authentic"—to represent the sentiments of the committee conducting the cultural revolution, which is led by a fifth-ranking Politburo member, Chen Po-ta, and by Chairman Mao's wife, Chiang Ching.

Other posters may be the work of youth groups disloyal to Mr. Mao and eager to confuse the situation or to cast doubt on the authenticity of "authentic" posters.

The posters reported in the Nanking incident said that Tao Chu, the Propaganda Minister, had incited Nanking party officials to attack the headquarters of the Mao-Lin faction there.

Mr. Tao, who had been party boss of the south-central region, rose rapidly last year, being elevated to the Politburo and to fourth place in the party rankings after Mr. Mao, Mr. Lin and Premier Chou En-lai.

On Dec. 13, he made the first speech reported by any top leader denouncing the chief of state, Mr. Liu, and the party's General Secretary, Mr. Teng, as opposing Chairman Mao.

But since then, Mr. Tao has himself been denounced in Red Guard posters as a "bourgeois" and as a supporter of Mr. Liu, the man he denounced.

Purge of the Purgers

One possible explanation is that the two top leaders of the cultural revolution, Mr. Chen and Miss Chiang, had decided to purge their own group of those suspected of less than total loyalty to Chairman Mao.

Another possible explanation is that Mr. Liu and Mr. Teng have lost influence and that Mr. Tao believed he should take their place as protector of the party organization, which all three men had labored so many years to build.

Another possible explanation is that there is no longer effective control over wall posters.

Last week a poster appeared attacking Premier Chou, charging he was trying to shield other Government officials. The anti-Chou posters were taken down promptly.

From posters and other evidence it appears that the hard core of the Mao-Lin faction at the top level in the party is rather small.

A speech by Miss Chiang listed only Mr. Lin, Premier Chou, Mr. Chen Po-ta and Kang Sheng, another official elevated from 20th to seventh place in party ranking this year.

January 9, 1967

January 9, 1967

414

CONTROL OF ARMY TIGHTENED BY MAO AMID DISSENSION

Special to The New York Times

HONG KONG, Friday, Jan. 13—Mao Tse-tung and Lin Piao took steps today to insure the army's loyalty to their faction in the bitter power struggle that has plunged Communist China into a political crisis.

They reshuffled the committee in charge of the "cultural revolution" in the army and placed it directly under the Military Commission of the Communist party's Central Committee, which is controlled by Defense Minister Lin, and the central group in charge of the cultural revolution, which is headed by Chen Po-ta, Chairman Mao's protégé.

Miss Chiang Ching, Mr. Mao's wife, was appointed adviser to the new army committee.

Chieh Fang Chun Pao, the armed forces publication, commenting on the change, confirmed the existence of military opposition to the Mao-Lin faction. This had been implied in Peking wall posters attacking senior army personnel.

The People's Liberation Army, which incorporates China's navy and air force, could play a key role in resolving the conflict if the opposing factions fail to find a political solution, according to Western analysts here.

The change in the army's Cultural Revolution Committee was viewed as a move by the Mao-Lin faction to tighten political control over the army. Miss Chiang is also first deputy head of the central group in charge of the cultural revolution. A former actress, she has had a sudden rise to prominence in the course of the cultural revolution, launched early last year to reshape China according to the dictates of her husband and to purge his enemies.

An editorial published jointly by Jenmin Jih Pao, the main party newspaper, and by Hung Chi, a journal on ideology, asserted that opposition citadels were being captured one by one. But it also said that in capturing each fortress, Mao supporters would meet "frenzied resistance."

Announcing the army committee's reorganization, the Peking radio said that Hsu Hsiang-chien would head the new group. A Vice Chairman of the National Defense Council, he is a career soldier who was one of 10 marshals before China abolished military ranks.

Last year Liu Chi-chien, a deputy director of the army's General Political Department, was reported to be in charge of the cultural revolution in the army. He was denounced in Red Guard posters seen recently in Peking.

The armed forces publication said the committee had been formed in accordance with a directive ratified by the Central Committee and Mr. Mao, who is Chairman of the party.

Chieh Fang Chun Pao called for the launching of "fierce attacks on the handful of those persons within the army who are in authority and who are taking the capitalist road."

Upheavals in the Army

The opposition faction in the party has been similarly described. Red Guard posters have specified Liu Shao-chi, head of state, and Teng Hsiao-ping, General Secretary of the party, as leaders of the opposition.

The army's role would be crucial in the event that violence became widespread. The extent of its loyalty to Mr. Mao and Mr. Lin is an unknown factor, as far as observers have been able to discern. It has undergone several upheavals, including the purge of Defense Minister Peng Teh-huai in 1959 and the Chief of the General Staff, Lo Jui-ching, last year, which have been interpreted as manifestations of discontent.

A message sent to Shanghai yesterday in the name of the Central Committee and other bodies, calling on the people to "beat back the new counter-attack" by opposition elements, was interpreted by the armed forces newspaper as a directive intended for the army also. It said "commanders and fighters" had responded warmly.

The joint editorial attributed the message sent to Shanghai to a decision by Chairman Mao. The message disclosed that economic and political sabotage had been carried out by opponents of the Mao-Lin faction and it denounced members of the Shanghai Municipal Committee of the party.

The editorial said Mr. Mao's supporters were "launching a full-phased general offensive against the bourgeois reactionary line" and were "growing in scale and strength."

The editorial also summed up the charges that the Mao-Lin faction has made against its opponents. It accused them of arbitrarily increasing wages and amenities and of instigating "violent struggle."

"Reactionary elements" have incited a number of workers to desert their posts in production, "thus bringing some factories to a standstill and disrupting railway and road traffic," it added. "They even incite harbor personnel to stop work," it said, and "some leading members of the railway departments use similar means to disrupt rail transport in a vain attempt to sabotage the great proletarian cultural revolution."

The editorial hinted at the widespread nature of similar incidents by stating that the appeal to others to study the experience of "Revolutionary Rebel groups" in Shanghai was "undoubtedly great encouragement to the working class and revolutionary people throughout the country."

Also in the editorial was a warning that the opposition "cunningly takes over revolutionary slogans raised by the party Central Committee and Chairman Mao and distorts them to serve their counter-revolutionary political purposes."

January 13, 1967

TROOPS INCREASED IN CENTRAL PEKING AFTER MAO'S CALL

The following dispatch is by a correspondent of Agence France-Presse in Peking.

PEKING, Jan 24 — Troops in the center of Peking were sharply increased today.

Military guards, some of whom wore the Red Guards' arm band, were strengthened outside Communist party headquarters and the Central Telegraph Office. Trucks with military registration plates carried troops along the main roads.

The growing military presence seems to be a direct result of a directive to Defense Minister Lin Piao from Mao Tse-tung, the party chairman.

The directive, posted on walls yesterday, called for the direct participation of the army in the "cultural revolution."

The order condemned as "intolerable and erroneous" the army's previous policy of non-intervention.

Chou Also Issued Order

Similar instructions are attributed by another poster to Premier Chou En-lai. The poster said that in a speech on Jan. 22 Premier Chou said that troops must help "leftist" organizations to seize power and must fight with them against the "reactionary bourgeois line."

The intervention of the armed forces apparently corresponds to a new phase in the cultural revolution involving the seizure of power in all Government and party bodies by what are officially called "revolutionary minorities."

Ministries that have already been taken over include the Ministry of Culture, two machine-building ministries and the Ministries of Reclamation, Middle and Higher Education and Public Health.

Officials from these ministries, driven slowly through the streets in trucks to confess their faults, were more numerous than usual today. They wore paper dunce's caps and carried placards expressing their shame. Their errors were broadcast from loudspeaker vans that followed closely behind.

The Hsinhua press agency, reporting the army's support for the rebel movement, lists garrisons that have already taken this line.

The agency mentions garrisons at Canton and Foochow in the south, Nanking and Wuhan in the center, Kunming in the southwest, Lanchow in the northwest, Chengtu in Szechwan, Tsian in Shantung and the three autonomous regions of Tibet, Sinkiang and Inner Mongolia, as well as Peking itself. The towns are those where local parties were previously said to have been purged.

A Red Guard newspaper in Peking said the party's Central Committee and the Government had decided that students whose schools were closed must undergo short periods of military training. This measure is already in effect in Peking.

Not all the humiliated officials have necessarily lost their jobs. Some posters recommend political criticism of all executives without causing excessive interruptions in production and administration.

This pragmatism appears to have been inspired by Premier Chou at a meeting last Wednesday. According to the party newspaper, Jenmin Jih Pao, Mr. Chou called on industrial and commercial workers to control taxes, recover salary rises or bonuses wrongly paid, return to the state objects confiscated by the Red Guards and eliminate bottlenecks blocking foreign trade.

The army and the security services were called upon to cooperate in these measures. They were warned that if they did not comply they would be treated as counterrevolutionaries.

Meanwhile, the two children of President Liu Shao-chi attacked today their father's private life in a special number of Hung Chi, organ of the Red Guards at the Peking Aeronautics Institute.

Father Called Inhuman

The President's son, Liu Yun-chen, and his daughter, Liu Tao, both about 20 years old, said that after their first self-criticism in front of their comrades in class, they were advised by Chairman Mao's wife, Chiang Ching, to break with their family and to support the party chairman in the cultural revolution.

Attacking President Liu and his present wife, Wang Kwang-mei, they said:

"On Jan. 1 we visited our mother, Wang Chi-en, who lifted the veil on Liu Shao-chi's past. According to her, the hypocritical and inhuman Liu took 10 years off his age to marry her in 1945 when she was only 16 while he was 42."

During this marriage Mr. Liu was said to have used party funds for a golden belt buckle and shoehorn made to his order. He gave the buckle to his wife when they were divorced, but later accused her of stealing it, the children wrote.

Recently Wang Chi-en was said to have sent the buckle to the party's Central Committee group responsible for the cultural revolution.

"Liu Shao-chi, you must also give back the shoehorn," the children wrote.

The children charged that in 1949 their stepmother gave Wang Chi-en two boxes of trick chewing gum that took on a bitter taste after it had been chewed.

The children seem to have a special grudge toward their stepmother. They said that after having been elected "Queen" of Fujen University of Peking, a Roman Catholic institution under the Chinese Nationalists, she became an interpreter in English. She did not go to Yenan, headquarters of the Communist leaders before they took power in 1949, until urged to do so by Yeh Chien-ying, a Red Army leader.

The children accused their father of trying to create "Liuism," a political philosophy intended to supplant Chairman Mao's thoughts, and to take his place at the head of the party.

They said that Mr. Liu had adopted an attitude of capitulation during the civil war against the Nationalists. The children said his philosophy did not differ from that of former Premier Nikita S. Khrushchev of the Soviet Union.

January 25, 1967

Anti-Maoists Are Reported Encircled in Sinkiang

By JOSEPH LELYVELD
Special to The New York Times

TOKYO, Monday, Jan. 30 — Army units loyal to Mao Tse-tung have encirclued dissident forces in Sinkiang in western China, according to Japanese resports from Peking based on wall posters.

Other posters told of the spread of clashes to Szechwan with "dozens" killed, but gave no indication of the date or outcome of the fighting.

The loyal units in the Sinkiang-Uigur Autonomous Region demanded that the dissidents surrender and turn in their arms but the demand was spurned, the posters said. The correspondent of the Japanese newspaper Tokyo Shimbun reported that the posters were based on a telegram from Sinkiang that arrived in Peking yesterday.

The two sides in Sinkiang apparently met Friday for a truce talk but failed to reach an agreement. The dissidents were said to be elements of the Second Motorized Division reinforced by former servicemen.

They have taken the name of the "August 1st Field Army," an apparent allusion to the anniversary of the Red Army's formation Aug. 1, 1927.

Chou Appeal Unheeded

Earlier reports said that seven of eight divisions in Sinkiang were opposing the Maoist faction. Premier Chou En-lai was said to have ordered loyalist forces to intervene after 100 persons were reported killed in clashes last week.

A poster reported by Kyodo, the Japanese news agency, indicated that some military authorities in Sinkiang were wavering.

"The masses are pinning great hopes on the military district representatives," it said, "but their attitude is not clear. They are not on the side of the rebels. But certain leaders are not acting according to Chou's instructions."

The Peking radio, monitored here, said that the lunar New Year holiday had been canceled for all Chinese workers. It said "reactionaries" were planning to use the holiday to incite opposition to Chairman Mao.

"To achieve victories in revolution and production so that the proletarian cultural revolution may advance," the broadcast said, "the State Council has decided to consider the lunar New Year as no holiday. The problem of holidays will be considered later on."

Meantime, posters announced the official beginning of a new form of government in Peking. A "people's regime," taking the name of "Peking Revolutionary Corporation," was said to have come into existence.

Plea for Moderation

By CHARLES MOHR
Special to The New York Times

HONG KONG, Jan. 29. — The republication in Communist China over the weekend of a 37-year-old essay of Mao Tse-tung, the party's Chairman, is interpreted by observers here as an appeal for moderation in the Cultural Revolution.

The 1929 essay, titled "On Correcting Mistaken Ideas in the Party," called for greater organizational discipline and less "impetuosity" and warned against the "ultra-democratic" approach of heeding demands from lower levels.

The party newspaper, Jenmin Jih Pao, which printed the essay in yesterday's editions, reported today that the publication had met "nationwide acclaim."

In publishing Mr. Mao's essay, Jenmin Jih Pao said in an editorial note that revolutionary elements supporting him should seriously study the text to correct faults within their ranks.

"There exist in our revolutionary mass organizations some mistaken tendencies that hinder a great alliance of the proletarian revolutionaries," said the editorial note. "These include selfish departmentalism, cliquism, ultrademocracy, disregard of organizational discipline, subjectivism and individualism.

"Only by firmly correcting these mistaken tendencies can we form a resolute and powerful proletarian revolutionary force," it added.

Open to Interpretation

The 1929 essay seemed open to any number of interpretations and it was unclear how it might be used.

The text warns of the dangers of a "purely military viewpoint" in the army and insists that politics must be supreme. This accords with the recent Maoist plea that the army must not adopt a hands-off policy in the Cultural Revolution.

Another passage said some comrades "suffer from the malady of revolutionary impetuosity." Recent press articles have said extreme actions were necessary parts of the Cultural Revolution.

The essay says inner-party criticism is meant only to strengthen the party organization and "should not be used as means of personal attack." It also says that such criticism should be confined to party meetings.

Public attacks in the form of wall posters and struggle meetings in sports stadiums have been major features of the Cultural Revolution up to now.

Mr. Mao's essay warned against the "ideology of roving rebel bands," saying that reliance on such bands was only an excuse for avoiding hard spadework in fixed localities. China has been crisscrossed by roving Red Guard contingents for many months.

The essay describes as "erroneous" demands that "higher levels" should base their actions on discussion and demands from "lower levels." Such a principle "damages or even completely wrecks the party organization," Mr. Mao wrote.

In recent days the nation has been urged to form committees patterned on the Paris Commune of 1871 to "seize power from below" and to run industries through elected committees subject to recall by the masses.

Some observers were tempted to see the use of the 1929 essay as an attempt to moderate the Cultural Revolution, but they remembered that previous advice of moderation was followed by a new intensification of the campaign.

Meanwhile, the Chinese army seemed to be slow to implement Chairman Mao's order of a week ago to take an active part in the Cultural Revolution. There have been few substantiated reports of army action on the side of Maoist revolutionary organizations.

Some analysts thought it possible that the army was trying to avoid the Chairman's instructions to assist the Red Guards and Revolutionary Rebel Committees in seizing power from established party committees in the provinces.

The analysts associated such possible hesitation with the character of the provincial power structure where top party officials frequently hold high political or even military positions in the armed forces.

Party-Army Link Shown

An examination of the Chinese party's regional bureaus showed that at least 16 top officials held important jobs in the regional party structure and in the army. Five of them are commanders of military regions, one is the commander of the Canton garrison and 10 are political commissars of military regions or of the lesser provincial military districts.

Sung Jen-chiung, First Secretary of the Northeast party bureau, is also first political commissar of the Mukden military region, which embraces all of Manchuria.

One of the secretaries in Mr. Sung's bureau is Chen Hsi-lien, who is also commander of the Mukden military region.

Three other secretaries of the Northeast bureau are concurrently political commissars or deputy commissars of military districts.

In the Northwest China bureau, the First Secretary, Wang En-mao, is also the commander and political commissar of the Sinkiang military region and First Secretary of the Sinkiang Uigur Autonomous Region.

One of Mr. Wang's fellow secretaries in the Northwest bureau is Chang Ta-chih, commander of the Lanchow military region.

Similar patterns prevail elsewhere.

End to Excesses Urged

PEKING, Jan. 29 (Agence France-Presse) — Posters issued with Chairman Mao's authorization appeared here today calling on the army to show moderation and end excesses in carrying out the Cultural Revolution.

The printed posters were issued by the Military Commission of the party's Central Committee.

Arbitrary arrest and searches, parading supporters of the "bourgeois reactionary line" while forcing them to wear paper dunce caps, and punishment obliging persons to remain kneeling are forbidden, the posters said.

The Military Commission stressed the need to distinguish between repression of "real counterrevolutionaries," against whom legal measures should be taken, and "leftist elements" guilty of political errors.

Coming after Chairman Mao's official request for the army to intervene in the Cultural Revolution, the posters seemed to reflect the wish of the military leaders, and particularly Defense Minister Lin Piao, that the army's political participation be orderly and disciplined.

MOSCOW PROTESTS CHINESE VIOLENCE AGAINST EMBASSY

Warns of Retaliation Unless Harassment Is Stopped— Liu Reported Humiliated

By RAYMOND H. ANDERSON
Special to The New York Times

MOSCOW, Feb. 4—The Soviet Government warned China today to halt a campaign of violence and humiliation against Russians in Peking or face retaliatory action by the Soviet Union.

The warning was contained in a note delivered to the Chinese Embassy. Moscow did not stipulate what steps it might take, but it was assumed that the warning meant that diplomatic relations might be severed.

Denouncing "anti-Soviet hysteria" in China, the Soviet note cautioned that "the restraint and patience of the Soviet people are not boundless."

[Peking wall posters described by Japanese correspondents said that President Liu Shao-chi, considered a leading opponent of Chairman Mao Tse-tung, was publicly humiliated by a crowd in the capital Jan. 26.]

Chinese Make Charges

The Soviet message was made public at a news conference in the Foreign Ministry. Shortly before, correspondents were called to the Chinese Embassy to hear charges against the Soviet Union in an incident outside the embassy last night.

The Chinese asserted that about 170 Soviet plainclothes men had committed a "barbaric, fascist act" in tearing down propaganda display cases and beating 31 Chinese who tried to resist them.

The Chinese charged that the Russians had violated the diplomatic immunity of the embassy grounds by removing the six glass display cases, one of which contained photographs of fighting on Red Square Jan. 25 between Russians and Chinese students.

A Foreign Ministry spokes-

man declared that the Soviet Government "categorically denied" Chinese allegations that Soviet citizens had intruded onto the embassy territory.

Balustrade Is an Issue

The display cases stood on stilts about a foot and a half inside a marble balustrade in front of two embassy buildings flanking the chancery.

The Chinese asserted that the Russians had crossed the balustrade and used electric saws to cut the stilts. The Foreign Ministry spokesman and Russians who were at the scene last night insisted that the display cases had been pulled down from the sidewalk.

The Russians also denied Chinese accusations that the embassy's chargé d'affaires, An Chih-yuan, had been beaten during the incident. A Soviet policeman posted at the embassy said at the Foreign Ministry news conference that the chargé d'affaires had not emerged from the embassy when about 30 Chinese staff members rushed out, hatless and coatless, into the below-zero cold to defend the propaganda displays.

Tass, the Soviet press agency, said today that the propaganda displays had been removed by "Soviet citizens" who had taken matters into their own hands after the embassy had refused to take down the "slanderous materials" in the cases.

The Soviet Foreign Ministry's note to Peking charged that the Chinese Government was fanning "hostile anti-Soviet hysteria, carrying it to the extreme form of rude highhandedness and direct physical encroachment on officials of the Embassy of the U.S.S.R., employes of other Soviet institutions and Soviet citizens in the People's Republic of China."

Tass reported that thousands of Chinese tried yesterday to lynch nine Russians, including three diplomats and six advisers, returning to the Soviet Union from North Vietnam.

According to the press agency, the Chinese detained the Russians aboard a bus for three hours, spat on them, splashed them with glue and subjected them to abuse.

"They demanded that the Soviet citizens leave the bus and tried to lynch them," Tass said. It did not report how the Russians had escaped.

Moscow said the demonstrations outside the Soviet Embassy in Peking for the last week and a half were "without precedent in the history of diplomatic relations."

The demonstrations followed an incident in Moscow's Red

Square in which Chinese students passing through Moscow on their way home from Western Europe attempted to place wreaths at the Lenin Mausoleum and the nearby grave of Stalin.

"The Soviet Government lodges with the Government of the Peoples' Republic of China resolute protest over the lawlessness and arbitrary behavior toward Soviet people in Peking," today's note said.

"It categorically insists that the Chinese authorities, in conformity with generally accepted standards of international law, take the most urgent steps to insure the full safety of officials of the Embassy of the U.S.S.R., other Soviet institutions in Peking and members of their families."

The Soviet protest came shortly after the departure from Peking of a planeload of Soviet wives and children in an emergency evacuation.

The 40 women and children arrived in Moscow at 7 P.M. and were greeted with flowers and tears by relatives.

Sixty Men Will Remain

The spokesman said that about 200 women and children would be evacuated and about 60 men would remain to staff the besieged embassy.

Today's hint by Moscow that it might break diplomatic relations with Peking if the violence there continued followed months of determined forbearance by the Soviet Government as the Chinese increased the virulence of their campaign of harassment of Soviet diplomats and denunciation of the Soviet Government's policies and leaders.

Diplomats in Moscow believe that the Soviet Government feels it must maintain relations while it is committed to assist North Vietnam. Soviet supplies to Hanoi are still moving by train through China and Soviet aircraft have been flying advisers to North Vietnam over China.

A break in relations with Peking, diplomats say, would compel the Russians to move all supplies and advisers by sea, thus increasing the risk of a confrontation with United States warships.

Furthermore, according to these analysts, Moscow is hopeful that the anti-Soviet disorders in China will die down within a reasonable time when the faction of Mao Tse-tung, Chairman of the Communist party, or his opposition emerges victorious in the country's power struggle.

According to this interpretation, the Russians will try to keep their embassy open and thereby avoid the cumbersome procedures of negotiating a reestablishment of diplomatic relations when calm has been restored in China.

Red Guard Is Told To Cease Marches And Return Home

By ALFRED FRIENDLY Jr.
Special to The New York Times

TOKYO, Wednesday, Feb. 8—Red Guards, the shock troops of China's Cultural Revolution, have been ordered to suspend their marches around the countryside and return to their homes, Japanese correspondents in Peking reported yesterday.

They said the order, issued by the Central Committee of the Chinese Communist party and by the State Council (Cabinet), had been posted in wall notices in the capital.

According to the Peking correspondent of the newspaper Mainichi Shimbun, a wall poster ordering the Red Guards home said this signified a "new stage" in the Cultural Revolution.

That is the name given to a campaign led by Mao Tse-tung, the party chairman, to introduce a more puritanical form of Communism in China and to overcome the opposition of party leaders whom he accuses of taking the "capitalist road." The Peking wall poster called on the Red Guards to "return to the places and schools from which they came and take part there in the great, historical, decisive battle."

Despite a ban on railroad transportation for Red Guards in effect since November, the youngsters continued to crowd into the capital on foot and move around the country in bands "exchanging revolutionary experience."

The wall bulletin said too many Red Guards, estimated to number up to 10 million, had crowded into Peking and such "sacred revolutionary places" as Shaoshan, a village in Hunan Province where Chairman Mao was born, and Yenan in Shensi Province, where he headed the Chinese Communist movement before it came to power in 1949.

"These places are jammed, and the weather is very cold and arrangements for food, lodging and transportation are very difficult to make," the poster said. The local economies in these regions have been hard hit and "in some places epidemics have spread," the notification added.

Because of these considerations, the bulletin ordered:

"1. The exchange of experiences on foot over long distances shall be suspended all over the country. Those expeditionary units who have stayed more than five days and have attained their objectives should return to the places from which they came. The exchange of experiences within county borders shall be suspended in the revolutionary sacred places to avoid congestion of transportation.

"2. In returning to their hometowns, the Red Guards shall go on foot. Those Red Guards who have come from places that are more than 500 kilometers [300 miles] away may be given free tickets for trains and steamers within 15 days.

"3. Chairman Mao Tse-tung told the people 'Let us economize and carry out the revolution.' Let us respond to this. During the exchange-of-experiences period and the period of returning to hometowns, the Red Guards should pay their own food and transportation expenses in the cities. The food ration can be increased appropriately. Necessary expenses for clothes should be held to a minimum.

"4. Until now the Red Guards in Peking have been given free meals. However, beginning Feb. 8, expenses for food will be charged and food will not be given free from now on."

February 8, 1967

CHINA BIDS TROOPS RETURN TO UNITS

Special to The New York Times

TOKYO, Saturday, Feb. 11—All members of the Chinese Communist Army and its supporting agencies who are away from their posts for political activity have been ordered to return to their units by Feb. 20, according to Japanese reports from Peking.

Quoting wall posters in the capital, the Japanese dispatches said that the order, signed by Defense Minister Lin Piao and dated Feb. 8, had gone to all provinces by telegraph.

Also from Peking, a correspondent of Mainichi Shimbun reported that all civil aviation in Communist China has been placed under control of the army.

'Providing Against War'

An order issued by the State Council and the Military Affairs Committee of the Communist party on Jan. 26 said that the militarization of international and domestic air transport was a step taken "in providing against war" and to assist in "the smooth progress of the Cultural Revolution," the newspaper dispatch said.

The Lin Piao order was said to have included students of military schools, munitions workers, hospital staffs and all others connected with the army. They were instructed to abandon propaganda efforts and to return to their regular stations "as quickly as possible."

According to the Japanese account, the posters said that the orders had been issued on behalf of the Military Affairs Committee of the party. The Defense Minister is also Vice Chairman of the party and the designated political heir to Mao-Tse-tung, the party chairman.

The order banned trips away from stations by military personnel to "exchange revolutionary experiences," a practice that had been encouraged earlier by the Mao-Lin faction as a means of mobilizing support in a struggle with President Liu Shao-chi and Teng Hsiao-ping, the party's General Secretary.

A Government order issued recently barred further travel by the Red Guard. These teen-aged backers of the austere brand of Communism preached by Chairman Mao had poured into Peking by the millions, taking advantage of free accommodation on railroads.

February 11, 1967

Chinese Concern Over Harvest Said to Slow Mao Revolution

By CHARLES MOHR
Special to The New York Times

HONG KONG, Feb. 15 — Some Western analysts of politics in China said today that increasing concern about the food supply might have forced a slowdown in the Cultural Revolution led by Mao Tse-tung, Communist party chairman.

A broadcast from Nanning in South China, monitored here yesterday, said "all places, particularly disaster areas" in Kwangsi-Chuang Autonomous Region must work hard to make up for "insufficiency" in the grain ration and "to overcome a spring famine."

Such phrases may describe fear of a food shortage rather than an existing shortage.

There have been many signs in recent days that compromises may have been made by Mr. Mao and allied leaders in the drive to revolutionize China and purge more pragmatic party bureaucrats, in the analysts' view.

Ideological exhortation of the masses in the name of the Cultural Revolution is likely to continue, the observers thought.

The Chinese press in recent days has stressed the need for hard work to prepare for the spring crop.

The Nanning broadcast said political enemies of the Cultural Revolution had engaged in "a lot of monkey business" and "reckless misdeeds" in attempting to sabotage the state's distribution of grain and edible oils.

Suggesting that granaries had been raided by mobs, the radio said that "if the storehouses are found to be stormed, the first thing to do is to carry out political and thought work among the misled masses to convince them by persuasion."

It said that the new Maoist officials of public security organizations "must make a success of grain protection."

"All places, particularly disaster areas, must strengthen the tending of the winter crops, plant more early crops to make up for insufficiency in the grain ration, implementing the spirit of self-reliance to overcome spring famine," the broadcast said.

There have been suggestions in the official press that work, administration and even the collective system in the countryside are being disturbed by the Cultural Revolution campaign against party and government officials considered by the Maoists to be "pro-Soviet" and following a "capitalist line."

Mr. Mao has announced a goal of "destroying" the old machinery of government and replacing it first with "provisional" organs of power responsive to his mass organizations and finally by elected committees modeled on the insurrectionary Paris Commune, which briefly ruled Paris for two months in 1871 at the end of the Franco-Prussian War.

February 16, 1967

MAOISTS WEAKEN ON COMMUNE IDEA

By Agence France-Presse

PEKING, Feb. 28—The Maoist communes of Shanghai and Peking, hailed at their birth this month as glorious successors of the short-lived Paris Commune of 1871, both seemed today to have been abandoned.

A poster signed by Security Minister Hsieh Fu-chih warned that the setting up of communes in China's big cities would raise the danger of federalism by threatening "to transform the People's Republic of China into an assemblage of people's communes."

The Chinese city communes, which were supposed to seize power from established local party and government authorities, were said to have been patterned after the Paris Commune, an insurrectionary government that briefly ruled the French capital at the end of the Franco-Prussian War.

Reports in the Peking press of a big rally held in Shanghai Friday by the revolutionary municipal committee, described as "the highest provisional power organ" in Shanghai, omitted any reference to the Shanghai Commune.

The Shanghai committee is headed by Chang Chun-chiao and Yao Wen-yuan, members of the Central Committee's steering group for the Cultural Revolution. This is the name given to Mao Tse-tung's campaign to introduce a more austere type of Communism in China and oust party officials considered "pro-capitalist" or pro-Soviet from positions of authority.

Delegated by Mao

The new Shanghai group apparently replaces the provisional committee of the Shanghai Commune. Formation of the commune committee was announced in the Shanghai press on Feb. 7 but was never reported by the press in Peking.

Mr. Chang told the rally crowd Friday that his activity in Shanghai was based on instructions received from Mr. Mao, who is the party chairman. The speaker insisted on the need for a "triple alliance" grouping representatives of the masses, Maoist party officials and army delegates.

The rally adopted a resolution providing that the armed forces be "the supporting pillar of provisional power organs at all levels" and that "no mass organization or individual may give orders on his or its own initiative to the armed militia."

The three organizational sectors should meet together at all levels to decide "whether it is necessary to take power, how to do so and how to act after power is seized," the resolution said.

It contrasted with official appeals earlier this month, inciting Maoists to "seize power" indiscriminately.

The resolution invited mass organizations to "conform strictly with the state plan and the state system," recommended "rectification campaigns" and warned against such deviations as "anarchy, ultra-democracy, sectarianism and fractionism."

Mr. Chang told the rally that Chairman Mao was in "excellent health."

Shanghai Events Recalled

Recent posters here quoted Wang Li, the Central Committee's new propaganda chief, as having said that Chairman Mao refused to recognize the Shanghai commune on the ground that it was not sufficiently representative.

Reports of Friday's rally by the party newspaper, Jenmin Jih Pao, and the Hsinhua press agency amounted to an official consecration of the new Shanghai municipal committee.

The events in Shanghai began with a Maoist revolution in January, hailed at the time as a model for all China. A purge swept most of the city leadership from power. Dignitaries were driven through the streets wearing paper dunce caps.

A provisional commune committee announced Feb. 7 that it had taken all power from the party and city administration. The committee represented 38 organizations, but apparently comprised only two army delegates and one from the city administration.

As late as Feb. 15, posters were still appearing with the pledge that "all dog heads opposed to the Shanghai Commune will be crushed." But about Feb. 20, new posters described the commune as a "fascist organization."

In another development President Liu Shao-chi was accused here tonight of fomenting "a new counteroffensive of the bourgeois reactionary line" in opposition to Chairman Mao.

Mr. Liu and the party's general secretary, Teng Hsiao-ping, were also charged with complicity with the ousted Mayor of Peking, Peng Chen, who is said to have been the leader of a plot aimed at overthrowing Mr. Mao last year.

The accusations against President Liu and Mr. Teng were made in Red Guard posters that reported a clash between 3,000 workers and students of People's University here last Friday and Saturday. The violence was attributed to "a handful of monarchists" among the students.

The posters demanded the exclusion of Mr. Liu and Mr. Teng from the party's Central Committee.

March 1, 1967

Trouble in Wuhan

Military officers and mass public organizations in the Chinese city of Wuhan have dealt Mao Tse-tung the most humiliating rebuff he has suffered since he began a purge of Chinese Communism 14 months ago.

Two important emissaries of the party Chairman were apparently "seized," detained and humiliated in that central China industrial center, before being released last weekend. Since then the Chinese press and radio have been full of denunciations of "power holders" in Wuhan and of expressions of support for pro-Maoist "revolutionary" groups in the area.

When the cultural revolution began rolling in the summer of 1966, it was with two stated objectives. Mr. Mao wanted to drive out of power and influence party leaders at every level suspected of harboring "revisionist" ideas likely to foster a "capitalist restoration.". Mr. Mao also wanted to remold the minds of the people, get them to accept more austerity and greater collectivization. In practice the cultural revolution quickly degenerated into a witch-hunt.

By late February, even Mao Tse-tung was apparently ready to admit his purge had lost direction, gotten out of control and become a danger to China's stability and economic health. The Chinese Army was ordered to intervene nationwide in the growingly chaotic power struggles between Red Guard and other "revolutionary rebel" organizations, on the one hand, and Communist party officials on the other.

The orders given to the army, however, were extremely difficult to implement—or even to understand. The army was to identify the "true revolutionary," or pro-Mao, groups and to support them. But it was also to carry out "rectification" campaigns among these Maoists to stamp out "anarchism" and violations of discipline.

In such circumstances, the army had to do the best it could. Not all of its decisions met with favor with the left wing of the Maoist faction in Peking. In fact, only in four Chinese provinces was the "revolutionary three-way alliance" of army, party and Maoist elements given official sanction.

In other areas, like Wuhan and the surrounding Hupeh province, some fanatical "Maoist" organizations have refused to accept the working arrangements made by army.

By May, Peking Red Guard wall posters began to appear attacking Chen Tsai-tao, commander of the Wuhan military area and the effective boss of the region since February. Mr. Chen's crime was not giving sufficient support to the "true" leftists.

Street fighting of serious proportions broke out in Wuhan. It was a struggle for power. By late June at least 250 "bloody" clashes were reported, in which some 350 persons were said to have died and 1,500 were believed injured.

Two high officials were sent from Peking to Wuhan July 14 with instructions to end the violence. They were Hsieh Fu-chih, the Minister of Public Security, and Wang Li, a Maoist intellectual.

Some political observers in Hong Kong believe that the two emissaries must have shown favoritism for the most fanatical, left-wing Maoist faction in Wuhan. In any case, something they did angered the more orthodox Communist and public groups in that city.

Maoist wall posters in Peking said Mr. Wang was "kidnapped" by "conservative" elements on July 20 and Mr. Hsieh the next day. Some reports were that Mr. Wang was paraded with a dunce cap on his head—much like the treatment meted out by Red Guards to Mr. Mao's opponents. How the release of Mr. Hsieh and Mr. Wang was negotiated last weekend is not clear, but the two men were given a hero's welcome when they returned to Peking.

At week's end the Peking Radio announced that the military leaders of Wuhan had made an "open confession of errors in orientation and political line" and of failing to support the "revolutionary left." But the broadcast indicated that these leaders were still in power. It predicted that they would regret their errors in the future and "return to Mao's revolutionary line."

To Western observers in Hong Kong this denoted a compromise that hold little promise of improving the position of fanatic, left-wing Maoists in Wuhan. The whole episode seemed to be the most dramatic example yet of the tendency of the cultural revolution to make more enemies for Mao Tse-tung.

July 30, 1967

SOVIET EMBASSY STORMED IN CHINA

By Reuters

BELGRADE, Yugoslavia, Aug. 17 — Chinese demonstrators forced their way into the Soviet Embassy compound in Peking tonight and smashed furniture and set fire to files in a consular department building, Tanjug, the Yugoslav press agency, reported from the Chinese capital.

The demonstrators also smashed the windows of the main building in the compound but did not break in.

Tanjug, quoting Soviet Embassy officials, said that Chinese troops and policemen stationed outside the embassy did not take steps to prevent the disorders, which lasted for about an hour.

Earlier in the day, a Soviet Embassy car was set on fire in the center of Peking in front of a department store for diplomats, the agency reported.

The Soviet Embassy lodged a protest with the Chinese authorities, Tanjug said.

The outburst took place after the Chinese, in a note delivered to the Soviet Embassy on Sunday, charged that seamen aboard the Soviet freighter Svirsk had been instructed to insult Mao Tse-tung while at port in China.

The Svirsk docked at the Manchurian port of Dairen on July 22 and was detained by the Chinese. It was allowed to leave on Monday after Premier Aleksei N. Kosygin indicated that Moscow might sever trade relations with Peking if the vessel was not released.

The Chinese charged that a Soviet seaman had insulted Mr. Mao, the Communist party chairman, by throwing overboard a Mao lapel badge.

August 18, 1967

A CURB ON VIOLENCE ORDERED IN PEKING

PEKING, Sept. 4 (Agence France-Presse—A big crowd carrying red flags and streamers massed in front of the headquarters of the city revolutionary committee today. Apparently the crowd was hailing the committee's newly published resolution condemning violence.

The eight-point document adopted by the committee Friday was published today in the committee's newspaper. It calls for severe punishments for those who have been guilty of looting and murder. It says all persons who stopped work, in order to take part in "violent struggles" will receive no salary until they resume work.

It emphasizes the necessity of immediately putting an end to "violent struggles," thus apparently confirming reports that serious disturbances involving killing, rioting, looting and work stoppages have taken place.

September 5, 1967

CHINA REINSTATES LOWER OFFICIALS

Special to The New York Times

HONG KONG, Nov. 6—Peking has reinstated many of the country's old-line officials who were pushed aside by Red Guards and other revolutionary militants during the upheaval of the Cultural Revolution.

These officials were given the largest share of the blame for the consequences of the "great leap forward," China's disastrous economic experiment of the late nineteen-fifties. They have been a popular target of the Red Guards during the Cultural Revolution, set in motion early last year to sweep away all opposition to Mao Tse-tung, Communist party leader.

Now Peking has called for rehabilitation of all officials denounced during the Cultural Revolution except for a few "incorrigible" enemies of Chairman Mao.

This development coincides with a new effort by Peking to get the youth of the country back into classrooms that they were permitted to leave in June of last year to roam the country in Red Guard bands.

Both operations appear to be intended to end the turmoil created by the excesses of the Cultural Revolution.

Mao Witnessed Turmoil

Mr. Mao had an opportunity to see some of the turmoil at first hand when he toured central and east China recently and his impressions, together with pressure from the armed forces, is believed to have dictated the hierarchy's decision to slow down the Cultural Revolution. Red Guards and other revolutionaries have been directed to end factional fighting and to make peace with the officials.

The focus of the campaign at the moment appears to be on rehabilitation of managerial experts, officials with special skills needed to extricate China from social and economic confusion created by the Cultural Revolution.

No top officials have been publicly rehabilitated and press attacks are continuing against Liu Shao-chi, the head of state, and other key figures accused of opposing Mr. Mao.

Some political observers believe the campaign may be partly aimed at preserving the status of senior officials who have been subjected to severe Red Guard assaults but have held on to their jobs. Chen Yi, the Foreign Minister, falls into this category. Coincidental with the present climate of conciliation he has come into public prominence after a period of eclipse and was at Peking Airport with Premier Chou En-lai to meet Chinese diplomats withdrawn from Indonesia.

Lower Aides Benefit

But lower officials are the prinicpal beneficiaries of the campaign. Chinese papers have been publicizing officials at the level of factories, hospitals, mines, rural communes and schools.

The Peking radio broadcast a report about a middle school in Tientsin at which the army took a hand in establishing rapport between students and officials. Just how much pressure the troops had to apply to this end was not revealed, but the report said that after "study and some discussion, students came to the realization that the majority of the cadres were good."

The radio said: "Now when students find that a cadre has made some mistake they no longer attack him but instead help him to correct his mistake. In the past they would have unleashed a severe attack upon him."

The press and radio reveal that many officials who lost their authority to Red Guard groups or self-appointed committees have been reinstated in virtually the same positions they held before. The only difference usually is a change in their titles.

November 12, 1967

ARMY IN RED CHINA TO AID COMMUNES

Plans to Support Rural Units Favored by Mao

The following dispatch is by David Oancia of The Globe and Mail, Toronto.
© 1966 by The Globe and Mail

PEKING, Dec. 18—The Peking garrison is reported to have mapped a program for the armed forces to continue to participate in food production and in striving to halt the drift away from the commune ideal as envisaged by Mao Tse-tung, the Communist party chairman.

The upshot of a recent conference of 500 commanders appears to be that the army will seek to strengthen the position of those loyal to Mr. Mao's ideals and, at the same time, strengthen and cultivate the loyalty of the militia (local forces) in the countryside.

This suggests that the Cultural Revolution, which has caused upheavals in schools, factories and other sectors of urban society, will be carried out with greater control in rural areas.

The commune system was launched during the Great Leap Forward era of 1958 and almost immediately it ran into difficulties, officially attributed to natural disasters and Soviet sabotage.

Incentives Reintroduced

In the period of adjustment that followed these setbacks, material incentives were reintroduced, the size of the communes was reduced and the center of power passed from the commune to the production-brigade level. A commune is made up of several brigades.

The central leadership headed by Mr. Mao now has signaled that it wants to halt the backsliding in the countryside, eradicate the material incentives and other manifestations it feels are essentially private enterprise and attempt to rekindle the selfless dedication to the public interest that the commune was intended to engender.

"The rural people's communes are the primary units in the countryside of our socialist society and also the primary units of socialist power," said a recent editorial in the newspaper Peking Jih Pao.

"The question of whose hands leadership will be in is a fundamental question involving whether the Chinese countryside will follow the socialist or the capitalist road.

"In the suburbs not only units at the county level should establish revolutionary committees, but communes also should follow the principle of a three-way combination and establish revolutionary, representative provisional organs of power with proletarian authority — that is, revolutionary committees to further consolidate proletarian dictatorship."

The Peking garrison meeting reported in yesterday's newspapers made it plain that the armed forces hoped to rely on the local militia to help them

December 19, 1967

CHINA'S PUPILS GIVEN NO WINTER VACATION

Special to The New York Times

HONG KONG, Jan. 22—Peking has decreed that Communist China's students will have no winter vacation this year in a move to keep them in school in order to prevent a resurgence of the turmoil that prevailed last year.

The order will also enable teachers to make up some of the ground lost while their students were taking part in the Cultural Revolution. Actually, China's schools are imparting little practical knowledge because of the emphasis on political education.

Reporting the vacation ban, which was issued in the name of the Communist party's Central Committee, a broadcast from Hweichow Province, in southwest China, said that 20 colleges and secondary schools in Kweiyang, the provincial capital, had pledged support.

Since early last year Peking has repeatedly appealed to students to return to their classrooms, but many schools remain unopened.

January 23, 1968

PEKING SETTING UP NEW YOUTH CORPS

The following dispatch is by David Oancia of The Globe and Mail, Toronto.

© 1968 by The Globe and Mail

PEKING, March 18 — The memory of Communist China's Red Guards is to be perpetuated in the name of a new organization for youngsters, but the new groups will have little of the power that the teen-agers wielded in their struggle to establish the primacy of Mao-Tse-tung's policy line.

The Red Guards were the first shock troops used in the onslaught against President Liu Shao-chi and others labeled as followers of the capitalist road. But they are being subjected to increasingly rigorous discipline as the central leadership turns its attention to production and the development of a new power structure.

Those meeting the rigorous recruiting standards of the regular army are being drafted. Thousands of them, wearing uniforms but without the identifying red star on their caps, can be seen in the suburbs of Peking, where experienced soldiers teach them how to march.

Among their other tasks are pruning or cutting down trees along the streets and highways or working in the fields with the peasants.

Other secondary-school and university students have been given limited military training to instill the sense of organization and discipline needed to get on with the task of reopening the schools. That goal is now being given top priority by the leadership.

A major hurdle, however, is continuing factional strife and anarchic behavior.

The schools closed almost two years ago to permit students to participate in the Cultural Revolution, Mr. Mao's attempt to purge his opponents. When classes resume tens of thousands of teen-agers will be absent, though, because they have been assigned to work in frontier areas or in a variety of other jobs. The number involved has not been published.

The new Red Guards are to be primary students, those in the first six grades.

The Peking leadership has called on all primary schools to set up Young Red Guard Corps. The new entity appears to be a replacement for the discredited Young Pioneers League, an organization said to have been permeated by the

"poisonous influence of the revisionist line."

The old league accepted children between the ages of 9 and 15. Those considered sufficiently advanced could then seek membership in the Young Communist League. As a result of the Cultural Revolution the pattern has now been disrupted and the two organizations are being subjected to a purge and to reconstruction.

March 19, 1968

NEW ARMY CHIEF NAMED IN CHINA

PEKING, March 29 (Agence France-Presse)—Posters in central Peking declared today that Huang Yung-sheng had been named Chief of Staff of the Chinese Communist armed forces.

The new commander, who is 62 years old, replaces Yang Cheng-wu, whose removal has raised a new political storm according to the posters.

"Let's support the decision of Mao Tse-tung, Lin Piao and Chou En-lai in making Huang Yung-sheng chief of the general staff," the posters said. Mr. Huang was ranked eighth on Wednesday on a list of 11 persons who held a reception here for 10,000 military aides.

Others Are Dismissed

During this reception it was apparently announced that Yu Li-chin, the political commissar of the air force, Fu Chung-pi, the commander of the Peking garrison, and Mr. Yang had been dismissed.

The posters in Peking did not say whether Mr. Huang would keep his job as chairman of the Revolutionary Committee in Kwangtung Province. He has held that post since the committee was set up Feb. 21.

The committees are being established throughout China to replace the administrative structure that was shattered during the purges of Mr. Mao's Cultural Revolution.

Mr. Huang, the commander of the Canton Military Region since 1955, was himself a subject of violent criticism by Red Guards last year. The region exercises military authority over the provinces of Kwangtung, Kwangsi and Hunan.

Sporadic Strife Reported

The province of Kwangtung, including its capital at Canton, has proved particularly difficult for the Peking leadership to control. Sporadic and sometimes bloody clashes have been reported since early last summer as factional strife erupted in the area.

A Canton radio broadcast in November indicated that Mr. Huang had visited Peking and his trip may have had a bearing on the ensuing slowdown in the Cultural Revolution.

Mr. Yang's predecessor as chief of staff, Lo Jui-ching, was one of the first casualties of the purges.

The new chief of staff, a native of Kiangsi, which borders Kwangtung, has been an alternate member of the Communist party's Central Committee since September 1956.

In February, 1964, he became a member of the Secretariat of the party bureau for Central-South China, and thus became a collaborator of Tao Chu, the former First Secretary of the bureau. Mr. Tao was promoted to propaganda chief of the Central Committee and became the regime's fourth-ranking member in August, 1966, but he was suddenly removed four months later.

March 30, 1968

421

A Group of 'Ultraleftists' Is Accused in China

By CHARLES MOHR

Special to The New York Times

HONG KONG, April 18 — A group of Chinese Communist "ultraleftists" who were close to the inner circle around Mao Tse-tung until last fall has been accused of plotting against Chairman Mao's wife and Premier Chou Enl-lai.

One of them was accused of a sinister attempt to collect information detrimental to Chair-Mao's wife, Chiang Ching. All were accused of having tried to unseat Premier Chou and the Cabinet.

The accusations that reached Hong Kong recently cannot be independently substantiated.

The three most important leftists under attack are Wang Li, Kuan Feng and Chi Pen-yu. All were formerly members of the Central Cultural Revolution Group, responsible for directing the purge.

Chen Po-ta—a member of the Politburo and a close associate of Mr. Mao—is the director of the group. Chiang Ching is the deputy director and, perhaps, dominant figure.

The three leftists have been deputy editors of the ideological journal Hung Chi, which was founded and supervised by Mr. Chen. The magazine has not appeared since Nov. 22.

Analysts also noted that Mr. Chi was the author of the attack on the chief of state, Liu Shao-chi, last spring that signaled the start of a still continuing denunciation of Mr. Liu as the "top party person taking the capitalist road."

The unofficial publications attacking the leftists were published last month by Red Guard organizations in a Canton university.

The articles accuse Mr. Wang, Mr. Kuan and Mr. Chi, and a large group of followers, of responsibility for having disrupted Chinese foreign policy last year and having stirred up such outrages as the burning of the office of the British chargé d'affaires in Peking and attacks on the Soviet and Burmese embassies.

Mr. Chi was accused in one publication of having sent underlings to Government departments "to buy information about the several vice premiers and Premier Chou so as to seize power from the center."

He was also accused of having instructed some members of the literary and art subcommittee of the Central Cultural Revolution Group to "vigorously collect information against Comrade Chiang Ching" and of having defended one man caught in such activity.

It was also said that Mr. Chi had sent a man "in the capacity of a representative of the People's Liberation Army to the State Bureau of Archives to see Comrade Chiang Ching's dossier under the pretext of writing an autobiography for Chiang Ching, so as to sinisterly collect information against her."

Another article concentrated on the "crimes" of Mr. Wang, Mr. Kuan and their associates. "They vigorously oppose Premier Chou and sabotage and split the leadership of the party Central Committee," the article said.

Mr. Wang, Mr. Kuan and Mr. Chi fell into disgrace last year after they had mounted an open attack on the army, charging that it contained some "capitalists" who should be "dragged out." This mistake evidently gave the moderates under Premier Chou and regional army commanders the opportunity to force the leftists out of public life.

April 19, 1968

Gains for Peking's Moderates Seen in Provincial Regimes

By PETER GROSE

Special to The New York Times

WASHINGTON, April 18 — Analysts of Chinese affairs say that the efforts of moderates in the Peking leadership to rebuild Communist China's local governments have brought new provincial administrations to more than two-thirds of the country's population.

But installation of the new administrations, in which the armed forces structure largely replaces the shattered apparatus of the Communist party, has not always damped down the turmoil stirred by radical Red Guards.

In at least seven provinces, the local leadership seems to be encouraging the more extreme partisans of the Cultural Revolution.

The analysts' conclusions are based on evidence from the official press and radio, Red Guard wall posters and reports from diplomats and other foreigners in Peking.

China has the appearance of a checkered confederation, no longer a tightly unified state. Each province is undergoing a power struggle among local leaders, closely parallel to the one that has shaken the Peking regime for the last two years.

Each at Its Own Rate

In each province, the political process is evolving at its own speed, governed more by local circumstances than any directives from the center.

Analysts drawing these conclusions minimize suggestions that centrifugal forces may be pulling outlying regions away from Peking's control. The issue in the provinces does not seem to be pro-Peking versus anti-Peking.

Rather, according to these analysts, each of the provincial factions has its patrons in the central leadership. The issue is which of the Peking factions, all of them invoking the name of Mao Tse-tung, can prevail in the local administrations.

After the purges of the Cultural Revolution, starting in 1966, overturned the existing party apparatus, the instrument of local government became the so-called revolutionary committee.

Theoretically, these committees were to be made up of representatives of three factions: the armed forces, the remnants of the party hierarchy and the Red Guards. The first committees were formed in early 1967.

There are now 20 revolutionary committees; two provinces, Szechwan and Kwangsi, have formed preparatory groups prior to a full-fledged committee, and seven regions remain under a de facto military administration—Liaoning, Anhwei, Fukien, Yunnan, Shensi, Tibet and Sinkiang.

Establishment of a revolutionary committee provides a mechanism for local government, but does not necessarily restore law and order.

Analysts point to seven provinces in which the chairmen of the revolutionary committees seem to be encouraging the local Red Guards to continue the protests, denunciations and even violence that have marked the Cultural Revolution from the start. These are: Shansi Honan, Kiangsu, Kweichow, Shantung, Tsinghai and Inner Mongolia.

The other revolutionary committees seem to be more of a double alliance than a triple alliance, with the Red Guard only tolerated by the more powerful military and unpurged Communist party administrators.

Army Heads Most Groups

In fact, though the revolutionary committees are called instruments of civil administration, most of them are headed by the army representatives. Civilians head the local governments of only three provinces and two autonomous municipalities: Heilungkiang, Hopeh, Honan, Tientsin and Shanghai

The differing complexion of the existing revolutionary committees is believed to reflect the jockeying for power among the various factions represented in the Peking leadership.

Since the composition of each committee must be approved in Peking, analysts believe that the factional leaders bargain over the committees to try to enhance their own positions.

The committees formed since last September seem to have been dominated by more conservative or moderate figures, suggesting the enhanced power of Premier Chou En-lai.

Renewed tensions in Peking in the last three weeks, however, lead some analysts to believe that both in the capital and the provinces the proteges of the more radical Cultural Revolution leaders are trying to resist being squeezed out of positions of authority.

April 19, 1968

MAOISM CHANGES THE FACE OF CHINA

Leader's Thought Dominates Public and Private Life

The following dispatch is by David Oancia of The Globe and Mail, Toronto.

©1968 by The Globe and Mail

PEKING — China's Cultural Revolution activists have renewed efforts to fashion what they describe as the new era of Mao Tse-tung's thought.

The activities take many forms. Some seem relatively permanent, others are quietly dropped after a trial. In the process, the outward appearance of the city has been transformed in the little more than 2½ years that this correspondent has lived here.

Chairman Mao's statue, usually sculptured out of white marble, stands in the square just beyond the entrance gates of virtually every school, university, factory and office building. His portraits, and quotations from his works, are everywhere. In private dining rooms of some restaurants there are as many as four portraits in a single room, supplemented by a variety of quotations.

In one restaurant, famed for its Mongolian shashlik, one of the quotations reminds diners that a revolution is not a dinner party, but an act of violence in which one class overthrows another.

Schools Are Scarred

In the streets, columns of school children guided by their teachers and often by soldiers march up to huge billboards portraying Chairman Mao in military garb. They open their red books and, led by their teacher or by a soldier, select appropriate quotations and read them reverently while they bow to the portrait.

This is part of the effort to rebuild the educational system along still unspecified "revolutionary" lines. The schools, with their statues or portraits of Mr. Mao, still bear the scars of the earlier period of turmoil. Windows that have been shattered and furniture that has been smashed still await replacement. In some schools, the students are using wooden packing cases and thin plastic to cover holes.

In factories, restaurants, offices and schools, tens of thousands of people are preoccupied with group study classes. They not only try to find ways of applying Chairman Mao's thought to their work, but they also strive as individuals to eradicate unwholesome "revisionist" cravings for such things as shorter work weeks and more wages or rations. A primary goal is to turn the overwhelming majority of Chinese into individuals dedicated to the concept of public service.

It is not only the newspapers, radios and neighborhood loudspeaker systems that take Mr. Mao's thoughts into every room and every home. The newspapers in recent months have been filled with reports of how neighborhood committees have been leading residents in group study classes.

Those considered outstanding are singled out for special praise, often by name in the official propaganda media. At the top of the list are the families who gather before Chairman Mao's portrait every morning before work to consult him and every evening to report to him.

PEKING CALLS LIU AGENT OF CHIANG

Maoist Attack Bitterest to Date on Chief of State— 'Factual' Proof Claimed

By Agence France-Presse

PEKING, May 17—Communist China's chief of state, Liu Shao-chi, was accused by the official press today for the first time of "representing the interests of the Kuomintang."

The Kuomintang was the governing party of Nationalist China under President Chiang Kai-shek, who withdrew to Taiwan when the Communists took power in 1949. The party now rules Taiwan.

The accusation against Mr. Liu was made on the second anniversary of the Cultural Revolution, an attempt to purge the Communist party and Government of opponents of the party chairman, Mao Tse-tung.

The charges apparently indicated that there was no longer any possibility of a compromise between Mr. Liu and the present leaders of China.

'Factual Proofs' Claimed

The Communist press agency distributed a long article that said, "Numerous factual proofs have been gathered that establish that the Chinese Khrushchev, along with other party leaders taking the capitalist road, form a gang of counter-revolutionaries representing the interests of the Kuomintang."

The "Chinese Khrushchev" is the Maoist way of identifying Mr. Liu. Nikita S. Khrushchev, the former Soviet Premier, has long been a target for bitter attacks by the proponents of the Cultural Revolution.

The accusations against Mr. Liu were made in connection with the second anniversary of the "May 16 Directives," drawn

United Press International
Liu Shao-chi

up by Chairman Mao. These directives, which were not made public until a year later, touched off the Cultural Revolution, with the dismissal of many top-ranking leaders of the party and the Government.

The directives called for the ouster of "representatives of the bourgeoisie who have infiltrated the party and have not yet been discovered." A general attack was opened against Mr. Liu several weeks later.

But today, the Chinese Khrushchev is accused not only of being a "representative of the bourgeoisie" but also of being a representative of the Kuomintang.

Among Chinese Communist class enemies, "Kuomintang agents" are the lowest form.

Such agents are considered to be hopeless cases, which cannot be saved through re-education or rehabilitation.

The reason for the newest charges against Mr. Liu are not known. But some observers think it may be linked with the failure of attempts of the present leaders to reach a compromise with him on problems connected with preparations for a proposed Communist party Congress.

April 28, 1968

May 18, 1968

China Reshapes Police Forces
in the Provinces

Special to The New York Times

HONG KONG, May 6 — New paramilitary organizations of soldiers and civilians have taken over the functions of the old public security forces and the militia in some areas of Communist China.

Most of the new security organizations have been formed under the direction of the revolutionary committees that have assumed administrative control of 19 provinces and many major cities. All have pledged support for the revolutionary committees to which they owe allegiance.

Provincial radio broadcasts have given credit to the Army for helping to arm and organize the new security organizations. In most provinces the military commanders are the key officials within the revolutionary committees.

The emergence of the new groups, which appear to be similar throughout the nation and to have the approval of Peking, follows strong criticism of the old public security system by Chinese Communist leaders.

Mao's Wife Coined Phrase

Many groups have taken their name from a phrase used by Chiang Ching, wife of Chairman Mao Tse-tung, when, in an address last July, she called for "attack by nonviolence and defense by force." Now the cities of Shanghai and Hofei, capital of Anhwei Province, each have an "attack by nonviolence and defense by force command."

Miss Chiang, who has become increasingly prominent in day-to-day political affairs in China, was one of the first Peking leaders to denounce the old public security system. She declared that the public security forces of Chekiang Province should be "thoroughly smashed" and attacked the public security bureau for Szechwan Province.

A recent broadcast from Chengtu, capital of Szechwan, called for a purge of the public security bureau, accusing certain members of wanting to rehabilitate discredited provincial officials. Szechwan is still without a revolutionary committee and a Peking-sponsored group in charge of its establishment has come under steady fire from factions within the province.

Premier Chou En-lai and even the Minister of Public Security, Hsieh Fu-chih, have been critics of the public security system. Mr. Hsieh was recently reported to have said that the majority of public security employes supported conservative groups.

In Kwangtung a "worker provost corps" both for the province and Canton, the capital, was "set up in accordance with the suggestion put forward by the provincial and municipal revolutionary committee," according to a broadcast monitored here.

The broadcast said the worker provost corps had played an important part in the "struggle for strengthening the proletarian dictatorship and defending the Cultural Revolution" and it called for heightened vigilance against "the plot of class enemies" to overthrow it.

The worker provost corps, the broadcast said, has scored "great achievements in protecting law and order" but because it is newly established, "it will make various kinds of mistakes."

Some of the new organizations have been in existence for several months but their existence has only recently been disclosed.

In Kweichow an organization was formed last August. The Kweichow radio recently gave details of the birth of this organization in the wake of "frenzied attacks" by "class enemies" against the provincial revolutionary committee, which was formed in February 1967.

LEFTISTS IN CHINA SCORE MAO POLICY

Demand Return to Initial Paris Commune Aims

By CHARLES MOHR
Special to The New York Times

HONG KONG, June 12 — A new form of anti-communism has come into being in China, expressed by young radicals disenchanted with 17 years of rule by Communist bureaucrats.

These ultraleftists envision a new, violent revolution to establish an austere, egalitarian form of socialism, in which officials would be popularly elected and easily impeached.

The movement was originally encouraged by Mao Tse-tung, the Chinese leader, in the opening days in 1966 of the Cultural Revolution, or political purge, as an expression of Mr. Mao's dissatisfaction with a party hierarchy that had resisted his own radical policies.

In recent months such visionary views have been denounced and several leading ultraleftists have been disgraced.

Threat to Regime Seen

Some experts on China think that the ultraleftists threaten the Communist regime in China. Others are not so sure, but it is generally agreed that Mr. Mao let loose dangerous forces in 1966 by encouraging rebellion against his political enemies.

An ultraleftist group in Hunan Province, known as the Sheng Wu Lien, was denounced earlier this year by Chiang Ching, Mr. Mao's wife, possibly because of the group's refusal to work with the province's regular Revolutionary Committee, the administrative body.

However, there is an affinity between the ideas of Mr. Mao

and the ultraleftists, and for this reason the latter will probably be a threat to party discipline for some time to come.

A statement of aims of the Hunan ultraleftists, published Jan. 6 by Canton Red Guards, has become available here.

Better written, more coherent and more deftly reasoned than the prose in the official press, the article has evoked interest among Western analysts.

Of special interest is that the ultraleftists of Hunan are as hostile to the army as they are to such old party officials as Premier Chou En-lai.

They call for an armed seizure of power and an internal revolutionary war by peasants and workers who have seized arms from arsenals, and eventually the complete remolding of the army.

The article, titled "Whither China," reflects in extreme form the disenchantment of many Chinese with the faltering direction of the Cultural Revolution and with the present governing revolutionary committees dominated by military men and party officials. These men are virtually indistinguishable from their old comrades who have been officially condemned as persons "taking the capitalist road."

The article remarked: "As the masses have said, 'Everything remains the same after so much ado.'"

The article recalls that in both the summer of 1966 and in January, 1967, Mr. Mao said that the Cultural Revolution would result in a commune-type government modeled after the Paris Commune. This was an egalitarian insurrectionary government that briefly ruled Paris in 1871 after the withdrawal of German forces at the end of the French-Prussian war.

Although people in general regarded the commune idea as utopian, the article said, intellectual youths want it "because they realize that only a new society, different from the existing society, is the society in

which they may have liberation."

'Red Capitalists'

Such startling talk of liberation reflects the dislike of some
Chinese youths for the Communist party, observers said.
The article refers to party officials other than Mr. Mao as
"Red capitalists," "bourgeoisie" or "bureaucrats."

The article said relations between party leaders and the
masses had become relations
"between the rulers and the
ruled, the exploiters and the
exploited."

The article said people found
it hard to understand why Mr.
Mao had withdrawn his ad-
vocacy of the Paris Commune
idea and substituted the present Revolutionary Committees,
which give Maoist mass organizations only subsidiary power
under generals and rehabilitated party leaders.

The revolutionary committees
are "bourgeois reformist,"
the article said, and "the fruit
of revolution has been, in the
final analysis, reaped by the
capitalist class."

A basic problem, the article
added, is the army, which it
said had degenerated politically
since the Communist take-over
in 1949.

"If the first Great Proletarian
Cultural Revolution is to succeed, a radical change in the
army will be necessary," the
article said.

Adding that a "revolutionary
war in the country is necessary," it went on to praise the
seizure of weapons that took
place in various parts of China
last year, at first with the approval and encouragement of
Mr. Mao's wife.

The article said the seizures
of weapons by the populace
had led to "local wars of varying magnitude" that left a deep
impression on the Chinese.

The article also discussed the
possible need for a new political party to represent the ultraleftists or at least revolutionary
changes in the party that would
enthrone leftists.

The article asserted that, in
time, consideration must be
given to the possibility of
"winning a pure, thorough victory" in one or more of China's
provinces as a first step toward
overthrowing the present Revolutionary Committees and Premier Chou's governmental
structure.

The article interpreted a
speech given last November by
Miss Chiang as one that "tells
us that the real revolution, the
revolution to negate the past
17 years, has basically not yet
begun."

Under the Paris Commune
system eventually to be established, present party bureaucrats would be replaced by
cadres with no special privileges, the article said. It added:

"They would get the same
economic treatment as the
masses in general. They would
be dismissed or changed at any
time in accordance with the
demands of the masses."

"Let the new bureaucratic
bourgeoisie tremble . . . the
China of tomorrow will be the
world of the Commune," the
article said in summary.

The article said Mr. Mao
had retreated from the leftist
positions he took early in the
Cultural Revolution and had
made concessions to the bourgeoisie.

However, such retreats were
strategically necessary, the article said, because the people
as a whole did not fully understand or support the original
goals of the Cultural Revolution.

By slowing down temporar-
ily, the article said, Mr. Mao
had avoided the mistake of
"left adventurism," or trying
to accomplish what was temporarily impossible. It indicated a belief that he would,
sooner or later, again call for
the smashing of the old state
structure.

Whether these explanations
for the Chinese leader's tactics
were meant sincerely or as
irony was not clear.

RED GUARDS TOLD TO JOIN WORKERS

Students' Power, at Height
Two Years Ago, Is Fading

By TILLMAN DURDIN
Special to The New York Times

HONG KONG, Aug. 18—The
famous mangoes with which
Chairman Mao Tse-tung recently conveyed his approbation to
a worker-peasant propaganda
team engaged in straightening
out ideological kinks among
student Red Guard factions at
Tsinghua University in Peking
have been enshrined with a
portrait of Mr. Mao on an altar
at Peking airport.

Arrivals here from the Chinese Communist capital say the
mangoes—two of them—were,
at least as of late last week,
the chief attraction at the airport.

One mango, travelers report,
is in a bottle of liquid, very
possibly a preparation of for-
maldehyde, and is beginning to
look dark and mushy. The
other appears to be in a somewhat better state of preservation and is enshrined in a glass
case and encircled with a red
ribbon tied with a bow knot.

2 Militiamen Keep Vigil

Standing vigil before the
mangoes are two militiamen,
sternly erect and pressing to
their bosoms with one hand
copies of little red books of
quotations from Chairman Mao.

Mr. Mao's presentation of the
mangoes—a gift to him from
a foreigner leaving Peking—to
the worker-peasant team has
been hailed throughout the
country during the last week.
Newspaper editorials have
been written on the significance of the presentation, and
mass meetings have been held

in cities and towns to celebrate
the event.

Propaganda regarding the
mangoes has driven home the
lesson that they exemplify the
new Peking policy of relying
principally on the workers, including farm workers, to carry
forward the program of the
Maoist Great Proletarian Cultural Revolution.

Base of Militant Factions

The fact that the mangoes
were presented to a worker-
peasant propaganda team at
Tsinghua, the base of some of
the country's most militant factions of the youthful Red
Guards, is being used to point
up the fact that the Red
Guards have faded as a political
force in China and that the
students are to learn from
workers and peasants and subordinate themselves to them.

The situation was made plain
in an editorial in Jenmin Jih
Pao, the official Peking paper,
relayed here today by Hsinhua,
the Chinese Communist press
agency.

Written to commemorate the
review on Aug. 18, 1966, by
Chairman Mao of hundreds of
thousands of Red Guards in
Peking, the editorial praised the
vanguard role played by the
millions of Red Guards over the
country in attacking revisionists, imperialists and exploiters.

But the editorial added that
the hallmark today of whether
a youth is a revolutionary is
"whether or not he is willing
to integrate himself with the
broad masses of workers, peasants and soldiers and does so in
practice."

The editorial said that the
laboring masses, the workers
and peasants, are the most reliable and resolute revolutionary group and together with
the army are "the main force."

"Ours is a state of the dictatorship of the proletariat," the
editorial said, "and it does not
need intellectuals who look
down upon the workers and
peasants."

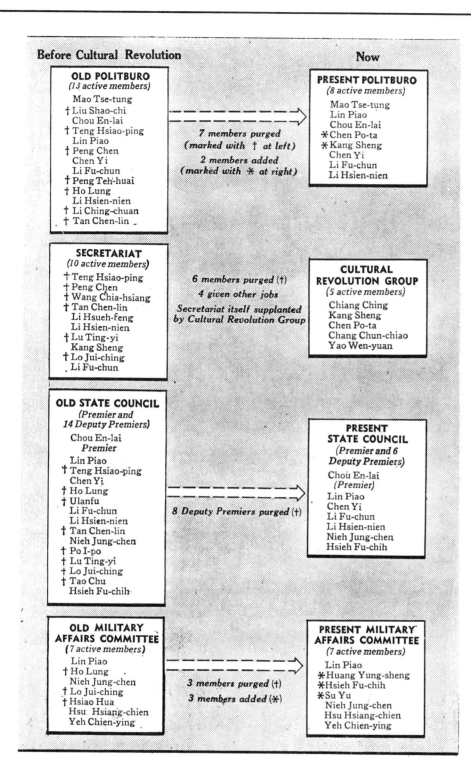

Before Cultural Revolution

Now

OLD POLITBURO
(13 active members)
Mao Tse-tung
† Liu Shao-chi
Chou En-lai
† Teng Hsiao-ping
Lin Piao
† Peng Chen
Chen Yi
Li Fu-chun
† Peng Teh-huai
† Ho Lung
Li Hsien-nien
† Li Ching-chuan
† Tan Chen-lin

PRESENT POLITBURO
(8 active members)
Mao Tse-tung
Lin Piao
Chou En-lai
✳Chen Po-ta
✳Kang Sheng
Chen Yi
Li Fu-chun
Li Hsien-nien

*7 members purged
(marked with † at left)
2 members added
(marked with ✳ at right)*

SECRETARIAT
(10 active members)
† Teng Hsiao-ping
† Peng Chen
† Wang Chia-hsiang
† Tan Chen-lin
Li Hsueh-feng
Li Hsien-nien
† Lu Ting-yi
Kang Sheng
† Lo Jui-ching
Li Fu-chun

*6 members purged (†)
4 given other jobs
Secretariat itself supplanted
by Cultural Revolution Group*

**CULTURAL
REVOLUTION GROUP**
(5 active members)
Chiang Ching
Kang Sheng
Chen Po-ta
Chang Chun-chiao
Yao Wen-yuan

OLD STATE COUNCIL
*(Premier and
14 Deputy Premiers)*
Chou En-lai
Premier
Lin Piao
† Teng Hsiao-ping
Chen Yi
† Ho Lung
† Ulanfu
Li Fu-chun
Li Hsien-nien
† Tan Chen-lin
Nieh Jung-chen
† Po I-po
† Lu Ting-yi
† Lo Jui-ching
† Tao Chu
Hsieh Fu-chih

8 Deputy Premiers purged (†)

**PRESENT
STATE COUNCIL**
*(Premier and 6
Deputy Premiers)*
Chou En-lai
(Premier)
Lin Piao
Chen Yi
Li Fu-chun
Li Hsien-nien
Nieh Jung-chen
Hsieh Fu-chih

**OLD MILITARY
AFFAIRS COMMITTEE**
(7 active members)
Lin Piao
† Ho Lung
Nieh Jung-chen
† Lo Jui-ching
† Hsiao Hua
Hsu Hsiang-chien
Yeh Chien-ying

*3 members purged (†)
3 members added (✳)*

**PRESENT MILITARY
AFFAIRS COMMITTEE**
(7 active members)
Lin Piao
✳Huang Yung-sheng
✳Hsieh Fu-chih
✳Su Yu
Nieh Jung-chen
Hsu Hsiang-chien
Yeh Chien-ying

June 25, 1968

NUCLEAR PROGRAM SLOWED IN CHINA

Peking Arms Chief Involved in Ideological Conflict

By TILLMAN DURDIN
Special to The New York Times

HONG KONG, Oct. 27—Fresh details have been received here of ideological conflicts that have slowed the development and production of nuclear and other armaments in Communist China during the last year.

The conflicts involved not only political activists throughout the defense industry but also Nieh Jung-chen, director of the Scientific and Technological Commission for National Defense. The commission has charge of Communist China's weapons development programs.

A Canton Red Guard bulletin that has reached here says that Mr. Nieh was under such a cloud in Peking last April that he had to submit written self-criticisms to Mao Tse-tung, chairman of the Chinese Communist party.

The bulletin says that Mr. Mao assigned Premier Chu En-lai to take personal charge of Mr. Nieh and to help him with repeated revisions of his self-examination.

Report of Meeting

The bulletin consists of a verbatim report of an all-night meeting in Peking April 20 between Premier Chou and representatives of political factions in the Scientific and Technological Commission, the Seventh Ministry of Machine Building, the Academia Sinica and other organizations.

In his remarks at the meeting, Mr. Chou said that he had been asked by Mr. Mao to find a solution to the problem of factionalism in the defense agencies.

The Premier emphasized the urgency of the situation and indicated that production was lagging.

"We can wait no longer," he said. "Seen in terms of foreign aid or war preparedness, or viewed from other angles, such organs as the Scientific and Technological Commission and the Office of National Defense Industry cannot allow the dispute to drag on. Just now some comrades have deplored the failure to promote production."

It has already been reported that factional and ideological differences generated by Chairman Mao's "Cultural Revolution" had slowed defense production. But the Canton bulletin provides fresh authentication of these reports. It indicates that political disaffection has possibly been more widespread than previously suspected.

No Visible Progress

Political disaffection and technical problems in defense agencies are believed here to be responsible for Communist China's failure to show progress in nuclear-weapons and missile development in more than a year. There has been no successful test of a nuclear device for 16 months and no test-firing so far of a long-range missile.

The Canton bulletin indicated that Mr. Nieh had sought to promote his domination of the Scientific and Technological Commission by barring the election of persons not loyal to him to represent the commission in revolutionary affairs.

Mr. Nieh, 69 years old, is a member of the Politburo and the Military Affairs Commission and is a Vice Premier.

He was present on the rostrum with leaders of the Peking regime on the Oct. 1 National Day, indicating that he has not been purged. It might also be evidence that with the recent general calming down of the Cultural Revolution, the agencies that Mr. Nieh heads have been stabilized politically.

The Cultural Revolution was started by Chairman Mao in 1966 to purge his opponents within the bureaucracy of the Communist party and the Government.

October 28, 1968

KWANGSI CLASHES SAID TO BE BRUTAL

By TILLMAN DURDIN
Special to The New York Times

HONG KONG, Sept. 21—Savage fighting between rival Maoist factions in Kwangsi in the first half of 1968 cost the lives of more than 50,000 people on one side alone, according to Tachun Pao, a newspaper of the April 22 Kwangsi Faction, which was published in Canton in July.

A copy of the paper that reached here recently portrayed the fighting in the autonomous region in the most brutal terms.

The paper reported that the hostilities ranged from small clashes to major battles, which, in some instances, were waged with artillery and tanks.

The engagements, the paper said, were often brutal massacres of captives, "even worse than those of the Kuomintang and the Japanese devils."

Heavy Fighting Indicated

The April 22 Faction was the loser in the Kwangsi strife and Tachun Pao's account is doubtless exaggerated. But even a sharp discounting of the paper's report would still indicate a scale of fighting in Kwangsi over a period of months rivaling that of hostilities in the Vietnam war.

Other accounts that have reached here, some from reasonably reliable people who witnessed the events, have portrayed the Kwangsi clashes in roughly the same terms as those used by Tachun Pao. Persons on the spot, for example, have confirmed the paper's accounts of fighting that went on for weeks at Wuchow, a city of half a million people on the West River. The paper said that destruction in the area had been enormous and that thousands of people had been killed.

Hong Kong experienced a grim aftermath of the Wuchow fighting in July when more than 50 bodies that had drifted 200 miles downstream from Wuchow appeared over a period of weeks in Hong Kong waters.

Foe's Losses Not Cited

The Tachun Pao report told only of casualties and travails suffered by April 22 partisans and said nothing about losses suffered by opposition forces.

After describing small battles at Lingyun and Tsingsi, which it said caused hundreds of casualties, Tachun Pao told of fighting that went on in March at Ishan, near Nanning, in which hundreds were killed and large parts of the town burned.

The paper reported that sporadic fighting went on through February and March at other towns and that whole families had been killed if one member was found to belong to the April 22 Faction.

The paper stated that "the number of revolutionary masses killed was too large to count." In the protracted fighting for Wuchow, it added, opponents of the April 22 Faction killed men, women and children with machine guns and set large sections of the city afire with napalm.

Faction Believed Shattered

Fighting in Kwangsi went on after the period covered by Tachun Pao and all indications are that the April 22 Faction was shattered as an effective force.

The faction has claimed to have the support of persons around Mao Tse-tung, the Communist party chairman, including Mr. Mao's wife and Premier Chou En-lai.

Opposition to the April 22 Faction in Kwangsi was led by Wei Kuo-ching, governor of Kwangsi and Communist party

chief of the province for many years. Mr. Wei and his supporters have been branded by the leftists around Mr. Mao as "power-holders following the capitalist road."

But it appears that Mr. Wei and his supporters proved too strong for the Peking-backed forces. He and a good number of his followers, all swearing loyalty to Mr. Mao, were confirmed in power recently as members of the new governing revolutionary committee in Kwangsi.

September 22, 1968

Chinese Reds Expel Liu From the Party

By TILLMAN DURDIN
Special to The New York Times

HONG KONG, Nov. 1 — At an unheralded plenary session in Peking, the Central Committee of the Chinese Communist party formally expelled Liu Shao-chi, the country's disgraced head of state, from the party and from all party and other posts, Communist China announced today.

The committee denounced Mr. Liu by name as a "traitor, renegade and scab" and a "lackey of imperialism, modern revisionism and the Kuomintang," or Chinese Nationalist party. There was no indication what punishment, if any, he would receive.

A surprise Peking report that the Central Committee had met was received here tonight from Hsinhua, the Chinese Communist press agency. The report said the committee was in session from Oct. 13 to Oct. 31 for its first plenum since August 1966.

The meeting hailed the Great Proletarian Cultural Revolution, launched and led by the party chairman, Mao Tse-tung, as a sweeping success and declared all policies laid down and actions taken under the leadership of Mr. Mao and his deputy, Lin Piao, have been correct.

Indicating that a new party congress, the first since 1956, will be held soon, the plenary session announced that "through the storms of the Great Proletarian Cultural Revolution ample ideological, political, organizational conditions have been prepared for convening the ninth national congress of the party."

The meeting was described in a communiqué as the "enlarged 12th plenary session of the Eighth Central Committee."

Its action against Mr. Liu, who until August, 1966, was a deputy leader of the party, was the first formally announced official party move to oust him. The Cultural Revolution, launched to purge the party of what Chairman Mao considered revisionist policies and personalities, made Mr. Liu its chief target in late 1966.

Today's announcement was the first time that Mr. Liu was identified by name in an official party declaration since late 1966. He was identified simply as "China's Khrushchev" or one of the other insulting descriptions that have been applied to him for the last two years.

Action Appears Definitive

On previous occasions official Peking press organs have stated that "China's Khrushchev" has been "overthrown," "smashed" and "deprived of rights and powers." Today's announcement supersedes all the figurative allusions and indicates a final, definitive action.

The statement said the plenary session "expressed its deep revolutionary indignation" at Mr. Liu's "counterrevolutionary crimes" and unanimously adopted a resolution, based on an investigation by a special party group, to expel him from the party "once and for all" and "to dismiss him from all posts both inside and outside the party and to continue to settle accounts with him and his accomplices for their crimes in betraying the party and the country."

The Maoists charge that the 70-year-old Mr. Liu had steered Chinese Communist policy into moderate or revisionist policies and was the "top party person following the capitalist road."

Usually the party's secretary general, Teng Hsiao-ping, has been bracketed with Mr. Liu as equally guilty of carrying out revisionist policies.

Today's statement made no reference to Mr. Teng although there was a general denunciation of the "handful of other top party persons in authority following the capitalist road" whose "counterrevolutionary revisionist ideas" were said to need repudiation and eradication along with Mr. Liu's.

Mr. Teng has not yet been mentioned by name as a target of the Cultural Revolution. He has been described as the second-ranking party person in authority following the capitalist road.

The third most important target of the Cultural Revolution, Tao Chu, a Politburo member and former party propaganda chief, has been attacked by name. Other high party officials attacked have also been referred to by name.

Mr. Liu was first made a target of the Cultural Revolution in the August, 1966, meeting of the Central Committee. At that time the tall, reserved party leader, who had served for 20 years as Mr. Mao's chief aide, was demoted from second position to seventh in party ranking and replaced as Mr. Mao's deputy by Mr. Lin, the Defense Minister.

Specialists on China believe that the August, 1966, meeting was a rump session from which Mr. Mao had excluded many of Mr. Liu's supporters and over which Mr. Mao exercised domination by packing the meeting with Red Guards, the militant students who were used as the spearhead of the Cultural Revolution.

The latest Central Committee meeting was described as not only an enlarged meeting but also attended by "principal responsible comrades of the revolutionary committees of the provinces, municipalities and autonomous regions" and "principal responsible comrades of the Chinese People's Liberation Army."

This could mean that the meeting was also packed with outsiders and in this way was made subject to domination by Mr. Mao and his supporters.

The announcement said Mr. Mao presided and "made a most important speech" on the Cultural Revolution. Mr. Lin, who since August, 1966, has

been the party's only vice chairman, was also said to have made an important speech.

As if to underline the identification of the party with the Cultural Revolution and its proclaimed success, the announcement reported that all members of the so-called Cultural Revolution Group, which has played a major role in charting the course of the revolution, were present at the meeting. The Cultural Revolution Group is headed by Chen Po-ta. Chiang Ching, Mr. Mao's wife, is his chief deputy, and Kang Sheng is top-ranking "adviser" to the group.

The Maoists have on a number of occasions proclaimed all-round success of the Cultural Revolution, most notably in September when the process of forming revolutionary committees to administer the various provinces was completed.

Mr. Liu, besides being a Central Committee member, was also a vice chairman of the Politburo. He has been chief of state since 1959.

Theoretically, the Central Committee does not have the authority to remove Mr. Liu as chief of state, a post filled through election by the National People's Congress. There has been no meeting of the congress since 1965.

The committee's announcement today ratified the whole course of the Cultural Revolution and Mr. Mao's role in it. It called the revolution necessary and timely for "consolidating the dictatorship of the proletariat, preventing capitalist restoration and building socialism."

Mr. Mao was lauded for his theory of continuing revolution under the dictatorship of the proletariat.

The statement approved the phases through which the Cultural Revolution has gone. It called for continued revolutionary struggle, strengthening of the armed forces and the "liberation" of Taiwan.

It predicted that "imperialism, revisionism and all other counterrevolutionary forces" would be smashed by the "revolutionary people" of the world backed by Communist China. It said China was not isolated but had the support of revolutionary forces "comprising over 90 per cent of the world's population."

November 2, 1968

Communist China Is 'Purifying' Its 'Class Ranks' in Wide Purge

By TILLMAN DURDIN
Special to The New York Times

HONG KONG, Dec. 7—Communist China is experiencing a period of intense political purging known as "purifying the class ranks."

Under this slogan, so-called "class enemies" are being uncovered on a large scale and penalized in varying ways after repeated denunciations at mass rallies.

"Class enemy" is a designation that can cover a multitude of sins.

It can be applied to anyone with an even remotely bourgeois background or pinned on individuals who have been opponents of the military-dominated revolutionary committees, the new ruling bodies in the cities and villages of China.

Radio broadcasts from China list as special targets of the campaign the "seven black elements." These are identified as former landlords, former rich peasants, rightists, former capitalists, counterrevolutionaries, bad elements and black gangsters.

A large proportion of the bourgeoisie and former officials of the Kuomintang, or Chinese Nationalist, regime were dealt with by the Communists in the years after they took power in 1949. Millions were killed in countrywide upsurge of mass trials a d executions, millions of others were consigned to forced labor or a pariah status as workers "under the surveillance of the masses" in their home communities.

Some Became Agents

Over the years, many of the bourgeoisie who survived the early liquidations managed to find niches along with their children in the new society. Some changed their names, melted into the general population and got themselves classified as workers or peasants.

When controls broke down at times in the last two years during the Cultural Revolution, some of these people succeeded in having their dossiers destroyed; others even achieved a "reversal of verdicts," that is, getting decisions against them expunged from the records or altered.

Some former bourgeoisie and Kuomintang officials were able

to take a hand in the intrigues and the factional fighting that marked phases of the Cultural Revolution. Some influenced events as behind-the-scenes manipulators, some became active agents of the Kuomintang regime on Taiwan, a role for which they had been tapped when the Nationalists evacuated the mainland.

One of the aims of the present purges seems to be to root out these elements. Another is to crack down on detractors and opponents of the new power-holders.

In many instances the purging is simply a way for one faction to pay off scores against groups and individuals that opposed them in past factional struggles. In some cases targets of the purges are student Red Guards who have been unwilling to subordinate themselves to workers and peasants, as Peking had directed.

'Drag Out Class Enemies'

An article in the newspaper Shensi Jih Pao of Sian, broadcast last Saturday, called on the masses to "drag out all class enemies who have sabotaged the grasping of revolution and production, incited struggles among the masses, created incidents in production, consistently propagated counterrevolutionary economic principles, sabotaged the collective economy and indulged in speculation."

A Nanchang radio broadcast recently quoted Yang Tung-liang, vice chairman of the Kiangsi Revolutionary Committee, as having said at a public rally that the masses of the province had been fully aroused in carrying out the task of purifying the class ranks. As a result, he said, "many renegades, secret agents, die-hard capitalists and counterrevolutionaries have been laid bare."

Similar reports have come from all over the country. Worker-soldier and peasant-soldier propaganda teams take the lead in exhorting the masses until public accusations are brought against individuals and mass meetings can be held at which these persons are repeatedly accused and denounced.

Radio broadcasts indicate

428

that some get death penalties, usually carried out on the spot after mass denunciations; some get prison terms, but most appear to be sentenced to periods of forced labor, often in remote frontier regions, or to labor in their native places "under the supervision of the masses."

The new campaign is adding to the number of those in Communist China who are undergoing penalties of some kind for political reasons. The total is generally estimated in the millions, but exact figures are impossible to come by.

PARTY REMOLDING SEEN AS MAO AIM

By CHARLES MOHR
Special to The New York Times

HONG KONG, April 4—The congress of the Chinese Communist party now under way in Peking appears to be an attempt by Mao Tse-tung not only to rebuild the party but also to insure its future ideological purity.

It was the party chairman's conviction that the old party bureaucracy was riddled with men who opposed him personally and ideologically. That conviction is believed to have led him to undertake in 1966 the prolonged purge known as the Cultural Revolution.

The party congress has met without press publicity since it opened Tuesday. It is believed to be deliberating on a political report given by Defense Minister Lin Piao, Mr. Mao's hand-picked heir apparent.

A draft of a new party constitution that reached Hong Kong in January defines a party congress as "the highest leading organ of the party," and 1,512 delegates have gathered in Peking for the meeting.

One of their jobs will be to adopt the new charter, the Peking radio has said. The draft document suggests much about the tactics that Mr. Mao evidently intends to follow in restructuring the party.

He is believed to have been obsessed in recent years with a belief that a "socialist" state is in danger of a restoration of capitalism and of "revisionist" ideas as it proceeds toward pure "communism."

The preamble, or "general program," of the draft constitution reflects this view when it says that in the stage of transition from socialism to communism "there will throughout exist classes, class contradictions and the class struggle, there will exist the struggle of the two roads between socialism and capitalism, there will exist the danger of a capitalist restoration."

A number of measures are planned to forestall these dangers.

Article 5 of the draft says the whole party must "obey a unified discipline," but then goes on to encourage party members to protest and appeal any local branch decisions that may be in violation of Mr. Mao's policies.

"If a party member does not agree with the decisions or directives of the party organization, he may reserve his opinions and has the right to pass over his superiors and report directly to the Central Committee and the chairman of the Central Committee," the draft charter said.

'Slavish Obedience' Scored

This provision is clearly meant to deal with what the Maoist press calls the concept of "slavish obedience." The Maoists say that men such as the former chief of state, Liu Shao-chi, and the party's former general secretary, Teng Hsiao-ping, used the concept of unwavering obedience to spread anti-Maoist policies, such as the extension of private land in agriculture.

It was the party secretariat headed by Mr. Teng that allowed the Liu forces to usurp so much day-to-day power from Mr. Mao, and the draft charter reflects suspicion of such bureaucracy.

It alludes to replacement of the old secretariat by saying that "there shall be established the necessary competent organs to unify and expedite the daily operations of party, government and army."

Article 3 of the draft also says that a party member "must particularly guard against careerists, plotters and two-faced persons and must prevent bad persons of this sort from usurping party or state leadership at any level."

This will probably encourage zealots to continue to bring their complaints of "bourgeois thinking" and revisionism to Mr. Mao and the group around him.

The preamble also asserts that the "party must unceasingly get rid of the old and absorb the new" and another article says that one must be a "revolutionary element" to gain admittance to the party.

A reading of the press in recent years shows that nothing has disturbed Mr. Mao more than the possibility that his old enemies would succeed in gaining political rehabilitation. An example is former Defense Minister Peng Teh-huai, who struggled for four years to be rehabilitated after his dismissal in 1958. In present jargon, this is called "the evil wind of reversing verdicts."

To prevent it, the new draft provides for no appeal procedures at all and says that "renegades" who stubbornly refuse to reform "must be purged from the party and **never** allowed to rejoin it."

CHINA'S REDS VOTE CHARTER MAKING LIN HEIR TO MAO

Party Congress Approves New Policy Program — Discloses No Details

By CHARLES MOHR
Special to The New York Times

HONG KONG, April 14—The ninth congress of the Chinese Communist party unanimously adopted today a new party charter that stipulates that Defense Minister Lin Piao will eventually succeed Mao Tsetung as China's leader.

A communiqué made public today by the official press agency Hsinhua said the congress also unanimously adopted a political report by Mr. Lin that will probably become a blueprint for policy in foreign, economic and domestic political fields. But it gave no details of the report.

The communiqué added that the party congress would begin tomorrow to elect a new Central Committee. During the Cultural Revolution initiated by Mr. Mao three years ago, about two-thirds of the members of the old Central Committee were dismissed as "power-holders taking the capitalist road."

Unusual Occasion

A congress is described by Chinese Communists as the highest governing organ of their party, and such convocations are both rare and important. The ninth congress is only the second held since the Communists won control of China in 1949. The last congress was elected in 1956 and last met in 1958.

The 1,512 delegates to the present, or ninth, congress met in Peking 14 days ago on April 1. Until tonight there had been no further news on their deliberations, but today's communiqué indicated that the congress would soon adjourn.

The first two items on the congress agenda, as announced April 1, were the adoption of Mr. Lin's political report and a

December 8, 1968

April 5, 1969

429

new party constitution. These tasks have been completed.

Politburo to Be Selected

Tonight's communiqué said the congress would begin electing a new Central Committee "starting from April 15." It was unclear how long this process would take.

The Central Committee will then meet to select a new Politburo, which, in turn, will elect a standing committee. This will be the supreme ruling party body in China.

The new Central Committee would technically be empowered also to elect a new chairman of the committee, but most analysts in Hong Kong assume that Mr. Mao will be re-elected to his post with Lin Piao the sole vice chairman.

Some observers in Washington have speculated that Mr. Mao may be elevated in title to something approximating "Great Leader" and Mr. Lin named party chairman.

In either case it seems clear that as long as the 75-year-old Mr. Mao is fit he will remain the paramount figure in the leadership.

Because of its ambiguity and lack of details, tonight's communiqué gave no real indication of any new departures in policy by China.

However, it said that the congress had entrusted the secretariat of its presidium, which is headed by Premier Chou En lai, with publishing "two documents after making modifications in wording." From the context of the announcement, it seemed that these would be the texts of the new party constitution and of Mr. Lin's political report.

The announcement that the new constitution "clearly stipulated that Comrade Lin Piao is the successor of Chairman Mao" came as no surprise.

A draft of the new constitution that reached Hong Kong in January had specified Mr. Lin as Mr. Mao's closest comrade and political heir. Soon after the Cultural Revolution began in 1966, Mr. Lin dis-

placed the former chief of state, Liu Shao-chi, as China's second-ranking Communist.

The draft constitution also declared the "thoughts of Mao Tse-tung" to be the guiding doctrine of Chinese communism. The test was worded with the clear intent of attempting to perpetuate Mr. Mao's militant and "left-wing" version of communism.

If the discussions of the congress had resulted in any important realignment of personal power in China, tonight's communiqué did not revail it.

The list of persons that showed the ranking of major delegates was the same as the one issued when the congress opened on April 1.

On the basis of past experience, specialists on China have speculated that the top names among the delegates to this congress will probably be selected to serve on the new Politburo.

PEKING, Tuesday, April 15 (Agence France-Presse) — The congress delegates appeared relaxed and smiling yesterday when they named Lin Piao as future successor to Chairman Mao.

The delegates, who have been meeting behind closed doors since April 2, seemed in excellent humor when they appeared on television shortly after midnight today in a program devoted to the second plenary session of the congress.

The program offered viewers domestic, family-like shots of Chinese leaders—Premier Chou En-lai arranging the microphones for Chairman Mao, Chairman Mao drinking tea, wagging an admonishing finger at the audience and being enthusiastically applauded by his wife, Chiang Ching.

Viewers were able to see Lin Piao giving an extemporaneous speech, being applauded by Mr. Mao, Premier Chou and the whole congress, and Mr. Chou reading his speech and being applauded by Mr. Mao, Mr. Lin and the congress.

The delegates approved the new party statutes by brandishing their little red books.

CHINA'S MILITANTS TERMED STRONGER

Analysts Also Believe Army Gained at Party Congress

By CHARLES MOHR
Special to The New York Times

HONG KONG, April 29 — Militant supporters of Mao Tse-tung's theory of continuous revolution emerged from the ninth congress of the Chinese Communist party with impressive strength, some political analysts said today.

The Chinese Army also gained strength as a result of the election of a new Central Committee and Politburo, but it was still unclear to what extent the army would support— or try to thwart—any new Maoist policies meant to put political purity ahead of public order and pragmatic economic policy.

After electing a Central Committee of 170 full and 109 alternate members, the congress adjourned last Thursday. The Central Committee yesterday elected, or possibly ratified, a new Politburo and Politburo standing committee.

The Politburo election tended to diminish the already badly shattered ranks of experienced, able administrators in China who have generally been identified with "moderate" political positions.

Listing of Those Dropped

Dropped from the Politburo were such figures as Foreign Minister Chen Yi; Chairman of the State Planning Commission Li Fu-chun; Chen Yun, an economic planner who has been largely inactive lately; Nieh Jung-chen, a military man who heads China's nuclear weapons development, and Hsu

Hsiang-chien, another military man.

Premier Chou En-lai, who is probably China's most gifted high-level administrator and a consistent if cautious voice of moderation during the three years of the Cultural Revolution, lost his clear ranking as China's No. 3 Communist after Chairman Mao and Deputy Chairman Lin Piao, Mr. Mao's designated heir as party leader.

The official list of new Politburo members was painstakingly careful to list only Mr. Mao and Mr. Lin in order of precedence. After that the members of the standing committee and the full Politburo were listed in the Chinese equivalent of alphabetical order — by the number of strokes in the Chinese characters of their surnames.

3 Associated With Lin

Thus, besides Mr. Mao and Mr. Lin, the three other members of the standing committee were listed as follows: Chen Po-ta, Chou En-lai and Kang Sheng.

This five-man committee is empowered to make decisions when the Central Committee or full Politburo is not in session, which is most of the time.

Mr. Chou is the only member Western analysts generally regard as a moderate. The others have sometimes shown a considerable flexibility and have even occasionally turned savagely on "ultraleftists," but are all closely associated with Mr. Mao and with support for the Cultural Revolution, the political purge that sent more than two-thirds of the former Central Committee into political oblivion.

On the full Politburo, consisting of 21 members and four alternates, the shift further left was also apparent. At least 11 persons are confirmed "Maoists" and only seven can be termed moderates, in some cases doubtfully.

The exact orientation of some new members who were rather unexpectedly elevated to Politburo status is still in question, some analysts conceded.

These include the commanders of the Shenyang and Nanking military regions, the navy's political commissar and the army's rear service commander.

Although the army commanders in the provinces have sometimes taken relatively conservative positions hostile to excesses of the Cultural Revolution, at least three of these men have been closely associated with Mr. Lin, who is also Defense Minister, and may be considered reliable followers by Mr. Mao and Mr. Lin.

Chen Yi, Nieh Jung-chen and others had appeared twice on the rostrum of the ninth congress near Chairman Mao but had not been named to the Politburo.

"Everyone must have been conscious that this is probably the last party congress that will take place before Mao dies," said one specialist on Chinese affairs today. "Every faction must have been concerned to make sure that their point of view was preserved in the Central Committee and Politburo and that there would be no chance of turning China around politically if Mao does die. Evidently, in the end, they just wouldn't take men like Chen Yi, Nieh and Li Fu-chun."

Men like Mr. Nieh and Mr. Chen remain on the Central Committee. There is no way to know yet whether the Politburo will allow them to continue to exercise their technicians' talents on behalf of China or whether they will also lose their administrative jobs.

"The one thing that all this makes clear is that political purity is going to be put ahead of other factors," said one observer.

AT FIRE IN PEKING, THOUGHTS OF MAO

But Regime Seems to Shift to More Pragmatic Line

HONG KONG, Oct. 26—The Peking fire brigade recently received a call to the mission of the Vietcong's provisional revolutionary government of South Vietnam. Although the blaze was well established by the time the first engine arrived, the fire fighters stood in a group reading quotations from the works of Mao Tse-tung, the Communist party chairman, before tackling the fire.

This incident, reported by visitors to Peking, indicates that "Mao thought" continues to be regarded in Communist China as an inspirational invocation with something of the power of prayer. But there are signs that the authorities are encouraging a relatively more pragmatic approach to situations in which lives might be endangered or public property damaged.

This is especially apparent in the field of medicine where over the last few years the thought of Mao Tse-tung have been credited with miracle cures.

Medical Aid Stressed

An article on health work recently broadcast from Nanking, capital of Kiangsu Province, declared: "Ideological and political work can aid a patient's recovery but cannot replace medical treatment."

This was in contrast to the attitude in previous years. Last year, for example, an article published in Peking proclaimed: "Mao Tse-tung's thought—key to success in rare abdominal operation."

Any statement questioning the efficacy of ideological or political work would have been regarded as something akin to heresy. The Chinese authorities now appear to be prepared to acknowledge that the previous preoccupation with political indoctrination could lead to incorrect diagnosis and treatment.

The Nanking article said a patient should be given "necessary ideological education according to his needs" but at the same time hospitals should "diagnose his disease correctly and treat it correctly."

It stated: "With correct diagnosis and treatment, plus the patient's strong fighting will, the effectiveness of medical treatment will be enhanced."

The article disclosed that patients were expected to undertake not only political activities but also physical labor as a form of educational therapy. But it cautioned that they should not be "put on the same basis as medical personnel" and that "a distinction should be made between patients who are very sick and those not so sick."

Another article broadcast by the same station stressed the different roles of nurses and doctors. This contrasted with the attitude expressed last year in the official Peking newspaper Jenmin Jih Pao. It acclaimed nurses who were undertaking operations, including brain surgery, "which formerly could only be done by doctors who had received special training and had a suitably long period of experience."

The Nanking article stressed the need for a reasonable division of labor between doctors and nurses "for many years to come." It said incorrect diagnosis, inappropriate medicines or inappropriate dosages could "impair the effectiveness of treatment or even endanger the life of the patient" and asserted that in this area doctors had more experience than nurses.

In case of necessity, the article said, "nurses can have their say, but their suggestions cannot be a substitute for the doctors' experience." When doctors have laid their plans for treatment, it added, "nurses should conscientiously fulfill the plans."

Peking Note Scores Soviet On Its Ouster of Students

Special to The New York Times

HONG KONG, Oct. 23—Peking has protested against the Soviet order expelling all Chinese students, declaring that the move has "further worsened relationships between the two countries." This was reported today by Hsinhua, the Chinese Communist press agency, which said a note lodging the "strongest protest" against the Soviet action was handed to the Soviet chargé d'affaires ad interim yesterday.

The Soviet diplomat refused to accept the note.

The Soviet expulsion order was issued on Oct. 7 in retaliation for the Chinese decision to suspend the studies of all foreign students. The 65 Chinese students in the Soviet Union were given 24 days to leave the country and Peking's protest note said they would all depart for home on Oct. 27.

Peking's move against foreign students was made as a consequence of the vast social and political upheaval occurring in China in the name of the "great proletarian cultural revolution."

Classes in institutions of higher education have been suspended to enable the students to devote their energies to the study of the works of Mao Tse-tung, Chairman of the Chinese Communist party's Central Committee, or to join China's new militant youth movement, the Red Guards.

Peking Offered Negotiations

Since there was no role for foreign students in the cultural revolution, Peking suspended their studies for a year. According to the protest note, Peking was prepared to negotiate on a graduation arrangement for students nearing the end of their studies, but the Soviet Government "recalled on its own Soviet students in China."

"On the very next day following the departure of the Soviet students," the Chinese note said, "the Soviet Government went so far as to falsely accuse the Chinese Government of having unilaterally decided to suspend the studies of Soviet students, and on the pretext of what it called the principle of reciprocity suddenly announced the decision ordering all Chinese students to leave the Soviet Union within a set time limit."

This is a "grave incident," the Peking note said, in which the Soviet Government has "flagrantly violated the agreement on cultural cooperation between China and the Soviet Union."

The end of contacts through the exchange of students severs one of the last important cultural ties between Peking and Moscow. It also marks a new low point in their steadily declining relations.

The issues of Vietnam and the cultural revolution have provoked the bitterest exchanges in their long quarrel. Peking has accused Moscow of forming an "anti-China holy alliance" with the United States, while the Soviet leaders have accused the Chinese of weakening the Communist effort in Vietnam.

Incitement Charged

Peking's protest note said the Soviet Union had created all kinds of difficulties for Chinese students. It alleged that Moscow had "even tried to incite them to betray their own country."

"It is futile," the note said, "for you to turn things upside down and try to shift on to us responsibility for sabotaging the exchange of students."

Peking said that the latest development was "by no means an isolated incident" and that lately the Soviet leadership had "painstakingly engineered a fresh worldwide campaign against China."

It added that the Soviet press had "poured out a huge amount of anti-Chinese material, viciously slandering and attacking the Chinese people, the Chinese Communist party and Chairman Mao Tse-tung, great leader of the Chinese people," and had spread rumors about the cultural revolution.

The Chinese note asserted: "All this once again reveals that your glib talk about 'united action' against imperialism is sheer twaddle designed to deceive people. But your 'united action' with U.S. imperialism against China is real stuff."

Red Guards Demonstrate

MOSCOW, Oct. 23 (AP)— Red Guards demonstrated outside the Soviet Embassy in Peking tonight, shouting "Out with the modern revisionists!" Tass reported from the Chinese capital.

The official Soviet press agency said the crowd blocked cars going in and out of the embassy and posted anti-Soviet slogans nearby.

October 24, 1966

Prestige of Red China Plummets

By MAX FRANKEL

Special to The New York Times

HONG KONG, Nov. 13—Whatever urgent domestic requirements inspired Communist China's "cultural revolution," the spectacle of yet another convulsion in the world's most populous nation has done great damage to its prestige and influence around the world.

A journey around the western Pacific and reports by correspondents of The New York Times throughout the world not only support this conclusion; they show no significant doubt about it.

In just a year the upheavals inside China have changed its reputation from that of a formidable challenger of the United States throughout Asia and of the Soviet Union inside the Communist world to that of a hobbled giant riddled by dissent and thus incapable of sustained growth and self-assertion.

Startled, bemused or just plain confused by strife among the Chinese leaders and their inability to settle the conflict within the institutions of their Government and party, the non-Communists of Asia have become less awed by their giant neighbor, Communists have become more ashamed, and Russians and Americans have been moved in Asia and elsewhere to try to exploit Peking's loss of glamour.

Prestige, of course, is often a transitory attribute, especially in international politics, where governments tend to judge others only through distorting lenses of their own interests. Nevertheless, officials and diplomats sense particular significance in the fact that China's reputation has discernibly diminished, not only among non-Communist nations but among communities of Chinese living outside China and among parties and front organizations of the Communist world.

From Nathan Road here in Hong Kong, where the sentimental attachment of the Chinese to their homeland has always been formidable, to Leninallee in East Berlin, where there has always been a modicum of admiration for the Spartans of Peking, there are now signs of deep disappointment and disaffection.

The overseas Chinese, often feared by their host countries as a potential fifth column responsive to Peking, are said to have been dismayed by the sacrifices of economic progress and orderly government to the drive for ideological purity and the purge.

The spectacle of weakness and division in China has more than vitiated the pride and encouragement these same communities derived only recently from Chinese development of nuclear weapons and other attributes of big-power status.

The Communists of most nations are described as dismayed by the fact that China is contributing so vividly to the reputation of all Communists as dogmatic, totalitarian, violent and even irrational. At a time when most Communists had decided to concentrate on providing a better life for the people of their own countries and avoiding military conflict, Peking is found to be an embarrassing liability.

In the world at large the turmoil in Peking is thought also to have damaged the Communist cause in two specific ways.

First, by aggravating their conflict with Moscow and straining relations even with North Vietnam, the Chinese have blocked all chances of international Communist cooperation for either military or diplomatic support of North Vietnam.

And by their own militant conduct and refusal to coexist even with Communist nations, the Chinese are thought to have given greater credence to the American argument that Peking is a threat to stability and peace and therefore a proper object of containment.

Non-Communists in Asia such as the Japanese, who have sought to find their own path to good relations with China, have been particularly startled by the emotional extremism unleashed in Peking.

For Asian Communists the "cultural revolution," the stridency of Peking's propaganda and the spectacle of Red Guard excesses appear to have been taken as yet another indication that the Soviet Union, though white and European, makes a better claim to leadership of the Communist movement.

The Japanese Communists, already alienated by Chinese nuclear tests and opposition to joining the treaty forbidding most nuclear tests, have broken sharply with Peking recently. The North Koreans have continued their swing away from association with China and back toward alignment with Moscow.

And the North Vietnamese, though dependent on Chinese

432

support in their war, have firmly rejected Peking's contention that the Soviet Union is acting in collusion with the United States. By their neutrality in the dispute between their bigger allies they have greatly strained relations with the Chinese and made themselves increasingly dependent upon Soviet assistance.

The decline in China's prestige began last year after the failure of the coup by the pro-Chinese Indonesian Communist party and after the expulsion of Peking's envoys from several African countries.

Yet China's test of nuclear weapons and its encouragement of the guerrilla war against the United States in Vietnam tended to offset the damage. At least in its own sphere in Asia, China continued to loom as a great power, demanding not only recognition but subservience by other nations. Small countries such as Cambodia still felt that their safety depended more upon the Chinese than on the Americans or anyone else.

Today, with the war in Vietnam no longer so one-sided—indeed, with the Communist drive blunted—with the United States increasingly committed to containment of Chinese influence and, above all, with the Chinese proving themselves deeply divided about their own future course, the pendulum has clearly swung the other way.

Not one report from Times correspondents found the Chinese to be enhancing their position. Following is a digest of some of those reports.

JAPAN

Chinese Communist prestige began to decline among Japanese intellectuals when well-known figures such as Kuo Mo-jo, the intellectual leader, and Peng Chen, the mayor of Peking, were struck down by the cultural revolution. The activities of the Red Guards have appalled the Japanese, who compare their juvenile excesses and the general atmosphere in China to those produced by Japanese Fascism in the late thirties. China's refusal to support negotiations on Vietnam and its insistence on developing nuclear weapons are other sources of disaffection, although the Japanese still want to expand trade with China both for its own sake and for its ameliorating effect on the Chinese.

AUSTRALIA

Communist China has long been regarded as an aggressive revolutionary force and a long-term threat. But it still seems far away to South Pacific nations and thus events inside China do not significantly affect day-to-day judgments. Nevertheless, recent signs of factional conflict in China and failure of the North Vietnamese to make progress in the war have brought a feeling of relief. The Chinese nuclear tests always produce shudders of alarm, but Peking's nuclear

power is generally seen only as part of its long-range bid for power.

INDONESIA

Peking is viewed as an inevitable source of agitation and friction by the new Indonesian Government but not as a direct military threat now. Recent events in China have disturbed Chinese intellectuals and their attachment to the homeland, but the Chinese are being treated so harshly by the Indonesians that many young people who are being repatriated go with a strong commitment to Peking's ideology.

SINGAPORE

China's prestige, which had soared among the largely Chinese population, seems to have fallen as a result of the "cultural revolution" and the Red Guard movement. These events have plainly nullified the effects that China's fourth nuclear test and announcement of a guided missile last month would have had otherwise. The Singapore Chinese look on the upheaval as a reversal of all previous progress and believed it is damaging China's reputation more than anything that has happened in the 17 years since the Communists achieved power. China's stock, so far as the Vietnam war is concerned, is also thought to have dropped sharply. At least there is a marked diminution in the demands for a halt in the bombing of North Vietnam and withdrawal of American troops. Most people would prefer that Asians settle the conflict by themselves, but they plainly do not want the Chinese Communists to settle it in their way.

MALAYSIA

The Government fears China less than it fears its own Chinese population. Malaysian officials insist that the local Chinese have remained loyal to Peking and that therefore the American efforts in Vietnam and commitments to all Southeast Asia, are essential to their own survival. The Malaysians say that Peking's prestige among the Chinese is so great that nothing short of civil war will shake it. But they do not consider China a direct military threat in the foreseeable future.

SOUTH VIETNAM

Few South Vietnamese look far beyond their war to events in Communist China, but Dr. Tran Van Do, the Foreign Minister, finds comfort in what he calls a conflict of the generations in Peking. He believes the Red Guard revolution has eroded China's standing in Asia. "She is more and more isolated and her 700 million people are not so great a threat as we have all been taught to think," he says. He doubts that China will enter the war unless the United States adopts altogether different tactics toward North Vietnam. He also believes that North Vietnam is now in a position to resist Chinese

pressure against negotiations if it wishes.

THAILAND

The Thai Government regards China as a long-term threat to itself and other Asian nations unless the United States provides a counterforce. While there is a certain amount of cheering in the press for Peking's internal difficulties, the Government's basic view has not been influenced by either the problems or the achievements of the Chinese Communists.

INDIA

Chinese credibility suffered heavily last fall after Peking's threat to intervene in the war over Kashmir on Pakistan's side turned out to be idle. The recent Chinese nuclear test with a guided missile, however, forced the Indians to take stock again and recognize China's potential as a threat. Yet, the general belief is that China is unlikely to move soon against India or elsewhere in Southeast Asia, and now it is expected that China will concentrate on internal problems for some time.

SOVIET UNION

The Russians have sensed a serious loss of China's prestige since the collapse of the attempted coup in Indonesia and especially during the last year's cultural revolution. They appear to have decided in mid-August to take the offensive to exploit the disillusion in other Communist parties. In this effort the Russians are emphasizing Peking's refusal to join in the common front in Vietnam. But they are also concentrating on portraying internal unrest, which the Russians picture as action hostile to the mass of Chinese Communists and to party institutions. The Chinese nuclear tests contribute to the apprehensions of the average Soviet citizen. The Government takes the line that the current Chinese leadership is a transitory aberration from the Communist family and will change for the better after Chairman Mao Tse-tung is replaced.

WEST GERMANY

There have been no official assessments of events in China because of a feeling that the situation is too confused. There is some concern, however, about Chinese progress in nuclear weaponry and about the effect this will have in diverting American attention to Asia. The Germans feel that Washington already is too preoccupied with the Far East to attend to the problem of German reunification.

FRANCE

Chinese prestige has undoubtedly slipped during the recent excesses, but some of the ridicule has abated recently. It is still, however, the domestic turmoil in China, and not the atomic bomb or Vietnam, that

dominates French thinking about the Chinese. However, the French Government, eager to play up its own burgeoning nuclear arsenal, has attached greater importance than others to Chinese strides in nuclear technology.

AFRICA

The Soviet Union has been doing better diplomatically than Communist China in the last year, virtually supplanting Chinese influence in Algeria and Somalia and profiting elsewhere from Chinese excesses. Peking, which has diplomatic relations with 14 of the 38 independent African nations, has opened no new embassies on the continent in more than a year. In the meantime, Dahomey and the Central African Republic have broken off relations and Peking pulled out of Ghana only last week. Even in the half-dozen countries that receive aid from China officials prefer to retain the Soviet presence as competition and insurance.

LATIN AMERICA

Communist parties throughout the continent have been split for some time into pro-Soviet and pro-Chinese factions. The latter profited somewhat from the prestige of Chinese nuclear tests, but are still clearly in a minority everywhere. Chinese extremism has aroused fear in some places that pro-Soviet Communists might become more active to compete with pro-Chinese factions. Ironically, the Cubans, though in many ways following an analogous party line, have had their own troubles with the Chinese. Because they, too, tried to strike a balance between Peking and Moscow, the Chinese have denounced Premier Fidel Castro as a revisionist and Cubans have scolded the Chinese for making fools of themselves and trying to subvert the Cuban armed forces.

UNITED STATES

Washington analysts stress the inconclusiveness of their theories about what is going on in China. They believe that China's nuclear advances have, in the short run, been nullified by the internal dissension but will, nonetheless, present a serious challenge to China's neighbors in the long run. And if the internal troubles are resolved as most observers expect, short of civil war or collapse of the regime, it is thought that China's stature will rise again. The real damage done by the current upheaval, it is thought, depends on how much more serious the situation becomes—whether the top leadership is irreparably split or whether Mr. Mao is simply trying to shake up the bureaucracy and instill a more revolutionary spirit, and whether the Red Guards will get out of hand or split into rival groups.

November 14, 1966

Peking's Xenophobia

By CHARLES MOHR
Special to The New York Times

HONG KONG, Aug. 24—Communist China's foreign relations are becoming more and more xenophobic and violent.

The pugnacity of Peking's international relations has been exemplified by the beating of British diplomats this week, the maltreatment of Soviet women and children last winter and an almost endless series of denunciations of other governments. One highly qualified student of Chinese affairs has remarked that China is behaving like a "rogue elephant" with a sore tooth, lashing out at former friends as well as its many declared enemies.

News Analysis

But the official Chinese view is that the "ruling circles" of the rest of the world are trying to forge an "unholy anti-China alliance" to prevent the spread of the thoughts of Mao Tsetung, the Chinese Communist party's Chairman.

"United States imperialism and Soviet revisionism have lined up reactionaries, public enemies of the people, renegades to the revolution, national scums, dregs of society, political mummies of all shades and hues and filthy and contemptible die-hards to perform one mad act after another in the anti-China farce."

Statement in Party Paper

This explanation of the events of recent months was made in the Communist party newspaper, Jenmin Jih Pao.

"This is in fact a good thing," Jenmin Jih Pao added, saying that the hostility of other nations "cannot in the least harm towering Socialist China."

The isolation of China has increased in the course of the Cultural Revolution, or purge of Mr. Mao's opponents.

To the already long list of declared enemies, such as the United States, the Soviet Union and India, have been added Burma, Kenya, Mongolia, Ceylon, Britain, Japan, most of the Communist states of Eastern Europe and such diverse targets as the Communist government of the Indian state of Kerala and the Japanese Communist party.

Few Escape Wrath

Only a handful of nations have escaped China's recent wrath. They include Albania, Rumania, North Vietnam, Cambodia, Yemen, Syria, Mali, Tanzania and Somalia.

Peking does not acknowledge this growing isolation, arguing that the "anti-China chorus" is the work of ruling cliques and not the world's peoples. Jenmin Jih Pao also asserted recently that "we have comrades and friends all over the world."

It said that 90 per cent of the world's population loved Chairman Mao and China and that the more "reactionaries of all countries curse us, the bigger the number of people who support China."

One problem that has worsened international relations is that the Chinese have a double standard on the question of diplomatic immunity and accepted diplomatic practice. They frequently complain about any infringement on the freedom of action of their own diplomats or nationals abroad, even those in violation of local laws.

Moscow Attack Protested

When Russians destroyed some outdoor display cases mounted with anti-Soviet polemics outside the Chinese Embassy in Moscow last winter, Peking protested that "minimum protection" for the embassy no longer existed and said: "No sovereign state can tolerate this grave state of affairs."

But a few days later, wives and children of Soviet personnel in Peking were forced to crawl under portraits of Mao to reach an airplane — a modern version of the kowtow, or prostration, of imperial times. Both the Soviet and British mission's grounds were invaded and damaged this month.

These acts are justified, Peking argues, because they are "revolutionary acts."

Last February, an official of the Chinese Foreign Ministry was reported to have told a complaining Mongolian diplomat that "diplomatic immunity is a remnant of bourgeois institutions and a country carrying out revolution cannot recognize bourgeois norms."

Chen Yi Also Criticized

The atmosphere prevailing in China since the Cultural Revolution began last summer has made normal diplomacy difficult.

Foreign Minister Chen Yi and many of his subordinates have been under unrelenting criticism by Red Guards for following a "bourgeois" line. There have been wild brawls, witnessed by foreigners, in the ministry, including one in which Red Guards ransacked files shouting, "What's so terrific about secrets, anyway?"

Another problem is that one of the premises of the Cultural Revolution is that Chinese abroad have a sacred duty to propagate the thought of Chairman Mao. It was such propaganda action that led to the serious crisis with Burma, set off bloody riots and has caused China to proclaim that it now actively supports the violent overthrow of Gen. Ne Win's Government.

There are some parallels between the Maoist style indiplomacy and that of imperial China. In the late 18th and early 19th century, the Ching Dynasty sometimes ended edicts to the British with the words, "Heed this and tremblingly obey."

August 25, 1967

CHINESE BATTLE POLICE IN LONDON

Swinging Clubs and Axes, They Brawl in Street— Peking Sets New Curbs

By EDWARD COWAN
Special to The New York Times

LONDON, Aug. 29—Chinese swinging clubs, iron bars and axes fought with British policemen today in a narrow, dead-end alley behind the Chinese diplomatic office. There were two clashes, one at about 11:20 A.M. and one close to 1 P.M.

According to bystanders and a Foreign Office account, the clashes began when groups of Chinese rushed from the faded yellow building that houses the Chinese mission.

Three policemen, three Chinese and a British newspaper photographer were taken to nearby Middlesex Hospital. One officer and the three Chinese were kept overnight for observation. The hospital said this evening that they had head injuries and that their condition was "fully satisfactory."

[China issued a strong protest Wednesday over the fighting outside its mission building, the Peking radio announced. It declared that all personnel of the British mission in Peking were barred from leaving China without permission of the Chinese Foreign Ministry. All exit visas already issued to British diplomats were declared null and void.]

Tonight, the Foreign Office called the clashes "a deliberate attempt by the Chinese mission to provoke violence in order to try to justify action which Chinese have taken" against the British diplomatic mission in Peking.

A man who answered the telephone at the Chinese office said the fighting was "another serious provocation planned by the British Government and the British Government should be prepared for all the consequences." He then hung up.

While the man refused to answer questions, his statement was unusual in that Western reporters usually get only the click of the telephone from the Chinese office.

China's acting chargé d'affaires, Shen Ping, personally protested at the Foreign Office what he called the "beating up" of a Chinese official by the police. The Foreign Office indicated that it had denied the accusation and brushed off the protest.

The British Government has been taking a tough line toward Chinese diplomatic and trade officials in this country since a mob of Chinese Red Guards burned the British diplomatic building in Peking last Tuesday night and roughed up British diplomats. Britain said the Chinese Government had "deliberately instigated" the attack, which also extensively damaged the house of the British chargé d'affaires, Donald C. Hopson.

In reprisal for the sacking of the British mission, officials here have ordered the 50 or 60 Chinese with official passports to remain within five miles of Marble Arch, in the center of London.

Britain has been trying unsuccessfully since then to arrange the evacuation from China of 35 secretaries, wives and children. The Foreign Office is plainly worried and incensed by Peking's refusal so far to let the women and children leave.

This afternoon, Sir John Waldron, assistant commissioner of the metropolitan police, signed an order forbidding loitering and demonstrations in seven streets in front of and near the Chinese office. The order took effect at 5 P.M. and at that hour the police began directing away several hundred spectators, journalists and photographers.

434

Relative calm had been restored by early evening, although extra policemen were stationed around the building. They have been keeping it under heavy surveillance since last week and individual Chinese have been followed about town.

There were no arrests today. Chinese diplomats would be immune from prosecution, anyway, under traditional diplomatic practice.

The Chinese office stands at the corner of Portland Place and Weymouth Street, two blocks south of Regent's Park and five blocks north of Oxford Street, the busy shopping thoroughfare.

Behind the office is Devonshire Close, a mews that comes to a dead end behind the office and is entered from Devonshire Street. The mews, about 15 feet wide and lined with two-story brick cottages, is used by Chinese leaving and arriving at the office by car.

The Chinese building is an "office" and not an "embassy" because the senior Chinese diplomat accredited here is a chargé d'affaires, not an ambassador. Britain has felt that China's conditions for full ambassadorial representation are excessive.

Of the two clashes between the Chinese and the police, the more serious was the second. It began, according to accounts by the Foreign Office, Scotland Yard and witnesses, after an unmarked police car had been parked in front of the Chinese garage doors in the mews.

Two Chinese argued with officers about removing the car. As the police radioed for reinforcements, about 30 Chinese poured out of the back door of the office. They jumped on the car and knocked off its aerial.

The police agreed to move the car, but then the Chinese, it appears, changed their minds and said that the car should not be moved.

More Chinese came out. Swinging two axes, two baseball bats, iron bars, broom handles and staves, the Chinese fought with the police, who were armed with 18-inch wood truncheons. Bottles and garbage pail covers were hurled by the Chinese, the police said.

One of the Chinese brandished a revolver, according to policemen, but did not fire it. The police, as is their custom, did not carry firearms.

How the Chinese had obtained baseball bats in a country where baseball is not played was not clear.

The first clash occurred after a youth emerged from the side door of the Chinese office, carrying a copy of the little red book, containing the thoughts of Mao Tse-tung, chairman of the Chinese Communist party. A bystander knocked the book from his hand and someone shouted "Long live Chiang Kai-shek." Generalissimo Chiang is the president of the Republic of China, on Taiwan.

The ensuing scrap was filmed by the Chinese.

About 20 Chinese rushed from the house. They knocked over a policeman, kicked another and stepped on the hand of a third. One Chinese was injured on the nose.

It was after this incident that the Chinese chargé, Mr. Shen, went to the Foreign Office. He was received by Arthur J. De La Mare, an Assistant Under Secretary in charge of the Far Eastern Department.

Policemen repulse members of mission who had attacked an unmarked police car parked in front of building's garage

TURMOIL HAMPERS RED CHINA'S TRADE

Exports Drop Faster Than Imports—Slump in Last 3 Months Is Pronounced

HONG KONG IS AFFECTED

Colony Develops Shortages of Food as Normal Supply From Mainland Shrinks

By TILLMAN DURDIN
Special to The New York Times

HONG KONG, Sept. 3 — The damaging consequences of the turmoil caused by the great proletarian cultural revolution in Communist China are beginning to be conspicuously evident in the country's foreign trade.

The trade slump is being felt with special acuteness in Hong Kong, which normally depends for half of its food on supplies from Communist China.

Chinese Communist exports have dropped more sharply than imports, with the decline especially pronounced in the last three months.

If the present lower rate of exports continues, imports must inevitably follow suit since Peking by the end of this year will have appreciably less foreign exchange to spend for the purchase of products from abroad than in former years.

Other Supply Sources

The drop in exports to Hong Kong, Communist China's principal foreign market, has been so large-scale that a shortage of some basic foods is developing here.

The colony is turning to other sources of supply for products that heretofore have mainly come from Communist China.

T. D. Sorby, the Director of Commerce and Industry in Hong Kong, today sent a letter to some 200 food importing firms drawing attention to the recent reduction in supplies of many commodities normally imported from Communist China.

Mr. Sorby said the purpose of his letter was to "point out the facts so that importers could "make appropriate changes in their pattern of orders," or, in other words, buy from other places than Communist China.

Drastic Drop

Mr. Sorby's figures showed that the river boats and junks delivering goods to Hong Kong had brought in only 259,159 tons for June, July and August compared with 463,821 tons for these months last year.

August 30, 1969

435

Only 56,765 tons of products arrived by boats and junks in August this year compared with 159,339 tons for August last year.

The commerce director's report on rail traffic into Hong Kong revealed an even more drastic drop. His figures showed only 3,496 loaded railway freight cars rolled into the colony from Kwangtung in June, July and August this year compared with 10,553 last year, and the number slumped last month to a mere 369 compared with 4,084 for August, 1966.

Ordinarily Communist China earns up to half its foreign exchange through exports to Hong Kong. Last year exports reached a value of $480,770,000.

Because of continued high exports to Hong Kong for the earlier part of this year, the total of Communist China's exports here this year up through the end of July, the last month for which figures have been released, were still marginally higher than for the first seven months of 1966.

But the July figures this year dropped to almost half the amount for July, 1966, and August figures are expected to show an even bigger decline. If exports to Hong Kong were to continue at the level of July and August, Communist China's sales to this little British colony for 1967 would amount only to roughly three-quarters of the 1966 total. Peking would, in short, earn only $360-million in hard currency foreign exchange here instead of $480-million.

Figures for trade by other territories with Communist China are not as up-to-date as those of Hong Kong's but have begun to show the same trends as the Hong Kong figures.

Available figures show a decline in exports for every country except Italy, and the Italian figures only cover the first four months of 1967. It is believed recent Italian returns indicate a decline.

Japanese Trade Dips

Japan's trade with Communist China is off particularly sharply. Figures show Communist China's exports to Japan for the first six months of this year were worth $145-million compared with $156-million for 1966 and Communist China's purchases from Japan were down to $133-million for this year compared with $164-million for 1967.

Communist China's trade slump appears to be the result of disruption in interior transportation and production and of labor troubles and political interference at seaports, all stemming from the confusion and turbulence produced by the cultural revolution.

The severe curtailment of train traffic to Hong Kong, with no trains at all arriving on some days, is a reflection of what is happening also in other parts of the country in railway traffic.

Regular stevedoring labor of ports seems virtually to have vanished. Port authorities have tried to use Red Guards for substitute workers but the result has been slow and cargo damage extensive.

Shipping Delays

Reliable sources estimate average delays for ships into Tsingtao of more than four weeks and for ships in Shanghai and Dairen of more than three weeks. Ships at other ports take up to at least two weeks for loading and unloading.

The drop in exports to Hong Kong, officials here say, reflects no unwillingness, because of the Communist insurgency inside the colony, of the Kwangtung Chinese to sell products to Hong Kong.

Sales have slumped, they say, simply because curtailed and disrupted transportation facilities are unable to deliver products to Hong Kong in normal quantities.

The disruption of railway traffic from Kwangtung into the Yangtse Valley is indicated by the state of hog shipments into Hong Kong. These have fallen to less than a third of the normal 35,000-to-40,000 usually exported here monthly and those that are coming are from Kwangtung and not from the main sources of supply in Hunan, Hupeh and other Yangtse Valley Provinces.

Because it now has to turn to Australia, Taiwan, South Korea and Thailand for food supplies, Hong Kong faces a much higher food bill than it has been paying for the cheap food that has been coming from Communist China.

September 4, 1967

Soviet and Chinese Clash on Border;
Each Lists Deaths in Siberian Incident

Two Sides File Protests Charging Violations of River Frontier

By HENRY KAMM
Special to The New York Times

MOSCOW, March 2—The Soviet Union announced tonight that a Chinese military unit crossed the border on a river in the Far East this morning and fired on Soviet border guards, causing an unspecified number of dead and wounded.

The intruders were driven back by the guards, Tass, the official press agency, said. The Soviet Government has protested the action in a note to China.

[The Chinese rejected the Soviet protest, the Peking radio said, and in turn charged that Soviet border guards had crossed into Chinese territory and had killed and wounded several Chinese soldiers.]

Despite occasional unconfirmed reports of clashes in the last 10 years, this was thought to be the first time that either government had reported an armed incident. It was also believed to be the first acknowledgment of casualties in a Chinese-Soviet conflict.

This is how Tass described the incident:

"At 4:10 A.M. Moscow time [10:10 A.M. Far Eastern time] on March 2, the Chinese authorities staged an armed provocation in the area of the border post of Nizhnemikhailovka (Damansky Island) on the Ussuri River. An armed Chinese unit crossed the Soviet state frontier and proceeded toward Damansky Island.

"The Chinese side suddenly opened fire at Soviet border guards guarding the area. There are killed and wounded. By the resolute actions of Soviet border guards the violators of the frontier were chased from Soviet territory."

The account gave no further details on the casualties and did not make clear whether they were suffered by the Russians or the Chinese or both.

Presumably the Ussuri River was frozen at this time of year and the alleged border violation occurred on the ice.

The Soviet protest note declared that "any provocative actions by Chinese authorities on the Soviet-Chinese border will be rebuffed and resolutely cut short by the U.S.S.R."

The incident came at a time when Chinese-Soviet relations appear to observers to be at a low state. Nothing new has appeared in the exchange of recriminations between the two nations for some time. Diplomatic and commercial relations are at a minimum and cultural and other contacts almost nonexistent.

Islands in the Ussuri River, which forms the border between Chinese Manchuria and the Soviet Union's Maritime Territory are disputed. Presumably Damansky Island, near Nizhnemikhailovka, 140 miles south of Khabarovsk, is one of the disputed islands.

Aside from the local frontier disputes, Peking contends that the entire Soviet Far Eastern region was seized from China by the Czars in the 19th cen-

436

cury through a series of unequal treaties.

Moscow has accused China of expansionism in seeking to detach from the Soviet Union about 500,000 square miles of territory.

As tension mounted along the 4,150-mile-long border, divided into two nearly equal sections but Soviet-dominated Mongolia in the middle, China tightened restrictions on travel on the Amur and Ussuri rivers in the Far East.

Observers speculated that the shooting incident might have been occasioned by a local dispute involving river traffic. Vague language in the treaties on the Ussuri border is believed by geographers to be conducive to disputes over the islands in the river.

Soviet leaders in public statements have left no doubt that they consider the Far East a vital border zone kept in a constant state of alert and military preparedness.

had fired first and killed and wounded a number of Chinese border guards. The note said that, after having given the Soviet border guards repeated warnings in vain, the Chinese guards had returned fire in self-defense.

March 3, 1969

CHINESE AFFIRM HARD-LINE STAND IN PARTY REPORT

By TILLMAN DURDIN
Special to The New York Times

HONG KONG, April 27 — The Chinese Communist party has adopted as its basic program a plan for continued hard-line revolutionary action, at home and abroad.

The program was set out in a 24,000-word report by Lin Piao, the party's deputy chairman, and adopted at the ninth party congress, which met in Peking the first 24 days of this month. It was made public tonight by Hsinhua, the official Chinese Communist press agency.

Mr. Lin, who is also Defense Minister, denounced the United States and the Soviet Union, and said that China must pre-

pare for the eventuality of nuclear war with either country. He pledged continued support for revolutionary movements everywhere and called on nations to form a united front to resist Soviet and United States efforts to divide up the world.

Kosygin Offer Disclosed

The report said that the Chinese had rejected an offer by the Soviet Premier, Aleksei N. Kosygin, to discuss the Chinese-Soviet border dispute over the telephone. [Page 14.]

It asserted that the Cultural Revolution, initiated by the party chairman, Mao Tse-tung, in 1966 to purge Communist China of revisionist leaders and influences, had achieved a smashing victory. However, it declared that the revolution was not yet over and that further struggle lay ahead before complete political transformation in China and world revolution were attained.

The report underlined the new primacy of the military in the affairs of Communist China by quoting Chairman Mao as having said, "The main component of the state is the army." It proclaimed Mao Tse-tung's thoughts, in equal status with Marxism-Leninism, as the basis for all the actions of the people of China.

Mr. Lin gave his report, which sums up the genesis, development and future perspectives of the Maoist Cultural Revolution, on April 1. It was adopted by the congress after protracted discussion and some emendations on April 14.

The report is the basic document for policy and action to come from the congress of 1,512 carefully selected delegate—the first party congress held since 1958. In addition to adopting the report, the congress approved the draft of a new party constitution, the text of which has not been made public, and named a new governing party Central Committee. A majority of the members on the previous Central Committee were purged in the Cultural Revolution, which shattered the party and government structure.

The holding of the party congress was intended to represent a consolidation of a purged and renovated Communist system. Delegates to the congress were selected by the new Revolutionary Committees, which have emerged as the organs of control for provinces,

cities and lower social units.

A large percentage of the delegates were military men or political commissars of military units. The new Central Committee, consisting of 170 regular and 109 alternate members, has roughly 40 per cent military men among the regulars and 35 per cent among the alternates.

Report Is Revolutionary

The report was, on the surface at least, a tougher and more revolutionary document than had been expected by many specialists in Chinese affairs here. It not only contained a clarion call for revolution and opposition to the world status quo, but also proclaimed continued conformity to Maoist doctrine and pursuit of Maoist economic and social policies internally.

However, aside from prescribing further internal struggle against opposition elements, the report was not specific about economic or social programs. It gave no indication of what role the new Revolutionary Committees, which combine both party and governmental functions, would play in the new party system.

Continuation of the production drive now under way was indicated by injunctions that the people must "firmly grasp revolution and energetically promote production and fulfill and overfulfill our plans for developing the national economy."

Mr. Lin did not call for another Great Leap Forward—the drive in 1958-59 to achieve rapid industrialization, which seriously set back the economy — but used a slogan of that time: "Going all out, aiming high and achieving greater, faster, better and more economical results in building socialism," to emphasize the demand for intensive production efforts.

He repeated charges that have frequently been made from Peking about the aggressiveness of the United States and the Soviet Union, their "paper tiger" weakness caused by internal economic and social problems and their aims to collaborate to oppose and encircle China. He denounced the United States because Americans, "still occupy" Taiwan and said that Chinese troops "are determined to liberate their sacred territory of Taiwan and resolutely, thoroughly, wholly and completely wipe out all aggressors."

Mr. Lin pledged Communist China's support for revolutionary movements in the United States, the Soviet Union and elsewhere, citing in particular backing for Albania, the Vietnamese people "in their struggle against the United States"

and "the revolutionary struggles of the people of Laos, Thailand, Burma, Malaya, Indonesia, India, Palestine and other countries in Asia, Africa and Latin America."

The report reviewed the history of the Chinese Communist party in the light of struggles to maintain proletarian predominance against continued threats of bourgeois, counterrevolutionary influences and, quoting Marx, Engels and Lenin, portrayed Mr. Mao as having consistently advocated the correct party line.

Liu Shao-chi, Chairman Mao's former deputy who since 1959 has been China's head of state, was denounced as "a hidden traitor, scab and a crime-soaked lackey of the imperialists, modern revisionism and Kuomintang reactionaries." Accusations against Mr. Liu were the same as those that have already been made repeatedly in the last two years.

No other person was referred to by name as associated with Mr. Liu, but he was called the "archrepresentative" of "renegades, enemy agents and capitalist-roaders in power" who formed an underground bourgeois headquarters and schemed against Mr. Mao to restore capitalism and serve the interests of the "U. S. imperialists, the Soviet revisionists and the reactionaries of various countries."

Leniency Is Backed

There was no indication what punishment, if any, would be meted to Mr. Liu, but in discussing policy toward opposition elements, Mr. Lin again endorsed leniency toward those who confess and can be reformed.

He said "the policy of killing none and not arresting most should be applied to all except the active counterrevolutionaries against whom there is conclusive evidence of crimes, such as murder, arson or poisoning and who should be dealt with in accordance with law."

Calling attention to the continued presence of class enemies and revisionist influence, Mr. Lin said that though the establishment of Revolutionary Committees marked a "great decisive victory" for the Cultural Revolution, the "revolution is not yet over." He said the proletariat must continue to advance, "carry out the tasks of struggle - criticism - transformation, and carry the socialist revolution in the realm of the superstructure through to the end."

He cited a quotation from Mr. Mao that was new to China-watchers here, quoting the party chairman as having stated in October, 1968, presumably at the meeting that month of the old Central Committee, that the defeated class enemy was still around and would still struggle. In view of this, he quoted Mr. Mao as having said "we cannot speak of final victory, not even for decades."

Mr. Lin depicted the road to continued success as lying in absolute reliance on the thoughts of Chairman Mao and his leadership. He said the wide dissemination of Chairman Mao's thoughts in Communist China "is the most significant achievement of the Great Proletarian Cultural Revolution." He called for a further "deep-going" mass movement for the study of the thoughts.

Mr. Lin repeatedly emphasized the congress was a demonstration of victory and unity. He praised the military forces as the "pillar of the dictatorship of the proletariat" and said the solidarity of the people and the army had insured the defeat of the opposition elements.

April 28, 1969

CHINESE APPOINT ENVOY TO ALBANIA

Move Considered First Step in Restaffing Embassies

By IAN STEWART
Special to The New York Times

HONG KONG, May 16—Communist China has sent a new ambassador to Albania, in what is presumably a first step toward bringing its diplomatic missions back to full strength. For th last two years, only the Chinese Embassy in Cairo has been continuously in the charge of an ambassador.

The new Ambassador to Albania is Keng Piao, who served as Peking's Ambassador to Denmark, Sweden and Pakistan in the nineteen-fifties and who was elected a member of the Central Committee last month at the ninth congress of the Chinese Communist party. His appointment was announced by Hsinhua, the Chinese press agency, which said he left Peking for Tirana, the capital of Albania, yesterday.

The appointment followed signs that China was preparing to resume normal diplomatic activities, which were curbed by the Cultural Revolution, the purge initiated in 1966. The most notable sign occurred during May Day celebrations in Peking, when Mao Tse-tung, the Communist party chairman, and Lin Piao, his designated successor, received eight ambassadors newly accredited to China.

Albania, Communist China's chief ideological ally, was a natural choice as the country to receive priority in the sending of senior diplomats abroad again.

After most of China's ambassadors were recalled early in the Cultural Revolution, Chinese foreign policy took on an exceptionally unpredictable and xenophobic character. Much of this was attributed to pressure from the Red Guards, the youthful shock corps of the Cultural Revolution.

The Foreign Ministry is believed to have been heavily purged, and an important victim may have been its head, Chen Yi. He was dropped from the Politburo last month and has been missing from a number of functions that he would have been expected to attend as Foreign Minister.

For example, he was not present when Chairman Mao, Mr. Lin and other leaders met the eight ambassadors on May Day.

As Ambassador to Albania, Mr. Keng replaces Liu Hsiao, a former Ambassador to the Soviet Union, who may have been purged. A Red Guard publication reported that he had been severely criticized.

Mr. Keng was one of two ambassadors elected to the Central Committee. The other was Huang Chen, who was Ambassador to France before the Cultural Revolution. Further appointments of ambassadors are expected to reveal how well the rest of Peking's senior diplomats have weathered the purges.

Although China's basic foreign policy pronouncements during the last few months have continued to denounce the United States, the Soviet Union, "imperialists" and "revisionists," there have been signs of moderation in specific policy matters.

In Hong Kong, two years after Chinese Communists led rioting against the Government, they are at peace with the authorities and are busily developing new outlets for trade. Criticism of the Hong Kong Government in the local Communist press is quite mild in comparison with its tone of two years ago.

May 17, 1969

After Moscow's Summit

The international Communist Congress just concluded in Moscow is, almost by inadvertence, a milestone in the evolution of world Communism. For the first time since Stalin two generations ago captured control of the main current of international Marxism-Leninism, a major summit meeting has been held under conditions in which it immediately and publicly became known that there was fundamental disagreement among the participants. The practical result is to legalize public dissent in international Communism and to end the dream of restoring the monolithic unity that Stalin prized so much.

Roughly two decades ago, Yugoslavia was expelled from the Cominform and subjected to a coordinated political, economic and propaganda attack from the Soviet Union and its satellites because Tito refused to obey Stalin's orders. At this month's Moscow meeting, Mr. Brezhnev had no such means of compulsion. He was able to persuade most of the parties in attendance to sign the principal statement of the conference only by making it so ambiguous that even such avowed heretics as the Rumanians could accept it. The resultant declaration is so bland that it does not even condemn China, though such condemnation was the main point of Brezhnev's own lengthy speech.

Even the attempt to paper over the differences at Moscow was not entirely successful. It is indicative of the change in world Communism that the militant but weak Dominican Communist party dared to refuse to sign the final document altogether, while the Italians and some others accepted only one part of the statement and rejected the rest. And the most independent Communist parties—the Chinese, the Albanian, the Yugoslav, the Japanese and others—did not even bother to come to Moscow.

Perhaps most important, the Soviet press had to inform its readers that unanimity did not exist at this summit. The question must occur to many Soviet minds why dissent is legal at an international Communist meeting, but illegal and punishable by prison sentences within the Soviet Union.

When Nikita Khrushchev began the drive for a world Communist summit in the early 1960's, his goal was to expel the Chinese from the movement and to reinstitute Moscow's control over the majority of Communist parties. His successors continued to pursue that goal. But the meeting just ended has neither expelled the Chinese nor re-established Russian hegemony. The Kremlin has to face the likelihood that the strong forces backing genuine independence for Communist parties will grow stronger now that the precedent has been set at the summit of 1969.

June 19, 1969

Soviet-Chinese Talk On Border Rivers Begun in Far East

MOSCOW, June 21 (Reuters) —Talks between the Soviet Union and Communist China on border river navigation opened in Khabarovsk Wednesday, Tass the Soviet press agency, reported tonight.

The agency said the 15th meeting of the mixed Soviet-Chinese Commission for Navigation on Boundary Rivers had begun in the Soviet Far Eastern city "in accordance with the agreement between the two sides."

The Chinese Government an-nounced last month it had accepted a Soviet proposal to hold the talks.

The commission, set up 18 years ago, last met in Harbin, Manchuria, in 1967, and China blamed the Russians for the "fruitless outcome." Another meeting was scheduled for last year in Khabarovsk, but it did not take place and each side blamed the other.

The Russians asked for the current meeting after Chinese and Soviet troops clashed twice last March on a disputed island in the Ussuri River, on the border between the two countries. Several soldiers from each side were killed in the encounters. Since then both countries have reported clashes along their 4,500-mile border, charging each other with provocation and intrusion.

June 22, 1969

NIXON PLANS CUT IN MILITARY ROLE FOR U.S. IN ASIA

By ROBERT B. SEMPLE Jr.
Special to The New York Times

MANILA, Saturday, July 26— President Nixon declared yesterday that the United States would not be enticed into future wars like the one in Vietnam and would redesign and reduce its military commitments throughout non-Communist Asia.

Mr. Nixon promised, however, that the United States would continue to play a sizable role in the Pacific and would not forsake its treaty commitments.

This was the essence of views put forward by the President in an informal news conference before he set forth from Guam on the diplomatic leg of his global journey.

President Exhilarated

The President, who seemed exhilarated by the successful moon venture of Apollo 11, arrived here today for the first foreign stop of a tour taking him to Indonesia, Thailand, India, Pakistan, Rumania and, briefly, Britain.

During his short stop in Guam, Mr. Nixon set forth in considerable detail the purposes of his week-and-a-half trip and disclosed major points he would be making to the Asian leaders. He spoke for publication but asked that his words not be directly quoted.

The President defined his Asian policy in more specific and forceful terms than at any time since taking office. Some of his views had been expressed earlier in articles and in the political campaign last fall, but he went further today in emphasizing his intention of limiting United States commitments.

New Aid Is Hinted

Specifically, he said he might order a reduction of military operations in South Vietnam if that would help the negotiations to end the war.

The President also hinted that new forms of economic aid to the Asian nations might soon be forthcoming, but — perhaps mindful of growing ill will toward foreign aid at home and the constraints that inflation has placed on new Government spending—he carefully avoided promising an increase in aid.

The President spent the major part of his news conference, held at the naval officers' club in Guam, on questions relating to Vietnam and Asia, demonstrating that despite all the early publicity devoted to visit he will pay to Rumania Aug. 2, he himself was placing highest priority on the Asian part of the journey. Yet in the course of his unusually relaxed and unusually long session—it last 52 minutes, compared with his average news-conference length of 30 minutes—Mr. Nixon also made these points:

¶He remains willing to participate in a top-level meeting with the Soviet Union to talk about the Vietnam war, the Middle Eastern crisis and the arms race, but only if such a meeting were to be preceded by lower-level consulations and held out some promise of success.

¶While he most wishes for a summit meeting to enlist the Soviet Union in the search for an end of the war, he doubts that Moscow would work for a settlement, even if it wants one, in so public and highly visible a forum.

¶There is no basis for what he called speculation that his visit to Rumania would be an affront to either the Soviet Union or Communist China; instead, it is designed to develop communication with Eastern European nations.

¶Recent charges by some Senators that the United States had struck a secret defense agreement with Thailand are without foundation.

Mr. Nixon acknowledged at the outset his consuming interest in the future of Asia after the end of the war in Vietnam. He said further that the Asians were equally interested in whether the United States would continue to play a significant role in their area or whether, like the French, British and Dutch, it would withdraw from the Pacific and play a minor part.

He conceded that many Americans were extremely frustrated by the Vietnam war and, in their frustration, wished for a substantial reduction of America's Pacific commitments. He indicated by his tone that he understood these frustrations and to a certain extent sympathized with them.

But he argued that the United States could not withdraw from its Asian commitments, first because withdrawal might well pave the way for other wars; and second, because the United States itself is a Pacific power with a major stake in Asian stability.

In answering subsequent questions, however, Mr. Nixon sought more clearly to define the future dimensions of that commitment. He asserted, for example, that except when Asian nations were threatened by a nuclear power such as Communist China, the United States would insist that both internal subversion and external aggression be dealt with increasingly by the Asians themselves.

Collective Security Urged

He said it was foolish to believe that the non-Communist Asian nations could soon devise collective security arrangements enabling them to defend themselves against Communism. Collective security now is a weak reed to lean on, he said, and it will take five to 10 years for the non-Communist Asian nations to devise adequate collective security arrangements among themselves.

This blunt assessment of the prospects for collective security prompted a question on what the United States would do in the event of another Vietnam situation in the five to 10 years in which the Asian nations would be struggling to devise mechanisms for self-protection. The President replied that such incidents would have to be judged case by case.

But he will consider each case very carefully, he asserted, with an eye to avoiding what he called creeping involvements that eventually submerge a great nation, as, he said, the Vietnam conflict has submerged the United States in emotional discord and economic strain.

To illustrate his point, the President recalled a line from his election campaign that he said he had used in every speech, drawing loud applause each time. He said the statement had been made to him by Mohammad Ayub Khan, former President of Pakistan, in 1964.

"The role of the United States in Vietnam or the Philippines, or Thailand, or any of these other countries which have internal subversion," the statement went, "is to help them fight the war but not fight the war for them."

Mr. Nixon then declared, in answer to a question, that military assistance of all kinds, including the commitment of United States troops, would be reduced. He did not say how large such reductions would be, or how soon they would be carried out.

To compensate in part for the reduced military assistance, Mr. Nixon indicated that the United States would soon be suggesting initiatives on the economic side designed to add fresh momentum to what he said was the developing economic strength of non-Communist Asia. He promised that United States aid would be adequate to meet the challenge of Asian economic problems.

The President professed to see several hopeful signs that non-Communist Asia had recently become stronger, including rapid economic development. He rattled off an impressive list of statistics showing the economic growth of

South Korea, Japan, Thailand, Indonesia, India and Pakistan.

Another sign, he said, was the dwindling capacity of Communist China to foment internal insurgencies in other countries. Early in the news conference, Mr. Nixon declared that China was the single biggest threat to stability in Asia, but later he expressed a conviction that the appeal of the Communist philosophy had dwindled in some Asian countries in the last 16 years. He cited Pakistan, India, Indonesia and Japan as examples.

The President returned to the same themes on his arrival at the Manila International Airport, where he was greeted by President and Mrs. Ferdinand E. Marcos and a large delegation of Filipino officials.

"I want to convey throughout the trip," he said, "the great sense of respect and affection which the people of the United States feel for their Asian neighbors and the readiness of my country to support the efforts of Asian nations to improve the life of their peoples. I will also offer the view that peace and progress in Asia must be shaped and protected primarily by Asian hands and that the contribution which my country can make to that process should come as a supplement to Asian energies and in response to Asian leadership."

2 ANZUS PARTNERS BACK U.S. ON CHINA

Australia and New Zealand Support a Bid for Talks

By ROBERT TRUMBULL
Special to The New York Times

CANBERRA, Australia, Aug. 8—Australia and New Zealand voiced their support today for the United States' conciliatory policy toward Communist China, enunciated here by Secretary of State William P. Rogers.

The endorsement came in a joint communiqué at the end of the one-day annual meeting of the Anzus Treaty Council, the mutual security organization formed in 1951. Mr. Rogers represented the United States on the council.

Earlier today Mr. Rogers said that Washington would soon undertake new approaches to Peking for a resumption of the periodic conversations between their ambassadors in Warsaw. Last February Peking broke off the series of talks, held intermittently over several years.

In one of the most explicit statements yet by a member of the Nixon Administration on the China problem, Mr. Rogers said: "We recognize, of course, that the Republic of China on Taiwan and Communist China on the mainland are facts of life."

View of 'Two Chinas'

The statement was one of the United States' clearest definitions so far of its view of "two Chinas."

Such a policy abandons the long-held concept that the Nationalist regime of President Chiang Kai-shek on Taiwan is the true government, though dispossessed, of all China.

Mr. Rogers, in a luncheon address to the National Press Club here, also said that the United States would remain neutral in the conflict between Communist China and the Soviet Union "while persisting in efforts to engage in a constructive dialogue with both" of the Communist nations.

Mr. Rogers will leave tomorrow for Auckland, New Zealand, where he will stop overnight before proceeding to Pagopago, in American Samoa, and then home.

'Isolation Self-Imposed'

Australia was represented at the Anzus meeting by Gordon Freeth, the Minister for External Affairs, and New Zealand by Prime Minister Keith J. Holyoake, who also serves as his Government's Minister of External Affairs.

"The ministers discussed the problem of Communist China's continued isolation from the world community," the communique said. "They considered that this isolation was essentially self-imposed and that the situation was unlikely to improve unless there was a change in the attitude of the Peking regime itself."

"Nevertheless," the communique continued, "the Anzus Council members agreed that efforts should be continued to resume a dialogue with the regime. They noted the recent decision by the United States Government to relax its restrictions on travel and commercial relations with Communist China and expressed the hope that the Communist Chinese might be prepared to re-

sume conversations with United States representatives."

The representatives called for "a serious response" by Hanoi to the reduction in United States forces in South Vietnam. Australia has about 8,000 troops in Vietnam, and New Zealand has a token contingent of about 500 men.

"It was also agreed that the Anzus partners would continue to consult on such matters as the rate at which forces of the Republic of Vietnam are going to be increasingly able to take over," the communiqué said.

The three countries deplored "the deteriorating military situation in Laos," charging North Vietnam with "continued unwillingness to stop its military attacks against that country and its use of Laotian territory to support aggression against South Vietnam."

"The representative of the United States commended the decisions of the Governments of Australia and New Zealand to continue maintaining elements of their armed forces in Malaysia and Singapore after the British withdrawal in 1971," the statement added.

The Australian and New Zealand contribution to the defense of Malaysia and Singapore, though criticized in Kuala Lumpur as insufficient, and the decision of Britain to continue training activities in the area after the bulk of British forces withdraw, were hailed as a significant part of the trend toward regional cooperation in Asia and the Pacific.

The communiqué went on to say, however, that Australia and New Zealand endorsed the view of the Nixon Administration and some Asian leaders that Asian countries should be left to control internal subversion.

KOSYGIN AND CHOU CONFER IN PEKING IN SURPRISE MOVE

By BERNARD GWERTZMAN
Special to The New York Times

MOSCOW, Sept. 11 — Premier Aleksei N. Kosygin, on his way home from Ho Chi Minh's funeral in Hanoi, made an unexpected visit to Peking today and met with Premier Chou En-lai.

Tass, the Soviet press agency, said tonight that Mr. Kosygin and Mr. Chou "frankly made known their positions and had a conversation useful for both sides."

The announcement of the meeting was made shortly before Mr. Kosygin arrived back in Moscow after the unexpected visit.

[A broadcast from Peking, monitored in Hong Kong said the meeting took place at the airport. In Eastern Europe Communist diplomats credited Rumania with having arranged the talks.]

It was the first time top Soviet and Chinese leaders had met since February, 1965, when Mr. Kosygin stopped in Peking both on his way to and from Hanoi.

There was no indication from the short Tass report of what the two leaders discussed, or the prospects for future Soviet-Chinese relations, which have fallen to extremely low depths in recent months.

The initial reaction here was that the two leaders, while not coming to any substantive agreements, at least indicated they were not displeased by the meeting.

In Communist jargon the word "frankly," used in the Tass report, generally indicates that the two sides are not in agreement. The phrase "useful for both sides" could indicate a desire to take some of the heat out of the rather tense state of Soviet-Chinese relations, which this year erupted several times into border clashes.

Just yesterday, apparently before Mr. Kosygin's visit to Peking was known, Tass distributed a long statement accusing the Chinese of 488 border violations and repeating charges that China was threatening the Soviet Union with war.

Diplomatic observers, who were generally surprised by the Peking meeting, assumed that Mr. Kosygin called on the Chinese to stop border "provocations" and to enter into negotiations on differences. Mr. Kosygin was assumed to have also repeated the Soviet assertion that it wants good relations with the Chinese people but will deal firmly with any attempt to "speak with the language of force."

The meeting apparently was arranged in the last 24 hours or so. The Soviet leader traveled to Peking by a rather unusual route, and the Chinese side had appeared to go out of its way to avoid a meeting on the occasion of President Ho's funeral in Hanoi.

Mr. Chou flew from Peking to Hanoi last Thursday to pay his Government's last respects to Mr. Ho, but had returned to Peking before Mr. Kosygin's delegation arrived in Hanoi on Saturday.

Avoided Flight Over China

And, as if to emphasize the strained state of Soviet-Chinese relations, Mr. Kosygin's plane flew to Hanoi by way of New Delhi rather than the conventional Peking route.

China was represented at Mr. Ho's funeral two days ago by Vice Premier Li Hsien-nien, who recently has been acting as Foreign Minister in place of the apparently discredited Chen Yi. It is possible that Mr. Li discussed the details of the meeting with Soviet representatives in Hanoi.

But yesterday, when the Soviet delegation left Hanoi for Moscow there was no indication that a Peking visit was planned. The Soviet plane stopped first in Calcutta and then went on

to Dushanbe, the capital of Soviet Tadzhikistan in central Asia.

Yesterday afternoon Tass reported the arrival of Mr. Kosygin in Dushanbe, but when the morning newspapers said nothing of the landing there, speculation began in the Soviet capital on Mr. Kosygin's whereabouts, since he normally would have arrived in Moscow this morning.

It is considered possible that Mr. Kosygin, on landing at Dushanbe, received word of an agreement for the talks. His flight to Peking took him some 2,700 miles across China.

Tass said that Mr. Kosygin was accompanied in his session with Mr. Chou by the other members of his delegation to the Ho funeral, Konstantin Katushev, the party secretary in charge of relations with ruling Communist parties and Mikhail Yasnov, vice chairman of the Presidium of the Supreme Soviet. With Mr. Chou were Vice Premier Li and Vice Premier Hsien Fu-chin. Tass said the talks had been arranged by "mutual agreement."

The Soviet Union in a note to the Chinese Government on March 29, proposed diplomatic consultations on border disputes, but stressed that it would not negotiate more than minor border adjustments and delinaations.

The Chinese have insisted that the Far Eastern border areas of the Soviet Union were annexed by the Russian czars in the 19th century through "unequal treaties" and have pressed the Soviet Union to acknowledge this. But the Russians have flatly refused to discuss the historical basis of their territories and have called the Chinese claims provocations.

September 12, 1969

China Said to Be Moving Nuclear Plant to Tibet

By SYDNEY H. SCHANBERG
Special to The New York Times

NEW DELHI, Sept. 12 — The Indian Foreign Ministry reported today that Communist China had been moving its nuclear installations in Sinkiang Province to a "safer place" in northern Tibet, farther from its border with the Soviet Union.

A spokesman for the Foreign Ministry said at the regular weekly briefing for newsmen

that the movement of the installations to Tibet, which borders India on the north and has been occupied by China since 1950, started about a year ago and that the pace of the transfer operation from northwest China had been increased in recent months.

The facilities involved, the spokesman said, were mainly in the Lob Nor area of what the Chinese call the Sinkiang-Uighur Autonomous Region. He said they included a "gaseous

diffusion plant" and a plant for the manufacture of nuclear bombs.

The official, who gave no details of how this information had been obtained by New Delhi, said that the shift of the Sinkiang nuclear establishment to Tibet indicated the serious nature of the dispute between China and the Soviet Union.

Border tensions have risen sharply in recent months. Soviet and Chinese military forces have engaged in a series of

clashes this year at various points on their 4,500-mile frontier. The most recent and apparently most severe clashes have occurred in remote areas where the Soviet Central Asian republic of Kazakhstan meets Sinkiang.

Immediately after the latest battle, on Aug. 13, each country accused the other of mobilizing for nuclear war. Heavy troop build-ups by both sides have been reported along their common border.

The United States acknowledged last month that it had received reports that Soviet officials had been sounding out fellow Communist leaders in Eastern and Western Europe on what they would think of a pre-emptive air strike by Moscow against Peking's expanding nuclear facilities.

The Indian Foreign ministry spokesman said his Government had no details of either Chinese or Soviet preparations for a major confrontation.

But other Indian officials said that New Delhi was apprehensive about a nuclear war be-

The New York Times   Sept. 13, 1969

Chinese nuclear plants were reported being moved from Lob Nor (1) to the northern part of Tibet (2). Clashes with Soviet forces have erupted along Sinkiang border with Kazakhstan (3).

tween the two Communist countries, adding, "We consider a conflict in this region will affect us seriously."

These officials said that the Chinese decision to shift the nuclear installations to a place out of reach of the Soviet Union was clearly a defensive measure, apparently taken in anticipation of a pre-emptive attack.

The Indian Foreign Ministry spokesman said the exact location in Tibet of the new site for the nuclear facilities was not known. But it was believed, he indicated, that the Chinese have probably chosen a valley surrounded by mountains in a range north of the Himalayas that would be difficult for the Russians to bomb or hit with missiles.

The Lob Nor area in Sinkiang is more than 500 miles south of the site of the recent border clashes. The nearest point in Tibet is 300 miles farther south—and away from the Soviet border.

The Foreign Ministry spokesman said that because of increasing tension between the Soviet Union and China, India welcomed yesterday's meeting in Peking between Premier

Aleksei N. Nosygin and Premier Chou En-lai.

As for India's own dispute with China, the spokesman said that Prime Minister Indira Gandhi had made it clear on several occasions that New Delhi was prepared to talk and had "always kept the door open."

September 13, 1969

CURB ON U.S. BASES IN JAPAN IS EASED BY OKINAWA PACT

By RICHARD HALLORAN
Special to The New York Times

WASHINGTON, Nov. 21 — President Nixon and Premier Eisaku Sato of Japan, in arranging for the return of Okinawa to Tokyo's control, agreed today that United States forces based in Japan would have new freedom of action to fulfill American security commitments in South Korea, Taiwan and other countries of Asia.

The basic conditions for the return of Okinawa to Japan in 1972, which was formally announced today, included relatively flexible stipulations for the use of the United States troops who remain on the island.

These stipulations will also apply to combat operations of American forces stationed in Japan proper. Previously the forces in Japan were in effect restricted to operations in defense of that country alone.

U. S. Freedom Enlarged

Administration officials said that while American military operations from the vast complex of bases in Okinawa would theoretically be curtailed after 1972, the freedom of the United States to use its bases in Japan itself would be considerably enlarged.

These officials said this was a major conclusion that emerged from a joint communiqué issued by Mr. Nixon and Mr. Sato at the White House and from a speech by Mr. Sato at the National Press Club. The officials stressed that the two messages were interlocking and made up a single policy statement.

Pledges Made on Trade

Both Mr. Nixon and Mr. Sato said the three-day negotiations that they completed today constituted a historic turning point in American-Japanese relations. Mr. Sato said they marked the beginning of a "new Pacific age," in which "a new order will be created by Japan and the United States."

Mr. Sato also used the occasion to emphasize his continuing effort to bring about a Japanese national consensus that would support a more positive political, economic, and security role for Japan in Asia. "In the real international world," he said, "it is impossible to maintain adequately the security of Japan without international peace and security in the Far East."

Mr. Sato's attempt, which began about two years ago, to project Japan into a position of greater international influence has been vigorously opposed by the Japanese pacifist, neutralist left. Demonstrators tried to prevent his departure for the United States earlier this week, claiming that he would give away too much and not get enough from the United States in the negotiation over Okinawa. Leftist leaders have warned that anything less than the withdrawal of all American bases from Japan and Okinawa will lead to more demonstrations.

In the communiqué, Mr. Nixon "reaffirmed the commitment of the United States to the principle of freer trade." Mr. Sato, in turn, pledged to "accelerate the reduction of Japan's trade and capital restrictions."

Specifically, Mr. Sato stated "the intention of the Japanese Government to remove Japan's residual import quota restrictions over a broad range of products by the end of 1971 and to make maximum efforts to accelerate the liberalization of remaining items." Administration officials said American import quotas on Japanese textiles were not mentioned because they were being negotiated in Geneva.

In their communiqué, the two leaders agreed to maintain indefinitely the Mutual Security Treaty of 1960, the fundamental document defining the commitment of the United States to defend Japan and the obligation of Japan to permit American bases to remain there. Officials said this was the first formal statement by the two nations that the treaty, which can be renounced on a year's notice beginning next June, would continue in force.

They also agreed that after Okinawa reverts to Japanese control, the provisions of the treaty will apply to American

bases that will be retained there. The most important of these is the agreement that all major military movements are subject to "prior consultations" between the United States and Japanese governments. In effect, American officials said, this means obtaining Japanese approval. It also means that nuclear weapons will be withdrawn from Okinawa and will not be redeployed there without the consent of the Japanese Government.

The communiqué and Mr. Sato's speech, Administration officials said, are an expression of the public attitude of the Japanese on prior consultations and the standards they will apply to situations requiring such consultations.

In the communiqué, Mr. Sato expressed for the first time a Japanese "recognition that, in the light of the present situation, the presence of United States in the Far East constituted a mainstay for the stability of the area." The Premier, in his speech, added that "Japan and the United States agree in their basic recognition of the importance of United States military bases on Okinawa. The peace-keeping function of the bases on Okinawa must continue to be kept effective."

Specifically, the Premier said in the communiqué that "the security of the Republic of [South] Korea was essential to Japan's own security." He elaborated in his speech, saying that if an attack on South Korea required the United States to use bases in Japan "for military combat operations to meet the armed attack, the policy of the Government of Japan towards prior consultation would be to decide its position positively and promptly."

Mr. Sato said in the communiqué that "the maintenance of peace and security in the Taiwan area was also a most important factor for the security of Japan." He added in his address that an armed attack from the outside "would be a threat to the peace and security of the Far East, including Japan," and the decision on the use of bases in Japan would be made in light of American treaty commitments to Nationalist China.

The issue of using bases in Okinawa and Japan to support American operations in South Vietnam, Japanese sources said, was the most difficult for Japan to handle because of the political opposition at home to the war there. The communiqué said the two governments would agree, before the reversion of Okinawa, on how reversion would be accomplished without affecting United States efforts in South Vietnam.

The Nixon-Sato Communique

Help in Peace-Keeping

Mr. Sato told his luncheon audience at the Press Club that Japan would be prepared to participate in "any international peace-keeping machinery which may be set up after cessation of hostilities." He also pledged Japanese help in rebuilding the South Vietnamese economy.

On Japan's enlarged role in Asia, Mr. Sato said that "Japan's self-defense capabilities are already filling an important role in securing the primary defense of Japan and it is our policy to continue to consolidate such capabilities."

He said that "the responsibilities that must be shouldered by Japan and the Western European countries in the 1970's will also be great."

Administration officials said that the commitments made by Mr. Sato in his address were not negotiated by Mr. Nixon and Mr. Sato. But they said the Premier informed Mr. Nixon of what he intended to say and that was taken into account by the United States in accepting the communiqué.

Special to The New York Times

WASHINGTON, Nov. 21— *Following is the text of the joint communiqué issued today by President Nixon and Premier Eisaku Sato of Japan:*

[1]

President Nixon and Prime Minister Sato met in Washington on Nov. 19, 20 and 21, 1969, to exchange views on the present international situation and on other matters of mutual interest to the United States and Japan.

[2]

The President and the Prime Minister recognized that both the United States and Japan have greatly benefited from their close association in a variety of fields, and they declared that, guided by their common principles of democracy and liberty, the two countries would maintain and strengthen their fruitful cooperation in the continuing search for world peace and prosperity and in particular for the relaxation of international tensions. The President expressed his and his Government's deep interest in Asia and stated his belief that the United States and Japan should cooperate in contributing to the peace and prosperity of the region. The Prime Minister stated that Japan would make further active contributions to the peace and prosperity of Asia.

[3]

The President and the Prime Minister exchanged frank views on the current international situation, with particular attention to developments in the Far East. The President, while emphasizing that the countries in the area were expected to make their own efforts for the stability of the area, gave assurance that the United States would continue to contribute to the maintenance of international peace and security in the Far East by honoring its defense treaty obligations in the area. The Prime Minister, appreciating the determination of the United States, stressed that it was important for the peace and security of the Far East that the United States should be in a position to carry out fully its obligations referred to by the President. He further expressed his recognition that, in the light of the present situation, the presence of United States forces in the Far East constituted a mainstay for the stability of the area.

[4]

The President and the Prime Minister specifically noted the continuing tension over the Korean peninsula. The Prime Minister deeply appreciated the peace-keeping efforts of the United Nations in the area and stated that the security of the Republic of Korea was essential to Japan's own security. The President and the Prime Minister shared the hope that Communist China would adopt a more cooperative and constructive attitude in its external relations. The President referred to the treaty obligations of his country to the Republic of China which the United States would uphold. The Prime Minister said that the maintenance of peace and security in the Taiwan area was also a most important factor for the security of Japan. The President described the earnest efforts made by the United States for a peaceful and just settlement of the Vietnam problem. The President and the Prime Minister expressed the strong hope that the war in Vietnam would be concluded before return of the administrative rights over Okinawa to Japan. In this connection, they agreed that, should peace in Vietnam not have been realized by the time reversion of Okinawa is scheduled to take place, the two Governments would fully consult with each other in the light of the situation at that time so that reversion would be accomplished without affecting the United States efforts to assure the South Vietnamese people the opportunity to determine their own political future without outside interference. The Prime Minister stated that Japan was exploring what role she could play in bringing about stability in the Indochina area.

[5]

In light of the current situation and the prospects in the Far East, the President and the Prime Minister agreed that they highly valued the role played by the Treaty of Mutual Cooperation and Security in maintaining the peace and security of the Far East including Japan, and they affirmed the intention of the two Governments firmly to maintain the treaty on the basis of mutual trust and common evaluation of the international situation. They further agreed that the two Governments should maintain close contact with each other on matters affecting the peace and security of the Far East,

including Japan, and on the implementation of the Treaty of Mutual Cooperation and Security.

[6]

The Prime Minister emphasized his view that the time had come to respond to the strong desire of the people of Japan, of both the mainland and Okinawa, to have the administrative rights over Okinawa returned to Japan on the basis of the friendly relations between the United States and Japan and thereby to restore Okinawa to its normal status. The President expressed appreciation of the Prime Minister's view. The President and the Prime Minister also recognized the vital role played by United States forces in Okinawa in the present situation in the Far East. As a result of their discussion it was agreed that the mutual security interests of the United States and Japan could be accommodated within arrangements for the return of the administrative rights over Okinawa to Japan. They therefore agreed that the two Governments would immediately enter into consultations regarding specific arrangements for accomplishing the early reversion of Okinawa without detriment to the security of the Far East, including Japan. They further agreed to expedite the consultations with a view to accomplishing the reversion during 1972, subject to the conclusion of these specific arrangements with the necessary legislative support. In this connection, the Prime Minister made clear the intention of his Government, following reversion, to assume gradually the responsibility for the immediate defense of Okinawa as part of Japan's defense efforts for her own territories. The President and the Prime Minister agreed also that the United States would retain, under the terms of the Treaty of Mutual Cooperation and Security, such military facilities and areas in Okinawa as required in the mutual security of both countries.

[7]

The President and the Prime Minister agreed that, upon return of the administrative rights, the Treaty of Mutual Cooperation and Security and its related arrangements would apply to Okinawa without modification thereof. In this connection, the Prime Minister affirmed the recognition of his Government that the security of Japan could not be adequately maintained without international peace and security in the Far East

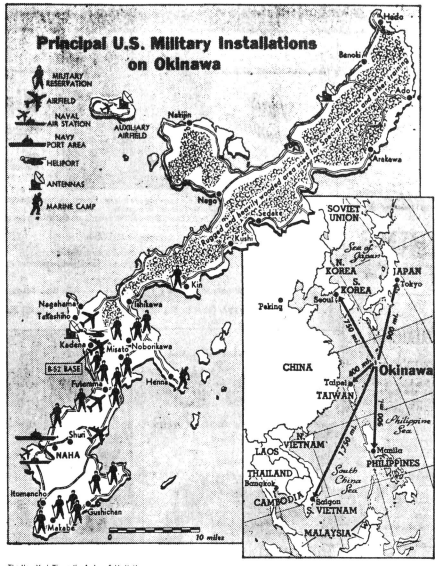

Principal U.S. Military Installations on Okinawa

MILITARY RESERVATION
AIRFIELD
NAVAL AIR STATION
NAVY PORT AREA
HELIPORT
ANTENNAS
MARINE CAMP

AUXILIARY AIRFIELD

Heda
Benoki
Ado
Nakijin
Arakawa
Nago
Sedake
Kushi
Kin
Nagahama
Takashiho
Ishikawa
Kadena
Misato—Noborikawa
B-52 BASE
Futenma
Henna
Shuri
NAHA
Itomancho
Gushichan
Makabe

Rugged and heavily wooded area used for Special Forces and other training

0   10 miles

SOVIET UNION
Sea of Japan
N. KOREA
JAPAN
Tokyo
S. KOREA
Seoul
Peking
CHINA
Okinawa
Taipei
TAIWAN
LAOS
N. VIETNAM
THAILAND
Bangkok
CAMBODIA
Saigon
S. VIETNAM
MALAYSIA
Philippine Sea
Manila
PHILIPPINES
South China Sea

The New York Times (by Andrew Sabbatini)   Nov. 22, 1969

The American installations cover nearly one-fourth of Okinawa. Besides the 28 shown on map there are 92 smaller ones. B-52 missions to Vietnam are staged from Kadena airfield.

and, therefore, the security of countries in the Far East was a matter of serious concern for Japan. The Prime Minister was of the view that, in the light of such recognition on the part of the Japanese Government, the return of the administrative rights over Okinawa in the manner agreed above should not hinder the effective discharge of the international obligations assumed by the United States for the defense of countries in the Far East, including Japan. The President replied that he shared the Prime Minister's view.

[8]

The Prime Minister described in detail the particular sentiment of the Japanese people against nuclear weapons and the policy of the Japanese Government reflecting such sentiment. The Pres-

ident expressed his deep understanding and assured the Prime Minister that, without prejudice to the position of the United States Government with respect to the prior consultation system under the Treaty of Mutual Cooperation and Security, the reversion of Okinawa would be carried out in a manner consistent with the policy of the Japanese Government as described by the Prime Minister.

[9]

The President and the Prime Minister took note of the fact that there would be a number of financial and economic problems, including those concerning United States business interests in Okinawa, to be solved between the two countries in connection with the transfer

of the administrative rights over Okinawa to Japan and agreed that detailed discussions relative to their solution would be initiated promptly.

[10]

The President and the Prime Minister, recognizing the complexity of the problems involved in the reversion of Okinawa, agreed that the two Governments should consult closely and cooperate on the measures necessary to assure a smooth transfer of administrative rights to the Japanese Government, in accordance with reversion arrangements to be agreed to by both Governments. They agreed that the United States-Japan Consultative Committee in Tokyo should undertake over-all responsibility for this preparatory work. The President and the Prime Minister decided to establish

in Okinawa a preparation commission in place of the existing advisory committee to the High Commissioner of the Ryukyu Islands for the purpose of consulting and coordinating locally on measures relating to preparation for the transfer of administrative rights, including necessary assistance to the government of the Ryukyu Islands. The preparatory commission will be composed of a representative of the Japanese Government with ambassadorial rank and the High Commissioner of the Ryukyu Islands, with the chief executive of the government of the Ryukyu Islands acting as adviser to the commission. The commission will report and make recommendations to the two Governments through the United States-Japan Consultative Committee.

[11]

The President and the Prime Minister expressed their conviction that a mutually satisfactory solution of the question of the return of the administrative rights over Okinawa to Japan, which is the last of the major issues between the two countries arising from World War II, would further strengthen United States-Japan relations, which are based on friendship and mutual trust and would make a major contribution to the peace and security of the Far East.

[12]

In their discussion of economic matters, the President and the Prime Minister noted the marked growth in economic relations between the two countries. They also acknowledged that the leading positions which their countries occupy in the world economy impose important responsibilities on each for the maintenance and strengthening of the international trade and monetary system, especially in the light of the current large imbalances in trade and payments. In this regard, the President stressed his determination to bring inflation in the United States under control. He also reaffirmed the commitment of the United States to the principle of promoting freer trade. The Prime Minister indicated the intention of the Japanese Government to accelerate rapidly the reduction of Japan's trade and capital restrictions. Specifically, he stated the intention of the Japanese Government to remove Japan's residual import-quota restrictions over a broad range of products by the end of 1971 and to make maximum efforts to accelerate the liberalization of the remaining items. He added that the Japanese Government intends to make periodic reviews of its liberalization program with a view to implementing trade liberalization at a more accelerated pace than hitherto. The President and the Prime Minister agreed that their respective actions would further solidify the foundation of over-all U.S.-Japan relations.

[13]

The President and the Prime Minister agreed that attention to the economic needs of the developing countries was essential to the development of international peace and stability. The Prime Minister stated the intention of the Japanese Government to expand and improve its aid programs in Asia, commensurate with the economic growth of Japan. The President welcomed this statement and confirmed that the United States would continue to con-tribute to the economic development of Asia. The President and Prime Minister recognized that there would be major requirements for the postwar rehabilitation of Vietnam and elsewhere in Southeast Asia. The Prime Minister stated the intention of the Japanese Government to make a substantial contribution to this end.

[14]

The Prime Minister congratulated the President on the successful moon landing of Apollo 12, and expressed the hope for a safe journey back to earth for the astronauts. The President and the Prime Minister agreed that the exploration of space offers great opportunities for expanding cooperation in peaceful scientific projects among all nations. In this connection, the Prime Minister noted with pleasure that the United States and Japan last summer had concluded an agreement on space cooperation. The President and the Prime Minister agreed that implementation of this unique program is of importance to both countries.

[15]

The President and the Prime Minister discussed prospects for the promotion of arms control and the slowing down of the arms race. The President outlined his Government's efforts to initiate the strategic arms limitations talks with the Soviet Union that have recently started in Helsinki. The Prime Minister expressed his Government's strong hopes for the success of these talks. The Prime Minister pointed out his country's strong and traditional interest in effective disarmament measures with a view to achievement of general and complete disarmament under strict and effective international control.

November 22, 1969

PEKING MAY SEND ENVOY TO MOSCOW

Agreement Is Reported on Ambassador Exchange

Special to The New York Times

MOSCOW, July 15 — Diplomatic sources said today that Communist China had agreed to send a new ambassador to Moscow.

Soviet and Western sources said the agreement by the Chinese was part of an agreement under which the two governments would exchange envoys. The two countries have not had ambassadors in each other's capital since 1966.

Western diplomats said such an exchange would signal an improvement in relations, which have been strained in recent years.

Reliable diplomatic sources said earlier this month that the Chinese had agreed to accept Vladimir I. Stepakov, a 58-year-old party ideologist, as the Soviet ambassador. At the time, it was not clear whether the Chi-nese would also send an ambassador to Moscow.

The diplomats said the identity of the Chinese ambassador was not known, although he was believed to hold the rank of deputy foreign minister.

May Take Posts Soon

Western diplomats said that if the agreement were enacted, it was probable that the new ambassadors would take their posts this summer.

In 1966, when the ideological dispute between the Chinese and the Russians accelerated, Moscow withdrew Ambassador Sergei G. Lapin and Peking recalled Pan Tzu-li. Since then the two nations have maintained relations at the level of chargés d'affaires

Polemics between the two countries have subsided recently. The last Soviet attack on China was on May 18. The last Chinese attack was a month later.

The two governments have been negotiating their border disputes since October in Peking. The Soviet representative at the talks has been the First Deputy Foreign Minister, Vasily V. Kuznetsov, who returned to Moscow last month. Soviet officials have indicated that his place may be taken by a Deputy Foreign Minister, Leonid F Ilyichev.

July 16, 1970

CHAPTER 9

Reconstruction Era
1970–72

*Nixon's meeting with Mao
in Peking, February 1972.*

China: Maoist Man

By SEYMOUR TOPPING
Special to The New York Times

PEKING, June 19 — The doctrines of the Cultural Revolution have been translated into new Communist dogma. Under Mao Tse-tung that dogma has propelled China into a continuing revolution that is producing a new society and a new "Maoist man."

Relative stability, prosperity and surface tranquillity have been restored with the end of the convulsive mass conflicts and great purge generated by the Cultural Revolution, which began in 1966 as a power struggle between Chairman Mao and Liu Shaochi, then Chief of State and since deposed amid charges that he had deviated from revolutionary principles.

Mr. Mao believes that he has interrupted an evolution that was turning China into a society on the Soviet model, characterized by a privileged bureaucracy and tendencies toward a rebirth of capitalism in industry and agriculture.

The gigantic Maoist thought-remolding program has profound implications not only for the 800 million Chinese but also for the world. It is producing a highly disciplined, ideologically militant population that is taught that Mr. Mao is the sole heir of Marx and Lenin and the interpreter and defender of their doctrine and that each Chinese must be committed to fostering a world Communist society.

Even so, underlying tensions persist in the party hierarchy and at the grass roots as the ideological struggle to resolve what Mr. Mao describes as "contradictions among ourselves" goes forward.

"We have won a great victory," the leader says, echoed by his designated successor, Vice Chairman Lin Piao. "But the defeated class will still struggle. These people are still around and this class still exists. Therefore, we cannot speak of final victory, not even for decades."

In virtually every factory and on every agricultural commune toured by this reporter during a five-week visit, army propaganda teams originally sent three or four years ago were still struggling to root out what they regard as subversive thinking. All economic enterprises and schools were festooned with posters denouncing "the renegade traitor Liu Shao-Chi," who took the capitalist path by encouraging money incentives.

Corrosion and Individualism

"Material incentives corrode man's soul and make up a hotbed for creating individualism," said Tien Chi-ching, a party leader in Anshan, the big iron and steel center in the northeastern region.

To sustain what the Maoists consider to be ideological purity and progress toward the eventual classless society, a tighter nationwide system of ideological surveillance, purge and re-education has been instituted.

Government administrators and managers of economic enterprises have been locked into a "revolutionary committee" system of supervision under which their work is monitored by delegates of the army, the reconstituted Communist party and militant workers or peasants. Deviation from Maoist principles can land them in peasant villages or special schools, where they stay for several months to several years doing manual labor while undergoing ideological re-education.

An entire generation of students, young people attending secondary schools and universities when the Cultural Revolution began, have been ideologically screened, purged and re-educated. Hundreds of thousands have been sent to the villages to do manual labor under the surveillance of peasants and to be reindoctrinated, many without any hope of resuming their formal educations.

Hundreds of the so-called May 7 schools—the date appears on a letter from Mr. Mao to Mr. Lin, who pioneered them — have been established throughout the country and members of the bureaucracy, intellectuals and technicians are being run through in rotation.

At a school in Peking's eastern suburbs there are such "students" as Ming Kuai-san, 38, a former deputy chief of the education division of the Cultural Bureau in Peking. He works as a laborer in a rice paddy while undergoing reindoctrination. Mrs. Hsu Ying, 26, a teacher, labors as a masonry worker. Tien Chi-chen, former vice chairman of now-disbanded trade unions in the eastern district of the capital, makes water pails in a school-run factory.

The ideological atmosphere is intense. For a Westerner there is something frightening about the Peking regime's ability to summon as many as half a million people in a major city, red banners flying and drums beating, to shout tirelessly in unison and, given the slogan, welcome a friend or denounce an enemy.

There is no convincing evidence that Premier Chou Enlai's recent pragmatic gestures toward non-Communist states, including his Ping-Pong flirtation with the United States, represent any retreat from the underlying Maoist objective of world revolution.

There is also no evidence of an inclination at any level toward involvement in foreign military adventures. The prime emphasis in domestic propaganda is on consolidating the Cultural Revolution and building the economy.

During a tour of cities and countryside, in discussions with party and government officials, with managers of factories and farms, with professional men and women and ordinary peasants and workers, the writer gained the impression that Maoist principles were taking effective hold.

Apart from the influence of unending propaganda and organizational disciplines, the peasants and workers who make up the great bulk of the population are apparently favorable to the system because they believe they have a stake in it. Many members of this class say that their material living standards have never been better.

Ordinary Chinese carry themselves with a new dignity and respond to the exhortations of the party, which tells them, "You are the masters of the new society." The memory of foreign privilege—such as the restrictions in clubs and the old park sign in the Shanghai foreign concession saying "No dogs or Chinese"— have receded before new pride in China's unity and its status in the world.

The improvement in the physical condition of the people since the Communist takeover in 1949 is staggering.

Hordes of beggars and of the starving and diseased that once were familiar are gone. The people look healthy and are obviously adequately fed and clad although clothing is often worn and there is uniform dullness in blue and gray tunics over inevitable baggy pants.

Basic Income Is Assured

As the hot June days settled on Peking a few bright long cotton skirts appeared and some of the girls fluffed their hair a bit instead of wearing it severely short or in tight braids.

The state assures each family a basic income sufficient to feed and house itself. Living standards are below those of Japan or Taiwan but seem uniformly adequate in the Asian context. The writer wandered unescorted down some back streets and village lanes without seeing sanitary conditions as bad as in New York ghettos.

Although tremendous improvements have been wrought by the Communists, the favorable contrast with the past is also attributable simply to a period of peace and unity.

Prior to the Communist victory China had been a victim of Japanese invasion and of civil war for 27 years. Brutal living conditions resulted from the constant turmoil as well as from the shortcomings of the Government of Generalissimo Chiang Kai-shek.

The great coastal cities look more drab than before largely because Western adornment and consumer goods have vanished and the bright lights have gone out. The cities are more typically Chinese, integrated closely with the economy of the interior rather than dependent on foreign luxury trade.

Construction Is Spread

Chairman Mao, determined to reduce the gap in living standards between city and village, has had investment in new construction spread throughout the country. "In the interior most of our factory equipment is new," Premier Chou, day-to-day manager of government affairs, said.

With the notable exception of Peking, which has been spruced up for the role of a great world capital, the cities have lagged in housing construction. Old foreign and Chinese buildings have been painstakingly preserved but many still look scruffy.

Pressure on the cities has been eased by Peking's policy of moving surplus workers and ideological unreliables, particularly students, en masse into the countryside. Nearly a million from Shanghai alone have been shipped to the villages.

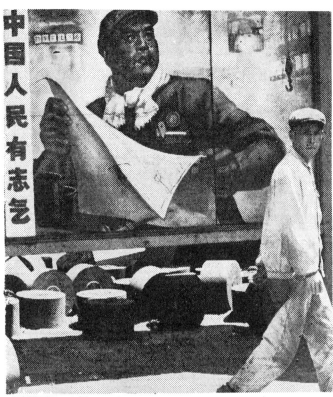

POSTER outside Anshan steel complex proclaims the Chinese have the drive to excel

The New York Times/Audrey Topping

In a flight over central China, the new construction a visitor observes is mainly factories and central agricultural commune buildings. Otherwise the clusters of mud and brick houses with thatched and tile roofs that stand beside pampered fields —vivid green rice paddies in the south, then brown wheat beyond the Yellow River — look unchanged, though the landscape is gashed by great water-conservation projects.

The markets in towns and villages are full of food and there seems to be a plentiful supply of basic consumer goods, though high prices on more choice consumer items impose a form of indirect rationing.

The process of leveling up the living conditions of the masses has been accompanied by a leveling down of the status and material rewards of the political and managerial bureaucracy.

According to Government sources, monthly wages in urban areas range from 34 yuan to 108 yuan (about $14 to $45 at the going rate). In factories wages are fixed in eight grades according to skill, length of experience and ideological reliability. Only a relatively few technicians, managers and senior officials get salaries substantially higher than this scale.

The head of a mine in Anshan was earning 108, while a political chief of a big Shenyang machine-tool plant was getting 140. A master iron carver in Peking who had worked at his bench for 30 years was earning 100 yuan. In a Chengchow textile plant the chief engineer is paid 188 yuan while the head of the plant gets 166.

If a skilled worker has a wife holding a job, family income may exceed that of the head of a factory.

Specific titles—and elegant manners and fine dress—are frowned upon. A manager of a big enterprise, unless pressed, will identify himself solely as "a responsible member" of a revolutionary committee.

In Anshan a visitor was received by the head of a factory producing alarm clocks for export. He wore a brown tunic and dark trousers of slightly better texture than those of his workers.

Dressed for the Occasion

An accompanying party official glanced at the factory chief, who had been through a rigorous course of criticism for ideological failings and said that he had put on his best clothes to receive visitors. While the factory chief flushed and nodded, the party man said he would put on his working clothes as soon as the visitors left.

In Peking top Government and party officials live at secret locations, presumably in the fine state residences that can be seen around the capital. However, they all entertain in public buildings. They arrive at receptions in chauffeured cars that usually are several years old. In public there is no display of affluence and their dress is austere.

Mr. Mao has put the bureaucracy into a vise out of the conviction that the corruption of his society may begin with the emergence of new Mandarin classes. He is often suspicious of intellectuals and technicians, believing that only workers and peasants as a class can be fully trusted.

Foreign experts ask how long the members of the bureaucracy, who are required to perform periodic manual labor as part of the process of "integrating with the masses," can stand the situation.

Some of the experts say that many members of the bureaucracy are simply "bending like young bamboo" in the ideological wind, waiting for another change. With the most virulent phase of the Cultural Revolution over, a restoration of Mandarin attitudes is detected.

To allow Mr. Chou to get on with the business of pushing the country forward again economically and of coping with the imperatives of foreign policy, extreme leftist tendencies have been curbed.

Two Politburo members in the extremist faction, Chiang Ching, wife of Mr. Mao, and Kang Sheng, who had been concerned with security matters, seem to have lost some influence. A third, Chen Po-ta, formerly Mr. Mao's secretary, has not been seen publicly since August, 1970.

Although there has been some easing of pressures, Chairman Mao has not deviated from his fundamental line—egalitarianism and self-reliance, all in a spartan manner. Despite some rumble deep in Chinese society, Mr. Mao and his supporters are firmly in command as the Chinese Communist party prepares to celebrate the 50th anniversary of its founding on July 1.

Mr. Mao is 78 years old and is believed to be in failing health, but his disciples have already enshrined "the great helmsman" and his ideology in much the same way that Lenin lives in the Soviet pantheon. Mr. Mao's voluminous writings have become scripture not only for ideologues but also for peasants in their daily life.

However, the regime may have a problem of succession because virtually all the top leaders are in their sixties and seventies.

Mr. Lin, Mr. Mao's "close comrade in arms" who was designated his successor in the 1969 party constitution, is 63. Bouts of tuberculosis have left him in poor health. Mr. Chou, a tireless dynamo, is 72.

The rising star is Huang Yung-sheng, 64, army chief of staff and Politburo member. A tough disciplinarian who has been close to Mr. Lin, he was brought to Peking from Canton during the Cultural Revolution after he had crushed rampaging extremist Red Guards.

Presumably he would have the support of the army should Mr. Lin die. Army men already occupy powerful posts in every phase and on every stratum of economic and political life.

There is no reason to believe that Mr. Huang would deflect China from the course set by "the great helmsman."

Leftists in China Seeking Power By Rebuilding Party Structure

Special to The New York Times

HONG KONG, July 12—Ultraleftists in Communist China, who formed a militant force that had its headiest moments in the heyday of the Red Guard movement, are making a strong bid for a bigger share of power from their old base, Shanghai, in the view of political analysts here.

The medium through which they are seeking more power is the Communist party. Today the left, which played a vanguard role in the destruction of the old party apparatus during the early period of the Cultural Revolution, which began in 1966, is the political group most keen to see it rebuilt. It hopes to insure that the leftist "rebels" will be well represented in the party structure.

The top leaders in Shanghai are Chang Chun-chiao and Yao Wen-yuan. Both of them are close associates of Chiang Ching, the wife of Chairman Mao Tse-tung, who has been identified with the political left. Shanghai is still more leftist than any other city in China and is pushing ahead with party reconstruction while most of the country is only talking about it.

2 Committees in Shanghai

Top municipal officials in Shanghai celebrated the formation of a party committee in a factory on July 1. This was the second factory to form a party committee in Shanghai in less than two weeks.

The left's bid for power is meeting with little support in Peking and strong resistance in most provinces. When Revolutionary Committees were formed to fill the power vacuum resulting from the destruction of the party apparatus, the left was prevented by the army and party officials who had survived the purges from gaining significant power. Today, the military and top civilian officials are continuing to resist leftist pressures.

In Peking, there is still something of a power vacuum because the contending elements appear to have reached something of a stalemate. This is a vacuum that leftists may yet fill if they gain enough support in the hierarchy, perhaps from Chairman Mao himself, to counter moderate forces.

These leftists are an amalgam of many radical elements, including students and younger bureaucrats with little or no power before 1966 who had hoped to benefit from the Cultural Revolution. Two of their most prominent members are Mr. Chang and Mr. Yao, both of Shanghai, who helped Chairman Mao start the Cultural Revolution to strengthen his own position and purge his enemies. Both were elected to the ruling Politburo of the Central Committee in April during the ninth party congress.

Press Shows Differences

The differences between Peking and Shanghai are reflected in the press of the two cities. China News Analysis, a weekly Hong Kong newsletter, noted in a recent issue that the chief party newspaper in Peking, Jenmin Jih Pao, seemed empty, containing "no directives about essential lines of national life nor about the economy."

It added: "The impression is given that the party congress decided nothing, that the men on top could not agree."

The difference between the Shanghai and Peking press is noticeable in their respective treatment of Chiang Ching. Shanghai treats her with more respect than Peking. An item from Peking reported that "revolutionary" theatrical works had been staged in the capital to mark the party anniversary but did not mention the name of Miss Chiang, who in the past had been praised for her role in introducing these new art forms.

However, an item from Shanghai reported that a Peking opera and a ballet with revolutionary themes had been staged in that city and paid tribute to Miss Chiang's leadership in the cultural fields.

A recent issue of the Shanghai paper Wen Hui Pao carried a story about the "revolution in Peking opera, ballet and symphony," which it described as a "life and death, close, hand-to-hand struggle."

The paper declared: "Despite the devious attempts by Liu-Shao-chi and his accomplices to oppose and sabotage this revolution, a final and magnificent victory was won in the revolutionary literature and art field after repeated and hard struggles under the leadership of Comrade Chiang Ching."

July 13, 1969

Chinese Reds Emphasizing Unity of Leadership

By TILLMAN DURDIN
Special to The New York Times

HONG KONG, Oct. 9—Communist China has begun to show a new concern with emphasizing the collective unity of the country's top leadership.

Observers here are uncertain just what this means. Some believe it could be an effort to counteract the effect of continued factional differences known to exist in the leadership. Others think it may be designed to present to the Soviet Union an impression of Chinese unity at a time of friction over their common frontier.

The new approach was first indicated Sept. 21 in a quotation from an editorial in a newspaper in Tibet that was broadcast from Lhasa. The broadcast, monitored here, urged everyone to give prominence to "unified and collective leadership."

And last Friday, the Lhasa radio broadcast a speech by Tseng Yung-ya, head of Tibet's Revolutionary Committee, in which the phrase again appeared. A similar phrase, "cen-tralized and unified leadership," appeared Friday in a broadcast from Hunan and Saturday in a broadcast from Canton.

The two phrases are new and have attracted the attention of specialists in Chinese affairs here.

The word "collective" caused special interest because Communist China has not used the term to describe its leadership since 1957.

Although there has been a diminishing lately in the amount of adulation lavished on Chairman Mao Tse-tung, there has been no decrease in references to his primary role in national affairs.

His leadership and the supremacy of his thought were emphasized over and over again in the speeches, editorials and slogans that were a part of celebrations of the 20th anniversary of Communist rule on Oct. 1.

There is therefore a reluctance here to believe that the sudden appearance of the new phrases represents any lessening of Mr. Mao's importance.

October 10, 1969

CHINA IS ADAMANT ON INTELLECTUALS

Says They Must Work as Peasants or in Factories

By TILLMAN DURDIN
Special to The New York Times

HONG KONG, May 23—A policy editorial made public by Peking today emphasized that there would be no easing of the drive to keep millions of intellectuals and officials laboring as peasants and factory workers.

The editorial, published jointly in Jenmin Jih Pao, the official Peking newspaper, Chiehfang Chun Pao, the army newspaper, and the Communist party's ideological journal, Hung Chi, told intellectuals and cadre members that they must "completely shift their stand to the side of the proletariat" through "a long and even painful process of tempering."

The editorial, relayed here by Hsinhua, the Chinese Communist press agency, was written to commemorate the 28th anniversary of a series of talks given at Yenan in 1942 by the Communist party chairman, Mao Tse-tung, on literature and art.

Many Sent to Countryside

The talks dealt with the necessity for writers, artists and other intellectuals to accept the proletarian viewpoint, destroy the bourgeois outlook and remold their ideology in class struggle.

In a movement inaugurated during the political purges of the Cultural Revolution, which began in 1966, intellectuals were assigned to settle in rural areas or to work in industrial establishments. Many party and government officials were ordered to similar activity, usually carried out in special schools in which they follow a routine of manual labor on farms and in industrial enterprises while undergoing political re-education.

Since the term intellectuals in China can apply to anyone with only a moderate amount of formal schooling, the number of people sent to labor as intellectuals is believed to total many hundreds of thousands and possibly millions.

In addition, three million officials are known to be undergoing the process of remolding through manual labor and ideological study, chiefly in the thoughts of Mao Tse-tung.

'Remold World Outlook'

The joint editorial today reminded the intellectuals and officials that they must carry out their new activities wholeheartedly and not think it is to be for just a short time.

"We must be resolute," the editorial stated, "do away with bureaucratic, apathetic, arrogant and finicky airs, go into the midst of workers, peasants and soldiers. throw ourselves into the revolutionary movements of class struggle, the struggle for production and the struggle for scientific experiment, persist in taking part in productive labor, criticize and repudiate the bourgeoisie and remold our world outlook."

The fact that the policy statement was published as a joint editorial in the three major official publications indicates the extent of the problems that the authorities are having with the intellectuals and officials and emphasizes the importance attached to the issue.

Many of those sent to rural areas are known to have deserted their lifetime assignments and drifted back to cities. Others pursue their new lives apathetically and feel they no longer have any satisfying future.

May 24, 1970

Debate in China on Economics Turning Into Political Struggle

Special to The New York Times

HONG KONG, March 28—A debate that could have far-reaching political repercussions is in progress in the Chinese Communist press over fundamental economic issues.

The debate centers on whether China should follow pragmatic policies, aimed at increasing production by giving workers material incentives, or adhere to the Maoist precepts that political indoctrination is the key to economic progress.

While the issues are essentially economic, the debate is developing into a political struggle in which the conservative elements of China's leadership are ranged on one side and the more radical elements on the other.

The debate began with an article that appeared in the official Peking newspaper Jenmin Jih Pao on March 12. The paper's main article, it was spread over the top half of the first page. It explained how workers in Tientsin, a leading industrial center and port, had learned through study to make a distinction between "what is right and wrong." It offered a semantic compromise by couching pragmatic policies in ideologically acceptable.

Seek to Curb Army

The radicals appear to have a two-fold purpose of imposing Maoist economic doctrines on factories and other industrial enterprises and undermining the influence of the army "propaganda teams" stationed there. The army's influence is believed to have been conservative and pragmatic.

This tactical maneuver conforms with the radicals' overall strategy of attempting to increase their political power through the party apparatus, largely destroyed in the Cultural Revolution, which is now slowly being rebuilt. They have stressed the importance of party leadership over factories and discounted the role of the army teams.

The present debate underlines the dissension that continues to exist within the hierarchy of China in the wake of the Cultural Revolution, which began in 1966. The Cultural Revolution was partly aimed at resolving political and economic differences by eliminating the chief opponents of Mao Tse-tung, the Communist party chairman. While many top officials, including Liu Shao-chi, the former head of state, were purged, the Cultural Revolution generated new conflicts and created new power groupings.

The debate comes at a time when China's economic controls have been bypassed by speculators and black-marketeers on a wide scale throughout the country. Complaints about "corruption, speculation and theft" have been repeatedly aired in broadcasts from many provinces. Black-market trading has even been reported in grain and cotton, items that were formerly handled only by the state under rigid controls.

Solutions to Problem Differ

The conservative or pragmatic elements among China's leaders apparently believe the problem should be tackled by giving greater care and consideration to the workers' welfare in conjunction with the imposition of necessary discipline by the authorities. The radical elements see the present "anarchistic" trend as a threat to China's socialist structure and advocate more strict adherence to Maoist policies, ideological indoctrination and production "innovations" by the workers instead of relying on experts.

Another article in Jenmin Jih Pao on March 16 continued the pragmatists' argument, saying that while it is wrong to "put money prizes in command" or advocate "material incentives," it is quite another matter to recommend the "socialist system of rewards and penalties" and "caring for the mass livelihood."

A counterattack against the pragmatism inherent in the two articles came in the form of an editorial first published in Liaoning Province and reprinted in Jenmin Jih Pao.

The editorial delivered a sweeping attack on the "sinister trash of putting profit in command, putting professional work in command, putting technique in command and putting bonus in command."

Linking these ideological heresies to Liu Shao-chi, the editorial said they were "the chief measures of the revisionist line in controlling enterprises and they must be exposed, criticized and resolutely eliminated."

March 29, 1970

LOCAL ARMY ROLE WIDENED IN CHINA

Military Leaders Gain Even More Power in Provinces

By TILLMAN DURDIN
Special to The New York Times

HONG KONG, June 13—Recent changes in the ruling provincial Revolutionary Committees of Communist China show continued gains by military men at the expense of those who were the earliest and most ardent supporters of the Maoist Cultural Revolution.

Reports on provincial radios of recent provincial rallies, notably those summoned to hail the May 2d statement of Chairman Mao Tse-tung, the party leader, calling for world revolution against "U. S. imperialism," have enabled specialists in Chinese affairs here to get a better reading on provincial power structures.

Scores of new names have appeared on provincial committee lists, and many are military men. The new assignments reflect, in particular, a tightening of military influence in border provinces adjoining the Soviet Union.

In many instances changes of personnel in the Revolutionary Committees, which were formed in 1967-68 to perform administrative functions of the shattered party and governmental bodies, show that individuals who were purged in the early days of the Cultural Revolution are back in office, seemingly rehabilitated but always in posts geographically remote from those they occupied originally.

Major Shifts in 3 Areas

Provincial lists show major shake-ups appear to have occurred in Shantung, Shansi and Kweichow with a loss of position for Maoist activists who early in the Cultural Revolution gained power by turning against alleged "revisionists" leaders.

In Shansi, Liu Ko-ping appears to have been removed as chairman of the Revolutionary Committee. He has not been mentioned on recent lists from Taiyuan, the provincial capital. The same is true of Chang Jih-ching, who became political commissar during the Cultural Revolution, and Chen Chin-yu, the provincial military commander and a member of the Revolutionary Committee.

Mr. Chang and Mr. Liu had long been at odds, and this is believed to be one of the reasons why Shansi in 1968 and 1969 had factional strife bordering on open warfare.

The new commander for Shansi, recent lists show, is Hsieh Chen-hua, who has also been identified as "principal responsible member of the provincial Revolutionary Committee." This seems to make him the equivalent of provincial chairman. Formerly he was deputy political commissar of Shansi.

In Kweichow, Li Tsai-han, the Revolutionary Committee chief, has dropped from public view, and Lan Yi-nung, described as a leading member of the Kunming regional military command with authority over Kweichow, has recently been performing the functions of chief of province.

Mr. Lan appears to be working with Ho Kuang-yu, provincial commander in Kweichow and vice chairman of the Revolutionary Committee, in exercising control over the province.

In Shantung Wang Hsiao-yu has dropped from view and Yang Teh-chih, commander of the Tsinan military region, appears to be the chief executive of the province.

In Hunan, Li Yuan has not appeared in listings at provincial rallies recently, and Pu Chan-ya, a deputy political commissar of the Canton military region, which embraces Hunan, is being shown with the new title of vice chairman of Hunan and May, in fact, be exercising the functions of chairman.

Scene Close to Lin Piao

The majority of provincial committee chairmen have all along been military men. Recent changes have added to the military coloration.

Important changes in the power structures have also occurred in Fukien, Szechwan, Yunnan, Sinkiang and Heilungkiang, strategic border provinces. In these provinces high ranking military men, shifted from other posts, serve in provincial or regional commands and concurrently on provincial Revolutionary Committees.

A number of the military men who have appeared in the provinces have had long associations with Defense Minister Lin Piao.

The pattern that emerges seems to suggest continued gains by more law-and-order-minded individuals as opposed to those inclined to agitational, radical activty.

In Shanghai, a municipality equal in administrative importance to a province, leftist power still seems strong. There

Chang Chun-chiao has not only kept his position as chairman of the Revolutionary Committee but, as a member of the Politburo of the Communist party. was listed recently in the No. 6 position in the national rankings, ahead of Huang Yungsheng, chief of staff of the armed forces.

June 19, 1970

PEKING RESHAPES ITS STATE COUNCIL

Some Ministries Merge and a New Minister Is Named

Special to The New York Times

HONG KONG, Aug. 1—Evidence has appeared in the press of Communist China that the State Council, or Cabinet, has undergone a reorganization. A new minister has been appointed while the work previously undertaken by four ministries is now in the hands of two.

The reorganization is the first sign of any attempt by Chinese leaders to rebuild the state administrative apparatus, which was seriously weakened by the convulsions and purges of the Cultural Revolution.

The first sign of change within the State Council was contained in a report by Hsinhua, the Chinese press agency, on the departure of a Chinese Government delegation for Iraq. The report said the delegation was headed by Chien Chih-kuang, who was identified as "Minister of Light Industry." He was formerly a deputy minister of the textile industry.

The report disclosed not only Peking's first ministerial appointment since the Cultural Revolution, which was launched in 1966, but also the merger of two ministries. A single Ministry of Light Industry has now replaced the former First and Second Ministries of Light Industry.

Another Change Reported

Another change was disclosed in a broadcast from Hunan Province, which reported the opening of a national symposium on rice-transplanting machines in a town near Changsha, the provincial capital. According to the broadcast, the symposium was convened by the First Ministry of Machine Building and Hsu Pin-chou, who was

identified as a "responsible person of the First Ministry of Machine Building," made an important speech.

Formerly there were eight ministries of machine building. The first was held responsible for machinery and equipment for civilian use while the second to seventh were concerned with military equipment and the production of armaments. The eighth ministry was responsible for agricultural machinery and equipment.

As the symposium on rice-transplanting machines was convened by the First Ministry of Machine Building, it is assumed here that the first and eighth ministries have been merged. Confirmation for this assumption is seen in the fact that Mr. Hsu, now described as a "responsible person of the First Ministry" was a deputy minister of the Eighth Ministry

New Congress Possible

These developments have been interpreted among some political analysts here as a possible prelude to a meeting of the

National People's Congress— Communist China's equivalent of a legislature—which has not convened for more than five years. The congress gives official endorsment to State Council appointments and other senior positions, including that of head of state, a position that remains unfilled.

The last session of the congress concluded in January, 1965, with the re-election of Liu Shao-chi as head of state. But in October, 1968, Peking announced that the Communist party's Central Committee had divested Mr. Liu of all party and state positions.

Much has yet to be done in reorganizing the state apparatus before it will function normally again. The last National People's Congress approved the appointment of 16 deputy premiers. One has died and eight were victims of the Cultural Revolution purges. Of the remaining seven, only two, Lin Piao and Li Hsien-nien, are still accorded the title of deputy premier and are active in public

August 2, 1970

Chinese Reds Rebuilding Shattered Youth League

By NORMAN WEBSTER
© 1970 The Globe and Mail, Toronto

PEKING, Aug. 22—Like its parent, the Chinese Communist party, the young Communist League is gradually rising from the ashes. Both were destroyed as functioning bodies during the Cultural Revolution, which began in 1966.

Membership of the youth league in its previous incarnation was estimated at more than 25 million, ranging in age from 15 to 25, and the organization was an important part of the party machine.

In 1966, however, with the full backing of Mao Tse-tung, the party chairman, the student Red Guards became the most important movement in China, and both party and league fell before their onslaught.

The country's central leadership seems to have decided the league would eventually be reconstructed along with the party and not replaced by the Red Guards. Since the ninth party congress last year, party and league have been rebuilding concurrently, although reports about the junior organi-

zation have been scattered and few.

'Worthy Successors' Cited

Indeed the party theoretical journal, Hung Chi, has not taken up the question of the youth league until now. Its latest issue firmly endorses the need to reconstruct the league "to train worthy successors to the revolutionary cause of the proletariat."

Chairman Mao's belief that the heirs to his revolution were not being correctly molded and tempered was one of his motives in launching the Cultural Revolution.

Hung Chi reported on the rebuilding of the youth league branch in a farming production brigade in Shensi Province. The decision to highlight a rural unit was undoubtedly deliberate.

Millions upon millions of young people have been sent to live in the countryside in the last few years, and it is important to the Peking leadership that their enthusiasm be roused and channeled, leisure time organized and potential discontent allayed.

Not surprisingly, the article concludes with a vision of young people who have fostered the concept of farming for the revolution wholeheartedly, thus bringing into play the role of the youth league as a shock force in building the new socialist countryside.

Potential members, it is emphasized, must "have a strong sense of revolutionary organization and discipline and have done good work in enhancing revolutionary unity." The anarchistic tendencies of the Red Guard will obviously not be allowed in the new league.

Another echo of the moderate line being taken is the instruction that old league members who made mistakes in the past —even serious ones—are to be allowed to re-educate themselves and regain their membership.

The results in the Shensi production brigade are said to have been good. But, the Hung Chi article concedes, opposition and apathy had to be overcome.

It said: "Some youth league members had a lack of revolutionary vigilance against the disruptive activities of the class enemy. Some were not concerned about the socialist collective economy owing to the pernicious influence of the spontaneous bourgeois trend. Some lacked revolutionary vitality and vigor and feared hardship."

This was one of several passages in the Chinese version that does appear in excerpts that have just been published in English by Hsinmua, the Chinese press agency.

Chinese Army Gets an Ideological Chief

Special to The New York Times

HONG KONG, Sept. 7—Peking has disclosed a new senior appointment within Communist China's armed forces that came as a surprise to specialists in Chinese military affairs here.

Reports by Hsinhua, the Chinese press agency, on officials present at two recent functions in Peking marking the 25th anniversary of North Vietnam's independence from France identified Li Teh-sheng, a former army corps commander who was elected an alternate member of the Politburo last year, as director of the general political department of the Peoples Liberation Army.

In this capacity, Mr. Li, who was lifted from obscurity to national prominence by the Cultural Revolution, wields considerable power as the ideological watchdog of the armed forces.

The general political department is responsible for supervising political work and ideological indoctrination within all military units.

Never in Politics

Mr. Li has not previously had experience in handling political affairs. He has always been a commander of troops and never a political commissar. Military specialists accordingly regarded his appointment as a departure from normal procedures.

Some military specialists expressed a belief that his appointment represented a tactical gain for the leftist forces in China and their mentor, Chiang Ching, wife of the Communist party chairman Mao Tse-tung. They said Mr. Li had no known historical affiliations with either the Defense Minister, Lin Piao, or Huang Yung-sheng, chief of the general staff of the Peoples Liberation Army, the two key figures within the military establishment, which is considered a conservative stronghold.

The specialists said he did, however, have links with Chiang Ching and with Shanghai, the leftist stronghold and headquarters of the central core of radical thinking.

Commanded a Corps

Mr. Li is military and administrative chief of Anhwei Province, which together with Chekiang and Kiangsu falls under the jurisdiction of the Nanking military region. He was a corps commander in Chekiang as the Cultural Revolution got under way, and was sent with his unit to Anhwei early in 1967 when that province was the scene of Red Guard turmoil and heavy armed fighting between rival factions.

Subsequently he was appointed commander of the Anhwei provincial military district and in April of 1968 became chairman of the new provincial revolutionary committee. A year later he was elected by the Communist party's Central Committee to the Politburo.

Some specialists in military affairs said they did not believe that the leftists were strong enough to push through a military appointment that Lin Piao or Huang Yung-sheng would object to. However, they described Mr. Li as a surprising choice and added that he could represent a compromise acceptable to the left and moderate elements.

Chiang Ching, who as a rule appears in public in a military uniform, has in the past extended her influence into the sphere of military affairs.

The General Political Department ceased functioning in 1967 after the former director, Hsiao Hua, and Deputy Director Liu Chih-chien were purged. Both men survived the early stages of the Cultural Revolution but were later reported to have quarreled with Chiang Ching, who at that time was playing a role within the armed forces as adviser to its Cultural Revolution group.

Last November, Hsinhua disclosed that the General Political Department was functioning normally again by reporting that a deputy director was among other Chinese leaders welcoming the arrival in Peking of an Albanian art troupe.

While Mr. Li's appointment may represent an effort by one faction or another to establish new checks and balances within the armed forces, most analysts believe that the military man exerting the most influence today, below the ranks of Mao and Lin, is the Army chief, Huang Yung-sheng.

Communist theaters in Hong Kong are currently screening films of two public appearances by Mao and other top leaders during May. On each occasion Huang appeared as a dominant, self-assured personality, who strode confidently to one side or slightly ahead of Mao, clearing a path for the leader or introducing him to others present.

September 8, 1970

PEKING BOLSTERS MILITARY IN PARTY

By TILLMAN DURDIN
Special to The New York Times

HONG KONG, Nov. 28—Evidence from Communist China is growing that the Communist party, now being slowly reconstituted after the purges of the Cultural Revolution, will have a military component in its controlling organs from the highest to the lowest level.

The role of the military is borne out by the composition of additional hsien (county) party committees that have been set up recently. Such committees began to be formed about a year ago in an effort to re-establish party agencies at the local level, but the reconstitution has been slow.

New committees in Honan Province are being formed in accordance with the principle of a "dual three-way alliance," consisting of a grouping of youths, middle-aged and oldsters and of military representatives, rehabilitated former party officials and of new leaders of the masses.

Top-level organs, the Central Committee and the Politburo are already organized with a military component. This was done at a party congress in April, 1969.

Factions Are a Problem

The efforts to establish party organs at lower levels seem to have been slowed by factional differences and the leadership's feeling that protracted indoctrination and the weeding out of undesirable elements were still necessary.

Of the 21 full members of the Politburo, 12 are military men. Of the 170 full members of the Central Committee, roughly 50 per cent are military.

The three-way-alliance concept grew up during the Cultural Revolution and permitted the leadership to integrate antagonistic factions into new governmental administrative

August 23, 1970

agencies called revolutionary committees.

The draft of a new Constitution due to be adopted at a forthcoming National People's Congress (legislature) enshrines the three-way principle as a permanent feature of all governmental agencies. Article 11 states: "Leadership organs must practice the revolutionary three-in-one combination between army personnel, cadres and masses and between the old, the middle-aged and the young."

It now seems evident that the same combination is being applied to the rebuilding of a parallel party structure from top to bottom. In the lowest-level party committees, those in industrial establishments, collective farms and social institutions, the military are usually represented by militia leaders, but at county level the military men are believed to be in many cases commissars accustomed to serving in political posts.

Instruments of Control

Military representatives were installed in ministries and other central government agencies as instruments of control during the turbulent 1967-68 period of the Cultural Revolution. They also sit in provincial and lower-level revolutionary committees. Of the 29 chairmen of ruling provincial revolutionary committees, 20 are military.

In ministries and other central government bodies the position of the military representatives, at first regarded as temporary, appears to be increasingly permanent.

If the party organization pattern at lower levels that seems to be developing turns out to be national in scope, it will dispose of the speculation as to which group will run China in the future, the rehabilitated Communist party or the military. The answer is both—with the military in probably the pivotal and decisive role.

However, it must be empha- sized, the military men in party and government agencies are highly politicized and far different from the career regulars commonly envisaged in the West when military men are thought of.

In any case, putting together "three-way combinations" for party committees seems to be marked by difficulties. For a year and a half of effort, organizers have less than a hundred committees in operation at a level as high as the hsien, and there are more than 2,000 hsien in China.

No party committees have yet appeared at the level of special district, a subprovincial unit comprising several hsien, or at the level of province.

November 29, 1970

Chinese Reds Complete Rebuilding of Party at Provincial Level

By TILLMAN DURDIN
Special to The New York Times

HONG KONG, Thursday Aug. 26—Peking announced today that Communist party committees had been formed in Szechwan, Tibet, Ningsia and Heilungkiang. The move completed the process of rebuilding the party at province level, where party committees were smashed during the Cultural Revolution, and many of the party leaders were purged.

Until today the four provinces were the only major administrative districts in Communist China in which party committees had not been organized.

The announcement may have brought nearer the holding of a National People's Congress. Observers here believe the slow pace of party rebuilding has held up the convening of a

MILES 1,000
SOVIET UNION
MONGOLIA
HEILUNGKIANG
CHINA
Peking
NINGSIA
TIBET
SZECHWAN
INDIA
South China Sea
BURMA

The New York Times   Aug. 26, 1971

Congress which Peking has often said was near.

It is expected that the Con- gress, when held, will adopt a new national constitution, elect a new chief of state and adopt measures with regard to government structure and personnel.

Both the Communist party and the organs of government were shattered during the Cultural Revolution, which began in 1966. Thousands of members of the party and of government agencies were purged, including the chief of state, Liu Shao-chi, and the old constitutions of the party and nation were discarded.

A revamped governing structure is now functioning although it is still incomplete both in terms of personnel and framework. A new party Central Committee and Politburo were organized in 1969, but progress has been slow in rebuilding the party at provincial and local levels.

Rivalries between factions and the protracted nature of efforts to flesh out the party with loyal Maoists have delayed plans to produce a new party organization.

Before today's announcement, the last provincial party committee formed was that in Yunnan on June 3. The 50th anniversary of the party was observed on July 1 with four provinces still without party committees.

The membership of the new committees, disclosed in dispatches from Peking by Hsinhua, the Chinese press agency, shows they are dominated by military men and by individuals who can be categorized as moderates or pragmatists. This has been the pattern for provincial - level committees throughout the country.

Radicals who advanced to positions of importance during the Cultural Revolution are missing from the four new party committees, showing that they have lost out in the factional jockeying.

The new party chief in Tibet is Jen Jung, acting chairman of the Revolutionary Committee and a political commissar for the area. Mr. Jen replaced Tseng Yung-ya, a leftist, on the Revolutionary Committee in June, and Mr. Tseng has not been heard from since.

Three of the six secretaries under Mr. Jen are military men and, like Mr. Jen, are ethnic Chinese. The three civilian secretaries are Tibetans.

The party chief in Szechwan is Chang Kuo-hua, who is also chairman of the provincial Revolutionary Committee and first political commissar of the military region that embraces Szechwan and Tibet.

The head of the Ningsia committee, Kang Chien-min, is a military man, as is the head of the Heilungkiang committee, Wang Chia-tao.

August 26, 1971

CHINA STILL FINDS TROUBLE IN TIBET

A Rebellious Population and Power Struggles Reported

Special to The New York Times

HONG KONG, Sept. 4 — Twenty years after the Chinese Army marched into Lhasa, the capital, Tibet remains one of China's most troubled regions. In establishing control over Tibet, Peking has had to cope with a sensitive border, a rebellious population and contending factions among the Chinese sent to settle there.

Last month the Tibet Autonomous Region held its first Communist party congress and established a regional party committee. A power struggle preceded the formation of the committee, and recent broadcasts have stressed the continued need to distinguish between "enemies" and "friends."

The composition of the new party committee reflects recent problems in the region. It confirmed that the former military commander and chairman of the revolutionary committee, which was established in September, 1968, had been removed from power. It revealed that the top official of Tibetan origin is a person who has been more closely associated with Szechwan Province than with Tibet.

Nobody has been found to replace Tibet's two traditional leaders, the Dalai Lama, who fled to India in 1959, and the Panchen Lama, who has been reported to be a prisoner, a fugitive or dead.

Chairman Loses Out

In most of China's 29 administrative units, the men appointed as chairman of the revolutionary committees — which were formed during the Cultural Revolution to replace the old governing bodies — were also elected recently to head the new party committees. But in eight areas, including Tibet, the chairmen lost out in power struggles.

A broadcast from Tibet following the formation of the party committee said that after the establishment of the regional revolutionary committee "the whole course of affairs was imbued with fierce struggle between two classes, two roads and two lines."

During the Cultural Revolution Red Guards poured into Tibet to overthrow "capitalist power holders" among the Chinese party and Government officials. Local leaders formed their own Red Guard factions, and reports of fighting between the rival organizations were still coming out of Tibet long after order had been restored in other areas.

Chang Kuo-hua, the regional military commander and party chief before the Cultural Revolution, was the principle target of radical Red Guards attacks and was transferred to Szechwan Province in 1967. Tseng Yung-ya, a deputy military commander, replaced him. He was elected chairman of the revolutionary committee and appeared to be the logical new party leader until his disappearance from the public scene late last year.

Moderates Said to Gain

In June, Jen Jung, the regional political commissar and an old associate of Mr. Tseng, was identified as acting chairman of the revolutionary committee while Chen Ming-yi, an associate of Chang Kuo-hua, was named as commander of the Tibet military region. Last month Jen Jung became first secretary of the regional party committee while Chen Ming-yi appeared at the head of the list of six secretaries.

Chang Kuo-hua's appointment as first secretary of Szechwan party committee was announced simultaneously with the formation of the Tibet party committee. The indications are, therefore, that moderate elements are now in control of both Szechwan and Tibet.

While the factional problems in Tibet appear to have been resolved to a point that a party committee could be established, unrest continues among the Tibetan people. There has been strong opposition to Chinese efforts to introduce communal farming and to replace Tibetan cultural Buddhism with Communism and the thoughts of Chairman Mao Tse-tung.

A report from Hsinhua, the official press agency, on the establishment of the new party committee in Tibet said that communes had been set up on about 60 per cent of Tibet's townships and declared that total grain output had doubled between 1958 and 1970. But refugees report that grain is severely rationed and that living standards have fallen.

Sabotage Reported

According to refugee reports, Tibetan resistance to the Chinese has continued sporadically, and this appears to be supported by official broadcasts from Lhasa, which have made repeated references to subversion and sabotage.

Speaking at the party congress last month, Jeng Jung praised the army for its success in "putting down rebellion."

He also acclaimed them for their contributions in "maintaining the security of the southwestern frontiers and in the self-defense operations on the Sino-Indian borders."

The signing of a 20-year treaty of peace and cooperation between India and the Soviet Union has given China new cause for concern about the security of its southwestern frontier.

September 5, 1971

RED CHINA FORMS ECONOMICS BODY

New Ministry Evidence of Emphasis on Development

By TILLMAN DURDIN
Special to the New York Times

HONG KONG, Sept. 12—A new Ministry of Economic Affairs has been added to the growing number of Government organs in Communist China.

The formation of the ministry, possibly with wide powers over the country's economic development, comes as another indication of rebuilding efforts since the Government was disrupted during the turbulent Cultural Revolution from 1967 to 1969.

The ministry's establishment also provides new evidence of the importance attached to building up the economy after the slump caused by the Cultural Revolution.

The existence of the ministry was made known in a broadcast last week from Shihkhiachwang, the capital of Hopeh Province, in a report on a conference about improved gasoline engines.

Many Officials Present

Representatives of the ministry were at the conference along with officials of the Ministry of Fuel and Chemical Industry, the Ministry of Commerce and other Peking-based groups.

The officials had come to praise and propagandize an engine that, the broadcast said, uses less fuel with greater power, is more durable and is lighter than conventional engines.

The broadcast called the engine "of major importance economically, scientifically, technologically and strategically." Judging from the broad representation, reported to include representatives of the automobile industry, members of the armed forces logistics department, the armed forces railway corps and others, the conference was of great importance to the Chinese.

The conference was also indicative of the importance attached to getting the most out of petroleum products and practicing economy in general.

It is likely that the Ministry of Economic Affairs has been created from the former State Economic Commission, which apparently ceased functioning during the Cultural Revolution. The State Economic Commission was headed by Po Yi-po, formerly an alternate member of the Communist party's Politburo and a Vice Premier who was purged during the Cultural Revolution.

Mr. Po, who is 64 years old, was a key figure in economic planning. He had served in earlier years as Minister of Finance. The Shihkhiachwang broadcast gave no indication of who heads the new Ministry of Economic Affairs.

Before the Cultural Revolution there were 40 ministries in the central Government, but this number seems to have been greatly reduced through suppression and merging of state organs. At present only 17 ministries are known to be in operation and of these the ministers of only eight have been identified. Six of the eight ministers are military men. Some former ministries have become bureaus.

September 13, 1971

Mao Becomes Less In the Public Places Of Tourist's China

PEKING, Sept. 19 (Agence France-Presse) — A statue of Chairman Mao Tse-tung has been removed from the lobby of the Hsin Chiao hotel, one of Peking's two big hotels for foreigners.

The removal by the authorities of the white plaster statue, more than six and a half feet high, is the latest sign of a new policy that seems to call for the toning down of the "personality cult." Since the beginning of the summer, numerous portraits and quotations of Chairman Mao have disappeared from public places.

This has been notable in Shanghai, Nanking, Canton and Peking, where the Mao effigies and directives appear to have been left only on official buildings, on billboards, and in factories and communes. They are no longer in hotel rooms, trains, restaurants and other places where foreigners had learned to expect the face of the leader.

Frequently, portraits and quotations have been replaced by modern Chinese paintings, mainly landscapes where the only "political" note is a red flag or a red sun.

It has also been noted that the hospital in Peking used by people from European Communist countries, which had been renamed during the Cultural Revolution the Anti-Revisionist Hospital has resumed its old name, Friendship Hospital. However, the Anti-Imperialist Hospital has not been renamed.

As Peking prepares for China's National Day Oct. 1, people have been repainting the fronts of their houses, often in lively colors. One also sees a fresh coat of red paint on big billboards carrying slogans.

Near Tienanmen Square, until a few days ago, there was a poster that said: "Long live the great leader, great helmsman, great supreme commander and great teacher, Chairman Mao."

Now it reads: "Long live our great leader, Chairman Mao."

September 20, 1971

MAO DEATH RUMOR DENIED BY PEKING

By TAD SZULC

The Peking Government denied last night widespread rumors that Chairman Mao Tse-tung may be ill or dead.

An official of the Foreign Ministry in Peking, reached by telephone, said in reply to a question that the 77-year-old leader was in "very good health," contrary to rumors that spread yesterday on his illness or possible death.

There was no explanation, however, of the cancellation of the annual Oct. 1 parade, marking the Chinese National Day and usually attended by Mr. Mao, and of a reported suspension for three days last week of all flights of civilian and military aircraft over mainland China.

Earlier, Chinese Communist sources, commenting on diplomatic and press reports from Peking that the National Day parade had been called off, said that this year's celebrations would take "another form."

No Explanation Given

They did not clarify, however, why the parade itself was being called off. This is the first time since the Communist regime came to power 21 years ago that the parade will not have been held.

Speculation over possible major political events taking place in China spread yesterday following the reports of the cancellation of the parade, the reported suspension of the flights over China last week and a broadcast yesterday by the French state radio saying that Mr. Mao was seriously ill.

This speculation included the possibility of a political power struggle, conceivably related to the succession problem in China.

The reports that the Oct. 1 parade was being canceled came yesterday from French and Canadian news correspondents in Peking.

They were later confirmed by at least one Western embassy in Peking in communications to its home government, according to diplomatic sources.

A Western embassy in Pe-king notified its country's foreign ministry yesterday that "internal flight problems" were continuing and were preventing airline connections in China. This report said that a group of visitors scheduled to leave Peking on Monday by air for Canton on their way to Hong Kong were forced instead to take a train, thus delaying their departure from China.

Party Meeting Reported

The Agence France-Presse correspondent in Peking reported that despite the cancellation of the parade, commemorative events would take place in Peking's parks along the lines of May Day celebrations and including entertainment on revolutionary themes and sporting displays.

Reports from Taipei early today quoted Chinese Nationalist sources as saying that "abnormal air activity" had been occurring over China this week, including an increase in special flights that may have carried high-ranking party or Government officials.

Intelligence sources in Washington said that these flights might be related to a special session of the Communist party's Central Committee. Western press reports from Peking have said that such a meeting might be under way or about to begin.

However, the Peking radio, monitored in Hong Kong and Tokyo, offered no suggestion that anything unusual was afoot in China.

The Taiwan sources also said that from Sept. 13 to Sept. 15, the period during which all flying over China was reportedly banned, Nationalist aircraft on regular patrols near the Fukien Province coast were not challenged by Communist fighters as usually happens.

They said that the challenges were resumed last Thursday, the 16th. Fukien Province lies across the Taiwan Strait from Taiwan.

Air France said in Paris that its regular weekly flight to Shanghai, via Cairo, Karachi and Rangoon, arrived on schedule yesterday as it had a week earlier.

American intelligence sources in Washington said they had only scanty information on possible developments in China.

They expressed the view, however, that the reports of the banning of flights last week and the cancellation of the annual Peking parade could even reflect a domestic political power struggle whose gravity remained uncertain.

September 22, 1971

Chou and Other Officials Attend National Day Rites

By Agence France-Presse

PEKING, Oct. 1—Premier Chou En-lai and other Government leaders, along with tens of thousands of ordinary Chinese, took part in National Day celebrations here today. The celebrations, with the customary giant parade omitted, took place in the capital's parks.

Jenmin Jin Pao, the Communist party newspaper, omitted its usual editorial comment and did not publish the customary large photos of Chairman Mao Tse-tung and Deputy Chairman Lin Piao. A giant photo of Mr. Mao adorned Tienanmen Square, the heart of the capital.

Tens of thousands of Chinese and several hundred foreigners, warmly applauded by the crowds, watched performances by revolutionary theater groups, folk dancers, acrobats and conjurers. Clusters of red flags waved in the warm sun.

Boat Trip for Chou

At midday, as the stands were taken down and the foreign groups left, Mr. Chou went for a boat trip on the Summer Palace lake with Prince Norodom Sihanouk, deposed leader of Cambodia, and his wife.

Others present were Deputy Premier Li Hsien-nien, Yeh Chien-Ying, a Politburo member who is deputy chairman of the Central Committee's Military Commission, and by Kuo Mojo, deputy chairman of the National Assembly.

Absent were the Politburo members in command of the army, air force and navy, respectively Huang Yung-sheng, Wu Fa-hsien and Li Tso-peng, who have not appeared in public for nearly three weeks.

The Soviet Ambassador, Vasily S. Tolstikov, was greeted by smiling girls waving flowers when he arrived at the Summer Palace.

Among groups of "friendly foreigners" who joined the Chinese at the festivities were Aiichiro Fujiyama, a former Japanese Foreign Minister, and his delegation, which favors the normalization of relations between Japan and China.

Also present were the writer Han Suyin, three American Black Panther leaders led by Huey Newton, and a French chef, Sam Letrone, who is here at the invitation of Prince Sihanouk.

Jenmin Jih Pao, printed in red, had a front-page slogan reading: "Let us celebrate the 22d anniversary of the foundation of the People's Republic of China. Long live our great leader Mao Tse-tung. May he live a very long time."

The front page also included an article on the progress of the economy. On the back page were two songs: "Chairman Mao Tse-tung is the Red Sun of Our Heart" and "Long Life to the Great Chinese Communist Party."

The parks were recently renovated, and bars and ice-cream stands contributed to the festive atmosphere. Huge red banners bore slogans including, "Peoples of the world, unite to destroy the American aggressors and their lackeys." Quotations from and poems by Chairman Mao, as well as photographs on his life and on the history of the Chinese revolution, were on display.

Other slogans, the product of the ninth party congress in April, 1969, stressed unity between the people and the army and among the country's nationalities and social classes.

One of the most striking spectacles was a performance of the revolutionary ballet "The White-Haired Girl."

October 2, 1971

Mao Meets With Selassie And Is Said to Appear Fit

By Reuters

PEKING, Oct. 8 — Chairman Mao Tse-tung made a public appearance today for the first time in two months as he greeted Emperor Haile Selassie of Ethiopia. Mr. Mao looked fit and he told jokes.

After posing for photographers in the Great Hall of the People, Mr. Mao, who is 77 years old, took the Emperor, who is 79, by the hand and led him to another room for talks. The talks lasted an hour and 40 minutes, sources close to the Ethiopian entourage said.

"This will end speculation elsewhere in the world about the Chairman's health," said China's Ambassador to Ethiopia, Yu Pei-wen, according to the sources. Mr. Mao was last seen in public on Aug. 7, when he received Ne Win, the Burmese chief of state.

As Mr. Mao led his visitor away today, he said, "Let us liberate ourselves from photographers and have a talk."

Chairman Mao was joking and was in a jovial mood during the public part of the meeting, and he posed for photographers with various Ethiopian visitors, according to the sources.

Premier Chou En-lai was among the leaders meeting Emperor Haile Selassie, but members of the Ethiopian delegation could not say for certain whether Vice Chairman Lin Piao, Mr. Mao's heir apparent, was present.

Tonight the Emperor and Premier Chou went to the capital stadium to watch a gymnastics and table-tennis demonstration.

Haile Selassie spent much of the day inspecting the Great Wall of China and touring Peking's Imperial Palace before he met Chairman Mao.

The Emperor arrived on Wednesday for a six-day visit. A reception was given for Emperor Selassie by African ambassadors resident in Peking.

Peking Denounces Plotters in Party; Attack on Lin Seen

By TILLMAN DURDIN
Special to The New York Times

HONG KONG, Dec. 1—A joint editorial in Peking's leading publications, apparently connected with the recent disappearance of Defense Minister Lin Piao from public view, charged today that "chieftains of opportunist lines" were intriguing against Communist unity in China.

The editorial was the sharpest and most outspoken attack so far to come from official quarters in Peking in connection with the protracted absence of Mr. Lin.

Others who have disappeared from public view include Mr. Lin's wife, Yeh Chun; Huang Yung-sheng, chief of staff of the armed forces; Wu Fa-shien, the air force commander; Li Tso-peng, the navy political commissar; Hsu Shih-yu, the Nanking military commander, and Chiu Hui-tso, chief of logistics for the armed forces—all members of the Communist party's ruling Politburo—and numerous other lesser military figures.

Defense Minister Lin, who is also deputy party chairman, was designated Chairman Mao Tse-tung's successor in the 1969 party constitution.

The editorial appeared yesterday in two Peking dailies, Jenmin Jih Pao and Chiehfang Chun Pao, and the ideological journal Hung Chi. It was relayed here in English today from Peking by Hsinhua, the Chinese press agency.

The editorial follows two months of oblique denunciations in Chinese news media of undesignated "bourgeois careerists," "splittists" and "sham Marxist schemers," all in context of references that have seemed to point to Mr. Lin and his associates.

Unofficial and unverified reports from China have said that Mr. Lin is under house arrest or dead. Travelers from China say stories are current there that he had led attempts to assassinate Chairman Mao, and numerous lurid accounts of these attempts, all unsubstantiated, have appeared in the Hong Kong press.

The crash of a Chinese jet in Mongolia the night of Sept.

12, killing all nine persons aboard, has given rise to reports that the 64-year-old Defense Minister and deputy to Mr. Mao was aboard with his wife. Other accounts, citing Soviet sources, say all the unrecognizable burned bodies in the shattered aircraft were those of persons younger than Mr. Lin and his wife.

The thesis of yesterday's joint editorial was the necessity for greater party strength and unity to deal with problems of deviation from correct party policies under the leadership of Chairman Mao.

The editorial quoted a 1964 injunction by Chairman Mao to "beware of those who engage in conspiracies and intrigues" and said: "As chieftains of opportunist lines are engaged in splitting activities they are bound to resort to conspiracies and intrigues."

The editorial continued: "Some persons are bent on plotting. They want to do this, so what can be done? Even now there are persons at it.

"That there are persons plotting is an objective fact. It is not a question of whether we like it or not.

"In our party's history those bourgeois careerists, conspirators and persons having illicit relations with foreign countries who clung to opportunist lines and engaged in conspiracies could not but bring ruin, disgrace and destruction upon themselves in the end."

The editorial said that by dealing with opposition in its ranks the party had become "stronger, more unified and thriving."

The editorial maintained that "hidden antiparty and antisocialist counterrevolutionaries are very few in number" and added, "the overwhelming majority of good people who committed mistakes in political line are able to return to the correct line through criticism and self-criticism.'

Taking up a theme that has been often used in recent attacks seemingly directed at Mr. Lin, the editorial said party members, particularly senior party officials, should speak out their views openly and frankly. It seemed to imply that Mr. Lin had concealed his differences with Mr. Mao and had plotted against him.

It said bourgeois representatives in the party always attempted to turn it from a proletarian into a bourgeois party to "achieve their criminal aim of abolishing party leadership and undermining the Chinese revolution."

The editorial and other recent articles seem to indicate that Mr. Lin had led the armed forces, opposing Mr. Mao's intention to re-establish the

The Lin Piao Mystery

By JACK CHEN

HONG KONG—All China-watchers have noted recent signs of shifts and changes and particularly the nonappearance of such prominent personages as Vice Chairman Lin Piao, Chief of Staff Huang Yung-sheng and other top army men.

In the last few weeks on those occasions when they would usually have been present they have been represented by Marshal Yeh Chien-ying, vice chairman of the military commission of the Communist party's Central Committee. This has led to a flurry of speculation.

At this date, few will be taken in by a picture of China coming apart at the seams under stress of a power struggle, yet serious observers seek some rational explanation of what all this really means.

The explanation, of course, is very simple. The Cultural Revolution is now in its final stages and the whole administrative and management apparatus of the country is undergoing final readjustments necessitated by the conclusion of this phase of the Chinese revolution.

China's administration before the Cultural Revolution was based on the system of elected people's congresses. These rose from the communes and county congresses through the provincial congresses to the National People's Congress, the supreme organ of state power. The congress elected its standing committee and its chairman, the head of state. That job is now vacant with the deposing of Liu Shao-chi. It approved the choice of Chou En-lai as Premier of the State Council (cabinet) and its members.

The political backbone of the congress is, of course, the Chinese Communist party. Its top organ is the national Party Congress with its elected Central Committee, the political bureau and a five-man standing committee.

On the eve of the Cultural Revolution, the system of unified party leadership prevailed. Political and executive leadership was concentrated in the person of the party secretary. This ensured party leadership of the dictatorship of the proletariat. The "mass line" of constant consultation with the people was designed to prevent bureaucracy and "commandism."

At the height of the Cultural Revolution from 1966 to 1968 and even later, this state and management structure was in disarray. From the ministerial level down, the Government apparatus functioned only in parts.

The party structure was also fractured. Power was taken over in many units by spontaneously organized revolutionary mass organizations. These were supposed to obey party and Government instructions sent to them direct from the top. Some did. Others were infiltrated by anti-Mao elements both from the right and the extremist ultraleft. Implementation of party instructions depended mainly on the loyalty of the revolutionary masses and the army. The army was directed by Mao's "closest comrade-in-arms," Minister of Defense Lin Piao.

Where mass organizations failed to join in "great alliances," army teams were sent in to help them overcome factional squabbles. Finally, revolutionary committees were formed everywhere as the new organs of government and management. These were composed of three-in-one combinations of representatives of the mass organizations, the army teams and the best of the old cadres. The army played a key role at this stage.

In the twenty months from January 1967 to September 1968 all 29 new provincial-level revolutionary committees were formed. In the last few months the last of the new provincial party committees and their subordinate branches and groups were also re-established. Their ranks have been purged of die-hard Liu Shao-chi revisionists, counter-revolutionary elements like the "516" leaders and unrepentant ultraleftists.

This has provided the basis for the re-establishment of unified party leadership operating through the revolutionary committees. Now state and party can return to normal reliance on the new party-government structure.

This is one of the big shifts taking place in China, and that is behind the recent editorials and exhortations to observe unified party leadership, collective responsibility and the mass line in the revolutionary committees.

Another shift is the long-term campaign to de-escalate the personality cult that during the Cultural Revolution grew up around Mao and his "closest comrade-in-arms," Lin Piao. Recent articles and speeches have stressed the metaphysical nature of the role of the hero and the genius spread by Liu Shao-chi, Lu Ting-yi, his man in education and culture, and other "political swindlers" who were "attempting to portray a handful of careerists, including themselves, as incomparable geniuses" and the "embodiment" of truth.

Quite a bit of fur is flying in this debate. But it would be wrong to imagine that this, no matter who is involved, is going to cause the breakup of China and the present effective leadership.

The military side of the three-in-one renovated Communist party structure, instead of the armed forces, as the controlling element in the country.

Evidence is slowly emerging that Mr. Mao began more than a year ago to trim back the extensive power network Mr. Lin had built up.

It now seems likely that Mr. Lin gradually came to realize that Mr. Mao and his supporters were moving to downgrade him and that Mr. Lin's actions to combat this led to confrontation in September that Mr. Lin lost.

Mr. Lin's fall from power, if such is the case, follows the purge earlier this year of another intimate of Mr. Mao's, Chen Po-ta, the fourth-ranking member of the Politburo.

Mr. Chen has not been attacked by name, but his name has been dropped from Politburo listings and he has been missing from public view for more than a year. He was allegedly too leftist and had schemed with ultraleftists to oust Premier Chou En-lai and others and establish an ultraleftist leadership, keeping Mr. Mao as a figurehead only.

revolutionary committees and in the top leadership is not being phased out but put in its proper place. In the event of military danger from without, that side, as during the Cultural Revolution, can be given a more prominent stress. This built-in maneuverability of the revolutionary committee structure is one of its advantages.

It should also occasion no surprise if there are further changes in the top ranks of leadership in China. Since the Ninth Party Congress in 1969, there have been many personnel changes at lower levels and these have not yet been fully reflected in the top leadership. Adjustments will obviously have to be made here too and in the National People's Congress when it meets.

October 9, 1971

Mao Is Quoted as Saying Lin Was Killed in Crash

By JOHN BURNS
The Globe and Mail, Toronto

PEKING, July 27—Chairman Mao Tse-tung has broken months of official silence on the fate of former Defense Minister Lin Piao by telling two foreign statesmen in recent weeks that Mr. Lin was killed in an air crash last year while fleeing the country in the wake of an attempted coup.

Authoritative diplomatic sources here report that the leader of the Chinese Communist party made the revelation in meetings in his Peking residence with Mrs. Sirimavo Bandaranaike, the Prime Minister of Ceylon, and Maurice Schumann, the French Foreign Minister.

According to the diplomatic accounts, which were corroborated in part by Chinese sources, the 78-year-old Chairman told his visitors that Mr. Lin had plotted to assassinate him as part of a conspiracy aimed at replacing the civilian leadership of China with a military dictatorship.

Officials Had Been Secret

The Chairman's account tallies closely with stories that have been circulating outside China for months. However, there has been no previous confirmation of the accounts from officials here. They have steadfastly refused to discuss the whereabouts of the former Defense Minister, or the events

that led to his disappearance last summer.

The Mao account also fits one of the few independently verifiable features of the whole affair — the crash of a Chinese Trident jetliner deep inside Mongolia on Sept. 13, 1971.

There have been numerous reports that Mr. Lin was among those killed in the crash, but—until now, at least—no confirmation.

The crash coincided almost exactly with the last mention of Mr. Lin in the Chinese press. Though still officially designated as the eventual successor to the Chairman, he has since become a nonperson, his quotations expunged from public places, all portraits of him removed.

In his talk with the visiting statesmen, the Chairman is said to have given a surprisingly full account of what happened. Diplomats reconstructing the talk, do not hesitate to quote his exact words, as conveyed by the participants.

According to the diplomat the Chinese leader told h itors that Mr. Lin's install "milita began with Mini

July 27, 1972

Chen Yi's Successor as Foreign Minister Named

Special to The New York Times

HONG KONG, Tuesday, Jan. 20—Chi Peng-fei, a former army medical officer who became a diplomat, has been appointed China's Foreign Minister. He succeeds Chen Yi, who died in Peking earlier this month at the age of 71.

The appointment of Mr. Chi, who had been acting Foreign Minister for about a year, was disclosed in a report by Hsinhua, the Chinese press agency, listing officials present at a performance in Peking by a Japanese drama group. Mr. Chi was described for the first time as Minister of Foreign Affairs.

Mr. Chi, a 61-year-old native of Shensi, is the third Foreign Minister since the Communists came to power in China in 1949. The first was Chou En-lai, who was concurrently Premier. Chen Yi took over in 1958.

Mr. Chen was an active and outspoken Foreign Minister who is believed to have exerted considerable influence on the conduct of China's foreign relations during the height of his career.

During the Cultural Revolution, Mr. Chen was subjected to severe personal abuse and suffered a political decline. His

health began to fail about the same time. In 1969 he was dropped from the Politburo.

Mr. Chen was never officially replaced as Foreign Minister and, at his death, was still accorded this ministerial rank.

Mr. Chi, who was first named Acting Foreign Minister in April last year, ranks far below Premier Chou and Mr. Chen in party status, not being a member of the Central Committee. Accordingly, Premier Chou is still believed to be the person most directly responsible for foreign policy.

Mr. Chi, a tall man with close-cropped hair who bears a somber expression on most of his published photographs, graduated from a military medical college and worked a warlord before joining the Communist forces in 1931.

He took part in the famous Long March of the Red Army from southern China to northern Shensi as a medical officer in 1934-35.

In 1950 he was appointed chief of Peking's mission in East Germany with the rank of ambassador. He remained in East Germany until 1955 when he became Deputy Foreign Minister.

January 30, 1972

Peking Discloses Acting Chief of State Is Tung Pi-wu, 86

TOKYO, Feb. 24 (AP)—China has named 86-year-old Tung Pi-wu acting chief of state, filling the vacancy created by the ouster of Liu Shao-chi, a Peking broadcast disclosed today.

Mr. Tung served in a presidential capacity as far back as October, 1969 But the designation of acting head of state was accorded him today for the first time in an official report by Hsinhua, the Chinese press agency, of a congratulatory message to Kuwait on her National Day.

The message, addressed to

the Emir of Kuwait, was signed "Tung Pi-wu, acting chairman of the People's Republic of China."

Since Mao Tse-tung, the Chairman of the Communist party, deposed Mr. Liu during the Cultural Revolution, the post has been considered a largely ceremonial one.

Mr. Tung has been one of the two deputy chiefs of state and is a member of the Politburo of the Communist party Central Committee. The other deputy chief of state is Soong Ching-ling, widow of Dr. Sun Yat-sen, the founder of the Chinese Republic.

The broadcast did not indicate whether the National People's Congress, which has not been in session since 1965, will be called on soon to name a new chief of state.

February 25, 1972

China Stockpiling Strategic Materials

Special to The New York Times

HONG KONG, Jan. 27—The Chinese Communist authorities have launched a new austerity drive in the country in conjunction with programs for stockpiling food and strategic materials and developing regional self-sufficiency.

The campaigns have all been linked to the war threat that the Soviet Union is said to pose and the nationwide call for "combat readiness," but they also appear to be aimed at strengthening the Chinese economy and countering widespread black-market operations, corruption and theft, which have become a serious problem in recent months.

While the Chinese authorities seem seriously concerned that a war danger exists, many political analysts here believe that Peking is taking advantage of the external threat to tighten political and economic controls.

Provincial radio stations throughout the country have been reporting new achievements in reducing consumption of coal, petroleum and electricity. A broadcast from Chengchow, capital of Honan Province, said the campaign for practicing economy must be looked at "from the viewpoint of combat readiness."

Peking has publicly called for the storage of grain reserves as a measure against war and famine. Reports on the stockpiling of strategic materials have come from travelers and trade sources here.

Steel prices have risen in Hong Kong because supplies from China have dropped. The South China Morning Post, a Hong Kong newspaper, reported that China had failed to honor commitments made last year to export steel and was instead buying on the local market.

Metal buyers at the Canton trade fair last October found the Chinese unwilling to make big commitments, according to trade sources here. A drop in exports of tungsten ore by China — the leading producer of the metal — has sent the world price soaring.

Economic analysts point out that China cut down on imports of some key metals in 1968 to offset a trade imbalance and to some extent may be replacing depleted stocks. However, the present stockpiling policy appears to go beyond resolving a depletion problem, they say.

The present campaigns, from a defense viewpoint, will create self-sufficient bases for the "people's war" envisaged by Chairman Mao Tse-tung in the event of an invasion of China. The Communist party leader asserts that an invader will be "drowned in the vast ocean" of China's 700 million people.

A broadcast from Fukien Province said Chairman Mao had directed that "various localities should endeavor to build up independent industrial systems." The broadcast added that both industrial and agricul-

tural production should "serve the purpose of preparedness against war."

The provincial authorities in Chekiang recently announced a "battle to seize coal" in order to "achieve self-sufficiency in coal for this province and promptly put an end to the practice of transporting coal from the north to the south."

"This battle to seize coal is being organized to meet the requirements of war preparedness and of building an independent industrial system in this province," the announcement, which was broadcast from Hangchow, said.

Throughout China the people have been told to keep in mind Chairman Mao's teaching of "saving every cent for the war effort, for the revolutionary cause and for our economic construction."

The army has been hailed as a leader in the movement for "practising economy and opposing waste." Hsinhua, the Chinese press agency, reported that last year military administrative expenses were cut by 6 per cent. The agency stated that many units had made strenuous efforts to save timber, rolled steel, cement and other building materials as well as coal, petroleum, and cotton textiles.

"The medical and health departments enthusiastically save great quantities of cotton and gauze by sterilizing old dressings and using them again," the agency reported.

contributed to heavy volume and soaring prices on the London metal exchange. But dealers are divided in their interpretation of the buying spree.

Some, such as officials at Rudolf Wolff & Co., a big metals trading company, conjecture that the Chinese are building up their stockpiles against the possibility of war with the Soviet Union. Others, such as Philip Smith, chairman of the London exchange, think the big purchases are fueling an industrial upsurge. Still others say it is impossible to tell what the Chinese are doing.

The method of paying is also baffling, according to Mr. Smith. He said Chinese purchases in the past had been financed by Chinese sales in the West of antimony and tungsten. Sales of these metals have dried up, he said, and present Chinese sources of Western currency are obscure.

London metal exchange dealers often do not deal directly with Chinese traders but execute various contracts on the exchange that reflect purchases and sales elsewhere. Thus London dealers are not necessarily involved in Chinese financial arrangements.

Mr. Smith said that although the Chinese had been more active recently, the purchases were apparently relatively small if viewed in terms of stockpiling. For this reason, he suggested that the metals were earmarked for industrial use. He said Chinese purchases come in short bursts, which have a big influence on prices.

January 28, 1970

COMMUNIST CHINA ORBITS SATELLITE; SPACE GAINS SEEN

By TILLMAN DURDIN
Special to The New York Times

HONG KONG, April 25 — Communist China announced today that it launched its first space satellite yesterday.

A communiqué received here from Peking's Hsinhua press agency said the satellite, weighing 380 pounds, was orbiting the earth every 114 minutes along a trajectory the perigee of which is 263.4 miles and the apogee 1,430 miles.

Hsinhua reported that the satellite was broadcasting "Tung Fang Hung" (The East Is Red), a popular song that has been virtually adopted as the national anthem.

The announcement gave no indication of where the launching took place.

[The launching of China's first satellite was greeted by United States space and defense officials as a long-anticipated event that underscores China's growing technological capability. The satellite, which cannot be seen by the unaided eye, will pass over the United States five times on Sunday. Page 2.]

A Big Advance

Although such a feat has been expected for several years,

the launching represents a big advance in Communist China's capability in rocket and general space technology.

Specialists here point out that technologists who can make a rocket that can propel a 380-pound vehicle into space can also make a missile for delivering the nuclear weapons that China is now producing.

The Chinese Communists are believed to have developed an intermediate missile with a 1,000-mile range but so far have not given any evidence of having an intercontinental missile.

Test-firing of an intercontinental ballistic missile would require firing into the Pacific or the Indian Oceans, and ships to monitor the shot.

China's launching of a space

satellite comes just a little more than two months after Japanese scientists orbited a satellite—a much smaller vehicle weighing only 50 pounds.

Peking attacked the Japanese space shot as indicative of an undercover Japanese intention to develop missiles for nuclear warheads and "unleash wars of aggression."

Today's announcement from Peking was short on concrete details but long on propaganda, praise and exhortation.

Hsinhua said the launching was "a great victory for Mao Tse-tung thought, a great victory for Chairman Mao's proletarian revolutionary line and another fruitful result of the great proletarian revolution."

Hsinhua reported that the Central Committee of the Chinese Communist party "extends warm congratulations to the workers, the commanders and the fighters of the people's liberation army, the revolutionary cadres, the scientists, engineers and technicians and the people's militia who have been engaged in the research, manufacture and launching of the satellite."

The launching was called a result of the leadership of the Communist party chairman, Mao Tse-tung, and his deputy, Lin Piao, adherence to the principle of independence and self-reliance, promoting production and preparing against war with concrete action.

Hsinhua said the Central Committee urged "the comrades" to continue to exert themselves and "strive to further develop China's science and technology, accelerate socialist construction and make still greater contributions to mankind."

The launching made China the fifth nation to put a satellite in orbit with its own rockets. The others are the United States, the Soviet Union, France and Japan. The United States launched its first satellite in 1958, a few months after the first Soviet launching in 1957.

The launching of a satellite by China strengthened predictions by observers here that Peking would soon test-fire an intercontinental missile and possibly increase the testing of nuclear weapons.

China has exploded 10 nuclear devices since its first in 1964. One explosion appears to have been abortive and was not reported by Peking. The last nuclear test, of a hydrogen bomb, was carried out last October.

Peking's announcement of yesterday's space satellite said nothing about its having any military significance but the military connection is obvious.

There was also no indication that the launching was connected with the centenary of Lenin's birth earlier this week but the timing could have been fixed for the approximate date of the centenary, with the intention of distracting from the Soviet Union's celebrations.

In a message received here two hours after the announcement of the launching, Hsinhua announced the times that the satellite will pass over the larger Chinese mainland cities.

The angle of its orbit to the Equator was given as 69.5 degrees. Its music was being broadcast on a frequency of 20.009 megacycles.

Hsinhua reported that the satellite would pass over Peking at 11:11 A.M. tomorrow, local time; over Taipei at 9:09, and over Hong Kong at 11:04.

April 26, 1970

FRUGAL WORKER A MODEL IN CHINA

By NORMAN WEBSTER

© 1970 The Globe and Mail, Toronto

PEKING, Oct. 24 — Should a Chinese inventor come up with the throwaway bottle, it is unlikely the Orient would beat a path to his door. He would more probably receive a visit from his local revolutionary committee telling him to forget it.

This is a frugal society. That miracle of capitalist ingenuity, planned obsolescence, would be known in China by its other name — waste. Old equipment here is repaired and used to set up new small-scale factories. Industrial wastes are reclaimed and made into something else. Clothes are patched and repatched. Paper, boxes and cans are saved.

Chinese society has traditionally been thrifty and short of consumer goods. The habit is reinforced in modern days by constant exhortations about front-line fighters in the frugality war. Chao Yuan-show, for example.

Mr. Chao, a Communist party member, works at the Yichang No. 1 People's Hospital in Hupeh Province. His philosophy is that, just as "high buildings are built brick by brick and tile by tile, so is the mansion of Communism — one must be frugal bit by bit." His labors of economy can have few equals anywhere.

When Mr. Chao was put in charge of hospital supplies, he began to consider the possibilities for things usually discarded after use. Examining used cotton balls, he concluded that they could be washed out and sterilized.

He began collecting, drying and washing the hospital's discards. In seven or eight years he has collected more than 400 pounds. After sterilizing and processing, the cotton was made into 62 quilts for hospital beds.

Mr. Chao's attention has not been confined to cotton. In the same period he collected 120 pounds of aluminum by saving small bottle caps; 40 such caps weigh a fraction over one ounce.

The hospital used to throw away needles when they became dull. Mr. Chao collected 40,000 over the years. After grinding, more than 20,000 could be reused, and the state was saved $880.

"Waste and nonwaste are relative terms, not absolutes," says Mr. Chao. "Waste in one place may not necessarily be waste in another."

Applying this theory, he sorted discarded medicine bottles by size and called other institutions to see whether they could use them. It was found that small penicillin bottles could be used by a food company for condiments, larger bottles by a hardware company for furniture paint.

On frugality, Mr. Chao takes no narrow view: "Only when a country practices frugality can the country become prosperous and mighty," he says.

October 25, 1970

Go Out and Toil, Peking Tells Women

Special to The New York Times

HONG KONG, Sept. 18— Pointing to the exploits of a host of heroines, the Peking press has proclaimed that "what men can do, can also be done by women."

The catch phrase is not, as it might seem, the slogan for a women's liberation movement in Communist China but simply a selling point in a drive to enlarge the country's labor force by increasing the number of working women.

While women are expected to undertake the same heavy manual work performed by men, many have used marriage as an excuse to forgo this Peking-style equality.

An article in Peking's Jenmin Jih Pao complained that some women had been "loafing around in the cities, thinking of nothing but their families and household chores and talking only of better days." The admission that some people think of "better days" sometimes slips into the Chinese press.

The article also criticized women who "stayed at home all day long" and blamed this trend on the "pernicious influence of the counterrevolutionary revisionist line pushed by the renegade, hidden traitor and scab Liu Shao-chi."

Mr. Liu, former head of state, who was the chief victim of the Cultural Revolution purges, has become the scapegoat for virtually all of China's shortcomings.

Condemned Liu

The paper called for the "organization of workers' dependents for collective productive labor" as a "great revolution directed against old habits, customs." It condemned the view said to be held by Mr. Liu that as women took good care of their husbands and households "they would be serving the people in the best possible way."

"This is a counterrevolutionary revisionist fallacy," the Jenmin Jih Pao article said. It added that many women had "stepped out of the narrow confines of their houses into the vast battlefield of labor."

Jenmin Jih Pao, the official Communist party newspaper, noted that women formed half the population and were therefore "an immense source of man-power." But it warned that the "pernicious influence" of the past had not yet been completely wiped out and said that the old society's "habit of belittling women" continued to cause mischief.

"Therefore, penetrating sustained revolutionary mass criticism is still necessary to remove all these erroneous ideas and to eliminate all obstacles to the dependents participation in collective productive labor," the paper said.

One of China's current heroines is a 71-year-old Communist party official named Tsung Tsai-pao, who lives in a village in Chekiang province. Hsinhua, the Chinese press agency, gave an account of her exploits, which included resistance to capitalist tendencies and selfless activities on behalf of the state.

Recently, after a party meeting, she forgot her fatigue and joined the peasants in transplanting rice shoots, declaring: "Don't think I'm so old. I still can climb a mountain and work in the fields and contribute my share to the revolution."

For the younger generation of women, Hsinhua recounted an exploit rivaling the tale of the Dutch boy who heroically stemmed the flow of water through a hole in a dyke. The agency reported that in Liaoning Province four young girls used their bodies to plug a breach in a container to prevent the waste of manure stored there.

Childbirth, the agency reported, is only a temporary inconvenience to China's "revolutionary women." It said that a woman laborer resumed work on a building site "only six days after giving birth to a child."

PEKING REPORTS ECONOMIC GAINS

By HARRY SCHWARTZ

Official figures disclosed by Premier Chou En-lai indicate that Communist China has made significant, though limited, economic progress in the last decade.

The figures were received with great interest by Western specialists since they appear to be the first official comprehensive statistics made public by Peking since 1960. Premier Chou disclosed the data in an interview with the American writer Edgar Snow, who published them in a recent issue of the Italian magazine Epoca. Mr. Snow has had frequent access over the years to Chinese Communist officials.

Premier Chou's disclosures indicate that Communist China still has only a relatively narrow industrial base for the production of modern weapons though it has exploded atomic and hydrogen bombs and built missiles that have put two satellites in orbit. The Chinese industrial capacity implied by the Premier's statistics is still very small compared with that of the United States, the Soviet Union, Japan, West Germany, Britain and France.

Implicit in Premier Chou's revelation, too, is the acknowlegement that the hopes of rapid industrial advance voiced during the late nineteen fifties proved illusory. The modest industrial gains indicated in Premier Chou's figures apparently reflect the fact that agricultural production enjoyed top priority during all or most of the nineteen sixties in Communist China.

Steel Output Cited

Steel production, Premier Chou told Mr. Snow, averaged between 10 million and 18 million metric tons a year over the last five years. In 1960, a Chinese economic official, Li Fuchun, said that the 1959 steel production of his country was more than 13 million metric tons.

Mr. Li's figure for 1959 apparently included almost five million tons of steel produced by primitive techniques in socalled backyard furnaces, steel having little value for that metal's normal uses. Premier Chou told Mr. Snow that Chinese steel production is expected to increase, since capacity is being expanded, but it is uncertain what proportion, if any, of the steel he reported as having been produced consists of low-value metal produced by primitive methods.

The Chinese Premier said his country's oil output amounted to more than 20 million metric tons last year and said China was now self-sufficient in petroleum. This figure is higher than earlier foreign estimates, but it had long been taken for granted abroad that Chinese oil production far surpassed the 1959 figure of less than four million tons.

Premier Chou released no statistics on the production of coal, China's chief source of fuel.

The Premier told Mr. Snow that last year China produced 14 million metric tons of chemical fertilizer and 8.5 billion meters of cotton cloth. A decade ago official sources put China's 1959 output at 1.3 million tons of chemical fertilizer and 7.5 billion meters of cotton cloth.

Increased output of chemical fertilizers to aid Chinese agriculture has been a high priority objective for Peking since the early nineteen-sixties. But some observers expressed skepticism that a ten-fold increase had taken place, noting that the nutritive quality of much of the present Chinese fertilizer—made in small and technically backward plants—is poor.

Premier Chou said that China's total grain output in 1970 was 240 million metric tons and that China now had state grain reserves of about 40 million tons. The 1970 grain figure is well below the output of 270 million tons that official Chinese sources reported a decade ago had been produced in 1959.

Some specialists noted that the precise accuracy of Premier Chou's statistics was less important than the fact that he had disclosed them to a foreigner. This suggests, they noted, that the Chinese leaders feel more confident about their economic situation than they did during the nineteen-sixties when comprehensive economic figures were considered secret.

China's Changing Society Seems to Cut Birth Rate

By TILLMAN DURDIN
Special to The New York Times

SHANGHAI, April 20—Mrs. Hu Fang-tsu was emphatic about it. "Children are a lot of trouble," she said. "Nobody wants very many of them any more." The leader of a production team in the Machiao commune in the countryside 18 miles west of Shanghai, the 35-year-old Mrs. Hu has one child, and she and her husband have no plans to add another.

Other couples in her team feel as the Hus do, she said, and their reasoning is incisive and practical.

Both husband and wife work in the fields or at other jobs on the collective farm. Two very young children can be left at nurseries during the day while the parents are at work but they need home care and feeding and this is a burden.

And as children grow up in the society of the Machiao commune, there is progressively less and less interdependence between them and their parents. The children are taken into the activities of schools and youth programs and by the age of 16 are on their own in the communes as self-supporting workers.

By the time they are teenagers, the children have little need of their parents and the parents have little material need of their children, for the elderly in China today rely not on their offspring for support in their old age but on the organization to which they are attached.

Petite and attractive despite her garb of padded trousers and jacket of faded blue, Mrs. Hu gave her views on children and birth control in the clean, plain but neatly furnished upstairs bed-living room of her two-room home in an apartment building near the fields in which she works.

"The old idea that parents should have lots of children to honor and support them is finished," she said. "Most parents in this production team have one or two children. The largest family has only four."

Mrs. Hu's team forms a collective that is roughly the equivalent of the traditional Chinese village with its surrounding fields. Out of 248 persons in the team, 80 are married women, and Mrs. Hu said 20 had had sterility operations while others were taking birth-control pills or using contraceptive devices so they would have no more children.

At the commune hospital nearby, the doctor in charge said he not only was operating on women to make them sterile but was performing vasectomies on men at the rate of three a week.

Steady Decline Indicated

The evidence provided at the Machiao commune, where a group of foreign newsmen visited today as part of a four-day stay at Shanghai, and at other institutions in the Shanghai area where the correspondents have asked questions about birth control, points to the probability that a steady decline is taking place in the birth and population growth rates in China.

The vice chairman of the commune, Wu Chiu-ling, with whom the newsmen talked, had no comparative figures from

The present life style in China does not encourage large families, as did the old. Here, a young woman holds her baby, but children spend much time away from parents.

earlier years. But he said the present birth rate in the commune, which consists of 196 collective farms and 35,000 people, was 15 to 17 per 1,000. He had no figures on the death rate, so a population growth rate for the commune could not be calculated.

Factories and other establishments the newsmen have visited also reported declining

birth rates. The so-called extended Chinese family of former times seems to have virtually disappeared, replaced by just a man and wife with one, two or three children.

Officials queried here have no information on national population growth or the effectiveness of birth control on a nationwide basis, and the lack of statistics in the Machiao com-

mune would indicate that social organizations throughout the country are not recording very good population growth information for forwarding to a central authority.

Thus it seems doubtful that Peking has at present any very exact data on the rate of population increase. It is clear, however, that the central Government is encouraging birth control without making an intensive publicized campaign out of it.

Late Marriage Favored

The encouragement consists, for one thing, of constant pressure on the young not to marry before the age of approximately 28 for men and 26 for women. Additionally, birth-control pills and other contraceptive means are made available free. Vasectomies for men and sterilization for women can be had at nominal cost in hospitals.

China's population is usually estimated today at around 800 million. Peking itself has used a peak figure of 750 million.

The growth rate has for years been estimated at about 2 per cent annually, but it is possibly below this figure now.

Growth in China's enormous population has been one of the basic problems of the Communist Government. The increase has steadily curtailed the effects of economic expansion in improving the livelihood of the people.

Now it appears, as much because of factors stemming from the new way of life in China as because of the use of artificial contraception, that the birth rate and population growth rate are dropping appreciably.

April 21, 1971

China's Shiny Airports Await Planes

By TILLMAN DURDIN
Special to The New York Times

HONG KONG, May 11—Neat, well-furnished and shiny, the big international section of the Hungjao Air Terminal in Shanghai is mostly an empty showpiece.

Used by international air services only three times a week, the terminal, which this correspondent saw last week, symbolizes the near-isolation of China from world air traffic. However, its readiness for greater use may be a harbinger of future links that could result from the new Peking policy of opening doors to the outside world.

Similar big international terminals in Canton and Peking are also infrequently used. In fact, the only foreign airlines that fly into China are the Soviet Union's Aeroflot, the North Korean airline, Air France and Pakistan International Airlines. Peking's own Civil Aviation Administration of China runs international flights to Moscow, to Hanoi, to Rangoon, the capital of Burma, and to Pyongyang, North Korea.

Aeroflot has two flights a week to Peking, Pakistan International Airlines flies twice a week into Shanghai and Canton, Air France has one flight a week to Shanghai and the North

Korean airline has once-a-week service to Shenyang and Peking. The Chinese airline flies twice a week to Hanoi, once a week to Pyongyang by way of Shenyang and once a week to Rangoon.

Traffic Said to Be Light

Both Air France and Pakistan International Airlines give the Chinese a chance to view American planes. Both fly Boeing 707's into China. Traffic on all the international flights to and from China is said to be light.

China's airline isolation from the areas to the east is most striking. The hundreds of Japanese, for example, who go to

Peking annually have to fly almost 2,000 miles southwest from Japan to Hong Kong and, after an overnight stay, take a train to Canton where, if they are lucky, they can get a domestic Chinese flight the day after their arrival for the journey of nearly 1,000 miles northward to the capital.

If a jet air service existed between Osaka and Peking, the journey could be made in less than four hours.

Canada Also Seeks Link

The Pakistani airline and Air France have long sought to extend their Shanghai services on to Japan, but the Japanese Government will not permit this. The Japanese, who have no official diplomatic relations with China, want to make this link themselves, and one of the few levers they have for getting Peking to approve is to block any other international airline from operating a service from the Chinese mainland to Japan.

Canada has been seeking a service into China, but Peking has been noncommittal so far in responding to Canadian representations. Canada might also face Japanese opposition if landings in Japan en route to and from China were planned.

Peking's dispatch of a civil aviation mission last year to Europe and other places seemed to indicate plans for extension of China's international air services, but there have been no definite signs that any new flights will start soon.

The Communist Govern-

ment's domestic air services are also limited, though considerably more developed than the international services.

All the main cities are linked, but the frequency of service, even for the big coastal cities, is not great. There is, for example, only one nonstop flight each week from Shanghai to Canton. The daily flights operated on this route make two stops.

The Civil Aviation Administration of China still operates no pure jet aircraft. The mainstays of its fleet for longer flights are British Viscounts and Soviet Ilyushin-14's, both turbojet aircraft. The Chinese themselves manufacture a big single-engine biplane that is used for short hauls but build

no larger transport planes.

Peking last year acquired four British-made three-jet Hawker-Siddeley Tridents from Pakistan, but these planes have not yet been put into service. When questioned, officials say that a training program for the crews that will fly and maintain the planes is still going on.

Actually, air travel does not appear to be very popular in China. Railway services are good and people generally seem to prefer the trains.

Rail fares were raised recently, and air travel is now cheaper than first-class train travel, but many planes still fly with empty seats.

Pilots on the Chinese planes wear no special uniform, not

even distinctive caps. They dress in the same ill-fitting khaki trousers and jackets as military men.

Ground and cabin hostesses are helpful and courteous and especially single out foreigners to say, "Huangyin, Huangyin," which means "Welcome, welcome." They too have no special uniforms.

Facilities for instrument landings are meager, and if there is bad weather flights are simply delayed until visibility improves. Planes have Mao Tsetung slogans painted along the sides, but the loudspeakers that blared inside the cabins during the Cultural Revolution a few years ago have been turned off and sweet Chinese symphonic music has been substituted.

May 12, 1971

'Revolutionary Committees' Insure Discipline in China

By SEYMOUR TOPPING

Special to The New York Times

PEKING, June 1—At Peking's heavy electric machinery plant, Wei Ching-shen, the 50-year-old chairman of the Revolutionary Committee that runs the big factory, listened patiently as a young woman worker criticized his record.

Mr. Wei did not seem greatly perturbed by her unexpected outburst although he was being interviewed by an American reporter and top management officials of the factory, which employs 5,300, were also in the room.

The incident was revealing of the profound changes that have taken place since the eruption of the Cultural Revolution in management techniques and the style of operation of the Chinese Communist production system. Throughout the country, extending to the grassroots levels in farm communes, factories and other economic enterprises and schools, a new uniform structure of control and administration has been imposed.

Each economic unit and school is managed by a Revolutionary Committee that insures tight political control, ideological discipline and work methods in keeping with the Maoist philosophy.

Army Man Has Role

Mr. Wei, a small, gentle-looking man wearing a plain

gray cap and tunic, was flanked during the interview by Ma Kuei-tang, head of the 16-man army propaganda team, and Miss Yeh Ya-hua, 33, a design worker who voiced the criticism of the committee chairman.

The triumvirate, all members of the Revolutionary Committee, was typical of the prevalent "three-in-one combination" that always includes management officials in responsible positions, representatives of the People's Liberation Army and workers or peasants.

When Mr. Wei was asked if he had been the director of the factory before establishment of its Revolutionary Committee on Feb. 14, 1968, Miss Yeh interrupted by saying: "Yes, he was formerly general secretary of the Communist party of the plant. He is now the same man physically but he has greatly changed since the Cultural Revolution."

Miss Yeh, a handsome, confident woman wearing braids and a worn olive-drab jacket over a gray blouse, glanced at Mr. Wei. As an aide took notes, the committee chairman confessed that before the Cultural Revolution his staff "had been divorced from production and the masses."

"We did not take part in manual labor and we had bureaucratic airs," he said.

In dress, it is difficult to distinguish Mr. Wei or any other senior manager from other

workers in the plant. Possession of a wrist watch is sometimes an indication that a man or woman has a key job. Virtually everyone in the factory insists on describing himself or herself as "an ordinary worker."

The reception room in which the interview took place, the equivalent of the board room in the executive suite of an American corporation, was bare except for plain wooden chairs and a long narrow table on which jasmine tea and cigarettes were served. The walls were of unfinished white plaster but like the stone floor were scrubbed clean.

Mr. Wei said that the "pernicious revisionist influence of Liu Shao-chi," the former chief of state, had influenced the factory. Material incentives and rewards had been put in command and development of technology had been emphasized rather than production, he explained.

Changes Carried Out

The chairman added that with the help of the workers and the army propaganda team, the factory had passed through a period of struggle and criticism and now was being run completely according to Maoist doctrine.

In early 1967 when Mao Tsetung, the party chairman, was locked in a power struggle with Liu Shao-chi, he first issued his call for establishment of Revolutionary Committees.

"Proletarian revolutionaries, unite and seize power from the handful of party persons in power taking the capitalist road," Mr. Mao declared.

Unleashing millions of Red Guards — young militants — to smash the party and Government bureaucracy, which constituted Mr. Liu's power base, Mr. Mao sought control of the farm communes, factories and schools through Revolutionary Committees. The struggle and purge continued through 1969 and the "re-education" period is now in its final phase.

Hundreds of thousands of intellectuals, students, government and party officials and production managers are going through special schools where through manual labor and propaganda courses they are "integrated with the masses." Depending on the individual and how the school directors decide he is faring, a student may remain in the course anywhere from several months to several years.

To assure the most trustworthy framework of control, Chairman Mao has put the army, which he regards as the "main component of state," into the factories, communes and schools.

In some state establishments such as the Peking Experimental Chemical Works, an army representative has become chairman of the Revolutionary Committee and the former plant director has been relegated to a more junior post.

Mr. Ma, the uniformed 33-year-old head of the army propaganda team in the Peking electrical machinery factory,

464

said his men had been there since June, 1967, to "safeguard and defend our red political power and to consolidate the dictatorship of the proletariat."

After factory sessions, members of the team go to the apartments of the workers who live in the housing complex nearby for further discussion with the families.

Mr. Ma said that his men spend one-third of their time in productive manual labor in the factory.

Ready to Fight 'Aggression'

An infantry officer, Mr. Ma, like all army commanders, wears no identification of rank on his baggy olive-drab uniform with red collar epaulets.

He declared that he was ready to go to the front if "imperialists or revisionists impose aggression on our country." The term "imperialists" was an allusion to the United States while "revisionists" alludes to the Soviet Union.

The 20-member Revolutionary Committee, which has a standing committee of 10, nine of whom are members of the Communist party, has put into effect the Maoist precept: "Better

troops and simpler administration." The factory's administrative staff has been reduced from 500 to about 200, Mr. Wei said.

Other enterprises visited in a number of Chinese cities reported similar cuts in their administrative personnel.

Touring the electrical factory, this writer saw propaganda posters everywhere stressing the central theme of self-reliance and innovation. In every workshop, workers proudly exhibit equipment, ranging from simple power-driven wheels that wrap generator coils to heavy

presses and lathes, that had been designed and manufactured in the plant.

"The imperialists and revisionists have imposed a boycott on us and if we wait for the state to supply us, it would take too long," one shop foreman said. An intensive effort is being made through Maoist indoctrination to obtain a creative release of energy from the workers since such material incentives as pay bonuses have been eliminated.

June 2, 1971

Chinese Welfare Plan Seeks to Assure Minimum Living Standard

By SEYMOUR TOPPING
Special to The New York Times

PEKING, June 2—The Chinese Government has put into effect a welfare system designed to assure every family a minimum standard of living.

Since the reform of the wage structure during the Cultural Revolution, which began in 1966, new subsidies have become available to urban workers and peasants when their income is inadequate to feed their families.

Foreign observers have not recently seen any evidence of hunger in urban or rural areas of China they have visited.

The framework of the new wage structure and the welfare system became apparent during a series of interviews with senior officials of agricultural communes, factories and commercial enterprises in the regions of Peking, Shanghai, Hangchow and Canton. The pattern is said to be uniform for the country, although the decreed changeover has not yet been completed in some areas.

Incentive Bonuses Ended

The old incentive bonuses and overtime pay have been eliminated as having been an expression of the "revisionist thinking" of the purged chief of state, Liu Shau-chi. A new graduated scale of wages for urban workers has been substituted, with revolutionary criteria for determining how a worker should be classified.

Factories are grading all employes in eight categories ranging from 34 yuan to 108 yuan monthly, with apprentices

earning from 18 to as much as 30 yuan. The value of the yuan, according to the official Chinese exchange rate, is 2.4 to the dollar.

"We determine the category of a worker by his total contribution to the country, including length of service and development of skills," Chen Chang-yi, a member of the Revolutionary Committee that runs the Peking Experimental Chemical Works, said. What is described as the ideological ability of the worker is also taken into account.

Men and women receive equal pay.

A worker can move up in grade but he is not demoted. Skill tests for promotion are given each year by committees of workers. An apprentice can graduate to Grade 1 at 34 yuan after two to three years.

Under this system, a skilled worker with long experience may be earning more than his younger department head.

In visits to factories, it is difficult to get responsible officials to state their rank and responsibilities. Responding to Chairman Mao Tse-tung's dictum that intellectuals must integrate with the masses, senior administrators usually describe themselves as "ordinary workers."

Rent Is Low

The welfare system comes into play when a worker in a lower wage category has a large number of dependents and, with the common expenditure for food amounting to 10

yuan a person each month, finds his total outlay exceeding his income. Rent in state-owned apartments is only about 3 to 4 yuan a month.

There is no personal income tax in China. Government revenue comes from a 6 per cent tax levied annually on income of farm communes as a fee for land use and from profits accumulated by other state enterprises such as shops. Individual taxes are concealed in state-pegged prices of consumer goods.

In each region of the country, a minimum per-capita income has been fixed. Around Peking the cost-of-living scale is pegged at 12 to 14 yuan a person per month. When family income is below the per-capita minimum, the factory where the worker is employed is required to pay a subsidy that brings it up close to the general standard.

System Not Overtaxed

The subsidy system evidently is not overtaxed, because many families have more than one person working.

There is said to be virtually no unemployment in China although underemployment is reported in some areas. Since the Cultural Revolution, hundreds of thousands of surplus workers and their families as well as many students have been moved from urban areas into rural communes.

In the countryside the welfare system works somewhat differently.

Wages in communes are based upon the share of earn-

ings of a production team. Each peasant is awarded work points for each day's labor according generally to one of four categories, established under criteria similar to those applicable for urban workers.

When a peasant, because of low income or because of physical incapacity, cannot feed his family from his earnings and the output of his small private vegetable plot, the commune assigns him a subsidy. The money comes from a welfare fund accumulated by a 2 per cent deduction taken annually from the total earnings of the commune.

Every peasant family is entitled to free medical attention, usually through membership in a medical collective with dues of 1 to 2 yuan a year. Children, like those in urban areas, are entitled to universal education, generally including access to the first three years of secondary school.

The state has established uniform social benefits for factory workers.

Each worker is guaranteed free medical service, but members of his family are entitled only to payment by the factory of 50 per cent of their medical costs.

Some Form Cooperatives

In some factories, such as the Peking Experimental Chemical Works, and at the Shanghai Pungpo housing development, which serves a complex of 15 plants, the workers have founded cooperatives to pay the additional 50 per cent of the medical costs of family dependents. Each family gets complete coverage by contributing one-fifth of a yuan a month. This system seems to be spreading to most factories.

When a worker suffers an occupational accident or illness, the factory pays all medical costs and his full salary. Safety arrangements in Chinese workshops seem to be less comprehensive than in the West and there is probably a higher incidence of industrial accidents.

For other extended illnesses, workers get 60 per cent to full payment of their salary, according to length of service, during the first six months of the illness and thereafter 60 per cent. Subsidies are available to ease family hardships.

At the Peking No. 3 cotton textile mill, where 70 per cent of the 6,000 workers are women, excellent free nurseries and kindergartens are provided for children who cannot be left at home.

"In the old society we were fired if we got married or had a child, but here we get 56 to 72 days of paid maternity leave and special rest periods for the first seven months after returning to the job," Mrs. Chang Wen-lan, a 45-year-old worker, said.

Most large factories operate around the clock on three shifts, with each shift working eight hours including a half hour of rest added to the midshift break for lunch. Workers get one day a week off and seven days a year vacation, divided among the main festival holiday periods.

Two weeks a year are granted for a husband or wife, if separated, to visit the spouse, or for unmarried workers to visit parents who live at a considerable distance. A three-day holiday is granted for marriage.

The state stipulates retirement for women workers at the age of 50 and men at 60, at 70 per cent of regular salary. They may at the discretion of the factory continue on the job at full salary.

Most Chinese grandparents at retirement prefer to live with one of their children in traditional manner, caring for the young grandchildren. The factory does permit them, if they prefer, to retain their apartments in its housing projects.

June 3, 1971

China: Economic Policy Stresses Local Self-Help

By SEYMOUR TOPPING
Special to The New York Times

PEKING, June 21 — In the Mukden mini-tractor factory, all the machines are painted either green or gray, revealing the unique Chinese Communist approach to industrialization.

Green designates a piece of equipment that has been manufactured by the plant's own resources while gray means it has been produced with state funds. Many, if not most, of the smaller machines are painted green.

The plant, which was turning out water faucets in 1964 with 200 workers, now has more than 1,000 workers and factory officials say it is producing about 450 12-horsepower tractors monthly in a drive to modernize agriculture.

Since the start of the Cultural Revolution, heavy

emphasis has been on self-reliance, innovation and local self-sufficiency. This was the slogan on every farm visited and in factories ranging from small neighborhood workshops to large textile, steel, chemical and machine-tool plants.

In the Soviet Union and other Communist countries of Europe, the emphasis is on economic centralization and specialization. In China Mao Tse-tung has opted for decentralization and local diversification. Each hsien, or county, has been given the target of becoming self-sufficient in food and light industrial products.

"See the country as a chessboard," each square self-sufficient but related, the people are told.

Peking's policy is not moving China dramatically and quickly into the ranks of the

advanced industrial nations. In fact China has not yet fully entered the industrial age while the United States, Japan and some European countries are well into the postindustrial electronic era of automation and computerization.

Presumably at Chinese nuclear installations and in research institutes there are advanced computers. Those seen by this writer in factories were primitive models that, apart from a serial production model for operating lathes, seemed installed largely for training and experimentation.

Backwardness Conceded

Chinese officials, while showing off their agricultural communes and factories, tell you that in general the country remains backward economically and has a long way to go.

Agriculture, moreover, remains the foundation of the economy despite the drive to industrialize. Many imports needed to nurture the industrial base are financed by exports of such products as animal hides, soybeans, vegetable oils and canned fruit. Only recently have the Chinese begun to compete seriously with textiles and other light industrial products, largely in Asian and African markets.

The shortage of goods to export to industrial countries limits foreign exchange earnings and is a major factor in the relatively slow growth of heavy industry and explains the dependence on local efforts and innovation.

Nevertheless, the evidence of construction, the lush, well-tended fields, the markets full of food and consumer necessities and the energy exhibited everywhere add up to the impression that the basic needs of the people are being met and the foundation is being laid for a modern industrial country.

The policy of decentralization not only has compensated for inadequacy of the transport system but has given China the capacity to absorb a strong nuclear blow without suffering total paralysis.

The drive for local self-sufficiency can be illustrated by the industrial complex of Mukden, Anshan and Fushun in Manchuria.

In Anshan, the Chitashan open strip mine atop two mountains was opened last year and is producing four million tons of iron ore for the nearby iron and steel plant. The mines are being expanded so that production soon will be up to eight million tons. The ore is of a 30-per-cent grade and requires

concentration before use in blast furnaces.

More Local Ore Use

Previously Anshan drew on mines as far away as Hainan Island. The drive to tap low-grade iron-ore deposits near by is bringing Anshan, Fushun, the coal-mining center, and Mukden, with its machine-tool, tractor and electrical equipment plants, closer to self-sufficiency.

Mukden, whose official Chinese name is Shenyang, has doubled in population in the last 20 years with about two million inhabitants in the city and another two million in suburbs. With a short growing season of about 150 days, the region was dependent formerly on grain imports. Now it is close to self-sufficiency in grain with the introduction of rice fields and new techniques of intensive cultivation of wheat, corn, soybeans and vegetables.

Every agricultural commune, even if it used to grow specialty crops, is now seeking self-sufficiency in grain so as not to diminish central state reserves. At the West Lake tea commune near Hangchow, peasants recounted how for months they had fought back the swift waters of the Chientang River, building dikes and reclaiming land so that rice could be planted without diminishing the cultivation of tea, an important cash crop.

Births Are Declining

The central problem of the economy now seems within reach of a solution. Formerly the population was increasing at a rate—probably 15 million a year—that so consumed farm output that little was left for capital development or for export to pay for badly needed foreign machinery and raw materials.

Now agricultural production is increasing while the birth rate is dropping because of a policy of encouraging late marriage and such birth control measures as the pill and sterilization. Abortion is also legal if both man and wife approve.

Peasants no longer feel the need for several sons as security for their old age. The commune provides welfare funds where needed and a coffin at death. Families with two or three children seems to be the rule in the new generations.

While other foods seem plentiful, grain still is rationed in amounts adequate for the average family's needs.

According to Premier Chou En-lai, China's grain output

466

The New York Times/Audrey Topping

Factory chimneys are background in view of Shanghai harbor. China's industry lags while agriculture advances.

in 1970 was a record 240 million metric tons, a figure that foreign experts traveling in the country and observing the bumper harvests tend to accept.

The country imported 5 million tons of wheat last year but this year has contracted for only 2.5 million tons from Canada, saving about $100-million in foreign exchange. The imports will compensate for higher-priced rice shipped abroad to bring in foreign exchange and to feed such aid beneficiaries as North Vietnam.

The upsurge in grain production is attributable to new water-management projects, more intense cultivation employing new techniques, greater use of fertilizer and mechanization and the incredible industry of the peasant.

Climate's Impact Reduced

The water-management projects completed with mass labor in every section of the country are a shield against the weather cycle, which in the past brought famine through drought or floods.

Many millions of trees have been planted in the countryside and in cities to guard against soil erosion

and beautify the landscape.

In the countryside one sees peasant production teams marching out to work in the fields with a red banner fluttering at the head of the column. There are glimpses of army propaganda teams lecturing peasants beside paddy fields to spur them to greater efforts.

Army propaganda teams also have been trying to combat some dissatisfaction among the peasantry and tendencies toward the "capitalist road" that came under attack during the Cultural Revolution when Mr. Mao ousted former President Liu Shao-chi.

In the August First Commune near Mukden, San Kwang-ta, a tall, tough-looking party man who became chairman of the revolutionary committee a year ago, said serious ideological problems had developed in the grain-growing commune because of the "capitalist influence" of the renegade Liu Shao-chi."

Private Plots Cut Back

Mr. San asserted that the private plots that each peasant family of collective production teams is allowed, together with ownership of a house, had mushroomed in size. The plots, on which a pig and a few chickens also are kept, now have been cut

back.

Free markets and speculation have also been ended, Mr. San said. Peasants now buy and sell their domestic side products such as handicrafts through a commune cooperative. Loans and savings deposits are made at a commune loan and credit cooperative at 4 per cent interest.

In factories there is heavy propaganda emphasis on a United States strategic ban on shipments of machinery to China and the abrupt termination of Soviet aid in 1960 as spurs to workers to build their own equipment. President Nixon's recent relaxation on trade has not been mentioned in the Chinese press.

Decentralization of the economy has paralleled changes in the structure of the national Government. Since the Cultural Revolution, central government administrative personnel has been pared from 60,000 to about 10,000, according to Premier Chou. About 80 per cent of those removed, many of whom were linked to former President Liu, were sent to re-education schools. Thousands are still in these schools or in villages awaiting reassignment.

Departments Merged

The Government's 90 departments have been consolidated into 26, each under a revolutionary committee made up of members of the army, which Mr. Mao regards as a "key component of the state," and of party and staff workers.

Throughout the country, responding to Mr. Mao's injunction to simplify the administrative structure, similar personnel cuts, often exceeding 50 per cent, have been made by local governments, factories, communes and other enterprises.

Mr. Mao seems to have boundless faith that through indoctrination the ordinary workers can be roused to increase production and through innovation renew the antiquated and makeshift character of much of the Chinese industrial plant. Each factory now keeps an official count of the number of innovations by workers. In many factories army propaganda teams still grapple with resentments and dislocations caused by a decision taken in the Cultural Revolution to eliminate such material incentives as bonuses, payment for piecework and overtime pay.

Letters From China: IV

By JAMES RESTON

TIENTSIN, China, Aug. 5—You hear a lot about the Chinese theory of "people's war" and "protracted war" these days but what does it all mean?

Well, frankly, we don't know and the Chinese won't tell, but the 196th Infantry Division of the People's Liberation Army operates out of a flat agricultural plain at the village of Yang Chun, and for the first time since the Cultural Revolution of 1966-69, it is now open to inspection by invited guests. One thing is sure: That old country boy from Wisconsin, Secretary of Defense Melvin Laird, never saw a base like this. It does all the routine stuff, basic training, discipline, marksmanship, and particularly the techniques of guerrilla warfare, but in addition, it is a political school, a vast farm, producing its own fodder, a pharmaceutical factory, and a machine shop, making tools, spare parts, and repairing weapons and vehicles.

In short, it concentrates on political motivation, integration with the peasants and their work, simple weapons that can be carried quickly from one place to another, and self-reliance and self-sufficiency.

We were received at division headquarters by the deputy commander, Keng Yu-chi, who explained that the main purpose of his command was to help defend Peking. His division had been formed in 1937 during the early part of the anti-Japanese war, he said, and since that time "under the guidance of Chairman Mao," had killed 38,000 Japanese, Chiang Kai-shek "traitors" and American imperialists in the Korean war. All this very politely.

His division, he explained, had three principles and three main tasks. The principles were to maintain unity between his officers and men, with each group teaching the other, to develop a common purpose between his division and the civilian population and to disintegrate the enemy, undefined.

His three main tasks, he continued, were to develop his division into a fighting force, a work force in the fields and factories, and a production and political force. His division numbered "over ten thousand men," plus their dependents who helped run the farms and factories, schools, and nurseries of his command.

He took us first to the barracks and club of Two Company of the 587th Regiment of the 196th Division. The club was a propaganda room with maps of the company's battles, photos of its heroes, exhibits of its captured weapons and citations, and a Ping-Pong table.

We went back to Peking a little sad thinking about memory. Maybe we have to learn to forget, we said as we left. How could we forget the past, the Chief of Staff asked—forget the Japanese, forget Korea, forget Taiwan? we would like to ask Nixon to think about that.

The barracks in the plain red brick buildings were immaculately clean with bare double-decker bunks fitted with mosquito netting, at the end of each row of beds were neatly lettered company "newspapers" composed of letters of gratitude to Chairman Mao. Each man had his battle roll on his bed for instant action, and automatic rifles, carbines and machine guns were racked neatly at a clear space beyond each double row of sixteen beds.

After a tour of the pig pens, rice paddies, and pharmaceutical sheds, we were shown how the pig bristles were used to make brushes to clean the rifle bores, taken to the machine shops and then given or offered a lunch of wine, mao tai (a clear distillation of sorghum and dynamite) and enough food to paralyze a regiment.

In the afternoon, the division produced a concert and series of propaganda skits, remarkably good and even amusing, after which we were taken to a vast artillery range where Two Company put on a demonstration of marksmanship by rifle, automatic and machine-gun fire, antiaircraft, mortar, antitank and rocket fire, and man-to-man combat and house-to-house guerrilla tactics. It was an impressive performance.

We were then invited to come back and discuss "the international situation." Asia, Africa, and Latin America, we were told, were fighting in unison against the American imperialists. Men, the deputy commander insisted, were more important than weapons. Any enemy invading China would be "drowned in oceans of people," he added, and did we have any comment?

We said we had come to China to report and not to argue and suggested that things were changing in the world and America was looking now to the future and to peace and understanding in the Pacific. This proved to be a disastrous gesture.

The past could not be forgotten, the deputy commander insisted. The main trend in the world was against the U.S. imperialists and all their running dogs. All nations wanted independence and liberation, all peoples wanted revolution and this was the irresistible trend of history.

China was friendly toward all peoples including the American people, he concluded, but imperialist and reactionary governments "never change," so the danger of a new world war still exists. Nixon, as he called the President, must get out of Taiwan and Vietnam and give China its rightful place in the United Nations.

He continued in this vein until an official of the Foreign Office intervened to say the sun was going down and we had to get back to Peking. The Chinese people and the American people were friends, he said, but the American Government was something else. It said it wanted to normalize relations with the People's Republic of China, but Secretary Rogers had suggested a two-China formula for the United Nations which was "a new brand with the same old stuff."

A Job for The Birth Control Teams

A girl on her way to work steps briskly from her Shanghai apartment, pokes her head in a door down the street and says, "mark me down for today!" then continues on.

It is a procedure repeated countless times each day in the urban areas of China—and to some extent in rural communes. The girl is letting the local "barefoot doctor" or other health worker know that her monthly period has begun. The fact is noted in her record and is used to help her keep on schedule in taking contraceptive pills for 20 to 22 days of her monthly cycle.

This is but one of the various ways in which China is trying to stem its ever-expanding population. The program is aimed not only at improving the standard of living for the average Chinese, but also at freeing women from the burdens of prolonged childbearing.

According to a study by the Population Reference Bureau in Washington, D. C., birth control was frowned on in the early years after the Chinese Communist revolution because of the Marxist view that the Malthusian doctrine of population control by hunger was reactionary. Productivity, it was argued, could outstrip population growth.

However it became obvious that, to improve living standards, the population growth would have to be checked. Only in the so-called national minority areas is there no attempt to check the birth rate. These are the sparsely inhabited regions, such as Inner Mongolia, where it is believed a larger population can be accommodated.

But to what extent has Peking's program been successful in altering the growth rate? For Western demographers the margin of uncertainty in estimating the population of China is enormous.

For example, an estimate by the United States Bureau of the Census puts the 1970 population of mainland China at about 871 million. Yet two other studies, one under United Nations auspices, put it closer to 753 million. The margin of difference, as noted in an issue of the Population Bulletin circulated last week, is almost 120 million — more than half the total population of the United States and Canada combined.

The Population Bulletin, published by the Population Reference Bureau, notes that, despite current difficulties in estimating China's population, the country's historical population statistics are the most abundant of any nation, reaching back almost 2,000 years. In 2 A.D. the population was recorded at 60 million.

Presumably it then expanded, but 12 centuries later, after the Mongols had been driven out and the Ming Dynasty was founded, it was again back to 60 million. It reached a peak of more than 430 million in the middle of the last century, only to be devastated by the Taiping Rebellion. In 1953, China underwent its first modern census. The result was a count of 582,603,417 on the mainland, 7,591,298 on Taiwan Chinese—a total of more than 600 million.

The problem in estimating the current population centers on birth and death rates. Birth control efforts are said to have begun under the Communists as early as 1956, but the problems of mass producing birth control pills and devices, getting them to the vast Chinese populace, and persuading them to use the devices have been formidable. In 1964 Premier Chou En-lai told Edgar Snow, the author, who died in Switzerland last week, that his Government hoped to see the birth rate drop below 2 per cent by 1970.

Mr. Snow was later told that it had dropped that low as early as 1966, but had then shot up during the cultural revolution. Millions of Red Guards went on the march, the sexes mingling freely, and many early marriages resulted. Now, however, reports from many sources indicate that marriage before the age of 28 for men and 25 for women is discouraged. Marriage before the ages of 20 and 18, respectively, is illegal.

However, a number of sources report that the tendency of some women to forget their pill-taking has troubled the Chinese birth-control effort. It is for this reason that local check-off lists are used. For several years the Chinese have been experimenting with a once-a-month pill, but, so far, it seems to produce more side effects than the daily pill.

Mr. Snow was told by Dr. Lin Ch'iao-chih, a female gynecologist trained in England: "We are experimenting with a once-in-three-months pill and we now believe we can develop a pill or vaccine effective for about a year." It was reported to him that in Peking 70 per cent of the women of child-bearing age use contraceptives with two thirds of them taking the pill.

Apart from the oral contraceptives, intra-uterine loops are said to be used extensively. The writer Han Suyin, who is a doctor of medicine, has reported that in every commune that she visited in 1969 both the pill and intra-uterine devices were available at no charge.

In the rural communes, however, the figure for pill-takers is only about 40 per cent. Couples are encouraged to limit their families to two children and abortions are available to women who do not wish additional children. Girls pregnant for the first time are said to be discouraged from having an abortion.

The aspiration technique is used in the early weeks of pregnancy. The method, widely favored in the West as well, employs suction and avoids surgical procedures.

Key figures in all of these efforts are the so-called "barefoot doctors." A description of their role—based in part on a communication from Mr. Snow—appeared in a report last year by the Victor Bostrom Fund Committee and the Population Crisis Committee, both in Washington. The report described the barefoot doctors as paramedical personnel of both sexes who average 20 years in age. They receive three months' training in hospital schools and may return for further instruction after assignment to a commune or urban block organization where they dispense contraceptives and supervise their use.

—WALTER SULLIVAN

PEKING INDICATES CUT IN SCHOOLING

By TILLMAN DURDIN
Special to The New York Times

HONG KONG, Sept. 16—Peasant-soldier teams engaged in taking over the schools of rural Communist China have been given a model that provides for nine years of schooling, from the first grade through high school, a reduction of three years.

The model system allows plenty of time for farm labor and emphasizes practical matters as well as intensive attention to the thoughts Mao Tse-tung.

The new system consists of five years of primary study, two years of junior high school and two years of senior high school.

The take-over of rural schools by peasant-soldier teams, which is proceeding parallel with the take-over of city schools by worker-soldier teams, was ordered by Peking two weeks ago. It is part of a new policy of subordinating teachers and other Intellectuals, including student Red Guards, to the over-all supervision of workers, peasants and military men.

Article Broadcast Widely

The description of the model rural school system appeared yesterday in Jenmin Jih Pao and Hung Chi, two official organs of the Peking regime, and was relayed here today by Hsinhua, the Chinese Communist press agency. The importance of the model was indicated by the fact that radio stations throughout the country broadcast the article.

The change from the 12-year program required until recently is clearly intended for general adoption. It conforms with ideas for revisions in the school system put forward during the last two years by leaders of the Cultural Revolution, chairman Mao's effort to purge his opponents and bolster his strict brand of Communism.

Mr. Mao said recently that higher education should be devoted mainly to the study of engineering and science for two to three years and should be provided for industrial workers and peasants who would return to labor after finishing their higher schooling.

All schools, even primary schools, were closed down late in 1966. In March, 1967, the resumption of schooling was ordered, but only the primary schools reopened—and not all of those. With some exceptions, high schools and higher schools have not been operating.

Millions of students of the 1966 and 1967 classes who have had no formal education for some time are being sent to factories, mines and the countryside for lifetime assignments at manual labor. Waiting for schooling in the higher classes of high schools and the still-to-be established higher educational institutions are millions who have come of age since the Cultural Revolution started in 1966.

The Peking report condemned the old system as revisionist because it emphasized intellectual training and good grades. The report said this discriminated against the children of poor and lower middle peasants because they could not learn as fast and as well as the children of parents who were better off and could help their children at home.

The old system was also denounced because it inculcated the idea that with education rural children could escape the peasant's lot and move to the city.

September 17, 1958

RED CHINA YOUTHS SERVE AS DOCTORS

Peking Improvises in Effort to Overcome Shortages

Special to The New York Times

HONG KONG, Nov. 9 — Chinese Communist newspapers recently carried a photograph of a young, smiling girl, sitting in a dry paddy field together with a group of peasants. At her bare feet was a tin box marked with a red cross.

The girl looked barely old enough to be a trained nurse, but the caption identified her as one of a new breed of "barefoot doctors" assigned to care for people living in the countryside of Communist China.

The term doctor is used loosely. Young people fresh out of high school, or at best with a year or two of medical training at college, are given a short period of instruction in the field under an offically qualified doctor and are then expected to "apply what they have learned in practice."

This is just one way in which China is improvising in an effort to overcome a chronic shortage of doctors, which has been aggravated by power struggles in medical colleges

during the Cultural Revolution of Chairman Mao Tse-Tung.

Factional fighting and the spread of disease through the mass movement of Red Guards led to a sharp increase in the number of patients requiring medical attention in the more heated periods of the Cultural Revolution. The situation was made worse by a shortage of modern drugs as well as doctors.

Old Methods Stressed

Apart from short-cut training methods, Peking is meeting the problem with a renewed emphasis on traditional Chinese medicine and the use of herbs.

To generate public confidence in makeshift medical methods, the Chinese Communist press has reported extraordinary achievements in the field of medicine, with particular emphasis on major feats of surgery.

Acupuncture, in which the skin is pierced by needles at various specified areas, is the miracle treatment for deafmutes, according to a report by Hsinhua, the Chinese Communist press agency. An army medical team, after studying the teachings of Chairman Mao Tse-tung, tried using a needle at a point previously regarded as "forbidden" and to a depth formerly considered dangerous, the agency said.

The treatment was successful, and now 128 students at the Liaoyuan School for Deaf-Mutes in Kirin province can hear and 125 can speak, Hsinhua said.

Surgery in China is no longer the prerogative of doctors. In order to serve the peasants well, "nurses are diagnosing complaints, making out prescriptions and performing surgery, according to a report in the Peking organ, Jenmin Jih Pao.

Ta Kung Pao, a Communist paper published in Hong Kong, carried a report that illustrated the primitive conditions existing still in the rural areas of China. But the paper's emphasis was on the ability of doctors to provide some medical care despite great difficulties .

The medical team, sent from Shanghai to a mountainous region, "borrowed some stools and boards to make some beds and fetched water from a well some half a kilometer away," the report said. The operating table was a wooden board bed, and "child delivery was carried out in a bamboo reclining chair," it said.

November 10, 1968

CHINESE SCHOOLS STRESS POLITICS

Thoughts of Mao Are Given Precedence Over 3 R's

By NORMAN WEBSTER
© 1969 The Globe and Mail, Toronto

CANTON—A Chinese teenager's main course of study is the thought of Mao Tse-tung. His education is, first and foremost, political.

Take Canton's No. 32 Middle School. Here more than a quarter of the formal curriculum is dedicated specifically to studying the thoughts of Chairman Mao, and the political content of the school's total program is much higher.

The institution has 136 teachers and 3,300 students, most aged 12 to 16, but its main features seem to provide an outline of the new pattern emerging in the Chinese educational system, disrupted and reformed from top to bottom during the Cultural Revolution, the move by the Maoists to impose a more austere form of Communism on China.

Those features are the unchallenged primacy of political studies and activity, the integration of schooling and practical work, under the direction of workers and peasants; and a shortening in the period of schooling.

Its Pattern Set by Mao

It is a pattern that fits Chairman Mao's declaration: "The period of schooling must be shortened, education must be revolutionized, and the domination of our schools by bourgeois intellectuals must not be allowed to continue any longer."

The new curriculum, as outlined by Mrs. Chen, a Chinese language teacher and head of the teachers group, was as follows:

Politics (the study of Mao Tse-tung thought), eight periods a week; mathematics, six periods; physics, two; chemistry, two; Chinese, five; English, two; history and geography, one; military training, two; agricultural knowledge, two; and revolutionary literature and arts, one.

Thirty-one periods in all, eight of them reserved for study of the chairman's writings and almost all the other subjects — especially history, English and Chinese—have political content.

As Mrs. Chen said: "All our work is toward putting politics in command, so that politics commands every field in all subjects."

This is not all. The school week is six days long and there are seven 45-minute periods daily. Time not spent on the formal curriculum is given over to further study of revolutionary literature and arts, criticism and repudiation of the "revisionist education line" of Chairman Mao's vanquished opponent, Liu Shao-chi, preparation of lessons and sports and physical training.

Criticism Taken Seriously

The criticism and repudiation tasks are taken very seriously. All over the schoolyard are bulletin boards to which are tacked the repudiation essays, in neat characters, of individual students.

Pupils Assemble Flashlights

The school has close ties with the Canton Flashlight Factory and its two key officials are former workers at the factory—Mr. Peng, the 37-year-old head of the school's revolutionary committee, and Mrs. Lin, head of Mao Tse-tung thought propaganda team.

The Revolutionary Committee was established in February, 1968, and the thought propaganda team of workers and soldiers entered the school that same year, in December.

In one large room at the school there is an assembly operation with students putting together parts of flashlights sent from the factory. This is done in their spare time, and it is considered an important part of their education.

Considered equally important is the time the students spend every year on farming communes near Canton. There they gain practical experience of the life of the vast majority of China's population.

China Tightens Curbs on Student Rebels

Special to The New York Times

HONG KONG, June 17—Communist China, which has enthusiastically endorsed the anti-Establishment activities of young people around the world, is adopting increasingly repressive measures against its own student rebels.

Chinese authorities have been calling for greater efforts in the indoctrination of young children "to raise their class awareness" and "to deepen their love" for Mao Tse-tung, chairman of the Chinese Communist party.

The aging Peking leaders' preoccupation with the younger generation appears to reflect a continuing concern that the present political system might not endure when they step down. They are attempting to foster generations of "revolutionary successors," who will not succumb to the "sugarcoated bullets" of enemies at home or abroad.

A recent public meeting at Changchun, capital of Kirin Province, was told by a municipal official that class enemies were "trying by every means to win over to their side the young people and children."

Must Obey Unquestioningly

"Imperialist conspirators also pin their hopes for a peaceful evolution on our young generation," he said. "It is imperative for us to smash this illusion of the imperialists."

In these circumstances, the young must follow Peking's edicts unquestioningly. Posters seen recently by travelers in China stated: "Decisively liquidate bad elements who fan the wind of criminal opposition among the youth."

A large proportion of the many hundreds recently executed in Kwangtung Province

for various alleged crimes were young people. Many of them were students who had rebelled against being sent to work in the countryside and had turned to crime to feed themselves.

Most high school graduates are expected to undergo "reeducation" at the hands of the peasants. Millions have been sent from cities and towns to the countryside. In this way, the Chinese authorities have removed potential or known rebellious elements from the centers of power, reduced the urban population pressures and increased the rural labor force.

Hsinhua, the Chinese press agency, reported that "several million graduates from senior and junior middle schools" had settled down in the countryside since December, 1968. The students are expected to spend the rest of their lives with the peasants.

Some Swim to Hong Kong

The campaign has met with persistent resistance. Many refugees who swim to Hong Kong are former students who were sent from Canton, capital of Kwangtung Province, to work in the countryside.

Many students from Canton and other urban areas in Kwangtung have been assigned to Hainan Island. A broadcast from Hainan Island recently complained that some workers "brought all kinds of nonproletarian ideas from their old schools."

It stated: "Some said: 'To study in school for over 10 years and to work as a docker is a waste of our talents.' Others feared hardship and fatigue."

The broadcast said that "class education" and study of the works of Chairman Mao "proved highly effective" in overcoming

these tendencies and other "anarchist trends."

For the very young, a new program of "red children's classes" has been introduced "to cultivate the children into successors to the proletarian revolutionary cause" by giving them daily doses of Mao's thought.

5-Year-Old Is Example

A broadcast from Hofei, capital of Anhwei Province, reporting on the results of these classes, said a 5-year-old boy from a certain peasant production team used to pick up rice from the field and take it home.

The broadcast stated: "After attending the red children's class, he has come to realize that to take home the team's crops means acting from self-interest. With this new understanding in mind, he has not brought home any more crops picked up from the fields."

Hsinhua also had high praise for five children ranging in age from 10 to 15 who "died heroically in the course of putting out a forest fire."

"People saw them run into the flames and heard them recite Chairman Mao's great teaching 'When we die for the people it is a worthy death'," the agency said.

"In an instant, the five young heroes were surrounded by the conflagration, but people still heard shouts of 'Long live Chairman Mao!' loud and clear."

June 18, 1970

China Reopens Universities, Shut 4 Years

By TILLMAN DURDIN
Special to The New York Times

HONG KONG, Sept. 24—Three weeks ago a weary, dust-covered contingent of young men and women, some carrying hoes and shovels to symbolize their peasant origin, arrived on foot at Peking's Tien An Men Square after having walked 50 miles from Tientsin in four days.

December 2, 1969

The group was typical of the thousands who are arriving these days at universities that are resuming regular classes for the first time since the start of the Cultural Revolution in 1966.

The admission process and curriculum of the universities have been radically revised according to directives of Mao Tse-tung, putting class background ahead of academic

achievement and emphasizing technical subjects over liberal arts courses.

Bow Before Portrait

Waving red banners and little red books containing quotations from Mr. Mao, the young people from Tientsin bowed before the giant portrait of Mr. Mao affixed to Tien An Men, the Gate of Heavenly Peace, which fronts on the square, and intoned:

"We 221 workers, peasants and soldiers from the banks of the Hai river have arrived at your side to enter the university. This greatest happiness is given by you, and we must do honor to you and to the great socialist motherland.

"We reject blind belief in bourgeois authorities, we do not worship foreigners and men of old, we do not want to make a name for ourselves, we do not want to make money. We dare to wage revolution, are audacious in creativity and will resist corruption. We are resolved that the true nature of working people will never change, the working style of hard struggle will never change. Our red hearts, loyal to you, will never change."

Primary and secondary schools have gradually resumed classes since 1967. Higher institutions remained open for political struggle aimed at rectifying the thoughts of students and teachers, but it was not until late this year that arrangements were concluded to begin regular classes.

Engineering Stressed

In July the Peking ideological journal Hung Chi reported plans to start regular classes at Tsinghua University, a Peking center for science and engineering studies.

Reports in recent weeks have shown that other institutions are emulating the Tsinghua example and enrolling students for studies on the basis detailed in the Hung Chi article.

The account about the student contingent from Tientsin appeared in a Hsinhua dispatch printed in Ta Kung Pao, Communist daily of Hong Kong.

It disclosed that Peking University as well as Tsinghua was now taking in students and that the two universities together had enrolled 4,000 students so far.

Before the Cultural Revolution, Peking University was a liberal arts institution. Nothing was said in the Hsinhua dispatch about what the new student body would study there, but it is believed courses would be vocational and technological, as at Tsinghua.

The example set by Tsinghua provides for engineering and other technological courses to last two to three years. Classroom study is to be interspersed with work in factories and on farms, and even in classes the practical approach is to be emphasized through the actual building of equipment by students and teachers. The Tsinghua model includes short courses for peasants and workers as well as some graduate study and research work.

Political guidance and study

aimed at preventing students from developing attitudes of superiority are to be stressed. Teachers, many of whom are charged with still retaining bourgeois ideas, are to be watched and reindoctrinated to guard against their influencing students with bourgeois ideas.

A directive of Mr. Mao in July, 1969, laid down that higher education should be mainly in engineering and physics. He said periods of schooling should be shortened, control should be in the hands of the proletariat, classroom study should be combined with physical labor and students should be workers, soldiers and peasants.

The Hsinhua article today in Ta Kung Pao told of workers and peasants from all over China setting forth, after send-off rallies by the people of their home towns and cities, to attend university. The article said the students were selected as meritorious workers, soldiers and peasants after repeated discussion among the masses.

Many of those selected, the article makes clear, have meager educational qualifications but rate highly in proletarian credentials. One old coal miner, Sun Teh-yu, according to the article, has not had a single day of formal schooling.

September 25, 1970

China's Factories Mind the Children

By NORMAN WEBSTER

PEKING—Day care centers, a cause celebré for women's liberation groups in the United States are an established way of life for working mothers here and all over mainland China. Some mothers, in fact, leave their children in the care of the communal nurseries not only for the day, but for the week.

The center at the Peking Number Three Textile Mill and one in a sewing machine plant in Canton, both of which were visited recently, are two examples; there are others in cities all over China, for a majority of mothers of young children hold steady jobs.

A group of children, 5 and 6 years of age, were sitting attentively at their desks when a visitor arrived at the textile mill's center. The teacher was leading them through their numbers. First she used an apparatus with colored beads, and the youngsters counted the beads.

Math and Politics

Then came a subtraction problem—along with a political lesson. The teacher put 10 airplane cutouts on a board. "The United States imperialists have sent 10 planes to bomb Vietnam," she said. She brought out a toy automatic rifle, took aim and fired. The weapon's ratatatatat echoed around the room. The teacher removed nine of the planes.

"Our heroic Vietnamese brothers have shot down

nine planes," she said. "How many are left?"

Several children raised their hands, a little boy in front was recognized, answered correctly and was congratulated.

Other activities for the older children include coloring, games, stories, recitations, singing and dancing.

All over Peking in the warmer months, one sees groups of 5- and 6-year-olds sitting on little chairs outdoors with their ahyis ("aunties," who are really teachers). There are usually 12 to 15 children assigned to an ahyi.

In general, the nursery facilities are provided by the company for which the mother works, and they are said to be free except for the cost of the child's food. Children who are 3 or older can stay for the week, going home for part of Saturday and all of Sunday. This arrangement is especially convenient for mothers who work a night shift.

The programs range from crib care for 2 month-old infants to kindergartens for

preschoolers. (Chinese children enter the regular school system at age 7.)

Babies in Cribs

In Canton, which also has a medical clinic, the babies were in cribs in a noisy nursery attended by white-garbed women. Some babies are put there the day their mothers return to work after their 56-day maternity leave. The mothers get an hour off each shift to nurse the babies until they are about a year old.

Molding of the Socialist man begins when the child is barely more than a toddler. In almost identical words, the ahyis at the textile mill and sewing machine factory said that their goal was to train the children "to love Chairman Mao and be loyal to the Socialist motherland."

A group of 5-year-olds at the sewing machine plant informed a visitor that should they dare to attack China, American imperialism and Soviet social-imperialism would be soundly thrashed—indeed, completely wiped out.

"What I sing are Chairman Mao's quotation," rang out the piping voices in unison.

"What I read is Chairman Mao's red book.

"Follow Chairman Mao closely and make revolution forever."

November 19, 1970

PEKING STRESSING PHYSICAL FITNESS

New Exercises Ending a Long Period of Neglect

By TILLMAN DURDIN

HONG KONG, Sept. 4 — Sports and physical fitness are getting major official emphasis again in China after a long period of neglect during the turbulent years of the Cultural Revolution.

Exemplifying the new attitude, the State Council, or Cabinet, and the Central Committee of the Chinese Communist party are sponsoring a new set of physical exercises that the mass of the population throughout the country will be expected to perform every morning.

The calisthenics routines are being broadcast over the national radio network to musical accompaniment daily and over television in Peking.

News of the physical-training project was reported here in a dispatch from Peking by Hsinhua, the Chinese press agency.

The set of exercises, which takes five minutes, was worked out by calisthenics specialists of the Chinese Physical Culture and Sports Commission. Musical accompaniment was devised by the Peking Central Philharmonic Society.

Athletes Were Assailed

Sports and physical culture on an organized basis were virtually dropped during the hectic years of the Cultural Revolution, which began in 1966. Athletes with outstanding rec-ords were often singled out for condemnation as having bourgeois tendencies and sent to farms and factories to do physical labor.

Ho Lung, the veteran military leader who headed the sports commission in 1966, and his deputy, Jung Kao-tang, were subjected to public criticism sessions and eventually purged not only from the sports commission but other high posts. Mr. Ho was dropped from the Politburo of the party.

Sports and physical culture began to make a tentative comeback last year. The Physical Culture and Sports Commission was reconstituted and a Chinese table tennis team was sent to Japan to play, the first time a Chinese team ventured abroad in years.

Momentum has built up, and now there is a return to the centrally directed nationwide campaign to promote sports and physical culture that characterized Communist China before the Cultural Revolution.

City and provincial sports meetings are now regularly held and outstanding soccer, basketball, swimming, table tennis, volleyball and other teams are touring the country.

There has so far not been a resumption of the national athletic meets that were held before the Cultural Revolution.

Trend Toward Workouts

Calisthenics have also been getting more stress, and the national program, launched this week, follows a trend toward development of daily physical workouts at factories, schools, business establishments and other institutions.

The sports build-up received a tremendous impetus from the tour earlier this year by American, British, Australian, Japanese and other table tennis teams. Since then other foreign soccer, table tennis and volley-ball teams have visited China and Chinese table tennis teams have toured abroad. Teams are scheduled to visit the United States, Britain, Canada and other countries later this year.

Peking may well have in mind the next Olympic games in its build-up of athletes. The presence of teams from Nationalist China has heretofore kept the Chinese Communists out of Olympic competition, but with the Nationalists facing possible loss of their United Nations seat and the decline in their international status this year Peking may be thinking of participation in the 1972 games.

September 5, 1971

Peking In Autumn

By HAN SUYIN

PEKING—By early September the weather in Peking has cooled from the "tiger heat days"; already everywhere there is cleaning and painting; the little hutungs are swept clean; every hand seems busy; whether it is grandmothers who run bicycle stands and public telephones, or vegetable sellers with their carts.

The shops are full of shoppers from all parts of the country. This is the time for young students to return home to visit their parents. It is also the time at which the cadres who are in the new May 7 cadre schools in the countryside visit their families.

There is an effervescence about Peking which is very stimulating; the cultural revolution has been a success; but what to someone like me (on my sixteenth visit) is most striking is the new sense of freedom, a real grass-roots democratic spirit, which is evident everywhere.

The implementation of "let the masses speak, arouse the masses, listen to their opinions"; the fact that I have personally seen how this new democracy works in a new outspokenness may account for a good deal of this exhilaration. But it is also the lack of bureaucracy, the heightened efficiency and the sense of public responsibility which strikes one as so "comfortable to live in."

Brian Brake/Rapho Guillumette

People on the streets now volunteer help and information; children volunteer to take care of the traffic as some cyclists still persist in ignoring the red lights (there are no fines, only a "telling off" by the policeman).

I visited Tsinghua University which had just had its new batch of students; 2,500 new enrollments. The enrollment is along new lines; no longer by examinations. Tsinghua University announces its vacancies. These are distributed to each province. The province distributes "empty places" to each county and each county to factory and commune.

So there has been enormous debate in each factory, production brigade, production team, as to who should be sent to university; the only specification was that it should be a middle school graduate. Apart from that it was left to the communes and factories to choose, by debate and by election, the lucky youngsters who would go to university. They were chosen by their "three revolutionary" assets, that is, their politics (which is translated as behavior, intelligence, leadership qualities, ability to stimulate, to energize and to initiate, and *not* by mere recitation of quota-

473

tions), by their production, which is their hard work and assiduity, and by their "technical innovation."

The bunch I saw certainly seemed extremely alert; and highly conscious and eager to learn. Quite different from the apathy and lack of interest in studies one often finds in other Asian universities.

The kind and quality of meetings one now gets into is altogether different; they are much more closely linked to the concrete problems discussed. I remember a small factory in a commune where electronic machinery was being made by women, and where every step of how this small factory grew up was related. Some criticism we made was accepted not only with good temper, but with touching gratitude; one was very far from the bureaucratic "tin god" touch of previous visits.

But it is quite certain that the touchstone for this tremendous energy and vitality is "the little Red Book"; the scientific thinking, analysis from cause to effect, sober assessment, and recommendations to "see reality" and

"tell the truth" it contains.

I was told of several cases where some irregularities had been committed; the masses (which means the people involved) had appealed over the heads of their revolutionary committee (guilty of "bureaucratic" ramming through of measures without previous consultation) to higher echelons. Investigations teams set forth. Now instead of holding rectification meetings behind closed doors, all was done in public and wrongs were redressed speedily.

At the moment I write I have just seen an army colonel sewing at a sewing machine together with some girls in the bazaar repair shop. He is a member of the revolutionary committee of the bazaar and doing his manual labor, for revolutionary committee members are not exempt from doing their work.

Another facet of life in Peking today (as it is in other cities I visited) is the preparation for being attacked by air. This, it must be emphasized, is *self-defense. Self-defense* consists

not only in digging shelters (they are being dug everywhere), in storing food and supplies, in creating a network of first aid posts all over the country, in storing medicines, but in the mobilization of the population.

It is this aspect which repels so many hasty tourists who have no idea of what is going on in the world, and who have not read books on the possibility of war. It is certain that war today being total war, it is the population which is hit; genocide is now all too common. So the population must be trained in self-defense; in remaining at their own spots; in each region being as self-sufficient as possible. There must be no panic as in May 1940 in France, or mass exodus of helpless people then being slaughtered from the air or napalmed. Groups of marching and singing and drilling youngsters are everywhere. If war comes, it will be a long war, and it is better that the young should know what to expect than to become helpless victims, as in Vietnam, as in Cambodia today.

September 21, 1970

Mao's Wife Shapes Operas Anew to Fit Ideological Needs

By TILLMAN DURDIN
Special to The New York Times

HONG KONG, June 2— Chiang Ching, the wife of Chairman Mao Tse-tung, is again in the limelight.

She is being hailed in the Chinese Communist press for reshaping theatrical works produced under her direction to serve political needs during the turbulent early period of the Cultural Revolution.

These theatrical works—primarily Peking operas with voluntary themes—are again being revised to suit new ideological requirements.

In the original revisions, Miss Chiang's aim was to eliminate themes and ideas considered traditional, bourgeois or revisionist and to make them reflect the Maoist concept of struggle against "revisionist" officials, of self-denying service to society and of loyalty to the state and to the teachings of Mr. Mao, the Communist party leader.

Miss Chiang's new revisions portray proletarian heroes as even more brave, resourceful, devoted to the masses, ardently patriotic and loyal to the teachings of Chairman Mao. All human weaknesses on the part of the proletarian heroes have been eliminated.

There is more emphasis on selflessness for the sake of the masses and on discipline than in the earlier versions.

The revised works are clearly

meant to inspire the Chinese people to carry out what the authorities see as the needs of today. The people, through the theatrical productions, are being exhorted to work harder, fulfill the tasks set for them by their leaders, serve the state and the people, pay rigorous attention to the directives of Chairman Mao and be prepared to fight in case of war against the Soviet "revisionists" or the American "imperialists."

The themes are designed, in short, for a time of internal consolidation and external threat, and not a time of struggle for political power, as was the case in 1967 and 1968.

The new productions, a number of which deal with fighting against the Japanese during

the last war, emphasize military struggle and glorify the armed forces.

All the new Peking operas, which combine music and drama, are about relatively recent events, such as fighting against the Japanese or the Chinese Nationalists. All traditional Peking operas, based on stories about emperors, concubines, generals and scholars, have been suppressed.

Hsinhua, the Chinese Communist press agency, praised Chiang Ching recently, saying that "literary and art fighters led by Comrade Chiang Ching have painstakingly improved model revolutionary theatrical productions" so that they "give prominence to the propagation of Chairman Mao's brilliant thinking."

June 3, 1970

The Music: Movie-Like

By HAROLD C. SCHONBERG

The ballet that President Nixon and his entourage saw yesterday in Peking is a prime example of socialist realism, Chinese style. For whatever else it may be, "Red Detachment of Women" is a work that extols party doctrine, and that is its prime reason for being. Chairman Mao Tse-tung himself approved in 1964. "The orientation," he wrote, "is correct, the revolutionization successful and the artistic quality good."

Western musicians may have a somewhat lower estimate of the artistic quality than does Chairman Mao. A full score of "Red Detachment of Women" is available. It is a huge score, with no composer's name given.

The music sounds like Russian academism with a touch of Oriental exoticism. It is close to the kind of thing that Aram Khachaturian was writing in such socialist-realballets as "Spartacus."

Harmonically, "Red Detachment of Women" is unadventurous. It stays close to D minor and related keys. It uses a few leit-motifs that represent various characters. The scoring is competent but unimaginative Largely the score is poster music, of a movie background nature, with a great climax toward the end that sings the praises of the workers and peasants.

Whatever interest there is in the music of "Red Detachment of Women" comes from its native elements. The composer, or arranger, has made full use of Chinese percussion instruments. One can only imagine their quality of sound, for they are familiar only to ethnomusicologists, but they probably provide an unusual touch to an otherwise conventional example of Moscow Conservatory scoring, 1935 vintage.

February 23, 1972

Maoist Ballet

The writer of the following article is a critic specializing in the arts of the Far East.

By FAUBION BOWERS

Whatever the Chinese may feel toward the Russians nowadays, one debt of gratitude (two, if you include the atomic bomb) remains. It was the Russians who made it possible for the Chinese to combine toe slippers and rifles, and with splendid effect.

Whenever distinguished foreigners visit China—the United States table-tennis team in April last year, or President Nixon on George Washington's birthday yesterday—the Chinese trot out their best ballet, "Red Detachment of Women," one of the two "model" or "exemplary productions" approved by Chairman Mao Tse-tung in accordance with his axiom, "Art is to serve workers, peasants and soldiers." To this a rider could be added, "and foreign visitors." The other approved ballet is "The White-Haired Girl."

Performances in the cities of China begin and end not with the national anthem but with "Long live Mao Tse-tung" shouted three times by audience and cast.

Film Show Here

In October, the movie version of this three-hour ballet, exported from Hong Kong, was shown in New York's Chinatown.

In 1951, the Soviet Union sent some of its best teachers from the Bolshoi to start ballet in Peking. Under the Minister of Culture, Mao Tun, the great novelist whose works have been translated in European languages, the Russians trained a few dozen "recruits," picked for their dancing potential and for their school records.

Today, the Peking Ballet Troupe — there's a rival troupe in Shanghai—numbers about 110 graduates, who perform all over the country and who have replaced their former colleagues as instructors.

There are no stars in China, since the star system is eschewed as bourgeois, but there is little doubt that young Shih Ching-hua, who played the lead in "Red Detachment of Women" for Mr. Nixon, and in the movie version, is a prima ballerina.

Versatile Dancer

She can do anything—a split during a leap in the air, combining a back bend in which her head nearly touches her knee, for example — and do as well as any dancer with a Russian name.

Mao Tun was retired in February, 1966, and during the Cultural Revolution so were most of the ballets that the Russians had taught—"Swan Lake," "Sleeping Beauty" and "The Hunchback of Notre Dame."

"Red Detachment of Women," however, survived. It was created in 1964 by a committee of performers and advisers under the direct supervision of Chiang Ching, Chairman Mao's wife.

'Couldn't Understand'

"The people couldn't understand the stories of those Russian ballets, couldn't identify personally with what was going on on the stage," said Chen Yuanchi, an actress with the People's Art Theater in Shanghai who now lives in the United States. "Besides," she added explaining the generally cold reception of the proletariat to tutus, "we objected to the girls being bare-legged."

Now the heroines dance in shorts to cover the upper part of their thighs and they wear knee-length socks, which suit the banner-waving, gun-toting plot more realistically. The ballet shoes remain, and so do the entrechats, arabesques, and attitudes on point.

Politically, "Red Detachment of Women" tells of progress from servitude to leadership. A slave girl, tortured by the "Tyrant of the South," one of Chiang Kai-shek's wicked landlords during the war against Japanese aggression, is abandoned as dead.

Rain revives her, and she joins the Red Army and falls in love with one of its political commissars. Together they attack the landlord, but she spoils the plan when her hatred for the landlord overwhelms her and she fires her pistol too soon. The landlord escapes.

Then follows a tricky scene. She recognizes the error of her ways in confusing personal vengeance with party discipline. After some self-criticism she matures politically. The commissar gives her all his secret papers and she replaces him as leader of the company after his immolation.

"Red Detachment of Women" provides an opportunity for ethnic dance by being set on the large southern island of Hainan, where the Lis, a national minority, have a graceful arm-waving, body-swaying dance form.

The men retain the elegant classical movements of clenched fists and leg extensions at right angles to the hip, carried over from Chinese opera, including the famous acrobatics and dazzling sword fights. The marvelous mime of the past is preserved, too—in one ballet, snow troops move convincingly on invisible skis.

Hero's Death Realistic

Scenically, even the Bolshoi would be satisfied, with the hero being burned to death in realistic flames, smoke and ashes.

The heartstrings are tugged by the heroine's vicissitudes, and good triumphs over evil.

As Miss Chiang said at the start of the Cultural Revolution: "New works have to be written. Old ones must be drastically revised. Villains should be more villainous. Heroes more heroic."

February 23, 1972

SCENES FROM A BALLET, "Red Detachment of Women," performed at the Great Hall. From left: Wu Ching-hua, the oppressed slave girl; Hung Chang-ching, Red Army commissar in disguise; women of the Red Army practicing marksmanship; their target—a caricature of Gen. Chiang Kai-shek of the Kuomintang. In last panel, soldiers of Red Army learn that Kuomintang troops have launched a major offensive. Action takes place in Hainan, about 1937.

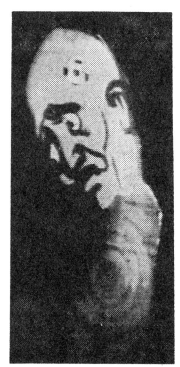

C.B.S. News

China's Very Unstarchy Army

By JOHN S. SERVICE

BERKELEY, Calif. — The old saying was that "good iron is not forged into nails: good men do not become soldiers." Now the army in China is a calling of pre-eminent prestige. A senior cadre tells of his daughter's (and his own) disappointment at her failure to qualify for enlistment—not as an officer, but in the ranks.

Interviewing high school seniors, one finds that "to serve with the People's Liberation Army" is the most popular career goal (one serious girl, though, hopes to "benefit mankind" by making a great, scientific discovery).

It is, however, an oddly unmilitary army. No one, for instance, wears any insignia of rank. The middle-aged man sitting across from me in the airplane must be an officer of some seniority, or else he would not be flying. But there is no sign in his dress or manner, nor is he accompanied by orderly, aide or armed bodyguard. Everyone, in fact, wears the same shapeless, unstarched and unpressed cotton uniform. No hint of spit and polish, of swagger and strut. There are guards at some Government buildings (and at our hotel, because some diplomats had been assaulted—"by ultraleftist troublemakers"—during the frenzied days of the Cultural Revolution). Off-duty, unarmed P.L.A. men are in great numbers on the streets, in parks and theaters, and in the stores (where they clearly have money and expect to pay for their purchases). But one never sees units of marching men, or hears a military band or even the fumbling army bugle practice that used to make dawn hours hideous in inland Chinese cities.

Also new, of course, is Mao's persistent drive against élitism and bureaucracy; his efforts to eliminate the old chasm between mental and physical work, between city and country, and between intellectuals and the workers and peasants. This, in large part, is what the Cultural Revolution was all about—but one can trace it back at least to Yenan days. It is not all negative—against élitist intellectuals, bureaucratic cadres, and bourgeois technicians; it also rests on a populist faith in the innate abilities and creativeness of the common people.

This insistence on the dignity of manual labor and the benefits of physical fitness has brought a new revolution in the schools. Every student spends some time in shop work —schools in Chungking seemed to be producing simple parts for motor trucks; some time in military training, usually field marches by school or class—including the girls—lasting for one or several days; and some time in farm work, generally going to the

communes at harvest or sowing—unless the school has its own fields. The same is true of universities.

In 1943, I traveled by bus from Chungking to Kansu with a party of Chinese Government officials, engineers, college professors and newspaper correspondents. They were "modern" intellectuals. None, of course, had the long fingernails proudly worn by the earlier Confucian scholars. Most wore Western clothes; indeed, a good many had studied in foreign universities. It was midsummer and oppressively hot on the Chengtu plain. After several days, we came to the Chialing River, flowing smooth, cool and clear as it emerged from the mountains. Our bus had to be ferried across the river. There was a line of trucks ahead. We settled down to a hot wait. The river was inviting. I suggested a swim. When I showed signs of being serious, excuses began to be made. I ended by swimming alone. We traveled together for two more months, and my companions' inaptitude for physical exercise was fully confirmed.

In October, 1971, I revisited some warm springs about twenty miles from Chungking. In World War II days it had been a favorite site for country

homes of high Kuomintang officials. Now the whole area has become a public park—including a large, outdoor, warm-water pool. We were a group of eleven or twelve: three drivers, the rest middle-level or senior cadres. The leader asked whether I liked to swim. I said I had not been in the water for several years. "Come on," was the reply. "None of us is expert." So I swam and, presumably because of the long absence of foreigners from Szechwan, before an undeservedly large and enthusiastic audience. But every member of the party was in the water with me. There was only one man, the eldest, not actually able to swim.

Perhaps swimming is a special case: Mao has set the example by his fondness for swimming the Yangtze. But it was obvious, in bathing trunks, that the bodies of these men were used to physical work and activity.

Egalitarian confidence and self-assurance might be accompanied, one supposes, by some self-importance and arrogance. Actually, what one finds everywhere are courtesy, cheerful good humor and cooperative helpfulness.

The atmosphere is comfortable, relaxed and free of tensions. Everyone works hard. If any people have a work ethic, it must be the Chinese. But the pace is not frenetic. It was new, for instance, to find that a long lunch-break, from noon to 2 P.M. or 2:30, seems now to be a general habit.

The police, unlike the past, are now unarmed—without even a stick. And, except for the men and women on traffic duty, they are few and inconspicuous. One does not hear the night watchman of old times, striking his clapper as he makes his rounds. Crime and robbery do not seem a problem. No longer are the walls around a new home or factory topped by jagged broken glass set in cement.

In all our traveling, we never saw an adult strike a child; and only very seldom did we hear a child cry.

In fact, after we had been a month in China, I realized that I had not heard any swearing and cursing. Our interpreters said there had not been any campaign against cursing, but it no longer seemed "appropriate."

This new civility may owe something to the example of a state and party that seem to prefer governing by persuasion and propaganda rather than by command and force. One wonders, though, if it does not also have some foundation in the much more comfortable, stable life enjoyed by most people, the broader sense of community that has been created, and the ending of the old, bitterly competitive scramble for a bare existence.

January 27, 1972

The Good Deed Of Dai Bee-lun

The cover of a comic book distributed to children in Communist China. The heroine is a schoolgirl in the Hunan Province town of Zhu Zhou. On these and the following pages are excerpts from the narrative.

"Her father works on the railway, but in the oppressive days of the old society, he was a beggar and a farm hand. Bee-lun will never forget how hard life was in the old society. Ever since she was very small, she has resolved always to follow the teachings of Chairman Mao, and to be his good little girl.

"In school, she loves listening to the stories of heroes. Once, the teacher tells her class the story of Uncle Wang Jie, who, to save the lives of his comrades, sacrificed his own life by throwing himself onto a package of explosives. From then on, Bee-lun is determined to learn from Uncle Wang Jie's example.

"Bee-lun has saved her pocket money to buy 11 notebooks. After writing in them Chairman Mao's directive, 'Be concerned about the affairs of our country, and carry out the Great Proletarian Cultural Revolution to the end,' she offers them to 11 little friends. She tells them: 'We must follow Chairman Mao closely.'

"She and her friends often go into the streets to read the big character posters, and with the workers, their 'uncles,' expose and criticize a small group within the party that has taken the 'capitalist road.'

"During the summer holidays, Bee-lun and her friends often help the aged of the neighborhood in their daily chores. They organize discussion groups and give revolutionary cultural performances of the thoughts of Mao Tse-tung.

"On Sept. 14, 1968, Bee-lun has gone to gather water cress by the Zhu Zhou railway station. There she sees three small children, Hong-hong, An-an and Qui-qui, playing in the middle of the tracks.

"All of a sudden, a runaway freight car comes rolling toward the children. Bee-lun sees it and shouts: 'Hong-hong, An-an, Que-qui! Get off! The train is coming!" But the three children, absorbed in their game, can't hear her call.

"The freight car is speeding toward the children. At this crucial moment, Bee-lun remembers the teaching of Chairman Mao Tse-tung: 'When we die for the people, it is a worthy death.' She rushes toward the tracks with only one thought in mind—to save the children.

"The freight car is coming nearer and nearer. Bee-lun first grabs Qui-qui and then Hong-hong off the tracks. But little An-an is still standing petrified in the middle of the tracks, staring at the oncoming freight car. For the third time, Bee-lun rushes onto the tracks. An-an is plump and heavy; she . . .

. . . can't move him an inch. The story of Uncle Ou Yang-hai pulling a horse off the railway track to save a trainload of passengers flashes across her mind. Bee-lun musters all her strength and just manages to push An-an to safety, but she herself is hit.

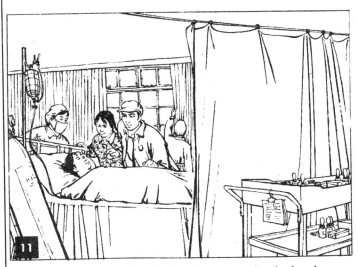

"Bee-lun is hospitalized with a broken arm and a broken leg. When her father and sister come to visit her, she comforts them by saying: 'Daddy, Sister, don't feel sorry for me. I still have one arm to write the thoughts of Chairman Mao. I can still serve the people.'

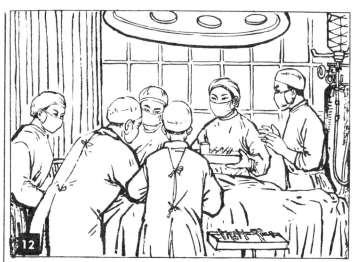

"Bee-lun has to undergo an operation which lasts more than three hours. As soon as she begins to regain consciousness, she sings 'The East Is Red.'"

"Every day, she opens her book with the bright red cover and studies diligently. Each time Chairman Mao's latest directive comes over the radio, she writes it out and learns it by heart."

"Soon, Bee-lun can help in sweeping the hospital grounds and doing other light chores. Both doctors and nurses praise her, saying that she really is Chairman Mao's good little girl."

"Bee-lun has left the hospital. She says: 'Though I am handicapped, my heart remains loyal to our great leader, Chairman Mao. I will follow his teachings and serve the people.'" ■

February 20, 1972

CHOU BEGINS VISIT TO NORTH KOREA

Trip Is Viewed as a Move to Improve Relations

TOKYO, Sunday, April 5 (AP) — Premier Chou En-lai of Communist China arrived today in Pyongyang, capital of North Korea, for a friendship visit, the Pyongyang radio reported.

In a brief broadcast monitored in Tokyo, the radio said that Mr. Chou had been greeted at the airport by Premier Kim Il Sung and other Government officials.

Move to Bolster Ties

Special to The New York Times

HONG KONG, April 4 — The recent announcement by Communist China that Premier Chou would visit North Korea marked a significant shift in Peking's policy toward Pyongyang.

Earlier developments indicated that the chill in China's relations with North Korea during the Cultural Revolution was giving way to a new warmth. Mr. Chou, whose visits abroad are rare, now appears to be making a special effort to bring the two countries closer.

The announcement from Peking underlined China's gradual return to moderation in the field of foreign policy after the xenophobic excesses of the Cultural Revolution. The transition has not been swift or smooth but it has apparently been effected, despite pockets of resistance within China, because of the guiding influence of Mr. Chou.

Englishwoman Is Freed

The hand of Mr. Chou was also seen in another development in the field of foreign policy. In Hong Kong, the Government announced the release by China of a 72-year-old Englishwoman, Mrs. Constance Martin, who was arrested last October in Shanghai, where she had been a resident for many years.

Signs of an improvement in China's relations with North Korea have coincided with attacks by Peking and Pyongyang on the Japanese Government. Japan's growing military and economic importance is believed to be a key element in the new friendliness between China and North Korea.

Relations between China and North Korea began to cool in 1965 and reached a low point in 1967 when travelers in China reported the appearance of wall posters critical of the North Koreans in general and Premier Kim Il Sung in particular. In July of that year China's ambassador to North Korea was recalled and in September the North Korean ambassador returned to Pyongyang.

Last October North Korea sent a delegation to China's National Day celebrations. It was headed by President Choi Yong Kun, who was given a place beside Mao Tse-Tung, chairman of the Chinese Communist party, on the reviewing stand at Tienanmen Square.

April 5, 1970

Hanoi Party Chief Sees Anti-U.S. Front

By JAMES F. CLARITY
Special to The New York Times

MOSCOW, April 21 — Le Duan, First Secretary of the North Vietnamese Communist party, said here today that the people of Vietnam, Laos and Cambodia would unify their efforts against "American imperialists."

He implied that such unity was necessary because "the socialist camp" in Southeast Asia had come under a new threat from the "American imperialists," who he said intend to widen the war throughout Indochina.

Mr. Duan, in a speech at the Kremlin during Lenin centennial ceremonies, seemed to be hinting that the Government in Hanoi was considering a united military front against United States and other anti-Communist forces in Southeast Asia.

ands of troops in all three countries.

As Soviet and other Communist leaders from around the world listened, Mr. Duan said: "In order to defend sacred national rights, the peoples of the brotherly countries of Vietnam, Cambodia and Laos will carry on the struggle against the common enemy, the American imperialists, and by strengthening their cohesion they will tighten their ranks in order to undermine decisively the adventuristic plans of aggression in Indochina. The peoples of the three countries will undoubtedly be victorious."

Mr. Duan also attacked the Nixon Administration policy in Southeast Asia.

"Nixon's group still stubbornly carries on an aggressive war against South Vietnam, trying to deceive world and American public opinion with phrases about peace," he said.

Mr. Duan is believed to be discussing the situation in Southeast Asia which Soviet and other Communist officials during his visit here.

Strategy Meeting Planned
© 1970 The Globe and Mail, Toronto

PEKING, April 21—Leaders of the "socialist and progressive governments and movements in Indochina will hold a conference to coordinate strategy in their fight against United States imperialism and its lackeys, according to the North Vietnamese Ambassador.

Ambassador Ngo Thuyen said at a news conference Monday that the site and agenda of the conference were under discussion. He said Prince Norodom Sihanouk, the deposed Cambodian Chief of State, and representatives of the Vietcong and the Pathet Lao would attend.

United Front Reported

TOKYO, April 21 (AP)— Truong Chinh, head of the National Assembly, said at a celebration of the Lenin centenary today that the people of Vietnam, Laos and Cambodia had formed an "Indochinese People's United Front," according to a North Vietnamese radio broadcast monitored here.

April 22, 1970

Big Allied Sweep Aimed At Enemy's Sanctuaries

By TERENCE SMITH
Special to The New York Times

SAIGON, South Vietnam, Thursday, April 30—South Vietnamese forces supported by United States warplanes and artillery and accompanied by United States advisers swept across the border into Cambodia yesterday in a big operation against North Vietnamese and Vietcong sanctuaries inside Cambodia.

The operation, which involves thousands of troops backed up by armor and heavy artillery, was announced last night in a statement issued here by the South Vietnamese Ministry of Defense and confirmed later by the United States command.

First Announced Operation

It was the first time that either the South Vietnamese or American military commands openly reported operations across the Cambodian border, although at least six such sweeps are known to have been carried out since the overthrow of Prince Norodom Sihanouk as Cambodian Chief of State six weeks ago.

United States officials said the American assistance was in the form of "advisers, tactical air strikes, medical evacuation and some logistics assistance."

A brief statement issued early this morning by the United States military command elaborated slightly, saying that Americans were also providing helicopters and artillery support for the operation.

The current operation appears to be much the largest yet undertaken. It is also the first in which American support has been provided openly. Reliable South Vietnamese sources said several regiments of South Vietnamese troops were involved, along with armored cavalry units and several battalions of Vietnamese rangers.

'The Lid Is Off'

Although United States military spokesmen declined to give any details of the American assistance, sources said that United States advisers had gone in with the South Vietnamese troops and were assisting them in the planning and execution of the operation.

"The lid is finally off," one United States officer said with obvious satisfaction. "The advisers will be doing everything on this operation that they normally do on an operation inside South Vietnam."

This means Americans will probably staff the forward command posts of the different units involved in the operation and accompany the South Vietnamese troops in combat, perhaps down to the battalion level.

The more senior American advisers will fly overhead in helicopters, assisting their South Vietnamese counterparts mapping strategy and relaying requests for air strikes and artillery.

The advisers on the ground customarily carry weapons, but their principal mission is to assist the infantry commanders and provide an English-speaking liaison with the command post. If air or artillery strikes are needed, it is usually the American adviser who gets on the radio and calls them in.

The sources said the force crossed into Cambodia from Tayninh Province at 8 A.M. yesterday and reached the Cambodian district town of Bavet by early afternoon. Bavet is located on Route 1, the main highway between Saigon and Pnompenh. The area around the town is said to me a stronghold for Vietcong and North Vietnamese units, which reportedly use it as a base for forays into Tayninh Province.

The South Vietnamese Army reported that 375 enemy soldiers had been killed as of mid-

night last night. Some 300 were reported killed by American and South Vietnamese air strikes.

In addition, the South Vietnamese reported capturing weapons, ammunition and rice and destroying 350 bunkers. Casualties among the allies were listed as 3 killed and 51 wounded.

The operation is expected to last the better part of a week and reliable American sources said that the south Vietnamese commanders hoped to sweep the length of the "Parrot's Beak"— a long, narrow extension of Cambodia that juts 30 miles into South Vietnam west of Saigon.

Judging from the statements released last night, Americans will also be ferrying troops in helicopters during the current operation, as well as flying the medical evacuation helicopters and providing forward aerial reconnaissance for artillery and air strikes.

Because the operation is a large one, it may well involve over 100 Americans in various advisory and support roles.

The plans for the operation were reportedly discussed by President Nguyen Van Thieu and Ellsworth Bunker, the United States Ambassador, at a series of meetings at the Presidential Palace. Sources said Mr. Thieu had personally reviewed and approved all the battlefield plans.

The United States decision to participate only in the operation caught a number of American diplomats by surprise.

"I never thought he (President Nixon) would decide to do it," one ranking American official said last night.

Although the actual fighting in Cambodia will, according to the plan, be done by South Vietnamese, the American participation in the operation was thought by observers to be sufficiently great as to commit the United States to extensive military support of the new Cambodian regime, headed by Lieut. Gen. Lon Nol.

"In essence," one Western diplomat said, "the United States has decided to widen the war by proxy. The South Vietnamese may do the fighting, but everyone knows who will be providing the weapons and the ammunition."

April 31, 1970

CHOU PLAYED ROLE IN LEFTIST PARLEY

By TILLMAN DURDIN
Special to The New York Times

HONG KONG, April 30 — A major role for Communist China in last weekend's conference of Cambodian, Laotian and Vietnamese Communist and pro-Communist leaders was disclosed in official reports reaching here today from Peking and Hanoi.

The reports showed the conference took place somewhere in China and that Premier Chou En-lai and his wife, Teng Ying-chao, flew from Peking Saturday, the last day of the two-day conference, to give a banquet for conference delegates at the conference site. They honored the Chou En-lais the following evening.

Earlier reports had indicated that the site was somewhere in the area of Laos, North Vietnam and China.

The Indochinese conference, initiated by the deposed Cambodian Chief of State, Prince Norodom Sihanouk, brought together a Cambodian delegation under the Prince; a North Vietnamese delegation under Premier Pham Van Dong; a Vietcong delegation under Nguyen Huu Tho and a Pathet Lao delegation under Prince Souphanouvong.

Mutual Aid Pledged

The delegation pledged cooperation and mutual support in combating the United States and other forces opposed to them in Vietnam, Laos and Cambodia.

The role of China in the conference was disclosed in part in a letter written by Prince Sihanouk to Premier Chou.

The main purpose of the letter, made public today by Itsinhua, the Chinese press agency, was to convey Prince Sihanouk's congratulations to Mr. Chou over the launching last Friday of Communist China's first earth satellite. It also made public, obviously with Peking's approval, details of Mr. Chou's activities over the weekend.

Prince Sihanouk referred to "the banquet of April 25 which your excellency kindly gave in honor of the delegations of the three Indochinese peoples to their summit conference" and additionally quoted from a a speech the Prince said he gave at "the banquet of April 26 given by the Khmer Laotian and Vietnamese delegations in your excellency's honor."

In addition, a North Vietnamese broadcast from Hanoi reported that in a speech at the second banquet, Prince Sihanouk and thanked Premier Chou and "the local leaders and people" for providing conference facilities. This indicated the local leaders were Chinese and that the conference was held in China probably near the Vietnam border.

Chou Denounces U.S.

According to the broadcast Mr. Chou in a speech at the first banquet, denounced the "U.S. imperialists" for indicating their "flunkeys, the traitorous rightist Lon Nol-Sirik Matak clique, to stage a reactionary coup d'état" with the thought they could "place Cambodia under their sway, thwart the resistance of the Vietnamese people and thereby materialize their foolish ambition of occupying Indochnia as a whole."

The premier said the United States could never succeed in the face of the new unity of the Indochinese people and China's support for the participants.

"The three fraternal Indochinese people can rest assured," Mr. Chou stated, "that in the common struggle against U.S. imperialism the Chinese people will forever unite with them and fight shoulder to shoulder with them and win victory together."

Top Hanoi Aides Present

The North Vietnamese delegation included Truong Chinh, member of the Communist party's Politburo; Hoang Quoc Viet and Hoang Minh Giam, members of the presidium of the Central Committee of the Vietnam Fatherland Front; Nguyen Co Thach, Vice Minister for Foreign Affairs, and Nguyen Thuong, former Ambassador to Cambodia.

The Vietcong group under Nguyen Huu Tho, a non-Communist who is titular head of the National Liberation Front of South Vietnam, included more important Communist leaders such as Nguyen Van Hieu, a former Ambassador to Cambodia, and Trinh Dinh Thao, head of the Alliance of National, Democratic and Peace Forces.

The Cambodian delegation, besides Prince Sihanouk, included Penn Nouth, former Premier; Huot Sambath, former Cambodian delegate to the United Nations, and Chau Seng, former Minister of Information.

Prince Souphanouvong was accompanied by Phoumi Vongvichit, secretary general of the Laotian Patriotic Front, and Khamsouk Keola, a neutralist leader who has thrown in his lot with the Pathet Lao.

May 1, 1970

HANOI-PEKING TIES APPEAR STRONGER

Soviet Role Seems Reduced by Events in Indochina

By TILLMAN DURDIN
Special to The New York Times

HONG KONG, May 16—Recent developments appear to have left the Soviet Union more than ever an outsider in Indochina.

Communist China's adroit exploitation of new circumstances has, for the time being at least, strengthened the ties between Hanoi and Peking.

Peking has emerged as the big power champion of a new Communist-run revolt in Cambodia and a new Indochina "people's front" that promises to coordinate the struggles of Communist and Communist-front forces in Vietnam and Laos as well as Cambodia.

These two ventures are of vital concern to North Vietnam, particularly at this time when the allies say the loss of a sanctuary and supply dumps in Cambodia for Vietnamese Communist forces has severely damaged Communist prospects in the war in South Vietnam.

Vietnamese Communist hopes for regaining their former position in Cambodia are said to lie in stepping up as quickly as possible the Cambodian insurrection for which Prince Norodom Sihanouk, the deposed Cambodian head of state, is serving as leader in Peking.

Hanoi is thus, along with Peking, a firm supporter of an all-Indochina front and especially of its Cambodian component, and this has forged new bonds between the Vietnamese and Chinese Communists.

At a meeting last month of Communist and pro-Communist leaders from Cambodia, Laos and Vietnam initiated by Prince Sihanouk, cooperation and mutual support was pledged in combatting the United States and its allies in Vietnam, Laos and Cambodia.

The Soviet Union has expressed sympathy and support for the front and Prince Sihanouk's efforts but is an outsider in what has developed as a Peking-fostered, essentially Asian Communist initiative, and apparently has reservations that prevent full rapport with North Vietnam and its allies in Indochina.

Soviet Gives Most Aid

The Russians, for example, have not recognized the new Sihanouk government of Cambodia formed in Peking and continue to have relations with the Government in Pnompenh of Premier Lon Nol, who overthrew Prince Sihanouk in a coup on March 18.

It is believed that the Russians want to retain freedom of action and not be bound too closely to a situation in which Peking is so prominent.

In dollar value, Russia provides more military supplies and other aid to the Communist forces in Indochina than the Chinese do. However, the nearness of China makes close ties with the Indochinese Communists both necessary and unescapable.

It is the need of the Indochinese Communists for Soviet material aid and for a Soviet counterbalance to China that gives the Soviet Union most of its leverage.

The Vietnamese Communists continue to play the dominant role in the war in Indochina and there are no signs that either Peking or Moscow will cease to provide support for Hanoi.

Communist China's geographical proximity, its material interests and its ideological commitment to prolonged "people's wars" make the Chinese Communists more concerned with keeping the fighting going in Indochina until a Communist victory is achieved than the Russians are, but the Soviet Union has shown no sign it is unenthusiastic about the war to the extent of actively trying to bring it to an end.

May 17, 1970

Cambodia War Said to Cause Major Peking Shift

By HARRISON E. SALISBURY

Information reaching New York from sources close to Communist leaders in Asia suggests that the United States move into Cambodia has transformed the Indochina situation more radically than originally estimated. This evaluation is being taken seriously in Washington.

United States specialists there say the evaluation conforms in many respects to other information becoming available concerning China and its role in Southeast Asia.

The key to the changed aspect in Indochina was said to be agreement by North Vietnam, the Vietcong, Prince Norodom Sihanouk and the Communist Pathet Lao organization in Laos on an all-for-one and one-for-all arrangement to which China has pledged full support.

Those who have had a first-hand opportunity to assess the situation in Peking and Hanoi describe it "as a wholly new ball game." What faces the United States now in Southeast Asia, they believe, is protracted war with virtually no possibility of arriving at a settlement in Vietnam unless there is a settlement covering Laos and Cambodia at the same time.

In fact, some who are close to Peking's thinking even suggest that the settlement would have to cover "all of Southeast Asia, including Thailand."

Change in Stance Seen

It is conceded by United States specialists that the sweeping description of changes in Hanoi's attitudes as well as in those of the others in the new Indochina association may be offered for bargaining purposes. But those who have been following Peking's attitudes with the greatest care believe that it has arrived at an entirely new posture since the opening of the Cambodian phase of the war.

Peking is said to have made it clear that the Indochinese people have its full backing. This goes not only for supplies and materials but for specialists and experts if needed, and for "volunteers" if requested. It does not mean a joint military command, it was said, but it does mean common strategy, military and diplomatic.

What China, North Vietnam and their associates now foresee, it was said, is a protracted war. According to this view, they see no possibility that a diplomatic move by Washington, even if couched in the most generous terms, would provide an answering response from Hanoi—except in the unlikely event that the United States was prepared to negotiate complete withdrawal from Southeast Asia.

Prior to the United States entry into Cambodia, it was said, it was possible to envisage a settlement embracing only North Vietnam and South Vietnam, with Cambodia and Laos left to one side, presumably continuing in their theoretically neutral status. Now, it was said, there is no question of such an approach.

May 26, 1970

PEKING ENHANCES ITS STATUS IN ASIA

By TILLMAN DURDIN
Special to The New York Times

HONG KONG, June 27—Communist China has successfully used the 20th anniversary of the outbreak of the Korean war to further enhance the appeal and solidarity of the Asian Communist front that has taken shape under Peking auspices in recent months.

"United States imperialism" and "Japanese militarism" have been the open targets of attack for the anniversary, but the whole exercise has been obliquely directed against the Soviet Union as well.

With the Chinese obviously in a coordinating role, leaders of Communist China, North Vietnam, North Korea, the provisional revolutionary government of South Vietnam, the exile Cambodian government of Prince Norodum Sihanouk and the Pathet Lao of Laos have not only joined in observances of the war anniversary in

485

Pyongyang, the North Korean capital, and their own territories, but have echoed each other in revolutionary themes and expressions of mutual support.

Russians Excluded

The Russians were excluded from the activity, which emphasized united Asian action to drive out "United States imperialism" and defeat "Japanese militarism," and were even subjected to indirect attack in front of Korean, Vietnamese and other officials by Chinese leaders.

In a speech before a mass rally Thursday in Pyongyang, for example, Huang Yung-sheng, Chief of Staff of the Chinese armed forces, stated:

"United States imperialism and its partners and lackeys have committed innumerable crimes in Asia, and this is clear for all to see. The attitude one takes toward the aggressive acts of the United States and Japanese reactionaries—whether it is one of opposition or non-opposition, whether it is genuine opposition or opposition only in words but encouragement and connivance in fact—that is the watershed distinguishing between those who are truly anti-imperialist and those who are spuriously anti-imperialist and between those who are true revolutionaries and those who are sham revolutionaries."

The remarks of Mr. Huang, who headed a Chinese delegation to Pyongyang, used all the terms with which Peking has in the past characterized the Soviet Union, omitting only the name of the country. Premier Chou En-lai and Deputy Premier Li Hsien-nien used similar terminology in their speeches in Peking, criticizing Moscow by innuendo.

Dispatches by Hsinhua, the Chinese press agency, reporting the speeches of Vietnamese, Korean, Cambodian and Laotian representatives show they were circumspect in not saying anything overtly critical of the Soviet Union. However, they indicated that the new Asian Communist front had aims and characteristics that distinguish it from Soviet-bloc countries.

But for the omission of the oblique Chinese attacks on the Soviet Union, the speeches of the other Asians might well have been written in Peking. The Chinese speeches, moreover, said nothing of ideology; they based their appeal on nationalist and Asian hostility to the United States role in Asia.

June 28, 1970

PEKING AID PACT HAILED BY HANOI

HONG KONG, Oct. 8—Expressions of solidarity with Communist China and appreciation for Peking's assistance came from Hanoi today as the North Vietnamese Government devoted more than usual attention to a new agreement for military and economic aid announced in Peking yesterday.

Reporting the agreement in a radio broadcast heard here, Hanoi revealed that the aid, described as "covering assistance for 1971," would be "nonrefundable," that is, free. The Peking announcement that preceded Hanoi's report did not mention this aspect of the aid package.

The Hanoi broadcast said that Nguyen Con, a North Vietnamese Deputy Premier who headed the delegation that negotiated the agreement in Peking, had expressed joy over the aid and "sincere thanks to the Communist party, Government and great people of China."

The Hanoi radio said the Chinese Premier, Chou En-lai, who was present at the signing of the agreement, had stressed that "China and Vietnam are standing in the same combat trench" and that "the Chinese people are resolved to support the Vietnamese people's resistance against United States aggression until final victory."

The official Hanoi daily, Nhan Dan, elaborated on North Vietnam's appreciation of the aid in an editorial, heard here in a radio broadcast, that said the new aid package was "an eloquent manifestation of the Chinese people's determination to oppose United States imperialist aggressors and warmongers."

No details have come from Peking or Hanoi with regard to the scope of the latest aid program. The new accord follows up other agreements concluded annually for almost two decades.

Between last year's annual agreement and this year's, a special programs of grant aid was provided by China at midyear. This appeared to be the result of the Vietnamese Communists' loss of Cambodia as a sanctuary and import supply route for the Vietnam war through the port of Sihanoukville, now known as Kompong Som.

The announcement of last year's annual aid agreement, unlike this year's, made no mention of military aid, nor was there any statement that last year's aid was nonreimbursable.

October 9, 1970

KOREAN REDS EDGE CLOSER TO PEKING

Special to The New York Times

SEOUL, South Korea, Nov. 7 —North Korea has made plain that it is moving closer to Peking under its "independent line" policy.

The stand was expressed at the fifth congress of the Korean Workers (Communist) party, which opened in Pyongyang Monday. The party convention, the first full-scale one held in nine years despite party regulations calling for one every four years, is to continue until next Friday.

In a long report on party work delivered at the opening session, Marshal Kim Il Sung, the North Korean Premier and party leader, indirectly accused the Soviet Union of obstructing the unity of the world's Communist parties. The text of Marshal Kim's speech was broadcast by the Pyongyang radio and was monitored here.

Although he did not mention the Soviet Union by name, Premier Kim asserted that "revisionism appeared in the international Communist movement and obstructed its unity and cohesion, causing ideological confusion."

"Revisionism" is a term frequently used by pro-Peking Communist parties in criticizing Soviet Communism.

Premier Kim also criticized "revisionism" for "obscuring the line of demarcation between friend and foe, yielding to U.S. imperialism, scared at its policy of nuclear blackmail, and casting sheep's eyes at the imperialists while paying lip-service to an anti-imperialist position."

In another passage, Marshal Kim denounced Moscow obliquely, without naming it, for increasing the danger of war in Asia by promoting friendship with Japan without recognizing "the aggressiveness of Japanese militarism." He ignored the Soviet Union when he called for strengthening of a "united anti-U.S. front" in Asia by the peoples of Korea, Communist China, Vietnam and Cambodia.

Despite the indirect attacks on the Soviet Union, the party congress reaffirmed North Korea's "independent line," adopted in 1966.

South Korean analysts of North Korean affairs believe that Marshal Kim has no intention of breaking away from Moscow as he did in 1962. They said the Pyongyang Government could not afford any such step because it continued to need military and economic aid from Moscow as well as from Peking.

On the domestic scene, Premier Kim proposed a new six-year economic plan to start next year, succeeding the seven-year plan begun in 1961 and later extended three years to end this year.

More Consumer Goods

Although specific production goals for the 1971-76 plan are yet to be announced, he said the main goals included further industrialization, a technical revolution in factories, increased domestic production of industrial raw materials, development of the machinery industry and expansion of consumer goods industries to produce more household commodities, including television sets and refrigerators.

To expand agricultural production, the plan calls for the expansion of two-crop acreage, improved irrigation and increased use of chemical fertilizers.

Premier Kim called for continued emphasis on war industries by urging that "material preparations for war and revolution" in South Korea should be given top priority.

In reviewing the results of the old economic plan, he reported that North Korea's gross industrial output had increased 11.6 times since 1956. This meant that industrial production attained an average annual increase of 19.1 per cent throughout that period, he said.

Calling for increased defense preparations, Marshal Kim warned that "the danger of war is further increasing with every passing day." He asserted that peaceful reunification of Korea was "utterly unthinkable" so long as United States military forces remained in the south and the present Seoul Government, headed by President Chung Hee Park, continued in power.

November 8, 1970

MAJOR DRIVE NEAR LAOS BY G.I.'S AND VIETNAMESE IS ANNOUNCED IN SAIGON

By ALVIN SHUSTER
Special to The New York Times

SAIGON, South Vietnam, Thursday, Feb. 4—United States and South Vietnamese troops have launched a major operation into the northwest corner of South Vietnam, the United States command announced. This cleared the way for a possible South Vietnamese strike against the Ho Chi Minh Trail in Laos.

The operation, involving 9,000 Americans from three divisions and 20,000 South Vietnamese troops, has been under way since early Saturday morning, when a column of American tanks and armored troop carriers started moving west across Quangtri, the northernmost province of South Vietnam, toward the Laotian border.

The U.S. military command had embargoed all news from Saigon on the operation until 4:30 P.M. today Saigon time, 3:30 A.M. today New York time.

Reopen Khesanh Base

The American troops cleared and repaired key roads, reopened the former Marine Corps base at Khesanh, established new airstrips there and opened a forward support base at Langvei, just three miles from Laos.

Some American units moved directly to the border on reconnaisance missions and established a "screen" between the border and the American bases.

It was unclear this morning whether the South Vietnamese would move into Laos to try to cut the Ho Chi Minh Trail. Hanoi's main supply line to Laos, South Vietnam and Cambodia.

Sources here said that President Nixon had still not decided on whether to order an assault across the border.

Advance Approval by Thieu

It was understood that President Nixon had received advance approval from President Nguyen Van Thieu of South Vietnam to order a cross-border operation.

But some informed sources said that the President, although aware of the long-term military benefits from such an operation, was apprehensive over the furor an incursion would create among antiwar critics at home even though American support would not include ground troops.

Whatever the final decision, a vast American military machine, moved to the north in a round-the-clock airlift opera-

The New York Times   Feb. 4, 1971

New sweep was reported in Fishhook section of Cambodia (1). Allied operation continued in northwest corner of South Vietnam (2). In Laos, Muong Soui (3), a nearby post and positions near Luang Prabang (4) fell.

tion, stands poised to provide air and logistical support for a South Vietnamese effort to attack the trail and destroy huge **stockpiles of supplies flowing into the supply network from North Vietnam.**

The Americans would also participate in attacking an estimated 30,000 enemy troops said to be in the northern provinces.

So far enemy resistance has been described as light. The command here said that three Americans had been wounded and five enemy soldiers had been killed.

The operation, called Dewey Canyon II, is the largest military effort in nearly three years in South Vietnam and the largest in Indochina since last spring, when Americans and South Vietnamese attacked Communist sanctuaries in Cambodia.

Since Friday, the skies over South Vietnam have been filled with an army on the move. Giant C-130 cargo planes have been landing as often as every 15 minutes at the Quangtri combat base, about 50 miles east of Khesanh. Columns of American armor pushed across the twisting and muddy road to Khesanh, where work began to repair the old marine airstrip and to build a new one.

Three battalions landed by helicopter at the base, deserted by the Americans after the 1968 siege.

The operation was supported by B-52 bombing strikes and up to 30 sorties a day by smaller fighters and bombers, and by helicopter gunships, cargo planes and troop-carrying aircraft.

Artillery Fired into Valley

Elements of the 101st Division fired artillery shells into the Ashau Valley and probably into Laos.

Military spokesmen would not confirm that the artillery reached across the border.

The spokesmen, who provided briefings here daily on the operation since Saturday night, would not comment on whether the South Vietnamese would drive to the trail.

They said only that the operation was ordered after a reported build-up of enemy forces and supplies in Laos threatened 'the security of allied forces" in South Vietnam.

They also said that Quangtri province was a major infiltration route for the enemy war effort in South Vietnam.

They said this posed a threat, not only to the allied troops in South Vietnam but also to the populated areas of Hue and Danang and other coastal cities.

Quangtri province, part of Military Region I, abuts the demilitarized zone straddling North and South Vietnam. The terrain is mountains and dense jungle, and many military experts and observers had written off the possibility of clearing it of enemy troops before the Americans withdraw.

Senators Assail Secrecy
Special to The New York Times

WASHINGTON, Feb. 3—The official embargo on news reports from Saigon about the South Vietnamese operation at the Laotian border was severely criticized today by several leading Democrats and Republican Senators.

Expressing the frustration felt by many on Capitol Hill at the six-day embargo on news reports, the Senate Democratic leader, Mike Mansfield of Montana, charged that the secrecy was "creating a very difficult situation and a certain amount of apprehension as to what is in the offing."

Senator George D. Aiken, the senior Republican on the Senate Foreign Relations Committee, told reporters that his office was receiving a heavy flow of mail from constituents alarmed by the continuing reports of an allied attack into Laos.

"So long as the blackout continues," he said, "they fear and expect the worst."

Even Senator Robert C. Byrd, the assistant Democratic leader, who has been a steady supporter of the administration's

Vietnam policy, described the embargo as "inexcusable bungling."

Meanwhile, the Soviet Union charged for the third consecutive day that United States and South Vietnamese troops had invaded southern Laos.

Tass, the Soviet press agency, said, "The Soviet Union strongly denounces the armed intrusion of the United States and their Saigon puppets into Laos." It went on to charge that the situation in Indochina had become "greatly aggravated in recent days," as a result of the "invasion."

February 4, 1971

RED CHINA WARNS ON MOVE IN LAOS

Special to The New York Times

HONG KONG, Saturday, Feb. 13—Communist China declared yesterday that it "will not remain indifferent" to the recent incursion into Laos by "large numbers of U.S. and puppet forces."

A government statement transmitted by Hsinhua, the Chinese Communist press agency, denounced the United States for "savage crimes of aggression against Laos" and declared that the Chinese people would "take all effective measures" to aid the Communist forces in Laos, Cambodia and Vietnam.

It was the third official declaration from Peking this month on the Laos situation. Denunciations of American and South Vietnamese moves affecting Laos were issued by the Chinese Foreign Ministry on Feb. 4, a few days before the South Vietnamese incursion, and on Feb. 8, the day it began.

Grave Provocation Charged

In these statements Peking said it would not allow the United States to do what it pleased in Indochina and described the incursion into Laos as a grave provocation against China as well as the peoples of Indochina and the whole world.

The statements were seen here as reflections of Peking's concern that the war in Indochina might be carried closer to its own borders either as a result of the present offensive in Laos or through a South Vietnamese attack against North Vietnam. But all three statements have expressed confidence in the ability of the "Indochinese peoples" to handle the situation. There have been

no suggestions so far that Peking's promise of support would go beyond the supply of arms and ammunition.

U.S. Sees No Intervention
Special to The New York Times

WASHINGTON, Feb. 12—United States officials said today there were no indications that Communist China intended to intervene in the fighting in Laos.

The State Department brushed aside a report from Vientiane that Premier Souvanna Phouma of Laos was worried about possible Chinese intervention. The report published today by The Washington Post, said the Premier had told foreign diplomats he was afraid that Communist China would send in volunteers if the allied operations succeeded in choking off Communist supply lines in southern Laos.

A State Department spokesman said the Premier had "not communicated that reported attitude or concern to any United States official."

Other officials said that Washington detected no other indications that the Chinese intended to put troops into combat in Laos.

Ziegler Denies Threat to China
Special to The New York Times

KEY BISCAYNE, Fla., Feb. 12 — Ronald L. Ziegler, the White House press secretary, said here today that the Nixon Administration did not believe that the South Vietnamese effort to cut the Ho Chi Minh Trail network would provoke Chinese Communists into crossing the Laotian border in force.

"These operations," he said, "pose absolutely no threat to Communist China, and we can therefore see no reason for them to be interpreted as such."

February 9, 1971

A Chinese Puzzle in the Jungle: Work Stops on New Laos Road

By TILLMAN DURDIN
Special to The New York Times

VIENTIANE, Laos, Feb. 14— Highway One, the mystery road the Chinese Communists are building from Yunnan Province of China into northern Laos, has become more of a puzzle than ever.

Although surveying continues, extension of the route has been stopped. The halt may be temporary — sources here who keep track of activities on the road assume that it is — but it is nevertheless puzzling since the present dry season would be a logical time for construction to be pushed as fast as possible. It has aroused speculation that the road will not be completed to the point for which it appears headed on the banks of the Mekong River before the year's rains come in June or July.

Earlier progress led observers here to predict last year that the road would reach the Mekong village of Pak Beng by the end of this dry season.

The highway, on which construction has been proceeding for several years, now extends from Mengla in Yunnan Province 100 miles into Laos as far south as Muong Houn. Muong Houn is 30 miles from Pak Beng.

Road Is Well Guarded

A branch of the road cuts off northeast at Muong Sai, a point about 40 miles into Laos from the China border, seemingly aiming for a linkup with a road into North Vietnam that leads to Dienbienphu.

But work has also stopped on this branch. A gap of several miles and the Nam Ou River, still unbridged, separate the end of the branch and the beginning of the road on the other side of the Nam Ou.

The Chinese road, as far as it goes, is reported by aerial reconnaissance to be a fine, broad, laterite-topped, two-lane artery. Pilots who occasionally fly planes over or near it and get shot at attest to the fact that it is well guarded by anti-aircraft batteries.

A charter plane that got too close to the road recently just managed to get back to Luang Prabang in Laos with several holes in its wings and fusilage made by the Chinese guns.

If the road is eventually pushed to Pak Beng it will provide trucks with an overnight route from the Chinese border to a navigable waterway over which cargoes could be transported north to where the Mekong becomes the Thai border

The New York Times   Feb. 21, 1971
Communist China has held up the construction of road that now extends from Muong Houn (1) in Laos to Mengla (2).

or east toward Luang Prabang.

If the road's builders chose they could continue the road from the south side of the Mekong to the Thai border, which is 25 miles below the Mekong in this area.

The fact that surveying continues from the present end of the road to Pak Beng would seem to indicate the Chinese plan to build this stretch.

Many perfectly ordinary considerations could explain the suspension of construction. Building materials may have run short or the Chinese may simply have decided the project is not as pressing as they once thought it was and have slowed down their building program.

But observers, who have always wondered what role the road was intended to fulfill, cannot help but speculate that the Chinese may have decided it is not very important after all and never finish what must be a very costly venture. It runs through a mountainous, sparsely-populated jungle region.

"Right now in the state it is in," one American observer here remarked, "it looks to me like a road built simply for the convenience of those who are building it."

Those who are building it are Chinese Army engineers with a good assortment of modern equipment. If they were now to resume work at full steam they could reach the Mekong by mid-year. Maybe they will, maybe they won't.

February 21, 1971

Chou Attacks U.S. but on a Mild Note

By TILLMAN DURDIN
Special to The New York Times

PEKING, April 25—Premier Chou En-lai struck a relatively mild note in a speech at a banquet held here tonight to mark the first anniversary of the summit conference of Vietnamese, Cambodian and Laotian regimes at war with the United States and its allies in Indochina.

The host for the occasion was Prince Norodom Sihanouk, who still upholds the status in Peking of head of state of Cambodia. Other principals for the occasion besides Premier Chou were Kaysone Phomvihan, vice chairman of the Lao Patriotic Front; Hyon Jun Guk, Ambassador of North Korea; Nam Tranh Binh, chargé d'affaires of the Communist-led provisional revolutionary government for South Vietnam, and Ngo Thuyen Thuyen, Ambassador of North Vietnam.

The Indochina spokesmen denounced the United States presence in Indochina, pledged mutual support and affirmed continuation of their fight until victory and the expulsion of the United States from the Peninsula.

Chou Stresses Support

Premier Chou stressed the support of the People's Republic of China for these aims and said, "The Chinese Government and people firmly oppose the U.S. imperialist frenzied aggression against the three countries of Indochina and firmly support and assist the heroic peoples of Vietnam, Laos and Cambodia in their war against U.S. aggression and for national salvation."

He said, "The U.S. aggressor troops and their vassal troops must withdraw completely from Indochina so that the three Indochinese peoples may respectively settle their problems by themselves."

The Premier voiced support for North Korea, opposition to what he termed the revival of Japanese militarism and backing for national liberation struggles of Asian, African Latin American, North American, European and Oceanian peoples, and for "the American people in their just struggle against the U. S. Government's policies of aggression and war and racial discrimination."

But these statements of time-honored positions were not accompanied by any harsh invective against the United States and there was no reference in the Premier's speech or any of the other speeches to the United States role in Taiwan, usually made on such occasions. Backing for China's stand on Taiwan by the Indochina countries and North Korea was a prominent feature of joint statements at the time of the summit meeting of Indochina last April.

Many Officials Present

Tonight's banquet for several hundred guests of countries that have recognized the Peking-based Cambodian Government under Prince Sihanouk was attended by a stellar list of Chinese officials. Besides Premier Chou, others present included Huang Yung-Sheng, Chief of Staff of the armed forces; Yeh Chine-Ying, Chang Chun-Chiao, Yan Wen-Yuan, Li Hsien-nien, Li Tso-peng and Chiu Hui-tso, all members of the Politburo, and Kuo Mo-jo, prominent in foreign relations.

The banquet was held in the huge social hall of the National Peoples Congress Building. Premier Chou, looking fit despite his 73 years, exchanged banter with foreign photographers who circulated freely around the head table to take pictures.

He and Prince Sihanouk invited newsmen to come to Pnompenh when it has been occupied by the forces fighting the Government of Premier Lon Nol.

April 26, 1971

Peking Renews Advocacy of Revolution

By TILLMAN DURDIN
Special to The New York Times

HONG KONG, May 24—Recent Chinese moves for a thaw in relations with non-Communist countries have been accompanied in the last few days by a splurge of propaganda from Peking reaffirming its commitment to revolution, particularly in Southeast Asia.

The new declarations have caused analysts here to speculate that the Chinese may be trying to reassure worried foreign revolutionary allies that Peking's new posture in foreign affairs does not mean any diminution of support for the Communist cause abroad.

The Chinese reaffirmations highlight the old problem posed for a Communist power over the extent of the help it can or should give to Communist movements abroad when its immediate national interests are involved in improving relations with governments and peoples opposed to these movements.

Trade Deals Negotiated

Both North Vietnam and North Korea are reported to have expressed displeasure recently with Peking's new people-to-people contacts with Americans and its seeming readiness, even to improve its relations' with the United States Government.

Peking's new moves for better relations with the Philippines, Burma, Thailand and India may have prompted similar expressions of concern from the Communist movements in Southeast and South Asia that have been relying on assistance from China.

China has recently played host not only to American visitors but also to trade delegations from the Philippines and Malaysia, with which trade deals were made and preparations were begun for what could eventually be the establishment of diplomatic relations.

Meanwhile, reports from Bangkok say there have been contacts between Thai and Chinese officials, through third parties, that the Thais regard as favorable. In Rangoon, a new Chinese ambassador has been energetically cultivating friendly relations with the Burmese Government.

Simultaneously, Peking has marginally downgraded its propaganda support for Communist revolutionists in Thailand, Malaysia, Burma and India. Regular reports that used to be made by Peking's official Hsinhua press agency about the progress of revolutionary activities in these counties have been dropped and Hsinhua now limits itself to relaying reports and statements from the radio stations and other publicly organs of the revolutionists themselves.

The occasion for the increase in Peking's declarations of support for revolution during the last few days was the first anniversary of a statement made by Mao Tse-tung, the Chinese Communist party chairman, on May 20 last year.

At a mass rally in Peking on that occasion, Mr. Mao called on the peoples of the world to unite in revolution against the "U.S. aggressors and their running dogs." He predicted victory for revolutionary movements and promised Chinese support.

A joint anniversary editorial printed in the Peking dailies Jenmin Jih Pao and Chieh Fang Chun Pao and the fortnightly Hungchi hailed the pronouncement as having become "a program for the anti-imperialist struggle waged by the Chinese people together with the revolutionary people throughout the world."

Indochina was called the main battlefield of the "anti-imperialist" struggle, and there, the editorial said, great victories have been won in the last year, landing the Nixon Government "in a blind alley."

The joint editorial was followed by a succession of articles in Jenmin Jin Pao and Hsinhua specifically hailing revolutionary movements in the United States, Japan, the countries of Indochina, New Zealand, Australia and Latin-American nations. Other articles have denounced the Government of Japan and Japanese "militarism."

May 25, 1971

China Rejoins Korean Talks After 5 Years

By SAMUEL KIM
Special to The New York Times

PANMUNJOM, Korea, July 9 —A Chinese Communist delegate returned to the Korean truce village of Panmunjom today, after his country's absence of five years, to attend a meeting of the Korean Military Armistice Commission.

The United Nations Command at once challenged the qualifications of the delegate, Ho Chu-jo, on the ground that his credentials failed to say whether he was a military officer.

Peking has not had a delegate here since North Korea's announcement in August, 1966, that it was not dependent on China or the Soviet Union. Most observers agreed that the delegate's return reflected the current thaw between China and the United States. They also saw a clear indication of improved relations between Pyongyang and Peking.

Some, however, said that the move was merely part of China's policy of refilling diplomatic posts vacated at the time of the Cultural Revolution.

Comments on Seating

Representing the United Nations Command at the 318th session of the commission, Maj. Gen. Felix M. Rogers of the United States Air Force told his North Korean counterpart: "I note for the record that you have seated on your side of the table an individual who lacks the necessary qualifications to attend these meetings."

He said that the armistice agreement, signed in 1953, requires that members of the commission, five from the United Nations side and five from the North Korea-Chinese side, be military officers.

The credentials appointing the new Chinese delegate were received by the United Nations side on June 14 but did not state his military rank and referred to him only as "Comrade Ho Chu-jo."

"Our side takes note of this

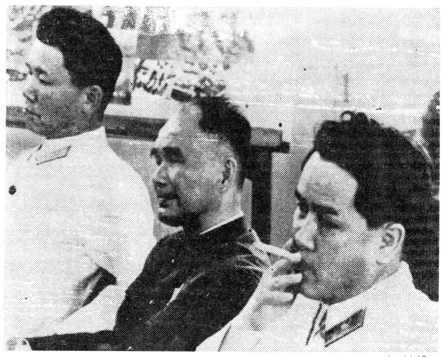

Associated Press

Ho Chu-jo, center, of Communist China, with Maj. Gen. Han Yong Ok, right, chief of North Korean delegation, and unnamed member, left, at Panmunjom session yesterday.

deviation from the provisions of the armistice agreement," General Rogers said. But he did not object to the seating of the Chinese delegate.

Complaint Rejected

Maj. Gen. Han Yong Ok, the chief North Korean delegate, rejected General Rogers's complaint by asserting that "whom and by what procedures we appoint our members is entirely the internal affairs of our side and therefore, it is not a business your side should meddle in."

The Chinese delegate remained silent while arguments about his attendance were exchanged. Dressed in an olive green Chinese military uniform without rank or insignia, the delegate took a seat next to General Han at the green felt topped conference table. Two other North Korean officers were seated flanking them.

On the United Nations side, there were two South Korean generals, a British brigadier and a Turkish colonel, besides General Rogers.

According to South Korean intelligence sources, the new delegate was a ranking official at the Chinese Foreign Ministry before appointment to the Panmunjom post. He was said to be 53 years old and to have fought in the Korean war as a commander of a Chinese unit.

Today, he wore a white badge with Chinese characters reading "the Chinese People's Volunteers." Above it was a star-shaped metal badge with Mao Tse-Tung's picture at the center.

General Han made no introduction of the Chinese delegate when he started today's six-hour meeting. He accused the United Nations side of having delayed the meeting for 18 days. The United Nations Command had boycotted the session, which was originally called for June 21, on the ground that the North Koreans had permitted groups of their foreign visitors to stage anti-American demonstrations here on 11 occasions.

Smoking cigarettes frequently, the Chinese delegate did not talk with North Korean delegates throughout the meeting. From time to time he listened to a young Chinese officer seated behind him, who was apparently interpreting.

CHINA AGAIN FILLING AMBASSADOR POSTS

HONG KONG, April 25—Communist China has sent four ambassadors abroad within a period of a month, resuming the reorganization of diplomatic representatives that it began last May and suspended in July.

The latest deployment of ambassadors brings to 22 the number of mission chiefs sent abroad since May. This includes 21 ambassadors and one chargé d'affaires.

Forty-four of Peking's 45 ambassadors were recalled in 1967, when radical elements were attempting to reorganize the Foreign Ministry during the Cultural Revolution.

The posting of ambassadors abroad again began last year when Keng Piao was sent to take charge of China's embassy in Albania, Peking's foremost ally. Ambassadors have also been sent to France, North Vietnam, Cambodia, Pakistan, Tanzania, Guinea, Zambia, Rumania, Sweden, Congo (Brazzaville), Syria, Nepal, the Sudan, Mauritania, Afghanistan, Finland, Mali, North Korea, Algeria and Yemen, and the chargé d'affaires to South Yemen.

April 26, 1970

NEW RUSSIAN AIDE IN CHINA FOR TALK

Ilyichev Replaces Kuznetsov in Border Negotiations

By BERNARD GWERTZMAN
Special to The New York Times

MOSCOW, Aug. 15 — Leonid F. Ilyichev, a Soviet Deputy Foreign Minister, arrived in Peking today as the new delegate at the 10-month-old talks with Communist China on border problems and other questions.

The news of Mr. Ilyichev's appointment as the replacement for the First Deputy Foreign Minister, Vasily V. Kuznetsov, had been rumored but was not officially confirmed until today's report by Tass, the Soviet press agency.

Mr. Kuznetsov, who had led the Soviet delegation since the Peking talks began Oct. 20, returned to Moscow about July 1 "on the advice of doctors," Tass said today, and 'has resumed his duties" in the Foreign Ministry. It was reported at the time that Mr. Kuznetsov, who is 69 years old, had problems with his urinary tract.

Fresh Effort Likely

The arrival of Mr. Ilyichev, a former party ideologist who participated in talks with the Chinese in Moscow in July, 1963, appears to signal a fresh effort by Moscow to obtain some results from the drawn-out parley.

Although Mr. Ilyichev lacks the diplomatic stature of Mr. Kuznetsov, the fact that he was sent to Peking indicates that Moscow is not ready to give up on the talks.

The most authoritative word on the progress remains Premier Aleksei N. Kosygin's speech in June in which he said that the talks had failed to make progress because of obstacles placed by the Chinese side.

Nevertheless, Mr. Kosygin stressed that Moscow would continue to make efforts to reach an accord both on border problems, the heart of the controversy, and on other questions. It is reliably reported that the Soviet side has proposed an expansion of cultural and trade relations as well as an exchange of ambassadors.

China Shifts Officers on Border

By TILLMAN DURDIN
Special to The New York Times

HONG KONG, July 4 — Recent personnel changes in Chinese provinces bordering the Soviet Union reflect a steady strengthening in these areas of military commands and administrative structures that were disrupted by the purges of the Cultural Revolution.

Coupled with military preparations in north, northeast and northwest China, the changes indicate a continuing preoccupation in Peking with the development of the country's defense capabilities against the Russians.

In many instances the changes put into key positions men with long records of association and presumably of personal loyalty to Lin Piao, Minister of Defense, who is deputy of Chairman Mao Tse-tung.

Scene of Soviet Clashes

Recent reports of top officials present at public occasions in Manchuria, in the northeast, list a new "leading officer" for Heilungkiang Province, Li Shao-yuan. Mr. Li, who was listed directly after Pan Fu-Sheng, chairman of the provincial Revolutionary Committee, is believed to be in direct charge of defense along one of the most important provincial fronts on the Soviet border.

The Heilungkiang front on the Amur River, was the scene of a number of bloody clashes with the Russians last year. The recent incorporation of the northernmost district of Inner Mongolia into Heilungkiang province extends the provincial border to the Chita region of the Soviet Union and increases the responsibility of the provincial military command.

Mr. Li is listed as Mr. Pan's chief deputy in the province's Revolutionary Committee, the administrative body. Militarily he operates under the over-all command of Chen Hsi-lien, chief of the Mukden military region, which includes the provinces of Liaoning and Kirin as well as Heilungkiang.

Mr. Li, who has a long record of service under Lin Piao is one of two new deputy political commissars under Mr. Chen. The other is Liu Kuang-tao, who has also been listed as a deputy political commissar of military forces in Heilungkiang.

There is no indication of what has happened to Wang Chia-tao, who became the top military man in Heilungkiang early in the Cultural Revolution in 1966. His name has not been mentioned for a long time. It is possible he still has the title of commander in Heilungkiang, but it is believed here that Mr. Li is in charge.

Changes in Sinkiang

Other important changes have taken place on the western end of the Chinese-Soviet border. There Chang Chieh-cheng, another long-time colleague of Deputy Chairman Lin, is being listed as the new deputy commander for Sinkiang and concurrently commander of the 600,000-man Production and Construction Corps in Sinkiang, a paramilitary group.

Mr. Chang serves under Lung Shu-chin, who is head of the Sinkiang Revolutionary Committee as well as military commander. Mr. Lung is also an old colleague of Mr. Lin.

The new commander of the Production and Construction Corps in Sinkiang replaces Tao Chih-yueh, a 78-year-old former Kuomintang general who defected to the Communists with his troops in Sinkiang during the civil war.

Changes have also taken place in the Lanchow military region, which is responsible for a long section of the Chinese frontier with Soviet-aligned Outer Mongolia. There a new "leading officer," Kuo Peng, has appeared, and it is believed he may be the new commander of the region, replacing Chang Ta-chih, who has been appointed head of the Armed Forces Artillery Command in Peking. Mr. Kuo was transferred from Sinkiang, where he had been deputy commander.

The Lanchow command takes in Shensi, Tsinghai, Ningsia and Kansu as well as a large section of the western end of Inner Mongolia that was believed to have been recently made a part of Kansu Province.

No important recent personnel changes have been noted in the Peking military region, which includes a large section of the border with Outer Mongolia. But there is some evidence that the importance of the Peking garrison command, which is responsible for the defense of Peking and its environs, may have been upgraded and put, not under the Peking regional command, but directly under the general headquarters for the armed forces.

There is some speculation that an over-all special command has been created for Soviet border areas, but evidence for this is not conclusive.

July 5, 1970

491

Rumors on New Envoy

On the last point, there have been unconfirmed reports that Vasily S. Tolstikov, the Communist party leader for the Leningrad area, was nominated as ambassador to Peking after a previous designate, Vladimir I. Stepakov, became ill. The Chinese have reportedly proposed a Deputy Foreign Minister, Liu Hsin-chuan, to Moscow. Both countries have lacked ambassadors for nearly five years.

Tass said Mr. Ilyichev had been welcomed at the Peking airport by Chiao Kuan-hua, the Deputy Foreign Minister, who has headed the Chinese side at the talks since their beginning, and Tsai Chang-wen, the deputy head of the Chinese delegation.

V. G. Gankovsky, the deputy head of the Soviet team, and F. Potapenko, the Soviet chargé d'affaires in Peking, were also reported at the airport by Tass.

Except for occasional statements by Soviet leaders about the lack of progress, there has been little solid information on the substance of the talks.

Polemics between the two countries have continued this year, but below the vituperative level reached in 1969 when the two sides engaged in several border clashes.

According to reliable sources, the Soviet Union has offered to make slight border concessions to the Chinese, if Peking renounces its oft-stated historical claims to large areas of the Soviet Far East and Central Asia. The Chinese, these sources have said, have refused to negotiate

on the borders until the Russians pull back their forces.

Peking Editorial Quoted

The heavy deployment of Soviet forces along the frontier, equipped with modern missilery and aircraft, has apparently troubled Peking leaders who do not want, they say, to negotiate with "a gun at their head."

Earlier this month, the Peking press printed an editorial that said "social-imperialism," the Chinese current euphemism for the Soviet Union, "greedily eyes Chinese territory."

"It has not for a single day relaxed its preparations to attack China," the editorial says. "In words, it contends that it poses no threat to China. Why then, does it mass its troops in areas close to the Chinese borders?"

Moscow denies that it has aggressive designs on China and some press articles have accused the United States of starting rumors about a "Soviet attack" to sabotage the talks in Peking.

Mr. Ilyichev, 64, was named a Deputy Foreign Minister in March, 1965. His appointment represented demotion for Mr. Ilyichev, the former chief of ideological matters under Nikita S. Khrushchev, who was ousted in October, 1964. A man of apparently conservative tastes in the arts, Mr. Ilyichev, as party secretary for ideology, was unpopular with many Soviet intellectuals.

He worked from 1953 to 1958 as head of the Foreign Ministry's press section. In the Stalin years, he was editor of Izvestia, the Government paper, and Pravda, the party paper.

CANADIANS SET UP TIE TO RED CHINA AND DROP TAIWAN

Ottawa Recognizes Peking as 'Sole Legal' Regime but Not Its Claim to Isles

TAIPEI'S AIDE DEPARTS

Nationalist Embassy Closed as Ambassador Deplores Yielding to Communists

By JAY WALZ
Special to The New York Times

OTTAWA, Oct. 13—Canada and Communist China, after 20 months of negotiations, established diplomatic relations today. At the same time, Canada broke relations with the Chinese Nationalist Government on Taiwan.

"The Canadian Government recognizes the Government of the People's Republic of China as the sole legal Government of China," said a joint communiqué issued here and in Peking.

Hsueh Yu-chi, the Chinese Nationalist Ambassador in Ottawa for three and a half years, left immediately for New York, where he has also represented his Government at the United Nations. In a farewell statement, he "deplored" Canada's decision, which he said had been made "regardless of its adverse affect on the interests of the Chinese people and on the international situation in Asia and the Pacific."

'Friendly Relations' Recalled

He also deplored Canada's yielding to "the demands of the Communist regime at the expense of the friendly relations of a long standing" between Canada and his Government.

Ambassador Hsueh declared his embassy in Ottawa closed immediately, and announced that the Chinese Nationalist Consulate-General in Vancouver, where a large Chinese population resides, would be shut.

The Chinese-Canadian communiqué, which was read to

the House of Commons by Mitchell Sharp, Secretary of State for External Affairs, said that the Canadian Government had "noted" the Peking Government's claim to the Nationalist-ruled island of Taiwan as an "integral part" of the territory of Communist China but had not accepted it.

"Our position," Mr. Sharp declared, "is that the Canadian Government does not consider it appropriate either to endorse or to challenge the Chinese Government's position on the status of Taiwan." Mr. Sharp expressed hope that a Canadian Ambassador might be in Peking in six months. An envoy will leave for the Chinese capital in a few days to plan for an embassy, which officials here hope will be ready for occupancy within two or three months. It will be headed initially by a chargé d'affaires.

Mr. Sharp called Ambassador Hsueh to his office Sunday to receive a memorandum informing him that Canada would cease to recognize nationalist China at 11 A.M. today. The communications requested Mr. Hsueh "therefore to close the Chinese Embassy in Ottawa and the Chinese Consulate-General in Vancouver," Mr. Sharp further asked the ambassador "to withdraw from Canada within a reasonable time."

In a formal note of response, Ambassador Hsueh called Canada's decision an 'unfriendly act" and declared that it would help perpetuate tyrannical rule in the Chinese mainland.

The issue of Taiwan's status had been the chief element delaying the agreement on mutual recognition. The Chinese negotiators at the ambassadorial meetings held by the two Governments in Stockholm long insisted that Canada, in recognizing the Communist regime as the "sole legal Government" of China, include jurisdiction for the territory of Taiwan.

Peking's ultimate approval of the Canadian position produced a recognition agreement similar to that concluded by France with Communist China in January, 1964. This time the Communist diplomats reportedly had tried to improve the terms of that accord.

Ottawa yielded reluctantly on Peking's insistence that Canada break off relations with the Nationalist Government of Chiang Kai-shek even as the legal government ruling the island of Taiwan.

Answering a question in the Commons, Mr. Sharp said that Canadian and Chinese Nationalist leaders had previously agreed that "it is not possible to recognize simultaneously more than one Government as the Government of China." The Chinese Nationalist administration has always refused to concede that it represents only Taiwan.

On the basis of past official statements, it is expected that Canada will vote for the seating of Communist China in the United Nations when the issue comes up in the General Assembly in a few weeks. China has always been represented by the Nationalists, and Canada for many years voted with nations opposing a change, including the United States.

In the last two years, however Canada has abstained from voting on this question. Recently Mr. Sharp said that if Canada extended recognition to Communist China, her vote in the United Nations would be "consistent." This has been taken to mean that Canada would support Peking membership for the first time.

Both Canadian and United States diplomats here voiced doubt today that Ottawa's switch to diplomatic relations and support for Peking would materially damage United States-Canadian relations, although Washington has always opposed such a move.

A high Canadian official said today: "We always knew that Washington was against what we were doing, but there were no formal declarations or threats." An official at the United States Embassy described the various exchanges on the subject as "conversations." President Nixon and Prime Minister Pierre Elliot Trudeau held such conversations when they met for the first time in Washington 18 months ago.

In the past United States officials have expressed concern that Chinese Communist diplomats would come to Canada with eyes and ears trained mainly on the United States. But Canadian diplomats have argued that a Canadian Embassy in Peking would provide a listening post, too, and serve as a much-needed line of communication in the capital of a country of 800 million people.

In recent years the principal Chinese-Canadian communications have been through an exchange of newspaper correspondents. At present Norman Webster of The Toronto Globe and Mail reports from Peking and Tu Chao-min represents Hsinhua, the official Chinese press agency, in Ottawa. Li Yueh has represented the Central News Agency of Taiwan in Ottawa's parliamentary press gallery, and his presence there has caused Mr. Tu to boycott proceedings in Parliament.

Canadian officials began talking about recognizing Communist China in 1949, shortly after Mao Tse-tung's forces took control on the mainland. Until the start of the Korean war in June, 1950, it seemed that Canada might be the first major Western nation to have diplomatic relations with the Communist Government.

Serious talks resumed seven years ago when the two Governments, without formal diplomatic channels, found ways to negotiate a huge cash purchase of Canadian wheat.

Since 1963 Canada has sold more than 500 million bushels of wheat to China. The second three-year contract expired one year ago. This was followed by a supplemental one-year contract calling for sale of 86 million bushels, deliveries of which now being completed. Last week a Canadian grain mission left for Peking to conclude new nam, Pakistan, Syria, Yemen speculated that today's announcement of diplomatic relations might expedite the transaction.

Mr. Sharp noted today that establishment of diplomatic recognition was only a "first step" in the development of relations.

"We have already indicated to the Chinese in our Stockholm discussions our interest in setting up cultural and educational exchanges, in expanding trade between our two countries, in reaching an understanding on consular matters and in settling a small number of problems left over from an earlier period," he told the Commons.

Cultural Revolution Led To Diplomatic Isolation

By TILLMAN DURDIN
Special to The New York Times

HONG KONG, Oct. 13—Communist China's establishment of diplomatic ties with Canada marks another stage in the reconstitution of foreign relations that the Peking Government embarked upon early last year.

During 1967 and 1968 the turmoil of the Cultural Revolution disrupted most of Peking's foreign relations, almost isolating China diplomatically from the outside world.

Before that upheaval, Peking had 41 diplomatic missions abroad headed by ambassadors. The Government called home all but one ambassador, the envoy in Cairo, and the lower-level officials who were left in charge of the foreign missions reduced their diplomatic activities to a bare minimum.

In many countries with which Communist China had relations, the fever of the Cultural Revolution spilled over either into clashes by Chinese with local authorities or into harsh exchanges between Peking's representatives and officials of the host country.

In Hong Kong, Peking partisans attempted an uprising, while in Burma pro-Peking Chinese went on a rampage of violence. Foreign envoys in Peking and some foreign missions were subjected to attacks. China's relations with other Communist countries became strained and animosities against the Soviet Union widened into border clashes and strident propaganda warfare.

Envoys Return to Posts

As the Cultural Revolution cooled down in 1969, Peking's authorities started the road back to restoration of the previously prevailing situation. Ambassadors began to go back to embassies abroad—28 are now at their posts—and more flexible and customary diplomatic maneuvering was resumed.

The talks in Warsaw between the United States Ambassador and the Chinese chargé d'affaires were resumed, trade and courtesy missions started going abroad again and friendly overtures brought about easier contacts with most of the states—except for the Soviet Union and its closer associates—with which Peking has relations.

Canada's offer of recognition fitted in with the new Peking program and has led to the formal establishment of Chinese Communist ties for the first time with a country on one of the American continents.

China's moves to rehabilitate its foreign relations have not led to any discernible expansion of its overseas role, except for the new ties with Canada. The Chinese still have fewer ambassadors and other diplomatic representatives abroad than before the Cultural Revolution.

Ties With 45 Countries

The number of states with which Communist China has diplomatic relations stands at 45, one fewer than before the Cultural Revolution and less than half the total number of countries in the world. Fourteen of these countries are in Asia, 16 in Europe, 13 in Africa, one in Latin America and now one in North America.

The Asian countries are Afghanistan, Burma, Ceylon, India, Iraq, Laos, Mongolia, Nepal, North Korea, North Vietnam, Pakistan, Syria, Yemen and South Yemen. Peking also has relations with the Cambodian exile regime of Prince Norodom Sihanouk and the provisional government set up by the Vietcong in South Vietnam.

The European countries are Albania, Britain, Czechoslovakia, Denmark, East Germany, Finland, France, Hungary, the Netherlands, Norway, Poland, Rumania, the Soviet Union, Sweden, Switzerland and Yugoslavia.

The African countries are Algeria, the former French Congo, Guinea, Kenya, Mali, Mauritania, Morocco, Somalia, the Sudan, Tanzania, Uganda, the United Arab Republic and Zambia. Western Hemisphere countries are Cuba and Canada.

Eight countries recognize but do not have relations with Communist China — Tunisia, Ghana, Burundi, Senegal, Nigeria, Indonesia, Israel and Mauritius. Fifty-one of the nations that recognize Peking are United Nations members.

The Chinese Nationalist Government on Taiwan is recognized by 67 countries. Two countries recognize both Chi-

493

nas and 14 do not recognize either Chinese Government.

Communist China, more than other countries, uses recognition and diplomatic relations with foreign countries as an instrument of political policy and for advancement of national interests.

In Africa and the Middle East, for example, Peking openly uses diplomatic relationships to promote revolutionary causes and counter Soviet and United States interests. When Indonesia was governed by President Sukarno, Communist China carefully nurtured its ties with Jakarta while assisting a Communist movement that sought to take control.

In the case of Canada, recognition strikes another blow at the status of the Nationalist Government in Taipei, promotes Peking's effort to oust the Nationalists from the United Nations and gain their seat and makes the official United States policy toward China more difficult.

Governments' Foes Backed

The fact that China has diplomatic representation with a country does not necessarily mean that it strives for good relations with that country's government. Peking has relations with Burma and India while simultaneously helping

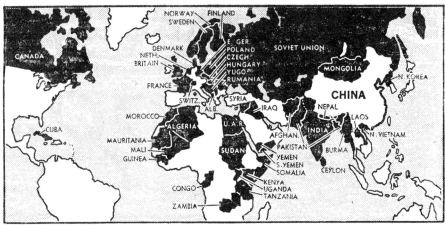

The New York Times   Oct. 14, 1970

TIES WITH RED CHINA: The 45 countries shown on the map in black have diplomatic relations with Peking. The Communist regime of Mao-Tse-tung also recognizes the Cambodian exile regime of Prince Sihanouk and the Vietcong's provisional government.

revolutionary movements that are opposed to the two governments. In both Britain and France, with which Peking has relations, printed Chinese Communist materials and agents for the Chinese Government support outbreaks of anti-government violence.

Nor do diplomatic relations appear to give any preference in trade with Communist China. The Peking Government's biggest trading partner is Japan,

a country that is a prime target for hostile Chinese propaganda these days and against whose government Peking is openly encouraging revolutionary activity.

Britain was the first major non-Communist power to recognize Communist China in 1949, but has continuously had troubled dealings with Peking and has gained no trade advantages. West Germany, which does not recognize Peking, has for years exported more goods

than Britain to Communist China.

Communist China's relations with Pakistan were bitter while Pakistan was a close ally of the United States, but are now cordial because Pakistan is hostile to India and standoffish toward Washington.

In a return to its old, pre-Cultural Revolution flexibility, Peking now cultivates Rumania and Yugoslavia because they show independence of the Soviet Union.

October 14, 1970

Moscow and Peking Conclude One-Year Agreement on Trade

MOSCOW, Nov. 23 — The Soviet Union and Communist China today signed a trade and payments agreement in Peking.

A Soviet dispatch from the Chinese capital said that Ivan T. Grishin, a Soviet Deputy Minister of Foreign Trade, and Li Chiang, his Chinese counterpart, had signed the accord.

Mr. Grishin arrived in Peking on Wednesday, and met yesterday with Li Hsien-nien, a Deputy Premier. Trade between the two countries, which reached a peak of more than $2-billion in 1959, steadily diminished as

relations worsened. Last year's trade was $55-million.

Increased trade was one of the items urged by the Soviet Government as a way of improving relations between the two governments, which were strained by the border clashes last year.

[A Reuters dispatch from Moscow, quoting Chinese sources, said the new trade pact was for one year. It is reported to have been 18 months in negotiation.]

In another development, Li Hsin-chuan, the new Chinese ambassador, arrived here last

night to take up his duties. He was received promptly this morning by Foreign Minister Andrei A. Gromyko. The envoy is expected to present his credentials to President Nikolai V. Podgorny and will probably see Premier Aleksei N. Kosygin.

The new Soviet ambassador to China, Vasily S. Tolstikov, saw Premier Chou En-lai on Wednesday.

Although there has been no words of progress in the 13-month-long talks on border questions, much of the tensions in relations between the two states has been reduced in recent months.

Ambassadors Left in 1966

HONG KONG, Aug. 23—With the arrival in Moscow today of its new Ambassador, Liu Hsin-chuan, Communist China repaired a breach of more than four years in relations at the ambassadorial level.

Each nation withdrew its ambassador in 1966 as the anti-Soviet passions of the Cultural Revolution worsened existing animosities.

The exchange of ambassadors is one of a number of recent developments that indicate there has been some abatement in hostility.

November 24, 1970

Communist China Recognized by Chile

Special to The New York Times

HONG KONG, Jan. 5—Communist China announced today the establishment of diplomatic relations with Chile, where a Marxist president, Dr. Salvador Allende, came to power last year.

The move gave Peking a third foothold on the American continent and a second in Latin America. The Chinese Communists established relations with Cuba shortly after Fidel Castro came to power in 1959. Last October relations were established with Canada.

A joint communiqué said the Chilean accord had been concluded in Paris by Huang Chen, the Chinese ambassador in France, and Enrique Bernstein Carabantes, the Chilean ambassador.

Canadian Formula Used

Following a formula used in the agreement with Canada, the communiqué said that Peking had affirmed that Taiwan was "an inalienable part of the territory of the People's Republic of China and that the Chilean Government had taken note of this statement.

The communiqué added: "The Chilean Government recognizes the government of the People's Republic of China as the sole legal government of China."

Chile has maintained diplomatic relations with the Chinese Nationalist Government on Taiwan, which is now expected to break these ties as a result of the agreement between Santiago and Peking.

During the last few months Communist China has sought to broaden its diplomatic and trade ties after an isolationist attitude that prevailed during the Cultural Revolution starting in 1966. In the last quarter of 1970 Peking established diplomatic relations with Canada, Equatorial Guinea, Italy and Ethiopia. The new link with Chile brings to 50 the number of countries with which Peking has diplomatic ties.

China's interest in establishing ties with Chile became apparent after the election of Dr. Allende as President when Premier Chou En-lai sent a congratulatory message. A Chinese workers' delegation attended Dr. Allende's inauguration ceremony. In November a Chilean delegation arrived in Peking for a visit.

When the question of Chinese representation came before the United Nations General Assembly in November, Chile voted in favor of Peking's admission.

Communist China has recently been making a significant effort to improve its relations with Cuba. The two countries engaged in angry exchanges in 1966. In November, it was announced that Cuba had agreed to the appointment of Chang Teh-chun as a new Chinese ambassador to Havana, the first since the former ambassador was recalled in 1967.

Last Saturday, Premier Chou attended a Cuban embassy reception in Peking marking Cuba's National Day.

January 6, 1971

Sato Stresses Desire for Better Relations With Peking

By TAKASHI OKA
Special to The New York Times

TOKYO, Jan. 22 — Premier Eisaku Sato reiterated today his Government's desire to improve relations with the Chinese Communists and referred to their country for the first time as the People's Republic of China.

His remarks came in a state-of-the-nation address delivered at the opening of the Diet's 65th session today. Emperor Hirohito inaugurated the session with a brief Speech from the Throne, expressing gratification at progress the nation had made and calling for further efforts "to raise national prosperity and to increase the confidence of the world."

Both the Emperor and Mr. Sato will turn 75 this year. Both have lived through some of the most tumultuous decades in the nation's history: from the era of the rickshaw and the silkworm, through a brief experiment with parliamentary democracy, into economic depression, rising militarism and territorial expansion, Pearl Harbor and World War II, Hiroshima and shattering defeat and the postwar era with a new emphasis on pacifism abroad and single-minded concentration on economic growth at home.

Throughout these decades, China and the United States have been among Japan's foremost foreign policy concerns.

Cabinet Debate Inducted

Mr. Sato's speech, and Foreign Minister Kiichi Aichi's address on foreign policy, which followed it, showed evidence of agonizing debate within the Cabinet's inner councils on how to offer friendship to mainland China without gravely offending the Republic of China on Taiwan.

As one Cabinet source close to the Premier put it, Japan's approach to the mainland can take place only to the extent that it does not damage irreparably her diplomatic ties with Taiwan.

"We cannot go so far as diplomatic recognition of Peking, and Peking must know this," the source declared.

Mr. Sato's speech acknowledged the difficulty. "The most difficult aspect of the China problem," he said, "lies in the fact that the Government of the Republic of China in Taipei and the Government of the People's Republic of China in Peking are both claiming sovereignty over the whole of China."

Stresses Amity With U.S.

Turning to the United States, Mr. Sato said that what happened in Japanese-American relations had a greater influence "on our people's livelihood than relations with any other country."

Mr. Aichi echoed his words, saying that from both the economic and security viewpoint, "our relations with the United States are more important to us than those with any other country."

Both the Premier and the Foreign Minister voiced hope that the negotiations on textile quotas with the United States would produce an amicable settlement and both expressed gratification that procedures to implement the 1969 agreement on the reversion of Okinawa to Japan in 1972 were moving ahead smoothly.

Foreign policy, however, occupied only about a fourth of Mr. Sato's half-hour speech, which was designed mostly to offer his 105 million countrymen the prospect of peace and prosperity through continued hard work and determination in the 1970's.

His outline was general rather than specific, calling for the construction of 9.5 million housing units, the expenditure of $7-billion for sewers and treatment works, and the building of 780 miles of superhighways in the next five years.

He also spoke of measures to cope with pollution and to utilize land in a manner designed to promote human welfare rather than helter-skelter industrial growth.

Mr. Sato has been Premier for more than six years and there are recurrent reports that he will step down before his present term expires in 1972.

Several commentators described his speech today as one designed not so much to show what his own Government intended to accomplish as to give the nation goals that future leaders should try to fulfill.

January 23, 1971

Tanzania-Zambia Railway: a Bridge to China?

Special to The New York Times

DAR ES SALAAM, Tanzania—The biggest economic event in this East African country last year was the start of construction by Communist China of the much-discussed, long-awaited Tanzanian-Zambian railway.

The 1,056-mile, single-track line, known as the Tanzam Railway, will link this Indian Ocean port with landlocked Zambia's northern copper belt. The work, which is expected to be completed in five years, will employ 7,000 to 8,000 Chinese engineers and technicians and some 14,000 Tanzanian and Zambian laborers. The cost is presently estimated to be nearly $406-million.

Western countries have speculated about how much political significance the undertaking may have. But there can be no doubt that the project—by far Communist China's most ambitious and costliest foreign-aid effort—is expected to gain Peking considerable prestige and influence in Africa. Both have diminished sharply in recent years, along with the volume of Communist Chinese economic aid to Guinea, Mali and a few other African countries.

So far, there has been little evidence of the Chinese "presence" here. Most of the Chinese construction workers, now numbering 7,000, are housed in camps some distance from town and along the 300 miles of right-of-way that have already been cleared. Actual work on the line began in July and the cornerstone-laying ceremonies were held in October at the future terminal at Yombo.

The few Chinese administrative personnel and their families hardly cause any raised eyebrows in this multiracial city, where in addition to Africans, and a variety of Asians and Westerners, there are many long-time Chinese residents, who appear to have little interest in the newcomers.

As described here, the Tanzanian view of the project, which is said to be shared by the Chinese, is that it be regarded simply as another foreign-contractor operation to be carried out in routine, unobtrusive fashion. President Kenneth Kaunda of Zambia has denied there is any political motivation.

World Bank Rejection

The main benefit of the Tanzanian Railway is to provide Zambia with a further northern shipping outlet that will completely free her from any dependence on transportation through white-ruled southern Africa. The Tanzam highway and oil pipeline built from here in recent years already has filled much of this need and raised some question about whether a rail link is either necessary or economical. Other road-building projects are underway.

In the early sixties, the rail project was rejected by the World Bank as unfeasible and later efforts to interest other governments and private groups in the undertaking fell through. Communist China offered to build the railway in 1965, and an initial agreement of the three governments was reached in 1967. A further two years was needed for surveying and design.

The Chinese terms basically are generous. The $406-million loan is interest-free and with a five-year grace period dating from 1968, repayment — shared 50-50 by Tanzania and Zambia—is to extend to 2013.

However, local costs of the work, estimated at 52 per cent of the total, are to be met from proceeds of the sale of $16.8-million of Communist Chinese consumer goods to be imported annually by each of the African countries. The proceeds are to be debited to the Peking loan account.

While Zambia probably can absorb $16.8-million a year of Chinese products, Tanzania may face some problems. Tanzania already imports about $9.5-million of Chinese products annually and raising this by $16.8-million would increase competition for her own small consumer-goods industries.

Both President Kaunda and Tanzanian President Julius K. Nyerere, however, are determined to have the railway. There have been questions about whether any of the countries, including China, can really afford the undertaking and also whether the Chinese could build the railway.

On the latter point, one American here commented, "After all, Chinese laborers built some of the first American railroads, so why shouldn't they be able to build this one?"

January 29, 1971

China Discovers a New Friend In Africa—Equatorial Guinea

WASHINGTON, Jan. 30—China appears to have found a new African friend in the tiny but strategic Republic of Equatorial Guinea.

The elaborate reception in Peking last week for a delegation of Equatorial Guinean Cabinet officials, the first since the two countries established diplomatic relations last October, suggested to United States experts on Chinese affairs that the new republic was regarded as a member of a small group of China's closest friends.

Peking radio, describing a banquet given for the delegation by Vice Premier Li Hsiennien, listed as attending only diplomats from Africa and from governments intimately linked to China.

It mentioned diplomats from Albania, which is China's only European ally, North Korea, North Vietnam, South Vietnam's provisional revolutionary government and officials associated in Peking with Prince Norodom Sihanouk of Cambodia.

Absent were diplomats from the Soviet Union, European Communist countries and Cuba.

American specialists said that Peking, whose policies in Africa had been fairly inactive since the Chinese Cultural Revolution in the middle 1960's, may have selected Equatorial Guinea as its new center of African influence along the lines of the relationship with Albania in Europe.

Equatorial Guinea, having won independence from Spain in October, 1968, severed most of her Spanish ties early in 1969, following a violent dispute with Madrid. Since, the economically bankrupt infant republic with a population of 260,000 has been undergoing a steady process of political radicalization.

Equatorial Guinea's importance is largely due to her location on Africa's west coast. Her mainland section, the former territory of Rio Muni, is squeezed between Cameroon and Gabon. The island of Fernando Po makes up the rest of the country, which is well to the southeast of two other Guineas on the west coast—Portuguese Guinea and the Republic of Guinea.

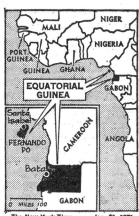

The New York Times   Jan. 31, 1971

During the Nigerian civil war, Fernando Po served as a crucial air transshipment point for foodstuffs and weapons for the breakaway Biafra province. The island is still a point of aerial access to much of West Africa with a modern jet airport built by Spain before independence.

Equatorial Guinea's attitude toward China was expressed in a talk by the Minister of Public Work, Housing and Transport, Jesus Alfonsa Oyono Alogo. He said at the banquet that, "through the joint efforts of our two Governments, the friendly relations and cooperation between our two countries will be consolidated and developed day by day."

January 31, 1971

PEKING WIDENING TIES WITH ARABS

Chinese Making a Political and Economic Comeback

By IHSAN A. HIJAZI
Special to The New York Times

BEIRUT, Lebanon, Feb. 9—After more than three years of self-imposed isolation because of the Cultural Revolution, Communist China is making both a political and economic comeback in Arab countries.

Statistics published by the Damascus office of Hsinhua, the Chinese press agency, showed that Chinese exports to Arab markets last year increased 10 per cent over the period of 1967 to 1969. The increase totaled about $200-million.

The main rise was in exports to Southern Yemen, the Sudan and Lebanon, although Kuwait remained the chief Arab importer of Chinese Communist goods.

In Lebanon's free market, goods marked "Made in the People's Republic of China" include such items as fly swatters and pencil sharpeners.

The statistics indicated an increase of 58 per cent in Chinese exports to Lebanon and as much as 72 per cent to Southern Yemen in the last half of 1969 and the first half of 1970. For the Sudan, the rise was 63 per cent.

Iraq Is Second

Iraq is second to Kuwait in the volume of exports from China, and is followed by Syria and Libya. While in 1967, the United Arab Republic's imports from China dropped by about 38 per cetn, they are expected to be doubled in 1971 under an agreement signed last month in Cairo

Tea, frozen foods, chemicals and some industrial products are China's main exports to the Arab world.

The upsurge in Chinese trade was accompanied by the recent return to a number of Arab capitals of Chinese Communist Ambassadors, most of whom had been recalled in 1967 for indoctrination in the Cultural Revolution.

Last week, on the eve of the scheduled expiration of the Middle East cease-fire, the Chinese Ambassador in Damascus called on Syrian head of state, Ahmed al-Khatib, and according to the Damascus radio, assured him of China's "full backing to the Arabs" in their battle "against Israel and the imperialists led by the United States."

The Government of Lebanon, which has maintained diplomatic relations with Nationalist China, is currently considering recognizing Peking.

Lunch Publicly in Beirut

Chinese Communist diplomats from the Embassy in Damascus lunch publicly with Lebanese leftists and Palestinian commando intellectuals at Beirut's leading restaurants.

Another new effort by the Chinese is an attempt to establish themselves in the Persian Gulf region. Statistics show that Chinese exports to Bahrain have increased 45 per cent in 1969 and 1970.

Through their foothold in Southern Yemen, which is becoming the strongest in the Arab world, the Chinese have become the sponsors of the revolt in Dhofar against Sultan Qabus of Oman, who is backed by British military advisers.

The Chinese have been helping the Palestinian guerrillas, but there has been less talk lately about this aid. One explanation given by informed sources here is that the Palestinians are beginning to learn the difference between Chinese promises and deeds.

The sources said that the Chinese assistance delivered so far to the guerrillas was less than a quarter of the aid promised to then leaders during visits to Peking in the last two years.

Chinese statistics indicate that as much as 26 per cent of Peking's aid to foreign countries goes to the Arabs. This aid was put at $212-million in the last decade.

The largest promise of Chinese aid in the last two years was made to the Southern Yemen, but so far all the Chinese have done was to study that country's assistance requirements. When southern Yemeni officials asked last month that this aid be delivered, a Chinese delegation arrived to make a further study of Southern Yemen's economy.

In 1962, Peking agreed to lend Syria about $6-million, but it only two years ago that Peking began to channel part of the money into building a yarn factory in Hama, a town in central Syria.

February 10, 1971

State of Our Asia Policy

By O. EDMUND CLUBB

In his State of the World Message, President Nixon sought to demonstrate a non-hostile disposition toward China. There were amiable references to "a dialogue with Peking," and the possibility of China's playing "a constructive role in the family of nations." But Washington would continue to oppose the seating of Peking's delegation in the U.N. at the expense of Taipei's representation, and we stand by our 1954 treaty with "the Republic of China on Taiwan." In sum, no change.

And so it was, too, in the President's passages on the Indochina war. He found no fault on our side; it was not we but the North Vietnamese who had expanded the war, and they who set up unreasonable conditions for a negotiated peace. So they have our answer—"Vietnamization."

This is a dreary, thrice-told tale, and we are far from hearing the end of it. The President's earlier State of the Union Message indirectly suggests the reason. In that communication, he proposed that a reinspired U. S. Government should effect, at home, a "peaceful revolution in which power was turned back to the people': the keynote was—democratic change.

Consideration of the merits of that view can be omitted here, but it is to be remarked that, with respect to Asia, the United States for a full quarter century has undeviatingly supported autocratic regimes and followed a counter-revolutionary policy.

We began by trying to help the Nationalists turn back the revolutionary tide in postwar China. In the course of the Indochina War, the Korean War and two Formosa Strait crises, our policy evolved all too naturally into one of direct intervention. The United States is now entering upon the tenth year of a military effort aimed at winning decisive victory for "anti-Communist" parties of its choice in Southeast Asia. The strategy designed first to "contain" the Chinese revolution has been expanded to embrace all Asia.

There is indeed a massive revolution in course in Asia. The achievement of independence from colonial rulers did not always bring good government and social justice in its train; and most Asians continue plagued by age-old poverty. The underprivileged of the earth are becoming ever more resentful of a state of affairs which permits the richest country in particular to command the lion's share of the world's natural resources and material goods.

Washington's thinking neglects the essence of the situation. The contemporary Asian revolution derives

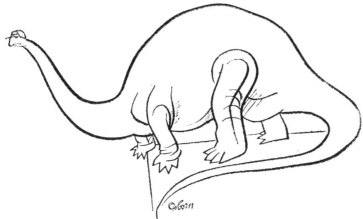

The American Way in Asia as seen by Robert Osborn

its strength from native sources, not from Peking. "Our" Chinese, trained, equipped and advised by us, lost out to the revolutionaries in the Chinese civil war of 1946-49. Similar attempts to impose our will in revolutionary situations elsewhere in Asia through the use of mercenary forces are also doomed to failure. And when the "Vietnamization" device fails, nothing would remain, by our present strategy of interventionism, but to wage wars of annihilation against whole populations —the "Communist infrastructure."

That mad way leads to disaster. All logic dictates a turnabout of our grand strategy. Such a fundamental shift is admittedly difficult for an ideological power possessed of as many politicized commitments (and myths) as the United States, but it is entirely feasible.

Basically, it would be essential to grant that the United States has no divine call to act as the world's mentor and policeman. And, as regards Asia in particular, there would be required:

• The acquisition and entertainment at the highest levels of government in Washington of a deeper apprecia-

tion of the prime motivations (shall we say, "driving dreams"?) of Asian peoples.

• *Full* abandonment of our military intervention in Indochina.

• The demilitarization of our Asia policy, with progressive withdrawal of U.S. military forces from Asian bases.

• The adjustment of our treaty relations with Taiwan, while undertaking the re-establishment of regular diplomatic and commercial relations with China.

• The conversion of a sizable fraction of our overseas military investments and activities into an expansive undertaking for global economic cooperation for the benefit of the poor of the earth.

If we were really to turn from the ways of war and help to "open wide the doors of human fulfillment" (again borrowing the President's words) for Asians as well as for Americans, the Asian revolution, paradoxically enough, would in all certainty soon be seen to offer distinctly less of that fearsome "threat to our national security" than officially imagined at present.

March 1, 1971

Nixon was on the last day of his long Florida wekend, the White House press secretary, Ronald L. Ziegler, said that "it is the President's policy to carefully examine further steps we may take for broader contacts between Red Chinese and Americans and it is his intention, wherever possible, to remove needless obstacles to the realization of these opportunities."

The United States keeps all aspects of its China policy under constant review. Besides possible measures to establish a trade relationship with Peking, the Administration is seeking to evolve a formula that may allow Communist China's admission to the United Nations without the expulsion of the Chinese Nationalist Government on Taiwan.

It is considered doubtful here whether Peking would accept such an arrangement—for one thing it would not gain a veto-wielding seat on the Security Council under the formulas now under discussion — but State Department officials pointedly remarked today that discussions on the future of Taiwan should properly be conducted between the two Chinese Governments and not by the United States.

This comment was offered in connection with a recently published report that Premier Chou En-lai had indicated Peking's willingness to discuss the Taiwan issue with the United States.

Mr. Bray said that private diplomatic channels had been used to convey to the Chinese the United States readiness to resume the ambassadorial talks in Warsaw.

The last session between American and Chinese diplomats was held on Feb. 20, 1970. The next meeting was scheduled for May 20, but Peking cancelled it in protest against the United States incursion into Cambodia.

'No Response From Peking'

The new efforts to revive the talks have met with "no response from Peking," Mr. Bray said.

Having dropped the 20-year-old requirement that American passports be especially validated for China, the United States now bans travel only to North Vietnam, North Korea and Cuba.

The ban on travel in those three countries was extended today for six more months under an existing law requiring that travel bans be either extended or dropped every half year. The restriction on travel to China expired today when the Administration chose not to renew it.

U.S. Lifts Ban on China Travel

By TAD SZULC
Special to The New York Times

WASHINGTON, March 15 — The United States today lifted its ban on travel by Americans to Communist China and disclosed that it was working through private diplomatic channels to bring Peking's Ambassador back to the Warsaw talks interrupted more than a year ago.

Both steps are a part of the Nixon Administration's continuing policy of seeking im-

proved relations with China, but the State Department conceded that no rapid response was expected here.

Officials noted that Peking was known to have granted only three entry visas to Americans in the last 18 months, even though a thousand persons have had their passports validated for travel to China for purposes the United States Government has termed "legitimate." Thus it was considered doubtful that the Chinese would throw their doors open to Unit-

ed States citizens as a result of today's State Department action.

In announcing the decision on authorizing travel to China, the State Department's press officer, Charles W. Bray 3d, said it was in line with President Nixon's promise in his message to Congress on foreign affairs last month "to create broad opportunities for contacts between the Chinese and American people."

In Key Biscayne, where Mr.

March 16, 1971

PEKING AND KUWAIT TO EXCHANGE ENVOYS

Special to The New York Times

HONG KONG, March 29 — Communist China and Kuwait have established diplomatic relations, Hsinhua, the Peking press agency, reported today.

A joint communiqué signed by representatives of both Governments in the small oil-producing Arab state at the head of the Persian Gulf on March 22 said that they had decided to establish relations at the ambassadorial level and exchange ambassadors "within the shortest possible period."

The decision was also made, the communiqué said, because of Kuwait's recognition of China as the legal Government of China and because of China's support for "the Arab struggle against imperialism and Zionism."

Peking was represented in the talks and at the signing ceremony by Kung Ta-fei, its Ambassador to Iraq, who was sent to Kuwait on March 8.

March 30, 1971

The New York Times — April 9, 1971

Communist China, competing with Nationalist China for influence in Africa, is recognized by 20 nations but does not have ties with all. Nationalists have links with 21.

China Quietly Renewing An Active Role in Africa

By WILLIAM BORDERS

Special to The New York Times

LAGOS, Nigeria, April 8—A Chinese Communist diplomat, Chang Li, came to this sultry capital the other day to open an embassy, establishing diplomatic relations with Nigeria and marking what many regard as a turning point in the Peking Government's relations with Africa.

"The Chinese had been quiet and stagnant all over the continent since the middle sixties," explained a Western diplomat who counts China-watching among the principal duties of his post in East Africa. "Now, suddenly, they're really back in business."

The Nigerian recognition of Communist China, which was announced earlier this year after negotiations in Cairo, is considered especially significant because Nigeria is Africa's most populous country and, increasingly, one of its leaders.

The last six months have brought the Chinese several other attainments in Africa, including these:

¶Diplomatic recognition last December by Ethiopia, another large and influential country.

¶The emergence of Equatorial Guinea, the newest independent country in Africa, as a tiny and strategically situated ally.

¶The inauguration of a $400,- million Chinese railway project in Tanzania and Zambia, illustrating renewed aid potential.

Peking is winning new friends among the Africans, from the rice paddies of Mauritania, where Chinese agronomists are improving the yield, to the whitewashed Lenin Hospital overlooking the Indian Ocean in Zanzibar, 4,000 miles away, where Chinese doctors are fighting disabling tropical diseases.

With a zeal that often surpasses that of advisers from other countries, teams from Peking are digging wells in Somalia, erecting radio towers in Zambia, making shoes in Mali and building a river dockyard in the former French Congo.

The reassertion of China's diplomatic and aid offensive in Africa is part of its emergence, worldwide, after self-imposed isolation during the Cultural Revolution. Late last year Peking also won the diplomatic recognition of Canada, Chile and Italy, and all the world over its ambassadors have returned to posts vacated during the domestic turmoil of 1967 and 1968.

In Africa China's presence now reflects a change in the style and image that its diplomats and aid advisers are trying to project.

"They tell us that this time they have come simply as friends, to help and not to subvert, as they used to do," said a Government official in Tanzania, which has more mainland Chinese than any other country in the world outside Asia. "I am inclined to believe them, but still we are watching very closely," the official added, expressing a prevailing caution.

In the early days of independence 10 years ago, Chinese accredited as diplomats to African countries often spent most of their time fomenting rebellion, giving expensive backing in hard currencies to the most radical group they could find.

In 1965 the Chinese Embassy in the Central African Republic, an obscure land of a million people, had a staff of 30 men, some of them advising the leftist Government the country had then and others training a secret "people's army" for ultimate use against it.

In Niger at about the same time the Chinese were secretly backing the anti-Government Sawaba party, sending its guerrilla fighters to Nanking for training and, reportedly, financing an unsuccessful coup d'état.

In Burundi the Chinese were generally believed to have been involved in the assassination of the Premier, and their presence in Ghana when Kwame Nkrumah was President was pervasive.

Next came a period of reaction against the Chinese role, dating roughly from the overthrow of Mr. Nkrumah in 1966 while he was on a visit to Peking. Several countries, including the Central African Republic and Niger, broke relations with China; Burundi and Ghana suspended them.

Staffs Sharply Reduced

Other states followed the course of Kenya, which let the Chinese stay but sharply limited the size of their embassy staff. The Kenyans also outlawed the distribution of Chinese propaganda, and just the other day two men in Nairobi received 18-month jail sentences for having some books by Chairman Mao Tse-tung in their home.

One place being watched closely for evidence that the Chinese have changed since the middle nineteen-sixties is Tanzania, where they have gone in great numbers to build the Tanzam Railway, Peking's largest aid project, which got under way in October.

By June, there will be 13,000 Chinese working on the 1,100-mile railroad, which is to link the Zambian copper mines to the Indian Ocean, bypassing white-ruled Rhodesia and Mozambique. Other Chinese in Tanzania are advising the army, planning a naval base and building a plant outside Dar es Salaam for the manufacture of smallpox vaccine.

How many are also proselytizing is not known, but Chinese literature is ubiquitous, including the little red books of quotations from Chairman Mao. Teen-agers buy copies for 14 cents and, in a display of budding capitalism, sell them to tourists at the Hotel Kilimanjaro for 75 cents.

Some observers fear that President Julius K. Nyerere of Tanzania, who is widely regarded as an idealist, has been naive in accepting so much from the Chinese, particularly the 30-year loan for the railway. But others insist that he has sacrificed no more than, say, President Félix Houphouët-Boigny of the militantly capitalistic Ivory Coast, whose economy is almost controlled by Frenchmen.

The Chinese, almost none of whom have families with them in Tanzania, live in austere work camps cut out of the dense tropical forest. In Dar es Salaam most of them live in rough barracks and keep to themselves.

They can be seen in groups of two or three shopping or riding in the backs of trucks. Few speak English or Swahili and their contacts with the people are limited.

Informed Westerners report that, so far at least, the Chinese have just been doing the jobs they went to do and showing no signs of trying to sell their political ideas. President Nyerere says: "People's China will soon learn that she will have a job if she wishes to pocket us."

The extensive aid program in Tanzania has attracted envious attention from poor African Governments that do not recognize Communist China.

Sixteen African countries have diplomatic relations with Peking or are establishing them. Four others recognize the Communist Government but do not have relations with it.

Twenty-two countries recognize the Chinese Nationalist Government on Taiwan, which gives it a numerical edge—although the 20 Governments that recognize the Communists represent more than two-thirds of the people and half the territory.

Shift in Vote at U.N.

The numbers are important in the United Nations, where the vote among African states on the question of a seat for Peking was 19 to 18 in favor last year, compared with 20 to 15 opposed two years ago.

Observers here believe that the United Nations votes have become a less central consideration in the aid offensive by the Chinese than their desire to assume the role of a well-meaning and disinterested friend.

"They'll stay on their good behavior, in contrast to the Americans, who try to run things, or the French, who succeed in running them," said a diplomat in Nouakchott, the desert capital of Mauritania, where the Chinese presence is second only to that of the French. "Their goal is to hear the Africans say to the other big powers, 'Why can't you be like the Chinese?'"

The Chinese come into Africa emphasizing their differences not only with the West but also with the Soviet Union, which the Peking radio regularly accuses of "following the example of United States imperialism" in Africa.

Exhorting African-Asian solidarity in a common struggle against the white man, Russian as well as Western, the Chinese stress that they are colored too and that their land is also poor.

Long-time observers of their projects in Africa say that they have managed to avoid some mistakes of the Soviet aid program, like sending snow tires or heavy wool uniforms to the tropics. And unlike United States aid officials, who usually live conspicuously in relative luxury, the Chinese genuinely live at the level of the people they are advising.

Small by Big-Power Standard

The Chinese are spending four or five times as much on African aid as the Nationalists, whose program here consists largely of agricultural assistance. But Peking's aid is still small by big-power standards, often concentrating on symbolic projects.

The Communists are still willing to offer support in battles that they consider promising. Premier Gaafar al-Nimeiry of the Sudan, which is trying to put down a rebellion in the South, announced on his return from a visit to Peking last August that he was grateful for China's "friendship in arms."

Not counting the Tanzam Railway, Peking's aid to Africa since the nineteen-fifties has totaled about $250-million, most of it in the five countries that China seems to have selected as special allies: Algeria, the former French Congo, Guinea, Mauritania and Tanzania.

Although the Chinese, acting through brokers in Hong Kong, are believed to be big trading partners of Rhodesia and South Africa, they also make a special effort to help the guerrillas fighting against the white-dominated Governments in those countries and in the Portuguese territories.

Most observers of African politics consider it inevitable that those lands will eventually be ruled by blacks, perhaps by the blacks now fighting for them in the swamps and jungles.

"When the time comes the Chinese want to have been on the right side, helping, not on the wrong side, where the Americans often are," said an American diplomat in one of the black countries from which the so-called liberation fighters stage their strikes against Africa's southern tier.

The Soviet Union is also giving money and guns to nationalist groups, and, to the distress of some black Africans, the rivalry between the two Communist powers is often reflected in a debilitating split. Two groups are fighting the white minority Government of Rhodesia, and Angola has three liberation movements, which

often battle one another instead of the Portuguese.

An exception is in Portuguese Guinea, where both the Chinese and the Russians are supporting the African Party for the Independence of Guinea and Cape Verde, headed by Amilcar Cabral, perhaps because it is Africa's most successful rebel organization, controlling half the embattled territory.

Not only in the bush villages and back roads where these wars are being fought but also in such cities as Bamako and Brazzaville, where French economic influence is still strong, the Chinese are allying themselves again with the African nationalist spirit against vestiges of colonialism, and the support is often reciprocated.

Nigeria, for example, is fiercely proud of her independence, but most of the corporations here are headed by white Englishmen, and the country had been widely regarded, in the words of Dr. Okoi Arikpo, Minister of External Affairs, "as being nonaligned, but in a pro-Western manner.'

"We wanted to get away from that, asserting a positive neutrality, a real nonalignment, and that played a part in our decision to recognize China," he explained in an interview.

Asked about the possibility of Chinese subversion, Dr. Arikpo said he was not apprehensive and hinted strongly that guarantees against it had been an explicit part of the agreement with Peking.

"This move is nothing against the West," he said, expressing a view that is often heard from African leaders discussing China, "but we are trying to build a truly Nigerian society, and having normal, friendly relations with the Government of China fits in with that plan."

April 9, 1971

15-Man U.S. Table Tennis Team Crosses Into China From Hong Kong

HONG KONG, Saturday, April 10—Members of the United States table tennis team crossed from Hong Kong into Communist China this morning, walking over a railway bridge that marks the border between this British Crown Colony and Chinese Communist territory.

The 15 members of the team —nine players, one a sportswriter as well, four officials and two wives—were the first Americans to visit China as a group since the mid-nineteen-fifties.

The team accepted an invitation, given during the world table tennis championship in Nagoya, Japan, earlier this week to spend a week in China playing exhibition matches.

As the Americans crossed the bridge, walking in bright sunshine, they could be seen from the British side receiving a cordial welcome from Chinese officials, who shook hands with the visitors. Loudspeakers on the Chinese side were playing soft orchestral music as a background to the event.

The Americans were escorted to a waiting train, which will take them to Canton, about 40 miles northwest of Hong Kong.

From Canton they will fly to Peking, where the rest of their itinerary will be decided.

The team arrived last night in Hong Kong, which they were given a friendly reception by representatives of Communist China.

The Americans were welcomed at Hong Kong's airport by representatives of Hsinhua, the Chinese Communist press agency, and the China Travel Service, an official agency of Peking, which makes all the arrangements for those invited to China.

Those in the United States team are Graham B. Steenhoven, 59 years old, of Detroit, the team president; Rufford Harrison of Wilmington, Del.; the deputy team leader; George Buben of Detroit, an official; Richard Miles of New York, a nonplaying member; Tim Boggan, 40, of Merrick, N.Y., the writer; Jack Howard, 36, of Seattle, player, captain and coach of the team; John Tannehill, 18, of Middleport, Ohio; Glenn Cowan, 19, of Santa Monica, Calif.; Errol Roseck, 29, New York; Olga Soltesz, 18, of Orlando, Fla.; George Braithwaite, Brooklyn; Connie Sweerts, 23, of Grand Rapids, Mich.; Judy Bochenski, 15, of Eugene, Ore.; Mrs. Reseck and Mrs. Buben.

Teams from four other countries, Britain, Canada, Nigeria and Colombia—have also accepted invitations to tour China.

Associated Press

Group boarding plane at Tokyo, with Graham B. Steenhoven, the leader, at lower left

April 10, 1971

3 U.S. NEWSMEN ENTER RED CHINA FOR WEEK'S VISIT

By IAN STEWART
Special to The New York Times

HONG KONG, Sunday, April 11—Three American newsmen entered Communist China from Hong Kong this morning as part of a group of seven men who will be allowed to cover the current visit of an American table tennis team.

The Government of Communist China granted visas to the men yesterday in a surprise move that was a marked departure from the Communists' basic and long-standing policy of excluding American journalists since they took power 22 years ago. It was interpreted here as more significant than the invitation to the table tennis players five days ago.

[In Washington, United States officials viewed the granting of the visas as a further sign that China was moving to discard its policy of self-isolation. In Peking, the American team arrived after a flight from Canton. Page 2.]

A.P., N.B.C. Represented

The Americans are John Roderick of The Associated Press and two National Broadcasting Company representatives, John Rich and Jack Reynolds, all based in Tokyo. The N.B.C. team also includes two Japanese, Hiromasa Yamanaka and Masaaki Shihara. The others in the group were John Saar, an Englishman, and Frank Fischbeck, a German, both of whom will cover the tour for Life magazine.

A Hong Kong government spokesman said the correspondents had crossed into China at Lowu, a border railway station, at 10:15 A.M.

Mr. Roderick said that he had been informed that the visas were granted only to allow the correspondents to cover the week-long tour of the United States table tennis team, which entered China yesterday. The American team was invited by the Peking delegation that took part in the world table tennis championship tourament that ended Wednesday in Japan.

The invitation to the team and the granting of the visas represent the first positive response by Peking to the Nixon Administration's action in removing restrictions on visits to China by citizens of the United States. They are major events in what has been a sterile history of relations between the United States and Communist China and could lead to a broad range of exchanges in many fields.

There were indications here that applications for visas by other American correspondents might be favorably received, and an informed source said that local Communist officials appeared "shell-shocked" by the sudden shift in Peking policy.

Although the three Americans granted visas were the first full-time correspondents with United States citizenship to visit China since 1949, other American journalists have visited China since then. William Worthy traveled to China in 1957 for the Afro-American newspapers and the Columbia Broadcasting System, and Edgar Snow has made two trips to China since 1949, the latest in 1970.

Ten years ago negotiations between Peking and Washington for an exchange of correspondents ground to a halt as a result of charges and countercharges by the two sides.

A Chinese Foreign Ministry statement in March, 1961, said that any exchange of correspondents between China and the United States "must help eliminate estrangement between the Chinese and American peoples," make a preliminary improvement in the existing relations between the two countries and impel them to settle peacefully "the question of the withdrawal of all U.S. armed forces from China's territory, Taiwan, and the Taiwan Straits areas."

Speaking as Assistant Secretary of State for Far Eastern affairs in December, 1963, Roger Hilsman summed up the American position in a speech before the Commonwealth Club in San Francisco. He said that the United States had been "striving for years to arrange an exchange of correspondents" but had been put off with China's assertion that so long as the principal issue of Taiwan was unresolved there could be no progress on "secondary issues."

In February, 1964, Mr. Hilsman renewed the American call for an exchange of newsmen, and in 1966 the United States advised China through their Warsaw meetings that Chinese reporters would be allowed to visit the United States despite the Chinese ban on American reporters. These moves produced no response from Peking.

April 11, 1971

COMMUNIST CHINA BACKS PAKISTAN AND WARNS INDIA

KARACHI, Pakistan, April 12 — The Pakistani Government announced today that it had received a note from Premier Chou En-lai of Communist China strongly supporting its efforts to put down a movement for autonomy in East Pakistan.

The Government said that Premier Chou had denounced the United States, the Soviet Union and India for "carrying out gross interference in the internal affairs of Pakistan" and had promised China's support "should the Indian expansionists dare to launch aggression against Pakistan."

[United States officials said that they did not believe that the Chinese message presaged any direct involvement by Peking in the Pakistani situation. In Moscow, Premier Aleksei N. Kosygin met with the Pakistani and Indian Ambassadors.]

A Letter to Yahya

In reporting Mr. Chou's statements, the Pakistani Government's news agency said that they had come in a letter to President Agha Mohammad Yahya Khan.

The message was welcomed here as China's firmest and most specific declaration of support for Pakistan since the military crackdown in East Pakistan began on March 25. No formal comment on the message was immediately forthcoming from the Pakistani Government, but news of it was broadcast by the Pakistani radio.

As quoted by the news agency, the letter ended: "Your Excellency may rest assured that should the Indian expansionists dare to launch aggression against Pakistan, the Chinese Government and people will as always firmly support the Pakistani Government and people in their just stuggle to safeguard their state sovereignty and national independence.

No details about the eventual support were given.

"Of late," Premier Chou was quoted as having said, "the Indian Government has been carrying out gross interference in the internal affairs of Pakistan by exploiting the internal problems of your country. And the Soviet Union and the United States are doing the same, one after another."

Since the fighting broke out. In the East, Pakistan has made repeated allegations — denied by India—that Indian armed infiltrators had entered East Pakistan to aid the independence forces of Sheik Mujibur Rahman, head of the Awami League, the major party in the East.

In his letter, the Chinese Premier praised President Yahya, saying "Your Excellency and the leaders of various quarters in Pakistan have done a lot of useful work to to uphold the unification of Pakistan and to prevent it from moving toward a split."

"In our opinion" the letter continued, "the unification of Pakistan and the unity of the people of East and West Pakistan are basic guarantees for Pakistan to attain prosperity and strength. The Chinese Government holds that what is happening in Pakistan at present is purely an internal affair of Pakistan which can only be settled by the Pakistani people and which brooks no foreign interference whatever."

April 13, 1971

Indonesia Seeks Renewal Of Relations With China

By JAMES P. STERBA

Special to The New York Times

JAKARTA, Indonesia, May 17 — After a warm love affair followed by a nasty separation, Indonesia is once again dropping her handkerchief in front of China. Peking has responded by stepping on it, but there is hope here that as China makes friends with the rest of the world it will make up with Indonesia.

Relations between the two countries were suspended in 1967 following an attempted Communist coup in 1965 in which the Chinese were implicated, and the fall from power of one of Peking's best friends in Asia, the late President Sukarno.

The present Government under President Suharto first proposed "normalizing relations" under certain conditions nearly a year ago. In response to China's recent gestures toward the West, Foreign Minister Adam Malik has restated the proposal and followed up with diplomatic overtures.

Indonesia's conditions are that Peking recognize the Suharto Government, that it pledge not to interfere in Indonesia's internal affairs and that it stop beaming Indonesian - language propaganda broadcasts into the country.

China has agreed to none of these conditions so far, Government officials say, and the powerful broadcasts, originating from southern China, continue to denounce Indonesia's Government as a "fascist military clique."

Change of Attitude Foreseen

"Unlike the Soviet Union, China is now still like a child who enjoys aggressive attitudes but I am sure that changes will emerge there," Mr. Malik said in an interview late last year.

Since then he has softened his language. He recently held talks at the Rumanian Embassy, which takes care of China's diplomatic affairs here, and he has scheduled a trip to Eastern Europe next month, primarily to settle some national debts but presumably also to discuss possible relations with Peking.

Indonesia has no representation in Peking now. Cambodia had responsibility for Indonesian affairs there until Prince Norodom Sihanouk was overthrown as the Cambodian Chief of State last year. Both Indonesia and China had full embassy missions in each other's countries before relations were suspended. But in a series of violent demonstrations before the suspensions, each mission was sacked and burned.

Indonesia is especially eager to restore normal trade relations with the Chinese. Trade now passes through third parties in Singapore and Hong Kong.

"If relations are normalized, we can sell 100,000 tons of rubber annually to counter the release of American rubber from its stockpile," Mr. Malik said last month. Some Indonesian rubber now goes to China by way of Singapore.

According to Indonesian Government statistics, China is already the seventh largest supplier of Indonesian imports, ranking behind Japan, the United States, West Germany, Singapore, the Netherlands and Taiwan. Indonesian markets and shops display many Chinese - made articles, mostly smaller items ranging from bicycles and carpentry tools to teacups and underwear.

More than a million dollars worth of such goods a month flow into Indonesia from Hong Kong, constituting nearly half of Hong Kong's exports here. But middlemen in both Hong Kong and Singapore take their cuts from both imports and exports, which means less profit for Indonesians on goods bound for China and higher prices for goods coming from China.

Since the attempted coup on Sept. 30, 1965, which was followed by the slaughter of hundreds of thousands of suspected Communists and outlawing of the Communist party, China has treated Indonesia coldly. Even though the Jakarta Government describes Indonesia's foreign policy as nonaligned, China appears to consider it in the clutches of the "imperialist capitalists."

China's influence in Indonesia was at its peak at the time of the coup attempt in 1965. A 45-man Indonesian delegation was in Peking to celebrate China's National Day on Oct. 1. Diplomats and reporters referred to the relationship as "the Peking-Jakarta axis." Military and other aid worth millions of dollars flowed from Peking, along with advisers and technical teams.

Once when President Sukarno fell ill, a team of specialists in acupuncture — an Oriental treatment involving piercing the skin with needles — came from China to treat him.

In a book about that period, a Soviet diplomat was reported to have said: "Those Chinese are everywhere. But we can never find out what they are doing."

After the attempted coup, the Government reported that arms caches intended for the Indonesian Communists had been found in construction materials sent from China, and that the Communists had expected a shipment from Peking of 100,000 rifles.

For China, the close association with Indonesia had obvious advantages. Indonesia had the oldest Communist party in Asia, an outgrowth of the Indies Social Democratic Association of the early nineteen-twenties. By 1965 the party claimed a membership of three million, with an additional 16 million supporters in a total population of 115 million. This made it the third largest Communist party in the world, behind those of the Soviet Union and China.

There is some fear in Indonesia that normal relations with Peking would eventually lead to another period of subversion, and that with approximately three million ethnic Chinese living in this country, in addition to the remnants of the Indonesian Communist party, old relationships and networks could quickly be reestablished.

But Government officials say they believe Indonesia is now strong enough to make a start toward reconciliation, perhaps starting with exchanges in sports. Mr. Malik suggested the other day that it might be a good idea for Indonesia to send Rudy Hartono to China. He is a world champion badminton player.

May 18, 1971

Chou, at a Dinner, Describes Birth of Rift With Soviet

By AUDREY TOPPING
Special to The New York Times

PEKING, May 5—Premier Chou En-lai said today that the split between Moscow and Peking developed because Nikita S. Khrushchev took the road of revisionism and peaceful coexistence rather than continuing vigorous revolution after he came to power in the nineteen-fifties.

Mr. Chou said that he had tried to dissuade Mr. Khrushchev and his successors but that the split had persisted and even deepened.

Those views were expressed at a small dinner party the Premier gave for Chester A. Ronning, a retired Canadian diplomat, and his daughters, Mrs. Sylvia Cassady and myself. Asked after dessert if he would mind if I wrote about our discussion, he replied, "That is your freedom."

The 12-course dinner, attended by 12 people in all, began with numerous toasts and an exchange of Chinese jokes and riddles. Then the conversation took a more serious **tone.**

Chou Looks Fit

In reply to a question whether he had ever imagined that China would accomplish what it has in the course of his lifetime, Mr. Chou, looking relaxed and very fit for his 73 years, smiled and said that the Chinese had not yet reached the goal by far. "We still have a long way to go," he said.

During his youth, he went on, he only imagined that the revolution would attain victory. At that time he thought that revolution was quite simple; it was only after suffering several setbacks that he learned how to make revolution from the teachings of the Communist party Chairman, Mao Tse-tung.

After the triumph of the revolution, according to Marxist-Leninist principles and Chairman Mao's thoughts, he said, the revolution must be carried on continuously to win complete victory over the reactionaries.

Discussing the circumstances that led to the Chinese-Soviet breach, which became public in 1961, the Premier said that China tried fruitlessly at a conference in Moscow in 1957 to dissuade Mr. Khrushchev from going too far along the path of revisionism — the Chinese Communists' term for the Soviet policy of coexistence with capitalist states and for what the Chinese view as a revival of capitalism in the Soviet Union.

Pacts Reported Broken

Then in 1959, Mr. Chou said, Mr. Khrushchev tore up the agreements between the two countries on atomic energy cooperation. Moreover, he went to the United States and met with President Dwight D. Eisenhower to begin his exercise in flirtation with the United States that, Mr. Chou said, was the so-called spirit of Camp David.

When the Chinese-Indian border dispute broke out in 1962, Mr. Chou said, the Soviet Union went so far as to side with Prime Minister Jawaharlal Nehru and to condemn China. The Chinese leader also said that in 1960 the Soviet Union broke agreements and contracts for both industry and construction and all Soviet experts and technicians were withdrawn.

Nevertheless, Mr. Chou explained, in 1961 China sent a delegation headed by himself to the 22d Congress of the Soviet Communist party. It was at that conference that the Russians expelled the Albanian Communists and the public polemics began.

Mr. Chou recalled that Mr. Khrushchev was ousted in October, 1964. It was a coincidence, he added, that China's first atomic bomb was exploded the following day. His eyes sparkled when he remarked that some foreigners had said that the explosion was deliberately arranged as a sendoff for the Soviet leader.

With a bright smile, the Premier added that, after all, the explosion of the Chinese bomb was thanks to the Russians' behavior since Soviet experts had been withdrawn and the Chinese were compelled to rely on their own strength.

Mr. Chou went on to relate that when Leonid I. Brezhnev came to power in Moscow China had hoped for a change in policy and sent a delegation to Moscow in 1964 to celebrate the anniversary of the October Revolution even though it was not a five-year celebration. China also persuaded other reluctant Communist parties to attend, he said.

Chinese Were Disappointed

They discovered that the change in leadership in Moscow was not a result of a change in party policy, Mr. Chou said, but was motivated by a struggle for power in the leadership, which was very disappointing to the Chinese.

The following February, Mr. Chou related, Chairman Mao met the new Soviet Premier, Aleksei N. Kosygin, who was in Peking. Mr. Mao told him that because China and the Soviet Union had differences in principle, the polemics would go on for 10,000 years.

Mr. Kosygin commented that it would be too long, Mr. Chou said, and the Chairman replied that since the Soviet leader had said so, 1,000 years was taken off, which would still leave 9,000 years for polemics.

Nevertheless, Mr. Chou went on, state relations between the two countries could have been improved, but instead of doing so the Soviet Union prepared to go to war with China and by 1969 had stationed over a million troops along the northern frontiers of China and had even dispatched its troops into the Mongolian People's Republic.

Three-Hour Talk at Airport

Faced with the situation, Premier Chou continued, China had no alternative but to make preparations against war. (There were exchanges of fire between border troops at the time.)

He went on to tell of the conference he had with Mr. Kosygin in 1969, when the Soviet leader was on his way home from the funeral of President Ho Chi Minh of North Vietnam. Mr. Kosygin had requested a meeting at the airport, to which China agreed, and Mr. Chou talked with him there for three hours.

Mr. Kosygin agreed with Mr. Chou's view that in order to improve relations the two countries could start with boundary negotiations, Mr. Chou said, and the two leaders reached an understanding on certain questions:

¶The dispute on principle should not hamper the normalization of state relations.

¶The two countries would meet in Peking at the vice-ministerial level on the question of disputed boundaries in the Issuri-Amer region.

¶The negotiations should be free of any threat. To this end, before the negotiations on the boundary alignment, the two sides should reach agreement on provisional measures to maintain the status quo and halt armed conflict.

The boundary negotiations began on Oct. 20, 1969, and are still going on.

In referring to the boundaries, Mr. Chou noted that a great area of China had been ceded to Czarist Russia as a result of unequal treaties. In spite of that, he said, China is still willing to take the old treaties as the basis for defining the boundary line.

PRESIDENT ENDS 21-YEAR EMBARGO ON PEKING TRADE

By ROBERT B. SEMPLE Jr.

Special to The New York Times

WASHINGTON, June 10 — President Nixon ended a 21-year embargo on trade with Communist China today. He authorized the export of a wide range of nonstrategic items and he lifted all controls on imports from China.

At the same time, he announced a decision to suspend certain shipping requirements that have inhibited the export of wheat and other grains to the Soviet Union and other Eastern European countries as well as to China.

Officials here refused to speculate on what the lifting of the embargo would mean in dollar terms to American industry, but the list released at the White House set forth 47 categories of exportable, nonstrategic items and covered a wide variety of goods including farm products, household appliances, automobiles and basic metals, such as steel.

The list carefully omitted several major items of possible strategic value, such as locomotives, trucks, high-grade computers, advanced telecommunications equipment, petroleum products and commercial aircraft. But the White House statement suggested that "consistent with the requirements of U. S. national security" such items might well be granted special licenses on a case-by-case basis after review by the Department of Commerce and other agencies.

Officials conceded that initially the relaxation of trade would probably do little to increase United States exports. They noted that all Chinese imports now total about $2-billion, of which $1.5-billion — little more than two weeks' worth of total American exports—comes from non-Communist countries. American trade with China amounted to about $200-million annually in 1950. Following China's entry into the Korean war, Washington imposed the embargo.

The disclosure of the list of items that can be exported to China was marked by more fanfare than usually accompanies trade decisions, in part because it represented perhaps the most significant in a series of diplomatic efforts by the President to improve relations with Peking.

It also followed a series of less dramatic efforts over the last two years to ease restrictions on trade with and travel to China.

On April 14, for example, following Premier Chou Enlai's invitation to an American table tennis team to visit China, Mr. Nixon announced a series of minor amendments to present shipping restrictions and also disclosed his intention to lift the embargo on trade pending a final review of exportable items by the National Security Council.

Addressing himself to the significance of today's announcement of the items chosen for export, Ronald L. Ziegler, the White House press secretary, declared:

"President Nixon looks upon these measures as a significant step to improve communications with a land of 800 million people after a 20-year freeze in our relationships.

"The President will later consider the possibility of further steps in an effort to re-establish a broader relationship with a country and a people having an important role for future peace in Asia."

As for Chinese exports to the United States, some officials predicted that business would be slow at first, but that the Chinese could conceivably develop markets worth between $100-million and $200-million for such products as bristles, tungsten, ceramics, art objects and textiles.

The prospect of a surge in the importation of relatively inexpensive Chinese textiles was noted with apprehension by Howard Richmond, president of Crompton Company, speaking on behalf of American manufacturers. He said in part:

"We have reason to believe that Red China has a very large textile industry, and this simply opens up another vast source for low-wage imports added to those which already are displacing hundreds of American jobs. Chinese products are sold at a political price without regard to cost."

Some observers here believed that the short-range economic impact of Mr Nixon's decision to lift restrictions on the export of grain to certain Communist countries would be as great as, if not greater than his steps relaxing trade with China.

What the President did, in effect, was to lift a requirement imposed by President Kennedy in 1963 that 50 per cent of grain shipments to China, the Soviet Union and Eastern Europe be carried in United States ships.

Because American shipping costs are higher than those of foreign shippers, American grain producers have found themselves at a competitive disadvantage.

On April 14 President Nixon announced that United States-owned foreign-flag carriers may now call at Chinese ports. There has been no mention as whether American-flag ships will be permitted to do so.

The Commerce Department could not furnish today a detailed list of nonstrategic items that may be exported to the Soviet Union. The United States exported $118.5-million worth of goods to the Soviet Union last year, a tiny fraction of its total of $40-billion trade with other countries.

However, officials said that the Chinese list was slightly smaller than the Soviet list, largely because Peking's relatively smaller technological capacity meant either that the Chinese could not usefully absorb certain items or that the export of such items would materially improve their military potential at this time.

NIXON IS EXPECTED TO VISIT CHINA AROUND END OF YEAR; TO SEE BOTH MAO AND CHOU

By JOHN HERBERS
Special to The New York Times

SAN CLEMENTE, Calif., July 16—Officials at the Western White House said today that President Nixon's trip to China could be made late this year at the earliest and that he would confer with Mao Tse-tung as well as Premier Chou En-lai.

In announcing last night that he would visit China, Mr. Nixon said only that he would make the trip before next May.

The officials also disclosed some details of Henry A. Kissinger's 49-hour visit to Peking July 9 to 11 during which, in intensive discussion with Premier Chou, he worked out the final agreement for the visit.

There are "certain risks" in the visit, the officials said, because of the enormous differences between the United States and China, especially on American support for the Nationalist Government on Taiwan and the Peking Government's insistence that this support be withdrawn.

Briefing for Press

In a one-hour briefing for the press, the White House officials also said:

¶President Nixon in his brief but dramatic television appearance last night set May of 1972 as the "outside date" for the trip because he did not want it to become mixed up in the 1972 Presidential campaign in which Mr. Nixon is expected to seek re-election. Campaigning for the election already has started and by May several Presidential primaries will have been held.

¶Preliminary plans for the Presidential trip were made before Mr. Kissinger's Peking visit, during intensive negotiations that took place between the United States and China starting in April. What remained to be determined in Peking was whether the President's trip "would be useful, whether it would contribute to peaceful conditions in the world." The officials refused to discuss what was decided at Peking that would make the trip useful.

¶The State Department will announce in "the near future" what position the United States will take in the United Nations regarding possible membership for Communist China.

¶The China developments have no direct relation to the war in Vietnam, and the White House does not expect the President and Chinese leaders to settle current problems, but to work out a long-range basis for peaceful relations between the two governments.

Earlier this week, Gough Whitlam, the Australian Labor party leader, said Premier Chou had expressed interest in Chinese participation in a new Geneva conference on Indochina. Today, however, United States officials refused to predict whether China might now be prepared to use its influence to terminate the war.

Mr. Kissinger, who had been in seclusion with the President since his arrival on Tuesday, appeared in the press room this morning with a broad smile on his face, obviously pleased with the outcome of his trip.

July 17, 1971

As China Sees It, The Enemy Is Japan

For some time Peking has been emitting shrill sounds of alarm over revived Japanese militarism. Now James Reston, in his remarkable recorded interview with Premier Chou En-lai, made public last week, has spelled out this major Chinese anxiety. Fear of Japan, it now seems, may well be one of the main motives for Peking's recent moves toward détente with the United States.

"The Japanese people are a diligent and brave people and a great nation," Mr Chou said. But the "reactionaries" among them, he contended, were strengthened by the United States after World War II, "and when they have developed to the present stage they are bound to develop militarism."

It is not hard to see the reasoning behind the Chinese worries. Japan's skyrocketing economy — third-largest in the world, close to three-times that of China, and carrying a foreign trade wallop 10 times as big — seems to be creating in economic terms the Japanese-dominated "Greater East Asia Co-Prosperity Sphere" that Japanese arms failed to hold in World War II.

The Japanese economy already dominates areas of great sensitivity to Peking, such as Taiwan and South Korea. Its spreading influence throughout Southeast Asia is predictable. Such economic strength, based as it is on one of the world's greatest industrial concentrations, could easily be transformed into military power, including a nuclear capacity.

The historical record is not reassuring to the Chinese. They traditionally have paid scant and largely contemptuous attention to Japan, which in their eyes is a late and distorted offshoot of China's ancient civilization. What has drawn their notice has been the marauding of medieval Japanese pirates, Hideyoshi's attempted conquest of Korea on the way to attack China in the 16th Century, Japan's humiliating defeat of China in 1894-95, its joining the Western imperialist game of cutting up the "Chinese melon," its detachment of Manchuria in 1931, and finally the aggression of 1937-45, which all but snuffed out Chinese independence.

This history, when combined with Japan's present industrial power, is perhaps good reason for Chinese nervousness. Similar though less intense anxieties are to be found in Korea and in Southeast Asia. If Japan were in fact to combine its economic capacities with a resurgent militarism, world tensions would greatly increase, and Americans, too, would feel very uneasy.

In the Reston interview, Mr. Chou laid stress on Japan's $16-billion defense budget for the five-year period of 1972-76, a 148 per cent increase over the $6.5-billion spent on defense during the previous five years. These figures, however, must be seen in perspective. The Japanese defense budget is going up rapidly, but only in step with the total budget and economy. It remains in proportional terms the smallest military budget of any important country in the world — less than 1 per cent of gross national product and only a small fraction of China's own rate of military investment.

The armed forces stand at fewer than 250,000 men, and, though well-trained, their armament and abilities are geared to the narrowest definition of self-defense. For a tide of national self-confidence is running strongly in Japan, and the people as a whole remain the most thoroughly pacifistic in the world, proud of their no-war Constitution and understandably "allergic" to nuclear weapons. Their democratic form of government, moreover, precludes any sudden shift toward militarism.

All this was reflected in some unusually blunt language by the Japanese Ambassador to Washington, Nobuhiko Ushiba, in an appearance before the National Press Club last week. Citing Chou En-lai's reference to alleged Japanese "ambitions of aggression against Korea and China's Taiwan," the Ambassador called it "the biggest nonsense I have ever heard."

Still, one can see why Peking

might wish an understanding with the United States through which we could be deflected from what they assume to be our intent of encouraging rapid rearmament for Japan and a larger military role. The fuzziness of some Washington pronouncements and the ambiguities of the Nixon Doctrine may be to blame for Chinese anxieties on this score. Defense Secretary Melvin Laird's visit to Japan last month, in which he was reported to have asked the Japanese to assume a greater share of the defense burden, appears from Mr. Chou's remarks to have contributed to these anxieties.

The other aspect of China's approach to the Japanese problem is less understandable. Peking is clearly doing its best, through pressures and enticements aimed at both Washington and Tokyo, to split the Japanese-American defense alliance, which is embodied in the Mutual Security Treaty and the American bases in Japan and Okinawa. The irony of the situation is that, if the Japanese-American defense alliance were destroyed or seriously weakened, the chances that Japan might drift toward militarism would greatly increase.

Without the support of Japan and bases on its soil, the United States would almost inevitably withdraw its military power from the Western Pacific. The Japanese then, without the comforting presence of American naval power in their surrounding seas and with no automatic umbrella, might well move to a more rapid rearmament. This would cause greater tensions with China and other East Asian nations, which in turn might further stimulate the Japanese military buildup.

While Chinese and Americans may agree on the desirability that Japan remain nonmilitaristic and nonnuclear, nothing would be more likely to spark a trend in the opposite direction than a Sino-American deal over Japan's future. That is not the way an incipient superpower can be treated. But a joint Japanese-Chinese-American understanding on such matters might well prove a cornerstone for a general détente in East Asia.

—EDWIN O. REISCHAUER

Peking Is Seeking to Erode Soviet and U.S. Influence

By TAD SZULC
Special to The New York Times

WASHINGTON, Aug. 17— United States officials said today that they believed Peking had opened a worldwide diplomatic offensive concentrating on countries where the Soviet Union has had a dominant influence and on those with close relationships or alliances with Washington.

This assessment was made in the light of China's establishment of diplomatic relations with Iran today, a week after the establishment of similar ties with Turkey and Peru. There were also indications in diplomatic chircles here that Greece, Lebanon and additional Latin-American countries might soon recognize Peking.

American officials said they found particularly interesting China's emphasis on new or improved relations in the Middle East, the Balkans and parts of Africa.

Officials here believe that Mr. Nixon's acceptance of the invitation to visit China influenced a number of governments, including allies of the United States, to decide in favor of establishing ties with Peking sooner than they might have otherwise.

American officials, acknowledging surprise over the speed and intensity of the Chinese diplomatic effort, which was intensified after President Nixon's announcement that he would visit Peking, said the Chinese seemed guided by long-range strategic considerations as well as by immediate tactical ones.

A major objective, they said, was Peking's determination to strengthen its political position and influence in strategic areas of the world.

The assessment here was that Peking was also trying to weaken Soviet positions wherever possible, notably taking advantage of Moscow's new problems in the Balkans and the Middle East.

Tactically, officials here said,

Peking appeared to be engaged in an attempt to marshal enough votes to expel the Chinese Nationalist Government on Taiwan from the United Nations this fall and be seated in its place.

American analysts cited the scope of the Chinese effort in the Middle East and contiguous African areas as evidence of Peking's desire to challenge the Soviet Union there as well as to undermine American influence.

Egypt and Sudan Targets

With the recognition of Iran and Turkey, they said, China now has formal relations with all four members of the American-supported Central Treaty Organization, which includes Pakistan and Britain. Turkey is also a member of the North Atlantic Treaty Organization and Iran is the recipient of much military aid from both the United States and Britain. In addition, the Russians have for some time been courting the Turks and the Iranians.

In the Middle East, the Chinese have paid special attention to the United Arab Republic and the Sudan as relations between these two nations with the Soviet Union have deteriorated as a result of restrictions on local Communist parties.

The Egyptian Minister of Economy and Foreign Trade, Muhammed Abdullah Marzaban, visited Peking early this month and was treated as a distinguished guest. And when President Gaafar al-Nimeiry of the Sudan regained power last month after a short-lived pro-Communist coup, he and Chairman Mao Tse-tung exchanged what were described as "important messages."

American officials also noted the new emphasis given by China to the Balkan countries. A Chinese military mission visited Bucharest en route to Albania this week and talks were held with Rumanian defense officials. In addition, China's relations with Yugoslavia have become increasingly warm.

Peking Reported in Drive to Play Key Role in Mideast and Africa

By TAD SZULC
Special to The New York Times

UNITED NATIONS, N.Y., Oct. 16—China recently asked Iran and Turkey—two nations with whom she has just established diplomatic ties—to let Chinese airliners refuel there along planned new routes from Peking to Albania and Rumania. It is courting the Persian Gulf states of Kuwait and Bahrain, strengthening its new relations with Ethiopia, financing development projects in Sudan, helping to build houses in Algeria, and even quietly flirting with Israel.

In the view of diplomats of the governments in the area, China has launched a determined and sophisticated long-range program to play a major role in the Middle East and Africa—and the countries of those regions are now fitting the Chinese plans and activities into their own political calculations.

In the most immediate sense, this new reality is affecting the policies of a dozen governments—from Israel to Iran and Burundi—toward the forthcoming votes in the General Assembly on the question of Chinese representation in the United Nations.

Decisions Still to Be Made

With the China debate opening here on Monday, such governments as Israel and Bahrain—always considered supporters of American efforts to keep Nationalist China in the United Nations — have yet to make up their minds on how to vote.

In the close battle over the fate of Nationalist China, each vote is priceless—and diplomatic observers feel surprise actions by Middle Eastern countries could affect the outcome.

A significant example is Israel. For years she has voted with the United States to keep Peking out of the United Nations through the device of the "important question," requiring a two-thirds majority for admission.

When Washington shifted policy this year to seek "dual representation" for China—the admission of Communist China and the retention of the Nationalist seat — its strategy called for declaring any attempt to expel the Nationalists an "important question" necessitating the two-thirds vote.

But Israel surprised Washington when she indicated that she had serious doubts about the American strategy.

In the first place, the Israelis had decided that Peking was fated to play a major role in the Middle East and that there was little advantage in their antagonizing it on a crucial United Nations vote.

"If we seemed to be siding with the Nationalists," a senior Israeli remarked recently, "a legend would develop that the Jews had a chance to help the Chinese in 1971 and failed to do it. We don't need legends: We must be pragmatic."

He noted that Israel never had diplomatic relations with Nationalist China and that she offered to recognize Peking in 1952, but received no response. He said Israel had reservations about the principle of "dual representation" because a Palestinian "exiled" government could some day conceivably claim United Nations membership.

Hesitation is also the lot of Bahrain, Oman and Qatar, the newly independent Persian Gulf states that entered the United Nations this month.

It had originally been assumed that all three would support the United States on the "important question" on behalf of the Nationalists.

But powerful new pressures in the Persian Gulf may force one or more of them to switch. Peking established relations with Kuwait earlier this year and now has Kuwaiti support in the United Nations. Premier Chou En-lai sent Bahrain a warm message of congratulations on her independence last month. Bahrain's response may come in the United Nations vote.

Rapidly spreading opinion in the foreign ministries from Jerusalem to Addis Ababa and Teheran is that China has made a "geopolitical decision" to challenge the Soviet influence in the Middle East, in the Persian Gulf and in Western Asia at the approaches to the Indian Ocean.

This view is that, unlike in the early nineteen-sixties, when Peking tried subversion and poorly planned foreign aid, the present Chinese campaign is serious and well thought out.

Diplomats point out that in the last year Peking established diplomatic and trade relations with such key nations in the region as Iran, Turkey, Kuwait, Libya and Ethiopia.

With China firmly established in Pakistan, diplomats said, relations with Iran and Turkey were a logical step in the westward move in the Middle East.

Iran and Turkey provide stepping stones for Chinese operations both in the Balkans and the Middle East.

China has already requested —and, in principle, obtained— rights to fly over Iran and Turkey. When Peking is ready, it will have a direct air route to its allies in Rumania and Albania—bypassing the Soviet Union—and into the Middle East.

Relations with Ethiopia, improved this month by Emperor Haile Selassie's visit to Peking, are a natural element in the apparent Chinese strategy to establish positions in the south.

The Chinese have had an important foothold in the People's Republic of Yemen for a decade. Now, they are challenging Soviet influence in Ethiopia on the other side of the Red Sea.

Early this week, China and Ethiopia signed an agreement providing for $84-million in Chinese loans for farm development. Additional interest-free loans are expected.

Late in August—shortly after Sudan and the Soviet Union became embroiled in a dispute—China provided the Sudanese with a $35-million loan for highways, bridges and a textile factory.

Chinese experts went to Algeria last month to assist with public housing. Other experts are in Equatorial Guinea, Burundi and Rwanda.

Quiet meetings have been held in Paris recently between Israelis and Chinese diplomats. And, symbolically, chinese envoys were in Persepolis this week to help Iran celebrate the 2,500th anniversary of the Persian Empire.

"This is the opening of the road from Cathay," a diplomat here observed this week.

October 17, 1971

China's Neighbors Reassess Attitudes In Wake of Thaw

By TERENCE SMITH
Special to The New York Times

WASHINGTON, Oct. 23—The Nixon Administration's overtures toward Peking and the prospect of a Presidential visit there have set off a series of political shifts and realignments in countries all around China, from North Korea to Burma.

Reports from Peking today said that Henry A. Kissinger's mission preparing for the President's visit was drawing to a close. The President's adviser on national security affairs has spent some 10 hours in talks with Premier Chou En-lai since his arrival Wednesday and the impression was that all had gone well in arranging a date and the agenda.

The changes in Asian countries range from overt moves by some to improve relations with China to more subtle modifications in rhetoric and attitude.

While the impact of the new American policy is most obvious in Japan and Taiwan, the smaller, less powerful nations in the area are also profoundly affected.

The most dramatic example is in Korea, where the competing regimes in the North and South have begun the first direct negotiations on a quasi-official level in two decades.

The Administration's Asian specialists believe these talks —between the two sides' Red Cross societies—were prompted directly by the new communication between Washington and Peking.

U.S. Relaxes Attitudes

"Both sides can see their principal benefactors moving toward one another," one analyst said, "and neither wants to be left out in the cold."

The Korean talks and many of the other changes have occurred since July 15, when President Nixon startled the countries in the region with the announcement of his intention to visit Peking. Other changes have been under way longer and are outgrowths of the more gradual relaxation of American attitudes toward mainland China that has been obvious since 1969.

So far, officials here seem pleased by what they call the

507

"fallout" of the new policy. They believe the political realignments bode well for the United States role in Asia and for the Nixon Doctrine, under which this country, while keeping its treaty commitments, expects its allies to handle their defense themselves.

They concede, however, that the changes are taking place with such speed that, as one official said with a rueful smile, "It's impossible to say whether we'll still be proud of our handiwork when the dust finally settles a year or two from now."

Some Allies Are Worried

In some cases, in fact, the prospect of serious Washington-Peking negotiations has stirred fears among America's allies, such as Cambodia, about the consequences of a big-power settlement of the Indochina problem. In other cases, such as that of Thailand, the Nixon overtures are being interpreted as a green light for more overt dealings with Peking.

For opposite but related reasons, both North and South Vietnam are also apprehensive about the consequences of improved relations between the United States and China.

The South Vietnamese privately fear that Mr. Nixon, in the interests of big-power politics, might bend to some of China's demands that the withdraw support from Saigon. President Nguyen Van Thieu has been assured that this will not pen, but diplomatic sources here believe he still feels considerable concern.

The North Vietnamese have yet to comment directly on the planned Presidential trip, but they have indicated their dismay in editorials warning the Chinese to be wary of American efforts to split the Communist camp. Hanoi has also been assured by Peking that none of its interests will be compromised, but specialists here believe the North Vietnamese like the South Vietnamese, are still skeptical.

Country by country, the changes that officials here believe are at least in part attributable to the new American policy toward China include the following:

KOREA

In addition to agreeing to join the Red Cross talks on the problem of divided families which began on Aug. 20, North Korea has softened its rhetoric about Seoul dramatically in recent weeks. Premier Kim Il Sung has dropped his denunciations of the South Korean President, Park Chung Hee, as a "lackey of the imperialist aggressors," and has officially "welcomed" the relaxation of tensions that might result from a Nixon visit to China.

In the North Korean context, where every American move had routinely been rejected as a perfidious maneuver, this represents a remarkable change, in the view of analysts here.

The South Koreans have also exhibited a new willingness to discuss a reduction of tensions with the North in recent weeks. The assumption of specialists here is that both sides wish to remain one step ahead of the big-power discussions of the Korean problem that may be on the agenda in Peking.

In recent days the South Koreans have expressed apprehension that the United States and China might conduct substantive negotiations on the issue.

BURMA

After a three-year break, the Burmese are in the process of resuming full relations with China. Gen. Ne Win, the absolute leader of Burma, visited Peking in August for the first time since 1967, when relations between the two countries all but collapsed after the propaganda of Chinese Red Guards had caused rioting.

THAILAND

Officially, the Thais have adopted a wait-and-see attitude toward the new American policy, but privately Thai officials have said that it will help their own efforts to improve communication with China. These efforts have been under way for some time, but, again, analysts here believe that Thailand is essentially responding to the shifts in American policy.

MALAYSIA

Despite China's long-standing support of the Communist rebels operating along the Malay-Thai border, the Government has taken steps to improve its standing with Peking. An official trade delegation visited China in April. A Chinese delegation repaid the visit in August and signed agreements that will sharply increase Chinese purchases in Malaysia. Officials here expect the two countries will soon establish normal diplomatic relations, at least partly in response to the Peking-Washington trend.

SINGAPORE

This ethnically Chinese city-state, which already does a brisk commercial business with China, is carefully studying what its Foreign Minister, Sinnathamby Rajaratnam, recently described in an interview as the "most fundamental change in Asian political realities since 1945." **His Government believes that improved relations between Peking** and Washington could do more than anything else to secure peace in Southeast Asia.

CAMBODIA

For the record, officials of the Lon Nol Government have applauded the Nixon policy and the upcoming trip. Their private concern, expressed in interviews here, is that the visit might lead to the convening of an all-Indochina peace conference at a time when the North Vietnamese occupy more than half their territory. In such circumstances, they fear, their bargaining position would be hopelessly weak. Despite American assurances of support, they remain wary.

LAOS

Of all the Indochinese nations, Laos probably stands to gain the most from a new understanding between the United States and China. Premier Souvanna Phouma has applauded the new policy, presumably on the assumption that **an agreement between the United States, his principal benefactor, and his dominant neighbor can do nothing but improve his country's precarious situation.** Specifically, the Laotians hope that the Chinese will prevail upon the North Vietnamese to withdraw their troops from Laotian territory.

The attitudes of other Southeast Asian nations, such as the Philippines and Indonesia, are less well-formed, but all are grappling with the consequences of the Nixon policy.

"If Washington and Peking can come to an understanding," Mr. Rajaratnam, the Foreign Minister of Singapore, said last week, "all the variables in the Asian formula will change. No country can be oblivious to it."

October 24, 1971

Peking Charges Indians Annexed East Pakistan

Special to The New York Times

HONG KONG, Dec. 18—Peking said today that the Indian occupation of Dacca represented "annexing East Pakistan with armed forces."

In a dispatch from the Chinese Capital, Hsinhua, the Chinese press agency, said thata fter taking over Dacca "the Indian aggressor troops will hang on in East Pakistan and impose military occupation there."

The dispatch, dated Dec. 17, a day after the Indian capture of Dacca, said nothing about the surrender of the city's Pakistani defenders.

December 19, 1971

ARGENTINA INITIATES TIES WITH CHINESE

Special to The New York Times

BUENOS AIRES, Feb. 19—Argentina and China announced jointly today the establishment of diplomatic relations.

But Argentina's military Government, while recognizing Peking as "the only legal Government in China," announced in a Foreign Ministry note that this "does not imply suspending all ties with Taiwan," the seat of the Chinese Nationalist Government.

The note said that commercial relations with Taiwan could be maintained and that Argentina would continue to recognize passports issued by Taiwan.

Argentina is the fifth Latin-American country to establish diplomatic relations with Peking. The others are Cuba, Chile, Peru and Mexico.

In the joint communiqué, China recognized Argentina's claim to territorial waters of 200 miles, as it did in the case of Chile and Peru when establishing diplomatic relations.

February 20, 1971

PEKING SEAT IN U.N. EXPECTED IN FALL

Some Diplomats Also Feel '2-China' Plan Will Fail— See Ouster of Taiwan

By HENRY TANNER
Special to The New York Times

WASHINGTON, July 16—Some diplomats here and in the United Nations predicted today that Peking would obtain admission to the United Nations this fall, replacing the Chinese Nationalists.

Administration officials here said that President Nixon had been on the verge of reaching a decision, on the basis of a report submitted to him earlier this year by a commission headed by Henry Cabot Lodge, favoring a "two-China" policy aimed at seating Peking in the United Nations without expelling the Nationalists.

The officials would not predict what the President's final decision would be, but many diplomats with a special interest in the United Nations said that they felt his freedom of maneuver had been sharply reduced by the announcement that he would visit China.

Secretary General Thant, who until a few weeks ago had frequently predicted that the matter would not be settled before 1972, said today that "it seems that the chance for the solution of the question at the next session of the Assembly is brighter." The session starts in September.

If the United States wants to put up a fight, there are two ways of doing so.

It can try to block Taiwan's expulsion and Peking's admission as it has in the past, giving all-out support to a procedural resolution stating that the China representation issue is an "important question" that can be changed only by a two-thirds majority.

Or, it can throw its full support behind a proposal for "dual representation,"—admission of Peking without expulsion of Taiwan.

The "important question" resolution was passed by a majority of 14 last year. But many diplomats believe that at least seven nations that voted for it last year are likely to switch to opposition.

They are Austria, Britain, Bolivia, Canada, Iceland, Italy and Malta. Several others, including Iran and Turkey, are in doubt. And Cameroon, which abstained last year, is certain to vote "no."

Dual Representation Doubted

Similarly, dual representation also might face defeat. This spring, Japan surveyed members to find out whether there was support for a move to make the "important question" provision, and hence the two-thirds majority, apply only to the expulsion of Taiwan, thus permitting dual representation.

The response was almost uniformly negative, according to informed sources.

Most governments are understood to have pointed out that Peking and Taiwan each says it is China's sole legal Government.

The impression that the President's announcement had enhanced the chances of Peking's admission and Taiwan's expulsion was implicit in many comments.

A European diplomat called it "the coup de grace for Taiwan."

One Eastern European diplomat noted that the official announcement that was read by Mr. Nixon spoke of the visit to Peking as a "meeting between the leaders of China and the United States."

"How much further can you go in recognizing that Peking is China?" he asked.

Several diplomats said that while they thought that Mr. Nixon's policy of creating a "new relationship with Peking might be hastening Taiwan's defeat in the United Nations, the United States would continue to guarantee the defense of Taiwan.

"The two things are not comparable," one of them said. "Even if the Administration takes the relatively low hurdle of accepting a change in the United Nations, it will balk at the high hurdle of withdrawal from Taiwan."

U.S. Backs Its China Stand With Soft and Hard Sell

By TAD SZULC
Special to The New York Times

UNITED NATIONS, N. Y., Oct. 13—With the China debate scheduled to open on Monday, the United States is applying the full weight of its diplomacy and prestige in scores of foreign capitals for its policy of dual Chinese representation in the United Nations.

The American campaign, known here inelegantly as "arm-twisting," is aimed at the so-called uncommitted governments—those that either have not said how they will vote or have not yet reached a decision. The ingredients of the campaign range from soft persuasion to hard-sell, sometimes with a touch of threat.

Although the United States favors for the first time in 21 years the admission of Communist China, it opposes the attempts to oust the Chinese Nationalist Government on Taiwan. It is willing, however, to grant to Peking the Security Council seat now allocated to China.

The United States, working through its ambassadors abroad and its mission at the United Nations, is seeking commitments for support in a series of complex procedural and substantive votes expected to be cast in the General Assembly before the final decision is made, perhaps not until early next month.

Two of these votes could be the most significant—one on whether to grant priority to the American proposals for "dual representation" here for Communist China and Nationalist China, the other, immediately afterward, on whether to declare the issue of the ouster of the Nationalists an "important question," requiring a two-thirds majority.

Washington strategists assume that moves to expel the Nationalists cannot command a two-thirds majority, though they could win a simple majority, and thus the pressure on the uncommitted countries is to vote for the "important question" resolution.

Diplomats here say, however, that the American effort involves the prevention of continuing defections from the pro-Nationalist camp and, when such defections occur, to search for compensatory votes.

In the words of a European delegate, the American strategy is a "finger-in-the-dike" approach in the face of a gathering pro-Peking wave in recent months.

But the situation here is so murky that diplomats do not always know whether a defection is really a defection or a feint.

Americans here, sharply aware of the importance of the psychological climate surrounding the United States campaign to save membership in the United Nations for the Chinese Nationalists, have on occasion argued with foreign diplomats and with newsmen that a tendency to see defections where, they say, none have occurred is perilously developing in the United Nations corridors.

20 to 25 Votes Involved

As far as can be determined, there is a bloc of 20 to 25 governments that are either undecided on the "important question" or that oppose it but can be won back.

In some situations, the United States seeks to tell a friendly or neutral government that the expulsion of the Chinese Nationalists would be an immoral act in international politics. This message has been personally conveyed to dozens of foreign ministers by Secretary of State William P. Rogers over the last three weeks.

In other situations, the hard-sell comes in.

A number of governments have been warned that the expulsion of the Nationalists may mean Congressional action to curtail American financial support for the United Nations.

However, many diplomats believe this approach has brought more resentment than support.

An argument that seems to be having greater effect—it has been used with Israel, among others—states that once the United Nations establishes the precedent of expulsion, a weapon will have been developed that can be turned against anybody.

The Israelis, known to be leaning away from the Chinese Nationalists, were told that some day, an African-Asian coalition might decide to seek Israel's expulsion. Secretary Rogers said on television Sunday that 10 or more nations also might be faced with the threat of expulsion some day.

The American strategists are still worried about such countries as Italy, Turkey, Iceland, Austria and Iran. Most observers list these countries as defectors but Washington considers them to be uncommitted.

U.N. SEATS PEKING NATIONALISTS WALK U.S. DEFEATED ON TWO

SESSION IS TENSE

Washington Loses Its Battle for Taipei by 76 to 35

By HENRY TANNER

Special to The New York Times

UNITED NATIONS, N. Y, Tuesday, Oct. 26—In a tense and emotion-filled meeting of more than eight hours, the General Assembly voted overwhelmingly last night to admit Communist China and to expel the Chinese Nationalist Government.

Moments before the vote, Liu Chieh, the Chinese Nationalist representative, announced from the rostrum that his Government would take no further part in the proceedings of the Assembly. He received friendly applause from most delegations, and then led his delegation out of the hall.

The vote, which brought delegates to their feet in wild applause, was 76 in favor, 35 opposed, and 17 abstentions. The vote was on a resolution sponsored by Albania and 20 other nations, calling for the seating of Peking as the only legitimate representative of China and the expulsion of "the representatives of Chiang Kai-shek."

Voting Is Sudden

Thus, the United States lost — in the 22d year—its battle to keep Nationalist China in the United Nations. This development, which came with dramatic suddenness, was denounced by the chief American

United Press International

Liu Chieh, right, Nationalists' chief U.N. delegate, and delegation walk out of the hall

delegate as a "moment of infamy."

The key decision that signaled the United States defeat came an hour and a half earlier, when the Assembly voted, 59 to 55 with 15 absentees, to reject the American draft resolution that would have declared the expulsion of the Nationalists an "important question" requiring a two-thirds majority for approval.

The United States had successfully used such a resolution since 1961 to keep the Chinese

Communists out and the Chinese Nationalists in. Before that time, a simple majority would have admitted Peking, but no majority could be mustered.

Pandemonium Breaks Out

Last night as the electrical tally boards flashed the news that the "important question" proposal had failed, pandemonium broke out on the Assembly floor. Delegates jumped up and applauded.

The American delegation, also in the front row, sat in total

dejection. George Bush, the United States delegate, who had been leading the fight for Nationalist China with considerable energy, half turned away from the rostrum, looking silently at the turbulent scene.

An analysis of the voting showed that the abstention of eight nations that had been thought almost to the last to be leaning toward the United States position had been fatal to the American cause. Had they voted with the United States, the American "import-

AND EXPELS TAIPEI; OUT BEFORE VOTE; KEY QUESTIONS

ant question" resolution would have been adopted, 63 to 59.

The eight nations were Belgium, Cyprus, Laos, Qatar, Senegal, Togo, Trinidad and Tobago, and Tunisia.

However, the 76 members who voted for the Albanian resolution to admit Peking and expel the Nationalists constituted a two-thirds majority of those voting. While this majority would have permitted the admission of mainland China even if the American "important question" motion had won, many observers expressed the opinion that the final vote had been swelled by the pattern of the earlier voting.

Meeting with newsmen shortly before midnight at the United States Mission across the street from the United Nations, Mr. Bush said he hoped the world organization would "not relive this moment of infamy."

"The United Nations crossed a very dangerous bridge tonight," he said. Expressing surprise at the vote, he added: "I thought we would win and it would be very, very close."

Mr. Bush said that he expected a very bad reaction from the American public.

When he was asked when he thought Peking's delegates would be arriving, he said: "It's hard to believe that a few hours ago we didn't think we had anything to worry about."

But Mr. Bush said the United States would "cross that bridge when we get to it" as he replied to a question as to how the United States would act regarding Peking's Security Council seat.

During last night's meeting, Adam Malik of Indonesia, who presides as this year's Assembly President, announced that he would notify the Peking Government immediately of its admission. Communist China had said repeatedly that it would accept a seat in the United Nations only if the Chinese Nationalists were expelled.

The suddenness of the voting came as a surprise to all. As late as the afternoon, as the long China debate was in its final phase, it had been expected that the vote would come sometime in the next day.

Time, many here believed, might have worked in favor of the American position. As late as the morning, it was reported, the 131-member assembly was close to being evenly divided. Therefore, the Albanian delegation, which for years has sponsored the resolution that would admit Communist China and expel the Nationalists, made it known that it would try to force a quick decision.

This precipitated an attempt by the supporters of Nationalist China to delay the proceedings. Jamil M. Baroody of Saudi Arabia proposed that all voting be postponed for one day, but his proposal lost, 53 to 56, with 19 abstentions.

In the parliamentary maneuvering that ensued, the United States experienced a short-lived victory. By a vote of 61 to 53, with 15 abstentions, the Assembly adopted an American proposal that priority be given to the "important-question" resolution.

Earlier in the day, both Saudi Arabia and Tunisia had put forward compromise proposals for settling the China issue. The Saudi proposal included a call for a plebiscite on self-determination for the people on Taiwan.

Mr. Baroody, who made many trips to the rostrum during the eight-hour session, made his proposal for a delay in the voting so as to give time for the Assembly to study the American, the Albanian, the Tunisian and the Saudi Arabian resolutions.

The overwhelming vote for the Albanian resolution to seat Communist China and unseat the Nationalists contrasted with last year's bare majority —51 to 49. That was the first majority that advocates of admitting the Communists had obtained since the China item was first taken up by the Assembly in 1950.

U.N. Roll-Calls on China

Special to The New York Times

UNITED NATIONS, N. Y., Oct. 25—Following are two roll-call votes taken in the General Assembly tonight on seating Communist China and expelling Nationalist China.

On Two-Thirds Requirement

Resolution declaring the expulsion of Nationalist China an "important matter" and thus requiring a two-thirds vote rather than a simple majority for passage.

IN FAVOR—55

Argentina	Ghana	New Zealand
Australia	Greece	Nicaragua
Bahrain	Guatemala	Niger
Barbados	Haiti	Panama
Bolivia	Honduras	Paraguay
Brazil	Indonesia	Philippines
Cambodia	Israel	Portugal
Cent. Afr. Rep.	Ivory Coast	Rwanda
Chad	Jamaica	Saudi Arabia
China	Japan	South Africa
Colombia	Jordan	Spain
Congo (Kinsh.)	Lebanon	Swaziland
Costa Rica	Lesotho	Thailand
Dahomey	Liberia	United States
Dominican Rep.	Luxembourg	Upper Volta
El Salvador	Madagascar	Uruguay
Fiji	Malawi	Venezuela
Gabon	Mauritius	
Gambia	Mexico	

OPPOSED—59

Afghanistan	Ethiopia	Norway
Albania	Finland	Pakistan
Algeria	France	Peru
Britain	Guinea	Poland
Bulgaria	Guyana	Rumania
Burma	Hungary	Sierra Leone
Burundi	Iceland	Singapore
Byelorussia	India	Somalia
Cameroon	Ireland	So. Yemen
Canada	Kenya	Soviet Union
Ceylon	Kuwait	Sudan
Chile	Libya	Sweden
Congo (Brazza)	Malaysia	Syria
Cuba	Mali	Tanzania
Czechoslovakia	Mauritania	Trinidad-Tobago
Denmark	Mongolia	Uganda
Ecuador	Nepal	Ukraine
Egypt	Nigeria	Yemen
Eq. Guinea		Yugoslavia
		Zambia

ABSTENTIONS—15

Austria	Italy	Qatar
Belgium	Laos	Senegal
Botswana	Malta	Togo
Cyprus	Morocco	Tunisia
Iran	Netherlands	Turkey

Absent—Maldives, Oman.

On Seating Peking

Resolution to seat Communist China and expel Nationalist China.

IN FAVOR—76

Afghanistan	Guyana	Portugal
Albania	Hungary	Rumania
Algeria	Iceland	Kwanda
Australia	India	Senegal
Belgium	Iran	Sierra Leone
Bhutan	Iraq	Singapore
Botswana	Ireland	Somalia
Britain	Israel	So. Yemen
Bulgaria	Italy	Soviet Union
Burma	Kenya	Sudan
Burundi	Kuwait	Sweden
Byelorussia	Laos	Syria
Cameroon	Libya	Tanzania
Canada	Malaysia	Togo
Ceylon	Mali	Trinidad-Tobago
Chile	Mauritania	Tunisia
Cuba	Mexico	Turkey
Czechoslovakia	Mongolia	Uganda
Denmark	Morocco	Ukraine
Ecuador	Nepal	Yemen
Egypt	Netherlands	Yugoslavia
Eq. Guinea	Nigeria	Zambia
Ethiopia	Norway	
Finland	Pakistan	
France	Congo (Brazza)	
Ghana	Peru	
Guinea	Poland	

OPPOSED—35

Australia	Gambia	Nicaragua
Bolivia	Guatemala	Niger
Brazil	Haiti	Paraguay
Cambodia	Honduras	Philippines
Cent. Afr. Rep.	Ivory Coast	Saudi Arabia
Chad	Japan	South Africa
Congo (Kinsh.)	Lesotho	Swaziland
Costa Rica	Liberia	United States
Dahomey	Madagascar	Upper Volta
Dominican Rep.	Malawi	Uruguay
El Salvador	Malta	Venezuela
Gabon	New Zealand	

ABSTENTIONS—17

Argentina	Greece	Mauritius
Bahrain	Indonesia	Panama
Barbados	Jamaica	Qatar
Colombia	Jordan	Spain
Cyprus	Lebanon	Thailand
Fiji	Luxembourg	

Absent—China, Maldives, Oman.

Texts of U.N. Resolutions on China Issue

Reaction to China Vote Is Emotional and Angry

By JOHN W. FINNEY
Special to The New York Times

Special to The New York Times

UNITED NATIONS, N. Y., Oct. 25—Following are the texts of the resolutions on the question of China's representation in the United Nations.

On Seating Peking

Sponsored by Australia, Chad, Costa Rica, Dominican Republic, Fiji, Gambia, Haiti, Honduras, Japan, Lesotho, Liberia, New Zealand, Philippines, Swaziland, Thailand, United States and Uruguay.

The General Assembly,

Noting that since the founding of the United Nations fundamental changes have occurred in China,

Having regard for the existing factual situation,

Noting that the Republic of China has been continuously represented as a member of the United Nations since 1945,

Believing that the People's Republic of China should be represented in the United Nations,

Recalling that Article 1 Paragraph 4 of the Charter of the United Nations establishes the United Nations as a center for harmonizing the actions of nations,

Believing that an equitable resolution of this problem should be sought in the light of the above-mentioned considerations and without prejudice to the eventual settlement of the conflicting claims involved,

Hereby affirms the right of representation of the People's Republic of China and recommends that it be seated as one of the five permanent members of the Security Council;

Affirms the continued right of representation of the Republic of China;

Recommends that all United Nations bodies and the specialized agencies take into account the provisions of this resolution in deciding the question of Chinese representation.

On Expelling Taipei

Sponsored by Albania, Algeria, Ceylon, Congo [Brazzaville] Cuba, Equatorial Guinea, Guinea, Iraq, Mali, Mauritania, Nepal, Pakistan, Rumania, Somalia, Southern Yemen, Syria, Sudan, Tanzania, Yemen, Yugoslavia and Zambia.

The General Assembly,

Recalling the principles of the Charter of the United Nations,

Considering that the restoration of the lawful rights of the People's Republic of China is essential both for the protection of the Charter of the United Nations and for the cause that the United Nations must serve under the Charter,

Recognizing that the representatives of the Government of the People's Republic of China are the only lawful representatives of China to the United Nations and that the People's Republic of China is one of the five permanent members of the Security Council,

Decides to restore all its rights to the People's Republic of China and to recognize the representatives of its Government as the only legitimate representatives of China to the United Nations, and to expel forthwith the representatives of Chiang Kai-shek from the place which they unlawfully occupy at the United Nations and in all the organizations affiliated to it.

On Two-Thirds Vote

Sponsored by Australia, Bolivia, Colombia, Costa Rica, Dominican Republic, El Salvador, Fiji, Honduras, Japan, Lesotho, Liberia, New Zealand, Mauritius, Nicaragua, Philippines, Swaziland, Thailand, United States and Uraguay.

The General Assembly,

Recalling the provisions of the Charter of the United Nations,

Decides that any proposal in the General Assembly which would result in depriving the Republic of China of representation in the United Nations is an important question under Article 18 of the Charter.

October 26, 1971

WASHINGTON, Oct. 26—In an emotional, often angry reaction to the expulsion of Nationalist China from the United Nations, a strong sentiment developed in Congress today to reduce American contributions to the organization's various agencies.

The initiative was coming from the conservative side where Senator James L. Buckley of New York teamed with Senator Peter H. Dominick of Colorado in drafting an amendment to the foreign aid authorization bill to reduce United States contributions to specialized agencies of the United Nations.

The movement was supported by the Senate Democratic leader, Mike Mansfield of Montana, and the Republican leader, Hugh Scott of Pennsylvania, both of whom stressed that their position was not related to the ouster of the Taiwan Government.

A coalition appeared to be developing of Senators who want to take reprisal for expulsion of the Nationalists and those who have felt for some time that the United States is carrying too much of the financial burden of the United Nations.

In the current Congressional mood an amendment reducing United States contributions, in the opinion of Senate leaders, probably would be adopted. The effort of the Republican leadership, therefore, was to attempt to persuade all sides to let emotions cool before the issue was raised on the Senate floor.

Senator William B. Saxbe, Republican of Ohio, moved at one point to recommit the $3.2-billion authorization bill to the Foreign Relations Committee for a few weeks so that the Senate would not legislate in "hot blood." But he withdrew his motion when the Senate leaders protested that a delay would upset the legislative schedule aimed at adjournment by Dec. 1.

Bill on Senate Floor

The foreign aid measure, brought to the Senate floor today, authorizes $141-million in contributions to various United Nations agencies, such as the Development Program, the Children's Fund and the World Health Organization.

It is such contributions rather than the assessment for the support of the United Nations that are expected to be the target of any amendment offered by Senator Buckley, a Conservative-Republican, and Senator Dominick, a Republican.

Congress has approved an appriation bill for $115-million in contributions to the United Nations, including $52-million in annual dues. Senator Buckley emphasized through an aide that he was not interested in "destroying" the United Nations but rather on reducing contributions to the specialized agencies.

With its annual dues, the United States pays about 31 per cent of the annual budget of the United Nations but with many of the specialized agencies, United States contributions amounts to 40 per cent and more.

Going back to the early days of the United Nations, the annual contributions have been assessed by the General Assembly according to a formula based on a country's ability to pay, such as its population and gross national product.

The United States, therefore, is not bound under the United Nations Charter to make any set annual contribution, but in principle it could reduce its contribution only with the approval of Assembly as it passes on the annual budget. The United Nations does have certain punitive powers to force contributions, since under Article 19 of the Charter a nation two years in arrears in its annual assessments loses its vote in the General Assembly.

Senator Mansfield told reporters that he had "felt for a long time we are contributing too much" to the United Nations and suggested the United States share should be reduced to around 25 per cent. Similarly, Senator Scott told reporters he had long believed the United States contribution was too high.

There was no demand for United States withdrawal, except from a few conservatives, such as Senator Barry Goldwater, Republican of Arizona, and Representative Robert L. F. Sikes, Democrat of Florida, who called for a reassessment of United States support.

"The time has come," Senator Goldwater said, "to recognize that the United Nations for the anti-American, anti-freedom organization that it has becomes. The time has come for us to cut off all financial help, withdraw as a member, and ask the United Nations to find a headquarters location outside of the United States that is more in keeping with the philosophy of the majority of voting members, some place like Moscow or Peking."

In contrast to the outpouring of comments from the conservatives. Congressional moderates and liberals were relatively reticent. One of the few to stand up on the floor was Senator Adlai E. Stevenson 3d, Democrat of Illinois, who observed, "It would be better now if the hysterics on the right were disregarded and instead we calmly accepted our defeat."

Among the liberals and moderates, there was a commonly expressed regret over the expulsion of Nationalist China and no criticism of the position taken by the Administration in the United Nations debate. At the same time, such liberals as Senators Alan Cranston, Democrat of California, and Clifford P. Case, Republican of New Jersey, warned against retaliation.

In the House, where conservatives consumed nearly an hour deploring the United Nations action, Speaker Carl Albert said, "It would be heaping one irresponsibility on another to diminish our support of the U.N. because of our displeasure with this vote."

Indicative of the Congressional reaction was what was described as the virtually unanimous sentiment among 25 Republican Senators at the weekly luncheon of the Republican Policy Committee. This was that the time had come to review United States contributions to the United Nations and its agencies as well as voting procedures in the Assembly.

It was apparent that the United Nations action could have a profound impact on long-held Congressional tenets, such as the concept that foreign aid bought friendship and votes of other countries or that allies were joined with the United States in common cause against Communism.

Expressing a common resentment, Senator Scott observed that "a good many nations we have helped generously with foreign aid over many years have shown a classic lack of appreciation."

Senator J. W. Fulbright, chairman of the Foreign Relations Committee, suggested that rather than cutting back on United States contributions to the United Nations, Congress might reduce aid to countries that had voted against the United States position on China.

A list compiled by the Foreign Relations Committee staff showed that 43 countries had voted in favor of the Albanian resolution on the admission of Peking were scheduled to receive $1.5-billion in aid in the current fiscal year and that 12 other countries that abstained on the resolution were to receive $813-million.

Noting that most of the North Atlantic Treaty allies had voted against the United States, Senator Gordon P. Allott of Colorado, chairman of the Republican Policy Committee, said, "This is going to make it more difficult to get contributions for for NATO." He said he would also have to take a "hard look" now at proposed aid for Laos, which voted for the Albanian resolution.

Senator George D. Aiken of Vermont, the ranking Republican on the Foreign Relations Committee, said, "If I understand what Western European countries said yesterday, they want us to get our troops out of Western Europe, and I am for just that."

October 27, 1971

Taipei Hopes to Continue Active International Role

By TILLMAN DURDIN
Special to The New York Times

TAIPEI, Taiwan, Oct. 27 — While conceding that the status of their Government has plummeted, Chinese Nationalist officials stressed their determination today to make the most of a new situation they called "tough but not irreparable."

Commenting on the sudden transformation of the Government from one of the five permanent members of the Security Council to a nonmember of the United Nations, Tsai Wei-ping, a Vice Minister of Foreign Affairs, said in an interview:

"We are not going to draw back into a shell. Our approach will be positive and outgoing, we are prepared to have relations wherever we can, and these will be extensive.

"We are still recognized by 59 members and nonmembers of the United Nations and expect many will stay with us.

Will Continue World Role

"We will continue to play a constructive role in promoting international cooperation and understanding.

"It is in our Constitution that we abide by the principles upon which the United Nations was founded, and we feel we did not desert the United Nations but that it deserted us.

"We will continue to have economic, cultural and technological relations and visitor exchanges all around the world, irrespective of whether we have diplomatic relations."

Mr. Tsai repeated the comment made by President Chiang Kai-shek in his statement last night on Monday's events in the United Nations by saying, "We are not small and weak; we still intend to count in the world."

The people of Taiwan remained worried and apprehensive of the future but were not markedly depressed as a result of the Nationalist Government's forced withdrawal from the United Nations.

Yesterday's statement by President Chiang voiced confidence, stressed self-reliance, appealed for fresh dedication and vowed a "no compromise" continuation of his Government's mission to free Chinese in the mainland from Communist rule.

The Taipei press this morning echoed the President's sentiments but some papers sharply criticized the United States for its role in the events that led up to the General Assembly's vote to expel the Nationalists and seat the Chinese Communists.

U.S. Is Blamed for Defeat

Conceding United States sincerity in the final fight for a Nationalist Assembly seat, the newspapers pointed to the United States plan to give the Security Council seat to Peking, President Nixon's forthcoming trip to Communist China and the visit last week to Peking by his adviser, Henry A. Kissinger, at the height of the United Nations debate on the China question, as being at the root of the Nationalist defeat.

"The Communist regime's ad-

mission into the United Nations is the making of United States appeasement and mistakes," said the United Daily News, Taipei's largest newspaper.

It said that what had happened "has also degraded America's position in the United Nations and leadership in the free world" and added, "Communist China's flame is raised higher and America's image and reputation ruined."

The paper predicted a weakening of efforts in non-Communist Asian countries to combat Communist aggression, infiltration and subversion and increased difficulties in preserving "democracy and freedom."

Rogers Gets Thanks

The paper, like a number of officials here, expressed appreciation for Secretary of State William P. Rogers's statement yesterday that United States-Nationalist ties are unaffected by Taipei's departure from the United Nations.

Referring to the United States defense treaty with Nationalist China, the paper said, "We think at this moment it is necessary for President Nixon to reiterate this commitment, to express America's determination in defending Taiwan, the Pescadores, Quemoy and Matsu and safeguarding the security of the Pacific."

The paper proposed a Taipei-Washington meeting on Pacific defense.

Aside from one brief gathering by a small group last night before the American Embassy, there have been no public anti-American manifestations, and in general the attitude toward Americans is friendly.

Despite his visit to Communist China five months ago, this correspondent has had no difficulty in entering Taiwan and has been received with special cordiality.

Annual Savings Seen

Other points made by Mr. Tsai in the interview were:

The Taipei Government will not withdraw from any specialized agencies of the United Nations until the Chinese Communists take part in them and make an issue of Nationalist participation. Withdrawal from agencies based directly on United Nations membership may then occur, but the Nationalists will not retire from those where United Nations membership is not a requirement.

By forfeiting United Nations membership, the Nationalist Government will save the $5-million a year it has been assessed as the representative of all China.

Aid projects here financed by United Nations specialized

agencies will not appreciably diminish. Those that will eventually be terminated will be small-scale, and the biggest one —$1-million from the United Nations Development Program —will continue because it is not governed by membership in the United Nations.

Taipei's aid programs in Africa will be terminated in countries that recognize Peking and possibly in some others because the countries concerned have failed to put up matching funds according to agreements or have poorly administered their programs.

Trade offices with the right to issue visas will be opened where they are needed and permitted. Maximum trade and other contacts will be used to build up support for the Nationalist regime.

The Government expects the Chinese Communists to attempt to whittle away at Nationalist China's support around the world and promote internal political divisions. However, it sees Peking as being too preoccupied with its main worries, the Soviet Union and Japan, to seriously threaten Taiwan for an indefinite period.

October 28, 1971

Soviet Union as to the United States."

An article in the current issue of Red Flag, theoretical journal of the Chinese Communist party, discussed at length the "contradiction" between industrialized and developing countries. It concluded that China may be capable of "exploiting" it in the "interest of world revolution."

Forum for Campaigns

A diplomat here said, "The Chinese have been saying all these things for years in their press and radio, but now they will have the respectable United Nations forum to push their campaigns."

The wide scope of the Chinese involvement in the underdeveloped countries in recent months has ranged from the signing on Sept. 14 of a mili-

tary aid agreement with the Congo Republic to the reception for Ethiopia's Emperor, Haile Selassie, in Peking and this week's "third-world" table tennis tournament attended by 500 youths from 51 Asian, African, Middle Eastern and Latin-American countries.

China's new role as the leading Communist supplier of economic aid to underdeveloped countries results mainly from $400-million in credits given to Tanzania and Zambia for the 1,000-mile Tanzam railway, which the West refused to finance, and $200-million to Pakistan for economic development and imports. In the last year, Peking also supplied credits to Ceylon, Ethiopia, Southern Yemen and the Sudan. It has arranged for special imports from Ceylon, Malaysia, Peru and Chile to help their balances of payments.

China Expected to Champion Underdeveloped Lands at U.N.

By TAD SZULC
Special to The New York Times

UNITED NATIONS, N. Y., Nov. 6 — Peking has left no economic or political stone unturned this year in its effort to assert itself as the undisputed champion of the world's underdeveloped nations, an effort that probably will be enhanced by its entry in the United Nations.

Peking has become the principal donor among Communist countries of economic aid to developing countries. Its offers in mid-1971 exceeded $750-million as compared with $500-million by the Soviet Union and the Eastern European countries together. This figure does not include annual Soviet aid to Cuba covering food and fuel deliveries and estimated at $400-million.

Dealing with economically weak nations in Africa and Asia, China provides credits that often are interest-free and call for long-deferred payments, in sharp contrast with Soviet loans, given on harder, businesslike terms.

China, always responding to the grievances of the underdeveloped countries against the industrialized powers, recently engaged in politically motivated trade with Ceylon, Malaysia, Chile and Peru, among other countries.

Peking has also publicly supported Latin - American countries' claims to a 200-mile territorial-waters limit. These claims have been rejected by the United States, leading to bitter controversies between Washington and half a dozen Latin-American countries.

"Peking is quickly outstripping Moscow as the champion

of nationalism and 'anti-imperialism,'" an experienced diplomat here remarked today.

Other diplomats noted that the current Chinese campaign for leadership of the "third world" is the latest phase of the new foreign policy begun by Peking at the end of the cultural revolution.

This policy is concentrated on the economically underdeveloped countries of Asia, Africa, the Middle East and Latin America and such "nonaligned" countries as Yugoslavia.

Experts here believe that on entering the United Nations— the Chinese delegation is scheduled to arrive here next week—Peking will further seek to formalize its attempts to act as the "third-world" champion.

"Being here, able to hold meetings, propose resolutions, deliver speeches, vote and so on, the Chinese can really make a bid for 'third-world' leadership," a Western diplomat said.

Specifically, diplomats here believe that the Chinese will attempt to establish a permanent relationship at the United Nations with the 55-member caucus of the "nonaligned" countries.

This group formed the core of the conference of 94 underdeveloped countries last week in Lima, Peru, which protested the new United States economic policy, especially the 10 per cent surcharge on dutiable imports.

"China would be the natural leader of a coalition of underdeveloped nations against the world's industrialized powers," a diplomat said. "And this would be as much of an irritant to the

November 7, 1971

President Calls On Taipei And Peking to Negotiate

Reduced Tension Sought

By TAD SZULC
Special to The New York Times

WASHINGTON, Feb. 9—President Nixon encouraged the Chinese Communists and Nationalists today to settle directly the fate of Taiwan.

With his trip to Peking only a week away, Mr. Nixon said in his annual foreign policy report to Congress that a peaceful resolution of the Taiwan problem "by the parties would do much to reduce tension in the Far East."

This question is certain to loom large in the President's conversations with the Chinese leadership. The island's political unification with continental China is one of the main tenets in Peking's policies. Mr. Nixon noted pointedly in his State of the World Message that "the ultimate relationship between Taiwan and the mainland is not a matter for the United States to decide."

But President Nixon promised Nationalist China the maintenance of "our friendship, our diplomatic ties and our defense commitment."

The United States is committed by treaty to Taiwan's military defense, in the event of a Communist attack, and the Nixon Administration has no known plans to lift this obligation even though an invasion from the mainland is considered improbable at this point.

Mr. Nixon also recognized in his report that the new American dialogue with Peking "cannot help but be painful for our old friend on Taiwan, the Republic of China," and he recalled that last fall, "we exerted the maximum diplomatic efforts to retain its seat in the United Nations."

Although the President emphasized that the United States was not urging either Chinese faction "to follow any particular course" over Taiwan, a high White House official left no doubt at a meeting with the press during the day that the Administration favored direct negotiations between them.

Kissinger Favors Course

Henry A. Kissinger, the President's national security adviser, said, "This is obviously the course which we think has the greatest promise." He was replying to a question as to whether the Administration could envision any course other than direct talks.

Mr. Kissinger visited Peking twice last year—once secretly in July to arrange for President Nixon's forthcoming journey, then openly in October—and it is known that on both occasions he discussed the Taiwan issue at length with Premier Chou En-lai.

The President's pledge of continued support for the Nationalist Government was a repetition of the American position as it was reportedly conveyed to Premier Chou by Mr. Kissinger.

Peking insists on an immediate "return" of Taiwan. However, Mr. Nixon's journey to China was planned with full understanding of United States policy on the part of Premier Chou and his associates.

Peking, on the other hand, has advised the Nixon Administration that it would not establish diplomatic relations with the United States so long as Washington maintains any ties with Taiwan.

But, in his report, Mr. Nixon listed the developing relationship with China, after a quarter of a century of mutual "implacable hostility," as the principal United States "breakthrough" in its dealings with its adversaries.

Mr. Nixon observed that "fragile as it is, the rapproachement between the most populous nation and the most powerful nation of the world could have greater significance for future generations than any other measure we have taken this year."

"Contact now might help avert a disastrous catastrophe later," the President said, while warning at the same time against expectations that his visit to China might bring "a quick resolution of the deep differences which divide us."

Mr. Nixon made it clear that a range of subjects, from the question of Taiwan to the Indochina war, could be part of his discussions with Chairman Mao Tse-tung and Premier Chou. He said in his report that "either side is free to raise any subject it wishes, and, of course,

issues affecting the general peace are of bilateral concern."

Frankness Is Expected

"Both sides can be expected to state their principles and their views with complete frankness," the President said. "We will each know clearly where the other stands on the issues that divide us. We will look for ways to begin reducing our differences."

In the report, Mr. Nixon offered a fairly detailed but still far from complete account of the complex public and secret diplomacy he undertook in 1969, immediately after his inauguration, to open the dialogue with Peking.

"No other United States foreign policy move in the past three years has been approached more meticulously," he said.

Mr. Nixon preserved the secrecy surrounding the channels and techniques he had used to communicate with Peking—it remains one of Washington's best-kept secrets—but tantalizingly, he outlined his process in broad strokes.

At the outset, he said, "It was necessary to find an intermediary country which had the full trust of both nations, and could be relied upon to promote the dialogue with discretion, restraint and diplomatic skill."

"After a period of cautious exploration and gathering confidence," he said, "we settled upon a reliable means of communication between Washington and Peking"

February 10, 1972

The China Negotiations, From a Hope to Reality

By TAD SZULC
Special to The New York Times

WASHINGTON, Feb. 14—On Friday, Feb. 20, 1970, the United States conveyed to China in secrecy a proposal from President Nixon that a senior Administration official travel to Peking as a demonstration of the American seriousness about improving relations between the two countries.

This proposal marked the opening of the active phase in the long diplomatic process that is to culminate next Monday with President Nixon's arrival in Peking, two years and a day after he first offered the Chinese a high-level contact.

The Nixon message—stating that the President wished to send a personal representative to Peking and asking whether this would be agreeable to the Chinese leadership—was presented by Walter J. Stoessel Jr., the American Ambassador to Poland, to Lei Yang, the Chinese charge d'affaires, in the course charge d'affaires, in the course of a meeting at the United States Embassy in Warsaw.

A 14-Month Effort

But the final affirmative reply, transmitted through a different confidential channel, came almost 14 months later, in the first half of April, 1971, setting the stage for the secret visit to Peking in July by Henry A. Kissinger, the President's adviser on national security.

Mr. Kissinger and Premier Chou En-lai worked out the agreement leading to the joint announcement by Washington and Peking that Mr. Nixon would go to China "at an appropriate date before May, 1972."

Secrecy Continues

Except for a few tantailzing remarks in Nr. Nixon's State of the World Message in Congress last week about unidentified "mutually friendly countries" helpful in the Chinese-American rapprochement, the Administration remains secretive about all the channels and contacts involved in the various stages of the preliminary negotiations.

But private interviews in the Presidential entourage and a close study of the Administration's public utterances on the subject over the last three years have permitted at least a partial reconstruction of this diplomatic process.

It has confirmed the longheld belief here that the heads of state of France, Rumania and Pakistan have played key roles in what Mr. Nixon called in his policy report the "period of cautious exploration and gathering confidence" between the United States and China, and, subsequently, in practical arrangements.

However, the record shows that the first step toward improving relations was taken by Peking on Nov. 26, 1968, in publicly proposing that the Warsaw ambassadorial talks, inter-

515

rupted since Jan. 8 of that year, be resumed in February, 1969, one month after President Nixon's inauguration.

Mr. Nixon, as President-elect, accepted the Chinese suggestion for the two countries to resume the ambassadorial conversations —the only direct link between Washington and Peking—held on and off since 1955.

American diplomats were particularly interested at the time in Peking's invitation for a discussion in Warsaw over a possible agreement on the "five principles of peaceful coexistence." This was seen here as a signal of moderation from China as she emerged from the Cultural Revolution of 1966-67.

The meeting planned for February, 1969, in Warsaw was never held because of a sudden dispute over a Chinese diplomatic defector in the Netherlands to whom the United States promised asylum, but the Nixon Administration quietly went ahead with its efforts to establish a dialogue with Peking.

Contact Is Sought

"Within two weeks of my inauguration I ordered that efforts be undertaken to communicate our new attitude through private channels, and to seek contact with the People's Republic of China," Mr. Nixon recalled last week in his report.

The President undertook this task personally in France during his first European tour when he met on March 1, 1969,

with President de Gaulle in Versailles.

Administration sources have indicated in recent private conversations that de Gaulle agreed to transmit Mr. Nixon's views to Peking.

In the course of a world tour in the summer of 1969, Mr. Nixon conferred with Gen. Agha Mohammad Yayha Khan, then Pakistan's President, and Rumania's President, Nicolae Ceausescu, taking up in considerable detail the question of Chinese-American relations.

Simultaneously, Administration spokesmen began voicing with growing frequency the American hopes for better relations with Peking, and the first steps were taken to remove restrictions on China in the fields of trade and travel.

In the autumn of 1969, the United States and China, in Mr. Nixon's words, "settled upon a reliable means of communication." He did not explain, but this was a foreign channel through which, late in October, word came that Peking was again ready to resume the talks in Warsaw.

The first diplomatic contact came on Dec. 3. Then on Dec. 12 Ambassador Stoessel met formally with Mr. Lei, the Chinese chargé d'affaires. This was the first direct contact since Mr. Nixon took office.

On Jan. 8, 1970, the two governments announced that the ambassadorial negotiations would resume later in the ffonth. In making the an-

nouncement, the State Department spokesman, Robert J. McCloskey, referred for the first time publicly to the Peking Government by its official name, the People's Republic of China. This was said to have been a calculated signal to the Chinese.

A meeting was held in Warsaw on Jan. 20, 1970, and the next one was called for Feb. 20. On the eve of the February meeting, Ambassador Stoessel pointedly said in a television interview that he would pursue President Nixon's goal of "improved practical relations" with Peking.

The next day, Mr. Stoessel reportedly surprised Mr. Lei with the Nixon message proposing that a high-level emissary be dispatched to China.

The Chinese reply was expected to be delivered at the Warsaw meeting scheduled for May 20, but the United States incursion in Cambodia and several other foreign policy situations led Peking to cancel the session on May 19.

Chou Gives the Word

Three weeks later, however, Premier Chou was reported to have told Emil Bodnaras, the visiting Deputy Premier of Rumania, that China hoped the talks with the United States could be resumed soon.

President Nixon wrote in his report last week that "by the fall of 1970, in private and reliable diplomatic channels, the Chinese began to respond" to

the American encouragement demonstrated through new trade and travel concessions.

These responses came chiefly through the Rumanian and Pakistani Presidents, both Mr. Ceausescu and General Yahya Khan visited the White House in October, 1970, before their respective trips to Peking and both carried oral messages from Mr. Nixon.

President Yayha Khan was in Peking between Nov. 10 and 15. Edgar Snow, the American writer who was in China late in 1970, said in an article describing his meeting with Chairman Mao Tse-tung in December that "go-betweens" were delivering messages from Washington to Peking.

On Oct. 26, the day after he received the Pakistani President at the White House, Mr. Nixon conferred at length with President Ceausescu, again with emphasis on China. The Rumanian Deputy Premier, Gogu Radulescu, met with Premier Chou in Peking late in November.

Early in 1971, the quiet exchange continued. Mr. Radulescu was again in Peking on March 22, and informed diplomats said he again served as a vital channel

As President Nixon described this final period, "the spring of 1971 saw a series of orchestrated public and private steps which culminated in Dr. Kissinger's July trip to Peking and the agreement for me to meet with the leaders of the People's Republic of China."

NIXON ARRIVES IN PEKING TO BEGIN AN 8-DAY VISIT; MET BY CHOU AT AIRPORT

United Press International

HONOR GUARD REVIEWED: Mr. Nixon and Mr. Chou passing part of 500-man contingent

By MAX FRANKEL
Special to The New York Times

PEKING, Monday, Feb. 21—President Nixon arrived in Peking this morning to mark the end of a generation of hostility between the United States and China and to begin a new but still undefined relationship between the most powerful and the most populous of nations.

The President received a studiously correct but minimal official welcome as he began his eight-day visit to China—the tribute due a chief of state but without any acclaim for a Government that still does not officially recognize the People's Republic of China.

Besides foreign correspondents and their interpreters and a few dozen Chinese officials, the Americans were met at Peking airport by a 500-man military honor guard. Two flags, one Chinese, one American, were raised a few minutes before Mr. Nixon's arrival, but there were no special decorations visible in this city, nor were any crowds of citizens, farmers or school children assembled for the welcome, as there usually are for visiting foreign dignitaries who are on good terms with the Chinese.

Overnight Stop in Guam

Mr. and Mrs. Nixon, leading an official party of 15 but a total contingent of more than 300 Americans, flew in from the Pacific across the muddy mouth of the Yangtze River and touched down at Shanghai's Hung Chiao Airport just before 9 A.M. (8:00 P.M. Sunday New York time). The President's plane had taken off three hours and 45 minutes earlier from Guam, where Mr. Nixon made a last overnight stopover on the long journey from Washington, which began Thursday.

After having tea and soup with officials and eating a tangerine at the terminal in Shanghai during a one-hour stay, the President and his party flew on, with a Chinese navigator aboard the plane, across the wintry North China plain and landed in Peking just before 11:30 A.M. (10:30 P.M. Sunday New York time).

Premier Chou En-lai led the reception committee at the airport. His handshake symbolized the end of American ostracism of his Communist Government. Mr. Nixon grasped the hand that Secretary of State John Foster Dulles spurned at the Geneva Conference in 1954, when the memories of conflict between China and the United States in Korea were still raw and their contest over Indochina had just been joined.

Upon its arrival, the President's plane taxied to the end of the Peking airport in front of the simple stone terminal building. The door swung open and Mr. Nixon stepped out atop the ramp.

He could survey a huge and motionless field. Two Chinese jet planes, almost the same size as the two planes that brought the official American party, were parked conspicuously in his line of sight—they were Ilyushin-62 four-engine jets.

517

In a remote corner off to the President's left was an American air transport plane, probably the one bearing his special back-up communications gear. All around the airport were large but relatively restrained slogans calling upon the "oppressed" peoples and nations of the world to unite and pay tribute to Marxism-Leninism and the Chinese Communist party.

Mrs. Nixon Wears Red Coat

Mrs. Nixon wore a fur-lined cloth coat of bright red—the same color as the giant billboards that ring the airport. She provided the only bright color in the official grouping that strolled past the honor guard.

After the official but informal greetings, the People's Liberation Army band played the anthems of the two nations—"The Star-Spangled Banner" and "The March of the Volunteers." Mr. Nixon and his official party reviewed the honor guard.

But there were no welcoming speeches for the small airport assemblage or for the worldwide television audience that could watch the arrival over a specially imported satellite communications system.

The moment that has been so elaborately labeled as historic by the President and by many other Americans passed swiftly into history. The arrival ceremonies were completed within a few minutes and the President and Premier Chou then drove swiftly off through a long avenue of poplars toward the capital on a crisp but clear and sunny winter day.

Premier Chou escorted the President to a black Hung Chi, or Red Flag, limousine, then walked around the car to Mr. Nixon's left, and joined him behind drawn silk curtains for the drive into town.

The people they passed along the 40-minute drive are best described as groups of onlookers. Many were cyclists and others held up on the sidestreets along the route. But many Peking citizens obviously knew of the special guest and a total of several thousand stood in random groups on the village lanes and on some of the city streets.

Chinese Officials Listed

The Chinese Government issued a formal list of 42 persons who constituted the official greeting party at Peking airport.

Besides Premier Chou, only two Politburo members were present. They were Yeh Chien-ling, vice chairman of the military commission and an old marshal who was present at all the preliminary meetings between Premier Chou and Mr. Kissinger here last year, and Li

Hsien-nien, a deputy Premier. Mr. Li's wife, Lin Chia-mei, acted as official hostess to Mrs. Nixon.

Other officials on hand included Kuo Mo-jo, president of the Chinese Academy of Sciences; Chi Peng-fei, the Foreign Minister; his wife, Hsu Han-ping; Wu Teh, who was identified as acting chairman of the Peking Municipal Revolutionary Committee; Pai Hsiang-kuo, the Minister of Foreign Trade; Hsiao Ching-kuang, the Deputy Defense Minister and Commander of the navy, and Li Chen, Deputy Minister of Public Security.

Nixon Seems in High Spirits

A few hours earlier at Shanghai, the President, on his first stop in China, was greeted by about 20 officials, who escorted him into the modern terminal building. There were an American and a Chinese flag on each side of the terminal door. The President and Mrs. Nixon wore overcoats in the 30-degree weather, but were hatless.

The first official to greet the President was deputy Foreign Minister Chiao Kuan-hua, who led the Chinese delegation to the United Nations last fall. Two other officials from Peking greeted him in Shanghai. They were Chang Wen-chin, director of the West European, American and Australasian Affairs Department of the Ministry of Foreign Affairs, and Wang Hai-jung, a woman deputy director of protocol in the Foreign Ministry.

Local leaders on hand included Wang Hung-wen, vice chairman of the Shanghai Municipal Revolutionary Committee and the city's third-ranking official. The two ranking Shanghai leaders, who are members of the Politburo, Chang Chun-chiao and his deputy, Yao Ken-yuan, had already flown to Peking for the official welcome.

Mr. Nixon appeared in high spirits, chatting in informal fashion with the Chinese officials who greeted him. There were no crowds at the Shanghai airport for the President's arrival, and commercial traffic was halted during the plane's stopover.

Mr. Nixon and Mr. Chou and high officials of the two countries are scheduled to meet this afternoon for at least one hour of formal talks. The two leaders will probably trade toasts at an official banquet this evening. But they intend to say next to nothing in public about their consultations until they issue a communiqué near the end of the eight-day visit.

The schedule for the rest of the week in Peking and for

brief visits to Hangchow and Shanghai next weekend has not been announced. But it appears that the American and Chinese leaders will meet almost every day, including one or two calls by Mr. Nixon on Chairman Mao Tse-tung, the founder and leader of China's Communist state.

Peking has been spruced up for the Presidential party, but all the repainting and restocking of supplies has been accomplished in the name of the just-concluded spring festival marking the Lunar New Year.

Most—but not all—of the slogans denouncing American imperialism have been replaced by less directly challenging wordings on the billboards. There is no way of knowing, however, whether China's energetic new campaign for good relations with non-Communist nations would not have inspired a similar toning-down in any case.

There is said to be a general air of relaxation among the Chinese people now that the turmoil of the Cultural Revolution seems spent. The glorification of Chairman Mao has also been de-emphasized. And while purges have left many senior positions unfilled, the Government seems to be addressing itself once again to the orderly conduct of business at home and abroad.

But there can be no question in Mr. Nixon's mind that he has come to a distant nation, far removed not only physically but also philosophically. Mr. Mao's portrait stares down upon visitors from prominent positions at both the Shanghai and the Peking airports and from many of the prominent buildings of the capital along the drive to the Government guest house, where the Nixons will be staying. The house is named Tiao Yu Tai, which means Angling Terrace. Also in view in several places were portraits of the universal giants of Communism—Marx, Engels and Lenin—plus the figure no longer worshiped in his own country—Stalin.

Huge red posters adorn the airport buildings, mostly with fairly neutral tributes to the Chinese Communist party and importunings to the "proletariat and the oppressed people and the oppressed nations" to unite. Awaiting the Nixon motorcade beside the road from the Peking airport were a series of calligraphic stanchions proclaiming support for the "struggles of the peoples of Asia, Africa and Latin America" against unnamed colonialists.

Posters and Stanchions

But none of this denies visitors a glimpse of the China

behind the slogans. Flying low into Shanghai, the President could see the vast stretches of rice paddies, green and gray patches around endless clusters of villages, many of whose residents stopped to stare at the gleaming jet aircraft from the West.

On the descent toward Peking, new arrivals find themselves over a bleak plain of wheat country, all ashen and brown, clear to the horizon and seemingly rolled right across the huddled homes of Chinese peasantry.

On the drive into Peking, the homes can be seen a little more plainly among the barren fruit and nut tree orchards. They are squat stone homes, with boards in the windows and mud walls around them. As the road widens, the visitor passes a series of brick factory buildings surrounded by rows of low brick houses, all of them a dull dark red that does little to enliven the scene.

Then the main avenue—the wide Changan Boulevard. It appears even broader than it is because most of its houses are hidden behind steel gray walls, with only the tiled roofs peeking over the top.

Only Tienanmen Square—the heart of the city and the country—conveys some of the spectacular grandeur of China, old and new, on this first passage by any official American party in 22 years, apart from the informal preparatory visits by Henry A. Kissinger, Mr. Nixon's adviser on national security.

The huge red Gate of Heavenly Peace stands on the right, the stark 100-acre square to the left, flanked by the Great Hall of the People and other big modern buildings thrown up by the new regime in the nineteen-fifties before it rebelled against Soviet thought and design.

As if to emphasize their new independence—and to reassure anxious allies about the Nixon talks—the Chinese have used this great square as the setting for their three most specific foreign policy slogan displays.

One complains of the "bullying by United States imperialism and social imperialism" —the latter expression being a euphemism for the Russians. A second "warmly hails the great victories of the three Indochina peoples in their war against United States imperialism." And the third promises support to the people of the Arab countries "in their struggle against United States imperialism and Zionism."

Five miles farther to the west is the Government guest house, actually a walled compound of small buildings in Jade Abyss Pool Park, which once housed Soviet technicians.

Among the more recent guests have been Premier Pham Van Dong of North Vietnam, who came here three months ago to protect his interests in Chinese-American talks, and, just two weeks ago, President Zulfikar Ali Bhutto of Pakistan, a country that China and the United States tried to protect from dismemberment late last year in the first major diplomatic action in which they have shared a joint position.

Separate but overlapping American and Chinese difficulties with the Soviet Union are thought to have provided the final impetus for this visit by Mr. Nixon.

In two preliminary conferences between Premier Chou and Mr. Kissinger, Peking and Washington appeared to have reached an understanding to begin a search for more communication and even limited co-ordination of their policies. They agreed to do so despite still strong differences over Taiwan and ways to end the war in Vietnam.

But that seems to be the extent of their understandings so far and there is no reliable evidence yet of the issues that they will stress in this week's get-acquainted sessions.

Rogers Also in Party

Besides Mr. Kissinger, the President also brought Secretary of State William P. Rogers and Marshall Green, the Assistant Secretary for East Asian Affairs, but their schedules and role in the main talks also remained undefined.

With no embassy in Peking to serve the traveling White House, Mr. Nixon has had to import everything from a hair-dresser for Mrs. Nixon to his own elaborate and multiple communications network. Many planeloads of gear and supplies preceded him into China in recent weeks, and one group of White House officials and private communications experts has been assisting in the technical preparations here since Feb. 1.

Two planeloads of correspondents and television crews arrived yesterday afternoon to try to satisfy the enormous interest that has been aroused among Americans by Mr. Nixon's unusual journey.

So far, however, they have established only that no such comparable excitement has developed among the Chinese people here. And today's courteous but modest welcome arrangements make it unlikely that any will be generated by the President's hosts.

Peking Announces Arrival
Special to The New York Times

HONG KONG, Monday, Feb. 21 — China's official press agency, Hsinhua, announced President Nixon's arrival in Peking this morning with a speedy but very brief dispatch from Peking.

For the first time in the memory of local newsmen Hsinhua designated its message "flash," the term often used by Western agencies for the first announcement of important news. The dispatch reached here within 30 minutes after the President had stepped from his plane in the Chinese capital.

In homes and offices all over Hong Kong people watched live television broadcasts of Mr. Nixon's arrival in Peking. The telecasts were the first ever to be transmitted from China to Hong Kong.

February 21, 1972

Transcript of the Toasts by Premier Chou and President Nixon

By Premier Chou

Mr. President and Mrs. Nixon. Ladies and gentlemen, comrades and friends.

First of all, I have the pleasure on behalf of Chairman Mao Tse-tung and the Chinese Government to extend our welcome to Mr. President and Mrs. Nixon and to our other American guests.

I also wish to take this opportunity to extend on behalf of the Chinese people cordial greetings to the American people on the other side of the great ocean.

President Nixon's visit to our country at the invitation of the Chinese Government provides the leaders of the two countries with an opportunity of meeting in person to seek the normalization of relations between the two countries and also to exchange views on questions of concern to the two sides.

This is a positive move in conformity with the desire of the Chinese and American people and an event unprecedented in the history of relations between China and the United States.

The American people are a great people. The Chinese people are a great people. The peoples of our two countries have always been friendly to each other, but owing to reasons known to all, contacts between the two peoples were suspended for over 20 years.

Now, through the common efforts of China and the United States, the gates to friendly contact have finally been opened.

At the present time it has become a strong desire of the Chinese and American people to promote the normalization of relations between the two countries and work for the relaxation of tension.

The people and the people alone are the most motive force in the making of world history.

We are confident that the day will surely come when this common desire of our two peoples will be realized.

The social systems of China and the United States are fundamentally different and there exists great differences between the Chinese Government and the United States Government.

The Five Principles Recalled

However, these differences should not hinder China and the United States from establishing normal state relations on the basis of the five principles of mutual respect for sovereignty and territorial integrity; mutual non-aggression; noninterference in each other's internal affairs; equality and mutual benefits, and peaceful co-existence. Still less should they lead to war.

As early as 1955 the Chinese Government publicly stated that the Chinese people do not want to have a war with the United States and that the Chinese Government is willing to sit down and enter into negotiations with the United States Government. This is a policy which we have pursued consistently.

We have taken note of the fact that in his speech before setting out for China, President Nixon, on his part, said that what we must do is to find a way to see that we can have differences without being enemies in war.

We hope that through a frank exchange of views between our two sides, to gain a clearer notion of our differences and make efforts to find common grounds, a new start can be made in the relations between our two countries.

In conclusion I propose a toast to the health of President Nixon and Mrs. Nixon, to the health of our other American guests, to the health of all our friends and comrades present and to the friendships between the Chinese and American people.

By President Nixon

Mr. Prime Minister and all of your distinguished guests this evening.

On behalf of all of your American guests I wish to thank you for the incomparable hospitality for which the Chinese people are justly famous throughout the world. And I particularly want to pay tribute not only to those who prepared the magnificent dinner but also to those who have provided the splendid music: Never have I heard American music played better in a foreign land.

Mr. Prime Minister, I wish to thank you for your very gracious and eloquent remarks.

At this very moment, through the wonder of telecommunications, more people are seeing and hearing what we say than on any other such occasion in the whole history of the world.

Yet what we say here will not be long remembered. What we do here can change the world.

As you said in your toast, the Chinese people are a great people. The American people are a great people. If our two peoples are enemies, the future of this world we share together is dark indeed.

But if we can find common ground to work together, the chance for world peace is immeasurably increased.

In the spirit of frankness

519

which I hope will characterize our talks this week, let us recognize at the outset these points. We have at times in the past been enemies. We have great differences today. What brings us together is that we have common interests which transcend those differences.

As we discuss our differences, neither of us will compromise our principles. But while we cannot close the gulf between us, we can try to bridge it so that we may be able to talk across it.

'Let Us March Together'

And so let us, in these next five days, start a long march together. Not in lockstep, but on different roads leading to the same goal: the goal of building a world structure of peace and justice in which all may stand together with equal dignity and in which each nation, large or small, has a right to determine its own form of government free of outside interference or domination.

The world watches, the world listens, the world waits to see what we will do.

What is the world? In a personal sense, I think of my eldest daughter, whose birthday is today. And as I think of her I think of all the children in the world, in Asia, in Africa, in Europe, in the Americas, most of whom were born since the date of the foundation of the People's Republic of China.

What legacy shall we leave our children? Are they destined to die for the hatreds which have plagued the old world? Or are they destined to live because we had the vision to build a new world?

'No Reason' to Be Foes

There is no reason for us to be enemies. Neither of us seeks the territory of the other. Neither of us seeks domination over the other. Neither of us seeks to stretch out our hands and rule the world.

Chairman Mao has written: "So many deeds cry out to be done, and always urgently. The world rolls on. Time passes. Ten thousand years are too long. Seize the day." Seize the hour. This is the hour. This is the day for our two peoples to rise to the heights of greatness which can build a new and a better world.

And in that spirit I ask all of you present to join me in raising your glasses to Chairman Mao, to Prime Minister Chou and to the friendship of the Chinese and American people, which can lead to friendship and peace for all people in the world.

February 22, 1972

NIXON SPENDS AN HOUR WITH MAO AND THEN, AT A BANQUET, HEARS CHOU TOAST HIS TRIP AS 'POSITIVE'

By MAX FRANKEL
Special to The New York Times

PEKING, Tuesday, Feb. 22—President Nixon's week-long summit conference in China quickly reached a high point yesterday in a surprise meeting with Chairman Mao Tse-tung.

The session was followed by an exchange of banquet toasts with Premier Chou En-lai in which both leaders stressed common interests, and by extensive rounds of itinerant glass-clinking in the Great Hall of the People.

The meeting with Chairman Mao, the enshrined leader of the Communist rulers of China, lasted an hour and appeared to have been added hurriedly to Mr. Nixon's schedule on his first afternoon here. Both sides later described it as "frank and serious," but nothing is known about what was said. Major attention was therefore focused on the remarkable banquet given for the visiting Americans by the Premier last night.

Greetings to America

After a banquet dish called shark's fin in three shreds, Premier Chou rose to send greetings across the ocean, by television, to the American people and to describe Mr. Nixon's long journey here as a "positive move" responding to the wishes of the people of both countries.

Mr. Chou said the reasons for 20 years of tension without contacts were "known to all"—meaning primarily American support for an independent Taiwan. He credited both Governments with "common efforts" to improve contacts. And he expressed confidence that further pressure from the people—who "alone" shape world history—would surely bring the day when China and the United States could establish "normal state relations."

"Now, through the common efforts of China and the United States, the gates to friendly contact have finally been opened," he said.

President Replies Expansively

Mr. Nixon responded, also in an expansive tone, after the fried and stewed prawns. Rising from Table 1, where he had eaten with chopsticks after his hosts had loaded his plate with a serving of each dish in succession, he described the hospitality as incomparable, the dinner magnificent and the American music, as rendered by the People's Liberation Army band, unsurpassed in any foreign land.

Although the Chinese have made it plain that they still harbor suspicions about American policy and what they call its "imperialism," the President did his best to bury the American fears of a Chinese menace that he himself had once helped to arouse.

"There is no reason for us to be enemies," he said. "Neither of us seeks the territory of the other; neither of us seeks domination over the other; neither of us seeks to stretch out our hands and rule the world."

There were enmities in the past and there are differences today, Mr. Nixon asserted, but the "common interests" of the moment transcend everything else. Using the most vivid image of Chinese, the President said:

"And so let us, in these next five days, start a long march together. Not in lockstep, but on different roads leading to the same goal: the goal of building a world structure of peace and justice in which all may stand together with equal dignity."

He defined the goal as a structure in which all nations would determine their own form of government without interference.

And using a quotation from Mao the President said it was time to seize the day and to seize the hour "for our two peoples to rise to the heights of greatness which can build a new and a better world."

After each toast before the

800 guests seated at round tables in the huge reception hall, the principal conferees went roaming, thimble-size glasses in hand, clinking this way and that from table to table and sipping or pretending to, as Mr. Chou is nited for pretending.

The Americans warmed up gradually to this routine. The band offered a bouncy tune and Mr. Nixon, Secretary of State William P. Rogers and Henry A. Kissinger were soon scattered far from their own sumptuous table. The Premier and his principal Politburo colleagues for this visit, Yeh Chien-ying, who is in charge of the military, and Li Hsiennien, the deputy premier who is in charge of most other domestic matters, moved in orbits of their own.

Table-Hopping on Signal

By the time Mr. Nixon had spoken the magic word "friendship" at the end of his toast, everyone had learned the routine. Powerful spotlights encouraged the cameras forward and the table-hopping began as if on signal. The army band, which had already drawn applause for "Home on the Range" during the course of spongy bamboo shoots and egg-white consommé, now rendered an original and sweet version of "America the Beautiful" that went on and on and on while the principals smiled, clinked, milled and sipped from sea to shining sea.

It was a particularly striking exercise for the men of the Nixon Administration who had so long and earnestly deplored the diplomacy of mere "atmospherics." (Mrs. Nixon, in a wine-red dress, stood demurely in her place during these commotions.)

Each of the leading diners offered two or three dozen toasts during each round of wandering. They seemed to be consuming more snoe leather than mao tai — the Chinese sorghum firewater that was in their glasses. But bottle bearers were close at hand and Mr. Kissinger, among others, was seen taking at least two refills.

Curiosity About Reception

It was a striking celebration also because it occurred only eight hours after a rather minimal welcome ceremony for the President in Peking. Premier Chou and his colleagues provided an honor guard and a high-ranking welcoming committee of Government leaders, but they allowed no suggestion of popular enthusiasm and only a few signs of public curiosity.

The Presidential party was

annoyed not so much by this welcome, aides said, as by news and television accounts that portrayed the arrangements as modest. The group's spokesmen contended that nothing more had been expected. But the party was in fact intensely curious about the caliber of reception the Chinese would stage on its arrival and was informed of the situation by walkie-talkie from the airport only moments before the President's plane touched down in Peking.

Much of this visit had been elaborately planned, with the advance parties camping here since Feb. 1. But much also had been left entirely to the Chinese hosts. So very little had actually been disclosed about the quality of the reception. Moreover, the two governments had agreed to keep their formal schedule of conversations deliberately flexible so that they might be moved or extended as the discussions warranted. In any case, high-level talk on short notice is part of the regular routine to which foreigners in Peking have long been accustomed.

Disagreements Indicated

In any case, whatever irritations there were passed quickly when Mr. Nixon's hosts arranged for a furtive change of schedule yesterday afternoon and gave the President the relatively rare honor of an opening audience at the home of Chairman Mao.

This was later described as a one-hour visit, from 3 to 4 P.M. In Communist parlance, "serious and frank discussion," means more than courteous conversation, but it also means that the talk was punctuated by disagreement. And the White House refused to go beyond that formula of the host to explain how the talk went.

Nor would the White House give the location of Mr. Mao's home. But it is known to be a graceful old one-story, yellow-roofed residence along the lakes in the old Imperial City, one of a group of palace buildings formerly occupied by mandarins.

The President went with Mr. Kissinger, his assistant for national security, who arranged the trip in two visits here last year. Sitting with Mr. Mao were Premier Chou, Wang Hai-jung, the deputy director of protocol, and Miss Tang Wen-sheng, an interpreter. The White House did not explain the absence of Secretary Rogers. It said it was fair to assume that tea was served.

Mr. Mao, the 78-year-old revolutionary, poet, Marxist theoretician and founder of the People's Republic in 1949, has

usually held himself in reserve until well into the program of a distinguished visitor. The President had been planning on an audience and had expected it to turn to more philosophical talk than some of the concrete policy discussions with Premier Chou. Although the top-level meetings are said to be on no fixed schedule, there is now a distinct possibility that Mr. Nixon will meet with the Chairman a second time, either here or at his vacation home in Hangchow.

The unexpected detour delayed the first Nixon-Chou conference for 90 minutes, until 6 P.M., and delayed the banquet by a half hour, to 7:30. But the conference was largely an opening formality anyway, for picture-taking and introductions of the two delegations.

The President and the Premier are to meet in a small group this afternoon while Secretary Rogers and others meet separately with their counterparts.

Beads of bulbs lit the tiled rooflines of the colossal Hall of the People last night to signal the celebration inside. Premier Chou had invited the entire American press corps, the air-line crews and other technicians traveling with the President. From the Chinese side came their hosts and interpreters and many scholars and journalists, military officers and other distinguished citizens. Most of them appeared to have some professional interest in American affairs.

Foreign Diplomats Absent

As at the airport, there were no invitations for members of the diplomatic corps. This was to emphasize the "bilateral" and unusual nature of an affair of state between two governments that do not have diplomatic relations.

By drawing his subtle distinctions between the United States Government and the American people, Premier Chou carefully held to this formula. The central and obvious purpose of the Chinese formula has been to suggest that popular pressures are forcing changes in American policy and that the Chinese can encourage the process by meeting with Mr. Nixon without in any way betraying their claims of struggle against American "imperialism."

Mr. Nixon, by contrast, offered a much looser statement. He himself observed that "more people are seeing and hearing what we say than on any other such occasion in the whole history of the world" and thus he spoke not only to his hosts but to the vast audience beyond — perhaps principally to that audience.

February 22, 1972

Peking's View:

Seeking Peace on At Least One Front

Inscrutable? No, the meeting in Peking is not inscrutable to any Chinese who saw his beloved Chairman with broad smile and bright eye clasp the hand of President Nixon. Through photographs far more meaningful than any formal communiqué, Mao Tse-tung reassured his 800 million countrymen they need not fear war with the United States. This was no emperor haughtily acknowledging tribute from a foreign barbarian. Instead, the ideological godhead of the People's Republic of China sat joking in the relaxed informality of his personal study, waving ceremony aside as he put his visitor at ease. Through press, radio and television the message was out: The American President is here as the honored guest of the Chairman.

Mysterious? Not to any Chinese who appreciated the important difference between "U.S. imperialism" as an international problem and the "U.S.-Chiang gang" as a threat to mainland China. Ever since the shock of war with the United Nations (read United States) burst upon Chinese consciousness in October, 1950, the nightmare of an American attack has recurrently haunted the populace. The Taiwan Strait crises of 1958 and 1962, the spreading Indochina War, the recurrent shootdowns of United States-supplied reconnaissance and fighter aircraft and the museum displays of captured American guerrilla equipment all gave credence to the incessant propaganda which depicted Uncle Sam aiming his bombs and bayonet at China. Now that President Nixon has journeyed half way around the world after virtually removing United States interests from the resolution of Taiwan's future, clearly this long nightmare is over.

Unpredictable? Not to those in Peking who remembered 1969 as the year Moscow raised its fist while Washington held out its hand. Since then, millions of Chinese have dug air-raid shelters and vast tunnel networks from fear of Russian, not American, attack. In March, 1969, bloody clashes on the Soviet border sounded the alarm in every Chinese village. At higher levels attention focused on the doubling of Russian manpower along the frontier,

new airfields in Mongolia and the concentration of nuclear missiles around Manchuria. In June, 1969, as the Chinese Nationalists later revealed, Soviet long-range bombers redeployed from Europe to stage exercises which simulated attacks on major targets in north China, including key nuclear facilities.

Whether Moscow was still making up its mind or merely engaging in a massive bluff, the "worst case" was a sufficiently serious possibility for the Chinese to undertake whatever countermeasures lay at hand. Unfortunately the true "worst case" threatened China with a two-front attack, from Russia in the north and west and from United States-Chinese Nationalist forces in the south and east. Washington realized the full implications of the Russian military moves as seen from Peking, and acted swiftly to damp such fears.

Secretary of State Rogers and Under Secretary Richardson warned publicly against either side escalating border incidents to war. Covertly, United States diplomats sought to reopen the ambassadorial exchanges at Warsaw, broken off earlier by Peking. From the partial lifting of restrictions on trade and travel in July, 1969, to termination of the Taiwan Strait patrol by the United States Seventh Fleet in December of the same year, Peking received a series of signals which showed that the Nixon Administration had begun a systematic abandonment of past policy.

From Mr. Mao's perspective, Moscow stayed its hand of war as Washington offered its hand in peace. The warm greeting in his home last week means no less — and at this stage no more — than that. Whatever influence the American moves may have had on Russian military calculations, they clearly freed China of one threat when faced with another.

On the other hand, both Peking and Washington know they cannot actively collude against any third country, least of all the Soviet Union. However much they may have increased their separate bargaining advantages by talk of "common agreement," their interests remain separate and, in some instances, conflicting.

A Sino-American détente cannot take priority over United States-Soviet negotiations on arms control, Europe, the Middle East and outer space. Mr. Mao's ideological struggle against "Soviet revisionism" has no relevance for President Nixon. Nor does President Nixon's interest in preserving the Thieu regime in Saigon and the Lon Nol government in Pnompenh converge in any way with Mr. Mao's commitments.

But it is enough to a nation that has felt threatened by either or both of the superpowers for more than 20 years to win a credible promise of peace on one front. A recent visitor

queried teenage youths engaged in military exercises in China. Asked who was the possible attacker, they replied, "Soviet revisionists." Pressed further, one of them said, "Japanese militarists." Only after prodding and delay did "U. S. imperialists" come to mind as a potential menace. Last week's events, and Mr. Mao's meeting with Mr. Nixon in particular, should remove even that remnant of pre-1969 indoctrination.

Not all Chinese think alike; interests vary, as do perceptions. Some undoubtedly see the President's visit as a subtle humiliation of American pretensions to power manifested in the ring of bases and security treaties designed to "contain Communist China." Others may feel that their professed role as leaders of world revolution has been degraded for the sake of expediency and token gains on the Taiwan question. Still others, perhaps a majority, are trying to sort out the harsher "study-group" briefings for the Chinese populace that have been portraying "U.S. imperialism" as a declining but continuing menace that had been forced to "accept reality."

But whether one chooses a "Middle Kingdom" perspective of tributary relations or a Communist perspective of implacable conflict, within which "talk-fight" tactics alternate negotiations with struggle, there is no mistaking the change in signals for Chinese attitudes toward President Nixon, the United States and the American people. How long those signals remain strong depends as much on Washington as on Peking. Conceivably they will continue and even increase in their intensity at least for the duration of President Nixon's goal: a "generation of peace."

—ALLEN S. WHITING

Professor Whiting teaches political science at the University of Michigan.

CHINA VISIT ENDS

President Presents a Pledge to Build Pacific 'Bridge'

By MAX FRANKEL
Special to The New York Times

SHANGHAI, Monday, Feb. 28 —President Nixon and Premier Chou En-lai concluded a week of unusual negotiations here today and parted with an American pledge to arrange a gradual withdrawal of United States forces from Taiwan and a joint pledge for a gradual increase in American-Chinese contacts and exchanges.

Mr. Nixon, contending that "This was the week that changed the world," headed home with a conviction that both governments were committed to "build a bridge" across the Pacific and 22 years of hostility. The President took off from Shanghai at 10:12 A.M. (9:12 P.M. Sunday New York time) and was scheduled to reach Washington, after a stopover in Alaska, at 9 P.M. Monday, New York time.

Chou at Airport

Premier Chou saw his guests off at the airport in an informal farewell, warm and high-spirited but without any ceremony. He held to the President original vow to let their joint communiqué "speak for itself."

The communiqué alternated between statements of agreement and separate statements of divergent positions—a technique that is not uncommon in diplomacy but that was employed rather extensively by the two leaders.

The United States committed itself not to challenge the contention of both the Communist and Nationalist Chinese that "Taiwan is part of China." It reported Washington's desire for a peaceful settlement "by the Chinese themselves" and with that "prospect" in mind asserted the President's "ultimate objective of the withdrawal of all United States forces and military installations from Taiwan."

United Press International

IN SHANGHAI: President and Mrs. Nixon under statue of Mao Tse-tung at industrial exhibition hall. With them are Premier Chou En-lai and Secretary of State Rogers.

In the meantime, but without timetable, Mr. Nixon promised progressively to reduce the 8,000-man American contingent on the island "as the tension in the area diminishes." Almost all of the American forces in Taiwan are operating in support of the troops in Vietnam, but the Nixon Administration appears now to be earmarking their presence for diplomatic use in the developing relationship with China.

Taiwan Issue Held Crucial

American officials here insisted, however, that the United States would maintain the defense commitment to Taiwan that exists under the 1954 Mutual Defense Treaty. But this commitment was not mentioned in the communiqué.

On behalf of the Peking Government, the communiqué said that the Taiwan issue remained "the crucial question obstructing" normal relations with the United States. But it agreed to several steps, also without timetable, toward closer contacts.

The Chinese promised to stay in touch with the United States Government through various official channels, including the occasional dispatch to Peking of a senior American representative for diplomatic discus-

sions. They agreed to "facilitate" further unofficial contacts in science, technology, culture, sports and journalism. And they agreed to permit the progressive development of trade with the United States.

These provisions on Taiwan and contacts formed the core of the bargain struck by Mr. Nixon and Premier Chou in 15 hours of formal talks last week, mostly in Peking. The two leaders, in their communiqué, touched on many other subjects, some of them concrete and some of them rather general. But the success of the collaboration they sought hinged on the central compromise.

The President had wanted an even faster pace of diplomatic

and private communications and exchanges. The Premier had wanted a firmer recognition of Peking as the sole and legal government on Taiwan.

Movement by Both Sides

Both sides moved somewhat from past positions, but their concessions were in the realm of future action. Therefore, the degree to which they are actually carried out can be regulated to match the performance of the other side. The withdrawal from Taiwan and the contacts with China were not directly linked in the accord, but Henry A. Kissinger, the President's principal adviser, acknowledged that they could "become interdependent again" at any time.

Mr. Kissinger's use of the word "again" was the clearest indication of the trade-off that was arranged. But the President and the Premier had indicated their contending objectives on many other occasions, including the public toasts that they exchanged at alternately warm and restrained banquets through the week.

They parted in high spirits, at least outwardly. They downed a number of thimble-sized drinks in mutual tribute at a dinner here last night and stood to shake hands warmly on impulse when their host at the dinner, Chang Chun-chiao, the chairman of the Shanghai Revolutionary Committee, celebrated the agreement in his city.

The desire to cooperate in the search for stability in Asia after the Vietnam war was plainly a major impulse for the meeting in the first place. The communiqué said both sides had benefited from the candid discussions at a time of "important changes and great upheavals" in the world.

Look to the Future

Mr. Nixon said in his toast that the fact of agreement here and the future conduct of the two nations were even more important than the letter and the words of the communiqué.

Mr. Kissinger, commenting on the accord at a news conference, took the same approach. He said that the direction of the new relationship was more important than the accomplishments of the last week because the two sides had agreed to begin a process of coordinating when their interests converged and of reducing frictions when their interests differed.

A desire to help each other relieve the pressures generated by the Soviet Union was deemed to be another important stimulus toward agreement. On behalf of China and also as an expression of shared attitudes, the communiqué twice vowed opposition to any effort to es-

tablish "hegemony" in the Asia-Pacific region.

It did not mention the Soviet Union, which Mr. Nixon will visit late in May, and Mr. Kissinger insisted that the language here was not aimed against any specific country. But this disavowal is widely described by American officials as merely a polite dodge for an effort to suggest to the Soviet Union that China and the United States would not let their relations with Moscow interfere with their own diplomatic prospects.

And presumably, the President and the Premier also found important domestic political advantages in the accord and in the elaborately televised public fellowship that accompanied the negotiations.

'Generation of Peace'

Mr. Nixon is returning home ready to argue that he had laid the basis for his "generation of peace." Premier Chou has re-enforced the moderate line by which he is trying to lead China from the convulsions of the Cultural Revolution toward more orderly and profitable development of industry at home and trade and contacts abroad.

The 1,800-word communiqué, issued last evening after two nights of intensive last-minute bargaining — presumably over the Taiwan issue—was divided into five separate but unmarked sections.

The first section was a straightforward account of Mr. Nixon's sojourn in China and his meetings with Mr. Chou and Chairman Mao Tse-tung. Mr. Kissinger said later that the one-hour talk with Mr. Mao, the 78-year-old patriarch of Chinese Communism, had been general but not merely philosophical and that the American delegation had reason to believe that the Chairman was consulted by the Premier "at every step along the way."

The second section was made up of long and separate statements by the two sides of their divergent views on Indochina, Korea, Japan and South Asia. They offered statements of support for the rival positions of Hanoi and Saigon in the deadlocked negotiations for a settlement in Vietnam. They recited support for South and North Korea, with the United States stressing the need for "relaxation" of tensions and China stressing the aim of "unification." Neither mentioned its military defense commitments in Korea, where the two countries fought their only war, 22 years ago.

They recorded Washington's pre-eminent desire for "friendly relations" with Japan, and

China's concern about Japanese "militarism."

And they reaffirmed their separate but overlapping policies in South Asia, alluding to their collaboration in support of a cease-fire during the recent war between India and Pakistan, a war in which both countries were seen to be leaning toward the defense of Pakistan. The Chinese also deplored "great power rivalry" in the subcontinent.

An agreement on general principles of international conduct made up the third section. Mr. Nixon subscribed fully to the Premier's long-standing definition of peaceful coexistence, as first defined at the Bandung Conference of nonaligned nations in 1955, and Mr. Chou accepted an American statement that international disputes should be settled without threat or use of force.

This did not amount to a renunciation of the use of force against Taiwan, which Peking deems to be a province of China and therefore a strictly internal problem.

Statements on Taiwan

In the fourth section, separate Chinese and American statements were made concerning Taiwan, the first calling for an American withdrawal and the second promising withdrawal by stages, but conditionally. Mr. Kissinger would not specify the "tension in the area" that he said would delay the American force reduction for yet some time.

He had previously indicated that nearly all the troops on Taiwan were necessary mostly in support of war efforts in Vietnam. Before the build-up in Indochina, there were only a few hundred American troops in Taiwan, engaged in naval activities and on advisory and aid missions to the Chinese Nationalist Government.

But Mr. Kissinger avoided any suggestion today that an end of the fighting in Indochina would permit—or assure—the promised pullout. On the contrary, the Nixon Administration appears eager to extend the process of withdrawal to retain some leverage in the unfolding relationship with China. Its definitions of policy have already eroded the diplomatic position of the Nationalists — in the United Nations and in many other countries. This is expected to set in motion a form of political erosion on Taiwan and it is doubtful that Mr. Nixon will pull out American forces altogether until he has seen the pace of political change there and in Taiwan's dealings with Peking.

The United States had previously urged the Chinese sides to resolve the Taiwan issue by

themselves and had promised not to interfere in this vestige of the Chinese civil wars. But in taking that step toward Peking, the President had also pledged to maintain diplomatic relations with and defense commitments to the Nationalists—pledges that were not mentioned in the communiqué.

Repetition Avoided

They were last made in the President's State of the World Message earlier this month and Mr. Kissinger said they remained active. But it was embarrassing on the Chinese mainland to repeat commitments with such an unpleasant ring to the hosts, he indicated, and so they were left out of the joint declaration. Mr. Kissinger asked that the issue not be raised further in this setting.

He also contended that the gradual withdrawal of American troops had been indicated on "innumerable" previous occasions. He could not cite any precedents and reporters remembered only a statement to that effect by him last fall. And the pledge of an eventual total withdrawal of American forces had never been given before.

The fifth section of the communiqué consisted of expressions of agreement that the two nations would promote more exchanges of private groups, more trade and some continuous diplomatic link.

Mr. Kissinger indicated that the Chinese would refuse to send official representatives to Washington as long as the Chinese Nationalists maintained diplomatic status there. For the same reason, the Peking Government appears determined to move more slowly and in largely indirect ways on all forms of exchange and contact.

The communiqué did not mention it directly, but Mr. Kissinger said he thought a "contact point" between Washington and Peking would be established in the "reasonably near future," though not in the United States. He cited the precedent of the occasional and slow-paced ambassadorial talks between the United States and China in Warsaw over the last 15 years. He appeared to have in mind a more active channel, such as those he developed in Canada and elsewhere to arrange his and the President's trips here.

The official representatives who would be sent to Peking "from time to time" could have ambassadorial or even Cabinet rank, Mr. Kissinger indicated. Now that the President and the Secretary of State, William P. Rogers, and Mr. Kissinger have all been here, such a mission would obviously be well within the bounds of precedent.

Over all, however, Mr. Kissinger contended that the agreement took the two countries far beyond their positions of a year ago when the American table tennis team received its invitation to Peking and when Chairman Mao first indicated through Edgar Snow, the late American journalist, that the President would be received here if he wished to come.

At that time, Mr. Kissinger said, China envisioned only low-level people-to-people exchanges. China's decision to encourage much broader exchanges, to create a diplomatic mechanism for continuing contact and to join the United States in the definition of policy principles were all still "unthinkable" a year ago, he added.

The talks here last week also ranged beyond his own conversations with Premier Chou, in July and October, Mr. Kissinger said, in that he had none of the President's ability to make commitments and to speak with authority on a variety of topics.

This defense of the value of Mr. Nixon's personal involvement was also offered by Ronald L. Ziegler, the President's press secretary, in a television statement before American cameras here. The very fact of the communiqué between the governments "is symbolic of the greater understanding produced" by the participation of Mr. Nixon, Mr. Ziegler said.

The President's concluding comment on the communiqué was an expression of gratitude for the "gracious hospitality" shown him by the Chinese Government. Encompassed in that remark was gratitude not only for the food and the comfortable quarters made available to the American visitors

but also for the security and communications arrangements, and the extraordinary efforts to facilitate live-color transmission of television coverage of many of Mr. Nixon's activities here.

The Chinese allowed hundreds of technicians and newsmen to run through their cities in every direction to manage this technological extravaganza, with the help of two ground stations that fed the television signals to a satellite over the Pacific for relay to New York.

Mr. Nixon's host thus provided him with a massive stage, from the Great Hall of the People in Peking to the Great Wall of China, 35 miles away, and other attractions in Hangchow and Shanghai. Apparently the Chinese understood Mr. Nixon's political desire for exposure at home in this election year and deemed it an accommodation that could be made without significant loss of control in their own territory. They may even have calculated that the vast coverage only further committed the President to a successful outcome here, thus easing their negotiating task somewhat.

Mr. Kissinger insisted that the American delegation and not look upon the relationship here with a scoreboard mentality, registering points for or against one side or the other on various issues. But the Presidential aide, who has been the impresario for the entire undertaking, was unusually tense in addressing the news conference.

This was probably due in part to the inhibitions imposed by the need to address sensitive subjects on Chinese soil. But the nervousness appeared also

to derive from a sense in the American delegation that some of its concessions might not be favorably received at home or in allied capitals.

As one diplomatic reporter observed, the negotiating side that feels it is coming out ahead does not usually disdain a look at the scoreboard.

Also appearing at the news conference was Marshall Green, the Assistant Secretary of State for East Asia, who will now fly to Tokyo, Taipei and other allied capitals in Asia to report on the discussions here and to avoid resentment or charges of diplomatic betrayal.

Mr. Kissinger was the principal "go-between" at the conference, negotiating difficult issues with Chiao-Kuan-hua, a deputy foreign minister, on behalf of the principals. Secretary Rogers and the Chinese Foreign Minister, Chi Peng-fei, met for a total of 10 hours with their aides to consider more specific aspects of the same issues. They apparently dealt with the problems posed by more extensive contacts without diplomatic recognition and appeared to have concluded that easiest progress would come in places where unofficial groups such as academies of sciences or universities were available to deal directly with their counterparts and without government involvement in China.

Some of the negotiators were up until 5 A.M. Saturday and again until 3 A.M. yesterday to prepare the final communiqué. At the very end they were juggling such minor issues as whether the Chinese view of some questions or the American view should be listed first. They decided in the end to run some paragraphs one way in

the English version and in a different order in the Chinese text.

Premier Chou called on Mr. Nixon at his guest house for an hour before the departure, just reviewing their conversations and saying good-bye.

Then at the airport, the Premier, in an obviously good mood and appearing to be very pleased with the outcome of the talks, dealt warmly with all the American officials. When Chou said good-bye Marshall Green, who is flying out separately from Shanghai, the Premier, obviously aware of the Assistant Secretary's upcoming mission, said "You have a difficult job."

After the President's plane took off, Mr. Chou surprised the American correspondents by remaing on the airport apron bantering with them for about 10 minutes.

There were some trivial exchanges. But there were also a couple of half-serious questions that he fielded alterly.

One newsman said that people hoped to see him at the United Nations or in the United States one day. He indicated that he had no plans to come to the United States, that this was work for his United Nations delegation.

Foreign Ministry officials at the airport would not talk much about the accord, but they did indicate that they thought the discussions a "positive" experience and they seemed happier than that with their outcome.

These officials clearly interpreted the communiqué and the week of talks as yet another step in American disengagement from involvement with Chiang Kai-shek and the Nationalists.

Text of U.S.-Chinese Communiqué

SHANGHAI, Feb. 27 (AP)—Following is the text of the communiqué issued today at the conclusion of the meetings between President Nixon and Premier Chou En-lai:

President Richard Nixon of the United States of America visited the People's Republic of China at the invitation of Premier Chou En-lai of the People's Republic of China from Feb. 21 to Feb. 28, 1972. Accompanying the President were Mrs. Nixon, U.S. Secretary of State William Rogers, Assistant to the President Dr. Henry Kissinger, and other American officials.

President Nixon met with Chairman Mao Tse-tung of the Communist party of China on Feb. 21. The two leaders had a serious and frank exchange of views on Sino-U.S. relations and world affairs.

During the visit, extensive, earnest and frank discussions were held between President Nixon and Premier Chou En-lai on the normalization of relations between the United States of America and the People's Republic of China, as well as on other matters of interest to both sides. In addition, Secretary of State William Rogers and Foreign Minister Chi Peng-fei held talks in the same spirit.

President Nixon and his party visited Peking and viewed cultural, industrial and agricultural sites, and they also toured Hangchow and Shanghai where, continuing discussions with Chinese leaders, they viewed similar places of interest.

The leaders of the People's Republic of China and the United States of America found it beneficial to have this opportunity, after so many years without contact, to present candidly to one another their views on a variety of issue. They reviewed the international situation in which important changes and great upheavals are taking place and expounded their respective positions and attitudes.

The U. S. side stated:

Peace in Asia and peace in the world requires efforts both to reduce immediate tensions and to eliminate the basic causes of conflict. The United States will work for a just and secure peace: just, because it fulfills the aspirations of peoples and nations for freedom and progress; secure, because it removes the danger of foreign aggression. The United States supports individual freedom and social progress for all the peoples of the world, free of outside pressure or intervention.

The United States believes that the effort to reduce tensions is served by improving communications between countries that have different ideologies so as to lessen the risks of confrontation through accident, miscalculation or misunderstanding. Countries should treat each other with mutual respect and be willing to compete peacefully, letting performance be the ultimate judge. No country should claim infallibility and each country should be prepared to re-examine its own attiudes for the common good.

The United States stressed that the peoples of Indochina should be allowed to determine their destiny without outside intervention; its constant primary objective has been a negotiated solution; the eight-point proposal put forward by the Republic of Vietnam and the United States on Jan. 27, 1972, represents the basis for the attainment of that objective; in the absence of a negotiated settlement the United States envisages the ultimate withdrawal of all U.S. forces from the region consistent with the aim of self-determination for each country of Indochina.

The United States will maintain its close ties with and support for the Republic of Korea. The United States will support efforts of the Republic of Korea to seek a relaxation of tension and increase communications in the Korean peninsula. The United States places the highest value on its friendly relations with Japan; it will continue to develop the existing close bonds. Consistent with the United Nations Security Council Resolution of Dec. 21, 1971, the United States favors the continuation of the cease-fire between India and Pakistan and the withdrawal of all military forces to within their own territories and to their own sides of the cease-fire line in Jammu and Kashmir; the United States supports the right of the peoples of South Asia to shape their own future in peace, free of military threat, and without having the area become the subject of big-power rivalry.

The Chinese side stated:

Wherever there is oppression, there is resistance. Countries want independence, nations wants liberation and the people want revolution—this has become the irresistible trend of history. All nations, big or small, should be equal; big nations should not bully the small and strong nations should not bully the weak. China will never be a superpower and it opposes hegemony and power politics of any kind.

The Chinese side stated that it firmly supports the struggles of all oppressed people and nations for freedom and liberation and that the people of all countries have the right to choose their social systems according to their own wishes and the right to safeguard the independence, sovereignty and territorial integrity of their own countries and oppose foreign aggression, interference, control and subversion. All foreign troops should be withdrawn to their own countries.

The Chinese side expressed its firm support to the peoples of Vietnam, Laos and Cambodia in their efforts for the attainment of their goals and its firm support to the seven-point proposal of the Provisional Revolutionary Government of the Republic of South Vietnam and the elaboration of February this year on the two key problems in the proposal, and to the Joint Declaration of the Summit Conference of the Indochinese Peoples.

It firmly supports the eight-point program for the peaceful unification of Korea put forward by the Government of the Democratic People's Republic of Korea on April 12, 1971, and the stand for the abolition of the "U.N. Commission for the Unification and Rehabilitation of Korea." It firmly opposes the revival and outward expansion of Japanese militarism and firmly supports the Japanese people's desire to build an independent, democratic, peaceful and neutral Japan. It firmly maintains that India and Pakistan should, in accordance with the United Nations resolutions on the India-Pakistan question, immediately withdraw all their forces to their respective territories and to their own sides of the cease-fire line in Jammu and Kashmir and firmly supports the Pakistan Government and people in their struggle to preserve their independence and sovereignty and the people of Jammu and Kashmir in their struggle for the right of self-determination.

There are essential differences between China and the United States in their social systems and foreign policies. However, the two sides agreed that countries, regardless of their social systems, should conduct their relations on the principles of respect for the sovereignty and territorial integrity of all states, nonaggression against other states, noninterference in the internal affairs of other states, equality and mutual benefit, and peaceful coexistence. International disputes should be settled on this basis, without resorting to the use or threat of force. The United States and the People's Republic of China are prepared to apply these principles to their mutual relations.

With these principles of international relations in mind the two sides stated that:

¶Progress toward the normalization of relations between China and the United States is in the interests of all countries.

¶Both wish to reduce the danger of international military conflict.

¶Neither should seek hegemony in the Asia-Pacific region and each is opposed to the efforts by any other country or group of countries to establish such hegemony; and

¶Neither is prepared to negotiate on behalf of any third party or to enter into agreements or understandings with the other directed at other states.

Both sides are of the view that it would be against the interests of the peoples of the world for any major country to collude with another against other countries, or for major countries to divide up the world into spheres of interest.

The sides reviewed the long-standing serious disputes between China and the United States.

The Chinese side reaffirmed its position: The Taiwan question is the crucial question obstructing the normalization of relations between China and the United States; the Government of the People's Republic of China is the sole legal government of China; Taiwan is a province of China which has long been returned to the motherland; the liberation of Taiwan is China's internal affair in which no other country has the right to interfere; and all U.S. forces and military installations must be withdrawn from Taiwan. The Chinese government firmly opposes any activities which aim at the creation of "one China, one Taiwan," one-China, two governments," "two Chinas" and "Independent Taiwan" or advocate that "the status of Taiwan remains to be determined."

The U.S. side declared: The United States acknowledges that all Chinese on either side of the Taiwan Strait maintain there is but one China and that Taiwan is a part of China. The United States Government does not challenge that position. It reaffirms its interest in a peaceful settlement of the Taiwan question by the Chinese themselves. With this prospect in mind, it affirms the ultimate objective of the withdrawal of all U.S. forces and military installations from Taiwan. In the meantime, it will progressively reduce its forces and military installations on Taiwan as the tension in the area diminishes.

The two sides agreed that it is desirable to broaden the understanding between the two peoples. To this end, they discussed specific areas in such fields as science, technology, culture, sports and journalism, in which people-to-people contacts and exchanges would be mutually beneficial. Each side undertakes to facilitate the further development of such contacts and exchanges.

Both sides view bilateral trade as another area from which mutual benefits can be derived, and agree that economic relations based on equality and mutual benefit are in the interest of the peoples of the two countries. They agree to facilitate the progressive development of trade between their two countries.

The two sides agree that they will stay in contact through various channels, including the sending of a senior U.S. representative to Peking from time to time for concrete consultations to further the normalization of relations between the two countries and continue to exchange views on issues of common interest.

The two sides expressed the hope

that the gains achieved during this visit would open up new prospects for the relations between the two countries. They believe that the normalization of relations between the two countries is not only in the interest of the Chinese and American peoples but also contributes to the relaxation of tension in Asia and the world.

President Nixon, Mrs. Nixon and the American party express their appreciation for the gracious hospitality shown them by the government and people of the People's Republic of China.

February 28, 1972

Historic China Journey

By MAX FRANKEL
Special to The New York Times.

ANCHORAGE, Feb. 28— President Nixon returns from his "long march"—an arduous retreat that in Chinese Communist history became a legendary victory—urgently offering the American people the claim that he is, after all, the great peacemaker, that he has found his mission for four more years in the White House, that **News** he has over-**Analysis** whelmed the agony of Vietnam with the promise of reconciliation in China and that the youth of America, which never suffered his own fierce hatred of Communism, has reason to celebrate the new China lobby led by the new Nixon.

Premier Chou En-lai stays behind, pretending that the official communiqué about useful and frank discussions says it all, and that it is for the offending party in diplomacy to wrestle with the consequences of a turnabout. But in the memorable slogan of the current phase of China's Cultural Revolution, Chou En-lai is now steering his nation of 800 million in a period of "struggle, criticism and transformation"—back from the chaos of three years of "perpetual revolution" and xenophobia toward the normalization of life and foreign affairs.

So they found each other, these masters of survival and self-preservation.

They found each other useful, sharing parallel concerns

about the Russians, holding common concerns about the Japanese, groping for a new post-Vietnam balance in Asia and wondering why they had ever permitted themselves to become such passionate and obsessed enemies.

The Event Is Threatened

Now, in the afterglow, the pretenses of politics and the pretensions to allies and the obsession with the negotiated semantics of the communiqué are already threatening to overwhelm the event.

For it was an event. Mr. Nixon and Henry A. Kissinger have done what they have always deplored in their predecessors by committing the prestige of the Presidency to the diplomacy of goodwill and what used to be contemptuously known as "atmospherics."

There were the table-hopping toasts of Richard Nixon & Co. in the Great Hall of the People that first night in Peking, in full view of those nervous allies in Japan and even Europe and practically in earshot of the sinking Chinese Nationalists on Taiwan. And there was Chou En-lai celebrating the President as a courageous man and working for his place in history by offering the Great Hall and the Great Wall as stages for television drama. He was playing his part in the drama by giving China the televised new image of a nation of genteel, hospitable, hard-working and long-suffering innocents lured out of their isolation by the dear old Americans who used to fly the Hump and who fought the Japanese and who stared down the Russians and dutifully learned the error of their ways in Taiwan and Vietnam on this one jet journey to Peking.

All this, and not the communiqué of soberly balanced disagreement and modestly circumspect agreement, was the essence of the China caper.

Results as Expected

There was little in the final definition of future relations that had not been anticipated by the long hours of talk beween Premier Chou and Mr. Kissinger last July and October. And there was even less that the traveling horde of broadcasters and newsmen could see of China in eight days than had been seen by their individually guided colleagues over the months since the famous table tennis match of last April.

It is just that this time the world was finally startled into giving the attention that the coming together deserves. The President and the Premier had to meet to ratify and to reveal the diplomatic bargain and psychological breakthrough that they had already arranged at long distance over the last three years.

The essential agreement was that China and the United States now shared enough common interests on the world scene to forget their ideological obsessions and fears of each other. They agreed that their conflict in Korea had all been a ghastly miscalculation, fomented by irresponsible men in the Kremlin.

They agreed that China had not really been the aggressor that Americans imagined in her war with India in 1962. They agreed that, with the exception of Taiwan, they had no real dispute between themselves.

So over the long months of climb to the summit, they beat a largely semantic path out of the Taiwan labyrinth. Since both the Communists and the Nationalists deem the island to be an integral part of China, President Nixon was prepared to grant precisely that and to state the United States no longer challenged that fact. Since the 8,000 American troops on Taiwan are there largely because of the conflict in Vietnam, the President was ready to promise also their gradual but certain withdrawal.

Since China lacks the means to conquer the island by force, the Premier was ready to let the President see a "prospect" for peaceful settlement of the

dispute, by the Chinese themselves, with no further American interference in what has been all along a civil war.

And since there is no real prospect of military action across the Taiwan Strait—in either direction—there was no difficulty about assuring the diplomatic purists, though not in the Peking communiqué itself, that the American defense commitment and diplomatic recognition of Taiwan would be honored until the final settlement (anomalous though it might appear for Washington to be thus committed to what it now concedes to be merely a province of China).

The trip was proof enough that Americans know the location of the real Chinese capital and tribute enough for the government that now reigns there

What the Chinese 'Gave'

In return for these recognitions of reality, the Chinese leaders allowed Mr. Nixon to represent as great concessions the "opening" of communications and exchanges of people, ideas and goods, which they seemed quite eager to have in any case.

Actually, they did not give the President the level of official contact and the pace of exchanges for which he had hoped on the way into China.

Having achieved a new American litany on Taiwan, they now pressed for more, from Tokyo as well as from Washington. Premier Chou refused to come to Washington or to send his officials there as long as some other Chinese embassy functions in the United States and he promised to be rather fastidious about managing most of the new exchanges through unofficial contact with American institutions and individuals.

But he wants those troops to get off Taiwan and he wants to inspire political change on the island by making its eventual absorption appear now to be inevitable.

He will succeed in this. Even in their first hours on American soil, the American travelers back from Peking can sense the feeling of inevitability about this incredible week, which a year ago would have been dismissed as unthinkable.

Thus are great moments demeaned into mere drama and the tortured language of communiqués.

The real record of this journey is not the communiqué. The picture that ought to linger is the one of President Nixon, seated between Premier Chou En-lai and Mrs. Mao Tse-tung, in the Great Hall of the People,

watching women soldiers in ballet shoes shooting target practice at a caricature of Chiang Kai-shek. The President said the next day that he loved

the dancing and the music and he called it a play with a powerful message.

It has been a most remarkable week.

February 29, 1972

Taipei Says Nixon's Trip Will Not Result in Peace

By TILLMAN DURDIN
Special to The New York Times

TAIPEI, Taiwan, Feb. 28—Nationalist China today expressed strong disapproval of the communiqué issued in Shanghai yesterday by President Nixon and Premier Chou En-lai. In an 850-word statement the Foreign Ministry said that contrary to President Nixon's hopes his visit would not bring a generation of peace and relaxation of tensions in the Asian and Pacific region but was causing "diametrically" the opposite.

Referring to the Shanghai document as a "so-called 'joint communiqué,'" the Foreign Ministry statement said the Nationalist Government would consider "null and void" any agreement "which has been and which may not have been published, involving the rights and interests of the Government and people of the Republic of China" reached between Washington and Peking.

[In Washington, Defense Department sources disclosed that two American fighter-bombers, equipped to carry nuclear bombs, were removed from Taiwan before President Nixon's China trip. Page 16.]

Nationalist China's statement, referring to the Peking leadership, called it "a rebel group which has no right whatsoever to represent the Chinese people."

But the statement avoided any invective toward the United States or Americans and Taiwan continued today to go calmly about its usual activities with no display of any anti-American feeling.

The general populace was as cheerful as usual and showed no indications of any alarm or pessimism as a result of the President's visit to mainland China.

The Foreign Ministry statement said the question of Taiwan to which the communique addressed itself could be solved only when "the Government of the Republic of China, the sole legitimate government elected by all people of China, has succeeded in its task of the recovery of the mainland, the unification of China and the deliverance of our compatriots."

"There is definitely no other alternative," the statement said.

The statement made no reference to the declaration in the communiqué of United States interest in a peaceful settlement of the Taiwan question "by the Chinese themselves," that is, by negotiation between the Chinese Communists in Peking and the Nationalists in Taipei. However, the statement's reiteration of the Nationalist Government's determination to recover the mainland —which it lost to the Communists in 1949—amounted to a rejection of the idea of negotiating an agreement.

The Foreign Ministry statement was issued 24 hours after the Shanghai communiqué was made public, and the length of time it took to appear is indicative of the trouble Government officials had in drafting it.

The statement had originally been expected last night and newsmen were advised only near midnight that it had not been completed. Today they were first told it would probably be ready by late morning, then by late afternoon. It finally was read out by the Foreign Ministry spokesman, Ho-tu Liu, at 9:30 this evening.

Loosely organized, often vague as to meaning and less than smooth in its English version, the statement did not attempt a detailed rejoinder to the Shanghai document or a detailed presentation of the Nationalist view. It dealt with only a few major points and some of these only tangentially.

Despite its undertones of bitterness, the statement was less vehement than the comments in the press here. The commentaries, all following pretty much the same line and therefore indicating coordination of views by some official agency, can be taken as a more faithful reflection of the feelings of the Government and at least that section of the population here that came from the China mainland with the Government 23 years ago.

Soviet Shows Relief At Results of Talks

Special to The New York Times

MOSCOW, Feb. 28—The Soviet Union, in a marked shift of its treatment of China, gave indications of relief tonight that President Nixon's talks with Chinese leaders had evidently achieved only modest results.

In a delayed but extensive and straightforward account of the Chinese-American communiqué, the Soviet press agency Tass gave Peking credit for the first time in several months for having opposed the American position on the Vietnam war.

The Tass dispatch, from Washington, reported Chinese support for the Vietcong peace plan, although lately the Soviet press has been accusing Peking of selling out the Communist cause in Indochina, ignoring Peking's denunciations of American air attacks on North Vietnam on the eve of Mr. Nixon's arrival in China.

In another reversal of recent Soviet propaganda charges that Peking was engaged in collusion with Washington, Tass reported the declaration that there remained "essential differences between China and the United States" on foreign policy issues and in their social systems.

At another point, Tass noted that the communiqué had set out "not common positions but the positions held by each side," citing Taiwan, Korea and Japan as other areas on which China and America differed.

The straightforward account in the Government-controlled media gave the Soviet public the first significant indication in weeks of American-Chinese differences, and it represented the most favorable treatment of Peking's positions on key issues.

Moreover, the 1,000-word Tass dispatch on the communiqué represents by far the most extensive treatment given to any aspect of the Nixon visit by the Soviet media.

The treatment given the communiqué suggested that after a high-level review Soviet officials were taking a somewhat more relaxed view of the American-Chinese talks and were surer of the obstacles in the way of any serious collaboration against Moscow than they had been in the weeks leading up to the visit.

In those weeks, some well-placed Russians were speaking fearfully of some new power grouping directed against Moscow and, during the visit, the Soviet press reprinted foreign Communist commentaries to that effect.

By modifying the picture of active collusion and near-complete agreement between its two major rivals now that the visit to Peking is over, the Kremlin could also be preparing the way for its own negotiations with the United States before and during President Nixon's visit to Moscow late in May.

Nonetheless, Tass noted warily, as it did yesterday, that the communiqué had been couched in general terms and that China and the United States had stated some of their views with "insufficient clarity," meaning that some of the content of the talks was being "kept secret."

The delay in reporting the communiqué extensively is not unusual for an issue of such paramount importance to the Kremlin, given the fact that the new developments occurred on a Sunday when top leaders were not all at work.

Soviet citizens as well as foreign diplomats assume that any such issue requires review at the highest levels before any official press account is published, thereby adding importance to the neutral and relaxed treatment of the communiqué.

SAIGON PLEASED BY COMMUNIQUE

By CRAIG R. WHITNEY
Special to The New York Times

SAIGON, South Vietnam, Feb. 28—"We felt at ease," said a senior official of the South Vietnamese Foreign Ministry, describing his colleagues' initial reaction to the Chinese-American communiqué from Shanghai.

"The communiqué seemed to indicate that both sides had to agree that no negotiated settlement of the war was in sight," the official continued. "That is a comfort to us, because it means that they were unable to make a deal behind our backs."

Although the South Vietnamese Government has not yet made an official statement on the communiqué issued by President Nixon and Premier Chou En-lai, the general reaction seems to be cautious and favorable.

"We wished the United States had been as strong in the Indochina issue as in the Korean issue, where it explicitly stated its closes ties and strong support of the Republic of Korea," the Foreign Ministry official said. "But aside from that, the communiqué does not show that the United States has changed its position in any way about the Vietnam issue."

Thieu in Nhatrang

President Nguyen Van Thieu has not met with Ambassador Ellsworth Bunker since the communiqué was issued, but he went today to Nhatrang, on the central coast, where he met with senior military commanders and predicted a Communist offensive in July and August in the northern military regions.

Mr. Thieu said that the Communists would try to prove the failure of Vietnamization and to defeat President Nixon in the American elections this fall, "because President Nixon helps South Vietnam fight the Communists." He did not talk specifically about the communiqué from Shanghai. American officials here believe the South Vietnamese Government's reaction will be favorable.

The Foreign Minister, Tran Van Lam, was with Mr. Thieu in Nhatrang and was reported to be preparing a statement about the communiqué, which is expected to welcome the position taken by the United States.

President Thieu is scheduled to be briefed next weekend by the Assistant Secretary of State for Far Eastern and Pacific Affairs, Marshall Green, who accompanied Mr. Nixon to Peking, but Mr. Thieu has sent an adviser, Hoang Duc Nha, to the United States anyway to try to find out how South Vietnam fared during Mr. Nixon's discussions in China last week.

Attention on Moscow Trip

Attention here is now being focused on Mr. Nixon's trip late this spring to Moscow, which supplies the North Vietnamese with most of their arms. An article in the Government paper Tin Song today bore the headline: "United States, China maintain their respective positions on Indochina." But an editorial said "the Indochina war will only be finally settled between the United States and the Soviet Union," a somewhat ambiguous statement that reflects nevertheless a basic helplessness felt by most Vietnamese about their ability to determine their own fate.

An article in the opposition newspaper Dien Tin, which supports the retired general Duong Van Minh, said "the Peking summit marked the start of a new era, and Messrs. Nixon and Chou En-lai have played the role of pioneers. But for us Vietnamese, we wonder why the United States should continue to intervene in the internal affairs of South Vietnam while the principle of people's self-determination has once again been restated in the joint communiqué." The article was accompanied by an unflattering cartoon of President Nixon with the Chinese Premier.

February 28, 1972

TOKYO IS RELIEVED BY LIMITED RESULT

By JOHN M. LEE
Special to The New York Times

TOKYO, Monday, Feb. 28—The Japanese Government, fearful of being undermined by President Nixon's visit to China, reacted last night with almost visible relief to the limited concrete achievements set out in the communiqué.

Foreign Minister Takeo Fukuda, meeting newsmen at the Ministry of Foreign Affairs shortly after the communiqué was made public, praised the President's visit as fruitful and said it would serve as a lubricant for Japan to normalize her relations with China.

He said, as if relieved, that the visit had produced no more than he had expected.

However, this morning, the highly critical Japanese press spoke of "betrayal" by the United States and assailed Premier Eisaku Sato for having let himself be outstripped by Washington in forging ties with Peking.

Asahi Shimbun, a leading Tokyo daily, noting that China has agreed to receive American diplomats in Peking, said, "The Japanese Government is forced to think seriously why Peking has utterly disregarded the Japanese Government endeavor to make a Government-level contact with China."

Japanese Is Hopeful

However, a spokesman for Premier Sato, Noboru Takeshita, the chief cabinet secretary, said business and other private contacts between China and Japan had already produced "considerable results" and he expressed hope that a Government - level dialogue would begin soon.

"The distance between Washington and Peking is now shorter than that between Tokyo and Peking," he said. "But Japan is now in a better position to close that distance."

Although gratified that the United States did not make too great a leap forward in its relations with China, some officials expressed concern that there might be undisclosed secret agreements affecting this country.

The Government is thus eagerly awaiting a briefing tomorrow by Marshall Green, Assistant Secretary of State for the Far East, who accompanied the President. Mr. Green is expected in Tokyo tonight. Some officials have expressed annoyance that the President is not sending his national security adviser, Henry A. Kissinger.

The Japanese fear in Mr. Nixon's approach to China was that this country was being ignored while a new order was taking shape in Asia. The Government fears that its cautious approach to China and its close ties to Taiwan would be made to look ridiculous and outmoded by some dramatic Presidential breakthrough.

February 28, 1972

U.S. SAYS JAPAN REMAINS KEY ALLY

By JOHN M. LEE
Special to The New York Times

TOKYO, Tuesday, Feb. 29—The United States told the Japanese Government today that President Nixon had made no secret deals with Peking during his visit to China.

The message was conveyed to Premier Eisaku Sato by Marshall Green, Assistant Secretary of State for East Asian Affairs, at a meeting this morning, official American sources said.

The sources said also that President Nixon had sent Mr. Sato a personal letter reassuring him that Japan remained a key ally of the United States. The letter was apparently intended to calm any Japanese fears of being undermined by the expanding contacts between the United States and China.

Mission of Assurance

Mr. Green arrived in Tokyo yesterday on an American diplomatic campaign to reassure Asian allies that President Nixon had not sacrificed their interests during meetings with China's Communist leaders.

Mr. Green, accompanied by John H. Holdridge, the Far Eastern specialist on the National Security Council staff of Henry A. Kissinger, is to visit 11 countries to brief such leaders as President Park Chung Hee of South Korea, President Chiang Kai-shek of Taiwan and President Nguyen Van Thieu of South Vietnam, besides Premier Sato.

The American officials, who accompanied Mr. Nixon to China, left the Presidential party at Shanghai yesterday and flew directly to Tokyo. Last night they met with Foreign Minister Takeo Fukuda, and later today they are to confer with other Foreign Ministry officials before leaving for Seoul tomorrow.

According to Foreign Ministry sources, Mr. Green told Mr. Fukuda that the United States had maintained in Peking that it would retain its military and other commitments to its allies and that the Chinese leaders must have realized this.

Mr. Green was also reported to have said that most of the talks in China had been devoted to "historical and philosophical discussions" and that the personal exchanges envisioned between China and the United States would take time to develop because of the language barrier and other factors.

According to the reports, Mr. Green assured Mr. Fukuda that the American delegation had refused to accept Chinese charges of a revival of Japanese militarism.

After the meeting, Mr. Fukuda told Japanese newsmen he saw no reason to revise his earlier favorable assessment of the United States-Chinese talks. The Foreign Minister said he now understood the Chinese attitude toward Japan better.

Sato's View on Taiwan

Earlier yesterday, Premier Sato came under sharp questioning in Parliament on the Government's China policy. He tried to clarify his views by making what many termed his most clear-cut statement so far that Taiwan was part of China.

Noting that the People's Republic of China is now a member of the United Nations, he said: "Based on this situation

530

we can say Taiwan is part of the People's Republic of China. It is a natural assertion that the Chinese mainland and Taiwan are inseparable and it is not a question a third country argues."

Mr. Sato said later that Japan had concluded a peace treaty with the Chinese Nationalist Government in 1952 because that regime was among the founders of the United Nations. But he said the situation had changed with the seating of Peking as the representative of China.

Mr. Sato's statement was seen here as representing a departure from his earlier position, which held that Taiwan's status was still undetermined or that rival regimes existed in China.

There appears to be great confusion in Asia over the passage in yesterday's United States - Chinese communiqué dealing with Taiwan, and there is uncertainty whether the United States has loosened its commitment to defend the Nationalist Government there. There are rumors of a reduction in American forces on the island as a token of goodwill toward Peking.

It will be Mr. Green's job to take up these issues with President Chiang and a Taipei Government that is incensed over Mr. Nixon's actions.

In Japan, Mr. Green is presumably seeking to bolster Premier Sato, who is coming under increased attack for clinging too long to Taiwan at the expense of improving relations with Peking. Mr. Sato, a deeply conservative politician, cooperated for years with American efforts to keep the Nationalists in the United Nations and keep the Peking Government out.

First Flight From Shanghai

Other allies of the United States are clearly perplexed over what their relations with China should be now that the years of cooperation with American containment have apparently come to an end.

Mr. Green and Mr. Holdridge flew into Yokota Air Force Base, an American installation outside Tokyo, in the Boeing 707 that had been used as the back-up plane on the President's flight across the Pacific. The direct flight here from Shanghai was the first Shanghai-Tokyo flight since 1949 when Pan American World Airways and Northwest Orient Airlines suspended their service as China fell to the Communist forces.

Another problem facing the Presidential envoys is the widespread belief in Asia that there were secret agreements or understandings in Peking that were left out of the communiqué.

Besides Japan, South Korea, Taiwan and South Vietnam, Mr. Green is scheduled to visit the Philippines, Indonesia, Singapore, Malaysia, Thailand, Australia and New Zealand.

China Since 1949: Seeking the Road to National Greatness

By O. EDMUND CLUBB

When the Communists came to power in China in 1949 the nation was agonizingly weary of decades of strife and the backward economy was near collapse. The last half century had seen the abortive imperial Reform Movement of 1898, the Boxer Rebellion, the 1911 Revolution, the violent warlord era and the foreign and civil wars of the Nationalist rule. The Chinese nation was more than ready for a new order of things.

Mao Tse-tung's promise was not peace, stability and homely bliss but fundamental social change and national greatness. In the next 20 years the nation was taken over a rugged, arduous course. In the beginning the regime demonstrated political will and imagination in repair of the economy, consolidation of political controls and initiation of social reforms. In foreign affairs China made her weight felt in both the Korean and Indochina wars and then came out as a proponent of the Bandung principles of peaceful coexistence and economic cooperation. Smaller underdeveloped countries began to view the Chinese experience as offering patterns worthy of imitation.

After the impressive beginning, China attempted to speed up her economic development by the "Great Leap" tactic, but that approach to the towering hurdle of economic backwardness failed disastrously. In foreign relations Peking soon departed from the Bandung line to follow a zigzag course of aggressive "revolutionary diplomacy," even vis-à-vis the Soviet Union, her ally.

The radical undertaking to mobilize a worldwide revolutionary following in opposition to both the United States and the Soviet Union collapsed. Deepening divisions in the party leadership resulted finally in the launching of the biggest of all Chairman Mao's purge movements — the Great Proletarian Cultural Revolution. The social fabric was torn apart, the political apparatus shattered, the leadership structure badly weakened. China emerged from her domestic travail. She again embraced the principle of peaceful coexistence for foreign relations but still stood antagonistically independent alike of the Soviet Union, Japan and the United States. The balance of power in Asia shifts strongly as President Nixon visits Peking. The two nations, of East and West, meet at a strategic crossroads.

As of 1949 the military victory that had been won by the People's Liberation Army was clearly decisive and the new regime attained quick diplomatic recognition not only from the Soviet Union and the rest of the Communist bloc but also from such Asian states as India, Indonesia and Burma, and from Britain and other European countries. France, engaged in her colonial war in Indochina, held off; so did the United States, to "let the dust settle."

Tasks of vast dimensions confronted the new regime. First and foremost, it was essential to rehabilitate the wrecked transport system and the debilitated economy, so that the country might function again on the basic level. The Peking Government also faced the general task of employing the nation's natural and human resources so as to turn China into a modern economic power that could wield a major political force and thus resume her traditional position of dominance in Asia.

Finally, the Communist leadership had proposed that, after victory, there should be social and political reorganization to advance the nation into first, socialism, and then Communism.

The Government headed by Mao Tse-tung had already given vivid demonstration, on the long hard road to victory, of its military and administrative capacities. The Chinese Communist party, to all outward appearances, was tightly knit and disciplined, seemingly monolithic, a coordinated team that operated by ready consensus.

February 29, 1972

Rights for 'People' Only

The Government as established in October, 1949, was not a Communist "proletarian dictatorship" but, as sketched by Mao a few months before, a "people's democratic dictatorship." In that system, he said, "the right of reactionaries to voice their opinions must be abolished and only the people are allowed to have the right of voicing their opinions." Mao asked and answered the natural question:

"Who are the people? At the present stage of China, they are the working class, the peasant class, the petty bourgeoisie, and national bourgeoisie."

Certain classes (landlords, bureaucratic capitalists, and "Kuomintang reactionaries and their henchmen"), while still bearing the duties of citizenship, had already been deprived of the rights granted "the people." The Communist party, for its part, was of course identified with the proletariat — the workers and peasants.

The central Government established in Peking on Oct. 1 was provisional in form. Outwardly, it was a "united front" composed of Communists and representatives of other parties, including bourgeois carryovers from the Kuomintang period. In 1954 a National People's Congress approved a Constitution that gave more permanent form to the Government. Notably, the Congress itself was designated "the highest organ of state authority in the People's Republic of China."

With passage of a Land Reform Law in 1950, the landlord class was brought under concentrated attack and eliminated, with division of confiscated land among the peasantry — and the killing of many landlords as "enemies of the people." There was a sign of impending events in the organization of mutual-aid teams, and in the initial organization of agricultural producers' cooperatives. Even as the land was being divided, the stage of collectivization was being introduced.

Another piece of major legislation was the 1950 Marriage Law. The Nationalist Civil Code had accorded equal legal status to men and women within the family, but that statute, like the Nationalist land reforms, had remained in good part a dead letter. The Communists, on the contrary, actively promoted the provisions of their Marriage Law and, with many instances of personal anguish, the position of woman was

brought closer to that of man than ever before in Chinese society.

Mao had set a pattern, in 1942, in carrying out a "rectification" movement for the correction of a variety of "erroneous" administrative practices in the political apparatus. In 1951, there was a "three-anti" movement against certain bad practices of party members, and this was followed shortly by a "five-anti" movement aimed at unsocial behavior on the part of the national bourgeoisie. As in the land reform movement, there were accusations and accusation meetings, people's tribunals, confessions and recantations, and condemnations. By its purge of the national bourgeoisie, the Government substantially advanced the process of taking over private enterprise.

During this period, Peking effectively consolidated its control over border regions, buttressing the national security. Sinkiang had been won over to the Communist side in September, 1949. Chinese control was re-established in Tibet, which had maintained effective autonomy since 1912. Other terra irredenta, such as Hong Kong, Taiwan and Outer Mongolia, remained for the moment beyond Peking's reach.

China showed herself ready to take strong action in critical sectors of her frontier. The Korean war and the Indochina war alike saw Chinese intervention (in different forms) on the side of Communist forces fighting respectively against "U. S. imperialism" and French colonialism.

China was able safely to intervene in the Korean war because in February, 1950, she had entered upon a treaty of alliance with the Soviet Union. That tie induced caution in United Nations councils confronted with the issue of whether the war should be carried to Manchuria (as proposed by Gen. Douglas MacArthur); it also brought the Chinese needed Soviet military equipment.

But the supply of arms was not gratis. China went in debt to her ally to get that matériel. And although the economy was put into working order again in the period 1950-52, the country was hardly in a position to proceed rapidly with new construction.

For all of the confiscations and the penalties levied, the country was poor in capital. It was poor in technology too, and its foreign trade was even below its usual low level.

Mao's assertion of July, 1949, that China was going to "lean to one side," the side of the Soviet Union, because imperialist states could not be expected to aid a "people's state," had

not been richly rewarded. By the agreement of 1950, China was accorded a Soviet credit of only $300-million, to be extended over five years. But this was not the sum total of Soviet aid. Soviet experience, technical skills and blueprints were made available In addition, there were profitable trade exchanges.

On Road to Socialism

The Formosa Strait crisis of early 1955, which led China and the United States to what some Americans judged was the brink of war, served only to enhance China's prestige when Premier Chou, at the Bandung Conference in April, presented an amiable countenance to the assembled African and Asian nations—and subscribed more formally to the rinciple of peaceful coexistence as incorporated in Bandung's Ten Principles. The soft answer made the voicing of wrath against China seem grossly out of order.

China was now leaving the people's democracy stage and embarking on the road to socialism. At this juncture, a note of urgency was introduced into developments by Mao, the impatient millenarian. There had been widespread withdrawal of peasants from the budding agricultural producers' cooperatives.

In a speech in July, 1955, Mao called for a speed-up of the collectivization process, to the end that half of the peasantry should be organized into cooperatives or collectives by 1957, and the rest by the end of 1960.

Fifty million additional households were in fact brought into the cooperatives by December. And a draft 12-year development plan for agriculture as presented to the Supreme State Conference in January, 1956, revealed that the full socialist stage of collectivization was to be completed by 1958. Mao announced that China was "witnessing the flood tide of the great socialist revolution."

By the end of the first five-year economic development plan in 1957, remarkable progress had been made in the industrial sector; but it was evident also that, despite the report that the over-all agricultural goals had been overfulfilled, agriculture was falling

behind the country's consumption needs, the demands of an expanding industry and the servicing of the external debt.

The economic "scissors gap" widened to the accompaniment of various important political developments. In 1956-57, during the Hundred Flowers movement, the Government invited liberal criticism, only to be confronted with clear evidence that the party and its leadership were by no means held in the esteem that had been assumed.

A rift that had been introduced into the Chinese-Soviet relationship by the "de-Stalinization" process of 1956 was widened when Mao, in Moscow the next year for the celebration of the 40th anniversary of the Bolshevik Revolution, made demands on the Soviet leadership for major changes of bloc strategy in both the economic and political sectors.

But Moscow had been forewarned with respect to China's growing ambition to become again pre-eminent in Asia. In 1954, when Moscow had been led to grant Peking additional economic aid, the Chinese had demanded, and obtained, the liquidation of various Chinese-Soviet joint-stock enterprises. Mao had gone on to ask for the "return" of Outer Mongolia to China—but had been given no satisfaction. In 1957, Mr. Khrushchev, the Soviet party leader, rejected Mao's latest propositions.

The second five-year plan began formally in 1958. The carrying out of the plan, in the circumstances, promised to be a slow and arduous task. The decision, which was clearly Mao's, was instead in favor of a Great Leap Forward.

The new "movement" saw a nationwide introduction of backyard workshops and, notably, the transformation of the agricultural producers' cooperatives into some 26,000 rural communes in which all rights of joint ownership and withdrawal were terminated. The land that had been distributed to the peasantry so short a time before was taken back by the state—it was now viewed as belonging to "the whole people."

The peasants worked in quasi-military formations and in a further move toward regimentation the Government reported it had mobilized 230 million of the population into the "people's militia." The nation strove to leap over an entire economic stage in one tremendous frenzied effort.

On Oct. 1, the official newspaper Jenmin Jih Pao announced that "with the Great Leap Forward in production Communism has already begun to push forth sprouts in our actual life." And at the end of the year it was officially claimed that vast increases in both agricultural and industrial production had been achieved.

But the Great Leap and the coincident mobilization of "the masses" into militia formations had been accompanied by rash and unprofitable adventures in the field of foreign affairs. Another Formosa Strait crisis brought China face to face once more with American military power—and the Soviet Union did not interpose its might to protect its ally.

In 1958, also, China broke off commercial ties with Japan. In neither case did China benefit.

And doubts regarding the results of the Great Leap seemingly began to permeate inner party circles. A party Central Committee plenary meeting held in December issued a resolution asserting that "We should not declare that people's communes will enter Communism immediately . . . this distorts and vulgarizes the great ideal of Communism, strengthens the petit-bourgeois trend toward equalitarianism, and adversely affects socialist construction."

After the session, there came clearer evidence of division in the Communist leadership: it was announced that Mao had decided to retire from his position as chief of state (while retaining his position as head of the party).

Liu Shao-chi, termed Mao's "close comrade-in arms," was duly elected in the spring of 1959 to succeed Mao as chief of state. That year was one of grave economic and political crisis, and the party's Central Committee met in August to wrestle with the pressing problem of restoring order. There had been dislocation of transport, labor utilization and foreign trade. Economic planning and control had been effectively wrecked; the second five-year plan was heard of no more.

It was now publicly acknowledged that the amazing production figures issued in late 1958 had been grossly inflated. At the Central Committee meeting Defense Minister Peng Teh-huai challenged Mao and his Great Leap policies. At Mao's demand, the Defense Minister was replaced by Lin Piao. The rift in the leadership between the voluntarist "Reds" and pragmatist "experts" crystallized.

Adventurism in China's foreign affairs continued. In 1959, with the flight of the Dalai Lama from his native Tibet to India, the amiable Chinese-Indian relationship went sour. Worse was to follow. In February, 1959, Moscow agreed to help China construct 78 more industrial projects, to cost $1.25-billion, for a grand total of 336 agreed upon since 1950. But China was to pay on the barrelhead: no new Soviet credits were forthcoming.

In April, 1960, Mao sought to bring pressure to bear on the Soviet leadership by causing publication in the official journal Hung Chi of an article entitled "Long Live Leninism!" which in essence challenged the Soviet ideological position with respect to the world situation.

A confrontation took place between Premier Khrushchev and the Chinese delegation at a Communist gathering at Bucharest in June. Those developments presumably contributed to a critical decision by Moscow—in the summer of 1960, all Soviet technicians left China, taking their skills and blueprints with them. China had been dealt a severe economic blow, and was now on her own.

From 1960 to 1963, to the accompaniment of bitter polemics, the quarrel between the two Communist giants worsened.

Peking savored one victory in January, 1964, when France extended recognition. About the same time, the Peking leadership showed a shift in tactics by proclaiming the "intermediate zone" doctrine. Mao in 1949 had proclaimed that "in the world, without exception, one either leans to the side of imperialism or to the side of socialism. Neutrality is a mere camouflage and does not exist." Now the Chinese were inferentially prepared to theorize that many states occupied an uncommitted position between the socialist bloc and United States imperialism, and China's collaboration with them was permissible as being in the common cause against imperialism. This in essence was a return to the Comintern's "united front" policy of the nineteen-thirties.

The deviation from "revolutionary diplomacy" was brief. It was hardly compatible with Mao's urge to exercise leadership of the world revolutionary movement to the exclusion of Moscow, which was now viewed as being the home of "modern revisionism."

In October, 1964, the explosion of China's first nuclear device and Khrushchev's fall from power created a new situation for Peking. By becoming a nuclear power, China automatically became a first-strike target in any nuclear war and thus faced new danger; on the other hand, Khrushchev's departure suggested possible weakness in Moscow, and consequently new opportunity. Peking continued to strive for leadership of the African-Asian nations, indeed of the whole of the Third World, in its drive against both "imperialism", and "modern revisionism."

In 1965, the strategy to gain leadership of the Third World met definitive failure. The United States escalated its war in Vietnam, but China obviously felt compelled still to limit her support for the revolutionaries. Peking's strenuous efforts to prevent the Soviet Union from participating in the projected second conference of Africans and Asians failed, and the project itself was abandoned. Then, in October, Peking's policy and Mao's revolutionary theory met disaster when the Indonesian Communist party was effectively wiped out in the aftermath of the abortive coup.

Mao's Double Discontent

It is now clear that, as soon as the economy had begun to recover from the disastrous Great Leap, Mao began to bow to a double discontent. He was distressed by the pragmatism—one might say "revisionism"—being displayed by the Liu Shao-chi leadership in rehabilitation of the shaken economy; he also experienced the urge to recover full political power.

After the Central Committee meeting of September, 1962, Mao resumed his "class struggle" in a drive on domestic "revisionism." Lin Piao undertook to implement Mao's voluntarist ideas in the military and in early 1964 the People's Liberation Army began to be extolled as a model for all society in its self-abnegation, its spirit of sacrifice—and its single-minded devotion to Mao's thought. In July, 1964, a Cultural Revolution movement was launched, as a new purge of the academic realm.

The foreign-policy defeats of 1965 would have deepened Mao's discontents. At an extraordinary meeting of the Central Committee in September that year, he demanded an intensification of the fight against "reactionary ideology," but was rebuffed. This can only have convinced him that both revisionism, and his enemies, had become so firmly entrenched in the party as to threaten both the revolution and his place in history.

He crossed his Rubicon. That very fall, with the collaboration of a small number of associates that included, notably, Defense Minister Lin Piao, Mao struck out on the biggest "movement" of his career—the Great Proletarian Cultural Revolution. He proceeded with care in the beginning, but in the spring of 1966 advanced boldly to attack the party's powerful Peking municipal committee. In June, China's schools were closed. In August, with students mobilized into Red Guards, the Great Proletarian Cultural Revolution was formally launched. In theory, it was to rid China of "revisionist" traces and evil "old" influences; in fact, its chief aim was the destruction of Mao's opposition within the party, and his restoration to full leadership of the Chinese Revolution.

The Cultural Revolution followed a chaotic, devastating course for two full years, zigzaging from extremist left to moderate and back time and again. In response to Mao's command to "bombard the headquarters," various outstanding party figures were brought under attack, and many fell disgraced before the onslaught.

The whole operation was characterized, however, by dangerous factional fighting among the various Red Guard groups, and in the summer of 1968 the army was finally loosed against the now truly rebellious leftists, and they were suppressed.

At a Central Committee meeting in October, 1968, however, Mao's prime purpose was achieved: it was decided that Liu Shao-chi should be ousted from all party and governmental posts. A party congress was held in April, 1969, and there Lin Piao, serving as Mao's mouthpiece, confirmed that action in fine disregard of the constitutional provision allocating to the National People's Congress authority for selection (or dismissal) of the head of state. And a new party constitution designated Lin as "Comrade Mao's close comrade-in-arms and successor."

Rebuilding the Party

The final accounting of the massive convulsion that had wracked the country was still to be made. In response to Mao's drive toward social egalitarianism, there had indeed been a great leveling, with the bourgeoisie practically eliminated as a class. Now the rule was described not as a people's democratic dictatorship, but (in the constitution particularly) as a "dictatorship of the proletariat."

The rebuilding of the party and the government apparatus, both badly damaged in the course of the Cultural Revolution, had been undertaken but was still to be completed. At the time Lin Piao spoke, the armed forces, which had shouldered ever broader functions during the revolution and had grown correspondingly stronger, was discovered to be in a dominant position in both party and Government

China's foreign relations during the Cultural Revolution reflected the domestic disorders, with assaults on diplomats and diplomatic establishments, and extravagant behavior by Chinese diplomats and students abroad. At the end of the Cultural Revolution, the country's foreign affairs were in sad disorder. Worse, dangerous situations had developed on two major sectors of China's frontiers—those bordering on the Soviet Union and facing Japan. Moscow, after suffering numerous provocations from the Chinese side, built up its military positions along the Chinese border and in 1969 began to strike back sharply. Japan, now the third greatest economic power in the world, was steadily rearming; and in November, 1969, Premier Eisaku Sato, in a visit to Washington, joined with President Nixon in a communiqué proposing in substance American-Japanese collaboration for the maintenance of peace and order in East Asia.

Shortly before, Peking and Moscow had agreed that, although party differences between them might persist, amicable state-to-state relations were nevertheless feasible, and political negotiations began at Peking in October. China returned diplomats to the foreign posts abandoned by chiefs of mission during the Cultural Revolution, and once more presented a benign aspect to the outside world. Peking had returned to the Bandung policy of peaceful coexistence.

China soon reaped rich fruits from her policy shift. From October, 1970, to October, 1971, 14 more countries recognized Peking; and last October the United Nations' General Assembly, where the United States for a full decade had vigorously campaigned on behalf of its Chinese Nationalist ally, voted to seat a delegation from Peking as the true representative of China. And now President Nixon himself is in Peking.

As Mao would be the first to tell him, China's revolution is not yet over; her drive for wealth and power remains unsatisfied. In 1971, in theory, China embarked upon her fourth 5-year plan—but nothing is known of its dimensions. In 1971 also, the nation was to have convened its long overdue fourth National People's Congress, which in all logic will be called upon to draw up a new constitution and sanction the acts of Mao since the last Congress sat in 1964-65. In actuality, the Congress was not convened, and mysterious events in September, 1971, seemed to indicate that a new crisis had arisen in the party leadership, and that this time it was Lin Piao and some of his close lieutenants who were purged in their turn.

Nor were the fates kind to Peking in the international field after the October victory in the United Nations. In the Indian-Pakistani war of November-December, China even as the United States shared the defeat of the reactionary Islambad Government. And the escalation of American bombings in Vietnam in December and February were as much in defiance of Mao's revolutionary purposes as of Hanoi's recalcitrance.

President Nixon visits a China which, under Mao's autocratic rule, achieved great advances in some fields; but it is also a China with an aging shattered leadership, and still far from being the great economic and political power of Mao's dreams. In a real sense, the country is indeed "encircled," as it charges, by the United States, the Soviet Union and Japan. It is also "contained" by its great weaknesses and great needs.

In those circumstances, will the American President perhaps offer long-anathematized "Red China" extended credits dwarfing those granted by Stalin two decades ago? And might Mao's China, which chose in 1949 to "lean" to the side of the Soviet Union, now decide to lean to the side of "the greatest imperialist of them all," the United States? Granted the tantalyzing theoretical possibilities inherent in the situation, a healthy skepticism is clearly in order.

China, 1900-72: A Brief Chronology

1900-01	Boxer Rebellion
1904-05	Russo-Japanese War and partition of Manchuria
Nov. 1908	Deaths of the Emperor Kuang-hsu and the Empress Dowager Tzu-hsi
Oct. 1911	Outbreak of the 1911 Revolution
Dec. 1911	Sun Yat-sen elected provisional president
Feb. 1912	The ruling house abdicates; Yuan Shih-kai elected President; Sun Yat-sen steps down
May 1913	U.S. grants diplomatic recognition
Sept. 1914	Japan, going to war with Germany, violates China's neutrality
Jan. 1915	Japan presents her Twenty-one Demands
Dec. 1915	Yuan Shih-kai accepts imperial office, but cancels plan, March 1916, in the face of rebellion; dies June 1916
Mar. 1918	Society for the Study of Marxist Theory organized in Peking under the leadership of Li Ta-chao
1919	May Fourth Movement (in response to Versailles settlement)
Feb. 1921	China Socialist Youth Corps founded, Paris
July 1921	Chinese Communist Party founded
1916-28	Warlord era. Wars between local military chiefs disrupt national government
Jan. 1923	Sun Yat-sen, seeking aid for a Kuomintang government, turns to Russia; meeting with adviser Adolph Joffe; Dr. Sun reaffirms Three People's Principles (nationalism, democracy, people's livelihood) in more revolutionary expression
Oct. 1923	Michael Borodin and other Russian advisers arrive Canton
Mar. 1925	Sun Yat-sen dies
July 1925	Nationalist government formed at Canton
June 1926	Chiang Kai-shek becomes commander-in-chief of National Revolutionary Army
Mar. 1927	Chiang breaks with Nationalist government at Wuhan, and, April, establishes opposition Nationalist government at Nanking
July 1927	Launching of Northern Expedition; Wuhan proscribes Communist Party; Russian advisers expelled
Aug. 1927	Part of Fourth Army mutinies and forms Red Army
Jan. 1928	Chiang returns to power
June 1928	Overthrow of warlord regime, Peking
Oct. 1928	Formal establishment of national government at Nanking
Dec. 1930	Nationalists begin "bandit-supression" campaigns against Communist military forces
1931-32	Japanese occupation of Manchuria
Feb. 1932	Manchukuo (Manchuria) declared independent
1934-35	Communist troops and civilians, pressed by Chiang's army and blockade, accomplish Long March from Kiangsi to north Shensi
Dec. 1936	Kidnapping of Chiang Kai-shek, Sian
1937-41	Sino-Japanese War
1941	Sino-Japanese War merges into World War II as China declares war on Japan, Germany, Italy
Aug. 1945	Nationalist government concludes 30-year Treaty of Friendship and Alliance with USSR; Japanese surrender
Dec. 1945	General George C. Marshall arrives to mediate Nationalist-Communist differences
Jan. 1946	Truce, followed by political agreements
July 1946	Third Revolutionary Civil War begins with expiration of June 30 truce
Jan. 1947	U.S. abandons mediation efforts
Nov. 1948	Fall of Manchuria to Communists
1949	Chiang Kai-shek retires in favor of Vice President Li Tsung-jen
Aug. 1949	U.S. publishes White Paper
Oct. 1949	People's Republic of China proclaimed
Oct. 1949- Jan. 1950	Recognition of new state granted by USSR, Hungary, Czechoslovakia, Poland, Yugoslavia, North Korea, Mongolian People's Republic, Albania, Burma, India, Great Britain, Pakistan, Ceylon, Denmark, Finland, Sweden, French Indochina (Ho Chi Minh regime), Afghanistan, Israel, Switzerland, Netherlands
Dec. 1949	Nationalists move capital to Taiwan (Formosa)
Jan. 1950	U.S. consular offices at Peking confiscated
Feb. 1950	Soviets conclude 30-year Treaty of Friendship and Alliance and trade agreements with People's Republic, rescinding '45 agreement with Nationalists
Apr. 1950	New marriage law promulgated; U.S. consular and diplomatic offices in China closed
June 1950	Land reform law adopted; beginning of Korean War, President Harry S Truman orders Seventh Fleet to defend Taiwan
Oct. 1950	Chinese volunteers intervene in Korean War (1950-53)
1951	Three-Anti and Five-Anti movements launched against political and economic corruption
Jan. 1953	Inauguration of First Five-Year Plan
June 1953	Population census taken
July 1953	Truce, Korean War
Dec. 1953	Resolution on agricultural cooperatives
Apr. 1954	Geneva Conference on French Indochina War begins with China a participant

July 1954 End, Indochina War

Sept. 1954 First Taiwan Strait Crisis begins as Communists shell Quemoy Islands; First National People's Congress convenes

Dec. 1954 Defense treaty signed by U.S. and Taiwan

Apr. 1955 Bandung Conference of African and Asian nations

May 1956 Mao Tse-tung speech "Let a Hundred Flowers Bloom"

May 1957 Open criticism of government

June 1957 Party rectification movement

Aug. 1957 Anti-"rightist" movement: intellectuals sent to villages and factories

Nov. 1957 Mao Tse-tung in Moscow says "East Wind prevails over West Wind"

Feb. 1958 Chou En-lai gives up post of Foreign Minister; Chen Yi succeeds him; National People's Congress proclaims Great Leap Forward

Apr. 1958 Drive for backyard furnaces and workshops; organization of first agricultural communes

May 1958 Trade with Japan canceled nominally because of Premier Kishi's "hostile attitude"

Aug. 1958 Politburo approval of commune program; Second Taiwan Strait Crisis begins

Sept. 1958 People's Militia established

Dec. 1958 Mao Tse-tung retires from chairmanship of the People's Republic

Apr. 1959 The Dalai Lama flees to India; Liu Shao-chi elected chairman of the People's Republic of China

Aug. 1959 Shortcomings of the Great Leap Forward acknowledged

Sept. 1959 Lin Piao replaces Peng Teh-huai as Minister of Defense

Apr. 1960 Publication of "Long Live Leninism!"—challenge to Soviet leadership

June 1960 Khrushchev openly attacks Mao Tse-tung

Aug. 1960 Soviet technicians withdraw from China

Jan. 1961 Economic policy liberalized

Mar. 1961 U.S. sends special forces to South Vietnam

Nov. 1961 At Twenty-second Party Congress in Moscow, Khrushchev denounces Albania; Chou En-lai defends her

Dec. 1961 UN General Assembly opens first full-scale debate on China representation

1962 Sino-Indian border conflict

Apr. 1963 Directive circulated on political work by the People's Liberation Army

Dec. 1963 Roger Hilsman, Jr., speaks on need for change in U.S. China policy

Jan. 1964 France grants diplomatic recognition

July 1964 Launching "Cultural Revolution"

Oct. 1964 Khrushchev is ousted from Party and premiership; China explodes first nuclear device

Nov. 1964 Party urges people to study Mao's thought and exalt him as an immortal

Dec. 1964 Third National People's Congress convenes; Chou En-lai calls for elimination of capitalism and the bourgeoisie

Mar. 1965 Chinese and Vietnamese students demonstrate in Moscow against war in Vietnam

July 1965 Second Afro-Asian Conference collapses, Algeria

Sept. 1965 Lin Piao's essay "Long Live the Victory of the People's War"

June 1966 Great Proletarian Cultural Revolution erupts with purges of Peking University and Communist Party

Aug. 1966 Red Guards mass in Peking, carry Cultural Revolution to major cities

Dec. 1966 Discrediting of Liu Shao-chi begins

Apr. 1967 Official attacks against Liu Shao-chi

July 1967 Clash at Wuhan between Maoists and army forces

Aug. 1967 Red Guard attacks on Soviet and British embassies, Peking; actions against embassies in London and Moscow; Three-in-One (soldier-worker-peasant) Teams formed to guide Cultural Revolution

Oct. 1968 Central Committee Plenum expels Liu Shao-chi from Party and other posts; Party rebuilding begins

1969 Peking begins returning ambassadors to foreign posts

Mar. 1969 Sino-Soviet conflict on Ussuri River

Apr. 1969 Ninth Congress, Chinese Communist Party; approval new Party constitution; Lin Piao named as successor to Mao

1969 Millions sent to rural areas to intersperse manual labor with ordinary life

Sept. 1969 Meeting, premiers Kosygin and Chou at Peking airfield

Oct. 1969 USSR and China begin talks on border dispute

Nov. 1969 Nixon-Sato accord allows U.S. free use of military bases, Okinawa, in return for Japanese administration of island

Feb. 1970 Pathet Lao and North Vietnamese soldiers retake Plaine des Jarres, Laos; U.S. Congress protests American involvement; Nixon reveals details of involvement

Mar.-
May 1970 Norodim Sihanouk overthrown, Cambodia; Peking offers him shelter and recognizes government in exile; Nixon sends U.S. combat troops into Cambodia

Aug. 1970 Tsinghua is first major university to reopen

Oct. 1970 Canada offers diplomatic recognition; by 1972 recognition of Peking by Equatorial Guinea, Italy, Ethiopia, Chile, Nigeria, Kuwait, Cameroon, San Marino, Austria, Libya, Sierra Leone, Turkey, Iran, Togo, Belgium, Peru, Lebanon, Rwanda, Cyprus, Senegal, Iceland, Malta, Mexico, Argentina

Apr. 1971 Nixon eases trade barriers with China; U.S. lifts ban on newsmen to China; American table-tennis team visits China

July 1971 Nixon announces forthcoming visit to Peking

Sept. 1971 Political crisis in Peking; Lin Piao disappears, seemingly purged (July 1972, Mao announces Lin died in plane crash over Mongolia in Sept. 1971)

Oct. 1971 China admitted to the United Nations; Taiwan expelled

Feb. 1972 Nixon visit to Peking

Biographical Sketches of

Leading Chinese Personalities,

1900-72

Chang Tso-lin, 1873-1924, the "Old Marshal," ruled Manchuria from 1919 to 1928 and after 1924 controlled Peking. Born into a peasant family, uneducated, he fought in the Sino-Japanese War of 1894-95 and shortly afterwards organized a military force in Fengtien. One of the numerous "bandits" in China at the time, he increased his power by allying himself with the Japanese in the Russo-Japanese War (1904-05). In 1912 he was promoted to divisional command in Manchuria and eventually became military governor of southern Manchuria. With the indirect support of the Japanese, he extended his grip over all of Manchuria and came to dominate much of northern China through alliances with other warlords. Several attempts by Sun Yat-sen to bring him into the Nationalist fold met only brief success in 1922. In 1924 when the Peking government concluded a treaty with Russia concerning the Chinese Eastern Railway which crossed Manchuria, Chang won *de facto* recognition of his autonomous control of the region by a separate agreement with the Soviets. He later tried to interfere with Russian operation of the railroad, but was forced to back down in 1926.

Chang's attempts to extend his control over all China eventually collided with the Nationalist Northern Expedition. He retreated from Peking in 1928, proposing to consolidate his power in Manchuria. On his way north his railway car was blown up by a Japanese military man who was plotting the seizure of Manchuria, and Chang was killed.

Questions remain as to who used whom the more profitably in the relationship between Chang and the Japanese. His positive contribution lay in maintaining a harsh stability in Manchuria during a troubled period of China's history.

Chen Po-ta, b. 1905, was a leading spokesman for international Communist affairs and an interpreter of Mao's Thought. He was born to a poor peasant family in Fukien and received his early education by the benevolence of an overseas Chinese who established a school for poor children of his native district. Since college was out of his reach, Chen joined the local army, but by 1927 had become a member of the Chinese Communist Party and was studying in Moscow. On his return to China in 1930, he began teaching in China College in Peking, a hub of political activity at that time; when war with Japan broke out in 1937 he joined Mao's forces in Yenan. He taught in the Central Party School and after 1937 served in the propaganda section, becoming director in 1949. According to rumor, Mao was not immediately impressed by Chen, a good scholar and writer, but a poor speaker and socializer. But Mao came to respect Chen's talents; Chen became the Chairman's political secretary and the chief extoller of his virtues. By 1946 Chen became a member of the Central Committee and in 1956 of the Politburo. This prolific writer has contributed books and articles attacking the Republican leaders, praising Mao, criticizing the Soviets, and has edited the theoretical journal *Red Flag* since its inception in 1958.

His career reached a new peak in the mid-sixties when he headed the important Cultural Revolution Group of the Central Committee. Since he was then Mao's personal secretary, it is believed that he acted as Mao's agent in the purges of the time. Chen himself was purged in 1970 or 1971 when moderation became Party policy.

Chen Yi, 1901-72, was born to a family of scholars in Szechwan, but spent his year of study in France (1919) in political agitation. By 1923 he had joined both the Chinese Communist Party and the Kuomintang and become an expert in military affairs. His career received an early boost when, as a political commissar with the Fourth Red Army, he sided with Mao in an early Party struggle. Elected to the Central Executive Committee of the Kiangsi Soviet, Chen remained behind with his troops while other Communists made the Long March. During the Sino-Japanese War, Chen's troops were active in the southeast; from 1941 to 1944 he commanded the Party's New Fourth Army. After a brief assignment in Yenan, he returned to distinguish himself and his army in the Third Revolutionary Civil War by campaigns in Shantung province and by capturing the Shanghai region. He became mayor of Shanghai and took on responsibilities in the national government as well. He formally joined the Peking government in 1954, received the title of marshal the following year and was elected to the Politburo in 1956. In 1958 he succeeded Chou En-lai as foreign minister, which gave him the opportunity to travel abroad extensively. He ran afoul of the Cultural Revolution in the mid-sixties; although he retained the title of foreign minister, he was in failing health and remained politically inactive thereafter.

Chiang Ching, b. 1914, was a Shanghai actress when she joined the Party in 1933. She studied in Yenan, where she fell in love with one of her teachers—Mao Tse-tung. Mao was married at the time and in order to get a divorce and marry her had to pledge that Chiang Ching would stay out of politics. The years of obscurity were apparently bitter ones for her; she built up many grudges, especially against Party wives who had achieved prominence. Chiang has always taken an interest in the arts. In 1964, fearing that Mao was losing power, she helped convince him that the play *Hai Jui Dismissed from Office* had a treacherous theme and thus played a role in launching the Great Proletarian Cultural Revolution. She became second to Chen Po-ta in commanding the Cultural Revolution Group and made use of her position to settle some old scores, particularly against the wife of Liu Shao-chi. She played a prominent role in directing the Red Guards at the height of the purges and made herself the supreme arbiter of socialist art. Her place in the Party heirarchy has fluctuated since then between sixth and third; however, she has been less active politically since the 1967 trend toward moderation. Although seriously ill through much of the 1950's, she appears to be in good health now and served as hostess to the Nixons in 1972.

Chiang Ching-kuo, b. 1909, the eldest son of Chiang Kai-shek, was expelled from school and arrested for participating in Nationalist agitation as a youth. He traveled to study in the Soviet Union in 1925 and remained there when his father broke with the Communists in 1927. He continued his studies for some time, but later worked in mines and factories. He was permitted to return to China in 1937 after negotiation of a Nationalist-Communist united front. At the age of 28 he arrived home with a Russian wife and two children. His father approved his appointment as an administrator in Kiangsi, where the son, who became known as the "iron commissioner," began a vigorous program of social reform and political consolidation. Chiang attempted various assignments for his father, notably negotiating with the Soviet military in Manchuria in 1945, for which he was criticized, and stabilizing the runaway inflation in Shanghai in 1948, in which he understandably failed. As his father's personal representative, he twice returned to Moscow after World War II to negotiate with Stalin. After the retreat to Taiwan, Chiang Ching-kuo established and directed a political department of the ministry of national defense. He controlled the secret police and created a ruthless but effective security apparatus. He became a member of the Central Committee of the Kuomintang and eventually defense minister. In 1969 he was named Deputy Premier and thus became heir apparent.

Chiang Kai-shek, b. 1887, son of a Chekiang merchant family, early decided to pursue a military career. His first participation in military action in Shanghai, 1911-12, won him important friendships and promotion to regimental commander. In 1918 Sun Yat-sen suggested his participation in the newly established Canton regime. In 1923 Sun appointed Chiang head of a delegation to the Soviet Union to explore the chances for Soviet aid and in 1924 made him head of the Whampoa Military Academy, which was established to train cadets for military action in unifying China. Although not viewed as the likely successor to Sun, who died in 1925, Chiang managed to grasp the reins of power. In 1927 he set up a rival Nationalist government in Nanking and began to purge Communists from the Kuomintang. The Wuhan gov-

ernment merged with the Nanking organization, and in 1928 the rejuvenated Nationalists under Chiang's leadership broke the power of the northern generals and Chiang became chairman of the national government formally inaugurated at Nanking in October 1928.

China was nominally unified, but the power of the Communists was growing in the country and Japan constituted an external threat. In Chiang's mind, the Communists were the more dangerous. While Japan occupied Manchuria, Chiang pursued the Communist "bandits," managing to expel them from their principal base in Kiangsi in 1934. In 1936 he was kidnapped in Sian by Chang Hsueh-liang and others, who compelled him to terminate civil war and form a united front against Japan. A Communist delegation to the kidnapping negotiations promoted the Soviet line of preserving Chiang as the national leader of China. Through that incident, Chiang became the symbol of a united front against Japan—a policy he had opposed for years.

Chiang had proposed marriage to the widowed Mme Sun Yat-sen; when she refused him he successfully proposed marriage to her sister Soong Mei-ling in 1927, and thus established ties with a family of political and social influence and was converted to Christianity, which won him some favor in the West. (His first wife, whom he didn't divorce, died in 1937.)

In the summer of 1937 the Sino-Japanese war began and the national government moved first to Wuhan and then to Chungking before the Japanese advance. Early in the war the Soviets sent aid, but when the USSR was engulfed in the European war by the Nazi attack of June 1941, China became isolated politically. By that time the Japanese had occupied over half the area of China and controlled half her population and resources; the Communist government at Yenan controlled another sizeable portion. In December 1941, after Japan's attack had brought the U.S., Britain and the Netherlands into the conflict, Chiang declared war on Japan, Germany and Italy, and brought China aid from the U.S. and Britain and status as a world power, largely through U.S. urging. For his own strategy, Chiang resolved to contain the Communist-held areas and strengthen the national government.

Clarence E. Gauss, American ambassador to Chungking, and Lt. General Joseph W. Stilwell, commander of American forces in the China-Burma-India theater, looked upon Chiang's government and military effort as apathetic. In October 1944 Washington recalled Stilwell; in November Gauss resigned. Maj. General Patrick J. Hurley was dispatched to increase cooperation with Chiang and bolster Chinese morale and succeeded Gauss as ambassador. After him, in 1945, General George C. Marshall continued the hopeless task of trying to reconcile Nationalists and Communists.

Corruption and an inability to cope with China's social problems led to Chiang's defeat in the civil war and at the end of 1949 he retreated with his followers to the island of Taiwan and there purported to govern still as President of the Republic of China. The Korean War brought him the protection of the U.S. Seventh Fleet and in 1954 a treaty of alliance was signed with the U.S., but his predictions of the imminent collapse of the People's Republic have drawn less attention as the years pass. Ruling with an absolute grip on his island, he has been elected president repeatedly, most recently in 1972. He, like Peking, rejects the two-Chinas concept, and has regularly asserted his intent to reestablish Nationalist rule over the mainland. But as more and more countries extend recognition to the People's Republic, signs mount that Peking is more likely to win authority over Taiwan than Taiwan over Peking.

Chou En-lai, b. 1898. Chou's parents were wealthy landowners in Kiangsu province. He was early acquainted with the writings of reform-minded political thinkers and returned from study in Japan in 1919 to participate in the May Fourth Movement. He was jailed briefly for agitating against police treatment of student demonstrators. In the next year he wrote and edited student publications, encouraging among other things work-and-study programs, and in 1920 left for Paris to enter such a program. In 1922 in Paris he joined the Chinese Communist Party and in 1924 the Kuomintang, the latter membership then important to students who wished to return home. Returning to China in 1924, he began political work in Canton, notably in the political department of the Whampoa Military Academy.

In 1927 Chou was made a member of the Politburo and the Central Committee; he maintained his position of power during several intra-Party struggles and even, reportedly, during a falling-out with Mao, whom he joined in Kiangsi in 1931 and accompanied on the Long March (1934-35). During early years in the Party, Chou had served primarily in military posts, but now his skills as a negotiator were put to use—in the Sian incident of Chiang's kidnapping; as liaison officer to the Nationalist government after 1938, where Chou made contact with the non-Communist left in Chungking and impressed foreign journalists and diplomats favorably; and in talks with American mediator General George C. Marshall after World War II.

Chou En-lai became premier of the Central People's Government set up at Peking in October 1949. His formidable administrative talents notwithstanding, Chou became known to the outside world primarily as a diplomat, especially for his performances at Geneva in 1954 and the Bandung Conference in 1955. Although he gave up the foreign ministry in 1958, he retained his influence over Chinese foreign policy. Chou's particular contribution to government has been to sense the need for moderation and compromise, which has been for his own and the country's good. Though not breaking openly with Mao on the Great Leap Forward, he advised a slower pace; and he attempted to curb the excesses of the Great Proletarian Cultural Revolution. With the fall from power of Lin Piao, Chou became second to Mao in the Party hierarchy; and he is premier in fact as well as in name of the governmental hierarchy. In that capacity, he acted as chief negotiator for the Chinese on the occasion of President Nixon's 1972 visit.

Chou's wife, Teng Ying-chao, whom he married in 1925, is politically active in her own right.

Chu Teh, b. 1886, brought to the Party military skills learned from years of campaigning. The offspring of a farming family in Szechwan, Chu studied at the Yunnan Military Academy and participated in the military strife that followed the overthrow of the Manchu dynasty. In the morass of warlord struggles, Chu sank into dissolute habits; but by 1920 he resolved to take a new hold on life, partly influenced by his friendship with the scholarly revolutionary Sun Pingwen. He broke the opium habit, met Sun Yat-sen, and applied for membership in the Chinese Communist Party—and was rejected. In 1922 he traveled to France and later Germany, where he met Chou En-lai who apparently acted as his sponsor for Party membership. He returned home in 1926, joined the Northern Expedition as head of the political department of Yang Sen's Twentieth Army, and fled to Kiangsi when Yang became apprehensive of Communist influences in the ranks.

Chu took part in planning the 1927 Nanchang uprising, from which he retreated with his enfeebled rebel troops. In 1928 he joined Mao in western Kiangsi where the two merged their forces to form an army of about 10,000 men, formally establishing the Red Army with Chu as commander. Chu became the Communists' most prominent military figure and was given command of the Eighth Route Army in 1937. He encouraged his troops to self-sufficiency and was known for his closeness to his men. He commanded the People's Liberation Army in the last phase of the civil war.

Though technically high in the Party, Chu was not politically oriented; but he was elected to the post of vice chairman of the People's Republic in 1954. In 1959, at age 73, by which time he had given up all ties with the military, Chu relinquished the vice chairmanship to become an elder statesman.

Kung, H. H. (Kung Hsiang-hsi), 1881-1967, was born in Shansi province to a banking and commercial family that traced its lineage to Confucius. His early Christian education in China, followed by degrees from Oberlin and Yale, prompted in him a strong attraction to Westerners and their culture; one of his first political acts was to give haven to foreigners threatened by the Boxer Rebellion.

He admired Sun Yat-sen, whom he met in the United States in 1905, but his main concern until the 1920's was the Christian school he established upon his return to China in 1908. Kung's marriage (his second) to Soong Ai-ling in 1914 gave him an important tie with Sun and in the future with another brother-in-law Chiang Kai-shek. By the late twenties Kung was prominent in the Kuomintang. As a financial aide to Chiang, he negotiated some much-needed foreign financial assistance for the Nationalists in the early 1930's. He became minister of finance in 1933 and in that capacity helped to strengthen the central banking system and bolster the currency.

Kung traveled abroad in 1937 seeking military and financial aid for China. During World War II he served as president of the Executive Yuan, but continued at the same time as finance minister, while Chiang directed the military effort. He retired in 1945; because of his wife's poor health, he moved to the United States in 1948 and there spent the rest of his life.

Lin Piao, 1907-71, a military man once named successor to Mao, fell victim to a purge in 1971. This son of a small land-owner in Hupeh was early attracted by radical movements and at the age of 18 enrolled in the Whampoa Military Academy to prepare himself for revolution. His first assignment in the beginning stage of the Northern Expedition won him the rank of company commander.

Lin was admitted to Party membership in 1927, the year of the unsuccessful Communist assault upon Nanchang. Lin, who participated in that attack, managed to salvage the supplies and equipment of his unit and join Chu Teh in Kiangsi. Chu was impressed by the 20-year-old soldier and assisted his rise in the military heirarchy. Lin commanded troops on the Long March, headed the Red Army Academy at Yenan and achieved a decisive victory over the Japanese in 1937 on the Hopei-Shansi border. He was wounded in action and spent the years 1939 to 1942 recuperating in Moscow.

He was elected to the Central Committee in 1945 and successfully commanded troops in Manchuria during the civil war. Lin was an administrator in south China in the early 1950's, but was ill much of the time. He was elected to the Politburo in 1955 and became minister of defense in 1959. Late in 1961 he was instrumental in creating a set of tenets on which the political activities of the People's Liberation Army were based: the so-called Four Firsts, between weapons and men, political and other work, routine political work and ideological work, and theory and practice. He was also significant in emphasizing the omnipotence of Mao's Thought. In 1965 Lin was chosen to make a major policy statement "Long Live the Victory of the People's War," which urged all Third World countries to adopt Mao's strategy of forging rural bases to encircle the cities—and the cities were broadly interpreted as Western industrialized (capitalist) nations.

At the Ninth Communist Party Congress of April 1969, Lin was named Mao's "close comrade-in-arms and successor." But in September 1971 a Chinese plane, apparently headed for the USSR, was shot down over Mongolia; for about two weeks all civil and military flights over the mainland were canceled; National Day ceremonies were called off; and Lin was heard of no more. In July 1972 Mao announced that Lin had died in the plane crash.

Liu Shao-chi, b. 1898, like Mao, was the son of well-to-do peasant farmers in Hunan and the two young men were fellow students at the provincial normal school. He was one of several students chosen by the Comintern in 1920 to study at the Communist University for Toilers of the East in Moscow (where no Chinese interpreters were available) and there in 1921 joined the Chinese Communist Party.

Liu's specialty was labor organization. When Chiang began his purge of Communists, Liu was driven underground and so reports of his early Party work is fragmentary. His importance is known by his election to the Politburo in 1934 and by Party praise for him in 1945 for his underground work. Liu became an expert on Party organization and a spokesman

for Party policy. In *How to Be a Good Communist* (1939), he argued that many Party members come from nonproletarian and thus tainted backgrounds; therefore, each member must train himself by continual study of Marxism-Leninism and by participation in revolution. His removing of Communism from its socioeconomic base was significant to the nationalistic Chinese. He was influential in the rectification movement of 1942 to 1944 and at the Seventh Party Congress of 1945 delivered a speech "On the Party" that became a guide to Party organization. He presided over the conference that drafted the land-reform law promulgated in 1950. His 1949 speech to an international trade union conference set forth Peking's early foreign policy concept that China was to be taken as a model for militant revolution.

When the People's Republic was declared, Liu ranked third in the government; in 1959 he replaced Mao as chief of state. Following the failure of the Great Leap Forward he took the position that Mao's attempt to achieve communism in their lifetimes was unrealistic.

The Great Proletarian Cultural Revolution seems to have been instigated largely to purge Liu and his followers; he was held up to public ridicule, in 1967 the journal *Red Flag* called for his overthrow, and the Party Congress of 1969 proclaimed the *fait accompli*. Some observers hold that the purge movement flowed from Mao's discontent with the "revisionism" discovered in the Communist Party structure, a product of Liu's efforts, but plain personal rivalry also manifestly played a part.

Mao Tse-tung, b. 1893, leader of the Chinese Communist Party and founder of the People's Republic of China, is one of the major political figures of the twentieth century and an important revolutionary theorist. He was born in Hunan province to a peasant family of modest prosperity; his father opposed his reading of novels and curtailed his schooling at age 13, but Mao rebelled successfully against both. In 1911 he enthusiastically joined a rebel army, but left within a year, believing the revolutionary fervor was spent, to enter school at Changsha. His first publication, an essay on physical fitness and bristling with nationalism, appeared in 1917. Mao, occupied in forming student groups and editing reform publications, was so successful that he was compelled to flee Hunan province to escape the local warlord's wrath. In Peking and Shanghai in 1918 and 1919 he encountered Marxist thought and began a budding commitment to communism. After the warlord was driven from Hunan, Mao returned to a teaching position in Changsha and to ripe opportunity for political activity among students.

Mao was a Hunan representative in the organizational meeting of the Chinese Communist Party (CCP) in 1921 and in 1923 was elected to the Central Committee. When the CCP obedient to Kremlin policy cooperated with the Kuomintang and as individuals entered the national government, Mao became director of the Peasant Movement Training Institute. In 1927 he presented a report to the Party arguing that the Chinese peasants were ripe for revolution. After the purge of Communists in that same year, Mao returned to Hunan and began building a peasant-based organization. He attempted to mobilize peasant discontent over landlord abuses in what is known as the Autumn Harvest Uprising (1927), but that effort collapsed and Mao and his small force of soldiers retreated to the mountains of Kiangsi where they were joined the next year by Chu Teh and his troops who together formed the Chinese Workers' and Peasants' Red Army. The Party criticized Mao for emphasis on country over city; although Communist membership grew strong in Mao's Kiangsi region and Mao headed the government created there in 1931, he was unable to secure power within the Party.

Beginning in the winter of 1930, Chiang Kai-shek launched the first of five "bandit-suppression" campaigns to annihilate the Communists. Although their force was inferior, the Communists were skillful at strategic withdrawal and counterattack. Not until 1934 could Chiang by combined blockade and attack expel them from their stronghold and drive them into the Long March. Of the 100,000 who set off, almost two-thirds were lost on the march to Shensi; on the way Mao asserted his leadership and further developed his strategy of a mobile and guerrilla warfare.

From headquarters in the caves of Yenan from 1935 to 1945, Mao built a powerful administrative and military structure. He also wrote political and theoretical tracts and exercised his talents as a poet. His role was formally confirmed in 1943 when he was elected Chairman of the Central Committee and Politburo.

With victory over the Nationalists, a People's Republic was established in 1949, and Mao faced overwhelming problems in resurrecting a country ravaged by war and in asserting his authority. Stern measures were imposed: the landlord class was wiped out; campaigns were mounted against businessmen and the corrupt within the government; peasants were first given land and then herded from their family plots into new collectives. By Mao's later admission, 800,000 people lost their lives during the early years of rehabilitation.

However, the country was rehabilitated, and observers agree that the Chinese people today enjoy a life far superior to what they knew under Republican rule.

Many of Mao's decisions reflect a man in a hurry. Chinese "volunteers," weary from civil war, charged into the Korean conflict to support the people's army there. The Great Leap Forward of 1958 was designed to hasten the country toward communism; too great haste and calamitous natural disasters spoiled that plan, and in its wake Mao had to step down as chief of state. In 1957 Mao began to challenge Moscow's leadership in international Communism, thus sacrificing for his country valuable aid. The Great Proletarian Cultural Revolution beginning in 1966 purged the country of Mao's political opponents, but apparently failed in its aim of molding a fresh young leadership to step into the shoes of the aging leaders. The Cultural Revolution also marked the height of the campaign to deify Mao. His image became as familiar to the Chinese as Lenin's is to the Russians. In recent years this has modified somewhat, but his sayings are still quoted as scripture and his hour-long meeting with Nixon in February 1972 seemed to some more significant than Nixon's several days of conferences and meetings with Chou En-lai. The Thought of Mao will doubtless continue to influence China's future when he is no longer physically present to exhort his people to greater leaps.

Pu-yi, 1906-67, a nephew of the Emperor Kuang-hsu, was two years old when the Empress Dowager maneuvered him onto the throne under the reign name Hsuan-tung. The last Manchu ruler, he was forced to abdicate in 1912. Since an emperor (ruling or otherwise) could not be addressed by name, he took the name Henry to facilitate communication with his English tutor; hence he became known in the West as Henry Pu-yi. When Pu-yi was forced from the Forbidden City in 1924 by the military leader Feng Yü-hsiang, he took refuge in the Japanese legation. In 1932 he was installed as chief of state in the Japanese-controlled Manchukuo and proclaimed Emperor Kang-teh in 1934; his power was nominal. At the end of World War II he was captured by the Russians. He testified at the Tokyo war-crimes trial that he had been the unwilling agent of the Japanese. In 1950 the Russians returned him to the Communist Chinese government, which imprisoned and "reeducated" him. Released and rehabilitated in 1959, he worked in Peking on his memoirs for the rest of his life.

Soong Ching-ling (Mme Sun Yat-sen), b. 1890. One of three daughters of the wealthy, American-educated businessman Charles Soong, Mme Sun was born in Shanghai and educated at the Wesleyan College for Women in Macon, Georgia. She met Sun in 1912, followed him into exile in Japan and married him in 1915. (One sister, Mai-ling, married Chiang Kai-shek; another, Ai-ling, married H. H. Kung, a wealthy descendant of Confucius; their brother, T. V. Soong, served variously as finance minister, foreign minister and premier in the Nationalist government.) After Sun's death, Mme Sun gravitated toward the left wing of the Kuomintang. When Chiang turned on the Communists, she left for Russia (1927) and remained there and in Europe until 1931, except for a brief visit to China in 1929. She was elected to the Kuomintang Central Executive Committee in 1926 and continued her association with the party until the Communist victory in 1949. As Sun's widow, she survived Chiang's drives against the left and was able to criticize his government without jeopardy. In 1949, by invitation from the Communists, she joined the Chinese People's Political Consultative Conference, but has never become a Party member. She has lent her name to many international-front organizations and attended various peace conferences; in 1951 she was awarded the Stalin Peace Prize. She took part in drafting a constitution for the People's Republic and became chairman of the Sino-Soviet Friendship Association. In 1959 she was elected one of two vice chairmen of the People's Republic, a largely ceremonial post which qualified her to accept the credentials of foreign diplomats in the absence of the chief of state (then Liu Shao-chi). Mme Sun was harassed by Red Guards during the Cultural Revolution, but protected by Chou En-lai. She symbolizes for the Communist Party the continuity of the Chinese revolution.

Soong Mei-ling, b. 1897, another of the offspring of Charles Soong, was born in Shanghai and received a Christian education like that of her brothers and sisters. She attended college in Georgia and Massachusetts where she acquired a familiarity and community with American life that helped her in later years. In 1927 she married Chiang Kai-shek whom she urged to become a Christian and prompted to include moral uplift in his program for China. Among her tasks in the government were the leadership of women's groups and relief work. From 1936 to 1938 she also headed the National Aeronautical Affairs Commission. During World War II she toured the United States and addressed the U.S. Congress, seeking aid for the Nationalist government. She made a good impression on Americans who were charmed by her graciousness. After Chiang was forced from the mainland she became a frequent visitor to this country and became closely allied with the China Lobby in efforts to bolster the Nationalists and prevent U.S. recognition of the People's Republic. Her enmity for the Communists led to her estrangement from her sister Ching-ling.

Soong, T. V., 1894-1971. Soong's career in the Nationalist government followed a Harvard education and a brief stint as a New York banker. He became brother-in-law to Sun Yat-sen in 1915 and the latter made considerable use of Soong's economic talents. He became finance minister of the Nationalist government at Canton in 1925 and although he later quarreled with Chiang Kai-shek, that Nationalist leader in 1927 also became his brother-in-law. Soong helped to modernize China's finances and devoted special attention to currency reform. He headed the Bank of China from 1935 to 1943. He became Chiang's personal ambassador to the U.S. in 1940 and played an important role in securing loans and other assistance for his government. Soong was also minister of foreign affairs during World War II and headed the Chinese delegation to the San Francisco Conference in 1945. He handled preliminary negotiations for the treaty with the Soviet Union after the war and from 1945 to 1947 served as president of the Executive Yuan. Soong fled to the U.S. after the Nationalist's defeat and lived quietly there till his death.

Sun Yat-sen, 1866-1925, was born to a farming family in Kwangtung province. He attended a missionary school in Hawaii and continued his education in Hong Kong, where he was baptized. In 1892 he graduated from medical school, but the science to which he dedicated his life was revolution.

As a youth Sun was expelled from his native village for breaking an idol—an omen of his future. Following an unsuccessful attempt to incite revolt in Canton in 1895, he fled China and toured the world several times seeking aid from overseas Chinese to finance his revolutionary activities. During this time he read widely in Chinese and Western writings, defined his own social thought, and became strongly influenced by the work of Henry George in particular.

In Japan in 1897, with support from Japanese liberals, he drew dissident Chinese to his cause. In 1905 he welded several radical groups into the Tung-meng-hui, an organization based on his Three People's Principles: nationalism, democracy and the people's livelihood. He was expelled from

Japan in 1907 and shortly thereafter from Indochina; renewed efforts to spark a rebellion in south China were defeated; more travel and further expulsions from Japan and Malaysia followed. He fell out of touch with his colleagues in China and was traveling in the United States when he heard of the 1911 Revolution. He returned to China and in December was elected president of the provisional republic, but resigned in favor of Yuan Shih-kai and unity. He soon broke with Yuan and returned to Japan to head a new version of his party, the Komingtang (Revolutionary Party). Following Yuan's death, he returned to his power base in the south where he set up his own government, transformed the Komingtang into the Kuomintang (Nationalist Party) and began the long push to the north and unification. His plans were thwarted by problems of organization and the erratic loyalty of his military forces. Denied help from Japan and the West, he turned to the Soviet Union for aid and advice. He adopted a more revolutionary political platform and opened his government to members of the nascent Chinese Communist Party.

Sun failed in his attempt of 1923 to 1924 to forge an alliance with the warlords Chang Tso-lin and Tuan Chi-jui, and his goal of unifying China remained unfulfilled when he died of cancer in 1925. Sun Yat-sen is considered the father of modern China by Communists and Nationalists alike, both claiming him as a source of legitimacy.

Tung Pi-wu, b. 1886, came from an urban middle-class background in the province of Hupeh. He fought briefly with the rebel forces after the Wuhan revolt of 1911. He was a classical scholar and teacher and broadened his education by study in Japan, becoming especially knowledgable in the field of law. Tung helped to organize the Communist Party in 1921. Following Chiang Kai-shek's turn against the Communists in 1927 he fled first to Japan and then to the Soviet Union. He rejoined his comrades in Kiangsi in 1932 and served the Party in various capacities. Following the Long March he was a liaison officer to the Kuomintang and was the only Communist in the Chinese delegation to the San Francisco Conference in 1945. Tung participated in relief efforts in China after World War II and helped organize the legal structure of the new government, eventually becoming chief justice of the Supreme People's Court. He left that post in 1959 to become one of two vice chairmen of the People's Republic. With the disgrace and purge of Liu Shao-chi, "elder statesman" Tung Pi-wu, despite his age, became acting chairman of the People's Republic.

Wang Ching-wei, 1883-1944, struggled unsuccessfully with Chiang Kai-shek for leadership of the Kuomintang after Sun Yat-sen's death and in 1940 established a separate regime at Nanking and sought peaceful accommodation with the Japanese. His long association with Sun began with his membership in the Chinese patriotic society Tung-meng-hui during student days in Japan. Skilled in debate, he was a prime interpreter of nationalism, one of the Three People's Principles. In 1910 Wang attempted to assassinate the prince regent Tsai-feng, hoping his sacrifice would rouse the Chinese to revolution; but Manchu authorities were so impressed by his forthrightness under interrogation, as well as weak in their position, that Wang the would-be assassin was only imprisoned. Released following the 1911 Revolution, he found himself a national hero. He was elected chairman of the national government formed at Canton in 1925 and seemed Sun's most likely successor; however, Chiang Kai-shek forced his resignation in 1926 by identifying Wang with leftist elements. In 1927 when the Kuomintang split over the issue of Communist collaboration into a rightest group surrounding Chiang at Nanking and a leftist group at Wuhan, the leftist government recalled Wang from abroad. Wang soon severed relations with the Communists on the grounds that their policies were inimical to Sun's principles, but he was still unable to overpower Chiang's position. Wang again went abroad, only to return in 1930 to help set up an opposition government in challenge to Chiang's rule at Nanking. The Japanese occupation of Manchuria in 1931 and 1932 united the quarreling factions of the Kuomintang, and in early 1932 Wang became president of the Executive Yuan. Until 1935 he balanced his governmental functions with Chiang's military ones. Administration under Wang's guidance made those years the most progressive of the Nationalists' rule, but his task of appeasing the Japanese, although performed with integrity and ultimately traceable to Chiang's decisions, discredited him in the eyes of patriotic Chinese. In late 1935 he was wounded in an assassination attempt, resigned and went abroad for medical care. After the outbreak of open hostilities with Japan in 1937, Wang doubted China's ability to withstand protracted war; that doubt and a Nationalist attempt upon his life, which resulted in the death of a close associate, drove him permanently from the Nationalist government. In 1940 he became head of a separatist government at Nanking, advocating a pan-Asian, anti-Western policy. In 1943 his government declared war on the U.S. and Great Britain. The Japanese had hoped to use the puppet Nanking regime and the factor of the "Communist menace" to seduce the Nationalist government at Chungking into capitulation to the Japanese position, but Wang died in 1944 with his mission unaccomplished. The Nanking government did not long survive his departure, for the war he had misjudged was nearly over.

Yeh Chien-ying, b. 1898, advanced his career by siding with Mao over questions of strategy in the 1930's and has managed to survive the purges that have punctuated Mao's rule. He was born to a wealthy merchant family in Kwangtung and attended the Yunnan Military Academy. He was a field commander in the Northern Expedition and an instructor at Whampoa. Yeh traveled in Europe for several years following the Nanchang uprising and the disaster of the Canton Commune (in which he played an important role), returning to China in 1931 to become chief of staff of the First Front Army in Kiangsi. Later, in the War of Resistance against Japan, he worked under Chou En-lai as a liaison officer to the Nationalists and became chief of staff of the Eighth Route Army. With the advent of the People's Republic he served variously as mayor of Peking and Canton and governor of Kwangtung

province. He has been active in the National People's Congress since 1954 and served as Inspector General of the People's Liberation Army. Since the fall of Lin Piao in late 1971 he has been acting defense minister and was one of the officials serving as host to President Nixon during his 1972 visit.

Yen Hsi-shan, 1883-1960, Shansi warlord, was one of the most adroit political strategists of the Republican era. He maintained control of at least part of his native province from 1912 to 1949 and after the retreat to Taiwan continued to be a member of Kuomintang ruling circles until his death. When his father, a banker, was bankrupted during the depression of the early century, Yen entered a government military college, received a government scholarship for further study in Japan and returned in 1910 to a military career in Shansi. He proclaimed the province's independence when word of the 1911 uprising reached him; Yuan Shih-kai, upon assuming the presidency of the Republic, appointed Yen military governor of Shansi, but excluded him from civil government. Yen remained unaligned with Yuan's monarchial ambitions or his opposition, and a year after Yuan's death drove the civil government from Shansi, leaving himself sole ruler of the province. His reform program won Shansi the designation "model province." In the tumultuous decade following Yuan's death, Yen skillfully shifted allegiances, always siding with the winning coalition. When Chiang Kai-shek returned to power in 1928, Yen Hsi-shan's forces led the drive on Peking; among other rewards for this service, Yen was named governor of Shansi. Joining with Feng Yü-hsiang in the so-called northern coalition against Chiang (1930), Yen chose a losing tactic; he withdrew from Peking, sent his army back to Shansi and announced his retirement from public life. When the Japanese occupied Manchuria, where Yen had retired, he returned to reassert his authority in Shansi, even receiving appointment from the Nationalist government as pacification commissioner; but now both Japanese and Communists were encroaching on his domain. His efforts to balance between the two forces in the Sino-Japanese war that began in 1937 led to charges of collaborationism against him, but he returned to power in Shansi after the war was over and his was one of the last of the northern provinces to fall before Communist attack. He then became premier of the tottering Nationalist government and served in that capacity for a short time after the Nationalist retreat from the mainland at the end of 1949.

Yuan Shih-kai, 1859-1916. Yuan's opportunism in a period of imperial decay brought him to the verge of emperorship in 1915. He began his career as a soldier in 1880. Taking advantage of the imperial army's interference in Korean affairs, he managed to work his way up to the position of commissioner of commerce in Seoul (1885-94). After the war with Japan, he established a military academy in Peking; as reward for his part in stymieing the reform movement of 1898, he obtained an important command.

As his influence at court increased, he was appointed governor of Shantung. For putting down the Boxer movement in that province he was made governor general of Chihli and high commissioner for north China. He enlarged and modernized his army and instituted civilian reforms, but in 1907 was transferred to the post of minister of foreign affairs, in good part because he was growing too powerful for the liking of rivals in the Manchu court.

The death of the Empress Dowager in 1908 brought his enforced retirement from public affairs until the 1911 Revolution. With the Manchu empire crumbling, he regained power as premier and chief of the imperial forces and from that strategic position manipulated the Manchu abdication and simultaneously blocked the revolutionary will. The revolutionaries were forced to agree to his assuming the presidency in 1912. Yuan rode out a second revolution in 1913 and then in January 1914 dissolved Parliament and began an autocratic rule. He next aimed at restoration of the monarchy, but proclamation of his intent to become emperor led various provincial leaders to rise in armed revolt at the end of 1915 and beginning of 1916. Yuan canceled his monarchical scheme, but resistance to him continued to mount and he died in June 1916, leaving the country divided.

Suggested Reading

Clubb, O. Edmund. *Russia and China: The Great Game.* New York: Columbia University Press, 1971.

———. *Twentieth-Century China.* 2nd rev. ed. New York: Columbia University Press, 1972.

Fairbank, John K. *The United States and China.* 3rd ed. Cambridge: Harvard University Press, 1971.

Hinton, William. *Fanshen: A Documentary of Revolution in a Chinese Village.* New York: Monthly Review Press, 1966.

Hsü, C. Y. *The Rise of Modern China.* New York: Oxford University Press, 1970.

Lifton, Robert Jay. *Revolutionary Immortality: Mao Tse-tung and the Chinese Cultural Revolution.* New York: Random House, 1968.

Liu, F. F. *A Military History of Modern China, 1924-49.*

MacFarquhar, Roderick, ed. *China under Mao: Politics Takes Command. A Selection of Articles from* The China Quarterly. Cambridge: The MIT Press, 1966.

Mao Tse-tung. *Quotations from Chairman Mao Tse-tung.* Peking: Foreign Languages Press, 1966; reprinted in New York: Bantam Books, 1967.

Myrdal, Jan. *Report from a Chinese Village.* New York: Pantheon Books, 1965.

Schurmann, Franz. *Ideology and Organization in Communist China.* Berkeley and Los Angeles: University of California Press, 1966.

Schurmann, Franz, and Orville Schell, eds. *Communist China: Revolutionary Reconstruction and International Confrontation, 1949 to the Present.* New York: Vintage Books, 1967.

Tuchman, Barbara W. *Stilwell and the American Experience in China, 1911-45.* New York: Bantam Books, 1972.

Yang, C. K. *The Chinese Family in the Chinese Communist Revolution.* Cambridge: Technology Press, 1959.

Index

Felt, Adm. Harry D., 398
Feng Kuo-chang, 29, 33, 43
Feng Yu-hsiang, 50, 54-55, 57
Feng Yu-hsiang, Mme., 251
Feng Yu-lang, 282
Fischbeck, Frank, 501
"Five-anti" campaign, 129-33, 532
Five-Year Plan: first, ix, 133, 136, 175, 244-61, 532; second, 258, 260, 292, 302, 353, 532-33
Flag, Chinese Communist, 126
Flood control, 245, 279
Flying Tigers, 88; see also Claire L. Chennault, American Volunteer Group
Fong Kuo-chang, 42
Food: production, (1949) 165, 167, (1951) 171, (1953) 176; cost of, 255
Formosa, see Taiwan
Formosa Resolution, 222-23, 310, 312, 318
Formosa Strait Crisis, see Taiwan Strait Crisis
Forrestal, James V., 93, 101
France: and the Boxer Rebellion, 3; Chinese laborers and World War I, 35-36; and loan to Yuan's government, 26-28, 37-38; and U.S. Korean strategy, 201; and the French Indochina War, 209-15; recognition of China, 379-80; reaction to Cultural Revolution, 433
Freeman, Fulton, 105
French Indochina War, the, 209-15
Fu Chung, Gen., 297
Fu Chung-pi, 421
Fu Tso-yi, Gen., 111-13, 289
Fujiyama, Aiichiro, 308, 311
Fukuda, Takeo, 530
Fulton, James G. 118, 212
Gaafar al-Nimeiry, 500, 506
Gaselee, Gen. Sir Alfred, 5
Gauss, Clarence E., 538
Geneva Conference, 214-15, 236-41
George, Lloyd, 38
George, Sen. Walter F., 236
Germ warfare, 180
Germany, 4, 26-28, 34, 37-38; see also West Germany
Ghana, 323, 499
Goldberg, Arthur J., 380
Gold Coast, 233
Goldwater, Sen. Barry, 512-13
Gomulka, Wladyslaw, 336-37
"Good Deed of Dai Bee-lun, the," 478-82
Gordon, Right Rev. Frederick D., 238
Goulart, Joao, 324
Grain production, 173, 466-67
Grandt, M., 50
Great Britain: and the Boxer Rebellion, 3-5; and loan to Yuan's government, 26-28, 37-38; concession at Hankow, 61; and fall of Mandalay, 86-87; recognition of Peking, 145-47; closing of Chinese concerns, 173; and U.S. Korean strategy, 200-01; and sacking of Chinese mission, 434
Great Leap Forward, the, IX, 290, 292-305, 351, 532-33
Great Proletarian Cultural Revolution, the, ix-x, 402-45, 464-65, 493-94, 533
Greece, 201
Green, Marshall, 530-31
Green, Theodore Francis, 121
Greenslade, Capt. John F., 218
Grew, Joseph C., 163
Gromyko, Andrei A., 144
Gross, Ernest A., 139, 180, 189
Gymnastics, 172

Hai Jui Dismissed from Office (Wu Han), 403
Han Yong Ok, Maj. Gen., 490
Han Yu-tung, Mrs., 364
Hankow government, 58-61
Hankow Rebellion, 111
Harrison, Lt. Gen. William K., Jr., 207
Hart, Sir Robert, 7
Hatoyama, Ichiro, 232

Hay, John, 3
Hayashi, Baron, 10
Henne, W., 22
Herb therapy, 278
Herod, W.R., 88
Hickenlooper, Bourke B., 119
Hien-fung, Emperor, 18
Hilsman, Roger, Jr., 402, 502
Hiss, Alger, 120, 160
Ho Chi Minh, 209
Ho Chu-jo, 490
Ho Hsiang-ning, 127
Ho Lung, Marshal, 127, 399
Ho Ying-chin, Gen., 103, 142, 153
Hoashi, Kei, 311
Hodgson, Sir Frederic, M., 4
Hong Kong, 305, 393
Hoo Pi Teh, 40
Hoover, Herbert, 163
Hopkins, Harry, 97
Hoppenot, Henri, 224
Hopson, Donald C., 434
Housing, 253, 255-58
Houphouët- Boigny, Félix, 500
Howard, Hungerford B., 105
Hoxra, Enver, 359
Hsi Chung-hsun, 127
Hsi Liang, 21
Hsia Yen, 393
Hsiang Ming, 135
Hsieh Fu-chih, Gen., 291, 419
Hsieh Hsueh-hung, Mme., 289
Hsien Cheuh-tsai, 299
Hsiung Shih-fei, Gen., 88
Hsu Chien, 56
Hsu Chung-yi, 290
Hsu Han-ping, 518
Hsu Hsiang-chien, 127, 415, 430
Hsu Mao-yung, quoted, 271
Hsu Shih-chang, 22-23, 29
Hsu Shih-yu, 457
Hsu Teh-li, 127
Hsu Teh-seng, 251
Hsueh Yu-chi, 492
Hsueh Yueh, Gen., 95
Hu Chuen-wen, 167
Hu Feng, 245-46, 285
Hu Lien, Lt. Gen., 161
Hu Shih, Dr., 85, 88
Hu Tsung-nan, Lt. Gen., 117, 161
Huang Ching, 251, 289
Huang Ho-sen, 288
Huang Hua, 166
Huang Ko-cheng, 291, 407
Huang Shao-hsiung, Gen., 113
Huang Shao-ku, 112
Huang Sing, 21
Huang Yen-pei, 127
Huang Yung-sheng, 421, 449, 457, 486
Hughes, Secretary, quoted, 41
Hull, Cordell, 85, 101
Hundred Flowers Movement, the, ix, 282-91, 532
Hungary, 334-35
Hurley, Maj. Gen. Patrick J., 96, 98-99, 104-05, 115, 538
Hutchison, John Colville, 146
Hwang Sing, Gen., 29
Hyde, Rev. Joseph Eugene, 238
Hyon Jun Guk, 489

I Kuan Tao Society, 246
Illiteracy, 257
Illsley, Walter, 173
Ilyichev, Leonid F., 491-92

Mongolian People's Republic, 104, 184-85, 248, 343-44, 375-76
Morse, Wayne, 225
Mountbatten, Adm. Lord Louis, 90, 94
Muccio, John J., 188-89
Muniz, Joao Carlos, 151
Muravieff, Count, 5
Mutual-aid teams, 172, 176

Naim, Prince, 321
Nam Tranh Binh, 489
Nasser, Gamal Abdel, 230-33
"Nasakom," 331, 333
Nasution, Gen. Abdul Haris, 329
National anthem, Chinese Communist, 126
National Day Rites (1971), 456
Nationalist government, *see* Republic of China, Taiwan
National liberation movements, Sino-Soviet dispute on, 356-58
National People's Congress, 133-36, 249, 252, 289, 353, 428, 454
Nehru, Jawaharlal, 138, 182-83, 230-36, 272, 294, 321, 384
Nelson, Donald M., 97-98
Nepal, 233, 321
Nepotism, 269
Netherlands, the, 7, 201
New Democracy, ix, 165-66, 169, 254-55, 334
New Democratic Youth League, 288
Newsmen, 145, 274, 501-02
New Zealand, 440
Ngabo, Sawang, 140
Ngo Thuyen Thuyen, 489
Nieh Jung-chung, 111, 127, 426, 430
Nigeria, 499
Nincitch, Djuro, 190
Nixon, Richard M., 439, 442-45, 497-98, 504-05, 514-34
Nkrumah, Kwame, 323
Nomura, Adm. Kichisaburo, 85, 102
North Atlantic Treaty Organization, 206, 232
North China People's Government, 111
North East (India) Frontier Agency, 382
North Korea, 187, 208, 483
North Vietnam, 233, 484-85, 487
Norway, 146
Nuclear program (China), 341, 365-66, 396-98, 426, 441
Nuclear weapons, 225-26, 235-36
Nyerere, Julius K., 328, 500

Obata, Minister, 40
Ochab, Edward, 335
O'Conor, Sen. Herbert R., 118
Offshore islands, 222-29, 368-69
Oil production, 258
Okamura, Gen. Ysauji, 103
Okinawa Pact, the, 442-45
Oku, Gen. 12-14
Olive, William M., 166
Olympic Games, 257
On Dealing with the Communist World (Kennan), 371-72
Open door policy, 39
Opera, 172, 474
Organization of American States, 322
Orloff, M., 54
Osborne, Brig. Gen. R.N., 207
Outer Mongolia, *see* Mongolian People's Republic
Overseas Chinese, 324-25, 432
Oyama, Field Marshal, 11

Pai Chung-hai, 153
Pai Chung-hsi, 117
Pakistan, 146, 502, 508
Panchen Lama, the, 138-41, 299, 383-84
Pao Kuei-ching, 36
Paperworkism, 175
Paris Commune, 419, 424
Park Sung Hee, 508
Paxton, J. Hall, 105

Peaceful coexistence, 240-41, 247, 282, 354, 356-58, 360
Peaceful Coexistence, Five Principles of, 183, 232, 235, 334, 366
Peace Restoration Army, 57
Peasant-soldier teams, 428, 470
Peasants: Soviet advice on organizing, 54; and the Hankow government, 61; as revolutionary class, 126; unionization of, 257; earnings of, 170, 256; pressure on to collectivize, 263-64; resistance to family planning, 304; subsidies for, in communes, 465-66
Peasants' Association, 168
Peking University, 272, 405, 419
Peng Chao-hsien, 113
Peng Chen, 127, 129, 134, 404-05, 419
Peng Teh-huai, 127, 208, 291: and Quemoy ceasefire, 319; purge of, 359; dismissal of, 395-96, 399, 407; arrest of, 413; rehabilitation of, 429; challenging of Mao, 533
Peng Tse-min, 127
People's Democratic Dictatorship, ix
People's Democratic Republic of Korea, 187, 208, 483
People's Liberation Army: "volunteers" for Korean War, 195, 197, 207; advance on Tibet, 137-41; and conflict with civilians, 284; civil labor by, 297, 396, 406; ranks and insignia of abolished, 399; and the Cultural Revolution, 415-16, 418-21, 437; power of in revolutionary committees, 451-52; appointments to, 453; unit of described, 468; end of elitism, 477; as model for Maoism, 533-34
People's liberation movements, 394
People's tribunals, 170
Perkins, Sarah, 238
Perry, Harold G.B., 167
Peru, 506-07
Pescadores Islands, 218
Philippines, the, 232-33, 324-25
Phomvihan, Kaysone, 489
Physical fitness, 256-57, 472-73, 477
Pi Shou-chen, 55
Pichon, M., 9
Piecework wage system, 170
Pignon, Leon, 209
Plimsoil, James, 151
Public denunciation, 268-70
Public health, 251
Public security, 251, 396, 424
Punyaratabhan, Khenjati, 181
P'u Lun, Prince, 42
Pu-yi, vii, 16-18, 20, 32, 541
Po Chung-Chang, 127
Po I-po, 134, 244, 260
Po Yi-po, 127, 166, 175, 251
Podgorny, Nikolai V., 359
Poland, 334-36
Poletti, Father Ambrose, 277
"Police action," 226
Political commissars, 399
Political Consultive Council, Chinese People's, 125
Polk, Frank, L., 36-37
Population, 143, 177, 244, 256, 303-05, 338, 342, 469
Port Arthur, 104, 247
Portugese Guinea, 500
Potsdam Declaration (1945), 101, 103, 152
Prisoners of war, 236
Production brigades, 353
Proletarian dictatorship, 334
Propaganda teams, 467

Quadros, Janio, 324
Quemoy Island, 222-29, 368-69
Quo Tai-chi, Dr., 42, 153

Radford, Adm. Arthur W., 163
Railroads, 173-74, 244, 248, 253
Rao, Dr.K.L., 279
Rationing, 246, 352
Rau, Sir Benegal N., 190
"Red Detachment of Women," 475-76
Red Guards: destruction of art works, 407; storming of Soviet

Byline Index